For 100% Success in Competitive Exam

Comprehensive English Grammar & Composition

SC Gupta
BSc, MA, MCom. LLB, DLL, CA/IB

ARIHANT PUBLICATIONS (INDIA) LIMITED

arihant

ARIHANT PUBLICATIONS (I) LTD

ADMINISTRATIVE & PRODUCTION OFFICES

Regd. Office
'Ramchhaya' 4577/15, Agarwal Road, Darya Ganj, New Delhi -110002
Tele: 011- 47630600, 43518550; Fax: 011- 23280316

Head Office
Kalindi, TP Nagar, Meerut (UP) - 250002
Tele: 0121-2401479, 2512970, 4004199; Fax: 0121-2401648

SALES & SUPPORT OFFICES

Agra, Ahmedabad, Bengaluru, Bhubaneswar, Bareilly, Chennai, Delhi, Guwahati, Hyderabad, Jaipur, Jhansi, Kolkata, Lucknow, Meerut, Nagpur & Pune

Price : ₹ 300.00

PO No. : TXT-59-T071430-6-26

Printed & Bound By
ARIHANT PUBLICATIONS (INDIA) LTD. (PRESS UNIT)

For further information about the books published by Arihant log on to www.arihantbooks.com or email to info@arihantbooks.com

PREFACE

For a number of the candidates appearing in competitive examinations, the subject of English is a frightening object. They find themselves incapable to understand and make the practical use of the Grammatical rules. Most of them suffer from the phobia of English learning. I have kept these points in mind while writing this book. This book is mainly written for those who are taking competitive examinations but find themselves in a state of utter frustration due to low or marginal marks secured by them in the paper of English. In this book all kinds of Grammatical, Compositional and Word power related segments are covered. One part is solely comprises Specific Questions usually asked in various competitive examinations. This is indeed a comprehensive guide for Competitive English.

This book is divided in four parts.

Part-I : Competitive Grammar

Part-II : Essential Word Power

Part-III: Specific Exercises for Competitive Examinations

Part -IV: Compositional English

Part-I This part as the name suggests comprises the important rules of grammar along with illustrations and examples, describing the practical usage of the rules. A plenty of solved exercises are given in each Chapter.These would be extremely helpful for the students in checking and testing their acquired knowledge and also while attempting the questions in competitive examinations. These exercises cover all types of questions usually asked about Grammatical rules and their applicabilty, in various academic and competitive examinations. In this way, students would become well conversant with the traditional and modern concepts of English Grammar and they would be surely in a position to answer the questions correctly in various competitive examinations.

Part-II This part of Essential Word Power is the most desirable requirement of the students who are preparing for the competitive examinations. This part contains thousands of words, used in daily routine and asked in various examinations. The part comprises the varied segments of word power that would surely be much helpful for the students in improving their word power and in answering the questions appeared in competitive examinations.

Part-III This part contains 'ready to use' material for the students appearing in competitive examinations. In this part we have given a number of Specific Exercises for Competitive Examinations, covering almost all kinds of questions usually asked in competitive examinations. By solving these exercises the candidates will be able to test their acquired knowledge and be well confident in attempting such questions in the examinations.

Part-IV This is a very important part, consists of various segments of compositional English. In this part valuable tips to attempt the comprehensions, writing precis, reports and letters including essays, expansions, paragraphs etc.,have been given.This part contains almost all kinds of compositional questions asked in various competitive examinations. This part also contains 51 essays on important topics and 79 expansions and paragraphs that will facilitate the candidates in preparing for the competitive examinations.

It has been the utmost endeavour on the part of the author to make the book really helpful for the students studying in schools,colleges, universities and for the candidates making preparations for various competitive examinations.

Remember

"Something one finds difficult,
doesn't mean, one shouldn't try.
It means one should try harder,
with double vigour and triple confidence."

Sagacious suggestions, and constructive criticism are welcomed. I shall like to convey my sincere thanks to M/S Arihant Publications, especially to Mr. Deepesh Jain for bringing this book in the market, in the present shape and size.

Author

S C Gupta

129-South West Block, Near Eid Gah Alwar (Rajasthan), Tel: 0144- 2700438

CONTENTS

PART - II

ESSENTIAL WORD POWER

PART - III

SPECIFIC EXERCISES FOR COMPETITIVE EXAMINATIONS

PART - IV

COMPOSITIONAL ENGLISH

Unit

1

You Should Know!

Basics of English Language

CAPITALS & smalls (English Alphabet)

English language has 26 letters in its alphabet. Each letter can be written as a 'small letter' or as a 'large letter'. Large letters are also called 'capital letters' or 'capitals'.

Small letters are sometimes called 'lower case' and large letters 'upper case'.

A	B	C	D	E	F	G	H	I	J	K	L	M	CAPITAL
N	O	P	Q	R	S	T	U	V	W	X	Y	Z	LETTERS
a	b	c	d	e	f	g	h	i	j	k	l	m	small
n	o	p	q	r	s	t	u	v	w	x	y	z	letters

Grammatical Terms of English Language

Sentence

A sentence is a group of words that conveys some meaning. It means a sentence consists of words, but not every string of words constitute a sentence, as we can see in the following example :

(a) To he market goes.

A possible analysis is that if we look at this example we know the meaning of the individual words, but the sequence as a whole does not make sense or does not convey any meaning. So we cannot consider this structure a sentence. Thus, we can affirm that if a sequence of words is to constitute a sentence, it must be meaningful; for instance :

(a) He goes to market.

Subject

The subject is the person or thing 'performing' the action. The noun, pronoun or group of words act as a noun that performs the action indicated in the predicate of the sentence or clause.

Predicate

Basically, it is the rest of the sentence or clause other than the subject. It usually has a verb and thus indicates some action, but may have other functions such as modifying the subject. What is said about the subject is called 'predicate'.

Declarative Sentence

A declaration is a statement or observation that states an idea. Narrative and descriptive passages are written using declarative sentences, for instance :

(a) I did not abuse him.

(b) We warned him.

Interrogatives

Questions are interrogatives. Grammarians like to use jargon, while telling writers to avoid it, so we have to deal with words like interrogative.

(a) Have you taken your lunch?
(b) Did you complete your work?

Imperatives

Imperatives are command, request, advice or emergency pleas.

(a) It is imperative that you leave today.
(b) Go there.
(c) Please, open the door for me.

Exclamations

Most exclamations stand alone, making for very short sentences. Sentences can be exclamations, if they contain a strong emotion or opinion.

(a) Wah! (b) Wow! What a great fall.

Sentence Complements

A sentence complement is a word or phrase adding meaning to the subject or verb. A complement clarifies the sentence. Complements usually appear after the simple predicate verb in a sentence, forming the complete predicate. Simply remember that complements complete predicates.

Direct Objects

These are objects, which receive directly the actions described by the verbs. A direct object answers the question 'Who or What?' and is being acted upon by the subject of a sentence.

Indirect Objects

In addition to taking direct objects, some verbs also take indirect objects. In the following examples, the direct objects are printed in bold type, and the indirect Objects are underlined. An indirect object answers 'To/For Whom/What?' Indirect objects usually refer to living things.

(a) She gave the child a pen.
(b) He sent the man the information.

Clause

Clause is a group of words that forms part of a sentence and contains a subject and a finite verb. A clause contains both a subject and a predicate.

Principal Clause

An independent clause has a subject and a finite verb. It can stand alone as a sentence. The independent clause is a short sentence.

Subordinate Clause A subordinate clause modifies the sentence by acting as an adjective, adverb or noun. Usually a dependent clause is introduced by a subordinate conjunction.

Phrase

A phrase is a group of words, without subject a verb or a complete thought. For example, red tapism, ins and outs, hand in gloves, etc.

Simple Sentence

The most basic type of sentence is the simple sentence, which contains only one clause with one finite verb. A simple sentence, contains a subject and a verb (finite), and it expresses a complete thought.

Compound Sentence

A compound sentence is a sentence formed by two or more independent clauses.

Complex Sentence

A complex sentence has an independent clause joined by one or more dependent clauses. Unlike a compound sentence, however, a complex sentence contains clauses which are not equal.

Look at the following example

(a) Do you know that Smt. Indira Gandhi was the first lady Prime-Minister of India?

Parts of Speech

Traditional grammar classifies words, based on eight parts of speech. These are : verb, noun, pronoun, adjective, adverb, preposition, conjunction and interjection. Each part of speech explains not what the word is, but how the word is used. In fact, the same word can be a noun in one sentence and a verb or an adjective in the next.

Colloquial

Colloquial means conversational, informal, everyday, casual, familiar, etc.

Cognate Object

Some verbs take an object after them that are similar in meaning to the verb. Such objects are called cognate objects, For example, :

(a) He **sighed** a deep **sigh.**
(b) Our army **fought** a fierce **fight.**

In the above sentences the verbs and the objects, (cognate) are in bold letters.

Syllable

A syllable is a part of a word that contains a single vowel sound and that is pronounced as a unit. So, for example, 'book' has one syllable, and 'reading' has two syllables.

One syllable word : run, sit, come, go, my, he, etc.

Two syllable words: Mon-day, four-teen, fa-ther, Sun-day, etc.

Words with more than two syllables :
won-der-ful, beau-ti-ful, de-mo-cra-cy, im-po-ssi-ble.

Slang

Slang consists of words, expressions and meanings that are informal and are used by the people who know each other very well and are quite familiar with one another. (Generally abusive language).

Tense

Tense is that form of a verb which shows not only the time of an action but also the state of an action or event.

Sequence of Tense

The sequence of tenses are the principles which govern the tense of the verb in subordinate clause vis-a-vis the tense of the verb in a principal clause. The rules which determine the tense of the sub-ordinate clause, if the tense of the principal clause is present or past or future, are studied under the Sequence of Tense.

Noun

A noun is a word used as name of a person, place or thing. Types of noun are following:

(1) **Proper Noun** Proper noun refers to the name of a person, place or thing. For example, Ram, Delhi, Nike, etc.

(2) **Common Noun** A common noun refers to persons, things or places of the same kind or class, For example, king, boy, girl, city, etc.

(3) **Collective Noun** A collective noun is the name of a group of persons or things taken together and spoken of as a whole, as unit. For example, team, committee, army, etc.

(4) **Abstract Noun** Abstract noun in general refers to the quality, action or state that cannot be seen but expressed as ideas or feelings, for example, honesty, bravery (quality), hatred, laughter (action), poverty, young (state), art, etc.

The Noun Case

The relation of noun with other words in a sentence is determined by its case.

(1) **Nominative Case** When a noun is used as subject of the verb in a sentence, it is nominative case.

(2) **Objective Case** When a noun is used as an object of the verb in a sentence, it is objective case.

(3) **Nominative of Address** When a noun is used to address, it is nominative of address.

(a) Boys, don't make a noise.

(b) Harish, wait for me.

In the above sentences, boys and Harish are nominative of address.

(4) **Case in Apposition** If two nouns referring to the same person or thing are in apposition, one is placed immediately after the other, with no conjunction joining them. For example,

(a) Her father, Naresh Chandra, left home three months ago.

Conjunction

A conjunction is a word that joins words or sentences together. It is also called a joiner, a word that connects (conjoins) parts of a sentence.

Adverb

An adverb is that word in a sentence which modifies the meaning of verb or adjective or another adverb or adverbial phrase.

Pronoun

Generally, but not always, pronouns stand for (pro + noun) or refer to a noun, an individual or individuals or things or thing (the pronoun's antecedent) whose identity is made clear earlier in the text.

Preposition

Preposition is a word placed before a noun or a pronoun, which denotes the relation, the person or thing referred to, has with something else.

A preposition is followed by a noun. It is never followed by a verb.

Subject-Verb Agreement

The verb must agree with its subject in number and person. For example,

(a) A kite flies.

(b) Birds fly.

Weak Verbs

Verbs which require -ed, -d or -t to be added to the present tense to form the past are called 'weak verbs'. They are also called 'regular verbs'.

Present	Past	Past Participle
sell	sold	sold
burn	burnt	burnt
think	thought	thought
lend	lent	lent
talk	talked	talked
live	lived	lived

Strong Verbs

Verbs that form their past tense by merely changing the vowel in their present form, without adding and ending are called 'Strong Verbs'. As...

Present	Past	Past Participle
abide	abode	abode
bear	bore	borne
become	became	become
find	found	found
see	saw	seen
go	went	gone
come	came	come

These are also called irregular verbs.

Inchoative Verbs

The term inchoative verb is used for a verb that denotes the beginning, development or final stage of a change of condition.

Some of these verbs are :

get, became, grow, etc.

(a) My father is getting weaker.

(b) It is getting dark.

Transitive Verbs

Transitive verbs take objects. These verbs carry the action of a subject and apply it to an object. They tells us what the subject (agent) does to something else (object).

Intransitive Verbs

Intransitive verbs do not take an object, they express actions that do not require the agents doing something to something else.

Linking Verbs

A linking verb connects a subject to a subject complement, which identifies or describes the subject.

The following sentences are descriptive, using linking verbs :

(a) The house **is** green.

(b) The house **was** white, until we painted it.

In the above sentences bold letters are linking verbs.

Causative Verbs

Causative verbs show that somebody or something is indirectly responsible for an action. The subject does not perform the action itself, but causes someone or something else to do it instead. For example, :

(a) I made her sing a song.

(b) I made him polish my shoes.

Modals

Modal auxiliaries are special auxiliary verbs that express the degree of certainty of the action in the sentence, or the attitude or opinion of the writer or speaker concerning the action. These are verbs which help other verbs to express a meaning. It is important to note that 'modal verbs' have no meaning by themselves.

Non-Finites

Non-finite verb forms are those that do not show number (they are not singular or plural) or tense (they do not make the sentence past or present).

Non-finites are of three kinds :

1. infinitive 2. gerund 3. participle

(1) **Infinitive** In grammar, the infinitive is the form of a verb that has no inflection to indicate person, number, mood or tense. Infinitives are also defined as 'to + base' form of the verb.

(2) **Gerund** Gerund is that a form of verb that ends in 'ing' and has the force of a noun and a verb.

(3) **Participle** A participle is a non-finite verb, called a 'verbal adjective', which means that

it has characteristics of both verbs and adjectives. Since they function as adjectives, participles modify nouns or pronouns. A participle most often ends in -ing or -ed.

Unattached or Dangling Participle

A participle is a verbal adjective, so it must be attached to some noun or pronoun. It means it must have a proper subject of reference. If the participle is not attached to some noun or pronoun it is called dangling participle.

Inversion

Certain adverbs and adverb phrases, most with a restrictive or negative sense, can for emphasis be placed first in a sentence or clause and are then followed by the inverted (*i.e.*, interrogative) form of the verb. It is called inversion.

Synonym

A synonym is a word or expression which means the same as another word or expression.

The term 'industrial democracy' is often used as a synonym for worker participation.

Antonym

The antonym of a word is a word which means the opposite. 'day' and 'night' are antonyms.

Heteronym

A heteronym is a word that has the same spelling as another word but with a different pronunciation and meaning. These words are sometimes also called homographs.

Autograms

A self-referencing sentence describes itself. For example, 'This sentence has five words.' An autogram is a self-referencing sentence that describes its letter content.

Contronym

The word contronym (also, synonym or antagonym) is used to refer to words that, by some freak of language evolution, are their own antonyms. Both contronym and antagonym are relatively recent neologisms. However, there is no alternative term that is more established in the English language.

(a) fast—quick, unmoving
(b) fix—restore, castrate

Palindrome

A palindrome is a word or sentence that reads the same forward as it does backward. The words a and I are perhaps the simplest and least interesting palindromes. The word 'racecar' and the name 'Hannah' are more interesting and illustrative.

Palingram

A palingram is a sentence in which the letters, syllables or words read the same backward as they do forward. The sentence, 'He was, was he?' is a word palingram, because the words can be placed in reverse order and still read the same. The sentence, 'I did, did I?' is not only a word palingram but also a letter palingram (or palindrome) as well.

Pangram

A pangram is a sentence that contains all letters of the alphabet. Less frequently, such sentences are called 'holalphabetic sentences'. For example,

(a) The quick brown fox jumps over a lazy dog.

Eponym

An eponym is someone or something whose name is or thought to be the source of something's name (such as a city, country, era or product). Xerox is a brand of photocopy machine. But this word has also been since adopted to refer to any brand of photocopy machine and, moreover, also employed as a verb to describe the act of photocopying.

Adjunct

An adjunct is a word or group of words which indicates the circumstances of an action, event or situation. An adjunct is usually a prepositional phrase or an adverb group.

Contraction

A contraction is a shortened form of a word or words.

(a) It's (with an apostrophe) should be used only as a contraction for 'it is'.
(b) Can't is the contraction form of cannot.

Elementary Questions About English Language

Q. 1 *How many words are there in the English language?*

Ans. About a million, may be more.

It is difficult to calculate the exact number of words. If we include all scientific nomenclature, this could easily double the figure. For example, there are apparently some one million insects already described, with several million more awaiting description. The two largest dictionaries—the Oxford English Dictionary and MCerriam Webster's Third New International Dictionary—each include around half a million words.

Q. 2 *What is the longest word in the dictionary?*

Ans. It might be supercalifragilistic-expialidocious (which appears in the Oxford English Dictionary), unless we want to count names of diseases (such as pneumonoultramicrosco-picsilicovolcanoconiosis, defined by the Oxford English Dictionary as 'a factitious word alleged to mean' a lung disease caused by the inhalation of very fine silica dust, but occurring chiefly as an instance of a very long word), places (such as air pwllgwyngyll go gery chwyrnd robwlll Lantysiliogogogoch, a village in Wales), chemical compounds (apparently there is one that is 1,913 letters long) and also a few words found only in Joyce's Finnegans Wake.

Other famous words sesquipedalian: antidisestablishmentarianism (opposition to the disestablishment of the Church of England), floccinaucinihilipilificationhonorificabilitudinitatibus (Which appears in Shakespeare's Love's Labour's Lost, and which has been cited as [dubious] evidence that Francis Bacon wrote Shakespeare's plays).

Q. 3 *What does 'floccinaucinihilipilification' mean?*

Ans. It means 'the estimation of something as worthless.'

But it is usually used only as an example of a very long word, considered to be the longest. The Oxford English Dictionary labels it 'humorous' and gives the following citations for it.

I loved him for nothing so much as his floccinaucin ihilipilification of money. —William Shenstone' Letters

They must be taken with an air of contempt, a floccinaucinihilipilification of all that can gratify the outward man.—Sir Walter Scott, Journal

Q. 4 *What does 'pneumonoultramicro-scopicsilicov olcanoconiosis' mean?*

Ans. It is defined by the Oxford English Dictionary as 'a factitious word alleged to mean "a lung disease caused by the inhalation of very fine silica dust" but occurring chiefly as an instance of a very long word.'

Q. 5 *How can I figure out what a Roman numeral stands for?*

Ans. **Conversion Table**

1 = I	2 = II	3 = III
4 = IV	5 = V	6 = VI
7 = VII	8 = VIII	9 = IX
10 = X	20 = XX	30 = XXX
40 = XL	50 = L	60 = LX
70 = LXX	80 = LXXX	90 = XC
100 = C	500 = D	1000 = M

You should add the numbers together if numbers of the same size are placed next to each other or if a smaller number is placed to the right of a larger number. For example, :

II = 2, III = 3, VI = 6, VIII = 8, XX = 20, XXI = 21, CC = 200

You should subtract the smaller number from the larger if a smaller number is placed to the left of a larger number. For example, :

IV = 4, IX = 9, XL = 40, CD = 400, CM = 900

Sometimes you are to perform both operations. For example,

XIV = 14, XIX = 19 , XXIV = 24 , XCI = 91 , XCIX = 99 , MCM = 1900, MCMXLVII = 1947, MCML = 1950, MCMLXVIII = 1968

Q. 6 *Does bimonthly mean twice a month or every two months?*

Ans. Every two months (usually).

Bi-means 'two', so bimonthly means 'happening every two months'—but it also means 'happening twice a month'. Another word for the latter is semimonthly.

Q. 7 *What is a linking verb?*

Ans. A linking verb is usually a form of 'be' or 'seem' that identifies the predicate of a sentence with the subject.

Example 'Achilles is a lion.'

'Is' links Achilles with lion, indentifies Achilles with a lion. Achilles is the subject of the sentence and is a lion is the predicate.

A linking verb is also called a copulas.

Q. 8 *What is ambiguity in writing?*

Ans. Ambiguity in writing means when its meaning cannot be understood by its context.

Ambiguity may be introduced accidentally, confusing the readers and disrupting the flow of reading. If a sentence or paragraph jars upon reading, there is lurking ambiguity. It is particularly difficult to spot one's own ambiguities. It is strongly recommended that one should let another person read one's writing before submission for publication.

Q. 9 *What is redundancy in writing?*

Ans. The use of language that can be eliminated without incurring a loss of meaning, is called redundancy in writing. Redundancy in writing usually comes from these sources : Wordy phrases.

Example 'in view of the fact that' instead of 'since' or 'because'. Employing obvious qualifiers when a word is implicit in the word it is modifying.

Example 'completely finish.' If you have incompletely finished something, you haven't finished it at all.

Using two or more synonyms together.

Example 'thoughts and ideas.'

Q. 10 *What is the difference between its and it's?*

Ans. Its is the possessive form of it. It's is a contraction of 'it is' or 'it has'.

Examples

(a) It's a common mistake.

(b) The boat has a hole in its hull.

The confusion arises from the dual function of the's ending, which can indicate either possession or contraction, as in : John's Pizzas are the best ('The Pizzas which are John's—that is, in that he makes them—are the best'); John's going to have to buy some more files soon (='John is going to have to buy some more files soon'). However's is never used to indicate possession in pronouns. We do not write hi's (instead of his).

Q. 11 *What is the difference between i.e. and e.g.?*

Ans. i.e. means 'that is' (to say). e.g. means 'for example', i.e. is an abbreviation for Latin id est, 'that is.' e.g. is for exempli gratia, 'for the sake of example.' So you can say, 'I like citrus fruits, e.g., oranges and lemons' or 'I like citrus fruits, i.e. the juicy, edible fruits with leathery, aromatic rinds of any of numerous tropical, usually thorny shrubs or trees of the genus citrus.'

Q. 12 *What is the difference in usage of 'like' vs 'as' ?*

Ans. The rule is 'as' comes before a clause.

If the word is followed by a clause, a group of words with both a subject and a verb, use as : He liked the restaurant, as any gourmet would.

If no verb follows, choose like: He walks like a platypus.

However, in casual usage, like is gaining steadily as in 'He tells it like it is, or 'She eats ice cream like it's going out of style.' The informal use of like to introduce a clause is fine in conversation or casual writing, but to be grammatically correct, remember 'as comes before a clause' rule.

Q. 13 *What is the difference between 'there' and 'their'? 'Your' and 'you're' ? How can I remember these?*

Ans. 'Their' and 'your' are possessive forms used as modifiers before nouns. They basically mean: 'belonging to them' and 'belonging to you', respectively. You're is a contraction of 'you are: 'You're doing fine.'

Q. 14 *What is the only word in the English language that has three consecutive sets of double letters?*

Ans. Bookkeeper. Also bookkeeping. If you are willing to accept a hyphenated word, sweet-toothed is another.

Q. 15 *What is the difference, if any, between using 'once in a while' and 'once and a while'?*

Ans. These two idioms mean the same thing—occasionally. The latter, might well have grown up as a misunderstanding of 'once in a while' or a confusion of that phrase and 'once and for all'. Use 'once in a while'.

Q. 16 *What is the rule for determining whether or not to write out a number as a word?*

Ans. In general, write out the first nine cardinal (1-9) numbers; use figures for 10 and above.

In general, write out the first nine cardinal (1-9) numbers (except for address numbers 2–9, dates, decimals, game scores, highways, latitude/longitude, mathematical expressions, measurement/weight, money/financial data, percentages, proportion, scientific expressions, statistics, technical expressions, temperature, time, unit modifiers, votes and numbers not written out in a proper noun) and any number that begins a sentence. Use figures for 10 and above. The first nine ordinal (1st-9th) numbers are usually written out, especially when describing order in time or location.

Q. 17 *What is the word meaning 'to throw out of a window'?*

Ans. Defenestrate : Its roots are Latin de-, 'out of' and fenestra, 'window'.

Defenestration is the noun form of the word. It is also a computing jargon term for 'the act of exiting a window system in order to get better response time from a full-screen program' or 'the act of discarding something under the assumption that it will improve matters' or 'the act of dragging something out of a window (onto the screen)'. source: Jargon File.

Q. 18 *What is the plural of virus?*

Ans. Viruses.

It is not viri or (which is worse) virii. True, the word comes directly from Latin, but not all Latin words ending in -us have -i as their plural. Besides, viri is the Latin word for 'men' (plural of vir, man, the root the English virile). There is in fact no written attestation of a Latin plural of virus.

Q. 19 *What one English word ends in 'mt' ?*

Ans. There are five words ending with mt—daydreamt, dreamt, outdreamt, redreamt, undreamt.

Q. 20 *Can I use 'and' (or 'but', etc.) at the start of a sentence?*

Ans. Yes.

The old 'rule' that we should not begin a sentence with a conjunction (and or but) has actually gone by the wayside these days. Occasionally, especially in casual writing, you can begin a sentence with 'and' or 'but'. These words are mainly used to join elements within a sentence, but they have begun sentences since long.

Q. 21 *What two words make the contraction 'ain't'? Is it proper?*

Ans. 'Ain't' is a contraction of 'am not'. It is not considered proper.

'Ain't' is not accepted by many as it suggests illiteracy and the inability to speak properly. It can be used jokingly. The widely used aren't I?, though illogical (noone says I are), is used in speech, but in writing there is no acceptable substitute for the stilted am I not?

Q. 22 *What is the difference between main and helping verbs?*

Ans. A helping verb accompanies the main verb in a clause and helps to make distinctions in mood, voice, aspect and tense.

A helping or auxiliary verb such as have, can or will, accompanies the main verb in a clause and helps to make distinctions in mood, voice, aspect and tense. The main verb represents the chief action in the sentence.

Q. 23 *When do you use lie and lay?*

Ans. To lay is to place something; to lie is to recline.

To lay is to place something. It is always followed by an object, the thing being placed. To lie is to recline. For example: He lays the book down to eat. She lies quietly on the chaise.

Part of the source of the confusion is the past tense of lie, which is lay: She lay on the chaise all day. The past participle of lie is lain, as in—She has lain there since yesterday, as a matter of fact.

The past tense of lay is laid, as is the past participle.

Q. 24 *When do you capitalise words like mother, father, grandmother and grandfather when writing about them?*

Ans. When they are used as proper nouns you should capitalise these, when referring to your own relatives 'Hello, Mother.' A good rule to follow is to capitalize them if they are used as proper nouns. If used as common nouns, don't capitalise: 'We honour all mothers in May.'

Q. 25 *When do you use 'well' or 'good' ?*

Ans. In general, use 'well' to describe an activity, 'good' to describe a thing.

When it is an activity being described, use well, as in 'He did well in the spelling bee.' Well is an adverb here, describing the verb.

When it is a condition or a passive state being described, use good, as in 'You're looking good tonight!'. Good is an adjective here, describing the noun.

With feel good/feel well, it is more complicated. In this case, the word well is being used an adjective meaning 'healthy'—so it is correct to say, 'I feel well.' You can say 'I feel good' also, but it is more informal.

Q. 26 *When was the first dictionary made?*

Ans. The western tradition of dictionary making began with the Greeks when changes in the language made many words in literature unintelligible to readers. During the Middle Ages, when Latin was the language of learning, dictionaries of Latin words were compiled.

The first dictionary of English appeared in 1604—Robert Cawdry's **A Table Alphabetical.** This work contained about 3,000 words but was so dependent upon three sources that it can rightly be called a plagiarism. Early dictionaries were generally small and defined 'hard' words and were made by men in their leisure time as a hobby. John Kersey the Younger is regarded as the first professional lexicographer whose introductory work, **A New English Dictionary**, appeared in 1702. Kersey's accomplishments were superseded in the 1720s by Nathan Bailey's innovative work, **An Universal Etymological English Dictionary.** For the rest of that century, it was actually more popular than Dr. Samuel Johnson's dictionary!

Q. 27 *Which is right: 'I wish it were...' or 'I wish it was...'?*

Ans. 'I wish it were...'

There is often confusion about were (a past subjunctive) and was (a past indicative). In conditional sentences where the condition is unreal or not yet real, use were : 'I wish it were true that he loved me' or 'If anyone were to ask me to stay, I would refuse.' Were is also used following 'as if' and 'as though' : 'The toddler wore the towel proudly, as though it were a Superman cape'. Were is also part of these fixed expressions: as it were, if I were you.

Q. 28 *What is the difference between the word 'into' and the words 'in to?' Which is the most appropriate and when?*

Ans. Whenever the 'to' is a particle of the infinitive, be sure to keep them separate:

See the following sentences :

(a) We dropped in to visit my friend.
(b) He just stepped in to pay the bill.
(c) You wouldn't want people walking into your dinner.

We use 'into' to express motion or direction as per following:

(a) He stared into her eyes.
(b) She walked into the store to say hello.
(c) She drove into the side of the garage.
(d) Let's invite them into dinner. Of course, I hope that helps.

Q. 29 *A misogynist hates women. What do you call a person who hates men?*

Ans. A misandrist. The word misandrist comes from Greek, mis-, a prefix meaning 'hate' + andr-, 'man' + -ist.

Q. 30 *Does a comma go after i.e. or e.g.?*

Ans. By rule, they are preceded by a mark of punctuation, usually a comma. Generally both are followed by a comma in American English, though not in British English. E.g. may also be followed by a colon, depending on the construction. In British English, it is often written as e.g. with comma omitted after it.

Q. 31 *Are there any English words that do not have vowels ?*

Ans. It depends what you mean by 'vowel' and 'word'. There are two things we mean by the word 'vowel': a speech sound made with the vocal tract open a letter of the alphabet standing for a spoken vowel (look up vowel for a more detailed definition). Cwm and crwth do not contain the letters a, e, i, o, u, or y, the usual vowels (*i.e.*, the usual symbols that stand for vowel sounds) in English. But in those words the letter 'w' simply serves instead, standing for the same sound that 'oo' stands for in the words boom and booth. Dr., nth (as in 'to the nth degree') and TV also do not contain any vowel symbols, but they, like cwm and crwth, do contain vowel sounds.

Shh, psst, and mm-hmm do not have vowels, either vowel symbols or vowel sounds. There is some controversy whether they are in fact 'words', however. But if a word is 'the smallest unit of grammar that can stand alone as a complete utterance, separated by spaces in written language and potentially by pauses in speech' (as it is according to The Cambridge Encyclopedia of Language), then those do qualify. Psst, though, is the only one that appears in the Oxford English Dictionary.

» Unit

2

Articles

Articles are members of determiners family. Articles are used before nouns.

Use of 'A' or 'An'

Article 'a' or 'an' is used before a singular noun. The choice between 'a' or 'an' is determined by **the first sound of pronunciation** (not by the letter of alphabet even it may be a, e, i, o, u) of the noun. If the first sound is a vowel, an, is used.

Look at the following sentences

(a) He is an honest man.
(b) He is a European.
(c) He is an MLA
(d) He is an SDO

The choice between a or an is determined by the word which immediately follows a or an. If it is pronounced with vowel sound, use an otherwise a.
(a) It was an extremely difficult situation.
(b) I need an eighty-feet-long iron rod.

Please note the following words and the use of 'a' or 'an' before them. Students generally commit mistake using them before these words:

Note the correct use of article a or an

1. an hour **2.** an hourly meeting
3. an hour's daybreak **4.** an honour
5. an honorary post **6.** an honourable person
7. an honest man **8.** an heir
9. an honorarium **10.** a house
11. a historical fair **12.** a humble person
13. a husband **14.** a heinous crime
15. a young man **16.** a ewe
17. a university **18.** a unity
19. a union **20.** a eulogy
21. a one rupee note **22.** a one eyed man
23. a uniform **24.** a useful book
25. a useful feature **26.** a unique decision
27. a united front **28.** a unified plan
29. a year **30.** a USA allay
31. an FO **32.** a forest officer
33. an MP/MLC **34.** a member of society
35. an IAS/IPS/ILO **36.** an SP/SDO
37. an M.A./M.Sc **38.** an RTS/RTC
39. an RC worker **40.** a UK ship/European

'A'/'An' and 'One'

Used as measure or numbers

When we are counting or measuring time, distance or weight, etc, then we can use either a/an or one for the singular.

$1 = a/one dollar $1000000
= a/one million dollars

But note this in the following sentence

(a) The rent is $100 a month.

(b) The a before month is not replaceable by one.

In other types of statement a/an and one are not normally interchangeable, because one + noun normally means one only not more than one and a/an does not mean this.

(a) A pen is no good. (It is the wrong sort of thing.)

(b) One pen is no good. (I need two or three.)

Special uses of 'One'

(a) One (adjective/pronoun) is used with **another/others.**

One (girl) wanted to read, another/others wanted to watch TV.

One day she wanted her lunch early, another day she wanted it late.

(b) One can also be used before day/week/month/year/summer/winter, etc. or before the name of the day or month to denote a particular time when something happened. Note the use of 'one' in the following sentenes

(i) One night there was a terrible earthquake.

(ii) One winter the snow fell heavily.

(iii) One day a message arrived.

(c) One day can also be used to mean at some future time or date, as following sentences

(i) One day you'll be sorry.

(ii) One day you will realise your mistake.

A/An and One (pronoun)

One is the pronoun equivalent of a/an.

(a) Did you get a ticket?

Yes, I managed to get one.

The plural of one used in this way is some, as in the following sentences

(a) Did you get tickets?

Yes, I managed to get some.

Definite Article : 'The'

The definite article 'the' is used in the following cases

1. **While speaking of a particular person or thing or one already referred to.**

(a) **The** purse contained a gold chain. **The** golden chain is very precious.

(b) **The** book you referred is out of print.

(c) I dislike **the** fellow who came here yesterday.

Exceptions

First and subsequent reference: When we first refer to something in written text, we often use an indefinite article to modify it. Read the following examples

(a) "I'd like a glass of orange juice, please," John said.

(b) "I put the glass of juice on the counter already," Shilpa replied.

When a modifier (adjective) appears between the article and the noun, the subsequent article will continue to be indefinite.

(a) "I'd like **a big glass** of orange juice, please," John said.

(b) "I put **a big glass** of juice on the counter already," Shilpa replied.

2. **When a singular noun is meant to represent a whole category or class**

(a) The dog is a faithful animal.

(Or we say: Dogs are faithful animals.)

(b) The banyan is a kind of big tree.

3. **'The' is used before superlatives.**

(a) She is the most beautiful girl in our college.

4. **'The' is used with the names of building, gulf, river, ocean, sea, etc.**

the Taj Mahal	the Persian Gulf
the Char Minar	the Pacific
the Ganga	the Red Sea
the Yamuna	the Thames

5. **'The' is placed only before the plural names of islands and the mountain ranges, chains of mountains, plural names of countries.**

the Netherlands, the Phillipines,
the Bahamas, the Lakshadweep islands
the Himalayas,
the Alps, and before certain other names.

'The' is not used before the name of countries but if the name of countries contains words like: States, Kingdom, Republic. For example, the USA, the USSR, the UK, the Republic of Ireland, the Domonican Republic.

(a) He went to Mexico.
(b) He is from the United States.
(c) The USA and the UK both agreed on this point.

6. 'The' is used before names consisting of adjective + noun (provided the adjective is not east, west etc.)
the Arabian Gulf, the New Forest,
the High Street

7. 'The' is also used before names consisting of noun + of + noun.
the Cape of Good Hope, the Bay of Biscay,
the Gulf of Mexico

8. 'The' is used before the adjectives east, west etc. + noun in certain names:
the east, west end the east,
West/Indies, the North/South Pole

9. 'The' is also used before the name of directions.
the east, the west, the north, the south

10. 'The' is used before the name of persons (family) in plural.
the Raymonds, the Ambanis, the Birlas

11. 'The' is used before the names of important, renowned books.
the Quran, the Ramayana, the Mahabharata
But we say:
Homer's Iliad, Valmiki's Ramayana,
Jaidev's Geet Govind.

12. 'The' is used before such common nouns that are names of things unique of their kind.
the sun, the earth, the sky, the world, the sea, the environment
(a) The sky is dark and the moon in shinning.
(b) The sea seems calm today.

1. In some cases we do not use 'the' before 'sea'.
   (a) We go to sea as sailors.
   (b) He is at sea now a days (on a voyage)
2. We can use 'the' before 'space' if it means place.
   (a) He tried to park his car there but the space was too small.
3. But if it means area beyond the earth's atmosphere, do not use the before it.
   (a) There are lacs of stars in space.

13. 'The' is used before terms referring to nationality or community.
the Indian, the French, the American,
the English

14. 'The' is used before a proper noun, only when it is qualified by an adjective.
the great Caesar, the immortal Shakespeare,
the brave Napolean.

15. 'The' is used with ordinals like
(a) He was the first man to stand up.
(b) The sixth chapter of this book is very interesting.
First, second, third ..... are called ordinals.
One, two, three.........are called cardinals.

16. 'The' is used before musical instruments and name of inventions.
(a) He can play the flute/the tabla/the harmonium well.
(b) Who invented the telephone?

17. 'The' is used before an adjective, when the noun represents a class of persons.
(a) The young will support the motion.
(b) The poor can be trusted.

18. 'The' is used before a common noun to give it the meaning of an abstract noun.
(a) The moralist in Gandhi, revolted against the injustice.
(b) The judge in her prevailed upon the wife and she sentenced her husband to prison..

19. 'The' is used before name of newspaper, community, political party, historical event, train, ship, aeroplane, etc.
(a) the Hindus, the Muslims, the Sikhs
(b) the BJP, the Congress, the Communist party
(c) the French Revolution, the Quit India Movement
(d) the Hindustan Times, the Indian Express
(e) the Intercity, the Rajdhani Express
(f) the Boeing, the Vikrant

20. When two or more nouns refer to one person, put 'the' before the first noun only. If both the nouns refer to two different persons or things, 'the' is used before both of them.
(a) The producer and financier was present there.
(producer and financier is one person)
(b) The producer and the financier were present there.
(producer and financier are two different persons)

21. 'The' is used as an adverb with a comparative.
(a) The more she gets the more she demands.
(b) The sooner you complete the better it is.

22. 'The' is used before comparative degree being used for selection or comparison.
(a) He is the stronger of the two.
(b) This is the better of the two novels.

23. When a person is referred by his designation, 'the' is used.
the Chairman, the Director, the President.
(a) All financial decisions will be taken by the chairman.
(b) It is the president who will take final decision in this case.

24. When the thing referred is understood, 'the' is used.
(a) Kindly return the book.
(That I gave you.)
(b) Can you turn off the light?
(The light in the room.)

25. 'The' is used in the following phrases also.
(a) What is the matter?
(b) Come to the point.
(c) She came to the rescue.
(d) Keep to the left.
(e) The market is hot with the rumour.
(f) He is in the wrong.

26. In phrases : go to the cinema, go to the theatre, 'the' is used.
(a) He went to the cinema yesterday.
(b) She is going to the theatre.

27. Before names of committee, club, foundation and trust, 'the' is used.
the Lions Club, the Rotary Club,
the United Nation, the WHO,
the Ford Foundation,
the Rajiv Gandhi Trust, etc.

28. When letters addressed to two or more unmarried sisters jointly, 'the' is used.
The Misses + surname
+ The Misses Smith.

Zero Article Situations

Students should learn the following points carefully to avoid the wrong use of articles.
Article is omitted in following cases

1. Before a proper noun
(a) Akbar was a great king.
(b) Bombay is a beautiful city.

When 'Article' is used before a proper noun, it becomes a common noun. Examples
(a) mumbai is the manchester of india.
(b) this man is a second sachin.

2. Before a common noun, used in its widest sense
(a) Man is mortal.
(b) What kind of bird it is?

3. Before Plural nouns referring a class in a general sense
(a) Bankers are generally honest.
(b) Lawyers are generally intelligent.

4. Before Abstract nouns that express qualities, state, feeling, actions
(a) Honesty is the best policy.
(b) Virtue is its own reward.

When abstract nouns, instead of referring qualities, express person or things possessing such qualities or express qualities of definite objects. They are preceded by article. **Examples**
(a) She possesses the cunningness of a fox.
(Here cunningness refers the quality of a definite object that is 'fox')
(b) He is a justice of peace ('Justice' stands for judge)
(c) He possesses the swiftness of a tiger.

5. Before material nouns
(a) Iron is a hard metal.
(b) Silver is a semi-precious metal.

When material noun express things instead of matter of which they are made they are representing' common noun', so they can be preceded by the article.
Examples
(a) He threw a stone on the cow.
(b) She threw a stick at the pig.

6. Before names of diseases like Fever, Cholera, Consumption, etc.
(But if the names of diseases are plural in their form, the article is generally uses as: the measles, the mumps.)

7. Before name of regular meals
breakfast, lunch, dinner
(a) He was invited to dinner.
But if the meal becomes particular article is used.
(b) The dinner hosted by the queen was superb.

8. **Before name of singlular things in kind: hell, heaven, God, Parliament, paradise (but, 'the Pope', the Devil are exceptions).**
   (a) He was condemned to hell.
   (b) The Pope delivered a religious speech.
   (c) He raised the question in Parliament.
   (d) May God grant him success!
9. **Before names of 'languages' or 'colours'.**
   (a) I do not know Hindi but know English.
   (b) He is learning French.
   (c) He likes red and blue.
10. **Before certain titles and names indicating the relationship.**
   Emperor Ashoka, Presidoent Bush, Dewan Bahadur.
   (a) Prince Charles is Queen Elizabeth's son.
   (b) President Kennedy was assassinated in Dallas.
   (c) Dr. Watson was Sherlock Holmes' friend.
   (d) He is Duke of York.

The Queen of England, the Pope are exceptions.

11. **Before a noun following the expression 'kind of'.**
   (a) What kind of girl is she?
   (b) What kind of boy is he?
12. **In certain phrases: to take breath, to set sail, to leave school, to lay seige, to catch fire, at home, in hand, at school, by water, at sunset, on earth, by land, by train, by car, on demand, in debt, in jest, etc.**
13. **Before nouns, which are plural in their meaning, though singular in form.**
   cattle, gentry, furniture, scenery, advice, information.
14. **Before names of public institutions (church, school, university, prison, hospital, court, etc.) if they are used, for the purpose they exist rather than actual building.**
   (a) He went to church (means, he went to church for saying his prayer).
   But note:
   He went to the Church and from there he took a bus. (Means he went to the place where building of the Church is situated)
   Ram goes to school daily at 10 a.m.
   He goes to college at 8 a.m. daily.
   (Here the purpose of going is for study.)
   I am going to the college, wherefrom I will catch the bus for Jaipur. (Here the purpose of going to college is not for the purpose the college is established.)
15. **When two or more descriptive adjectives qualify the same noun and adjectives are connected by 'and', the article is used before the first adjective only:**
   (a) This is a Hindi and English dictionary. (Here only one dictionary is referred to.)
16. **If two nouns refer to the same person or thing, the article is used before the first noun only, but if they refer to different persons or things, the article must be used with each noun.**
   (a) He is a better soldier than statesman.
   (b) He was a greater soldier than a statesman.
17. **Article is omitted after the 's possessive case.**
   (a) His brother's car, Peter's house.
18. **Article is omitted with professions:**
   (a) Engineering is a useful career.
   (b) He'll probably go into medicine.
19. **Article is omitted with years:**
   (a) 1947 was a wonderful year.
   (b) Do you remember 2000?
20. **No article is used before name of games, sports.**
   (a) I am playing cricket.
   (b) He is fond of playing tennis.
21. **No article is used before a noun when it is modified by either a possessive adjective or a demonstrative adjective.**
   (a) Do you like my shirt? (possessive adjective 'my')
   (b) I like this pen. (demonstrative adjective 'this')
22. **No article is used before a noun when it is preceded by a distributive adjective.**
   (a) Every student got a prize. (distributive adjective 'every')
   (b) Each student was present in the hall. (distributive adjective 'each')
23. **No article is used before number + noun.**
   (a) The train arrives at platform 7.
   (b) I want shoes in size 10.
24. **Work (= place of work) is used without definite article 'the'.**
   (a) He is on his way to work.
   (b) She is at work.
   (c) They haven't got back from work yet.
25. **Office (= place of work) needs 'the': He is at/in the office.**

(a) To be in office (without the) means to hold an official (usually political) position.
(b) To be out of office = to be no longer in power.

26. Definite article 'the' is omitted when speaking of the subject's or speaker's own town.
(a) We go to town sometimes to meet our mother.
(b) We went to town last year and remained there for a week.

27. 'Nature' when means environment, do not use article before it.
(a) If you interfere with nature you will suffer for it.

28. No article is used before name of 'season'.
(a) In spring we like to clean the house.
(b) She is planning to visit her parents in winter.

29. Definite article the is not used before 'Time of day' For example,
(a) We travelled mostly by night.
(b) We'll be there around midnight.

30. We can use definite article 'the' before sea in following cases:
We go to sea as sailors. To be at sea = to be on a voyage (as passengers or crew)
But to be at the sea = to be at the seaside.
We can also live by/ near the sea.

31. Names without 'the' : Names of many places especially names of important buildings and institutions consist of two words. First word is usually the name of a person or a place, we do not use 'the' before such names usually.
For example: Delhi Airport, Victoria Station, London Zoo, Jaisingh Palace, Indira Gandhi Airport, Edinburgh Castle, Jaipur Palace, etc.

32. Usually no article is used with the name of airlines, companies.
British Airways, Sony, IBM, KODAK, Indian airlines, etc.

» Exercises

Exercise 1

Fill in the blanks with articles where necessary.

1. He went to .... college to meet .... class teacher.
2. I will take .... tram from .... church.
3. He came and sat on .... bed.
4. He has already gone to .... bed.
5. Ram was appointed .... clerk.
6. Suresh was declared .... captain of our team.
7. Ramesh invited Sarla for .... dinner yesterday.
8. He organised .... nice lunch in honour of .... President.
9. .... dinner hosted by Ram was superb.
10. .... measles is .... contagious disease.
11. He died of .... cholera.
12. She has been suffering from .... fever for three days.
13. He can speak .... Hindi, but I can't speak .... English.
14. I like .... blue colour.
15. When I went .... home, Raja was watching .... TV.
16. I heard .... news on .... radio.
17. He is .... rich man, he always go by .... car.
18. Three per cent posts are reserved for .... disabled and two per cent for .... ex-servicemen.
19. He first went to .... Mexico and then to .... USA.
20. Ram took .... action with ....swiftness of .... tiger.

Solutions

(1) the, the (2) a, the (3) the (4) x (5) x (6) the (7) x (8) a, the (9) The (10) x, a (11) x (12) x (13) x, x (14) x (15) x, x (16) the, the (17) a, x (18) the, the (19) x, the (20) the, the, a

Exercise 2

Rewrite the following sentences after filling up the blanks with suitable articles, where necessary.

During .... first two years .... village project had .... awful time. .... mission had accepted .... use of .... farm from .... affluent landowner, and ....natives believed .... story that this land would be returned to ....owner after ten years. .... project never started.

Solutions

During the first two years the village project had an awful time. The mission had accepted the use of a farm from an affluent landowner, and the natives believed the story that this land would be returned to the owner after ten years. The project never started.

Exercise 3

Insert suitable articles wherever they are missing.

1. Pt. Jawahar Lal Nehru was .... first Prime Minister of free India.
2. Indian government wants to build......... strong India.
3. She has never touched .... onion.
4. After discussing this matter for .... hour or two we are sure to arrive at .... decision.
5. Pt. Nehru was...............great man. He struggled hard to attain freedom from ..... Britishers.

Solutions

1. the 2. a 3. an 4. an 5. the

Exercise 4

Rewrite the following sentences after filling up the blanks with suitable articles, where necessary.

Once there were elections. .... entire polling station seemed to be .... huge mass of humanity. Men and women all seemed to be quite conscious of their votes. I had seen .... old man insisting on the polling officer and he would not even return .... identity slip. Women had come in groups and were putting on colourful clothes .... polling stations assumed .... shape of .... fair and .... crowd also behaved likewise. It was really .... pleasure to see them in such .... jolly mood. It was ..... nice scene.

Solutions

Once there were elections. The entire polling station seemed to be a huge mass of humanity. Men and women all seemed to be quite conscious of their votes. I had seen an old man insisting on the polling officer and he would not even return the identity slip. Women had come in groups and were putting on colourful clothes. The polling stations assumed the shape of a fair and the crowd also behaved likewise. It was really a pleasure to see them in such a jolly mood. It was a nice scene.

Exercise 5

(A) Put appropriate articles in the blanks. **[*RAS 91*]**

...... businessman of ..... colony was shot dead by...... armed intruder on Sunday night. .... dead man's wife also received .... gunshot, but she is said to be progressing in ..... Civil Hospital. ..... murder is said to be ...... result of .... old dispute over some agricultural land between ...... killer and his victim.

(B) Put appropriate articles in the blanks. **[*RAS 92*]**

India is one of .... very big countries in the world. If a man takes ..... quickest train, he will take nearly............week to go from one end of India to the other. One who leaves Ramnad in ...... South on .... first day of .... month will perhaps get to Srinagar in .... North only about .... sixth of .... same month.

(C) Fill in the blanks with appropriate articles. **[*RAS 94*]**

Number..... hundred and two .... house, next door to us, is for sale. It's quite .... nice house with .... big rooms........ back windows look out on ....park. I don't know what......... price .... owners are asking. You could give them .... letter and make them .... offer.

Solutions

(A) a, the, an, The, a, the, The, the, an, the.
(B) the, the, a, the, the, a, the, the, the.
(C) x, the, a, x, the the/a, x, the, a, an.

Spotting the Errors

Find the errors and justify your answer.

1. Of the two (A)/solutions the second was (B)/definitely better (C).
2. I have been (A)/informed that (B)/Mr. Clinton visits Rajasthan (C)/following month (D). **(*RRB*)**
3. In the field of invention (A)/the credit goes to a man (B)/who convinces the world (C)/with his arguments (D)/not to the man who simply thinks (E).
4. He claims to be a scientist (A)/but in reality he (B)/does not know even (C)/A B C of science (D).
5. Her father (A)/forbade her to go (B)/to cinema (C)/with Mohan (D).
6. It is an impossile task (A)/to calculate number (B)/of creatures living (C)/on earth (D).
7. The man (A)/is the only living creature (B)/that can speak (C)/and smile (D).

8. He is an atheist (A)/but today he is going (B)/to the Church (C)/for offering prayer (D). **(CDS)**
9. You should not spend (A)/good part of the day (B)/in marketing only (C).
10. Whatever little (A)/milk left in the bottle (B)/was drunk by your cat (C).
11. She leads (A)/a luxurious life (B)/so she visits everywhere (C)/by a car (D).
12. The principle instructed (A)/the girls to return (B)/to the college (C)/before the sunset (D).
13. You must (A)/be true to your words (B)/in order to enjoy (C)/the real reputation in the life (D). **(CDS)**
14. Sarla is the (A)/most beautiful girl (B).
15. It was an insight (A)/and perseverance of the lady doctor (B)/that many women were (C)/able to lead normal life (D).
16. It is a pity (A)/that the daughter of millionaire (B)/is involved in (C)/the bank robbery (D).
17. He was in a trouble (A)/when he saw (B)/a truck running (C)/towards his car (D). **(RRB)**
18. The fruits of (A)/all the modern luxuries (B)/lie in the science (C).
19. I advised him (A)/to take the heart (B)/in all odd circumstances (C).
20. Little knowledge (A)/of computers that she possessed (B)/proved a boon for her (C)/in getting a job (D). **(Bank PO)**
21. We (A)/saw (B)/a elephant (C)/in the zoo (D)/No error (E).
22. It is (A)/a most (B)/beautiful (C)/painting of the gallery (D).
23. Mr. Gaurav Sharma (A)/is (B)/coming to (C)/dinner (D).
24. I (A)/go (B)/to cinema (C)/every sunday (D)/No error (E).
25. He (A)/went there (B)/a hour (C)/ago (D)/No error (E).
26. He (A)/always speaks (B)/truth (C).
27. Kashmiri (A)/shawls (B)/are made of (C)/the hair of sheep (D).
28. The Tajmahal (A)/is (B)/situated (C)/at the Agra (D)/ No error (E)/.
29. Bible (A)/said that (B)/the sun (C)/goes round the earth (D).
30. An horse (A)/is (B)/running (C)/in the ground (D)/No error (E).
31. An European (A)/dish (B)/is (C)/very famous (D)/No error.
32. Rome (A)/was (B)/not built (C)/in a day (D)/No error (E).
33. Ritika (A)/helps (B)/poor and (C)/the sick people (D)/No error (E).
34. The Sapna (A)/is a very (B)/beautiful (C)/girl (D)/No error (E).
35. I (A)/saw (B)/an one rupee note (C)/on the road (D)/No error (E).
36. The boy (A)/is (B)/swimming (C)/in the pool (D)/No error (E).
37. Here is a red (A)/shirt (B)/which Sapna gave me (C)/ yesterday (D)/No error (E). **(Bank PO)**
38. Shatabdi express (A)/runs (B)/very (C)/fast (D)/No error (E).
39. Parul (A)/was also invited (B)/to the lunch hosted by the queen, (C)/at her cottage yesterday (D)/No error (E). **(BSRB)**
40. My uncle (A)/is (B)/a (C)/S.P. (D)/No error (E).
41. Gold (A)/is (B)/an useful (C)/metal (D)/No error (E).
42. This is (A)/a good dress (B)/but (C)/that's a better one (D)/No error (E).
43. Rupam (A)/presented me (B)/a ring (C)/. The ring is lost (D)/ No error (E). **(CDS)**
44. The Punjabi (A)/is (B)/a sweet language (C)/of Punjab (D)/ No error (E). **(Bank PO)**
45. Adnan Sami (A)/is the (B)/most popular (C)/singer in Indian film industry (D)/No error (E). **(CDS)**
46. The sun (A)/rises (B)/in (C)/east (D)/No error (E).
47. The teaching (A)/profession (B)/is (C)/good for women (D)/ No error (E). **(Bank PO)**
48. The milk (A)/is (B)/good (C)/for health (D)/No error (E).
49. I (A)/think (B)/a baby (C)/is crying (D)/No error (E).
50. Kunal (A)/was (B)/sent to (C)/a prison (D)/No error (E).
51. I (A)/will go (B)/there (C)/by train or by bus (D)/No error (E).
52. My parents (A)/sometimes (B)/comes to school (C)/to see the principal (D)/No error (E). **(RRB)**
53. Riya (A)/went home (B)/very late (C)/last Monday (D)/No error (E).
54. The winters (A)/are (B)/generally very (C)/cold here (D)/No error (E).
55. The monkeys (A)/jump (B)/on (C)/the trees (D)/No error (E).

56. The dog (A)/is (B)/a (C)/faithful animal (D)/No error (E).

57. Chief Minister (A)/will (B)/decide (C)/the matter (D)/No error (E).

58. Kshitiz (A)/is (B)/a (C)/honest boy (D)/No error (E).

59. The sun (A)/rises in (B)/the east (C)/is an universal truth (D)/No error (E).

60. Times of India (A)/is a most popular (B)/news paper (C)/of these days (D)/No error (E). **(RRB)**

61. Three children (A)/died (B)/in a (C)/bus accident yesterday (D)/No error (E).

62. The Mahatma Gandhi (A)/was (B)/also called (C)/ 'Bapu' (D)/No error (E). **(BSRB)**

63. Chinese (A)/are (B)/fondof (C)/chowmin (D)/No error (E).

64. Taj Mahal (A)/is a (B)/beautiful (C)/building in Agra (D)/No error (E). **(BSRB)**

65. The capital (A)/of (B)/U.K.is (C)/London (D)/No error (E).

66. My mother (A)/is cooking (B)/in a (C)/kitchen (D)/No error (E).

67. The teacher (A)/called a (B)/last boy (C)/standing in the queue (D)/No error (E).

68. The apple (A)/a day (B)/keeps (C)/the doctors away (D)/No error (E).

69. The more (A)/I learn history (B)/the more (C)/I get bored (D)/No error (E). **(RRB)**

70. The intelligent (A)/should (B)/help (C)/the duffer (D)/No error (E).

71. Shreya (A)/gave (B)/me (C)/the watch (D)/No error (E).

72. In the conclusion it (A)/may be said (B)/that the writer has surpassed (C)/the ethical norms (D). **(RRB)**

73. It is the most (A)/important point that (B)/you have to (C)/understand well (D). **(BSRB)**

74. He said to me, (A)/I think you (B)/will never (C)/a turn a traitor (D).

75. Ramesh told me (A)/that he first went (B)/to the Mexico and (C)/then to the Netherlands (D). **(BSRB)**

» Answers

1. (C) Place the before better.

2. (D) Place the before following.
Here following month has become particular.

3. (B) Replace a man, by the man.
Here man has become particular.

4. (D) Place the before ABC, to emphasise 'the' is necessary.

5. (C) Place the before cinema.

6. (B) Place the before number.

7. (A) Delete the before man.

8. (C) Delete the before Church.

9. (B) Place a before good part. Note that here a good part of the day is used as a phrase.

10. (A) Place the before little.

11. (D) Delete a before car, (by car, by water, by plane etc.)

12. (D) Delete the before sunset. Note that before sunset, before noon, after day break, are some phrases that don't take the in between.
He returned home after sunset.
He returned home after the sun had set.

13. (D) Delete the before life.
He is leading a happy life.

14. (A) Replace 'the' by 'a'
Here most is used in the sense of 'very'.

15. (A) Replace 'an' by 'the'.

16. (B) Place a before millionaire.
Millionaire is a countable noun.

17. (A) Delete a before trouble. Note: in danger, in trouble, in detail, in debt, in compasion, infact are some of the phrases that don't take article between.

18. (C) Delete the before science.

19. (B) Delete the before heart.

20. (A) Place the before little.

21. (C) Here 'a' is used with elephant instead of 'an'. An elphant is correct.

22. (B) It is a most beautiful painting. Use the before most, being superlative.

23. (E) no error.

24. (C) I go to the cinema every Sunday. When 'club', 'cinema', 'pictures', 'theatres', are used for their primary purpose of entertainment. 'The' is used before them.

25. (C) Replace 'a' by 'an'. Here "an" will be used instead of 'a' because 'h' is silent.

26. (C) He always speaks the truth.

27. (A) The Kashmiri shawls 'The' is used before nouns which name the inhabitants of a country or city collectively.

28. (D) Delete 'The' before Agra, being proper noun.

29. (A) The Bible said. 'The' is used before the names of renowned books of religion or literature.

30. (A) A horse is running in the ground. 'A' is used with the singular countable nouns which pronounced with the consonant sound.

31. (A) 'A' European dish is very famous. Here 'European' begin with vowel 'E' even then its sounds 'yoo' or 'u'.

32. (E) 'A' is used with certain numerical terms to give the sense of 'one'.

33. (C) Ritika helps the poor and the sick people.

34. (A) Sapna is a very beautiful girl. 'The' is not used before proper noun.

35. (C) I saw a one rupee note on the road. 'A' is used with nouns pronounced with consonant sound.

36. (A) A boy is swimming in the pool. 'A' is used with the singular countable nouns.

37. (A) Here is the red shirt which Sapna gave me yesterday. Red shirt has become particularised.

38. (A) The Shatabdi Express. 'The' is used before the names of well-known trains.

39. (E) No error. 'The' is used before particular meals.

40. (C) My uncle is an S.P. Here, 'An' is used before a consonant which sounds like a vowel.

41. (C) Gold is a useful metal. Before useful we should put a instead of an.

42. (E) 'A' is used with positive and comparatives but not with superlatives.

43. (E) 'The' is used before a noun which is repeated after it has been introduced once.

44. (A) Punjabi 'The' is not used before name of the language.

45. (E) No error. 'The' is used with the superlative degree of adjective.

46. (D) in the east. 'The' is used with the name of 'directions' like east, west, north, south.

47. (E) 'The' is used with the professions like the nursing ,the medical profession.

48. (A) Milk is good for health. 'The' article are omitted before proper nouns, uncountables etc. in general.

49. (C) the baby.

50. (D) Kunal was sent to prison. The article is omitted before Church, prison, hospital, college, school and bed, when the visit to these place is for the purpose they are primarily built.

51. (E) The Article is omitted before modes of transportation or travel. Always use by bus,by car, by train, etc.

52. (C) Insert 'the' before school. When the visit to places : school, church, hospital, prison are for the purpose other than they are primarily built, always use 'the' before these nouns.

53. (E) no error 'The' is not used before name.

54. (A) Remove the before 'winters'. Do not use article before name of the seasons.

55. (A) Monkeys jump on the trees. The article is omitted before plural countable nouns when they tell about class or cast etc.

56. (E) 'The' is used before a singular countable noun meant to represent a whole class or kind.

57. (A) Insert 'The' before Chief Minister. Use the before designation.

58. (C) Kshitiz is an honest boy. Here 'an' is used before as word beginning with silent 'H'.

59. (D) The sun rises in the east is a universal truth. 'A' is used before a word beginning with the sound 'u' (pronounced as 'yoo' or 'u')

60. (A) The 'Times of India' .... 'The' is used before the name of the newspapers and magazines.

61. (E) No Error.

62. (A) Delete 'the' before Mahatma Gandhi. Article is not used before proper noun.

63. (A) The Chinese........... 'The' is used before nationality.

64. (A) The Taj Mahal .... 'The' is used such name of Monuments.

65. (C) 'The' is used before name of country UK, USA, etc.

66. (C) My mothor is in the kitchen. Here 'The' is used before the noun which can be understood easily.

67. (B) The teacher called the last boy.......... 'The' is used before the ordinals.

68. (A) An apple...... 'An' is used here before a word beginning with a vowel (a, e, i, o, u) sound.

69. (E) 'The' is here used twice, with comparative to show that two things increase or decrease in the same proportion.

70. (E) Here 'the intelligent means intelligent person and the 'duffers' means duffer persons.

71. (D) Shreya gave me a watch. 'A' is used before a word beginning with a consonant.

72. (A) Delete the before conclusion.

73. (A) Replace the by a most used in the sence of 'very'.

74. (D) Delete a before turn. Turn is an inchoative verb.

75. (C) Delete the before Mexico.

» Unit

3

The Rules and Sequence of Tense

In English, there are three basic tenses : present, past, and future. Each has a perfect form, indicating completed action; each has a progressive form, indicating ongoing action; and each has a perfect progressive form, indicating ongoing action that will be completed at some definite time.

Tense and Time

Tense is a grammatical concept. It indicates time of an action or state. Present tense usually refers to present time. Past tense refers to past time. Time unlike tense is not a grammatical concept. It is a natural thing. Tense is related to the language (English). Time does not have any relation as such. Hence tense and time are different things. There are many sentences of present or past tense that may indicate future time actions. Many sentences of future tense may denote present time action.

Look at the following examples

1. He leaves for USA next month.
   (Sentence of simple present, refers future time)
2. She is coming on next Sunday.
   (Sentence of present progressive, indicating future time)
3. I wish I knew his address.
   (Sentence of past tense, indicate present time)
4. Will you have a cup of tea?
   (Sentence of future simple, indicate present time)

Forms of Verbs

Verb is classified into regular and irregular verbs.

Regular Verbs Those verbs which form their past tense and past participle by adding 'ed' are called regular verbs.

Irregular Verbs Those verbs which form their past tense and past participle in a different way. We are giving below three lists of irregular verbs.

List I Verbs which have all the three forms same.

List II in which two forms are same.

List III Verbs which have all the three forms different.

List I All three forms are the same

Base Form	Past Tense	Past Participle
bet	bet	bet
burst	burst	burst
cast	cast	cast
cost	cost	cost
cut	cut	cut
hit	hit	hit
hurt	hurt	hurt

Base Form	Past Tense	Past Participle
let	let	let
put	put	put
read	read	read
rid	rid	rid
set	set	set
shut	shut	shut
split	split	split
spread	spread	spread

List II Two of the forms are the same

Base Form	Past Tense	Past Participle
abide	abode	abode
awake	awoke	awoke
beat	beaten	beaten
become	became	become
bend	bent	bent
bleed	bled	bled

List III All three forms are different

Base Form	Past Tense	Past Participle
arise	arose	arisen
be	was/were	been
bear	bore	born
begin	began	begun
bite	bit	bitten
blow	blew	blown
break	broke	broken
choose	chose	chosen

Following verbs have a different past participle (adjectival) form, which can only be used as adjective.

Verb	Normal Past Participle	Adjectival Past Participle
drink	drunk	drunken
melt	melted	molten
prove	proved	proven
shave	shaved	shaven
shear	sheared	shorn
shrink	shrunk	shrunken

For the sake of convenience two more forms of verbs are in use these days. These are :

1. Present participle form (V-4) : Base form (V-I) + ing. For example—going, playing, writing etc.
2. Infinitive (V-5) : To + base form (V-I). For example— to play, to go, to write, etc.

Tense : Important Rules

Rule 1 In present indefinite sentences, the number and person of the subject play very important roles.

If the subject is singular number third person, affix 's' or 'es' to the verb. If the verb ends in any of the following :

ss, o, x, z, sh, ch

add, es instead of s with the verb.

Like : pass, miss, do, mix, fix, whiz, buzz, catch, fetch, clash, rush, etc.

(a) I **fetch** a glass of water.
He **fetches** a glass of water.

(b) I **pass.**
She **passes.**

Rule 2 When the main verb is in future, use present simple in clauses with if, till, as soon as, when, unless, before, until, even if, in case and as.

(a) We shall wait till she arrives.
(b) I shall not go there even if it rains.
(c) I shall go to market, if it rains.
(d) I shall go to Jaipur in case she asks me.

Rule 3 Present simple must be used instead of the present continuous with verbs of perception (feel, hear, smell, etc.), verbs of cognition (believe, know, think, etc.), verbs of emotion (hope, love, hate, etc.) which cannot be used normally in the continuous form.

	Incorrect	Correct
1.	We are seeing with our eyes.	We see with our eyes.
2.	Are you hearing a strange noise?	Do you hear a strange noise?
3.	We are smelling with our nose.	We smell with our nose.
4.	I am feeling you are worng.	I feel you are wrong.
5.	The water is feeling cold.	The water feels cold.
6.	The coffee is tasting bitter.	The coffee tastes bitter.
7.	How much am I owing you?	How much do I owe you?
8.	I am hating it.	I hate it.

9. He is resembling his brother.	He resembles his brother.
10. I am believing in God.	I believe in God.
11. I am loving her.	I love her.
12. I am remembering him.	I remember him.

But these verbs can be used in progressive form in following cases :

1. The session judge is hearing our case.
2. We are thinking of going to USA next year.
3. He is minding (looking after) the children, while his wife is away.
4. I am seeing my lawyer today.
5. I am having some difficulties with this puzzle.
6. Are you forgetting your manners? (A reminder)
7. The dog is smelling the packet of food.
8. She is tasting the sauce to find out whether it is tasteful or not.
9. The doctor is feeling the pulse of the patient.
10. He is looking for his glasses.

Important : Stative verbs when used in progressive form become dynamic verbs.

1. We see with our eyes. (permanent stative verb 'see')
2. I am seeing the teacher tomorrow. (temporary dynamic verb)
3. I have a maruti car. (permanent stative verb 'have')
4. I am having a nice time (temporary dynamic verb)

Rule 4 One must not use adverbs of past time like yesterday, last year, last month, ago, short while ago, etc. with present perfect tense.

(a) He has completed his book yesterday.

Incorrect

He completed his book yesterday.

Correct

(b) I have met her three days ago.

Incorrect

I met her three days ago. *Correct*

Rule 5 Use of since/for. Students commit mistake in using 'since' or 'for'. Please note, 'for' is used for 'period of time' and 'since' is used for 'point of time'. With morning, evening, etc. use since and with 'some time', 'hours', 'months' ,etc. use 'for'

Rule 6 If two or more actions take place in sequence, we use simple past to denote the actions. (Otherwise past perfect is used to denote the earlier action.) This is usually used with conjunction 'before'.

(a) He switched on the light before he opened the door.

(b) The train started just before I reached the station.

(c) He changed his dress before he went to bed.

Rule 7 The use of simple past with 'wish' and 'if only' shows 'unreal past' and present state of things.

(a) I wish I were a millionaire. (I am not a millionaire.)

(b) I wish I knew her. (I don't know her.)

(c) If only I knew her. (I don't know her.)

Rule 8 In following structure the use of simple past denotes 'unreal past' and present time situation.

(a) It is time we went home.
(It is time for us to go home.)

(b) It is time you finished.
(It is time for you to finish.)

(c) It is high time we left.
(It is proper time for us to leave.)

Rule 9 Use of past continuous with 'when' and 'while'.

'When' is usually used when one action was completed and another action was going on.

(a) When he arrived, his wife was washing her clothes.

(b) Where were you living, when the war broke out?

'While' is used when two actions were going on at a time.

(a) While she was cooking, I was washing the clothes.

(b) While I was singing, Ramesh was reading.

Rule 10 Past perfect is used when we look back on earlier action from a certain point in the past.

(a) I had just poured myself a glass of milk when the phone rang.

(b) She had completed her work, before I reached there.

Rule 11 The past perfect is also used for an action which began before the time of speaking in the past and which stopped some time before the time of speaking.

(a) He had served in a bank for twenty years, then he retired and established his business. His children were now well settled.

Here we cannot use 'either' 'since' or the past perfect continuous.

Rule 12 Past perfect continuous is used when the action began before the time of speaking in the past, and continued up to that time.

(a) It was now eight and she was tired because she had been cleaning the house since dawn.

Rule 13 Simple future is used for an action that will take place in future and for habitual actions.

(a) I shall write a letter.
(b) He will go to Delhi on next Monday.
(c) Winter will come again.
(d) Everyone will die one day.

Rule 14 When two actions are to take place on some future time, we use future Perfect for the action completed first and present simple for the action to be completed afterwards.

(a) The student will have left the class before the teacher comes.
(b) The Principal will have started before I reach there.

Rule 15 Future perfect is also used for such incidents and actions which we presume that another person already had the knowledge of that incident or the action is already completed by that time.

(a) You will have heard about Mother Teresa.
(b) He will have read the newspaper so far.
(c) They will have heard about the accident by this time.

Sequence of Tense

Sequence of Tense The sequence of tenses are the principles, which govern the tense of the verb in subordinate clause vis-a-vis the tense of the verb in the principal clause. The rules which determine the tense of the subordinate clause, if the tense of the principal clause is present or past or future, are studied under sequence of tense rules, as mentioned below.

Rule 1 If the principal clause is in the past tense the subordinate clause should also be in the past.

(a) My father assured me that he would buy a bike for me.
(b) He failed because he didn't work hard.
(c) He asked me what she was reading.
(d) I thought that I could win the race.
(e) Ram said that he would come on Monday.

Exceptions

(i) A past tense in the principal clause may be followed by a present tense in the subordinate clause when the sub ordinate clause expresses a universal truth, mathematical calculation, historical fact, moral guidelines, habitual fact or something that has not yet changed. In such cases the tense of the subordinate clause is not governed by the tense of principal clause (The subordinate clause is usually in the present tense in such cases.) For example :

(a) He said that the earth revolves round the sun.
(b) We learnt at school that the truth always triumphs.
(c) He said that two and two is four.
(d) Krishna told in Geeta that life is not victory but battle.
(e) Ram said that man is mortal.
(f) I was happy to note that India is progressing.
(g) Newton discovered that the apple falls because of gravitational force of earth.

(ii) If the subordinate clause is introduced by a conjunction of comparison such as 'than', 'as well as' etc. then a past tense in the principal clause may be followed by any tense in the subordinate clause as per the sense of the statement. Furthermore any tense in the principal clause can be followed by any tense in the subordinate clause. For examples :

(a) He loved me more than he loved you.

(b) he loved me more than he loves you.
(c) He loved me more than he will love you.
(d) He will love you more than he loved me.
(e) He has loved you more than he loved me.
(f) He will love you more than he loves me.
(g) She helps you as well as she helped me.
(h) She will help you as well as she has helped me.

(iii) If the subordinate clause is an adjective clause, in that case it may be in any tense even if the Principal clause is in past tense.
(a) I visited the place where the accident took place.
(b) I visited the village where he lives.
(c) I visited the hotel where she will stay.

Rule 2 A present or future tense in the principal clause may be followed by any tense.

(a) He says that she passed the examination.
(b) He says that she will come tomorrow.
(c) Ram says that he likes that girl.
(d) Ram will say that Sita is a beautiful girl.
(e) Ram will say that he didn't like that girl.
(f) He will say that he will pass the examination positively.

Exception

If the subordinate clause is introduced by if, till, as soon as, when, unless, before, until, even if, as, etc. and the principal clause is in simple future, in that case the verb in the subordinate clause must be in present simple.

(a) We shall not go to market if it rains.
(b) He will wait till she comes.
(c) We will start as soon as the taxi arrives.
(d) I shall ask him, when he meets me.
(e) I shall not go before he comes.
(f) I shall not help him unless he asks me.
(g) I shall help him even if he doesn't ask me.
(h) He will start as the taxi arrives.

» *Exercises*

Exercise 1 (Present Tense)

Correct the following sentences

1. Sarita dule go to office at 10 a.m. daily
2. She has been cooking meal from 7 a.m.
3. Nisha is playing tabla for 2 hours.
4. Rani have just come from college.
5. They have been residing here since four years.
6. They goes to field at 5 a.m.
7. Ram do his work in time.
8. He drink coffee in the morning.
9. Mr Sharma teachs us English grammar.
10. Sakshi catchs the train at 8 o'clock.
11. He flys kite on Sunday.
12. We takes bath together in the river.
13. We have been playing for 12 o'clock.
14. Raheja has been singing since one hour.
15. He pass all the tests without fail.

Solutions

1. change 'go' to 'goes'
2. change 'from' to 'since'
3. change 'is' to 'has been'
4. change 'have' to 'has'
5. change 'since' to 'for'
6. change 'goes' to 'go'
7. change 'do' to 'does'
8. change 'drink' to 'drinks'
9. change 'teachs' to 'teaches'
10. change 'catchs' to 'catches'
11. change 'flys' to 'flies'
12. change 'takes' to 'take'
13. change 'for' to 'since'
14. change 'since' to 'for'
15. change 'pass' to 'passes'

Exercise 2 (Past Tense)

Correct the following sentences

1. Tejpal and his friends were playing chess for two hours.
2. Sita had been cooking for 2 o'clock.
3. Rahim gone to the market.
4. The teacher was taught us Hindi at that time.
5. Ramesh had took your purse.
6. The girl had been crying since an hour.
7. We had been playing chess since two hours.
8. The train arrived before we reached there.
9. The patient had fainted than the doctor came.
10. My friends was coming by bus.

Solutions

1. change 'were' to 'has been'
2. change 'for' to 'since'
3. change 'gone' to 'went'

4. change 'taught' to 'teaching'
5. change 'took' to 'taken'
6. change 'since' to 'for'
7. change 'since' to 'for'
8. insert 'had' after 'train'
9. change 'than' to 'before'
10. change 'was' to 'were'

Exercise 3 (Future Tense)

Following sentences have some errors/mistakes. Correct them.

1. The students will have left the school before the principal came.
2. The train will have arrived before I reaches the station.
3. He would have reached here before the sunset.
4. Will he has completed his work by tomorrow?
5. Will he have not repaired the car by 7 p.m.?
6. He will has been waiting for you for three days.
7. Will not he have been waiting for you since morning?
8. Ram will have not been playing at this time tomorrow.
9. Will the girls have played the game at 7 p.m?
10. He will have finish the work by 8 p.m.

Solutions

1. Change 'came' to 'come' will.
2. Change 'reaches' to 'reach'.
3. Change 'would' to 'will'.
4. Change 'has' to 'have'.
5. Change 'has' to 'not have' ?
6. Change 'has' to 'have'.
7. Change 'will not' to 'Won't' ?
8. Change 'have not' to 'not have'.
9. Change 'at' to 'by' ?
10. Change 'finish' to 'finished'.

Spotting the Errors

Find the errors and justify your answer :

1. I came to (A) / know that (B)/ his father has died (C)/ three days ago (D)/.
2. When you will find (A)/ out a solution (B)/ to this problem (C)/ you will be awarded a prize (D)/.
3. Before the alarm had stopped (A)/ ringing (B)/ Nisha had telephoned (C)/ the police (D)/. **(BSRB)**
4. This is (A)/ the first time (B)/ that I see such (C)/ an interesting movie (D)/. **(NDA)**
5. Whenever he is coming (A)/ here, he brings (B)/ many (C)/ gifts for me (D)/.
6. Nowadays (A)/ he teaches English (B)/because the teacher of English (C)/has gone for a month's leave (D)/. **(Bank PO)**
7. 'It is high time (A)/ you are starting (B)/ this, business' (C)/ said Ram to Mahesh. (D)/.
8. I will let you know (A)/ as soon as I (B)/will get (C)/ any news in this regard (D)/.
9. When I will (A)/ cross fifty, my (B)/ wife will cross (C)/ forty-five (D)/.
10. The secret of his good health (A)/ lies in the fact (B)/ that he is getting up early (C)/ and goes to bed early (D)/. **(NDA)**
11. The students sitting on the dais (A)/ studied here (B)/for three years, but (C)/they have never created any problem (D)/. **(BSRB)**
12. A philogynist is a person (A)/ who loves woman (B)/ but a mysogynist is a person (C)/ who is hating woman (D)/. **(CDS)**
13. It is appearing to me (A)/ that you are (B)/ trying to destabilise (C)/ the presen committee (D)/.
14. I have been knowing her (A)/ for many years (B)/ but I don't know (C)/ where she works (D)/.
15. If he would have done this, (A)/ he would have done wrong (B)/ and would have deceived (C)/ many of his relatives (D)/.
16. The victim tried to tell us (A)/ what has happened (B)/ but his words (C)/ were not audible (D)/. **(BSRB)**
17. I want you to (A)/ pick up the box of eggs gently (B)/ and kept it in (C)/ the corner carefully (D)/.
18. She came to (A)/ the party much (B)/ later than (C)/ I expect (D)/.
19. I lived here (A)/for five years (B)/ so I know about the (C)/ problems of this colony (D)/. **(NDA)**
20. The chairman had not taken (A)/ any decision until (B)/ he had studied (C)/ the case thoroughly (D)/.
21. They got everything (A)/ ready for the visitors (B)/ long before (C)/ they reached there (D)/. **(NDA)**
22. He switched on (A)/ the light before (B)/ he entered (C)/ the room (D)/. No error (E).

23. I have been admiring (A)/ her for the (B)/ voice with which (C)/ she is gifted (D)/. **(CDS)**
24. He was with me (A)/ uptil now, (B)/so don't (C)/ punish him for the delay (D)/.
25. Several survey reports (A)/indicate that (B)/the number of (C)/ drug addicts is grown gradually. (D)/. **(Bank PO)**
26. 'Here is coming up Bachchan!,' (A)/ said he (B)/ when he was (C)/ waiting for him (D)/.
27. I could not recall (A)/ when she has told me (B)/ about her (C)/ affair with Gopal (D)/.
28. Four and four (A)/ always made eight (B)/ cannot (C)/ be questioned by anyone (D)/. **(Bank PO)**
29. She hopes to (A)/ become an engineer (B)/ after she will complete (C)/ her education (D)/.
30. I have been working (A)/ in this firm (B)/ for the last twenty years (C). No error (D).
31. When you will find (A)/ a solution to this problem (B)/ you will be able (C)/ to get this project (D). **(CDS)**
32. The teacher told us (A)/ that we should remain (B)/ in the hostel (C)/ if it rains (D).
33. I could not recall (A)/ what she has advised me (B)/ in this matter (C).
34. By this time tomorrow (A)/ she has had reached (B)/ there positively(C).
35. I will inform (A)/ you as soon as (B)/ I will get any news (C)/ about his health (D). **(BSRB)**
36. A recent survey (A)/ indicates (B)/ that the number of drug addicts (C)/ grew day by day (D).
37. Before the alarm (A)/ had stopped ringing (B)/ Reena had pulled up the shade (C).
38. If I was you (A)/ I would have told (B)/ the Principal (C)/ to keep his mouth shut (D). **(CDS)**
39. I want you (A)/ to pick up the box (B)/ of glasses gently (C)/ and kept it on the table carefully (D).
40. The victim tried (A)/ to tell us what has happened (B)/ but his words (C)/ were not audible (D). **(BSRB)**
41. It is appearing to me (A)/ that you are working against (B)/ your friends (C).
42. A misogynist is (A)/ a person who is hating woman (B)/ but a philogynist is a person (C)/ who loves woman (D).
43. The secret of his (A)/ good health lies (B)/ in the fact (C)/ that he is getting up before sunrise (D).
44. He said to me, (A)/ 'It is high time (B)/ you are starting (C)/ this new business' (D). **(BSRB)**
45. I came to know (A)/ that your father (B)/ has died (C)/ last month (D).
46. If we had Ramesh (A)/ in our team, we (B)/ would have won the match (C). **(Bank PO)**
47. My friend said to me, (A)/ 'When have (B)/ you come here?' (C).
48. I have been knowing (A)/ him for the last five years (B)/ but now I don't know (C)/ where he lives (D).
49. He lived here (A) since 1998 (B)/ so he knows everything (C)/ about this town (D). **(Bank PO)**

» Answers

1. (C) Replace 'has died' by 'died'. Don't use past time adverbs with present perfect.
2. (A) delete 'will'. We should not use 'will' after when in such sentences.
3. (A) Replace 'had stopped' by 'stopped'.
4. (C) Replace 'I see' by 'I have seen'. Present perfect tense is used in such constructions. For example,
   (a) This/that/it is the first/second/third .... time/chance.
   (b) That/this/ it is the only ....
   (c) This/that/it is the best/worst/finest/most interesting.
5. (A) This is a habitual act, use present indefinite. Whenever he comes here....
6. (B) Replace 'he teaches' by 'he is teaching'.
7. (B) 'You started' is the correct phrase.
8. (C) Replace 'will get by 'get'.
9. (C) Replace 'I will cross' by 'I cross'.
10. (C) Replace 'he is getting up' by 'he gets up' a habitual act use present indefinite.
11. (B) Replace 'studied' by 'have studied'.
12. (D) Replace 'who is hating' by 'who hates'.
13. (A) Replace 'It is appearing' by 'It appears'.
14. (A) Replace 'I have been knowing' by 'I have known'.
15. (A) Replace 'If he would have done this' by 'If he had done this'.
16. (B) Replace 'has happened' by 'had happened'.
17. (C) Replace 'kept it' by 'keep it'.
18. (D) Replace 'I expect' by 'I had expected'.
19. (A) Replace 'I lived' by 'I have lived'.

20. (A) Replace 'The chairman had not taken' by 'The chairman did not take'.
21. (A) Replace 'They got' by 'They had got'.
22. (E) No error.
23. (A) Replace 'I have been admiring' by I admire. Please note that normally, know, admire, adore, trust, believe, rely, hope, etc. are not used in continuous form.
24. (A) Replace 'He was with me' by 'He has been with me'. The use of uptil now shows present tense.
25. (D) Replace 'is grown' by 'is growing'.
26. (A) Replace 'Here is coming' by 'Here comes'. In exclamatory sentence present indefinite is usually used. For Example,
    Here comes the tram! There works Rita!
27. (B) Replace 'she has told' by 'she had told'. The whole sentence is in past.
28. (B) Replace 'made' by 'makes'.
29. (C) Replace 'she will complete' by 'she has completed'.
30. (D) No error.
31. (A) Delete 'will'. In such construction we should not use will after; when, it, before, after, until.
32. (D) Replace 'if it rains' by 'if it rained'.
33. (B) Replace 'she has' by 'she had'.
34. (B) Replace 'has had reached' by 'will have reached'. This is sentence of future perfect tense.
35. (C) Delete 'will'.
36. (D) Replace 'grew' by 'is growing'. The sentence is in present tense.
37. (B) Replace 'had stopped' by 'stopped'.
38. (A) Replace 'If I was' by 'If I were'.
39. (D) Replace 'kept' by 'keep'. The whole sentence is in present tense.
40. (B) Replace 'What has happened to' by 'What had happened'.
41. (A) Replace 'It is appearing' by 'It appears'. Appear is a verb of perception, avoid its use in progressive form.
42. (B) Replace 'is hating' by hates. Hate is also a verb of perception, avoid its use in progressive form.
43. (D) Replace 'he is getting up' by 'he gets up'.
44. (C) Replace 'You are starting' by 'You started'.
45. (C) Replace 'has died' by 'died'.
46. (A) Replace 'we had' by 'we had had'. For example,
    If he had come to me, I would have helped him.
    If he had had in our group, we would have won the shield.
47. (B) Replace 'when have' by 'when did'.
48. (A) Replace 'I have been knowing' by 'I have known'. Verbs: know, see, appear, believe should not be used in progressive form in normal course.
49. (A) Replace 'lived' by 'has been living'.

»Unit

4

Noun

Noun : Rules

There are certain rules to be followed for the correct use of nouns.

Rule 1 Some nouns always remain in plural form. They take plural verb. These nouns have no singular form. These are

assets, alms, amends, annals, archives, ashes, arrears, athletics, auspices, species, scissors, trousers, pants, clippers, bellows, gallows, fangs, eyeglasses, goggles, belongings, breeches, bowels, braces, binoculars, dregs, earnings, entrails, embers, fetters, fireworks, longings, lees, odds, outskirts, particulars, proceeds, proceedings, riches, remains, shambles, shears, spectacles, surroundings, tidings, tactics, tongs, vegetables, valuables, wages, etc.

(a) The proceeds were deposited in the court.
(b) He sees dissidents as the dregs of society.
(c) Alms were given to the beggars.
(d) The embers of the fire were still burning.

'Means' in the sense of 'income' always takes a plural verb. In the sense 'way to achieve some end' means takes a singular verb .When 'a' or 'every' is used before 'means' it is singular.

(a) My means were reduced substantially.
(b) Every means is good if the end is good.

Rule 2 Some nouns look plural in form but have singular meaning. Some nouns take singular verb. These are : news, innings, politics, summons, physics, economics, ethics, mechanics, mathematics, measles, mumps, rickets, billiards, draughts, etc.

(a) No news is good news.
(b) Draughts is a good game.
(c) Economics is a good subject.
(d) Ethics demands honesty in working.

Rule 3 Some nouns look singular but have plural meaning. Such nouns take plural verbs. These are : cattle, clergy, cavalry, infantry, poultry, peasantry, children, gentry, police, etc.

(a) Cattle are grazing in the field.
(b) Our infantry have marched forward.
(c) There are no gentry in the colony.
(d) Police have arrested the thieves.

Rule 4 Some nouns are always used in singular. These are uncountable nouns. We should not use article 'a' and 'an' with such nouns. These are

scenery, poetry, furniture, advice, information, hair, language, business, mischief, bread, stationery, crockery, luggage, baggage, postage, knowledge, wastage, money, jewelry, breakage, etc.

(a) The scenery of Darzeeling is very charming.
(b) I have no information about her residence.
(c) He transported his furniture by train.
(d) The mischief committed by him is unpardonable.
(e) His hair is black.
(f) He has no knowledge of grammar.

We cannot pluralise such nouns by adding 's' or 'es'. For example: It is incorrect to write sceneries, informations, furnitures, hairs.
We can make such nouns countables in the following way :
(a) He gave me a piece of information.
(b) All pieces of information given by her were reliable.
(c) Many kinds of furniture are available in that shop.
If hair is used as countable it can be pluralised. For example : one hair, two hairs.
(a) I need your two grey hairs.
(b) I need three hairs of a black horse.

Rule 5 Some nouns have the same form in singular as well as in plural. For example : deer, fish, crew, family, team, jury, carp, pike, trout, aircraft, counsel, swine,vermin, etc.

(a) Our team is the best.
(b) Our team are wearing their new uniform.
(c) The jury is considering its judgement.

Rule 6 Some nouns have plural meaning. If a definite numeral adjective is used before them they are not pluralised. For example : pair, score, gross, stone, hundred, dozen, thousand, million, billion, etc.

(a) I have two pair of shoes.
(b) I have two hundred rupees only.

Otherwise these nouns can well be pluralised: dozens of women, hundreds of people, millions of dollars, scores of shops, many pairs of shoes, thousands millions, etc.

Rule 7 If the same noun is repeated after preposition, the noun will be singular.

(a) Town after town was devastated.
(b) Row upon row of pink marble looks beautiful.

Rule 8 If a numeral adjective and a fraction are used with a noun, the noun is used with the numeral and the noun will be in sigular. For example:

(a) He gave me one rupee and a half.
(b) She gave me two rupees and a quarter.

Avoid the following structure

(a) He gave me one and a half rupees. *Incorrect.*
(b) She gave me two and a quarter rupees. *Incorrect.*

If the numeral adjective and the fraction refer to the multiplication, the noun be placed in the end (after the fraction) and must be plural.
(a) Your deposits has grown two and a half times within two years.
(b) My salary has increased three and a quarter times within three years.

Rule 9 Some nouns are known as *common gender* nouns. They can be used for either sex : male or female. These are called dual gender nouns. Such nouns are : teacher, student, child, clerk, candidate, advocate, worker, writer, author, leader, musician, politician, enemy, client, president, person, neighbour, etc. When these are used in singular, use third person singular masculine (his) pronoun with them.

(a) Every candidate should write his (not her) name.
(b) Every person should perform his (not her) duty.
(c) No one should abuse his (not her) neighbour.

each, either, everyone, everybody, no one, nobody, neither, anybody are also common gender pronouns.

Rule 10 Some nouns are used for specifically for feminine gender only. Like: blonde, maid, midwife, coquette, virgin, etc.

Nowadays nouns 'bachelor' and 'virgin' are being used for masculine and feminine gender as well.
(a) Ram is a bachelor.
(b) Sita is a bachelor.
(c) Rahim is a virgin.
(d) Rehana is a virgin.

Rules of Changing Masculine Noun to Feminine Noun

Rule 1 Some nouns can be changed to feminine by adding 'ess' with its masculine form. For example

Masculine	Feminine
author	authoress
baron	baroness
count	countess
giant	giantess
host	hostess
heir	heiress

Rule 2 Some nouns can be changed to feminine by removing the vowel and consonant, and adding 'ess' as per following :

Masculine	Feminine
actor	actress
tiger	tigress
benefactor	benefactress
director	directress
hunter	huntress
negro	negress

Rule 3 In some cases some words in its masculine forms are changed and 'ess' is added as per following

Masculine	Feminine
abbot	abbess
duke	duchess
emperor	empress
god	goddess
governor	governess
master	mistress

Rule 4 In case of compound masculine nouns, some changes are made in first or second word.

Masculine	Feminine
man-servant	maid-servant
milk-man	milk-maid
doctor	lady-doctor
peacock	peahen
washerman	washerwomen
land-lord	land-lady
buck-rabbit	doe-rabbit
father-in-law	mother-in-law
brother-in-law	sister-in-law
step-father	step-mother

Rule 5 Masculine and Feminine genders of some important foreign words are given below. There is no rule for such nouns.

Masculine	Feminine
administrator	administratis
shepherd	shepherdess
beau	belle
czar	czarina
executor	executrix
hero	heroine
lad	lass
monsieur	madam
prosecutor	prosecutrix
signor	signora
sultan	sultana
testator	testatrix

Some Typical Plural Nouns (Number)

Latin words Some Latin words ending in 'um' are pluralised by dropping 'um' and adding 'a'.

Singular	Plural
addendum	addenda
agendum	agenda
datum	data
dictum	dicta
ovum	ova
memorandum	memoranda
erratum	errata
stratum	strata

Agenda and data are used in singular as well as in plural :

(a) The agenda has been finalised.

(b) The agenda of the meeting are drawn to day.

(c) The data is incomplete.

(d) More data are required.

Medium when used in the sense of means or agency, its plural form is media.When used in the sense of spiritual its plural form is mediums.

Important : Note the following Latin words, which are pluralised by adding 's' only.

Singular	Plural
asylum	asylums
forum	forums
museum	museums
pendulum	pendulums
premiums	quorum quorums
petroleum	petroleums
formula	formulae/formulas

1. Some Latin words ending in 'us' are pluralised by changing 'us' to 'i'.

Singular	Plural
radius	radii
locus	loci
syllabus	syllabi
genius	genii

2. Some Greek words ending in 'is' are pluralised by changing 'is' to 'es'.

Singular	Plural
analysis	analyses
basis	bases
crisis	crises
thesis	theses
hypothesis	hypotheses
parenthesis	parentheses

3. Some Greek words ending in 'on' are pluralised by changing 'on' to 'a'.

Singular	Plural
phenomenon	phenomena
criterion	criteria

4. Other Important nouns

Singular	Plural	Singular	Plural
If	Ifs	But	Buts
I	I's	T	T's
5	5s	10	10s
P	P's	MP	MPs
BA	BAs	MA	MAs
ATM	ATMs	UPC	UPCs

5. Compound nouns are pluralised by adding 's' with the main word.

Singular	Plural
brother-in-law	brothers-in-law,
bed-room	bed-rooms
commander in-chief	commanders in chief,
step-daughter	step-daughters
maid-servant	maid-servants,
peahen	peahens
peacock	peacocks
mother-in-law	mothers-in-law
sister-in-law	sisters-in-Law
member of Parliament	members of Parliament
man servant**	men servants
woman conductor**	women conductors
man nurse**	men nurses
woman engineer**	women engineers
man hater*	man haters
woman lover*	woman lovers
man lover*	man lovers

There is difference among the plurals of nouns with single star (*) and with double stars (**)

6. There are twelve nouns, ending in 'f' or 'fe', which drop the f or fe and add 'ves'.

Singular	Plural	Singular	Plural
calf	calves	life	lives
half	halves	leaf	leaves
wife	wives	self	selves
thief	thieves	knife	knives
wolf	wolves	shelf	shelves
loaf	loaves	sheaf	sheaves

Hoof, scarf and wharf take either 's' or 'ves' in their plural form.

hoofs hooves, scarfs scarves, wharfs wharves

Exceptions

Singular	Plural	Singular	Plural
belief	beliefs	proof	proofs
chief	chiefs	roof	roofs
cliff	cliffs	safe	safes

7. Following eight nouns are pluralised by changing inside vowels in them.

Singular	Plural	Singular	Plural
man	men	mouse	mice
woman	women	louse	lice
foot	feet	goose	geese
tooth	teeth	dormouse	mormice

8. Some nouns have two plurals with different meanings.

brother	- brothers	sons of the same parent
	brethren	members of a society or community.
cloth	- cloths	unstitched cloth
	clothes	stitched clothes (garments)
die	- dies	stamps used for printing and coining
	dice	small cubes used in games
index	- indexes	tables of contents in a book
	indices	signs used in algebra

Use of Apostrophe with 's'

1. You can form the possessive case of a singular noun that does not end in 's' by adding an apostrophe and 's'. We should use apostrophe in the following situations only :

living things → Mohan's book
a cow's horn
a woman's purse

thing personified → week's holiday
earth's surface

space time or weight → a day's leave
well's water
a pound's weight

certain dignified objects → the court's orders
at duty's call
a razor's edge
a needle's point

familiar phrases → at his wit's end
at a stone's throw

If there are hissing sounds (sounds of 'sh' or 's') ending a word, use apostrophe without 's' with such words. For example : For Jesus' sake, for conscience' sake, the roses' fragrance, etc. (It can be noted that if we use apostrophe with 's' with such words it couldn't be pronounced well.)

2. You can form the possessive case of a singular noun that ends in 's' by adding an apostrophe alone or by adding an apostrophe and 's', as in the following examples

(a) The bus's seats are very comfortable.
(b) The bus' seats are very comfortable.
(c) The film crew accidentally crushed the platypus's eggs.
(d) The film crew accidentally crushed the platypus' eggs.

3. You can form the possessive case of a plural noun that does not end in 's' by adding an apostrophe and 's' as in the following examples

(a) The children's books were scattered on the floor of the porch.
(b) The men's cricket team will play as soon as the women's team is finished.

4. You can form the possessive case of a plural noun that does end in 's' by adding an apostrophe.

(a) The concert was interrupted by the dogs' barking, the ducks' quacking and the babies' squalling.
(b) The janitors' room is downstairs and to the left.
(c) My father spent many hours trying to locate the squirrels' nest.

5. Do got use apostrophe with possessive pronouns like his, hers, yours, mine, ours, its, theirs, etc.

yours faithfully, yours truly, ours garden, his pen, hers purse, their room.

6. Use apostrophe with the last word in following titles.

(a) Governor-general's instructions.
(b) Commander-in-chief's orders.
(c) My son-in-law's sister.
(d) Ram and Sons's shop.

7. Avoid double apostrophe in a sentence.

(a) My wife's secretary's mother has expired. *Incorrect*
The mother of my wife's secretary has expired. *Correct*
(b) Mrs Kuwrani's now chairperson of society's proposal was rejected. *Incorrect*
The proposal of Mrs Kuwrani, now chairperson of society was rejected. *Correct*

8. Apostrophe with 's' is used with anybody, nobody, everybody, somebody, anyone, some one, no one, every one.

(a) Everyone's concern is no one's concern.
(b) Every body's business is nobody's business.

If else is used after these words, use apostrophe with else as per following :
(a) I can rely on your words, not somebody else's.
(b) I obey your orders and nobody else's.

Exercises

Exercise 1

Correct the following sentences

1. Her hairs are curly.
2. Our elders gave us many advices.
3. I have many work to do.
4. Sita has sold all her furnitures
5. She gave me informations about this bank.
6. The sceneries of Himachal Pradesh are very charming.
7. The peoples are hard working.
8. The cattles are grazing in the field.
9. I want a paper.
10. I bring fruits and vegetables from the market.
11. You must continue your study.
12. These news are false.
13. They go to Agra during the summer vacations.
14. Her spectacle is very nice.
15. She has a twenty rupees note.

Solutions

1. Her hair is curly
2. Our elders gave us many pieces of advice
3. I have much work to do.
4. Sita has sold all her furniture.
5. She gave me information about this bank.
6. The scenery of Himachal Pradesh is very charming.
7. The people are hard working.
8. The cattle are grazing in the field.
9. I want a piece of paper.
10. I bring fruit and vegetables from the market.
11. You must continue your studies.
12. This news is false.
13. They go to Agra during the summer vacation.
14. Her spectacles are very nice.
15. She has a twenty rupee note.

Exercise 2

Correct the following sentences

1. He got only passing mark.
2. Ram was true to his words
3. Ten miles are a long distance.
4. They want two dozens apple.
5. I want two pairs of white shoes.
6. Rahul has finished two-third of his work.
7. The chair's legs are broken.
8. Good night, I am so glad to meet you.
9. There is no space in the car.
10. We should help the poors
11. She left for Delhi by 8.30 'o'clock bus.
12. One of his son is a teacher.
13. Amazing stories are an interesting book.
14. This is my son's in law house.

Solutions

1. He got only pass marks.
2. Ram was true to his word.
3. Ten miles is long distance.
4. They want two dozen apples.
5. I went two pair of white shoes.
6. Rahul has finished two-thirds of his work.
7. The legs of the chair are broken.
8. Good evening, I am so glad to meet you.
9. There is no room in the car.
10. We should help the poor.
11. She left for Delhi by 8.30 bus.
12. One of his sons is a teacher.
13. Amazing stories is an interesting book.
14. This is my son-in-law's house.

Exercise 3

Correct the following sentences

1. I brought my furnitures by goods train
2. I saw two beautiful fishes in the pond.
3. Thomson's poetries are very charming.
4. Is your scissors dull?
5. Light travel faster than sound.
6. All the furnitures of my house have been stolen.
7. A poet and writer are dead.
8. The committee was divided on this issues.
9. Mathematics are not a dificult subject.
10. My sympathies are always with the poor.
11. The mother both carried her son and daughter from the burning house.
12. My sister serves in boy's school.
13. Rohan's and Mohan's house is very far from here.
14. There are many news published in local paper.
15. The teacher has taught the alphabets.

Solutions

1. I brought my furniture by goods train.
2. I saw two beautiful fish in the pond.
3. Thomson's poetry is very charming.

4. Are your scissors dull?
5. Light travels faster than sound.
6. All the furniture of my house have been stolen.
7. A poet and writer is dead.
8. The committee was divided on this issue.
9. Mathematics is not a dificult subject.
10. My sympathy is always with the poor.
11. The mother carried both her son and daughter from the burning house.
12. My sister serves in boys' school.
13. Rohan and Mohan's house is very far from here.
14. There are many items of news published in the local paper.
15. The teacher has taught the letters of alphabet.

Exercise 4

Correct the following sentences

1. Please reply your's faithfully.
2. I go for a two miles walk daily.
3. She loves either you or I.
4. There are four breads in the kitchen.
5. One should not hate the poors.
6. The magistrate passed order of his release.
7. She has committed not one but many mischiefs.
8. The first inning is going to over now.
9. There is no place in this compartment.
10. He bought some stationeries.
11. My mother's brother's son has come.
12. There are a few peoples who are really honest.
13. Give me ten pices.
14. There were no gentries in that function.

Solutions

1. Please reply, yours faithfully.
2. I go for a two-mile walk daily.
3. She loves either you or me.
4. There are four pieces of bread in the kitchen.
5. One should not hate the poor.
6. The magistrate passed orders of his release.
7. She has committed not one but many acts of mischief.
8. The first innings is going to be over now.
9. There is no room in this compartment.
10. He bought some stationery.
11. The son of my mother's brother has come.
12. There are few people who are really honest.
13. Give me ten pice.
14. There were no gentry in that function.

Exercise 5

Correct the following sentences

1. He is a sixty years old man.
2. A five men committee had a three hours meeting yesterday.
3. An all parties meeting was called to consider the drought situation in the country.
4. There is two ways traffic here, so no problem of traffic blockage.
5. How can our country accept the two nations theory?
6. He has gone to market to purchase vegetable.
7. He said, 'Riches has wings'.
8. I asked him where was his spectacles.
9. She said that she was suffering from measle.
10. She said, 'Please give him an alm'.

Solutions

1. He is a sixty-year old man.
2. A five men committee had a three-hour meeting yesterday.
3. An all party meeting was called to consider the drought situation in the country.
4. There is two-way traffic here so no problem of traffic blockage.
5. How can our country accept the two-nation theory.
6. He has gone to market to purchase vegetables.
7. He said, 'Riches have wings'.
8. I asked him where were his spectacles.
9. She said that she was suffering from measles.
10. She said, 'Please give him alms'.

Exercise 6

Correct the following sentences

1. Shelley's poetries are great.
2. I saw beautiful sceneries in Kashmir last year.
3. He has purchased new machineries.
4. He said, 'He has purchased very costly crockeries'.
5. There were very heavy traffics on the road.
6. She has bought very beautiful furnitures.
7. He gave me many informations.
8. I am going to purchase some stationeries.
9. Ram said, 'The hair of Sita are black'.
10. This house is made of bricks and stones.

Solutions

1. Shelley's poetry is great.
2. I saw beautiful scenery in Kashmir last year.
3. He has purchased new machinery.
4. He said, 'He has purchased very costly crockery.'
5. There was very heavy traffic on the road.
6. She has bought very beautiful furniture.
7. He gave me a lot of information.
8. I am going to purchase some stationery.
9. Ram said, 'The hair of Sita is black'.
10. This house is made of brick and stone.

Exercise 7

Correct the following sentences

1. Cities after cities were destroyed by the army.
2. Hours after hours were passed, but she didn't turn up.
3. Ram said, 'I beg from doors to doors daily'.
4. Ships after ships were sailing by those days.
5. Rows upon rows of pink marble are soothing to the eyes.
6. I gave her three and a half apples.
7. The meeting was held for three and a quarter hours.
8. The length of this hall is three times and a half to that hall.
9. His salary is two times and a half to that of mine.
10. I have two and a half rupees only.

Solutions

1. City after city was destroyed by the army.
2. Hour after hour was passed but she didn't turn up.
3. Ram said, 'I beg from door to door daily.'
4. Ship after ship was sailing by those days.
5. Row upon row of pink marble is soothing to the eyes.
6. I gave her three apples and a half.
7. The meeting was held for a three hours and a quarter.
8. The length of this hall is three and a half times to that hall.
9. His salary is two and a half times to that of mine.
10. I have two rupees and a half only.

Exercise 8

Correct the following sentences

1. What the peoples think, I can't say?
2. Who owns these poultries?
3. He is my cousin brother.
4. How many 3s are there in 31313.
5. How many cattles you have?
6. I have only ten five rupees's notes.
7. He has written a nice poetry.
8. Today I have received two month's wages.
9. What is this book's price.
10. There are only two females in the garden.

Solutions

1. What the people think, I can't say?
2. Who owns these poultry?
3. He is my cousin.
4. How many 3's are there in 31313.
5. How many cattle you have?
6. I have only ten five-rupee notes.
7. He has written a nice poem. or
He has written nice poetry.
8. Today I have received two months wages.
9. What is the price of this book?
10. There are only two women in the garden.

Exercise 9

Correct the following sentences

1. There are three childrens in the park.
2. He gave me many informations.
3. Ram brought his furnitures by goods train.
4. Every candidate should write their names neatly.
5. Your's faithfully
P. K. Sharma.
6. I want to purchase ten knifes.
7. Three young mans and two young womans were present in the hall.
8. How many MP's were present in the meeting.
9. This is a girl's hostel.
10. My son's-in-law sister is coming tomorrow.

Solutions

1. There are three children in the park.
2. He gave me many pieces of information.
3. Ram brought his furniture by goods train.
4. Every candidate should write his name neatly.
5. Yours faithfully
P. K. Sharma.
6. I want to purchase ten knives.
7. Three young men and two young women were present in the hall.
8. How many MPs were present in the meeting.
9. This is a girls' hostel.
10. My son-in-law's sister is coming tomorrow.

Spotting the Errors

Find the errors and justify your answer

1. He acted not (A)/ as per my advice (B)/ but somebody else (C).
2. Pakistan's problems (A)/ are also as (B)/ serious as (C)/ that of India (D).
3. When I reached (A)/ at the gate of his (B)/ house I found his (C)/ locking up the gate (D). ***(Bank PO)***
4. Many of the question (A)/ appeared in this question paper (B)/ are too difficult (C)/ to solve (D).
5. I visited (A)/ Ram's and Sita's house (B)/ and found the couple missing (C). ***(SSC)***
6. All the girls students (A)/ are advised to (B)/ attend the meeting positively (C).
7. She gave me (A)/ two important informations (B)/ I had been waiting for(C)/ the last two months (D).
8. The English teacher(A)/ gave him a home work (B)/ to complete that (C)/ by night positively (D). ***(BSRB)***
9. She could not complete (A)/ even the two-third (B)/ of the book (C)/ owing to her busy schedule (D).
10. All the woman teachers (A)/ are agitating (B)/ against the haughty attitude (C)/ of the Principal(D).
11. He informed that (A)/ he had lost a packet (B)/ of the hundred (C)/ rupees notes (D). ***(CDS)***
12. He has ordered (A)/ bricks for the proposed (B)/ shopping complex (C).
13. She has ordered (A)/ two dozens of copies (B)/ of English Book by Mr. Gupta (C).
14. She uses a good (A)/quality of shampoo (B)/so her hairs are (C)/black (D). ***(Income Tax)***
15. I known nothing (A)/ about her (B)/ whereabout (C).

» Answers

1. (C) Replace else by else's. Use of apostrophe is necessary here.
2. (D) Replace India by India's. We are to compare the problem of Pakistan with the problems of India, so use of apostrophe is necessary.
3. (C) Replace 'his' by 'him'. Here locking is used as a participle, so objective case pronoun will be used. For examples :
   Swimming is a good exercise.
   I found him swimming in the pool.
4. (A) Replace question by questions. After phrases : 'of the' like 'one of the','many of the', plural noun is used.
5. (B) Replace Ram's and Sita's by Ram and Sita's. When two nouns showing the possession of one thing only, we should use apostrophe at one noun and that is the latter noun.
6. (A) Replace girls students by girl.
7. (B) Replace two important informations by two important pieces of niformation. Please note that 'information' is a uncountable noun, we can't use it like; one, two or three informations.
8. (B) Replace 'gave him a home work' by 'gave him home work'. Please note 'home work' is uncountable, so we can't use a with it.
9. (B) Replace two-third by two-thirds.
10. (A) Replace woman teachers by women teachers. For examples :

Man supervisor	Men supervisors
Woman cleaner	Women cleaners

11. (D) Replace rupees by rupee.
12. (B) Replace bricks by pieces of brick. Please note, brick, stone, iron chalk are uncountable material nouns.
13. (B) Replace two dozens of copies by two-dozen copies.
14. (C) Replace hairs by 'hair'. Normally hair is used in singular.
15. (C) Replace 'whereabout' by 'whereabouts' (address).

Unit

5

Pronouns

Pronouns are words which are used in the place of nouns. Normally pronoun stand for (pro + noun) or refer to a noun, an individual or individuals or thing or things (the pronoun's antecedent) whose identity is made clear earlier in the text.

Kinds of Pronouns

Personal Pronouns

Personal pronouns refer to persons or things. Personal pronouns change form according to their different uses in a sentence.

Personal Pronoun : Use and Rules

1. **A pronoun should clearly refer to the noun it stands for.**

When it is not obvious to which antecedent a pronoun refers, the sentence should be corrected. This can be done either by repeating the noun or by rewriting the sentence to make the meaning clear.

(a) My friend was there with her aunt. She was wearing a red saree. *Incorrect*
My friend was there with her aunt. My friend was wearing a red saree. *Correct*
or My friend, wearing a red saree, was there with her aunt. *Correct*

(b) The children stared at the dogs. They were ready to jump. *Incorrect*
The children stared at the dogs. The dogs were ready to jump. *Correct*
or The children stared at the dogs, which were ready to jump. *Correct*

2. **When the verb 'to be' is immediately followed by a personal pronoun, the pronoun must be in the subjective case.**

It is I. That was he.

Nowadays this rule is usually ignored. The verb 'to be' is also being followed by the objective form of the pronoun. Thus, in informal English the sentence 'It is I' would usually be expressed 'It is me', and the sentence 'That was he' would usually be expressed 'That was him'. Both are also acceptable these days. Strictly speaking the use of subjective form of pronoun is grammatically correct.

3. **When a personal pronoun is the object of a verb, the pronoun must be in the objective case.**

They like me. We respect you.

4. **A noun or pronoun which forms part of a prepositional phrase is said to be the object of the preposition. Personal pronouns in the objective case are used as objects of prepositions.**

(a) Please give the copy to him.
(b) They went with her.

The underlined pronouns are the objects of the prepositions **to, with.**

5. **Possessive adjectives : The personal pronouns have two possessive forms. One form shows possession by preceding a noun, it is referred as a possessive adjective, since, like an adjective, it describes the thing to which the noun refers. The possessive**

adjectives must agree with their antecedents.

Look at the following sentences :

(a) The boy obeys his father.

(b) The girl likes her mother.

(c) The bird sat on its nest.

6. **Possessive adjectives used with gerunds : When a gerund is preceded by a personal pronoun, the pronoun must be in the form of a possessive adjective.**

(a) The girl said that **her** writing had improved.

(b) The boy entertained the guests with **his** singing.

In the above examples, the gerunds are underlined, and the possessive adjectives are printed in bold type.

7. **Possessive pronouns : The possessive form of a personal pronoun which is called a possessive pronoun, can be used in place of a noun.**

(a) He did not bring his briefcase, but I brought mine.

(b) Because I forgot my pen, she lent me hers.

In the above sentences, the possessive pronouns are underlined.

Except for the pronoun **mine**, all of the possessive pronouns end in **s**. However, it should be noted that, unlike possessive nouns, the possessive personal pronouns are not spelled with an apostrophe. Care should be taken not to confuse the possessive form its with the contraction it's, which stands for it **is** or **it has.**

8. **Pronoun follows 'let': When a pronoun follows 'let', we use the objective form of the pronoun. We should not use subjective form after 'let'.**

Let you and I decide the matter once for all.

Incorrect

Let you and me decide the matter once for all.

Correct

9. **Different person pronouns with the same verb : If pronouns of different persons are used with the same verb in a sentence, they should be placed in the following sequence :**

If all the pronouns are in singular form then the good manners demand that second person pronoun should come first and then the third person.The first person should take the last position, i.e. 2 + 3 +1.

(a) You, he and I are partners.

(b) He and I are good friends.

If pronouns are in plural forms then the sequence should be 1+2+3, it means the first person plural pronoun is followed by second and third person plural pronouns.

(a) We and you cannot live together.

(b) We, you and they can purchase that complex.

(c) Sometimes the sentence have some apologetic sence or negative sense or sense of some errors committed, etc., in such sentence the good manners demand; to accept the guilt first by the speaker that means by the first person. In such case the sequence should be 1+2+3.

(a) I and you are responsible for the loss.

(b) You and he spoiled the party.

(c) I and he will beg sorry for the misconduct.

10. **If a pronoun refers to more than one noun or pronoun of different persons, it must be of the first person plural in case, nouns or pronouns are first and second person and if nouns or pronouns referred by the pronoun are second and third person, it must be second person plural. In case of nouns or pronouns of first and third person, the pronoun must be first person plural.**

II + I	--------------	I person plural
II + III	--------------	II person plural
III + I	--------------	I person plural

Example :

(a) You and I have done our job.

(b) You and he have completed your job.

(c) He and I have done our duty.

(d) You he and I have completed our duty.

11. **If a collective noun is used as a unit denoting a unitary action as a whole, the pronoun used is singular and in neutral gender.**

(a) The crew revolted and murdered its captain.

(b) After three days, the jury gave its verdict.

If the collective noun denotes separation or division, the pronoun used is plural.

(a) The jury were divided in their opinions.

(b) The Government decided to revise their plans outlays.

12. When two or more nouns are joined by 'and' the pronoun used would be plural.

(a) Ram and Mohan went to their school.
(b) Suresh and his family members have completed their work.

If both the nouns joined by 'and' denotes the same person, the pronoun used would be sigular.

The collector and magistrate is negligent in his duty.

13. When two singular nouns are joined by and, and preceded by each or every, the pronoun used would be singular.

(a) Every teacher and every boy was in his room.
(b) Each officer and each clerk has joined his duty.

14. Singular pronoun and singular verb is used with; Each, Either and Neither.

(a) Each of the students is ready to do his duty.
(b) Either of the two students gets his gift.
(c) Neither of them gets his turn.

15. Singular pronoun is used when two or more singular nouns are joined by 'or', 'either.....or', 'neither.....nor'.

(a) Ram or Shyam should deposit his dues.
(b) Either Ramesh or Ganesh lost his purse.
(c) Neither Ram nor Shyam has completed his work.

But if one noun is plural, then the pronoun should be plural and plural noun should be placed near the verb.
(a) Either the principal or the teachers failed in **their** duty.
(b) Neither the teacher nor the students have done **their** work.

Pronoun : 'It'

'It' is used

1. **For thing without life**
   (a) Here is your pen. Please take it.
2. **For Animals**
   (a) He has a cat. It is very beautiful.
   (b) I have a dog. It is very faithful.
3. **For young child (if sex differentiation is not referred)**
   (a) When he saw the child, it was playing.
   (b) The baby has spoiled its dress.
4. **'It' is used to emphasise a noun in following type of sentences :**
   (a) It is you, who can solve this problem.
   (b) It was I, who called you.
   (c) It was at Shimla, where the agreement was signed.
   (d) It is the place where he was murdered.
5. **'It' is also as Indefinite nominative :**
   (a) It rains. (b) It snows.
   (c) It thunders. (d) It blows.
6. **'It' is also used for time, whether, etc.**
   (a) It is 7 'o'clock.
   (b) It is fine.
   (c) It is winter.
   (d) It is summer.
7. **'It' is also used in exclamatory expressions.**
   (a) What a beautiful bird it is!
   (b) What a large building it is!
8. **'It' is also used in following type of expressions.**
   (a) It is easy to find faults with others.
   (b) It is confirm that he is wrong.
   (c) It is doubtful whether she will join here.
   (d) It is uncertain that she will come.
   (e) He is telling what is not true : as he knows it.
   (f) He deserved the award : as we knew it.
   (g) I think it is wrong to travel without proper ticket.
   (h) I consider that it is pity to waste time.

   It is also called an Impersonal pronoun.

'It' and 'This'

'This' is used for introducing a person or for things. 'This' also refers to things that are nearby either in space or in time. We also use 'this' for informing telephone numbers to the caller and introducing the broadcasting channels. 'This' shows intimacy.

(a) This is my friend.
(b) This is a cat.
(c) This is All India Radio.
(d) This is my brother.
(e) This is 2345714.
(f) This is BBC/Voice of America.

We cannot use 'this' for time, weather, etc., 'it' is used for the purpose.

(a) It is 7 o'clock.
(b) It is very cold today.
(c) It is morning.
(d) It is winter.
(e) It is raining.
(f) It is 7:30 by my watch.

Reflexive Pronouns

The reflexive pronouns (ending in -self) are used when the action denoted by the verb is directed towards the thing referred to by the subject. The reflexive pronouns shows that the subject also receives the action of the verb. This use of reflexive pronouns is illustrated in the following examples.

(a) She washed herself thoroughly before putting on new dress.

(b) Did you hurt yourself?

This means that whenever there is a reflexive pronoun in a sentence there must be a person to whom that pronoun can 'refer'.

Avoid the use of reflexive pronoun (ending in -self) where they are neither appropriate nor necessary.

(a) Ram and I are responsible for this decision.

(b) This matter will be decided by me.

(c) If you have any questions, please contact me or Ramesh.

Reflexive Pronouns : Use and Rules

1. **When pronouns are combined, the reflexive will take either the first person or, when there is no first person, the second person.**

(a) Ram and I have deceived ourselves about purchasing a house.

(b) You and Ram have ruined yourselves.

2. **Transitive verbs take object with them. If a transitive verb has no object, the reflexive pronoun fills the place of object. Such commonly used verbs are: avail, absent, enjoy, resign, apply, revenge, exert, etc.**

(a) I absented myself from the office.

(b) I revenged myself upon her.

(c) He availed himself the opportunity.

(d) They enjoyed themselves the pleasure of weather.

3. **Verbs when used intransitively do not need an object. In such case we should not use any reflexive pronoun as object. Such commonly used verbs are : keep, break, set, bathe, make, stop, steal, qualify, move, open, draw, rest, roll, burst, hide, feed, gather, etc. These verbs are commonly used intransitively.**

(a) He kept away from the function. *Correct*

He kept himself away from the function. *Incorrect*

(b) Let us rest at the bed. *Correct*

Let us ourselves rest at the bed. *Incorrect*

4. **The indefinite pronoun one has its own reflexive form ('One must have faith in oneself.'), but the other indefinite pronouns use either himself or themselves as reflexives.**

'One' as Pronoun

Sometimes the pronoun one functions as a numerical expression :

(a) Those are goodlooking shirts. I think I'll buy one.

(b) One is red, the other green.

(c) The four brothers get along quite well; in fact they respect one another.

(d) One of the student will lead the group to the parliament.

(e) The white jeep is fast, but I think the green one will win.

As a pronoun, one can also function in an impersonal, objective manner, standing for all the people in general who belong to a class.

(a) The young actress was awful, one felt embarrased for her.

(b) If one fails, then one must try again.

When the pronoun one is used in the numerical sense, a different pronoun can be used in a subsequent reference.

(a) We watched as one [of the birds] dried its feathers in the sun.

(b) One [person] pulled her car over to the side.

We should not mix the impersonal one with another pronoun, especially in the same sentence.

(a) If one fails, then **he/you** must try again. *Incorrect*

(b) If one fails then one must try again. *Correct*

'One's Reflexive and Possessive Forms

In the United States, the possessive and reflexive forms of one—one's and oneself—are often replaced by other pronoun forms. In British English, they are commonplace :

One must be conscientious about one's dental hygiene.

Oneself is used in formal writing and speech as the proper reflexive form of one :

If one slipped on this icy walk, one could hurt oneself badly.

There is usually no apostrophe used in the spelling of oneself.

Plural of 'One'

As a singular numerical pronoun, we do not have trouble with one. It is possible, sometimes, to pluralize one.

(a) I really like the chocolate ones.
(b) Are these the ones you want?
(c) Do you want these ones?

When the word ones is preceded by a plural determiner (like these), we usually drop the ones and the determiner turns into a demonstrative pronoun : 'Do you want these?'

The phrases 'one in [plural number]' and 'more than one' always take a singular verb :
(a) One in four doctors recommends this medicine.
(b) One out of every six instructors gets this question wrong.
(c) There is more than one reason for this.
(d) More than one lad has lost his heart to this lass.

Emphatic Pronouns

The emphatic pronouns (such as myself, yourself, herself, ourselves, themselves) consist of a personal pronoun plus self or selves. The emphatic pronoun is used to emphasise a noun.

It is possible (but rather unusual) for an emphatic pronoun to precede the noun it refers to. (Myself, I don't believe a word she says.)

Usually emphatic pronoun is placed after the noun it refers.

(a) I myself solved this question.
(b) She herself found the solution.

Reciprocal Pronouns

Reciprocal pronouns refer to persons or things which are acting on each other. 'Each other' and 'one another' are only two reciprocal pronouns. These are always used objectively.

Both phrases may be used to refer to either persons or things.

(a) You and I saw each other last week.
(b) The two friends helped one another with their work.

They are used for combining ideas.

If Ram gave Sita a book, and Sita gave Ram a book, we can say that they gave each other books (or that they gave books to each other).

Each other is usually refers idea of 'two'.

(a) My mother and I give each other a hard time.

If more than two people are involved (let's say a large book club), we would say that they gave one another books.

(a) The two friends quarrelled with each other.
(b) They all gave gifts to one another.

As per traditional theory each other is used for two and one another for more than two, but now the rule is not strictly adhered to.
(a) For you and I are foreigners to one another.
—*Aldous Huxley*
(b) The artistic result of Volpone is not due to any effect that Volpone, Mosca, Corvino, Corbaccio, and Voltore have upon each other. —*T.S.Eliot.*
Reciprocal pronouns can also take possessive forms
(a) They both borrowed **each other's** ideas.
(b) The students in this lab often use **one another's** equipment.

Demonstrative Pronouns

The family of demonstratives (this/that/these/those/such) functions either as pronouns or as determiners.

As pronouns, they identify or refer to nouns.

(a) That is incredible! (referring to something you just saw)
(b) I will never forget this. (referring to a recent incident)
(c) Such is my belief. (referring to a statement just made)

The words **this, that, these** and **those** are demonstrative pronouns. These are used to denote specific persons or things.

Note : When these words (**this, that, these** and **those**) are used immediately preceding a noun, the function as demonstrative adjectives (determiners).

(a) This umbrella is made of Swiss cotton.
(b) That idea seems workable.
(c) These people are my friends.
(d) Those shops are ours.

In the preceding examples, **this, that, these** and **those** act as adjectives, modifying the nouns.

Indefinite Pronouns

A pronoun that refers to person or thing in a general way (not in a definite way) is called indefinite pronoun. The indefinite pronouns (everybody/anybody/somebody/all/ each/every/so me/none/one) do not act for specific nouns but function themselves as nouns.

Indefinite pronouns may be used without antecedents.

Look at the following sentences

(a) **One** cannot get everything one desires.
(b) I will try to think of **somebody** who can help you.
(c) **Nobody** will believe it!
(d) Is there **anyone** here by the name of Sujak?

All of the pronouns listed above take verbs in the **third person singular.** The phrase **no one** is used like the other indefinite pronouns, but is spelled as two separate words.

The pronoun **one** can refer to persons or things.

(a) One of the boys will help you.
(b) Please hand me one of the boxes.

'One' when used in a general sense, the pronoun one is usually understood as referring to persons.

Interrogative Pronouns

The Interrogative pronouns are used for making querries or asking questions. The pronouns who, what and which are used as interrogative pronouns.

(a) Who telephoned?
(b) What did you say?
(c) Which is your brother?

The interrogative pronouns are 'who', 'whom', 'which', 'what' and the compounds formed with the suffix 'ever' ('whoever,' 'whomever,' 'whichever' and 'whatever').

'Who' and 'whom' usually refer to people and 'which' too can refer to people occasionally. 'Which' and 'what' usually refer to things and animals. 'Who' acts as the subject of a verb, while 'whom' acts as the object of a verb or preposition.

Which is generally used with more specific reference than what. If we're taking a test and I ask 'Which questions do you find the most difficult?', I am referring to specific questions on that test. If I ask 'What questions do you find most difficult'? I could be asking what kind of questions on that test (or what kind of question, in general) you find difficult.

'Which' or 'what' can also be used as an interrogative adjective, and that 'who', 'whom', or 'which' can also be used as a relative pronoun.

Relative Pronouns

A **relative pronoun** is a word such as 'who', 'whom' 'that', or 'which' that is used to introduce a relative clause. These words are called **relative pronouns.** The compounds 'whoever', 'whomever', and 'whichever' are also relative pronouns.

In other words stet pronoun which is used to begin a subordinate clause can be referred to as a **relative pronoun,** since it indicates the relationship of the subordinate clause to the rest of the sentence.' A subordinate clause which is introduced by a relative pronoun is often referred to as a **relative clause.**

Look at the following sentences :

(a) The woman *who* is wearing red saree is a doctor.
(b) The door, *which* is dark blue, is very tight.
(c) Have you found the magazine **that** was missing?

In the above sentences the words in bold type are relative Pronouns.

We can use a **relative pronoun** to link one phrase or clause to another phrase or clause. You can use the relative pronouns 'who' and 'whoever' to refer to the subject of a clause or sentence, and 'whom' and 'whomever' to refer to the objects of a verb or a preposition.

Kinds of Relative Pronouns

Who **Who** is used as the subject of a verb, **whom** is used as the object of a verb or the object of a preposition, and **whose** is used as an adjective denoting possession. The relative pronouns **who, whom** and **whose** generally refer only to persons, and are used either in defining or non-defining relative clauses.**Who** refers to the subject of the sentence, **whom** referes to the object of a verb or a preposition, while **whose** refers the possession and it is used as adjective.

In the following examples, **who** introduces the defining relative clause **who secures the highest marks** and the non-defining relative clause **who is learning Russian.**

(a) The child **who secures the highest marks** will receive a trophy.

(b) My brother, **who is learning Russian**, wants to travel to Kazhakistan.

In these examples, **who** has the antecedents **child** and **brother**, and acts as the subject of the verbs **secures** and **is learning.**

Whom In the following examples, **whom** introduces the defining relative clause **whom we visited** and the non-defining relative clause **whom we will meet tomorrow.**

(a) The girl whom we visited is her sister.

(b) Mr Francis, whom we will meet tomorrow, will be our guide.

In these examples, **whom** has the antecedents **sister** and **Mr Francis**, and acts as the object of the verbs **visited** and **will meet.**

In the following examples, **to whom** introduces the defining relative clause **to whom you gave your umbrella** and the non-defining relative clause **to whom we send a birthday card every year.**

(a) The girl to whom you gave your umbrella lives near my house.

(b) His aunt, to whom we send a birthday card every year, is ninety-eight years old now.

In these examples, **whom** has the antecedents **girl** and **aunt**, and is the object of the preposition **to**.

Whose In the following examples, **whose** introduces the defining relative clause **whose house was sold** and the non-defining relative clause **whose family lives in America.**

(a) The man whose house was sold will leave this town.

(b) My brother, whose family lives in America, will visit us for a few days.

In these examples, **whose** has the antecedents **man** and **brother**, and modifies the nouns **house** and **family.** In the case of **whose,** it should be noted that it is the antecedent which must be a person; the noun being modified may be a person or a thing.

We may find use of **whose** at the beginning of a clause occasionally. **Whose** can also be used to referring to things, in order to make a simpler sentence.

For example

(a) The tree, the branches of which overhung the street, was laid with fruit. *Correct*
The tree, whose branches overhung the street, was laid with fruit. *Incorrect*

However, this use of whose is considered to be grammatically incorrect in formal English.

That As a relative pronoun, **that** can refer to either persons or things. The relative pronoun **that** is generally used only in defining relative clauses.

(a) The girls that were here yesterday will return in a week.

(b) The bag that was on the steps belongs to our tenant.

In these examples, **that** has the antecedents **girls** and **bag**, and introduces the defining relative clauses that were here **yesterday** and **that was on the steps.** Here, **that** acts as the subject of the verbs **were** and **was**. When **that** acts as the object of a verb or preposition, it is usually omitted.

(a) The magazines that we bought are very useful.

(b) The city that this road leads to is twenty kilometres away.

In the first sentence, **that** acts as the object of the verb **bought.** In the second sentence, **that** acts as the object of the preposition **to.** These sentences can also be written as following :

(a) The magazines we bought are very useful.

(b) The city this road leads to is twenty kilometres away.

Here **that** can well be omitted.

That can be used for living and non-living nouns, for singular as well as plurals.
(a) I have lost the book that you gave me.
(b) He that is content is happy.

No preposition is used before that, if any preposition is required to be used, it is used in ending position.

(a) We know the hotel that she lives in.

(b) This is the lady that I told you about.

In a sentence after the following words that is generally used : all, any, anybody, anything, much, nothing, little, somebody, no one, none,
the same + noun + that,
the only + noun + that etc.

(a) All that glitters is not gold.
(b) There was none that didn't support the cause.
(c) It is for nothing that I have been trying to find.
(d) There is much that he needs.
(e) There was not any that could be followed.
(f) There was somebody that raised the matter.
(g) This is the same girl that we met yesterday.
(h) This is the only girl that secured more than 90% marks.

After interrogative pronoun 'who' and 'what' that is used.

(a) What is it that you can't solve.
(b) Who was there that you were talking with.

Which It is important to note that when used as a relative pronoun, **which** refers only to things, when used as an adjective or interrogative pronoun, **which** can refer to either persons or things.

The relative pronoun **which** can be used in either defining or non-defining relative clauses.

(a) The book which I purchased last week is very useful.
(b) The bag, which was full of coins, was very heavy.

In the first example, **which** has the antecedent **book**, and introduces the defining relative clause **which I purchased last week**. In the second example, **which** has the antecedent **bag,** and introduces the non-defining relative clause **which was full of coins.**

Preferring 'that' to 'who' or 'which'

That is preferably used after Superlative degree instead of who or which.

(a) He is the most eloquent speaker that I have ever heard.
(b) Patel was the greatest man that India produced.

After two antecedents one referring a person and the other referring an animal or a thing, use that instead of who or which.

(a) The boy and his dog that entered the temple were caught by the people.
(b) The lady and her cat that created the nuisance were arrested by the police.

After 'same' or 'such' use 'as' or 'that' not 'who' or 'which'.

(a) This is the same fellow that came yesterday also.
(b) My books are same as yours.
(c) His reply was such as we never expected from him.

What Relative pronouns **what** is used without antecedents. When used as a relative pronoun, **what** has the meaning - **the thing or things that.**

(a) What you say is not true.
(b) What he did was not wrong.

In the above examples, **what** introduces the clauses **what you say** and **what he did.** Such clauses are called as noun clauses, since they serve the functions of a noun. For instance, in the preceding sentences, the clause **what you say** acts as the subject of the verb is and the clause **what he did** acts as the subject of the verb **was.**

Whatever and Whoever **Whatever** and **whoever** are also normally used without antecedents. **Whatever** means **no matter what** or **anything which. Whoever** means **no matter who** or **anyone who.**

(a) You can tell me whatever you think fit.
(b) Let in whoever comes to our house.

In these examples, the noun clauses **whatever you think fit** and **whoever comes to our house** act as the objects of the verbs in the main clauses.

Whomever **Whomever** refers to the objects of a verb or a preposition.

Look at the following sentences :

(a) You may invite **whomever** you like to the function.

The relative pronoun **whomever** is the direct object of the compound verb **may invite.**

(a) The coach will select **whomever** he pleases.

Here the relative pronoun **whomever** is the direct object of the compound verb **will select.**

The expanded form of the relative pronouns—**whoever, whomever, whatever**—are known as indefinite relative pronouns.

The antecedent of a relative pronoun should not be in possessive case.

(a) These are chairman's instructions that must be followed. *Incorrect*

(b) I went to Sarla's house, who is my class fellow. *Incorrect*

It is an incorrect structure. These sentences should have been written as following:

(a) These are the instructions of the chairman that must be followed.

(b) I went to the house of Sarla who is my class fellow.

The relative pronoun should be of same number and person as its antecedent. It means the verb should agree with the number and person of the antecedent.

(a) The girl who was late was fined.

(b) The girls who were late were fined.

(c) I, who am responsible for the loss, shall pay.

(d) They who live in glass houses should not throw stones.

(e) This is the only one of his books that is worth reading.

(f) We who seek your help, are new to this place.

Distributive Pronouns

Each, either and neither are classified as distributive pronouns. They denote person or thing one at a time. These pronouns are always treated as singular and take singular verbs.

Look at the following sentences :

(a) Each of the students gets a prize.

(b) Each got his turn.

(c) Either of the two will win the race.

(d) Neither of those two students can secure first position.

(e) Every one of the students was happy.

(f) Each of the two students received a medal.

Each (adjective and pronoun) and every (adjective) :
Each means a number of persons or things considered individually.
Each student got a prize.
Every can have this meaning but with every there is less emphasis on the individual.
Every is an adjective only. Every man knows about the incident.

Each can be used for two or more persons or things and is normally used for small number. Every is not normally used of very small numbers. Each can be used for more than two when the number is usually definite. Both take a singular verb.

Neither and Either : Either Is the *Negative of Neither*

1. **Neither means 'not one and not the other'. It takes an affirmative singular verb.**

It can be used by itself or followed by a noun or by of + the/these/those/possessives or personal pronouns

(a) I tried both keys but neither (of them) worked.

(b) Neither of them knew the way (neither boy knew).

(c) I've read neither of these (books).

2. **Either means 'any one of the two'. It takes a singular verb and like neither can be used by itself or followed by a noun/pronoun or by of + the/these/those, etc.**

3. **Either + negative verb can replace neither + affirmative except when (b) above but could in (c) :**

(a) I haven't read either of these (books).

Though either cannot be the subject of a negative verb, it can be subject or object of an affirmative or interrogative verb.

(a) Either (of these) would do.

(b) Would you like either of these?

Either and **neither** is used for speaking of two persons or things. For more than two, **any, no one** or **none** is usually used.

With 'distributive pronouns' the third person, singular pronoun, masculine gender (he, his, him) is used.
(a) Everyone should obey **his** parents.
(b) Neither of there two students **has** received his prize.

If feminine gender noun follows the distributive prououns use personal pronoun 'her' is used'.

(a) Neither of these two girls has deposited her fees.

(b) Either of the two girls has received her gift.

(c) Each of the girls has donated her pocket money.

(d) Everyone of the women has a choice of her own.

If a plural pronoun (us/them/you) follows the distributive pronoun use singular masculine gender pronoun.

(a) Neither of them has done his duty.

(b) Each of them has forgotten his purse.

Position of Pronoun 'Each'

Where to put **each** in a sentence is an important point. Each can have three positions.

(a) I bought each of these books for rupees fifty. *Incorrect*

I bought these books each for rupees fifty. *Incorrect*

I bought these books for rupees fifty each. *Correct*

Each is used after a numeral.

(b) These tables cost each two hundred rupees. *Incorrect*

These tables cost two hundred rupees each. *Correct*

When there is no numeral.

(c) These men received each a prize. *Incorrect*

These men received a prize each. *Incorrect*

Each of the men received a prize. *Correct*

In such cases begin the sentence with each.

Exclamatory Pronoun

A pronoun used as an exclamation is called an exclamatory pronoun.

(a) What! You don't know Sonia Gandhi ?

(b) What! You lost the chain ?

In the above sentences **what** is functioning as an exclamatory pronoun.

Who/Whom

For persons Who and whom are normally reserved for persons, but they may be used for animals when they are referred to in a semi personal way.

My dog, who is getting old now.

And of countries, when the people rather than the territory are referred to :

India, who feels very strongly on this matter... .

Who/whom as relative pronouns As relative pronouns, **who and whom** are preceded by a comma when they introduce a nondefining clause, but the comma must not be used when the clause is a defining one.

Who as subject, **whom** as object : **Who** is used for the subject and the complement of a verb.

(a) My father, who works in a bank, is retiring soon.

(b) My father, who will be sixty next year, works in a bank.

Whom is used for the object and when governed by a perposition.

(a) The man whom you rescued from the sea has recovered.

(b) The newspaper editor, to whom we all owe so much, is leaving the company.

But in questions introduced by an interrogative pronoun which is governed by a preposition which comes at the end of the sentence it is more usual to use who.

(a) Who is that letter from?

(b) Who has written this poem ?

In spoken English or colloquial written style, **who** is now almost universally used. But even here, **whom** must always be used after a preposition at the beginning of a sentence.

(a) To whom do I send it?

(b) To whom shall I sheak ?

In relative clauses A frequent source of trouble is sentences of this type.

(a) The person **who (or whom?)** we thought was guilty proved to be innocent.

(b) The man **who (or whom?)** we feared we had injured proved to be unharmed.

The temptation is always to use **whom,** presumably because it is felt that tho word is the object of thought and feared (or whatever verb takes their place in other sentences); but it is not. In the first sentence, it is the subject which guilty, hence **who** is correct, and in the second, the object of had injured hence **whom** is required.

If there is any doubt, a useful test is to substitute the personal pronoun he or him; if he would be used, the correct relative is who; if him, it is whom.

(a) We thought he was guilty (therefore who).

(b) We feared we had injured him (therefore whom).

(c) We thought him to be guilty (therefore whom).

Difficulty may arise with questions.

(a) Who (not whom) do you think we saw? (because it is the object of saw).

Whom is never indirect object Whom is not used as an indirect object. We do not say the boy whom I gave the book, or ask whom did you give the book? It must be to whom (or the preposition may be placed at the end).

The verb after who Who is the same number and person as its antecedent, and takes its verb accordingly.

(a) It is I who am to blame.

The rules regarding the use of the coordinating conjunctions **and** and **but** before **who** are the same as those for which

—Current English Usage by F.T. Wood

» Exercises

Exercise 1

Correct the following sentences

1. Let you and I go to play.
2. There is close relation between he and I.
3. You, he and I have done their job.
4. You and he could not complete his work.
5. He and I have fastened his belts.
6. I, you and he were present in the function.
7. I and you are strangers.
8. You and I are responsible for this loss.
9. He and I were the main accused.
10. You, he and I must beg sorry for the misconduct.

Solutions

1. Let you and me go to play.
2. There is close relation between him and me.
3. You, he and I have done our job.
4. You and he could not complete your work.
5. He and I have fastened our belts.
6. You, he and I were present in the function.
7. You and I are strangers.
8. I and you are responsible for this loss.
9. I and he are the main accused.
10. I, you and he must beg sorry for the misconduct.

Exercise 2

Correct the following sentences

1. Neither of these four vehicles will do.
2. Anyone of the two girls can solve this puzzle.
3. Either of the three students is responsible for the loss.
4. None of the two girls could complete the job.
5. One should obey his elders.
6. One should respect not only his own parents but also others.
7. One should take care not to make himself obnoxious to others.
8. Each girl and every madam tried their best to finish the work before 7 p.m.
9. Every man and every woman have their own fascinations.
10. Every leader and every citizen have a duty towards their country.

Solutions

1. None of these four vehicles will do.
2. Either of the two girls can solve this puzzle.
3. Anyone of the three students is responsible for the loss.
4. Neither of the two girls could complete the job.
5. One should obey one's elders.
6. One should respect not only one's own parents but also others.
7. One should take care not to make oneself obnoxious to others.
8. Each girl and every madam tried her best to finish the work before 7 p.m.
9. Every man and every woman has his own fascinations.
10. Every leader and every citizen has a duty towards his country.

Exercise 3

Correct the following sentences

1. Each of the employees have to arrange their own vehicle.
2. Every one of them were given their table and chair.
3. Either Ramesh or Sita have left their tiffin box.
4. Either the teacher or the students have left his classroom unlocked .
5. Please take the buffalo to her shed.
6. The cow has hurt her legs.
7. This is easy to get her agree.
8. This was he who arrived first in the meeting.
9. It is to certity that Mr. A is our employee.
10. This is 8 o'clock by my watch.

Solutions

1. Each of the employes has to agrrange his own vehicle.
2. Every one of them was given his table and chair.
3. Either Ramesh or Sita has left his tiffin box.
4. Either the teacher or the students have left their classroom unlocked.
5. Please take the buffalo to its shed.
6. The cow has hurt its legs.
7. It is easy to get her agree.
8. It was he who arrived first in the meeting.
9. This is to certify that Mr. A is our employee.
10. It is 8 o'clock by my watch.

Exercise 4

Correct the following sentences

1. All which she said was incorrect.
2. Who was the girl which came to meet you?
3. What is his opinion about the work which you have completed?
4. I always purchase the item which is best in the market.
5. This is the same shirt which I saw in the shop.
6. Who is she who can abuse me like this?
7. Only those employees should be promoted whom are sincere.
8. The leaders which do not love their country are not respected.
9. Those whose live in glass houses should not throw stones at others.
10. What was the reply, which she submitted?

Solutions

1. All that she said was incorrect.
2. Who was the girl that came to meet you?
3. What is his opinion about the work that you have completed?
4. I always purchase the item that is the best in the market.
5. This is the same shirt that I saw in the shop.
6. Who is she that can abuse me like this?
7. Only those employee should be promoted who are sincere.
8. The leaders who do not love their country are not respected.
9. Those who live in glass houses should not throw stones at others.
10. What was the reply that she submitted?

Exercise 5

Correct the following sentences

1. It was me who telephoned you yesterday.
2. The girl whom you spoke to in the office is my friend.
3. My brother and myself are glad to get your greetings.
4. I am not one of those who cannot keep his promise.
5. It is not us who are responsible for the delay.
6. They admired his wife and he.
7. What place are you going?
8. Which house do you live?
9. She has absented from duty today again.
10. I could not avail of the opportunity I got last year.
11. The treatment received by me was such, which I never expected.
12. His expectation is the same which is hers.
13. One cannot bear his insult like this.
14. My house is bigger than their.
15. This is a secret between you and I.

Solutions

1. It was I who telephoned you yesterday.
2. The girl who you spoke to in the office, is my friend.
3. My brother and I are glad to get your greetings.
4. I am not one of those who cannot keep their promise.
5. It is not we who are responsible for the delay.
6. They admired his wife and him.
7. What place are you going to?
8. Which house do you live in?
9. She has absented herself from duty today again.
10. I could not avail myself of the opportunity I got last year.
11. The treatment received by me was such as I never expected.
12. His expectation is the same as is hers.
13. One cannot bear one's insult like this.
14. My house is bigger than theirs.
15. This is a secret between you and me.

Exercise 6

Correct the following sentences

1. Everyone should obey their parents.
2. Sita must do their duties.
3. Each girl and every student was busy in her their work.
4. Either Pramod or Narendra has learnt their lesson.
5. Nisha or Sushma was teaching their son.
6. Either Rohan or his friends forgot his books.
7. You, he and I am friends .
8. He, I and you went to Nehru Garden yesterday.
9. Manish and I should learn my lesson.
10. You and Sushma should read her book.

11. He, you and I must do my work.
12. Ram and Shyam help one another.
13. Three children love each other.
14. Two friends love one another.
15. It is I who is your friend.

Solutions

1. Everyone should obey his parents.
2. Sita must do her duties.
3. Each girl and every student was busy in work.
4. Either Pramod or Narendra has learnt his lesson.
5. Nisha or Sushma was teaching her son.
6. Either Rohan or his friends forgot their books.
7. You, he and I are friends.
8. You, he and I went to Nehru Garden yesterday.
9. Manish and I should learn our lesson.
10. You and Sushma should read your book.
11. You, he and I must do our work.
12. Ram and Shyam help each other.
13. Three children love one another.
14. Two friends love each other.
15. It is I who am your friend.

Exercise 7

Correct the following sentences

1. That is one of the girls who has stolen eggs.
2. It is me, who am speaking on this topic.
3. That is one of the interesting books that has appeared this year.
4. This is the only one of his stories that are worth reading.
5. It is I, who is answering the question.
6. The boy which is sitting in the corner reads is my class.
7. She who walk in the evening gets energy.
8. The sun whom rays give life to earth is a source of energy.
9. This is the same toy which I gave you.
10. Uneasy lies the head which wears the crown.
11. All which glitters is not silver.
12. Man is the only animal which can use his intelligence.
13. That is the best which you can do.
14. The girl and his cat who had entered my house were locked.
15. I have read Milton's poems who was a romantic poet.

Solutions

1. That is one of the girls who have stolen eggs.
2. It is I, who am speaking on this topic.
3. That is one of the interesting books that have appeared this year.
4. This is the only one of his stories that is worth reading.
5. It is I, who am answering the question.
6. The boy who is sitting is the corner reads is my class.
7. She who walks in the evening gets
8. The sun whose rays give life to earth is a source.
9. This is the same toy that I gave you.
10. Neasy lies the head that wears the crown.
11. All that glitters is not silver.
12. Man is the only animal that can use his intelligence.
13. That is the best that you can do.
14. The girl and his cat that had entered my house were locked.
15. I have read poems of Milton who was a romantic poet.

Exercise 8

Correct the following sentences

1. You self did this work?
2. Who do you want?
3. Neither Sushma nor Indu were wanted.
4. The girls absented from the class.
5. One should do his duty.
6. I was not so rich as him.
7. This is the boy whose all admire.
8. This is the girl whom marks are highest.
9. Either of these roads lead to the hospital.
10. Yourself admitted the guilt.
11. You, he and I are in the wrong.
12. You are stronger than me.
13. It is me.
14. Only you and him can do that work.
15. If I were him, I should help you.

Solutions

1. You yourself did this work?
2. Whom do you want?
3. Neither Sushma nor Indu was wanted.
4. The girls absented themselves from the class.
5. One should do one's duty.
6. I was not so rich as he.
7. This is the boy whom all admire.
8. This is the girl whose marks are highest.
9. Either of these roads leads to the hospital.
10. You yourself admitted the guilf.
11. I, he and you are in the wrong.
12. You are strenger than I.
13. It is I.
14. Only you and he can do that work.
15. If I were he, I should help you.

Exercise 9

Correct the following sentences

1. This is mine pen.
2. Between you and I Mohan is a thief.
3. Let me take your leave.
4. He cannot bearing separation from me.
5. Good girls like you and she should not abuse others.
6. This pen is superior to your.
7. Every man and every woman should obey their elders.
8. He availed of the chance.
9. He will not object to me going there.
10. He is a good player is not it?

Solutions

1. This is my pen.
2. Between you and me, Mohan is a thief.
3. Let me take leave of you.
4. He cannot bear separation from me.
5. Good girls like you and her should not abuse others.
6. This pen is superior to yours.
7. Every man and woman should obey his elders.
8. He availed himself of the chance.
9. He will not object to my going there.
10. He is a good, player isn't it?

Spotting the Errors

1. The board of directors (A)/ want the facilities (B)/ of car and accommodation (C)/ for itself (D). ***(Bank PO)***
2. Every teacher (A)/ and every student (B)/ of this school is determined to do their best (C)/ for the benefit of all (D). ***(BSRB)***
3. The officer (A)/ as well as the (B)/ clerks absented themselves (C)/ from the office (D). ***(CDS)***
4. There were (A)/ five active workers (B)/ and three lazy one (C)/ in the factory (D).
5. There is none (A)/ who can support you (B)/ in this crucial period (C).
6. Any of the (A)/ two photos which reflect (B)/ the natural beauty of Kashmir (C)/ is worth seeing (D). ***(CDS)***
7. The guests (A)/ whom we were talking (B)/ about have arrived (C)/ are my relatives (D). ***(BSRB)***
8. He introduced (A)/ to the chairman as (B)/ the president of the (C)/ workers association (D). ***(Bank PO)***
9. As a student (A)/ of arts (B)/ you are much better (C)/ than him (D).
10. He hates everybody (A)/ and everything who (B)/ reminds him (C)/ of his blunder (D).
11. Whomever (A)/ does not come in time (B)/ will not be allowed (C) / to mark his presence (D).
12. The six partners (A)/ are at daggers drawn (B)/ so they do not talk (C) to each other (D). ***(BSRB)***
13. If some one has (A)/ completed the work (B)/ he may leave (C)./ No error (D)
14. She lent me (A)/ some money with the condition (B)/ that I should return (C)/ the same within a month (D). ***(BSRB)***
15. The teacher instructed (A)/ the peon to let (B)/ the students and I (C)/ go into the office of Principal (D).
16. The candidate (A)/ being a commerce graduate (B)/ she is eligible (C)/ for the post of accountant (D). ***(Bank PO)***
17. In all circumstances (A)/ I have helped him (B)/ and he knows (C).
18. I don't appreciate (A)/ him who laugh (B)/ at others without (C)/ any reason (D). ***(BSRB)***
19. You and myself (A)/ will enjoy the function (B)/ being arranged in honour of (C)/ the new Principal (D). ***(CDS)***
20. He asked for (A)/ permission to go to the cinema (B)/ but his mother (C)/ did not give (D). ***(Bank PO)***

» Answers

» Answers

1. (D) Replace 'itself' by 'themselves'.
2. (C) Replace 'their' by 'his'.
3. (C) Replace 'themselves' by 'his'.
4. (C) Replace 'lazy one' by 'lazy ones'. Ones is used for plurals.
5. (B) Replace 'who' by 'that'. For example :
   All that glitters is not gold.
   He is the same man that supported me.
6. (A) Replace 'any' by 'either'. Either is used for two.
7. (B) Replace 'whom' by 'who'.
8. (A) Place himself after introduced.
9. (D) Replace 'him' by 'he'.
10. (B) Replace 'who' by 'which' or 'that'.
11. (A) Replace 'whomever' by 'whoever'.
12. (D) Replace 'each other' by 'one another'.
13. (D) No error.
14. (D) Replace 'the same' by it.
15. (C) Replace 'I' by 'me'.
    (1) Let you and me go there.
    (2) Let you and him prepare a proposal.
16. (C) Delete 'she'.
17. (C) Place 'it' after 'knows'.
18. (B) Replace 'laugh' by 'laughs'.
19. (A) Replace 'myself' by 'I'.
    Myself is Suresh. *Incorrect*
    I am Suresh. *Correct*
20. (D) Place 'it' after 'give'.

» Unit

6

Adjectives and Determiners

Determiners

Determiners are not found in traditional grammar books. Half of what we now call determiners used to be a separate class, the articles. The other half, even though they work in the same way as articles do, used to be categorised with adjectives. So we had 'real' adjectives and also things called demonstrative adjectives, possessive adjectives, etc.

Modern grammarians and linguists make a clear distinction between adjectives and determiners, because they have different meanings and different uses. Adjectives tell us about the qualities of the thing referred to (red pens, a black dog, beautiful girls).

The most common determiners are as follows

1. **articles** : a, an, the
2. **quantifiers** : all, few, many, several, some
3. **possessive** : her, his, its, my, our, their, your
4. **demonstratives** : this, that, these, those
5. **numerals** : one , three, hundred
6. **negative** : no

The determiner, along with the adjective, usually indicates whether a noun is singular or plural, masculine or feminine. In other words, it indicates number and gender. This means that most determiners have several different forms.

Determiners are words which quantify or identify nouns. Determiners are followed by a noun.

Adjectives

An **adjective** modifies a noun or a pronoun by describing, identifying, or quantifying words. An adjective usually precedes the noun or the pronoun which it modifies.

Adjective Clause If a group of words containing a subject and verb acts as an adjective, it is called an adjective clause.

(a) My sister, **who is much younger than I am,** is a nurse.

Adjective Phrase If an adjective clause is stripped of its subject and verb, the resulting modifier becomes an adjective phrase.

He is the man (who is) **keeping his family in a hotel.**

In the above sentence, the underline phrase is an adjective phrase.

Some Important Determiners and Adjectives

Farther/farthest and Further/furthest

Both forms (Farther/farthest and further/ Furthest) can be used for distances.

(a) New York is farther/further than Lincoln or Selby.

(b) New York is the farthest/furthest town.
(c) New York is the farthest/furthest of the three.

Further is usually used with abstract nouns to mean additional or extra.

(a) No further action is needed in this matter.
(b) Further discussion would be pointless.

Furthest can also be used with abstract nouns.

(a) This was the furthest point they reached in their discussion.
(b) This was the furthest concession he would make.

Elder, Eldest/Older, Oldest

Elder, and **eldest** are chiefly used for comparisons within a family. They imply seniority rather than age. Elder and eldest are used for persons, while older and oldest are used for persons as well as for things. Elder is not used with 'than', it takes 'to'. Older and oldest is used for age.

(a) Ram is my elder brother.
(b) My mother is the eldest member of our family.
(c) Ram is older than Shyam.
(d) Sunder and Purinder are real brothers. Sunder is elder to Purinder.
(e) This is the oldest college in our city.
(f) The older people should be respected.

Later/Latest/Latter/Last

Later and **latest** are used with reference to time. **Latter** and **last** is used with reference to order. Latest refers to new (last up to now) or very recent things. Last means final or nothing new after that. In talking about events, inventions, productions, etc. we use latest. Latter is used for comparison of two in order, for more than two we use last.

(a) He came later than Ram.
(b) He came in the last.
(c) Between Ram and Shyam, the latter is more intelligent.
(d) Of iron and silver, the latter is known as white metal.
(e) This is the latest fashion.
(f) This is the latest technology.
(g) At last the chairman distributed the prizes.
(h) Lord Mountbaten was the last Governor General of India.

Many and Much (Adjectives and Pronouns)

Many (adjective) is used before countable nouns.

Much (adjective) is used before uncountable nouns.

(a) She didn't buy many books.
(b) We haven't much sugar.

The comparative and superlative of **much** and **many** are same, **more** and **most.**

Much and **many** can be used quite freely with negative verbs, but with affirmative or interrogative verbs they have a restricted use.

(a) I haven't much patience.
(b) She hasn't much money.

Use of many and much with affirmative verbs

Many is used when it is modified by a good/ a great. Both (much and many) can be used when modified by so/as/too.

(a) Ram has made a good many friends there.
(b) She has had so many jobs that......
(c) He studied as much as he could.
(d) She drinks too much (wine).

We use a **lot/lots of** (+ noun) or a lot or lots (pronouns) instead of many, when it is not modified and used as object or part of the object. Much is also replaced by a great/good deal of (+ noun) or a great/good deal (pronouns) as object or part of the object.

(a) I saw a lot/ lots of animals. I expect you saw a lot too.
(b) She spends a lot/lots of/a great deal of money on her new bungalow.
(c) I know many persons. *Incorrect*
(d) He bought much sugar. *Incorrect*

Use of much and many in affirmative sentence as object or part of object must be avoided.

Look at the following sentences : (negative and affirmative sentences)

(a) He hasn't won many competitions.
(b) You've won a lot/ lots of competitions.
or You've won a lot or
(c) You've won a great many (competitions).
(d) She didn't eat much fruit.
(e) He ate a lot/ lots of fruit/ a great deal of fruit.
(f) He ate a lot/ a great deal.

Use of many and much in interrogative sentences

Both can be used with **how.** How many times? How much?

In questions where how is not used, **many** is possible but **a lot (of)** etc. is preferred when an affirmative answer is expected.

(a) Did you take a lot of photos? I expect you did.

We can use much without how but the other forms are a little more usual.

(b) Did you have a lot of rain/much rain last year?

Less, Fewer and Lesser

When we talk about countable things, we use the word **fewer,** when we talk about uncountables we use the word **less.** She had fewer chores, but she also had less energy. We do, however, definitely use **less** when referring to statistical or numerical expressions.

(a) It's less than fifty kilometres to Delhi.
(b) He's less than five feet in height.
(c) Your essay should be five hundred words or less.
(d) We spent less than two thousand rupees on this trip.

Lesser means less important.

(a) Many lesser speakers also came to speak.
(b) Many lesser leaders were present in the function.

Taller than I/Me : Which is correct?

He is taller than I, or He is taller than me.

The correct answer is 'taller than I'. We are looking for the subject form : "He is taller than I am". (except that we leave out the verb in the second clause, "am") Some writers, however, will argue that the word "than" should be allowed to function as a preposition. If we can say, "He is tall like me/her," then (if "than" could be prepositional like like) we should be able to say, 'He is taller than me/her." It's an interesting argument, but—for now—in formal, academic prose, use the subject form in such comparisons.

More Than/Over

In the United States, we usually use "more than" in countable numerical expressions meaning "in excess of" or "over". In England, there is no such distinction. For instance, in the US, some editors would insist on "more than 40,000 traffic deaths in one year," whereas in the UK, "over 40,000 traffic deaths" would be acceptable. Even in the US, however, you will commonly hear "over" in numerical expressions of age, time or height : "His sister is over forty; she's over six feet tall. We've been waiting well over two hours for her."

Good versus Well

In both casual speech and formal writing, we frequently have to choose between the adjective **good** and the adverb **well.** With most verbs, there is no contest. When modifying a verb, use the adverb.

(a) She swims **well.**
(b) She knows only too **well** who the thief is.

However, when using a linking verb or a verb that has to do with the five human senses, you want to use the adjective instead.

(a) How are you? I'm feeling **good**, thank you.
(b) After a bath, the baby smells so **good.**
(c) Even after my careful paint job, this room doesn't look **good.**

Many careful writers, however, will use **well** after linking verbs relating to health, and this is perfectly all right. In fact, to say that you are **good** or that you feel **good** usually implies not only that you are OK physically but also that your spirits are high.

How are you? I am **well**, thank you.

Bad versus Badly

We use bad to indicate that something is unpleasant or undesirable.

(a) He had a bad accident two years ago.
(b) We have been going through a bad time.

If something is done **badly** or goes **badly,** it is not very successful or effective..

(a) I was angry because I played so badly.
(b) The whole project was badly managed.

If someone or something is **badly** hurt or **badly** affected, means they are severely hurt or affected.

(a) The bomb destroyed a police station and badly damaged a church.
(b) One man was killed and another badly injured.
(c) It was a gamble that went badly wrong.

If a person or their job is badly paid, it means they are not paid very much for what they do.

You may have to work part-time, in a badly paid job with unsociable hours.

In the case of nouns which are uncountable or plural, no article is required.
(a) We produce sweeter honey than they do.
(b) They are better actors than we are.
(c) She has warmer gloves than her friend does.

3. **The comparative form of an adjective followed by than can also be combined with longer phrases and clauses.**
(a) The air is fresher in the mountains **than** in the valleys.
(b) The work seems easier once one becomes familiar with it **than** it does at first.

4. **The use of the subjective case : In comparisons using than, personal pronouns following than should be in the subjective case.**
(a) I am taller than he is.
(b) She is a better student than I am.
In formal English, the final verb of such sentences is sometimes omitted.
(a) I am taller than he.
(b) She is a better student than I.
In informal English, the objective case of a personal pronoun is often used after **than.**
(a) I am taller than him.
(b) She is a better student than me.
However, this use of the objective case is considered to be grammatically incorrect.

5. **Progressive comparisons : As well as being used in combination with than to compare objects which differ in some respect, the comparative form of an adjective can also be used to describe a characteristic which is becoming progressively more pronounced.**
(a) The waves are growing rougher and rougher.
(b) The sounds became fainter and fainter.
(c) The noise is becoming louder and louder.

In informal English, the verb **to get** is often used in this type of construction.
(a) The noise is getting louder and louder.
(b) The lights got brighter and brighter.

6. **While comparing an object with others, it is necessary to exclude it from the comparison.**
(a) Iron is harder than any metal. *Incorrect*
Iron is harder than any other metal. *Correct*
(b) This building is larger than any building in the town. *Incorrect*
This building is larger than any other building in the town. *Correct*
(c) He is more intelligent than any student of his class. *Incorrect*
He is more intelligent than any other student of his class. *Correct*

7. **Two comparative adjectives are not normally used in a sentence.**
(a) He is more wiser than you. *Incorrect*
He is wiser than you. *Correct*
(b) I am comparatively better today. *Incorrect*
I am better today. *Correct*
I am comparatively well today. *Correct*
If one adjective is in comparative degree the other should be in positive.
We should also not use any comparative degree adjective with the word'comparatively'.

But we can use rather with the adjective of comparative degree.
(a) She is rather better today.

8. **Some comparative degree adjectives, ending in 'or' are followed by the preposition 'to' instead of 'than'. Such adjectives are : senior, junior, posterior, superior, inferior, anterior. All these adjectives are borrowed from Latin. Likewise, Elder, prefer and preferable also take preposition 'to' with them.**
(a) He is superior to me.
(b) She is junior to me.
(c) Ram is senior to Shyam.
(d) He came prior to me.

Major, minor, exterior, interior, outer, lower, ulterior, upper, former, inner are some words that resemble with comparative degree adjectives are no comparatives.

9. **When we compare two qualities in the same person or thing we should not use comparatives in 'er', instead we should use 'more'.**
(a) Ram is more strong than intelligent. *(not stronger)*
(b) She is more clever than intelligent. *(not cleverer)*

10. **Superlative forms of adjectives : The superlative form of an adjective is used to describe something which possesses a characteristic in the greatest degree.**
(a) Dhiraj is the youngest boy in our class.
(b) She is the best actress I have ever seen.

1. **The superlative form preceded by 'the'. The superlative forms of adjectives are usually preceded by the, and followed by the nouns they modify.**
   (a) Shyam is the tallest boy in the class.
   (b) Nisha is the fastest runner in the team.
2. **The comparison of one or more things with a group. When one or more things are compared with a group to which they do not belong, the comparative form of an adjective is normally used.**
   (a) The girls are cleverer than the boys.

The girls are being compared with **the boys**, a group to which they do not belong. Therefore, the comparative form **cleverer** is used.

In contrast, when one or more things are compared with members of a group **to which they belong,** the **superlative** form of an adjective is normally used.

(a) Ashok is the **youngest** of all the boys in the class.

In this example, Ashok is being compared with members of the group identified as **all the boys** in the class. This is a group to which he belongs. Therefore, the superlative form **youngest** is used.

3. **Logical comparison: While making comparisons, care must be taken, particularly in formal English, to ensure that the comparisons are logical and that the appropriate objects are in fact being compared.**
   (a) Life in the country is different from the city. *Incorrect*

The sentence is logically incorrect, because it compares **life in the country** to **the city.** In order to be logically correct, the sentence must be changed so that similar types of things are being compared.

(b) Life in the country is different from life in the city. *Correct*

This sentence is logically correct, since it compares **life in the country** to **life in the city.**

4. **Comparative degree of adjectives is used for the comparison of two, for more than two we should use the superlative. Likewise we should not use superlative for comparing two objects.**
   (a) Which is better tea, coffee or milk? *Incorrect*
   Which is the best tea, coffee or milk? *Correct*
   (c) He is the best of the two students. *Incorrect*
   He is the better of the two students. *Correct*
5. **Normally two superlatives are not used in a sentence.**
   (a) He is the most strongest of all. *Incorrect*
   He is the strongest of all. *Correct*
6. **We should also not use 'other' or 'else' with superlatives.**
   (a) She is the most beautiful of all girls. (not all other girls)
   (b) He is the strongest of all students. (not all other students)
7. **We usually use 'of' with superlative but while referring 'place' we should use 'in'.**
   (a) Kolkata is the dirtiest city in India.
   (b) Udaipur is the most beautiful city in Rajasthan.
8. **The superlative with 'most' is sometimes used to denote the possession of a quality of a very high degree. In such cases no comparison is made.**
   (a) This is a most interesting book.
   (b) She is a most beautiful girl.
9. **With 'like' we use superlative, 'best' and 'most'. In such case we do not use 'the' before the superlative.**
   (a) Which of the story do you like most?
   (b) Which of the magazine do you like best?
10. **When more than one adjectives are connected with 'and', they should be either in comparative or in superlative degree.**
    (a) Ram is wise and stronger than Shyam *Incorrect*
    (b) Ram is wiser and stronger than Shyam *Correct*
11. **Some adjectives expressing qualities of highest order or for their extreme meanings cannot be compared. Such adjectives are :** absolute, perfect, full, complete, entire, whole, chief, extreme, unique, universal, circular, square, round, ideal, flat, impossible, etc.

A thing cannot be more round, more square.

Though we can see some writers using full, fuller, fullest and perfect, more perfect, most perfect and also most impossible.

12. Kind and sort refer to singular number. We can use 'this' and 'that' with them , but we cannot use 'these' and 'those' with them.

(a) I donot like these kind of shirts. *Incorrect*

I donot like this kind of shirt. *Correct*

(b) He does not like those kind of shirts. *Incorrect*

He does not like this kind of shirts. *Correct*

Note the structure of the following sentences

One of ....if not ....superlative....

(a) He is one of the greatest writers, if not the greatest writer.

(b) This is one of the largest buildings, if not the largest in the world.

(c) This is one of the longest rivers, if not the longest in the world.

Use plural noun in first part and singular noun in second part of the sentence.

One of the + superlative + plural noun...... if not the+ superlative + singular noun

Note the following structure also.

(a) She runs as fast as, if not faster than Shyam.

(b) He is as good as if not better than you.

(c) The house is as large as if not larger than that.

» Exercises

Exercise 1 *(RAS 96)*

Fill in the blanks with suitable determiners

1. Small cars are more economical than big.....
2. I bought ..... mangoes.
3. Have you .... sugar ?
4. .... knowledge of English is essential for all of us.
5. Clean .... floor properly.
6. .... room is airy.

Solutions

1. (i) ones (ii) some (iii) any (iv) A little/Some (v) the (vi) The.

Exercise 2 *(RAS 97)*

Fill in the blanks with suitable determiners

1. Will you have ...... cake?
2. There isn't....... sugar in the bowl.
3. I'll have a cigarette; will you have ..... too?

Solutions

(i) a (ii) any (iii) one

Exercise 3

Fill in the blanks with suitable determiners *(RAS 98)*

1. Uneasy lies...... head that wears .... crown.
2. .... women of India are as beautiful as .... of Europe.
3. He got admission in .... university in.......... USA.
4. He started learning .... piano at .... age of ten.

Solutions

(i) the, a (ii) x, those (iii) a, the (iv) the, the.

Exercise 4

Fill in the blanks with appropriate determiners

1. .... people have car. (a few/a little)
2. Give me .... time to decided the matter. (a few/a little)
3. He drank...........the water. (all/whole)
4. Delhi is .... from Alwar than Jaipur. (further/farther)
5. He is senior .... me . (than/to)
6. There are .... children outside the room. (some/any)
7. Have you .... question? (some/any)
8. Please give me .... water. (some/any)
9. Has he bought .... dress? (some/any)
10. He can't find .... banana tree. (some/any)
11. She has .... flowers of rose. (some/any)
12. I could not get .... notebook there. (some/any)
13. Nisha did not eat .... mango. (some/any)
14. Will you please lend me .... money. (some/any)
15. She must give me .... time to finish this work. (some/any)

16. Is there .... money in your pocket? (some/any)
17. .... dreams are very romantic. (some/any)
18. Sorry, I am stranger here, I have .... knowledge about this place. (few/little)
19. She has .... clothes. (some/any)
20. He has not .... car. (some/any)

Solutions

1. A few 2. a little 3. all
4. farther 5. to 6. some
7. any 8. some 9. any
10. any 11. some 12. any
13. any 14. some 15. some
16. any 17. Some 18. little
19. some 20. any

Exercise 5

Fill in the blanks with near or next

1. Mr. Sharma lives .... to Ram's house.
2. Radhika will speak .... to Sarla.
3. The railway station is .... to my school.
4. I will meet you at the .... crossing.
5. This matter will be discussed again in the .... meeting.

Solutions

1. near 2. next 3. near
4. next 5. next

Exercise 6

Fill in the blanks with much or many

1. How .... students are there in the hostel.
2. .... people comes to see this temple daily.
3. He doesn't have .... money to donate.
4. I love you very ....
5. There are .... balls in the store room.
6. I am .... obliged to you for your timely help.
7. .... girls were absent yesterday.

Solutions

1. many 2. many 3. much
4. much 5. many 6. much
7. many

Exercise 7

Fill in the blanks in the following sentences with elder, eldest, older or oldest

1. Ram is .... than me.
2. My father is the .... member of our family.
3. My father is .... than your father.
4. My brother is .... to me.
5. This is the .... building in our village.
6. How .... are you?
7. My ....brother is an IAS officer.
8. This building is .... than that.
9. We should respect to our ....
10. The .... he grew, the more demands he made.

Solutions

1. older 2. eldest 3. older
4. elder 5. oldest 6. old
7. elder 8. older 9. elders
10. older

Exercise 8

Fill in the blanks with last, later, latest or latter

1. At .... the president gave thanks to the audience.
2. Ram came .... than Shyam.
3. This is the .... technology in the field of computer science.
4. Between Ram and Shyam, the .... is more intelligent.
5. The .... half of the century saw many revolutions.
6. Ram was promoted as officer at a .... date.
7. The ....chapter of this book is very interesting.

Solutions

1. last 2. later 3. latest
4. latter 5. latter 6. later
7. last

Exercise 9

Correct the following sentences

1. Whole girls were present in the function.
2. All the third books are in our course.
3. This is mine bed, which is your?
4. None of these two books are useful.
5. A good deal of persons were present at the railway station.
6. All the sides of the coin are shining.
7. He alone lives in such a large house.
8. The both girls have arrived.
9. She is among the four first merit holders.
10. Lord Ram was an incarnate God.

Solutions

1. All the girls were present in the function.
2. All the three books are in our course.

3. This is my bed, which is yours?
4. Neither of these two books are useful.
5. A number of persons were present at the railway station.
6. Both the sides of the coin are shining.
7. He lives alone in such a large house.
8. Both the girls have arrived.
9. She is among the first four merit holders.
10. Lord Ram was God incarnate.

Exercise 10

Correct the following sentences

1. Our all members are very cooperative
2. His all books have been burnt in fire.
3. I bought tickets three for Delhi.
4. The Great Ashoka was a brave king.
5. This custom has been observed since immemorial time.
6. Have you new anything to tell me about the incident?
7. Ram is as taller as his brother.
8. Sita is not more beautiful as Rita.
9. Gold is more precious than any metal.
10. She is not that all reliable.

Solutions

1. All our members are very cooperative.
2. All his books have been burnt in fire.
3. I bought three tickets for Delhi.
4. Ashoka the Great was a brave king.
5. This custom has been observed since time immemorial.
6. Have you anything new to tell me about the incident.?
7. Ram is as tall as his brother.
8. Sita is not as beautiful as Rita. or Sita is not more beautiful than Rita.
9. Gold is more precious than any other metal.
10. She is not all that reliable.

Exercise 11

Correct the following sentences

1. To drive is as difficult as fishing.
2. It is as difficult to swim as driving.
3. It is not as easy to write as reading.
4. They had better died than surrender before the enemy.
5. I had rather read than wasting my time here.
6. He is junior than me.
7. According to Ram milk is preferable than tea.
8. She is more wiser than her brother.
9. My house is better than Ram.
10. The climate of Udaipur is better than Jaipur.

Solutions

1. Driving is as difficult as fishing.
2. It is as difficult to swing as drive.
3. It is not as easy to write as read.
4. They had better die than surrender before the enemy.
5. I had rather read than waste my time here.
6. He is junior to me.
7. According to Ram, milk is preferable to tea.
8. She is wiser than her brother.
9. My house is better than Ram's.
10. The climate of Udaipur is better than that of Jaipur.

Exercise 12

Correct the following sentences

1. There are lesser rooms in this hotel than mentioned.
2. Take this tablet with a few milk.
3. Your problem is comparatively easier than that of mine.
4. The quality of this detergent powder is comparatively better.
5. He runs as faster, if not fast than you.
6. Sita is as beautiful as her sister if not beautiful.
7. The more you hide something, the most you expose yourself.
8. This is all the more better.
9. The valley goes deep and deep after this point.
10. Ram said, 'I am very better now.'

Solutions

1. There are fewer rooms in this hotel than mentioned.
2. Take this tablet with a little milk.
3. Your problem is comparatively easy than that of mine.
4. The quality of this detergent powder is comparatively good.
5. He runs as fast, if not faster than you.
6. Sita is as beautiful as if not more beautiful than her sister.
7. The more you hide something, the more you expose yourself.
8. This is all the better.
9. The valley goes deeper and deeper after this point.
10. Ram said, 'I am much better now.'

Spotting the Errors

Find the errors and justify your answers

1. Kolkatta is further (A) /from Alwar (B) /than Jaipur (C) /the capital of Rajasthan (D). ***(Bank PO)***
2. Ramesh is smarter (A) /enough to get (B) /selected for this (C) /post, without any recommendations (D). ***(NDA)***
3. He said, 'Priyanka (A) /is the most unique (B) /singer of (C) /our college (D).'
4. This shirt is (A) /comparatively better (B) /than that (C) /we saw in corner shop yesterday (D). ***(BSRB)***
5. Everyone was surprised to note (A) /that Rahim married a girl (B) /who was more beautiful and more tall (C) /than he (D).
6. A lots of books (A) /on English grammar are (B) /available with me but (C) /this one is the best (D). ***(BSRB)***
7. I told her (A) /that it would be all (B) /the more better (C) /if she herself talked to the groom (D).
8. She does not have (A) /some money to buy (B) /a new refrigerator (C) /so she is worried (D). ***(CDS)***
9. Now a days (A) /the weather (B) /is getting more cold (C) /and colder (D).
10. All the books (A) /were indeed interesting (B) /but that one was (C) /the more interesting (D).
11. There were only two (A)/warriors but each and every (B)/warrior was equal (C)/to six persons (D). ***(CDS)***
12. Whole the chapter (A) /of this grammar book is full of errors (B) /that shows the (C) /carelessness of the proof reader (D).
13. Can we rely (A) /on this agency (B) /for the last news (C) /of the day (D)?
14. Ram is junior than (A) /Shyam and (B) Ram is older (C) /than Ganesh (D). ***(Bank PO)***
15. The militants (A) /entered the palace (B) /from the utmost gate (C) /with guns hidden in their clothes (D). ***(BSRB)***
16. "She can't sing (A) /much than (B) /four songs at (C) /a stretch", he informed (D).
17. It is well know (A) /that Mrs Indira Gandhi (B) /was the first statesman (C) /of her time (D). ***(Bank PO)***

» *Answers*

1. (A) Change further to farther. Farther is the comparative degree of far.
2. (A) Replace smarter by smart.
3. (B) Delete most. Some words like unique, full, whole, square, universal are used as superlatives so we should not use most here.
4. (B) Write either 'comparatively good' or 'better'.
5. (C) Replace 'more tall' by taller.
6. (A) Replace 'A lots of' by 'Lots of' or 'A lot of'.
7. (C) more better is incorrect. Avoid double comparative. Delete more.
8. (B) Replace some money by any money. Any is used in negative sentences.
9. (C) Replace more cold by colder.
10. (D) Replace more by most.
11. (B) Change each and every to 'each'.
12. (A) Replace whole the by 'The whole'.
13. (C) Replace last by latest.
14. (A) Replace than by 'to'.
15. (C) Replace utmost by outermost.
16. (B) Replace much by more.
17. (C) Replace first by foremost.

Unit

7

Adverb

What Is an Adverb?

An adverb is that word in a sentence which modifies the meaning of verb or adjective or another adverb or phrase, or a clause.

(a) He ran fast.
Modifies the verb, ran.

(b) These are very sweet magoes.
Modifies the adjective, sweet.

(c) She speaks very loudly.
Modifies the adverb, loudly.

(d) He was sitting close beside her.
Modifies the phrase, beside her.

If an adverb is used in the beginning of a sentence, it modifies the whole sentence.

(a) Unfortunately, the bank closed at two today.

(b) Certainly she is right.

(c) Fortunately we escaped unhurt.

In the above examples, the adverb modifies the entire sentence.

Some Important Adverbs

Fairly and Rather

Fairly is used with favourable adjectives and adverbs while **rather** is used before unfavourable adjectives and adverbs.

(a) Ram is fairly clever, but Ramesh is rather foolish.

(b) Ram walks fairly fast but Anil walks rather slowly.

(c) Harish was fairly relaxed; Sita was rather tense.

(d) It was a fairly interesting film.

(e) It is rather a boring book.

With adjectives and adverbs like fast, slow, thin, thick, hot, cold, etc. which do not indicate in themselves either favourable or unfavourable, the use of fairly reflects approval and use of rather, disapproval .

(a) This coffee is fairly hot.
(implies that the speaker likes hot coffee)

(b) This coffee is rather hot.
(implies that it is a little too hot for him)

Rather when used before alike, like, similar, different etc. and before comparatives, means 'a little' or 'slightly'.

(a) These cats are rather like cubs in some ways.

(b) The weather was rather hot than we had expected.

Rather a is possible with certain nouns like disappointment, disadvantage, nuisance, pity, shame and sometimes joke.

(a) It's rather a nuisance (= a little inconvenient) that we can't play here.

(b) It's rather a disappointment (= a little unfortunate) that he failed again.

When rather is used before favourable adjectives/ adverbs like clever, good, pretty, well, amusing, etc. then its meaning changes; it becomes nearly equivalent to very and expresses complimentary feelings.

(a) She is rather clever.
(means she is very clever)
(b) It is rather a good movie.
(means better than our thoughts, it is a recommendation)
(c) I rather like the smell of petrol.
(d) He rather enjoys queueing.

The use of rather + like or enjoy often expresses a liking.

Hard and Hardly

The adverb **hard** means as adjective.

(a) He works hard.
(b) She looked hard at me.
(c) He was running as hard as he could.
(d) She was working hard.

Hardly, Scarcely, Barely

The adverbs hardly, scarcely and barely are almost negative (almost not) in meaning. **Hardly** is usually used with any, ever, at all, or the verb 'can'.

(a) She has hardly any money.
Very little money)
(b) We hardly ever go out.
(We very seldom go out)
(c) It hardly rained at all summer last year.
(Almost no rain)
(a) The bag is so heavy that he can hardly lift it.
(Unable to lift the bag)

Hardly can also be used with other verbs :

(a) I hardly know him.
(I know him only very slightly)

One should not be confused with adverbs 'hard' and 'hardly'.
(a) He looked hard at it. (He stared at it)
(b) She hardly looked at me. (She gave me only a brief glance or didn't look)

Scarcely means 'almost not' and can replace 'hardly' as used above.

But scarcely is usually used to mean not quite.

(a) There were scarcely ten people in the meeting. (probably fewer)

Barely means 'not more than'/'only just'.

(a) His voice was barely audible. (It was only just audible)
(b) There were barely ten people in the meeting. (only just ten)
(c) I can barely see it. (I can only just see it)

Yet and Still

Both are adverbs of time. **Yet** means up to the time of speaking. It is usually used with the negative or interrogative.

Still emphasises that the action continues. It is mainly used with the affirmative or interrogative. It can also be used with the negative to emphasise the continuance of an action.

(a) He hasn't completed (his work) yet.
(b) He hasn't yet applied for the licence I told him about.
(c) He is still in bed.
(d) Has she come? Not yet.
(e) The jeep hasn't arrived yet.
(f) Is lunch ready yet?
(g) Has the jeep arrived yet?
(h) It is still raining.
(i) She still doesn't understand.
(Action of not understanding continues)
(j) She doesn't understand yet.
(The positive action of understanding hasn't yet started)

Yet is normally placed after verb or after verb + object. If the object consists of a large number of words yet can be placed before the verb also.
Still is placed after the verb 'be' but before other verbs

Since and Ever Since

Since and **ever since** are used with perfect tenses. Since can be placed after the auxiliary or in end position after a negative or interrogative verb; ever since (adverb) is usually placed in the end position.

Phrases and clauses with since and ever since are usually in end position though front position is also possible.

(a) I first met her three years ago and have remembered her face ever since.
(b) I saw her five years ago and had been trying to meet her ever since.
(c) He's been in bed since his accident.
(d) It has been raining since I came.

Somehow and Anyhow

Somehow (means in some way or other) can be placed in the front position or after averb without object or after the object.

(a) Somehow they managed.
(b) They managed somehow.
(c) They raised the money somehow.

(d) I wasn't qualified to apply for this job really but I got it anyhow.

Anyhow is an adverb of manner. It is often used to mean in any case/anyway.

Badly and Well

Badly and **Well** can be used as adverbs of manner or degree. As adverbs of manner they come after an active verb, after the object or before the past participle in a passive verb.

(a) He behaved badly.
(b) He read well.
(c) He paid her badly.
(d) She speaks French well.
(e) She was badly paid.
(f) The trip was well organised.

Badly as an adverb of degree usually comes after the object or before the verb or past participle :

The door needs a coat of paint badly. *Incorrect*

The door badly needs a coat of paint. *Correct*

(a) He was badly injured in the last match.

Well (degree) and well (manner) have the same position rules.

(a) I'd like the steak well done.
(b) He knows the town well.
(c) Shake the bottle well.
(d) The children were well wrapped up.

The meaning of **well** may depend on its position. Note the difference.

(a) You know that I can't drive well. (I'm not a good driver)

Well can be placed after may/might and could to emphasise the probability of an action.

(a) He may well refuse = It is quite likely that he will refuse.
(for may/might as well, see 288)

Too

Too is different from 'very'. Too means 'excess' ('more than enough' or 'more than necessary' or 'more than is wanted')

(a) He is too weak to walk.
(b) She is too poor to pay her fee.
(c) It was too cold to go out, so we stayed at home.

We can use an infinitive structure after too + adjective/adverb/determiner.

(a) She is too old to work.
(b) It is far too cold to play tennis.
(c) We arrived too late to have lunch.

If the infinitive has its own subject, this is introduced by for.

(a) It's too late for the shops to be open.
(b) The runway's too short for planes to land.
(c) There was too much mud for us to go walking.

The subject of a sentence with too can also be the object of the following infinitive. Object pronouns are not normally used after the infinitive in such cases.

The water is too hot to drink it. *Incorrect*
The water is too hot to drink. *Correct*

However, object pronouns are possible in this structures with 'for'.

The water is too hot for us to drink (it).

The two possible meanings of sentences like.
(a) He's too stupid to teach. (He's too stupid to be a teacher.)
(b) He's too stupid for anyone to teach. (He can't be taught.)

Too is not normally used before adjective + noun.

(a) I put down the too heavy bag. *Incorrect*
I put down the bag because it was too heavy. *Correct*
(b) She doesn't like too tall men. *Incorrect*
She doesn't like men who are too tall. *Correct*
(c) Let's forget this too difficult problem. *Incorrect*
Let's forget this problem, it's too difficult. *Correct*

In a rather formal style, 'too' can be used before adjective + a/an + noun.

(d) It's too cold a day to go out.
(e) He was too clever a businessman to accept the offer initially.
(As a businessman he was too clever to accept the offer initially.)

too + adverb + infinitive
(a) It is too soon (for me) to say whether the plan will succeed.
(b) She spoke too quickly for me to understand. (for me is necessary here.)

Too and Too Much

Before adjectives without nouns and before adverbs we use too, not too much.

(a) You're too much kind to me. *Incorrect*
You're too kind to me. *Correct*
(b) I arrived too much early. *Incorrect*
I arrived too early. *Correct*

Far, Farther, Farthest and Further, Furthest

Far is usually used in the comparative and superlative.

(a) He travelled farther than we expected.
(b) He travelled the farthest of all and so got the first prize.

In negative and interrogative sentences the positive form of 'far' is more usual.

(a) How far can you see?
(b) I can't see far.

In the affirmative 'a long way' is more usual than 'far' and a 'long way away' is more usual than 'far away'.

(a) They went a long way.
(b) Jack sailed a long way.
(c) Ram lives a long way away.

Far can be used in abstract terms also.

(a) The new law doesn't go far enough.
(b) You've gone too far!
(You've been too insulting/overbearing etc.)

'Far' is also used with comparatives or with too/so + positive forms.
(a) He explains far better than I do.
(b) She eats far too much.

Further, Furthest Further, Furthest can be used as adverbs of place/distance.

(a) It doesn't appear safe to go any further/farther in this fog.

Further and Furthest can also be used in abstract terms.

(a) Ramesh said that these biting toys should not be on sale.
(b) Mahesh went further and said that no biting to should be sold.
(c) Ganesh went furthest of all and said that no toys of any kind should be sold.

Much and Very Much

Much (meaning a lot) modifies comparative or superlative adjectives and adverbs.

(a) The dinner was much better.
(b) Nisha is much the best girl in the college.
(c) He completed the task much more quickly than we expected.

'Much too' can be used with positive forms.

(a) He spoke much too fast.

Much (meaning a lot) also modifies negative verbs.

(a) He doesn't walk much nowadays.

In interrogative sentences, much is mainly used with how. In questions without how, **much** can also be used but a lot is more common.

(a) How much has she walked?
Has she walked a lot/much?

In affirmative sentences, the construction **as/ so/ too + much** is possible, but a lot/a good deal/ a great deal is preferable.

(a) He shouts so much that it causes irritation.
(b) He talks too much.
(c) She writeh feelings like admire, amuse, approve, dislike, distress, enjoy, impress, like, object, shock, surprise, etc.
(a) Thans a lot/a great deal.

Very much (meaning greatly) is used more widely in affirmative. It is used with; blame, praise, thank and with a number of verbs concerned witk you very much.

(b) I admire her very much.
(c) They object very much to the noise we make.

Much (means greatly) with or without very can also be used with the participles like admired, amused, disliked, distressed, impressed, liked, shocked, struck, upset, etc.

(a) I was (very) much admired.
(b) He was (very) much impressed by her good manners.
(c) She was much shocked to hear the sad news.
(d) I was much upset to hear about the accident.

Much and Very

Generally participles are modified by **much** and adjectives by **very**. Certain participles which have largely lost their verbal force and are felt to be adjectival, however, take **very**.

(a) The law has been much abused. *(participle)*
(b) Her dress was much admired. *(participle)*
(c) It is a very good book. *(adjective)*
(d) This is a very old building. *(adjective)*
(e) She is a very clever girl. *(adjective)*
(f) I was very interested in his story. *(adjective)*

(g) We are very worried about the position. (*adjective*)

(h) I feel very concerned about him. (*adjective*)

Conversely, participles used before a noun to make a compound adjective with a modifying adverb, take **much**: a much abused privilege, a much travelled person, a much discussed question.

Quite : Has Two Meanings

Quite means completely when it is used with a word or phrase which expresses the idea of completeness (such words or phrases are all right, certain, determined, empty, finished, full, ready, right, sure, wrong, etc.) and also when it is used with a very strong adjective/adverb like amazing, extraordinary, horrible, perfect, etc.

(a) The container was quite empty.
(b) You're quite right.
(c) It was quite amazing. I can't believe it at all.

Quite means slightly less, when it is used with other adjectives/adverbs. It has a slightly weakening effect. Quite good is normally less complimentary than good. Quite used in this way has approximately the same meaning as 'fairly' but its strength changes a lot according to the way it is stressed.

(a) quite good (weak quite, strong good) is slightly less than good
(b) quite good (equal stress) means moderately good
(c) quite good (strong quite, weak good) is much less than good

The position of a/an with **quite**:
(a) We had quite a long walk.
(b) It is quite an old castle.

Seldom

Seldom is an adverb. We may say 'I seldom go to London,' but not 'My visits to London are seldom,' for here we are treating the word as a predicative adjective. It can be used after a verb in this way (and then as an adverb) only in the following types of construction.

After 'it is'. and followed by a 'that' clause in apposition to the anticipatory pronoun 'it'.

(a) It is seldom that we get such an opportunity as this.

In a relative clause : that refers back to the whole notion expressed in a preceding clause of time.

(a) When she lost her temper, which was seldom.
(b) Whenever I take a day off from work, which is seldom.

In a parenthetic clause referring back to the entire notion expressed in a preceding adverb clause of time.

(a) Whenever I take a day off from work, which is seldom.

Modify seldom : Seldom is a negative word meaning 'not often' and should not, therefore, be modified by another negative.

The phrases 'seldom if ever' and 'seldom or never' are possible but not 'seldom or ever'.
(a) She seldom if ever asks the boys the reason of their absence.
(b) She seldom or never tells lies.

Enough

Adjective/adverb + enough : When enough modifies an adjective or adverb, it normally comes after the adjective/ adverb.

(a) Is that music loud enough?
(b) These shoes are not big enough.
Is it warm enough for you?
(Not ..... enough warm ....)
(a) You're not driving fast enough.
(b) We haven't got a big enough house.
(c) We'll go swimming if we get warm enough weather.
(d) You could wear my shoes, you've got big enough feet.

Position with adjective + noun : Enough follows an adjective which it modifies (see paragraph I above). But when enough modifies an adjective and noun together, it comes before the adjective.

Compare:

(a) We haven't got big enough nails.
(we need bigger nails—enough modifies big)

Enough + infinitive

The adverb enough is often followed by an infinitive.

(a) She didn't run fast enough to win.
(b) She's old enough to do what she wants.

Infinitives can be introduced by for + noun/pronoun. Object forms of pronouns are used.

(a) It's late enough for the staff to stop work.
(b) There was just enough light for us to see what we were doing.
(c) The radio's small enough to put in your pocket.
(d) Those tomatoes aren't ripe enough to eat. (Not .... to eat them.)

Close and Closely

Close is used as an adverb meaning 'near'.

(a) Keep yourself close to me.
(b) He was following close behind.

Closely is used with other meanings like stiricitly,carefully etc.,

(a) The militants were closely (= strictly) guarded.
(b) Watch closely (= carefully) what she does.

He explained the theory in six closely written pages. (i.e. with the words and lines close together.)

Dead and Deadly

Dead as an adverb means 'completely', 'absolutely': dead level; dead straight; going dead slow (almost stopped, very very slowly); dead certain; dead drunk.

(a) I found him dead drunk.
(b) I am dead certain that Shyam has taken the purse.
(c) I am dead against the legalisation of prostitution.
(d) The wind was blowing dead against our desired direction.

Deadly is otherwise an adjective. It is used as an adverb meaning like 'death' in deadly pale and (figuratively) deadly dull.

(a) The news was accurate and reliable but deadly dull.

Direct and Directly

When used as adverb, **direct** means straight, without detours, intermediaries, etc.

(a) This train goes direct to New Delhi.
(b) He went direct to the hospital.

I shall have direct communication with you. (not through any intermediary)

Directly is used meaning either 'at once', 'immediately, or 'after a short time', 'very soon'.

(a) She left directly after lunch.
(b) I'll be with you directly.

Other meanings :

(a) I am not directly affected by the changes in policy.
(b) He's directly descended from Indira Gandhi.

Easy and Easily

The use of **easy** as adverb is found in a few phrases only.

(a) Stand at ease (a military command)
(b) Take it easy.
(Don't be worried about it or don't work too hard)
(c) Go easy with the cheese.
(means, 'use it with moderation')

Easily means without difficulty or with ease.

(a) He solved the problem easily.
(b) She's not easily satisfied.
(c) He won the match easily.

High and Highly

High is used adverbially in a numer of phrases like fly high, aim high, fix one's hopes high dream high, play high.

(a) One should dream high. (have lofter aims)
(b) He aims high.

It is also used after run in following kind of sentences:

(a) Feelings there have been running high, in the wake of last week's killings.
(means, the people were angry or excited)
(b) The sea was running high. (Sea was trubulent)
(c) Passions were running high.(Excitement)

Highly is used adverbially before participles like highly interesting, highly paid, a highly educated, highly qualified, highly amusing, highly intelligent, speak highly of someone, esteem someone highly, think highly of someone.

(a) He is highly educated.
(b) She is a highly intelligent woman.
(c) I esteem my father highly.

Right and Rightly

Right has a wide use as an adverb.

(a) It serves you right.
(It is in your benefit)
(b) She answered right. (Answered correctly)

(c) Nothing goes right with me.
(I feel unlucky)
(d) You will come right away. Immediately or at once).

Rightly usually means 'correctly', and has mid position, with the verb.
(a) He rightly answered that question.
(b) I am unable rightly recollect if she brought anything.
(c) The president rightly pointed out the mistake.

Just and Justly

The adverb **just** is used in many phrases like only just, just now then just here there just as you say or just so. It has no resemblance with the adjective just and the noun justice.
(a) We only just managed to catch the plane.
(b) He has arrived just now.
(c) They earn just enough for their needs.

The meaning of adverb **justly** is linked with the adjective just and the noun justice.

Justly usually means 'rightly' or 'as per demand of justice'.
(a) As you justly (rightly) notice.
(b) He was justly punished by the court.

Late and Lately

The meaning of adverb **late** is the opposite of the adverb 'early' : go to bed late, get up late, stay up late, arrive late, marry late.

Lately means recently.
(a) He came late today.
(b) I haven't seen her lately (recently).
(c) She has finished her work lately.
(d) You are late.

Position of Adverbs

Adverbs of Manner

1. Generally adverbs of manner is placed after the verb.
(a) He played **beautifully**.
(b) He wrote **quickly**.
If there is an object the adverb is placed after it
(c) She gave him a pen **reluctantly.**
(d) Ramesh speak English and Hindi **well.**

2. If the structure of the sentence is verb + preposition + object, the adverb can be placed either before the prepostion or after the object.
(a) She looked at me surprisingly.
(b) She looked surprisingly at me.

In case the object contains a number of words then put the adverb before the preposition.
(a) She looked surprisingly at everyone who got off the car.

In case of sentence structure **verb + object,** if the object is long, put the adverb before the verb and for short object the adverb should be placed after the object.
(a) He carefully picked up all the bits of broken mirror.
(b) She hastily denied that she had stolen the purse.

Adverbs of Place

The most commonly used adverbs of place are away, everywhere, here, nowhere, some where, there, abroad, upstairs, etc.

In sentences with object or object + preposition structure, adverb comes after the verb.
(a) Ramesh sent his wife away.
(b) I searched for her everywhere.

In sentences with no object, adverbs are placed after the verb.
(a) The thief fled away.
(b) He lives abroad.
(c) Jack is upstairs.

Adverbs of Time

Adverbs of time such as **eventually, afterwards, lately, now, recently, soon, then, today, tomorrow**, etc. and adverb phrases or time like **at once, since then till (6.00 etc.)** are usually placed at the very beginning or at the very end of the clause.
(a) Eventually she came.
(b) She came eventually.
(c) Then they went home.
(d) They went home then.

Adverbs of time such as **before, early, immediately** and **late** are usually placed at the end of the clause.

(a) Ram came late.
(b) He will go early.

If 'before' and 'immediately' are used as conjunctions, they are placed at the beginning of the clause.
(a) Immediately the rain stops we will go.
(b) I had left the house before he came.

Adverbs of time such as **since and ever since** are used with perfect tenses. Since can be placed after the auxiliary verb or in the end after a negative or interrogative verb and ever since (adverb) is usually placed in the end.

(a) He's been in bed since his accident.
(b) I have been working here since last January.
(c) She had an accident last month and has been on leave ever since.
(d) He hadn't turned up since.

Adverbs of Frequency

The adverbs of frequency are divided in two groups to understand their use.

1. always, continually, frequently, occasionally, often, once, twice, periodically, repeatedly, sometimes, usually, etc.

2. ever, hardly ever, never, rarely, scarcely ever, seldom, etc.

All the above adverbs in Group 1 are placed after auxiliary 'is, am are' in simple sentences.

(a) He is always ready.
(b) She is often late.
(c) He is occasionally late.
(d) They are usually happy.

Adverbs in Group 2 are placed before the verbs (if there is no auxiliary).

(a) His mother never cooks food.
(b) He always speaks the truth.
(c) He often comes late.
(d) He has never advised me.
(e) We have never seen an aeroplane.
(f) He can never understand.
(g) You have often been told not to do that.

If the sentence contains auxiliary verbs has, have, can, etc. these adverbs are placed after first auxiliary as in sentences (d), (e), (f), (g) above.

These adverbs are used after auxiliary + subject in interrogative sentences :

(h) Have you ever taken meat?
(i) Have you ever visited Agra?

Exceptions

With 'used to' and 'have to' place the adverb before them.

(a) I hardly ever have to remind him; he always remembers.
(b) He is always used to smoke before going to bed.

Adverbs in Group 1 above (except always is not used with imperatives) can also be placed at the beginning or end of a sentence or clause.

The adverb 'often' if put at the end normally requires the use of 'very' or 'quite' with it.

(a) Often he walked.
(b) He walked quite often.
(c) She visits here very often.
(d) She often visits here.

Adverbs in Group 2 above; hardly ever, never, rarely etc. (but not ever alone) can also be placed at the beginning of a sentence.

1. If these are used at the beginning of the sentence , inversion of the verb is necessary.

Negative verbs are not used with hardly/ scarcely ever, never, rarely and seldom, as these are themselves negative in meanings.

(a) Hardly ever did we manage to meet unobserved.
(b) Never before had I been asked to do this work.
(c) I hardly ever go out.
(d) It hardly rained at all last summer.
(e) There were scarcely twenty girls there.

Adverbs of Degree

The most commonly used adverbs of degree are almost, absolutely, barely, completely, enough, entirely, extremely, fairly, far, hardly, just, much, nearly, only, quite, rather, really, scarcely, so, too, very, etc.

The adverb **only** modify verbs. Usually it is placed next to the word to which it qualifies. It is placed before the verbs, adjectives and adverbs. It is also placed before and after the nouns and pronouns. The meaning of the sentence changes with change of position of adverb 'only'.

(a) He had only four chairs. (not more than four)
(b) He only lend the umbrella. (he didn't sell it)
(c) He gave the pen to me only. (not to anyone else)

(d) I believe only half of what he said.
(not everything what he said)

Note the difference in meaning

(a) Only she can speak. (she alone can speak)
(b) She can only speak. (she can't write or read)
(c) She can speak only.
(she can't do any other work like cooking or washing)

The adverb **just** like **only**, should also be placed before the word it qualifies.

(a) I'll just buy one.
(b) I had just enough money.

It can also be placed before the verb.

(c) I'll just buy one.
(b) I just had enough money.

The change of position would change the meaning.

(e) Just sign. it means,
(you are to sign only or this is all you have to do)
(f) Sign just here means. (Sign at this particular spot)

An adverb of degree usually modifies an adjective or another adverb. It is placed before that adjective or adverb.

(a) You are **absolutely** correct.
(b) I was **almost** ruined.

Exception

The adverb **enough** is placed after the adjective.

(a) The house isn't large enough.
(b) She didn't work quickly enough.
(c) He is tall enough to reach the fan.

Some adverbs of degree can also modify verbs like; **almost, barely, enough, hardly, just, little, much, nearly, quite, rather, really and scarcely.** These are placed before the main verb like adverbs of frequency.

(a) She almost/nearly slipped.
(b) He is just coming.

The adverb far usually needs a comparative, or ' too + positive'.

(a) It is far better to keep mum.
(b) She drives far too fast.

Order of Adverbs

If two or more adverbs are used in a sentence then it becomes important to place them in a certain order.

When there are two adverbs of time, the adverbs indicating a point of time (e.g. 3 'o'clock, 4 P.M.) or the shorter period of time is usually placed first. In some cases position can also be reversed.

(a) I saw the movie on Sunday evening last week.
(b) I'll meet you at 4 'o'clock on Monday.
(c) She arrived at 3 'o'clock yesterday evening.
(d) She was born at 6 'o'clock in the evening on Sunday in 1987.

The adverb showing a period of time may have front position for emphasis, prominence or contrast.

(a) Yesterday I went there at four 'o'clock but tomorrow I'll go there at 6 'o'clock.
(b) Yesterday evening she arrived at 6 'o'clock, but tomorrow she'll arrive at 7 'o'clock.

When there are two such adverbs, one indicating point of time another indicating period of time, the adverb showing point of time cannot have front position in isolation.

(a) At 4 'o'clock I'll meet you tomorrow. Incorrect

But if both are used, front position is possible.

(a) At 4 'o' clock tomorrow I will meet you at the hotel.

If, however, the larger unit of time is considered to be more important or for the sake of emphasis or if the smaller is an afterthought this order may be reversed.

(a) She arrived yesterday evening, about 6 'o'clock.

When there are two adverbs of place, the smaller unit is usually placed first. The order is often a matter of style and balance. It is not a mandatory rule.

(a) Ram lives in a small village in Rajasthan.
(b) We spent the holidays in cottage in the mountains.
(c) We spent the holidays in the mountains in a small cottage we rented from a friend.

When a sentence contains both an adverb of place or direction and an adverb of time, the adverbial of time is usually placed last.

(a) We're going to Agra next month
(b) I expect to be back home by Sunday.

(c) Meet me outside the church at 6 o'clock on Sunday.

(d) We went to a party last month.

Variations in this order are possible. The adverbs of **time** may also have front position. The adverbs of **place** or **direction** are not placed normally in front position.

(a) Last month we went to Kashmir; next month we're going to Nainital. (adverbs of time in front position)

(b) On Monday they sailed from Sri Lanka; on Saturday they landed in India.

Adverbs of place and direction usually precedes the adverbs of frequency. Adverbs of frequency usually precede the adverbs of time.

(a) I have been to USA several times this year.

(b) He strolled round the park twice before supper.

(c) She gave lectures at the school three days a week last term.

(d) I passed him in the street twice last month.

(e) She goes to USA every other year nowadays.

Variations in this order are possible. We can place adverbs of time in front position for emphasis or contrast.

(a) Before supper she strolled round the park twice.

(b) Last term she gave lectures at the school three days a week; this term she is lecturing there two days a week.

When adverbs of manner, place and time occur in one sentence adverb of manner usually precedes adverb of place.

(a) He climbed swiftly on the roof.

(b) He will stay happily there.

But some adverbs like away, back, down, forward, home, in, off, on, out, round and up usually precede adverbs of manner.

(a) He went back happily.

(b) She turned back anxiously.

(c) Ram went home sadly.

(d) She rode on confidently.

Adverbs of time usually follow adverbs of manner and place.

(a) We worked hard in the office today.

(b) They lived there happily for two years.

But they can also be placed in front position for the sake of emphasis.

(a) Every day he queued silently at the railway station.

Look at the following sentences also :

(a) She spoke loudly at the meeting yesterday.
1 2 3

(b) He is crying loudly at the field now.
1 2 3

(c) He was going hurriedly to Jaipur yesterday.
1 2 3

(d) She comes regularly at the ground daily.
1 2 3

1=adverb of manner, 2=adverb of place, 3= adverb of time

» Exercises

Exercise 1

Correct the sentences

1. She takes generally her breakfast at 8 A.M.
2. Ram only came here last Saturday.
3. Ramesh was too tired when he came here.
4. Sita came quicker than I expected.
5. We wanted a better and efficient office assistant.
6. It was much cold last night.
7. I visited her frequently while in New York.
8. He will be quite sorry to know that.
9. The water of this tank is too cold.
10. He ran very fastly.

Solutions

1. Generally she takes her breakfast at 8 A.M.
2. Ram came here only last Saturday.
3. Ramesh was much tired when he came here.
4. Sita came quickly than I expected.
5. We wanted a better and more efficient office assistant.
6. If was very cold last night.
7. I frequently visited her while in New York.
8. He will be very sorry to know that.
9. The water of this tank is very cold.
10. He ran very fast.

Exercise 2

Correct the sentences

1. Hari was fortunately not available in the hostel.
2. It was nothing else than her arrogance.
3. He feels comparatively better today.
4. Come at seven o'clock to my office.
5. I seldom or ever refused the leave.
6. He quickly ran away from the site.
7. Firstly you think over the words and then speak.
8. I go often to the Shani Temple.
9. No one hardly goes to church daily.
10. I care a straw for it.

Solutions

1. Fortunately Hari was not available in the hostel.
2. It was nothing else but her arrogance.
3. He feels better today.
4. Come to my office at 7 o'clock.
5. I seldom or never refused the leave.
6. He ran away quickly from the site.
7. First you think over the words and then speak.
8. I often go to the Shani Temple.
9. Hardly any one goes to church daily.
10. I do not care a straw for it.

Exercise 3

Correct the sentences

1. We were very delighted to get the news.
2. Call me anything else than a fraud.
3. They could not find her nowhere.
4. I only solved two sums.
5. She peacefully died yesterday.
6. Do you know to drive?
7. I went directly to Meerut.
8. It is very cold to go for a walk today.
9. Parul runs fastly than Nalini.
10. If you run fast, you would have won the race.

Solutions

1. We were much delightful to get the news.
2. Call me anything else but a fraud.
3. They could not find her anywhere.
4. I solved only two sums.
5. She died peacefully yesterday.
6. Do you know how to drive?
7. I went direct to Meerut.
8. It is too cold to go for a walk today.
9. Parul runs faster than Nalini.
10. Had you run fast you would have won the race.

Exercise 4

Correct the sentences

1. They have gone to Jaipur yesterday.
2. He has left this place five minutes ago.
3. Do you know him? Yes, I do not.
4. Do you know him? No, I do.
5. The teacher asked him to not sleep in the class.
6. Could you lend me your umbrella? Oh, no, I can.
7. She will today go to Mumbai.
8. With most humbly and respectfully, I beg to apprise.
9. I have not pen with me.
10. There was no an intelligent student to solve that question.

Solutions

1. They went to Jaipur yesterday.
2. He left this place five minutes ago.
3. Do you know him? Yes, I do.
4. Do you know him? No, I don't.
5. The teacher asked him not to sleep in the class.
6. Could you lend me your umbrella? Oh no, I can't.
7. She will go to Mumbai today.
8. Most humbly and respectfully, I beg to apprise.
9. I have no pen with me.
10. There was not an intelligent student to solve that question.0

Spotting the Errors

Find the errors and justify your answers

1. 'Under no circumstances (A)/ we can help you (B)/ in this immoral project' (C)/ said the chairman (D). **(BSRB)**
2. Somebody informed (A)/ the contractor that his (B)/ brother had only died (C)/ five days before (D). **(Bank PO)**
3. She is very senior(A)/ to me, so I (B)/cannot defy her orders (C).
4. Who can believe (A)/ that she was not (B)/ hardly hit (C)/ by the death of her son (D).

5. Hardly she likes (A)/ to hear my name (B)/ after the dispute which occurred (C) / between us last year (D). ***(CDS)***
6. Only by discussing with (A)/ the officer concerned (B)/ they found out (C)/ the person behind the fraud (D). ***(BSRB)***
7. The house is very good (A)/ but too much small (B)/ to accommodate (C)/ the full family (D).
8. He does not (A)/ know to make (B)/ friends so he is leading (C)/ a lonely life (D). ***(BSRB)***
9. Every member of the family (A)/ is addicted to drinking (B) and so Asha is (C).
10. He was very tired (A)/ of work so he said (B)/ that he would (C)/not accompany us (D). No error
11. Shakshi was exorbitantly paid (A)/ for how skilful she (B)/ welcomed the visitors (C). ***(CDS)***
12. She is almost quite competent (A)/for the post of marketing executive (B)/so if given a chance (C)/ she can show the results (D).
13. The student requested (A)/ the principal to be enough kind (B)/ to grant him seven days leave (C). ***(BSRB)***
14. He has been trying (A)/ to persuade her for several months (B)/ but he has (C)/ not still succeeded (D).
15. Before the game he felt surely (A)/ of wining, but within five minutes (B)/ he realised that he was wrong (C).
16. The amount which the company (A)/ paid to the dependents of (B)/ the deceased was (B)/ fairly unjustified (D). ***(NDA)***
17. Although he only earns (A)/ sixteen hundred rupees per month (B)/ yet he manages his (C)/ family well (D). ***(BSRB)***
18. I liked that opportune moment (A)/ where the workers proved themselves (B)/ and came out victorious (C). ***(Bank PO)***
19. Where else (A)/ did you go besides (B)/ the bank (C)?
20. I hardly ever (A)/ see him (B)/ because in my opinion(C)/he is not a reliable man (D).
21. He is a linguist (A)/ and always tries to (B)/ make his students (C)/ pronounce the words correctly (D). ***(Bank PO)***

» Answers

1. (B) Replace 'We can' by can we. In sentence beginning with 'Under no circumstances', verb comes before subject. (inversion is applied)
2. (C) Put 'only' after 'died'.
3. (A) Replace 'very senior' by 'much senior'. Please note that very is used before the adjectives of positive degree, while much is used before adjectives of comparative degree.
   He is a very strong boy.
   He is much stronger than you.
4. (C) Replace 'Hardly' by 'hard'.
5. (A) Write 'Hardly does she'. Inversion is applied here.
6. (A) Write 'only' before 'with'. By discussing only with.
7. (B) Replace 'Too much' by 'much too'. Much too is used before an adjective.
   It is much too pleasuresome.
8. (B) Replace 'know to make' by 'know how to make'.
   I know how to swim
   He knows how to cook.
9. (C) Replace 'so Asha is' by 'so is Asha'. Inversion is applied here.
   I don't like such cheap things nor does she.
10. (E) No error.
11. (B) Write 'how skilfully'.
12. (A) Here use of almost is wrong. We should not use any adverb before 'quite'.
13. (B) It should be 'to be kind enough'. The adverb enough is placed after the word it qualifies.
    He is intelligent enough to solve this problem.
14. (D) Replace still by yet. Normally still is used in affirmative while yet is used in negative sentence.
15. (A) Replace 'surely' by 'sure'.
16. (D) Replace 'fairly' by 'rather' or 'quite'. Fairly is used in good sense.
17. (A) It should be 'he earns only'.
18. (B) Replace 'where' by 'when'.
19. (A) delete 'else'.
20. (E) No error.
21. (B) It should be 'and so he always tries to'.

Unit

8

The Verb

Importance of Verb

We cannot frame a sentence without a verb. Verbs indicate thoughts and actions. We need nouns to name things and verbs to express what those things do. Verbs do more than just show action. They indicate when the action happened, how many things were acting and can describe the action.

Classification of Verb

Verb can be classified as following

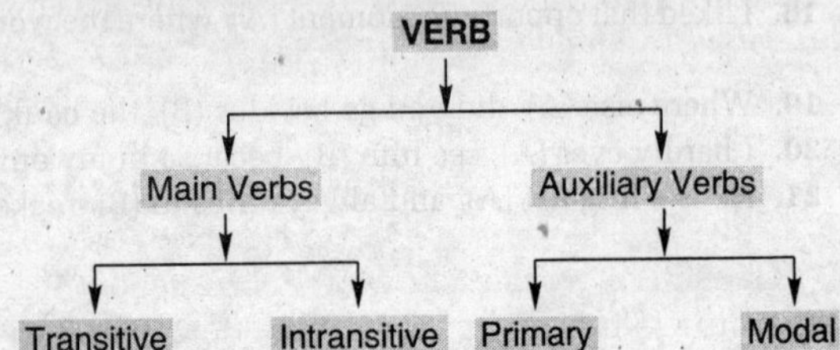

Transitive and Intransitive Verbs

Verbs can be divided into two categories, transitive and intransitive. **Transitive verbs** take objects. That is, these verbs carry the action of a subject and apply it to an object. They tell us what the subject (agent) does to something else (object).

Intransitive verbs do not take an object; they express actions that do not require the agent's doing something to something else.

Example : Sita danced.

The **intransitive verb** 'danced' is a complete action by itself and does not require a direct object to receive the action.

Some verbs can function as both transitively and intransitively. So it is not reasonable to classify a verb as **transitive** or **intransitive,** instead we should say that the verb is used transitively or intransitively.

Verbs used transitively	**Verbs used intransitively**
(a) He **speaks** the truth.	(a) Sita **speaks** slowly.
(b) The students **rang** the bell.	(b) The bell **loudly.**
(c) He **flies** kites.	(c) A bird **flies.**

Cognate Objects

Some intransitive verbs take an object after them that are similar in meaning to the verb. Such objects are called **cognate** objects.

(a) He **sighed** a deep **sigh.**

(b) Our army **fought** a fierce **fight.**

(c) I **dreamt** a sweet **dream.**

In the above sentences the verbs and the objects **(cognate)** are in bold type.

Direct and Indirect Objects

Direct Objects

When a verb is in the active voice, the **subject** of the verb refers to the person or thing 'performing' the action described by the verb; the **object** of the verb refers to the person or thing 'receiving' the action described by the verb.

In the following examples, the objects of the verbs are in bold.

(a) She read the **magazine.**

(b) I did not see the **car.**

(c) He ate the **apples** quickly.

In these sentences, the verbs **read, see** and **ate** are in the active voice; and the words magazine, car and **apples** are the objects of the verbs. These objects are said to be **direct** objects, because they refer to things which receive directly the actions described by the verbs.

Indirect Objects

In addition to taking direct objects, some verbs also take **indirect** objects. In the following examples, the direct objects are printed in bold type, and the **indirect** objects are underlined :

(a) She gave the child a **pen.**

(b) He sent the man the **information.**

In above examples, the words **child** and **man** are said to be the indirect objects of the verbs **gave** and **sent.** Indirect objects refer to things which receive indirectly the actions described by the verbs. In the above examples, the words pen and **information** are the direct objects of the verbs. **Indirect objects usually refer to living things.**

Causative Verbs

Causative verbs show that somebody or something is indirectly responsible for an action. The subject does not perform the action itself, but causes someone or something else to do it instead.

Yesterday I had my hair cut.

(I didn't cut my own hair, but I made someone else do it for me instead—I 'caused' them to cut my hair.)

(a) I made her sing a song.

(b) I made him polish my shoes.

(c) I got my clothes washed by him.

(d) I got my thesis written by him.

Such commonly used verbs are get, make, have, keep, etc.

(a) I made him laugh.

(b) I made him write a letter.

(c) He made me polish his shoes.

(d) I kept her waiting.

(e) He keeps me away from the office.

(f) I shall make him complete the project today.

The causative verbs **make, keep** are used in active voice while **have, got** are used in passive voice.

Auxiliary Verbs

Auxiliary verbs can be divided into primary and modal auxiliary verbs. Primary auxiliary verbs can be further divided as following :

Verbs **to be** : is, am , are ,was , were

Verbs **to have** : have, has ,had

Verbs **to do** : do, does, did

Auxiliary Verb 'to be' (Is/Am/Are/Was/Were)

Is, am and **are** are used in present tense while was / were are used in past tense. **Am** is used with I only, while **is** is used with other singulars. **Are** and **were** are used with plurals. **Was** is used in past with singular subject .

'To be' form of verbs are also used in continuous tense and in active and passive structures.

Auxiliary Verb 'to have' (Have/Has/Had)

Have, has and **had** are used in continuous form in perfect structures. **Have, has** and **had** are also used to show possession or ownership. **Have** is used with plural and **has** is used with singular subject. With pronoun I, use **have. Have** and **has** refer to present while **had** refers to past tense.

(a) I have a car.
(b) I have got a car.
(c) He has a book.
(d) He has got a book.
(e) He had a beautiful house.
(f) I had two sons.

The use of got with have merely emphasise the point.

Have and had are also used for take, receive, experience.

(a) I have my dinner at 9 P.M. (take)
(b) I have my bath in the morning. (take)
(c) I had no problem in searching his house. (experience)
(d) I had many messages from my past employer. (receive)

Auxiliary Verb 'to do' (Do/Does/Did)

Do, does and **did** are used in framing negative and interrogative questions in present and past tenses.

Emphatic **'do'** : The so-called emphatic do has many uses in English :

To add emphasis to an entire sentence.
(a) He does like me. He really does!

To add emphasis to an imperative.
(a) Do come in. (actually softens the command)

To add emphasis to a frequency adverb.
(a) He never did understand his mother.
(b) She always does manage to hurt her mother's feelings.

To contradict a negative statement.
(a) You didn't do your homework, did you? Oh, but I did finish it.

To ask a clarifying question about a previous negative statement.
(a) Raju didn't take the purse. Then who took the purse?

To indicate a strong concession.
(a) Although the Jack denied any wrong-doing, they did return some of the presents.

'Do' is also used to show suitability or adequacy.

(a) Have you a torch?
I haven't got a torch.

Will a match box do? (Whether the matchbox will be suitable?)

No a matchbox won't do.

(No matchbox won't be suitable.)

I am trying to find out the gas leak.

(b) Could you lend me rupees one thousand?
Would one hundred do? (= be adequate)

No it wouldn't. I need 1,000 Rs. to deposit my annual fees.

One Principal Verb + Two Auxiliaries

When two auxiliaries are used with a principal verb, the principal verb need not be repeated if the sames form (of principal verb) serve the purpose with both the auxiliaries. But if the same does not serve the purpose with both the auxiliaries, we must use different forms of the principal verbs with each auxiliary.

(a) She neither **can** nor **will** help him.
(b) He **did** not and **should** not talk to him.
(c) He neither **will** nor can solve it.
(d) They **did** not and **will** not help you.

Words in bold type are auxiliaries and words italicised are principal verbs.

(a) He neither has **talked** nor will **talk** to me.
(b) They have not **helped** and will not **help** you.

In the above sentences different forms of principal verbs are used with each auxiliary. These sentences cannot be written in following way :

(a) He neither has nor will talk to me. *(Incorrect)*
(b) They have not and will not help you. *(Incorrect)*

Linking Verbs

Linking verbs link the relationship between the agent and the rest of the sentence. They explain the connection between the subject and its complement or that which completes the subject's description.

The most common linking verb is 'to be'. Some other linking verbs are :

appear	feel	remain	sound
become	grow	seem	stay
continue	look	smell	taste

Examples :

Opera seems overly dramatic to the music novice.

'Overly dramatic' describes the agent or subject 'opera' but it does not express an action that 'opera' performs.

(a) He **appeared** jubilant at the news of the inheritance.

(b) I **am** pathetically inept in such situations.

(c) He **is** a doctor of bioethics.

While 'a doctor' answers the question 'What?' the verb is not an action verb, but rather a 'state of being' verb. Therefore it is not a transitive verb; it links the subject (he) with his state of being (doctor).

Linking verbs are always followed by nouns called **predicate nouns** or adjectives called **predicate adjectives.** They are never followed by direct objects.

Linking verbs followed by a predicate noun :

Because he had a great voice, he **became** a singer.

Linking verbs followed by a predicate adjective :

As the sun **shined** on the water, it looked beautiful.

Wow, that pie **smells** good!

However, sometimes a verb that is used as a **linking verb** in one sentence can be an **action verb** in another. When a verb is followed by an direct object, it is an **action verb.** When it is followed by an predicate adjective or noun, it is a linking verb.

Linking verb : You're growing happier every day.

Action verb : The plant is growing fast.

Inchoative Verbs

Inchoative verbs are the verbs that denote the beginning, development or final stage, or a change of condition.

Get, became, grow, etc. are some commonly used inchoative verbs.

(a) My father is getting weaker.

(b) He has become the richest man in the town.

(c) It is growing dark.

(d) It is getting dark.

Other such verbs are come, go, turn, fall, run, wear.

(a) The paper of the book turns yellow.

(b) Will his dream come true?

(c) Ram soon fell asleep.

(d) The carpet is wearing thin.

(e) The supply of water is running low nowadays.

» Exercises

Exercise 1

Identify the underlined part of speech, choose the correct answer

1. The burglar disappeared with the cash.
   a. transitive verb b. intransitive verb
   c. linking verb d. auxiliary verb

2. The director told the actors, "Do your best, and we'll be a hit."
   a. transitive verb b. intransitive verb
   c. linking verb d. auxiliary verb

3. He would tell me if he thought we were in danger.
   a. transitive verb b. intransitive verb
   c. linking verb d. auxiliary verb

4. His ability to concentrate is legendary.
a. transitive verb b. intransitive verb
c. linking verb d. auxiliary verb
5. The campers hid inside the cabin when they saw the bear.
a. transitive verb b. intransitive verb
c. linking verb d. auxiliary verb
6. Alexis is swimming in the state championship next week.
a. transitive verb b. intransitive verb
c. linking verb d. auxiliary verb
7. Frustrated with the official's call, Ethan kicked the bench.
a. transitive verb b. intransitive verb
c. linking verb d. auxiliary verb
8. The student procrastinated too long and failed to finish the project.
a. transitive verb b. intransitive verb
c. linking verb d. auxiliary verb
9. The vegetarian burger tasted like salted cardboard.
a. transitive verb b. intransitive verb
c. linking verb d. auxiliary verb
10. Ellen nodded to the audience and sang her song.
a. transitive verb b. intransitive verb
c. linking verb d. auxiliary verb
11. Her brother likes bananas, but she likes peaches.
a. transitive verb b. intransitive verb
c. linking verb d. auxiliary verb
12. Adjunct faculty are teaching in several of the lower division courses.
a. transitive verb b. intransitive verb
c. linking verb d. auxiliary verb
13. The director told the actors, 'Do your best, and we'll be a hit.'
a. transitive verb b. intransitive verb
c. linking verb d. auxiliary verb
14. Regis Philbin, the host of 'Who wants to be a Millionaire,' smiled at her answer.
a. transitive verb b. intransitive verb
c. linking verb d. auxiliary verb
15. When the contestant completed the first test, she received another clue.
a. transitive verb b. intransitive verb
c. linking verb d. auxiliary verb
16. Dennis became impatient when Thomas took so long choosing a movie.
a. transitive verb b. intransitive verb
c. linking verb d. auxiliary verb
17. President Clinton pushed into the crowd and shook her hand.
a. transitive verb b. intransitive verb
c. linking verb d. auxiliary verb
18. The hiker turned quickly toward the noise behind him.
a. transitive verb b. intransitive verb
c. linking verb d. auxiliary verb
19. Our teacher gave each of us another chance to take the exam.
a. transitive verb b. intransitive verb
c. linking verb d. auxiliary verb
20. After the chef completed the demonstration, she left the students to clean the kitchen.
a. transitive verb b. intransitive verb
c. linking verb d. auxiliary verb

Solutions

1. b	2. a	3. d	4. c
5. b	6. d	7. a	8. b
9. c	10. b	11. a	12. b
13. a	14. b	15. a	16. c
17. b	18. b	19. a	20. a

Exercise 2

Underline the verb in each sentence and indicate whether it is being used as a transitive verb or an intransitive verb.

1. Many contemporary television program expose children to violence and vulgar language.
2. My exam grade will excludes me from the soccer game.
3. Alice imagined a world full of fascinating creatures.
4. James ran in the park every afternoon.
5. The tornado destroyed entire buildings when it struck.
6. I raked the yard on Saturday.
7. The boiling water scalded my hand.
8. We talked about the news all evening.
9. My mother washes clothes every Saturday.
10. I opened the door for the lady with the stroller.

Solutions

1. Many contemporary television programmes expose children to violence and vulgar language. T
2. My exam grade excludes me from the soccer game. T
3. Alice imagined a world full of fascinating creatures. T
4. James ran in the park every afternoon. I
5. The tornado destroyed entire buildings when it struck. destroyed T, struck I
6. I raked the yard on Saturday. T
7. The boiling water scalded my hand. T
8. We talked about the news all evening. I
9. My mother washes clothes every Saturday. T
10. I opened the door for the lady with the stroller. T

» Unit

9

Modals

Modal auxiliaries are special **auxiliary verbs** that express the degree of certainty of the action in the sentence, or the attitude or opinion of the writer or speaker concerning the action. Some common modal auxiliaries are *may, might, can , could,will, shall, would, should, must,need, dare, ought* to, used to (need, dare and used to are called semi modals)

Important Functions of Modal Auxiliaries

May

Used to show or ask permission.

(a) May I go now? (seeking permission)
Yes you may. (giving permission)

May is also used for informal request.

(a) May I have the salt please?

(b) May I borrow your pen?

May and might for present or future possibility. We can use either to express present or future possibility, but use of might slightly increases the doubt or uncertainty.

(a) The sky is cloudy, it may rain today. (*possibility*)

(b) The sky is not cloudy but a change in weather is always possible it might rain today. (*remote possibility*)

The use of **may** shows possibility while use of **might** shows remote possibility.

May is used for good wishes, desires in formal English.

(a) May God bless you!

(b) May you live long!

May can also be used to show astonishment and for seeking the knowledge of a thing.

(a) Who may be my friend here? (astonishment)

(b) How old she may be? (knowledge)

Might

The use of might for request expresses more politeness, hesitation or lack confidence of the speaker.

(a) Might I borrow your golden necklace?

(b) Might I talk to the P.M.?

Use of may and might in perfect tense.

'May' is used when you are not certain about a past action. When the uncertainty no longer exists in the present (i.e. something did not happen but it was possible) then only 'might' is used in perfect tense.

(a) He may have been wounded.
(We do not know so far, but he is perhaps injured, possibility exists.)

(b) He has not arrived so far. He may have taken a wrong way.
(We don't know the actual position, but as he has not arrived so far, so the prossibility is that he may have taken a wrong way.)

(c) He might have been wounded. That was a possibility in the past. He was not wounded.)

Can

Can is used to express physical or mental ability, capacity or capability.

(a) I can solve this puzzle.
(b) Can you lift this suitcase?

Can is also used to denote ability arising out of the circumstances. It is usually meant to express 'Are you in a position to do so?'

(a) Can you lend me ten lacs rupees?
(Are you in a position to do so? Are you having this much amount surplus?)
(b) Can you attend the meeting tomorrow?
(Are you free tomorrow?)

(4) Can also shows the circumstantial possibility.

(a) You can ski on the hills now-a-days.
(As there is enough snow.)
(b) You can go there by road now.
(As the road is repaired now.)

May and Can

May and can are used for permission in present and future.

With first person

(a) I can meet the chairman whenever I want.
(It means I have already been granted permission.)

We can also use **may** in above construction but the use of **can** is more common.

(a) I may purchase stationery items whenever I need.

With second person May is usually used when the permission is being given by the speaker.

(a) You may park your vehicle here.

(It means : I give you permission to park your vehicle here. It does not mean that you have authority to park your vehicle here.)

The use of can refers to the authority or right of the person.

(a) You can park your vehicle here.
(You have authority to park your vehicle here.)

With third person the use of may refers to the permission given by the speaker, as above.

(a) He may take my umbrella.
(b) He may take my scooter.
(c) I give him permission.

We can also use **can** in such sentences.

(a) He can take my car.
(b) He can use my phone.

The use of **can** denotes the right or authority of the subject or the relations are so informal that which doesn't need any permission, while the use of **may** usually denotes the permission granted by somebody else.

Note the difference in the following sentences :

(a) In certain circumstances an officer may ask a driver to take a vision test.
(b) An officer can ask a driver to take a vision test.

'May' shows the authority given by someone else. 'Can' shows authority lying with the subject.

May Not and Cannot

The use of **may not** denotes improbability or uncertainty, while **cannot** denotes impossibility.

(a) The news may not be true.
(may or may not be true)
(b) The news cannot be true.
(there is no possibility of its come out to be true)
(c) You may go from A to B, by changing train at C or you may go by way of D, but you cannot go direct. (as there is no direct route from A to B)

Can and Could

'Could you?' is a very good way of making a request. It denotes more politeness and courteousness.

(a) Could you lend me your car for a day?
(b) Could you lend me your sofa?

The use of could refers to past ability. It then means 'was able to'.

(a) When I was young, I could climb any tree.

Could is used in present context with conditions.

(a) Could you operate the machine by yourself?
(if it becomes necessary)
(b) Could you get another job?
(if you lose this)

The use of 'could' in perfect shows such a past possibility that did not take place or the action was actually not performed.

(a) He could have caught the train, if he had hurried. (but he didn't catch)
(b) He could have done it without much problem.
(but he didn't)

The use of could in the above construction can also express irritation at or reproach for the non-performance of an action.

(a) You could have informed me (means, I am annoyed/disappointed that you didn't inform me.)

Could is also used to express general permission in the past.

(a) On Sundays we could (were allowed to) stay up late.

(b) On holidays I could use company's car.

Could is also used to express presumption or probability.

(a) I wonder where Shyam is? He could be in the club. (perhaps he is in the club)

(b) I wonder why Sita isn't here so far? She could still be waiting for a taxi. (perhaps she is still waiting for a taxi)

Shall and Will

As per traditional grammar, **shall** is used with first person (I/we) and **will** is used with second and third person to denote pure future actions. As modals when **shall** is used with second and third person and **will** is used with first person, they denote determination, threat, warning or promise.

Shall

The use of **shall** in first person denotes a pure future action, while use of shall in second and third person denotes, promise, determination, threat or warning.

(a) I shall go to market tomorrow. *(future action)*

(b) He shall pay you on Monday. *(promise)*

(c) He shall work hard to achieve success. *(determination)*

(d) Anyone found involved shall be punished. *(warning/threat)*

(e) You shall be transferred it you don't work properly. *(warning/threat)*

(f) We shall play a hockey match tomorrow. *(future action)*

The use of shall with second and third person also expresses compulsion, bindings, or an idea of force.

(a) You shall go to meet him tomorrow. (You are instructed to go and meet him.)

(b) She shall complete her work by tommorrow. (She has to complete her work by tomorrow.)

The use of 'shall not' in second and third person denotes prohibition or a negative command.

(a) You shall not meet him.

(b) Nobody shall write on the table.

The use of shall with first person in interrogative form expresses the idea of knowing the willingness of the other person.

(a) Shall I open the door for you?

(b) Shall I carry this box into the room for you?

The use of shall in third person also expresses an idea of working as per the wish of the others.

(a) Shall Rahim wait for you? (Do you want him to wait for you?)

(b) Shall the messenger wait outside? (Do you want the messenger to wait outside?)

Will

The use of will in second and third person denotes pure future actions. With first person the will denotes threat, warning, promise or determination.

(a) He will go tomorrow.

(b) You will work here.

(c) I will see you. *(threat, warning)*

(d) I will pay you on Monday. *(promise)*

(e) I will achieve my goal. *(determination)*

Will is also used for formal request.

(a) Will you close the door please?

Will also expresses probability with all the persons. The negative form 'will not' (won't) denotes refusal.

(a) I won't go there.

(b) He will not sanction your leave.

(c) He will be in the park.

(d) Today is 15th Aug. Schools will be closed.

Won't (will not) in interrogative denotes 'invitation'.

(a) Won't you have a cup at tea? (invitation, I want you to have a cup of tea.)

(b) Won't you meet her?

(c) Won't you stay for a day?

Will is also used for commands and instructions.

(a) All the cadets will attend the parade. (instructions, command)

(b) The girls will not wear the shorts. (instructions, command)

'Will' in third person denotes a general habit.
(a) The women will not keep mum. (habit)
(b) The girls will talk. (habit)

Should and Would

Should can be used to express duty, responsibility, advice, probability, expectation, presumption, moral obligation and mild command.

(a) One should obey one's elders. (duty)
(b) You should obey your parents. (moral obligation)
(c) The rich should help the poor. (expectation)
(d) You should work hard. (advice)
(e) You should find her in the play ground. (probability)
(f) You should take care of your health. (advice)
(g) You should take care of four luief case. (responsibilily)
(h) You should complete your work everyday.
(mild command)
(i) He should be reading now. (probability)
(j) He should be worried about me. (presumption)
(k) They should be anxious about us. (presumption)

Should is also used for expressing purpose like may and might.

(a) I taught her so that she should pass.
(she might pass)
(b) I scolded him so that he should work hard.
(he might work hard)

The use of should in perfect denotes an obligation that was not fulfilled.

(a) He should have gone by the morning bus.
(but he didn't go)
(b) Ramesh should have submitted the bills.
(but he didn't submit)

Should is also used with 'lest' in following type of conditional sentences. Lest means 'in case' or 'so that...not'.

(a) Move fast lest you should miss the bus.
(b) Work hard lest you should fail.

Would

For request use of would, shows more politeness in comparison to will. Would is more commonly used for requests. Would is also used to know the wishes of the others.

(a) Would you accompany me to the railway station? (polite request)
(b) Would you send me an application form? (polite request)
(c) Would you sing at the concert tomorrow? (willingness query)

Would is also used to express likelihood, presumption and probability.

(a) He would be in the field now. (likelihood)
(b) She would be in the club at this time (probability)
(c) She would be about eighty now. (presumption)

The use of would with 'rather' shows preference.

(a) I would rather rest now.
(b) I would rather study than see a movie.

The use of would in following construction shows strong desire or willingness.

(a) I wish you would fight this election.
(b) I wish you would support her fully.

Would is also used in conditional sentences showing unreal imaginations.

(a) If I had one crore rupees, I would donate fifty lacs to the trust.
(b) If I had wings, I would fly to Europe.
(c) If I were the king, I would make you my chief adviser.

The use of would in conditional sentences denotes the action which did not take place.

(a) If he had come to me, I would have given him a job.
(He didn't come.)

Must

Must is a defective verb. It has no past form. It is used to express present or future obligation. In reported speech must is used for past time. Except in reported speech must is not used to express past obligations normally.

Must is used to express command, compulsion or order.

(a) Soldiers must obey orders without any question.
(b) All the girls must attend the function.

Must is also used to express moral duty or obligation.

(a) We must respect our elders.
(b) You must help your friends in need.

Must also expresses necessity, urgency or circumstancial compulsion.

(a) I must leave now, otherwise I may miss the train.

(b) The electricity will be cut off at 8 A.M. So I must complete my work before?

The use of 'must not' expresses prohibition or emphatic advice.

(a) Students must not resort to copying. (prohibition)

(b) You must not miss the classes. (emphatic advice)

Must expresses strong probability, likelihood or logical presumption.

(a) She must be eighty now.

(b) They have not arrived so far. They must have taken a wrong turning.

In questions introduced with 'must', if answered in affirmative we use must otherwise (in negative answer) need not.

(a) Must I attend the meeting?
Yes, you must.
No, you needn't.

The use of must with ' have + past participle of the main verb' shows a logical conclusion about a past event :-

(a) The roads are wet. It must have rained last night.

(b) You must have heard about the robbery in the bank in our locality.

The use of 'must + have been' shows certainty of a happening.

(a) He must have been living here.

(b) She delivered her speech quite fluently. She must have been a debater.

Need and Dare

Need and **dare** are considered semi-modals because they can be used either as modal auxiliaries or as main verbs. The modal verb construction is restricted to non-assertive contexts (i.e. mainly negative and interrogative sentences) whereas the main verb construction can always be used and is in fact the more common.

Need

As a modal **auxiliary verb** in negative terms, need indicates absence of obligation. It expresses the speaker's authority or advise, and is used for the present and the future.

(a) You needn't type this letter.
(The speaker is the authority, it could be his boss.)

But it can also take do (auxiliary) and in this case it expresses absence of obligation as well but in this case the speaker is not the authority.

You don't need to do this letter. (Here it could be a conversation among colleagues.)

As main verb 'need' means 'require'.

As modal, the forms of need are needn't or need and is used in negative and interrogative for all persons in present and future. Need in such construction takes a bare infinitive.

(a) He need not talk to her.

(b) Need he talk to her?

(c) You needn't wear a tie.

(d) Need I wear a tie?

The use of needn't in perfect denotes an unnecessary action which was nevertheless performed.

(a) He needn't have written such a detailed essay. (the essay was to be written is 300 words only)

(b) You needn't have bought such a costly gift.
(waste of money)

Need when used as ordinary verb in negative takes auxiliary 'do'. Need conjugated with will, shall, do, does, did etc. takes the full infintive. It sometimes occurs in affirmative also.

(a) I do not need to write him anything.

(b) He won't need to attend the court.

(c) She didn't need to remind me.

(d) She needs to be careful.

Dare

Dare is also called semi-modal as a it can be used as main verb as well as a modal verb.

In the affirmative dare is used like a main verb, i.e. dare or dares in the present and dared in the past. But in the negative and interrogative, it can be used either like a main verb or like a modal auxiliary, i.e. it is a semi-modal.

(a) He dares to oppose you.

(b) He does not dare to oppose you.

(c) You do not dare to speak against him.

(d) We do not dare to talk to the president.

In the above constructions, 'dare' is used as an ordinary verb.

Use of Dare as Modal

(a) He dare not say like this.
(b) I dare not talk to the chairman.
(c) Dare he not say like this?
(d) Dare I talk to the chairman?

The constructions; How dare you? How dare he/they? Express indignation.

(a) How dare you speak like this?
(I am indignant because you spoke like this.)
(b) How dare my wife leave without my permission?

Infinitives after 'dare'. In theory the negative and interrogative forms with do/did are followed by the infintive 'with to' but in practice the 'to' is often omitted.

(a) He doesn't dare (to) say anything.
(b) Did he dare (to) say anything.

Dare I/ he/ you/ they/we? etc. and 'dare not' constructions take the infinitive without 'to'.

(a) Dare we disturb you?
(b) They dare not go.

When dare is preceded by nobody, anybody etc. 'to' is optional.

(a) Nobody dare to comment like that.
(b) Nobody dare comment like that.
(c) Some body dare complain in the matter.
(d) Somebody dare to complain in the matter.

Dare is not often used in affirmative except in the construction 'I daresay'. Daresay has two meanings.

1. In the sense of 'suppose'.

(a) I dare say he will come. *(I suppose)*
(b) I dare say they will be happy to get this news. *(I suppose)*

2. To accept what is said.

Indian tourist : But I drive on the left in India!

Swiss Policeman: I dare say you do, but we drive on the right here.

Traveller : But the watch was gifted to me; I didn't buy it.

Customs officer: I dare say you'll have to pay duty on it .

> Daresay is used in this way with the first person singular only.

Used to

Used has no present tense. Used is followed by the full infinitive 'to'.

To express a discontinued habit or a past situation which is no more in the present.

(a) He used to drink daily.
(Now he does not drink.)
(b) I used to smoke one packet of cigarettes.
(Now I do not smoke)

It is also used as an adjective meaning 'accustomed'. It is then preceded by be form of verb or become or get in any tense and followed by the preposition 'to'.

(a) I am used to taking tea in the morning.
(b) He is used to read newspaper with morning tea.
(c) He would soon get used to living at Mumbai.
(d) I am used to the cooler's noise.

Note the use of 'used to' in negative and interrogative.

(a) I used not to smoke daily. *Negative*
I did not use to smoke earlier? *Negative*
(b) He used to may chess at college. *Affirmative*
He didn't use to play chess at college *Negative*
Used he to play chess at college? *Interrogative*
Did he use to play chess at college? *Interrogative*

For making negative of such sentences we can use either 'used not to' or 'did not use to'. In interrogative sentences we can use either 'used + subject + to' or 'did + subject + use + to' structure as shown above.

Ought to

Ought is also a modal verb. The same form 'ought' is used for present and future. It is also used in past when preceded by a verb in past tense or followed by a perfect infintive.

Ought is always followed by full infinitive 'to'.

(a) I ought to write to her today or tomorrow.
(b) I knew I ought to write to her.

The negative form of 'ought' is or 'ought not' or 'oughtn't'. The interrogative form is ought I / he / you ? etc.

Negative interrogative form is ought I not / oughtn't I? etc.

Ought is used for advice, moral obligation or duty.

(a) You ought to consult a physician. (advice)

(b) We ought to respect our parents. (moral duty)

(c) We ought to help our friends. (moral obligation)

The use of ought in perfect denotes an unfulfilled obligation or an action that didn't take place.

(a) She ought to have invited him in the function.
(But she didn't invite him.)

(b) He ought to have helped him in that matter.
(But he didn't help him.)

It is generally assumed that 'ought to' and 'should' have similar uses. But in formal notices or for information, etc. should (but not ought) is used.

(a) Students should be prepared to donate the blood.

(b) Travellers should be in possession of the following documents.

(c) On hearing the alarm bell, the students should leave their rooms immediately.

We cannot use ought in the above sentences.

» Exercises

Exercise 1

Fill in the blanks supplying the appropriate modals

1. You .... have watered the flowers, for it is going to rain.
2. If we had taken the other road, we .... have arrived earlier.
3. The bank closes at two but the manager .... allow you to get in. (remote possibility)
4. .... you please send me an application form? (request)
5. As John was the only person who visited us yesterday. It .... be he who left the main gate open. (probability)
6. You .... read his latest book.
7. She .... speak three languages when she was twelve.
8. I .... see quite clearly what the children are doing in the garden.
9. He .... be at least sixty.
10. Your job .... be very demanding, but at least it isn't boring.

Solutions

1. need not	2. would	3. might
4. would	5. might	6. should
7. could	8. can	9. must
10. may		

Exercise 2

Fill in the blanks with can, could, may, might

1. .... you live long!
2. .... you read when you were five?
3. My father .... speak and write five language.
4. You .... write on both sides of the paper.
5. We thought it .... rain.
6. He said he .... always come when called.
7. .... you ride your bicycle up to that hill?
8. I ran fast so that I .... catch the train.
9. He tried to solve the sum but he .... not.
10. Do not put off till tomorrow what you .... do today ?

Solutions

1. may	2. could	3. can
4. may	5. might	6. could
7. can	8. might	9. could
10. can		

Exercise 3

Fill in the blanks with shall, will, should, would

1. .... you do me a favour?
2. When .... I see you again?
3. .... we go to the pictures today ?
4. His daughter .... be sixteen next month.
5. The wound .... not heal in spite of all the treatment he had.
6. .... that I were rich!
7. Had you worked hard, you .... have passed the examination.
8. As you sow, so .... you reap.
9. Those who live in glass houses .... not throw stones at others.
10. If you .... see him, give him my regards.

Solutions

1. will	2. shall	3. shall
4. will	5. would	6. would

7. would 8. shall 9. should
10. should

Exercise 4

Fill in the blanks with appropriate forms of must, need, dare, ought to, used to

1. The door .... painting.
2. I .... smoking but I gave it up last year.
3. You .... come and have dinner with me.
4. He has lost your book and he .... not tell you.
5. You .... have written to him yesterday.
6. .... he wait any longer ?
7. He .... pay you the loan he owes you.
8. .... you speak rudely to your father?
9. I .... be a clerk, but now I am an officer.
10. What cannot be cured .... be endured.

Solutions

1. needs 2. used to 3. must
4. dare 5. ought to 6. need
7. ought to 8. dare 9. used to
10. must

Exercise 5

Use appropriate modals to fill in the blanks

1. .... you, please, stop talking?
2. you .... go only when you have finished your work.
3. .... you rather have tea or coffee?
4. I .... try again, if you wish.
5. You .... not hurry, there is plenty of time.
6. I .... like you to do as I tell you.
7. If only they .... keep quiet for a moment.
8. .... God bless you!
9. You .... be mad to do this.
10. I .... learn English, and none shall stop me.
11. I .... prefer not to give any explanation.

Solutions

1. Will you, please, stop talking?
2. You can (or should) go only when you have finished your work.
3. Would you rather have tea or coffee?
4. I will try again if you wish.
5. You need not hurry, there is plenty of time.
6. I should like you to do as I tell you.
7. If only they would keep quiet for a moment.
8. May God bless you!
9. You should be mad to do this.
10. I will learn English, and none shall stop me.
11. I should prefer not to give any explanation.

Exercise 6

Use appropriate modals to fill in the blanks

1. One .... obey one's parents.
2. You .... go home whenever you like.
3. I .... like you to answer my question properly.
4. My father says we .... buy some sweets.
5. .... God give you courage to face it!
6. .... you like to have lunch now?
7. .... you please tell me where the cinema house is?
8. It .... rain, it is so sultry.
9. The doctor said that the patient .... recover. (The doctor was not very sure about it.)
10. You .... insist on being given your share. (Note the stress on the word 'insist'.)
11. .... God bless you!

Solutions

1. One should obey one's parents.
2. You may go home whenever you like.
3. I should like you to answer my question properly.
4. My father says we shall buy some sweets.
5. May God give you courage to face it!
6. Would you like to have lunch now?
7. Will you please tell me where the cinema house is?
8. It may rain, it is so sultry.
9. The doctor said that the patient might recover.
10. You must insist on being given your share.
11. May God bless you!

Exercise 7

Use appropriate modals to fill in the blanks

1. You .... have given me a helping hand. It was your moral duty.
2. I .... try to get you a job. I promise.
3. Arun is not a weak student. He is also not a very good student. He .... however, pass.
4. The student politely said to the teacher, '......... have a word with you?'
5. You .... go now. (permission)
6. .... you please close the door ? (a polite request in the form of a question)
7. It .... rain soon. (it is likely to happen)
8. You .... see a doctor at once. (it is an advice)
9. We .... hurry. We are very late.
10. I'm afraid I .... tell you that. It is a secret.

Solutions

1. You should have given me a helping hand. It was your moral duty.
2. I will try to get you a job. I promise.
3. Arun is not a weak student. He is also not a very good student. He can however, pass.
4. The student politely said to the teacher, 'Could I have a word with you?'
5. You can go now.
6. Would you please close the door?
7. It may rain soon.
8. You should see a doctor at once.
9. We must hurry. We are very late.
10. I'm afraid I cannot tell you that. It is a secret.

Exercise 8

Questions, appeared in Rajasthan Administrative Services examinations in previous years

Identify the notion/concept expressed by each of the following sentences by choosing one of the three alternatives mentioned against each sentences.

1. No smoking! (advice/prohibition/threat)
2. I wish you'd be quiet. (request/wish/suggestion)
3. I'm seeing the principal this afternoon. (likelihood/determination/arrangement)
4. You needn't have hurried. (absence of necessity/ prohibition/suggestion of hesitation)
5. It might rain before evening. (possibility/strong possibility/remote possibility)

Solutions

1. prohibition
2. request
3. arrangement
4. absence of necessity
5. remote possibility.

Exercise 9

Restructure the following sentences using may, might, must, ought to, wish, only

1. Candidates are required to answer at least five out of ten questions.
2. He was not careful enough.
3. Perhaps he was hurt.
4. Please make a little less noise. (You can make it less if you wish to.)
5. Please be quiet. (request)

Solutions

1. Candidates must answer at least five out of the ten questions.
2. He ought to have been more careful.
3. He may have been hurt.
4. You might make a little less noise.
5. I wish you would be quiet.

Unit

10

Subject-Verb Agreement

- **If the subject is singular, the verb must be singular.**
- **If the subject is plural, the verb must also be plural.**

The subject of a sentence must agree with the verb of the sentence. They must agree in two ways.

In number: singular vs. plural

(a) I am reading.
(b) They are dancing.
(c) You are doing your work.
(d) We are swimming.

In the above sentences, the verb agrees with the person of the subject. With first person use 'am', while with second person use 'are' and with third person singular use 'is'.

In person: first, second, or third person

(e) Ram plays football.
(f) They play football.
(g) Sita sings a song.
(h) We go to movie.

In these sentences, the verb agrees with the subject in number. Use singular verb with singular subject.

Exceptions to the rule (subject singular/ plural—verb singular/plural)

In sentences expressing some imaginary wish, supposition, the verb used is plural as following

(a) I wish I were the Prime Minister.
(b) I wish I were a bird.
(c) She ordered as if she were my mother.
(d) Were he a king!

Verbs : bless, save, help, live, when used to express good wishes, desire, blessings etc. always take plural form.

(a) God save (not saves) the queen.
(b) Gop help (not helps) you.
(c) Long live (not lives) the king.
(d) God bless you with a son!

When 'dare' and 'need' are used as 'modal' (in negative and interrogative) these are not made singular by addinng 's' (dares or needs).

(a) He need not to go there.
(b) She dare not oppose your proposal.
(c) Need he go there?
(d) One need not write anything to him.
(e) Dare she oppose you?
(f) He dare not speak like this.

Rules of Correct Use of Verbs

1. If the two subjects are joined by 'and' the verb will be plural.

(a) He and she were present in the function.
(b) Ram and Rahim are friends.

2. When two nouns refer to the same person or thing, take singular verb.

(a) The poet and painter has died.
(b) The project director and additional collector is on tour.
(c) The clerk and counsellor was present in the meeting.

Please note in such case, article is used with the first noun only.

3. When two nouns almost identical in meaning, are used in a sentence, for the sake of emphasis, we use singular verb.

(a) The scheme and plan of my life differs from that of yours.
(b) His authority and command is indeed great.
(c) The benefit and advantage from this business is enormous.

4. When two nouns are not identical in meaning but part of the same idea and used as a phrase, the verb used is singular.

(a) Bread and butter is a good breakfast.
(b) Slow and steady wins the race.
(c) 'Early to bed, early to rise' is a good habit.
(d) Pen and ink is needed by me.

5. When two subjects are connected by or, either...or, neither...nor, and not only...but also, the subject which is closest to the verb determines whether the verb is singular or plural. Usually the plural subject is placed near the verb (it means if one subject is singular and the other is plural, the plural subject will be placed near the verb and the verb will be plural).

(a) Neither the principal nor the teachers were present in the function.
(b) Either Ramesh or his friends have stolen the watch.
(c) Ramesh or his friends are abusing him.
(d) Not only the principal but also the teachers were playing the match.
(e) Either you or I am to go there.
(f) Neither he nor you are to attend them.
(g) You or Ramesh is responsible for the loss.
(h) He or I am to go there.

6. With collective nouns like team, family, jury, crowd, class, committee, army, assembly, fleet, majority, mob, government, parliament council, staff, etc., the verb used can be singular or plural. If the collective noun functions as a unit the verb will be singular, but if the collective noun functions dividedly or not in unison, the verb used will be plural.

(a) The Parliament has passed the bill.
(b) Army was deployed at the border.
(c) The fleet has reached the port.
(d) The assembly is in session nowadays.

7. Some nouns end in 's' and look like plurals, but are actually singular in meaning, take singular verbs. Such commonly used nouns are; physics, mathematics, economics, news, gallows, billiards, innings, wages, alms, politics, measles, mumps, etc.

(a) No news is good news.
(b) Physics/economics/maths is a good subject.
(c) Billiards is a good game.
(d) First innings was spoiled due to rain.

8. A plural noun denoting quantity or measurements of time, money, distance and weight as a unit takes singular verb.

(a) Five kilograms is not a heavy weight.
(b) Hundered rupees is a big amount for him.

9. Some nouns appear singular but are plural in meaning take plural verbs. Such commonly used nouns are dozen, hundred, million, cattle, people, score, thousand, gentry, police, peasantry, company, alphabet, progeny, offspring, clergy, infantry, etc.

(a) The cattle are grazing in the field.
(b) The score were saved by him.
(c) Not less than a dozen were injured.

10. Sometimes a word that is actually an adjective is used as a noun. It is preceded by the and means 'people'. The poor = people who are poor, the old = people who are old, the young = people who are young.

(a) The poor are trustworthy.
(b) The rich are generally unkind to the poor.

11. Each and every take sigular noun and singular verb.

(a) Each boy and girl has to attend the function.
(b) Every man, women and child was happy to meet the president.
(c) Each minute and each second is precious.
(d) Each male and every female was protesting against that law.

12. Usually singular verb is used in sentences showing arithematical calculation. Also note the following views* of Norman Lewis.

(a) Four and four is eight.
(b) Four and four are eight.

*Five and Five is ten : Right—But don't jump to the conclusion that 'five and five are ten' is wrong both verbs are equally acceptance

Norman Lewis

(c) Three plus three <u>equals</u> six.
(d) Three plus three <u>equal</u> six.

13. One of, either of, neither of, none of, always take plural noun and singular verb. Note the construction

One of/none of/either of/neither of/none of + plural noun + singular verb.

(a) One of my friends <u>needs</u> some help.
(b) None of those reasons <u>is</u> valid.
(c) Either of those books <u>is</u> adequate.
(d) Neither of the girls <u>is</u> here.

14. Some nouns are uncountable in nature like; furniture, luggage, information, advice, work, knowledge, equipment, behaviour, scenery, traffic, fruit, electricity, music, progress, weather, nonsense, sense, etc. cannot be pluralised by adding 's'. Uncountable noun, take singular verbs.

(a) Work is worship.
(b) Knowledge is power.
(c) His behaviour was not proper.
(d) His advice in the matter is trustworthy.

15. When two nouns are joined together by besides, as well as, and not, in addition to, like, with, together with, including, accompanied by, the verb is governed by the former noun.

(a) Ram and not his friends was present there.
(b) The house with all its belongings was sold.
(c) The president as well as the members has come.
(d) The pigeon like other birds has wings.

16. Hair is used in singular and usually takes singular verb. But if hair is used as countable, use plural verb as following.

(a) His hair is black.
(b) Five hairs of the horse are needed by him.

17. If a countable noun follows 'all' or 'some' in a sentence, the noun as well as the verb used will be plural. But if the noun following is uncountable, the verb used will be singular.

(a) All tigers are wild animals.
(b) All the money was taken away by the thief.
(c) Some animals are faithful.
(d) Some milk is needed.

If the use of 'all' denotes a 'unit' the verb used will be singular.

(a) He informed the police all that happened last night.
(b) I would inform you all that was discussed in the meeting.

18. When used in sentences, the titles of books, plays, poems, movies, are singular and so take singular verb.

(a) Salman Rushdie's Midnight's Children is my favourite novel.
(b) The Untouchables was a very violent movie.

19. The verb used after 'there' will be singular or plural depends upon the subject follows. If it is singular, use singular verb, if plural use plural verb.

(a) There is a girl in the room.
(b) There are ten students in the class.

20. Some nouns consist of two parts, take plural verbs. Such commonly used nouns are scissors, paints, trousers, binoculars, tongs, spectacles, shorts, breeches, shoes, scales, glasses, etc.

(a) My shoes are new.
(b) The scissors are blunt.

If 'a pair' is used with such nouns, the verb used is singular.

(a) Only a pair of shoes is required.
(b) A pair of scissors was purchased by me.

21. Some sentences have following constructions singular noun + preposition + singular noun...... singular verb.
Use sigular verb in such constructions. It is important.

(a) Man after man was coming there.
(b) One month after another has passed.
(c) Ship after ship is arriving regularly.
(d) He begs from door to door.

22. Some nouns have the same form in singular as well as in plural. The verb is used according to what we mean to refer. Such nouns are sheep, fish, deer, pice etc.

(a) A sheep is a beautiful animal.
(b) Many sheep are grazing there.
(c) I found a pice.
(d) I found five pice.
(e) There are many fishes in the pond. *(Incorrect)*
There are many fish in the pond. *(Correct)*

23. If in a sentence; infinitive gerund, phrase or a clause, functions as subject use singular verb.

(a) Swiming is a good exercise. *Gerund*
(b) To swim is good for you. *Infinitive*
(c) How to start it is a big question. *Phrase*
(d) That she is poor is known to me. *Clause*

24. If phrase; a number of, lots of , a lot of, plenty of, a quarter of, part of, percent of, proportion of, none of, remainder of, two third of, most of, some of, majority of, much

of, many of, a good deal of, a great deal of, heaps of, etc., followed by a countable noun , it will be plural and the verb used will also be plural. If the noun followed is uncountable, the verb used will be singular.

(a) Most of the persons are dishonest.
(b) Most of people like the goverment jobs.
(c) Most of the milk was impure.
(d) Most of the sugar was wet with water.
(e) About half of the students were present there.

25. In 'number' and 'the number' a number means many and always takes plural verb. 'The number' means a definite number and s act as collective noun, takes singular verb.

(a) The number of students opted English in administrative services is generally small.
(b) The number of candidates appeared in SSC this year was very large.
(c) A number of English books are available in the library.
(d) There were a number of students waiting for their turn.

26. 'None' usually takes singular verb, but some renowned grammarians also use plural verbs with none.

(a) It is mistake to suppose that the pronoun 'none' is singular only and must at all costs be followed by singular verb.

—Fowler

(b) None was originally used only as singular but it has also acquired a plural meaning.

—Nesfield

(c) None is an abbreviated form of not one or no one and would therefore seem to be singular, but in its context it usually has a plural sense.

—Vallins

As such none can be used in singular as well as in plural.

27. The phrase 'nothing but' is treated as singular, so it takes singular verb, irrespective of the noun following it is singular or plural.

(a) Nothing but hill is seen.
(b) Nothing but birds is seen.

28. If 'no' precedes each of the two singular nouns in a sentence as following, singular verb is used.

(a) No boy and no girl was present in the party.
(b) No man and no woman was swimming at that time.

29. Following indefinite words require singular verbs : anybody, anyone, each, every, everyone, everybody, much, no one, one, other, someone, something, somebody .

(a) Has <u>anybody</u> seen my purse?
(b) <u>Anyone</u> is welcome.
(c) <u>Each</u> child gets a prize.
(d) <u>Every</u> dog has its day.
(e) <u>Everyone</u> is welcome.
(f) <u>Everybody</u> is welcome.
(g) <u>Much</u> has been made of his new book.
(h) <u>No one</u> was willing to try.
(i) <u>One</u> of them is lying.
(j) This is my painting. The <u>other</u> is my sister's.
(k) <u>Somebody</u> has stolen my car.
(l) <u>Someone</u> is waiting for you.
(m) <u>Something</u> is worrying Pluto.

30. Following indefinite words can have singular or plural verb. If the subject is singular verb will also be singular, if the subject is plural verb will be plural. Such commonly used words are all, any, enough, most, some.

(a) All she wants is to be happy.
(b) All her dreams have come true.
(c) friends of yours is a friend of mine.
(d) Any friends he had were few and far between.
(e) Enough has been said about that already.
(f) Enough people have been hurt already.

31. When the subject and verb are separated, find the subject and verb and make sure they agree. Ignore the words in between because they do not affect agreement.

(a) The quality of these goods is well known.
(b) Financial help from all the countries was received.
(c) The colour of this shirts is liked by all.
(d) Your views on this matter are supported by all.
(e) The details of the accident were not received by us so far.
(f) The cost of production of steel goods is increasing.

32. In some sentences some words or phrases in apposition are placed between subject and predicate, the verb will be governed in number and person by the subject's number and person.

(a) You, my friend, are not guilty of misconduct.

(b) I, manager of this company, am responsible for the loss.

33. The relative pronouns who, whom, which, and that are either singular or plural, depending on the words they refer to. If the word referred is singular, verb will also be singular, otherwise plural.

(a) It is I who am responsible for the loss.

(b) It is he who is responsible for this loss.

(c) The woman who is in black saree is my wife.

(d) The women who are standing there are my sister.

In above sentences the verb is governed by the antecedent (that comes before the relative pronoun).

34. If a sentence compounds a positive and a negative subject and one is plural, the other singular, the verb should agree with the positive subject.

(a) The staff members but not the principal have decided not to teach on Independence Day.

(b) It is not the teachers but the principal who decides this issue.

35. 'Many a' is distributive in nature and effect, so requires a sigular verb.

(a) Many a man has failed to do his duty.

(b) Many a girl has come to visit the temple today.

36. Some verbs are followed by 'as'. These are regard, describe, represent, portray, depict, mention, define, treat.

(a) You ought to have regarded him as your brother.

(b) He was described by his wife as the most harmless man.

(c) He portrayed him as a typical country farmer.

37. Verbs such as name, call, term, think, consider, nominate appoint are not followed by 'as'.

(a) The chairman nominated Hari secretary of the society.

(b) Ram called him a fool, a rogue and a crook.

(c) Ram calls his wife 'Site'.

Verb 'act' and 'pass' are followed by 'as' in following constructions.

(d) He acted as principal.

(e) He passed as a gentleman.

38. 'More than one', though its sense is necessarily plural, is treated as a sort of compound of 'one', following its construction and agrees with a singular noun and takes a singular verb. —*Fowler.*

(a) More than one worker was absent.

(b) More than one student was killed.

39. Note the construction more + noun + than one +··· Plural verb is used in following constructions.

(a) More books than one have been purchased by her.

(b) More girls than one were present in the party.

40. 'The following' and 'the undersigned' if used for singular subject or noun, the verb will be singular otherwise plural.

(a) The following are the new prices of the items.

(b) Undersigned S.K. Jain, has taken a decision.

(c) We the undersigned request the pleasure of your company.
S. K. Jain P.K. Jain.

(d) The following is the summary of the discussions held in the meeting.

41. Language V/S people.

(a) Chinese <u>is</u> a difficult language.

(b) The Chinese <u>are</u> friendly.

(c) French <u>is</u> spoken in many countries.

(d) The French <u>make</u> good wines.

In (a) Chinese = language takes singular verb. In (b) Chinese = people of China takes plural verb

Inversion

What Is Inversion?

In normal English sentences, subject comes before the verb with following constructions :

subject + verb + ...

In some situations, like in questions, the order is reversed with following constructions:

verb + subject + ...

Such type of constructions wherein verb comes before the subject is known as inversion.

Inversion of the verb : Certain adverbs and adverb phrases, most with a restrictive or negative sense, can for emphasis be placed first in a sentence or clause and are then followed by the inverted (i.e. interrogative) form of the verb.

—Thomson and Martinet.

Inversion can be of two types.

When 'auxiliary' comes before the subject but main verb comes after the subject.

(a) Never does he go to temple.
(b) Hardly does he come here.

When main verb comes before the subject.

(a) Round the corner went Jacob. main verb + subject
(b) Under a tree was sitting an old lady. auxiliary + main verb + subject

When to Use Inversion?

1. **When a sentence begins with hardly, rarely, scarcely, seldom, never, little, etc.**
   (a) Hardly does she go to charch.
   (b) Seldom had I seen such a healthy baby.
   (c) Never does she go to temple.
   (d) Scarcely ever did they manage to meet the deadline.
   (e) Rarely is she absent from duty.
   (f) Little do you know how much trouble you are in.
2. **Use of conjuction 'not only..............but also'**
   (a) Not only did she watch TV but she also cooked meal.
   (b) Not only does he rob her but he also smashes everything.
3. **With 'no sooner'**
   (a) No sooner had she seen her husband than she hugged him.
   (b) No sooner did he see the dead body of his wife, than he burst into tears.
4. **In sentences beginning with following phrases : under no circumstances, in no way, on no account, on no condition, at no time.**
   (a) Under no circumstances shall I accept this proposal.
   (b) On no condition will she sell the house.
   (c) In no way will I forgive her.
   (d) On no account must this button be pushed.
5. **With adverbial expressions with 'only' : only yesterday, only the day before yesterday, only last month, only last fortnight, only after a month/year, only then, only in this way, only when, only by doing this thing, only in a few schools/colleges/countries/ continents etc.**
   (a) Only yesterday did he buy that car.
   (b) Only by taking risk did he save the life of the minister.
   (c) Only by accepting the condition, did he join this job.
   (d) Only by shouting was she able to make herself heard.
6. **With adverbial expressions showing place : outside the gate, under the table, in the valley, along the border, round the corner, on a hill, etc.**
   (a) In the valley did I see a strange man.
   (b) Out side the gate did he notice something moving.
   (c) On a hill did he find a new revolver.

With adverbial expressions like : under a tree, on the bed, ten/five miles beyond the school/college/city, nowhere else, etc. inversion is used.

(a) Under a tree was sleeping an old lady.
(b) On the bed was sitting her friend.
(c) Five miles beyond the city was a mysterious palace.

7. **Sentences beginning with here, there, away, out, up, indoor, out doors, in and down.**
   (a) Down fell a dozen apples.
   (b) In came the child weeping.
   (c) Here comes the train.
   (d) There goes Sita.
   (e) Away went Ram.

When a pronoun is used as subject, no inversion takes place in such sentences.
(a) There she goes.
(b) Away he went.
(c) Here she comes.

8. **Sentences beginning with 'So + adverb of manner'.**
   (a) So well did he organise the function, that everyone started praising him.
   (b) So absurdly did he speak that everyone was offended.
   (c) So suspicious did he become that he couldn't talk to her properly.
9. **Sentences beginning with : to such a degree, to such an extent, to such a point, to such a length.**
   (a) To such an extent he made the investment that people started trusting him.
   (b) To such a degree they made a noise that principal had to call the police.
10. **The most common use of inversion is in the forming of questions. We use the auxiliary verbs 'be' (for progressive and passive forms), 'have' (for perfect forms) and 'do' (for most other forms). Modal verbs can also be inverted to form questions.**
   (a) Were they ready when you arrived?
   (b) Where was it made?
   (c) Have you ever visited France?
   (d) Where do you live?
   (e) What should we do now?
11. **When we are making wishes, we can use inversion.**
   (a) May you both live happily ever after!
   (b) May you live long!
12. **In question tags.**
   (a) Tomorrow is Sunday, isn't it?
   (b) She left yesterday, didn't she?
13. **In following type of sentences.**
   (a) Were I a bird! (imaginary hope/wish)
   (b) Had he come to me, I would have helped him. (conditional sentence—If he had come to me, I would have helped him.)
   (c) Soniya went to church, so did I.
   (d) She did not visit the Agra, neither did I.
   (e) He did not go there, nor did I.

The inversion takes place with so, neither, nor, when there is similarity of action as in sentence (c), (d), (e) above.
(f) 'Let us play cricket,' proposed Ram.
'Let us go to market,' said Sita.
(g) 'Do it for me,' said Krishna.
'Go there,' instructed Rahim.

When reporting verb placed after the reported speech inversion takes place. But if a pronoun is used as subject as in following sentences, no inversion takes place.
(h) 'Do it for me,' she said.
(i) 'Go there,' he instructed.

» Exercises

Exercise 1

Rewrite the following sentences after correction

1. Either he or I is to represent the school.
2. Neither you nor he are to go now.
3. The mob move towards the collectorate.
4. The second innings were spoiled due to fire.
5. Each hour and each minute are to be utilised by you.
6. Every young and every old were happy to receive a gift.
7. Not only the Taj Mahal but also other monuments is worth seeing.
8. The house with all its furniture were auctioned at a very low bid.
9. The peacock like other birds have wings to fly.
10. There is another schools better than this.
11. More than one girl were killed in the accident.
12. God blesses you with success!
13. Financial help from all the quarters were received.
14. The quality of these items are appreciated by everyone.
15. The fragrance of these beautiful flowers are liked by all.
16. More workman than one are not traceable.
17. He said, 'Plenty of milk are required for the party.'
18. A lot of books and magazines was destroyed by the fire.
19. The number of students opted Hindi in RAS are generally large.

20. A number of English magazines is available in the college library.
21. It is I who is responsible for the loss in the business.
22. The women who is standing there are my sisters.
23. He is one of those who does know anything about the incident.
24. It is one of the problems that was taken care of by the civil administration.
25. Nothing but monkeys are seen.
26. No man and no woman were allowed to enter without payment.
27. Much of the time were wasted by the students.
28. More than one man were killed there.
29. Economic cooperation between India and China are decreasing day by day.
30. More students than one has participated in the annual function.
31. About half of the girls was present in the hall.
32. Half of the sugar were spoiled due to heavy rains.
33. The apparatus purchased by the Nagar Parishad were very old.
34. The advice of his friend are indeed valuable.
35. Men after men were coming to visit the art gallery.
36. One month after another have passed.
37. His shoes is shining.
38. Approximately ten sheeps were grazing in the college ground.
39. A pair of shoes are purchased by her for her husband.
40. There are many fishes in the aquarium.
41. Each of the sports women were given a certificate.
42. I wish I will be the minister.
43. She ordered as if she is my elder sister.
44. God saves our queen!
45. He needs not go to market.
46. The poors are never reliable.
47. All the milk were used in the preparation of sweets.
48. All the animal were given the proper diet.
49. She apprised the inspector all that have happened yesterday night.
50. Most of the person are reliable.

Solutions

1. Either he or I am to represent the school.
2. Neither you nor he is to go now.
3. The mob moves towards the collectorate.
4. The second innings was spoiled due to fire.
5. Each hour and each minute is to be utilised by you.
6. Every young and every old was happy to receive a gift.
7. Not only the Taj Mahal but also other monuments are worth seeing.
8. The house with all its furniture was auctioned at a very low bid.
9. The peacock like other birds has wings to fly.
10. There is another school better than this.
11. More than one girl was killed in the accident.
12. God bless you with success!
13. Financial help from all the quarters was received.
14. The quality of these items is appreciated by everyone.
15. The fragrance of these beautiful flowers is liked by all.
16. More workman than one is not traceable.
17. He said, 'Plenty of milk is required for the party.'
18. A lot of books and magazines were destroyed by the fire.
19. The number of students opted Hindi in RAS is generally large.
20. A number of English magazines are available in the college library.
21. It is I who am responsible for the loss in the business.
22. The women who are standing there are my sisters.
23. He is one of those who do know anything about the incident.
24. It is one of the problems that were taken care of by the civil administration.
25. Nothing but monkeys is seen.
26. No man and no woman was allowed to enter without payment.
27. Much of the time was wasted by the students.
28. More than one man was killed there.
29. Economic cooperation between India and China is decreasing day by day.
30. More students than one have participated in the annual function.
31. About half of the girls were present in the hall.
32. Half of the sugar was spoiled due to heavy rains.
33. The apparatus purchased by the Nagar Parishad was very old.
34. The advice of his friend was indeed valuable.
35. Man after man was coming to visit the art gallery.
36. One month after another has passed.
37. His shoes are shining.
38. Approximately ten sheep were grazing in the college ground.
39. A pair of shoes is purchased by her for her husband.
40. There are many fish in the aquarium.

41. Each of the sports women was given a certificate.
42. I wish I were the minister.
43. She ordered as if she were my elder sister.
44. God save our queen!
45. He need not go to market.
46. The poor are never reliable.
47. All the milk was used in the preparation of sweets.
48. All the animals were given the proper diet.
49. She apprised the inspector all that has happened yesterday night.
50. Most of the persons are reliable.

Spotting the Errors

Spot the errors in the following sentences

1. He ordered (A)/ as if he (B)/ was my master (C).
2. God saves (A)/ the queen of Victoria (B).
3. If it was so (A)/ poetry (B)/would cease to matter (C).
4. The merit (A)/ of these books (B)/ are known to everyone (C).
5. The condition of (A)/ people living in (B)/ rural area (C)/ are very bad (D). ***(NABARD)***
6. The smell (A)/of these rose (B)/ flowers are (C)/ very sweet.
7. The condolence messages (A)/ received on the (B)/ death of Mrs. Gandhi (C)/ speaks highly of her greatness (D).
8. Economic cooperation (A)/ between the two countries (B)/have increased substantially (C).
9. A band of musicians (A)/ have been engaged (B)/ for the inauguration function (C).
10. The number (A)/of persons interested (B)/in psychology are (C)/generally small (D). ***(Bank PO)***
11. The manager's comments (A)/ on the preparation of the test matches(B)/ for this tour (C)/has been generally praised (D).
12. The details (A)/of the incident (B)/was not known (C)/to me (D).
13. The majority of (A)/ writers never (B)/ passes this stage (C).
14. A large part of (A)/ the distinctive features (B)/ of the mind is due to its being (C)/ an instrument of communication (D). ***(Bank PO)***
15. A part of (A)/ the mango (B) / are rotten (C).
16. A part of (A)/ the mangoes (B)/ are rotten (C). No error (D).
17. The governing body at (A)/ its first meeting (B)/have decided (C)/ to conduct the test again (D). ***(CDS)***
18. The banker's association (A)/ has submitted a memorandum (B)/for the fulfilment of (C)/ their demands (D).
19. Five quintals of wooden coal (A)/ are (B)/ his annual requirement (C) for the unit (D). ***(CDS)***
20. Dickens have criticised (A)/the philosophy (B)/in 'Hard Times'.
21. All his money (A)/ is spent (B)/ and all his (C)/ hopes ruined (D).
22. This rule may (A)/ and ought to be (B)/disregarded for the time being (C).
23. He is one of the (A)/ richest man (B)/ if not the richest man (C)/ in the world (D).
24. We can almost get (A)/ everything in (B)/ this market (C).
25. Every (A)/ Tom, Dick and Harry (B)/ drink wine these days (C).
26. He and I (A)/ is partners in (B)/ this firm (C).
27. He is one of the (A)/ great man (B)/ that have ever lived (C).
28. The magistrate and collector (A)/ were (B)/ present there (C)/on the spot (D).
29. Horse and Carriage (A)/are (B)/waiting there (C)/for the couple (D).
30. Rice and fish (A)/are (B)/ my favourite dish (C).
31. 'Under no circumstances (A)/I can help you in (B)/ this venture' (C)/, said Sita (D). ***(BSRB)***
32. 'I don't like (A)/ such a bright colour (B)/nor she does' (C)/, he said to Ram (D).
33. 'Every member of (A)/his family is (B)/addicted to gambling (C)/and so John is (D).
34. Never before (A)/ I had been asked (B)/ to go there (C)/by bus (D).
35. On no account (A)/ this switch must (B)/ be touched (C).

36. 'Seldom I had seen (A)/ such a (B)/beautiful girl',(C)/said Mohanti (D). **(BSRB)**
37. Under a tree(A)/was sleeping an (B)/ old lady (C)/with her young child (D). No error (E).
38. To such a degree (A)/ he created (B)/ the problems that (C)/people thrashed him (D). **(Bank PO)**
39. Not only she watched (A)/the news (B)/ but she also (C)/cooked food (D).
40. No sooner the plane landed at the (A) /airport than (B)/ a group of armed (C)/commandos surrounded it (D). **(Bank PO)**

» Answers

1. (C) Replace was by were. In sentences expressing some imaginary wish, supposition, the verb used is plural
2. (A) Replace saves by save. 'Verbs : bless, save, help, live, when used to express good wishes, desire, blessings etc., always used in plural.
3. (A) Replace was by were. See explanation of question (1).
4. (C) Replace are by is. Subject 'merit' is uncountable so singular verb is used.
5. (D) Replace are by is. Subject 'condition' is uncountable so singular verb is used.
6. (C) Replace are by is. Subject of the verb is 'small' which is singular.
7. (D) Replace speaks by speak. Subject, condolence messages is plural.
8. (C) Replace 'have' by 'has'. Subject—economic cooperation—singular.
9. (B) Replace have been by has been. A 'band' collective noun is used as singular.
10. (C) Replace 'are' by 'is'. 'The number' takes singular verb.
11. (D) Replace 'has been' by 'have been'. Subject, manager's comments—plural, so plural verb will be used.
12. (C) Replace 'was' by were. Subject of the verb—details—is plural.
13. (C) Replace passes by pass. The noun after 'of'(writers) is plural so the verb will also be plural.
14. (C) Replace 'mind is due' by 'mind are due'
15. (C) Replace 'are' by 'is'. The noun after 'of'(mango) is singular so the verb will also be singular.
16. (D) No error.
17. (C) Replace have by has. governing body is a collective noun so verb is singular.
18. (D) Replace 'their' by 'its'. The banker's association is a collective noun so pronoun, 'its' is singular.
19. (B) Replace 'are' by 'is'. 'Five quintals' refers a definite quantity (as collective noun) so verb will be singular.
20. (A) Replace have by has. Dickens is the name of a person.
21. (D) Insert are after hopes. Hopes is plural, so verb will be plural.
22. (A) Place be after may.
23. (B) Replace richest man by richest men.
24. (A) Replace 'We can almost get' by 'we can get almost'.
25. (C) Replace drink by drinks. Every or each takes singular verb.
26. (B) Replace 'is' by 'are'.
27. (B) Replace 'man' by 'men'.
28. (B) Replace 'were' by 'was'.
29. (B) Replace 'are' by 'is'. Horse and carriage refers to one thing as a unit so takes singular verb.
30. (B) Replace 'are' by 'is'. Rice and fish used as a unit takes singular verb.
31. (B) Replace 'I can help you' by 'can I help you'. With 'under no circumstances' inversion is applied.
32. (C) Replace 'nor she does' by 'nor does she'. Inversion is applied here.
33. (D) Replace 'so John is' by 'so is John'. Inversion is applied here.
34. (A) Write never had I been. Inversion is applied here.
35. (B) Write must this switch. Inversion is applied here.
36. (A) Write Seldom had I seen. With seldom/hardly/rarely/scarely/never, inversion is applied here.
37. (E) No error
38. (B) Replace he created by did he create. Inversion is applied here.
39. (A) Write—Not only did he watch. Inversion is applied here.
40. (A) Write—No sooner did the plane land. Inversion is applied here.

Unit
11
Non-Finites

Non-finites are of three kinds
1. Infinitive **2. Gerund** **3. Participle**

Infinitive

In grammar, the infinitive is the form of verb that has no inflection to indicate person, number, mood or tense. The most common form of an infinitive in English language is with the particle 'to', such as in 'to walk', 'to cry', 'to eat', 'to fear'. This is known as the 'to-infinitive.' Infinitives are also defined as to + base form of the verb. When this particle is absent, the infinitive is said to be a 'bare infinitive'. The bare infinitive and the to infinitive are not generally interchangeable, but the distinction does not generally affect the meaning of a sentence.

Rules

1. After following modal auxiliaries infinitive comes without 'to'.

These are : shall, will, should, do, did , may, might, must, can, could, need.

(a) I shall play.
(b) He will come.
(c) I should write.
(d) He would write.
(e) I may go.
(f) He might come.
(g) They must play.
(h) He can say.
(i) I could talk.
(j) He need not come here.

2. Following verbs when used in active voice, take infinitive without to : bid, let, make, feel, watch, behold, hear, overhear, notice, observe, see, know.

(a) She bade me go.
(b) Let her sing.
(c) I made him sing.
(d) I didn't notice him go.
(e) I feel her touch me.
(f) I observed him play.

In passive form these verbs take infinitive 'with to'.

(a) He was made to sing.
(b) I was bidden to go.

3. Following words take bare infinitive after them : had better, would rather, would sooner, sooner than, rather than, had sooner.

(a) He had better withdraw.
(b) You had better resign.
(c) He would sooner resign than fight with the boss.
(d) I would go rather than waste my time here.

4. The 'bare infinitive' is used after the conjunction 'than'.

(a) She is better able to speak than write.
(b) He is stronger than me.

5. **Have/has/had + noun/pronoun is followed by a bare infinitive.**
   (a) I will have him realise his mistake.
   (b) I had him know his mistakes.
   (c) They will have you accept your fault.
6. **'But' and 'except' take the bare infinitive when they follow do + nothing/anything/ everything.**
   (a) I can do nothing but protest.
   (b) He did nothing but cry.
   (c) They did nothing but weep.
   (d) The dog does nothing except bark.
7. **Infinitive after 'too'.**
   (I) ··· + too + adjective + infinitive.
   (a) He is too weak to walk. (he is so weak that he cannot walk)
   (b) He was too young to get married. (he is so young that he cannot get married)
   (II) ...+ too + adjective +a + noun + infinitive
   (a) He is too shrewd a man to rely on anybody.
   (b) He is too experienced a driver to mind what anybody say.
   (III) ...+ too + adverb + infinitive
   (a) It is too soon to say whether the plan will run or not.
   (b) He cried too loudly to understand by any one.
8. **Infinitive after enough**
   (I) ...+ adjective + enough+ infinitive
   (a) He is matured enough to take decisions.
   (b) She is bold enough to travel by herself.
   (II) ... + adverb + enough +infinitive
   (a) He jumped high enough to win the first prize
   (b) He spoke loudly enough to understand by all.
9. **So.......... as + infinitive**
   (a) He was so foolish as to leave his car unlocked.
   (b) He was so intelligent as to argue without any difficult.
10. **If two infinitives are joined by and, the 'to' of the second infinitive is usually dropped.**
   (a) I intend to sit in my room and read novels.
   (b) I want you to assist me and clean the room.

Split Infinitive

The general rule is that no word should separate the to of an infinitive from the simple form of the verb that follows. If a word does come between these two components, a split infinitive results. It used to be seen as a grammatical crime to split an infinitive, although the rationale for this view is not clear.

Henry Fowler in A Dictionary of Modern English Usage, write, 'Those who do not know but do care [about a split infinitive] would as soon be caught putting their knives in their mouths as splitting an infinitive, but have only hazy notions of what constitutes that deplorable breach of etiquette ...'

A split infinitive has another word placed between the to and the base verb, such as to sometimes fight and to never yield or to boldly go where no man has ever gone before.

This ban on the split infinitive was misguided. There are many adverbs that need to be placed immediately before the verb.

(a) I ought to flatly refuse.
(b) We have to always be careful.

If you put the adverb somewhere else, you change the emphasis, and the sentence is awkward.

(a) I ought flatly to refuse. I ought to refuse flatly.
(b) You have always to be careful.
(c) You have to be careful always.

Whether you put an adverb between the to and the verb is a matter of style and meaning. We have to sometimes reverse old grammatical terminology.

Gerund

Gerund is defined as the 'ing' form of a verb and has the characteristics of a noun also. For example, walking, running, reading, writing, etc.

Present Participle Versus Gerund

Every gerund, without exception, ends in 'ing'. Gerunds are not, however, all that easy to find out. The problem is that all present participles also end in -ing. What is the difference? Gerunds function as nouns. Gerunds are called verbal nouns. Present participles, on the other hand, act as modifiers and are also called verbal adjectives.

Gerund Versus Simple Infinitive

Gerunds and **infinitives** are forms of verbs that act like nouns.

A **gerund** is a **verb + -ing.**

An **infinitive is to + the verb.**

In both the examples above, the gerund and the infinitive are the objects of the verbs in the sentence. However, as noun substitutes, gerunds and infinitives can also be the subject of a sentence. We can use either gerund or infinitive with the following verbs

advise	hate	propose	used to
agree	intend	recommend	want
allow	like	regret	be ashamed
being	love	remember	afraid
can/could	cease	need	start
	sorry	prefer	continue
	go on	permit	stop

Gerund	Infinitive
(a) They began playing.	(a) They began to play.
(b) We prefer taking tea.	(b) We prefer to take tea.
(c) He never ceased quality.	(c) He never ceased to complain about complaining about the quality.
(d) I can't bear waiting so long.	(d) I can't bear to wait so long.
(e) I intend buying it.	(e) I intend to buy it.
(f) He advised me writing today.	(f) He advised me to write today.
(g) He doesn't allow parking here.	(g) He doesn't allow us to park here.

Specific Use of Gerund : Rules

1. **A preposition is always followed by a gerund not by an infinitive. This is a good rule that has no exceptions. If we want to use a verb after a preposition, it must be a gerund. It is impossible to use an infinitive after a preposition**
   (a) He is fond of fishing.
   (b) She is good at swimming.
   (c) He is too afraid of losing.
   (d) I am tired of arguing.
2. **Some verbs followed by preposition/adverb take the gerund. The most common are : be for/ against, care for, give up, keep on, leave off, look forward to, put off, see about, take to, etc.**
   (a) We do not care for standing in queues.
   (b) We are looking forward to meeting you in the party.
   (c) He has given up smoking since long.
   (d) At last the lion left off roaring.
3. **The word 'to' often causes confusion. It is either a part of an infinitive or a preposition. When 'to' is followed by a noun/pronoun or gerund it is a preposition. When used as preposition, it is always followed by gerund.**
   (a) I am looking forward to meeting you. ('to' used as preposition)
   (b) I am accustomed to smoking. ('to' used as preposition)
   (c) I want to go there. ('to' used as part of infinitive)
   (d) Will you like to come in? ('to' used as part of infinitive)
4. **Following verbs are followed by gerund.**

admit	keep (= continues)	anticipate	loathe
appreciate	mean (= involve)	consider	miss
avoid	mind (= object)	defer	pardon
dislike	propose (= suggest)	delay	postpone
enjoy	remember (= recollect)	deny	practise
detest	prevent	dread	recollect
escape	resent	excuse	resist
risk	fancy (= imagine)	imagine	suggest
finish	save	involve	understa nd
forgive	stop (= cease)		

(a) He admitted taking the bribe.
(b) You should avoid overeating.
(c) He detests waiting.

(d) I dislike standing here.
(e) We dreads getting old.
(f) I do not enjoy teaching.
(g) He kept crying.
(h) I do not want to risk getting wet.

5. Verb+ possessive adjective / pronoun object is followed by gerund and this gerund refers the person denoted by the possessive adjective or pronoun.

(a) He insisted on my reading the letter.
(b) He resented on my refusing the entry.

If the verb or verb + preposition is followed directly by the gerund, the gerund refers to the subject of the verb.

(a) Sarla insisted on reading the letter. (Sarla read it.)

Following verbs can take either of the constructions

dislike	propose	understand
dread	recollect	approve/ disapprove of
fancy	remember	insist on
involve	resent	it's no good/use
like (negative)	save	object to
mean	stop	there's no point in
mind	suggest	what's the point of

(b) She disliked working late.
(c) She disliked me/ my working late.
(d) I object to paying twice for the same thing.
(e) I object to his/ him making private calls on this phone.

6. Forgive, excuse, pardon and prevent are not followed directly by the gerund. These take either possessive adjective/pronoun + gerund or pronoun + preposition + gerund.

(a) Please forgive my/me calling you so early.
(b) We can't prevent him wasting his own money.
(c) I indeed appreciate your giving me so much of your time.

Participle

A participle is a non-finite verb, called a 'verbal adjective,' which means that it has characteristics of both verbs and adjectives. The term verbal indicates that a participle is based on a verb and therefore expresses action or a state of being. However, since they function as adjectives, participles modify nouns or pronouns. A participle most often ends in '-ing' or '-ed'. There are three types of participles: present participles, past participles and perfect participles.

Rules

1. When two actions are done simultaneously by the same subject, one of them can well be expressed by the present participle. The participle can be placed before or after the finite verb as following :

(a) She went away.
(b) She cried as she went.
She went away crying.
(c) She holds the rope with one hand and stretches out the other to the man in the river.
(d) Holding the rope with one hand she stretches out the other to the man in the river.

2. If one action is immediately followed by another, by the same subject the first action can also be denoted by a present participle.

(a) He opened the almirah. He took out a file.
Opening the almirah he took out a file.
(b) He takes off his clothes and creeps cautiously into the water.
Taking off his clothes he creeps cautiously into the water.

In the above sentences we can also use perfect participle and say : Having opened ...., having taken off ....,but this is not necessary except when the use of the present participle leads to ambiguity.

3. When the second action is the part or a result of the first action, we can express the second action by a present participle.

(a) He went out slamming the iron gate.
(b) He fired, wounding several persons in the crowd.

(c) I fell, striking my head against the wall and cutting it.
(Here are three actions, the last two expressed by participles.)

4. **The present participle can replace as/since/because + subject + verb, as following**
   (a) As he was a student he was interested in books.
   Being a student he was interested in books.
   (b) Because he was ill he didn't go to Jaipur.
   Being ill he didn't go to Jaipur.
   (c) Since he knew that he wouldn't be able to recognize her, he used an addressed plate.
   Knowing that he wouldn't be able to recognize her, he used an addressed plate.
5. **Two or more participles can also be used in a sentence, one after the other.**
   (a) Realising that he hadn't enough money and not wanting to borrow from his friends, he decided to sell his chain.
   (b) Not knowing the language and having no friends in the city, he found it hard to get a room on rent.

We should not use a present participle to express an action which is not consistent with the action of the principal clause.
(a) He sailed for Srilanka on Tuesday and arriving their on Saturday. *Incorrect*
(b) He sailed for Srilanka on Tuesday and arrived their on Saturday. *Correct*

Here 'sailed' is used in principal clause so we cannot use 'arriving' in subordinating clause. We should use 'arrived'.

Past Participle

Most of the past participles end in -ed, -en, -d, -t or -n, as in the words walked, eaten, gone, saved, dealt, and seen.

1. **Past participle is used in passive structures.**
   (a) This is the book written by me.
   (b) Learn the lessons taught by her.
2. **Past participle can replace passive verbs.**
   (a) She was aroused by the noise and leapt to her feet.
   Aroused by the noise she leapt to her feet.
   (b) He enters. He is accompanied by his sister.
   He enters, accompanied by his sister.

Perfect Participle

1. **As mentioned in present participle, if one action is immediately followed by another, by the same subject the first action can also be denoted by a perfect participle.**
   (i) Opening the almirah he took out a file. present participle
   Having opened the almirah, he took out a file. participle
   (ii) Taking off his clothes he creeps cautiously into the water. present participle
   Having taken off his clothes he creeps into the water. perfect participle
2. **The perfect participle is used when there is an interval of time between the two actions.**
   (a) Having failed thrice, she didn't want to apply again.
   (b) Having passed his M.A, he enrolled for Ph.D.
3. **Perfect participle is also used when the first action covered a period of time.**
   (a) Having been his own boss for many years, he found it unusual to accept orders from others.
   (b) Having been a boxer for six years, he knew where to punch.
4. **The perfect participle passive structure (having been + past participle) is used when it is necessary to clarify that the action expressed by the participle happened before the action expressed by the another verb.**
   (a) Having been warned about the bandits they deposited the valuables in the lockers.
   (b) Having been bitten twice, the courier man refused to deliver the goods, unless the dog is chained up.

Unattached or Dangling Participle

A participle is a verbal adjective, so it must be attached to some noun or pronoun. It means it must have a proper subject of reference. If the participle is not attached to some noun or pronoun it is called dangling participle.

(a) Waiting for the train, a brick fell on my feet.

It appears that the brick was waiting for the train, which is nonsense.

A participle linked in this way to the wrong noun/pronoun is said to be misrelated or the participle 'waiting' has no noun or pronoun to which it is attached.

The above sentence should have been written as following

While I was waiting for the train, a brick fell on my feet.

See more such examples.

(a) Standing near the gate, a dog caught her. *Incorrect*
While she was standing near the gate, a dog caught her. *Correct*

(b) When using this machine it must be remembered to unlock it first. Incorrect
When using this machine, you must remember to unlock it first. *Correct*

(c) Deciding to join the navy, the recruiter happily pumped Jack's hand. *Incorrect*
(The recruiter is not deciding to join the navy Jack is.)
The recruiter happily pumped Jack's hand after learning that Jack had decided to join the navy. *Correct*

(d) When watching films, commercials are especially irritating. *Incorrect*

How to Correct This Sentence?

One option would be to change the subject so that it names the actor that the modifier implies :

(a) When watching films, I find commercials especially irritating.

Another option would be to turn the modifier into a word group that includes the actor :

(b) When I am watching films, commercials are especially irritating.

Both (a) and (b) are correct.

(c) Being a cold morning I didn't go to office. *Incorrect*
It being a cold morning I didn't go to office. or *Correct*
The morning being cold, I didn't go to office. *Correct*

(d) Being a rainy day, the school remained closed. *Incorrect*
It being a rainy day, the school remained closed. or *Correct*
The day being rainy, the school remained closed. *Correct*

As you can see, a **dangling participle** is one that either has no noun or pronoun to modify or else is not close enough to the word it is supposed to modify to prevent it from attaching to another element. In either case, the sentence is both ambiguous and nonsensical. Even if a sentence is not rendered nonsense by a dangling participle, it will still be ambiguous, and that is almost as bad. Dangling participles are not considered acceptable in standard English, so they should be avoided in writing.

However, some participles : considering, regarding, concerning, taking, speaking, touching, do not need to agree with the subject of the sentence:

(a) Considering the price, the quality of the cloth is good.

(b) Speaking roughly, the distance between Delhi and Alwar is 150 Kms.

(c) Taking every point into consideration, the proposal is very attractive.

» Exercises

Infinitive

Exercise 1

Correct the following sentences

1. English is difficult to be learnt.
2. Do you dare refuse me?
3. I watched her to cross the road.
4. The act is easy to be performed.
5. He is better able to act than to sing.
6. She can do nothing but to abuse him.
7. Stop to write.
8. I had sooner run than to walk.
9. I have decided helping her.
10. Better to reign in hell than to serve in heaven.
11. I made him to polish my shoes.
12. She avoids to do her duties seriously.
13. I am looking forward to meet you soon.
14. I got a mechanic repairing my car.
15. A brave man does not fear dying.
16. The river is very deep to be crossed by the army.

Solutions

1. English is difficult to learn.
2. Do you dare to refuse me?
3. I watched her cross the road.
4. The act is easy to perform.
5. He is better able to act than sing.
6. She can do nothing but abuse him.
7. Stop writing.
8. I had sooner run than walk.
9. I have decided to help her.
10. Better reign in hell than serve in heaven.
11. I made him polish my shoes.
12. She avoids doing her duties seriously.
13. I am looking forward meeting you soon.
14. I got a mechanic to repair my car.
15. A brave man does not fear to die.
16. The river is very deep to cross by the army.

Exercise 2

Correct the following sentences

1. Please tell me to close it.
2. I know swim.
3. I can't decide to get out of this trouble.
4. I chanced meeting her in the art gallery.
5. She appears recognising me.
6. Could you tell me to explain the situation?
7. There was no board to write.
8. She hopes of passing with distinction.
9. She is eager to meeting me.
10. He went to Jaipur seeing the Jantar Mantar.
11. She failed winning the prize.
12. I shall be glad meeting you.

Solutions

1. Please tell me how to close it.
2. I know how to swim.
3. I can't decide how to get out of this trouble.
4. I chanced to meet her in the art gallery.
5. She appears to recognise me.
6. Could you tell me how to explain the situation?
7. There was no board to write on.
8. She hopes to pass with distinction.
9. She is eager to meet me.
10. He went to Jaipur to see the Jantar Mantar.
11. She failed to win the prize.
12. I shall be glad to meet you.

Exercise 3

Correct the following sentences

1. I have no pen to write.
2. She has a house for furnishing.
3. I have no house to live.
4. He requested me going to Jaipur.
5. He did nothing but to talk and to laugh.
6. I will have you to remember me.
7. She was known having hidden the jewellery box.
8. I would study rather than to waste my time.
9. The bade me to go.
10. Let I sing a song.
11. I observed him to play.
12. We had him to know his mistakes.

Solutions

1. I have no pen to write with.
2. She has a house to furnish.
3. I have no house to live in.
4. He requested me to go to Jaipur.

5. He did nothing but talk and laugh.
6. I will have you to remember me.
7. She was known to have hidden the jewellery box.
8. I would study rather than waste my time.
9. The bade me go.
10. Let me sing a song.
11. I observed him playing.
12. We had him know his mistakes.

Exercise 4

Correct the following sentences

1. He learned to operate the machine.
2. I asked him from where to buy shirts at reasonable rates.
3. I wonder whether go or not.
4. She pretended to look for some eatables.
5. Ramesh seems to follow us in his car.
6. He seemed to be a great musician.
7. His plan of rebuild the building was not approved by the municipality.
8. He made an effort to getting pass without copying.
9. She is too weak that she cannot walk.
10. She is enough matured to go alone.
11. She rån enough fast to catch the train.
12. He was so foolish as left his car unlocked.
13. Will you be so kind as sanction my leave?
14. She is the only one secure 95% marks.
15. She likes to completely change the colour.

Solutions

1. He learned how to operate the machine.
2. I asked him, where to buy shirts at reasonable rates ?
3. I wonder whether to go or not.
4. She pretended to be looking for some eatables.
5. Ramesh seems to be following us in his car.
6. He seemed to have been a great musician.
7. His plan to rebuild the building was not approved by the municipality.
8. He made an effort to get pass without copying.
9. She is too weak to walk.
10. She is matured enough to go alone.
11. She ran fast enough to catch the train.
12. He was so foolish as to leave his car unlocked.
13. Will you be so kind as to sanction my leave?
14. She is the only one to secure 95% marks.
15. She likes to change the colour completely.

Gerund

Exercise 5

Correct the following sentences

1. She is good at write.
2. He is afraid to lose the game.
3. I cannot forget you for you helping me.
4. It is totally useless to cry over the past misdeeds.
5. He said, 'Don't give up to try again.'
6. Would you mind to work with me?
7. She is fond of being admire.
8. I am sorry for me getting late.
9. I am happy at your arrival at schedule time.
10. To drink being his habit, we didn't go with him.

Solutions

1. She is good at writing.
2. He is afraid of losing the game.
3. I cannot forget you for your helping me.
4. It is totally useless crying over the past misdeeds.
5. He said, 'Don't give up trying again.'
6. Would you mind working with me?
7. She is fond of being admired.
8. I am sorry for my getting late.
9. I am happy at your arriving at schedule time.
10. Drinking being his habit, we didn't go with him.

Exercise 6

Correct the following sentences

1. I enjoy to travel.
2. Check the air before to start the generator.
3. It is no good to work with him.
4. Some people prefer to spend money to earn it.
5. I am thinking to leave my job and going back to my native place.
6. She said to me, 'Don't forget to lock the door before go to bed.'
7. I heard someone crying but I failed seeing anyone.
8. She has finished to wash the clothes.
9. I prefer to play football to reading my course books.
10. A novice can't learnt to spelling without being help.

Solutions

1. I enjoy travelling.

2. Check the air before starting the generator.
3. It is no good working with him.
4. Some people prefer spending money to earning it.
5. I am thinking of leaving my job and going back to my native place.
6. She said to me, 'Don't forget to lock the door before going to bed.'
7. I heard someone cry but I failed to see anyone.
8. She has finished washing the clothes.
9. I prefer playing football to reading my course books.
10. A novice can't learn to spell without being helped.

Exercise 7

Fill in the blanks with appropriate words

1. Try .... being late for office. (to avoid/avoiding)
2. We have nothing to do but .... for her. (waiting/to wait/wait)
3. Does your wife object .... on holidays. (to work/to working/have worked)
4. Sita was charged and fined for .... without lights. (driving/have driven/drove)
5. When he spoke, it was very difficult for me .... (to understood/to understand/understanding)
6. .... an aim, the hunter shot the lion. (took/ to take/ taking)
7. .... his work, he went to market. (completing/having completed/after complete)
8. .... inside a bus is prohibited. (to smoke/smoking/have smoking)
9. The students refused .... the hostel. (leaving/to leave/lefting)
10. I had sooner .... than walk. (ran/run/to run/running)
11. Tell me .... this typical machine. (operation/how to operate/operating system)
12. Most of the students like .... cricket. (to play/playing/have playing)
13. He is too young .... this movie. (watching/watch/to watch)
14. He advised me "You had better .... now." (leaving/leave/left)
15. The office needs proper .... (cleanliness/cleaning/to clean)

Solutions

1. to avoid	2. wait
3. to working	4. driving
5. to understand	6. taking
7. having completed	8. smoking
9. to leave	10. run
11. how to operate	12. playing
13. to watch	14. leave
15. cleaning	

Participle

Exercise 8

Correct the following sentences

1. Being Sunday, I am thinking to go to a movie.
2. Remember the lessons teach by the teacher.
3. Where is the book wrote by Mr. Gupta?
4. Ploughing his fields some old statues were found.
5. I want a wrote complaint.
6. There is no drink water in the office.
7. Having satisfied with his reply, I didn't take any action.
8. Tired, I couldn't work any more.
9. Left from hand to month, he yet maintains his standard of living.
10. Having referred to your application, I beg to write...

Solutions

1. It being Sunday, I am thinking to go to a movie.
2. Remember the lessons taught by the teacher.
3. Where is the book written by Mr. Gupta?
4. While ploughing his fields he found some old statues.
5. I want a written complaint.
6. There is no drinking water in the office.
7. Having been satisfied with his reply, I didn't take any action.
8. Being tired, I couldn't work any more.
9. Living from hand to month, he yet maintains his standard of living.
10. Referring to your application, I beg to write.

Exercise 9

Correct the following sentences

1. In regard to my qualification I beg to submit...
2. Sleeping in the house, a thief entered their house.
3. Having injured he went to hospital.
4. Turn to the left you can see the palace.
5. Walking in the forest a lion was seen.
6. Don't get off a ran bus.

7. The ship has sunken.
8. Having been worked hard he got tired.
9. Having opened the drawer she took out a knife.
10. We must provide good education to grow children.

Solutions

1. Regarding my qualification I beg to submit...
2. While they were sleeping in the house, a thief entered their house.
3. Having been injured he went to hospital.
4. Turning to the left you can see the palace.
5. While I was walking in the forest I saw a lion.
6. Don't get off a running bus.
7. The ship has sunk.
8. Having worked hard he got tired.
9. Opening the drawer she took out a knife.
10. We must provide good education to growing children.

Exercise 10

Fill in the blanks with correct form of non-finite verbs (infinitive/gerund/participle)

1. His speech left me .... (to think/thought/thinking.)
2. Some boys like .... the TV. (to watch/watch)
3. Sita is good at .... (swim/swimming/to swim)
4. I had an aversion .... meet. (to eat/ to eating)
5. It is wrong .... a lie before the judge at least. (to tell/telling/have told)
6. He had rather .... than beg. (to starve/starve/starved)
7. My greatest pleasure is .... while alone. (singing/to sing/sung)
8. He wears a .... look today. (worrying/worried/to worry)
9. You had better .... nothing. (to say/saying/say/said)
10. .... is a good exercise for the young. (to swim/swimming)

Solutions

1. thinking
2. to watch
3. swimming
4. to eating
5. to tell
6. starve
7. to sing
8. worried
9. say
10. swimming

Exercise 11

Fill in the blanks with correct form of non-finite verbs (infinitive/gerund/participle)

1. I watched her .... and come often. (going/go/to go)
2. .... is easier than reading. (to play/having played/playing)
3. I found his daughter .... (to cry/crying/have cried)
4. She denied .... any force to get him accept his fault. (used/to use/using)
5. I hate .... and cheating. (to lie/lying)
6. He said, 'He has given up ....' (to smoke/smoking/have smoked)
7. I remember .... her in the park. (seeing/to see)
8. She stopped .... others. (to advise/advising/had advised)
9. They want us .... for the girls to arrive. (waiting/to wait)
10. .... many times, he doesn't want to try again now. (failing/failed/having failed)
11. .... that she was early, she went to meet her friends. (to know/having know/knowing)
12. The book .... on the chair is mine. (lye/lying)
13. Please excuse my .... early today. (leave/left/leaving)
14. She disliked my .... on Sunday. (work/working)
15. .... out of the window, she saw a strange creature. (looked/looking/having looked)

Solutions

1. go
2. playing
3. crying
4. using
5. lying
6. smoking
7. seeing
8. advising
9. to wait
10. Having failed
11. knowing
12. lying
13. leaving
14. working
15. looking.

Spotting the Errors

Find the errors and justify your answers

1. Being often ill (A)/ and frequently absent (B)/ she had no opportunity to complete his work (C)/ or do much of it in toto (D). **(Bank PO)**
2. Taking breakfast (A)/ he went to the office (B)/ and ordered the staff (C)/ to complete the work without any further delay (D).
3. Without taking proper care (A)/ the doctors would (B)/ not have been saved (C)/ the life of this patient (D). **(BSRB)**
4. Going towards the gate (A)/ with a cup of tea (B)/ somebody switched off (C)/ the light (D).
5. He does nothing (A)/ but to find faults (B)/ with others (C)/ and laugh at them (D). **(BSRB)**
6. The Chief Minister (A) should not let (B)/ the terrorist activities (C)/ to grow in our state (D).
7. Many persons are coming (A)/ to his concert (B)/ to hear him to sing (C)/ the religious songs (D).
8. Having had reached (A)/ the station, you (B)/ may make a telephone (C)/ to your boss (D).
9. It is better to stay (A)/ at home than to go to market (B)/ when it is raining (C). **(Bank PO)**
10. When he entered the home (A)/ he found the child sleeping (B)/ and the fan moves slowly (C).
11. He asked me to (A)/ completely forget her (B)/ but only I know (C) it is not possible (D). **(BSRB)**

» Answers

1. (D) Place to before 'do'.
2. (A) Either write 'After taking breakfast' or 'Having taken breakfast'.
3. (C) Delete been.
4. (A) The correct phrase will be 'While he was going towards the gate'.
5. (B) Use of 'to' after 'Nothing but' is incorrect. He does nothing but watch T.V.
6. (D) Delete 'to'. Do not use infinitive after let.
7. (C) Replace 'to sing' by 'sing'.
8. (A) Delete 'Had'.
9. (B) Delete to. Use of to after than is incorrect. It is better to study than wander here and there.
10. (C) The correct phrase will be 'fan moving slowly'.
11. (B) Replace 'completely forget her' by 'forget her completely'.

» Unit

12

Reported Speech
(*Direct-Indirect Narrations*)

Direct and Indirect Speech

Direct Speech : Saying exactly what someone has said is called direct speech (sometimes called quoted speech). What a person says appears within quotation marks ('...' or "...") and should be word by word.

(a) She said, 'Today's lesson is on presentations.'
or 'Today's lesson is on presentations,' she said.

Indirect Speech : Indirect speech (sometimes called reported speech), does not use quotation marks to enclose what the person said and need not be word by word.

Reporter/Reporting Verb/Reported Speech

Reporter : The speaker or narrator is called the 'reporter'.

Reporting Verb : The verb used by the 'reporter' is called reporting verb.

Reported Speech : Sentence enclosed within the inverted commas ('....' or "...") is called reported speech.

She said to me, 'I am going to Jaipur.'

In this sentence : She reporter, said is reporting verb and 'I am going to Jaipur' is reported speech.

Reported speech always begins with a capital letter and enclosed within the inverted commas (' ')

While we change a narration from direct to indirect, the inverted commas are removed.

Rules for Changing Direct Speech into Indirect Speech

For the sake of understanding we may broadly divide the rules of changing direct speech into indirect speech in two parts.

1. General rules applicable to all kinds of sentences.
2. Specific rules applicable to specific kind of sentences.

General rules and method of transforming a sentence into indirect narration.

1. First of all ascertain the tense of the 'Reporting verb'.

(a) If the reporting verb is in present or future tense, the tense of reported speech remains unchanged.

(b) If the reporting verb is in past, see the rules at next pages.

2. The reporting verb changes as following

Reporting verb in direct speech	Reporting verb in indirect speech
say	say
says	says
say to	tell
says to	tells
will say	will say
will say to	will tell
said	said
said to	told/asked

An object must follow 'tell' or 'told'.
He tells, 'Ram is playing.' *Incorrect*
He told, 'I am going.' *Incorrect*
He told that he was going. *Incorrect*

3. While changing into indirect speech the personal pronouns are changed as per following

(a) **First person pronoun** According to subject of reporting verb.

(b) **Second person pronoun** According to object of reporting verb.

(c) **Third person pronoun** No change

The number and case of the person do not change. Learn well the following to understand the change of personal pronouns.

4. Conjunction 'that' is commonly used while changing into indirect speech.

(a) He says, 'I am going to Jaipur". *Direct*
He says that he is going to Jaipur. *Indirect*

Reporting Verb in the Past

1. If the reporting verb is in 'past', the tense of the reported speech changes as following

Tense of Reported Speech

Direct Narration	Indirect Narration
Present Indefinite	Past Indefinite
Present Continuous	Past Continuous
Present Perfect	Past Perfect
Present Perfect Continuous	Past Perfect Continuous
Past Indefinite	Past Perfect
Past Continuous	Past Perfect Continuous
Past Perfect	No change of tense
Past Perfect Continuous	No change of tense

Change in Future Sentences (Reported Speech)

Will/shall	Would/should
Can	Could
May	Might
Could /should /would /might	No change

2. When the reporting verb is in 'past' words denoting time or place in reported speech change as following

Direct Narration	Indirect Narration
This	That
These	Those
Here	There
Hence	Thence
Hither	Thither
Now	Then
Ago	Before
Thus	So
Today	That day
Tomorrow	The next day/the following day
Yesterday	The previous day
Last week/month/year	The previous week/month/year
The last fort night	The previous fort night
The day before yesterday	The day before the previous day

3. If the reported speech contains universal truth, proverb, mathematical fact, historical fact, habitual act, an expression of morality or an unchanged fact, the tense of the reported speech remains unchanged.

(a) He said, 'The sun sets in the west'. (universal truth) *Direct*
He said that the sun sets in the west. *Indirect*

(b) The teacher said, 'A stitch in time saves nine'. (proverb) *Direct*
The teacher said that a stitch in time saves nine. *Indirect*

(c) The teacher said, 'India became Republic on 26th January 1950.' *Direct*
The teacher said that India became Republic on 26th Jan, 1950. *Indirect*

(d) She said to me, 'Honesty is the best policy. (morality) *Direct*
She told me that honesty is the best policy. *Indirect*

(e) She said, 'Two and two is four'. (mathematical fact) *Direct*
She said that two and two is four. - *Indirect*

(6) He said, 'London is the capital of UK.' (unchanged fact) *Direct*
He said that London is the capital of UK *Indirect*

(7) He said to me, 'I go for a walk daily.' (habit) *Direct*
He told me that he goes for a walk daily. *Indirect*

Specific Rules

Interrogative Sentences

Interrogative sentences can be classified into two types.

1. Sentences that have questions that can be answered in 'Yes' or 'No'.
2. 'Wh' questions that begin with words such as What, Where, Which, Who, How, etc.

Rules for Yes or No questions.

1. Use conjunction 'if' or 'whether' in place of 'that'. Whether is used when the question expresses an alternative.

She asked me, 'Do you like tea or coffee?'
She asked me whether I liked tea or coffee.

2. Remove the question mark (?) and the interrogative sentence (the question) is changed to assertive sentence (Subject + verb +...).

3. Reporting verb; ask, asks, asked—is used in indirect narrations. We can also use inquire or enquire of. Enquire of is used when an object follows it. For example: He enquired of me.

4. Other rules in respect to the change of pronouns and change of tense are also to be followed.

(a) She said to me, 'Are you going to college?" *Direct*
The asked me if I was going to college. *Indirect*

(b) She said to Shyam, 'Have you an extra copy?' *Direct*
She asked Shyam if he had an extra copy. *Indirect*

(c) He said, 'Am I looking smart?' *Direct*
He asked if he was looking smart. *Indirect*

Sometimes an answer is also attached with the main question. In that case 'Yes' is changed into affirmation and 'No' into negation.

(a) She said to me, 'Can you solve this question?' 'No,' I said.
She asked me if I could solve that question, I said, I couldn't or I replied in negative.

(b) He said to me, 'Do you know me ?, 'I said, 'Yes.'
He asked me if I know him, I said, I did or I replied in affirmative.

Questions beginning with 'Wh' words.

5. In questions beginning with Wh words, no conjunction (that, if, whether) is used, instead the Wh word itself functions as conjunction.

6. The interrogative sentence is changed into assertive (subject+ verb+...).

(a) He said to her , 'What do you want?' *Direct*
He asked her what she wanted. *Indirect*

(b) He said to me , 'Why are you happy?' *Direct*
He asked me why I was happy. *Indirect*

(c) Ram said to Hari , 'Where do you live?' *Direct*
Ram asked Hari where he lived. *Indirect*

(d) She said to Hari, 'When will you come?' *Direct*
She asked Hari when he would come. *Indirect*

7. Questions : Shall I/We + ...? Such questions can denote : speculation/request/advice/ offer of service/suggestion.

Read the following examples

When a speculation is expressed or an information is sought.

(a) 'Shall I ever see her again?' he said. (speculation) *Direct*
He wondered if he would ever see her again. *Indirect*

(b) 'When shall I know the result of the election?' Ram asked. *Direct*
Ram asked when he would know the result of the election. *Indirect*

Please note that 'shall' is as usual changed to would. Speculations are ordinarily introduced by 'wonder'.

In case of request or advice.

(a) He said to the customer, 'Shall we dispatch these letters?' *Direct*
He asked the customer if they should dispatch those letters. *Indirect*

(b) 'What shall I say father?' he said. *Direct*
Indirect : He asked his father what he should say. *Indirect*

Request and advice are expressed in indirect speech by 'ask', 'inquire' etc. Requests for advice are normally reported by 'should'.

When a choice is required we normally use 'whether' in indirect speech.

Whether + infinitive is also sometimes possible.

(a) 'Shall I lock the room or leave it unlocked?' Rajesh said. *Direct*

Rajesh asked whether he should lock the room or leave it unlocked. *Indirect*

When an offer is made.

(a) 'Shall I bring you something to eat?,' she said *Direct*

She offered to bring me something to eat. *Indirect*

When suggestion is made.

(a) 'Shall we meet again tomorrow?,' he said. *Direct*

He suggested to meet again the next day. *Indirect*

8. Questions beginning will you/would you/ could you?

Such questions may express invitations, commands, requests or may also be an ordinary question. The reporting verb is used according to the tenor/ theme of the statement.

(a) He said, 'Will you be there on Monday? *Direct*

He asked if he would be there on Monday. *Indirect*

(b) He asked, 'Would you like to do job in USA?' *Direct*

He asked if I would like to do job in USA. *Indirect*

Imperatives

Sentences expressing command, order, advice, request etc. are usually called imperative sentences. Imperative sentences have two characteristics.

First, imperative sentences make a command or request.

Second, imperative sentences end with a period.

Rules for Changing Imperative Sentences Into Indirect Speech

1. **Use conjunction 'to' instead of 'that'. Negative commands, requests, etc. are reported by not + infinitive.**
2. **In indirect speech expressions of commands, requests, advice are usually expressed by a verb of command /request/ advice + object + infinitive. Verbs : advise, ask, beg, command, encourage, entreat, forbid, implore, invite, order, recommend, remind, request, tell, urge, warn are normally used to express the notions of command/order/request/advice. (We do not use say or said in such sentences).**
3. **If a sentence contains words like; please, kindly etc. these are not mentioned in the indirect speech, as the notion is well expressed by the reporting verb request in such case.**

(a) She said to Ramu, 'Please bring my book.' *Direct*

She requested Ramu to bring her book. *Indirect*

(b) She said to me , 'Have a glass of milk'. *Direct*

She asked me to have a glass of milk. *Indirect*

(3) Ram said to Sita, 'Take medicines regularly.' *Direct*

Ram advised Sita to take medicines regularly. *Indirect*

(4) I said to Hari, 'Don't pluck the flowers.' *Direct*

I ordered Hari not to pluck the flowers. *Indirect*

Negative Imperatives

Negative commands, requests etc. are usually reported by not + infintive or forbid can also be used for prohibitions, but is more common in the passive than in the active.

(a) The teacher said to Hari , 'Don't write on the table'. *Direct*

The teacher forbade Hari to write on the table *Indirect*

or The teacher instructed Hari not to write on the table. *Indirect*

(b) The Principal said, 'Don't make a noise students.' *Direct*

The Principal forbade the students to make a noise. *Indirect*

or The Principal instructed the students not to make a noise. *Indirect*

Emphatic Imperative (Use of 'Do')

Look at the following sentences, where 'Do' is used to make the request more emphatic, more polite or courteous.

(a) He said to me, 'Do have a cup of coffee please'. *Direct*
He requested me to have a cup of coffee. *Indirect*

(b) She said to me, 'Do come again.' *Direct*
She requested me to come again. *Indirect*

(c) Rahim said to her, 'Do have a seat please'. *Direct*
Rahim requested her to have a seat. *Indirect*

Imperative and Tag Question

Sometimes tag questions are attached to the imperatives to make them more emphatic. Look at the following examples :

(a) He said to me, 'Open the door, will you?' *Direct*
He asked me to open the door. *Indirect*

(b) She said to Ram , 'Bring me a glass of water, won't you?' *Direct*
She asked Ram to bring her a glass of water. *Indirect*

A question tag at the end of an imperative sentence is left out in indirect narrations. Sometimes question tag is more important than the statement.
(a) He said, 'You don't love her, do you?'
He asked me if I loved her.
(b) She said to me, 'Do you like coffee, don't you?'
She asked me whether I liked coffee.

Imperatives with 'Let'

Sentences with 'Let' can be used to express suggestion, order, request and wish.

Let's/Let us for suggestions

(a) He said, 'Let's leave the bag at the hotel.' *Direct*
He suggested leaving the bag at the hotel. *Indirect*
or He suggested that they/ we should leave the bag at the hotel. *Indirect*

(b) She said, 'Let's stop now and finish it afterwards.' *Direct*
She suggested stopping then and finishing it afterwards. *Indirect*
or She suggested that we should stop then and finish it afterwards.

Negative sentences

(a) He said, 'Let's not do anything about it till we know the facts.' *Direct*
He suggested not doing anything about it till they knew the facts. *Indirect*
or He suggested doing nothing about it till they knew the facts *Indirect*
or He suggested that they shouldn't do anything till they knew the facts.

Let him/them for expressing command/order

(a) 'Let the boys clean the ground,' said the principal. *Direct*
The principal said that the boys were to clean the ground. *Indirect*

(b) The Principal said to the peon, ' Let the students come in'. *Direct*
The Principal ordered the peon to allow the students come in. *Indirect*

(c) 'Let the workers be given bonus,' he ordered. *Direct*
He ordered that the workers should be given bonus. *Indirect*

Very often the speaker has no authority over the person who is to obey the command.
'It's not my job,' said the clerk. 'Let the manager do something about it.'
Here, the speaker has no authority but expressing an obligation. Sentences of this type are therefore usually reported by ought/should.
He said that it wasn't his job and that the manager ought to/should do something about it.

Sometimes let him/them is used to express a suggestion. In such cases it is reported by suggest, or say + should.

(a) He said, 'Let them go to their advocate.' *Direct*
He suggested them going to their advocate. *Indirect*
or He said that they should go to their advocate. *Indirect*

Let him/them is also used to express an indifferent attitude.

(b) 'Ramesh will complain,' said Anita. 'Let him (complain),' said Tina.
Tina expressed indifference.
or Tina said she didn't mind (if he complained).

'Let there be' construction is used to order, advise, urge or beg.

'Let there be no further action,' said the union leader. *Direct*
The union leader urged/begged that there should be no further action. *Indirect*

Let can also be used to express 'wish'.

(a) The student said, 'Let me take food'. *Direct*

The student wished that he should take food. *Indirect*

(b) The lady said, 'Let me have an ice cream pack'. *Direct*

The lady wished that she should have an ice cream pack. *Indirect*

(c) She said, 'Let him be my friend.' *Direct*

She wished that he should be her friend. *Indirect*

Let for request : In such cases conjunction 'to' is used.

(a) The boy said to the teacher, 'Let me go home now.' *Direct*

The boy requested the teacher to allow him to go home then. *Indirect*

(b) The student said to the teacher, 'Let me complete this assignment'. *Direct*

The student requested the teacher to allow him to complete that assignment. *Indirect*

Optative Sentences

Sentences containing expressions of good wishes, prayer for someone or desires are called optative sentences.

Rule The reporting verb is changed according to the mood of the expression.

Usually 'that' conjunction is used in cases where the sentence is changed into assertive.

(a) My mother said to my friend, 'May you live long !' *Direct*

My mother wished my friend that he might live long. *Indirect*

(b) She said to Sita, 'May God bless you with a son !' *Direct*

She prayed that God might bless Sita with a son. *Indirect*

(c) She said, 'God grant you success!' (May God grant you success. May is hidden.) *Direct*

She prayed/wished that God might grant me success. *Indirect*

Expressions of salutations.

(a) He said to the teacher, 'Good morning!' *Direct*

He wished the teacher good morning. *Indirect*

(b) She said, 'Good morning, sir!' *Direct*

She wished the sir good morning. *Indirect*

Expressions of farewell. Reporting verb bid/bade is used.

(a) She said to me, 'Good bye.' *Direct*

She bade me good bye. *Indirect*

(b) The leader said, 'Farewell my friends.' *Direct*

The leader bade his friends farewell. *Indirect*

Exclamatory Sentences

Sentences containing sudden expressions of joy, sorrow, anger, applause, surprise and contempt are called exclamatory sentences.

Rules

1. **Reporting verb** : exclaimed with joy, sorrow, surprise, applause, anger, contempt, etc. is used according to the tenor of the sentence.
2. Conjunction 'that' is used as usual.
3. **Words such as** : Alas, Bravo, Oh, Wow, Wah, Hurrah used in direct speech are left out in indirect narration.
4. Exclamatory sentence is transformed into assertive.
5. **For any wish like** : If I were a bird, If I were the PM etc. reporting verb 'wish' is used.
6. All other rules regarding change of pronoun and change of tense also apply.

(a) She said, 'If I were a bird!'

She wished that she would be a bird.

(b) He said, 'If I were young again!'

He wished that he would be young again.'

(c) Ram said, 'Alas! I have been ruined.'

Ram exclaimed with sorrow that he had been ruined.

(d) The lady said, 'Oh! My dog is dead.'
The lady exclaimed with sorrow that her dog was dead.

(e) He said, 'What a beautiful girl Sita is!'
He exclaimed with praise that Sita was a beautiful girl.

(f) We said, 'What a nice place it is!'
We exclaimed with surprise that it was a nice place.

Note the change into indirect narrations in following sentences.

(a) He said to me, 'Congratulations!'
He congratulated me.

(b) I said to her, 'Happy Christmas!'
I wished her happy Christmas.

(c) She said, 'Thank you!'
She thanked me.

(d) They said to us, 'Welcome!'
They welcomed us.

Miscellaneous Sentences

When name of a person/sir/madam, is within inverted commas :

(a) He said, 'Rajeev, I am waiting for you.'
He told Rajeev that he is waiting for him.

(b) She said, 'Take your purse, Tony.'
She asked Tony to take his purse.

(c) Sheela said, 'Brother please help me.'
Sheela requested her brother to help her.

(d) He said, 'Kuku what are you doing?'
He asked Kuku what she was doing.

(e) He said, 'May I leave now Madam?'
He asked Madam if he might leave.

(f) She said, 'May I attend the class, Sir?'
She asked respectfully if she might attend the class.

Some sentence with well, okay, you see, you know, etc. are changed into indirect narration.

(a) The receptionist said, 'Well, what can I do for you ?'
The receptionist asked politely what she could do for me.

(b) 'Okay,' she said, 'I will consider your proposal.'
She said that she would consider my proposal.

Must

Must used for conclusion/deduction/command/prohibition and to express intention remains unchanged.

(a) She said, 'I usually meet him here; he must live near here.' *(deductions)*
She said that she usually met him there, he must live in that area.

(b) She said, 'This room must be kept locked.' *(command)*
She said that the room must be kept locked.

(c) She said, 'We must have a party to celebrate this.' *(intention)*
She said that they must have a party to celebrate it.

'Must' used for obligation usually changes to 'would have to' or 'had to'.

'Would have to' is used when the obligation depends on some future action or when the fulfillment of the obligation is not certain or appears remote or uncertain, i.e. when must means 'will have to'.

(a) Sarpanch said, 'If the floods get worse we must (will have to) leave this place.'
Sarpanch said that if the floods got worse they would have to leave this place.

(b) I said, 'When it stops drizzling we must start digging again.'
I said that when it stopped drizzling we would have to start digging again.

(c) She said, 'We must call the mechanic tomorrow.'
She said that they would have to call the mechanic the next day.

'Must' changes to 'had to' where times for fulfillments of the obligation either have been fixed or the obligation is fulfilled fairly promptly or at least by the time the speech is reported.

(a) She said, 'I must take a quick bath.' (and presumably did so)
She said that she had to take a quick bath .

(b) Harish said, 'I must be there by six tomorrow morning.'
Harish said that he had to be there by six the next morning.

Must I/you/he? can also change similarly but as 'must' in the interrogative usually concerns the present or immediate future so it changes to 'had to'.

(a) I said, 'Must you go so today?'
I asked him if he had to go that day.

'Must Not'

'I must not' and 'You must not' usually remain unchanged.

(a) She said to me, 'You mustn't talk anyone about it'.
She told me that I mustn't talk anyone about that.

Needn't

Needn't usually remains unchanged. It can be changed to didn't have to/wouldn't have to just as must changes to had to/would have to.

(a) Ram said to me, 'You needn't wait.'
Ram told me that I needn't wait.

(b) I said, 'If you can lend me the rupees five thousand I needn't go to the bank .
I said that if he could lend me rupees five thousand I needn't / wouldn't have to go to the bank.

(c) He said, 'I needn't be in office till next Monday'.
He said that he needn't /didn't have to be in office till next Monday.

(d) He said, 'You must not speak to anyone'.
He said that I must not speak to anyone.

Sometimes direct speech consists of statement + question or question + command or command + statement, or all three together.

Normally each comp requires its own reporting verb.

(a) He said, 'I don't know the way. Do you?'
He said he didn't know the way and asked me if I did.

(b) 'A stranger is coming,' he said. 'Get behind the wall.'
He said that a stranger was coming and told me to get behind the wall.

(c) 'I'm going shopping. May I get you anything?' he said.
He said he was going shopping and asked if he might get me anything.

(d) 'I can hardly hear the TV,' he said. 'Could you increase the volume?'
He said he could hardly hear the TV and asked her to high the volume.

In some cases, we use 'as' when the last clause is a statement which explains the first clause.

(a) He said , 'You'd better wear a woolen shirt. It's cold today.'
He advised me to wear a woolen shirt as it was cold that day.

(b) Hari said to her, 'You'd better not walk across the lane alone. People have been mugged there.'
Hari warned her not to walk across the lane alone as people had been mugged there.

In some cases the second reporting verb can be a participle.

(a) Sarla said to her husband, 'Please, don't drink too much! Remember that you'll have to drive home.'
Sarla begged her husband not to drink too much, reminding him that he'd have to drive home.

(b) He said to his wife, 'Let's shop on Monday. The shopping mall will be very crowded on Sunday.'
He suggested shopping on Monday, pointing out that the shopping mall would be very crowded on Sunday.

Would/ should/ could/ might remains unchanged usually in indirect speech.

(a) He said, 'She would/should/could/might attend the party.'
He said that she would/should/could/might attend the party.

'Had to' changes to 'had had to' in indirect speech.

(a) The poet said, 'After the function, I had to rush to my house.'
The poet said that after the function he had to rush to his house.

Indirect Commands

(a) She said, 'If I were you, I'd stop smoking.'
She advised me to stop smoking.

(b) He said, 'Why don't you change your clothes?'
He advised me to change my clothes.

(c) 'Would/could you show me your ticket, please?', the ticket collector said.
The ticket collector asked me to show him my ticket.

(d) The receptionist said, 'If you'd just sign the application form.'
The receptionist asked him to sign the application form.

(e) His wife said, 'Please, don't take risk.'
His wife begged/implored him not to take risk.

(f) Mrs Jacob said, 'Don't forget to order the whisky.'
Mrs Jacob reminded him to order the whisky.

(g) He said to me, 'If your brakes are bad don't drive so fast.'
He told me that if my brakes were bad I shouldn't drive so fast.
or He advised me not to drive so fast if my brakes were bad.

(h) He said to me, 'If she leaves the house follow her.'
He instructed me that if she left the house I was to follow her.

Joint Sentences

(a) She said, 'I am a girl. I cannot stay here at night.'
She said that she was a girl and added that she could not stay there at night.

(b) Ramesh said, 'Sita is going to Jaipur tomorrow. I can also go with her.'
Ramesh said that Sita was going to Jaipur the next day and he could also go with her.

(c) Payal said, 'I will not marry this year. I am preparing for IAS examinations.'
Payal said that she would not marry that year and further added that she was preparing for IAS examinations.

(d) He said, 'Do you know who is he ?'
He asked me if I knew who he was.

(e) She said, 'Can you find, where are the keys?'
She asked me if I could find where the keys were.

(f) He said, 'Sarla is coming, wait here.'
He said that Sarla was coming and asked me to wait there.

(g) He said, 'Where is your purse, I have lost mine?'
He asked me where my purse was and added that he had lost his.

(h) My father said, 'I am going to office, where are you going?'
My father said that he was going to his office and wanted to know where I was going.

(i) The leader said, 'Friends, my country men, lend me your support. I will take care of your problems.'
The leader addressed the people as friends, my country men and requested them to lend him their support. He further added that he would take care of their problems.

(j) 'Where are you going Sheela? Come here and we will talk about our marriage,' said he.
He asked Sheela where she was going and added that they would talk about their marriage.

(k) Sita said to Ram, 'No, no, I can't play with you. My father has, forbidden me to play with you.'
Sita told Ram that she could not play with him as his father had forbidden her to play with him.

Words such as accuse ...of/admit/apologise for/deny/ insist on + gerund construction can sometimes be used instead of 'say (that)'.

(a) She said, 'You took the money.'
She accused me of taking the money.

(b) He said,'I didn't steal the purse.'
He denied stealing the purse.

(c) Raj said , 'I'm sorry I'm late.'
Raj apologised for being late.

In some sentences we do not see object with the reporting verb. In such cases we can also choose an object.

(a) Sima said, 'I am waiting for you.'
Sima told me that she was waiting for me.
Or Sima told him that she was waiting for him.

(b) My mother said, 'You should take proper diet.'
My mother told me that I should take proper diet.

(c) He said, 'I do not like to talk to any of you.'
He told us that he did not like to talk to any of us.
Or He told them that he did not like to talk to any of them.

(d) The teacher said, 'You should learn the lessons well.'

The teacher told the students/me/him/her that they / I / he / she should learn the lessons well.

Some Specific Points about Reported Speech

As per the rules we have learnt so far, the past continuous tense changes to the past perfect continuous, but in practice usually remains unchanged except when it refers to a completed action.

(a) He said, 'When I saw her, she was playing football.'
He said that when he saw her, she was playing football.

(b) She said, 'When I saw them, they were swimming in the river.'
She said that when she saw them, they were swimming in the river.

(c) He said, 'When we were living in London we often saw Mr. James.
He said that when they were living in London they often saw/had often seen Mr. James.

A past tense describes a situation which still exists (unchanged) when the speech is reported, tense of the reported speech remains unchanged.

(a) He said, 'I decided not to purchase the house, because it was near the railway track.'
He said that he had decided not to purchase the house because it was near the railway track.

(b) They said, 'We decided not to buy the house as it was on the main road.'
They said that they had decided not to buy the house as it was on the main road.
(In the above sentences it was near the railway track, it was on the main road, the situation did not change.)

Unreal past tenses after wish, would rather/ sooner and it is time do not change.

(a) He said, 'I wish, I didn't have to take examination.'
He said he wished he didn't have to take examination.

(b) 'It is time we began planning for our examinations,' he said.
He said that it was time they began planning for their examinations.

(c) 'Kate wants to go alone,' said Amar. 'but I'd rather she went with her sister.'
Amar said that Kate wanted to go alone but that he'd rather she went with her sister.

Usually the construction I/ he/ she/ we/ they had better remains unchanged. 'You had better' can remain unchanged or can be reported by advise + object + infinitive.

(a) 'The children had better go to bed early,' said Ram.
Ram said that the children had better go to bed early.

(b) Sita said, 'You had better give up smoking.'
Sita said that you had better give up smoking.
Sita advised me to give up smoking.

(c) She said, 'The old had better go for a walk daily.'
She said that the old had better go for a walk daily.

(d) He said, 'You had better not drink the tea.'
He advised me not to drink the tea.
He said that I had better not drink the tea.

In following type of conditional sentences, no change of tense is needed.

(a) He said, 'If I had a permit I could get this job.'
He said that if he had a permit he could get that job.

(b) He said, 'If she had come to me, I would have helped her.'
He said that if she had come to him, he would have helped her.

(c) He said, 'If I had the tools I could mend the car.'
He said that if he had the tools he could mend the car.

(d) She boasted, 'I could read when I was there.'
She boasted that she could read when she was there.

(e) He said, 'When I was a boy, I could stay up as long as I liked.'
He said that when he was a boy he could stay up as long as he liked.

(f) He said, 'If my children were older would leave India.'
He said that if his children were older he would leave India.

Exercises

Exercise 1

Change the following sentences into indirect narration

1. Sumit said, 'Father, I want to go abroad after I finish my studies here.' **(RAS)**
2. I said to Sumit, 'Why do you want to go abroad? Where actually do you want to go?'
3. 'Don't go home yet,' I told my colleague, 'remember you promised to finish your week before leaving.' **(RAS)**
4. 'Please listen to me,' he answered, 'I must go now because my son is very ill.' **(RAS)**
5. 'What a relief to know that the girl has passed !' I exclaimed, 'Now she can get a job.'
6. The station master said to me, 'You are very late; it is one full hour since the train left.' **(Inspectors of Income Tax)**
7. Nitin said to me, 'Why don't you come with us? Why do you want to be so unsocial?'
8. The gang leader shouted, 'Keep together and run, the police are after us.'
9. I said to my companions, 'Let them not come with us if they don't want to let's not wait for them any longer.' **(RAS)**
10. 'What a pleasant surprise!' I exclaimed on seeing John in the room, 'I never expected to find you here.'
11. I said to Harish, 'The man who came to meet you asked if we could see his boss tomorrow.'
12. He said to his secretary, 'Why don't you carry out orders exactly?' Remember if you don't, you will be punished.'
13. I said to the boy, 'You have no ticket, get out before you are driven out.'
14. The lecturer paused and said, 'Those who are tired of listening to me can go. I shall not mind it.'
15. They said, 'How very awkward! What shall we say to him?' **(RAS)**

Solutions

1. Sumit told his father that he wanted to go abroad after he finished his studies here.
2. I asked Sumit why he wanted to go abroad and where he actually wanted to go.
3. I requested my colleague not to go home yet and to remember that he promised to finish his work before leaving.
4. He answered politely to listen to him and that he must go then because his son was very ill.
5. I exclaimed with joy that it was a great relief to know that the girl had passed and then she would get a job.
6. The station master told me that I was very late and it was one full hour since the train had left.
7. Nitin asked me why I did not come with them. He further asked why I wanted to be so unsocial.
8. The gang leader shouted to his followers to keep together and run because the police were after them.
9. I told the companions that they need not come with them if they didn't want to. He suggested that they should not wait for them any longer.
10. I exclaimed on seeing John in the room that it was a very pleasanst surprise, and I had never accepted to find him there.
11. I told Harish that the man who had come to meet him, had asked if we would see his boss the following day.
12. He asked his secretary why he did not carry out orders exactly, he warned him that if he did not (carry out orders) he would be punished.
13. I ordered the boy to get out (as he had no ticket) before he was driven out.
14. The lecturer paused and said that those who were tired of listening to him would go and that he would not mind that.
15. They cried out with contempt what they would tell him (by way of explanation), exclaimed that it was very awkward.

Exercise 2

Change the following sentences into indirect narration

1. Madhur said to his sister, 'Before I go to Delhi, I shall meet Sushila.' **(Assit Grade)**
2. Govind said to Mohit, 'Do not come here again or you will get a beating.'
3. John said to James, 'Have you come here just to see me or are there some other reasons?'
4. Abdul said, 'What a lovely morning for tennis?' **(Assit Grade)**
5. The teacher said to the boy, 'Since it is so warm let us go swimming.' **(Assit Grade)**
6. They said, 'Mother, we are not hungry; we shall eat later.' **(Assit Grade)**
7. He said angrily to his brother, 'Why don't you do as you are told.'

8. I said to the visitor, 'Don't sit on that chair, it is broken.'
9. My little brother said, 'I wish it rains hard, so I don't have to go to school.'
10. 'How steep the path is !' they said, 'We are quite tired.' ***(Income Tax)***
11. 'Neither a borrower, nor a lender be,' said the father to son. ***(Income Tax)***
12. 'And remember always that true education means the training of the mind,' said the VC addressing students. ***(Income Tax Inspectors)***
13. The teacher said to his students, 'Even in your life and conversation prove worthy of your glorious Alma Mater.' ***(Income Tax Inspectors)***
14. The son said to his father reverently, 'Do you expect me to have even done this sort of a mean thing.' ***(Income Tax Inspectors)***
15. 'Don't hang upon me, young man, I do not like flatterers' said the officer to his secretary.

Solutions

1. Mohan told his sister that before going to Delhi, he would meet Sushila.
2. Govind told Mohit not to come there or he would get a beating.
3. John asked James if he had come there just to see him or there were some other reasons.
4. Abdul exclaimed that was a lovely morning for tennis!
5. The teacher suggested the boys that they should go swimming since it was so warm.
6. They told their mother that they were not hungry, they would eat later.
7. He angrily asked his brother why he did not do as he was told.
8. I cautioned the visitor against sitting on that chair, (as) it was broken.
9. The little brother earnestly wished that it (should) rain so hard that he would not have to go to school.
10. They exclaimed that the path was very steep and they were quite tired.
11. The father advised his son neither to be a borrower, nor to be a lender.
12. Addressing the new graduates the Vic exhorted them to remember always that true education means training of the mind.
13. The teacher exhorted his students, ever in their life and conversation, to prove worthy of their glorious Alma Mater.
14. The son asked his father respectfully if he expected him to have ever done that sort of a mean thing.
15. Addressing the Secretary as young man, the officer advised him to wait there patiently till he returned with some food for him.

Exercise 3

Choose the best way to complete the sentences below

1. Please tell me ......
   A. where is the bus stop.
   B. where the bus stop be.
   C. where stops the bus.
   D. where the bus stop is.
2. I told him ......
   A. what the homework was.
   B. what was the homework.
   C. what was to be the homework.
   D. what is the homework.
3. I think .....
   A. will be the plane on time.
   B. the plane will be on time.
   C. the plane to be on time.
   D. it will be on time the plane.
4. I didn't know ...
   A. what he mean.
   B. what did he mean.
   C. what did he meant.
   D. what he meant.
5. He said ....
   A. that the weather colder than usual.
   B. the weather be colder than usual.
   C. the weather was colder than usual.
   D. the weather it is colder than usual.
6. I think ....
   A. today it is Wednesday.
   B. that is today Wednesday.
   C. today is Wednesday.
   D. today be Wednesday.
7. He said ....
   A. that yesterday he gone downtown.
   B. he goes downtown yesterday.
   C. he go downtown yesterday.
   D. he went downtown yesterday.
8. I believe ......
   A. him he is right
   B. he is right.
   C. he be right.
   D. that he right.
9. She said .....
   A. that she was hungry.
   B. she hungry.
   C. she be hungry.
   D. her was hungry.
10. He told us .....
    A. that he enjoy the movie.
    B. he enjoyed the movie.
    C. he be enjoying the movie.
    D. that enjoyed the movie.

Solutions

1. D 2. A 3. B 4. D
5. C 6. C 7. D 8. B
9. A 10. B

Exercise 4

Change the following sentences into indirect narration

1. He said, 'Two and two make four.'
2. She said, 'I saw a tiger here.'
3. Maneesh said, 'I may go to Delhi tomorrow.'
4. He asked me, 'Where has he gone?'
5. Sita said to me, 'Is it still raining.'
6. He said to me, 'When will she come?'
7. She said to me, 'Is Raju your friend?'
8. She said to me, 'Have you a car?'
9. She said, 'Do they play chess?'
10. Rahim said, 'Who are they?'

Solutions

1. He said that two and two make four.
2. She said that she had seen a tiger there.
3. Maneesh said that he might go to Delhi the next day.
4. He asked me where he had gone.
5. Sita asked me if it was raining till then.
6. He asked when she would come.
7. She asked me if Raju was my friend.
8. She asked me if I had a car.
9. She asked me if they played chess.
10. Rahim asked who they were.

Exercise 5

Change the following sentences into indirect narration

1. Kanika said to Suresh, 'Is the tea ready?'
2. She said to me, 'Is it my book?'
3. Tarmesh said to me, 'Will you keep shut?'
4. Chinkoo said to him, 'Get out?'
5. The teacher said, 'Hurry up, students .'
6. He said to the president, 'Please give me one chance.'
7. She said to him, 'Please cooperate me.'
8. The teacher said to the girls, 'Keep away from the wall.'
9. She said, 'What a pitiful scene?'
10. He said, 'Hurrah, I am the first'.

Solutions

1. Kanika asked Suresh if the tea was ready.
2. She asked whether it was her book.
3. Tarmesh asked me if I would keep shut.
4. Chinkoo ordered him to get out.
5. The teacher asked the students to hurry up.
6. He requested the president to give him one chance.
7. She requested him to cooperate her.
8. The teacher instructed the girls to keep away from the wall.
9. She exclaimed that it was a pitiful scene.
10. He exclaimed with joy that he was the first.

Exercise 6

Change the following sentences into indirect narration

1. The queen said, 'O, I were young again!'
2. The principal said, 'Well done! my boys.'
3. He said, 'God save the king.'
4. The mother said, 'Long live my son.'
5. She said to me, 'Do have some drinks?'
6. Rahul said to him, 'Will you go to Jaipur?'
7. The boy said, 'Sir, may I come in?'
8. Hari said to Rahim, 'You must obey your parents.'
9. He said, 'I must go to Jaipur next week.'
10. She said, 'You need not talk to me.'

Solutions

1. The queen eagerly wished that she were young again.
2. The principal exclaimed with applause that the boys had done well.
3. He prayed that God might save the king.
4. The mother wished that his son should live long.
5. She requested me to have some drinks.
6. Rahul asked him if he would go to Jaipur.
7. The boy respectfully asked whether he could come in.
8. Hari told Rahim that he must obey his parents.
9. He said that he had to go to Jaipur the following week.
10. She said that I need not talk to her.

Spotting the Errors

Find the errors and justify your answers

1. The Chief Minister assured the people (A)/ that the government (B)/will do its best (C)/for the welfare of the poor (D).
2. She exclaimed with sorrow (A)/that her younger (B)/son died (C)/six days before (D).
3. The father said to his daughter (A)/that if she wants to secure (B)/good marks, she (C)/had to work hard (D).
4. She asked me (A)/how could she (B)/help me in (C)/that situation (D).
5. The teacher forbade (A)/the students not (B)/to pluck the flowers (C)/in the school garden (D).
6. Sarla asked the teacher (A)/how many girls (B)/ were therein (C)/class X (D).
7. The boy requested (A)/the teacher to (B)/allow him to (C)/go to his home now (D).
8. The captain exclaimed with (A)/applause that (B)/the players played (C)/the match very well (D). **(Bank PO)**
9. My father asked me (A)/why you were (B)/taking that (C)/examination (D).
10. She asked Shyam (A)/if I could (B)/accompany him (C)/to the market (D).
11. Ram told me (A)/that he got up (B)/early in the (C)/morning daily (D).
12. The teacher told the students (A)/that (B)/India had attained freedom (C)/on 15th August, 1947 (D). **(Bank PO)**
13. He said that (A)/he was tired and (B)/that he wants (C)/to go to bed (D).
14. The mother asked (A)/her son where (B)/he was all (C)/the afternoon (D).
15. The magistrate asked the accused (A)/what was he doing (B)/with his hand (C)/in gentleman's pocket (D).
16. The old man advised his sons (A)/not to quarrel amongst themselves (B)/when he is dead (C)/but to remain united (D). **(Bank PO)**
17. He asked them (A)/whether he would (B)/listen to (C)/such a man (D).
18. He requested him (A)/ that to wait (B)/there till he returned (C)/from the office (D).
19. He urged them (A)/to be quite (B)/and listen to (C)/my words (D).
20. He asked him (A)/father when the (B)/next letter (C)/ will come (D).
21. He told that (A)/his father had gone (B)/to Mumbai (C)/the previous week (D).
22. Sumit told his father that (A)/he wanted to go aboard (B)/after the finishes (C)/his studies there (D).
23. The station master told me (A)/that I was very late (B)/and it was an hour (C)/since the train left (D).
24. He respectfully (A)/wished his teacher (B)/good morning sir (C).
25. He asked his son (A)/if he has seen (B)/the Taj Mahal earlier (C).
26. The child asked his mother (A)/whether (B)/she was going (C)/to office today (D).
27. The queen eagerly (A)/wished that (B)/she will be (C)/young again (D).
28. The officer warned him that (A)/he would be dismissed (B)/if he does not attend (C)/the office regularly (D). **(Bank PO)**
29. Ram asked (A)/me as if (B)/what (C)/I was doing (D).
30. Sarita said (A)/that a (B)/stitch in time (C)/saved nine (D).
31. He said that (A)/' Work hard (B)/if I want to (C)/ secure good marks (D).'
32. He tells me (A)/that he would go (B)/to Mumbai the (C)/next month (D).
33. Mohan told me (A)/that I was (B)/ doing his work (C).
34. John asked James (A)/if he had come there (B)/ just to see him or (C)/there is some other reason (D). **(Bank PO)**
35. He said that he had (A)/decided not to buy (B)/the house as (C)/it was on the main road (D).
36. My wife being ill sent (A)/a message to her boss (B)/informing why could she (C)/not attend the office on that day (D). **(BSRB)**
37. My mother prayed (A)/that God may granted (B)/ me success (C).
38. She reminded me (A)/that she has often (B)/told me not to (C)/play tricks with water (D).
39. The teacher told, (A)/'Never make mischief (B)/again (C).'
40. I asked Sumit (A)/why he wanted to (B)/join Navy and (C)/what he actually wants (D).

» Answers

1. 'C' Replace will by would.
2. 'C' Replace son died by son had died.
3. 'B' Replace wants by wanted.
4. 'B' Replace 'how could she'by 'how she could'.
5. 'B' Delete not.
6. 'C' Replace 'were there' by there were.
7. 'D' Replace now by then.
8. 'C' Replace 'played' by 'had played'.
9. 'B' Replace 'why you were' by 'why I was'.
10. 'B' Replace 'If I could' by 'If she could'.
11. 'B' Change it to 'that he gets up'. It is a habitual fact.
12. 'C' Replace 'had attained' by 'attained'.
13. 'C' Replace 'that he wants' by 'that he wanted'.
14. 'C' Replace 'he was all'by 'he had been all'.
15. 'B' Change to 'what he was doing'
16. 'C' Change to 'when he was dead'.
17. 'B' Change 'he'to 'they'.
18. 'B' Delete that.
19. 'D' Change my to his.
20. 'D' Change 'will' to 'would'.
21. 'A' Object is necessary with told or tell.
22. 'C' Replace 'finishes' byU finished.
23. 'D' Change to 'the train had left'.
24. 'C' Delete Sir.
25. 'B' Change 'he has seen' toU 'he had seen'
26. 'D' Change today to that day.
27. 'C' Change 'will be' to 'would be' or were.
28. 'C' Change 'does not' to 'did not'.
29. 'B' Delete as if.
30. 'D' Change 'saved' to 'saves'. It is a proverb.
31. 'A' Delete that.This is direct narration.
32. 'B'Change 'he would go' to 'he will go'.
33. 'B' Change 'I was' to 'he was'.
34. 'D' Change 'there is' to 'there was'.
35. E. No error.
36. 'D' Replace 'why could she' by 'why she could'.
37. 'B' Replace 'God may granted' by 'God might grant'.
38. 'B' Replace 'she has often' by 'she had often'.
39. 'A' Object is necessary after told.
40. 'D' Change wants to wanted.

Unit

13

Active and Passive Voice

Verbs are said to be either active or passive in voice. In the **active voice**, the subject and verb relationship is straightforward: the subject is a doer and the verb moves the sentence along. In the **passive voice**, the subject of the sentence is not a doer but is acted upon by some other **agent** or by something unnamed.

What Is Voice?

The voice of a verb tells whether the subject of the sentence performs or receives the action.

Active voice : In active voice, the subject performs the action expressed by the verb.

Passive voice : In passive voice, the subject receives the action expressed by the verb.

He sings a song *Active voice*

A song is sung by him. *Passive Voice*

General Rules to Change the Voice

If you want to change an active voice sentence to passive voice, consider carefully who or what (subject) is performing the action expressed by the verb, and then make that agent the object of the sentence 'by the...' phrase. Make what is acted upon the subject of the sentence, and change the verb to a form of be + past participle. Including an explicit 'by the...' phrase is optional, 'by' is used when the subject of active sentence is important.

Note the following points carefully : Make the object of the active sentence, the subject in the passive sentence.

I write a letter. *Active Voice*

Object of active sentence is 'a letter'. It becomes subject of the passive sentence.

A letter ....

Make the subject of the active sentence, the agent in the passive sentence. The agent will be in objective form. Use 'by' before it.' 'By' is used when the subject of active sentence is important to mention .

Subject of active sentence is 'I'. Its objective form is 'me'. So ... by me.

Always use third form of the verb (past participle) in passive structures. The past participle will be preceded by 'to be' form of verb, as per the tense of the sentence.

Please take care that the 'to be' form of verb is governed by the new subject (subject of the passive sentence).

(a) I write a letter. *Active Voice*
A letter is written by me. *Passive Voice*

(b) She is helping the students. *Active Voice*
The students are being helped by her. *Passive Voice*

In sentence (b) plural verb 'are' is used as per the new subject–students.

Change of subject of active sentence into object of passive is done as per the following table

Active Voice	Passive Voice	Active Voice	Passive Voice
I	me	she	her
he	him	they	them
you	you	it	it
we	us	who	whom

Only transitive verbs (those that take objects) can be transformed into passive constructions.

Furthermore, active sentences containing certain verbs cannot be transformed into passive structures. To have is the most important of these verbs. We can say "He has a new cycle," but we cannot say "A new cycle is had by him." Here is a brief list of such verbs: resemble, look like, equal, agree with, mean, contain, hold, comprise, lack, suit, fit, become. These verbs are intransitive in nature.

Sentences in 'present perfect continuous', 'past perfect continuous', 'future perfect continuous' and 'future continuous' be transformed into passive.

The change of verbs (tense-wise) take place as per following table.

Tense	Verb (active)	Verb (passive) To be form + V–III
Simple present	write/writes	am/is/are written
Simple past	wrote	was/were written
Simple future	shall/will write	shall/will be written
Present continuous	is/am/are writing	is/am/are being written
Past continuous	was/were writing	was/were being written
Present perfect	has/have written	has/have been written
Past perfect	had written	had been written
Future perfect	will/shall have written	will/shall have been written

Passive of Interrogative Sentences

Interrogative sentences are normally of two types.

1. Yes/No questions.
2. 'Wh' questions.

Yes/No questions are those questions which begins with an auxiliary.

(a) Questions beginning with Is/am/are. The passive structure of such questions will be as per following

Is/am/are/+ subject + V–III + by + agent?

Active	Passive
Is he writing a letter?	Is a letter being written by him?
Are they ploughing the field?	Is the field being ploughed by them?
Am I catching the thief?	Is the thief being caught by me?

(b) Questions beginning with do/does. The passive structure of such questions will be as per following

Is/am/are/+ subject + V–III + by + agent ?

Active	Passive
Does he need a pen?	Is a pen needed by him?
Do you like the rooms?	Are the rooms liked by you?

(c) Questions beginning with did. The passive structure of such questions will be as follows

Was/were + subject + V–III + by + agent ?

Active	Passive
Did he write a letter?	Was a letter written by him?
Did she help you?	Were you helped by him?

(d) Questions beginning with was/were. The passive structure of such questions will be as per following

Was/were + subject + being + V–III + by + agent ?

Active	Passive
Was she cooking food?	Was food being cooked by her?
Were they playing chess?	Was the chess being played by them?

(e) Questions beginning with have/ha/had. The passive structure of such questions will be as per following

Has/have/had + subject + been+ V–III + by + agent ?

Active	Passive
Has he written a book?	Has any book been written by him?
Have they played a match?	Have a match been played by them?
Had she written a letter?	Had a letter been written by her?

(f) Questions beginning with modal auxiliary verbs. The passive structure of such questions will be as follows

modal auxiliary + subject + be + V–III + by + agent

Active	Passive
Can she control the situation?	Can the situation be controlled by her?
May he cross the river?	May the river be crossed by him?
Should he cut the wood?	Should the wood be cut by him?

'Wh' words : Questions beginning with what, why, when, where, who, etc. The structures of many Wh questions in active voice is as follows :

Wh word + auxiliary +subject + main verb + object

The structure of such Wh questions in passive is as follows

Wh word + auxiliary + subject (object of active)+ to be + V-III + by + agent

Active	Passive
Why have you broken the mirror?	Why has the mirror been broken by you?
Why do you write a letter?	Why is a letter written by you?
When will you return my pen?	When will my pen be returned by you?
Why are you laughing at her?	Why is she being laughed at by you?
Where did he put the things?	Where were the things put by him?
What did he break?	What was broken by him?

Questions begining with 'Who'

Here 'Who' acts as subject. The passive of such questions is made as follows.

Active	Passive
Who broke this beautiful glass?	By whom was this beautiful glass broken?
Who solved that problem?	By whom was that problem solved?
Who can break this stick?	By whom can this stick be broken?
Who will help her in difficulty?	By whom will she be helped in difficulty?

Questions begining with 'Whom'

The passive of such questions is made as follows:

Active	Passive
Whom have you invited?	Who has been invited by you?
Whom has he abused?	Who has been abused by him?
Whom has she reported?	Who has been reported by her?

Passive Without Agent

In passive structures we should not use by + agent when the subject is understood or vague or unimportant to mention.

For example if the subject in active voice is—someone, somebody, nobody, people,etc.

Active	Passive
People speak English all over the world.	English is spoken all over the world.
Police arrested the thieves.	The thieves were arrested. (Subject is understood.)
Someone has stolen my watch.	My watche has been stolen
We execute all instructions without delay.	All instructions are executed without delay.
Robbers looted the shop.	The shop was looted.

"In all passive voice exercises the use of 'by' with an agent must be rigorously suppressed, except in those examples where our interest in the predicate has led us to use the pa0ssive voice—we should omit the agent where the agent is vague or unknown."

—*W. S. Allen*

Imperative Sentences

Imperative sentences are such sentences that contain expressions of order, request, advise, suggestions, etc.

Sentences with order! Command :

Active	Passive
Shut the window.	Let the window be shut.
Bring a glass of water.	Let a glass of water be brought.
Finish this work.	Let this work be finished.
Switch off the light.	Let the light be switched off.
Inform the police.	Let the police be informed.

The passive structure is usually as follows

Let + subject + be + V–III + ...

Sentences expresing command or order can be changed into passive as follows
(a) Get out of this office. Active
You are ordered to get out of this office. *Passive*
(b) Bring some glasses of water for them. Active
You are ordered to bring some glasses of water for them. *Active*

The passive structure will be as follows

You are ordered to + verb I + ...

Sentences containing request :

Active	Passive
Please open the door.	You are requested to open the door.
Please help that old lady.	You are requested to help that old lady.
Take this seat please.	You are requested to take this seat.
Please give me a book.	You are requested to give me a book.
Do it for me please.	You are requested to do it for me.
Please don't disturb me.	You are requested not to disturb me.

The passive structure will be as follows

You are requested to + V–I ...

Sentences with suggestion :

Active	Passive
Help the disabled.	The disabled should be helped.
Listen to me.	I should be listened to.
Help the needy and poor.	The needy and poor should be helped.
Always speak the truth.	The truth should always be spoken.
Love the kids.	The kids should be loved.
Hear him now.	He should be heard now.

The passive structure will be as follows

Subject + should be + V–III +...

Sentences with advice :

Active	Passive
Work hard.	You are advised to work hard.
Get up early.	You are advised to get up early.
Do not smoke.	You are advised not to smoke.

The passive structure will be as follows

You are advised to + V–I +...

Passive of Infinitive

Sentences with infinitive in active voice have following structures.

Subject + is/am/are/was/were/have/has/ had + to + verb -I + object.

The passive structure is as follows

Subject + is/am/are/was/were/have/has/ had + to be + V-3 + by + agent.

Active	Passive
I am to finish this work.	This work is to be finished by me.
You are to write an essay.	An essay is to be written by you.
They are to buy a TV.	A TV is to be bought by them.
He was to sell this freeze.	This freeze was to be sold by him.
We were to buy a car.	A car was to be bought by us.
I am to assist him.	He is to be assisted by me.
She has to help him.	He has to be helped by her.
You were to bring him here.	He was to be brought here by you.
The students have to write notes.	Notes have to be written by the students.

Miscellaneous Structures

It is time to + V-1 + noun ....
The passive structure is as follows
It is time + for + noun + to be + V-3 .....

Active	Passive
It is time to close the office.	It is time for the office to be closed.
It is time to supply food.	It is time for food to be supplied.
It is time to stop writing.	It time for the writing to be stopped.
It is time to give the final warning.	It is time for the final warning to be given.

Sentences beginning with 'There'
There + be form of verb + noun + infinitive ***Active Structure***
There + be form of verb + noun + to be + V-III ***Passive Structure***

Active	Passive
There is a lot of work to complete.	There is a lot of work to be completed.
There are six letters to write.	There are six letters to be written.
There is no time to lose.	There is no time to be lost.

Passive of verbs showing, state of mind or feelings

Some verbs do not express any action but simply state of mind or feelings. We should not use 'by' in passive structures of such sentences, instead an appropriate preposition is used.

Active	Passive
I know her.	She is known to me. (prep.-'to')
He annoyed her.	She was annoyed with him. (prep.- 'with')
Her behavior annoyed him.	He was annoyed at her behavior. (prep.-'at')
The news surprised all.	All were surprised at the news. (prep. - 'at')
The result amazed me.	I was amazed at the result. (prep. -'at')

Passive of verbs with appropriate prepositions.

Some verbs take preposition before an object. The preposition remains intact even in passive construction.

Active	Passive
He laughed at me.	I was laughed at by him.
The police is enquiring into the matter.	The matter is being enquired into by the police.
Sita smiled at Ram.	Ram was smiled at by Sita.
He looks after his parents.	His parents are looked after by him.
Rahim mocked at our class teacher.	Our class teacher was mocked at by Rahim.

Such commonly used verbs are : look at, look after, laugh at, smile at, deride at, mock at etc.

Some sentences have following constructions in active voice.

Subject + ask + object + if/whether + clause.

Active	Passive
I asked Rani, if she went to Jaipur.	Rani was asked if she went to Jaipur.
He asked me, when I would complete my work.	I was asked when I would complete my work.
They asked me, if I knew his address.	I was asked if I knew his address.

Rajesh asked me, when I would return.	I was asked by Rajesh when I would return.

Gerund constructions

Verbs such as : recommend, suggest, propose, insist, advise + gerund + object are converted into passive in following constructions :

Active	Passive
She insisted using steel mugs.	She insisted that steel mugs should be used.
He recommended using knife.	He recommended that knife should be used.

Other gerund constructions are expressed in passive as following:

I remember them taking me to the club. *Active*

I remember being taken to the club. *Passive*

Causative verbs

Active	Passive
I made him polish my shoes.	He was made to polish my shoes.
He made me sing a song.	I was made to sing a song.
I saw her go.	She was seen to go.
I let him go.	He was let go.

'To' is not used with 'let' even in passive constructions.

They made him king.	He was made king.
We elected him monitor.	He was elected monitor.
I found her crossing the road	She was found crossing the road.
We saw her sing a song.	She was seen to sing a song.

Sentences of the type : They believed..., People think..., People say..., We know..., Everyone knows.. etc. have two possible passive forms.

It was/is/.. believed that.............

He is/was/.. known/said/believed to be.........

Active	Passive
They believed that Mr Shukla was very rich.	It was believed that Mr Shukla was very rich.
	Mr Shukla was believed to be very rich.
We know that some children go wise early.	It is known that some children go wise early.
	Some children are known to go wise early.
People consider that she is intelligent.	She is considered to be intelligent.
	It is considered that she is intelligent.
People say that he is a thief	It is said that he is a thief.
	He is said to be a thief.
Everyone knows that he is a gangster.	It is known that he is a gangster.
	He is known to be a gangster.

Double passive

Active	Passive
They looted the shop and took away the money.	The shop was looted and the money was taken away.
She wrote the book and got published.	The book was written and got published by her.
The police arrested the thieves and sent them to jail.	The thieves were arrested and sent to jail

Verbs with two objects :

Some sentences have two objects; (i) Direct (non living)(ii)Indirect (living).We can use any of the object while converting these into passive. Generally indirect object is used.

Active	Passive
He gave me a purse.	I was given a purse by him.
	A purse was given to me by him.
Rahim teaches us English.	English is taught us by Rahim.
	We are taught English by Rahim
The principal asked him a question.	A question was asked him by the principal
	He was asked a question by the principal.
Rani gave him a letter.	A letter was given to him by Rani.
	He was given a letter by Rani.

Miscellaneous Sentences

Active	Passive
He likes people to call him, 'Don'.	He likes to be called 'Don'.
Someone will serve lunch.	Lunch will be served.
None must leave bicycles and scooters unlocked.	Bicycles and scooters must not be left unlocked.
Students may keep the library books for two weeks only.	The library books may be kept for two weeks only.
After that they must return them, otherwise they have to pay fine.	After that they must be returned otherwise fine has to be paid.
No one can do any thing unless someone gives us accurate information.	Nothing can be done unless we are given accurate information.
They threw him out.	He was thrown out (by them).
One must do one's duty.	Duty must be done.
The officer wants his subordinates to obey him.	The officer wants to be obeyed by his subordinates.
He wants that he should be treated as king.	He wants to be treated as king.
Ram desires his wife to respect his parents.	Ram desires his parents to be respected by his wife.
He wants someone to take photographs.	He wants photographs to be taken.
He recommended using the bullet proof car.	He recommended that the bullet proof car should be used. Passive
I remember them taking me to library.	I remember being taken to library.
We saw them go out.	They were seen go out.
They let us go.	We were let go.
When he arrived home, police arrested him.	When he arrived home he was arrested.
I saw her sing a song.	She was seen to sing a song.
Brutus accused Caesar of ambition.	Caesar was accused of ambition by Brutus.
We elected him secretary of the society.	He was elected secretary of the society.
Her reply shocked me.	I was shocked at his reply.
Honey tastes sweet.	Honey is sweet when (it is)tasted.
Thank God	God be thanked.
These oranges taste sour.	These oranges are sour when they are tasted.
The biscuits eat short and crisp.	The biscuits are short and crisp when they are eaten.
The flower smells sweet.	The flower is sweet when it is smelt.

» Exercises

Exercise 1

Change the Voice

Active: Simple Present

1. The movie fascinates me.
2. The movie bores Jack.
3. The movie surprises them.

Active: Simple Past

4. The movie bored me.
5. The movie fascinated Janu.
6. The movie surprised them.

Active: Present Continuous

7. I am helping Shanu.
8. June is helping Suresh and Lily.
9. I was cleaning the bathroom.

Active: Past Continuous

10. They were cleaning the bedroom.
11. Surabhi was cleaning the kitchen and gallery.

Present Perfect

12. I have mailed the gift.
13. Janu has mailed the gifts.

Past Perfect

14. Jack had directed the movie.
15. Prem had directed those movies.

Future Perfect

16. Johni will have finished the project next month.
17. They will have finished the projects before then.

Future with will

18. I will mail the gift.
19. Janu will mail the gifts.

Future with 'Going to'

20. I am going to make the cake.
21. Surabhi is going to make two cakes

Active : Will/Won't (Will not)

22. Shanu will invite Toni to the party.
23. Shanu won't invite Jack to the party.
(Shanu will not invite Jack to the party.)

Active : Can/Can't

24. Mata can foretell the future.
25. Toni can't foretell the future.
(Toni can not foretell the future.)

May to May not

26. Her company may give Kashyap a new office.
27. The lazy students may not do the homework.

Might'/'Might not'

28. Her company might give Kashyap new office.
29. The lazy students might not do the homework.

Should to 'Should not'

30. Students should memorize English verbs.
31. Children shouldn't smoke cigarettes.

Ought to

32. Students ought to learn English verbs.
(negative ought to is rarely used.)

Had better' to 'Had better not'

33. Students had better practice English every day.
34. Children had better not drink whisky.

Must' to 'Must not'

35. Tourists must apply for a passport to travel abroad.
36. Customers must not use that door.

Has to' to 'Have to'

37. She has to practice English every day.
38. Sarala and Mira have to wash the dresses every day.

'Doesn't have to' to 'Don't have to'

39. Mira doesn't have to clean her bedroom every day.
40. The children don't have to clean their bedrooms every day.

'Be supposed to' to 'Not supposed to'

41. I am supposed to type the composition.
42. I am not supposed to copy the stories in the book.
43. Jackii is supposed to clean the living room.
44. She isn't supposed to eat candy and gum.
45. They are supposed to make dinner for the family.
46. They aren't supposed to make dessert.

'Should' to Shouldn't have

47. The students should have learned the verbs.
48. The children shouldn't have broken the window.

Ought to have

49. Students ought to have learned the verbs.
(negative ought to is rarely used.)

Supposed to (past)

50. I was supposed to type the composition.
51. I wasn't supposed to copy the story in the book.
52. Jackii was supposed to clean the living room.
53. She wasn't supposed to eat candy and gum.
54. Frank and Jane were supposed to make dinner.
55. They weren't supposed to make dessert.

'May have' to 'May not have'

56. That firm may have offered Kakitana a new job.
57. The students may not have written the paper.

'Might have' to 'Might not have'

58. That firm might have offered Kakitana a new job.
59. The students might not have written the paper.

Solutions

1. I am fascinated by the movie.
2. Jack is bored by the movie.
3. They are surprised by the movie.
4. I was bored by the movie.
5. Janu was fascinated by the movie.
6. They were surprised by the movie.
7. Shanu is being helped by me.
8. Suresh and Lily are being helped by Janu.
9. The bathroom was being cleaned by me.
10. The bedroom was being cleaned by them.
11. The kitchen and gallery were being cleaned by Surabhi.
12. The gift has been mailed by me.
13. The gifts have been mailed by Janu.
14. The movie had been directed by Jack.
15. The movies had been directed by Prem.

16. The project will have been finished by next month.
17. The projects will have been finished before then.
18. The gift will be mailed by me.
19. The gifts will be mailed by Janu.
20. The cake is going to be made by me.
21. Two cakes are going to be made by Surabhi.
22. Toni will be invited to the party by Shanu.
23. Jack won't be invited to the party by Shanu. (Jack will not be invited to the party by Shanu.)
24. The future can be foretold by Mata.
25. The future can't be foretold by Toni. (The future can not be foretold by Toni.)
26. Kashyap may be given a new office by her company.
27. The homework may not be done by the lazy students.
28. Kashyap might be given new office by her company.
29. The homework might not be done by the lazy students.
30. English verbs should be memorized.
31. Cigarettes shouldn't be smoken by children.
32. English verbs ought to be learnt by students.
33. English had better be practised by students every day.
34. Whiskey had better not be drunk by children.
35. A passport must be applied for by tourists to travel abroad.
36. That door must not be used by customers.
37. English has to be practised by her every day.
38. The dresses have to be washed by Sarla and Mira every day.
39. Her bedroom doesn't have to be cleaned by Mira every day.
40. Their bedrooms don't have to be cleaned by the children every day.
41. The composition is supposed to be typed by me.
42. The stories in the book are not supposed to be copied.
43. The living room is supposed to be cleaned by Jackii.
44. Candy and gum aren't supposed to be eaten by her.
45. Dinner for the family is supposed to be made by them.
46. Dessert isn't supposed to be made by them.

Passive: Should have / Shouldn't have

47. The verbs should have been learned by the students.
48. The window shouldn't have been broken by the children.

Passive: Ought to

49. The verbs ought to have been learned by the students.

Passive: Be Supposed to (past time)

50. The composition was supposed to be typed by me.
51. The story in the book wasn't supposed to be copied.
52. The living room was supposed to be cleaned by Jackii.
53. Candy and gum weren't supposed to be eaten by her.
54. Dinner was supposed to be made by them.
55. Dessert wasn't supposed to be made by them.

Passive: May/May not

56. Kakitana may have been offered a new job by that firm.
57. The paper may not have been written by the students.

Might/Might not

58. Kakitana might have been offered a new job by that firm.
59. The paper might not have been written by the students.

Exercise 2

Choose the best way to complete these passive voice sentences.

1. Your jacket _____ over there.
   A. can be hang up
   B. can be hung up
   C. can be hung up
   D. can be hunged up
   E. can hung up
2. She _____.
   A. have never been heard of
   B. has never been hearing of
   C. has never been heared of
   D. has never been heard of
   E. has never be heard of
3. She _____ by a bus.
   A. was been knocking down
   B. was being knocked down
   C. was knocked down
   D. was knock down
   E. was knocking down
4. Nothing _____ me.
   A. can be hald against
   B. can be held against
   C. can be hold against
   D. can be holding against
   E. can held against

5. The protesters _____ by the police.
A. are holding back
B. are being holding back
C. are being hold back
D. are being held back
E. are being hald back

6. The flood water _____ by barriers.
A. was being kept back
B. was being keep back
C. was been kept back
D. was being keept back
E. was be kept back

7. Thirty more people _____ last week.
A. were laid off
B. were layed off
C. were laying off
D. were lie off
E. were lied off

8. The keys _____.
A. must have been left behind
B. must been left behind
C. must having been left behind
D. must have be left behind
E. must have been leaving behind

9. The criminal _____.
A. were locked up
B. were locked up
C. was locking up
D. was locked up
E. was lock up

10. The road _____.
A. was blocking off
B. was block off
C. was blocking off
D. was blocked off
E. was been blocked off

11. Our allies _____ support.
A. will be lend
B. will be lent
C. will be lent
D. will been lent
E. will being lent

12. _____ to you yet?
A. Has the book been given back
B. Have the book being given back
C. Have the book been gave back
D. Have the book been give back
E Have the books been given back

13. She _____ with a fine.
A. was let off
B. was letted off
C. was letting off
D. were let off
E. were let off

14. 3000 employees _____.
A. were lied off
B. were laying off
C. were layed off
D. were lain off
E. were laid off

15. The old cinema _____
A. being pulled down
B. is been pulled down
C. is being pull down
D. is being pulled down
E. is being pulling down

16. The inconvenience _____ by this money.
A. will made up for
B. will been made up for
C. will be made up for
D. will being made up for
E. will be mad up for

17. The candle _____ by the draught.
A. was being blown out
B. was blown out
C. was blewed out
D. was blow out
E. was blowed out

18. A story _____.
A. will be making up
B. will being made up
C. will be made up
D. will been made up
E. will be maked up

19. My bank loan _____ in five years time.
A. will paid off
B. will be being paid off
C. will be paying off
D. will be paid off
E. will be payed off

20. An idea _____ for discussion.
A. put forward
B. was put forward
C. was putted forward
D. was putting forward
E. were put forward

Solutions

1. C	2. D	3. C	4. B
5. D	6. A	7. A	8. A
9. D	10. D	11. C	12. A
13. A	14. E	15. D	16. C
17. B	18. C	19. D	20. B

Exercise 3

Correct the mistakes in these passive voice sentences.

1. A big chunk of his calf was being bitten off by the dog.
2. A plan to stop drug trafficking had been draw up.
3. He was running over by a bus as he was crossing the road.
4. His confidence will be build up by this.
5. I am being catched up by the stress of the last few weeks.
6. I have being done in by all that exercise. (informal)
7. More and more farmland is being eated up by cities.
8. Most of the land in the area has be bought up by property developers.
9. My money have been stolen.
10. One of the other prisoners was beat up.
11. Red meat have been cut out of my diet.

12. She are being brought up in a friendly atmosphere.
13. The engagement was being broken off just two days before the wedding.
14. The essays have be handed in on Monday.
15. The office had been being blown up by terrorists.
16. The rebels will being called on to stop fighting.
17. The road outside my house is being digged up.
18. The task is braked down into smaller, manageable mini-tasks.
19. This government could be bringing down by this scandal.
20. Unemployment must dealt with by the government.

Solutions

1. A big chunk of his calf was bitten off by the dog.
2. A plan to stop drug trafficking had been drawn up.
3. He was run over by a bus as he was crossing the road.
4. His confidence will be built up by this.
5. I am being caught up by the stress of the last few weeks.
6. I have been done in by all that exercise. (informal)
7. More and more farmland is being eaten up by cities.
8. Most of the land in the area has been bought up by property developers.
9. My money has been stolen.
10. One of the other prisoners was beaten up.
11. Red meat has been cut out of my diet.
12. She is being brought up in a friendly atmosphere.
13. The engagement was broken off just two days before the wedding.
14. The essays have to be handed in on Monday.
15. The office had been blown up by terrorists.
16. The rebels will be called on to stop fighting.
17. The road outside my house is being dug up.
18. The task is broken down into smaller, manageable mini-tasks.
19. This government could be brought down by this scandal.
20. Unemployment must be dealt with by the government.

Exercise 4

Change the following into passive voice

1. You should switch off the electricity when changing a fuse.
2. The Government is spending too much money on Operation Pink.
3. They have built six new helipads at Naila.
4. She always gives me calendars and diaries at new year.
5. You will have to amuse him with riddles and bed-time stories.
6. They discovered a new pill to stimulate the appetite.
7. It fascinated me.
8. A duke of the sixteenth century had killed his wife in this room.
9. The performed his symphony for the first time last week.
10. The owner himself showed them the house.
11. Have they carried out his imstructions ?
12. We have to pick the fruit very early in the morning.
13. They allowed Harry to go but they did not allow Dick.
14. Fear of death oppresses some old people.
15. The judge advised me to the settle the matter out of court.
16. Rajeev chose his words with care.
17. If in the sixteenth century they could make history by building monuments, in the twentieth century they can make it by selling and reselling them.
18. The promised Mary a new doll for her birthday.
19. No one ever taught me the rudiments of music.
20. They have proved all his calculations wrong.
21. No one has climbed this mountain before.
22. Did you grow these vegetables in your own garden ?
23. They answered me most rudely in the shop.

Solutions

1. The electricity should be switched off.
2. Too much money is being spent on Operation Pink.
3. Six new helepads have been built at Naila.
4. I am always given calendars and diaries at new year by her.
5. He will have to be amused with riddles and ....
6. A new pill to stimulate the appetite was discovered.
7. I was fascinated by it.
8. The wife of a duke of the sixteenth century was killed by him in this room.
9. His symphony was performed for the first time last week.
10. They were shown the house by the owner himself.
11. Have his instructions been carried out by them ?

12. The fruit have to be picked very early in the morning.
13. Harry was allowed to go but Dick was not (allowed to go).
14. Some old people are oppressed with the fear of death.
15. I was advised to settle the matter out of court by the judge.
16. Words were chosen with care by Rajiv.
17. It history could be made by building monuments in the 16th century it can be made by selling and reselling them in the twentieth century.
18. Mary was promised a new doll on her birthday.
19. I was never taught the rudiments of music.
20. All his calculations have been proved wrong.
21. This mountain hasn't been climbed before.
22. Were these vegetables grown in you own garden ?
23. I was most rudely answered in the shop.

Exercise 5

Rewrite the following sentences in the passive vocie **(RPSC Ajmer)**

1. They rejected his proposal and laughed at him.
2. Who is bothering you ?
3. One must do one's duty.

Rewrite the following sentences in the passive voice : **(RPSC Ajmer)**

4. Two oxen pull mthe plough.
5. The murderer hid the knife in the grass.
6. He will rob you if you are not careful.

Rewrite the following sentences into the passive voice **(RPSC Ajmer)**

7. He asked me to wait.
8. She is running a school these days.
9. Let them to it now.
10. Everyone knows that Mr.A is gang leader.
11. Has someone told you about your result?

Put the following sentences into the passive voice

12. Please sit here and wait till I return.
13. Has someone made all the necessary arrangements ?
14. It was clear that the parents had brought the child up well.
15. They can't put you in prison if they haven't tried you.
16. People say that tortoises live longer than elephants.

Put the following sentences into the passive voice **(RPSC Ajmer)**

17. They did not tell me the truth about the situation.
18. They will look after you well.
19. Did they not tell you to he here by six o'clock?
20. It surprised me to hear someone had robbed you.

Change the voice of the following **(RPSC Ajmer)**

21. Did you paint these pictures in your own studio?
22. They have decided to increase the school fees this year.
23. Anger provokes many people to take hasty decisions which they later regret very much.
24. You must understand clearly that this is the last time I shall allow it.
25. You can not expect children to understand these problems.

Solutions

1. His proposal was rejected and he was laughed at.
2. By whom are you being bothered.
3. Duty must be done.
4. The plough is pulled by two oxen.
5. The knife was hidden in the grass by the murderer.
6. You will be robbed if you are not careful.
7. I was asked to wait.
8. A school is being run by her these days.
9. Let it be done by them now.
10. Mr. A is known to be a gang leader.
11. Have you been told about your result ?
12. You are requested to wait here till I return.
13. Have all the necessary arrangements been made ?
14. It was clear that the child had been will brought up.
15. You can't be put in prison if you haven't been tried.
16. Tortoises are said to live longer than elephants.
17. I was not told the truth about the situation.
18. you will be well looked after be them.
19. Were you not told to be here by six o'clock?
20. I was surprised to hear you had been robbed.
21. Were these pictures painted in your own studio ?
22. It has been decided to increase the school fees this year.
23. Many people are provoked by anger to take hasty decisions which are very much regretted later.

Exercise 6

Change the following sentences into passive voice

1. He will have closed his shop by 8 O'clock.
2. They will have finished the paper by 11 O'clock.
3. I shall have saved enough money to buy a house by 1990.
4. He will have advised me.
5. He can help you.
6. The child could not climb the tree.
7. You may return the book next week.
8. They might win the match.
9. We should obey our parents.

10. He would make no promise.
11. We ought to respect our teachers.
12. You must do your duty.
13. You could have solved the sum.
14. He should have helped his friend.
15. I would have attended the meeting but for the rain.
16. Father must have taken away the purse.

Solutions

1. His shop will have been closed by him by 8 O'clock.
2. The paper will have been finished by them by 11 O'clock.
3. Enough money will have been saved by me to buy a house by 1990.
4. I shall have been advised by him.
5. You can be helped by him.
6. The tree could not be climbed by the child.
7. The book may be returned by you next week.
8. The match might be won by them.
9. Our parents should be obeyed by us.
10. No promise would be made by him.
11. Our teachers ought to be respected by you.
12. Your duty must be done by you.
13. The sum could have been solved by you.
14. His friend should have been helped by him.
15. The meeting would have been attended by me but for the rain.
16. The purse must have been taken away by father.

Exercise 7

Change the following sentences into passive voice

1. Post this letter.
2. Never tell a lie.
3. Tell him to go.
4. Do not pluck flowers.
5. Cut your coat according to your cloth.
6. Let him sing a song.
7. Please shut the door.
8. Kindly grant me leave.
9. Hurry up, please.
10. Work hard.
11. Do not smoke.
12. Stand up on the bench.

Solutions

1. Let this letter be posted.
2. Let a lie never be told.
3. Let him be told to go.
4. Let flowers not be plucked.
5. Let your coat be cut according to your cloth.
6. Let a song be sung by him.
7. You are requested to shut the door.
8. You are requested to grant me leave.
9. You are requested to hurry up.
10. You are advised to work hard.
11. You are advised not to smoke.
12. You are ordered to stand up on the bench.
13. You are requested to let me play now.

Exercise 8

Change the following sentences into passive voice

1. Do they like their teachers?
2. Does this shopkeeper sell grocery?
3. Did they win the match?
4. Did you grow vegetables?
5. Is he running a race?
6. Were they singing songs?
7. What does this word mean?
8. Why do you blame us?
9. Who teaches you English?
10. Can you solve this sum?

Solutions

1. Are their teachers liked by them?
2. Is grocery sold by this shopkeeper?
3. Was the match won by them?
4. Were vegetables grown by you?
5. Is a race being run by him?
6. Were songs being sung by them?
7. What is meant by this word?
8. Why are we blamed by you?
9. By whom are you taught English?
10. Can this sum be solved by you?

Exercise 9

Change the following sentences into passive voice

1. This bottle contains milk.
2. I know his father.
3. The report alarmed us.
4. My progress satisfied my teachers.
5. You cannot pleased everybody.
6. Satish married Kanika.
7. Her failure surprised us.
8. Stamp collection interested the boy.
9. His death shocked us.
10. His servant has offended him.
11. I want to buy a house.
12. Women like men to flatter them.
13. It is time to take tea.
14. It is now time to close the shop.
15. He ran fast to win the race.
16. Let me play now.

Solutions

1. Milk is contained in this bottle.
2. His father is known to me.
3. We were alarmed at the report.

4. My teachers were satisfied with my progress.
5. Everybody cannot be pleased with you.
6. Kanika was married to Satish.
7. We were surprised at her failure.
8. The boy was interested in stamp collection.
9. We were shocked at his death.
10. He has been offended with his servant.
11. I want a house to be bought.
12. Women like to be flattered by men.
13. It is time for tea to be taken.
14. It is now time for the shop to be closed.
15. He ran fast for the race to be won.

Exercise 10

Change the following sentences into passive voice

1. Honey tastes sweet.
2. The rose smells sweet.
3. He hopes to win a prize.
4. Thank God.
5. May you live long!
6. People take rice all over the world.
7. One should keep one's promise.
8. One must endure what one cannot cure.
9. God helps those who help themselves.
10. Those who live in glass houses should not throw stones at others.

Solutions

1. Honey is sweet when (it is) tasted.
2. The rose is sweet when (it is) smelt.
3. It is hoped that he will win a prize.
4. God be thanked.
5. It is prayed that you may live long.
6. Rice is taken all over the world.
7. Promise should be kept.
8. What cannot be cured must been endured.
9. Those who help themselves are helped by God.
10. Stones should not be thrown at others by those who live in glass houses.

Exercise 11

Change the following sentences into passive voice

1. Should we not obey our parents?
2. Must I help him?
3. How can I serve my country?
4. Could you have done it?
5. Have you finished the assignment?
6. Has he returned the books?
7. Had he obtained leave?
8. Will you have read the book by tomorrow?
9. What have you drawn?
10. Who has broken the bottle?

Solutions

1. Should our parents not be obeyed by us?
2. Must he be helped by me?
3. How can my country be served by me?
4. Could it have been done by you?
5. Has the assignment been finished by you?
6. Have the books been returned by him?
7. Has leave been obtained by him?
8. Will the book have been read by you by tomorrow?
9. What has been drawn by you?
10. By whom has the bottle been broken?

Exercise 12

Change the following sentences into passive voice

1. It is time to say prayers.
2. It is necessary to write this essay.
3. She told me a wonderful story.
4. Somebody gave her a box of chocolates on her birthday.
5. They laughed at the blind man.
6. A car ran over a child.
7. I am listening to you.
8. We must obey the laws of the land.
9. They are watching the sports.
10. Did you make a noise ?
11. Shalini threw the ball.
12. Shall I ever forget those happy days ?

Solutions

1. It is time for prayers to be said.
2. It is necessary for this essay to be written.
3. A wonderful story was told to me.
   Or I was told a wonderful story by her.
4. A box of chocolates was given to her on her birthday.
   Or She was given a box of chocolates on her birthday.
5. The blind man was laughed at by them.
6. A child was run over by a car.
7. You are being listen to by me.
8. The laws of the land must be obeyed.
9. The sports are being watched by them.
10. Was a noise made by you?
11. The ball was thrown by Shalini.
12. Will those happy days ever be forgotten by me?

Spotting the Errors

Find the errors and justify your answer

1. The bank robbery case was enquired two months ago but no report has published yet.
2. The lonely lady puzzled when she found some strange footprints near the door.
3. The poor boy was approached to the principal and requested him to forgive him for his mistake.
4. Two students were badly injured and a dog killed in the bus car accident that took place yesterday.
5. It was advised by our family doctor that the patient must be taken care.
6. A new TV serial is soon to be telecasted by the Star Channel.
7. Having found guilty of rape and murder, the accused was sentenced to life imprisonment.
8. Ram expelled his son from his house because he was married an other caste girl.
9. If you don't apologise for having committed the mistake you won't be forgave.
10. An officer sent to my house and all the documents and articles were thoroughly checked.
11. When he seriously wounded by a lorry he was immediately helped by an unknown person.
12. Stones should not be thrown others by those who live in glass.
13. I had never saw surch a magnificient building of a hotel.
14. The people was called him an imposter and regarded him as a 'Don'.
15. On 26th January all the streets was thronged with spectators.
16. Grammar is taught us by a lady teacher named Smt. Kumkum.
17. By whom were you taught to grammar.
18. The dog was killed by him by an iron road.
19. Why was such a nasty letter was written by your brother.
20. The wounded man was being help by some girls.

» Answers

1. 'B' Write 'into' after enquired. Some verbs take specific preposition with them.

   She laughed at me.................... Active

   I was laughed at by her.............Passive
2. 'A'Change 'it' to 'The lonely lady was puzzled'.
3. 'A' Delete 'was'. This is the sentence of active voice.
4. 'B' Change 'it' to 'a dog was killed'.
5. 'B' Write 'of' after 'care.' Some verbs take specific preposition with them.
6. 'C' Replace 'telecasted' by 'telecast'. The third form of telecast is telecast.
7. 'A' Change 'it' to 'having been found'.
8. 'C' Replace 'he was married' by 'he married'.This is the sentence of active voice.
9. 'D' Replace 'forgave' by 'forgiven'.
10. 'A' Write 'was' before 'sent'.
11. 'A' Change 'it' to 'when he was seriously wounded'.
12. 'B' Change 'it' to 'thrown at others'.
13. 'A' Replace 'never saw' by 'never seen'.
14. 'A' Delete 'was'. This is the sentence of active voice.
15. 'B' Change 'it' to 'the streets were'.
16. 'A' Change 'it' to 'taught to us'.
17. 'C' Change 'it' to 'taught grammar'.
18. 'C' Change 'it' to 'with an iron rod'.
19. 'C' Replace 'was written' by 'written'.
20. 'C' Change 'it' to 'helped some girls'.

» Unit

14

Preposition

Preposition is a word placed before a noun or pronoun or gerund, and denotes the relation the person or thing, referred by it, has with something else.

Rules Relating to Prepositions

1. A preposition cannot be followed by a verb.

If we want to follow a preposition by a verb, we must use the '-ing' form which is really a gerund or verb in noun form.

(a) I would like to move now.
(b) He used to smoke.

In these sentences, 'to' is not a preposition. It is part of the infinitive ('to move', 'to smoke').
It should be understood well that verbs placed immediately after preposition must be in gerund form.
(a) He prevented me from drinking cold water.
(b) He insist on trying again.
(c) He was debarred from taking examination.
(d) He succeeded in achieving his goal.
(e) They are afraid of loosing the match.

2. When 'object' of the preposition is an interrogative pronoun what, who, whom, which, where etc., the preposition takes end or front position.

(a) What are you thinking of ?
(b) Who were you talking to?
(c) What are you staring at?
(d) Which of these chairs did you sit on?

It was thought as ungrammatical, to end a sentence with a preposition, but it is now well accepted.

3. When 'object' of the preposition is relative pronoun 'that', the preposition takes end position.

(a) Here is the magazine that you asked for.
(b) This is the dish that she is fond of.

4. When 'object' of the preposition is infinitive (to + verb), the preposition is placed after infinitive.

(a) This is a good hotel to stay at.
(b) I need a pencil to write with .

5. In some sentences, preposition is attached with the verb. These verbs take appropriate preposition with them

(a) I hate being laughed at.
(b) This I insist on.

6. In some cases the preposition comes in the beginning. These are usually interrogative sentences.

(a) By which train did you come?
(b) For whom was instructions given?

Some Important Prepositions

At, In and On

These are very commonly used prepositions note the use of these prepositions is in reference with 'time' :

At is used for a PRECISE TIME.

In is used for MONTHS, YEARS, CENTURIES and LONG PERIODS

On is used for DAYS and DATES

AT	IN	ON
Precise Time	Months, Years, Centuries	Days, Dates
at 3 o'clock	in May	on Sunday
at 10.30 am	in summer	on Tuesdays
at noon	in the summer	on 6 March
at dinner time	in 1990	on 25th Jan. 2007
at bedtime	in the 1990s	on Christmas Day
at sunrise	in the next century	on Independence Day
at sunset	in the Ice Age	on my birthday
at the moment	in the past/future	on New Year's Eve

(a) I have a meeting at 10 am.
(b) That shop closes at midnight.
(c) Richa went home at lunchtime.
(e) Where will you be on Independence Day?
(f) Do you think we will go to Saturn in the future?
(g) There should be a lot of progress in the next century.
(h) Do you work on Sundays?
(j) Her birthday is on 26 April.

Note the use of these prepositions in reference of 'Place' :

(i) **At** is used for a point.
(ii) **In** is used for an enclosed space.
(iii) **On** is used for a surface.

At	In	On
Point	Enclosed space	Surface
at the corner	in the garden	on the wall
at the bus stop	in Delhi	on the ceiling
at the door	in India	on the door
at the top of the page	in a box	on the cover
at the end of the road	in my pocket	on the floor
at the entrance	in my wallet	on the carpet
at the crossroads	in a building	on the menu
at the entrance	in a car	on a page

(a) Rima is waiting for you at the bus stop.
(b) The shop is at the end of the lane.
(c) I live on the 4th floor at 21 diamond street in Kolkata.
(d) When will you arrive at the school?
(e) Do you work in a company?
(f) I have a meeting in Delhi .
(g) Do you live in India ?
(h) Saturn is in the solar system.
(i) The author's name is on the cover of the book.
(j) There are no prices on this menu.
(k) You are standing on my foot.
(l) There was a 'no smoking' sign on the wall.

At, In, To and Into

At shows stationery position or existing state while **in** shows movement.

(a) She is at home.
(b) The train is in motion.

At for small place, town etc., while **in** for big place , town, city, country etc.

(a) He lives at Alwar in Rajasthan.
(b) A temple is situated at Madurai in Chennai.

At is used for point of time and **in** is used for period of time.

(a) The train will arrive at six in the morning.
(b) He will meet you in the morning.

In and Into : In shows existing state of things while into shows movement.

(a) He jumped into the river.
(b) There are three students in the class.

In can also be used as an adverb:

Come in = enter. Get in (into the train).

To and Into : To and into is used as following :

To

(a) Direction : Turn **to** the right.
(b) Destination : I am going **to** Jaipur.
(c) From Monday to Friday; five minutes **to** ten.

(d) Compared with : They prefer hockey **to** soccer.
(e) With indirect object: Please give it **to** me.
(f) As part of infinitive: I like **to** ski; he wants **to** help.
(g) In order to: We went to the store **to** buy soap.

Into

(a) Inside of : We stepped **into** the room.
(b) Change of condition: The boy changed **into** a man.

On and Onto

On can be used for both existing position and movement.

(a) He was sitting on his bag.
(b) Snow fell on the hills.
(c) His number is on the gate.
(d) He went on board ship.

On can also be used as an adverb.

(a) Go on (b) Come on

Onto is used when there is movement involving a change of level.

(a) People climbed onto their roofs.
(b) He lifted her onto the table.

With and By

With is used for instruments and **by** is used for agents.

(a) The snake was killed by him with a stick.
(b) The letter was written by Suresh with a pencil.

Since, For and From

Since is often used with present perfect or past perfect tense. Since is used for point of time and never for place, as : Since 6 o'clock/last night/last Monday/since morning/evening/ Monday/January/2005 etc.

(a) It has been raining since 2 o'clock.
(b) He had been ill since Monday.

Since can also be used as an adverb.
(a) He left school in 1983. I haven't seen him since.
(b) It is two years since I last saw Tom.

For is used of a period of time : for two hours/two days/two years/a long time/some time/for ever etc.

(a) Boil it for two hours.
(b) He lived in this house for six months.

For is also used with a present perfect tense or past perfect tense for an action which extends up to the time of speaking.

(a) He has worked here for a year.
(b) It has been raining for two hours.

From is normally used with **to, till** and **until**.

(a) Most people work from eight to six.

From can also be used for place :

(a) He is from Mumbai.
(b) Where do you come from ?

During and For

During is used with known periods of time, i.e. periods known by name, such as Christmas, Easter or periods which have been already defined.

during the middle ages.
during the summer.
during his childhood.

(a) It rained all Sunday but stopped raining during the night.
(b) She was ill for a week, and during that week she ate nothing.

For may be used to denote purpose and may also be used before known periods.

(a) I went there for the summer.
(b) I rented my house for my holidays.
(c) I rented my car for the summer only.

For has various other uses.

(a) He asked for ten.I paid six for it.
(b) I bought one for Kuku.
(c) He has been ill for three days.

Below, Under and Beneath

Below and **under** both mean lower than (in level) and sometimes either can be used. But under usually denotes physical contact and below denotes space between the things.

(a) He put the books under the pillow.
(b) He placed the lamp below the almirah.
(c) They live below us. (We live at the second floor while they live at the first floor.)
(d) I was wearing a sweater also under the jacket.

Below and **under** may also mean junior in rank.

(a) He is under me means that I am superior to him.
(b) He is working under me.

Below is used meaning opposite to above.

(a) The temperature can fall below 15° Celsius.
(b) Rainfall has been below average this year.

Beneath is something under the other thing.

(a) I could see the muscles of his shoulders beneath his T-shirt.
(b) I found pleasure in sitting beneath the trees...
(c) ...the frozen grass crunching beneath his feet.

In and Within

In means the maximum time limit, while **within** means the period upto which the work will be completed. **Within** a particular length of time means before that length of time, while **in** refers to the maximum time requires for the completion of the job.

(a) I will complete the work in a month.
(b) I can repair the car within two hours.

Ago and Before

Ago is used for past events while before is used in reference to two events.

(a) He came three days ago.
(b) The train had left before he reached the station .

Beside and Besides

Beside and **besides** have altogether different meanings. One should not get confused with the two words.

beside = at the side of
(a) He was sitting beside Sarla.
besides = in addition to or as well as
(a) He has a car besides a motor cycle.

Between and Among

Between is normally used for two things or persons, but it can also be used of more when we have a definite number in mind and there is a close relationship or association within them.

(a) He distributed his property between his two sons.
(b) Luxembourg lies between Belgium, Germany and France.
(c) A treaty was signed between three parties.
(d) He inserted a needle between the close petals of a flower.

Among is usually used for more than two persons or things when we have no definite number in mind.

(a) He was happy to be among friends again.
(b) He distributed his property among the poor.

Among and Amongst

Both have same meaning. Either of them can be used if followed by 'the'. If followed by a word, beginning with a vowel 'amongst' be used. The use of amongst is usually found in literary writings.

(a) He distributed the toffees among/amongst the poor.
(b) He distributed the toffees amongst us.

Of and Off

Of and **off** are used in following situations referring :

(a) Location: east **of** here; the middle **of** the road.
(b) Possession: a friend **of** mine; the sound **of** music.
(c) Part of a group: one **of** us; a member **of** the team.
(d) Measurement : a cup **of** milk; two meters **of** snow.

Off

(a) Not on; away from: Please keep off the grass.
(b) At some distance from: There are islands off the coast.

Above and Over

Above and **over** both mean 'higher than' and sometimes either can be used.

(a) The helicopter hovered above/over us.
(b) White flags were waved above/over the buildings.

But over also mean covering/on the other side of/across.

(a) I put a cloth over her.
(b) He lives over this mountain.
(c) There is a bridge over the railway line.
(d) He put a blanket over the dead body.

Above can have none of these meanings.

Over can mean higher in rank.

He is over me. (means He is my immediate boss.)

Over is also used with meals/food/drink.

(a) We had a chat over a cup of tea. (while drinking tea)
(b) The matter was decided over the lunch.

Above is also used meaning 'earlier' or 'previous'.

(a) He lives at the above address. (previously mentioned)
(b) For details please see (P-1) above. . (previously mentioned)

Make of and Made from

Both refer to material used. **Make of** is used when the shape of the material is not changed.

(a) A notebook is made of papers.
(b) A house is made of bricks.

Made from is used when shape of the material has undergone a total change.

(a) Butter is made from milk.
(b) Paper is made from grass.

In and With

In is used in following situations.

(a) Place thought of as an area: **in** London; **in** Europe.
(b) Within a location: **in** the room; **in** the building.
(c) Units of time: That happened **in** March, **in** 1992.
(d) Within a certain time: return **in** an hour.
(e) By means of : write **in** pencil; speak **in** English.
(f) Condition: **in** doubt; **in** a hurry; **in** secret.
(g) A member of: He is **in** the orchestra; **in** the navy.
(h) Wearing: **in** the blue shirt.
(i) With reference to: lacking **in** ideas; rich **in** oil.
(j) Accompanying: came **with** her; my keys **with** me.
(k) Having; containing: book **with** a map of the island.
(l) By means of; using: repaired the shoes **with** glue.
(m) Manner : with pleasure; with ease; **with** difficulty.
(n) Because of: paralysed **with** fear.
(o) Agreement: I agree **with** you.

Opposite and In front of

Opposite is also called 'antonym' and is 'position in front. **Infront of** always means front position.

Ram and Shyam are having a meal. Ram is sitting at one side of the table and Shyam at the other side.

Ram is sitting opposite Shyam. (Ram is facing Shyam.)

People living on one side of a street will talk of the houses on the other side as the houses opposite rather than the houses in front of us.

His house is opposite to ours.

Infront of is used in following ways :

(a) He parked the car in front of the hotel.
(b) He put the plates on the table in front of us.

By and Before

By a time or by a date usually implies before that time or date.

(a) The train starts at 7.15 am so you had better be at the station by 7.00.

By + a time expression structure is often used with future perfect tense.

(b) By the end of July I'll have read all those books.

Before can used as a preposition or as a conjunction or as an adverb.

(a) Before signing this agreement let us discuss each and every point thread bare. (preposition)
(b) Before you sign this you can discuss it with your father. (conjunction)
(c) I've seen her somewhere before. (adverb)

After and Afterwards

After must be followed by a noun, pronoun or gerund.

(a) After breakfast he ordered a taxi.
(b) Don't run immediately after a meal.

If we do not like to use a noun/ pronoun or gerund, we cannot use after but we can use **afterwards** or then.

(a) Don't have a meal and run immediately afterwards.
(b) They bathed and afterwards played games.

But and Except

Both have the same meaning and are usually interchangeable.

After nobody/none/nothing/nowhere etc. 'but' is normally used.

(a) Nobody but Shyam knew the way.
(b) Nothing but the best is sold in our shop.

Except is used when the prepositional phrase comes later in a sentence.

(a) Nobody knew the way except Shyam.

After 'but' and 'except' bare infinitive (infinitive without to) is used.

To and Towards

The preposition **to** indicates movement with the aim of a specific destination, which can be a place or an event.

(a) I'm going **to** USA tomorrow.
(b) I need to go **to** the Bank.
(c) Can you tell me the way **to** the station?
(d) Are you going **to** the party?

Up to is often used to express movement **to** a person.

(a) She came **up to** me and asked me what the time was.

The preposition **to** is sometimes used to indicate a specific position, especially if a person or object is facing something, e.g:

(a) Thereis a door **to** your left.
(b) He stood with his back **to** the window.

Towards

The preposition **towards** indicates movement in a particular direction. e.g :

(a) Everyone sitting in the room turned **towards** me.
(b) She was carrying a suitcase and walking **towards** the railway station.

The contrast in the following two examples:
(a) I'm going **to** New York for a meeting.
(b) I think we're heading **towards** New York now, we must have gone wrong.
In the first example, **to** refers a specific destination.
In the second example with **towards,** the direction of movement is more importantly indicated.

Through and Into

The preposition **through** refers to movement within a space which can be thought of as three-dimensional. e.g:

(a) They drove **through** some spectacular countryside.
(b) The canal flows **through** the city centre.

Through usually suggests movement across an entire space, from one side of something to another, e.g :

(a) He cut **through** the wire.

The preposition **into** refers to movement from the outside to the inside of a three dimensional space, e.g:

(a) We got **into** the back of the car.
(b) She reached **into** her bag and found the keys.

With certain verbs **into** can be used to express the idea of movement in the direction of something, often resulting in actually hitting it, as in the second example below. e.g:

(a) He looked straight **into** her eyes.
(b) She swerved and crashed **into** the fence.

Across, Over and Along

The prepositions **across** and **over** are used to talk about movement from one side of a place to another. They usually refer to movement in relation to places which can be thought of as two-dimensional, such as surfaces (e.g a lawn) or lines (e.g a river) :

(a) I'll jump **over** the wall and open the gate.
(b) The aircraft flew low **over** the lake.
(c) How are we going to get **across** the stream?
(d) It's the first time I've flown **across** the Atlantic.

Over also functions as a preposition expressing position. It often has a similar meaning to the preposition above.

(a) There was a mirror **above/over** the sink.

One of its core uses however is to express position in relation to a two-dimensional surface, e.g:

(b) A white tablecloth was spread **over** the table.

Or to show when something is positioned on the opposite side of a 'line', e.g road, bridge, etc.

(c) The hotel is **over** the bridge.

Across is sometimes used to express position in relation to something which stretches from one side of a place to another.

(a) There was a barrier **across** the road.

Like **over** it is also used to show when something is positioned on the opposite side of a place in relation to the speaker.

(a) The bank is **across** the street.

The preposition **along** is used to show movement following a line.

(a) We walked **along** the river.
(b) I followed Mr Jackson **along** the corridor.
(c) Well-wishers began placing flowers **along** the railings.

It is also sometimes used to show a specific position in relation to a line.

(a) Somewhere **along** the path there's a signpost.

Or to show when a group of things are positioned in a line next to something.

(a) There were plenty of restaurants **along** the river front.

Unnecessary Use of Prepositions

In everyday speech, we fall into the bad habit, using prepositions where they are not required. It would be a good idea to eliminate these words altogether, but we must be especially careful not to use them in formal, academic prose.

(a) She met up with the new coach on the ground.

(b) The glass fell off **~~of~~** the desk.

(c) He threw the glass out **~~of~~** the window.

(d) He wouldn't let the cat inside **~~of~~** the house.
[or use 'in']

(e) Where did they **go ~~to~~**?

(f) Where is your college **~~at~~**?

Ellipsis in Preposition

When two words or phrases are used in parallel and require the same preposition to be idiomatically correct, the preposition does not have to be used twice.

(a) You can wear that outfit in summer and **~~in~~** winter.

(b) The female was both attracted **~~by~~** and distracted by the male's dance.

However, when the idiomatic use of phrases calls for different prepositions, we must be careful not to omit one of them.

(a) The children were interested **in** and disgusted **by** the movie.

(b) It was clear that this player could both contribute to and learn **from** every game he played.

(c) He was fascinated **by** and enamored **of** this beguiling woman.

	Incorrect	Correct
(a)	We should prevent damage and theft of public property.	We should prevent damage to and theft of public property.
(b)	He is neither ashamed nor sorry for his misdeeds.	He is neither ashamed of nor sorry for his misdeeds.

Preposition Omitted

Some transitive verbs do not take prepositions with them. Such commonly used verbs are : reach, resist, resemble, afford, accompany, attack, assist, pick, pervade, precede, obey, order, combat, benefit, inform, violate, etc.

Incorrect	Correct
He ordered for a cup of tea.	He ordered a cup of tea.
India attacked on Pakistan.	India attacked Pakistan.
He informed to me yesterday.	He informed me yesterday.

Nouns denoting time (Morning, evening, day, night, month,week, year) if preceded by objective like; this, that, next, every, last, etc. we should not use preposition with such words.

(a) She is going to Jaipur next morning.

(b) I met her last evening.

Yesterday, today, tomorrow are also used without preposition.

(a) Please meet me tomorrow.

(b) He is arriving today.

(c) He went yesterday.

Words denoting **time** and **place** like, last week, last month, abroad, minute, bit, inside, outside, etc. are also used without preposition.

(a) He came here last month.

(b) Sima is going abroad next week.

(c) Please wait a minute/bit.

If verbs showing movement like, go, get, etc. is used with **home**, we should not use any preposition before home.

(a) It took them three hours to get home.

(b) I went home by bus.

> If any pronoun, adjective or phrase is used immediately before home, the use of preposition is necessary.
>
> (a) She returned to her husband's home.
>
> (b) I went to his home.

The preposition **at** is also used with home.

(a) You can do this work at home.

(b) We can stay at home.

Verbs denoting command, request, invitation and advice, e.g. advise, ask, beg, command, encourage, implore, invite, order, recommend, remind, request, tell, urge, warn, can be followed directly by the person addressed without the use of preposition **to.**

(a) I advised her to wait.

(b) We urged him to try again.

(c) I reminded them that there were no trains after 8 p.m.

(d) She warned him that the ice was thin.

But note that recommend (means advise) when used with other constructions needs **to** before the person addressed.

(a) He recommended me to buy it.

(b) He recommended it to me.
(In this construction 'to' is required.)

(c) He recommended me. (It would mean that he said I was suitable.)

When 'ask' is used in following construction the preposition 'to' is never used here :

He asked* (me) about his health.

He asked * (me) if I liked that job.

Note : * 'to' is never used after ask in above constructions.

Use of Some Prepositions

A

1. **Abide by (decision)** She will abide by my decision positively.

   Abide with (person) He will abide with his friend Suresh in all circumstances.

2. **Angry at (thing)** He is angry at your way of questioning.

   Angry with (person) Sima is angry with Raj.

   Angry for (action) He is angry for your laughing at her wife.

3. **Arrive at (place)** The train is going to arrive at the station within ten minutes.

   Arrive in (country) He is scheduled to arrive in India on next Monday.

4. **Alight on (ground, thing)** A large number of birds alights on the roof of my house.

   Alight at (a place) The groom alighted from the elephant at her gate.

5. **Appeal to (person)** I earnestly appealed to the principal to consider the matter again.

   Appeal against (decision) He appealed against the decision of the lower court.

6. **Amuse at (thing)** He is greatly amused at the indifferent attitude of his father.

   Amused with (action) The boys amused themselves with throwing flowers at the girls.

7. **Ask for (a thing)** He asked me for some help.

   Ask from (person) He asked somehelp from me.

8. **Affiliated to (university, board)** Our college is affiliated to the University of Punjab.

   Affiliated with (a party) Bajrang Dal is affiliated with BJP indirectly.

9. **Annoyed at (thing)** He was annoyed at my laughing.

   Annoyed with (person) He is annoyed with you.

10. **Antipathy to (thing)** He has a great antipathy to wine.

    Antipathy against (person) You should not have any antipathy against your friend Jack.

11. **Answer to (person)** You have to answer to me for your conduct.

    Answer for (action) He was asked to answer for the misbehaviour.

12. **Arm against (danger)** We must arm ourselves against the danger of chemical weapons.

    Arm with (weapon) He armed himself with a revolver and a knife.

13. **Atone to (person)** He tried to atone to his new life.

    Atone for (action) He tried to atone for the mischief he had committed.

14. **Award for (action)** He got the award for his hard work.

    Awarded to (person) A silver medal will be awarded to the best sports girl.

15. **Antidote to (poison)** Diamond is regarded as an antidote to the poison of the snake.

    Antidote against (infection) Quinine is an antidote against malaria.

16. **Argue against or about (a matter)** He went to argue against the topic of debate.

He argued well about the newly introduced bill.

Argue with (person) Don't argue with me unnecessarily.

17. Agree in (opinion) Ganesh agrees with Ram in opinion expressed by him (Ram).

Agree to (proposal) I cannot agree to his proposal of dividing the property.

Agree with (person) I fully agree with you on this issue.

Agree on (subject) After a lot of discussion all agreed on the terms of agreement.

18. Accomplice with (person) Her wife was an accomplice with the murderer.

Accomplice in (act) His wife was an accomplice in the murder.

19. Authority for (action) You have no authority for instructing me as such.

Authority on (subject) She is indeed an unquestionable authority on Physics.

Authority over (person) He has no authority over me officially.

20. Accused of (a crime) He is an accused of murder.

21. Accused by (a person) He was accused by his wife.

B

1. Blush for (fault) She blushed for the misbehaviour of her husband.

Blush at (praise) She blushed at the comments of her husband.

2. Blind to (deeds, action) He should not be blind to the misdeeds of his son Rakesh.

Blind in (one eye) His husband is blind in the right eye.

3. Born of (parents) He was born of an orthodox mother.

Born at, in (place) He was born at a general hospital at Alwar.

4. Buy from (shop) You can buy this item from any grocery shop.

Buy for (person) I bought this ball pen for my son.

5. Beg of, from (person) I begged of him to give me some time to pay. I begged some rice from him.

Beg for (person) I begged him for some rice.

C

1. Close to (adjective) His house is very close to the railway station.

Close with (shut) She closed the door with a bang.

Close down (to terminate the operation) He close down his shop within six months.

Closeout (to reduce the price) There is a closeout, with fifty per cent discount.

2. Confer on (awarded) An honorary degree was confered on him.

Confer with (consult with a person) I will confer with my father in this matter.

3. Contend for (thing) Mr. S. S. Shekhawat will contend for a seat in Vidhan Sabha.

Contend with (person) You should not contend with any after.

4. Consist in (remain) The beauty of this building consist in its style and grandeur.

Consist of (composed of) Our body consists of flesh, bone and blood.

5. Condemn to (punishment) He was condemned to death by the judge.

Condemn for (crime) He was condemned for murder by the court.

6. Compare to (comparing two different kind of things) Don't compare water to milk.

Compare with (comparing two things of same class) Kalidas was compared with Shakespeare by several renowned scholars.

7. Care for (like) I does not care for drinks.

Care about (thing) She takes full care about her sarees and make-up.

8. Consult on (matter) We were not consulted on the new issue of debentures.

Consult with (person) You should consult with some expert before taking a final decision.

9. Controversy on (matter) A lot of controversy was raised on this issue.

Controversy with (person) I do not have any controversy with any of the members on this matter.

10. Confide to (to tell) You should not confide your secrets to anybody.

Confide in (to pose confidence) I confide in him, but he deceived me.

11. Complaint of (a thing) I complained of his misconduct to the boss.

Complaint to (person) I complained of his misbehaviour to his father.

12. **Compete with (person)** Can you compete with him ?

Compete for (job) I will try my best to compete for this job.

13. **Cause of (problem)** He is the main cause of all this trouble.

Cause for (anxiety) I do not have any cause for anxiety.

14. **Clothed in (dressing)** She was clothed in a silken dress.

Clothed with (quality) She was clothed with shame.

15. **Connect to (join)** Connect the end of this rod to the other.

Connect with (relation) I will connect with you soon.

D

1. **Displeased at (thing)** She does not displease at such humorous jokes.

Displeased with (person) Ram is greatly displeased with Sita.

2. **Disqualified for (post)** She was declared disqualified for the election .

Disqualified from (competing) He was disqualified from taking part in the competition.

3. **Dwell upon (to speak)** The chairman will dwell upon the importance of truth and honesty.

Dwell in (country) The French dwell in France.

Dwell at (place) These days Ram is dwelling at his friend's hotel.

Dwell among (people) He is dwelling among the tribal.

4. **Disgusted at (thing)** She became disgusted at your silly joke.

Disgusted with (person or life) I am very much disgusted with him.

5. **Deal with (to do with the matter)** This book deals with the population problem in India.

Deal in (trade) He deals in iron scrap.

Deal out (distribute) The principal should deal out equal treatment to all the teachers.

6. **Differ on (point)** I totally differ on this point.

Differ with (person) I differ with you on this point.

Differ from (thing) Your views entirely differ from that of mine.

7. **Die of (a disease)** He died of hunger.

Die from (some cause) He died from hard labour.

8. **Destined for (created for)** God had destined him for the post of President of India.

Destined to (subject) He is destined to such a pitiable condition.

9. **Dine with (person)** I am scheduled to dine with him to night.

Dine on (thing) I can't dine on the same kind of menu daily.

10. **Dispense with (do without)** Jack can't easily dispensed with her.

Dispense to (distribute) A judge must dispense equal justice to all.

11. **Dispose of (to sell)** She wants to dispose of all the goods at the earliest.

Dispose to (state of things) The news of his father's death disposed him to a deep sorrow.

12. **Dispute with (person)** Why are you disputing with your friends on such a trifle matter.

Dispute about (thing) There was a great dispute about the nomination of chairman.

E

1. **Embark on (a vessel)** She embarked on the ship for Sri Lanka.

Embark in (new business) He has embarked in the new business with full fervour.

2. **Enter into (thing)** They have entered into an agreement with Ramesh.

Enter upon (new course) After marriage I entered upon a new way of life.

3. **Exchange for (thing)** She exchanged a book for a piece of art.

Exchange with (person) I want to exchange my views with you.

4. **Exult at (success)** She was exulted at her brilliant success.

Exult over (an enemy) Our army exulted over the enemy's force.

Exult in (misery) One should not be exulted in the misery of others.

5. **Eager for (fame)** She is very much eager for making a name in society.

Eager in (to find) He has involved himself eagerly in pursuit of finding the cause of miseries in life.

6. **Equivalent for (word)** Write a word equivalent for 'fear'.

Equivalent to (money, thing) One million is equivalent to ten lacs.

7. **Exact from (person)** Heavy fines were exacted from the unruly students.

   Exact in (adjective) He is not exact in repayment.
8. **Expert in (doing)** He is expert in repairing automobiles.

   Expert at (thing) He is expert at English grammar.
9. **Enquire of (person)** I enquired of him the secret of his happiness.

   Enquire into (a matter) The police enquired into the case of bank robbery.
10. **Entrust with (a thing)** I entrusted him with my camera.

    Entrust to (person) I entrusted my camera to him.

F

1. **Fit out (equip)** The ship was fitted out for Sri Lanka.

   Fit up (furnishing) He fitted up his house with all necessary furniture.
2. **Fascinated with (person)** I was fascinated with Rekha.

   Fascinated by (thing) I was fascinated by her manners and looks.
3. **False to (person)** One should not be false to one's friends.

   False of (thing, heart) He is not false of heart.
4. **Fight for (depending)** Our army is ready to fight for the country.

   Fight with (together) We must not fight with our friends.

   Fight against (thing) We must fight against the evil of illiteracy.
5. **Familiar to (thing)** Your looks are quite familiar to that of Sachin.

   Familiar with (person) I am familiar with him.

G

1. **Gaze at (look attentively)** Don't gaze at these girls, they are the cops.

   Gaze on (look strangely) He stood gazing on the pathetic scene of accident.
2. **Grieve for (person)** She was extremely grieve for him.

   Grieve at (event) Everyone was grieved at the death of Rajiv Gandhi.

   Grieve over (thing) She grieved over my unfortunate loss.
3. **Good for (nothing)** He is a good for nothing fellow.

   Good at (something) She is good at swimming.

H

1. **Held by (person)** A condolence meeting was held by the staff yesterday.

   Held in (esteem of contempt) In the heart of every Indian. Gandhiji is held in great respect.

   Held at (place) A meeting was held at Hope Circus yesterday.
2. **Hear of (something)** I heard this robbery from sorla.

   Hear from (person) I heard of this robbery from Sarla.

   Hear by (post) I hear by this letter about your promotion.
3. **Happen to (person)** Please tell me what happened to you in New York.

   Happen at (place) This event happened at Red Square.

   Happen on (come across) While returning from market I happen to meet my teacher.
4. **Hidden from (view)** The neem tree has hidden your house from direct view.

   Hidden by (person, thing) My shoes were hidden by his sister.

I

1. **Introduce to (person)** Let me first introduce my friend to you.

   Introduce in (make modifications) The UPSC has introduced many changes into the syllabus of IAS.
2. **Invest with (authority)** The President invested him with the honour of Bharat Ratna.

   Invest in (business) I am ready to invest fifty lacs rupees in this business.
3. **Inquire for (a thing)** I went there to inquire for my lost brief case.

   Inquire into (matter) The police will inquire into the cause of death.

   Inquire about (concern) She came here to inquire about the health of her son.

   Inquire of (asking) First inquire of the way, then move.
4. **Involve in (thing)** She seems to be involved in some serious trouble.

   Involve with (person) Don't involve yourself with such unruly persons.

5. **Irritated at (thing)** I was greatly irritated at his unruly behaviour.
   Irritated with (person) She was extremely irritated with her husband.
6. **Impatient at (unexpected thing)** He became impatient at the unexpected delay.
   Impatient for (expected thing) She is very much impatient for the arrival of her husband.
7. **Indebted for (thing)** I was indebted for your timely help.
   Indebted to (person) He is greatly indebted to Rani for her timely help.

J

1. **Jest at (person)** I don't like to jest at a lunatic person.
   Jest with (thing) We should not jest with the communal thing.
2. **Judge of (giving opinion)** Without going in details, how can you be the judge of this matter.
   Judge by (observing) Judging by his qualifications, I think she is not fit for this job.

K

1. **Know by (recognise)** A man is known by his actions.
   Know for (quality) He is known for his foolish decisions.

L

1. **Live at (a small town)** He lives at Alwar in Rajasthan.
   Live in (in country, big place) He is living at Alwar in Rajasthan.
   Live on (food) He lives entirely on breads.
   Live for (devote) We must live and die for the cause of truth.
   Live with (a person) I live here with my parents.
2. **Liable for (crime)** You are liable for the death of your wife.
   Liable to (punishment) He was liable to imprisonment for three years.
3. **Listen for (sound)** You will have to listen for the heart beat of the baby.
   Listen to (hear attentively) We should listen to the advice of our elders.
4. **Laugh at (make fun)** We must not laugh at our friends.
   Laugh with (indulge with) Better to laugh with disabled than to laugh at them.

M

1. **Married to (a woman)** Ramesh was married to Sarla.
   Married with (a man) Sarla was married with Ramesh.
2. **Moved with (sorrow)** He was actually moved with a feeling of sorrow.
   Moved to (tears) On hearing the news of sudden death of his wife, all moved to tears.
   Moved from (one's determination) You can't move me from my decision with your logics.
   Moved at (a scene) He was greatly moved at her mother's dead body.

O

1. **Obliged to (person)** I am very much obliged to you.
   Obliged at (thing) I am obliged for your timely help.
2. **Occupied in (doing a job)** He is fully occupied in writing a book.
   Occupied by (thing) That house is occupied by a marriage party.
3. **Originate with (person)** All the planning originated with him.
   Originate in (place, cause) A fierce fire originated in Connaught Place yesterday.

P

1. **Part from (person)** I parted from my wife in Kumbh.
   Part with (thing) He is not ready to part with his furniture at any cost.
2. **Prepare for (be ready)** I am preparing for the IAS examination this year.
   Prepare against (danger) We must prepare ourselves against the danger of water pollution.
3. **Pray for (thing)** My wife prayed for my success.
   Pray to (make prayer) I prayed to God to help me in facing the unwarranted problems.
4. **Perish by (famine)** Our district was perished by drought last year.

Perish with (hunger) During drought the cattle are perishing with starvation.

5. **Plead with (person)** He pleaded with the principal for mercy.
   Plead for (thing) He pleaded with the king for mercy.
6. **Play at (cards)** They were playing at cards.
   Play on (musical instrument) Harish played on the violin in the party.

Q

1. **Quick in (doing)** He is quick in reasoning questions.
   Quick of (understanding) Ramesh is quick of understanding the questions.
2. **Quarrel over (thing)** You must not quarrel over the parental property.
   Quarrel with (person) We must not quarrel with our friends.

R

1. **Responsible to (person)** An MLA is responsible to work for welfare.
   Responsible for (action) She is responsible for the loss caused due to her negligence.
2. **Reason with (person)** I reasoned with him on each and every point in this matter.
   Reason about (thing) You can't reason about the importance of self respect.
3. **Ready for (action)** I am ready for the match.
   Ready with (something) I was totally ready with my arguments on that day.
   Ready in (replying) I always found her ready in her reply.
4. **Revenge on (person)** He revenged himself on his enemy.
   Revenge for (action) I will positively revenge for the insult inflicted on me by her.
5. **Reduced to (to decrease)** His salary was reduced to rupees four thousands only.
   Reduced by (decrease by an amount) His salary was reduced by three hundred rupees per month.

S

1. **Share of (thing)** I must be paid my share of profit.
   Share with (person) I do not share my lunch with anybody.
2. **Skilful at (thing)** He is skilful at numbers.
   Skilful in (doing a thing) He is skilful in mathematical calculations.
3. **Succeed to (property)** He succeeded to his uncle's empire.
   Succeed in (doing) This time she succeeded in IAS examination.
4. **Start at (time)** I started at 10 o'clock in the morning.
   Start from (place) I start at 10 o'clock in the morning from Delhi.
   Started for (place) I started at 7 o'clock in the morning for Delhi.
5. **Struggle for (thing)** We have to struggle hard for keeping peace in the country.
   Struggle with (person) We should not struggle with our neighbours.
6. **Serve out (distribute)** Sweets were served out to the audience.
   Serve up (to give food) A nice lunch was served up there in the function.
7. **Speak for (person)** You go there, I have already spoken for you to the secretary.
   Speak about (thing) He is speaking about 'Unemployment Problem'.
8. **Starved to (death)** She was starved to death by her husband.
   Starved with (hunger) He starved with hunger.
9. **Suited for (action)** She is not suited for the role of vamp.
   Suited to (occasion) Sad song does not suit to such an occasion.
10. **Supply to (person)** PHED is supplying water to all the colonies in the city.
    Supply with (thing) Government must supply poor with food and clothing.

T

1. **Thankful for (thing)** I am really thankful for your timely help.
   Thankful to (person) I am very much thankful to your kind favour.
2. **Think over (to consider)** The society agreed to think over the case in the next meeting.
   Think on (meditate) I have been thinking on this matter for the last many days.
3. **Trust in (person)** Trust in God and work hard.
   Trust to (thing) I trusted to his words, and he was right.
4. **Tired of (disgusted)** I am tired of your daily excuses.

Tired with (exhausted) You seems to be tired with the long run.

5. **Talk with (person)** I will talk with my father in this matter.
   Talk about (thing) I will talk about this matter with my parents.
   Talk over (discuss) All the members of the society talked over the issue for many hours.

U

1. **Useful for (thing)** The bag is very much useful for picnic parties.
   Useful to (person) I found that these directives are useful to me for success in exam.

V

1. **Vote for (person)** Vote for me please.
   Vote on (a resolution) After having cast votes on the resolution, all took lunch.
2. **Vexed with (person)** Why are you vexed with your wife ?
   Vexed at (thing) He is vexed at my jokes.

W

1. **Wait at (place)** I will wait at church near the hospital.
   Wait for (person) I will wait for you till tomorrow.
2. **Wake up (to get up)** She wakes up at 6 a.m. daily.
   Wake from (to be awaken) She waked from slumber and decided to take action.
3. **Warn against (an action)** I have already warn you, against your negligence.
   Warn of (danger) I have already warned you of the risk involved.

Z

1. **Zealous for (a thing)** A dedicated worker is always zealous for achieving the target.
   Zealous in (a cause) We must be zealous in the cause of humanity.

Appropriate Prepositions

1. abundance of (wealth)
2. assent to (a proposal)
3. accustomed to (work)
4. avail ourselves of (an opportunity)
5. attain to (a position)
6. addicted to (drinking , something)
7. accede to (a request)
8. abstain from (to keep away)
9. absolved from (a promise, a sin)
10. acquiesce in (proposal)
11. adhere to (principles)
12. afraid of (a ghost)
13. abhorrent to (good nature)
14. accession to (throne)
15. assure of (a thing)
16. absorbed in (study)
17. acquit (someone) of a charge
18. acquaintance with (a person)
19. beware of (cheating)
20. comply with (one's wishes)
21. condemn to (death)
22. cured of (a disease)
23. comply with (wishes)
24. conducive to (health)
25. despair of (success)
26. desirous (doing some thing)
27. deprive of (something)
28. devoid of (quality)
29. duty of (the country)
30. eligible for (a post)
31. exception to (a rule)
32. excuse for (a fault)
33. envious of (a person or a thing)
34. exchange a thing (with a person)
35. elder to (some family member)
36. fatal to (one's cause)
37. fearful of (death)
38. furnish with (clothes)
39. greedy of (money)
40. heir to (ancestral property)
41. healed of (a disease)
42. hopeful of (success)
43. hostile to (a person)
44. hunger after (fame)
45. innocent of (a crime)
46. intimate with (a person)

47. invite to (dinner)
48. insist on a (thing)
49. intimate with (Person)
50. impertinent to (elders)
51. invite to (dinner)
52. insight into (a matter or thing)
53. jealous of (a person)
54. keep to (the left, the point)
55. knock at (the door)
56. match for (a person)
57. key to (success)
58. mourn for (the dead)
59. match for (a person)
60. mad with (anger)
61. motive for (an action)
62. need for (help)
63. need of (a thing)
64. notorious for (drinking, doing)
65. occur to (mind)
66. overwhelmed with (sorrow, grief)
67. pay for (one's mistakes)
68. passion for (study)
69. peculiar to (a person or a thing)
70. persist in (doing)
71. pity for (poor, downtrodden)
72. pleased with (a person)
73. preface to (a book)
74. proud of (a thing)
75. pride on (a thing)
76. prefer to (a thing)
77. refrain from (doing some wrong)
78. repent of (a mistake)
79. respectful to (a person)
80. rob (a person) of (a thing)
81. sentence to (punishment)
82. short of (money)
83. side with (a person)
84. shocked at (a loss)
85. superior to (a thing)
86. sure of (some fact)
87. search for (a thing)
88. sacred to (a cause)
89. triumph over (difficulties)
90. trouble to (person)
91. vain of (beauty)
92. want of (money)
93. wanting in (wisdom)
94. worthy of (a reward)
95. yield to (an enemy)
96. search for (a thing)
97. sacred to (a cause)
98. work at (subject)
99. surrender to (enemy)
100. stick to (point)
101. suspect of (something)
102. translate into (language)
103. touch upon (subject)
104. slur on (character)

» Exercises

Exercise 1

Rewrite the sentences after correction

1. She was neither ashamed nor sorry for her misbehaviour.
2. She neither objected nor approved of it.
3. Ram has no interest and passion for cricket.
4. We must prevent damage and theft of public property.
5. Please listen and reflect on this topic afterwards.
6. He asked from her a silly question.
7. The police investigated into the case.
8. Ram resembles to his father.
9. She resigned from his post.
10. Ram signed to the agreement.
11. The poet described about the nature.
12. She must love to her children.
13. We have discussed on the merits of the issue.
14. In this article the author has described about poverty.
15. She criticised upon my action without logic.
16. A meeting was held on Hope Circus yesterday.
17. In the heart of every Indian, Gandhiji is held with great respect.
18. I was fascinated at her manners and looks.
19. I entrusted him by my camera.
20. The police will inquire in the cause of death.
21. You are liable to the death of your wife.
22. On hearing the news of sudden death of his wife, all moved in tears.
23. Why are you vexed at your wife?
24. His salary was reduced with four thousands rupees only.
25. He succeeded for his uncle's empire.

Solutions

1. She was neither ashamed of nor sorry for her misbehaviour.
2. She neither objected to nor approved of it.
3. Ram has no interest in and passion for cricket.
4. We must prevent damage to and theft of public property.
5. Please listen to and reflect on this topic afterwards.
6. He asked her a silly question.
7. The police investigated the case.
8. Ram resembles his father.
9. She resigned his post.
10. Ram signed the agreement.
11. The poet described the nature.
12. She must love her children.
13. We have discussed the merits of the issue.
14. In this article the author has described poverty.
15. She criticised my action without logic.
16. A meeting was held at Hope Circus yesterday.
17. In the heart of every Indian, Gandhiji is held in great respect.
18. I was fascinated by her manners and looks.
19. I entrusted him with my camera.
20. The police will inquire into the cause of death.
21. You are liable for the death of your wife.
22. On hearing the news of sudden death of his wife, all moved to tears.
23. Why are you vexed with your wife ?
24. His salary was reduced to four thousands rupees only.
25. He succeeded to his uncle's empire.

Exercise 2

Choose the correct alternative out of the four

1. The shopkeeper does not have the toys, I was looking.... ***(Income Tax Inspectors)***
   (a) by (b) about
   (c) for (d) to
2. Books are very often compared .... a granary. ***(Income Tax Inspector)***
   (a) with (b) to
   (c) by (d) at
3. Divide twelve mangoes .... three boys. ***(Income Tax Inspector)***
   (a) to (b) for
   (c) between (d) among
4. To reach their village, they have to change............ a small train at the junction. ***(Income Tax Inspector)***
   (a) on (b) to
   (c) over (d) into
5. Mohan will never pass his SSC examination .... he works hard. ***(Income Tax Inspector)***
   (a) if (b) unless
   (c) since (d) because
6. If you live in a corrupt society, you cannot easily rise ..... the prevailing corruption. ***(Income Tax Inspector)***
   (a) upon (b) over
   (c) above (d) beyond
7. It was the first time he had eaten a square meal ....he had left the village. ***(Income Tax Inspector)***
   (a) since (b) for
   (c) before (d) although
8. They are very grateful............ your kindness. ***(Income Tax Inspector)***
   (a) for (b) to
   (c) with (d) towards
9. His mother was 45 when she...... ***(Income Tax Inspector)***
   (a) had died (b) died
   (c) was dying (d) has died
10. There was nothing he could do .... wait. ***(Income Tax Inspector)***
    (a) and (b) except
    (c) otherwise (d) than

Solutions

1. c	**2.** b	**3.** d	**4.** d
5. b	**6.** c	**7.** a	**8.** a
9. b	**10.** b		

Exercise 3

Put the prepositions where they are required **(IFS)**

David felt sorry ....(1) Mrs. Micawber because he was always ....(2) debt. David took books ....(3) the invitation of Mrs. Micawber ....(4) the bookstall and sold them ....(5) whatever he could get. The wife ....(6) the booksellers usually paid ....(7) the books ....(8) shillings which David suspected she stole ....(9) her husband's pocket when he was lying ....(10) bed.

Solutions

1. for	**2.** in	**3.** at	**4.** form
5. for	**6.** and	**7.** for	**8.** some
9. from	**10.** in		

Exercise 4

Fill the blanks in each of the following sentences with the correct prepositions

1. Professor Krishna will take ......as the new Principal tomorrow.

2. We all have to adjust ourselves .... new circumstances. *(IIT Exam)*
3. Young fans clustered .... the film star. *(IIT Exam)*
4. My son is apprenticed .... Mr.Lal, Chartered Accountant. *(IIT Exam)*
5. You will always be short of money if you live .... your means. *(IIT Exam)*
6. He accused me ...... selling secret information .... the enemy. *(IAS)*
7. Please write .....ink and put your name ....the top of the page. *(IAS)*
8. The man .... pipe and long hairs is the brother..... the girl. *(IAS)*
9. If you do not comply .... the traffic regulations you will get .... the trouble............. the police. *(IAS)*
10. She is now married .... a rich merchant. *(IFS)*
11. I correspond ....her regularly. *(IFS)*
12. The patient died .... fever. *(IFS)*
15. This election is different .... mine. *(IFS)*

Solutions

1. over	**2.** with	**3.** round
4. to	**4.** on	**5.** of, to
6. in, at	**7.** with, of	**8.** with, in, with
9. to	**10.** to	**11.** of
12. from		

Spotting the Errors

Find the errors and justify your answers

1. He was sleeping (A)/ in his room when a thief (B)/ entered into his house (C)/ and took away a lot of things (D).
2. In her concluding speech (A)/ she said almost nothing (B)/ worth listening to (C).
3. It was apparent for (A)/ everyone present (B)/ that if the patient did not receive (C)/ immediate medical aid (D)/ he would die.
4. He proposed me (A)/ that we should go to the Disco (B) and then have (C)/ dinner at a restra (D). *(Bank PO)*
5. There appears (A)/ to be a little liaison (B)/ among the (C)/ two groups of the society (D) .
6. The team (A)/ complained to the manager (B)/ against the captain (C)/ and the poor facilities provided in the hotel (D) . *(Bank PO)*
7. Yesterday I met (A)/ a man (B)/ who was blind with the right eye (C).
8. The principal distributed (A)/ the sweet among our friends (B)/ who bade him forewell (C).
9. As per the invitation care (A)/ Rahim marries with Sayra (B)/ on 13 th December Monday (C) .
10. The debacle of the congress party (A)/ admit no other explanation (B)/ than its (C)/ poor performance during the last five years (D).
11. The society does not (A)/ hold itself responsible (B)/ for the loss or damage to (C)/ any item (D). *(BSRB)*
12. In spite of being (A)/ very busy at project work (B)/ he saves timer (C)/ to the relatives (D).
13. Some persons (A)/ get promotions (B)/ even if they are not (C)/ worthy for them (D) *(BSRB)*
14. While he was returning (A)/ from the office (B)/ a man attacked on (C)/ him with a dagger (D).
15. The decline of her moral (A)/ was caused by a lot of (B)/ factors that were once (C)/ fascinating to her (D).
16. He took me to a restra (A)/ and ordered for two cups (B)/ of cold coffee (C)/ which the waiter brought in an hour (D).
17. There are some animals (A)/ than can live both in water and land (C)/ without any difficulty (D). *(RRB)*
18. During his tour (A)/ to the south (B)/ he visited not only to Madras (C)/ but also Karnataka (D). *(RRB)*
19. The President Mr. Kalam (A)/ is much sought after (B)/ by school students and (C)/ is invited for many functions (D).
20. His mother is not well (A)/ but he (B)/ does not look for her/(C) properly (D) . *(BSRB)*
21. We may have to await for (A)/ a new political revival (B)/ to eradicate the (C)/ corruption from our economy.
22. When she was (A)/ in jail (B)/ she was debarred to send (C)/ a letter even to her son (D) .
23. Despite of the best efforts (A)/ put by the doctors (B)/ the condition of the patient (C)/ is detereorating from bad to worse (D).
24. The militant yielded for (A)/ the temptation and fell (B)/ into the trap (C)/ of police (D). *(RRB)*

25. Many people in India (A)/ are dying from hunger (B)/ but government seems (C)/ to be ignorant of such crude fact (D).
26. In difficult time (A)/ she prefers keeping her counsel (B)/ rather than wandering (C)/ here and there for relief (D).
27. The persons who are (A)/ suffering from diabetes are (B)/ advised to substitute (C)/ saccharin by sugar (D). ***(Bank PO)***
28. He always says (A)/ that he prefers to go (B)/ home to stay in (C)/ a hotel at night (D). ***(BSRB)***
29. Hardly had we settled down (A)/ for the rest (B)/ when we were startled by the (C)/ strange sound of trumpets (D).
30. He was able to (A)/ free himself with (B)/ the debts by (C)/ working day and night (D).

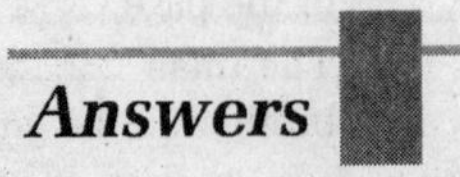

Answers

1. (C) Delete 'into'
2. (C) Delete 'to'
3. (A) Change it to 'apparent to'
4. (A) Change it to 'proposed to'
5. (C) Change among to between. Between is used for two.
6. (D) and about the poor
7. (C) Correct phrase is 'blind in'
8. (B) Replace 'among' by 'amongst'
9. (B)Delete with.
10. (B) Place of after admits.
11. (C) Place 'of' after 'loss'
12. (D) Change 'to' by 'for'
13. (D) Place of after worthy
14. (C) Delete 'on'
15. (A) Change 'decline of' to 'decline in'
16. (B) Delete 'for' after order
17. (C) Place on before 'land'
18. (C) Delete 'to' Madras
19. (D) Replace 'for' by 'to'
20. (C) Change 'look for' by 'look after'
21. (A) Delete for after await.
22. (C) debarred from sending is correct.
23. (A) Do not use of with despite. Despite means in spite of
24. (A) Change it to 'yielded to'
25. (B) dying of hunger is correct.
26. (C) Change than by 'to'
27. (D) Change 'by' to 'for'
28. (C) Change 'to stay in' by 'rather than stay in'. She prefers to write rather than to speak on telephone.
29. (C) Change 'startled by' to 'startled at'.
30. (B) Change 'with' to 'from'.

Unit

15

Conjunctions

What Is a Conjunction?

A **conjunction** is a word that joins words, phrases, clauses or sentences conjunctions can also be defined as a word that joins clauses together to make a sentence, and shows how the meanings of the clauses relate to each other. A conjunction is also called a joiner, connector or sentence linker.

Kinds of Conjunction

There are three types of conjunctions : **coordinating** conjunctions, **subordinating** conjunctions and **correlative** conjunctions.

Coordinating Conjunctions

Coordinating conjunctions may join single words, or they may join groups of words, but they always join elements of same kind : either subject and subject, or verb phrase and verb phrase, or sentence and sentence.

The most commonly used coordinating conjunctions are: **for, and, nor, but, or, yet, so.** Remember the acronym FANBOYS. Each of the letters in this word is the first letter of one of the coordinating conjunctions.

Subordinating Conjunctions

Subordinating conjunctions, the largest class of conjunctions, connect subordinate clauses to a main clause. A subordinating conjunction comes at the beginning of a subordinate clause and establishes a relationship between the dependent clause and the rest of the sentence. It also turns the clause into something that depends on the rest of the sentence for its meaning. Some most commonly used subordinating conjunctions are; *after, although, as, as if, as long as, as though, because, before, even if, even though, if, if only, in order that, now that, after, although, as, as if, as long as, as though, because, before, even if, even though, if, if only, in order that, now that, once, rather than, since, so that, than, that, though, till, unless, until, when, whenever, where, whereas, wherever, while, once, rather than, since, so that, than, that, though, till, unless, until, when, whenever, where, whereas, wherever, while.*

Correlative Conjunctions

Correlative conjunctions also connect sentence elements of the same kind. However, unlike coordinating conjunctions, correlative conjunctions are always used in pairs. Such conjunctions are *either.......or, neither....... nor, both.......and, whether ... or, not only........but also.*

When joining singular and plural subjects, the subject closest to the verb determines whether the verb is singular or plural.

Use of Coordinating Conjunction AND

To suggest that one work is sequential to another.

Kamini sent in her applications and waited by the phone for a response.

To suggest that one work is the result of another.

Ramesh heard the weather report and promptly went to his house.

To suggest that one idea is in contrast to another (frequently replaced by but in this usage).

Naresh is brilliant and Shalini has a pleasant smile.

To reflect an element of surprise (sometimes replaced by yet in this usage).

Mumbai is a rich city and suffers from many elements of urban blight.

To reflect that one clause is conditionally dependent upon another (usually the first clause is an imperative).

(a) Use your credit cards without care and you'll soon find yourself deep in debt.

(b) Waste your time carelessly and you will soon find yourself out of time to prepare for the examinations.

To suggest a kind of comment on the first clause.

Rajesh became addicted to gambling and that surprised no one who knew him.

BUT

To reflect a contrast that is unexpected in light of the first clause.

Jony lost a fortune in the stock market, but he still seems able to live quite comfortably.

To reflect in an affirmative sense what the first part of the sentence implied in a negative way (sometimes replaced by on the contrary).

The club never invested foolishly, but used the services of some intelligent counsellors.

To connect two ideas with the meaning of with the exception of (and then the second word takes over as subject).

Everybody but Jai Kishan is trying out for the team.

OR

To suggest that only one possibility can be realised, excluding one or the other.

You study hard for this exam or you will not get good marks.

To suggest the inclusive combination of alternatives.

We can cook dinner tonight, or we can just eat leftovers.

To suggest a refinement of the first clause.

Saraswati College is the premier all-girls' college in the State, or so it seems to most Saraswati College alumnae.

To suggest a restatement or correction of the first part of the sentence.

There are no tigers in this sanctuary, or so our guide tells us.

To suggest a negative condition.

Sayings of one of the freedom fighters was very imoportant 'do or die'.

To suggest a negative alternative without the use of an imperative (see use of and above).

They must approve his political style or they wouldn't keep electing him chairman.

NOR

The conjunction nor is not used as often as the other conjunctions. It is commonly used in the correlative pair, neither-nor (see below).

(a) He is neither sane nor intelligent.

(b) That is neither what I said nor what I wanted to say.

Nor can also be used with other negative expressions.

(c) That is not what I wanted to say, nor should you interpret my statement as an admission of guilt.

YET

The word **Yet** functions sometimes as an adverb. It can be used reflecting several meanings

1. in addition ('yet another cause of trouble' or 'a simple yet noble woman')
2. even ('yet more expensive')
3. still ('he is yet a novice')
4. eventually ('they may yet win')
5. so soon as now ('he's not here yet').

Yet also functions as a coordinating conjunction meaning something like 'nevertheless' or 'but.'

(a) Jack plays basketball well, yet his favourite sport is cricket.

(b) The visitors complained a lot about the heat, yet they continued to play golf here every day.

For

The word **For** is most often used as a preposition. It is also used, as a coordinating conjunction. Beginning a sentence with the conjunction 'for' should be avoided. Its function is to introduce the reason for the preceding clause.

(a) Ramesh thought he had a good chance to get the job, for his uncle was on the company's board of directors.

(b) Most of the visitors were happy just relaxing under the shade, for it had been a long, dusty journey on the cart.

SO

So, sometimes connects two independent clauses along with a comma, but sometimes it doesn't. For instance, in this sentence:

(a) He is not the only olympic athlete in his family, so are his brother, sister, and his niece Chetna.

Here the word so means 'as well' or 'in addition,'.

In the following sentence, 'so' means 'therefore,' the conjunction and the comma are adequate to the task.

(b) She has always been nervous in large gatherings, so it is no surprise that she avoids crowds of her fans.

When 'so' is used at the beginning of a sentence, it will act as a kind of summing up word, in that case comma is used after it as following:

(c) So, the judge peremptorily removed the child from the custody of the claimants.

Use of Subordinating Conjunctions

A **subordinating conjunction** comes at the beginning of a subordinate clause and establishes the relationship between the dependent clause and the rest of the sentence. Some of he subordinating conjunctions like : after, before, since, etc. are also prepositions, but as subordinators they are being used to introduce a clause and to subordinate the following clause to the main clause .

Always put a comma at the end of the adverbial phrase when it precedes the main clause.

Look at the following subordinate conjunctions and their use with different meanings:

as = because, when

(a) **because: As** he is my friend, I cooperate with him.

(b) **when: We** watched **as** the train departed.

after = later in time

(c) **Later in time: After** the train left, I went to my office directly.

Although or Though

(a) **In spite of the fact that : Although** he is poor, he is honest.

Before

(a) **Earlier than:** I arrived **before** the shops were open.

Because

(a) **For the reason that:** We had to wait, **because** the chief guest arrived late.

For

(a) **For, because** : He is happy, **for** he has a good job.

If

(a) **On condition** : **If** he is here, we will meet him.

Lest

(a) **For fear that:** We ran **lest** we should miss the train.

Providing or Provided

(a) **On condition that:** All will be well, **provided** you take interest in the function.

since = from a past time, as, because

(a) **From a past time:** I have been here **since** he came.

(b) **As, because:** Since you are here, we can discuss the matter.

So or **so that = consequently, in order that**

(a) **Consequently** : It was raining, so we did not go shopping.

(b) **In order that:** I am saving money **so** I can buy a car.

Supposing

(a) **If : Supposing** a monkey comes here, what will you do?

Than

(a) **Used in comparisons:** He is taller **than** you.

Unless

(a) **Except when, if not: Unless** he works hard, he will not succeed.

Until or till

(a) **Up to the time when:** I will wait **until** he comes. **whereas = because, on the other hand**

(a) **Because : Whereas** this is the temple, it is open to everyone.

(b) **On the other hand:** He is short, **whereas** you are tall.

Whether

(a) **If** : I do not know **whether** I was invited.
While = at the time when, on the other hand, although.

(a) **At the time when : While** it was raining, we were watching a movie.

(b) **On the other hand :** He is poor, **while** his friend is rich.

(c) **Although : While** I am not an expert, I will do my best.

In addition, the following phrases are often used at the beginning of subordinate clauses.

As if

(a) **In a similar way:** She behaves **as if** she is my sister.
as long as = if, while

(a) **If : As long as** we work fast, we can finish the work today.

(b) **While** : She has lived there **as long as** I have known her.

As soon as

(a) **Immediately when** : Inform me **as soon as** you reach there.

As though

(a) **In a similar way** : It looks **as though** it will rain today.

Even if

(a) **In spite of a possibility** : I am going out **even if** it rains.

In case

(a) **Because of a possibility** : Take a sweater **in case** it gets cold.

Or else

(a) **Otherwise** : Please be careful, **or else** you may have an accident.

So as to

(a) **In order to:** I hurried **so as to** be on time.

Some words, such as after, before, since and until may function as prepositions as well as subordinate conjunctions. However it should be noted that in some cases different words must be used as prepositions and subordinate conjunctions, in order to express similar meanings.

Use of Correlative Conjunctions

Correlative conjunctions are used in pairs, in order to show the relationship between the ideas expressed in different parts of a sentence. Correlative conjunctions join various sentence elements that must be grammatically equal.

The most commonly used correlative conjunctions are **both ... and, either ... or and neither ... nor, hardly ... when, not only ... but also,** etc. Note that in the construction **if ... then,** the word **then** can usually be omitted.

Correlative Conjunctions

both ... and	She is both intelligent and liberal.
either ... or	I will either go for a picnic or take rest.
neither ... nor	She is neither rich nor good natured.
hardly ... when	He had hardly begun to work, when it started raining.
if ... then	If that is true, then what happened can't be imagined.
no sooner ... than	No sooner had I reached the station, than the train arrived.
not only ... but also	She is not only clever, but also intelligent.
rather ... than	I would rather go swimming than go to the hospital.

Important : Parallel Construction

Correlative conjunctions (both, and; not, but; not only, but also; either, or; first, second, third; and the like) should be followed by the same grammatical construction. Thus, whenever possible, parallel construction should be employed when correlative conjunctions are used. Many violations of this rule can be corrected by rearranging the sentence. The repetition of a particular grammatical construction is often referred to as **parallel construction**. This is illustrated in the following examples.

(a) I am **neither** happy **nor** excited.

(b) The resort contains open bars, swimming pools and a library.

In the first example, the two phrases **neither happy** and **nor excited** show parallel construction. In the second example, the three phrases open bars, swimming pools and a library also show parallel construction.

Correlative Conjunctions and Parallel Constructions

Parallel construction should always be employed when correlative conjunctions are used. In the following example, the correlative conjunctions are printed in bold type.

She has **both** a good education, **and** she has good work habits. *Incorrect*

and good work habits. *Correct*

In first sentence **both** and **and** are followed by different grammatical constructions, so it is an incorrect sentence. **Both** is followed by the phrase **a good education**; whereas and is followed by the clause **he has good work habits**. The second sentence has been corrected by changing the clause **he has good work habits** into the phrase **good work habits**.

Conjunctive Adverbs

The **conjunctive adverbs** such as : however, moreover, nevertheless, consequently, as a result are used to create complex relationships between ideas. They show logical relationships between two independent sentences or between sections of paragraphs.

Such most commonly used conjunctive adverbs are : also, hence, however, still ,likewise, otherwise, therefore, conversely, rather, consequently, furthermore, nevertheless, instead, moreover, then, thus, meanwhile, accordingly.

Some Specific Conjunctions

'Neither.......nor.........nor........nor' and 'Either ....or........or........or'

Some grammarians feel that only one 'nor' can be used with 'neither' and only one 'or' can be used with 'either'. Please note the views of Mr Vallins in this matter.

The correct correlatives are 'either.....or' and 'neither.....nor'. Strictly speaking, we should not add another 'or' or 'nor' since either and neither imply two and two only.

But T.S. Eliot and H. Walker have opined differently.

(a) Either from the moralists point of view, or from the theologian's point of view or from the psychologist's point of view, or from that of the political philosopher, or judging by the ordinary standards of likeableness in human beings, Milton is unsatisfactory. *T.S. Eliot.*

(b) Neither the brilliancy of Haglitt, nor the harmony of De Quincey, nor the vigour of Macaulay, nor the eloquence of Ruskin, nor the purity of Goldsmith could for a moment be thought capable of expressing the meaning of lamb. *H. Walker.*

'No', 'Not' and 'Never'........or

Use **'or'** (but not 'nor') with not/never/no in a sentence if an alternative conjunction is needed.

(a) I have no chair or stool.

(b) I have never read about her or heard of her.

(c) She does not speak or weep.

(d) He did not say or write anything.

That

That is not used in 'direct narration'. It is usually used in 'indirect narration'.

(a) He said to me, 'That I will go there'. *Incorrect*

He told me that he would go there. *Correct*

After some verbs such as; agree, assert, avert, assume, hold, calculate, conceive, learn, maintain, state, **reckon**, suggest, understand, etc. it is incorrect to omit **'that'**.

Incorrect	Correct
I agree your proposal is very good.	I agree that your proposal is very good.
He asserted he could do that.	He asserted that he could do that.
He suggested we should go there.	He suggested that we should go there.

After some verbs such as; believe, hope, suppose, think, presume, afraid of, etc., it is appropriate to omit 'that'.

(a) I hope, he is right.
(b) We presume you are innocent.
(c) I suppose you have a good dictionary.
(d) I think he will come.

Omitting 'That'

The word **That** is used as a conjunction to connect a subordinate clause to a preceding verb. In this construction that is sometimes called the 'expletive that'. Indeed, the word is often omitted to good effect, but the very fact of easy omission causes some editors to take out the red pen and strike out the conjunction 'that' wherever it appears. In the following sentences, we can happily omit that (or keep it, depending on how the sentence sounds to us):

(a) Isabel knew [that] she was about to be fired.
(b) She definitely felt [that] her fellow employees hadn't supported her.
(c) I hope [that] she doesn't blame me.

Sometimes omitting the 'that' creates a break in the flow of a sentence, a break that can be adequately bridged with the use of a comma.

(a) The problem is, that production in her department has dropped.
(b) Remember, we didn't have these problems before she started working here.

As a general rule, if the sentence feels just as good without 'that', if no ambiguity results from its omission, if the sentence is more efficient or elegant without it, then we can safely omit that.

'However' and 'But'

However and **but** should never be used together in a sentence.

Incorrect	Correct
But his behavior, however has not changed.	His behavior however has not changed.
But that, however is not repairable.	But that is not repairable.

'Though', 'Although' and 'Even Though'

Though, although and even though are used to show a contrast between two clauses. Yet (not 'but') is used with 'though/although'.

(a) Our new neighbours are quite nice (this is good) though their two dogs bark all day long. (this isn't good.)

We can use though or although with no difference in meaning. But, some differences are:

Though is more common than although in conversation or writing.

Though (but not although) can come at the end of a sentence.

(a) My new bike is really fast. I don't like the colour, though.

Though (but not although) can also be used as an adverb.

(b) I'm not good at reasoning but I can help you with your geography, though, if you want.

The meaning of **though** is similar to however, but is much more common than however in conversation.

Even though can be used to make the contrast between two clauses stronger.

(a) My father got back from work really late, even though he had promised to take mum to the cinema.
(b) Although he is poor, yet he is honest.
(c) Though he is poor, he is honest.

Until/Unless

Until is used in reference to 'time' while unless refers to a condition.

(a) I will stay here until you return.
(b) He will wait until the train arrives.
(c) He can't succeed unless he works hard.
(d) You cannot achieve your goal unless you try for that.

'As', 'When' and 'While'

We can use as, when or while in situations or actions that take place simultaneously. Note the following points :

1. **We can use any of the these words to introduce a longer background action or situation, which is/was going on when something else also happens/ happened.**

(a) As I was walking down the street I saw Jack driving a jeep.

(b) The telephone always rings when you are having a bath.

(c) While they were playing cards somebody broke into the house.

As, when and **while** clauses can be used at the beginning or end of sentences, though **as** clause usually comes at the beginning.

A continuous tense is usually used for the longer background action or situation (was walking, are having, were playing). But **as** and **while** can be used with a simple tense especially with a verb like sit, lie or grow which refers to a continuous action or state.

(a) As I sat reading the paper the door opened.

2. We use while to say that two long actions or situation happened at the same time. We can use continuous or simple tenses.

(a) While you were reading the paper, I was watching TV.

(b) John cleaned the house while I watched TV.

As is used (with simple tenses) to talk about two situations which grow or change together.

(a) As he gets older he gets more liberal.

When is used to refer to ages and periods of life.

(a) When I was a child we wore half pants. (Not As : while I was a child ....)

(b) His father died when he was fourteen. (Not : ....while he was fourteen.)

3. As is used to denote two short actions or events that happened at the same time.

(a) **As** I opened my eyes I heard a loud noise.

(b) She always arrives **just as** I start work.

'As if' and 'As though'

1. As if and as though mean the same. We use them to say what a situation seems like.

(a) It looks as if/though it's going to rain.

(b) I felt as if/though I was dying.

(c) She was acting as if/though she was the owner.

2. We can use a past tense with a present meaning after as if or though. This shows that a comparison is unreal.

(a) She looks as if she's rich. (Perhaps she is rich.)

(b) He behaves as if he owned the palace. (But he doesn't own it.)

(c) He talks as if he was rich. (But he is not.)

(d) He orders me as if I were his servant.(But I am not.)

3. We use past perfect after, as if or as though, when referring to a real or imaginary action in the past.

(a) She talks about New York as if she had been there itself.

(b) He seems/seemed as though he hadn't had a nice meal for many days.

'Because', 'As' and 'Since'

Because, As and **Since** are used to answer the question: 'Why?' They join two clauses in the same sentence.

(a) I lost my job because I was often late.

(b) Ram resigned because he wanted to spend more time with his family.

Also, **because**, **as** and **since** show the relationship between the two clauses.

(a) Why did you resign from such a well-paid job, Ram ?

(b) **Because** I wanted to spend more time with my family.

Because is more common than 'as' and 'since' when the 'reason' is the most important thing. The **because clause** is usually placed after the main clause.

(a) I went to Madras for a holiday last October because I knew it would be warm and sunny every day I was there.

As and **since** are used when the reason is already well-known and/or less important. The **'as'** or **'since'** clause often comes at the beginning of the sentence and is separated from the main clause by a comma.

(a) As my family had finished dinner when I got home, I went to this really good beer bar. (I'm telling you about the beer bar. It's not so important 'why' I went there.)

(b) Since it's your birthday, I'll make you breakfast in bed. (I'm going to make you breakfast. (I know, and you know, it's your birthday) Since I have no money, I can't go to the movie.

» Exercises

Exercise 1

Join the following pairs of sentences using the connectors given in brackets

1. My father is ill. My wife is ill. (both............and)
2. The teacher was not in the class. The monitor was not in the class. (neither............nor)
3. He is poor. He is honest. (thought...........yet)
4. The book may be in the bag. It may be in the cupboard. (either ...... or)
5. There was a violent storm. Many trees were uprooted. (such......that)
6. The doctor reached. The patient died. (hardly .... when)
7. He is strong. He is brave. (not only .... but also)
8. Do not be a borrower. Do not be a lender. (neither............nor)
9. It was very dark. We could see nothing. (so............. that)
10. The thief saw the policeman. He ran away at once. (no sooner.... than)

Solutions

1. Both my father and my wife are ill.
2. Neither the teacher nor the monitor was in the class.
3. Though he is poor,yet he is honest.
4. The book may be either in the bag or in the cupboard.
5. There was such a violent storm that many trees were uprooted.
6. The doctor had hardly reached when the patient died.
7. He is not only strong but also brave.
8. Neither be a borrower nor be a lender.
9. It was so dark that we could see nothing.
10. No sooner did the policeman see the thief than he ran away.

Exercise 2

Combine each pair of sentences below into one sentence, choosing the right conjunction from the following

since, besides, lest, never the less, before, after, otherwise.

1. Walk carefully. You may fall.
2. It's raining. We won't play the match today.
3. Don't write.The bell has gone.
4. He was busy. He attended to me.
5. He is a rich man. He is an MP.

Solutions

1. Walk carefully lest you should fall.
2. Since it's raining,we won't play the match today.
3. Don't write after the bell has gone.
4. He was busy, nevertheless, he attended to me.
5. He is a rich man, besides,he is an M.P.

Exercise 3

Fill in the blanks by choosing the correct connector given in bracket

1. A student will fail ..... does not work hard. (because, if, until, though, unless)
2. He was late.........it was raining heavily. (while, after, so, that, when, because)
3. ....you have any doubt, please ask me. (in case, because,unless, until, though)
4. She is more intelligent .... her sister. (as, than, before, because, that)
5. She has changed a lot .... I saw her last. (when, before, while, as, since)
6. He could not get the prize, ... she tried hard for it. (yet, though, but, when, and)
7. We must leave now ...... it is getting dark. (as long as, as soon as, when, since)
8. I was taking a bath ... somebody rang the bell. (as, while, when, as soon as, than)
9. He failed in the examination;................, he didn't lose heart. (moreover, then,while, nevertheless, until)
10. She tried her best; ...., she couldn't succeed. (besides, in case, however, instead, as long as)

Solutions

1. if	2. because	3. In case
4. than	5. since	6. though
7. since	8. when	9. nevertheless
10. however		

Exercise 4

Fill in the blanks while choosing the correct connectors given in brackets

1. We want to respect our feelings................ , we should respect the feelings of others. (nevertheless, similarly, on the other hand)

2. We lost the key. We had .... to break the lock open. (still, for, therefore)
3. His parents were transferred to Agra ....he was five years old. (when, since, while)
4. A mechanic was sent for .... our car broke down. (since, as soon as, because)
5. The rent being very high he will not take that house; ....it is very far away from his office. (because, moreover, still)
6. The police asked the suspect question after question, ...he did not open his mouth. (yet, still, however)
7. I have been to the hanging garden four times,.......I won't mind going there again. (but, nevertheless, however)
8. .... much I tried, I could not help him. (though, however, as)
9. My uncle left for Mexico.......I was six years old. (when, since, while)

Solutions

1. similarly	2. therefore	3. when
4. because	5. moreover	6. still
7. but	8. However	9. when

Exercise 5

Correct the following sentences

1. I could neither contact Lila nor Sarla.
2. Neither he plays nor reads.
3. She both accused me and my friend Shyam.
4. Ram not only built a temple but also a mosque.
5. He has visited both to New York and Mexico.
6. English is not only difficult to speak but also to write.
7. She is as much noted for her beauty as for her wisdom.
8. I have both visited America and Russia.
9. He neither knows me nor my wife.
10. Ramesh neither went to Jaipur nor Delhi.

Solutions

1. I could contact neither Lila nor Sarla.
2. He neither plays nor reads.
3. She accused both me and my friend Shyam.
4. Ram built not only a temple but also a mosque.
5. He has visited both to Newyork and to Mexico. or He has visited to both Newyork and Mexico.
6. English is difficult not only to speak but also to write.
7. She is noted as much for her beauty as for her wisdom.
8. I have visited both America and Russia.
9. He knows neither me nor my wife.
10. Ramesh went neither to Jaipur nor to Delhi.

Exercise 6

Correct the following sentences

1. No sooner had he reached the station when the train arrived.
2. Though he is poor but he is trustworthly.
3. Hardly had she left the hospital, than it began to rain.
4. He had neither a car or a scooter.
5. There was much disturbance both in Jammu as well as in Pahalgaon.
6. One cannot be both present at New Delhi as well as at Jaipur.
7. He cannot either read nor write English.
8. She cannot run nor walk.
9. He has not any book nor any copy.
10. I have never seen her nor heard of her.

Solutions

1. No sooner had he reached the station than the train arrived.
2. Though he is poor yet he is trustworthly.
3. Hardly had she left the hospital, when it began to rain.
4. He had neither a car nor a scooter.
5. There was much disturbance both in Jammu and in Pahalgaon.
6. One cannot be present both at New Delhi and at Jaipur.
7. He cannot either read or write English.
8. She çannot run or walk.
9. He has not any book or copy.
10. I have never seen her or heard of her.

Exercise 7

Correct the following sentences

1. I do not know that when she will go.
2. I cannot say that where he is working nowadays.
3. I understand she will attend the function.
4. I hope that you are well now.
5. I can assert it is right.
6. I cannot explain that why I like her so much.
7. I asked my assistant that bring a chair and my mobile.
8. I agree it is a good oportunity to investment the money.
9. As she started late, she will miss the train.
10. Since Ram is a poor fellow, he couldn't buy a new dress.
11. The reason is because he is not well.

Solutions

1. I do not know when she will go
2. I cannot say where he is working nowadays.

3. I understand that she will attend the function.
4. I hope you are well now.
5. I can assert that it is right.
6. I cannot explain why I like her so much.
7. I asked my assistant to bring a chair and my mobile.
8. I agree that it is a good oportunity to investment the money.
9. As she started late, she missed the train.
10. Since Ram is a poor fellow he can't buy a new dress.
11. The reason is that he is not well.

Exercise 8

1. It was generally doubted that India would permit the use of her soil.
2. It is not doubtful whether she will atend the party.
3. Is there any doubt whether she will come ?
4. Keep your body fit like I do.
5. You are as dear to me as her.
6. Until he works hard, he can't pass.
7. Take an umbrella in case it may rain.
8. You wait here unless the train arrives.
9. You will succeed, if you will work hard.
10. It I had wings, I will fly to london.
11. It I won a lottery, I will buy a big house.
12. It he had worked hard, he would pass.

Solutions

1. It was generally doubted whether India would permit the use of her soil.
2. It is not doubtful that she will atend the party.
3. Is there any doubt that she will come ?
4. Keep your body fit like me or Keep your body fit as I do.
5. You are as dear to me as she.
6. Unless he works hard, he can't pass.
7. Take an umbrella in case it rains.
8. You wait here until the train arrives.
9. You will succeed, if you work hard.
10. It I had wings, I would fly to london.
11. It I won a lottery, I would buy a big house.
12. It he had worked hard, he would have pass.

Exercise 9

1. It is a year since I have met her.
2. It is a month since she has left for USA.
3. He speaks as if he was the master.
4. Ram orders as though he would be a millionaire.
5. Five years have passed since I had seen her.
6. A year passed since his wife died.
7. I was playing when he was watching TV.
8. I will go when he will come.
9. I went there while he awoke.
10. I will meet you before I shall leave for home.

Solutions

1. It is a year since I met her.
2. It is a month since she left for USA.
3. He speaks as if he were the master.
4. Ram orders as though he were a millionaire.
5. Five years have passed since I saw her.
6. A year has passed since his wife died.
7. I was playing while he was watching TV.
8. I will go when he comes.
9. I went there when he awoke.
10. I will meet you before I leave for home.

Spotting the Errors

Find the errors and justify your answers

1. She was not (A)/so well versed in English (B)/that they (C)/had expected (D). ***(RRB)***
2. He not only comes (A)/here for having lunch (B)/but also for having a glimpse of (C)/the beautiful sales girls (D).
3. I cannot permit you (A)/to leave the class (B)/unless the teacher comes (C)/and instructs me in the matter (D). ***(Bank PO)***
4. The patient would not (A)/have died (B)/when the doctor had (C)/come in time (D). ***(MBA Entrance)***
5. Three years have passed (A)/that I returned from (B)/USA and settled here (C). ***(RRB)***
6. The captain asked (A)/the players to go (B)/to market and buy some fruits (C)/as Apples, Oranges, Bananas etc (D).
7. Both the rich (A)/along with the poor (B)/are responsible for a great many vices (C)/with which our country is inflicted (D).

8. Since the festival of Diwali is approaching (A)/so my son has bought (B)/many fireworks (C)/as rockets, crackers etc. (D).
9. The thief had (A)/hardly put the cash (B)/in his pocket (C)/then the owner woke up (D). ***(MBA Entrance)***
10. No sooner did we (A)/find out a solution (B)/to the problem (C)/when another problem cropped up (D). ***(MBA Entrance)***
11. She has lots of money (A)/and she dare not (B)/purchase a new car (C). ***(Bank PO)***
12. She is not only (A)/sympathetic to the rich patients (B)/but also to the poor ones (C).
13. Because she is intelligent (A)/therefore she secures highest marks (B)/in her class (C).
14. It was almost five months ago (A)/since she wrote a letter (B)/to me (C)/to remind me of my promise (D).
15. The inspector was doubtful (A)/that the man who had been run over (B)/by the truck had (C)/lain there for more than a day (D).
16. He instructed me (A)/that I should do (B)/all the work as quickly (C)/like him (D). ***(Bank PO)***
17. Seldom or (A)/ever have I sent (B)/a beggar away without (C)/giving him something (D).
18. Seldom or ever (A)/have I tried my (B)/best to help my friends (C)/who are in need (D). ***(RRB)***
19. The teacher advised (A)/the students to (B)/go through the notes as many times as possible (C)/lest they would fail (D).
20. He asked me (A)/that why I was not appearing (B) in the examination (C).
21. Most of the founding fathers (A)/of our constitution are (B)/so reverend as Ambedkar (C)/if not more (D). ***(RRB)***
22. I don't know (A)/if any of the members (B)/of the society is conspiring (C)/against the chairman or not (D). ***(Bank PO)***
23. This is the same dog (A)/which bit her (B)/while she was going (C)/to the hospital (D).
24. This is not (A)/such a big problem (B)/which cannot be solved (C)/with some efforts (D). ***(BSRB)***
25. As he is (A)/a perfectionist (B)/so he always insists (C)/on regular practice (D). ***(BSRB)***

» Answers

1. (C) Replace 'that' by 'as'. The structure of the sentence is 'so....as'.
2. (A) It should be 'here not only for having lunch'.
3. (C) Replace 'unless' by 'until'.
4. (C) Replace 'when' by 'if'.
5. (A) Replace 'that' by 'since'. In perfect tence 'since' is used for point of time and 'for' is used for period of time.
6. (D) Replace 'as' by 'like'.
7. (B) Replace 'along with the' by 'and'.
8. (D) Replace 'as' by 'like'.
9. (D) Replace 'than' by 'when'.
10. (D) Replace 'when' by 'than'.
11. (B) Replace 'and' by 'but'.
12. (A) Use 'not only' before 'to the rich'.
13. (B) Use of 'therefore' is incorrect .
14. (B) Replace 'since' by 'that'. The sentence is of past indefinite.
15. (B) Replace 'that' by 'whether'.
16. (D) Replace 'like him' by 'as he'.
17. (B) Replace 'ever' by 'never'.
18. (A) Replace 'or' by 'if'.
19. (D) Replace 'would' by 'should'. Use should with lest.
20. (B) Delete 'that'.
21. (C) Replace 'so' by 'as'.
    Rahim is not so intelligent as Shyam.
    Rahim is as intelligent as Shyam.
22. (B) Replace 'if' by 'whether'. The sentence construction is : whether ...... as.
23. (B) Replace 'which' by 'that'.
    This is the same chair that was missing.
24. (C) Replace 'which' by 'as'. Such is followed by as or that. See the following examples :
    (a) Such + noun + as
    He is not such a person as I thought.
    (b) Such. that
    His behaviour was such that I felt hurt.
    (c) Such+ as + infinitive
    Her ailment is not such as to cause wories.
25. (C) Delete 'so'.

» Unit

16

Transformation of Sentences

Transformation of a sentence means to change it from one grammatical form to another, without changing its meaning. A sentence can be transformed to another grammatical form in various ways.

Ways of Transformation

Interchanging degree of adjective We can transform sentences by changing the degree of adjective in the following ways:

There are three degrees of adjectives:

1. Positive 2. Comparative
3. Superlative

Changing positive to comparative

Positive degree is used in three structures : Type-I : as..........as, Type-II : so...........as, Type-III : no other........as.........as.

Type-I : as........as

(a) Hira is as tall as Ram. *Positive*
Ram is not taller than Hira. *Comparative*

(b) Shalu is as intelligent as Ram. *Positive*
Ram is not more intelligent than Shalu. *Comparative*

Type-II : so..........as

(a) Ram is not so strong as Shyam. *Positive*
Shyam is stronger than Ram. *Comparative*

(b) Sita is not so beautiful as Rani. *Positive*
Rani is more beautiful than Sita. *Comparative*

Type-III : no other.......as.........as

(a) No other city in Rajasthan is as beautiful as Jaipur. *Positive*
Jaipur is more beautiful than any other city in Rajasthan. *Comparative*

(b) No other student in college is as strong as Rahim. *Positive*
Rahim is stronger than any other student in college. *Comparative*

Interchange of positive, comparative and superlative

(a) This is the most beautiful building in our town. *Superlative*
This is more beautiful than any other building in our town. *Comparative*
No other building in our town is so beautiful as this. *Positive*

(b) Ramesh is the strongest man in the village. *Superlative*
Ramesh is stronger than any other man in the village. *Comparative*
No other man in the village is so strong as Ramesh. *Positive*

Structure : one of the + superlative.

(a) Kalidas was one of the greatest poets. *Superlative*
Kalidas was greater than most other poets. *Comparative*
Very few other poets were as great as kalidas. *Positive*

Removal of adverb 'too'

Too means excess. The structure too....to, shows a negativity.

He is	too	weak	to run.
He is	so	weak	that he cannot run.
He was	too	tired	to do anything.
He was	so	tired	that he could not do anything.
The mountain is	too	high	to climb it up.
The mountain is	so	high	that one cannot climb it up.

Interchange of Affirmative and Negative Sentences

Using antonyms

Affirmative	Negative
He is a rich man.	He is not a poor man.
I am innocent.	I am not guilty.
The boss is always right.	The boss is never wrong.

Negative	Affirmative
He is not an honest person.	He is a dishonest person.
You do not trust him.	You distrust him.
He is not a wise fellow.	He is a foolish fellow.

Using double negatives

Affirmative	Negative
I love her.	I am not without love for her.
I have a car.	I am not without a car.

Negative	Affirmative
No gains without pains.	For gains one has to take pains.
I am not without money.	I have money.
He left no plan untried.	He tried every plan.

Using 'to fail'

Affirmative	Negative
He played the match.	He did not fail to play the match.
He delivered his speech.	He didn't fail to deliver his speech.
I saw the Taj Mahal.	I did not fail to see the Taj Mahal.

Miscellaneous sentences

Affirmative	Negative
Only the poor can beg like this.	None but the poor can beg like this.
Only a fool can say like this.	None but a fool can say like this.
As soon as I reached there,it started raining.	No sooner did I reach there than it started raining.
As soon as he saw the police, he ran away.	No sooner did he see the police.

Interchange of Assertive and Interrogative Sentences

Interrogative sentence beginning with helping verbs (auxiliaries)

Interrogative	Assertive
Am I not your friend?	I am your friend.
Isn't she beautiful?	She is beautiful.
Didn't I study?	I did study.
Can a blind see?	A blind can't see.
Don't I love her?	I love her.
Shall we ever forget you?	We shall never forget you.

Interrogative Sentence Beginning with Wh Words

Interrogative	Assertive
Who does not know Amitabh?	Everyone knows Amitabh.
Who does not love his mother?	Everyone loves his mother.
Who will tolerate such an insult?	No one will tolerate.
Who can live more than 100 years?	No one can live more than 100 year.
Who is more powerful than God?	No one is more powerful than God.

Interchange of Exclamatory and Assertive Sentences

Exclamatory sentences beginning with, What/How

Exclamatory	Assertive
What a bird it was!	It was a beautiful bird.
How fast she moves!	She moves very fast.
How hot it is!	It is very hot.
What a nice weather it was!	It was a very nice weather.

Exclamatory sentences beginning with, Oh that, O that, would that and alas

Exclamatory	Assertive
Would that I had not wasted my money!	I wish I had not wasted my money.
O that she were young again!	I wish that she were young again.

Exclamatory sentences beginning with Hurrah, Bravo and Well done

Exclamatory	Assertive
Bravo! You secured highest marks.	It is a matter of praise that you secured highest marks.
Hurrah! We have won the match.	It is a matter of joy that we have won the match.
Well done! you get selected!	It is matter of praise that you get selected.
Fie, fie! he is a thief.	It is a matter of contempt that he is a thief

Exclamatory sentences beginning with if only

(a) If only I could meet her once.
I wish to meet her once.
(b) If only I could once get selected.
I wish to get once selected.

Miscellaneous Sentences

Exclamatory	Assertive
How kind of you to help me!	You were kind enough to help me. It was kind of you to help me.
How foolish of him to abuse the chairman!	He was foolish enough to abuse the chairman. It was foolish of him to abuse the chairman.
A navyman! afraid of water .	It is strange that a navyman should be afraid of water.
An army man and such a coward!	It is shocking that an army man should be such a coward.
To think of our getting married!	It is strange that we should get married.

Interchange Parts of Speech

Changing into verb

Smoking is injurious to health. *Adjective*
Smoking injures health. *Verb*
You should give assistance to him. *Noun*
You should assist him. *Verb*
Graham Bell made the invention of telephone. *Noun*
Grahma Bell invented the telephone. *Verb*
Her action caused disgrace to the country. *Noun*
Her action disgraced the country. *Verb*
You must render help to her. *Noun*
You must help her. *Verb*

Changing into noun

Who discovered India? *Verb*
Who made the discovery of India? *Noun*
Who invented computer? *Verb*
Who made the invention of computer? *Noun*
Listen to him attentively. *Adverb*
Listen to him with attention. *Noun*
She is healthy. *Adjective*
She enjoys good healthy. *Noun*
Walk carefully. *Adverb*
Walk with care. *Noun*
He fought courageously. *Adverb*
He fought with courage. *Noun*

Changing into adjective

He confessed his guilt. *Noun*
He confessed that he was guilty. *Adjective*
Wine injures liver. *Verb*
Wine is injurious to liver. *Adjective*
Fortunately she escaped unhurt. *Adverb*
She was fortunate to escape unhurt. *Adjective*
He solved the puzzle easily. *Adverb*
It was easy for him to solve the puzzle. *Adjective*

Changing into adverb

(a) His success is sure. *Adjective*
He will surely succeed. *Adverb*
(b) He does not intend to speak. *Verb*
He does not speak intentionally. *Adverb*
(c) Sita sang a sweet song. *Adjective*
Sita sang a song sweetly. *Adverb*
(d) He fought with courage. *Noun*
He fought courageously. *Adverb*

Transformation of conditional sentences

(a) If you work hard, you will pass.
Unless you work hard you will not pass.
Work hard and you will pass.
Work hard in case you want to pass.
Should you work hard you would pass.
(b) Had he come to me, I would have helped him.

If he had come to me, I would have helped him.

(c) In case you support me, I will make a protest.
If you support me,I will make a protest.
Provided you support me, I will make a protest.

(d) One more try and you will achieve it.
If you make one more try, you will achieve it.

(e) If she does not turn up, you will get the job.
In case she doesn't turn up you will get the job.
Supposing she does not turn up, you will get the job.

Conversion of Simple/Compound/ Complex Sentences

Conversion of simple sentence into compound

A simple sentence has one principal clause and a compound sentence has two principal clauses which are joined together by a coordinating conjunction. A simple sentence can be converted into a compound sentence by enlarging a word or a phrase into a coordinate clause.

Simple	Compound
In spite of his poverty he is trustworthy.	He is poor yet he is trustworthy.
The sun having risen the fog disappeared.	The sun rose and the fog disappeared.
Besides being beautiful she is intelligent.	She is beautiful as well as she is intelligent.
The chief rewarded the officer for his excellent work.	The officer did excellent work and so the chief rewarded him.
Seeing a lion he fled away.	He saw a lion and he fled away.
Notwithstanding his problems he is trying again.	He has problems yet he is trying again.
You should work hard to achieve your gool.	You should work hard or you can't achieve your goal.
The officer punished the boy for his misbehaviour.	The boy misbehaved so the officer punished him.

Conversion of compound (double) sentences to simple sentences.

To change a compound sentence into simple, ensure that after conversion we have only one finite verb.

Compound	Simple
He finished his work and put away the tools.	Having finished his work he put away the tools.
Not only did her mother give her gift but her sister too.	Besides her mother giving her gift her sister also did the same.
She must not be late or she will be fined.	In the event of her being late she will be fined.
You must either pay the rent at once or vacate the godown.	Failing prompt payment the godown must be vacated by you.
You must eat or you cannot live.	You must eat to live.

Conversion of Compound Sentence into Complex Sentence

A compound sentence is composed of two simple sentences joined together by a coordinating conjunction. To convert a compound sentence into a complex one , we need to make one clause principal and another subordinate.

Compound	Complex
Run fast or you will miss the train.	Unless you run fast you will miss the train.
I am not well so I shall not come to the office.	I shall not come to the office as I am not well.
She was ill so I helped her.	I helped her because she was ill.
Check his room and you will find the money.	If you check his room you will find the money.
He is innocent and I know it.	I know that he is innocent.
She lost her child and she found it.	She found her child that she lost.

Conversion of Complex Sentences to Compound

To convert a complex sentence into a compound one, we need to use coordinating conjunction and the subordinate clause be changed to independent clause.

Complex	Compound
I am certain you have stolen my purse.	You have stolen my purse and of this I am certain.
I am glad that she has recovered from cholera.	She has recovered from cholera and I am glad of it.
We can prove that the sun rises in the east.	The the sun rises in the east and we can prove it.
I have found the bag that I had lost.	I had lost a bag but I have found it.
As soon as she got the message she left in a car.	She got the message and immediately she left in a car.
We sow so that we may reap.	We wish to reap so we sow.

Conversion of Simple Sentence into Complex Sentence

A simple sentence can be converted to a complex sentence by expanding a word or phrase into a subordinate clause. This clause may be a noun, adjective or adverb clause.

Simple	Complex
I know his address.	I know what his address is.
She accepted her guilt.	She accepted that she was guilty.
You should work hard to achieve your goal.	You should work hard so that you can achieve your goal.
I drink to enjoy.	I drink so that I can enjoy.
He is too poor to pay his fees.	He is so poor that he can't pay his fees.
This is my office.	This is the office where I work.

Conversion of Complex Sentences into Simple Sentences

While converting a complex sentence into simple sentence ensure that after conversion we have onlyone finite verb.

Noun clause

Complex	Simple
Tell me where you live.	Tell me your address.
It is informed that all students found with papers will be rusticated.	According to the information all students found with papers will be rusticated.
He commented how beautiful the girl was.	He commented on the girls's beauty.
How long he will stay is uncertain.	The duration of his stay is doubtful.

Adjective clause

Complex	Simple
I have no advice that I can offer her.	I have no advice to offer her.
We came upon the quarter where she lived.	We came upon hers quarter.
She died in the village where her parents were born.	She died in her parental village.
The time which is lost is lost for ever.	A lost time is lost for ever.

Adverb clause

Complex	Simple
The colonel was annoyed that I had not obeyed his orders.	The colonel was annoyed at my not having obeyed his orders.
You can eat as much as you like.	You can eat to your heart's content.
She will not pay unless she is forced.	She will pay only by force.
She has succeeded better than she hoped.	She has succeeded beyond her hopes.
He was so tired that he could not walk.	He was too tired to walk.

» Exercises

Exercise 1

Convert the following simple sentences into compound sentences **(RAS)**

1. The teacher punished the boy for disobedience.
2. Running at top speed, he got out of breath.
3. By his pleasant manners he gained many friends.
4. Raleigh, taking off his cloak politely, placed it in the muddy street.
5. In this tower sat the poet gazing on the sea.

Transforms the following sentences according of the directions given **[RPSC (RAS) Ajmer]**

6. If you do not take exercise, you will be ill.
   (Convert into a compound sentence)
7. The moment which is lost, is lost for ever.
   (Convert into a simple sentence)
8. Self-made men are always respected.
   (Convert into a complex sentence)
9. He will not pay unless he is compelled.
   (Convert into a simple sentence)
10. In the absence of the cat the mice will play.
    (Convert into a complex sentence)
11. To everyone's surprise, the enterprise completely failed.
    (Convert into a compound sentence.)
12. You must work hard to win the first prize.
    (Convert into a compound sentence)
13. He was very tired but he kept on working.
    (Convert into a simple sentence)
14. His silence proves his guilt.
    (Convert into a complex sentence)
15. Consult the dictionary and you will find the meaning of this word.
    (Convert into a complex sentence)

Solutions

1. The boy was disobedient, and so the teacher punished him.
2. He ran at top speed so he got out of breath.
3. He has pleasant manners and therefore he gained many friends.
4. Raleigh took off his cloak politely and placed it in the muddy street.
5. The poet sat in this tower and gazed on the sea.
6. Take exercise otherwise you will be ill.
7. The moment once lost is lost for ever.
8. The men who are self-made are always respected.
9. He will pay only under compulsion.
10. The mice will play when the cat is absent.
11. The enterprise completely failed and it surprised everyone.
12. You must work hard so that you many win the first prize.
13. In spite of being very tired he kept on working.
14. The fact that he is silent proves his guilt.Or
    His silence proves that he is guilty.
15. If you consult the dictionary you will find the meaning of this word.

Exercise 2

Join the following pairs into single sentences

[RPSC (RAS) Ajmer]

1. Storms may come. They may destroy the dam.
2. The girl has gone away. I wanted to marry her.
3. The king talked to a woman. The woman's four sons had been killed in the war.
4. He is very clever. He cannot be deceived.
5. Hiroshima was once a prosperous town. It is now a heap of ruins.
6. The moon rose. Their journey was not ended.

Solutions

1. Storms may come and destroy the dam.
2. I wanted to marry the girl who had gone away.
3. The king talked to the woman whose four sons had been killed in the war.
4. He is too clever to be deceived.
   Or He is so clever that he cannot be deceived.
5. Hiroshima, which was once a prosperous town, is now a heap of ruins.
6. The moon rose before the end of their journey.

Exercise 3

Rewrite the sentences using 'than'. (superlative to comparative degree)

1. Switzerland is the most beautiful country in the world. (use 'more beautiful')
2. Delhi is the biggest city of India. (use 'bigger')
3. Mahima is the most beautiful girl in the class. (use 'more beautiful')
4. Morning walk is the best exercise for us. (use 'better')
5. Anil Ambani is the richest man in India. (use 'richer')

Solutions

1. Switzerland is is more beautiful than any other country in the India.
2. Delhi is begger than any other city in the world.

3. Mahima is more beautiful than any other girl in the class.
4. Morning walk is better than any other exercise for us.
5. Anil Ambani is richer than any other man in India.

Exercise 4

Rewrite the sentences using 'as...............as' (Comparative to positive degree)

1. Nikita is taller than Babita. (use 'tall')
2. Reeta is more intelligent than Nita. (use 'intelligent')
3. America is richer than India. (use 'rich')
4. Kavita's hair is more beautiful than Vimla's hair. (use 'beautiful')
5. Alwar is larger than Tonk. (use 'large')
6. She is taller than any other girl in the school. (use 'tall')
7. Mohan is poorer than any other man in the village. (use 'poor')
8. My mother is more beautiful than any other lady in our colony. (use 'beautiful')
9. Ganga is more famous river than any other river in India.
10. Jodhpur is hotter than Shimla. (use 'hot')

Solutions

1. Babita is not as tall as Nikita.
2. Nita is not as intelligent as Reeta.
3. India is not so rich as America.
4. Vimla's hair is not as beautiful as Kavita's hair.
5. Tonk is not as large as Alwar.
6. No other girl in the school is as tall as she.
7. No other man in the village is as poor as Mohan.
8. No other lady in our colony is as beautiful as my mother.
9. No other river in India is as famous as Ganga.
10. Shimla is not as hot as Jodhapur.

Exercise 5

Change comparative to superlative

1. Subhash Chandra Bose was greater than any other leader of India. (use 'the greatest)
2. Kolkata is bigger than any other city of India. (use 'the biggest')
3. Iron is heavier than any other metal. (use 'the heaviest')
4. Everest is higher mountain in the world. (use 'the highest')
5. Sonu is fatter than any other boy in the house. (the fattest)
6. Rani is better than any other girl. (use 'the best')

Solutions

1. Subhash Chandra Bose was the greatest leader of India.
2. Kolkata is the biggest city of India.
3. Iron is the heaviest metal.
4. Everest is the highest mountain in the world.
5. Sonu is the fattest bay in the house.
6. Rani is the best girl.

Exercise 6

Interchange exclamatorry sentences to assertive sentences

1. How cute she is!
2. What a beautiful sight it is!
3. What a stupid question!
4. What a big building it is!
5. Oh that, I were the queen of Britain!
6. O that, I were a bird!
7. Alas! She died in an accident.
8. Bravo! You have done well.
9. Hurrah! I won the game.
10. What an attractive person he is!
11. What a good book it is!
12. How fast she reads!
13. What a fine weather it is!
14. What a sight it is!
15. How funny!
16. What a hut!
17. What a style!
18. Oh that, I had the wings of bird!
19. Oh, for a beautiful car to drive!
20. If I were Miss India!

Solutions

1. She is very cute.
2. It is a very beautiful sight.
3. The question is stupid.
4. It is a very big building.
5. I wish that I were the queen of Britain
6. I wish I were a bird.
7. It is sad that she died in an accident.
8. It is a matter of praise that you have done well.
9. It is joyful that I won the game.
10. He is a very attractive person.
11. It is a very good book.
12. She reads very fast.
13. It is very fine weather.
14. It is a lovely sight.
15. It is very funny.
16. It is a beautiful hut.
17. It is a good style.

18. I wish that I had the wings of bird.
19. I wish that I had a beautiful car to drive.
20. I wish that I were Miss-India.

Exercise 7

Use the following words as noun and as verb

1. close 2. court 3. back
4. head 5. light

Solutions

1. Close
The metting came to a close at 6 p.m. (Noun)
Please close the shop now. (Verb)
2. Court
I am going to attend the court of law tomorrow. (Noun)
She is regularly courting her boss. (Verb)
3. Back
He carried the load on his back. (Noun)
I am not going to back your arguments. (Verb)
4. Head
He has a big head full of white hair. (Noun)
She headed the list of investors. (Verb)
5. Light
There is no light in the corridor. (Noun)
Light the candle in the room. (Verb)

Exercise 8

Use the following words as noun and as adjective

1. fast 2. less 3. like
4. down 5. master

Solutions

1. Fast
She keeps fast on every Tuesday. (Noun)
He is a fast runner. (Adjective)
2. Less
I won't be contended with less. (Noun)
She paid less attention to sports. (Adjective)
3. Like
You cannot see her like again. (Noun)
They are man of like physic and stature. (Adjective)
4. Down
I have seen the ups and downs of business. (Noun)
The down train was very late yesterday. (Adjective)
5. Master
She is my master. (Noun)
He conceived a master strategy. (Adjective)

Exercise 9

Use the following words, as adverb and as adjective

1. round 2. next 3. near 4. well
5. slow

Solutions

1. Round
He brought her round to my point of view. (Adverb)
It is a round floor. (Adjective)
2. Next
What next are you planning? (Adverb)
I shall meet you at the next crossing. (Adjective)
3. Near
Come near and sit here. (Adverb)
She is my near relative. (Adjective)
4. Well
Well begun is half done. (Adverb)
You are well now. (Adjective)
5. Slow
She is working is a slow manner. (Adverb)
She is a slow worker. (Adjective)

Exercise 10

Transform the following simple sentences into compound sentences

1. He should work hard to pass the examination.
2. Besides making a promise, she keeps it.
3. For all the problems, he is happy.
4. The principal rusticated the boy for misbehaviour.
5. The sun having risen, the fog dispersed.
6. He did a brilliant death, leaving an example to the world.
7. Having finished his work, he went to market.
8. Owing to ill health, she could not prepare the breakfast.

Solutions

1. He should work hard or he will not pass the examination.
2. She not only makes a promise but also keeps it.
3. Though he is in great problems, yet he is happy.
4. The boy misbehaved so the principal rusticated him.
5. The Sun rose and the fog dispersed.
6. He died a brilliant death and left an example to the world.
7. He finished his work and he went to market.
8. She was in ill health and so she could not prepare the breakfast.

Exercise 11

Transform the following simple sentences into complex sentence

1. She owed her success to my support.
2. Wise persons do not talk nonsense.
3. His silence proves his guilt.
4. Nonvegetorians are not allowed to enter into the temple.
5. Listen to the elders.
6. We are sure to win the match.
7. Intelligent students always succeed.
8. His ambition is to become an engineer.
9. Tell me your address.
10. I have no money to spend.

Solutions

1. It was due to my support that she succeeded.
2. The persons who are wise do not talk nonsense.
3. The fact that he is silent proves his quilt.
4. If you are a non vegetarian, you can't be allowed to enter into the temple.
5. Listen to what the elders say.
6. We are sure that we shall win the match.
7. The students who are intelligent always succeed.
8. His ambition is that he wants to become a doctor.
9. Tell me where you live.
10. I have no money that I can spend.

Exercise 12

Transform the following compound sentences into complex sentences

1. He is a poor man, but he is honest man.
2. My brother gave me a watch and I have lost it.
3. She was very tired and so she didn't cook food.
4. She is still in teens, but she has the wisdom of a matured woman.
5. I have lost the purse but I have found it now.
6. She is very affable and so I love her.
7. He is doing his best and I am sure of it.
8. Be sincere and you will be respected by every one.
9. Send the money in advance or you will not get the magazine.
10. You are a teetotaller and I know it.

Solutions

1. He is a honest man although he is poor.
2. I have lost the watch which my brother gave me.
3. As she was very tired, she didn't cook food.
4. She has the wisdom of a matured woman, although she is still is teens.
5. I have found the purse that I had lost.
6. I love her because she is very affable.
7. I am sure that he is doing his best.
8. If you are sincare, you will be respected by every one.
9. You will not get the magazine unless you send the money in advance.
10. I know that you are a teetotaller.

Exercise 13

Transform the following affirmative sentences into negative

1. My sister is wise.
2. That is impossible.
3. I shall always remember your kindness.
4. He is always careful.
5. A true man is always right.
6. Sita's voice is harsh.
7. We like him.
8. This student is dull.
9. We are innocent.
10. She is always present.
11. They won the game.
12. I always treat her fairly.
13. This knife is blunt.
14. Everyone was hopeful.

Solutions

1. My sister is not foolish.
2. That is not possible.
3. I shall not forget your kindness.
4. He is your never careless.
5. A true man is never wrong.
6. Sita's voice is not sweet.
7. We do not dislike him.
8. This student is not intelligent.
9. We are not guilty.
10. She is never absent.
11. They did not lose the game.
12. I never treat her badly.
13. This knife is not sharp.
14. No one was without hope.

Unit 17

Conditionals

Conditional sentences have two parts.

1. If clause 2. Main clause

There are three kinds of conditional sentences.

1. If clause in present tense
2. If clause in past tense
3. If clause in past perfect tense

(A) Conditional Sentence

If clause in present tense

1. If + simple present + future

The verb in the if clause is in the present tense and the verb in the main clause is in the future simple.

(a) If it rains, he will not come in time.
(b) If he runs fast, he will reach in time.

2. Instead of if + present + future we may have If + present + may/might (possibility)

(c) If the fog gets thicker, the plane may be late.

3. If + present + may (permission) or can (permission or ability)

(d) If it stops raining, we can go to the top. (permission or ability)
(e) If your ticket is confirmed you may/can board the plane. (permission)

4. If + present + must/should/could etc.

(f) If you want to lose weight eat less potatoes.
(g) If you meet Sita in the party, could you tell her to ring me?
(h) If you want to lose weight, you should eat less potatoes.

The if clause may come after future clause also.

(i) He will reach in time if he runs fast.
(j) The plane may be late if the fog gets thicker.

This type of sentences denotes that the action in the if clause is quite probable.

The meaning here is present or future but the verb in the if clause is in present.

5. If + present + another present tense

(such construction shows automatic or habitual results)

(a) If you heat ice it turns to water. (the use of **will turn** is also possible)
(b) If you boil water it turns to vapours.
(c) If there is shortage of a commodity, its price goes up.

6. Instead of if + present tense we can also have
if + present continuous +...

(Such construction shows a present action or a future arrangement.)

(a) If you are waiting for a taxi (present action), you should better go there.
(b) If you are looking for Raju (present action), you may find him in the park.
(c) If you are staying for another day (future arrangement), I'll ask the manager to charge you at concessional rate.
(d) If you are going to purchase a car (future arrangement), I will ask my assistant to show you the dealer's shop.

7. If + present perfect conditional sentence

(a) If you have finished dinner, I will ask the waiter for ice cream.
(b) If she has written the thesis, I will send it to the professor.

(c) If you haven't seen the Victoria Palace we would better go there today.

(d) If there was short supply of any commodity, prices of that commodity increased.

(B) Conditional Sentence

If clause is in past

1. **If + simple past, + would + V-I**
   (a) If I had an umbrella I would lend it to you. (But I haven't an umbrella)
   (b) If I had a brief case, I would give it to her. (But I haven't a briefcase)

This construction refers to present or future, and the past tense in the if clause is not a true past but a subjunctive which indicates unreality.

2. **When we don't expect the action in the if clause to take place**
   (a) If he tried to threaten me I would inform his father.
   (But I don't expect that he will try to threaten me.)
   (b) If a thief came into my room I would call you.
   (But I don't expect a thief to come into my room.)
   (c) If she dyed her hair green every one would laugh at her.
   (But I don't expect that she will dye her hair green.)

The above construction refers to improbability.

'Might' or 'could' may be used instead of 'would'.
(a) If he tried again he would pass. (certain result)
(b) If he tried again he could pass. (ability)
(c) If he tried again he might pass. (possibility)

The use of **would** refers certainty, and might refers possibility, and could refers ability.

3. **If + past tense can also be followed by another past tense when we wish to express automatic or habitual reactions in the past.**
   (a) If anyone abused him he became angry.
   (b) If she interrupted him he got angry.
   (c) If there was scarcity of milk, its prices went up.

(C) Conditional Sentences

If clause is in 'Past perfect tense'

if + past perfect, would + have + past participle.

In this type of conditional sentences, the verb in the if clause is in the past perfect tense; the verb in the main clause is in the perfect conditional. The condition cannot be fulfilled because the action in the if clause did not happen.

(a) If he had come to me I would have helped him.
(But he didn't come to me.)
(b) If she had invited me I would have attended the function.
(But she did not invite me.)
(c) If he had tried to cheat me I would have dismissed him.
(But he didn't try to cheat me.)

Could or **might** may also be used instead of **would** in the same constructions.
(a) If we had found her earlier we could have saved her life. (ability)
(b) If we had found her earlier we might have saved her life. (possibilities)
(c) If you had got valid visa you could have left for USA. (ability or permission)

Had can be placed first and the if omitted.
(a) If he had come to me I would have helped him.
(b) Had he come to me I would have helped him.

We can also use past perfect continuous in the **if** clause.

I was wearing helmet. If I hadn't been wearing the helmet I would have been seriously injured.

Other Types of Conditional Sentences

Normally **will**, **would** and **should** is not used after **if** in conditional sentences; but there are certain exceptions.

For Making Request

If you will/would +.... is often used in polite requests would is the more polite form.

(a) If you will/would wait a moment I'll see your work is done. (please wait)
(b) I would be very grateful if you would accept the cash after 3 p.m. (more polite) ('would' is the more polite form for making request)

If you would + infinitive is used for the requests which would normally be complied as a matter of course.

(a) If you would fill up this form. (at a bank)
(b) If you would just sign the register. (in a hotel)
(c) If you'd put your address on the back of the cheque. (in a departmental store)

If you would like/care + ... is more polite than if + want/wish and is more common in use.

(a) If you would like to come I will arrange a party for you.
(b) If you would care to see the photos I will bring them for you.
(c) If he would like to leave his scooter here he can do so.

If + should +..... denotes that the action though possible is not very likely.
It is combined with an imperative and is mainly used in written instructions.

(a) If you should have any difficulty in getting newspaper, ring at this number.
(b) If these packets should arrive in a damaged condition please inform the company at once.

'Should' can also be placed first and the 'if' omitted.

Should these packets arrive in a damaged condition, please inform the company at once.

If + were/was +...construction is used for advice.

(a) If I were you, I would forgive him. (I advise you to forgive him.)
(b) If I were you, I would punish him. (I advise you to punish him.)

The use of 'otherwise'

Otherwise = if this doesn't happen/didn't happen/ hadn't happened'.

(a) We must reach there before 10 o' clock; otherwise we'll be debarred
(=If we do not reach there before 10 o' clock; we'll be debarred.)
(b) His father paid his dues; otherwise he wouldn't be in college.
(= If his father didn't pay his dues he wouldn't be in college.)
(c) I used my computer; otherwise I'd have taken many more hours.
(= If I hadn't used my computer I'd have taken many more hours.)

Unless + affirmative = if + negative

(a) You cannot pass unless you attend the college.
(=You cannot pass if you do not attend the college.)
(b) She cannot go to America unless she has a valid visa.
(= She cannot go to America if she does not have a valid visa.)

Use of 'in case' in conditional sentences.

(a) Inform me in case you need more money.
(b) Turn on the light in case you need my help.
(c) Ring my doorbell in case he comes here.

It appears similar to 'if' and is often confused with it. But the two are completely different. An 'in case' clause causes an action in the main clause.

Use of 'so long' in conditional sentences.
So long also imposes restriction or limitation.

(a) I shall support him so long he is here.
(b) You can stay here so long the owner is out of station.
(c) So long I am here I will assist in your work.

Use of 'provided' in conditional sentences.
Provided imposes restriction or limitation.

(a) I shall attend the meeting provided he also attends.
(b) We shall support you provided you favour us.
(c) I can pay you rent provided you get the roof repaired.

Use of 'suppose' in conditional sentences.

Suppose/supposing ....? = what if .... ?

(a) Suppose a monkey comes here what will you do?
(=What if a monkey comes here what will you do?)
(b) Suppose the train is late?
What if the train is late?

Use of 'but for' in conditional sentence.

But for = if it were not for/ if it hadn't been for

(a) But for his help Ramesh would have ruined.

(b) But for the flood, I would have arrived here yesterday.

(c) But for your company I would have been bored.

» Exercises

Exercise 1

Correct the following sentences

1. If he came to me, I would have given him a pen.
2. Had he invited me, I would attend the function.
3. If he had telephoned me, I would have gave him the address.
4. If a monkey came here, what you will do?
5. It I had an umbrella, I would have given it to her.

Solutions

1. It he came to me I would give him a pen.
or If he had come to me, I would have given him a pen.
2. Had he invited me, I would have attended the function.
3. If he had telephoned me, I would have given him the address.
4. If a monkey came here what would you do?
5. If I had an umbrella I would give it to her.

Exercise 2

Correct the following sentences

1. If he will work hard, he will get promotion.
2. Unless he will ask me, I shall not help him.
3. If I had a briefcase, I will have lend it to her.
4. If you will heat ice, it may turn to water.
5. If you are looking for Sita, you would find her with Ram.

Solutions

1. If he works hard, he will get promotion.
2. Unless he asks me I shall not help him.
3. If I had a briefcase, I would lend it to her.
4. If you heat ice, it turns to water.
5. If you are looking for Sita, you will find her with Ram.

Exercise 3

Correct the following sentences

1. If I was you, I would dismiss him.
2. Unless he comes back, wait for him.
3. Until you work hard, you can't beat him.
4. Suppose she does not agree, what could you do?
5. If he tried again, he can pass.

Solutions

1. If I were you, I would dismiss him.
2. Until he comes back, wait for him.
3. Unless you work hard, you can't beat him.
4. Suppose she does not agree, what can you do?
5. If he tried again he could pass.

Exercise 4

Fill in the blanks

1. I will stay here ...... you come. (until/unless)
2. .... you work hard, you can't secure first position. (until/unless)
3. If I .... you, I would forgive him. (was/were)
4. If I were him, I .... dismiss you. (will/would)
5. If it rains, he .... not come. (will/would)
6. If you boil water it .... to vapours. (turns/will turn)
7. If you are waiting for a taxi, you .... better go there. (should/would have)
8. If he had come here I .... given him a room to stay. (would/would have)
9. If she .... me, I would have attended the function. (had invited/invited)
10. If he tried again he .... pass. (will/would)

Solutions

1. until 2. unless 3. were
4. would 5. will 6. turns
7. should
8. would have
9. had invit
10. would

Exercise 5

Complete the conditional sentences (Type I). Remember to use the auxiliary verbs

1. If it doesn't rain, we (can/go) swimming tomorrow.
2. If you train hard, you (might/win) first prize.

3. If we go to Canada next year, we (can/improve) our English.
4. I (may/go) to the disco in the evening if I do the washing now.
5. If we go on holiday next week, I (not/can/play) tennis with you.
6. If you see Ganesh tomorrow, you (should/tell) him that you love him.
7. If my parents go shopping in the afternoon, I (must/look) after my little sister.
8. He (must/be) a good drummer if he plays in a band.
9. If you are listening to the radio after 10 pm, you (should/turn) the volume down.
10. If you like that shirt, you (can/have) it.

Solutions

1. If it doesn't rain, we can go swimming tomorrow.
2. If you train hard, you might win first prize.
3. If we go to Canada next year, we can improve our English.
4. I may go to the disco in the evening if I do the washing now.
5. If we go on holiday next week, I cannot play tennis with you.
6. If you see Ganesh tomorrow, you should tell him that you love him.
7. If my parents go shopping in the afternoon, I must look after my little sister.
8. He must be a good drummer if he plays in a band.
9. If you are listening to the radio after 10 pm, you should turn the volume down.
10. If you like that shirt, you can have it.

Unit

18

Un-English and Superfluous Expressions

India is the third largest English-speaking country in the world. The use of English in India dates from the trading 'factories' started by the Company at Surat in 1612. By 1928, English was accepted as the language of the elite, and after independence in 1947, its diffusion increased. Because English has become a language of a large number of people in India, its convergence with Indian languages and socio-cultural patterns have resulted in development of many un-English expressions and usage.

These expressions have no place in standard English but started being used in our country so widely and acquired so much acceptance among the masses, that we often hear and see their use in our routine life. Students must be aware of such pit-falls and avoid using them while writing and speaking English. In this chapter, we are giving a number of such expressions and usage, that are un-English and must be taken care of while writing and speaking English.

Some such expression, which are not proper, are dealt with in this chapter.

1. **'What to do?'** is not permissible in English. We should say : What am I to do?
2. **I enjoyed fully.** Enjoy must have an object, and therefore this expression is not correct. Instead we should say : I enjoyed myself fully.
3. **Family man is a wrong expresson.** Instead we should say : A man with a family.
4. **Fear for is often misused for 'afraid of'.** I fear for you means that I am anxious on your behalf. It does not mean that I am afraid of you.
5. **The word 'females' is often misused for women.** The word female actually indicates sex. A human being belongs either to the male or the female sex. It is incorrect to say : The females of this village ... instead we should say ... the women of this village.
6. **To take leave of**, means to part from someone or say good bye to a person. But take leave from is used in the sense of obtaining permission from one's employer to be absent from work for a time. The following sentences are wrong: Sadly, she took leave from her mother. (say, took leave of.)

   I took leave of my employer for ten days. (Say, took leave from.)
7. **One parts from people**, but parts **with** things. It is incorrect to say—She parted with her husband. (say, took leave from.)

   She was forced to part from her car. (say, to part with.)
8. **With a view to**: It must be noted that 'With a view to' is always followed by a gerund.

   He has called a meeting of all parties tomorrow, with a view to forming a national reconciliation government.

   These are commonly heard sentences :

   I hope to go over to your place next Monday.

   I will go to you tomorrow. The word 'come' should be used in such sentences.

I hope to come over next Monday; I hope to come to Jaipur next month.

I will come over tomorrow.

9. **I hope you are keeping good health**, is not proper English. (instead we should say : enjoying good health, I hope you are well or keeping fit.)

She seems very much reduced (Incorrect English) She looks much thinner, or she looks very thin (not lean). (Correct English)

I have been in (or on) sick bed. (Incorrect English) I have been ill in bed or I have been in bed with cholera. (Correct English)

10. **Hope** implies a happy news or some favourable anticipation. The following use of hope is wrong : I hope to get fever today. Instead we should say : I fear I am going to have fever today.

11. **The phrase family members** is incorrect and often misused : His family members are not here. Instead we should say : The members of his family are not here. It is also wrong to say Syndicate members or Council members. It is also wrong to say male members : The male members of my family did not agree to this. Instead we should say : The men in my family did not agree to this.

12. **May** is frequently misused for could or might. May implies that permission is granted. It should not be used by a subordinate to a superior—a junior advising his superior. You may ask them to prepare their notes at home. Instead we should use 'You might tell..........or You could tell.........would, of course, be the proper way of putting it.

13. **On the contrary and on the other hand.** When two statements or ideas are opposed to each other, and we want to draw attention to this opposition, the second of these statements is introduced by 'On the contrary'. 'On the other hand' merely implies a contrast. The phrase on the other hand is normally used when in the first part 'on the one hand' is expressed or understood.

(a) I intended no offence; on the contrary, I meant to congratulate you.

(b) He is not my supporter; on the contrary, he is my opponent.

(c) She has not finished her essay; on the contrary, she has just begun it.

(d) Failure on the one hand, and poverty on the other pained him much.

(e) Duty required her to obey her husband; on the other hand, love dictated a different course of action.

14. **Addicted to.** It is always used in a bad sense. It is never used in a good sense. We can never say, 'He is addicted to singing'. We can say : 'He is addicted to gambling.'

He is addicted to drink.

15. **All right.** These words should always be written as two separate words and never as 'allright'.

16. **Pulling on well**. Using 'pulling on well' in the meaning of 'getting on somehow' is not correct. 'Pulling well' is a correct English idiom which means 'working in harmony'. Instead of saying, 'They are pulling on well', we should say, 'They are pulling well together'.

17. **Say 'I am in the tenth class.'** I am reading in the tenth class is incorrect. We should say 'I am in the tenth class'.

18. Plurals such as **sceneries, drainages, advices, meats**, should be avoided. If a plural is required, say : bits of scenery or better scenes; dranage systems; pieces of advice or better, much advice.

19. **Sick** should not be used in the sense of physical disorder. It is wrong to say I am sick, my brother fell sick. We should say : I am ill, my brother fell ill.

Sick is used to denote 'the mental state of weariness, boredom, or disgust'. We can say 'He is sick of this life.'

20. **Used to** implies a past habit which has now been discontinued. Used to is frequently used wrongly as an auxiliary to form of present tense denoting habitual action. It is wrong to say 'We used to take our meals at ten.' Instead we should say, 'We generally dine at ten'.

21. **etc.** stands for 'et cetera', meaning and other things. If you want to begin with 'and', you must not end with etc. You must say 'and so on'. It is wrong to use statement like : Many kinds of fruits grow in Kashmir, such as apples, peaches, plums, pears, etc.

You may use either of these forms :

(a) Many kinds of fruits, such as apples, peaches, plums and pears, grow in Kashmir.

(b) Many kinds of fruits—apples, peaches, plums, pears, etc.—grow in Kashmir.

22. As follows. The verb is invariable in number never 'as follow' : 'His argument is as follows.' 'The rules and regulations are as follows.'

23. Broadcast. We never say 'broadcasted'. 'Soniya's speech was broadcast (not, broadcasted) from the National channel.'

24. 'Due to' and **'owing to'** A.B.C. of English Usage says : Unlike owing to, due (to) has never become a compound preposition, that is, due retains its adjectival function and must be properly related to the noun or pronoun it qualities. Thus in the sentence 'Due to the rainy weather, she cannot come,' due obviously does not qualify she, and therefore has an actual noun that has nothing left to qualify. If due is to be used, the only way is to provide it with an actual noun: 'Her inability to come was due to the rainy weather,' where due qualifies inability. But the obvious and idiomatic construction is, 'Owing to the rainy weather, she cannot come'.

It is a good rule to use due only as a predicative adjective (as in the sentence above—that is, not like a participle, as the first word of a phrse.). It is incorrect to say: 'Some goods have increased in price, due to the increasing demand.' We should say 'Owing to the increase in demand, some goods have increased in price.

25. An America-returned gentleman. It is a meaningless expression. We should say 'He has been to America.'

26. It is incorrect to say that **a ship swims**. A ship sails or floats; men and animals swim. Also do not say 'a ship is drowned'—a ship sinks; men and animals sink and are drowned.

27. Half. Half of them **is** or **are**? The rule is that when the noun or pronoun following **of**, is **singular**, half is considered singular. 'If half of a piece is genuine antique, then it is difficult to dismiss it as a fake'. When the noun or pronoun following **of is plural**, half is considered plural: 'Half of the oranges were rotten.' The same rule also applies to **lots of** and **heaps of**.

28. In possession of means 'holding' and is active; **in the possession of** means held by and is passive.

'The thief was found in possession of the golden bars'

'The golden bars were found in the possession of the thief.

29. Reason. At least three warnings are necessary in connection with the word reason:

(a) 'The reason is because' is a type of tautological expression that defies both grammar and logic. The correct expression is : The reason (why, etc.) is that......' the that introducing a noun clause as compliment of the verb is. So the sentence 'The reason why I am dealing with so many pictures tonight is because I happen to have seen them all just recently' may be written in two ways:

(i) The reason......is that I happen.......

(ii) I am dealing with so many pictures tonight because I happen......

Equally bad, and almost equally common are: 'The reason.......is due to'. The reason...........is on account of is correct.

(b) **Because of that reason:** a near relative of the error dealt with under (a), you act not because of but for a reason. Reason itself indicates cause.

(c) 'The reason for the increase may be attributed to the rapid development of science during the past two centuries.' The increase may be attributed, not the reason; the reason is the rapid development.

In all three types of sentence cited above the trouble arises from a confusion of ideas that leads to 'a double statement of cause.' (adapted)

30. It is wrong to say **'this man maintains his livehood by hard work'**. A man obtains his livehood, and maintains himself. Hence the expression should be :

(a) This man obtains his livehood by hard work.

(b) This man maintains himself by hard work.

31. It is a blunder to say that a man is **'good in health.'** The correct expression is, 'in good health'.

32. In case, if : 'In case' must be carefully distinguished from 'if'. It must not be used as equivalent to if. I shall take my umbrella in case it rains—is perfectly correct, but 'I shall take my umbrella if it rains' does not convey the same meaning.

33. Is it not? Indians are seen making an incorrect or unnecessary use of this interrogative phrase. 'You are going to Jaipur, is it not? or 'You will come to my rescue, is it not?'or 'He is a teacher is it not?' But in sentences the expression 'is it not ? is incorrect. In the first case it should be Are you not? or 'Aren't you?' In the second, 'Will you not?' or Won't you?' and in the third, 'Is he not?' or 'Isn't he'?

34. What to speak of ? is commonly used by Indian students for 'not to mention of' or 'not to speak of '. They would say: 'What to speak of salad and sweets, she had no bread even' or 'She can hardly rise from the bed, what to speak of walking'. The correct expresson is, 'She had no bread even not to mention of salad and sweets.

'She can hardly rise from the bed, not to speak of walking.'

35. To eat one's food : This is an un-english expression, very commonly used by Indian students. We should not say, 'I have eaten my food?' An Englishman always specifies the food or meal. He would say, 'I have had my lunch or dinner'? Also note that the verb 'have' not 'take' is used with reference to breakfast, lunch, tea, dinner and supper. Avoid saying, 'I take my breakfast at 7 o'clock', but 'I have my breakfast at 7 o' clock' etc.

36. Some words are wrongly by the students e.g. **any body, can not, post man, post master mad man, else where, not with standing, in as much, more over, some body, some times, other wise, in stead (of), work man, head master, foot ball, back bite, arm chair, tea spoon, half penny.** These words should be written as: anybody, cannot, postman, postmaster, madman, elsewhere, notwithstanding, inasmuch, moreover, somebody, sometimes, otherwise, instead (of), workman, headmaster, football, backbite, armchair, teaspoon, halfpenny.

37. Some words are worngly combined by Indian students e.g., **alright, everyone, someone, inspite (of), youngman.** These words should be written as, all right, every one, some one, in spite (of), young man.

38. To cut off means 'to remove by cutting'. The phrase cannot be used in place of 'strike off.' 'His name has been cut off from the roll-call' is incorrect. We cut off the upper end of the stick, or cut off a piece of paper, but not the name of a student from attendance register.

39. Success : The word 'success' has acquired a positive meaning of its own. It is incorrect to say 'good' or 'bad success'. Success may be great or small, important or trivial, according to its degree but never good or bad in its quality.

40. And oblige : In ending their letters, many students seem to think it necessary to insert at the end 'and oblige', followed by a full stop, e.g., 'I hope you will consider my request sympathetically and oblige'. This is incorrect. 'Oblige' being a transitive verb and so cannot thus do without an object. However, in a business letter but never in a friendly one, we can use it, if we want, without the full stop so that oblige has the author of the letter as its object, for example : 'and oblige'

Yours faithfully, Prakash

41. Rather very : Rather and very should not be used together. They do not strengthen each other, in fact they counter each other. 'Rather' means 'not very, a little, somewhat'. 'He was rather very happy'. This is meaningless.

42. Comparative and **better** should not be used together. Better is itself an adjective of comparative degree. Do not say, 'He is comparatively better'. Say either 'He is comparatively good', or 'He is better'.

43. Pass off : Often we hear, 'The days pass of happily', but it is incorrect. When we speak a thing passes off means something remains behind or takes its place. Illness passes off and leaves health; an event passes off and we resume our routine. But we cannot say that time, or a period of time, passes off. It is sufficient to say it passes or it passes away.

44. **'Find'** and **'find out'**: 'Find' ordinarily means 'merely to discover, whether by accident or upon search', but to find out means making deliberate efforts to discover, something which has been 'intentionally concealed'. So to find a man means merely to discover him; to find him out means to discover his true character or to detect some fault in him. In such sentences, it would be better if only find is used.

45. **Almost since:** Using both together looks awkward, because 'since' draws attention to the end, as well as to the beginning of the time, while 'almost' is meant to refer to the beginning only and not to the end. 'Almost from the day......' would be all right for there the intended force of 'almost' is clear' but in the sentence, The couple had been dating almost since last January, the use of almost is not correct.

46. **Generally** and **always** are contrary to each other, as 'generally' means 'usually but not always'. In the sentence, 'He always comes late generally. we should have either generally or always.

47. **Money-bag, bed-sheet** and **foot-path** are some of the peculiar instances of translation of vernacular terms into English. An Englisman would simply say purse, sheet and pavement for the these words.

48. **Fall down:** The use of this phrase in such sentences 'the empire fell down' or 'this political leader fell down from his high position' are absolutely incorrect. You may say : A house fell down under heavy monsoon rain; the child falls down when it tumbles over a stone; a book falls down from the table to the floor. But an empire can never 'fall down'. It can only 'fall'. The statesman fell from his hight position is also correct.

49. **'No mention' or 'no matter'** : The use of these expressions in return to 'thanks' is an unconscious translation of a vernacular phrase. The correct reply is 'all right' or 'that's all right'.

50. **'Better'** and **'more'** : In the sentence, 'I know him more than he does,' we should use 'better' instead of 'more'. Also note "I know more of him', means that I know more of his circumstances, not that I know the man better. It would also be right to say, "I know more French than he". In this instance 'more' is an adjective; in the first one it is a noun; in the second it is an adverb.

51. **Tomorrow morning** and **the next morning** : In speaking in the present, of the coming day, always use 'tomorrow'. In speaking in the past, 'next' is right. For example, 'He is coming tomorrow morning,' but 'He came the next morning'. In the sentence, 'We understand that the celebration is to take place next morning', 'next' should be changed to either 'tomorrow' or 'the following', according to the date of preceding event.

52. **It is happy to note that....** : The word 'happy' expresses a state of the mind, and may also be applied to anything tending to cause that state; but it is always applied directly to the thing itself, as 'a happy moment'. We cannot say 'It is happy to note that...........'; instead we should say 'It is pleasant to note that.......'

53. **Fair sex** : The expression 'fair sex' is frequently used by Indian writers as an equivalent for 'women'. It is, no doubt, much used colloqually, but it is not allowed as such in serious writings.

54. **Gentleman:** It is important to mention that the word 'gentleman' is far more frequently used by Indians than by Englishmen. It is,normally used by members of the lower grade of society in England in speaking of those whom they regard as of higher grade; but amongst Englishmen of equal rank, the term is mostly restricted to somewhat formal speech or ceremonial occassions. Speaking in a public meeting, a speaker will refer to the audience as 'gentlemen', but among intimate friends, or among ordinary acquaintances, one man will refer to another only as a 'man'. But in India, we usually say 'gentleman' when we should say 'man'.

55. **As best as he can** : We may say 'as well as he can' but we must not say 'as best as he can'. The reason is that 'well' is an adverb, so may be qualified by the adverb 'as' which is

'expressive of degree'; but the adverb 'best' being superlative excludes all question of degree and cannot, therefore, be qualified.

56. Young age : It is true that 'age' may mean period of life as well as actual oldness, and that Englishmen do say 'tender age'; but 'young age' is not appropriate. In a sentence like—'women who have not been able to attend school in their 'young age', we should say 'youth' and not 'young age'.

57. 'Lately' and **'latterly' :** The distinction between these two words (though they are sometimes interchangeable) should be understood well. 'Lately' means recently, without any suggestion as to a previous state of thing. 'Latterly' also means recently, but it expresses comparison, and suggests a change in situation or state of things. You can use **latterly** to indicate that a situation or event is the most recent one.

'Have you talked to her lately?'

He was to remain active in the association, latterly as vice president, for the rest of his life...

Of a single individual act, we should use lately, and not 'latterly', because no comparison is involved.

58. Another, any other and **other :** 'Another' is used with singular nouns and 'other' with plural ones. Both are used in affirmative statements. But 'any other' is normally used in negative statements, and with nouns in either number.

59. Idioms : Neglectful distortion of idioms results in some very peculiar effects.

(a) He found it hard to make his two ends meet (say, both ends meet).

(b) I am not on speaking terms with her (say, talking terms).

(c) There was unbroken silence (say, There was pin-drop silence).

(d) I wanted to run away, but he held me by the hand and would not leave off (say, would not let me go).

(e) You stick up to him no matter what happens (say, stick to).

(f) We aim to prove it (at proving is the correct idiom).

(g) With a view of establishing himself (say, with a view to establish himself).

(h) The subject of my essay is regarding politeness (say, 'is politeness').

(i) The subject of his speech was about taxation (say, the subject of his speech was Taxation, or his speech was about taxation.)

60. Note the following common errors also:

Incorrect (avoid)	**Correct (prefer)**
Take a visit.	Pay a visit.
Put a liberty.	Set at liberty.
Put a thing to test.	Put a thing to the test.
Make an injury to a person.	Do an injury to a person.
He put the opportunity to account.	He turned the opportunity to account.
The work is in the hand.	The work is in hand.
He acquired a name for himself as an engineer.	He made a name.....
It is probable to happen.	It is probable that it will happen.
Have you taken your meals?	Have you had your food? or Have you had your dinner?
Please do the needful.	Please do what is necessary.
He is a boy of seven years old.	He is a boy seven years old.
He disposed it off.	He disposed of it.
I had been to Delhi last week.	I went to Delhi last week.
I hope you would do it.	I hoped you would do it or, I hope you will do it. or I wish you would do it.
Do you know swimming?	Do you know how to swim?
When do you take to your bed?	When do you go to bed?
They worked whole the day.	They worked the whole day, or They worked all the day.
We go for walking.	We are going for a walk.
They played fairly.	They played fair.
The rose smells sweetly.	The rose smells sweet.
I am very much tired after my walk.	I am very tired after my walk.
I am very much pleased to see you.	I am very pleased to see you.
To give key to the watch.	To wind up the watch.

Superfluous Expressions and Unnecessary Wordiness

1. **Cousin brother or cousin sister:** brother or sister should not be used together with cousin. It's an example of superfluous expression.
   Ramesh is my cousin. Sarla is my cousin.
2. **Consensus opinion :** Here opinion is superfluous. Consensus means collective opinion.
3. **Consort husband or consort wife :** Here husband or wife is superfluous. Consort means husband or wife especially of a ruler.
4. **Supposing if :** If is superfluous.
5. **During the period of war or during the war period :** The correct phrase is during the war.
6. **Return back :** The use of back is superfluous. Return= go or come back.
7. **Reimburse back:** The use of back is superfluous. Reimburse=pay back.
8. **Retreat back:** Use of back is superfluous. Retreat= go back.
9. **Recede back:** Use of back is superfluous. Recede = go back.
10. **Recall back:** Use of back is superfluous. Recall= summon back, take back.
11. **Recapitulate back:** Use of back is superfluous. Recapitulate = repeat
12. **Recast back:** Use of back is superfluous. Recast = rewrite.
13. **reborn, rebuild, regain or recall again:** Use of again is superfluous. Reborn= born agains
14. **Equally as good as :** Either use equally or as good as. Both donote same meaning.
15. **Mutual agreement:** Use of mutual is superfluous. Agreement is always mutual.
16. **Mutual friend or interest:** The correct phrase is common friend or interest.
17. **Await for:** Use of for is superfluous. Await = wait for.
18. **Comprise of:** 'of' is superfluous. Comprise = consist of.
19. **Despite of:** 'of ' is superfluous. Despite = in spite of.
20. **Two twins:** Use of two is superfluous. Twins = two children.
21. **Coward man:** Man is superfluous. Coward = a cowardly man.
22. **Flee away:** Away is superfluous. Flee = run away.
23. **With bag and baggage:** Use of with is superfluous. Bag and baggage = with all belongings.
24. **An English teacher:** The correct phrase is teacher of English. An English teacher means a teacher native of England.
25. **Passing marks, linking road or linking language:** The correct phrase is pass marks, link road or link language.
26. **Spouse husband/wife:** Husband/wife is superfluous. Someone's spouse is the person they are married to.
27. **Kindly requested:** It is wrong to use kindly and requested together. Request is always kindly.

» *Exercises*

Exercise 1

Correct the following sentences

1. He has been sick since Monday.
2. I eat my food at 8 p.m.
3. There were many kinds of beg in the shop, such as paper, leather, cloth and canvass.
4. Ramesh said to me, 'Sita was rather very happy on that day.'
5. All his family members are planning to visit Jammu and Kashmir.
6. I give key to my wrist watch at 8 p.m. daily.
7. I eat my breakfast at 7 a.m. daily.
8. He said, 'Today I am feeling comparatively better.'
9. Sunita always wears blue saree on such functions generally.
10. She went to Delhi the tomorrow morning.

Solutions

1. He has been ill since Monday.
2. I take my dinner at 8 p.m.

3. There were many kinds of bag in the shop, such as paper, leather, cloth, and canvass.
4. Ramesh said to me, 'Sita was rather happy on that day'.
5. All the members of his family are planning to visit Jammu and Kashmir.
6. I wind my wrist watch at 8 p.m. daily.
7. I have my breakfast at 7 a.m daily.
8. He said, 'Today I am feeling better.'
9. Sunita always wears blue saree on such functions.
10. She went to Delhi the next morning.

Exercise 2

Correct the following sentences

1. We eat because we may live.
2. She didn't attend the meeting so that she was ill.
3. I took medicine, because I might get well soon.
4. Both he is a philosopher and a teacher.
5. Either he is a stupid or a rogue.
6. Others as well as Ram declares this an unethical act.
7. The females are not allowed to participate in the competition.
8. The days pass off happily.
9. With a view to study the urgent publications he joined the library.
10. Did you find your pen ? Yes, I didn't find it so far.

Solutions

1. We eat so that we may live.
2. She didn't attend the meeting because she was ill.
3. I took medicine, in order that I might get well soon.
4. He is both a philosopher and a teacher.
5. Either he is a stupid or a rogue.
6. Ram as well as others declares this an unethical act.
7. The women are not allowed to participate in the competition.
8. The days pass happily.
9. With a view to studying the current publications he joined the library.
10. Did you find your pen? No, I didn't find it so far.

Exercise 3

Correct the following sentences

1. I can not play football today.
2. He achieved good success in BA examination.
3. He some times comes to visit this parents.
4. Everyone will be given a certificate.
5. Have you found your lost purse? No, I have found.
6. It is not the men but the fair sex, responsible for the present trend in fashion.
7. Not with standing the present degradation in the society, he believes in fair means even today.
8. Inspite of increase in turn over, the profit remains the same.
9. Ram discussed the matter with so many another fellows.
10. Ram and his other friend Shyam went to Jaipur yesterday.

Solutions

1. I **cannot** play football today.
2. He achieved **great** success in B.A. examination.
3. He **sometimes** comes to visit this parents.
4. **Every one** will be given a certificate .
5. Have you found your lost purse? **Yes,** I have found it.
6. It is not the men but the **women,** responsible for the present trend in fashion.
7. **Notwithstanding** the present degradation in the society, he believes in fair means even today.
8. **In spite of** increase in turn over, the profit remains the same.
9. Ram discussed the matter with so many **other** fellows.
10. Ram and his **another** friend Shyam went to Jaipur yesterday.

Exercise 4

1. All the members (A)/of the club are (B)/kindly requested (C)/to attend the meeting (D). ***(BSRB)***
2. This is the wristwatch (A)/which my uncle (B)/brought it (C)/for you (D). ***(Bank PO)***
3. She asked me (A)/where I was going to (B)/and what I had done (C)/the previous day (D).
4. He will leave (A)/for Maxico (B)/on Monday (C)/with bag and baggage (D). ***(Bank PO)***
5. This idea of the (A)/Home Minister's (B)/has put everyone (C)/in serious thoughts (D). ***(BSRB)***
6. The teacher forbade (A)/the students not to(B)/make a noise (C).
7. Rita, cousin sister of the (A)/MP said that she would (B)/contest the next (C)/election certainly (D). ***(BSRB)***
8. 'Harish is comparatively better (A)/today and we hope that (B)/he will recover soon,' (C)/said Ramesh (D). ***(NDA)***
9. Yesterday in the night (A)/he came by bus (B)/and was disturbed (C).

10. In Jaipur she (A)/came across with many (B)/of her friends (C)/who settled there after marriage (D).

Solutions

1. (C) Delete 'kindly'. It is superfluous.
2. (C) Delete 'it'
3. (B) Delete 'to'
4. (D) Delete 'with'
5. (B) The use of apostrophe with Home Minister is superfluous.
6. (B) Delete 'not'. Use of forbade and not is wrong.
7. (A) Use of sister or brother with cousin is superfluous.
8. (A) Comparatively better is superfluous. Harish is comparatively good or Harish is better.
9. (A) Replace 'Yesterday in the night' by 'last night'.
10. (B) The use of 'with' is superfluous.

Exercise 5

1. Pakistan's support (A)/to the terrorists in India (B)/is universally condemned (C)/by all (D).
2. Within two hours (A)/we will approach (B)/near Agra (C)/by car(D).
3. Suppose if (A)/all problems are solved (B)/what would you do then ? (C)
4. When he lent me (A)/some money, he asked (B)/to return it back (C)/within a week (D). ***(NDA)***
5. Through out the whole year (A)/there was (B)/not a single day (C)/without any incidence of violence (D). ***(CDS)***
6. The recent incidents of corruption (A)/amply illustrate about (B)/ the characters of (C)/our political leaders (D).
7. The thing what (A)/ you like is (B)/available in (C)/that departmental store (D). ***(CDS)***
8. He denied that (A)/he was not present (B)/there at the time (C)/accident took place (D). ***(NDA)***
9. The P.M said (A)/that it was his decision (B)/and that nobody (C)/could get it changed (D).
10. The students (A)/requested the teacher (B)/to repeat the question (C)/again (D). ***(Bank PO)***

Solutions

1. (D) Delete 'by all'.
2. C) Delete 'near'. Use of near with approach is superfluous.
3. (A) Use of 'if' with suppose is superfluous.
4. (C) Use of 'back' with return is superfluous.
5. (A) Use of 'whole' is superfluous.
6. (B) Use of 'about' is superfluous.
7. (A) Replace 'what' by 'which' or delete 'the thing'.
   What you like most is this pen.
   The thing which you like most is this pen.
8. (B) Use of 'not' with 'deny is wrong.
9. (C) Use of 'that' is superfluous.
10. (D) The use of 'again' with 'repeat' is superfluous.

Exercise 6

1. The reason why (A)/most of the people commit crime (B)/is because they are unware (C)/of the legal complications (D). ***(CDS)***
2. He doesn't hardly know (A)/about the real factors (B)/that have created (C)/so many problems (D).
3. My mother asked me (A)/if I have sufficient enough money (B)/to buy the books C).
4. They were quite all right (A)/when they went to the police station (B)/to lodge an FIR (C).
5. He stayed in Jammu (A)/for a very short period of time (B)/and then went to (C)/Kolkata (D). ***(Bank PO)***
6. He reimbursed back (A)/the money which I spent (B)/on his medical treatment (C).
7. I have to attend (A)/the funeral service (B)/of my dear departed friend (C)/today(D). ***(Bank PO)***
8. Unless you do not (A)/pass this examination (B)/you cannot get the job (C).
9. I want to know (A)/whether it is (B)/the right and proper time (C)/to start this business (D). ***(Bank PO)***
10. The second project (A)/of this company was equally as (B)/sucessful as (C)/the first project (D).

Solutions

1. (C) Use of 'because' with 'reason' is superfluous.
2. (A) Use of 'not' with 'hardy' or 'scarcely' is superfluous.
3. (B) Don't use 'sufficient' and 'enough' together.
4. (A) The use of 'all' with 'quite' is superfluous.
5. (B) 'of time' is superfluous.
6. (A) Use of 'back' with 'reimburse' or 'return' is superfluous.
7. (B) Use of 'service' with 'funeral' is superfluous.
8. (A) Use of 'not' is superfluous.
9. (C) Use either 'right' or 'proper'.
10. (B) Use of 'equally' is superfluous.
    Ram and Rahim are equally successful.
    Ram is as successful as Rahim.

Exercise 7

1. He was (A)/very friendly enough (B)/to help me (C)/when I was in trouble (D).
2. My friend asked (A)/me if there was any place (B)/in the (C)/compartment for him (D). ***(CDS)***

3. I know (A)/that more than hundred (B)/students have applied (C)/for freeship (D).
4. Each competitor (A)/tried his best (B)/to defeat one another (C)/in the wrestling match (D).
5. He put his sign (A)/at the foot of the (B)/letter and posted it (C)/immediately (D). ***(CDS)***
6. She ran as (A)/fastly as she could (B)/to catch the train (C).
7. The officer advised me (A)/to talk to the concerned clerk (B)/in case I feel any (C)/problem in the matter (D).
8. Many pupils of this college (A)/are working as teachers (B)/in different (C)/public schools (D). ***(NDA)***
9. He was (A)/awarded cent percent (B)/marks in (C)/ mathematics (D)
10. All his family members (A)/are social (B)/and cooperative (C).

Solutions

1. (B) Use of 'very' is superfluous.
2. (B) Change 'place' to 'room'.
3. (D) Replace 'freeship' by 'freestudentship'.
4. (C) Replace 'one another' by 'the other'.
5. (A) Replace 'sign' by 'signature'. Sign is a verb.
6. (B) Replace 'fastly' by 'fast'.
7. (B) Replace 'concerned clerk' by 'clerk concerned'.
8. (A) Replace 'pupils' by 'students'.
9. (B) Replace 'cent percent' by 'hundred percent'.
10. (A) write 'All the members of his family'.

Exercise 8

1. To what has (A)/always puzzled me (B)/is your insincerity (C)/and carelessness (D).
2. According to me (A)/every student should (B)/go through the (C)/notes given by the professors (D).
3. One of my friends (A)/is in the teaching line (B)/and presently settled (C)/abroad (D).
4. Nowadays she (A)/is living in foreign (B)/but her husband (C)/is in India (D).
5. Our English teacher said (A)/that we should practice (B)/regularly if we wanted to improve (C)/our English (D).
6. I want to join (A)/lecturership (B)/because I think it is a (C)/peaceful profession (D).
7. As my neighbourers (A)/are very cooperative (B)/so I do not have (C)/any problem here (D).
8. The passing marks (A)/are thirty there (B)/but you have secured (C)/only thirty two marks (D).
9. Both of them (A)/have not (B)/turned up in (C)/the court today (D). No error (E)
10. We must wait (A)/for quiter time before (B)/the claims of civilization (C)/can over ride over the claims of the party spirit (D).

Solutions

1. (A) Use of 'to' is superfluous.
2. (A) Replace 'according to me' by 'in my opinion'.
3. (B) Replace 'teaching line' by 'teaching profession'.
4. (B) Replace 'in foregin' by 'abroad'.
5. (A) Replace 'English teacher' by 'teacher of English'. English teacher means the teacher whose nationality is English.
6. (B) Replace 'lectureship' by 'lecturership'.
7. (A) 'Neighbourers' is no English word. Change it to 'neighbours'.
8. (A) Replace 'passing marks' by 'pass marks'.
9. (E) No error.
10. (D) Use of 'over' after 'over ride' is superfluous.

Unit

19

Formation of Words

The basic part of any word is the **root.** Word formation is the process of forming new words usually by adding prefix or suffix to the root.

Ways of Formation of Words

1. **By prefix : Prefix is a syllable added before the root.**

un + lucky	unlucky
in + dependent	independent
im + polite	impolite

2. **By suffix : Suffix is also a syllable, added at the end of the root.**

great + ness	greatness
social + ism	socialism
leak + age	leakage

3. **Compounding of two words :**

drawing + room	drawing room
tax + paid	taxpaid
pre + paid0	prepaid

4. **Merging of two words:**

breakfast and lunch	brunch
hotel for motorist	motel

5. **Cutting or clipping:**

telephone	phone
teenagers	teens
picture with movement	movie

Prefix : im, is, ir, il, re, em, en, de, un, dis, mis, pre, non, mini, semi, vice, etc. used in the formation of words.

impolite	impotent	impure
indiscipline	incompetent	immaterial
irregular	irrelevant	immoral
illogical	illegal	illiterate
recast	refund	reclaim
empower	embody	embark
encourage	enrich	enlist
deform	defame	demoralise
unfortunate	untie	unexpected
disappear	dislike	discourage
miscarriage	mistrust	mismanage
premature	prepaid	prefix
noncooperation	non refundable	non sense
mini computer	mini-car	mini-skirt
semimodal	semicircle	semicolon
vice captain	vice chairman	vice president

Suffix : age, ed, ist, ing, em, ish, ful, en, ly, ship, ness, ment, etc. used in formation of words.

artless	cheerful	graceful
gifted	ruined	talented
socialist	artist	rightist
painting	gardening	watering
bolden	hidden	maiden
selfish	boyish	womanish
joyful	truthful	fearful
godly	manly	suddenly
friendship	membership	hardship
kindness	fasten	goodness
tasteless	colourful	powerful

Conversion of Words : One Form into Another

Changing Noun into Adjective

Noun	Adjective	Noun	Adjective
angle	angular	brass	brazen
adam	adamic	body	physical
ancestor	ancestral	beast	bestial
authority	authoritative	contempt	contemptuous
advice	advisable	coward	cowardly
brother	fraternal	cat	feline
blue	bluish	city	urban
beginning	initial	calamity	calamitous
bounty	bounteous	circle	circular
brute	brutal	college	collegiate
conscience	conscientious	nose	nasal
circumstance	circumstantial	ocean	oceanic
dog	canine	offence	offensive
emperor	imperial	omen	ominous
expectation	expectant	people	popular
example	exemplary	population	populous
enemy	inimical	professor	professorial
earth	earthen	patriot	patriotic
essence	essential	pathos	pathetic
elephant	elephantine	picture	picturesque
explanation	explanatory	prejudice	prejudicial
egg	oval	problem	problematic
eye	optical	punishment	penal
famine	famished	sentence	sententious
fraud	fraudulent	place	local
foot	pedal	palace	palatial
flower	floral	ruin	ruinous
fear	timorous	sedition	seditious
Fable	fabulous	service	serviceable
fever	feverish	secretary	secretarial
fate	fatal	study	studious
flesh	carnal	paradise	paradisiacal
grief	grievous	series	series
grass	grassy	salt	saline
hand	manual	serpent	serpentine
hypocrite	hypocritical	superstition	superstitious
island	insular	ship	naval
industry	industrious (industrial)	sky	etherial
spring	vernal	joy	joyous
sun	solar	joke	jocular
star	starry	judge	judicial (judicious)
tooth	dental	tribe	tribal
licence	licentious	town	urban
lustre	lustrous	talk	talkative
love	amorous	table	tabular
money	monetary	youth	juvenile

Noun	Adjective	Noun	Adjective
moon	lunar	vice	vicious
merchant	mercantile	voice	vocal
metal	metallic	village	rural
medicine	medicinal	war	martial
myth	mythical	title	titular
minister	ministerial	worth	worthy
muscle	muscular	watch	vigilant
merit	meritorious	wood	sylvan
night	nocturnal	year	annual
neighbour	neighbourly	zodiac	zodiacal
nihil	nihilistic	zenith	zenithal

Changing Noun into Verb

Noun	Verb	Noun	Verb
authority	authorise	hard	harden
assertion	assert	harmony	harmonise
apology	apologize	haste	hasten
allusion	allude	height	heighten
blood	bleed	idol	idolise
beauty	beautify	justice	justify
black	blacken	knee	kneel
brass	braze	loss	lose
bed	embed	list	enlist
body	embody	monopoly	monopolise
circle	encircle	magnet	magnetise
centre	centralize	memory	memorise
cipher	decipher	nature	naturalise
class	classify	notice	notify
certainty	ascertain	necessity	necessitate
colony	colonize	night	be night
collision	collide	origin	originate
company	accompany	office	officiate
conception	conceive	perception	perceive
custom	accustom	patron	patronise
character	characterize	peace	pacify
danger	endanger	person	personify
drop	drip	prison	imprison
enthusiasm	enthuse	power	empower
excellence	excel	relief	relieve
economy	economise	robe	enrobe
electricity	electrify	society	associate
furniture	furnish	sermon	sermonise
frost	freeze	spark	sparkle
food	feed	shrine	enshrine
force	enforce	slave	enslave
friend	befriend	title	entitle
fraud	defraud	tomb	entomb
grass	graze	utility	utilize
glory	glorify	vapour	evaporate
gold	gild	verse	versify
habit	habituate	vacancy	vacate
hand	handle	vice	vitiate

Changing Noun into Abstract Noun

Noun	Abstract Noun	Noun	Abstract Noun
beggar	beggary	machine	mechanism
coin	coinage	priest	priesthood
coward	cowardice	person	personage
cunning	cunningness	royal	royalty
creature	creation	regent	regency
elector	electorate	servant	service
hero	heroism	witch	witchery

Changing Adjective into Verb

Adjective	Verb	Adjective	Verb
abundant	abound	large	enlarge
able	enable	lamp	lamp
abusive	abuse	dramatic	dramatise
bitter	embitter	little	belittle
brief	abbreviate	long	prolong
brutal	brutalize	liquid	liquidise
base	debase	mad	madden
clear	clarify	moist	moisten
civil	civilize	noble	ennoble
clean	cleanse	public	publish
dense	condense	popular	popularise
different	differentiate	poor	impoverish
double	duplicate	perpetual	perpetuate
dramatic	dramatise	pure	purify
equal	equalise	real	realise
fat	fatten	rich	enrich
fertile	fertilise	safe	save
firm	confirm	stupid	stupidity
fresh	refresh	sweet	sweeten
feeble	enfeeble	solid	solidity

Changing Adjective into Noun

Adjective	Noun	Adjective	Noun
adequate	adequacy	intense	intensity
acid	acidity	just	justice
bankrupt	bankruptcy	merry	merriment
brief	brevity	magnificent	magnificence
busy	business	notorious	notoriety
chaste	chastity	obedient	obedience
civil	civility	pious	piety
compulsory	compulsion	public	publicity
dense	density	rival	rivalry
gay	gaiety	solitary	solitude
double	duplicate	perpetual	perpetuate
grand	grandeur	splendid	splendour
hot	heat	vain	vanity
humble	humility	wide	width
local	locality	worthy	worth

Changing Verb into Noun

Verb	Noun	Verb	Noun
acquit	acquittal	conceive	conception
bathe	bath	commit	committal
betray	betrayal	compare	comparison
deceive	deception	precise	precision
defy	defiance	predict	prediction
deny	denial	precede	precedence
do	deed	pursue	pursuit
prohibit	prohibition	yean	yeanling
heal	health	recede	recess
know	knowledge	rely	reliance
lend	loan	respond	response
give	gift	redeem	redemption
narrate	narration	steal	stealth
oblige	obligation	urge	urgency
move	motion	seize	seizure
please	pleasure	weave	web
persuade	persuasion	vary	variety

» Exercises

Exercise 1

Write the 'adjective' form of the following noun

1. calamity **2.** coward **3.** city
4. blue **5.** emperor **6.** brute
7. cat **8.** beast **9.** body
10. brass

Solutions

1. calamitous **2.** cowardly **3.** urban
4. bluish **5.** imperial **6.** brutal
7. feline **8.** bestial **9.** phyrical
10. brazen

Exercise 2

Write the 'noun' form of the following words

1. floral **2.** fatal **3.** populous
4. inimical **5.** penal **6.** saline
7. naval **8.** solar **9.** dental
10. jocular

Solutions

1. flower **2.** fate **3.** population
4. enemy **5.** punishment **6.** salt
7. ship **8.** sun **9.** tooth
10. joke

Exercise 3

Change the following noun into verb

1. hard **2.** loss **3.** magnet
4. centre **5.** bed **6.** circle
7. food **8.** grass **9.** collision
10. nature **11.** origin **12.** office

Solutions

1. harden **2.** lose **3.** magnetise
4. centralise **5.** embed **6.** encircle
7. feed **8.** graze **9.** collide
10. naturalise **11.** originate **12.** officiate

Exercise 4

Change the following verb into noun

1. bathe **2.** predict **3.** defy
4. please **5.** lend **6.** move
7. pursue **8.** steal **9.** oblige
10. respond **11.** yearn **12.** do

Solutions

1. bath **2.** prediction **3.** defiance
4. pleasure **5.** loan **6.** motion
7. pursuit **8.** stealth **9.** obligation
10. response **11.** yearned **12.** deed

Exercise 5

Form the words as directed from the following words

1. a noun form err (verb). **(*Inspectors of Income Tax*)**
2. A noun from flow (verb). **(*Inspectors of Income Tax*)**
3. a noun from precise (adjective). **(*Inspectors of Income Tax*)**
4. an abstract noun from witch (noun). **(*Inspectors of Income Tax*)**
5. A verb from office (noun). **(*Inspectors of Income Tax*)**
6. Adjectives from coast, home. **(*Inspectors of Income Tax*)**
7. Abstract noun from fool, poor, laugh. **(*Inspectors of Income Tax*)**

Solutions

1. error	**2.** flow	**3.** precision
4. witchery	**5.** officiating	**6.** coastal, homely
7. folly, poverty, laughter		

Exercise 6

Use each of the following words as a noun and as a verb in your own sentences **(*IAS*)**

1. quarrel	**2.** book	**3.** hand
4. lock	**5.** water	**6.** stand
7. field	**8.** chair	**9.** notes
10. sacrifice	**11.** train	**12.** work
13. present	**14.** Record	

Solutions

Use as noun

1. *Quarrels* take place over the property.
2. The *books* written by Mr. S.C. Gupta are very useful.
3. The *hands* of Mafia are many.
4. The *locks* of Aligarh are durable.
5. *Water* is necessary for life.
6. You should have taken a tough *stand*.
7. The *field* of Red Corner, China is plane.
8. This is a comfortable *chair*.
9. She has taken my *notes*.
10. The *sacrifice* made by Subhash Chandra Bose is indeed great.
11. The *train* is a good mode of travel.
12. Complete your *work* today positively.
13. This is a good *present* for her.
14. Sachin has made several *records*.

Use as a verb

1. You should not quarrel with your brother.
2. The scooter was booked for Alwar.
3. A representation was handed over to the Chairman.
4. Lock the house properly while going out.
5. He is watering the plants.
6. The inflation rate now stands at 4% only.
7. Sachin fields the ball very quickly.
8. The Home Minister chaired the meeting of MPs.
9. Please note down my telephone number.
10. Subhash Bose sacrificed his service and fought for independence.
11. Pakistan is suspected to be training militants.
12. He works in this office.
13. She presented a wrong information.
14. Please record my dissent in this matter.

Exercise 7

Fill in the blanks with the appropriate word in the second sentence of the following pairs of sentences

1. The corrupt politician is about to be exposed.
   The corrupt politician faces ....
2. Most of the cups broke in transit.
   Most of the cups suffered............ in transit.
3. The passengers were annoyed at the delay.
   The passengers expressed their .... at the delay.
4. The court ordered the building to be demolished.
   The court ordered .... of the building.
5. The strange word is repeated in all his poems.
   All his poems shows .... of the strange word.
6. He told me not to be in such haste.
   He told me not to ....so much.
7. My grandfather fell down.
   My grandfather had a ....
8. The visitor frightened the child.
   The visitor gave the child a ....look.

Solutions

1. exposure	**2.** breakage	**3.** annoyance
4. demolition	**5.** repetition	**6.** hurry
7. fall	**8.** frightening	

Unit 20

Spelling Rules

Here are a few rules to spell words. Keep the principles in mind—but do not get bogged down by them. (You'll do better simply memorising the words you misspell.) Actually, English spelling does follow specific rules. Knowing some basic rules of English spelling can eliminate many common errors even though there are some exceptions.

Basic Spelling Rules

1. **Whether ie or ei : Remember the following poem to decide if a word should be spelled ie or ei.**

   Put i before e, except after c
   Or when it sounds like a
   As in neighbour or neigh.

eg.
mischief believe field
receiver conceited eight weigh freight
Exceptions : friend, neither, leisure, foreign

2. **Doubling a consonant : Follow these steps to decide if a final consonant needs to be doubled when a suffix or verb ending is added.**

   (a) If the word is one syllable or is stressed on the last syllable

And has a single final consonant

And that single final consonant is preceded by a single vowel

And the suffix begins with a vowel

Then double the final consonant.

Control + able

- The stress is on the last syllable - **trol**
- There is a single final consonant - **l**
- The final consonant has a vowel before it - **o**
- The suffix, **able**, begins with a vowel.
- Therefore, you double the **l** before adding the suffix.
- Write **controllable**

Other examples : occur - occurring, swim - swimming, ship - shipping

Now see : **enter + ing**

- The stress is on the first syllable - **en** - not the last
- Therefore, you do not double the final consonant.
- Write **entering**

Other examples: visit-visiting, develop-developing, dread-dreading, appeal-appealing

3. **Handling final e when adding a suffix or verb ending.**

- If the suffix or verb ending is a vowel, drop the final letter.

Other amuse + ing = amusing

Examples : create-creating, type-typing, bake-baking

- If the suffix or verb ending begins with a consonant, keep the final **e**.

measure + ment = measurement definite + ly = definitely

4. **Adding a suffix or verb ending with words ending in y.**

- If the word has a consonant before the **y**, change the y to **i**.

  mercy + less = merciless
- If the word has a vowel before the **y**, keep the **y**.

  employ + ed = employed

5. Words ending in two vowels (a vowel + final e) retain the final vowel (e) before adding a suffix. (see/seeable; shoe/ shoeing; canoe/ canoeing)

6. For words ending in c, insert k before adding -ing or -y. (picnic/picnicking; traffic/ trafficking; panic/panicky.)

7. To retain the soft sound of the c (s sound) and of the g (j sound) in words ending in ce and ge, we keep the final e (peace/peaceable; replace/replaceable; arrange/arrangement; advantage/advantageous; notice/ noticeable; change/changeable)

8. Pluralising noun: Most of the nouns in English spell their plural by simply adding a final -s. Nouns that are noncount or abstract (e.g., cheese, sugar, honesty, intelligence) generally take a singular verb, but in some instances can be plural, in which case they follow the rules for plural based on their spelling. Also, there are some categories of words which are only plural, even though their spelling does not reflect this.

- Words that end in **ss, sh, ch** or x add **es.**

pass-passes, buzz-buzzes, coax-coaxes, wash-washes, watch-watches.

- Words that have a consonant before a final y, change the **y** to **i** before adding **es.**

  summary = summaries,

  cry= cries, try=tries
- Most nouns ending in **f** or **fe** add **s.** However, some change the **f** to **v** and add **s** or **es.**

There is no rule to follow here.

belief = beliefs

half = halves, calf = calves

- Most nouns ending in **o** add z However, some add es.

  there is no rule to follow in this case.

  studio = studios, cargo = cargoes

9. The spelling of a word does not change when you add a pbrefix to it even when the first letter of the word and the last letter of the prefix are the same.

mis + step = misstep

pre + eminent = preeminent

un + necessary = unnecessary

10. No rule for irregular plurals. These just need to be memorised.

child	children	foot	feet
goose	geese	louse	lice
man	men	mouse	mice
ox	oxen	tooth	teeth
woman	women		

11. Sometimes words have silent letters. These follow patterns that can be memorised.

gn, pn, kn= n

gnome, pneumonia, knife

rh, wr = r

rhyme, wrestle

pt, ght = t

ptomaine, height

ps, sc = s

psalm, science

wh = h

whole

List of Commonly Misspelt Words

autumn	conscience	irresistible	phenomenon
accommodate	cigarette	irrelevant	physique
accustom	colloquial	irreparable	psychology
agility	commemorate	indefatigable	potato
athlete	competition	indigenous	pharmaceutical
accommodate	convenient	incorrigible	pursue
acquaintance	conceive	juggler	quarrel
assailant	condemn	jealousy	queue
aggregate	curriculum	jubilee	quinine
acquiesce	deceive	juvenile	rogue
abbreviate	discernible	knave	routine
ascetic	deficiency	kitchen	regrettable

annihilate
appropriate
aerodrum
architecture
acquiesce
alcohol
adherent
abhorrence
accessible
acknowledgement
acquittal
apparatus
amateur
appetite
acclamation
affectionate
aesthetic
alienate
ambassador
ambition
assassin
bankruptcy
beneficent
behaviour
bequeath
besiege
bureaucracy
budget
buffoon
circumstance
commitment
committee
condescend
connoisseur
correspondence
counterfeit
catalogue
convalesce

dialogue
descendant
division
dilemma
deteriorate
dysentery
ecclesiastical
etiquette
erroneous
exaggeration
ecstasy
equilibrium
exchequer
extravagance
efficiency
efficacious
embarrass
fallacious
fascinate
facilitate
felicitate
freight
favourable
fourth
genuine
guarantee
gorgeous
grievance
grotesque
geometry
grammar
gazette
harassment
heinous
heterogenous
hygiene
inflammable
incarcerate

knee
knight
kneeled
knives
leniency
leisure
laurel
luxurious
lieutenant
manageable
magnificent
martyr
manoeuvre
misdemeanor
meagre
moustache
mosquito
missionary
millionaire
massacre
museum
mischievous
musician
noticeable
nuisance
neighbour
necessary
necessitate
occurrence
omitted
oscillate
ominous
parallel
pneumonia
proletariat
perceive
proprietor
perspicuous

restaurant
repetition
referee
rehearsal
rupee
sceptre
scissors
schedule
strategy
simultaneous
symmetrical
soliloquy
sovereign
stomach
technique
transience
tenacious
transgressor
utterance
vacation
vaccination
vicissitude
vocabulary
vicious
villainous
wednesday
weigh
woolen
written
writing
xenomania
xylography
yawning
yeoman
zodiac
zealous
zootomy
zythepsary

Spelling : American and British

Here are some general differences between British and American spellings:

1. **Words ending in–or (American) –our (British)**

   American - labor, color, rumor, humor, neighbor etc.

   British- labour, colour, rumour, humour, neighbour etc.

2. **Words ending in –ize (American) –ise (British)**

   American - recognize, patronize

   British - recognise, patronise

3. **Words ending in og (American), ogue (British).**

   American - catalog, dialog

   British - catalogue, dialogue

4. **Words ending in l (single or double):**

   American - Traveler, leveling

   British - Traveller, levelling

5. Words ending in ter (American English) and tre (British).

American – theater, meter, center
British – theatre, metre, centre

6. Spelling difference in some more words:

American	**British**
tire	tyre (on a vehicle)
program	programme
jail	gaol, jail
aluminum	aluminium
defense	defence
jewelry	jewellery

We Use British English in India

The best way to make sure that you are being consistent in your spelling is to use the spell check on your word processor (if you are using the computer, of course) and choose which variety of English you would like. As you can see, there are really very few differences between standard British English and standard American English. However, the largest difference is probably that of the choice of vocabulary and pronunciation.

» Exercises

Exercise 1

Insert 'ance' or 'ence' in the following words

(a) exist (b) attend
(c) correspond (d) magnific
(e) occurr... (f) persist...
(g) entr (h) emin
(i) prud (j) vigil
(k) compli (l) hindr
(m) acquaint (n) assure
(o) repent (p) differ
(q) refer

Solutions

(a) existence (b) attendance
(c) correspondence (d) magnificence
(e) occurrence; (f) persistance
(g) entrance (h) eminence
(i) prudence (j) vigilance;
(k) compliance (l) hindrance
(m) acquaintance (n) assurance
(o) repentance (p) difference
(q) reference

Exercise 2

Insert 'ant' or 'ent' in the following words

attend-; cog-; immigr-; complim-; disinfect-; immin-; serp-; inhabit-; serv-; brilli; monum-; pertin-; fragr-; promin-; perman-; vali-; adjac-; restaur- resist-; suffici-; excell-; benefic-.

Solutions

attendant; cogent; immigrant; compliment; disinfectant; imminent; serpent; inhabitant; servant; brilliant; monument; pertinent; fragrant; prominent; permanent; valiant; adjacent; restaurant; resistant; sufficient; excellent; beneficent.

Exercise 3

Add 'tion', or 'sion' to complete the spelling of the following words

applica-; discus-; deci-; colli-; posses-; profes-; combina-; explo-; confu-; permis-; sugge-; atten-; ambi-; ammuni-; associa-; determina-; divi-; exclu-; compul-; conclu-; commisi-; direc-; administra-; resolu-; reputa-; ses-; founda-; man-; excur-; popula-.

Solutions

application; discussion; decision; collision; possession; profession; combination; explosion ; confusion ; permission; suggestion; attention; ambition; ammunition; association; determination; division; exclusion; compulsion; conclusion; commission; direction; administration; resolution reputation; session; foundation; mansion; excursion; population.

Exercise 4

Insert 'ary', 'ery,' 'ory' or 'ry' in the following words

brav-; bound-; contra-; sal-; slav-; jewell-; gallant-; second-; prim-; secret-; cook-;coroll-; dai-; geomet-; laborat-; liter-; mercen-; milit-; mission-; monast-; myst-; necess-; satisfact-; machin-; fact-; begg-; carpent-; surg-.

Solutions

bravery; boundary; contrary; Salary; slavery jewellery; gallantry; secondary; primary; secretary; cookery; corollary; dairy; geometry; laboratory; literary mercenary; military; missionary; monastery; mystery necessary; satisfactory; Machinery; factory; beggary carpentry; surgery.

Exercise 5

Insert 'cial' or 'tial' in the following words

pala-; residen-; superfi-; ra-; par-; spe-; influen-; pruden-; provin-; sacrifi-; finan-; judi-; cru-; nup-; prejudi-; presiden-; preferen-; essen-.

Solutions

(a) palatial; residential; superficial; racial; partial; special; influential; prudential; provincial; sacrificial; financial; judicial; crucial; nuptial; prejudicial; presidential; preferential; essential

Exercise 6

Insert 'eous' or ious' in the spelling of the following words

nutrit-; courag-; court-; notor-; erron-; meritor-; supersitit-; bount-; industr-; licent-; prec-; prodig-; cur-; feroc-; grac-; conscient; luxur-;

Solutions

nutritious; courageous; courteous; notorious; erroneous; meritorious; superstitious; bounteous; industrious; licentious; precious; prodigious; curious; ferocious; gracious;conscientious; luxurious;

Exercise 7

Add the suffix 'able' or 'ible' with the following word

agree; love; resist; blame; move; access; value; eat; change; reduce; contempt;force; pay; profit;discern;

Solutions

agreeable; lovable; resistible; blamable; movable; accessible; valuable; eatable; changeable; reducible; contemptible; forcible; payable; profitable; discernible;

Exercise 8

Fill in 'age', 'dge' or 'ege' in the following words

pill-; coll-; carri-; mess-; man-; line-; ple-; dam-; bu-; bri-; he-; pres-; pack-; mortg-; post-; vill-; suffr-; lo-; pass-; cartri-;

Solutions

pillage; college; damage; message; manage; lineage; pledge; passage; budge; bridge; hedge; presage; package; mortgage; postage; village; suffrage; lodge; passage; cartridge;

Exercise 9

Insert 'cious' or 'tious' in the following words

mali-; fero-; supersti-; conscien-; ostenta-; ambi-; vi-; ficti-; deli-; perni-; atro-; vora-; sedi-; infec-; saga-; avari-.

Solutions

malicious; ferocious; superstitious; conscientious; ostentatious; ambitious; ferocious; fictitious; delicious; pernicious; atrocious; voracious; seditious; infectious; sagacious; avaricious;

Exercise 10

Insert 'ei' or 'ie' in the following

Perc-ve; hyg -ne; bel-f ; ach-ve; ch-f; dec-ve; rel-f; conc-t; th-f; v-l; n-gh; y-ld; br-f; n-ce; forf-t; I-ge ; surf-t; f-gn;retr-ve; rec-pt;gr-ve; pr-st;

Solutions

perceive; hygiene; belief; achieve; chief; deceive; relief; conceit; thief; veil; neigh; yield; brief; niece; forfeit; liege; surfeit; feign; retrieve; receipt; grieve; priest;

Exercise 11

Tick mark the following words with correct spellings

(Railways Apprentice)

1. (a) temperature (b) temprature (c) tempareter
2. (a) definate (b) definite (c) difinite
3. (a) expirience (b) exparience (c) experience
4. (a) incident (b) insident (c) insidant
5. (a) extasy (b) ecstasy (c) acstasy

Solutions

1. (a) 2. (b) 3. (c) 4. (a)
5. (b)

Exercise 12

Find out the wrongly spelt word

(Railways Apprentice)

1. (a) pompous (b) populous (c) prejudiced (d) pretentous
2. (a) exempleary (b) embarrass (c) envious (d) excellence
3. (a) dispose (b) dipose (c) demote (d) denote
4. (a) casual (b) candid (c) convercant (d) catastrophe
5. (a) procession (b) passion (c) posession (d) profession

Solutions

1. (d) 2. (a) 3. (b) 4. (c)
5. (c)

Exercise 13

Find out the wrongly spelt word

(Railways Apprentice)

1. (a) rein (b) neigh (c) neither (d) neice
2. (a) efficient (b) reticent (c) magnificient (d) deficient
3. (a) vocal (b) focal (c) mystical (d) vehical
4. (a) altogether (b) alrigt (c) almighty (d) allottee
5. (a) pretence (b) offence (c) dence (d) deference

Solutions

1. (d) 2. (c) 3. (d) 4. (b)
5. (c)

» Unit

21

Sentence Structure and Analysis

According to the traditional grammar, a sentence is a group of words that conveys some meaning. It means a sentence consists of words, but not every string of word constitute a sentence as we can see in the following example:

To he market goes.

A possible analysis is that if we look at this example we know the meaning of the individual words, but the sequence as a whole does not make sense or does not convey any meaning, so we cannot consider this structure a sentence. Thus, we can affirm that if a sequence of words is to constitute a sentence, it must be meaningful, for instance:

He goes to market.

The network of relations between the words of a sentence is called its structure. There are many different aspects that influence the structure of a sentence. Usually, however, the sentence has a subject as well as a predicate and both the subject and the predicate may have modifiers.

1. Subject **2. Predicate**

Subject

The subject is the person or thing 'performing' the action. The noun, pronoun, or group of words acting as a noun, which performs the action indicated, is the predicate of the sentence or clause.

Predicate

Basically, predicate is the rest of the sentence or clause other than the subject. It usually has a verb, and thus indicates some action, but may have other functions such as modifying the subject. What is said about the subject is called predicate.

Subject	**Predicate**
Ram	is a good man.
Rahim	plays football.
She	went to market.
He	is writing a letter.

Kinds of Sentences

There are four kinds of sentences.

1. Simple sentence
2. Compound sentence
3. Complex sentence
4. Mixed sentence

Analysis

Analysis means to identify different clauses (principal and subordinate clause) in the sentence and then find out the nature of the sentence whether is is a simple, compound or a complex sentence.

What Is a Clause

Clause is a group of words that forms part of a sentence and contains a subject and a finite verb.

A clause contains both a subject and a predicate. If a clause can stand by itself as a sentence, it is an **independent** or **principal clause.** If the clause is acting as a noun, adjective or adverb and cannot stand by itself, it is a **dependent** or **subordinate clause.**

Main, independent or principal clause : An independent clause has a subject and a finite verb. It can stand alone as a sentence. The independent clause is a short sentence. It is the primary clause because it contains the simple subject and simple predicate of the full sentence.

(a) This is the fan, which I bought yesterday.
(b) I will help her, as far as I can do.
(c) She went to dinner after she changed clothes.

In the above sentences all underlined clauses are principal or main clauses.

Dependent or Subordinate Clauses : A dependent clause, or 'subordinate clause,' modifies the sentence by acting as an adjective, adverb or noun. Usually a dependent clause is introduced by a subordinate conjunction. Look for either commas or conjunctions to identify dependent clauses.

(a) Rehana told us that her purse is missing.
(b) The magazine, which was her favourite, has a red cover.

In the first example, **'that'** introduces the dependent clause. Sentence (b) features a dependent clause marked by commas. Alone, the clause poses a question. In the **appositive** form, it adds a description of the magazine to the sentence.

Kinds of Subordinate Clause

Subordinate clauses are of three types.

1. Adjective clause
2. Adverbial clause
3. Noun clause

Adjective Clauses

An adjective clause acts as an adjective, modifying a noun or pronoun. Use an adjective clause when an adjective or two will not suffice. Often, the relative pronouns **who, whose, whom, which,** and **that** attach adjective clauses to their antecedents.

(a) She is the girl who secured first position.
(b) This is the house where I lived.
(c) That is the girl whom I love.

Adverb Clauses

An **adverb clause** (not adverbial) acts as an adverb and indicates the time, manner, or degree of an action. Adverb clauses often begin with subordinate conjunctions.

1. Adverb clause of time

(a) I get up before the sun rises.
(b) She cooked after her husband went to market.

2. Adverb clause of place

(a) This is the room, where I lived in.
(b) This is the hotel where she was murdered .

3. Adverb clause of manner

(a) She behaved as if she is known to me.
(b) He cried as though he was ruined.

4. Adverb clause of reason

(a) I am happy because my son passed in IAS.
(b) He is sad as he failed in the examination.

5. Adverb clause of purpose

(a) He worked hard so that he could succeed.
(b) Run fast lest you should miss the train.

6. Adverb clause of condition

(a) I will go if he comes.
(b) You can't pass unless you study sincerely.

7. Adverb Clause of contrast or concession

(a) Though he is poor, he is reliable.
(b) He didn't work hard, however he passed.

8. Adverb clause of comparison

(a) He is not so strong as his brother.
(b) She is as beautiful as her elder sister.

9. Adverb clause of result : (consequence)

(a) He is so poor that he cannot buy a pen.
(b) She speaks so slowly that I cannot hear her.

Noun Clauses

A noun clause is a clause acting as a noun, sometimes as the subject of a sentence. **If you can replace the clause with 'it,' you have identified a noun clause.**

How he thinks is a mystery to me.

It is a mystery to me. How he thinks is a noun clause.

Also, to recognise a 'noun clause' put question 'what ?' to the main verb,the answer is the noun clause.

(a) She asked me where I was going ?

She asked me--------- what?

Ans. Where I was going?

Subordinate noun clause

(b) I know that you are an intelligent student.

I know -------- what?

'That you are an intelligent student' is a subordinate noun clause.

Functions

(A) As subject of the verb

(a) What he does is not known to me?
what he does, is the subject of the verb 'is'?

(b) What I will do is uncertain?
what I will do, is the subject of the verb 'is'.

(c) That you abused him, surprised me.
That you abused him, is the subject of the verb 'surprised'.

(B) As object of the verb

(a) I asked him where he was going ?
Underlined clause, is the object of the verb 'asked'

(b) I can't say what does he do.
Underlined clause, is the object of the verb 'say'.

(c) She told me that she would resign.
Underlined clause is the object of the verb 'told'.

(C) As object of preposition

(a) Please listen to what he says.
Underlined noun clause is the object of the preposition 'to'.

(b) I have no problem, except that you should behave properly.
Underlined noun clause, is the object of the preposition, 'except'.

(c) I find no sense in what you spoke to her.
Underlined noun clause, is the object of the preposition, 'in'.

(D) As complement to a verb

(a) This is what I said ?
What I said is the complement of the verb 'is'.

(b) Life is how we enjoy it.
Underlined noun clause is the complement of the verb' is'.

(c) It is what I mean ?
Underlined noun clause, is the complement of the verb' is'.

(E) As case in apposition to the noun or pronoun

In each of the following sentences the noun clause is in apposition to a noun or pronoun :

(a) The news that Rajiv Gandhi was killed shocked everyone.
The news—principal clause ; that Rajiv Gandhi was killed—subordinate noun clause, which is in apposition to the noun news.

(b) The information that the Ossama Bin Laden is killed is wrong.
Underlined clause is in apposition to the noun, information.

(c) His wish that he may become an MLA is unreasonable.
Underlined clause is in apposition to the noun, wish.

(F) As object to a participle

Noun clause also functions as object to the participle.

(a) I reached there hoping that she would be there.

(b) He came to me, hoping that I would give him some money.

(c) She came to me thinking that I should help her.
Underlined clauses are objects to the participle (hoping, thinking).

(G) Object to an Infinitive

Noun clause also functions as object to the infinitive.

(a) I want to know what he thinks.

(b) I want to see how does he live.

(c) He wants to enquire where does he live.
Underlined noun clauses are object to the Infinitives (to know, to see, to enquire).

Phrase

A phrase is a group of words without a subject verb or complete thought.

(A) Noun phrases

A noun phrase is a group of words that does the work of a noun.

(a) She needs something.

(b) The girls want to go cinema.

The word 'something' is a noun. It is the object of the verb needs in sentence (a). Similarly, the group of words 'to go cinema' is the object of the verb 'want' in sentence (b). Hence this group of words does the work of a noun. The group of words to go cinema is therefore a noun phrase.

(B) Adjective phrase

An adjective phrase is a group of words that does the work of an adjective. Learn the following adjectives and the adjective phrases that are equivalent to them:

Adjectives	**Adjective Phrases**
Adjective Phrases	a medal made of silver
a purple dress	a dress of purple colour
a white tiger	a tiger with a white skin
a blue eyed girl	a girl with blue eyes

Look at the following examples, here a group of words (underlined) are doing the work of an adjective.

(a) The musician was a kind man.
The musician was a man with kind nature.

(a) The land lady was a wealthy woman.
The land lady was a woman with great wealth.

(C) Adverb phrases

An adverb phrase is a group of words that does the work of an adverb.

Like an adverb, it may modify, a verb, an adjective or a adverb.

Learn the following adverbs and the adverb phrases that are equivalent to them.

Adverbs	**Adverb Phrases**
cowardly	in a coward manner
quickly	with quickness.
beautifully	in a beautiful manner
carelessly	without any care.
rudely	in a rude manner

Look at the following examples, here a group of words (underlined) are doing the work of an adverb.

1. (a) Sapna ran quickly.
Sapna ran with great speed.
2. (a) She does his work carelessly.
She does his work without any care.

Simple, Compound, Complex and Mixed Sentences

Simple Sentence

The most basic type of sentence is the **simple sentence,** which contains only one clause or one finite verb. A simple sentence contains a subject and a verb (finite), and expresses a complete thought.

(a) Some girls like to study in the morning.

(b) Ram and Shyam play volleyball every afternoon.

(c) Anita goes to the library and studies there.

The three examples above are all simple sentences. Note that sentence B contains a compound subject, and sentence C contains a compound verb. Simple sentences, therefore, contain a subject and verb and express a complete thought, but they can also contain a compound subjects or verbs.

A simple sentence can be as short as one word.

(d) Run!

Usually, however, the sentence has a subject as well as a predicate and both the subject and the predicate may have modifiers. The following are the simple sentences, because each contains only one clause:

(a) The ice on the river **melts** quickly under the warm sun.

(b) Lying exposed without its blanket of snow, the ice on the river **melts** quickly under the warm sun.

As you can see, a simple sentence can be quite long—it is a mistake to think that you can differentiate a simple sentence from a compound sentence or a complex sentence simply by its length.

Compound Sentence

A **compound sentence** is a sentence formed by two or more independent clauses. Use a comma to separate long independent clauses joined by co-ordinating conjunctions **for, and, nor, but, or, yet, so.** (Helpful hint: FANBOYS.) **and, but, or** or **nor**. Place a comma before the conjunction.

(a) I tried to speak French, and Ram tried to speak English.
(b) Ram played football, so Mira went shopping.
(c) Ram played football, for Mira went shopping.

The above three sentences are compound sentences. Each sentence contains two independent clauses, and they are joined by a co-ordinator with a comma preceding it. Note how the conscious use of co-ordinators can change the relationship between the clauses.

A compound sentence is most effective when you use it to create a sense of balance or contrast between two (or more) equally important pieces of information :

Mumbai has better clubs, but Jaipur has better cinemas.

A compound sentence consists of two or more independent (principal) clauses joined together by a co-ordinating conjunction. A compound sentence in some cases includes one or more subordinate clauses also. Compound sentence is also called **double** when it is made up of two independent (principal) clauses. The term **multiple** is used for a sentence having more than two independent (principal) clauses.

1. The sun rose, and the fog dispersed. *(two principal clauses)*
2. She must weep, or she will be mad. *(two principal clauses)*
3. Either come in, or go out. *(two principal clauses)*
4. Walk fast, or else you may miss the train. *(two principal clauses)*
5. They found the dog, but distressed them to see it, for it was lame. *(three principal clauses)*
6. The mother asked her how she got the injuries but she refused to answer. *(two principal clauses + one subordinate clause)*
7. She asserts what she means and she means what she asserts. *(two principal clauses + two subordinate clauses)*

The relation between two principal clauses of a compound sentence depends upon the conjunction used to join these clauses.

Cumulative : If the two clauses are joined together by any of the following co-ordinating conjunctions the relation is cumulative. Such conjunctons are : **and, not only ..... but also, as well as, nor, also.**

1. The sun rose and the fog dispersed.
2. He is not only a great writer but also a great leader.
3. He as well as his father was present in the function.
4. She cannot write nor can she speak.
5. She plays the tabla she sings also.

Adversative: Conjunctions **but, nevertheless, yet, still,** etc. denote adversative relation between the two clauses.

1. He is rich but he is miser.
2. He did his best nevertheless he failed.
3. He is poor yet he is honest.
4. She is proudy still her husband loves her.

Alternative : Conjunctions **or, either ..... or, neither ...... nor, else,** etc. show the choice or alternate options available.

1. She must weep or she will go mad.
2. Either you come in or go out.
3. Neither a pen nor a pencil is required.
4. Walk fast or else you may miss the train.

Illative : (stating an inference) Conjunctions **therefore, so, for, consequently,** etc. show illative relationship between the two principal clauses.

1. She is intelligent therefore she secures good marks.
2. He has fever so he can't attend the office.
3. He is tired for he worked all the day.
4. The sides are equal consequently the angles are equal.

In some cases no conjunction is required or used to join two principal clauses. Discipline promotes punctuality, indiscipline spoils it.

In some cases two principal clauses can also be joined by a relative pronoun or adverb to form a compound sentence. In such cases the relative pronoun is used in a continuative sense (not in restrictive sense).

1. I went to Shimla where(and there) I stayed for three weeks.
2. He killed all the prisoners which (and this) was a cruel act.

Compound sentences are sometimes contracted.

1. When the subject is common.

(a) He went to hospital but (he) left soon.
(b) She came here but (she) didn't talk to anyone.

2. **When the predicate is common.**
   (a) He as well as you will be held responsible.
   (b) She is rich but (she is) miser.

Complex Sentence

A complex sentence has an independent clause joined by one or more dependent clauses. Unlike a compound sentence, however, a complex sentence contains clauses which are not equal. Consider the following examples:

Simple : She invited me to a party. I do not want to go.

Compound : She invited me to a party, but I do not want to go.

Complex : Although she invited me to a party, I do not want to go.

In the first example, there are two separate simple sentences: 'She invited me to a party' and 'I do not want to go.' The second example joins them together into a single sentence with the co-ordinating conjunction 'but,' but both parts could still stand as independent sentences—they are entirely equal, and the reader cannot tell which is the most important. In the third example, however, the sentence has changed quite a bit : the first clause, 'Although she invited me to a party,' has become incomplete, or a dependent clause. A complex sentence is very different from a simple sentence or a compound sentence because it makes clear which idea is the most important.

A complex sentence always has a subordinator such as because, since, after, although or when or a relative pronoun such as that, who, or which etc.

(a) When she handed in her homework, she forgot to give the teacher the last page.
(b) The teacher returned the homework after he noticed the error.
(c) The students are studying because they have a test today evening.
(d) After they finished studying, Ram and Mira went to the movies.
(e) Ram and Mira went to the movies after they finished studying.

When a complex sentence begins with a subordinating conjunction such as sentences (a) and (d), a comma is required at the end of the dependent clause. When an independent clause begins the sentence with subordinators in the middle as in sentences (b), (c) and (e), no comma is required.

Mixed Sentence

There are also mixed types of sentences which are neither compound nor complex. Rather than joining two simple sentences together, a co-ordinating conjunction sometimes joins two complex sentences, or one simple sentence and one complex sentence. Such sentence is called a compound- **complex or mixed sentence.**

The parcel arrived in the morning, but the courier left before she could check the contents.

» *Exercises*

Exercise 1

Pick out the principal clauses and the subordinate clauses in the following sentences

1. He runs as fast as possible.
2. Your shirt is better than mine.
3. She as well as I went there.
4. All that glitters is not gold.
5. He drew the revolver, took aim and fired.

Solutions

1. He runs - principal clause
   as fast as possible - subordinate clause
2. Your shirt is better - principal clause
   than mine - subordinate clause
3. She went there - principal clause
   as well as I went there - subordinate clause
4. All is not gold - principal clause
   that glitters - subordinate clause
5. He drew the revolver - principal clause
   He took aim - principal clause
   He fired - Principal Clause

Exercise 2

Pick out relative clause in the following sentences

1. This is the pen, that Ram bought yesterday.
2. He who helps the poor is helped by almighty.
3. I have found the purse, which I lost yesterday.

4. The dog that barks does not bite.
5. He who serves the helpless, is always happy.

Solutions

1. That Ram bought yesterday.
2. Who helps the poor.
3. Which I lost yesterday.
4. That barks.
5. Who serves the helpless.

Exercise 3

Pick out the adverb clause in following sentences

1. We eat that we may live.
2. The more she gets, the more she demands.
3. The tree is so tall that an old can't climb it up.
4. However hard she may work, she will not succeed.
5. Even if he doesn't cooperate me, I will fight alone.

Solutions

1. That we may live.
2. The more she gets.
3. That an old can't climb it up.
4. However hard she may work.
5. Even if he doesn't cooperate me.

Exercise 4

Find out the noun clause

1. Where he lives is not known to me.
2. She told me that she would not support me.
3. Please ask him, what he wants.
4. I can't say what he does.
5. It is useless to discuss, what he utters.

Solutions

1. Where he lives.
2. That she would not support me.
3. What he wants?
4. What he does?
5. What he utters?

Exercise 5

Pick out the adjective clause

1. I know the place, where she is hidden.
2. This is the place, where the murder was committed.
3. The idea why she spoke so is now clear.
4. This is the hotel, that my friend built.
5. One who lives in glass house, should refrain from throwing stone at others.

Solutions

1. Where she is hidden.
2. Where the murder was committed.
3. Why she spoke so is now clear.
4. That my friend built.
5. One who lives in glass house.

Exercise 6

State which of the following sentences are simple, compound or complex

1. Take whatever you like.
2. I am certain that she has gone mad.
3. I am very tired for I have been walking all the morning.
4. Honesty is the best policy.
5. He acted according to my advice.
6. God made the country and man made the town.
7. She wrote a letter and posted it through her brother.
8. Write as fast as you can.
9. She as well as her sister is guilty.
10. He is the leader whom we all respect.
11. I gave her the bag because she needed it.
12. He is sure of his success.
13. I like you no less than him.
14. I don't know the month of my birth.
15. She told me that she would come on Monday.

Solutions

1. complex	2. complex	3. compound
4. simple	5. simple	6. compound
7. compound	8. compound	9. compound
10. complex	11. complex	12. simple
13. complex	14. simple	15. complex

Exercise 7

State which of the following sentences are simple, compound or complex

1. Joe waited for the train, but the train was late.
2. I looked for Mary and Samantha at the bus station, but they arrived at the station before noon and had left on the bus before I arrived.
3. Mary and Samantha arrived at the bus station before noon, and they had left on the bus before I arrived.
4. Mary and Samantha had left on the bus before I arrived, so I did not see them at the bus station.
5. Because Mary and Samantha arrived at the bus station before noon, I did not see them at the station.
6. While he waited at the train station, Joe realised that the train was late.
7. After they left on the bus, Mary and Samantha realised that Joe was waiting at the train station.

8. Joe waited for the train.
9. The train was late.
10. Mary and Samantha took the bus.
11. I looked for Mary and Samantha at the bus station.

Solutions

1. compound 2. compound 3. compound
4. compound 5. complex 6. complex
7. complex 8. simple 9. simple
10. simple 11. simple

Exercise 8

State about whether the following sentences are simple, compound, complex, mixed and explain your answer

1. I do not own a Porsche.
2. When the train arrives and if Ms.Langlois is on it, she will be served with a subpoena.
3. Susanne wanted to be here, but she cannot come because her car is in the shop.
4. The football game was cancelled because of the rain.
5. The football game was cancelled because it was raining.
6. Unless my girlfriend postpones her visit from Calgary, I will not have time to study for my exam.
7. I ate the sushi and left the restaurant.
8. Call your father as soon as you arrive in Antigonish.
9. Democracy is a noble goal; it is important, however, to protect the minority from the tyranny of the majority.
10. Ottawa is the capital of Canada, but Toronto is the capital of Ontario.

Solutions

1. This is a simple sentence, containing only one independent clause.
2. This is a complex sentence. At first glance, it might look like a compound-complex sentence because of the conjunction 'and' joining the two dependent clauses 'when the train arrives 'and' if Ms. Langlois is on it'; however, there is only one independent clause in the sentence, so it cannot be compound.
3. This is a mixed (compound-complex) sentence. First, it contains two independent clauses—'Suzanne wanted to be here' and 'she cannot come because her car is in the shop'—joined by the co-ordinating conjunction 'but'; the second independent clause, however, contains the dependent clause 'because her car is in the shop,' making the sentence complex as well as compound.
4. This is a simple sentence: since it does not have a predicate, 'because of the rain' is a phrase rather than a clause.
5. This is a complex sentence since it contains the dependent clause 'because it was raining'.
6. This is a complex sentence, containing the independent clause 'I will not have time to study for my exam' and the dependent clause 'unless my girlfriend postpones her visit from Calgary.' Note the subordinating conjunction 'unless' at the beginning of the dependent clause.
7. This is a simple sentence. It is easy to see, however, why someone might think that this is a compound sentence, since it contains the co-ordinating conjunction 'and'; however, the conjunction actually joins two predicates—'ate the sushi' and 'left the restaurant'—within a single clause.
8. This is a complex sentence because it contains the dependent clause 'as soon as you arrive in Antigonish'. If that information were in a phrase instead of a clause, however, the sentence would be a simple sentence :

   Call you father upon your arrival in Antigonish.
9. This is a special type of compound sentence, where the two independent clauses—'democracy is a noble goal' and 'it is important, however, to protect the minority ...' are joined by a semicolon instead of a co-ordinating conjunction.
10. This is a compound sentence, because it contains two independent clauses joined by the co-ordinating conjunction 'and'.

Unit

22

Synthesis of Sentences

Synthesis means combining two or more different kind of sentences to form a new one. Two or more simple sentences can be combined into a simple, compound or complex sentence.

Combining Two or More Simple Sentences into One Simple Sentence

Learn the following ways of combining two or more simple sentences into one simple sentence

Using a participle.

1. (a) He saw a lion.
   (b) He fled away.
   Seeing a lion he fled away.
2. (a) She heard a noise.
   (b) She ran out.
   Hearing a noise she ran out.

Using a preposition with a noun or gerund.

1. (a) He was rusticated.
   (b) He had broken the school window.
   He was rusticated for breaking the school window.
2. (a) His wife died.
   (b) He heard the news.
   (c) He lost consciousness.

On hearing the news of his wife's death, he lost consciousness.

Using a noun or a phrase in apposition.

1. (a) I went to London.
   (b) London is the capital of Britain.
   I went to London, the capital of Britain.
2. (a) Gandhiji was a moralist.
   (b) He had once been a lawyer.
   (c) He struggled hard to attain freedom.

Gandhiji, a moralist and once a lawyer, struggled hard to attain freedom.

Using the nominative absolute construction.

1. (a) The police arrived.
   (b) The thieves fled away.
   The police having arrived the thieves fled away.
2. (a) The sun rose.
   (b) The fog dispersed.

The sun having risen, the fog dispersed.

Using an infinitive.

1. (a) I will go there.
   (b) I will settle the matter.
   I will go there to settle the matter.
2. (a) He came here
   (b) He signed the agreement
   He came here to sign the agreement.

Using an adverb or an adverbial phrase.

1. (a) He is intelligent.
   (b) He can solve this puzzle. He can solve this puzzle.
   He is intelligent enough to solve this puzzle.
2. (a) I have time.
   (b) I can go to hospital.
   I have time enough to go to hospital.

Using 'and'

1. (a) Harish played cricket.
   (b) Ramesh played cricket.
   Harish and Ramesh played cricket.
2. (a) Ram knows driving.
   (b) Shyam knows driving.
   Ram and Shyam know driving.

Several of the above methods may be combined in the same sentence. For example:

1. (a) The building caught fire.
   (b) All house hold articles burnt to ashes.
   The building having caught fire, all the household articles burnt to ashes.
2. (a) The job was completed.
   (b) He went on leave.
   The job having been completed he went on leave.

Combination of Two or More Simple Sentences into a Single Compound Sentence

Simple sentences may also be combined to form a compound sentence by the use of co-ordinating conjunctions. The coordinating conjunctions are four types: (1) cumulative (2) adversative (3) alternative and (4) illative.

Using cumulative conjunctions : and, both-and, as well as, not only-but also, not less than, etc. are called cumulative conjunctions.

using 'and'

1. (a) I watched TV.
   (b) He played football.
   I watched TV and he played football.
2. (a) The police came.
   (b) The thief ran away.
   The police came and the thief ran away.

Using 'both............and'

1. (a) He ate a biscuit.
   (b) He ate an orange.
   He ate both a biscuit and an orange.
2. (a) He is a student.
   (b) He is a painter.
   He is both a student and a painter.

Using as 'well.......as'

1. (a) Suresh is going to Jaipur.
   (b) Kuku is going to Jaipur.
   Suresh as well as Kuku is going to Jaipur.
2. (a) He is guilty.
   (b) She is guilty.
   He as well as she is guilty.

Using, 'not only......but also'

1. (a) He is a painter.
   (b) He is a student.
   He is not only a painter but also a student.
2. (a) Ram will go to Jaipur.
   (b) Sita will go to Jaipur.
   Not only Ram but also Sita will go to Jaipur.

Using Adversative Conjunctions : But, still, however, whereas, only, while, yet, etc., are adversative conjunctions. These are used to add two sentences having contrasting ideas.

Using 'but'

1. (a) He is smart.
   (b) He is not intelligent.
   He is smart but he is not intelligent.
2. (a) He worked hard.
   (b) He could not pass.
   He worked hard but he could not pass.

Using 'still' or 'yet'

1. (a) He worked hard.
   (b) He failed.
   He worked hard yet he failed.
2. (a) I don't support her.
   (b) She respects me.
   I do not support her still she respects me.

Using 'however'

1. (a) She did not prepare well.
   (b) She succeeded.
   She did not prepare well however she succeeded.
2. (a) Your leaves are not due.
   (b) You may go.
   Your leaves are not due however you may go.

Using 'nevertheless'

1. (a) He is a miser.
   (b) He spent one lac in the marriage.
   He is a miser nevertheless he spent one lac in the marriage.
2. (a) He is a rich man.
   (b) He is not contented.
   He is a rich man nevertheless he is not contented.

Using 'only'

1. (a) He could not solve it.
   (b) He became hopeless.
   He could not solve it only he became hopeless.
2. (a) Go anywhere you like.
   (b) You inform me.
   Go any where you like only inform me.

Using 'While' and 'Whereas'

1. (a) He was playing.
   (b) She was watching TV.
   He was playing while she was watching TV.
2. (a) Ram won the game.
   (b) Shyam lost this chance.
   Ram won the game whereas Shyam lost this chance.

Using Alternate Conjunctions : Conjunctions which express a choice between two alternatives are called alternative conjunctions. Conjunctions **or, or else, either ..... or, neither .... nor** express a choice between two alternatives.

Using 'or' and 'or else'.

1. (a) Go away.
   (b) Come in.
   Go away or come in.
2. (a) Run fast.
   (b) You will miss the train.
   Run fast or you will miss the train.

Using 'either...or' and 'neither ...nor'

1. (a) Come in.
   (b) Go out.
   Either come in or go out.
2. (a) Do not be a borrower.
   (b) Do not be a lender.
   Be neither a borrower nor a lender.
3. (a) A pen is not required.
   (b) A pencil is not required.
   Neither a pen nor a pencil is required.

Using Illative (causative) Conjunction : Conjunctions **therefore, so, for, hence,** etc. are called causative conjunctions.

Using 'therefore'

1. (a) He broke the glass.
   (b) He was punished.
   He broke the glass therefore he was punished.
2. (a) He is honest.
   (b) He was rewarded.
   He is honest therefore he was rewarded.

Using 'so'

1. (a) You are late.
   (b) You are fined.
   You are late so you are fined.
2. (a) We are late.
   (b) We should move fast.
   We are late so we should move fast.

Using 'for'

1. (a) Everyone has to die one day.
   (b) Man is mortal.
   Every one has to die one day for man is mortal.
2. (a) He forgave her.
   (b) She apologized publicly.
   He forgave her for she apologised publicly.

Using 'hence'

1. (a) It is very cold.
   (b) We purchased some winter wears.
   It is very cold hence we purchased some winter wears.
2. (a) He is a sincere worker.
   (b) He was promoted.
   He is a sincere worker hence he was promoted.

Using Who, When, Where, Which, in Continuative Sense.

1. (a) I went to London.
   (b) I got a job.
   I went to London, where I got a job.
2. (a) I killed a rat.
   (b) It was a cruel act.
   I killed a rat, which was a cruel act.

When relative pronoun who, where and which are used in continuative sense use comma before them.

Combination of Two or More simple Sentences into a Single Complex Sentence

Using noun clause as subordinate clause : A noun clause can be introduced by the conjunction 'that' or by some interrogative adverb.

1. (a) I do not know.
   (b) Who is he?
   I do not know who he is.
2. (a) I cannot say.
   (b) Has he come?
   I can not say whether he has come.
3. (a) Tell me.
   (b) Where does she live?
   Tell me where she lives.

4. (a) Inform him.
   (b) When will she go?
   Inform him when she will go.
5. (a) Do you know?
   (b) What does he do?
   Do you know what he does?

Using adjective clause as subordinate clause

1. (a) This is the magazine.
   (b) I want to purchase.
   This is the magazine that I want to purchase.
2. (a) This is the hotel.
   (b) I lived here for three months.
   This is the hotel where I lived for three months.
3. (a) This is the girl.
   (b) She secured first position.
   This is the girl who secured first position.

Using adverb clause

1. (a) I wrote a letter.
   (b) I posted it.
   I posted the letter after I had written it.
2. (a) I watched TV.
   (b) I went to market.
   I went to market after I had watched TV.
3. (a) He is so poor.
   (b) He cannot buy his books.
   He is so poor that he cannot buy his books.
4. (a) He is intelligent.
   (b) His sister is equally intelligent.
   He is as intelligent as his sister.
5. (a) He finished his work.
   (b) Then he watched a movie.
   He didn't watch a movie until he finished his work.

» Exercises

Exercise 1

Combine these simple sentences into a simple sentence

1. (a) She heard a noise.
   (b) She woke up.
2. (a) He saw a tiger.
   (b) He ran away.
3. (a) He was tired of playing.
   (b) He went to take bath.
4. (a) She sat on a chair.
   (b) She wrote a letter.
5. (a) He has two kids.
   (b) He has to nourish them.
6. (a) Turn to the right.
   (b) You will reach the railway station.
7. (a) I will go to market.
   (b) I want to buy a box.
8. (a) I received her message.
   (b) I was very happy.
9. (a) My parents were much delighted.
   (b) They got the news of my promotion.
10. (a) He was punished.
    (b) He had stolen my beg.

Solutions

1. Hearing a noise she woke up.
2. Seeing a tiger he ran away.
3. Tired of playing he went to take bath.
4. Sitting on a chair she wrote a letter.
5. He has two kids to nourish.
6. Turning to the right you will reach the railway station.
7. I will go to market to buy a box.
8. I was very happy to receive her message.
9. My parents wero much delighted to get the news of my promotion.
10. He was punished for stealing my bag.

Exercise 2

Combine simple sentences into a complex sentence

1. (a) He is a gangster.
   (b) Everybody knows it.
2. (a) I informed you yesterday.
   (b) You should rely on it.
3. (a) I met a girl.
   (b) She was very beautiful.
4. (a) I met a woman.
   (b) Whose purse was snatched by someone.
5. (a) Tell me the time.
   (b) You went there on Sunday.
6. (a) I have seen the place.
   (b) The accident had taken place there.

7. (a) The thief saw the constable.
   (b) He ran away.
8. (a) Ram is intelligent.
   (b) His brother Shyam is equally intelligent.
9. (a) He fled somewhere.
   (b) The police could not trace him.
10. (a) India is a powerful nation.
    (b) Pakistan is not so powerful.

Solutions

1. Everybody knows that he is a gangster.
2. You should rely on what I informed you yesterday.
3. I met a girl who was very beautiful.
4. I met a woman whose purse was snatched by someone.
5. Tell me the time when you went there on Sunday.
6. I have seen the place where the accident had taken place.
7. As soon as the thief saw the constable he ran away.
8. His brother Shyam is as intelligent as Ram.
9. He fled where the police could not trace him.
10. Pakistan is not so powerful as India.

Exercise 3

Combine these two simple sentences into a compound sentence

1. (a) He is slow.
   (b) He is sincere.
2. (a) He was annoyed.
   (b) He kept quite.
3. (a) He is a hardworker.
   (b) He is an intelligent man.
4. (a) I went to the market.
   (b) I purchased a pen.
5. (a) Get in.
   (b) You may fall ill.
6. (a) I shall try to help you.
   (b) I cannot make any promise.
7. (a) Do not walk so quickly.
   (b) You may fall.
8. (a) I went to the fair.
   (b) I bought a scenery.
9. (a) You may have some cold.
   (b) You may have some coffee.
10. (a) He got up.
    (b) He went to the college.

Solutions

1. He is slow but he is sincere.
2. He was annoyed but he kept quite.
3. He is not only a hard worker but also an intelligent man.
4. I went to the market and purchased a pen.
5. Get in or you may fall ill.
6. I shall try to help you but I can't make any promise.
7. Do not walk so quickly; you may fall.
8. I went to the fair and bought a scenery.
9. You may have some cold or some coffee.
10. He got up and went to the college.

Exercise 4

Combine the following sentences

1. (a) He was absent.
   (b) He was ill.
2. (a) He was cooking.
   (b) His wife arrived.
3. (a) He was washing the clothes.
   (b) She was watching TV.
4. (a) You must learn Grammar.
   (b) You will not pass.
5. (a) Hari cleaned the room.
   (b) Shyam washed the dishes.
   (c) Ram cooked the food.
6. (a) Jakob washed the clothes.
   (b) Jena ironed the clothes.
   (c) Rena put the clothes in the cupboard.
7. (a) Ram is my friend.
   (b) He is waiting for me.
8. (a) He lost his purse.
   (b) He lost his bicycle.
9. (a) Tell me.
   (b) How many times did you telephone her?
10. (a) This is the office.
    (b) I work here.

Solutions

1. He was absent because he was ill.
2. When his wife arrived he was cooking.
3. While he was washing the clothes, she was watching TV.
4. Unless you learn grammar you will not pass.
5. Hari cleaned the room, Shyam washed the dishes and Ram cooked the food.
6. Jackob washed, Jena ironed and Rena put the clothes in the cupboard.
7. Ram, my friend, is waiting for me.
8. He not only lost him purse but also his bicycle.
9. Tell me how many times you telephoned her?
10. This is the office where I work.

Exercise 5

Convert the following compound sentences into complex sentences

1. He is a poor man, but he is honest .
2. My brother gave me a watch and I have lost it.
3. She was very tired and so she didn't cook food.
4. She is still in teens, but she has the wisdom of a matured woman.
5. I have lost the purse but I have found it now.
6. She is very affable and so I love her.
7. He is doing his best and I am sure of it.
8. Be sincere and you will be respected by everyone.
9. Send the money in advance or you will not get the magazine.
10. You are a teetotaller and I know it.

Solutions

1. He is an honest man although he is poor.
2. I have lost the watch which my brother gave me.
3. As she was very tired, she didn't cook food.
4. She has the wisdom of a matured woman, although she is still in teens.
5. I have found the purse that I had lost.
6. I love her because she is very affable.
7. I am sure that he is doing his best.
8. If you are sincere, you will be respected by everyone.
9. You will not get the magazine unless you send the money in advance.
10. I know that you are a teetotaller.

Exercise 6

Combine the following sentences

1. (a) Are you an editor?
   (b) Are you an author?
2. (a) She is very weak.
   (b) She can't climb up the hill.
3. (a) He will pass.
   (b) It is certain.
4. (a) She is a thief.
   (b) She was sentences to prison.
5. (a) He heard the news.
   (b) He became sad..
6. (a) It may rain.
   (b) We may cancel our programme.
7. (a) He is a disabled
   (b) He is self confident of winning the race.
8. (a) He did not attend the function.
   (b) He did not inform me.
9. (a) He is a liar.
   (b) It is known to everybody.
10. (a) The tea is very hot.
    (b) One can not drink it.

Solutions

1. Are you an editor or an author?
2. She is too weak to climb up the hill.
3. It is certain that he will pass.
4. She is a thief so she was sentenced to prison.
5. When he heard the news he became sad.
6. If it rains, our programme may be cancelled.
7. Though he is a disabled yet he is self confident of winning the race.
8. He neither attended the function nor informed me.
9. That he is a liar is known to everybody.
10. The tea is too hot to drink.

» Unit

23

Synonyms

Frequently Used Words

Word	Synonyms
abandon	desert, forsake, leave, relinquish
abase	degrade, disgrace, humiliate, demean, dishonour,
abbreviate	curtail, abridge, compress, shorten, truncate
aberration	deviation, wandering, errant, irregular, weird,
abet	aid, assist, condone, favour, support, promote
abhor	hate, detest, loathe, abominate
abstain	refuse, renounce, avoid, shun
abstruse	recondite, hidden, difficult
absurd	ridiculous, silly, foolish, preposterous
abundant	ample, copious, plentiful, bountiful,
abut	adjoin, border, verge on, join
acclaim	applaud, cheer, celebrate, extol
accommodate	adapt, adjust, reconcile
acme	summit, apex, zenith, peak
acquiesce (in)	assent, rest, accede, comply, concur, consent,
adequate	enough, sufficient, proportionate
adherent	sticking to, follower, partisan, devotee
admiration	esteem, praise, respect, approval, approbation,
adversity	misfortune, calamity, catastrophe, hostility
affliction	distress, ordeal, suffering, sorrow

Word	Synonyms
ally	colleague, helper, partner, accomplice
alms	dole, gratuity, money, clothes and food that are given to poor people.
ameliorate	make better, improve, amend
antithesis	contrasting, reverse
aphorism	maxim, apothegm, axiom, proverb, motto, adage
appraise	evaluate, estimate
apprehend	seize, know, fear, arrest, understand
assiduous	painstaking, diligent, industrious, laborious,
assistance	help, aid, succor, collaboration, sustenance
astonish	amaze, surprise, astound, flabbergast
audacious	bold, brazen, impudent, daring
backlash	repercussion, reaction, recoil
bad	evil, wicked, devilish, naughty, worthless
bait	snare, trap, decoy
banal	dull, trite, hackneyed, prosaic
banish	exile, ostracize, deport,
barbaric	savage, uncivilised, primitive
base	ignoble, mean, low, foundation
bedlam	pandemonium, chaos, mayhem, clamor, confusion
beg	implore, solicit, supplicate, beseech, request, plead

Word	Synonyms
behaviour	conduct, demeanour, deportment, manner
belligerent	warlike, pugnacious, hostile
bewilder	confound, perplex, befuddle, befog, baffle, daze,
bigoted	biased, prejudiced, dogmatic, opinionated
bizarre	unusual, grotesque, fantastic
blame	censure, reprove, condemn, reproach
blessing	benediction, god's help or protection
bravo	fearless, intrepid, dauntless, valiant, bold
brittle	frail, fragile, hard but easily broken
browbeat	intimidate, bully, frighten, threaten
burlesque	mock, imitate, tease, satirize, ridicule, jeer, deride
cajole	persuade, flatter, wheedle, coax
calm	quiet, tranquil, peaceful, sedate, composed, placid,
captious	censorious, hypercritical, faultfinding
care	solicitude, anxiety, misgiving, foreboding
charlatan	impostor, mountebank, quack, chicane, trickster
choleric	irascible, petulant, bad-tempered
colossal	gigantic, huge, enormous, mammoth, vast
conceit	pride, vanity, ego, arrogance
concise	short, brief, abridged, compact
condign	due, merited, well deserved, due, suitablo
condone	pardon, forgive, excuse, overlook
confess	admit, apologise, own, acknowledge
constant	eternal, perpetual, incessant, continuous
contingent (on)	liable, possible, uncertain
conversant (with)	familiar, well versed, acquainted
crafty	cunning, artful, sly, calculating
cross	crusty, fretful, ill-humoured
cruelty	tyranny, persecution, brutality, oppression, ferocity
cursory	hasty, superficial, careless
cynical	misanthropic, moody, eccentric, sardonic, sarcastic

Word	Synonyms
damage	loss, harm, injury, detriment
dangerous	perilous, risky, hazardous, precarious
dear	expensive, costly, loved by somebody
decay	wither, fade, corrode, decline
definitive	limiting, final, positive
denounce	accuse, condemn, arraign, decry, censure
destitute	needy, forsaken, orphan
desultory	discontinuous, irregular, rambling
didactic	teaching, instructive, perfecting
diffident	modest, bashful, shy
discourse	lecture, sermon, exhortation, dissertation
dissipate	scatter, waste
divine	heavenly, celestial, graceful, godlike
economy	management, frugality, thrifty, judicious
effete	exhausted, old, worn out, tired
elicit	draw out, discover
elude	baffle, avoid, cheat, fool
emancipate	free, liberate, release, deliver, uplift
emulate	imitate, rival
entice	lure, persuade, allure, entrap
ephemeral	transient, short-lived
exacerbate	magnify, heighten, enlarge, overstate, amplify
exceptional	anomalous, unique, extraordinary
exculpate	absolve, vindicate
exigency	emergency, distress
exquisite	elegant, fine, matchless, exclusive
exterminate	uproot, eradicate, eliminate, destroy, annihilate
extravagant	prodigal, wasteful
extricate	disentangle, untangle
fallacy	imperfection, ambiguity, quirk, error
fallible	imperfect, erring, wrong
fascinate	charm, enchant, mesmerise, bewitch
fastidious	dainty, squeamish, hard to please
fatal	deadly, mortal, lethal, virulent
fate	lot, destiny, end
fatuous	silly, purposeless

Word	Synonyms
fecund	prolific, fertile, fruitful, luxuriant, productive
ferocious	savage, barbaric, fierce, wild, uncivilised
fictitious	false, imaginative, illusionary, fabricated, fanciful
fight	battle, contention, combat, struggle, conflict, strife
flagrant	notorious, outrageous, disgraceful
flamboyant	bombastic, ostentatious, ornate
flippant	pert, frivolous, impudent, saucy
forbid	prohibit, preclude, inhibit, debar
forerunner	precursor, herald, harbinger
fortitude	strength, firmness, valour, determination
fortuitous	chance, accidental
furbish	polish, spruce, renovate
fury	anger, rage, wrath, ire
garrulous	talkative, loquacious
gratification	satisfaction, enjoyment
guile	fraud, trickery, cunning
hamper	hinder, block, impede, prevent
haughty	arrogant, proud, egoist, obstinate
humane	kind, generous, benevolent, compassionate
humility	politeness, meekness, modesty
illiterate	unlearned, ignorant, uneducated
immaterial	unimportant, insignificant, useless, irrelevant
imminent	threatening, impending, approaching
impertinent	irrelevant, impudent, insolent, saucy
impotent	powerless, disabled, inadequate, incapable
inanimate	lifeless, dead, dormant, stagnant, extinct
indignant	angry, furious, irate, exasperated, outraged
inexorable	relentless, merciless, apathetic, harsh
ingenuous	artless, sincere, naive, innocent
insidious	cunning, clever, inventive, deceitful, sly
intimate	close, confidant, inform, cherished
irresolute	undecided, wavering, vacillating, unsettled
jolly	jovial, merry, cheerful, affable
joy	delight, pleasure, ecstasy, elation
jubilant	elated, triumphant
knave	fraud, cheat, scoundrel, rogue
lament	sorrow, mourn, grieve
lenient	forbearing, forgiving, compassionate, mild
lethargy	laziness, stupor, sluggishness, idleness
liberal	generous, kind, tolerant, permissive
likeness	similarity, resemblance, affinity
lively	active, enthusiastic, agile, brisk
loyal	devoted, faithful, trustworthy, honest
magnificent	splendid, grand, good, glorious
malice	bitterness, spite, ill-will, rancour, malevolence
meagre	small, tiny, inadequate, scanty
mean	low, petty, abject, selfish
melancholy	gloomy, sadness, sorrow, dejected
mighty	powerful, massive, strong, almighty
misery	sorrow, distress, affliction, grief
morbid	unhealthy, diseased, ghastly, horrid
mournful	sad, sorrow, gloomy, dejected
notable	memorable, remarkable, renowned, eminent
notorious	infamous, dishonourable, flagrant, blatant
obliterate	destroy, efface, demolish, erase
obscene	filthy, indecent, awful, bawdy, vulgar, gross, crude
obsolete	antiquated, old-fashioned, extinct, outworn
obtrude	thrust, pressure, importunate, interfere
opportune	timely, convenient, appropriate, well-chosen
pathetic	moving, touching, distressing, lamentable
patronize	condescend, stoop, snub
penalize	castigate, chastise, punish
pensive	thoughtful, rational, contemplative, reflective
perennial	perpetual, permanent, long lasting, constant
philanthropist	altruist, charitable, benevolent, kind
picturesque	charming, pictorial, scenic, sylvan

Word	Synonyms
pillage	plunder, loot, rob, destroy, steal
pious	religious, holy, devout, god-fearing
poignant	touching, moving, heart-rending
portray	delineate, depict, draw, sketch
possess	have, own, acquire, occupy, seize
prate	chatter, babble, tattle, talkative
precocious	premature, forward, advanced, developed
prerogative	privilege, advantage, exemption, right
prodigal	extravagant, wasteful, spendthrift, squander
prohibit	forbid, interdict, prevent, ban
quaint	queer, odd, singular, whimsical
qualm	scruple, doubt, uncertainty, suspicion
quarantined	separated, isolated, restrained
queer	strange, odd, indifferent, weird
quest	search, pursuit, inquisitive, crusade
questionable	doubtful, disputable, accountable, objectionable
quick	alive, swift, keen, fast
quip	retort, repartee, remark, jest
quirk	whim, caprice, fancy, peculiarity
radiant	brilliant, bright, intelligent, beaming
radical	fundamental, native, original, extreme, rebellious,
rash	impetuous, hasty, foolhardy, impulsive, heedless,
rebellion	mutiny, revolt, struggle, fight
refined	elegant, polished, cultured, sophisticated
refute	disprove, answer, deny
reiterate	repeat, do it again, rewrite, emphasis
rejoice	exult, delight, happy, glad
relevant	execute, applicable, pertinent, implement
remorse	repentance, regret, anguish, grief
remote	far, distant, interior place, aloof
renown	reputation, fame, famous, distinguished
resistance	opposition, hindrance, combat, struggle
ricochet	rebound, reflect, bounce, carom
ridiculous	absurd, silly, comical, ludicrous

Word	Synonyms
rigid	stiff, unyielding, stern
rimy	frosty, hazy, blurred
ruin	destruction, downfall, wreckage, devastation
rural	suburban, rustic, agrarian, country
rut	groove, hollow, furrow, habit, course, routine,
sacred	holy, consecrated, blessed, divine
sane	wise, sensible, sound, balanced
satiate	satisfy, surfeit, glut, happy
scanty	meagre, slender, insufficient, limited
scold	chide, rebuke, rail, complain
scorching	sweltering, searing, burning, fiery
scrutinize	examine, view, study, analyse, inspect
sensual	carnal, fleshy, voluptuous, attractive
servile	slavish, docile, timid, mean
shrewd	astute, perspicacious, canny, calculative
shy	bashful, coy, diffident, hesitant
solitary	single, hermetic, isolated, desolate
sordid	ugly, dirty, squalid, debauched
specimen	prototype, model, sample, dummy
spry	nimble, agile, animated, brisk, lively, quick
spurious	fake, counterfeit, artificial, false
static	firm, adamant, fixed
statute	law, decree, ordinance, edict, rule, act, bill
sterile	unproductive, barren, impotent, disinfected
stipulation	prerequisite, condition, qualification, clause
sublime	exalted, elevated, improved, magnified
substantiate	authenticate, validate, confirm, verify, corroborate,
subterfuge	ploy, scheme, stratagem, deceit, deception
succinct	brief, concise, terse, abbreviated
superficial	shallow, illusion, dream, outward
synonymous	identical, equivalent, alike, similar
taboo	forbidden, banned, prohibited

Word	Synonyms
temperate	moderate, balanced, controlled, sensible
temporal	worldly, materialistic, impermanent, ephemeral
tenacious	resolute, persistent, obstinate
tenet	belief, conviction, dogma, doctrine, creed,
tentative	temporary, transitory, brief
thankful	grateful, obliged, indebted, appreciative
therapeutics	curative, restorative, recuperative, remedial
thrive	flourish, succeed, grow
tirade	outburst, denunciation, harangue, speech, diatribe
tyrant	autocrat, despot, dictator, oppressor
tyro	amateur, novice, apprentice, neophyte
ulterior	concealed, shrouded, obscured
unique	unparalleled, single, peerless, unusual, matchless
urbane	sophisticated, suave, polite, refined, polished
urchin	waif, stray, foundling, orphan
urge	incite, press, implore, instigate, drive, impel, goad,
utopian	idealistic, perfect, visionary

Word	Synonyms
vehemence	force, passion, emphasis, obsession
veracity	truth, honesty, accuracy, exactness, correctness
veto	reject, discard, void, nullify, invalidate, dismiss
vigilance	watchfulness, alertness, attentiveness, caution
vilify	malign, slur, defame, slander
vindictive	revengeful, malicious, resentful, spiteful
vivacious	sprightly, spirited, energetic
waive	forgo, relinquish, defer, renounce
weary	exhausted, tired, devitalised, drained
wile	trickery, artifice, ruse
winsome	beautiful, captivating, comely, delightful,
wistful	melancholic, sentimental, plaintive, nostalgic
wreck	destroy, devastate, ruin, demolish
yearn	crave, desire, aspire, urge
yield	surrender, submit, admit, agree
zeal	zest, passion, enthusiasm, fervour, tempo
zenith	peak, apex, summit, acme

Unit 24

Antonyms

Word	Antonym	Word	Antonym
accurate	inaccurate	boisterous	placid
adequate	inadequate	bold	timid
advantage	disadvantage	borrow	lend
affected	unaffected	bottom	top
agree	disagree	brave	coward
appear	disappear	bright	dull
approve	disapprove	broad	narrow
armed	unarmed	build	destroy
articulate	inarticulate	busy	idle, lazy
ascend	descend	calculate	guess
attentive	inattentive	calculating	artless
avoidable	unavoidable	callous	kind
balance	imbalance	calm	stormy
baroque	plain	camouflage	reveal
barren	fertile	candid	evasive
barrier	link	captivate	repel
base	summit, noble	care	neglect
batty	sane	carnal	spiritual
bawdy	decent	casual	formal
beautiful	ugly	catholic	narrow-minded
beauty	ugliness	celebrated	unknown
befogged	clearheaded	cement	disintegrate
beginning	end	censure	praise
belie	justify	centralise	decentralise
believe	doubt	certain	uncertain
benevolent	malevolent	chartered	unchartered
benign	malignant, cruel	cheap	dear
best	worst	civilised	barbarous
bind	release	clandestine	open
birth	death	classic	romantic
bitter	sweet	clever	stupid
blame	praise	coarse	fine
bleak	bright, cheerful	comic	tragic
blunt	keen, sharp	common	rare, uncommon

Word	Antonym	Word	Antonym
common	uncommon	favour	disfavour
compact	diffuse	finite	infinite
compare	contrast	firm	infirm
compress	expand	flammable	nonflammable
conceal	reveal	gather	disperse
conceit	modesty	general	particular
concord	discord	generosity	stinginess
condemn	approve	gentle	rude
confess	deny	genuine	spurious
confidence	diffidence	gloomy	gay, bright
confident	diffident	glory	shame, disgrace
conformist	nonconformist	gorgeous	simple
consolidate	weaken	gratitude	ingratitude
contentious	noncontentious	hamper	expedite
continue	terminate	hamstrung	strengthen
contract	expand	happy	miserable, unhappy
country	town	harm	benefit
courtesy	rudeness	harmony	discord
create	destroy	harsh	melodious
creation	destruction	hasty	leisurely
credible	incredible	head	tail
credit	cash	healthy	diseased, unhealthy
credulous	sceptical	hear	ignore
cruel	kind	heaven	hell
cunning	naive	height	depth
curable	incurable	help	hinder
danger	safety	hide	divulge
deep	shallow	high	low
definite	indefinite	hollow	solid
demote	promote	honour	dishonour
denounce	defend	honour	shame, dishonour
dense	sparse	hospitable	inhospitable
derogatory	laudatory	human	inhuman
despair	hope	humble	proud
destructive	constructive	humility	pride
devil	god	hurry	delay
direct	indirect	hurt	heal
divide	multiply	hypocrisy	sincerity
docile	headstrong	imaginative	unimaginative
domestic	foreign	impenitent	repentant
doubt	trust	impulsive	cautious
dwarf	giant	increase	decrease
eager	indifferent,	indifferent	partial
early	late	indigent	rich
ease	disquiet	infernal	heavenly
eclipse	shine	inflate	deflate
efficient	inefficient	inhale	exhale
equal	unequal	inherit	disinherit
equivocal	unequivocal	innocent	guilty
expected	unexpected	insipid	tasty
familiar	unfamiliar	insult	esteem, honour

Word	Antonym	Word	Antonym
intentional	unintentional	noble	ignoble, base
interesting	dull, uninteresting	noise	quiet
interference	noninterference	normal	abnormal
jest	earnest	obedient	disobedient
just	unjust	obey	defy, disobey
keep	discard	obliging	mulish, obstinate
kind	unkind	obscure	prominent
knowledge	ignorance	observe	miss, disregard
known	unknown	obstinate	pliable, flexible
labour	rest, repose	obstruct	assist
languid	energetic	obtain	forfeit
law	anarchy	ominous	auspicious
lead	follow	optimist	pessimist
leader	follower	order	disorder
legal	illegal	orderly	disorderly
legible	illegible	ordinary	rare, unique
legitimate	illegitimate	orthodox	unorthodox
lenient	strict	pacify	irritate
lethargic	energetic	pack	unpack
liberty	slavery	painful	soothing
limit	stretch	particular	general
literate	illiterate	passionate	dispassionate
loud	soft	payment	nonpayment
lovely	hideous	permanent	temporary
loyal	disloyal	permission	refusal
major	minor	persuade	dissuade
majority	minority	pertinent	impertinent
make	mar	perturbed	calm
male	female	planned	unplanned
malice	goodwill	pleasant	unpleasant
mandatory	optional	poisonous	nonpoisonous
mark	erase	polite	impolite
masculine	feminine	political	nonpolitical
mask	unmask	popular	unpopular
material	immaterial	positive	negative
meek	arrogant	profit	loss
merit	demerit	progress	retrogress
mighty	weak	prohibit	permit
mild	stern	prologue	epilogue
miserly	generous	prolong	shorten
mix	separate	prompt	slow
moderate	immoderate	propagate	suppress
modest	immodest	proportionate	disproportionate
moral	immoral	prose	poetry
morbid	healthy	prudence	indiscretion
motion	rest	public	private
movable	immovable	punish	reward, forgive
native	alien	pursue	avoid
natural	unnatural	qualify	disqualify
neat	filthy	raid	retreat
nimble	lazy	raise	lower

Word	Antonym	Word	Antonym
rapidity	inertia	sympathy	antipathy
rare	common	synonym	antonym
real	unreal	system	chaos
reason	folly	tame	wild
rebellious	submissive	tangible	intangible
rectify	falsify	taste	distaste
refutable	irrefutable	teacher	student
relevant	irrelevant	temperate	intemperate
reliable	unreliable	terse	diffuse
religious	irreligious	thick	thin
reluctant	eager	thrifty	extravagant
remediable	irremediable	tolerable	intolerable
reparable	irreparable	tragedy	comedy
resident	nonresident	tranquil	agitated
resistible	irresistible	transparent	opaque
resolute	irresolute	trust	distrust
respect	disrespect	union	discord
responsible	irresponsible	vacant	occupied
restrain	incite	vain	modest
right	left, wrong	victory	defeat
sacred	profane	violent	gentle, peaceful
sad	cheerful	virtue	vice
safe	risky, dangerous	visible	invisible
savage	civilized	vision	blindness
save	spend	vivid	dull, dim
saviour	destroyer	voluntary	compulsory
scrupulous	unscrupulous	vulgar	cultured
secure	insecure	war	peace
severe	mild, lenient	warmth	coldness
shy	impudent	waste	save, hoard
significance	insignificance	weal	woe
sin	virtue	wealth	poverty
startled	waveringly	wicked	virtuous
steep	flat	wide	narrow
straight	curved	wind	unwind
stranger	acquaintance	wit	stupidity
sublime	ridiculous	zenith	nadir

» Unit

25

One Word Substitute

abdication — voluntarily renouncing throne.

aborigines — original inhabitants of a country

ablaut — a vowel change that accompanies a change in grammatical function. Same as 'gradation'. Sing, sang and sung

accismus — pretended refusal of something desired

acrolect — a variety of language that is closest to a standard main language, especially in an area where a creole is also spoken. Standard Jamaican English, where Jamaican Creole is also spoken

adianoeta — an expression that carries both an obvious meaning and a second subtler meaning

adynaton — a declaration of impossibility, usually expressed as an exaggerated comparison with a more obvious impossibility 'I will sooner have a beard grow in the palm of my hand than he shall get one of his cheek.'
—*William Shakespeare*

alexia — inability to read, usually caused by brain lesions; word blindness

alliteration — repetition of the same sound beginning several words placed close together, usually adjacent

alphabetism — the expression of spoken sounds by an alphabet

ambigram — a word, phrase or sentence written in such a way that it reads the same, upside down as right

anadiplosis — rhetorical repetition of one or more words, particularly a word at the end of a clause. 'Men in great place are thrice servants: servants of the sovereign or state; servants of fame; and servants of business.' —*Francis Bacon*

anagram — a rearrangement of a group of letters, especially a word that can be formed by rearranging the letters in another word

accessible — which can be approached

acclimatize — to accustom oneself in new climate

aggressor — who attacks first

alimony — Allowance paid to wife on legal separation

altruist — One who loves others

amateur — Who does things for pleasure and not for money

ambassador — person representing a State in a foreign country

ambidextrous — one who can use either hand without any problem

ambiguous — that can be interpreted in any way

amnesia — loss of memory

amphibia — animals that live both on land and sea
anaphora — repetition of a word or phrase at the beginning of successive phrases, clauses, or sentences
anarchy — absence of rule, or law and order
annual — which happens once a year
anomaly — deviation from common rule
anonymous — which does not bear the name of writer
antiseptic — medicine used to save plant and animals from being rotten or decaying
antonym — words opposite in meaning
aphasia — loss of speech
aquarium — vessel in which fish and water plants are kept
aquatic — animals that live in water
archeology — study of antiquities
aristocracy — government by the rich or aristocrats
ascetic — one who tortures himself for the good of soul
atheist — one who does not believe in existence of God
audible — sound which can be heard
auditor — one who audits the accounts
aurist — a specialist with regard to the ear
autobiography — life history written by oneself
autocracy — government by one man
autograph — getting signature of some important person in his handwriting
bachelorhood — State of being unmarried
bankrupt — one who can't pay the debts
bellicose — one who is fond of fighting
belligerents — nations engaged in war
billingsgate — coarsely abusive language
bibliophile — one who loves and collects books
biennial — happening every second year
bigamy — have two husband or two wives at a time
biography — life history of a person
biped — animal having two feet
blasphemy — speaking disrespectfully about sacred or religious things
bookworm — one who devotes full time in reading books
botany — study of Plants
brigand — a bandit or robber, esp. one of a band living by pillage and ransom
brittle — which can be easily broken
bullion — gold or Silver before using for manufacturing ornaments
bureaucracy — government run by officials
caducity — the infirmity of old age, senility
calligraphy — the art of beautiful handwriting; elegant penmanship
cannibal — one who eats human flesh.
centrifugal — anything tending to move awove towards centre
centripetal — anything tending to move away from centre
century — one hundred years
chrestomathy — a collection of choice literary passages especially to help in learning a language
coprolalia — uncontrolled, excessive use of obscene or scatological language, sometimes accompanying certain mental disorders
cruciverbalist — a constructor of crossword puzzles; also, an enthusiast of word games, especially crossword puzzles
colleagues — persons working in the same office
compatriot — belonging to same country
congenital — belongs to a person by birth
contemporaries — persons living at the same time
convalescence — period of gradual recovery after illness
cosmopolitan — a citizen of the world
credulous — who easily believes others
cryptography — study of secret writing and coded words
curable — which can be cured
cytology — study of cell
dead letter — an unclaimed letter
deaf — one who cannot hear
democracy — government of the people for the people by the people
dermatology — study of skin
digestible — that which can be digested
dilogy — an ambiguous speech
dittograph — a letter or word repeated unintentionally in writing or copying

dittology — two distinct interpretations of the same text
dipsomania — a strong desire to take liquor
divisible — that which can be divided
dotage — extreme old age when one behaves like a child
drawn — a game in which no party wins
dumb — one who cannot speak
dysgraphia — impairment of the ability to write, usually caused by brain dysfunction or disease
dyslexia — a learning disorder distinguished by impaired ability to recognise and comprehend written words
edible — a thing fit to eat
effeminate — womanish in habits
eligible — one who is fit for the post
elision — omission of a letter or syllable. 'don't instead of 'do not'
emigrant — one who goes to live in a foreign country
employee — one who is employed
employer — one who employs
endemic — a disease prevailing in a locality
entomology — study of insects
endophoric — characteristic of a reference to something outside the speech or text in which the reference occurs.
epic — a long narrative poem
epanorthosis — immediate rephrasing for emphasis, intensification or justification. 'you, young lad, are most brave! brave, did i say? no, heroic!'
epistrophe — repetition of the same word or phrase at the end of successive phrases, clauses or sentences
epicure — one who is fond of sensuous enjoyment
epilogue — a speech given after conclusion of drama
epitaph — words inscribed on the tomb of the dead
etymology — science deals with formation of words
encrasia — a good or normal state of health
etymon — an earlier form of a word in the same language or an ancestor language
examinee — one who takes examination
examiner — one who examines the copies of examinees
exonym — a name by which one people or social group refers to another but which is not used by said group to refer to themselves
expatriate — to send out of native country
expurgate — to remove all objectionable matter
extempore — a speech without previous preparations
extradite — to send back the criminal to the country of his origin
fanatic (bigot) — unreasonably enthusiastic about religion
fastidious — having very selective taste. hard to please
fatalist — one who believed in fate
feminist — one devoted to the welfare of women
foster child — child brought up by persons, who are not his parents
franchise — constitutional right to cast vote
fratricide — murder of brother
garage — a shed for motor car
geology — study of the earth
germicide — which destroy germs
glossolalia — fabricated, nonmeaningful speech, especially such speech associated with a trance state or some schizophrenic syndromes
glottochro nology — the determination of how long ago different languages evolved from a common source language
glutton — fond of eating too much
gratis — without any payment, free
gregarious — animals live in flocks
harangue — a noisy and loud speech before a large gathering
haplology — process by which a word is formed by removing one of the two identical or similar adjacent syllables in an earlier word
hearse — vehicle to carry dead bodies
herbivorous — animals that live on herbs
hendiadys — that use of a conjunction rather than the subordination of one word to another

heterography — a method of spelling in which the same letters represent different sounds in different words as in ordinary english orthography
heterophemy — unconscious saying, in speech or in writing, of some thing that one does not intend to say, especially when what is said is the reverse of what was intended
heterogeneous — things of different nature
histology — study of tissue
Hobson-Jobson — an anglicized word or phrase corrupted from one or more words of an asian language
holonym — a concept that has another concept as a part
homicide — murder of a human being
homogeneous — things of same nature
honeymoon — vacation taken by a newly married couple
honorary — a post without any remuneration
hydra — a serpent with many heads
hydrophobia — fear from water
hygienist — who cares fully of his health
hypallage — interchange of two elements in a phrase or clause from the order in which they would normally appear—'A mind is a terrible thing to waste,' instead of "to waste a mind is aterrible thing."
hypercorrect — characteristic of an incorrect linguistic construction in which the error is produced from a mistaken effort to be correct. 'between you and I,' which should be 'between you and me.'
hyponym — a word that is more specific than a given word
hypothesis — a tentative assumption made to drive a logical conclusion
iconoclast — breaker of art and literature.
idiosyncrasy — Peculiar temper of an individual
idolatry — worshipping of idols
ignorant — person having no knowledge of any happening
illegal — unlawful
illegible — which cannot be read
illiterate — one who can neither read nor write
illeism — the practice of referring to oneself in the third person
imitable — which can be imitated
immigrant — a person from another country comes to our country to settle
immovable — which can't be moved, fixed
imposter — one who assumes name or title of someone else for deceiving others
impregnable — a fort which one can not enter
incorrigible — cannot be corrected
ingressive — characteristic of a speech sound produced with an inhalation of breath
incredible — which cannot be believed
inevitable — that cannot be avoided
infallible — one who cannot make a mistake
infanticide — murder of an infant
infections — a disease spread by contact
inimitable — cannot be imitated
insomnia — loss of sleep
interpolate — inserting new matter in a book
intervein — anything pushed inside veins
invisible — that which cannot be seen
invulnerable — cannot be wounded
irreparable — that cannot be repaired
irrevocable — a decision that cannot be revoked
isocolon — a sequence of parallel structures, having the same number of words and sometimes the same number of syllables what else can one do when he is alone in a jail cell, other than write long letters, think long thoughts, and pray long prayers?
—Martin Luther King
itinerant — one who travels from place to place
kindergarten — a school for small children
kleptomania — an abnormal desire to steal
linguist — one who knows many languages
ligature — a character that combines two or more letters, such as

lipogram — writing composed of words lacking a certain specific letter or letters
litotes — understatement by negating the opposite; a type of meiosis. I was not disappointed with the news.
loquacious — a continuous talker
lunar — eclipse of moon
maiden speech — speech made for the first time
mammals — animals which give milk
manuscript — book written by hand
masochism — the condition or state of deriving (esp. sexual) gratification from one's own pain or humiliation
materialistic — one for whom money is the most important thing
matins — morning prayer in church
matricide — murder of own mother
matrimony — state of being married
maxim — an established principle
meadow — a low level tract of uncultivated grassland
meditation — the action or practice of profound spiritual or religious reflection or mental contemplation
melodrama — a sensational dramatic piece with crude appeals to the emotions and usually a happy ending
mercenary — one who fights for the sake of money
mesomorph — a person whose build is powerful, compact, and muscular
meteorology — study of climate or weather
metonymy — substitution of a word or phrase with another which it suggests—pen is mightier than the sword,' in which both 'pen' and 'sword' are substituted for 'written prose' and 'military'
meticulous — very particular even about small details
migratory — that moves from one place to another
misogamist — one who hates the custom of marriage
misogynist — hater of women
misologist — one who hates learning
mobocracy — rule by mob
morphology — the study of structure and form of words in language, including inflection, derivation, and formation of compounds
monogamy — marrying one at a time
morphology — study of animal and plant structure
narcotic — medicine which induces sleep
neologism — new word coined by an author
neology — study of formation of new words
notorious — a man with bad reputation
nosism — the practice of referring to oneself as 'we'; a type of enallage
numismatics — study of coins
obsolete — no longer in practice
oceanography — study of ocean
odontology — study of teeth
oligarchy — government by a few
omnipotent — one who is all powerful
omniscient — one who knows everything
omnivorous — who eats everything
opaque — that which cannot be seen through
ophthalmology — study of eye
optics — study of light
optimist — one who sees bright side of things
orthography — the study of corrcct spelling according to established usage
ornithology — study of birds
orography — study of mountain
orphan — a child whose parents are dead
orthodox — one who believes in traditional values
orthography — study of correct spelling of words
ostracize — to expel from society
pacifist — one who believes in total abolition of war
paleontology — study of fossils
panacea — a remedy for all ills
pantisocracy — government by all
pantomime — a dumb show

palilogy — repetition of a word or phrase in immediate succession, for emphasis

palindrome — a word, phrase, clause, or sentence that reads the same regularly as it does when its letters are reversed; a type of palingram

palingram — a word, phrase, clause, or sentence that reads the same backwards after rearranging segments—'workmate did teamwork'.

pangram — a sentence that uses all the letters of the alphabet; a holalphabetic sentence

paragoge — the process by which a new word is formed by adding a letter or syllable to the end of another word. same as 'proparalepsis'. 'Climature,' derived from 'climate.'

paraprosdokian — unexpected ending of a phrase or series

parasite — one who depends on others

parasol — a lady's umbrella

pathology — study of disease

patricide — murder of one's own father

patrimony — properties inherited from one's father

patriot — one who loves own country

pedagogy — study of art of teaching

pedantic — a style in which author displays his knowledge

perpilocutionist — one who expounds on a subject of which he has little knowledge

polyptoton — repetition of a word in different forms, cases, or with different inflection, in the sentence

purr word — a word with positive connotations and therefore desirable to use in building and sustaining good public relations

pedestrian — one who travels on foot

pessimist — one who sees dark side of things

philanderer — one who enjoys by love making

philanthropist — a lover of mankind

philately — study of stamp collection

philistine — who does not care for art or literature

philogynist — lover of womankind

philology — study of words and their roots

phonetics — acoustics study of sound

phrenology — study of skull with regard to human character

physiology — study of structure of human body

pioneer — one who leads others

plagiarism — literary theft using ideas and words of another person presenting them as own

platitudes — common place remarks

plutocracy — government by rich

polyandry — marrying more than one husband at a time

polygamy — marrying more than one wife at a time

post mortem — an examination of body after death

primogeniture — right of succession belonging to the first born

pseudonym — an imaginary name of author assumed to disguise himself

pugnacity — tendency to quarrel

purist — one who is particular about the purity of one's language

quadruped — animal having four foot

rebel — one who take up arms against government

redtapism — too much official formalities

regicide — murder of a king

reticule — a lady's purse

retrospective — which takes effect from some earlier date

sacrilege — violating sanctity of some religious place

sadist — a person who derives (esp. sexual) pleasure from inflicting pain, suffering, humiliation

shrew — a woman with peevish nature

simultaneous — happening at the same time

smuggle — importing goods illegally without paying custom duties

solar — eclipse of sun, related to sun

soliloquy — speaking himself when alone

sómnambulism — walking in sleep

somniloquism — talking in sleep

spokesman — one who speaks on behalf of other

stoic — one who is indifferent to pleasure and pain

suicide — killing of self

snarl word — a word with negative connotations and therefore not desirable to use lest good public relations be undermined

superordinate — a word that is more generic than a given word

syllogism — deductive reasoning in which a conclusion is derived from two premises. All human beings are mortal. I am a human being. Therefore, I am mortal

synesis — agreement of words to logic rather than grammatical form. The wages of sin is death

synchronize — occurring two or more events at a time

teetotaller — one who does not take alcoholic drinks

telltale — one who enjoys talking about others private affairs

thearchy — government by the god

theist — one who believes in the existence of god

theomania — a belief that one is god

transmigration — passing of soul from one body to another after death

transparent — that which can be seen through

truant — a student left school or class without permission

truism — an often repeated truth

twins — two child born together

usurer — one who lends money at higher rate of interest

utopia — a state of highest perfection

uxoricide — murder of wife

valetudinarian — one who always think that he is ill

venial — an excusable fault

verbatim — repetition word by word

verbicide — the destruction of the sense or value of a word

verbose — style full of words

vesper — evening prayer in a church

veteran — a well and long experienced person in a particular occupation

wardrobe — an almirah where clothes are kept

widow — a woman whose husband has died

widower — a man whose wife has died

xenoepist — one with a foreign accent

zoology — study of animals

» Exercises

Exercise 1

Give one word for each of the following expressions choosing from those given below each such expression

(*Income Tax Inspectors*)

1. Life history of a man written by himself.
(a) biography (b) autobiography
(c) calligraphy (d) bibliography

2. A statement that can have a double meaning.
(a) verbose (b) ambivalent
(c) epigraph (d) ambiguous

3. Work inscribed on the tomb.
(a) eulogy (b) epitaph
(c) epigraph (d) eloquence

4. The intelligent and educated class.
(a) literate (b) aristocrat
(c) educated (d) intelligentsia

5. Science of plants.
(a) zoology (b) geology
(c) anthropology (d) botany

6. List of headings of the business to be transacted at a meeting.
(a) minutes
(b) agenda
(c) excerpts
(d) proceedings

7. One filled with excessive and mistaken enthusiasm in a cause.
(a) pedant (b) patriot
(c) fanatic (d) marty

8. Regard for others as a principle of action.
(a) altruism (b) philanthropy
(c) nepotism (d) cynicism

9. One who promotes the idea of absence of government of any kind, when every man should be a law unto himself.
(a) agnostic (b) iconoclast
(c) belligerent (d) anarchist

10. Study of mankind.
(a) pathology (b) philology
(c) physiology (d) anthropology

Solutions

1. (b) 2. (d) 3. (b) 4. (d)
5. (d) 6. (b) 7. (c) 8. (a)
9. (d) 10. (d)

Exercise 2

Give one word for each of the following expressions choosing from those given below each such expression
(RRB ASM, Excise Inspector)

1. An office with no work but high pay.
(a) honorary (b) sinecure
(c) ex-officio (d) reticent

2. One who deserts his religion.
(a) deserter (b) apostate
(c) opportunist (d) turn coat

3. The act of looking back upon past events.
(a) introspection
(b) retrospection
(c) extrospection
(d) circumspection

4. Very vigilant and cautious.
(a) meticulous (b) fastidious
(c) anxious (d) alert

5. Matter written by hand.
(a) handwritten (b) manuscript
(c) amnesty (d) proof

6. A small shop that sells fashionable clothes, cosmetics, etc.
(a) store (b) dtall
(c) boutique (d) both

7. One who is honourably discharged from service.
(a) retired (b) emeritus
(c) relieved (d) emancipated

8. One who cannot be corrected.
(a) incurable (b) incorrigible
(c) hardened (d) invulnerable

9. One who is in charge of a museum.
(a) curator (b) supervisor
(c) caretaker (d) warden

10. The study of ancient societies.
(a) anthropology
(b) archaeology
(c) history
(d) ethnology

Solutions

1. (b) 2. (b) 3. (b) 4. (a)
5. (b) 6. (c) 7. (b) 8. (b)
9. (a) 10. (a)

Exercise 3

Give one word for each of the following expressions choosing from those given below each such expression
(SBI PO)

1. Responsible according to law.
(a) eligible (b) legitimate
(c) legalised (d) liable
(e) offensive

2. Constant effort to achieve something.
(a) patience (b) vigour
(c) enthusiasm (d) attempt
(e) perseverance

3. Opposed to great or sudden change.
(a) conservative (b) revolutionary
(c) evolutionary (d) static
(e) unalterable

4. Anything written in a letter after it is signed.
(a) corrigendum (b) manuscript
(c) postscript (d) post diction
(e) posterity

5. That which cannot be done without.
(a) impracticable (b) indispensable
(c) impossible (d) unmanageable
(e) irrevocable

Solutions

1. (d) 2. (e) 3. (a) 4. (c)
5. (b)

Exercise 4

Give one word for each of the following expressions choosing from those given below each such expression
(Bank PO)

1. He could not give a good explanation for his extraordinary behaviour.
(a) be satisfied with
(b) account for
(c) provide evidence for
(d) count for
(e) readily dispense

2. Those who pass through this gate without permission be prosecuted.
(a) bypassers (b) absconders
(c) thoroughfares (d) trespassers
(e) culprits

3. A careful preservation and protection of wild life is the need of the hour.
(a) management (b) embarkment
(c) enhancement (d) promotion
(e) conservation

4. I could achieve success through conscious efforts.
(a) tremendous efforts.
(b) efforts made with critical awareness.
(c) efforts done after gaining consciousness
(d) efforts done after being awakened
(e) efforts done without any desire

5. We are looking forward to a good monsoon this year.
(a) Getting (b) predicting
(c) hoping (d) visualising
(e) encouraging

Solutions

1. (b) 2. (d) 3. (e) 4. (b)
5. (d)

Exercise 5

Substitute one word for each of the following sentences **(IAS)**

1. A person in charge of a museum.
2. One who does not believe in the existence of God.
3. One who collects postage stamps.
4. One who goes on a journey to holy place.
5. One who abstains from alcoholic drinks.
6. That which can be understood.
7. One who studies the stars and sky.
8. A plant that draws sustenance from another.
9. A child whose parents are dead.
10. A dead body of a human being.
11. A child born after the death of his father.
12. Descending from parent to child.
13. The story of one's own life.

Solutions

1. Curator, 2. Atheist, 3. Philatelist,
4. Pilgrim, 5. Teetotaller, 6. Intelligible,
7. Astronomer, 8. Parasite,
9. Orphan, 10. Corpse. 11. Posthumous,
12. Hereditary, 13. Autobiography.

Exercise 6

Substitute one word for each of the following sentences

1. The science of words and language is known as
(a) philology (b) paleontology
(c) bibliography (d) entomology
2. One of the time-tested ways of remembering a series of items is known as a/an
(a) recollection (b) schematising
(c) mnemonic (d) ingenuity
3. Nations that do not trust each other look upon each other
(a) calmly (b) hopefully
(c) askance (d) retrospectively
4. If a person cannot be easily handled or dealt with, he will not be complimented for his
(a) domesticity (b) knowledge
(c) tractability (d) eulogy
5. A person who constantly thinks he is sick is a
(a) hypochondriac (b) misogynist
(c) misanthrope (d) hyperpituitary
6. But a person who is really sickly and is unduly solicitous about his health is a
(a) valedictorian (b) vegetarian
(c) valetudinarian (d) dialectician
7. The order to stay in one's own bailiwick means that a person should remain in his own
(a) room (b) district
(c) country (d) bed
8. Because the orator's speech was high-flown and pretentious, the reporters termed it
(a) bombastic (b) austere
(c) untruthful (d) vituperative
9. When the courtier had advanced to the highest positon attainable, he was said to have reached the
(a) vigil (b) precipice
(c) threshold (d) pinnacle
10. Accepting his fate with calmness, the camel driver said, 'It is....'
(a) growing late (b) kismet
(c) kiosk (d) suttee

Solutions

1. (a) 2. (c) 3. (c) 4. (c)
5. (a) 6. (c) 7. (b) 8. (a)
9. (d) 10. (b)

Unit 26

Phrasal Verbs

Phrasal verbs are part of a group of verbs called 'multi-word verbs'. Multi-word verbs, including phrasal verbs, are very common, especially in spoken English. A multi-word verb is like 'pick up', 'turn on' or 'get on with'. Generally people refer to all multi-word verbs as phrasal verbs. These verbs consist of a basic verb + another word or words. The other word(s) can be preposition or adverb. The two or three words that make up multi-word verbs form a short 'phrase'—which is why these verbs are often all called 'phrasal verbs'.

The important thing to remember is that a multi-word verb is still a verb. 'get' is a verb. 'get up' is also a, but with a difference verb. They do not have the same meaning.

There are three types of multi-word verbs

1. Prepositional verbs
2. Phrasal verbs
3. Phrasal-prepositional verbs

Prepositional Verbs

Prepositional verbs are made of

Verb + Preposition

As a preposition always has an object, so does all prepositional verbs have direct objects. Here are some examples of prepositional verbs:

Prepos. Verbs	Meaning	Example	Direct Object
believe in	have faith in the existence of	We believe in	God.
look after	take care of	He is looking after the	dog.
talk about	discuss	Did you talk about	me?
wait for	await	She is waiting for	Mira.

Phrasal Verbs

Phrasal verbs are made from a verb plus another word or words. Many people refer to all multi-word verbs as phrasal verbs.

Phrasal verbs are made of : Verb + Adverb

Phrasal verbs can be : transitive (direct object) or intransitive (no direct object).

Here are some examples of phrasal verbs :

Transitive phrasal verbs :

(a) put off (postpone) : We will have to put off the meeting *Direct Object*

(b) turn down (refuse) : They turned down my offer. *Direct Object*

Intransitive phrasal verbs :

(a) get up (rise from bed) : I don't like to get up.

(b) break down (cease to function) : He was late because his car broke down.

However, if the direct object is a pronoun we have no choice. We must separate the Phrasal verb and insert the pronoun between the two parts.

Look at this example with the separable phrasal verb 'switch on':

(a) John switched on the radio.

(b) John switched the radio on.

(c) John switched it on.

We can write any of the above sentences, but we cannot write the following :

John switchedless on it. *Incorrect*

Phrasal-Prepositional Verbs

Phrasal-prepositional verbs are made of : verb + adverb + preposition

(a) get on with (have a friendly relationship with): He doesn't get on with his wife.
(b) put up with (tolerate) : I won't put up with your attitude.
(c) look forward (to anticipate with pleasure): I look forward to seeing you.
(d) run out of (use up, exhaust) : We have run out of eggs.

Italic Words Are Direct Objects

Because phrasal-prepositional verbs end with a preposition, there is always a direct object. And, like prepositional verbs, phrasal-prepositional verbs cannot be separated. So, we can say that phrasal-prepositional verbs are inseparable.

(a) We ran out of fuel.
(b) We ran out of it. Phrasal Verbs and Their Uses

- **act up** [misbehave (for people); not work properly (for machines)]
  (a) The babysitter had a difficult time. The children *acted up* all evening.
  (b) I guess I'd better take my car to the garage. It's been *acting* up lately.
- **act on** [produce effect] : In general, acids *act on* metals.
- **act upon** [in accordance with] : The captain *acting upon* the secret information caught the militants.
- **act like** [behave in a way that's like ...] : What's wrong with Bob? He's *acting like* an idiot.
- **add up** [logically fit together.] :
  (a) His theory is hard to believe, but his research *adds up*.

  Note : This phrasal verb is often negative.

  (b) His theory seems, at first, to be plausible, but the facts in his research don't *add up*.
- **add up** [find the total] : What's the total of those bills? Could you *add* them *up* and see?
- **add up to** [to total] : The bills *add up* to Rs. 8570/- only. That's more than I expected!
- **ask out** [ask for a date] : Shalu has a new boy friend. Johny *asked* her *out* last night.
- **back down** [not follow a threat] : Tom was going to call the police when I told him I'd wrecked his car, but he *backed down* when I said I'd pay for the damages.
- **back off** [not follow a threat] : Tom was ready to call the police when I told him I'd wrecked his car, but he *backed off* when I said I'd pay for the damages.
- **back up** [move backward; move in reverse] :
  (a) You missed the lines in the parking space. You'll have to back up and try again.
  (b) The people waiting in line are too close to the door. We won't be able to open it unless they *back up*.
- **back up** [drive a vehicle backwards (in reverse)] :
  (a) You're too close! *Back* your car *up* so I can open the garage door.
- **back up** [confirm a story, facts, or information] : If you don't believe me, talk to Dev. He'll *back* me *up*.
- **back up** [make a 'protection' copy to use if there are problems with the original] : When my computer crashed, I lost many of my files. It's a good thing I *backed* them *up*.
- **backed off** [decline an invitation; ask to be excused from doing something] : At first Lily said she would be at the party. Later she *backed off.*
- **bear down** [to crush by force] : She was successful in *bearing down* the opposition group.
- **bear out** [verify or confirm] : Your arguments do not *bear out* the facts.
- **bear up** [to face hardships bravely] : He must try to
  bear up against this temporary phase of economic slump.
- **bear with** [endure to have patience] : A good wife *bear with* the habits of her husband.
- **beat down** [to crush] : He *beat down* the opposition with a single trick.
- **beat off** [to repulse, to drive back] : Indian army successfully *beat off* the enemy forces.
- **beat up** [to beat] : Ramesh was *beaten up* by Suresh for no reason.
- **blow up** [inflate] : We need lots of balloons for the party. Will you *blow* them *up*?
- blow up [explode; destroy by exploding] :
  (a) That old building really came down quickly!
  (b) That's because the construction company used dynamite to *blow* it *up*.

- **blow up** [suddenly become very angry] : When I told Jerry that I'd an accident with his car, he *blew up*.
- **bone up on** [review/study thoroughly for a short time] : If you're going to travel to the U.K., you'd better *bone up on* your English.
- **break down** [separate something into component parts] : We spent a lot of money at the supermarket. When we *broke* the total cost *down*, we spent more on cleaning supplies than food.
- **break down** [stop working/functioning] : Shalini will be late for work today. Her car *broke down* on the way.
- **break in** [enter by using force (and breaking a lock, window etc.)] :
  (a) John's apartment was burglarized last night. Someone *broke in* while John was at the movies.
  (b) Somebody *broke* in to John's apartment while she was at the movies.
- **break in** [wear something new until it's/they're comfortable] : These are nice shoes, but they're too stiff. I hope it doesn't take too long to *break* them *in*.
- **break in** [train; get someone/something accustomed to a new routine] : I hope I can learn my new job quickly. The manager hasn't scheduled much time for *breaking* me *in*.
- **break up** [disperse; scatter] : What time did the party *break up* last night?
- **broke up** [end a personal relationship] :
  (a) Tom and Jassi aren't going steady any more. They got really angry with each other and *broke up*.
  (b) Have you heard the news? Jassi *broke up* with Tom!
  (c) I'm sorry to hear that their marriage *broke up*. I'm sure the divorce will be difficult for the children.
- **bring/take back** [return something] :
  (a) Yes, you can borrow my pen, don't forget to *bring* it back to me when you're finished.
  (b) This book is due tomorrow. I guess I should *take* it *back* to the library.
- **bring off** [accomplish something difficult; accomplish something people had considered impossible or unlikely] : No one thought Raju could get an A in that course, but he *brought* it *off*.
- **bring up** [mention (as a topic of discussion)] : We planned to discuss overtime pay in the meeting. Why didn't someone *bring* that topic *up*?
- **bring up** [raise; rear] : Shalu's parents died when she was a baby. Her grandparents *brought* her *up*.
- **brush up on** [review/study thoroughly for a short time] : If you're going to travel to the UK, you'd better *brush up on* your English.
- **burn down** [become destroyed/consumed by fire] : **Note** : For upright things—trees, buildings, etc.- only. Lightning struck Mr. Kalhan's barn last night. It *burned down* before the fire fighters arrived.
- **burn up** [become destroyed/consumed by fire] :

For people and non-upright things only. All of Mr. Kalhan's hay *burned up* when his barn burned down.

- **burn up** [cause someone to become very angry] : Did you hear how rudely Golu talked to me? That really *burned* me *up*!
- **butt in** [impolitely interrupt (a conversation, an action)] : Hey, you! Don't *butt in*! Wait for your turn!
- **butter up** [praise someone excessively with the hope of getting some benefit] : I guess Mohan really wants to be promoted. He's been *buttering* his boss *up* all week.
- **call off** [cancel something that has been scheduled] : We don't have school today. The Collector *called* classes *off* because of the snow.
- **call on** [ask someone for an answer in class] : I don't know why the teacher never *calls on* you. You always know the answer.
- **calm down** [become calm/less agitated or upset; help someone become calm/less agitated or upset] :
  (a) Why are you so upset? Sheela didn't intend to spill orange juice on you. *Calm down*!
  (b) I know Raju is upset, but can you *calm* him *down*? He's making so much noise that he's irritating everyone in the office.

- **care for** [like; want] : **Note :** This phrasal verb is usually negative, though it may be used affirmatively in questions.
  (a) Would you *care for* something to drink? We have coffee, tea or orange juice.
  (b) Could I have water, please? I don't *care for* coffee, tea, or juice.
- **care for** [take care of; supply care to; attend/watch] : Ann's father got out of the hospital last week. The family is *caring for* him at home.
- **catch on** [develop understanding or knowledge of something] : Bholu had never used a computer until he took this class, but he *caught on* very quickly and is now one of the best students.
- **catch up** (with) [stop being behind] : Toshu stopped to rest for a few minutes. He'll *catch up/catch up* with us later.
- **check in (to)** [register for/at a hotel, conference, etc.; let someone know officially that you have arrived] :
  (a) My plane will arrive around 5:00 p.m. I should be able to *check into* the hotel by 6:00 or 6:30.
  (b) When you arrive at the convention, be sure to *check in* at the registration desk.
- **check off** [make a mark to indicate that something on a list has been completed] : Here are the things you need to do. Please *check* each one *off* when you've finished it.
- **check out (of)** [follow procedures for leaving a hotel etc.] : Don't forget to take your room key to the front desk when you check out (when you *check out* of the hotel).
- **check out** [follow procedures for borrowing something (usually for a limited period of time] : I'm sorry, but you can't take that encyclopaedia home. The library won't allow you to *check* reference books *out*.
- **cheer up** [help someone feel less worried/depressed/sad] : Shalu's brother was depressed about not getting a promotion, so she sent him a funny card to *cheer* him *up*.
- **chew out** [scold someone severely; berate] : Golu's father was really angry when Tom didn't come home until 3:00 a.m. He *chewed* Tom *out* and then said Tom had to stay at home for three weeks.
- **chicken out** [lose the courage or confidence to do something—often at the last minute] : Sahu said he was going to ask Tili for a date, but he *chickened out*.
- **chip in** [contribute/donate (often money) to something done by a group] : We're going to buy a birthday cake for our boss and I'm collecting donations. Do you want to *chip in*?
- **clam up** [suddenly become quiet/refuse to talk about something] : Lila wouldn't talk about the accident. When I asked her what happened, she *clammed up*.
- **come across** [find (unexpectedly)] : I've lost my extra car keys. If you *come across* them while your're cleaning the room, please put them in a safe place.
- **come down with** [become ill with _____] : George won't be at the office today. He *came down with* the flu over the weekend.
- **come to** [total] : Your charges *come* to $124.38. Will you pay by check, in cash, or with a credit card?
- **come to** [regain consciousness] : When I told Gita that she'd won a million dollars, she fainted. When she *came to*, I told her it was a joke and she almost hit me!
- **count on** [depend on; trust that something will happen or that someone will do as expected] : I'm *counting on* you to wake me up tomorrow. I know I won't hear the alarm.
- **cross out** [show that something written is wrong or unnecessary by making an X across it] : We can't afford to buy everything on your shopping list, so I've *crossed* all the unnecessary things *out*.
- **cut back** (on) [use less of something] :
  (a) You drink too much coffee. You should *cut back*.
  (b) You should *cut back* on the amount of coffee that you drink.
- **do in** [cause to become very tired] : Those three games of tennis yesterday afternoon really *did* me *in*. I slept for ten hours after I got home.
- **do in** [to kill; to murder] : The policeman said that the murdered man was *done in* between 10 and 11 o'clock last night.
- **do over** [do something again] : Oh, no! I forgot to save my report before I turned the computer off! Now I'll have to *do* it *over*!

- **drag on** [last much longer than expected or is necessary] : I thought the meeting would be a short one, but it *dragged on* for more than three hours.
- **draw up** [create a formal document] : Ajax and Tip-Top Banks have decided to merge. Their lawyers will *draw* all the official documents *up* sometime this month.
- **drop off** [deliver something; deliver someone (by giving him/her a ride)] :
  (a) Yes, I can take those letters to the post office. I'll *drop* them *off* as I go home from work.
  (b) You don't have to take a taxi. You live fairly close to me, so I'll be happy to *drop* you *off*.
- **drop in** (on) [visit informally (and usually without scheduling a specific time)] : If you're in town next month, we'd love to see you. Please try to *drop in*./Please try to *drop in* on us.
- **drop by** [visit informally (and usually without scheduling a specific time)] : If you're in town next month, we'd love to see you. Please try to *drop by* the house.
- **drop out** (of) [stop attending/leave school or an organization] : No, Parish isn't at the university. He *dropped out*./He *dropped out* of school.
- **draw out** [prolong something (usually far beyond the normal limits)] : I thought that speech would never end. The speaker could have said everything important in about five minutes, but he *drew* the speech *out* for over an hour!
- **eat out** [have a meal in a restaurant] : I'm too tired to cook . Why don't we *eat out*?
- **egg on** [urge/encourage greatly toward doing something (usually something negative)] : At first Boby and Kaku were just having a mild argument, but Boby's friends *egged* them *on* until they started fighting.
- **end up** [finally arrive at; arrive at an unexpected place] : We got lost last night and *ended up* in the next town.
- **end up** [arrive somewhere as a result or consequence] : You're working too hard. If you don't take it easy, you'll *end up* in the hospital!
- **face up to** [admit to; take responsibility for] : You can't pretend that you're doing OK in this course, John. Sooner or later, you'll have to *face up to* the fact that you're failing it.
- **fall through** [not happen. (Note : Describes something that was planned but didn't happen.)]: We had originally intended to go to Morocco for our vacation, but our trip *fell through* when I got sick.
- **feel up to** [feel strong enough or comfortable enough to do something] : I know the accident was a terrible shock. Do you *feel up* to talking about it?
- **figure out** [logically find the answer to a problem; solve a problem by thinking about it carefully] : For a long time I couldn't understand the last problem, but I finally *figured* it *out*.
- **figure out** [understand why someone behaves the way she/he does] : I can't *figure* marry *out*. Sometimes she's very warm and friendly and sometimes she acts as if she doesn't know me.
- **fill in** [add information to a form] : The office needs to know your home address and phone number. Could you *fill* them *in* on this form?
- **fill in** (on) [supply information that someone doesn't know] : I wasn't able to attend the meeting yesterday, but I understand that it was important. Could you *fill* me *in*?/Could you *fill* me *in* on what was discussed?
- **fill in for** [temporarily do someone else's work; temporarily substitute for another person] : Professor Neeraj is in the hospital and won't be able to teach for the rest of the term. Do you know who's going to *fill in for* her?
- **fill out** [complete a form by adding required information] : Of course I completed my application! I *filled* it *out* and mailed it over three weeks ago!
- **fill out** [become less thin; gain weight] : Jerry used to be really skinny, but in the last year he's begun to *fill out*.
- **find out** (about) [learn/get information (about)] : I'm sorry that you didn't know the meeting had been cancelled. I didn't *find out* (find out about it) myself until just a few minutes ago.

- **get across** [make something understood; communicate something understandably] : Alan is really intelligent but sometimes he has problems *getting* his ideas *across*.
- **get along** (with) [have a friendly relationship (with); be friendly (toward)] : Why can't you and your sister get along? Everyone else gets along with her just fine!
- **get around** [avoid having to do something] : Tisha *got around* the required math classes by doing well on a math proficiency test.
- **get around** [move from place to place] : She doesn't have a car. She *gets around* by bicycle, bus, or taxi.
- **get around to** [do something eventually] : I really should wash the dishes, but I don't feel like it. May be I'll *get around to* them tomorrow morning.
- **get by** [survive, financially, in a difficult situation] : It's going to be hard to pay the rent now that you've lost your job, but somehow we'll *get by*.
- **get in** [enter a small, closed vehicle] : I don't know where Jasmine was going. She just *got in* her car and drove away.
- **get in** [arrive] : Do you know what time Ted's plane *gets in*?
- **get on** [enter a large, closed vehicle] : I'm sorry, but you're too late to say goodbye to Anita. She *got on* the plane about 20 minutes ago.
- **get off** [leave a large, closed vehicle] : When you *get off* the bus, cross the street, turn right on Oak Street, and keep going until you're at the corner of Oak Hotel.
- **get off** [be excused (for a period of time) from work, class, or other regularly scheduled activities] : Some schools *got* President's Day *off* but ours didn't. We had classes as usual.
- **get off** [make it possible for someone to avoid punishment] : Everyone knew he was guilty, but his lawyer was clever and *got* him *off*.
- **get out of** [leave a small, closed vehicle] : There's something wrong with the garage door opener. You'll have to *get out of* the car and open it by hand.
- **get out of** [escape having to do something] : Liz said that she had a terrible headache and *got out of* giving her speech today.
- **get over** [finish (**Note** : as for individual activities, not ones that happen again and again)] : What time do your classes *get over*?
- **get over** [recover from an illness or painful experience] : Kelly was really upset when she failed the test. She thought she would never *get over* feeling so stupid.
- **get rid of** [dispose of; give away or throw away] : That shirt is really ugly. Why don't you *get rid of* it?
- **get rid of** [dismiss someone; fire someone from a job; cause someone to leave] : The treasurer of the ABC company was spending too much money so the company president *got rid of* him.
- **get up** [leave bed after sleeping and begin your daily activities] :
  (a) You'll have to *get up* much earlier than usual tomorrow. We have to leave by no later than 6:00 a.m.
  (b) I know I won't hear the alarm tomorrow morning. Can you *get* me *up* at 6:00 a.m.?
- **give up** [stop doing something (usually a habit)] : He knows smoking isn't good for his health, but he can't *give* it *up*.
- **give up** [decide not to try (unsuccessfully) to solve a problem] :
  (a) What's black and white and red all over?
  (b) I give up. What?
  (c) An embarrassed zebra!
- **go out with** [have a date with] : You *went out with* Shalini last night, didn't you?
- **go with** [look pleasing together (Note : for clothes, furniture etc.)] : You should buy that shirt. It will *go* well *with* your dark brown suit.
- **go with** [date regularly and steadily] : Is Hina *going with* Joe? I see them together all the time.
- **goof off** [be lazy; do nothing in particular] :
  (a) Do you have any special plans for your vacation?
  (b) No. I'm just going to stay home and *goof off*.
- **grow up** [spend the years between being a child and being an adult] : Did you know that Kallu *grew up* in Malaysia?
- **grow up** [behave responsibly; behave as an adult, not a child] :

(a) Lee really irritates me sometimes. He's really silly and childish.

(b) I agree. I wish he would *grow up*.

- **hand in** [submit homework, an assignment etc.] : You'd better get started on your report. You know that you have to *hand* it *in* at 8:30 tomorrow morning!
- **hand out** [distribute] : Why don't you have a course description and list of assignments? The teacher *handed* them *out* on the first day of class.
- **hang up** [end a phone conversation by replacing the receiver] : I'd like to talk longer, but I'd better *hang up*. My sister needs to make a call.
- **have to do with** [be about] : This class *has to do with* the behavior of people in groups.
- **hold up** [raise lift to a higher-than-normal position] : The winner of the race proudly *held* his trophy *up* for all to see.
- **hold up** [delay] : I'm sorry I'm late. There was an accident on the freeway and traffic *held* me *up*.
- **hold up** [rob threaten someone with harm unless he/she gives his/her money or other valuable things] : Shalu is very upset. When she was walking home last night, two men *held* her *up* and took her purse and jewellery.
- **iron out** [mutually reach an agreement; mutually resolve difficulties] : Yes, I know we disagree on lots of things, Susan, but we can *iron* them *out*.
- **jack up** [raise/life by using a jack] : We'll have to jack the back of the car up before we can change the tyre.
- **jack up** [raise (used for prices)] : The car dealer bought my old Ford for Rs. one lac and *jacked* the price *up* to Rs.1,50,000.00, when they sold it.
- **jump all over** [severely scold someone; berate someone] : Amar is really upset. His boss *jumped all over* him because he's been late for work three times this week.
- **keep on** [continue] : I'm not ready to stop yet. I think I'll *keep on* working for a while.
- **keep on (someone)** [continue to remind someone to do something until he/she does it (even if this irritates her/him)] : Jack's very forgetful. You'll have to *keep on* him or he'll never do all the things you want him to do.
- **kick out** [expel; force someone to leave because of his/her poor performance or unacceptable behaviour] : Jim's club *kicked* him *out* because he didn't pay his dues or come to beetings.
- **knock out** [make unconscious] :

  (a) The boxing match ended when one boxer *knocked out* the other one.

  (b) That medicine really *knocked* me *out*. I slept for 14 hours straight!
- **knock oneself out** [work much harder than normal or than what is expected] : We completed the project on time because of Jack. He *knocked himself out* to be sure we didn't miss the deadline.
- **lay off** [dismiss someone from a job because of lack of work or money (not because of poor performance)] : I feel really sorry Shalu's family. Her father was *laid off* yesterday.
- **leave out** [forget; omit] : Oh, no! When I made the list of those who attended the meeting, I left your name out!
- **let down** [disappoint] : I know I let you down when I didn't do what I promised. I'm really sorry.
- **let up** [become less intense or slower] : It's been raining hard for a long time. Will it ever *let up*?
- **look back on** [remember; reflect on/consider something in the past] : When they *looked back on* their many years together, they realized that their marriage had been a very happy one.
- **look down on** [hold in contempt; regard as inferior] : It's not surprising that Ted has few friends. He seems to *look down on* anyone who doesn't like the same things that he does.
- **look forward to** [anticipate pleasantly; think about a pleasant thing before it happens] : I'm really *looking forward* to vacation. I can't wait for it to begin!
- **look in on** [visit in order to check something's/someone's condition] : My father just came home from the hospital. I plan to *look in on* him today after I finish work.
- **look into** [investigate/get more details about something] : Someone said there was a meeting at 9:30 but I haven't heard anything about it. Shall I *look into* it?

- **look like [resemble** (in appearance)] : Does he *look like* his father or his mother?
- **look over** [check; review] : I think I may have some types in this report. Could you *look* it *over*?
- **look up** [find something in a reference work] : I'm sorry, but I don't know what that word means. I'll have to *look* it *up*.
- **look up** [find where someone lives or works and visit him/her] : Thanks for giving me your brother's address. When I'm in Chicago next month, I'll be sure to *look* him *up*.
- **look up to** [respect] : Everyone *looks up* to John because he always makes time to help others.
- **luck out** [be unexpectedly lucky] : Gloria was worried because she wasn't prepared to give a report at the meeting, but she *lucked out* because the meeting was postponed.
- **make fun of** [make jokes about (usually unkindly)] : I agree that Bob looks ridiculous since he shaved his head, but don't *make fun of* him. You'll hurt his feelings.
- **make up** [invent/create (imaginary) information] : Judy's story is hard to believe. I'm sure she *made* it *up*.
- **make up** [compensate for something missed or not done by doing extra or equivalent work] : I'm sorry I missed the test. May I *make* it *up*?
- **make up** (with) [re-establish a friendly relationship by admitting guilt] : "Jack and his girlfriend were very angry with each other, but last night they finally *made up*."
- **make out** [see/hear something well enough to understand what it means (Note: often negative.)]:
  (a) Kath's writing is very small. I almost need a magnify glass to *make* it *out*.
  (b) What were the last two examples that he gave? I couldn't *make* them *out*.
- **make for** [go to or toward] : Her teen-aged children are always hungry. As soon as they arrive home from school, they *make for* the refrigerator.
- **make for** [result in; cause] : Many hands *make for* light work. (If many people work together, there's less work for everyone.)
- **mark up** [increase the price (for resale)] : Mrs. Britt's import shop is profitable because she buys things inexpensively and then *marks* them *up*.
- **mark down** [reduce the price (as an incentive to buy)] : These shoes were really a bargain! The store *marked* them *down* by 40%!
- **mix up** [cause to become confused] : I didn't complete the assignment because I didn't know how the directions *mixed* me *up*.
- **nod off** [fall sleep (usually unintentionally)] : The speech was so boring that several people in the audience *nodded off* before it was finished.
- **pan out** [succeed; happen as expected (for plans)] : **Note :** almost always negative when in statements. I'll be here next week after all. My trip to Chicago didn't *pan out*.
- **pass away** [die] : I was very sorry to hear that your grandfather *passed away*.
- **pass out** [faint; lose consciousness] : When Kokila heard that she'd won a million dollars, she was so shocked that she *passed out*.
- **pass out** [distribute] : Everyone in the room needs one of these information sheets. Who will help me *pass* them *out*?
- **pick out** [choose; select] : Kelly's grandmother especially liked her birthday card because Kelly had *picked* it *out* himself.
- **pick up** [lift; take up] : Those books don't belong on the floor. Will you help me *pick* them *up*?
- **pick up** [arrange to meet someone and give her/him a ride] : Of course we can go there together. What time should I *pick* you *up*?
- **pick up** [get; buy] : The children just drank the last of the milk. Could you *pick* some more *up* on your way home this evening?
- **pick up** [refresh; revitalize] : He was feeling a little tired, so he drank a glass of orange juice. It *picked* him *up* enough to finish his work.
- **pick on** [bully; intentionally try to make someone upset] : You should be ashamed of teasing your little brother, Tony! *Pick on* someone your own size!
- **pitch in** [help; join together to accomplish something] : We'll be finished soon if everyone *pitches in*.

- **pull over** [drive a vehicle to the side of the rode] : When the policeman indicated that I should *pull over*, I knew he was going to give me a ticket.
- **put away** [return something to the proper place] : I just took these clothes out of the dryer. Will you help me *put* them *away*?
- **put off** [postpone; delay; avoid] :
  (a) I can't *put* this work *off* any longer. If I don't do it soon, it'll be impossible to finish it in time.
  (b) When will Mr. Jack agree to a meeting? I keep asking for an appointment, but he keeps *putting* me *off*.
- **put on** [begin to wear; don] : It's a little bit chilly outside. You'd better *put* a sweater *on*.
- **put on** [try to make someone believe something that is ridiculous or untrue] : Don't believe a word of what Jaru was saying. He was just *putting* us *on*.
- **put (someone) out** [inconvenience someone] : I hate to *put* you *out*, but I need a ride to the train station and hope you can take me.
- **put up** [return something to the proper place] : Your toys are all over the floor, Tinni. Please *put* them *up*.
- **put up** [provide someone with a place to sleep] : There's no need for you to check into a hotel. I'll be happy to *put* you *up*.
- **Put up with** [tolerate] : It's really important to come to work on time. The boss won't *put up with* tardiness.
- **Put back** [return something to the proper place] : I've finished with these books. Do you want me to *put* them *back* on the shelves?
- **rip off** [cheat; take advantage of; charge too much] : Don't even think about buying a car there. They'll *rip* you *off*.
- **round off** [change from a fraction to the nearest whole number] : *Round* all prices *off* to the closest whole rupee amount. For example, round Rs. 83.71 off to Rs. 84.00.
- **run into** [meet by chance] : Yesterday at the super market, Jan *ran into* her former roommate. Before yesterday, they hadn't seen each other for nearly five years.
- **run out of** [use the last of] : On the way home from work, Art *ran out of* gas.
- **set up** [make arrangements for something] : You'll see Mr. Kamas tomorrow. I've *set* a meeting *up* for 9:30 a.m.
- **set back** [cause a delay in scheduling] : We've had some problems with the project that have *set* us *back* at least two days. We'll give you a progress report tomorrow.
- **set back** [cost] : I wonder how much Am's new car *set* him back?
- **slip up** [make a mistake] : You *slipped up* here. The amount should be Rs. 54,172.00, not Rs. 54,127.00.
- **stand out** [be noticeably better than other similar people or things] : Good job, Ann! Your work really *stands out*!
- **stand up** [rise to a standing position] : When the Chairperson entered the room, everyone *stood up*.
- **stand up** [make a date but not keep it] : Angela was supposed to go to the dance with Fred, but she *stood* him *up* and went with Chuck instead.
- **show up** [arrive; appear] : The boss was very upset when you didn't *show up* for the meeting. What happened?
- **show up** [do a noticeably better job (often unexpectedly) than someone else] : Everyone thought Harsha would win, but Zean did. Actually, Zean really *showed* Harsha *up*.
- **stand for** [represent] : These letters seem to be an abbreviation. Do you know what they *stand for*?
- **stand for** [tolerate; permit (usually negative)] : I'm not surprised that Mrs. John rejected your report. She won't *stand for* shoddy work.
- **take after** [resemble; **Note :** used for people] : Both my sister and I take after our father.
- **take/bring back** [return] :
  (a) This book is due tomorrow. I guess I should *take* it *back* to the library.
  (b) Yes, you can borrow my pen, but don't forget to *bring* it *back* to me when you're finished.
- **take care of** [provide care for; watch one's health] :
  (a) Louis has been *taking care* of her father since he returned home from the hospital.

(b) You've been working too hard lately. You'd better *take care of* yourself!

- **take care of** [make arrangements (for something to happen); take responsibility for] : Will you *take care of* making reservations for our flight to London?
- **take off** [remove (something you're wearing)] : Please *take* your hat *off* when you go inside a building.
- **take off** [leave; depart (often suddenly or quickly)] :
  (a) Was something wrong with Kelly? She *took off* without saying goodbye.
  (b) When does your plane take off?
- **take off** [make arrangements to be absent from work] : Jusan isn't here today. She's *taking* today and tomorrow *off*.
- **take up** [begin (a hobby or leisure-time activity)] :
  (a) Do you like to ski?
  (b) I've never been skiing, but I think I'd like to *take* it *up*.
- **tell (someone) off** [speak to someone bluntly and negatively, saying exactly what she/he did wrong] : Julie was really angry at Bob; she *told* him *off* in front of all of us.
- **tick off** [irritate someone; make someone upset or angry] : It really *ticks* her *off* when someone is late for an appointment.
- **tick off** [show that something has been completed by putting a tick (check) beside it] : Here are the things you need to do. *Tick* each one *off* when you finish it.
- **throw away** [discard; put in the garbage] : You shouldn't throw *those* newspapers *away*; they're recyclable.
- **throw out** [discard; put in the garbage] : This food smells bad. You'd better *throw* it *out*.
- **throw out** [forcibly make someone leave (usually because of bad behavior)] : Those people are drunk and making everyone uncomfortable. The manager should *throw* them *out*.
- **throw up** [vomit] : Rau was so nervous about his job interview that he *threw up* just before he left for it.
- **try on** [wear something briefly to check its fit, how it looks etc.] : I'm not sure that jacket is large enough. May I *try* it *on*?
- **try out** [use a machine briefly to determine how well it works] : I really like the way this car looks. May I *try* it *out*?
- **try out** (for) [try to win a place on a team or other organization] :
  (a) I know you want to be on the football team. Are you going to *try out*?
  (b) If you like to sing, you should *try out* for the choir.
- **turn around** [move so that you are facing the opposite direction] : Everyone *turned around* and stared when I entered the meeting late.
- **turn around** [move so that someone/something is facing the opposite direction] : I don't want this chair facing the window. Will you help me *turn* it *around*?
- **turn around** [make changes so that something that was unprofitable is profitable] : The company was doing poorly until it hired a new president. He *turned* it *around* in about six months and now it's doing quite well.
- **turn down** [decrease the volume] : Your music is giving me a headache! Please *turn* it *down* or use your headphones!
- **turn down** [refuse] : I thought I could borrow some money from Joe, but when I asked, he *turned* me *down*.
- **turn in** [give/deliver/submit to someone] : I've written my report, but I haven't *turned* it *in*.
- **turn in** [go to bed] : I'm pretty tired. I guess I'll *turn in*.
- **turn in** [report or deliver wrongdoers to the authorities] : Two days after the robbery, the thieves *turned* themselves *in*.
- **turn off** [stop by turning a handle or switch] : I'm cold. Do you mind if I *turn* the air conditioner *off*?
- **turn off** [bore, repel (very informal)] : That music *turns* me *off*. Please play something else!
- **turn on** [start by turning a handle or switch] : It's cold in here. I'm going to *turn* the heater *on*.
- **turn on** [interest very much; excite (very informal)] : What kind of music *turns* you *on*?
- **turn up** [increase the volume] : I can barely hear the TV. Can you *turn* it *up* a little?

- **turn up** [appear unexpectedly] : We were all surprised when Rani *turned up* at the party. We didn't even know she was in town.
- **wait on** [serve (usually customers in a restaurant, shop etc.)] : I want to make a complaint. The person who just *waited on* me was very impolite.
- **wait for** [wait until someone/something arrives or is finished with something else] :
  (a) When will Jenny be finished with work? I've been *waiting for* him for almost an hour.
  (b) I'm tired of *waiting for* the bus. I guess I'll take a taxi instead.
- **wake up** [stop sleeping] : I usually *wake up* around 6:00 a.m. each day.
- **wake up** [rouse someone; cause someone to stop sleeping] : I have an important meeting tomorrow and I'm afraid I won't hear my alarm. Will you *wake* me *up* at 6:00 a.m.?
- **watch out for** [be careful of; beware of] :
  (a) There's a school at the end of this block. *Watch out for* children crossing the street.
  (b) If you take that road, *watch out for* ice during the winter.
- **wear out** [wear something/use something until it can no longer be worn/be used] :
  (a) I need a new pencil sharpener. I *wore* this one *out*.
  (b) I suppose I should get some new shoes. I've almost *worn* this pair *out*.
- **wear out** [cause to become exhausted; cause to become very tired] :
  (a) I had four different meetings today. They *wore* me *out*.
  (b) I suppose I should get some new shoes. I've almost *worn* this pair *out*.
- **work out** [exercise (usually in a gym etc.) to build muscles, tone body] : Instead of eating lunch on Monday, Wednesday, and Friday, Sheila goes to the recreation centre to *work out*.
- **work out** [solve a problem/resolve a difficult situation (usually by working together)] : I know we disagree on many points, but I believe we can *work* things *out*.
- **wrap up** [wear enough clothes to keep warm] : It's really cold today. Be sure you *wrap up* when you leave the house.
- **wrap up** [finish something; bring something to a conclusion] : We've been talking about the problem for nearly three hours. I hope we'll be able to *wrap* the discussion *up* soon.
- **write down** [record something in writing] : Could you tell me your e-mail address again? I want to *write* it *down*.
- **write up** [record, report in writing] : You'll need to make a report on your business meetings. Be sure you *write* them *up* as soon as possible after you return from your trip.
- **zonk out** [fall asleep quickly because of exhaustion] : I intended to go shopping after work, but I was so tired that I *zonked out* as soon as I got home.

Exercises

Exercise 1

1. *Give the meaning of phrasal verbs italicised in the following sentences and then use them in your own sentences* **(RAS)**
   (a) Don't worry, I shall try to *bring* him *round*.
   (b) You must *make up* your differences.
   (c) He has promised to *go into* the matter.
   (d) I shall *stand by* you through thick and thin.
   (e) You will have to *make good* this loss.
2. *Make sentences by using any five of the phrasal verbs given below :* **(RAS)**
   (a) bear out (b) take off
   (c) look into(d)make for
   (e) pick up (f)give in
   (g) come round
3. *Complete the phrasal verb in each of the following sentencess :* **(RAS)**
   (a) If the business continues to lose money, I'm afraid we'll have to close ....
   (b) You'd better ring her ...... and tell her you'll be late.
   (c) I invited her to drop ..... any time she was passing, and have a cup of tea.
   (d) He won't buy the car without trying it .... on the road first.
   (e) If you can't afford it, you'll have to do .... it.
4. *Complete the phrasal verbs in each of the following sentences :* **(RAS)**
   (a) They left the bomb in the street. Many people died when it ....

(b) The dacoits refused to give .... even though they were surrounded by the troops.
(c) The Prime Minister pulled .... his partymen for their rude behaviour.
(d) Each time a new problem cropped ...., he rushed to his parents for advice.
(e) She broke ..... when she heard the news of her son's death.
(f) The chief guest gave .... the prizes.

5. *Make sentences by using any three of the following phrasal verbs so as to bring out their meanings :* **(RAS)**
back up; look over; put out; put up; lay off; see back.

6. *Make sentences by using any four of the following phrasal verbs so as to bring out their meanings : hold up; lay off; call off; set back; calm down; bear with.*

Solutions

1. (a) persuade to accept something
(b) finish a quarrel
(c) investigate or go in detail
(d) support or help
(e) compensate
2. See the uses of Phrasal verbs.
3. (a) down (b) up
(c) in (d) out
(e) without
4. (a) up (b) in
(c) up (d) up
(e) down (f) away
5. See the uses of phrasal verbs.
6. See the uses of phrasal verbs.

Unit

27

Related Pairs of Words

In some competitive examinations, five to ten questions relating to related pairs of words are asked. In such questions a pair of word is usually given, having some associated relationship. Candidates are required to choose the answer out of the given options of pairs, which has the same relationship as that of the question pair.

For example

Choose the correct alternative given below to show close relation with the words given in capital letters :

trailer : picture ::

(a) truck : cargo

(b) theatre : play

(c) synopsis : thesis

(d) commercial: product

The correct answer is (c) synopsis : thesis.

Synopsis and thesis have same kind of relationship as that of trailer and picture.

Some Related Pairs of Words

as bald as a badger
as black as a gall
as black as a coal
as black as a crow
as black as ink
as black as midnight
as black as pitch
as blind as a bat
as blind as a beetle
as blind as a mole
as blithe as a bee
as blithe as a butterfly
as blithe as a lark
as bold as a lion
as brave as a lion

as bright as the day

as bright as the light

as bright as the silver
as brittle as glass
as brown as a berry

as hot as fire
as hungry as a horse
as innocent as a dove
as light as a feather
as loud as thunder
as mad as a hatter
as merry as a cricket
as merry as a lark
as mute as a fish
as nimble as a bee
as obstinate as a mule
as old as the hills
as pale as a ghost
as patient as an ox
as playful as a butterfly
as playful as a squirrel or a kitten
as plentiful as blackberries
as poor as lazarus
as proud as a peacock
as quick as lightning

as busy as a bee
as changeable as the moon.
as changeable as a weather cock
as cheerful as a lark
as clear as crystal
as clear as day, noon day
as cold as ice
as cold as marble
as cold as a cucumber

as cold as a stone
as cunning as a fox
as dark as midnight
as dark as pitch
as dead as a door-nail
as dead as a herring
as deep as a well
as drunk as a lord
as drunk as a fiddler
as dry as a bone

as quiet as thought
as quiet as a lamb

as rapid as lightning

as red as blood
as red as a cherry
as red as crimson

as red as rose
as red as scarlet
as regular as clockwork
as rich as croesus
as rich as a jew
as dumb as a statue
as fair as a rose
as false as a scot
as fast as a hare
as fat as big ben
as fierce as a tiger
as firm as a rock
as flat as a board

as dry as dust
as free as the air
as fresh as a daisy
as fresh as a rose
as gay as a lark
as gaudy as a butterfly
as gaudy as a peacock
as gentle as a lamb
as good as gold
as graceful as a swan
as grave as a judge
as greedy as a dog
as green as grass
as happy as a king
as hard as fling, marble
as hard as a stone
as harmless as a dove

as fleet as a deer
as soft as butter wax
as sound as a bell
as steady as a rock
as still as death
as strong as the grave
as stupid as a statue
as strong as a lion
as stupid as a donkey
as sure as death
as sweet as honey, sugar
as swift as an arrow
as swift as lightning
as tall as a may pole
as tall as a steeple
as tame as a hare
as timid as a hare

as heavy as lead, sand
as hoarse as a crow, a raven
as round as a ball or a globe
as sharp as a needle, a razor
as silent as the dead
as silent as the grave
as silent as the stars
as silly as a goose
as silly as a sheep
as slender as a gossamer
as slender as a thread
as yellow as saffron
as yielding as wax
she wept a flood of tears

as tricky as a monkey
as ugly as a scarecrow, a toad
as vain as a peacock
as warm as wool
as weak as a baby
as white as a sheet
as white as wool
as white as snow
as wise as a serpent
as wise as solomon
as smooth as a glass
as smooth as velvet
to spread like wild fire
to follow as a shadow

Exercises

Exercise 1

Choose the correct alternative from pairs given below to show close relation with the following words

1. we : our ::
(a) him : his (b) it : its
(c) you : you're (d) they : there
(e) who: whose

2. sleek : glossy ::
(a) contrite : unrepentant
(b) rapid : tepid
(c) vapid : complete
(d) dejected : jubilant
(e) credible : believable

3. astronomy : astrology ::
(a) symbolism : superstition
(b) geology : geometry
(c) magic : science
(d) chemistry : alchemy
(e) folklore : fable

4. dough : bread ::
(a) words : speech (b) paper : writing
(c) cold : ice (d) ink : pen
(e) sugar : cake

5. engineer : cab ::
(a) shepherd : flock
(b) passenger : taxi
(c) sailor : cabin
(d) driver : wheel
(e) aviator : cockpit

6. strings : violin ::
(a) wind : leaves
(b) air : flute
(c) pedal : organ
(d) membrane : drum
(e) plectrum : mandolin

7. scalp : violin ::
(a) Shoe : Foot
(b) Cloth : Table
(c) house : root
(d) curtain : window
(e) earth : grass

8. isthmus : land ::
(a) wire : pole
(b) strait : body of water
(c) neck : head
(d) bar : trapeze
(e) opening : tunnel

9. memorandum : memoranda ::
(a) insignia : insigne
(b) strata : stratum
(c) alumna : alumni
(d) automata : automata
(e) bacillus : bacilli

10. prone : supine ::
(a) likely : unlikely
(b) asiant : akimbo
(c) recumbent : prostrate
(b) face down : face up
(e) backward : forward

Solutions

1. (e) **2.** (e) **3.** (d) **4.** (a)
5. (e) **6.** (d) **7.** (e) **8.** (b)
9. (e) **10.** (d)

Exercise 2

Choose the correct alternative from pairs given below to show close relation with the following words

1. mule : burden ::
(a) scholar : books
(b) animal : oppression
(c) ship : cargo
(d) musician : cello
(e) house : tenants
2. although : nevertheless ::
(a) albeit : however
(b) because : therefore
(c) since : yet
(d) notwithstanding : if
(e) when : simultaneously
3. zenith : nadir ::
(a) high : higher
(b) zero : cipher
(c) perfection : baseness
(d) slough : despair
(e) pinnacle : bottom
4. spate : trickle ::
(a) much : little
(b) much : more
(c) copious : abundant
(d) much : many
(e) small : less
5. Ram : Ewe ::
(a) Doe : Hart
(b) Swan : Cygnet
(c) Marquis : Marquee
(d) Stallion : Colt
(e) Testator : Testatrix
6. facade : building ::
(a) drawer : desk (b) dial : watch
(c) page : book (d) fence : garden
(e) cork : bottle
7. pulsate : throb ::
(a) condone : condemn
(b) abate : increase
(c) disperse : gather
(d) expropriate : deprive
(e) accede : disagree
8. morass : swamp ::
(a) peak : mountain (b) desert : oasis
(c) sea : gulf (d) forest : tree
(e) prairie : plain
9. islands : archipelago ::
(a) stamps : philately
(b) stars : constellation
(c) nickels : follar bill
(d) hors d'oeuvre : banquet
(e) birds : apiary
10. serrated : saw ::
(a) mountain : jagged (b) sharpness : knife
(c) dappled : horse (d) pronged : fork
(e) incisor : tooth

Solutions

1. (c)	**2.** (a)	**3.** (e)	**4.** (a)
5. (e)	**6.** (b)	**7.** (d)	**8.** (e)
9. (b)	**10.** (d)		

Exercise 3

Choose the correct alternative from pairs given below to show close relation with the following words

1. fright : stampede ::
(a) flow of water : erosion
(b) clouds : tornado
(c) rain : snow
(d) haste : crowds
(e) wildness : cattle
2. guttural : throat ::
(a) venal : wine (b) mantle : cloak
(c) hair : hirsute (d) palmar : wrist
(e) brachial : arm
3. lobster : crustacean : :
(a) eagle : sparrow (b) reason : man
(c) tiger : cat (d) dolphin : whale
(e) lion : man
4. abominate : magnate ::
(a) noun : noun (b) adjective : noun
(c) noun : adjective (d) verb : verb
(e) verb : nouns
5. predatory : hawk ::
(a) contortion : grimace
(b) voracious : glutton
(c) tawny : lion
(d) speedy : cruiser
(e) ugly : vulture
6. minaret : mosque ::
(a) cross : basilica (b) muezzin : prayer
(c) have : cathedral (d) belfry : steeple
(e) campanile : church
7. incongruous : harmonious ::
(a) tall : short
(b) fickle : rebellious
(c) wearisome : tedious
(d) laughable : ludicrous
(e) nonplussed : distracted
8. cogent : convincing ::
(a) dubious : certain
(b) nonchalant : disturbed
(c) banal : unoriginal
(d) cunning : disingenuous
(e) insular : continental

9. decanter : carafe ::
(a) salver : tray (b) bottle : barrel
(c) cruet : kettle (d) cup : plate
(e) crystal : glass
10. intermittently : incessantly ::
(a) interminably : wearily
(b) slowly : rapidly
(c) strongly : weakly
(d) vicariously : frequently
(e) occasionally : continuously

Solutions

1. (a) 2. (e) 3. (c) 4. (e)
5. (b) 6. (e) 7. (a) 8. (c)
9. (a) 10. (e)

Exercise 4

Choose the correct alternative from pairs given below to show close relation with the following words

1. mercury : caduceus : :
(a) vulcan : forge
(b) pegasus : muses
(c) palladium : athena
(d) jupiter : thunderbolt
(e) neptune : trident
2. enervate : strengthen ::
(a) aver : attribute (b) divert : turn
(c) apprise : appraise (d) stultify : enliven
(e) invigorate : brighten
3. dolt : dour ::
(a) bolt : door
(b) escape : subterfuge
(c) reticent : silence
(d) numbskull : sullen
(e) infant : cry
4. exordium : peroration ::
(a) epilogue : prologue
(b) incipient : inchoate
(c) certain : uncertain
(d) alpha : omega
(e) exhortation : denunciation
5. mendacity : distrust ::
(a) begging : charity
(b) stupidity : failure
(c) truth : falsehood
(d) untruth : doubtful
(e) integrity : confidence
6. carelessness : jeopardise ::
(a) penalty : chastise
(b) failure : discouragement
(c) carefulness : security
(d) neglect : endanger
(e) crowding : discomfort
7. permeate : rueful ::
(a) truculent : merciful
(b) sadden : pitiful
(c) evaporate : mournful
(d) penetrate : sorrowful
(e) frighten : lamentable
8. flamboyant : rococo ::
(a) ornate : baroque
(b) inflammable : phlegmatic
(c) counterfeit : invaluable
(d) flagrant : flagitious
(e) florid : fragrant
9. hypertension : hypotension ::
(a) high : low
(b) excessive : deficient
(c) super : minimal
(d) abnormal : normal
(e) iso : sub
10. oaf : freshet ::
(a) lout : novice
(b) stupidity : impertinence
(c) fool : flood
(d) silly : brash
(e) gaucherie : elan

Solutions

1. (e) 2. (d) 3. (d) 4. (d)
5. (e) 6. (d) 7. (d) 8. (a)
9. (b) 10. (c)

Exercise 5

Choose the correct alternative from pairs given below to show close relation with the following words

1. implicate : complicate ::
(a) vitality : inevitable
(b) empathy : sympathy
(c) importune : construct
(d) imply : simplify
(e) belligerent : embellish
2. cupid : psyche ::
(a) zeus : aphrodite
(b) damon : pythias
(c) hero : leander
(d) apollo : cassandra
(e) venus : adonis
3. precedent : justification ::
(a) kindness : obedience
(b) authority : sanction
(c) usage : submission
(d) tradition : novelty
(e) orthodoxy : heresy
4. rachitic : rickets ::
(a) adulatory : adoration
(b) oxford : oxonian
(c) scorbutic : scurvy
(d) deification : deify
(e) therapy : therapeutic

5. laurel : victor ::
(a) chevrons : army
(b) oscar : movie star
(c) power : glory
(d) blue ribbon : cooking
(e) rabbit's foot : fuck

6. corvine : crow ::
(a) elephantine : dinosaur
(b) lioness : lion
(c) viceregal : viceroy
(d) corvette : automobile
(e) urbane : urban

7. zealot : fanaticism ::
(a) impostor : sham
(b) orator : frenzy
(c) umpire : game
(d) vagabond : vagrant
(e) parasite : food

8. pain : anodyne ::
(a) savagery : music
(b) grief : solace
(c) harshness : softness
(d) trifle : enormity
(e) accident : insurance

9. forgery : signature ::
(a) faked : genuine
(b) proxy : delegate
(c) carbon copy : original
(d) embezzlement : blank cheque
(e) Multigraph : Duplicate

10. philologist : language ::
(a) numismatist : stamps
(b) herbalist : tropical flowers
(c) philatelist : charms
(d) fish : ichthyologist
(e) conchologist : shells

Solutions

1. (b) 2. (d) 3. (b) 4. (c)
5. (b) 6. (c) 7. (a) 8. (b)
9. (a) 10. (e)

Exercise 6

Choose the correct alternative from words given below to fill in the missing word

1. donkey : brays :: wolf : ?
(a) bellows (b) howls
(c) whimpers (d) roars
(e) whines

2. anxiety : allay :: grief :.
(a) banish (b) condole
(c) heighten (d) assuage
(e) display

3. mosaics : words :: sentences: ?
(a) colours (b) small stones
(c) straw (d) papyrus
(e) bricks

4. minotaur : bull :: chimera : ?
(a) heifer (b) lion
(c) goddess (d) tiger
(e) dog

5. blandish : coax :: asseverate : ?
(a) affirm (b) cut
(c) repeat (d) complain
(e) twist

6. sylvan : woods :: terrestrial : ?
(a) urban (b) fear
(c) earth (d) planets
(e) stars

7. astronauts : space :: argonauts : ?
(a) fire (b) ship
(c) birds (d) treasure
(e) sea

8. scion : progenitor :: descendant : ?
(a) children (b) brother
(c) ancestor (d) progeny
(e) guardian

9. pediatrician : hair : : dematologist : ?
(a) children (b) feet
(c) plants (d) philosophy
(e) skin

10. sleazy : flimsy :: shoddy :
(a) tenable (b) despicable
(c) queasy (d) tenuous
(e) detrimental

Solutions

1. (b) 2. (d) 3. (b) 4. (b)
5. (a) 6. (c) 7. (e) 8. (c)
9. (a) 10. (d)

Exercise 7

Choose the correct alternative from words given below to fill in the missing word

1. genuine : simulated :: unaffected :
(a) elevated (b) bombastic
(c) dynamic (d) destructive
(e) emulated

2. actor : stage :: ? : rostrum
(a) pilot (b) acrobat
(c) soldier (d) rider
(e) orator

3. answer : test :: denouement : ?
(a) symphony (b) horse race
(c) mystery story (d) circus
(e) complete understanding

4. ? : Sullivan :: Hammerstein : Rogers
(a) Lerner (b) Bellini
(c) Gilbert (d) Mozart
(e) Purcell

5. recondite : abstruse :: banter : ?
(a) delay (b) tease
(c) bargain (d) exchange
(e) deceive

6. basilica : church :: dormer : ?
(a) movie (b) chapel
(c) room (d) window
(e) servant

7. cicerone : guide :: dragoman : ?
(a) cavalry officer (b) interpreter
(c) hauler (d) turnkey
(e) mythological monster

8. vilification : defamation :: ? : travesty
(a) parody (b) garment
(c) stripping (d) deterioration
(e) journey

9. supposititious : false :: spurious :
(a) inciting (b) duplicate
(c) exhilarating (d) not authentic
(e) not technical

10. mulct : defraud :: ratiocination : ?
(a) reasoning (b) bilk
(c) detective (d) proportion
(e) self-defenses

Solutions

1. (b) 2. (e) 3. (c) 4. (c)
5. (b) 6. (d) 7. (b) 8. (a)
9. (d) 10. (a)

Exercise 8

Choose the correct alternative from words given below to fill in the missing word

1. inveigle : cajole :: malign : ?
(a) slander (b) enlighten
(c) acclaim (d) eulogize
(e) compile

2. cygnet : swan :: ? : horse
(a) bridle (b) hoof
(c) mule (d) colt
(e) stallion

3. snake : reptilian :: lion : ?
(a) leotard (b) vulpine
(c) lemurine (d) tiger
(e) feline

4. hercules : ? :: cupid : arrow
(a) trident (b) spear
(c) club (d) poisoned bow
(e) hydra

5. sinecure : care :: intrepidity : ?
(a) hesitation (b) entanglement
(c) fear (d) support
(e) forethought

6. sancho panza : don quixote :: ? : sherlock holmes
(a) perry mason (b) don ameche
(c) maigret (d) john h. watson
(e) nero wolfe

7. ogle : eyes :: maneouver : ?
(a) fingers (b) human beings
(c) minds (d) machines
(e) hands

8. purloin : steal :: nebulous : ?
(a) frustrating (b) scanty
(c) dishonest (d) stormy
(e) vague

9. rubescent : red :: cerulean : ?
(a) sky (b) brilliant
(c) pale (d) seagreen
(e) blue

10. claptrap :: pithy : maxim : ?
(a) sincere (b) simple
(c) pretentious (d) thoughtless
(e) sccidental

Solutions

1. (a) 2. (d) 3. (e) 4. (e)
5. (c) 6. (d) 7. (e) 8. (e)
9. (e) 10. (c)

» Unit

28

Homonyms

Definition : Word similar in sound or pronunciation, but different in meaning, are called homonyms.

1. **affect** (to act upon, to pretend) :
   (a) She affects too much innocence.
   (b) The drought affected a large part of the district.
   effect (result) : Internet can produces a bad effect on the young generation.
2. **adapt** (accomodate) : One should adapt oneself to the new circumstances.
   adept (expert) : He is adept in folk dance.
   adopt (take up): One should not adopt unfair means to secure good marks.
3. **addition** (putting more) : I am to buy two more copies in addition to this one.
   edition (printing books) : The first edition of this book has sold like hot cakes.
4. **accede** (Agree) : He will not accede to your request.
   exceed (to be greater) : Write an essay not exceeding three hundred words.
5. **access** (approach, reach) : Now-a-days, every person has an easy access to the temples irrespective to his caste.
   excess (more than enough) : Excess of everything is bad.
6. **accept** (to take) : He cannot accept this gift.
   except (leaving out) : Except Nisha everyone was present in the party.
7. **alter** (change) : You cannot alter my opinion about her.
   altar (place of offering) :
   (a) S.C. Bose sacrificed everything at the altar of freedom.
   (b) In India incense is burnt at the altar in temples.
8. **antic** (odd, strange) : His behaviour on yesterday was antic.
   antique (ancient) : I am fond of collecting antique items.
9. **assay** (attempt, testing the purity of metals) :
   (a) He assayed hard to secure top position.
   (b) He assayed the gold ornaments.
   essay (a piece of composition) : Write a brief essay on 'Indian Films'.
10. **all ready** (all are ready) : They were all ready to welcome the groom.
    already (earlier) : I have already informed him.
11. **allusions** (Indirect reference) : The poem is full of allusions.
    illusion (a deceptive show) : Indian mythology regards the material world as an illusion.
12. **apposite** (proper) : his arguments were not apposite to the subject.
    opposite (contrary, in front of) : His house is opposite to the college.
13. **assent** (agreement) : He gave his assent to the new proposal.
    ascent (going up) : He pushed the button and the elevator began its slow ascent.
14. **arc** (part of circle) : If a straight line is drawn in a circle it will divide it into two arcs.
    ark (covered floating vessel) : He crossed the Black Sea **with** his family in an ark.

15. **aloud** (high volume) : I can't hear you well, please speak aloud.
allowed (permitted) : He was allowed to enter.
16. **angle** (An angle of degree) : This is a ninety degree angle.
angels (a divine messenger) : Angels reside in heaven while men reside on earth.
17. **advice** (noun) : I need your expert advice in this matter.
advise (verb) : Please advise me in this matter.
18. **amiable** (lovable) : She is not only beautiful but also an amiable girl.
amicable (friendly) : Finally they came to an amicable settlement.
19. **ail** (to be ill) : What ails the Industry is to be sorted out?
ale (a drink) : He has gone to the ale-house.
20. **all together** (wholly) : Let us move there all together.
altogether (completely) : It seems altogether impossible to cross the river in the night.
21. **aid** (to assist) : He has given aid of Rs 5000/- to the poor family.
aide (an assistant) : He is a close aide to the Prime Minister.
22. **aerie** (eagle's nest) : There is an aerie on this tree.
airy (breezy) : The house is quite airy.
23. **aisle** (walkway) :
(a) An aisle is a long narrow gap that people can walk along between rows of seats in a public building such as a church or between rows of shelves in a super market.
(b) The aisle is also used in expressions such as walking down the aisle to refer to the activity of getting married.
I am in no hurry to walk down the aisle.
isle (island) : I have seen many isles but this is the best isle.
24. **all** (everything) : He has donated all his property.
awl (A small pointed tool for pricking or piercing holes, esp. such a tool used by shoemakers) : An awl is a pointed too used by a shoemakers.
25. **ate** (past tense of eat) : He ate two apples.
eight (the number base of octal, seven, eight, nine) : I have eight pens.
26. **auger** (a drill tool) : I need an auger to make a hole.
augur (foretell) : The recent communal riots do not augur well for the smooth running of government.
27. **aural** (of hearing) : He became famous as an inventor of astonishing visual and aural effects)
oral (of the mouth) : He presented his ideas in a nice way orally.
28. **auricle** (external part of the ear).
oracle (seer) : He regards himself as an oracle on architecture.
29. **away** (distant) : Do not go far away from the house.
aweigh (just clear of the bottom).
30. **awed** (in a state of wonder) : Awedly she was unable to recall his name.
odd (not usual) : Find the odd word from the following passage.
31. **aye** (Aye means yes—used in some dialects of British English) :
'Do you remember your first day at school?'
'Oh aye. Yeah.'
eye (ocular organ) : Her eyes are very beautiful.
32. **bale** (package) : I received thirty bales of cotton last month.
bail (security) : The magistrate didn't grant him bail in theft case.
33. **berth** (sleeping place in train) : I have booked two berths in Shatabadi Express.
birth (coming to life) : This is not the birth place of Buddha.
34. **bare** (uncovered) : He came here bare footed.
bear (to tolerate) : I cannot bear your insulting remarks.
(an animal) : There are three bears in that circus.
beer (a kind of wine) : I prefer to take beer.
35. **blow** (to whistle) : A cool wind is blowing. Don't blow the whistle.
below (underneath) : Hitting below the belt is not allowed.
36. **born** (To take birth) : My wife was born in 1960.

borne (supported) : He is suffering from water borne disease.

37. **bad** (not good) : He is a bad man.
bed (sleeping place) : I go to bed at 11 P.M.

38. **by** (assistance) : A snake was killed by Ram with a stick.
buy (purchase) : I want to buy a car.

39. **beet** (A vegetable) : I prefer mango to beet.
beat (to thrash) : It is wrong to beat the students with a stick.

40. **borrow** (to take loan) : I have borrowed some money from Bank.
burrow (a hole in earth) : A mouse lives in this burrow.

41. **cell** (a small cottage) : There are more than twenty cells in that prison.
sell (to dispose off) : He sells fruits and vegetables.
sale (noun-act of selling) : I have purchased this dress from that shop.

42. **beach** (shore) : Many people like to walk along the sea beach.
beech (a kind of tree) : There are many beech trees near the railway station.

43. **brake** (lever) : I am going to get the brake wire changed.
break (To make a part) : Can you break this stick with your hands ?

44. **bow** (bend) : Let us bow to our motherland India.
bough (a branch of tree) : Many birds are sitting on the bough of the tree.

45. **bridal** (pertaining to marriage) : She is looking beautiful in her bridal dress.
bridle (reins) : It is not easy to bridle a vicious horse.

46. **baron** (a landlord) : There was a time when all powers rested in the hands of rich barons.
barren (not fertile) : In barren land you can't cultivate any thing.

47. **blue** (a colour) : I like blue colour.
blew (whistled) : The refree blew the whistle again and again.

48. **bait** (Food placed on a hook or in a trap to entice fish) :
Let your bait falls gently upon the water.
bate (to lessen) : We listened with bated breath the stories of grandmother's travel.

49. **bald** (hairless) : She is bald headed.
balled (carnal knowledge) : He picked up the sheets of paper and balled them tightly in his fists.
bawled (cried aloud) : Someone in the audience bawled out 'Once more'.

50. **band** (a group) : A band is a group of musicians.
banned (forbidden) : Drinking is banned in Gujrat.

51. **bard** (a poet) : People sometimes refer to William Shakespeare as the Bard.
barred (enclosed by poles) : The windows were closed and shuttered and the door was barred.

52. **basal** (forming the base) : The basal layer of the skin was also torn.
basil (an herb) : Basil is used in cooking also.

53. **base** (the bottom support for anything) : The base of the bottle is very narrow.
bass (the lowest musical pitch or range) : A bass is also a man with deep singing voice.

54. **bask** (to warm oneself pleasantly) : Crocodiles bask on the small sandy beaches.
basque (tight fitting bodice or tunic) : She was advised to wear basque.

55. **baud** (bits per second) : A unit of data transmission speed equal to one information unit per second.
bawd (brothel manager) : She is the bawd of that brothel.

56. **beau** (male friend) : A woman's beau is her boy friend or lover.
bow (a curve or bend) : He bowed slightly for taking her bag.

57. **bell** (ding ding) : Don't try to bell the cat.
belle (beautiful woman) : She was the belle in last night party.

58. **besot** (to get drunk) : He became so besotted with her that even he forgot his children.
besought (past tense of beseech) : She besought him to cut his drinking and reduce his smoking.

59. **better** (superior) : It is always better to drive carefully.
bettor (one who bets) : The person who bets is called a bettor.

60. **bight** (loop of a rope) : The is called bight.
bite (a mouthful) : You can have a bite of chocolates.
byte (eight bits) : Byte is a unit of storage in computers.

61. **bloc** (an alliance) : A bloc is a group of countries which have similar aims and interest and that generally act together over some issue.
block (a block in a town is an area of land with streets on all its sides) She walked four blocks down High Street.

62. **Boar** (wild pig) : We can find wild boars in the valleys.
boer (a South African of Dutch descent) : He is a boer.
boor (tasteless buffoon) : If we refer someone as a boor, we think his behaviour and attitude rough and rude.
bore (not interesting) : He bored me all through the meal with stories of the army life.

63. **bode** (an omen) : She says the way bill was passed bodes ill for the democracy.
bowed (curved) : He has bowed legs bold brave

64. **bole** (trunk) : He was standing behind the bole of a tree.
bowl (dish) : Put all the soup in a large bowl.

65. **boos** (disparaging sounds from audience) : Demonstrators booed and jeered him.
booze (whisky) : I have five empty bottles of booze.

66. **bough** (tree branch) : I rested my fishing rod against a pine bough.
bow (front of a ship; respectful bend) : I gave a theatrical bow and waved.

67. **bra** (brassiere) : She wears beautiful coloured bra.
braw (well-groomed) : He always keeps himself in braw shape.

68. **braid** (a narrow piece of twisted thread or cloth used to **decorate** clothes) : He was wearing a coloured uniform with lots of gold braid)
brayed (a donkey cried) : The donkey brayed and tried to bolt.

69. **braise** (cook with oil and water) : I like braised cabbage.
brays (loud, harsh cry of donkey) : A donkey is braying.

70. **bread** (a loaf) : Bread is necessary for the living.
bred (past tense of breed) : He is an ill bred fellow.

71. **brewed** (fermented) I like nicely brewed beer.
brood (family) : A brood is a group of baby birds that were born at the same time to the same mother.
If someone broods over something they think about it a lot seriously.

72. **bruise** (an injury) : How did you get that bruise on your cheek?
brews (making beer) : I brew my own beer.

73. **broach** (to raise a subject) : At last I broached the subject of her early life.
brooch (an ornament fastened to clothes which has a pin at the back) : I have five brooches.

74. **brows** (aiches of hair above each eye) : Your brows are on your forehead.
browse (grazing) : Three red deer were browsing near my lodge.

75. **burger** (meat sandwich) : I do not like eating burger.
burgher (merchant) : The burghers of a town are the people who live there especially the richer or more respectable people.

76. **but** (excepting) : He is but a good man.
butt (the thick end) : A number of cigarette butts are lying there.

77. **buyer** (one who purchases) : Only a prospective buyer can purchase this house.
byre (a cow barn) : A byre is a cowshed.

78. **check** (to verify, to stop) : He checked my passport. He checked me from leaving the function.
cheque (bank document) : I issued a cheque favouring PNB.

79. **calendar** (chart showing dates etc.) : I have only one calendar in my office.
calender (to press paper, cloth etc.) : Please calender my dress.

80. **cannon** (big gun) : A cannon of ancient time is placed near the railway station.
Canon (rule) He believes in canons of justice.

81. **canvas** (a kind of rough cloth) : My shoes are made of canvas.
canvass (to solicit votes) : Nowadays students are busy in canvassing for their friends.
82. **casual** (Accidental, occasional) : I was granted only one day casual leave.
Causal (showing cause) There is a causal link between balanced diet and sound mind.
83. **corpse** (dead body): The corpse was covered with a white bedsheet.
corps (a body of troops) : I want to join National Cadet Corps.
84. **coma** (state of senselessness) : The patient has been in coma since Monday.
comma (mark of punctuation) : One should be careful about proper use of comma.
85. **cession** (to yield) : India should not have made a cession of an inch of its land for the establishment of Pakistan.
session (sitting of assembly or court) : The winter session of Parliament will be over tomorrow.
86. **censer** (a pot in which incense is burnt) : Place some incense into the censer.
censor (an official examination) : The Censor Board has awarded 'U' certificate to this film.
censure (criticize adversely) : His conduct was censured by the Parliament.
87. **chord** (a string of musical instrument) : He is playing with the chords of the violin.
cord (a thin rope) : I need a fifteen fit cord for packing the luggage.
88. **cease** (Discontinue) : He resigned and thus ceased to be the Chairman of our society.
seize (to catch) : Heroin worth 2 lacs rupees was seized from his office.
sieze (surrounded) : Akbar's army siezed the castle of Chittorgarh.
89. **career** (profession) : For better career opportunities, join computer courses.
carrier (one who carries) : Mosquitoes are carriers of virus.
90. **coarse** (rough) : Do not use a coarse cloth to clean the glasses.
course (line of action) : A disciplined course of action is required to achieve success.
91. **collision** (clashing) : In a collision between train and bus, three persons died on thespot.
collusion (secret agreement for an evil plan) : He planned to execute a robbery in collusion with the clerk.
92. **cloth** (unstitched cloth) : I want to purchase cloth for a shirt and a trousers.
clothe (stitched cloth) : I have given my clothes to washerman for drycleaning.
93. **capital** (centre of administration) : Delhi is the capital of India
capitol (Roman temple of Jupiter, US Congress House) : A meeting of US Congress be held in capitol tomorrow.
94. **defy** (challenge) : One should not defy the orders of one's superiors.
deify (worship a God) : Mr. M.K.Gandhi is defied by all Indians.
95. **complacent** (self satisfied) : He seems complacent with his job and earning.
complaisant (polite) : He is a man of very complaisant nature.
96. **complement** (which completes) : Husband and wife are complementary to each other.
compliment (regards) : Please convey my best compliments to your parents.
97. **cautious** (aware) : I am quite cautious of his activities.
conscientious (careful, scrupulous) : My mother is very hard working, sincere and conscientious lady.
98. **council** (assembly) : He was nominated to the Council of State.
counsel (advice) : He counsels in a right way.
99. **credible** (believable) : He is not a credible person.
creditable (worthy of praise) : His achievements are indeed creditable.
100. **cymbal** (a musical instrument) : I like the melodious sound of the Cymbal.
symbol (sign) : What is the symbol of 2004 Olympic Games?
101. **current** (present) : What is the current news?
currant (dried grapes) : I am fond of currants.
102. **cite** (speak) : He cited the example of bravery of Maharana Pratap.

site (location) : In my opinion this site for the departmental store is commercially viable.

sight (view) : It was a pitiable sight.

(vision) Get your eyesight checked at the earliest.

103. **caste** (community) : He belongs to schedule caste.

cast (to give) : Please cast your votes in favour of me.

104. **cattle** (animal) : Cattle were grazing in the field.

kettle (vessel) : Put the kettle on the gas burner.

105. **corporal** (pertaining to body) : Corporal punishment are banned now-a-days in all schools and colleges.

corporeal (bodily) : God has no corporeal existence.

106. **cache** (hidden storage) : A huge arms cache was discovered by police.

cash (legal tender) : I do not accept cash, but cheque.

107. **canter** (a moderate gallop) : When a horse canters, it moves at a speed that is slower than a gallop but faster than a trot.

cantor (singer) : An official who sings liturgical music and leads prayer in a synagogue in called contor.

108. **carat** (unit of weight for precious stones, equal to 200 milligrams)

caret (proofreader's insertion mark)

carrot (edible orange root)

carrot contains aburdent iron.

Karat (one-24th part of otherwise pure gold)

109. **Carol** (Christmas song) Carols are Christian religious songs that are sung at Christmas day.

Carrel (Study enclosure) A small enclosure or study in a cloister.

110. **cause** (generative force) : Smoking is the biggest preventive cause of death.

caws (sounds of crows) : When a crow caws it makes a loud sound.

111. **cent** (one hundredth of a dollar)

scent (an aroma) : I like the aroma of freshly baked bread.

sent (dispatched) : I have sent you a packet of wool.

112. **cents** (hundredths of a dollar) : A dollar has hundred cents.

scents (many things to smell) : Flowers are chosen for their scent as well as their look.

sense (physical abilities of sight, smell, hearing, touch and taste) : She has a good sense of humour.

113. **cere** (waxy fleshy covering at the base of the upper beak in some birds)

sear (to sear something means to burn its surface with a sudden intense heat) : Grass fires have seared the land near the farming village.

seer (a prophet) : A seer is a person who foretells about the future.

114. **chalk** (calcareous earthy substance) : He writes on the board with a chalk.

chock (wedge to keep wheels from rolling) : The small roads are chock a block with traffic.

115. **chard** (spinach-like vegetable) : She is fond of chard.

charred (burnt) : In the fire broke out yesterday seven persons were charred to ash.

116. **chased** (quickly followed) : I chased the thief for 100 yards.

chaste (virgin) : If you describe a person or his behaviour as chaste, you mean that he does do not have sex with anyone, or he only has sex with his spouse.

117. **chews** (masticating) : Chew your food well and eat slowly.

choose (to select) : They will be able to choose their own leader through election.

118. **chile** (a South American country) : Keshavis living in Chile.

chilli (dried pod of red pepper) : Chillies are used in cooking.

chilly (uncomfortably cool) : It was a chilly night.

119. **choir** (church singers) : A choir is a group of people who sing together for example in a church or school.

Quire (the twentieth part of a ream of paper)

120. **collar** (around your neck) : The collar of this shirt has worn out.

choral (music sung by a choir) : His collection of choral music is very large and wonderful.

coral (a hard substance formed from the bones of very small sea animals).

corral (a space surrounded by a fence where cattle or horses are kept).

121. **clack** (a chattering sound) : The windshield wipers clacked back and forth.

claque (a group hired to applaud, sycophants) : Whenever our team scored a goal the claque made a superb clappings which further boosted the spirit of the team.

122. **claus** (fat, jolly guy with presents) : Santa Claus comes to town on every Christmas.

clause (clause is a group of words) : containing a verb, contractual unit

claws (big fingernails) : The cat tried to cling to the edge by its claws.

123. **click** (ticking noise) : You can check your e-mail with a click of your mouse.

clique (exclusive group) : Clique is a group of people that spend a lot of time together and seem unfriendly towards people who are not in the group.

124. **climb** (ascending) : He climbed up the stairs.

clime (climate) : She left Britain for the sunnier climes of Southern France.

125. **coal** (black mineral) : A number of families even today use he coal for cooking.

cold (opposite to warm) : I like tea neither too hot nor too cold.

126. **coax** (persuade) : The government coaxed them to give up their strike by promising them some temporary benefits.

coke (more than one soft drink) : Several kinds of cokes were available in the party.

cocks (more than one male bird) : I have two beautiful cocks.

cox In a rowing boat, the cox is the person who gives instructions to the rowers.

127. **coddling** (tenderly treating) : She coddled her younger daughter madly.

codling (small, unripe apple) : is also called codling.

128. **conch** (shellvish) : A conch is a shellfish with a large shell.

conk (blow to the head) : The dynamo conked out so we have no electricity.

129. **coo** (a soft murmuring sound) : 'Isn't she beautiful?' he cooed.

coup (a successful stroke) : He was sentenced to death for his part in the coup.

copes (gets along with adversity) : It was amazing how my mother coped with bringing up three children on less than one thousand a month.

copse (a stand of trees) : A copse is a small group of trees growing very close to each other.

cops (police officers) : I do not like the cops standing near my house.

130. **creak** (A short high pitched sound) : The door creaked open by the storm.

creek (small stream) : If someone is up the creek , he is in a difficult situation.

131. **desert** (a waste track of land noun, to forsake, verb) : churu is a desert area in Rajasthan. He has deserted his wife.

dessert (fruit served after dinner) : The dessert course after dinner was liked by all.

132. **decry** (to cry down) : The Iraq policy of the US government is decried by the Indian government.

descry (to see dimly) : Across the river you can descry a hut near the palm tree.

133. **dye** (a verb—to colour) : Dye my shirt in sky blue.

die (expire) : He died from cholera.

134. **dose** (quantity of medicine) : I have already taken four **doses** of this medicine by now.

doze (sleep) : You were dozing in the class yesterday.

135. **draught** (a quantity of liquid) : The patient was given a draught of medicine.

drought (want of rain) : Due to scanty rain whole of the district is in the grip of drought.

136. **dam** (surrounding area to stop flow of water): A dam is being built up here to storage the rainy water.

damn (condemn) : His behaviour is damned by all the members of the society.

137. **dear** (loving) : He is my very dear friend.

deer (an animal) : I saw many deer in that forest.

138. **deduce** (draw conclusion) : You can't deduce such a conclusion of the discussion.

deduct (to take something) : Deduct cash discount 3% and make the payment by tomorrow.

139. **deference** (respect) : I treat my elders with due deference.

difference (dissimilarity) : There was a difference of opinion on this point.

140. **decent** (good) : Because of his decent behaviour he was promoted to the post of General Manager.

descent (coming down) : That hill has a steep descent to the south.

dissent (to differ) : He recorded his dissent on this proposal.

141. **device** (noun-plan) : He used all devices to popularise the game.

devise (verb—to plan) : You are to devise a plan to increase the turn over.

142. **duel** (a fight between two) : There was a duel between Dara Singh and Kingkong.

dual (Double) : Dual system of governance is a bad governance.

143. **disease** (illness) : Malaria is a curable disease.

decease (death) : The sudden decease of his father forced him to abandon his studies.

144. **dam** (holds back water) : Government is building a dam on this river.

damn (a curse) : Don't be flippant, damn it! This is serious.

145. **darn** (to mend) : She is darning the old socks to wear in winter.

darne (a fish steak) : He had a darne with his lunch.

146. **dine** (to eat) : He dines alone most nights.

dyne (unit of energy) : Three dyne energy is needed to pull this pump.

147. **dire** (desperate) : He was in dire need of hospital treatment.

dyer (one who dyes) : Ram is working in the firm of drycleaners as dyer.

148. **do** (an auxiliary in grammar) : They do not know me. Do come tomorrow again.

doe (a female deer) : There are several does in the forest.

dough (uncooked bread) : Roll out the dough into one large circle.

dos (part of computer operating system) : He is learning dos now-a-days.

149. **done** (completed) : I have done my job.

dun (Something that is dun is in a dull grey-brown colour.)

150. **eruption** (bursting out) : There was an eruption of Volcano near Gujarat border.

irruption (Invasion) : The irruption of Mughals destroyed the glory of Rajput empire.

151. **emerge** (to come out) : He emerged successfully out of the miserable circumstances.

immerge (to plunge into) : He is immerged in mythological thoughts.

152. **eminent** (distinguish) : Indira Gandhi was an eminent politician.

imminent (impending) : Indian army is ready to face any imminent attack of Pakistan.

153. **eligible** (fit to be chosen) : He is eligible for the post.

illegible (that which cannot be read) : His writing is illegible.

154. **earn** (to come to deserve) : Companies must earn a reputation for honesty.

urn (a jar) : An urn is a container in which a dead person's ashes are kept.

155. **elude** (to escape from) : He eluded the police for ten years.

allude (refer) : She also alluded to her rival's post marital troubles.

156. **epic** (a narrative poem or story) : Like 'Gone with the Wind' it's an unashamed epic romance.

spoch (a noteworthy period in history) : The birth of Christ was the beginning of a major epoch of world history.

157. **eunuchs** (a castrated male person) : In India eunuchs are turning to politics.

unix (operating system) : Unix is a operating system in computers.

158. **ewe** (female sheep) : A ewe is an adult female sheep.

yew (a type of tree) : is a evergreen tree which has sharp leaves.

you (the second person) : Where are you going?

159. **eyelet** (small hole for laces) : My shoes have eight island.

islet (small island) : An islet is a small island.

160. **ere** (before) : Take the water ere the clock strikes four.
err (to make a mistake) : If you make a threat be sure to carry it out if he errs again.
heir (one who will inherit) : The younger prince was declared heir to the throne.

161. **facility** (ease, opportunity) : Facility of STD is also available in this hotel.
felicity (happiness) : True felicity can't be enjoyed by a dishonest man.

162. **foul** (unfair) : One can't achieve true success through foul means.
fowl (a bird) : He is fond of fowl's meat.

163. **find** (to get) : Go there you will find a tree near the river.
fined (to charge) : The court fined him Rs. 20000 for the offence.

164. **floor** (surface) : Clean the floor with dettol and water.
flour (wheat meal) : He has a flour mill.

165. **forth** (onward) : He alone came forth to assist that poor lady.
fourth (third-fourth) : April is the fourth month of the year.

166. **farther** (more distant) : Delhi is farther from Alwar in comparison to Jaipur.
furthr (next) : Please settle the case without any further delay.

167. **faint** (to swoon) : She fainted after taking wine yesterday.
feint (pretension) : She made a feint of reading the books.

168. **fain** (gladly) : She would fain on seeing me.
feign (pretend) : When his boss scolded him, he feigned as a deaf.

169. **fair** (pure, a show) :
(a) I believe in using fair means to achieve the target.
(b) Let us go to the fair.
fare (passage money) : A strike was called by the truckers demanding hike in minimum fare.

170. **feat** (an exploit) : A racing car is an extraordinary feat of engineering.
feet (plural of foot) : Do not put your feet on the table.

171. **forego** (go before) : We have already discussed this point in foregoing lessons.
forgo (to let go) : I cannot forgo my rights.

172. **fairy** (imaginary magic person) : Fairies are often represented as small people with wings.
ferry (river-crossing boat) : They crossed the river by ferry.

173. **fey** (whimsical) : If you describe someone as fey, you mean that they behave in a shy, childish, or unpredictable way, and you are often suggesting that this is unnatural or insincere. Her fey charm and eccentric ways were legendary.
fays (more than one fairy)

174. **faze** (to stun) : He was fazed to see such a big hall.
phase (a part of the sequence) : The crisis is entering a crucial phase.

175. **ferrate** : (a salt containing iron and oxygen).
ferret : (a domesticated polecat) A ferret is a small fierce animal which is used for hunting rabbits and rats.

176. **feted** (celebrated) : If someone is feted, they are celebrated, welcomed or admired by the public.
fetid (stinking) : Fetid water or air has a very unplesant smell.

177. **few** (not many) : I gave a dinner party for a few close friends.
phew (expression of relief) : Phew, what a relief I am feeling now!

178. **file** (a folder for holding papers) : Please put this paper in a file.
phial (a small glass bottle) : A phial is a small tube shaped glass bottle used to hold medicine.

179. **finish** (to complete) : I will finish my work by tomorrow.
finnish (from Finland) : Finnish is the language spoken in Finland.

180. **flair** (verve, talent) : If you have a flair for a particular thing , you have a natural ability to do it well.
flare (to spread) : Camp fire flares like beacons in the dark.

181. **flea** (parasitic insect) : A flea feeds on the blood of humans or animals.

flee (to run away) : He tried to flee from the sight, but he was caught.

182. **flecks** (many tiny specks) : His hair is dark grey with flecks of ginger.

flex (to bend) : He slowly flexed his muscles and tried to stand.

183. **flew** (past tense of fly) : He flew many kites yesterday.

flu (short for influenza) : I got flu day before yesterday.

flue (chimney pipe) : The flue of the chimney required to be changed.

184. **floe** (sheet of floating ice) : Ice floe is a large area of ice floating in the sea.

flow (to glide along) : A stream flowed gently down into the valley.

185. **for** (in place of) : It is enough for me.

fore (in front) : There is no direct damage in the fore part of the ship.

four (number after three) : I have four pens.

186. **frees** (releasing) : He frees the bird from the cage.

freeze (very cold) : (a) The trees are damaged by a freeze in December.

(b) We want the government to freeze the prices)

frieze (a wall decoration) : A frieze is a decoration high up on the walls of a room or just under the roof of a building. It consists of a long panel of carving or a long strip of paper with a picture or pattern on it.

187. **friar** (a monk) : He is a friar.

fryer (a utensil) : A fryer is a type of deep pan which is used to fry food in hot oil.

188. **gild** (thin coating of metal) : Gilded ornaments look more beautiful than the original.

guild (group of same profession) : Now-a-days all the workers have organised themselves into guilds.

189. **gage** (security) : I do not lend without sufficient gage.

gaze (to look attentively) : She stood gazing at herself in the mirror.

190. **gait** (manner of walk) : That model girl has a graceful and sexy gait.

gate (large door) : You should not enter through the main gate.

191. **goal** (aim) : To achieve this goal you are to work hard.

gaol (jail) : He has been to gaol earlier also.

192. **gaff** (a barbed spear) : A gaff is a pole with a point or hook at one end, which is used for catching large fish.

gaffe (a stupid mistake) : He made an embarrassing gaffe at the convention last weekend.

193. **galley** (ship's kitchen) : The galley of this ship is well maintained and full of eatables.

gally (to frighten or terrify) : He tried to gally the child with a mask of demon.

194. **gilt** (gold-plated) : This is a gilt ornament.

guilt (culpable) : You aren't convinced of Mr. Charles guilt.

195. **gnawed** (chewed) : He gnawed his long fingernail.

nod (head tilting) : 'Are you fine?' I asked. She nodded and smiled.

196. **gnu** (African deer) : I saw a Gnu in the zoo.

knew (past tense of know) : He knew me well.

new (not old) What is new in the market ?

197. **gored** (pierced by an animal's horns) : He was gored to death in front of his family.

gourd (fleshy fruit with hard skin) : I like gourd very much.

198. **gorilla** (large ape) : Gorilla has long arm, black fur and a black face.

guerrilla (irregular soldier) : The guerrillas threatened to kill their hostages.

199. **grade** : What grade are you going to get?

grayed (turned grey) : His hair grayed with tension.

200. **graft** (to attach) : The top layer of skin has to be grafted onto the burns.

gaphed (plotted) : You can see a graphed diagram of the progress made by the country in population control.

201. **grate** (a lattice) : A grate is a framework of metal bars in a fireplace which holds the coal or wood. A wood fire burned in the grate.

great (extremely good) : Gandhi was a great man.

202. **grill** (to sear cook) : A grill is a flat frame of metal bars on which food can be cooked

over fire. Place the omellete under agentle grill.

grille (an iron gate) : or door used to protect anything from the public.

203. **groan** (a long low sound uttered in pain) : He opened his eyes and he began to groan with pain.

grown (has gotten larger) : Dad, I am a grown woman. I know what I am doing.

204. **guise** (appearance) : She presented her dance in the guise of a rabbit.

guys (man) : Hi, guys! How are you doing?

205. **hail** (frozen rain) : It is hailing. It hailed yesterday.

hale (healthy) : May God keep you hale and healthy!

206. **horde** (a gang) : A horde of mischievous students attacked the shop keepers.

hoard (to store) : Hoarding of sugar beyond the prescribed limit is an offence.

207. **hair** : She has black hair.

heir (successor) : He is an heir apparent to the throne.

208. **hurt** (injury) : Your comments can hurt her feelings.

hart (a male deer) : I have a beautiful pair of harts.

heart (an organ in the body) : He is suffering from heart disease.

209. **humane** (kind) : UNO has advised the member countries to meet out humane treatment to Prisoners of war.

human (pertaining to mankind) : You will find almost the same human nature everywhere.

210. **heel** (part of shoe) : The heels of my shoe are pinching.

heal (to cure) : This medicine will help you in quick healing.

211. **hole** (a burrow) : A serpent lives in this hole.

whole (complete) : He ate whole of the breakfast.

212. **hall** (a large room) : He has hired a hall for the concert.

haul : If you haul something which is heavy or difficult to move, you move it using a lot of effort.

(a) crane had to be used to haul the car out of the stream.

(b) If someone is hauled before a court or someone in authority, they are made to appear before them because they are accused of having done something wrong.

He was hauled before the managing director and fired.

213. **hammock** (rope bed) : A hammock is a piece of strong cloth or netting which is hung between two supports and used as a bed.

hummock (low, rounded hill) : A hummock is a small raised area of ground, like a very small hill.

214. **hangar** (garage for airplanes) : Some repairing is going on in the hangar of the airport.

hanger (from which things hang) : I want to purchase a coat hanger.

215. **ho** (an expression of admiration or surprise) : Ho! you are here.

hoe (A garden tool) : Today he is hoeing in the vineyard.

216. **he'll** (contraction of 'he will') : He'll come tomorrow.

hill (smaller than a mountain) : There is a temple on that hill.

217. **hear** (to listen) : I hear his voice.

here (at this location) : Come here.

218. **heard** (listened to) : I heard a strange sound yesterday in the night.

herd (a group of animals) : They are individuals. They will not follow the herd.

219. **hi** (greetings) : 'Hi Luis,' she said.

high (way up) : I looked down from the high window.

220. **heroin** (narcotic) : Heroin is a powder drug.

heroine (female hero) : My favourite heroine is Aish.

221. **Hew** (to chop) : He fell, peeled and hewed his own timber.

hue (a colour) : The same hue will look different in different light.

222. **higher** (farther up) : He has gone to USA for higher studies.

hire (to employ) : Cars are available for hire.

223. **him** (pronoun) I know him.

hymn (religious song) I like singing hymns.

224. **hoard** (store) : They have begun to hoard food and sugar.

horde (a great many people) : This attracted hordes of tourists to Las Vegas.

225. **hoarse** (rough voice) : His voice is hoarse.
horse (equine) : He has a black horse.

226. **hold** (to grip) : Hold the bucket please.
holed (full of holes) : The wall seems to be holed by a drill.

227. **holy** (with religious significance) : Ayodhya is a holy place for the Hindus.
wholly (completely) : This approach for the urban area is wholly inadequate.

228. **hostel** (inexpensive lodging for travellers) : He is living in the college hostel.
hostile (unfriendly) : Pakistan has not yet changed its hostile attitude towards India.

229. **idle** (indolent) : An idle man can't make any progress.
ideal (visionary) : My teacher, Mr. Shrivastava, is my ideal.
idol (an image of a deity) : A section of the Hindus believe in idol worship.

230. **ingenious** (clever) : He is an ingenious engineer.
ingenuous (simple) : His ingenuous attitude is liked by all.

231. **incite** (to provoke) : His arrogant behaviour incited me a lot.
insight (a clear vision) : Do you know the insight story of this murder?

232. **indite** (to compose) : Though he indited the letter carefully, yet it was not liked by the chairman.
indict (to accuse) : He was indicted for theft and murder.

233. **in** (expressing inclusion) : He is in the room.
inn (hotel) : This is a well maintained inn.

234. **inc.** (short for incorporated) : Inc. is an abbreviation for 'Incorporated' when it is used after a company's name.
ink (writing fluid) : I have an ink pen.

235. **it's** (contraction of 'it is') : It's a large hotel.
its (possessive pronoun) : I know its true position.

236. **jealous** (envious) : He is not liked by anybody because of his jealous nature.
zealous (enthusiastic) : She is very zealous about her new book.

237. **jewel** (precious stone) : This watch contains many jewels.
joule (unit of energy measure) : In Physics joule is a unit of energy or work.

238. **juggler** (one who juggles) : He is a good juggler.
jugular (artery to head) :
(a) A jugular or jugular vein is one of the three important veins in your neck that carry blood from your head back to your heart.
(b) If you say that someone went for the jugular, you mean that they strongly attacked another person's weakest points in order to harm him.

239. **naughty** (mischievous) : She is a naughty girl.
knotty (difficult) : This was indeed a knotty problem.

240. **knap** (crest of a hill; break with a hammer) : We unfurled the flag at the knap of the hill at 6.30 p.m. He knapped the glass box to uncountable pieces.
nap (a short sleep) : You should use your lunch hour to have a nap in your chair.

241. **knead** (working bread dough) :
(a) He kneaded the mixture on a floured surface.
(b) She felt him knead the aching muscles.
need (must have) : He needs your help.

242. **knight** (chivalrous man) : He was knighted on the queen's birthday.
night (darkness) : Night comes after day.

243. **knit** (interlocking loops of yarn) : She has already started knitting baby sweators.
nit (louse egg) :
(a) Nits are the eggs of insects called lice which live in people's hair.
(b) If you refer to someone as a nit, you think they are stupid or silly. You'd rather leave the business than work with such a nit.

244. **knob** (handle) : He turned the knob and pushed against the door.
nob (rich person) : The nobs who live in that big house are very generous.

245. **knock** (to rap) : Someone had knocked him unconscious. I heard a knock at the front door.
nock (a notch in an arrow) : AV shape cut or indentation in an edge or across a surface.

246. **knot** (fastening in cord) : He tied a knot at the end of the lace.

naught (or nought is zero) : Sales rose by naught point four percent last month.

not (negation) : He was not present in the party.

247. **know** (to possess knowledge) : I know him.

no (negation) : I have no pen.

248. **knows** (only the shadow knows) : Everyone knows about Mahatma Gandhi.

nose (Plain as the nose on your face) : Clean your nose daily.

249. **lightening** (make lighter) : We had appealed to the court for lightening the punishment, but of no avail.

lightning (electric discharge in clouds) : There was occasional lightning in the sky last night.

250. **loath** (unwilling) : Nothing loath he did, as he was saying.

loathe (to dislike greatly) : I loathe her dressing pattern and arrogant way of talking.

251. **latter** (antonym of former) : Between Ram and Shyam, the latter (Shyam) is a diligent student.

later (comparative of late) : He came later than his friend.

252. **lose** (to part with) : Where did you lose your briefcase?

loose (to slack) : He was wearing a loose cotton shirt.

253. **lesson** (chapter) : Learn your lesson well.

lessen (to make less) : Even this medicine has not lessen my pain.

254. **last** (antonym to first) : Bahadur Shah was the last emperor of India

latest (superlative of late) : She always prefers latest design clothes.

255. **lacks** (does not have) : He lacks the judgement and political acumen for the post of General Manager.

lax (loose discipline) : One of the point of contention is the lax security for the airport personnel.

256. **lain** (past tense of lay or lie) : He has lain there for sometime.

lane (narrow road) : Shyam lives at the end of the lane.

257. **lam** (headlong flight) : If someone is on the lam or if they go on the lam, they are trying to escape or hide from someone such as the police or an enemy.

He was on the lam for seven years.

lamb (baby sheep) : A lamb is a young sheep.

258. **lay** (to recline) : Lay a sheet of paper on the floor.

lei (a flower necklace) : A garland made of flowers, feathers, shells, etc., often given as a symbol of affection.

259. **lea** (a meadow) : They live in a hut constructed in the lea.

lee (a sheltered position) : The lee of a place is the shelter that it gives from the wind or bad weather.

lease (rented) : She leased out her bungalow at a good rent.

260. **leach** (a dish consisting of sliced meat, eggs, fruits, and spices in jelly etc.

leech (sucking parasite) :

(a) A leech is a small animal which looks like a worm and lives in water. Leeches feed by attaching themselves to other animalsand sucking their blood.

(b) If you describe someone as a leech, you disapprove of them because they deliberately depend on other people, often making money out of them.

They're just a bunch of leeches cadging off others.

261. **leak** (accidental escape of liquid) : The roof is leaking.

leek (variety of onion) : I like leek vegetables.

262. **lean** (angle of repose) : They stopped to lean over the gate.

lien (a claim on property) : Please mark my lien over the property.

263. **liar** (tells falsehoods) : He is a liar and a cheat.

lyre (stringed instrument) : A lyre is a stringed instrument that looks like a harp.

264. **lichen** (a fungus) : Lichen is a group of tiny plants like moss and grows on the surface of things such as rocks, trees and walls.

liken (to compare) : If you liken one thing or person to another thing or person , you say that they are similar. The pain is often likened to being drilled through the side of the head.

265. **lie** (an untruth) : He is telling a lie.
lieu (instead) : He gave his TV. to the landlord in lieu of rent.
loo (British toilet) : I asked if I could go to the loo.

266. **low** (not high) : He put it down on the low table.
lo (an exprssion) : Lo and behold, the best is yet to come.

267. **limb** (tree branch) : The entire structure was hanging from the limb of an enormous leafy tree. She would be able to stretch out her cramped limbs for some time.
limn (illuminate) : His face was limned in the dim glow from the match.

268. **links** (pieces of chain) : I have no links with that man.
lynx (a lynx is a wild animal similar to a large cat) :

269. **literal** (taking words in their primary sense) : He was saying no more than the literal truth.
littoral (having to do with the shore) : In Geography the littoral means the coastal.

270. **load** (cargo) : I have just loaded my truck up.
Lowed (a cow mooed) : The cow lowed in agony.

271. **loan** (allow to borrow) : She has taken loan from a bank.
lone (by itself) : He was shot by a lone gunmen.

272. **loch** (a lake) : A loch is a large area of water that is almost surrounded by land.
lock (a security device) : I need a good lock.

273. **loot** (ill-gotten gains) : The troule began when the students began the looting of shops.
lute (stringed instrument) : A lute is a stringed instrument with a rounded body that is quite like a guitar and is played with the help of fingers.

274. **lumbar** (lower part of back) : Lumbar support is very important if you are driving along way.
lumber (dimensional wood) : (Noun) It was made of soft lumber. (Verb) : He turned and lumbered back to his chair.

275. **meat** (flesh) : I don't like eating meat.
meet (to assemble) : She came here only to meet me.

276. **mead** (meadow) : I met a beautiful girl in the meads yesterday.
meed (reward) : Kalidas has got a universal meed of praise.

277. **metal** (iron, brass etc.) : Silver is a white metal.
mettle (spirit, courage) : Our leaders have no mettle to fight against corruption.

278. **metre** (poetic rhythm) : Can you tell me in what metre Shelley's 'Skylark' is written?
meter (a measuring instrument =100 cm) : One meter is equal to hundred centimetres.

279. **minor** (underage) : Minors are not allowed to open current account in Banks.
miner (one who works in mine) : He is a miner, works in a coal mine.

280. **moat** (a ditch surrounding a castle) : There is a bridge over the moat near main gate.
mote (a particle of dust) : You cannot see small mote by naked eyes.

281. **monetary** (pertaining to money) : Have you any book on monetary theory?
monitory (giving advice) : He acted against the monitory advise of his friends and so failed.

282. **male** (opposite to female) : A male candidate can't be posted against the post reserved for a woman.
mail (post) : Have you received my mail ?

283. **mite** (small thing) : He contributed his mite for the service of mankind.
might (strength) : Your might will be tested in battle against the foreign power.
might (past of may) : He told me that he might come to attend the function.

284. **marry** (to get married) : I want to marry your sister.
merry (joyous) : Don't lose heart and be merry.

285. **main** (chief) : Ramesh is the main culprit in the bank robbery case.
mane (long hair of an animal's neck) : His horse had a fine mane.

286. **marshal** (a military officer) : He is a marshal of the court.

martial (war-like) : He has martial spirit and courage to fight in odd circumstances.

287. **maize** (corn) : I like to eat maize cake.

maze (labyrinth) : This castle has many hidden mazes.

288. **mach** (speed of sound) : Mach is used as a unit of measurement in stating the speed of a moving object in relation to the speed of sound. For example, if an aircraft is travelling at Mach 1, it is travelling at exactly the speed of sound.

mock (parody) : I thought you were mocking me.

289. **made** (accomplished) : The table is made of wood.

maid (young woman) She is our maid-servant.

290. **mall** (a large shopping area) : Branded shops are there in the mall.

maul (savage) : He had been mauled by a tiger.

moll (gangster's girlfriend) : She is the moll of the don.

291. **manner** (method) : I am a professional and I have to conduct myself in a professional manner. She smiled in a friendly manner.

manor (lord's house or a large private house) : The thieves broke into the manor at night.

292. **marc** (coarse brandy) : I don't like the taste of marc.

mark (a sign) : He made some peculiar marks with a pen.

293. **marquee** (a rooflike projection over a theatre entrance) :

(a) A marquee is a large tent which is used at a fair, garden party, or other outdoor event, usually for eating and drinking in.

(b) A marquee is a cover over the entrance of a building, for example, a hotel or a theatre.

Marquis a nobleman ranking between a duke and a count.

294. **marshal** (to organise) : He was marshalling the teachers and other officials, showing them where to go.

martial (warlike) : The newspapers were banned during martial regime.

295. **massed** (grouped together) : He could not escape the **massed** ranks of newsmen.

mast (sail pole) : The mast of a boat are the tall upright poles that support its sails.

296. **mews** (stables) : The house is in a secluded mews.

muse (creative inspiration) : (a) Noun : Once she was a nude model and muse to French artist Henri. (b) Verb : (think) Many scholars muse on the role of President in Indian polity.

297. **mince** (chop finely) : I'll buy lean meat and mince it mysef.

mints (aromatic candies) : Mint is a herb with fresh tasting leaves.

298. **mind** (thinking unit) : Mind your business, please.

mined (looked for ore) : The pit was shut down bcause it hadn't enough that could be mined economically.

299. **missal** (hymn book) : A book containing the service of the Mass for the whole year; loosely a Roman Catholic book of prayers,

missile (projectile) : The football supporters began throwing missiles one of which it the captain of the rival team.

300. **mist** (fog) : The mist made the flying impossible.

Missed (not hit) He scored four of the goals but missed a penalty.

301. **moan** (to groan) : She gave a low choking moan and began to tremble.

mown (the lawn is freshly cut) : He has mown the lawn today itself.

302. **mood** (emotional state) : She is in a jolly mood today.

mooed (what the loquacious cow did) : When cattle especially cows moo, they make a long low sound that cattle typically make.

303. **moor** (swampy coastland; to anchor) : I decided to moor near some tourist boats.

more (additional) : I need some more rice.

304. **moose** (a large elk) : Moose are large type of deer have big flat horns.

mousse (dessert of whipped cream and eggs) : Mousse is a sweet light food made from eggs and cream.

305. **morning** (a.m.) : I get up early in the morning.

mourning (remembering the dead) : On the death of Rajeev Gandhi, the whole of India was in the mourning.

306. **muscle** (fibrous, contracting tissue) : He is doing a lot of exercises to keep his muscles strong.

mussel (Mussels are a kind of shellfish that you can eat from their shells).

307. **mussed** (made messy) : His clothes are all mussed up.

must (required) : You must go there to get his support.

308. **mustard** (spicy yellow sauce) : This is fried in mustard oil.

mustered (assembled for roll call) : He travelled through out India to muster support for his movement.

309. **nice** (good) : She is a nice and beautiful girl.

niece (daughter of brother) : I am to attend the marriage of my niece positively.

310. **naval** (pertaining to ships and the sea) : He is captain in naval forces.

navel (pertaining to the belly button) : There is a black mole near her navel.

311. **nay** (no) : The Rajya Sabha can merely say yea or nay to such a bill.

neigh (a horse's cry) : The horse gave a loud neigh.

312. **our** (plural of 'my') : This is our house.

hour (a period of time) : I have been waiting for you for half an hour.

313. **oar** (used for rowing a boat) : Life without aim is like a boat without an oar.

ore (mineral from which metal can be extracted) : Iron is extracted from its ore by melting.

314. **ordinance** (a rule) : The President has promulgated an ordinance for administering the minority community.

ordnance (gun) : There is an ordnance factory in Jamshedpur Bihar.

315. **oohs** (informal) : People say 'ooh' when they are surprised, looking forward to something, or find something pleasant or unpleasant.

'Ooh dear me, that's a bit of a racist comment isn't it.'... 'Red? Ooh how nice.'

ooze : When a thick or sticky liquid oozes from something or when something oozes, the liquid flows slowly and in small quantities.

The lava will just ooze gently out of the crater.

The wounds may heal cleanly or they may ooze a clear liquid.

316. **overdo** (carried to excess) : It is important never to overdo new exercises.

overdue (past time for payment or some action) : The meeting is long overdue.

317. **pray** (entreat) : I pray to God everyday.

prey (hunt) : Do not prey upon the innocent animals.

318. **principal** (head of school or college) : R.C. Jha is the new Principal of our college.

principle (rule) : Do you understand anything about the principles of justice?

319. **prophecy** (noun-foretold) : It is his prophecy that America will not attack Iraq.

prophesy (verb—to foretell) : He prophesied that Iraq would attack Kuwait.

320. **proffer** (offer) : Many lucrative proposals were proffered to him for acceptance.

prefer (like) : I prefer coffee to tea.

321. **practice** (noun) Practice makes a man perfect.

practise (verb—to practise) : Don't preach but practise.

322. **plain** (easy, simple) : One should try to write his thoughts in plain language.

plane (to smoothen, level) : I use cream to plane my hair.

323. **peel** (to remove the skin) : You cannot eat a banana without peeling it.

peal (sound of thunder or Bells) : I am hearing peals of trumpets.

324. **pare** (to trim) : Pare your nails and then polish them.

pair (two) : I have only three pair of shoes.

325. **peace** (tranquility) : Peace of mind is more precious than the materialistic richness.

piece (fragment) : The dog found a piece of meat.

326. **price** (value) : What is the price of this shirt ?

prize (reward) : She could not win any prize this time.

327. **persecute** (to harass) : Pakistani soldiers persecuted the Hindus in a cruel manner.

prosecute (to bring before a court) : He was prosecuted for murdering his wife.

328. **physic** (medicine) : No physic can cure him of cancer.

physique (bodily fitness) : He possesses an attractive physique.

329. **prescribe** (to direct) : The doctor has prescribed three doses of medicine after four hours daily.

proscribe (to banish) : The minister was proscribed by the king.

330. **patrol** (going round) : A chowkidar was patrolling at the main gate.

petrol (oil) : Petrol is required to run vehicles.

331. **popular** (familiar) Rajeev Gandhi was a very popular leader.

populous (thickly inhabited) : Delhi is a highly populous city.

pail (bucket) : I have two pails full of water.

pale (yellowish appearance) : On seeing a lion, his face turned pale.

332. **paced** (measured by footsteps) : This excellent thriller is fast paced and unbelievable.

paste (thick glue) : I need a tooth paste.

333. **pain** (it hurts) : I felt a sharp pain in my lower back.

pane (a single panel of glass) : The left pane of this window required change.

334. **pair** (a set of two) : I need a new pair of socks.

pare (cutting down) : Local authorities were instructed to pare their budget.

pear (bottom-heavy fruit) : I am fond of red pears.

335. **palate** : The top part of the inside of your mouth is called palate.

pallet :

(a) A pallet is a narrow mattress filled with straw which is put on the floor for someone to sleep on.

(b) A pallet is a hard, narrow bed. He was given only a wooden pallet with a blanket.

(c) A pallet is a flat wooden or metal platform on which goods are stored so that they can be lifted and moved using a forklift truck. The warehouse will hold more than 90,000 pallets storing 30 million Easter eggs.

336. **pall** (to become wearisome) : Already the allure of meals in hotels and restaurants begun to pall.

pawl (locks a ratchet) : A pivoted, usually. curved, bar or lever whose free end engages with the teeth of a cog-wheel or ratchet so that it can only turn or move one way.

337. **pause** (to hesitate) : He talked for three hours regularly without pausing for a minute.

paws (cat transportation) : The cat has white front paws.

338. **pea** (round, green legume) : I like peas vegetable.

pee (piss) : The driver was probably having a pee. He needed to pee.

339. **peak** (mountain top) : He climbed up to the peak of the mountain.

peek (secret look) : On one occasion she had peeked at him through a hole in the door.

pique : (Pique is the feeling of annoyance you have when you think someone has not treated you properly).

(a) Simi had gotten over her pique at Rue's refusal to accept the job.

(b) If something piques your interest or curiosity, it makes you interested or curious. This phenomenon piqued Dr. Mohit's interest.

(c) If someone does something in a fit of pique, they do it suddenly because they are annoyed at being not treated properly. Lally , in a fit of pique, left the Army and took up a career in the town.

340. **pearl** (round, luminescent gem from an oyster) : She wore a string of pearls at her throat.

purl Thread or cord of twisted gold or silver wire, used esp. for edging; edging etc. made from this.

341. **pedal** (foot control) : I am too tired to pedal again.

peddle (to sell) : He attempted to peddle his paintings around the city.

342. **peer** : (if you peer at something, you look at it very hard, usually because it is difficult to see clearly).

(a) I had been peering at a computer print-out that made no sense at all.
(b) In Britain, a peer is a member of the nobility who has or had the right to vote in the House of Lords) Lord Swan was made a life peer in 1981.
(c) Your peers are the people who are the same age as you or who have the same status as you. His engaging personality made him popular with his peers.

pier : a pier is a platform sticking out into water, usually the sea, which people walk along or use when getting onto or off boats.

343. **pi** (3.1416) : Pi is a number, approximately 3.1416, which is equal to the distance round a circle divided by its width. It is usually represented by the Greek letter p.

pie (good eating) : A pie consists of meat, vegetables or fruit baked in pastry.

344. **pieced** (assembled from pieces) : We'll know the truth once the police have pieced all the facts together.

piste (a ski run of compacted snow) : A track of firm snow for skiing on.

345. **pincer** (claw-like gripping action) : The pincers of an animal such as a crab or a loberster are its front claws.

pinscher (terrier) : A short coated dog.

346. **pistil** : (seed-bearing organ of a flower) :

pistol (hand gun) : He was caught with a pistol.

347. **place** (a location) : This is a good place to live at.

plaice Plaice are a type of flat sea fish.

348 **Plait** (braid) : She parted her hair and then began to plait it into two thick braids.

plate (a dish) : She pushed her plate away. She had eaten nothing.

349. **plum** (purple fruit) : A plum is a small , sweet fruit with a smooth red or yellow skin and a stone in the middle.

plumb (straight up and down) : He knows how to plumb the pipe well.

350. **pole** (a person from Poland) : He is a Pole.

pole (big stick) : I need a pole to climb up that house.

poll (a voting) : More than 60 percent of those polled said that they approved of his record as Chairman.

351. **poor** (no money) : A poor man can't afford a car.

pore (careful study; microscopic hole) : We spent hours poring over the visa rules.

pour (to flow freely) : He poured himself another drink.

352. **precedence** (priority) : Enjoy fully but don't let it take precedence over work.

precedents (established course of action) : This case can set an important precedent for dealing with such cases in future.

presidents (The chief) : The President is all in all of this society.

353. **presence** (the state of being present) : The meeting took place in the presence of the Judge.

presents (gifts) : He gave a nice present to his friend on his wedding anniversary.

354. **pride** (ego) : We take pride in offering you the best services.

pried (opened) : I pried the top off a can of chilli.

355. **profit** (money earned) : The company has earned good profit in this quarter.

prophet (seer) : He did it as per the instructions of the prophet.

356. **pros** (benefits) : Motherhood has both its pros and cons.

prose (ordinary language) : Shute's prose is stark and chillingly unsentimental.

357. **quite** (altogether) : I am quite well now.

quiet (silent) : Please keep quiet.

358. **rein** (bridle) : Keep the rein tight, otherwise you may be thrown out by the horse.

reign (rule) : The reign of Akbar is known for communal harmony.

359. **rite** (ceremony) : Only a few rites were performed in his wedding.

write (compose) : I am to write a letter immediately.

right (antonym of left) : This is my right leg.

right (antonym to wrong) : You have taken a right decision.

wright (a worker) : He is a wonderful play wright.

360. **raise** (to life) : I will raise this issue in Parliament.

raze (to destroy) : The storm razed many buildings to the ground.

361. **route** (course) : By which route did you come here?

rout (flight) : The Pakistan armies were put to rout.

362. **rap** (a sharp blow) : He rapped her on the cheek.

rape (to ravish) : He raped a college girl.

wrap (to enclose) : The book was wrapped in a piece of white paper.

363. **reclaim** (to win back) : He was reclaimed from his bad habits by his devoted wife.

re-claim (to claim again) : He is thinking to re-claim the property on some other ground.

364. **recover** (regain) : He has now recovered a lot from the weakness.

re-cover (to cover again) : Re-cover the sweets with some clean cloth.

365. **road** (way) : The road has recently been repaired.

rode (past of ride) : He rode on the horse yesterday.

366. **ring** (an ornament for fingers) : This ring is made of gold.

wring (to twist, to squeeze) : Wring the clothes well and put them on the ground.

367. **rest** (respite) : I want some rest before starting the next assignment.

wrest (snatch by force) : Ram wrested a bag from Shyam.

368. **roll** (to run overy) : He rolled over the log to the right side of river.

role (part) : I am playing the role of Ravana in this serial.

369. **raise** (elevate) : He raised is hand in support of the resolution.

rays (thin beams of light) : The sun rays can penetrate water up to ten feet.

raze (to tear down completely) : Many of villages have been razed.

370. **read** (having knowledge from reading) : I have read this novel.

red (a primary colour) : I like red colour shirt.

371. **rede** (advice) : It is always fruitful to listen to the rede of your elders.

reed (tall, thin water plant) : He has a beautiful reed plant.

372. **real** (authentic) : Yes it is a real story.

reel (wavering move) : He lost is balance and reeled back.

373. **recede** (to move backward) : As he receded she waved goodbye.

reseed (to plant again) : He is trying to reseed the rose plant.

374. **reek** (smells bad) : Your breah reeks of stale cigar smoke.

wreak (to inflict) : She threatened to wreak vengeance on the men who toppled him some years ago.

375. **retch** (heave) : If you retch, your stomach moves as if you are vomiting. The smell made me retch.

wretch (Wicked) : Oh, what have you done , you wretch!

376. **review** (a general survey or assessment) : The PM reviewed the situation with his cabinet.

revue (a series of theatrical sketches or songs) : A revue is a theatrical performance consisting of songs, dances and jokes about recent events.

377. **rheum** (watery discharge of mucous) : A mucous discharge caused by infection with a cold.

room (partitioned space) : I need a three room set.

378. **rho** (seventeenth letter of Greek alphabet)

roe (fish eggs) : He is fond of cod's roe.

row (aisle; pull an oar) : They were standing in rows.

379. **rigger** (one who rigs) : A person who works with lifting-tackle; a person who erects and maintains scaffolding.

rigour (discipline) : He found the rigours of the tour too demanding.

380. **rise** (to stand up) : The sun rises in the east.

ryes (varieties of grain) : I am fond of cheese on rye.

381. **roam** (to wander) : Barefoot children roamed the streets.

rome (Italian capital) : Rome was not built in a day.

382. **roil** (to make turbid) : If water roils, it is rough and disturbed.

(a) The water roiled to his left as he climbed carefully at the edge of the waterfall.

(b) Something that roils a state or situation makes it disturbed and confused.

Times of national turmoil generally roil a country's financial markets.

royal (worthy of a king or queen) : He belongs to a royal family.

383. **rood** (across) : A cross as an instrument of execution; The cross on which Jesus suffered; the cross as the symbol of the Christian faith wears a golden rood.

rude (coarse) : He is rude to her friends and obsessively jealous.

384. **rot** (decay) : Sugary canned drinks can rot your teeth.

wrought (made) : The recent results of presidential elections in USA wrought a change in US policy towards India.

rote (by memory) : I am very sceptical about the value of rote learning.

385. **rough** (coarse) : His hands are rough.

ruff (pleated collar) : A ruff is a stiff strip of cloth or other material with many small folds in it, which some people wore round their neck in former times.

386. **rude** (impolite) : I am unable to understand as to why she behaved so rudely.

rued (regretted) :

(a) If you rue something that you have done, you are sorry that you did it, because it has had unpleasant results.

(b) If you rue the day that you did something, you are sorry that you did it, because it has had unpleasant results. You'll live to rue the day you said that to me, my girl.

387. **rye** (grain) : Rye is a kind of grain.

wry (twisted) :

(a) If someone has a wry expression, it shows that they find a bad situation or a change in a situation slightly amusing. He allowed himself a wry smile.

(b) A wry remark or piece of writing refers to a bad situation or a change in a situation in an amusing way.

There is a wry sense of humour in his work.

388. **sooth** (truth) : Sooth to speak, he is not a good boy.

soothe (to calm) : You can't soothe his anger with lame excuses.

389. **spacious** (enough space) : His office is quite spacious and well decorated.

specious (attractive) : With your specious look, you can't fool her.

390. **Stationary** (fixed) Earth is not stationary, it moves round the sun.

Stationery (writing material) I am going to market to purchase several stationery items for the office.

391. **straight** (opposed to curved) : I believe in straight talks.

strait (narrow)The lane is too strait to pass through for an elephant.

392. **sore** (painful) : I can't sing as my throat is sore.

soar (to fly high) : Birds soar in sky.

sour (not sweet) : The grapes were sour.

393. **suit** (an action in court) : Bank has filed a civil suit against you for recovery.

suite (a set of room) : I have reserved a suite for you in Ashoka Hotel.

394. **story** (a tale) : My grandmother told me a story of an oldman.

storey (floor of a building) : I have taken a room at first storey.

395. **serge** (a kind of cloth) : This suit is made of serge.

surge (move like waves) : The waves of ocean surge violently in night.

396. **shear** (to clip the wool) : He had to shear the sheep for wool.

sheer (downright) : He achieved success by the sheer force of his hard labour.

397. **sun** : The sun is a star.

son (a person's male child) : He is my son.

398. **sole** (lower surface of shoe) : The sole of the right shoe requires repairing.

The sole aim of my life is to earn reputation in the society.

soul (immaterial part) : You can't see soul. Soul is immortal.

399. **stair** (step) : Let us go up stairs.

stare (gaze) : It is wrong to stare at girls.

400. **sing** (melodious sound) : She will sing a sweet song.

swing (to oscillate) : She has gone to enjoy swing ride.

401 **sale** (to exchange for money) : This is not for sale.

sail (to travel in water) : Ships can sail in deep sea only.

402. **sachet** (a small bag containing perfumed powder) : I found twenty sachet of coffee.
sashay (to strut or flounce) : The models sashay down the catwalk.

403. **sacks** (bags) : I found twenty sacks for potatoes.
sax short for saxophone.

404. **sane** (mentally normal) He is perfectly sane.
seine (fishing net) A large fishing net having floats at the top and weights at the bottom so as to hang vertically in the water, the ends being drawn together to enclose the fish and the net usu. hauled ashore.

405. **saver** (one who saves) : Low interest rates are bad news for savers.
savour (to relish a taste) : People come here to savour the exquisite food provided by the owner.

406. **sawed** (cut timber) : He sawed the timber very quickly.
sod (to express anger) : If someone uses an expression such as 'sod it', 'sod you' or 'sod that', they are expressing anger or showing that they do not care about something.

407. **scull** (rowing motion) : Scull are small oars which are held by one person and used to move a boat through water.
skull (head bone) : He was treated for a fractured skull.

408. **seal** (to close) He sealed the envelope and put on a stamp.
seel (to close someone's eyes) : Close the eyes of (a hawk etc.) by stitching up the eyelids.

409. **seam** (row of stitches) :
(a) A seam is a line of stitches which joins two pieces of cloth together.
(b) If something is coming apart at the seams or is falling apart at the seams, it is no longer working properly and may soon stop working completely.
Britain's university system is in danger of falling apart at the seams.
(c) If a place is very full, you can say that it is bursting at the seams.
The hotels of New Dehi were bursting at the seams during Asia 1996 Trade Fair.
seem (appears) : Everyone seems very busy here.

410. **seamen** (sailors) : He emigrated to work as seaman.
semen (male discharge) : He is being treated for some semen problem.

411. **sear** (scorched) To sear something means to burn its surface with a sudden intense heat. Grass fires have seared the land near the farming villages of Haryana.
Seer (a person who sees). A seer is a person who tells what will happen in the future.

412. **serf** (slave) : In former times, serfs were a class of people who had to work on a particular person's land and could not leave without that person's permission.
surf (Surf is the mass of white bubbles that is formed by waves as they fall upon the shore) :
(a) If you surf, you ride on big waves in the sea on a special board.
I'm going to buy a surfboard and learn to surf...
I'm going to be surfing bigger waves when I get to Australia!
(b) If you surf the Internet, you spend time finding and looking at things on the Internet. (COMPUTING)
No one knows how many people currently surf the Net.

413. **sewer** (A sewer is a large underground channel that carries waste matter and rain water away, usually to a place where it is treated and made harmless).
sower (one who sows).
suer (one who sues).

414. **shell** (The shell of a nut or egg is the hard covering which surround it) :
They cracked the nuts and removed their shell.
she'll (contraction of 'she will') : She'll cooperate you positively.
shill (a decoy) : A decoy, an accomplice, esp. one posing as an enthusiastic or successful customer to encourage buyers, gamblers.

415. **sic** (You write sic in brackets after a word or expression when you want to indicate to the reader that although the word looks odd or wrong, you intended to write it like that or the original writer wrote it like that).
The latest school jobs page advertises a 'wide range (sic) of 6th form courses.'

sick (ill) : He is very sick. He needs medical treatment.

six (whole number) : I have six pencils.

416. **side** (lateral) : There is a park on the left side of the road.

sighed (breathed sorrowfully) : He sighed wearily.

417. **sign** (displayed board bearing information) : Equations are generally written with a two bar equals sign.

sine (reciprocal of the cosecant) : Find the sine value of this angle.

418. **sink** (to submerge) : A fresh egg will sink and an old egg will float.

synch (together in time) : If two things are out of synch, they do not match or do not happen together as they should. If two things are in synch, they match or happen together as they should. Normally, when demand and supply are out of sync, you either increase the supply, or you adjust the price mechanism.

419. **slay** (kill) : He slew a man with a sword.

sleigh (snow carriage) : A sleigh is a vehicle which can slide over snow. Sleighs are usually pulled by horses.

420. **slew** (past tense of slay).

slough (shed) : When a plant sloughs its leaves, or an animal such as a snake sloughs its skin, the leaves or skin come off naturally.

All reptiles have to slough their skin to grow...

sloe (blackthorn berries) :

A sloe is a small, sour fruit that has a dark purple skin. It is often used to flavour gin.

slow (not fast) The traffic is heavy and slow.

421. **solace** (comfort) : I found soalce in writting when my friend died three months ago.

soulless (lacking a soul) : If you describe a thing or person as soulless, you mean that they lack human qualities and the ability to feel or produce deep feelings.

He is a soulless person.

422. **some** (a few) : Please give me some money.

sum (result of addition) : The sum of all the angles of a triangle is 180 degree.

423. **soot** (black residue of burning) : Soot is black powder which rises in the smoke from a fire and collects on the inside of chimneys. This wall is blackened by soot.

suit (clothes) : I have a blue suit.

suite (A set of rooms) : We enjoyed our time during the week in a suite at London.

424. **spade** (shovel) : He used a spade for digging this pit.

spayed (to sterilize a female animal) : When a female animal is spayed, it has its ovaries removed so that it cannot become pregnant. All bitches should be spayed unless being used for breeding.

425. **spoor** (trail of an animal) : The spoor of an animal is the marks or substances that it leaves behind as it moves along, which hunters can follow.

spore (single cell reproductive body) : Spores are cells produced by bacteria and fungi which can develop into new bacteria or fungi.

426. **staid** (reserved) : If you say that someone or something is staid, you mean that they are serious, dull, and rather old-fashioned.

stayed (remained) : In the old days the woman stayed at home and the man earned the livelihood.

427. **stake :**

(a) If something is at stake, it is being risked and might be lost or damaged if you are not successful.

The tension was naturally high for that game with so much at stake.

(b) If you stake something such as your money or your reputation on the result of something, you risk your money or reputation on it.

He has staked his political future on this election victory.

(c) If you have a stake in something such as a business, it matters to you, for example because you own part of it or because its success or failure will affect you.

He was eager to return to a more entrepreneurial role in which he had a big financial stake in his own efforts.

(d) A stake is a pointed wooden post which is pushed into the ground, for example in order to support a young tree.

(e) If you stake a claim, you say that something is yours or that you have a right to it.
Jasmine is determined to stake her claim as an actress.
steak (slice of meat) : He hates eating steak.

428. **step** (a measure taken) : The next step is to put the theory into practice.
steppe (a level, grassy, unforested plain) : Steppes are large areas of flat grassy land where there are no trees, especially the area that stretches from Eastern Europe across the south of the former Soviet Union to Siberia.

429. **Stile** (narrow passage) : A stile is an entrance to a field or path consisting of a step on either side of a fence or wall to help people climb over it.
style (mode) : She had not lost her grace and style.

430. **stoop :**
(a) If you stoop, you stand or walk with your shoulders bent forwards.
She was taller than he was and stooped slightly.
(b) If you stoop, you bend your body forwards and downwards.
He stooped to pick up the carrier bag of groceries...
(c) If you say that a person stoops to doing something, you are criticizing him because he does something wrong or immoral that he would not normally does.
He had not, until recently, stooped to personal abuse...
How could anyone stoop so low?
(d) A stoop is a small platform at the door of a building, with steps leading up to it.
They stood together on the stoop and rang the bell.
stoup (a drinking cup) : She served wine in beautiful stoups.

431. **succour** (relief, assist) : Helicopters fly in appaling weather to succour ship wrecked mariners.
sucker (one who sucks) : If you call someone a sucker, you mean that it is easy to cheat him.

432. **suede** (split leather) : He wore asuede jacket and jeans.
swayed :
(a) When people or things sway, they lean or swing slowly from one side to the other.
The people swayed back and forth with arms linked.
The whole boat swayed and tipped.
(b) If you are swayed by someone or something, you are influenced by them.
Don't ever be swayed by fashion.
(c) If someone or something holds sway, they have great power or influence over a particular place or activity.
South of the Usk, a completely different approach seems to hold sway.
(d) If you are under the sway of someone or something, they have great influence over you.
mothers keep daughters under their sway is the subject of the next five sections.

433. **sundae** : A sundae is a tall glass of ice cream with whipped cream and nuts or fruit on top.
sunday (the first day of the week) : Today is Sunday.

434. **team** (a group of players) : Our college team has won the trophy.
teem (to be full of) : Rajasthan is a state teeming with natural resources.

435. **toe** (a part of foot) : She hurt her left toe in an accident.
tow (to draw by a rope) : The boat was towed with a tree near the shore.

436. **tail** (part of body) : Cow has a long tail.
tale (story) : My grandmother told me an interesting tale.

437. **their** (belong to they) : They have learnt their lessons.
there (at that place) : I am to go there now.

438. **throne** (royal seat) : All the brothers are fighting for the throne.
thrown (third form of throw) : She has thrown her certificates into the river.
thorn (impediment) : You need a needle to get the thorn out.

439. **tenor** (purpose) : The tenor of his speech was important from religious point of view.
tenure (right of holding an estate) : The Zamindari Abolition Act has finished the big problem of land tenure system in our country.

440. **tare** (the seed of a vetch used in refence to its small size) : When the harvest is gleaned the evil tares will be separated from the good wheat.

tear (salty drops from eyes) : Her eyes are filled with tears.

tier (a horizontal row) : I have booked your seats in two tier compartment.

441. **taught** (past tense of teach) : Who taught you English?

taut (stretched tight) : The clothes line is pulled taut and secured.

442. **tea** (herbal infusion) : I am fond of tea.

tee (golfball prop) : The tee was broken accidentally.

443. **tenner** (English slang for a ten pound note) : I have only a tenner in my pocket.

tenor (tendency) : The whole tenor of discussion has changed.

444. **tern** (a shorebird) : A tern is a small black and white seabird with long wings and a forked tail.

terne (alloy of lead and tin) : This plate is made of terne.

turn (rotate) : He turned left and went away.

445. **the** (denoting persons already mentioned) : The is the definite article.

thee (objective case of thou) : I missed thee, beloved mother.

446. **through** (from end to end) : Go straight through that door under the 'exit' word.

throe (a spasm of pain) : A violent physical spasm or pang, esp. in the pain and struggle of childbirth or death. Also, a spasm of feeling; mental agony; anguish.

throw (to discharge through the air) : The crowd began throwing stones.

447. **thyme** (herb) : Thyme is a type of herb used in cooking.

time (natures way of keeping everything from happening at once) : What is the time by your watch?

448. **tic** (twitch) : If someone has a tic, a part of their face or body keeps making a small uncontrollable movement, for example because they are tired or have a nervous illness.

tick (small noise; parasitic bug) : He sat listening to the **tick** of the clock.

449. **tighten** (to make tighter) : I use my nail to tighten the screw on my torch.

titan (a giant) : He is the richest business titan of our country.

450. **timber** (wood for building) : In Japan timber is used for construction of house.

timbre (musical quality) : The timbre of someone's voice or of a musical instrument is the particular quality of sound that it has. (formal)

His voice had a deep timbre...

The timbre of the violin is far richer than that of the mouth organ.

451. **toad** (frog) : A toad is a creature similar to frog.

toed (to conform a policy) : He tried to persuade the rivals to toe the line of his party.

towed (pulled ahead) : The policeman threatened to tow away my car.

452. **told** (what was spoken) : He told me how to do it.

tolled (a bell was rung) The pilgrims tolled the bell.

453. **track** (narrow path or road) : We set of once more, over a rough mountain track.

tract (a plot of land) : A vast tract of land is available for stadium.

454. **tray** (a platter) : I need a tray for six cups of tea.

trey (three) : The side of a die marked with three pips or spots; a throw which turns up this side.

455. **troop** (a company of soldiers) : Twenty thousands troops were deployed on the border.

troup (a company of actors) : She belongs to an acrobatic performing troup.

456. **trussed** (tied up) : She trussed him quickly with a rope and gagged his mouth.

trust (faith) : I trust you completely.

457. **umpire** (a referee) : You must not disobey the umpire.

empire (dominion The king was unable to manage his empire properly.

458. **vein** (a blood vessel) : Veins take the blood to all parts of body.

vane (weather cock) : There is a vane at the top of the temple.

459. **vale** (valley) : The beautiful vale of Manali is worthseeing.
veil (a cover) : Muslim ladies generally put a veil on her face.
wail (to lament) : Don't wail please, he is safe and sound.

460. **wave** (unevenness) : The waves of ocean are rising higher and higher.
wave (movement) : She waved her hand as the bus started.
waive (relinquish) : I request the officer to waive the punishment.

461. **waste** (useless) : Don't waste your precious time.
waist (part of body) : The boy had a chain round his waist.

462. **weather** (atmosphere) : It is cold weather today.
whether (which of two) : I asked her whether she would come.

463. **vain** (useless) : I made several request to our principal but all in vain.
wane (to decrease) : I see the moon waning these nights.

464. **vary** (to change) : Your actions vary from the promise you made.
very (more) : She is a very beautiful girl.
wary (cautious) : Because of his wary nature, he was saved.

465. **vacations** (holidays) : We are going to Delhi in summer vacations.
vocation (occupation) : What vocation do you intend to join after graduation?

466. **verses** (paragraphs) : This verse describes three reasons of his failure.
versus (against) : India versus Pakistan is a greatly contesting cricket match.

467. **vial** (narrow glass container) : A vial is a very small bottle which is used to hold something such as perfume or medicine. Please give me a vial of rose perfume.
vile (despicable, unpleasant) : She was in too vile a mood to work.
viol (stringed instrument) : Viols are a family of musical instruments that are made of wood and have six strings. You play the viol with a bow while sitting down.

468. **vice** (bad habit) : She described that those responsible for offences are connected with vice, like drugs or gaming.
vise (bench-mounted clamp) : I need a good vise while I repair the furniture.

469. **weigh** (to ascertain the weight) : I am to purchase one weighing machine.
way (passage) : This way leads to hospital.

470. **weight** (weight) : He gained ten kg. of weight within a month.
wait (to attend) : Don't wait for me, I will go myself.

471. **week** (period of seven days) : Monday is the first day of a week.
weak (feeble) : Ram is too weak to walk.

472. **ware** (article) : He has sold all his cook wares.
wear (to put on) : I like to wear silk sarees.
wear (to diminish) : My shirt has worn out.

473. **wine** (drink) : Drinking wine is harmful for lever.
vine (creeper) : The hut is covered with grapevines.

474. **wax** (candle stuff) : Candles had spread pools of wax on the furniture.
whacks (several blows) : He has the donkey a whack across the back with a stick. Someone whacked him on the head.

475. **wade** (walk in shallow water) : Rescuers had to wade across a river to reach them.
weighed (weight was measured) : He weighed approximately 270 kilos.

476. **vain** (too proud, futile) : The crow looked at the fox in vain.
wane (decrease, fade) : His interest in sports began to wane, a passion for golf developed.

477. **want** (desire) : I want to become a surgeon.
wont (inclined) :
(a) If someone is wont to do something, they often or regularly do it. Both have committed their indiscretions, as human beings are wont to do.
(b) (accustomed) If someone does a particular thing as is their wont, they do that thing often or regularly. Ram woke up early, as was his wont.

478. **war** (large scale armed conflict) : A war like situation is prevailed between India and Pakistan.

wore (past tense of wear) : She wore a silken saree last night.

ware (merchandise) : The box seems to contain glass wares.

479. **warship** (naval implement of destruction) : Warships played a decisive role in the victory of our forces.

worship (revere in a religious manner) : I enjoyed worshipping God.

480. **wary** (cautious) : People do not teach their wards to be wary of strangers.

wherry : A light rowing boat used chiefly on rivers and in harbours for carrying passengers.

481. **we** (us) : We are going to market.

wee :

(a) Wee means small in size or extent. He just needs to calm down a wee bit.

(b) To wee means to urinate. Wee is an informal word used especially by children. He said that he wanted to wee.

(c) Wee is also a noun. The baby has done a wee in his potty.

482. **we'd** (contraction of 'we would') : We'd meet you there positively.

weed (wild plants) : If you don't take care the garden it will be soon full of weeds.

483. **we're** (contraction of 'we are') : We're friends.

weir (a low dam, or a fence in a river for catching fish):

(a) A weir is a low barrier which is built across a river in order to control or direct the flow of water.

(b) A weir is a wooden fence which is built across a stream in order to create a pool for catching fish.

were (past tense plural of 'to be') : Where were you playing?

whir or whirr (prolonged swish or buzz) : When something such as a machine or an insect's wing whirrs, it makes a series of low sounds so quickly that they seem like one continuous sound. The camera whirred and clicked.

484. **we've** (contraction of 'we have') : We've twenty pencils only.

weave (to make cloth) : They were busy in weaving cotton fabrics.

485. **wheeled** (having wheels) : We wheeled her out on the stretcher.

wield (to apply or use) :

(a) If you wield a weapon, tool, or piece of equipment, you carry and use it.The assaitant was wielding a kitchen knife.

(b) If someone wields power, they have it and are able to use it.

He remains president, but wields little power at the company.

486. **weld** (to join metal by melting its edges) : Where did you learn to weld?

welled (pouring forth) : Her love for him welled stronger than ever.

487. **wet** (watery) : She towelled her wet hair.

whet (prime) : If someone or something whets your appetite for a particular thing, they increase your desire to have it or know about it, especially by giving you an idea of what it is like.

A really good catalogue can also whet customers' appetites for merchandise.

488. **which** (selection) : Which dress do you like most ?

witch : In fairy stories, a witch is a woman, usually an old woman, who has evil magic powers. Witches often wear a pointed black hat, and have a pet black cat.

489. **while** (during) : He was reading while she was cooking.

wile (A crafty, cunning, or deceitful trick; a stratagem, a ruse) : She used all her wiles to earn his favour.

490. **whine** (annoying cry) : I can hear my dog whining in the courtyard.

wine (fermented grape juice) : This is a nice wine.

491. **whit** (insignificant amount) : He cared not a whit for the social, political or religious aspects of literature.

wit (cleverness; sense of humour) : He was at his wit's end.

492. **whither** (to which place, point, condition) : They knew not whither they went.

wither (shrivel up) : The flowers withered away within three hours.

493. **whoa** (whoa is a command that you give to a horse to slow down or stop) : You can say whoa to someone who is talking to you, to indicate that you think they are talking too fast or assuming things that may not be true.

woe (despair) : She listened to my tale of woe very patiently.

494. **yearn** (to long) : I am anxiously yearning to meet my wife.

yarn (thread) : I have purchased three bundles of yarn.

495. **yoke** (slavery) : He is under the yoke of his master.

yolk (yellow portion of an egg) : Some people eat only the yolk of an egg.

496. **yore** (the past) : Yore is used to refer to a period of time in the past.

The images provoked strong surges of nostalgia for the days of yore.

you're (contraction of 'you are') : You're a great writer.

your (belonging to you) : Which is your house?

497. **you'll** (contraction of 'you will') : You'll be asked to explain your conduct.

yule (Christmas) : Everyone makes enjoyment in his own way during yule time.

» Exercises

Exercise 1

Fill in the blanks choosing the correct words given in the brackets

1. This remarks about the dominance of casteism in elections are quite...........to the present position. (apposite/opposite)
2. The..........to this mountain is not an easy task. (ascent/assent)
3. Yesterday his behaviour with the guests was.......... (antic/antique)
4. The boat man..........the boat with a chain. (tow/toe)
5. Bihar is a State..........with coal mines. (teeming/teaming)
6. She achieved this distinction by the....... force of hard work. (sheer/shear)
7. The reading of cheap books produce a bad......on the minds of youth. (affect/effect)
8. You cannot...........my opinion about her. (altar/alter)
9. This rhyme is full of.......... (allusions/illusions)
10. He says that the word to nothing but an..... (allusion/illusion)

Solutions

1. apposite 2. ascent 3. antic
4. tow 5. teeming 6. sheer
7. effect 8. alter 9. allusion
10. illusions

Exercise 2

Fill in the blanks choosing the correct words given in the brackets

1. He was kind enough to.........to my request. (accede/exceed)
2. Everybody should be given.......to this temple. (access/excess)
3. He refused to...........the gift. (accept/except)
4. She......hard to secured first position in the college. (assayed/essayed)
5. She is..........with malaria. (ailing/aleing)
6. Please keep.......... (quiet/quite)
7. What is the name of the....of this college? (principal/principle)
8. This house is near the...........of india. (border/boarder)
9. This world is nothing but an......... (allusion/illusion)
10. The property of the........was confiscated by the government. (deceased/diseased)

Solutions

1. accede 2. access 3. accept
4. assayed 5. ailing 6. quiet
7. principal 8. border 9. illusion
10. deceased

Exercise 3

Fill in the blanks choosing the correct words given in the brackets

1. India is now free from the....... of British empire. (yoek/yoke)
2. At last she left the house of her parents, knowing not.......... (whither/wither)
3. All the flowers have now........away. (wither/whither)
4. It is wrong to conclude that all............him are corrupt. (except/accept)

5. She is...........in the art of painting. (adapt/adept)
6. The drought........a large part of the state. (attected/effected)
7. This office is situated at the second.......... (storey/story)
8. This hotel has twenty A.C......... (suites/suits)
9. I am going to purchase........ items for the office. (stationery/stationary)
10. The earth is not..........., it revolves. (stationary/stationery)

Solutions

1. yoke 2. whither 3. wither
4. except 5. adept 6. affected
7. storey 8. suites 9. stationery
10. stationary

Exercise 4

Fill in the blanks choosing the correct words given in the brackets

1. Please..........my clothes. (calendar/calender)
2. He is on.........leave. (casual/causal)
3. The policeman........the thief by collar. (seized/seiqed)
4. We heard..........of trumpets. (peal/peel)
5. Through process of melting, iron is extracted from.......... (oar/ore)
6. He has some.........benefits in this project. (monetary/monitory)
7. You can show your............by fighting against injustice. (metal/mettle)
8. This wife came........than him. (latter/later)
9. An......................man always plans in a clever manner. (ingenious/ingenuous)
10. I have already clarified this point in..........paragraphs. (forgo/forego)

Solutions

1. calender 2. casual 3. seized
4. peal, 5. ore 6. monetary
7. mettle, 8. later 9. ingenious
10. foregone

Exercise 5

Fill in the blanks choosing the correct words given in the brackets

1. A good fellow will not..........a friend in need. (desert/dessert)
2. This house was......by earthquake. (wreck/wreak)
3. A good writes always uses..........at appropriate places. (comma/coma)
4. What he says is hardly.......... (creditable/credible)
5. He built his.............by hard work. (career/carrier)
6. The...........was covered with white sheet. (corpse/corps)
7. This bill has already been passed by legislative......... (council/counsel)
8. Pay my best...........to your parents. (compliments/complement)
9. He has............... to be the chairman of society. (cease/seize)
10. True........cannot be enjoyed by a man of jealous nature. (felicity/facility)

Solutions

1. desert 2. wrecked 3. comma
4. credible 5. career 6. corpse
7. council 8. compliment 9. ceased
10. felicity

Exercise 6

Fill in the blanks choosing the correct words given in the brackets

1. ....makes a man perfect. (practice/practise)
2. The..........of many pundits about destruction of the word didn't come true. (prophecy/prophesy)
3. He can...........many cases to prove his arguments. (site/cite)
5. Can you........this stick? (break/brake)
6. He defeated the earlier champion in....... (dual/duel)
7. We should not adopt.........means to achieve suceess. (fowl/foul)
8. She is a woman of..........nature. (jealous/zealous)
9. It is raining and.............in the sky. (lightning/lightening)
10. New Delhi is the.............of India. (capitol/capital)

Solutions

1. practice 2. prophecy 3. cite
4. berth 5. break 6. duel
7. foul 8. jealous 9. lightning
10. capital

Unit

29

Idioms and Phrases

- **A gentleman at large** (an unreliable person) : He is *a gentleman at large*, you must not trust him.
- **A man of straw** (a weak person) : The assistant being *a man of straw*, his advices were often discarded by his colleagues.
- **A bull in a China shop** (one who causes damage) : Many political leaders have proved *bulls in a China shop* in respect to the democratic fabric of the nation.
- **A damp squib** (complete failure) : The visit of our Foreign Minister to USA proved *a damp squib* on terrorist issue.
- **A green horn** (inexperienced) : Though *a green horn* in politics, he appears to win the election this time.
- **A stalking horse** (pretence) : The demands of the trade union seem only *a stalking horse* to blackmail the management.
- **A mare's nest** (a false invention) : The involvement of politicians in the developmental scheme proved to be *a mare's nest*.
- **A wolf in sheep's clothing** (a dangerous person pretending harmless): Charles Shobhraj is *a wolf in sheep's clothing* for general public.
- **ABC** (very common knowledge) : He doesn't know *ABC* of Physics.
- **Above board** (fair and honest) : He is a straight forward man. His financial dealings are *above board*.
- **Again and again** (repeatedly) : One who tries *again and again* gets success positively.
- **All and sundry** (without making any distinction) : He invited *all and sundry* in the marriage party of his younger brother.
- **All in all** (whole-sole, most important) : The Forest Minister is *all in all* of our department.
- **Alpha and omega** (First and last letter of Greek alphabet, means beginning and end) : The *alpha and omega* of British policy was to keep the Indians divided.
- **An eye wash** (a pretence) : He does nothing without self interest, all his excuses are but *an eye wash*.
- **An iron hand** (by force) : Indira Gandhi put down the opposition with *an iron hand*.
- **At odds** (in dispute) : The two groups of the society are *at odds* over the selection procedure of peons.
- **At sixes and seven** (persons who are having different opinions) : Economists are *at sixes and seven* on the policy of rationing.
- **Beck and call** (at the service) : Don't worry I am at your *beck and call*.
- **Bag and baggage** (with all goods) : He returned his village *bag and baggage*.
- **Bated breath** (in anxiety, expectancy) : Every Indian was waiting for the outcome of the cricket match with *bated breath*.
- **Bank on** (depend on, count on) : You can *bank on* me in odd times.
- **Between Scylla and Charybdis** (choice between two unpleasant alternatives) : Don't

make haste, take care so that in avoiding *Scylla* you don't fall in *Charybdis*.

- **Between the cup and the lip** (On the point of achievement) : Until I got the appointment letter in hand, I was not sure of the posting as there were many slips *between the cup and the lip*.
- **Black and white** (in writing) : It is always better to get every thing in *black and white*.
- **Blow hot and cold** (having no stand, shows favour at one time and unfavour at another) : He can't be relied upon as he *blows hot and cold* in this matter.
- **Body and soul** (entirely) : She devoted *body and soul* to win the medal.
- **By fits and starts** (irregularly) : Work done *by fits and starts* never completes in time.
- **By hook or by crook** (by any means) : I want to get this licence *by hook or by crook*.
- **By leaps and bound** (speedily) : The population is increasing *by leaps and bounds*.
- **By and by** (gradually) : She is recovering *by and by* after a long illness.
- **Call a spade a spade** (straight talks) : He believes in *calling a spade a spade*.
- **Cats and dogs** (heavy rain) : It has been raining *cats and dogs* for the last three hours.
- **Cock and bull story** (untrue story) : All his excuses seems a *cock and bull story*.
- **Confusion worse confounded** (be in further worse position) : Such demonstrations and communal speeches in present situation make *confusion worse confounded*.
- **Cut and dried** (readymade form) : There is no *cut and dried* method of learning draving.
- **Curtain lecture** (a reproof by wife to her husband) : My younger brother never pays any attention to his wife's *curtain lecture*.
- **Egg on** (to urge somebody) : The Captain **egged** the players **on** to continue the fight.
- **Ever and anon** (now and then) : She goes to temple *ever and anon*.
- **Fair and square** (honest) : He is *fair and square* in his dealings.
- **Fair field and no favour** (equal opportunity to all) : All the staff want *fair field and no favour* in the matter of transfer.
- **Far and wide** (everywhere) : Many tourists from *far and wide* come to see the Taj.
- **Fabian policy** (policy of delaying decisions) : Mr. Narsimha Rao always followed a *Fabian policy* in all political issues.
- **Few and far between** (very rare) : His visits to his parents are *few and far between* because of his busy schedule.
- **Fire and brimstone** (fearful penalties) : The USA has threatened Iraq with *fire and brimstone* if it refuses to follow the resolutions of UNO.
- **Fire and fury** (extreme enthusiasm) : The speech of the leader was full of *fire and fury*.
- **First and foremost** (highest priority) : To be sincere and devoted is the *first and foremost* requirement of a good employee.
- **Fishy** (doubtful) : Then seems to be something *fishy* going on in the hall.
- **Foot the bill** (bear expenses) : Although she hosted the feast, her father had to *foot the bill*.
- **Free and easy** (natural and simple) : The principal found his arguments *free and easy*.
- **Flesh and blood** (human nature) : I am only *flesh and blood* as anybody else.
- **Gall and wormwood** (source of irritation) : Her remarks about his father were *gall and wormwood* to him.
- **Gird up the loin** (to be ready) : We should *gird up the loin* to fight the poverty and menace of dowery.
- **Give in** (surrender) : He is a brave man , he will not give in easily.
- **Goods and chattels** (belongings of home) : On transfer he brought all *goods and chattels* by road.
- **Hand and gloves** (very intimate friends) : Ram and Rahim are *hand and gloves* to each other.
- **Hard and fast** (certain) : There no *hard and fast* rule to sanction the Loan in banks.
- **Haughty and naughty** (arrogant and naughty) : The *haughty and naughty* attitude of the president is not liked by any member of the society.
- **Heart and soul** (with full devotion) : He threw himself **heart and soul** into the game and tried to win it.

- **Head and shoulder** (superior) : Mr. Man Mohan Singh is *head and shoulder* above his counter parts.
- **Helter skelter** (here and there) : On arrival of the police the strikers ran *helter skelter.*
- **Herculean task** (a tedious job) : Getting selected in IAS is a *Herculean task* for everybody.
- **Hit below the belt** (contrary to principles of fairness) : By making his private secretes public he *hit* him *below the belt.*
- **Hither and thither** (here and there) : He is in the habit of putting his goods *hither and thither.*
- **Hornet's nest** (raise controversy) : The speaker of Lok Sabha stirred up *hornet's nest* by referring to impending changes in several rules.
- **Hole and corner policy** (a secret policy for an evil purpose) : The officer adopted *hole and corner policy* to get his P.A. transferred.
- **Hue and cry** (great noise) : A lot of *hue and cry* was raised in Parliament against this bill.
- **Hush money** (a bribe) : He managed to escape punishment by paying *hush money.*
- **Ins and outs** (full detail) : Before starting any new business you must know all *ins and outs* of it.
- **Intents and purposes** (practically) : My wife is the incharge of the house for all *intents and purposes.*
- **Ivory tower** (imaginary world) : Those who talk of non-violence as a useful tool in tackling the militants live in *ivory tower.*
- **Kith and kin** (blood relatives) : All *kith and kin* were invited in the marriage of his son.
- **Latin and Greek** (unable to understand) : His speech in English was *Latin and Greek* to the rural folk.
- **Law and equity** (legal and moral justice) : Law and *equity* demands that the reservation should be based on economic parameters.
- **Leave no stone unturned** (make all possible efforts) : I shall *leave no stone unturned* to get the promotion.
- **Length and breadth** (all over) : Anti English agitation spread through the *length and breadth* of the country.
- **Life and soul** (main support) : Soniya Gandhi is the *life and soul* of congress (I).
- **Like a fish out of water** (in every difficult and unsuitable situation) : Ram was given an unremunerative post. He is feeling *like a fish out of water.*
- **Live wire** (energetic) : India needs *live wire* scientists who can put the country on the fast track of progress.
- **Loaves and fish** (material interests) : Now-a-days Government servants are concerned with the *loaves and fish* of the office than to solve the problems of common public.
- **Lock and key** (in safe place) : He keeps jewellery under *lock and key.*
- **Might and main** (with all enthusiasm) : If you study with *might and main* you will positively secure the success.
- **Milk and water** (weak) : The foreign policy of India is nothing more than a *milk and water* policy.
- **Neck and crop** (completely) : The Pak army ruined the border village *neck and crop.*
- **Need of the hour** (necessity of time) : Providing full security for the residents of border area is the *need of the hour.*
- **Nook and corner** (everywhere) : I searched her in every *nook and corner.*
- **Not born yesterday** (worldly wise) : You can't befool me as I was *not born yesterday.*
- **Now and then** (occasionally) : I visit church *now and then.*
- **Null and void** (of no use, without force of application) : The law passed by legislature was declared *null and void* by the Supreme Court.
- **Odds and ends** (remaining goods) : Except *odds and ends,* all the items have since been arranged in order.
- **Often and often** (frequently) : She visits her parents *often and often.*
- **Once and again** (repeatedly) : I have told you *once and again* that I have no money to purchase the car at the moment.
- **One's Achilles'heel** (a weak point) : Her involvement in sex scandal has been *her Achilles'heel.*

- **Open and above board** (very clear, transparent) : He believes in *open and above board* discussion on every point before arriving at a conclusion.
- **Order of the day** (in fashion) : Sending greetings on all occasions has beome a *order of the day.*
- **Out of gear** (in disorder) : The strike of employees always put the government machinery *out of gear.*
- **Out and out** (completely) : Mahatma Gandhi was a great leader *out and out.*
- **Over and above** (besides) : I paid him rupees ten thousand *over and above* what he demanded.
- **Over head and ears** (excessively) : He is *over head and ears* in debt.
- **Oily tongue** (flattering words) : One should be aware of the persons with *oily tongue.*
- **Part and parcel** (being an important part of) : Each employee should feel himself *part and parcel* of the business enterprises.
- **Pell mell** (putting one upon the other, in confusion) : He was in such a hurry that he put all the articles *pell mell* and closed the room.
- **Pick and choose** (to choose selectively as per wish) : The management adopted *pick and choose* policy in the promotions from clerical to assistant cadre.
- **Pins and needles** (small items) : It is unwise to use swords and scissors where *pins and needles* can do.
- **Pin-money** (allowance given to housewife for personal use) : My wife asked me to enhance her *pin-money.*
- **Pros and cons** (merits and demerits) : Before signing this agreement you must understand all *pros and cons* well.
- **Queer fish** (strange person) : He is such a *queer fish* that we can't expect anything positive from him.
- **Rain or shine** (favourable or unfavourable circumstances) : *Rain or shine,* I will speak to oppose the proposal.
- **Rank and file** (everyone without discrimination) : For the actual prosperity of the nation, the economic conditions of *rank and file* should be improved.
- **Rank and ruin** (complete destructions) : The present drought has put the farmers at the verge of *rank and ruin.*
- **Rhyme or reason** (rational cause) : He resigned from the service without any *rhyme or reason.*
- **Right and left** (in all ways) : The robbers looted the village *right and left* and fled away.
- **Root and branch** (complete) : Poverty among the public is the *root and branch* of all the crimes.
- **Safe and sound** (quite well) : She reached their *safe and sound.*
- **Seamy side of life** (immoral side of society) : The present day cinema depicts the *seamy side of* life in our society.
- **Speck and span** (neat and smart) : Mr. J. L. Nehru was always *speck and span* in his dressing style.
- **Stuff and nonsense** (worthless) : The judge found all his arguments *stuff and nonsense.*
- **Sum and substance** (the actual theme) : The *sum and substance* of the paragraph must be reflected in a good precis.
- **Take bull by horns** (to meet the danger boldly) : One should have courage to *take bull by horns* if one wants to succeed in life.
- **The die is cast** (decided finally) : *The die is cast* there is not point of discussing over it now.
- **The last nail in the coffin** (The last action which resulted in the complete ond of something) : The reservation policy of V.P. Singh was *the last nail in the coffin* of Janta Party.
- **Thick and thin** (in all circumstances) : I shall support you through *thick and thin.*
- **Through fire and water** (in all sort of difficulties) : He can go *through fire and water* to achieve his goal.
- **Time and tide** (course of time) : *Time and tide* waits for none.
- **To and fro** (going and coming, backward and forward) : What are the *to and fro* taxi charges for Alwar to Delhi?
- **Toil and moil** (hard labour) : It require too much of *toil and moil* to secure first position.

- **Tom Dick and Harry** (everyone) : Every *Tom Dick and Harry* knows that Mohamend Kaif is the wonderful cricketer.
- **To lead up the garden path** (to cheat) : The tricky traders try *to lead* the customers *up the garden* path by assuring them of warranty and good discount.
- **Tooth and nail** (with all force) : Students of general caste opposed the reservation policy *tooth and nail* but of no avail.
- **Ups and downs** (prosperity and adversity) : There are *ups and downs* in every business.
- **Uphill task** (difficult task) : Passing CAT examination is an *uphill task.*
- **Warp and woof** (essential parts of a thing) : Blood and bones are *warp and woof* of human body.
- **Watch and ward** (careful guard) : At least three guards are required to have perfect *watch and ward* of the building.
- **Weal and woe** (prosperity and adversity) : I will abide by you in all *weal and woe.*
- **Whips and spur** (with greatest hurry) : He completed the project *whips and spur.*
- **Why and wherefore** (the basic roll season) : Please tell me the *why and wherefore* of your decision to take voluntary retirement.
- **Willy Nilly** (wish or nonish) : Willy mlly yio are to obey the orders of your boss.
- **Yellow press** (newspapers publishing sensational news) : These days *yellow press* is the order of the day.

Idiomatic Expressions

- **To add fuel to of fire** (to make matter worse or aggravated) : The arrest of the leader of agitators by the government only *added fuel to the flame.*
- **To assume airs** (to pretend superiority) : He is in the habit of *assuming airs* in the presence of his in-laws.
- **To add a new feather in one's cap** (additional success) : His success in his ICFAI exams has *added a new feather in his cap.*
- **To and fro** (forward and backward) : He was walking in the garden *to and fro.*
- **To be at sea** (a person confused) : My wife is quite *at sea* in maths.
- **To be in fix** (in a dilemma) : The police department was *in a fix* about the threatning calls sent by the militants.
- **To be in the good books** (to be in favour with a person) : A good student is always *in the good books* of his teachers.
- **To be under a cloud** (to be under suspicion) : His connections with the militants have brought him *under a cloud.*
- **To be at large** (free) : The man who tried to kill her is still *at large.*
- **To be not worth one's salt** (not deserving) :
- **To be in tune** (in agreement or mood) : The Principal asked the students if they were *in tune* with the rest of the class.
- **To be out of sorts** (to be unwell) : She had been *out of sorts* for several days and so could not do her office work.
- **To break the news** (to give bad news) : He *broke the news* of her husband's death very cautiously in order to lessen the shock.
- **To burn the midnight oil** (to work upto late hours) : I have to *burn the midnight oil* for several days in order to complete the work in time.
- **To be born with a silver spoon in one's mouth** (to be born in a rich family) : Indira Gandhi *born with a silver spoon* in her mouth.
- **To be worth its weight in gold** (something extremely valuable) : For a hungry man a piece of bread is often *worth its weight in gold.*
- **To be lost in clouds** (a person with confused or unclear thoughts) : Philosophers are often *lost in clouds.*
- **To be weak or vacant in the upper storey** (a feeble minded person) : I can't assign such work to him, as he is *vacant in the upper storey.*

- **To be under a cloud** (under suspicion) : The recovery of a revolver from his office has put him *under cloud.*
- **To be under one's thumb** (to be under control) : She is no more *under the thumb* of her mother in law.
- **To be at daggers drawn** (ready to fight) : Both the brothers are at daggers drawn.
- **To be at a loss** (to be puzzled or confused) : In interview he found himself *at a loss*, couldn't answer even very simple questions.
- **To be at one's wit's end** (unable to decid or explain the right course of action) : Seeing the income tax officer at his shop he was *at* his *wit's end.*
- **To be at the helm of** (enjoying the best position) : Until his father was a minister he was *at the helm of* affairs.
- **To be in a fix** (unable to decide) : He was *in a fix* when the inspector discovered many irregularities in the accounts book.
- **To be in the teens** (between the age of twelve and twenty) : Two girls still *in* their *teens*, were caught taking alcoholic drinks.
- **To be on one's last legs** (to be about to collapse) : It is wrong to say that caste system in India is *on* its *last legs.*
- **To be the tenter hooks** (to be very anxious, excited) : I have been on *tenter hooks* week, meating for result.
- **To be true to one's salt** (to prove faithful) : The Rajput soldiers in Akbar's army were *true* to their *salt.*
- **To be at loggerheads** (to quarrel) : The two brothers are now *at loggerheads.*
- **To bear the brunt of** (to bear the brunt) : The secretary has to *bear the brunt* of minister's wrath.
- **To beard the lion in his own den** (to attack a ferocious and powerful person in his own territory) : Only a person like Shivaji dared to *beard the lion in his own den.*
- **To bell the cat** (doing anything at a great personal risk) : When it came to asking for CEO no me wanted to blue he cat permission *bell the cat.*
- **To blow one's own trumpet** (to speak about self, boast about self) : You can't discuss with him, he is always *blowing* his *own trumpets.*
- **To break the ice** (make a beginning) : Everyone kept silence for sometime then Ramesh *broke the ice* by asking introductions.
- **To burn candle at both ends** (to become very third and get up early next morning) : Ram is working and studying it a college, he is *burning candle at both ends.*
- **To beat about the bush** (to talk in an ambiguous manner) : Don't beat about the bush, come to the point.
- **To build castles in the air** (to make visionary schemes) : He is in the habit of *building castles in the air* and so does not succeed in life.
- **To bring to book** (to call to account) : The corrupt officer was *brought to book* for his negligence of duty.
- **To get to the bottom of** (to find the main cause) : I had to investigate for five days to *get* at *the bottom of problem.*
- **To bury the hatchet** (to make peace forgetting the past enemity) : Hindus and Muslims should *bury the hatchet* for the development and prosperity of the nation.
- **To burn one's boats** (point of no return) : By migrating to USA, Raj had *burnt* his *boats.*
- **To blaze the trail** (to start a movement) : Bhagat Singh *blazed the trail* of Indian National Movement among Punjab youths.
- **To brow beat** (to bully) : He always tries *to brow beat* his colleagues who oppose to him.
- **To bite the dust** (to be defeated) : Pakistan had *to bite the dust* in the war with India.
- **To breathe one's last** (to die) : Pt. Nehru *breathed* his *last* in early sixties.
- **To be nipped in the bud** (to destroy in the very beginning) : All kind of evils must *be nipped in the bud.*
- **To buy a pig in a poke** (to purchase a thing without knowing its actual worth) : Please tell me full details of the company, so that I may think to purchase its shares otherwise I can't *buy a pig in a poke.*
- **To come home to** (to understand) : It *came home to* him that he was not fit for the post of police inspector as his eye sight is very weak.

- **To check by jowl** (very near to each other) : As the space was short, so he kept all the articles *check by jowl*.
- **To cool one's heels** (to be kept waiting) : We had *to cool* our *heels* before we could meet the Prime Minister.
- **To cross one's mind** (to occur to oneself) : In the examination hall it *crossed* my *mind* that I had left my admit card in the canteen.
- **To change hands** (passing from one hand to another) : That hotel has *changed hands* thrice within a short span of six months.
- **To cast a slur upon** (to disrepute) : He assured he would not to do anything which might *cast a slur upon* the reputation of the family.
- **To cast pearls before swine** (to offer to a person such valuable things, which he does not appreciate) : Presenting Shakespeare's book to an illiterate is *to cast pearls before swine*.
- **To catch a tartar** (to catch a person who is more powerful than the catcher) : Aurangzeb soon found out that he had caught a tartar in Shivaji.
- **To clip one's wings** (to deprive one of power) : The Prime Minister has *clipped* the *wings* of his minister by taking away the power of spending more than two lacs on a project.
- **To carry the day** (to win a victory) : After initial setback India *carried the day* in the hockey match against Pakistan.
- **To cut a sorry figure** (to give a poor show) : The organiser *cut a sorry figure* in the meeting for not giving proper feed back to the chief guest.
- **To cry over spilt milk** (to repent) : Careless students often have to *cry over spilt milk* during the examination days.
- **To come to a stand still** (to come to a stop) : As the car *came to a stand still* for want of petrol the thief ran away on foot.
- **To come off with flying colours** (to come out from a conflict with brilliant success) : Everyone was trying for ticket of Congress party but Ramesh *came off with flying colours.*
- **To count the chickens before they are hatched** (to anticipate gain prematurely, before time) : You will feel unhappy if you *count the chickens before they are hatched.*
- **To cross one's t's and dot one's i's** (to make minor changes) : His book is almost ready, he has just *to cross his t's and dot its i's.*
- **To cry for the moon** (to aspire for an impossible thing) : Your hope for marrying Aishwarya is like a *cry for the moon.*
- **To curry favour** (to win favour by gifts or flattery) : By giving presents and visiting again and again you are trying *to curry favour his.*
- **To draw the long bow** (exaggerate) : In calling her the best racer of the world, her admirers *draw the long bow.*
- **To dig the grave** (to tarnish, to destroy) : By taking the side of the thief he *dug the grave* of his honest image.
- **To end in smoke/fiasco** (come to nothing) : He spoke a lot about his new book but it all *ended in smoke*, when the book was in the market.
- **To feather one's own nest** (to look after one's own interest) : Our leaders are busy *feathering* their *own nests* and have no concern for the general mass.
- **To flag a dead horse** (to revive interest in old matters) : The rivals always *flag a dead horse* to insult their enemies.
- **To fall flat** (to have no effect) : The principal's speech fell flat on the students.
- **To get upper hand** (to get the better position) : Between the two rivals, each is trying *to get upper hand* in the local politics.
- **To get into hot water** (to be in a difficult situation) : The manager *got into hot water* participating in the union meeting.
- **To gild the pill** (to cover an unpleasant thing by a pleasant one) : Though he was issued charge sheet, the officer *gild the pill* by verbally praising his sincere working.
- **To give the devil his dues** (to give the credit to a bad man for his good work) : No doubt he is a haughty man, but to *give the devil his dues* he is dedicated and hard working.

- **To give chapter and verse for a thing** (to submit proof) : He can *give chapter and verse* for all the allegations he made against the minister.
- **To go on fool's errand** (to go on an expedition where only a fool can go) : The key was in his pocket and he *sent me on a fool's errand* to search the same at the shopping complex.
- **To gain ground** (to succeed slowly) : The belief in the abolition of Sati rites has *gained ground.*
- **To go with tail between the legs** (feel ashamed and embarrossed) : The minister was talking a lot about honesty, but when Ramesh reminded him about the money paid to him for the work, he *went* away *with* his *tail between the legs.*
- **To get off scot free** (to escape without punishment) : He *got off scot free* for lack of evidence.
- **To give one a long rope** (to let someone commit mistakes) : He never *gives* his employees a *long rope* and so you will find his office well-disciplined.
- **To give currency** (to make publicly known) : The Government refused to *give currency* to a number of secrets relating to national security.
- **To get down to brass tacks** (deal with the matter straight) : Instead of wasting time in discussion, please *get down to brass tacks.*
- **To give a wide berth** (to avoid) : I tried my best to *give a wide berth* to such a selfish person.
- **To get oneself into a mess** (to drift into trouble) : He seems to have *got* himself *into a mess* because of the involvement of his wife in a criminal case.
- **To go the dogs** (to be ruined) : He *went to the dogs* because of his son's involvement in the murder of a girl.
- **To grease the palm** (to bribe) : You cannot get this contract unless you *grease the palm* of the officials.
- **To have gift of the gab** (art of speaking) : Ram is simply middle pass but he *has the gift of the gab.*
- **To have an iron will** (strong will) : A person with *iron will* can achieve anything.
- **To hold a candle to** (match for, equal) : She is the daughter of a famous dancer, but she does not *hold a candle* to her mother.
- **To have brush with** (to have encounter) : Our neighbours *had a brush with* one another over the matter of throwing the garbage.
- **To hang fire** (remain unsolved) : The problem of poverty has been *hanging fire* for the last fifty-five years.
- **To have feet of clay** (full of faults) : The inquiry has revealed that most of the politicians *have feet of clay.*
- **To have thing at one's finger tips** (to know a thing thoroughly) : He has all the statistics of his employee *at his finger tips.*
- **To have an axe to grind** (to have a personal interest) : I am sure he *has an axe to grind* in this proposal.
- **To have no backbone** (to have no strength and support) : The movement against the reservation, based on caste, *had no backbone* and collapsed soon.
- **To harp on the same string** (to repeat the same arguments) : Every speaker had nothing new *to* say, *harped on the same string* of his predecessor.
- **To keep abreast of** (to have recent information) : It is very important for the young persons *to keep abreast of* all current events.
- **To keep one's fingers crossed** (to wait expectantly) : We should *keep* our *fingers crossed* till the last ball is bowled.
- **To knit the brow** (to frown) : My father always *knits the brow* at everything I do.
- **To kick the bucket** (to die) : She had *kicked the bucket* after suffering from cancer for several years.
- **To keep someone at arm's length** (to keep someone at a distance and not allow to get close) : She is not a good girl and must be *kept at arm's length.*
- **To keep body and soul together** (to maintain life) : Because of the inflation it has become difficult *to keep body and soul together.*
- **To keep the wolf from the door** (to avoid starvation) : In our country the poor have to struggle hard *to keep the wolf from the door.*

- **To lose ground** (fail to keep position) : He has *lost ground,* so his opponent has won the election.
- **To leave no stone unturned** (to make all possible efforts): The Prime Minister has assured the country that he shall *leave no stone unturned* to uplift the condition of the countrymen.
- **To live in a fool's paradise** (false hope) : It is wrong to *live in a fool's* paradise and do not work hard to achieve success.
- **To lie in the bed one has made** (to reap the fruits of one's acts) : He has made his fortune so he must *lie in the bed* he *has made.*
- **To move heaven and earth** (to make all possible efforts) : Prime Minister Man Mohan Singh is *moving heaven and earth* to find the solution of Kashmir problem.
- **To make light of** (not to care) : She is in the habit of *making light of* the advice of the doctors.
- **To make both ends meet** (to live within one's earning) : Sudden increase in prices has made it difficult for the employees *to make both ends meet.*
- **To make much ado about nothing** (to make a fuss over a small matter of no importance): He is a quarrelsome man, he *makes much ado about nothing.*
- **To make hay while the sun shines** (to seize the opportunity at the right time) : As the Congress party came into power, he became chairman of UTI, which rightly says *to make hay while the sun shines.*
- **To make the most of** (to utilize time) : Students should *make the most of* their time if they want to secure good marks.
- **To make sure** (to ascertain) : I went to college *to make sure* if the exams would commence from the next week.
- **To make neither head nor tail** (not to understand) : The leader spoke so fast that the audience could *make neither head nor tail* of his lecture.
- **To nip in the bud** (to destroy in the beginning) : The militancy must be *nipped in the bud.*
- **To play ducks and drakes** (to waste money) : He is *playing ducks and drakes* with his parental money.
- **To pass the buck** (to blame each other): Political parties *pass the buck* on to one another on all small or big matters.
- **To play the gallery** (to gain popularity) : Every action of the political leaders aimed *to play the gallery.*
- **To pull a long face** (to look sad) : My son *pulled a long face* when he was scolded by his mother.
- **To play truant** (to be absent without permission) : It is a bad habit of the students *to play truant* from class.
- **To put all eggs in one basket** (to risk all money in one enterprise) : It is not correct for a business *to put all eggs in one basket.*
- **To pour oil on troubled water** (to rectify the matter) : Both of them were fighting for the property but the justified decision of their mother *poured oil on troubled water.*
- **To play fast and loose** (repeatedly change one's attitude) : You should not trust her, she is used *to playing fast and loose* with her friends.
- **To pay off old scores** (to take revenge) : By suspending the clerk on frivolous grounds the officer *paid off old scores.*
- **To pay one back in the same coin** (to return like for like) : I believe in the policy of *paying back in the same coin.*
- **To put the cart before the horse** (being at the wrong side) : By making a contract with the publisher, without getting the book ready, he *put the cart before the horse.*
- **To put a spoke in one's wheel** (to create hindrance) : Every competitor in the market is trying *to put a spoke in* the *wheel* of others.
- **To ripe up old sores** (to revive forgotten quarrel) : Ramesh and his wife can't live in pleace; they are always *ripping up old sores.*
- **To rub one the wrong way** (annoy): If you *rub* him *the wrong way,* he will oppose the proposal.
- **To read between the lines** (to understand the hidden meaning) : If you go through the book seriously, you will be able *to read between the lines.*

- **To rule the roost** (to dominate) : Today the scheduled caste ministers *rule the roost* in the government.
- **To send about one's business** (to dismiss) : His employer *sent* him *about* his *business* when he was caught involved in forgery.
- **To stand ones ground** (remain firm) : He did not yield to pressure and *stood* his *ground* till he won the game.
- **To sail under false colours** (hypocrite) : We should not believe the politicians because they *sail under false colours.*
- **To set Thames on fire** (to achieve something impossible) : Qualifying civil services examination for you is like *setting Thames on fire.*
- **To say ditto to** (to agree) : You are bound *to say ditto to* what your boss says.
- **To see a thing through coloured glasses** (to judge a thing with prejudiced mind) : A prejudiced man will *see the thing through coloured glasses.* He cannot judge the things properly.
- **To show the white feather** (to act as a cowardice) : He will *show the white feather* when the real time of action comes.
- **To stem the tide of** (to put a check) : As a true social worker, first of all you should *stem the tide of* poverty and unemployment.
- **To speak volumes for** (to have abundant proof) : The sacrifice made by freedom fighters *speak volumes for* their truc lovc for the country.
- **To steal a march** (to get ahead secretly) : Shalini *stole a march* on her friend in marketing her products slowly and steadily.
- **To steer clear of** (to avoid) : You should try *to steer clear of* such nasty girls.
- **To take people by storm** (to surprise unexpectedly) : The refusal by Soniya Gandhi a to accept the prime ministership took the nation *by storm.*
- **To the backbone** (thoroughly) : We need leaders who are honest *to the backbone.*
- **To take wind out of another's sails** (to gain advantage by anticipation) : Intelligent generals can gather a lot of important information by *taking wind out of* enemy's *sails.*
- **To take heart** (feel bold) : You must take heart and face the failures boldly.
- **To take up arms** (to fight) : We must not shy from *taking up arms* against the misdeeds of the public departments.
- **To turn the corner** (to change the opinion) : He *turned the corner* by passing the examinations with good marks.
- **To take to one's heels** (to run away) : On seeing the police, the thief *took* to his *heels.*
- **To take up the cudgels** (to defend someone) : I *took up the cudgels* on behalf of my brother and proved him innocent.
- **To travel incognito** (to travel under a false name) : The freedom fighters used *to travel incognito.*
- **To throw out of gear** (not working properly) : Our small scale units have been *thrown out of gear* because of lack of infrastructure.
- **To throw cold water** (to discourage) : He tried *to throw cold water* on my plans.
- **To win laurels** (to win distinction) : Dr Kalam won laurels in the world of Missiles.
- **To worship the rising sun** (to respect a person who is becoming powerful) : Everyone *worships the rising sun.*
- **To wash hands of** (to have nothing to do) : I have *washed hands of* this affair because he has no relations with me.
- **To wrangle over an ass's shadow** (to quarrel over trifles) : Only foolish persons *wrangle over an ass's shadow.*
- **To wear the trousers** (dominant) : It is Shalu who *wears the trousers* and her husband simply obeys her.

Frequently Used Idioms and Phrases

Frequently used idioms with the following verbs—'break, carry, cast, catch, come, cut, do, fall, get, give, go, have, hold, keep, lay, make, play, put, set, stand, take, throw, turn.

Break

- To **break cover** is when you leave a place where you have been hiding or sheltering from attack, usually in order to run to another place :
They began running again, **broke cover** and dashed towards the road.
- To **break a fall** is to lessen the force of a fall.
- To **break ground** means to commence an undertaking.
- To **break the heart** means to afflict grievously, to cause to suffer seriously from grief.
- To **break the ice** means to start conversations by getting over the feeling of restraint which one may have in the presence of a new acquaintance.
- To **break the news to a person** means to communicate news quite unexpectedly to him in such a way as to diminish the shock :
He **broke the news to** his wife as gently as he could that he had lost all his money due to the failure of the bank.
- To **break the back of a job** is to have disposed of the main part of the task assigned to him.
- **Broken health** is impaired health or not in good health.
- **Broken sleep** is an interrupted sleep.

Carry

- To **carry one's point** is to achieve the desired goal, to overcome obstacles placed in the way to defeat the opposition in a public debate :
Most of the reformers find it very difficult to get people to give up a long prevailed custom, but they **carry their point** in the end.
- To **carry everything** is to win the victory or to overcome the opposition fully.
How is it that of these two persons engaged in the same business, one can scarcely get a living, while the other can **carries everything before him?**
- To **carry away captive** means to take away into captivity, as prisoners of war :
In ancient times, many prisoners of war were **carried away captive** and forced to live as slaves.
- **To carry a thing too far** means to continue it beyond what is logical or safe :
End the argument here, do not carry thing to far.
- **To carry matters with a high hand** means to take strong measures, to exercise authority with full force.
- The principal of the college had **to carry matter with a high hand** and expelled two students for a trivial offence.

Cast

- To **cast an eye upon** is to glance at :
He cast an eye upon the two persons sitting infront of him, trying to tease the girl at the reception.
- To **cast or throw light upon** means to illuminate : After a long investigation, a woman came forward and stated some facts which cast light upon the causes of suicide committed by the man.
- To **cast into the shade** means to pale the affect earlier act : A newspaper gives a thrilling account of Godhra carnage, next day's paper tells of more horrible things still—the latter account casting the other into the shade.
- To **cast a slur upon one** means to cast a slight reproach upon him :
Many men cast a slur on their own reputation by stooping to some mean or hateful act.
- To **cast in one's teeth** means to retort reproachfully, to make an insulting statement to one openly : She cast it in her husband's teeth that she had seen him drunk, whereas later on it turned out that she had mistaken another man for her husband.

Catch

- To **catch fire** is to become alight or ignited :
The dry grass soon caught fire.

- To **catch one's eye** means to attract one's notice by being seen or to come under one's notice :
  If I keep looking at a lady till her look meets mine, I am said to catch her eye.
- To **catch a train** means to arrive at the railway station in time to go by a train :
  If you want to catch the train, move at once.
- To **catch it** means to get a scolding or a beating or some other unpleasant treatment.
- To **catch at a straw.** There is a proverb 'a drowning man will catch at a straw'.
  When a man is in difficulties, finding nothing substantial to lay hold of, grasps at something trifling he is said to catch at a straw.
- To **catch a Tartar** is to seize or encounter an adversary who proves too strong for him :
  The story goes that in a battle with the Turks an Irish soldier shouted to his comrade, 'I've caught a Tartar.' 'Then bring him with you', said the comrade. 'But he won't come.' 'Then come along yourself.' 'But he won't let me.' The fact was that the Tartar had caught the Irishman. Hence the general meaning of the phrase as given above.

Come

- To **come to close quarters** means to tackle an enemy closely.
- To **come to light** is to become known.
- To **come to pass** is to happen, to occur.
- To **come to grief** is said of a person who meets with disaster or a scheme that proves abortive.
- To **come to hand** is idiomatic for, to reach one :
  Her letter came to hand yesterday, which means it reached me yesterday.
- To **come to be** means generally, to become important :
- He has come to be highly thought of means that he has so risen in people's esteem that they now think highly of him. His word has come to be considered of great value.
- To **come amiss** means to come in an inconvenient or improper time or way. When it is said of a man that nothing comes amiss to him, the meaning is that he is a very capable man, able to do any work or meet any difficulty that presents itself to him :
  A legacy seldom comes amiss to anybody.
- To **come home to a person** means to appeal successfully to his reason or his self-interest; to touch his feelings closely.
- To **come to age** means to become adult.
- To **come to a head** means to be ready to burst forth-said; e.g. of a conspiracy to make open. He allows his spiteful feelings to come to a head.
- To **come to a standstill** means to bring to a standstill : When the steam was shut off, the engine soon came to a standstill.
- To **come to his proper level** means to bring a man to his (proper) level. This expression means to bring a vain man down from his undue estimate of himself, and teach him to esteem himself at his true level.
- To **come to know** to get the knowledge or information :
  I came to know a thing, or a thing comes to my knowledge. It is the form of these idioms that needs to be noted.
- To **come to no good** means to come to a bad end :
  It can be said of an idle young fellow, 'Youth will come to no good.'
- To **come out of a business with clean hands** is sometimes said of a person who comes out perfectly innocent while others have done misdeeds. The phrase 'clean hands' in this phrase is synonymous with uprightness, innocence.
- To **come, or fall, under one's notice or observation :**
  If such conduct as you describe comes under my notice, I shall take serious notice of it.
- To **come short of or fall short of** means to be less than what is required or expected.
  When great deficiency is meant, the word 'far' is introduced into the phrase. And short of, which means 'less than', is sometimes used with other expressions. We have tried gold mining in India, but the results have come far short of or fallen far short of, our expectations.
- To **come off with flying colours** means to emerge from a conflict with brilliant success.

The idea behind this : A regiment goes into battle with its banner or colours displayed; it engages in the fight and emerges with banner unscathed in the conflict, with colours fluttering in the breeze.
At the recent examinations, Rajani came off with flying colours.

- To **come off second best** means to get the worst of it. These are similar in meaning. They mean to be defeated in a contest or in an argument or in a legal action.

Cut

- To **cut short** means to shorten or abridge what is likely to lengthen out.
A man is said to have cut short his speech when he ceases speaking sooner than he was expected to.
We also say of a person that his life was cut short meaning that he died prematurely.
- To **cut, or sting, to the quick**. The quick is the sensitive flesh, that which is susceptible of keen feeling. The phrase means to cause acute pain :
Your scoldings cut him to the quick.
A reputated man is often stung to the quick by baseless imputations and slanders.
- To **cut off in its prime** means to destroy a fair thing when in its prime :
Cholera cut him off in his prime.
- To **cut the Gordian knot :** Gordian knot is a knot tied by Gordias, king of Phrygia, in the thong which connected the pole of his chariot to the yoke, and which was so very intricate that there was no finding where it began or ended. An oracle declared that he who should untie this knot would be master of Asia. Alexander the Great, fearing that his inability to untie it would prove an ill augury, cut it as under with his sword. Hence a Gordian knot is an inextricable difficulty; and to cut the Gordian knot is to remove a difficulty by bold or unusual measures. And the phrase is sometimes used when an unexpected turn of affairs opens a way out of a serious difficulty.
- To **cut a figure** is to perform a conspicuous part, to attract attention either in wonder or admiration.
- To **cut a dash** means to make a flourish or a vain show.
Both the above two expressions, especially the latter, are slightly contemptuous and rather old-fashioned.
- To **cut and run** is to be off with all possible speed. The phrase was applied first to cutting a ship's cable and the ship sailing off immediately from her moorings.

Do

- It means to perform, to accomplish or to execute a work.
- **Do** your job.
- I cannot **do** more than indicate the line of thought which he pursued.
Will you kindly show me how to **do** (= solve) this problem?
- **Do** also means to finish or to complete : Done is often used in the sense of completeness; so that to be done is often mean to be used up, to be exhausted. For example, if a tailor says that his thread was done, we should understand him to mean that his supply of thread was used up and was exhausted. So, to have done, is to have finished. I have done writing means I have completed my writing work.
- To **have done with** is to have completed, to have no further concern with :
I have now done with this dis-respectful business.
- **Do** also means to bring about, to cause to happen :
Have the heavy rains done your house any damage ?
- **Do** is sometimes intransitive and means behave or act :
Be careful not to do such things again.
- **Do** has, in some particular context, the peculiar meaning of, to cook, to make ready a thing for eating. To do a mutton chop is to cook it and prepare it for eating. When it is done to a turn it is perfecly cooked.
- It sometimes means cooked; so that expressions like : Are the cakes done or the rice is done ? would mean Are the cakes exhausted? or Are the cakes cooked? The rice is all used up or the rice is cooked. In such cases, all ambiguity is removed by the

connection in which done stands in the sentence.

- **Do** is at times used in conversation for, to deceive, to play a trick upon, to outwit :
He felt he had been done by designing men. Be careful as to the terms of your bargain, for that man will try to do you if he can.
- **Do**, again, sometimes means to fare, to thrive, to profit. How do you do? The first do is the auxiliary verb.
- **'Do'** is also found with the meaning to answer an end, in such expressions as : 'That will do', meaning that will be enough to serve the purpose.
- 'It did very well', i.e. it suited very well, it was quite sufficient.
- To **do good** means to act in a manner that others are benefitted : Do good in all the ways you can, to all the people you can .
- He is **doing well** means succeeding in his new line of business.
- The **patient has been doing well** means progressing favourably.
- He is **doing good by his lecturing** means he is accomplishing good results.
- He is doing well by his lecturing means he is making a good deal of money by his lecturing.
- He is doing well in his lecturing means he is doing the work of a lecturer well.
- To **do well out of something** means to derive profit from the activity.
- Ramesh did well out of that investment.
- To **do one's best** means to put forth one's best efforts.
- To **be well to do** is to be in prosperous circumstances, to be well off.
- **Well-to-do** is sometimes put before a noun as a compound adjective, and is also used as a noun. He is a 'well-to-do man' means he is a prosperous man.
- To **do one good** means to be of advantage or benefit to one.
- These medicines did me good.
- To **do one a favour or a kindness.** A formally polite expression.
- Will you do me the favour of accepting this small gift ?
- You will do me a kindness if you will append your name to the list of donors.
- To **do a thing by fits and starts** means to do a thing impulsively and a small portion of it at a time.
To study by fits and starts is not the proper way to prepare oneself for the IAS examinations.
- To **do a thing off-hand** means to do it at once without delay or hesitation :
- To do it with ease and without preparation. I gave him a difficult problem in Algebra and he did it off-hand.
- To **do a thing by hook or by crook** means to do it by any means fair or unfair, no matter by what means.
- Nowadays every one wants to make money by hook or by crook.
It is said that a French admiral in the time of war once wanted to bring his warship into Waterford Bay, in the south of Ireland. At the entrance to the bay there are two headlands, one on each side, one called Hook Head and the other Crook Head.
The admiral declared that he would enter either 'by Hook or by Crook', meaning that he would pass in by keeping near to one or other of the headlands.
- To **do wrong** means to make a blunder or to commit an error of judgement.
In my opinion you have chosen the right course and you would do wrong to make a change.
- To **do honour to**, to **do reverence** to means to honour, to reverence.
- To **do the honours** means to act as host or hostess at a party or function.
- **Do to death** means to put to death. Byron uses the words, 'done to death by sudden blow'. Jack done himself to death for his love lost.
- To **do a city** or **do the sights** means to visit the city.
- 'Done!' said in response to a proposal means I assent, I agree.
- **'No sooner said than done!'** means that as soon as a thing is proposed to anyone, he immediately executes it and utters this phrase as his response.

- To **do a thing under the rose** is to do it in a secret manner. In ancient times, the rose was taken as a symbol of secrecy and was hung up at entertainments, to indicate that nothing said there was to be divulged.
- To **have to do with** is to have business with, to deal with. She tried to clear herself of all blame, but she did have something to do with that immoral act.

Fall

- To **fall foul of** means to come into collision with :
  If this new manager continues his criticisms, he will soon fall foul of the boss.
- To **fall in love** means to be in love :
  The young couple quickly fell in love with each other.
- To **fall out** means to quarrel :
  It is wrong to fall out for the ancestral property.
- To **fall into abeyance** means to cease to be exerted or used :
  This law has been allowed to fall into abeyance.
- To **fall out of use** means to cease to be used. We also say, drop out of use :
  As any language grows, new words are coined and many words fall out of use.
- To **fall to work** or **set to work** means to begin to do work. In these phrases work is a noun :
  We fell briskly to work and finished the job in two hours.
- To **fall a prey** to means to be the victim of :
  When people plot against a man to ruin him and succeed in their malicious attempts, he is said to fall a prey to their designs.
  Ramesh fell a prey to the ulterior designs of his colleagues and so he was not promoted.
- To **fall to the ground** means to prove useless or to become ineffective :
  The meeting was large, yet his motion found no support, and therefore fell to the ground.
- To **fall for** something means to yield to its charms : Mira fell for a pretty dress.
- To **fall flat** means to collapse.

Get

- To **get clear** of means to become free from difficulty or annoyance.
- To **get drunk** means to become drunk :
  Where are you going to get drunk ?
- To **get one's back up** is to become irritated.
- To **get on** means to advance; or to prosper :
  Let the men get on to the front.
  He is a hard working man. He is sure to get on in the world.
- To **get hold of** means to understand or to catch :
  I can't get hold of the meaning of this passage.With great difficulty the drowning man got hold of the rope.
- To **get rid of**; to be deprived of means quitting of a thing or to get free from a thing :
  To be deprived of a thing means to have a thing taken from you which you wish to keep. Hence we do not say that people are deprived of a tax; they get rid of a tax, or are relieved of it, or are freed from it. A man may be deprived suddenly of his property.
- To **get the upper hand;** to **get the better of** mean to get the superiority, to prevail over :
  Of the two rival textile firms, one is richer and better managed than the other, and therefore soon gets the upper hand.
  Trickery in trade may for the time being get the better of honesty, but losses lost its credibility.
- To **get into hot water;** to **be in hot water.** To be in difficulty, irritating circumstances :
  The school master got into hot water with the inspector for delivering a speech favouring a political party.
- To **get into a mess** means to get into a muddle : His accounts seem to have got into a mess.
- To **get into a scrape** means to find oneself in an awkward position.
- The opposite is, to **get out of a scrape :**
  It is easier to get into a scrape than to get out of one.
- To **get wind of** means to hear a rumour of or to get the clue of :
  I got wind of the plot after hearing their conversation.

Give

- To **give a person to understand** means to lead him to believe or to give him reason for believing a thing.

- To **be given to understand** means to be led to believe :
The officer gave me to understand that there would soon be a vacancy for an assistant in his office.
- To **give oneself to** means to devote oneself to it. This phrase expresses the habit :
Give yourself to study and you will certainly secure good marks.
If a man give himself to bad habits, nothing good can be expected of him.
- To **give oneself trouble about** or **over a thing** means to take pains about it :
He gave himself great troubles over the problem of his younger brother.
- To **give someone a bit** or **a piece of your mind** means to scold, to find fault with, to speak or write to :
He has treated me very badly, I intend to write a letter and give him a bit of my mind.
- To **give** or **show a person cold shoulder** means to treat him coldly, to receive him in cold manner :
- It is common to give a cold shoulder to one's poor friends.
- To **give chase** means to pursue something that is running away :
The police gave chase to the thief, but he escaped.
- To **give way** means to yield, to succumb :
Only once his faithful wife gave way to emotions.
His reason has given way means he has become insane.
- To **give someone the slip** means to avoid someone who is looking for you :
The thief saw the policeman and took care to give him the slip.
- To **give** a thing a **wide berth** means to keep at a distance from it :
A sailor gives a rocky headland a wide berth by keeping his ship at a safe distance from it.
- To **give good measure** means to give rather more than full, correct measure :
When a draper selling cloth, measures off the stipulated number of yards and then gives freely a little piece more, he is said to give good measure. So a man rebuking or scolding another is sarcastically said to give good measure when the rebuke or the scolding is more severe than the justice of the case demands.
- To **give chapter and verse for a thing** means to produce the proof of it :
- I can give you chapter and verse for every statement I am making.
- To **give coutenance** or **lend coutenance** to a project means to favour it, to give one's support to it :
Some of the greatest benefactors of mankind have had few friends at first to give countenance to their inventions or discoveries.
- To **give currency** to means to make publicly known :
It is wicked to give currency to a dead scandal.
- To **give place to** means to yield up one's place to. You give place to another when you allow him to take your place. The phrase is also used of inanimate things, custom etc.
Carriages have given place to motor cars and sailing vessels to steamers.
- A **give-and-take** policy means a policy involving mutual concessions : Nowadays people believe in give and take policy in maintaining their relations.
- To **give a false colouring** to means to misrepresent : A man who is known to give a false colouring to any statement will not be believed even when he speaks the truth.
- To **give loose rein to** means to give licence to, the leave without restraint.
The idea is derived from leaving a mettlesome horse unchecked by the reins.
A liberine is one who gives loose rein to his lusts.
- To **give rise to** means to be the cause of, to originate. The phrase is often applied to rumours or suspicions : What gave rise to this evil rumour?
I don't know what gave rise to the idea that the capital of country was to be changed.
- To **give vent to** means to allow to flow forth—usually said of one's own strong pent-up feeling, as anger and grief.
I rushed out of the room to give vent to my feelings.

He gave vent to his indignation in language more vigorous than polite.

- To **give tone to** means to invigorate. In this phrase tone commonly means the healthy state of the organs of the body. The phrase is also used metaphorically of the character or faculties. The word tonic is derived from this use of tone :
The chairman's opening speech gave fine tone to the meeting.
The Swiss, living among mountains, are a hardy and thrifty people. The very nature of their country gives tone to their character.
- To **give** or **lend dignity** to an occasion means to bestow social importance :
The attendance of the Queen gave dignity to the gathering.

Go

- To **go mad** means to become mad. To go crazy is to become crazy :
My dog went mad and bit several other dogs.
- To **go blind** means to become blind :
If you do not take care of your sight you will go blind.
- To **go hand in hand :**
When two or more persons cordially agree in pursuing the same course, they are said to go hand in hand.
In the matter of providing reservation to the scheduled castes and scheduled tribes most of the political parties go hand in hand.
- To **go a long way** means to go far, to go to a great length :
The newspapers went a long way in criticising the government.
- To **go to law** means to litigate, to seek redressal through a court of law :
Several people are too fond of going to law.
- To go halves; to (go) share and share alike :
When two persons agree to divide a thing equally between them, they are said to go halves, or to (go) share and share alike.
These phrases are commonly used for an enterprise, and the agreement to take equal shares—of both risk and advantage—would be made before hand :
A party of ten students set out on a fortnight's tour and agreed to go share and share alike in the expenses.
- To **go to great expense** means to be at great expense, both mean to expand much :
The city has gone to great expense to give a suitable welcome to the president.
- To **go out of one's way to do a thing** means to deviate from one's ordinary course of conduct in order to do something, generally a favour :
You should be willing to go out of your way to oblige your friend.
- To **go hard with** means to press heavily upon :
If dengue breaks out again, it will go hard with the general mass.
- To **go well with :**
When a person prospers, it is often said that things go well with him, or that everyone goes well with him.
Strictly speaking, to go well with means to agree with, to suit.
I can't go well with such a quarrelsome girl.
In harmonising colours, green goes well with red.
- To **go on (sick) leave :**
When an official obtains leave or absence from ordinary duty, he is said to go on leave.
- To **go on a fool's errand** means to go on an expedition which leads to a foolish end :
There were many failed expeditions to Mount Everest, Can we say that those who took part in them were sent on a fool's errand?
- To **go through fire and water for** a person or purpose means to ecounter any difficulty and undergo any risk, however great, for his sake :
This man would go through fire and water to save his wife.
- To **go to the wall** means to be hard pressed, to fail, to get the worst in a contest or in the struggle of life.
When the struggle comes, the weakest goes to the wall.
- To **go to the bad** means to become of depraved character, to associate with evil companions so as to lose character. To go to the dogs is also used with the same meaning :
He is sure to go to the bad because he has a company of such depraved people.
- To **go to rack and ruin.** Here rack has the same meaning as ruin, the meaning being intensified by using both words. The phrase

is used both with regard to one's outward circumstances and also with regard to character :
The house is going to rack and ruin for want of looking after.

Have

- To **have one's hands full (too busy)** : When a man is so busily engaged that he cannot attempt anything else, we say, he has his hands full :
  Do not expect him to help you; he has his hands full already.
- To **have clean hands** means to be perfectly innocent, to be a person of honesty and integrity. The phrase is commonly used in speaking of business transactions :
  One who receives bribes or engages in any nefarious scheme has not clean hands.
- To **have to do a thing** means to be forced to do it, either from necessity of circumstances or from the will of another person :
  He had to cut down the tree to save his house.
  I had to walk two hours before I could find any shelter.
- To **have (cash) in hand** means to have cash in possession to pay.
- To have a work **in hand** is to have undertaken it, to be busy in it.
- To **have a hand,** or **a voice in a thing** means to have some part in doing it, to have a role in doing it. To have a finger in the pie, also means the same for the same :
  I am glad to say I had no hand in getting him transferred from here.
  You always like to have your finger in everyone's pie means you are always meddling with the affairs of other fellows.
- To **have a thing** at one's finger ends means to be fully familiar with a thing or to be able to apply one's knowledge readily :
  She has the history of the World Wars at her finger ends.
- **To have a mind to do a thing** means to be willing to do it or to show willingness to do it.
  She could tell you the secret of the Mahal if she had a mind.
- **To have a way of one's own** means to have one's individual way of dealing with the thing.
  He has a way of his own in dealing with the subordinates.
- To **have one's eye upon a thing; have an eye to a thing.** Either of these phrases may be used when a man has set a thing before him as the goal he desires or which he tries to achieve. The latter phrase also means to supervise or to watch so as to take care of :
  The headmaster of school has his eye upon the principal's chair.
  Please have an eye on the child and see that he does not go stray.
- To **have the field before one** means to have full opportunity of showing what one can do, to be unopposed. To have the field to oneself means to be the sole worker in a particular field.
- To **have a short memory** is to be unable to remember a thing even after a short time. The phrase is often applied to a person who says he forgets a thing while at the same time you suspect that he cannot have forgotten it.
- To **have the face to do a thing** means to have the audacity to do it. Another slang expression is to have the cheek to do it.
- To **have a difference with a person** means to have mild quarrel (or difference of opinion) with him. When friendly relations are restored, the parties to the dispute, are said to have made up their difference.
- To **have a bone to pick with one** means to have a difference with him which has not yet been expressed.
- To **have a brush with** an opponent means to have a slight encounter :
  The president had a slight brush with one of the secretaries at the meeting.
- To **have had its day;** to **have seen better days.** When an item which has been much used falls into disuse now, we say of it that it has had its day. When an article, e.g. a car, has become worn and shabby, we say that it has seen better days. The phrase would be use also of a person who, having been well off, had come down in the world :

Men drawn palanquins used to carry the bride have had their day in India.

- To **have too many irons in the fire.** If a blacksmith puts many irons into the fire that he cannot attend to them all as they grow red hot, some will be wasted. The phrase means, to have so much work in hand that some part of it is left undone or is done very hastily.
He is sure to lose his health under the strain of overwork; he has too many irons in the fire.
- To **have no backbone** (used for a vacilliating person or one easily disheartened) :
At first there was a show of resistance to new act passed by the Parliament, but the movement had no backbone and speedily collapsed.
- To **have the true** or **right ring** means to be genuine. A perfect coin has a clear, metallic ring when let fall on something hard :
The speech of the home minister on Jammu and Kashmir had the right ring about it.

Hold

- To **hold one's tongue** means to be silent, not to speak :
- The militants ordered the captives to hold their tongue or they will be punished.
- To **hold oneself ready or in readiness** means to be ready, to be in a state of preparedness :
The commander ordered the soldiers to hold themselves ready to attack.
- To **hold in check** means to curb or restrain within limits :
It is always better to hold the children in check so that they are not spoiled by the miscreants.
- To **hold in play** means to keep a person's attention occupied in some other task while you are doing something which you do not wish him to know :
It is a right policy to hold the foe in play while accomplishing the actual task.
- To **hold one's own** means to maintain one's own position against opposition candidates; to keep what advantage one already has. The same meaning is expressed by to hold one's ground, keep one's ground or maintain one's ground.
In the present odd circumstances it is better to hold one's own position instead of making new advancement.
- To **hold up one's head** means to be able to look at every man in the face :
The phrase implies pride of one's character or position. He has no reason to be ashamed of so he can hold up his head among the so-called philantropists.
- To **hold one's head high** means to bear oneself proudly :
- To **hold true** means to regard as true, to continue to be true :
The principles of Newton holds true even today.

Keep

- To **keep within bounds** means to keep within due limits.
- To **keep happy** one should keep oneself within bounds. When his passion is roused, it is hard to keep him within bounds.
- To **keep out of the way** means to absent oneself intentionally, to avoid being in the way :
She tried her best to keep herself out of the way of her paramour.
- To **keep a thing to oneself; keep one's own counsel.** These are same and mean not to disclose the thing that one knows :
She never shares her problems with any body. She keeps things to herself.
- To **keep a thing dark** means to keep it hidden or concealed, not to disclose it or make it known to others :
She never discusses her plans with anybody but keeps everything dark.
- To **keep oneself to oneself** means to live apart, to shun society :
He does not mixes with any of his friends. He keeps himself to himself.
- To **keep company with** a person means to associate with him as a companion :
If you keep company with bad persons you will soon learn their ways.
- To **keep to the house,** the room or one's room is said of a person who is ill or of one who is obliged from any cause to remain indoors :

(a) She has had a severe illness, and still keeps to the house.

(b) A warrant is out for his arrest, and so Ramesh keeps to his room.

- To **keep house** means to manage the business of a household. This phrase is used of a woman who acts as a housekeeper.
- To **keep open house** is to be ready to entertain all guests :
  She is a very nice lady and keeps her house open for all the friends.
- To **keep a good table** means to entertain one's guests sumptuously and in the habit of providing food of excellent quality for one's own eating :
  No one ever sees poor dinners at her house; I can tell you from long experience that she keeps a good table.
- To **keep watch and keep watch and ward** means to be on the watch :
  We had better keep watch tonight against thieves.
- To **keep a sharp look-out** means to maintain a keen watch
  They **keep a sharp** look-out on boardship.
- To **keep pace with** means to keep abreast of the development, to advance or progress equally fast with :
  (a) How can you expect a child to keeps pace with a full-grown man?
  (b) You cannot keep pace with Renu in 'logics'.
- To **break the peace; to keep the peace.** These are contrary expressions :
  (a) Two men quarrel and fight; they are said to break the peace.
  (b) They were brought before a judge and were bound over to keep the peace, i.e. to refrain thenceforth from quarrelling.
- To **keep one's eyes on another person** means to keep watch on him, to observe his movements and actions :
  The policeman tried to keep his eye on the thief so that he might catch him stealing.
- To **keep someone at arm's length** means to keep someone at a distance and not allow him an opportunity of close contact :
  It is always better to keep the evil persons at arm's length.
- To **keep one's head above** means to avoid getting into debt or trouble so as to be overwhelmed by it :
  It is always prudent to keep one's head above in order to be happy and free from lot of troubles.
- To **get one's head above water** means to tide over difficulties successfully :
  He sold part of his property in order to get his head above water.
- To **keep good hours** means to be habitually early in returning home at night :
  The opposite is, keep bad hours or late hours :
  He always comes late in the night, he does not keep good hours.
- To **keep body and soul together** is to keep alive, to keep from starving :
  She happily eats as much as would keep her body and soul together.
- To **keep the wolf from the door** is to keep away extreme poverty, starvation, or death by hunger :
  In India thousands have a daily fight to keep the wolf from the door.

Lay

- To **lay waste** means to make desolate :
  A few of the finest cities of Europe have been laid waste by bombing.
- To **lay bare, lay open** means to disclose or reveal a secret thing :
  He did not rest till he laid bare the whole conspiracy of his friend Pratham.
- To **lay someone under an obligation** means to do a favour so that he feels indebted :
  You have laid me under a great obligation by helping me in my adversity.
- To **lay oneself open to** means to expose oneself to :
  By spending a lot of money on trifle occasion, he will lay himself open to the suspicion of tax authorities.
- To **lie in wait for** means to await in concealment, to be waiting as if in ambush :
  The murderer lady lies in wait for her victim as the tigress, for its prey.
- To **lay or set a trap** means to prepare a trap and place it in a position to catch prey. It also

means to prepare a scheme to deceive another and draw him in :

A hunter lays (or sets) a trap to catch elephants.

- To **lay on the shelf** means to lay aside as no longer fit for use, just as books and magazines not in use are put on the shelves of the book case :

A retired person is sometimes called as laid on the shelf. Also, a question or scheme moved and set aside, is said to be laid on the shelf, or shelved.

- To **lay down the law** means to speak in tones of authority.
- To **lay up for a rainy day** means to make provision for an adverse time and difficulty.
- To **lay their heads together** means to consult together or frame common opinion.

Make

- To **make peace** means to reconcile or to agree on a peace proposal by the parties at variance :

There had been feuds for ages between the rival groups, it was the effort of the great grand old man that finally made peace between them.

- To **make room** means to open a space or passage, to remove obstruction.

Room here means open space, while a room is an apartment :

There is enough room on this road for two cars to pass by.

- To **make way, make headway** or to make one's way means to progress slowly and steadily under difficult circumstances. To make way for is to allow space or room for :

I have the guts to make my own way.

These students are studying Russian, but they do not seem to be making much headway.

The crowd made way for the 'hero of the game' as he advanced.

- To **make a hash** of anything means to spoil it :

The secretary made a hash on the club accounts.

- To **make haste** means to hasten, to hurry :

Make haste or you will miss the train.

- To **make friends** means to win or secure the friendship of others :

This man is so genial, he makes friends wherever he goes.

- To **make a will** means to make a testamentary disposal of his property :

He made a will and entrusted the same to his advocate.

- To **make use of** means to use :

She has so many sandals and shoes that she will not be able to make use of them in her life.

- To **make love to** means to make love with a woman :

It was in vain that the young boy tried to make love to his girl friend.

- He **makes a good soldier** means he possesses qualities of a good soldier.
- **She will make you a good wife** means she possesses the qualities for becoming a good wife.
- To **make answer** means to reply.
- To **make sure** means to ascertain positively; also to make secure.
- To **make sure of** means to consider as certain.
- To **make terms** means to come to an agreement.
- To **make short work of** means to bring to a sudden end, or to dispose of speedily :

This lawyer will make short work of his adversary's arguments.

- To **make amends for** means to compensate for damage, injury or insult :

By helping her now, he is trying to make amends for his past misdeeds.

- To **make an example of a person** means to treat (punish) him so that the result will be a deterrent (warning) to others :

By suspending the subordinate for his misbehaviour the officer made an example of him to others.

- To **make a point of** means doing a thing, to set it before you as a thing to be certainly done :

Johny makes a point of writing ten English pages daily.

- To **make a clean breast of something** means to disclose fully and without reserve :

It is always better to make clean breast of the whole things before the lawyer.

- To **make a living** means to earn a livelihood for oneself.
- To **make (both) ends meet** means to be able to supply the necessaries of life while keeping expenditure within income. The phrase implies that the pinch of poverty is felt :
  It is far better to struggle and make both ends meet than to get into the clutches of an evil person for making quick bucks.
- To **make common cause with** means to co-operate with; to unite with and share the common risk, work, and reward :
  Nowadays political parties with different ideologies make a common cause temporarily to win the elections.
- To **make one's escape** means to escape by one's own efforts :
  He made his escape through water route.
- To **make one's mark** means to do some noteworthy thing, which brings honour or distinction :
  He made his marks by writing a very good book for the children.
- To **leave one's mark** means to leave behind the effect of one's work :
  He was not long at college before he made his mark.
  Men like Jai Prakash Narain and Lal Bahadur Shastri left their mark on the history of our country.
- To **make a mountain of a molehill** means to give great importance to trifle issues. A man through great timidity or sloth often exaggerates a small obstacle and makes a mountain out of a molehill.
- To **make a virtue out of necessity** means to do a very disagreeable thing, as though from compelled by duty, though not liking it :
  Knowing that the landlord would forcibly aks him to vacate the house, he himself delivered the key; making a virtue of out necessity.
- To **make much ado about nothing** is to make a great fuss about a trifle :
  Mr. Rehman made much ado about nothing when he again raised the matter of throwing waste papers in front of his house by someone.
- To **make no bones about a thing** means to make no scruple about doing it. The phrase implies that the thing is disagreeable :
  You need not raise imaginary difficulties, but just go and do the work and make no bones about it.
- To **make neither head nor tail** of a thing means not to understand it or any part of it; not to be able to see the thing clearly :
  She spoke so quickly and in such a confused manner that nobody could make neither head nor tail of her sayings.
- To **take no account of** a thing means to disregard it through oversight or because it is not worth notice :
  Government takes no account of such senseless agitation by the extremist.
- To **make a fool of oneself** means to act stupidly. To make a fool of someone is to dupe him :
  He went to meet the president without any appointment, so he was not allowd to enter. He made a fool of himself.
- To **make little of, light of, nothing of** means to disparage, to treat as of no account.
  To make nothing of, has another meaning too. If a person is too stupid to learn, we say the teacher can make nothing of him it means the teacher cannot succeed with him. If the phrase is used in reference to a passage in a book, it means I am unable to understand it.
  When I talked about his health, he made light of his illness.
  We can make nothing of what she says, i.e., we cannot understand her.
- To **make much of** means to value highly, to treat as of great importance.
- To **make too much of** means to over-estimate. The phrase to make enough of is commonly used with a negative expression.
- To **make the best** or **the most of** a thing means to reap the greatest advantage one can from it ; to reduce to the least possible inconvenience :
  The accident was very serious, but the surgeon made the best he could of the few appliances within his reach.

- To **make the best of a bad bargain.** When a man buys a thing which does not turn out according to his expection, that thing is often called a bad bargain. Hence the phrase means to turn a disappointment to the best possible account.
- To **make hay while the sun shines.** Sunshine is most suitable for making hay. Hence the phrase metaphorically means to take advantage of a favourable opportunity before it lasts, to use the opportunity to advantage :
When trade was brisk, he worked very hard, and made his fortune; he believes in making hay while the sun shines.
- To **make a tool,** or **cats paw of** someone, is to use him as a means of attaining or accomplishing your object :
The story goes that a monkey seeing nuts roasting at a strong fire and wishing to have them, but did not like to burn his own paw, laid hold of the paw of the cat and by means of it pulled the nuts to himself.
- To **make a man of someone** means to elevate him, to raise him from an inferior position into an independent and prosperous condition, so that he can act in a manly way :
A rich friend of mine took up this poor lad and kept him at school for seven years, and his education has made a man of him.
- To **make believe** means to pretend, to act under pretence :
He made believe he was going off for a month, and then unexpectedly returned in a week and found his wife messed with a fellow.
- To **make a shift** means to get along by some means, though with some difficulty :
A miser will always make a shift to save money.
- To **make faces** is to make grimaces :
Most of the people make faces while looking into a mirror.
- To **make merry** means to be happy and jovial; hence the word merry-making.
We spent our winter holidays in eating and drinking and merry-making.
- To **make free** means to take a liberty to which one has no right :
(a) No one should make free to open a letter addressed to someone else.
(b) I make free to say in this gentleman's presence, that his conduct has not been straightforward.
The phrase implies boldness or impertinence, whereas the phrase take the liberty of does not indicate anything disrespectful.
- To **make free with** means to treat freely or without formality.
- To **make oneself at home** means to act with as much freedom and with as little formality as if you were at home. The phrase is used of a person who is in another person's home so as feel at his ease in the house and move and act as freely as though he were in his own house.
- To **make one's mouth water.** If a hungry man smells food, the saliva gathers in his mouth and he longs to taste the food. So the phrase means to excite a longing for. It is generally used when the thing desired cannot be achieved and enjoyed. In this phrase, water is as used as verb :
The hungry man stood gazing at the baker's shop and it made his mouth water.

Play

- To **play** is generally used in the sense of, to act, to operate on, e.g. the fire engine played (= poured water) on the burning house. In such phrases as **call into play** or **bring into play,** the word **play** means active operation :
The guns of the fortress were called into play and the advancement of the enemy was checked.
- To **play truant** is to stay away, to loiter or to be idle. The phrase is commonly used for a schoolboy who when sent to school goes off to play. It also sometimes means to absent oneself from duty when one is supposed to be at his post :
Schoolboys playing truant should be punished.
- To **play into the hands of another,** is so to act as to be of advantage to another :
Two contractors come to me with estimates for a work; they seem to be perfectly independent. One estimate is much higher than the other, and even the lower one seems high; so I accept neither. Afterwards I come to know that the contractors are friends, and that he, who gave the higher estimate, was

only playing into the hands of the other; he meant by bringing his higher estimate to induce me to close at once with the other contractor.

- To **play at cross purposes** is said of two parties who oppose each other, or who have opposing plans but with the same end in view :
  The Congress and the Communist parties have been at cross purposes for several months, yet they are both working for the same object of keeping the BJP out of power.
- To **play fast and loose with** means to disregard one's promises or engagements.
- To **play second fiddle** means to take a subordinate part, like one who plays second to a leading performer on the violin. The phrase sometimes implies that he, who occupies the subordinate positon, is expected to further the designs of his superior. Sometimes the phrase is to be second fiddle, the instrument being taken for the performer.
  Even though he is the president of the party, he is content to play second fiddle.
- To **play with edged tools.** There is a saying, 'Children and fools should not handle edged tools.' Hence the phrase is applied to a man who has to do with a matter which requires delicate handling :
  To interfere in a quarrel between Ram and his wife is like playing with edged tools.
- To **play one false** means to be deceitful to him, to cheat him :
  I relied on her support and she played me false.
- To **play a double game** or **act a double part.** These mean to do one thing openly and a different thing in secret. The thing done openly is done to deceive, whereas the thing done in secret is the real object aimed at.
  (a) I do not believe in playing double game.
  (b) Generals often play a double game in war, but this is regarded as part of the war tactics.

Put

- **Put** is used in several idiomatic expressions as per following :
- To **put in mind** means to remind.
- To **put to the sword** means to slay with the sword.
- To **put to trial** or **to put trial** means to try to check.
- To **put a thing to the test** or **proof** means to try it to examine it sincerely.
- To **put to shame** means to make someone ashamed or to disgrace.
- To **put a thing to the vote** means to take a vote upon a proposal.
- To **put (or get) things ship-shape** means to settle them in an appropriate order.
- To **put to sea** means to start on a voyage.
- To **put one's oar in** means to interfere to meddle in something.
- To **put to use** means to make use of it.
- To **put one to silence** means to silence him.
- To **put in order** means to array in orderly fashion.
- A mother **puts** her children **to bed** means the children **go to bed.**
- A commander **puts** his enemies **to flight** means the enemies **take to flight.**
- A magistrate **puts** the law **in force** against a criminal means the magistrate dispense the justice.
- To **put** or **set** one **at his ease** means to free him from restrain.
- To **put one to it** means to press one hard, to press him to the utmost of his powers. 'It' in this phrase is impersonal :
  I felt so exhausted that I was put to it not fall over.
- To **put it to one** is to lay a matter before one for his consideration that he may form an opinion upon it. This phrase would be used by one who was trying to persuade others :
- I **put it to you,** Is it wise to remain indifferent while the government is making great efforts to extend education?
- To **put a case** is to set it forward for consideration.
- To **put down one's foot** is to make a decide stand, to resist further encroachments.
- To **put one on his guard** is to warn him.
- To **put one on his mettle** is to rouse him to do his best in trying circumstances :
  The cry of wolves behind put my horse on his mettle and he brought me in safety to the village.

- To **put one's hand to a thing** is to undertake it to begin.
- To **put a thing well** is to express one's meaning clearly and forcibly in speech or writing.
- To **put the screw on one.** This means to coerce him; particularly to restrain another with regard to expenditure or idling :
He could put the screw upon his son George.
- To **put the cart before the horse** is to begin at the wrong end to do a thing, to attempt a thing while neglecting to do first what ought to be done first.
You certainly do put the cart before the horse. You have actually brought the masons to build a house but have not yet got the bricks.
- To **put one's shoulder to the wheel** is to make a great effort oneself instead of looking to others for help.
- To **put a thing down in black and white** is to put it in writing, so that a record is available :
You tell me a long story; but put down what you want in black and white; and I will weigh its merits.
- To **put** or **set right,** or to **put to rights** means to adjust, regulate, correct put in correct order :
The engineer soon put the damaged TV to rights.
- To **put a good face** or the best construction on a thing means to regard it in the most favourable way. The phrases are applicable to conduct and commonly to unseemly conduct :
A lawyer generally tries to put the best face on the faults of his client.
- To **put one out of countenance** means to make him appear ashamed.
- To **put this and that together** is to infer from a conjunction of circumstances.
- To **put forth or throw out, a feeler** is when a person brings forward a proposal or makes an observation to elicit the opinions of others, he is said to put forth or throw out a feeler :
In his statement about Pakistan in the Lok Sabha, the Prime Minister threw out a feeler to test the opinion of the Parliament.
- To **put a spoke in one's wheel** means to obstruct progress, to prove a serious barrier or hindrance :
Rahim was getting on well in business till Rehman opened a rival establishment, and that put a spoke in Rahim's wheel.
- To **put something by for a rainy day** means to save money for the adverse circumstances.
- To **put someone through** it means to wear him out, e.g. by long interrogation.

Set

- To **set a scheme on foot** is to start it, to **set it going.**
- To **set a thing on fire** is to apply fire to it and make it burn; also to inflame (said of the passions).
- To set or **put** a thing **on the fire** means to place it upon the burning fire to heat or cook it. Use of 'the' implies that fire was already there. You may set a kettle on the fire but you cannot set it on fire.
The girl set the pot on the fire.
He set the withered leaves on fire.
- To set store by is to value highly.
- To **set the Thames on fire** means to do something extraordinary or brilliant :
Nisha is a steady worker but never likely to set the Thames on fire.
- To **set one's face against** means resolutely to resist :
Attempts were made to draw the prince into rebellion but he set his face against such intrigues.
- To **set one's house in order** means to arrange one's affairs :
When he joined the new office he found the affairs of the office in desperate confusion; it took several months to set the house in order.
- To **set people by the ears** means to provoke them to quarrel or wrangle.
- To **be well set up** means to have a good physique to have a strong and well-built body.
- To **set one's teeth** is to determine to endure hardship.

Stand

- To **stand in another man's shoes** means to occupy another man's place.
- To **stand in need of** means to be in need of :
The house stands in need of painting.

- To **stand in terror of means** to be in terror of, to be afraid of :
  The old person stood in secret terror of his son.
- To **stand in good stead** means to be of great advantage to one in a time of difficultly :
  The wolves were after the traveller but his horse stood him in good stead and the traveller was able to escape.
- To **stand one's ground** means to maintin one's position :
  He tried hard to stand his ground against the veteran lawyer but he failed.
- To **stand to one's guns** means to persevere when hardships press.
- To **stand in one's own light** means to act in a way that is disadvantageous to oneself :
  He stood in his own light when he refused this posting.
- To **stand to reason** means to be consistent with reason and propriety of action.
- To **stand one's trial** means to be tried in a court of law.
- He cannot stand it means He is not able to endure it.
- To **stand on ceremony with** means to be over punctilious in etiquette.
- To **stand on one's dignity** means to maintain a dignified and unbending attitude.
  He was offended or insulted, but he stands on his dignity and insists that an apology be made to him by the offenders.

Take

- To **take into account** means to regard, to consider :
  Before purchasing this house he has taken into account all the merits and demerits of the locality.
- To **take to task, call to account** means to reprove and require explanation : Take him to task for his negligence and unauthorised absent.
- To **take advantage of** means to use any benefit offered by; also, to get benefit by cunning means.
- To **take a thing in han**d means to undertake to do it, to attempt, to accomplish it :
  Several persons have taken in hand to write the history of the country, but only a few have been successful.
- To **take the law into one's own hands** means to punish a person supposed to be guilty without his being legally tried.
- To **take notice of** a thing means to observe it :
  He listened to my logics, objections patiently, but took no notice of them in submitting his report.
- To **take** a city **by storm** means to capture it through a fierce and surprised attack.
- To **take** people **by storm** means to captivate them unexpectedly :
  His singing took the audience by storm.
- To **take** one **by surprise** means to come upon him suddenly.
- To **take upon oneself** means to assume or undertake some work :
  She takes all the reponsibility upon herself.
- To **be taken aback** means to be taken by surprise, to be startled.
- To **take part with** means to unite or join with.
- To **take part in** is to unite or join in - said of things :
  Several good tennis players have consented to take part in this tournament.
- To **take another person's part** means to side with him, to defend him.
- To **take (pay, or give) heed to** means to attend to carefully :
  I will take heed to what my mother says.
- To **take in good part** means to receive without resentment—said of a disagreeable thing, as a rebuke, or admonition :
  I tried to give Johni some good advice, but instead of taking it in good part, he became unhappy.
- To **take to one's heels** means to run away :
  Seeing the police, the thief took to his heels.
- To **take to one's bed** means to be obliged to lie down in bed through illness.
- To **take in tow** means to drag along in water by means of a cable or chain.
- To **take a statement on trust** means to accept it as true without inquiry, to accept it as true believing that he who makes it is trustworthy :
  One should not take any statement on trust unless we have something to prove our contentions.

- To **take it into one's head;** to **come into one's head** means to occur to one, to suggest itself to one. The expressions sometimes imply whimsically :
  Jack took it into his head to wake up all the servants at midnight.
- To **take pride in** means to delight in, to be proud of :
  She takes pride in doing her stitching very neatly.
- To **take a leaf out of another's book** means to take a hint from another's mode of action, to adopt another person's plan in the hope of reaching a result like his :
  Ram took a leaf out of Shyam's book in the matter of dealing with the customers and got success.
- To **take the bull by the horns** is to grapple courageously with a difficulty that lies in your way :
  If you have factious opposition to deal with, do not avoid it but take the bull by the horns.
- To **take a leap in the dark** means to do a hazardous thing without any idea of what it may result in : It is wrong to leap in the dark without knowing the results.
- To **take things easy,** or **take it easy** means to pass through life without being worried by work or anxieties. The phrase to have an easy time of it means to be without worry or hard work. To have an easy time of it, is because of outward circumstances; to take it easy is because of inward disposition and way of living.
- To **take a fancy** or liking to a thing means to conceive an admiration for it or a desire to get it :
  She has taken a fancy to my car.
- To **take,** or **let, one into a secret** means to make known the secret to him, he also being expected to regard it as a secret :
  Two persons plan a theft but are not able to accomplish their object without a person; so they take a person into the secrecy and carry the nefarious business very cleverly.
- To **take the lead** to **get the start.** When several competitors, one at starting gets ahead of the others, he is said to get a start. In a competition when one gets ahead and takes the leading place, he is said to take the lead :
  All the boats started together, but Ramesh's soon took the lead.
- To **take one home** means to accompany one to his home.
- To **take care of** or look **after** means to look carefully :
  You should take care of your old parents.
- To **take the measure of a man** means to form after careful observation a due estimate of a man :
  I asked some irrelevant questions to her friend in order to take measure of him.
- To **take the cake** (or **the biscuit**). This is a slang expression meaning 'to take first prize'—usually in some absurdity.
- To **take the bread out of another's mouth** means to deprive him of his means of living.
  He is said to have taken the bread out of his friend's mouth by getting his job.

Throw

- To **throw cold water upon** a project means to discourage it, to disparage the project.
- To **throw dust in one's eyes.** The phrase means to deceive one :
  He talked glibly to me about his schemes and tried to show me that if I would lend him two thousand dollars he would soon be able to repay me the double; but I felt that he was only trying to throw dust in my eyes.
- To **throw off the mask** is said of one who, having acted a deceitful part for a time, suddenly declares his real intentions :
  His deceit was as a mask to conceal his intentions.
  The tenant soon threw off his masks and openly tried to dictate his terms to vacate the house.
- To **throw up the sponge** means to give up a contest, to surrender.
  Don't expect him to throw up the sponge so easily. Turn
- To **turn one's back upon** means to abandon, to reject or refuse unceremoniously, to change to a directly opposite course :
  I am happy to note that he had turned his back upon his former vices.
- To **turn one's coat** means to change sides, to change to the opposite party. One who does this is called a turncoat.

- To **turn over a new leaf.** This means to change completely one's course of action particularly changing from bad conduct to better :
After a long career of crime, the terrorist suddenly turned over a new leaf and became a model citizen.
- To **turn a matter over in one's mind** means to consider it carefully and look at it from allsides :
You have given a very important proposal to me; I will turn the thing over in my mind and tell you about my opinion tomorrow.
- To **turn the scale.** When an item is being weighed with beam and scales, a little thing will finally make one scale or the other go down. And when a man's judgement is divided between two opinions, and something arises which makes him decide to choose one rather than the other, this is said to turn the scale.
- To **turn one's hand to** is to engage oneself in :
This handy fellow seems to be able to turn his hand to anything.
- To **turn tail** means to retreat ignominiously. It is said when a person behaves like a coward.
- To **turn the day against one;** to **turn the fortunes of the day.** These mean to reverse superiority or success :
The fall of a king from his horse in a field of battle often turned the fortunes of the day.
- To **turn the tables** on someone is to reverse his success.
- To **turn a thing to account** is to utilise it :
She had kept the trinket ..... in the hope of turning it to better account.—Dickens
- To **turn one's nose at a thing** means to treat it with contemptuous dislike or disgust :
He has been reduced almost to beggary, and yet he turns up his nose at any suggestion that he should work.
- To **turn one's head** or **one's brain** means to confuse him that he seems to have lost his judgement; to make giddy or conceited, or wild or insane :
The sudden good fortune has turned his head.
- To **have a turn for** means to have capacity or fitness for :
This boy has a turn for classical music; send him to a good school of music.

Exercises

Exercise 1

Each of the following idiom is followed by four meanings. Indicate which one is correct

(RRB Ajmer, Bhopal)

1. To put two and two together
(a) To bear the brunt of
(b) to conclude from obvious fact
(c) To put off
(d) to put on a false appearance
2. To wash dirty linen in public
(a) to quarrel openly
(b) to clean solid lines
(c) to understand the hidden meaning of the word
(d) to wash dirty clothes
3. To read between the lines
(a) to suspect
(b) to read carefully
(c) to understand the hidden meaning of the word
(d) to do useless things
4. To face the music
(a) to prepare to give a music performance
(b) to suffer evil consequences
(c) to suffer hardship
(d) to change the things
5. To leave no stone unturned
(a) to keep clean and tidy
(b) to try utmost
(c) to work enthusiastically
(d) to change the things
6. Between the devil and the deep sea
(a) a deep sea diver
(b) to be evil tempered
(c) in a dilemma
(d) a man who is drowning
7. To fight tooth and nail
(a) to fight a losing battle
(b) to fight heroically
(d) to make every possible effort to win
(d) to fight cowardly

8. To flog a dead horse
   (a) to revive interest in a subject which is out of date
   (b) to beat a horse that is dead
   (c) to do interesting things
   (d) to try to take work from a weak horse
9. To bait the hook to suit the fish
   (a) to prepare a box to pack the fish
   (b) to do things to please others
   (c) to look at things from other person's point of view
   (d) to catch fish by providing suitable food
10. To meet one's waterloo
   (a) to meet a strong adversary
   (b) to meet with humiliation
   (c) to die fighting
   (d) to meet one's final defeat

Solutions

1. (b)	**2.** (c)	**3.** (c)	**4.** (b)
5. (b)	**6.** (c)	**7.** (c)	**8.** (a)
9. (b)	**10.** (d)		

Exercise 2

In the following, pick out the correct meanings of the following idioms ***(RRB Bhopal, Mumbai)***

1. Take exception to
   (a) different
   (b) to take with difficulty
   (c) object to
   (d) difficult
2. Through thick and thin
   (a) big and small
   (b) large object
   (c) under all conditions
   (d) thin and fat
3. Sitting on the fence
   (a) unbalanced
   (b) uncomfortable
   (c) coward
   (d) etween two opinions
4. An axe to grind
   (a) difficult job
   (b) hard labour
   (c) private ends to serve
   (d) punishment
5. His wit's end
   (a) finished (b) confused
   (c) comedy (d) very intelligent
6. To be born with a silver spoon in one's mouth
   (a) to be born in a rich home
   (b) to be born in a jeweller's home
   (c) to be fed milk with a silver spoon
   (d) to be a first born child
7. A hard nut to crack
   (a) difficult things require extra effort
   (b) a difficult problem to solve
   (c) a difficult problem solved effortlessly
   (d) costly things need careful handling
8. From hand to mouth
   (a) something repeated often
   (b) consuming food
   (c) to survive without saving
   (d) hitting someone by hand on the mouth
9. To beat about the bush
   (a) not to come to the poin
   (b) vigorous search for the culprit
   (c) easily achieved success without much effort
   (d) working hard to achieve the goal
10. To burn one's fingers
   (a) to get injured in an accident
   (b) to pay a heavy price
   (c) to suffer from meddling in something
   (d) to get a burn injury on the hands

Solutions

1. (c)	**2.** (c)	**3.** (d)	**4.** (c)
5. (b)	**6.** (a)	**7.** (b)	**8.** (c)
9. (a)	**10.** (c)		

Exercise 3

In the following questions, four alternatives are given for the idioms/phrases. Choose the one which best expresses the meaning of the given idiom/phrase ***(RRB Ajmer, Kolkata, Patna)***

1. To make mince meat
   (a) copy the appearance of somebody
   (b) take care of something
   (c) refute utterly
   (d) have the same opinion
2. To carry all before one
   (a) finish quickly
   (b) make a promise
   (c) be free from danger
   (d) be completely successful
3. To run riot
   (a) befool other
   (b) be violent in action
   (c) criticise other
   (d) behave in an undisciplined way
4. To carry the conviction
   (a) be extremely fond of anything
   (b) bear the proof of the truth
   (c) feel displeasure
   (d) make overtures of reconciliation
5. To hold
   (a) show unwillingness
   (b) keep at a distance
   (c) stop by threats of violence
   (d) endure hardship or danger

6. To come round
(a) To get well
(b) to reach a roundabout
(c) to succeed
(d) to complete a circle
7. A white elephant
(a) an elephant with white skin
(b) a costly thing
(c) a costly and useful thing
(d) a costly but useless thing
8. Merry as a cricket
(a) to enjoy a game of cricket
(b) to be carefree
(c) to dance and sing
(d) to be good at sport
9. To meet one's waterloo
(a) to meet a strong adversary
(b) to die fighting
(c) to meet one's final defeat
(d) to die an ignoble death
10. To set the Thames of fire
(a) to wreak evil on something
(b) to destroy with fire
(c) to do a heroic deed
(d) to try to do the impossible
11. To smell a rat
(a) to see hidden meaning
(b) to smell bad odour
(c) to misunderstand
(d) to suspect a trick or deceit
12. To rise like a phoenix
(a) to resemble a phoenician
(b) to get up with a start
(c) to rise with a new life
(d) to rise with anger

Solutions

1. (c)	2. (d)	3. (d)	4. (b)
5. (d)	6. (d)	7. (d)	8. (b)
9. (c)	10. (c)	11. (d)	12. (d)

Exercise 4

In the following questions, out of the given alternatives, choose the one which has meaning of sense of the idiom/phrase given at the question place

(RRB Bhopal, Income Tax Inspectors)

1. On the spur of the moment
(a) at once or without any kind of deliberation
(b) in accordance with the prevailing style
(c) open to blame
(d) on the side of something undesirable
2. To go hard with one
(a) to remain neutral
(b) to be busy over trifles
(c) to be unreliable
(d) to prove a serious matter
3. To snap one's finger at
(c) to continue doing anything
(d) to stay away from something
4. To keep house
(a) to keep pace with
(b) to be silent about one's own purpose
(c) to waste time
(d) to manage the business of the household
5. To talk over
(a) to consider (b) to discuss
(c) to understand (d) to think over
6. To show one's white feather
(a) to show arrogance
(b) to show signs of cowardice
(c) seek peace
(d) to become polite
7. To rule the roost
(a) to domineer (b) to surrender
(c) to run away (d) to fight
8. To turn down
(a) give up (b) reject
(c) follow (d) throw
9. He is out and out a liar
(a) surely (b) consistently
(c) basically (d) thoroughly
10. She is a clever girl and she can put two and two together.
(a) make a formal statement
(b) took very thoughtful
(c) draw a logical conclusion
(d) count very well

Solutions

1. (a)	2. (d)	3. (b)	4. (d)
5. (b)	6. (b)	7. (a)	8. (b)
9. (d)	10. (c)		

Exercise 5

In the following questions, out of the four alternatives, choose the correct meaning of the following idioms/phrases **(Income Tax Inspectors)**

1. To cut one short
(a) to insult one
(b) to criticise one
(c) to interrupt one
(d) to love one
2. To nail one's colours to the mast
(a) to understand the fact
(b) to refuse to surrender
(c) to mishandle something
(d) to accept the proposal

3. Beside the mark
(a) out of assumptions
(b) beyond the imagination
(c) beyond the reach
(d) irrelevantly
4. To put a good face on
(a) to smile graciously
(b) to be lucky in a business
(c) to bear up courageously
(d) to treat others politely
5. A far cry
(a) a disadvantageous thing
(b) an unfounded claim
(c) a long way off
(d) a thing which is neglected by all
6. I am pissed off with the behaviour of my employers.
(a) in a very delicate state
(b) annoyed or bored
(c) to delay inordinately
(d) very pleased or happy
7. He is really up in the creek without his friends and family members
(a) in serious difficulties
(b) forced to do a very hard work
(c) in a situation of failure
(d) shy or modest
8. Will you please stop beating about the bush and tell us the truth.
(a) to talk nonsense
(b) to talk endlessly without any purpose
(c) to talk about useless things without coming to the main point
(d) telling an interesting story about a situation
9. He is a silver tongued doctor and patients listen to him.
(a) speaking in a helpful but authoritative language.
(b) speaking in a way that make people angry
(c) speaking in a way that annoy or bore the people
(d) speaking in a way that charms of persuade people
10. Every piece of furniture in her house in an apple-pie order.
(a) very neatly arranged
(b) painted in light colours
(c) kept in a disorganised way
(d) very delicately arranged.

Solutions

1. (c)	2. (b)	3. (d)
4. (c)	5. (c)	6. (b)
7. (a)	8. (c)	9. (d)
10. (a)		

Exercise 6

Use the following idioms in your own sentences **(IAS)**

1. To play with fire
2. To come across
3. To burn one's boats
4. To read between the lines
5. To live in an ivory tower
6. To differ with
7. To carry the day
8. To skip over
9. To get along
10. To fall out

Solutions

1. USA is playing with fire by helping the government of Iraq.
2. I came across that girl while I was going to USA.
3. They have burnt their boats and taken the final plunge.
4. If you read between the lines, you will find that he never meant to over rule your decision.
5. If you describe someone as living in an ivory tower, you mean that they have no knowledge or experience of the practical problems of everyday life. They don't really, in their ivory towers, understand how pernicious drug crime is.
6. The opposition differed with the government over the question of disinvestment.
7. For the time being the Congress seems to have carried the day (To be winner).
8. She should skip over the past and should reinvented a new life.
9. They seemed to be getting along fine.
10. She fell out with her husband.

Exercise 7

Use the following idioms in your own sentences **(IAS, PCS, CDS)**

1. To have an axe to grind
2. To have many irons in the fire
3. To burn one's boat
4. To play second fiddle
5. To burn the candle at both ends
6. To laugh in one's sleeve
7. To bury the hatchet
8. To keep at an arm's length
9. Through thick and thin
10. Off and on
11. The Alpha and Omega
12. Tooth and nail

Solutions

1. He suspects that your friend *has an axe to grind* in this proposal.
2. He has too *many irons in the fire* means he is involved with many activities.
3. The freedom fighter will not go back now from their decision. They *nor burnt their boats* and taken the final plunge.
4. He hates the thought of *playing second fiddle* to Ramesh. *Playing second fiddle* to someone means to be treated as less important.
5. He will soon come to road for he is *burning the candle at both ends.* (To spend lavishly)
6. He *laughed in his sleeves* at the foolish behaviour of the wife of his close friend.
7. India and Pakistan must *bury the hatchet* for the prosperity and progress of both the countries.
8. Unloyal friends must be *kept at an arm's length.*
9. I will abide by my wife *through thick and thin.*
10. I have been visiting her *off and on* (occasionally).
11. The *Alpha and Omega* of Mahatma Gandhi's life was to improve the pitiable condition of the untouchables.
12. She opposed me *tooth and nail* but could not succeeded.

Exercise 8

Given below are four alternatives for the idiom/phrase in italics in the sentence. Choose the one which best expresses the meaning of the idiom/phrase in italic **(Assistant Grade Exam, Income Tax Inspectors)**

1. We *kept our fingers crossed* till the final results were declared.
   (a) kept praying (b) waited anxiously
   (c) felt sacred (d) kept hopeful
2. The smell from the kitchen *makes my mouth water.*
   (a) makes me giddy
   (b) makes me vomit
   (c) stimulates my appetite
   (d) makes me sick
3. My friend *got the sack from* his first job.
   (a) resigned
   (b) got tired of
   (c) was dismissed from
   (d) was demoted from
4. He is accused of *sitting on the fence.*
   (a) observing the scene
   (b) confused
   (c) resting on the fence
   (d) hesitating which side to take
5. I stepped forward fully determined *to take the bull by the horns.*
   (a) to act without any hesitation
   (b) to be fully alive
   (c) to meet the danger boldly
   (d) to act without preparation
6. He was unable *to account for* the deficit in the firm's bank balance.
   (a) for give a satisfactory explanation
   (b) speak the truth about
   (c) maintain accounts properly
   (d) give the accounts for

Solutions

1. (b)	2. (c)	3. (c)	4. (d)
5. (c)	6. (a)		

Exercise 9

Make the correct meaning of the idioms from the alternatives given below **(SBI PO, CDS)**

1. Will-o-the-wisp
   (a) to cut in a childish way
   (b) acting in a follish way
   (c) to have desires unbacked by effort
   (d) anything which eludes or deceives
   (e) yearning of the spirit
2. A snake in the grass
   (a) a hidden enemy
   (b) unforeseen happening
   (c) very ferocious enemy
   (d) unrecognizable danger
   (e) an reliable person.
3. To look down one's nose at
   (a) to show anger
   (b) to backbite
   (c) to insult in the presence of other
   (d) to regard with half-hidden displeasure or contempt
   (e) none of these
4. Hobson's choice
   (a) excellent choice
   (b) no choice at all because their is only one thing to take or not
   (c) choice to live or die
   (d) big man's choice
   (e) first choice
5. To have a chip on one's shoulder
   (a) to be boastful
   (b) to be deserving of piece
   (c) to have treated unfairly
   (d) to have deep cut wound on the shoulder
   (e) signs on the shoulder showing timidity
6. To meet one's Waterloo
   (a) to meet a strong adversary
   (b) to die an ignoble death
   (c) to meet one's final death
   (d) to die fighting
   (e) to meet with humiliation

7. To flog a dead horse
(a) to try to achieve an impossible thing
(b) to try to table work from a weak horse
(c) to beat a horse that is dead
(d) to revive interest in a subject which is out of date
(e) to act in a foolish way
8. To be lost in the cloud
(a) to be concealed from the view
(b) to find oneself in a very uncomfortable position
(c) to be perplexed
(d) to fly deep in the clouds
(e) to meet with one's clouds
9. To fish in troubled waters
(a) to indulge in evil conspiracies
(b) to aggravate the situation
(c) to be perplexed
(d) to catch fish in disturbed waters
(e) to make the most of a bad bargain
10. To make the wind out of another's sails
(a) to defect the motives of another
(b) to cause harm to another
(c) to anticipate another and to gain advantage over him
(d) to manoeuvre to mislead another on the high seas
(e) none of these
11. To wrangle over an ass's shadow
(a) to do something funny
(b) to quarrel over the possession of an ass
(c) to waste time on pretty things
(d) to quarrel over trifles
(e) to act in a foolish way
12. To fly off the handle
(a) to dislocate
(b) to be indifferent
(c) to lose one's temper
(d) to be airborne
(e) to act in a way unmindful of consequences
13. To bring one's eggs to a bad market
(a) to fail in one's plans because one goes to the wrong people for help
(b) to bring one's commodities to a market where there is no demand for them.
(c) to show one's talent before audience which is incapable of appreciating them
(d) tzo face a humiliating situation
(e) to act when the opportunity is lost

Solutions

1. (d) 2. d) 3. (d) 4. (b)
5. (c) 6. (c) 7. (a) 8. (c)
9. (e) 10. (c) 11. (d) 12. (c)
13. (a)

Exercise 10

Frame sentences to bring out the meaning of the following **(PCS)**

1. on the horns of a dilemma
2. a wild goose chase
3. take a leaf out of somebody's book
4. play into someone's hands
5. jack of all trades
6. to nip in the bud
7. in accordance with
8. to take to one's heels
9. to bear up
10. through trick and thin

Solutions

1. Mahatma Gandhi and other leaders were *on the horns of a dilemma* at the time of the division of the country in 1947.
2. He wondered if his boss had deliberately sent him on *a wild goose chase.* (Searching for a thing that have no chance to be found.)
3. The young generation must *take a leaf out of old generation's books* in the matter of observing moral values.
4. The terrorists are *playing into our enemy's hands.*
5. Ramesh is *jack of all trades* but master of none.
6. Unlawful activities must be *nipped in the bud.*
7. The Assam accord was not in *accordance with* the expectations of the common mass.
8. When he saw the police, he *took to his heels.*
9. In present time of uncertainty one must be ready *to bear up* against all disasters and misfortunes.
10. Good friends abide with each other *through thick and thin.*

Exercise 11

Frame sentences to bring out the meaning of the following **(PCS)**

1. to curry favour
2. to bury the hatchet
3. an apple of discord
4. to blow one's own trumpet
5. a man of show
6. a wild goose chase
7. take to heels
8. in the long run
9. to be up and doing
10. to make up one's mind

Solutions

1. It seems that by presenting such a costly gift, he is *trying to curry* favour with her.

2. It is believed that the Naxalites will *bury the hatchet* once the accord is reached.
3. Reservation to the Muslims is *an apple of discord* between the government and Hindup rotagonists.
4. One should not always *blow one's trumpet.*
5. He is merely a *man of show,* the real boss is his elder brother.
6. The police went to Assam in search of the killers, but the journey proved to *be a wild goose chase.*
7. As he saw her father, he *took to his heels.*
8. Honesty and sincerity pay *in the long run.*
9. One must be *up and doing* if one wish to achieve success in life.
10. Mrs Soniya Gandhi has made *up her mind* to fight the BJP.

Exercise 12

Frame sentences to bring out the meaning of the following ***(IAS, PCS)***

1. hold out an olive branch
2. read between the lines
3. to beat about the bush
4. off and on
5. win the rubber
6. out of the wood
7. to make a clean breast of
8. to be at loggerheads
9. to lose heart
10. bury the hatchet

Solutions

1. The Bush administration is *holding out an olive branch* in the matter of Iraq.
2. He was unable to *read between the lines* to get the true meaning of the letter.
3. It is of no use to *beat about the bush* before the interview board.
4. I visit my native place *off and on.*
5. The Australians have *won the rubber.*
6. Kashmir is still not *out of the wood.*
7. This militant *made a clean breast of* the secrets before the Suprintendent of Police.
8. USA and Iraq are *at loggerheads* now-a-days.
9. We should never *lose hearts* in adverse circumstances.
10. India and Pakistan must *bury the hatchet* for the peace and prosperity of both the nations.

Exercise 13

Frame sentences to bring out the meaning of the following ***(IAS, PCS)***

1. ill at ease
2. man of letters
3. prime of life
4. to fish in troubled waters
5. a burning question
6. to turn over a new leaf
7. to laugh in one's sleeves
8. a wild goose chase
9. toe the line
10. in full swing

Solutions

1. The Finance Minister is *ill at ease* in his new office under the present financial crisis.
2. Dr Abdul Kalam, the president of India, is a *man of letters.*
3. He is a young man. He is in the *prime of life.*
4. When two countries fight with each other, the other nations try to *fish in troubled waters.*
5. The Kashmir problem is a *burning question.*
6. The notorious terrorist Saudagar Lal *turned over a new leaf* of life by starting a new business.
7. He *laughed in his sleeves* at the foolish behaviour for his boss' wife.
8. India's effort to establish peace between Iraq and USA was *a wild goose chase.*
9. India refused *to toe the line* of USA in the matter of Iraq.
10. The trade fair is *in full swing* at Pragati Maidan.

Exercise 14

Frame sentences to bring out the meaning of the following ***(IAS, PCS)***

1. at the eleventh hour
2. bag and baggage
3. a red letter day
4. to play the second fiddle
5. to burn the candle at both ends
6. turn down
7. to show the white feather
8. an apple of discord
9. the sword of democles
10. at sixes and sevens

Solutions

1. The police party reached there *at the eleventh hour.*
2. People are leaving Kashmir *bag and baggage.*
3. 26th January is *a red letter day* in the history of India.
4. I do not like *to play the second fiddle* in any matter.
5. He will soon be in trouble for he is *burning the candle at both ends.*
6. My request for leave has been *turned down* by the boss.
7. When Ramesh asked him to argue in public he *showed the white feather.*
8. Kashmir is *an apple of discord* between India and Pakistan.
9. The fear of a war between India and Pakistan is hanging like a *sword of Democles* on the citizens of both the countries.
10. A thief entered my quarter and left everything *at sixes and sevens.*

Exercise 15

Frame sentences to bring out the meaning of the following **(PCS)**

1. null and void
2. on the horns of a dilemma
3. ad hoc
4. take your time
5. a cold war
6. hot line
7. a red letter day
8. to mince words
9. to have no axe to grind
10. a bone of contention
11. to have many irons in the fire
12. a public secret

Solutions

1. The recent Act for granting reservation based on religion was declared *null and void* by the court.
2. The political parties were on *the horns of a dilemma* on the point of granting reservation to the upper class.
3. She was given *ad hoc* posting.
4. You must take *your own time* to take final decision in the matter.
5. *A cold* war has been continuing between India and Pakistan since long.
6. There is a *hot line* (telephone line) between India and Pakistan.
7. August 15, is *a red letter day* in the history of India.
8. A sycophant always minces words of flattery before his boss.
9. He has *no axe to grind* in this project, whatever is being done by him, is in the name of humanity.
10. Kashmir has been *a bone of contention* betwen India and Pakistan since long.
11. He is a man of multiple business. He has *many irons in the fire.*
12. The murder of the college girl is a *public secret* now.

Exercise 16

Frame sentences to bring out the meaning of the following ***(IAS)***

1. break the ice
2. keep the wolf from the door
3. make hay while the sun shines
4. a rainy day
5. cry over spilt milk
6. kill two birds with one stone
7. a wet blanket
8. cold blood
9. blow one's own trumpet
10. fall upon
11. put the eggs in one basket

Solutions

1. India and Pakistan have *broken the ice by playing* cricket matches after a long interval.
2. The poor have to put a daily fight to *keep the wolf from the door.*
3. He is a successful businessman. He believes in making *hay while the sun shines.*
4. He is a prudent man. He believes in saving for *a rainy day.*
5. It is useless to cry *over spilt milk* now.
6. By asking the opposition to support the bill P.M. slapped his critics. Thus he *killed two birds with one stone.*
7. Ramesh is *a wet blanket,* do not include him in the list of picnic goers.
8. *Cold blooded* murders have become very common now-a-days.
9. Some leaders are in the habit of *blowing their own trumpet.*
10. He will have to *fall upon* me for help.
11. One must play safe and so must not *put* all *eggs in one basket.*

Exercise 17

Choose the correct meanings of the following idioms from the alternatives given below ***(SBI PO)***

1. To fight tooth and nail
   (a) making every possible effort to win
   (b) to fight cowardly
   (c) to fight heroically
   (d) to fight a losing battle
   (e) to lose every thing while engaged in fighting

2. To let the grass grow under one's feet *(SBI PO)*
(a) to miss the opportunity
(b) to let things go on in their natural way
(c) to be indolent and let others take advantage of one's indolence
(d) to idle away the time; to delay and linger
(e) to move very cautiously in order to avoid harming anything

3. Melting pot *(CDS)*
(a) an earthen vessel
(b) a cooking utensil
(c) an iron cauldron
(d) a witch's brewing pot
(e) circumstances in which things may changed greatly

4. To be a good Samaritan *(CDS)*
(a) a religious person
(b) a genuinely charitable person
(c) to be obedient
(d) a citizen of Samaritan
(e) to be law abiding

5. To fly off the handle *(CDS)*
(a) to dislocate
(b) to lose one's temper
(c) to take off
(d) to be airborne
(e) to be indifferent

6. The Alpha and Omega *(CDS)*
(a) a Shakespearean play
(b) beginning and end
(c) a Greek song
(d) a Swiss watch
(e) a beautiful object

7. To rise like a Phoenix *(CDS)*
(a) to resemble a phoenician
(b) rise with a new life
(c) to rise with anger
(d) to get up with start
(e) to stand up with royal gait

8. Merry as a cricket *(CDS)*
(a) to enjoy a game of cricket
(b) to dance and sing
(c) to be carefree
(d) to be extremely cheerful
(e) to be good at sports

9. Between the devil and the deep sea *(CDS)*
(a) in a dilemma
(b) a man who is drowning
(c) a deep sea diver
(d) near the coast line
(e) to be evil tempered

10. To make one's pile *(CDS)*
(a) to construct one's house
(b) to make a successful career
(c) to make a fortune
(d) to keep up rubbish
(e) to hit one's target

11. To blaze a trail *(CDS)*
(a) to set on fire
(b) to blow the trumpet
(c) to be annoyingly noise
(d) to initiate work
(e) to be vehemently opposed

12. Gift of the cab *(CDS)*
(a) talent for speaking
(b) to win a prize
(c) to get something free
(d) to distribute gifts
(e) talent for dancing

Solutions

1. (a)	**2.** (d)	**3.** (e)	**4.** (b)
5. (b)	**6.** (b)	**7.** (b)	**8.** (e)
9. (a)	**10.** (b)	**11.** (d)	**12.** (a)

Unit 30

Some Important Proverbs

- **Between the devil and the deep sea:** To choose between two equally bad alternatives in a serious dilemma.
- **Where there's a will there's a way:** When a person really wants to do something, he will find a way of doing it.
- **A burnt child dreads fire:** A bad experience or a horrifying incident may scar one's attitude or thinking for a lifetime.
- **First come, first served:** The first in line will be attended to first.
- **A friend in need is a friend indeed:** A friend who helps when one is in trouble is a real friend.
- **Discretion is the better part of valour:** If you say discretion is the better part of valour, you mean that avoiding a dangerous or unpleasant situation is sometimes the most sensible thing to do.
- **A hungry man is an angry man:** A person who does not get what he wants or needs is a frustrated person and will be easily provoked to rage.
- **Empty vessels make the most noise:** Those people who have a little knowledge usually talk the most and make the greatest fuss.
- **A man is as old as he feels:** A person's age is immaterial—it is only when he thinks and feels that he is ageing that he actually becomes old.
- **Great talkers are little doers:** Those people who talk a lot and are always teaching others usually do not do much work.
- **An idle mind is the devil's workshop:** One who has nothing to do will be tempted to do many mischievous acts.
- **An ounce of discretion is worth a pound of wit:** It is better to be careful and discrete than to be clever.
- **Faint heart never won fair lady:** To succeed in life one must have the courage to pursue what he wants.
- **A penny saved is a penny gained:** By being thrifty one will be able to save much.
- **A rolling stone gathers no moss:** A person who never settles in one place or who often changes his job will not succeed in life; one who is always changing his mind will never get anything done.
- **As you sow, so you shall reap:** One will either enjoy or suffer the consequences of his earlier actions or inactions.
- **Barking dogs seldom bite:** Those who make loud threats seldom carry them out.
- **Better late than never:** To do something that is right, profitable or good a little late is still better than not doing it at all.
- **A bird in hand is worth two in the bush:** Something that one already has is better than going after something seemingly more worthwhile that one may not be able to get.
- **Birds of a feather flock together:** People of the same sort of character or belief always go together.
- **Call a spade a spade:** If you say that someone calls a spade a spade, you mean that they

speak frankly and directly, often about embarrassing or unpleasant subjects; an informal expression.

- **Charity begins at home:** A person's first obligation should be to help the member of his own family before he can begin thinking of talking about helping others.
- **Dead men tell no lies:** Often used as an argument for killing someone whose knowledge of a secret may cause one loss or get into serious trouble.
- **A great talker is a great liar:** A smooth and persuasive talker may be a good liar.
- **Every cloud has a silver lining:** If you say that every cloud has a silver lining, you mean that every sad or unpleasant situation has a positive side to it. If you talk about silver lining you are talking about something positive that comes out of a sad or unpleasant situation.
- **All that glitters is not gold:** Do not be deceived by things or offers that appear to be attractive.
- **Eat to live, but do not live to eat:** Man was created for a divine purpose and he has a destiny with his Creator—he was not born just to enjoy food.
- **Don't put all your eggs in one basket:** One should not risk everything he has in a single venture.
- **Every dog has its day:** Everyone will get a period of success or satisfaction during his lifetime.
- **Every one can find fault, few can do better:** It is easier to find fault in other people's actions or methods than to do it properly or correctly.
- **Any time means no time:** When an event is not decided on or planned earlier it will never take place.
- **Fair exchange is no robbery:** A contract is fair as long as both the parties understand and agree to the conditions willingly; after a deal is closed neither side can turn around and say that he was unfairly treated.
- **Fire is a good servant but a bad master:** Fire, like any other manmade tool or device, will serve man well only when it is controlled and used wisely.
- **Actions speak louder than words:** Children usually learn more from the examples set by their elders than from what they are told; a person's character is judged by the thing she does and not by what he says; actions give evidence or proof of.
- **Fortune knocks once at every man's door:** Everyone gets at least one good opportunity in his lifetime; everyone has the opportunity to be successful in life.
- **Give the devil his due:** Be just and fair-minded, even to the one who does not deserve much or who is unfriendly or unfair; we should punish a person according to his wrongdoings.
- **God helps those who help themselves:** God only helps those people who work hard and make an honest effort.
- **It's an ill wind that blows nobody any good:** A bad or evil occurrence.
- **Great minds think alike:** Wise people will normally think and behave alike in certain situations.
- **Habit is second nature:** An act done repeatedly and often enough will sooner or later become a habit or second nature.
- **He laughs best who laughs last:** A person who does the best is the one who will get the greatest satisfaction in the end.
- **Never do things by halves:** One should not do an incomplete or imperfect job. Certain tasks must not be left half done; they must be done away with immediately.
- **Great haste makes great waste:** If one does things hastily he will make a lot of mistakes—he will need to spend a lot of time correcting those mistakes later.
- **It's never too late to mend :** It is never too late to correct one's mistakes or faults.
- **It's no use crying over spilt milk:** It is pointless to feel remorseful over a thing lost that can never be found or a mistake done that can never be corrected or rectified.
- **Still waters run deep:** One who is usually silent and goes about his business quietly may be a very wise person.
- **Jack of all trades and master of none:** A person who can do almost anything, but he rarely excels in any of them.

- **Let bygones by bygones** : One should consider forgiving and forgeting all the bad deeds done by others.
- **Let not the pot call the kettle black:** A person who has a fault should not point out the same fault in another; do not criticise another person as you may have the same weakness.
- **Let sleeping dogs lie :** One should preferably avoid discussing issues that are likely to create trouble.
- **No news is good news:** When there is no news, it is likely that everything is all right.
- **Look before you leap:** Avoid acting hastily, without considering the possible consequences.
- **Necessity is the mother of invention :** When a person is in great need of something, he will find a way of getting it.
- **Honesty is the best policy:** Being honest is believed to be the best route to take.
- **One man's meat is another man's poison:** No two persons are alike—every one has his own preferences, likes and dislikes.
- **Once bitten twice shy:** If a person has been tricked once he will more be careful and alert the next time.
- **Like father, like son; like mother, like daughter:** Used to describe a child's behavior when he or she acts like the father or mother.
- **Practice makes perfect :** It is believed that if one practices a certain skill often, he will excel in it.
- **Prevention is better than cure:** It is better to be careful beforehand than to try to solve a problem after it has arisen.
- **Rome was not built in a day:** Any great plan or big dream cannot be achieved overnight or easily.
- **Robbing Peter to pay Paul:** (this is quoted when one takes another loan to pay off an earlier loan) taking from one to give another.
- **Spare the rod and spoil the child:** A child who is not punished and showed the error of his ways will become unruly.
- **Speech is silver, silence is golden:** Talk may be beneficial, but sometimes acquiescence may be the best option to take.
- **It takes two to make a quarrel:** Both parties in a quarrel should share the blame or take responsibility for it; no one can start a quarrel all by himself.
- **Strike while the iron is hot:** Seize a good opportunity as quickly as possible.
- **There's no smoke without fire:** Rumours do not spread unless there is some element of truth in them.
- **Time and tide wait for none:** Time is precious, once it is past no one can go back and claim it thus everyone should be mindful of how his time is spent.
- **To err is human, to forgive divine:** It is only normal for man to make mistakes and do wrong, but for one to forgive another for his wrong is indeed great and gracious act.
- **What's done can't be undone:** In life there are some things once done or decisions once made cannot be changed; malicious words once uttered or harmful actions once done cannot be taken back.
- **Two heads are better than one:** It is always better to get the view of another than to rely entirely on one's own judgment.
- **When in Rome do as the Romans do:** When one is in a new place, country or situation he must adapt himself to the new manners and customs.
- **When the cat is away the mice will play:** When law enforcers are not present, certain public members will take the opportunity to break the law.
- **Absence makes the heart grow fonder:** One usually desires another more when he or she is far away.

Unit

31

Specific Use of Words (*Similar Meanings*)

- **Abstain (from a thing)** : Throughout one should abstain from smoking in public.
  Refrain (from doing) : One should refrain from making unwarranted comments.
- **Revenge (to return injury for injury)** : She revenged herself upon Ramesh, her former lover.
  Avenge (to punish the evil doers) : He has devoted the past three years to avenge his daughter's death.
- **Allow (giving permission for otherwise unreasonable thing)** : The girls were allowed to talk in the class by the Principal.
  Permit (to give a positive assent) : I was permitted to appear in the M.A. examination.
- **Anger (a sudden feeling of unhappiness)** : The people showed great anger at the news.
  Resentment (more lasting fooling of unhappiness) : My words could not lessen her resentment.
- **Atain (to get by labour)** : We attained a high degree of success through quality management.
  Acquire (to have something permanently) : The students of this section have acquired a thorough knowledge of Naturopathy.
- **Ancient (opposite to modern)** : We can learn a lot by the events of ancient history of India.
  Old (opposed to new and to young) : The old dressing pattern is liked by the people even today. Old people prefer simplicity to show.
- **Admit (to acknowledge as true)** : He did not admit that he was present in the house.
  Confess (to acknowledge responsibility or guilt) : He confessed that he had stolen the bike.
- **Anger (sudden feeling)** : He showed great anger on his sudden departure from the party.
  Resentment (more lasting feeling) : Your assurances cannot lessen his resentment.
- **Reply (to a letter)** : He always replies in time.
  Answer (to a question) : Answer only five questions.
- **Ability (intellectual quality)** : He is promoted on the basis of his ability to perform in a better way.
  Capacity (capable to hold or achieve) : His capacity to work, regularly is praiseworthy.
- **Surprise (when something unexpected happens)** : He was surprised to see the result.
  Astonishment (extreme surprise) : I was astonished to see my ex-peon maintaining a car.
  Wonder (surprise with admiration) : I wondered at his securing first position at all India level.
- **Bravery (in the blood)** : The bravery of Rajputs is well known.
  Courage (in mind) : He has the courage to speak the truth.
  Valour (a quality more than bravery or courage) : The black commandoes are known for their deeds of valour.
  Daring (rash) : He is daring but not prude

Boldness (a shortlived quality) : He showed his boldness in catching the robber single handed.

- **Battle (a contest between two opposing armies)** : The third battle of Panipat was the last nail in the coffin of the Mughal Empire.

  War (a series of contests continued for a long time) : The World War I and II saw the pinnacle of inhumane face of the weapons made by the men.

- **Begin (used on all occasions)** : The sooner you begin the better it is.

  Commence (used only in official and formal language) : The examinations will commence on the 25th of May.

- **Beautiful (used for girls)** : She is a beautiful girl.

  Handsome (used for man) : He is a handsome boy.

- **Custom (relates to community or society)** : Wearing kumkum after marriage is a custom among the Hindus.

  Habit (relates to individual) : Smoking is a bad habit.

- **Crime (against law of the state)** : Theft is a crime.

  Vice (offence against morals) : Drinking is a vice.

  Sin (against law of religion or society) : Abusing elders is a sin.

- **Ceiling (inner portion of roof)** : I want to purchase one ceiling fan.

  Roof (upper covering of house) : They are playing at the roof of their house.

- **Cite (is used for things or persons)** : He cited the authority of the Supreme Court Judgement.

  Quote (is used for things only) : He quoted passage after passage from Geeta.

- **Compulsion (is physical, what is generally against our wishes)** : He was compelled by the court to be present on the next date of hearing.

  Obligation (is moral; what is imposed on us as a duty) : We are obliged to maintain those who depend on us.

- **Confer (conferring is an act of authority)** : The government confers titles like Bharat Ratna, Padma Bhushan etc. on eminent persons.

  Bestow (an act of generosity/charity) : Many presents were bestowed on the refugees.

- **Character (mental or moral nature)** : A man of character overcomes all temptations.

  Conduct (one's actions) : None can blame you if your conduct is good.

- **Contentment (inner satisfaction when nothing more is required)** : Actual happiness consists in contentment.

  Satisfaction (fulfillment of one's desire) : She completed the preparations to my entire satisfaction.

- **Contagious (disease spread by contact)** : Small pox is a contagious disease.

  Infectious (disease spread through air or mosquitoes) : Malaria is an infectious disease.

- **Cool (pleasant feeling)** : A cool wind is blowing.

  Cold (unpleasant feeling) : Weather is very cold today.

- **Defend (against an attack)** : Indian army is capable of defending the nation against any attack.

  Protect (relates to an approaching injury) : Woollen clothes protect us from cold.

- **Deny (relates to a past a action)** : He denied his involvement in the murder.

  Refuse (relates to a future action) : He refused to lend me any money.

- **Doubt (a negative feeling)** : I doubt his loyalty (I think that he is not loyal).

  Suspect (a positive feeling) : I suspect his involvement in the crime. (I am thinking that he was not involvement.)

- **Discover (relates to thing already in existence)** : A new star was discovered by him.

  Invent (a new thing is created) : Who invented telephone?

- **Drown (relates to living beings)** : Many persons drowned in this river last year.

  Sink (relates to things) : A ship dashed against this rock and sank last year.

- **Wish (used in reference to a remote thing)** : I wish, I were a king!

  Desire (used in reference to achievable things) : I desire to have a beautiful house and a name in the society.

- **Want (relates to a thing, which is absent) :** I want to buy a car.
  Need (relates to necessary things) : I need a pen to write with.
  Require (to demand) : You are required to attend the meeting.
- **Envy (bad feeling) :** He is envious of his friend's prosperity.
  Jealousy (positive feeling of possessing something) : I am jealous of our ancestral heritage.
- **Sufficient (necessary for) :** Two persons are sufficient for this job.
  Enough (more than necessary) : I have enough money for the education of my children.
- **Accident (an unexpected happening) :** Train accidents have become common now-a-days.
  Incident (an ordinary occurrence) : Our newspapers are full of daily incidents.
  Event (an important happening) : The third battle of Panipat was an important event in the history of India.
- **Notorious (in bad sense) :** He is a notorious cheat.
  Famous (in good sense) : New York is famous for multi-storeyed buildings.
  Renowned (high reputation) : Shakespeare was a renowned dramatist.
- **Excuse (courteously used for trifle matters) :** Please excuse me for troubling you at this time.
  Forgive (used for comparatively big offences) : Please forgive me for my speaking ill about your friend.
  Pardon (generally used for asking repetition of something) : I beg your pardon (Please repeat, I was unable to understand earlier.)
- **Freedom (implies absence of restraint) :** We enjoy several kinds of freedom.
  Liberty (implies previous restraint) : The prisoners were set at liberty.
- **Falsehood (something said or done with wrong intentions) :** He was guilty of falsehood when he spoke against the character of the chairman.
  Lie (speak untrue words) : Never tell a lie.
- **House (refer to a dwelling unit) :** I am going to purchase a new house.
  Home (place to live with family association) : Men make houses, women make homes.
- **Listen (to hear attentively) :** The teacher asked the students to listen.
  Hear (to get through ears) : I am hearing your voice.
- **Hope (is used when what we anticipate is welcome) :** I hope to get selected this time.
  Expect (is used when what we anticipate is certain whether welcome or not) : Every student is expected to carry out the instructions given in the notes.
- **Hardly (refers to degree) :** You can hardly imagine how much I suffered because of her allegation.
  Scarcely (refers to quantity) : Don't ask me for milks, I have scarcely enough for my own use.
- **Idle (having nothing to do, due to circumstances) :** He has been sitting idle due to great slump in the market.
  Lazy (habit of not doing things in active manner) : He is too lazy to reply letters.
- **Sick (mental feeling) :** He is a sick man)
  Ill (out of health) : She is ill nowadays.
  Libel (written) : His statement in the press release amounts to libel.
  Slander (spoken) : His public speech was taken note of and an action for slander is being initiated.
  Oral (spoken words) : He was failed in oral examination.
  Verbal (written words) : Teachers were abused verbally and assaulted physically.
  Presume (pre decision of a thing) : I presume he is responsible for the loss in business.
  Assume (Assuming anything true) : I assume he will help you in case of need.
- **Place (to put) :** Place the keys on the chair.
  Keep (to put at some defined place) : Keep the books on the table.
- **Possible (can be done) :** It is not possible to reach there by car.
  Probable (likely to happen) : It is probable that she may agree with our proposal.
- **Blunder (a gross mistake) :** Disclosing business secrets to the rivals is a blunder on your part.
  Mistake (small act) : It is a mistake to go on leave without taking prior permission.
  Error (doing things against the recognise norms) : Your essay is full of grammatical errors.

- **Praise (for actions)** : His actions are praiseworthy.
  Admire (for qualities) : Everybody admires him for his benevolent nature.
- **Prohibit (has force of law)** : The government has prohibited the cow slaughter.
  Forbid (relating to personal life) : Forbidden fruits are more sweet.
- **Recollect (remember after some efforts)** : Can you recollect what exact words did he use?
  Remember (having in memory) : I remember his words well.
- **Regret (for a thing done or left undone)** : I felt regret for not completing the job in time.
  Sorrow (for big harm or evil) : Her husband's death caused her deep sorrow.
- **Redress (to correct something wrong)** : A victim looks to the court for redress.
  Relief (feeling happiness because something wrong did not happen) : I breathed a sigh of relief.
- **Rob (to take away by force)** : He was robbed of his money and jewellery.
  Steal (to take away secretly) : The thieves stole away all the goods of my house last Sunday.
- **Talk (speaking with others)** : I want to talk to him in this matter.
  Tell (to inform) : He tells me to wear neat dress.
  Speak (to say in ordinary way) : He speaks loudly.
  Say (to assert) : How did you say so ?
- **Seem (something assumed by our mind)** : The moon seems moving very fast.
  Appear (impression of objects on us) : The statue appears to be of ancient time.
- **See (in an ordinary way)** : I can see that house.
  Look (see with some attention) : Look at that house.
  Watch (to observe closely) : Keep a watch on that house.
- **Scenery (a view of landscape)** : The scenery of Manali is indeed beautiful.
  Scene (a place of any happening, a landscape) : He captured many beautiful scenes in his camera.
- **Treaty (a written or formal arrangement)** : India and the Usa have signed a treaty.
  Truce (a temporary suspension of conflict) : On New Year eve there was a truce between the fighting militant groups.
- **Trifling ('no importance' matter)** : She never neglects even a trifling matter.
  Trivial (a small matter, no seriousness) : Do not waste your time on trivial details.
- **Trade (small or large scale buying selling; it can be within or out of the country)** : India has a long history of trade with USA.
  Commerce (on a large scale; generally with foreign countries) : They have made their fortune from industry and commerce.
- **Empty (having nothing in it) : The briefcase is empty.**
  Vacant (having some occupancy) : Only one berth is vacant in this compartment.

Unit

32

Use of Words : Good and Bad Sense

Use of Words in Bad Sense

Certain words and phrases are never used in good sense. To use these words where a good sense is meant will be ridiculous. It would be ridiculous to say : 'He is a notorious scientist,' or 'He concocted a good plan for the welfare of the poor.' Some of such words in common use are given hereunder. Students should learn these words well and try to understand the difference. Mere Hindi meanings of these words is not sufficient to use these words properly.

accident — They met with an accident.

accomplice — Partner in some crime. He was an accomplice in the theft.

addicted — To some bad habit, drinking, gambling etc.

adversary — An opponent : one who can cause harm.

airs — He should not give himself airs (conceited = airs).

apprehensive — Of some danger, loss or injury.

artisan — Who practises some art of inferior nature.

blunder — A very serious mistake.

catastrophe — A disastrous happening.

coalition — Of men of divergent or opposite views : It refers a kind of partnership which is not homogeneous.

commit — To do something wrong : as to commit a suicide.

concoct — To make a plan for an evil purpose.
He concocted a false story to deceive her.

counterfeit — To imitate for a unlawful purpose.Counterfeit notes.

concubine — A woman having sexual relations with many persons.

cunning — Doing things cleverly but in a deceiving manner.

credulity — A simpleton readiness to believe easily.

dictator — A despot ruler , uses brutal force.

despot — A tyrannical kind of ruler.

demagogue — An unprincipled leader or a ring leader.

effeminate — Womanly ('feminine' and 'womanly are used in good sense).

fabricate — To invent with a bad motive. He fabricated a false story.

fancy — Imaginations which are not guided by reason.

fine figure — He cuts a fine figure (disgraceful or ridiculous figure)
(The phrase 'fine figure' is ironical.)

fulsome — Full or excessive, so as to produce disgust, hatred.

glaring — Conspicuous or something evil, as glaring error.

hasty — Quick to fault; rash, easily excited; patience less.

inveterate — Used for something bad, as 'an inveterate liar,' 'an inveterate enemy'.

loiter — To lin ger at a time when greater haste is required.

lonely — Depressed or sad from being alone.

minion — An unworthy favourite.
notorious — Evil reputation.
perpetrate — Used only for crimes or offences.
plight — A sad or painful condition. 'She is in a sad plight.'
pocket — To put into one's pocket fraudulently, as 'He pocketed the money fraudulently.'
prone — To some vice or weakness as 'He is prone to fever.'
sheer — Used as 'sheer nonsense', 'sheer folly'. We never say 'sheer virtue' but perfect or pure virtue.'
shrewd — Clever, but often in a sense implying some dishonesty or cunningness.
to a degree — 'He is insolent or dishonest to a degree (of high degree). This phrase is usually applied to some bad quality.
totally — Always used for something bad; as 'totally incompetent', 'totally blind'.
trivial — Things of little importance. A trivial or common place subject.
utter — An utter fool, an utter failure (always used for something bad).

Words Used in a Good Sense

Some words and phrases are used in a good sense only, so students should learn the proper use of these words and nouns. Mere knowledge of Hindi meanings of these words will not suffice to use them in proper manner. Students must learn the proper use of these words.

age — She is of age (= grown up). She is under age (= a minor).
breed — He is a man of (high) breed (= a well-breed man).
bosom — He is my bosom (fast friend) friend.
family — He is a man of (high) family.
feeling — He is a man of (tender and good) feeling.
famous — He is a famous artist.
form — The boatman pulled together in form (= in good form or style).
order — Everything is in (proper) order.
place — Everything was in place (= in its right place).
position — He is a man of (good) position.
principle — He is a man of (high) principles.
quality — He is a person of (good or high) quality.
renowned — Shakespeare was a renowned dramatist.
rank — Man of (high) rank.
taste — His remark was not in taste (= in good taste).
temper — He is out of temper (= ordinary or good temper). (But in 'temper' or in a temper' means in bad temper; as, 'She said all that in a temper = in a rage').
time — He arrived in time (= at the proper or right time).

Unit 33

Paronyms

In English we find several words which are derived from the same root word. These words differ slightly in form but in many cases the meaning differ a lot. Such words are also called Paronyms.

- **alternate** (by turn) : He comes here on alternate days.
  alternative (choice between two things) : There were alternative methods of travel available.
- **acceptance** (accepting a thing) : I am happy to learn that she has given her consent for the attending the court.
  acceptation (interpretation) : There are several acceptations of the word 'Nature'.
- **access** (approach) : I was not allowed access to a lawyer.
  accession (becoming sovereign) : Today is the 50th anniversary of the queen's accession to the throne.
- **act** (to do) : I shall act as per the wishes of my parents.
  action (doing things) : His timely action saved him from the loss.
- **admission** (being admitted) : He has taken admission in evening college.
  admittance (to let in) : He was denied admittance in the hall.
- **artist** (performer of fine art) : A poet is no less an artist than a sculpture.
  artiste (performer in singing, dancing etc.) : The group of five consists of several artistes.
- **artistic** (having aesthetic values) : This painting is indeed very artistic.
  artful (cunning, clever) : He wants to achieve success by artful means.
  artificial (antonym of natural) : City life is becoming more artificial day by day.
  artisan (well versed in hardicrafts) : The artisans of Nepal are very hardworking and efficient.
- **appropriation** (to take possession of) : He was charged for appropriation of Bank's fund.
  appropriateness (suitability) : The work of Harivansh Rai Bachchan is renowned for its appropriateness in style.
- **affecting** (touching, pathetic) : The movie has many affecting scenes and situations.
  affectation (false pretense) : Political leaders speak with affectation and artfulness.
- **besides** (in addition) : Besides paying my debt he also gave me money for the medicines.
  beside (by the side) : In Republic Day function none was sitting beside President.
- **barbaric** (simple, used in good sense) : I like her barbaric simplicity.
  barbarian (primitive) : 'Johar' and 'Sati' are the barbarian customs.
  barbarous (cruel : used in bad sense) : War is indeed a barbarous act.
- **barbarism** (uncivilised condition) : In some part of Bihar, absolute arbarism prevailed even now-a-days.
  barbarity (cruelty) : Aurangzeb was notorious for his barbarity.
- **confident** (certain) : I am confident that she will come.

confidant (reliable) : He is a cheat, don't make him your confident.

- **completion** (end) : After completion of this work you are to go to Kolkata.
  completeness (perfection) : None can claim completeness of knowledge in any field.
- **ceremonious** (overdone formalities) : His greetings and salutations are too ceremonious.
  ceremonial (pertaining to ceremony) : Diwali is a ceremonial occasion for Hindus.
- **comprehensive** (involves all aspects) : This book gives us comprehensive knowledge of English.
  comprehensible (understandable) : His views on this subject are not only clear but comprehensible also.
- **considerable** (much) : I have spent a considerable time in solving this problem.
  considerate (thoughtful) : He being a considerate man, can't refuse to sign this proposal.
- **continuous** (uninterrupted) : He has been continuously working on computer for the last three hours.
  continual (occasional breaks) : There has been continual raining since yesterday.
- **child-like** (in good sense act like a child) : Her child-like face attracts everybody.
  childish (in bad sense : silly act) : His childish habits annoyed everybody.
- **complacent** (pleasing look) : Indian farmer are complacent in their look.
  complaisant (polite) : She is a complaisant and intelligent girl.
- **dependent** (to rely on) : I am not dependent on anybody for my livelihood.
  dependant (depend on others) : My younger brother is dependant on me.
- **disinterested** (without self interest) : Mother Teresa rendered disinterested service to downtrodden.
  uninterested (indifferent) : Amitabh is uninterested in politics.
- **divers** (who swim under the water) : Divers are trying to reach the top.
  diverse (dissimilar, different) : Diverse opinions were given by the members on this proposal.
- **decided** (past form of decide) : He decided to go to Europe the next week.
  decisive (that which decides some thing important) : The battle of Plassey was a decisive one.
- **destination** (the place to reach) : The last destination of this train is Puri.
  destiny (fate) : One can make his destiny with hard labour.
- **envious** (feeling envy) You should not be envious of your friend's progress.
  enviable (a rousing envy) : His enviable posting made many jealous of him.
- **effectual** (creating desired effects) : He adopted the effectual means and so got the contract.
  efficacious (sufficient to have desired result) : Quinine nowadays is not efficacious in malaria.
- **egotist** (self conceited) : I cannot discuss anything with an egotist like you.
  egoist (selfishness, self interested) : He is an egoist, he believes that self interest is the base of all actions.
- **especially** (pertaining to exceptional degree) : Her mother was especially invited on the occasion.
  special (for the purpose) : I came specially to attend the function.
- **exceptional** (unusual) : J.L. Nehru was a man of exceptional qualities.
  exceptionable (objectionable) : His speech was full of exceptionable remarks.
- **exposition** (description) : Tennin's exposition of Ramayan is incomparable.
  exposure (no protection from open air, cold etc.) : Protect yourself from exposure otherwise you may catch cold.
- **economic** (relating to economy) : The economic condition of our country is not so good.
  economical (thrifty) : He is very economical in spending the money.
- **funeral** (ceremony after death) : More than ten thousand persons attended the funeral of his father.
  funereal (gloomy) : He came to the office with a funereal countenance.

- **fatal** (deadly) : He received a fatal wound in his chest.
  fatalist (believes in fate) : I am not a fatalist.
  fateful (lucky, important) : Fifteen August is a fateful day in Indian History.
- **forceful** (commanding force) : He enjoys a forceful personality.
  forcible (under compulsion) : Police made a forcible entry in his house.
- **godly** (pious) : Mahatma Gandhi led a godly life.
  God-like (like God) : Mahatma Gandhi was a God-like man.
- **graceful** (handsome-smart) : She has a graceful appearance.
  gracious (kind) : God is gracious.
- **honorary** (without any remuneration) : He was nominated 'Honorary' Chairman of the society.
  honourable (deserve honour, respected) : I request the honourable Principal to come on the dais.
- **imaginary** (not real) : Equator is an imaginary line.
  imaginative (pertaining to imagination) : A good writer must have imaginative ideas.
- **industrious** (laborious) : Nothing is impossible for an industrious and sincere student.
  industrial (relating to Industry) : Bhiwani is an industrial town.
- **intelligent** (wise) : He is an intelligent guy.
  intelligible (understandable) : He delivered an intelligible speech on educational necessities of rural area.
- **judicial** (pertaining to legal system or Judge) : Government has ordered a judicial enquiry in the matter.
  judicious (prudent , wise) : Going for a war is not a judicious decision.
- **loudly** (high volume) : Please do not speak so loudly in library room.
  aloud (audible voice) : He spoke aloud so that all could hear him.
- **luxuriant** (refer more growth) : There is a luxuriant growth of vegetables in our kitchen garden.
  luxurious (luxury) : He is leading a luxurious life after the death of his father.
- **lovable** (worthy of love) : He is a lovable person.
  lovely (charming) : What a lovely girl she is!
- **limit** (boundary) : Keep yourself within the limits, otherwise you have to face the music.
  limitation (restrictions) : Being a girl, I have many limitations.
- **memorial** (statue, building to commemorate) : You can find many memorials at Rajpath New Delhi.
  memorable (rememberable) : 26th January is a memorable day in Indian History.
- **momentary** (for a moment) : His anger is momentary, soon things will be okay.
  momentous (important) : The battle of Plassey was a momentous event in the history of India.
- **negligible** (unimportant) : There is a negligible difference between this shirt and the shirt we saw in that shop.
  negligent (careless) : She is generally negligent about her health.
  neglectful (careless about a thing) : She is so neglectful that she does not care even for her career.
- **officious** (over kind) : His officious attitude towards her creates doubts.
  official (relating to office) : As a responsible official of a company you must behave properly.
- **practical** (antonym of theoritical) : He failed in practical examination.
  He is a practical businessman.
  practicable (capable of being carried out) : This is not a practicable plan.
- **political** (relating to politics) : We should not trust the political statements of leaders.
  politic (sagacious, prudent) : It is not politic to argue with an intoxicated person.
- **pitiable** (relating to pity) : His condition is indeed pitiable.
  pitiful (feeling pity) : Seeing her pitiable condition everyone became pitiful.
- **prophecy** (noun-forecast) : He made a prophecy that the whole world would be destroyed in 2202.
  prophesy (to forecast) : These is a prophesy that within five years India will be a very powerful country.

- **respective** (particular thing or person) : After prayer, students should join their respective teams.
  respectful (full of respect) : One should be respectful to one's teachers, elders.
- **righteous** (just) : Her anger was righteous as no girl could tolerate such insult.
  rightful (just claim) : I am the rightful owner of this car.
- **regrettable** (causing regret) : It is quite regrettable that you are not taking care of your father.
  regretful (full of regret) : I am not at all regretful for my actions.
- **servility** (flattery) : I cannot adopt an attitude of servility to get promotion.
  servitude (slavery) : Try to come out of this state of servitude.
- **sociable** (fond of getting social) : She has a sociable nature.
  social (relates to society) : She is not only social but also very cooperative.
- **sensuous** (used in good sense for appreciation of beauty) : Keats was a sensuous poet.
  sensual (used in bad sense means voluptuous) : He was jailed for his sensual advancement towards his college friend.
- **sensitive** (touchy) : Cow slaughter is a sensitive matter for Hindus.
  sensational (exciting) : There are many sensational stories of murder in this magazine.
- **spirituous** (alcoholic) : Gujarat has banned the use of spirituous drinks in restaurants.
  spiritual (pertaining to soul) : She is a spiritual lady.
- **tolerant** (refer to a person, who respects different opinion also) : Akbar was regarded as a tolerant king.
  tolerable (bearable) : Because of his tolerable nature, he didnot lodge FIR against you.
- **temperament** (disposition) : Because of his violent temperament, he gets into trouble.
  temperance (sobriety) : He should observe temperance in drinking and dancing.
- **temporal** (antonym to spiritual) : Nowadays people are ready to do anything for temporal gains.
  temporary (a short time) : I offered her a temporary job.
- **transitory** (short lived) : The life is not eternal but transitory.
  transient (of short duration) : The world is transient.
- **union** (to be united) : Union is strength.
  unity (oneness) : There is no unity among different classes of the society.
  unison (harmony) : There was a good unison of Tabla and Violin in the cultural programme.
- **virtual** (in effect) : Sanjay Gandhi was the virtual head of Congress Party.
  virtuous (of good moral values) : Sita was a virtuous lady.
- **wilful** (knowingly) : He was charged for wilful negligence.
  willing (ready) : I am willing to help her.
- **womanly** (used in good sense, affectionately) : My wife possesses all womanly qualities.
  womanish (used in bad sense, means cowardly and weak like woman) : Everyone likes to dominate a man of womanish temperament.
- **wait** (generally used intransitively) : Please wait for me.
  await (line in wait) : A surprise awaited them at their home..
- **weary** (tired) : You look pale and weary.
  wearisome (tiring) : The journey was wearisome.
- **yield** (return) : What is the annual yield from the fields?
  yielding (submissive) : He is a man of yielding nature.

» Unit

34

Restricted Phrases

The use of some phrases or expressions are restricted to certain specific connections, and where no other words or expressions can substitute them. See the following phrases :

- **bevy of ladies**—We never say 'a bevy of gentlemen'.
- **bosom friend**—We never speak of 'bosom enemy'.
- **broad daylight**—We do not speak of 'broad moonlight,' but 'bright moonlight.'
- **burning question**—We should not say 'burning problem'.
- **drawn battle**—We never say 'a drawn fight.' But we can say 'a drawn match'.
- **fast friend**—We do not speak of 'a fast enemy'or 'a fast foe'.
- **foregone conclusion**—We never speak of 'a foregone result'or 'a foregone consequence'.
- **forlorn hope**—We never say 'forlorn success' or 'forlorn expectations'.
- **golden age**—We do not speak of 'the golden time or period'.
- **gratuitous insult**—We do not speak of 'gratuitous abuse'.
- **honest penny**—We do not speak of 'an honest six pence'.
- **implicit confidence, faith or reliance**—We do not say, 'implicit love or hatred'.
- **leading question**—We should not say 'a leading inquiry'.
- **livelong day or night**—We cannot say 'a livelong hour, or week, or year'.
- **maiden speech**—We cannot say 'a maiden song' or 'a maiden attempt'.
- **market rate or market value**—We cannot say 'trade rate' or 'trade value'.
- **moot point**—We cannot say 'a moot question.'
- **open question**—We cannot speak of 'an open point'.
- **open secret**—We cannot say 'an open point'.
- **out of doors**—We never say 'out of door' 'or 'out of gates'.
- **retrench expenditure**—We cannot say 'retrench trade of business'.
- **sinews of war**—We cannot say 'the muscles of war'.
- **snail's pace**—We cannot say 'snail's movement'.
- **spin in yarn or yarns**—We never say 'spin a thread'.
- **standing army**—We never say 'standing navy or regiment'.
- **standing joke**—We never say 'a standing jest'.
- **standing nuisance**—We never say, 'a standing trouble.' We may say 'a constant trouble'.
- **standing water**—We can never say 'standing need'.
- **standing rule**—We can never say 'standing practice or custom or habit'.
- **standing orders**—Generally we do not say 'standing instructions.' (In some offices we use 'standing instruction').
- **stubborn fact**—We can never say 'an obstinate fact' or 'a stubborn truth'.
- **sworn friends**—We can never say, 'a sworn enemy.' We may say 'an avowed enemy'.
- **stone's throw**—We never say 'pebble's throw' or 'brick's throw'.
- **tall talk**—We never speak of 'lofty talk'.
- **vials of wrath**—We cannot say 'vials of anger or fury.'
- **Whirligig of time**—We cannot say 'whirligig of period'.
- **white lie**—We do not say 'white falsehood' or 'black lie'.
- **willing slave**—We do not speak of 'willing servant'.
- **watery grave**—We do not say ' a watery tomb' or 'watery burial'.

» Unit

35

Phobias

- **ablutophobia** : fear of washing or bathing
- **aerophobia** : fear of swallowing air
- **ambulophobia** : fear of walking
- **anablephobia** : fear of looking up
- **anemophobia** : fear of wind
- **anthrophobia** : fear of flowers
- **arachibutyrophobia** : fear of peanut butter sticking to the roof of the mouth
- **arithmophobia** : fear of numbers
- **aulophobia** : fear of flutes
- **auroraphobia** : Fear of Northern Lights
- **barophobia** : fear of gravity
- **basophobia** : fear of walking
- **batophobia** : fear of being close to high buildings
- **bibliophobia** : fear of books
- **blennophobia** : fear of slime
- **bogyphobia** : fear of the bogeyman
- **cathisophobia** : fear of sitting
- **catoptrophobia** : fear of mirrors
- **chaetophobia** : fear of hair
- **chionophobia** : fear of snow
- **chromatophobia** : fear of colours
- **chronophobia** : fear of time
- **chronomentrophobia** : fear of clocks
- **cibophobia** : fear of food
- **clinophobia** : fear of going to bed
- **cnidophobia** : fear of string
- **deciophobia** : fear of making decisions
- **dendrophobia** : fear of trees
- **dextrophobia** : fear of objects at the right side of the body
- **eleutherophobia** : fear of freedom
- **eosophobia** : fear of daylight
- **epistemophobia** : fear of knowledge
- **ergophobia** : fear of work
- **ereuthophobia** : fear of the red colour
- **geliophobia** : fear of laughter
- **geniophobia** : fear of chins
- **genuphobia** : fear of knees
- **geumaphobia** : fear of taste
- **gnosiophobia** : fear of knowledge
- **graphophobia** : fear of writing
- **heliophobia** : fear of the sun
- **helmintophobia** : fear of being infested with worms
- **hemophobia** : fear of blood
- **hippopotomonstrosesquippedaliophobia** : fear of long words
- **homichlophobia** : fear of fog
- **hypnophobia** : fear of sleep
- **ichthyophobia** : fear of fish
- **ideophobia** : fear of ideas
- **kainophobia** : fear of anything new
- **kathisophobia** : fear of sitting down
- **lachanophobia** : fear of vegetables
- **levophobia** : fear of objects to the left side of the body
- **melanophobia** : fear of the black colour
- **melophobia** : fear of music
- **metrophobia** : fear of poetry
- **mnemophobia** : fear of memories
- **mottephobia** : fear of moths
- **nebulaphobia** : fear of fog
- **neophobia** : fear of anything new
- **nephophobia** : fear of clouds

- **nomatophobia** : fear of names
- **octophobia** : fear of the number 8
- **ommetaphobia** : fear of eyes
- **oneirophobia** : fear of dreams
- **ophthalmophobia** : fear of opening one's eyes
- **ostraconophobia** : fear of shellfish
- **panophobia** : fear of everything
- **papyrophobia** : fear of paper
- **paraskavedekatriaphobia** : fear of Friday the 13th
- **peladophobia** : fear of bald people
- **phengophobia** : fear of daylight
- **photophobia** : fear of light
- **phronemophobia** : fear of thinking
- **pogonophobia** : fear of beards
- **sciophobia** : fear of shadows
- **scolionophobia** : fear of school
- **selenophobia** : fear of the moon
- **siderophobia** : fear of stars
- **sitophobia** : fear of food
- **sophophobia** : fear of learning
- **stasibasiphobia** : fear of walking
- **thaasophobia** : fear of sitting
- **trichopathophobia** : fear of hair
- **triskadekaphobia** : fear of the number 13
- **verbophobia** : fear of words
- **xanthophobia** : fear of the color yellow

Unit

36

Manias

Word	Definition
ablutomania	mania for washing oneself
aboulomania	pathological indecisiveness
agromania	intense desire to be in open spaces
andromania	nymphomania
anglomania	craze or obsession with England and the English
anthomania	obsession with flowers
aphrodisiomania	abnormal sexual interest
arithmomania	obsessive preoccupation with numbers
balletomania	abnormal fondness for ballet
bibliomania	craze for books or reading
bruxomania	compulsion for grinding teeth
cacodemomania	pathological belief that one is inhabited by an evil spirit
catapedamania	obsession with jumping from high places
chinamania	obsession with collecting china
choreomania	dancing mania or frenzy
clinomania	excessive desire to stay in bed
copromania	obsession with feces
cytheromania	nymphomania
dacnomania	obsession with killing
demonomania	pathological belief that one is possessed by demons
dinomania	mania for dancing
dipsomania	abnormal craving for alcohol
discomania	obsession for disco music
doramania	obsession with owning furs
doromania	obsession with giving gifts
drapetomania	intense desire to run away from home
dromomania	compulsive longing for travel
ecdemomania	abnormal compulsion for wandering
egomania	irrational self-centered attitude or self-worship
eleutheromania	manic desire for freedom
empleomania	mania for holding public office
enosimania	pathological belief that one has sinned
entheomania	abnormal belief that one is divinely inspired
epomania	craze for writing epics
ergasiomania	excessive desire to work; ergomania
ergomania	excessive desire to work; workaholism
erotomania	abnormally powerful sex drive
etheromania	craving for ether
ethnomania	obsessive devotion to one's own people
eulogomania	obsessive craze for eulogies
flagellomania	abnormal enthusiasm for flogging
florimania	craze for flowers
francomania	craze or obsession with France and the French
gallomania	craze or obsession with France and the French

Word	Definition
gamomania	obsession with issuing odd marriage proposals
Graecomania	obsession with Greece and the Greeks
graphomania	obsession with writing
gynaecomania	abnormal sexual obsession with women
habromania	insanity featuring cheerful delusions
hagiomania	mania for sainthood
hellenomania	obsession with Greece and the Greeks; Graecomania
hexametromania	mania for writing in hexameter
hieromania	pathological religious visions or delusions
hippomania	obsession with horses
hydromania	irrational craving for water
hylomania	excessive tendency towards materialism
hypermania	severe mania
hypomania	minor mania
hysteromania	nymphomania
iconomania	obsession with icons or portraits
idolomania	obsession or devotion to idols
infomania	excessive devotion to accumulating facts
islomania	craze or obsession for islands
Italomania	obsession with Italy or Italians
kleptomania	irrational predilection for stealing
klopemania	kleptomania
logomania	pathological loquacity
lypemania	extreme pathological mournfulness
macromania	delusion that objects are larger than natural size
megalomania	abnormal tendency towards grand or grandiose behaviour
melomania	craze for music
methomania	morbid craving for alcohol
metromania	insatiable desire for writing verse
micromania	pathological self-deprecation or belief that one is very small
monomania	abnormal obsession with a single thought or idea

Word	Definition
morphinomania	habitual craving or desire for morphine
musomania	obsession with music
mythomania	lying or exaggerating to an abnormal extent
narcomania	uncontrollable craving for narcotics
necromania	sexual obsession with dead bodies; necrophilia
nosomania	delusion of suffering from a disease
nostomania	abnormal desire to go back to familiar places
nymphomania	excessive or crazed sexual desire
oenomania	obsession or craze for wine
oligomania	obsession with a few thoughts or ideas
oniomania	mania for making purchases
onomamania	mania for names
onomatomania	irresistible desire to repeat certain words
onychotillomania	compulsive picking at the fingernails
opiomania	craving for opium
opsomania	abnormal love for one kind of food
orchidomania	abnormal obsession with orchids
parousiamania	obsession with the second coming of Christ
pathomania	moral insanity
peotillomania	abnormal compulsion for pulling on the penis
phagomania	excessive desire for food or eating
phaneromania	habit of biting one's nails
pharmacomania	abnormal obsession with trying drugs
phonomania	pathological tendency to murder
photomania	pathological desire for light
phyllomania	excessive or abnormal production of leaves
phytomania	obsession with collecting plants
planomania	abnormal desire to wander and disobey social norms
plutomania	mania for money
polemomania	mania for war
politicomania	mania for politics

Word	Definition
polkamania	craze for polka dancing
polymania	mania affecting several different mental faculties
poriomania	abnormal compulsion to wander
pornomania	obsession with pornography
potichomania	craze for imitating oriental porcelain
potomania	abnormal desire to drink alcohol
pseudomania	irrational predilection for lying
pteridomania	passion for ferns
pyromania	craze for starting fires
rhinotillexomania	compulsive nose picking
rinkomania	obsession with skating
satyromania	abnormally great male sexual desire; satyriasis
scribbleomania	obsession with scribbling
sebastomania	religious insanity
sitiomania	morbid aversion to food
sophomania	delusion that one is incredibly intelligent
squandermania	irrational propensity for spending money wastefully
stampomania	obsession with stamp-collecting

Word	Definition
syphilomania	pathological belief that one is afflicted with syphilis
technomania	craze for technology
teutomania	obsession with Teutonic or German things
thanatomania	belief that one has been affected by death magic, and resulting illness
theatromania	craze for going to plays
theomania	belief that one is a god
timbromania	craze for stamp collecting
tomomania	irrational predilection for performing surgery
toxicomania	morbid craving for poisons
trichotillomania	neurosis where patient pulls out own hair
tulipomania	obsession with tulips
typhomania	delirious state resulting from typhus fever
typomania	craze for printing one's lucubrations
uranomania	obsession with the idea of divinity
verbomania	craze for words
xenomania	inordinate attachment to foreign things
zoomania	insane fondness for animals

Unit

37

Sounds and Cries

- Apes : gibber
- Asses : bray
- Bears : growl
- Bees : hum
- Birds : sing, twitter, chirp or warble
- Bulls : bellow
- Camels: grunt
- Cats : mew purr caterwaul
- Cattle : low
- Cocks : crow
- Cows : low
- Crickets : chirp
- Crows : crow
- Dogs : yelp, bark, whine, eq. growl, howl, bay
- Doves : coo
- Ducks : quack
- Foxes : yell bark
- Frogs : croak
- Goats : bleat
- Hawks : scream
- Hens : cackle cluck
- Horses : neigh snort, whinny
- Hyenas : laugh.
- Jackals: howl
- Kittens : mew
- Lambs : bleat
- Larks : sing, warble
- Lions : roar.a
- Magpies : chatter
- Mice : squeak
- Monkeys: chatter, gibber
- Nightingales : sing warble
- Eagles : scream
- Elephants : trumpet
- Flies : buzz
- Puppies : yelp
- Ravens : croak
- Serpents : hiss
- Sparrows : chirp, twitter
- Swallows: twitter
- Swabs : cry
- Tigers : growl, roar
- Vultures : scream
- Wolves : howl, yell
- Arms : clang
- Babies : lisp
- bells : ring, jingle or tinkle
- bugles : blow
- chains : clank
- clouds : thunder
- doors : creak or bang
- drums : beat
- footsteps: sound
- Owls : hoot, screech scream
- Oxen : low, bellow
- Parrot : talk
- Pigeons : coo
- Pigs : grunt, squeal
- Hoofs : clatter
- Leave : rustle
- Railway engines roar or whistle
- Silk : rustles
- Steel : clinks
- Trees : sigh
- Water : ripples
- Rivors : murmur
- Wind : whistles or sighs
- teeth : chatter
- hands : clap
- wings : flap
- coins : jingle
- old or discontented persons : mutter
- persons in agony : moan
- guns : roar or explode

» Unit

38

Homes and Abodes

Below are the name of homes and abodes of the different objects, animals, plants, etc. The study of the names of such homes and places will help the students in enhancing their power of expression and enriching their vocabulary.

- Aerodrome is the place for aeroplanes.
- Aquarium is the place for fish and water plants.
- Asylum is the place for lunatic, for political refugees.
- Arena is the place for wresting conflict.
- Arsenal is the place for ammunition and weapons.
- Barracks is the place for soldiers or army men.
- Bakery is the place for bread and biscuits.
- Castle is the place for noblemen.
- Cottage is the place for peasants.
- Cell is the place for prisoners.
- Cloakroom is the place for luggage at a railway station.
- Cage is the place for birds and animals.
- Cemetery is the place for corpses to be buried.
- Crematory is the place for corpses to be burnt.
- Den is the place for lions.
- Dockyard is the place for ships.
- Dispensary is the place for medicines to be dispensed.
- Granary is the place for grains.
- Garage is the place for vehicles.
- Godown is the place for goods for storing.
- Gymnasium is the place for appliances for gymnastic exercises.
- Hive is the place for bees.
- Hole is the place for mice and serpents.
- Kennel is the place for dogs.
- Library is the place for books.
- Laboratory is the place for scientific experiments.
- Lavatory is the place for washing hand and face.
- Laundry is the place for washing dirty clothes.
- Lair is the resting place of animals.
- Monastery is the place for monks.
- Museum is the place for historical curiosities and arts.
- Menagerie is the place for wild animals and birds.
- Mint is the place for coins to be manufactured and currency notes to print.
- Nursery is the place for young plants to be grown, and a room for children.
- Nest is the place for birds.
- Orchard is the place for fruit trees.
- Pharmacy is the place medicines to be prepared.
- Play ground is the place for playing games.
- Pantry is the place for provisions in the house.
- Prison is the place for convicts.
- Restaurant is the place for meals or refreshment to be had for payment.
- Ring is the place for boxing.
- Sanitorium is the place for invalids to enjoy good climate.
- Stadium is the place for athletic competitions.
- Studio is the place for artists.
- Study is the place for scholars.
- Sty is the place for pigs.
- Stable is the place for horses.
- Tannery is the place for leather polishing.
- Track is the place for races.

» Unit

39

Important Group Terms

A herd of antelope

A shrewdness of apes

A culture of bacteria

A shoal of bass

A colony of beavers

A flock, flight, congregation or volery of birds

A sounder of boars

A brace or clash of bucks

A clowder or clutter of cats

A brood or peep of chickens

A bed of clams

A rag of colts

A kine of cows (twelve cows are a flink)

A sedge or siege of cranes

A murder of crows

A herd of curlews

A herd of deer

A dule of doves

A clutch of eggs

A pod of elephant seals

A gang of elks

A business or fesnyng of ferrets

A school, shoal, run, haul, catch or draught of fish

A skulk or leash of foxes

A colony or an army of ants

A herd or pace of asses

A cete of badgers

A sleuth or sloth of bears

A swarm, grist or hive of bees

A sedge or siege of bitterns

A herd of buffalo

An army of caterpillars

A herd or drove of cattle

A clutch or chattering of chicks

A quiver of cobras

A cover of coots

A band of coyote

A float of crocodiles

A litter of cubs

A cowardice of curs

A pack of dogs

A brace, paddling or team of ducks

A herd of elephants

A weaner pod is yearling elephant seals

A mob of emus

A charm of finches

A swarm of flies

An army or colony of frogs

A flock, gaggle or skein (in flight) of geese

A herd, tribe or trip goats

A band of gorillas

A down or husk of hares

A brood of hens

A drift, or parcel of hogs

A pack, mute or cry of hounds

A troop or mob of kangaroos

An ascension or exaultation of larks

A pride of lions

A tiding of magpies

A stud of mares

A labour of moles

A barren or span of mules

A yoke, drove, team or herd of oxen

A company of parrots

A muster or ostentation of peacocks

A nest, nide (nye) or bouquet of pheasants

A litter of pigs

A string of ponies

A covey or bevy of quail

A pack or swarm of rats

An unkindness of ravens

A bevy of roebucks

A cloud or horde of gnats

A charm of goldfinches

A leash of greyhounds

A cast or kettle of hawks

A hedge of herons

A team, pair or harras of horses

A smack of jellyfish

A kindle or litter of kittens

A leap of leopards

A plague of locusts

A sord of mallards

A richness of martens

A troop of monkeys

A parliament of owls

A bed of oysters

A covey of partridges

A litter of peeps

A flock or flight of pigeons

A wing or congregation of plovers

A pod of porpoises

A nest of rabbits

A rhumba of rattlesnakes

A crash or herd of rhinos

A building or clamour of rooks

A herd or pod of seals
A nest of snakes
A host of sparrows
A murmuration of starlings
A flight of swallows
A flock of swifts
A spring of teal
A hover of trout
A pitying or dule of turtledoves
A pod of walrus
A nest of vipers
A fall of woodcocks
A stack of wood
A pair of shoes
A herd of deer
A flock of geese
A tribe of Arabs
A shower of rain
A flock of sheep
A bunch of keys
A sheaf of wheat
A pack of hounds
A bundle of hay
A bundle of sticks
A hoard of gold
A leash of hounds
A litter of puppies
A regiment of soldiers
A box of cigars
A pile of arms
A nursery of plants
A stud of horses
A yoke of oxen
A brood of hens
A team of oxen
A basket of fruits
A galaxy of beauties
A museum of art
A cellar of wine.
A family of sardines

A drove or flock of sheep
A walk or wisp of snipe
A dray of squirrels
A mustering of storks
A bevy, herd, lamentation or wedge of swans
A sounder or drift of swine
A knot of toads
A rafter of turkeys
A bale of turtles
A school, gam or pod of whales
A pack or route of wolves
A descent of woodpeckers
A stack of arms
A herd of swine
A shoal of fish
A stack of corn
A flight of birds
A suit of clothes
A flight of steps
A swarm of flies
A pack of wolves
A series of events
A sheaf of grain
A group of islands
A horde of savages
A host of men
A gang of labourers
A bunch of plantains
A brew of beer
A muster of peacocks
A posy of flowers
A team of players
A board of directors
A flock of birds
A staff of officials
A fight of stairs
A kennel of dogs
A muster of soldiers
A faggot of sticks
A packet of cigarettes

A clique of people
A colony of people
A heap or mass of ruins
A fall of snow or rain
A convoy of partridges
A nest or swarm of ants
A sheaf of arrows
A brood or flock of chickens
A herd of cattle (i.e., cattle pasturing)
A crowd, or throng, or concourse, or A bunch of grapes
A cluster or galaxy of stars
A range of hills or mountains
A collection of relics or curiosities
A bevy of ladies
A fell of hair
A gallery of pictures
A nosegay of flowers
A string of camels
A brace of pistols
A posse of arrows
A flotilla of boats
A suite of rooms
A parade of soldiers
A troupe of actors
A company of actors
A shrubbery of shrubs
A detachment of soldiers
A constellation of delegates
An orchard of fruit trees
A syndicate of merchants
An assembly of people
A jamboree of boy scouts
A tuz of hair

A clutch of eggs
A squad of soldiers
A heap of stones or sand
A clump or grove of trees.
A chain of mountains
A hive or swarm of bees
A flight or swarm of locusts
A gang of thieves or robbers
A drove of cattle (i.e., cattle being driven)
Multitude of people
A bunch or bouquet of flowers
A group of figures in a painting
A brace of pigeons
A crew of sailors
A council of advisers
A library of books
A division of troops
A band of musicians
A panel of jury
A quiver of arrows
A squadron of cavalry
A bench of magistrates
A throng of people
A battery of guns
A gathering of people
A party of people
A conference of delegates
An outfit of clothes.
A fleet of cars or ships
A commission of enquiry
A genus of animals or plants
A congregation of worshippers

Unit

40

Male, Female and Young Ones (Animals)

Animal	Female	Male	Young
alligator	cow	bull	hatchling
ant	queen, princess, worker	prince, drone	
antelope	cow	bull	calf, fawn, kid
ass	jenny	jack, jackass	foal
badger	sow	boar	cub
bear	sow, she-bear	boar, he-bear	cub
beaver	-	-	kit, kitten, pup
bee	queen, queen-bee	drone	larva
bird	hen	cock	nestling, hatchlin,
bison	cow	bull	calf
boar (wild)	sow	boar	boarlet, farrow
bobcat	-	-	kitten or cub
buffalo	cow	bull	calf, yearling,
camel	cow	bull	calf or colt
canary	hen	cock	chick
caribou	cow, doe	bull, stag, hart	calf or fawn
cat	tabby, queen	tom, tomcat,gib	kit, kitling, kitten
chicken	hen, partlet	cock, rooster	chick, chicken,
cicada	-	-	nymph
cod	-	-	codling, scrod
cougar	lioness, she-lion	tom, lion	kitten or cub
coyote	bitch	dog	whelp, pup
crocodile		bull	hatchling
deer	hind, doe	buck, stag	fawn
dog	bitch	dog	whelp or puppy
dolphin	cow	bull	calf, pup
dove	hen	cock	pigeon or squab
duck	duck	drake	duckling, flappe
eagle	-	-	eaglet, fledgling
elephant	cow	bull	calf
elk	cow	bull	calf
ferret	hob	jill	kit
fox	vixen, bitch, dog-fox, stag	kit	pup,cub
frog	-	-	tadpole, froglet
giraffe	cow	bull	calf
goat	she-goat, nannie	billy,buck,he-goat	kid
goose	goose, dame	gander, stag	gosling
gorilla	-	silverback	infant
grouse	-	-	chick, poult
guinea pig	sow	boar	pup
hare	jill	jack	leveret
hawk	tiercel	hen	eyas
hedgehog	sow	boar	pup, piglet

Animal	Female	Male	Young
hippopotamus	cow	bull	calf
horse	mare, dam	stallion, stag, stud, colt, foal, stat,	filly, hog-colt
impala	ewe	ram	-
kangaroo	doe	buck	joey
leopard	leopardess	leopard	cub
lion	lioness, she-lion	lion, tom	cub or lionet
lobster	hen	cock	-
louse	-	-	nit
manatee	cow	bull	calf
mink	sow	boar	kit or cub
monkey	-	-	suckling, yearling
moose	cow	bull	calf
mosquito			larva, flapper,
mouse	doe	buck	Pup, kitten
mule	she-ass, hinny	stallion, jackass	foal
muskrat	-	-	kit
opossum	jill	jack	joey
ostrich	hen	cock	chick
otter	bitch	dog	pup, kitten, cub
owl	jenny, howlet	-	owlet or howlet
ox	cow, beef	ox, steer, bullock	stot, calf
oyster	-	-	set seed, spat
partridge	hen	cock	cheeper
peacock	hen, pea-hen	cock, peacock	chick, pea-chick
pelican			chick, nestling
penguin	hen	cock	fledgling, chick
pheasant	hen	cock	chick, poult
pig	sow	boar	shoat, piglet
pigeon	hen	cock	squab, nestling
platypus	-	-	puggle
possum	jill	jack	joey
quail	hen	cock	cheeper, squealer
rabbit	doe	buck	kitten, bunny
raccoon	sow	boar	Kit, cub
rat	doe	buck	kitten, pup
reindeer	doe	buck	fawn
rhinoceros	cow	bull	calf
robin	hen	cock	-
salmon	hen	jack	salmon parr, fry
sea lion	cow	bull	pup
seal	cow	bull	whelp, pup, cub
shark	-	bull	pup
sheep	ewe, dam	buck, ram	lamb, lambkin,
skunk	-	boar	kitten
squirrel	doe	buck	dray
swan	pen	cob	cygnet, flapper
swine	sow	boar	shoat, trotter, piglet
termite	queen	king	nymph
tiger	tigeress	tiger	whelp, cub
toad	-	-	tadpole
trout	hen	jack	fry
turkey	hen	gobbler, tom	chick, poult
walrus	cow	bull	cub
weasel	bitch, doe, jill	dog, buck	kit
whale	cow	bull	calf
wolf	bitch	dog	cub, pup
woodchuck	she-chuck	he-chuck	kit, cub
zebra	mare	stallion	colt, foal

Unit 41

Foreign Words

Given below are a number of foreign words used in newspapers, standard books and magazines. students are advised to learn these words. These words are often seen in competitive examinations papers.

A

- **Ab aeterno** (L.), from eternity
- **Ab ante** (L.), from before
- **Ab antiquo** (L.), from olden time
- **Ab initio** (L.), from the beginning
- **Ab intra** (L.), from within
- **Ab irato** (L.), in a fit of passion
- **Abonnement** (Fr.), subscription
- **Ab origine** (L.), from the beginning
- **Ad arbitrium** (L.), at pleasure
- **Ad extra** (L.), outward
- **Ad finem** (L.), to the end
- **Ad infinitum** (L.), up to infinity
- **Ad interim** (L.), for the meantime
- **A' discretion** (Fr.), without restriction
- **Ad modum** (L.), after the method of
- **Ad valorem** (L.), according to value
- **Ad verbum** (L.), word for word
- **Advivum** (L.), to the life
- **Aequanimiter** (L.), calmly
- **A' fond** (Fr.), thoroughly
- **A' gauche** (Fr.), to the left
- **Age quod agis** (L.), do with all your power what you have to do
- **Alinude** (L.), from another place
- **Allons!** (Fr.), come along, let us go!
- **Alter ego** (L.), one's second self, intimate friend
- **Alter ipse amicus** (L.), a friend is another self
- **A' maximis ad minima** (L.), from the greatest to the smallest
- **Amicus curiae** (L.), a friend of the law-court
- **Amicus humani generis** (L.), a friend of humanity
- **Anglice** (L.), in English
- **Anima mundi** (L.), the soul of the world
- **Animo et Jide** (L.), by courage and faith
- **Annus mirabilis** (L.), year of wonders
- **Ante bellum** (L.), before the war
- **Ante mer idiem** (L.), before noon
- **Antiquarium** (L.), collection of antiquities
- **A posteriori** (L.), from the effect to the cause
- **A' propos** (Fr.), to the point
- **Arbitrium** (L.), power of decision
- **Arcana imperii** (L.), state secrets

B

- **Bella, horrida bella** (L.), wars, horrible wars
- **Bellum lethale** (L.), deadly war
- **Biennium** (L.), period of two years
- **Bona fides** (L.), good faith
- **Bona mobilia** (L.), movable goods

C

- **Cadeau** (Fr.), a present , a gift
- **Caeca est invidia** (L.), envy is blind
- **Casus belli** (L.), whatever involves a war
- **Caveat actor** (L.), let the doer beware
- **Centum** (L.), a hundred
- **Cito** (L.), quickly
- **Compos mentis** (L.), of sound mind, sane
- **Consilio et animis** (L.), by wisdom and courage
- **Con spirito** (It.), with spirit
- **Contra bonos mores** (L.)
- against good manners or morals
- **Coram populo** (L.), in the presence of the public
- **Coup de hasard** (Fr.), a lucky chance
- **Crimen falsi** (L.), crime of perjury
- **Culpa levis** (L.), a slight fault
- **Currente calamo** (L.), with a running pen

D

- **Data et accepta** (L.), expenses and receipts
- **De bon augure** (Fr.), of good omen
- **De die in diem** (L.), form day to day
- **De facto** (L.), really, in fact, actual
- **Dei gratia** (L.), by the grace of God
- **De integro** (L.), afresh, anew
- **De jure** (L.), by right, in law
- **Deo favente** (L.), with God's favour
- **Deo gratias** (L.), thanks to God
- **Deus avertat!** (L.), God forbid!
- **Deus det** (L.), God grant!
- **Dictum de dicto** (L.), hearsay, report
- **Domine, dirige nos !** (L.), God, direct us!
- **Dum spiro, spero** (L.), while I breathe, I hope

E

- **Editio princeps** (L.), original edition (of a book)
- **Eo nomine** (L.), by that name
- **Erenata** (L.), according to the exigencies of the case
- **Et, tu, Brute** (L.), and you too Brutus
- **Ex curia** (L.), out of court
- **Ex delicto** (L.), owing to crime
- **Ex dono** (L.), as a gift
- **Ex officio** (L.), by virtue of his office
- **Ex parte** (L.), on one side only
- **Expressis verbis** (L.), in express terms
- **Ex tacito** (L.), silently
- **Ex utraque parte** (L.), on either side
- **Ex voto** (L.), according to one's prayer.

F

- Facta non verba (L.), deeds not words
- **Factum est** (L.), it is done
- **Fadaise** (Fr.), a silly talk
- **Fait accompli** (Fr.), a thing already done
- **Fata obstant** (L.), the gate opposes it
- **Fecit** (L.), made or executed
- **Fide et amore** (L.), by faith and love
- **Fidus et audax** (L.), faithful and bold
- **Fillius nullius** (L.), a bastard

G

- **Gaillard** (Fr.), lively
- **Garcon** (Fr.), a boy, bachelor
- **Gloria in excelsis** (L.), glory to God is the highest

H

- **Hoc age** (L.), attend to what you do
- **Hoc anno** (L.), in this year
- **Hoc loco** (L.), in this place
- **Hoc tempore** (L.), at this time
- **Hominis est errare** (L.), to err is human

I

- **Impromptu** (L.), without study
- **In abstracto** (L.), in the abstract
- **In camera** (L.), in the private room
- **In curia** (L.), in court
- **In equilibris** (L.), in equili brium
- **In esse** (L.), in fact
- **In extenso** (L.), at full length
- **Infra dignitatem** (L.), below one's dignity

- **In pace** (L.), in peace
- **In statu quo** (L.), in the former state
- **Inter alia** (L.), among other things
- **In terrorem** (L.), as a warning
- **Inter se** (L.), amongst themselves
- **In toto** (L.), in the whole, entirely
- **Ipso facto** (L.), really

J

- **Jure divino** (L.), by divine law
- **Jure humano** (L.), by human law

L

- **Labor ipsev oluptas** (L.), labour itself is pleasure
- **Lapsus calami** (L.), a slip of the pen
- **Lapsus linguae** (L.), a slip of the tongue
- **Lapsus memoriae** (L.), a slip of the memory
- **Lese majeste** (Fr.), high treason
- **Lingua Franca** (It.), a mixed language spoken by the Europeans
- **Locus standi** (L.), place for standing, right of interferrin
- **Lucri causa** (L.), for the sake of gain
- **Lusus naturae** (L.), a freak of nature

M

- **Magnum bonuni** (L.), a great good
- **Magnum opus** (L.), a great work
- **Mala fide** (L.), faithlessly, treacherously
- **Memento mori** (L.), remember that thou shalt die
- **Mirabile dictu** (L.), wonderful to tell
- **Mirabile visu** (L.), wonderful to see

N

- **Nolens volens** (L.), willing or not willing, whether he will or not
- **Noli me tangere** (L.), do not touch me
- **Nota bene** (L.), abbr. NB take notice, mark well
- **Nulli secundus** (L.), unparalleled, second to none
- **Nunc est bibendum** (L.), now is the time for drinking

O

- **Omnia bona bonis** (L.), all things are good to the good
- **Onus probandi** (L.), the burden of proof

P

- **Pari passu** (L.), with equal pace, together
- **Particeps criminis** (L.), an accomplice
- **Per annum** (L.), per year
- **Per centum** (L.), by the hundred
- **Per diem** (L.), per day, daily
- **Per se** (L.), by itself
- **Populus vult decipi** (L.), the people wish to be fooled
- **Post mortem** (L.), after death
- **Post obitum** (L.), after death
- **Prima facie** (L.), on the first view
- **Primo** (L.), in the first place
- **Pro rata** (L.), in proportion
- **Pro tempore** (L.), for the time being, temporarily

Q

- **Quid pro quo** (L.), something given or taken as equivalent to another
- **Qui tacet consentit** (L.), he who keeps silence consents

R

- **Res gestae** (L.), exploits
- **Resume** (Fr.), a summary or abstract

S

- **Sine die** (L.), without a difinite day, of a meeting adjourned for an indefinite period
- **Sine odium** (L.), without hatred
- **Sine qua non** (L.), without which not, an indispensable condition
- **Sponte sua** (L.), of one's own accord
- **Status quo** (L.), the state or condition in which a thing is existing

- **Sub judice** (L.), under consideration
- **Suus cuique mos** (L.), everyone has peculiar habits

T

- **Terra incognita** (L.), an unknown country
- **Tu quoque Brute!** (L.), and thou too Brutus!

U

- **Ultima thule** (L.), the utmost limit
- **Ultra vires** (L.), beyond one's powers

V

- **Vale** (L.), farewell
- **Veni, vidi, vici** (L.), I came, I saw, I conquered
- **Versus** (L.), (abbr.V.), against
- **Vice** (L.), in place of
- **Vice versa** (L.), the order being reversed, the terms being exchanged
- **Vis-a-vis** (Fr.), opposite, facing
- **Volente Deo** (L.), God willing
- **Vox populi, vox Dei** (L.), the voice of the people is the voice of God

X

- **Xystum** (L.), a shaded walk in a garden

Z

- **Zonam perdidit** (L.), he has lost his wealth he is in need of money

» Unit

42

Spotting the Errors

Exercise 1

Read the following sentences to find error. The error will be in one part of the sentence. If there is no error, then the answer is E

1. Her and the (a)/other members of the group (b)/spoke to the person (c)/after their final victory. (d)
2. In early India (a)/there has been very little to read (b)/except for the books sent (c)/from Britain. (d)
3. Still remaining in the ancient castle (a)/are the Duke's collection of early Dutch paintings (b)/which will be (c)/donated to a museum. (d)
4. Most students preferred (a)/courses in the classical arts to (b)/courses in science unless (c)/they are science majors. (d)
5. When she comes (a)/to see us (b)/she usually will bring (c)/some thing with her. (d)
6. Why did you (a)/not told me (b)/that the meeting (c)/was postponed? (d)
7. I did not want (a)/him to have spent (b)/all the money at (c)/the fair yesterday. (d)
8. The assistant (a)/is never found (b)/wherever the manager (c)/want him. (d)
9. He picked up (a)/the books (b)/and put it (c)/on the table. (d)
10. They decided (a)/to talk it over (b)/at dinner. (c)

Solutions

1. (a) Replace 'Her' by 'She'. Her is a pronoun in objective case, so can't be used as subject.
2. (b) Replace 'has been' by 'was'. The sentence is in past tense.
3. (b) Replace 'are' by 'is'. Subject, Duke's collection of early Dutch paintings is functioning as collective noun so verb should be singular.
4. (a) Replace 'preferred' by 'prefer'. The sentence is in Present tense.
5. (c) Replace 'will bring' by 'brings'.
6. (b) Replace 'told' by 'tell'. In past interrogative Ist form of verb is used.
7. (b) Replace 'to have spent' by 'to spend'. Use of have spent is illogical.
8. (d) Replace 'want' by 'wants'. With manager (singular number IIIrd person) wants will be used.
9. (c) Replace put it by 'put them'. Here them is used for books.
10. (E) No error.

Exercise 2

Read the following sentences to find error. The error will be in one part of the sentence. If there is no error, then the answer is E

1. I am not hungry (a)/beside (b)/I do not like eggs. (c)
2. Economics are (a)/now-a-days included as a subject (b)/in all colleges. (c)
3. When he (a)/had got what (b)/he wanted (c)/he has gone home. (d)
4. Of the two proposals (a)/we think (b)/the second is (c)/the most attractive. (d)
5. If I wrote (a)/to my father now (b)/he will receive (c)/the letter tomorrow. (d)
6. This road is (a)/worst than (b)/any other road (c)/of the city. (d)
7. The driver as well as (a)/the conductor are (b)/responsible for this accident. (c)
8. Some peoples (a)/feel that (b) no progress is possible (c)/without discipline. (d)
9. She told (a)/her mother that (b)/she is busy. (c)
10. After listening to (a)/little songs (b)/she switched off (c)/the radio. (d)

Solutions

1. (b) Replace 'beside' by 'besides'.
2. (a) Economics is name of a subject so is will be used.
3. (d) Replace 'has gone' by 'went'. The sentence is in past.
4. (d) Replace 'the most' by 'more'. More is used for comparison of two.
5. (a) Replace 'wrote' by 'write'.
6. (b) Replace 'worst' by 'worse'. For comparison use comparative degree.
7. (b) Replace 'are' by 'is'. Noun 'driver' is singular.
8. (a) Replace 'peoples' by 'people'.
9. (c) Replace 'is' by 'was'.
10. (b) Replace 'little of' by 'some of'.'little' is used for uncountables.

Exercise 3

Read the following sentences to find error. The error will be in one part of the sentence. If there is no error, then the answer is E

1. We erect monuments (a)/in the memory of great leaders (b)/lest their achievements (c)/align be forgotten. (d)
2. He will not escape (a)/punishment unless (b)/he does not speak (c)/the truth. (d)
3. Being a cold day (a)/neither my friend (b)/nor I was (c)/in a mood to go to market. (d)
4. Such students (a)/who have not submitted (b)/their TC will not be allowed (c)/to appear in the examinations. (d)
5. I went to the librarian and cashier (a)/and they gave me (b)/all facilities required (c)/to complete the project. (d)
6. Milk is (a)/the most perfect (b)/food in the world. (c)
7. What is there (a)/ which is a secret (b)/between you and me. (c)
8. With the death of Rajiv Gandhi (a)/a great statesman and politician (b)/were lost. (c)
9. You had better (a)/to stop (b)/your work (c)/for some time. (d)
10. A severe cold (a)/prevented the president (b)/being present (c)/at the function. (d)

Solutions

1. (d) Replace 'might' by 'should', 'lest' is always followed by 'should'.
2. (c) Replace 'does not speak' by 'speaks', unless is itself negative.
3. (a) Place 'It' before 'Being'. This is the problem of unrelated participle.
4. (b) Replace 'who' by 'as' or 'that'. With such, 'as' or 'that' is used.
5. (b) Replace 'they' by 'he'. Librarian and cashier refers to one person.
6. (b) Delete 'most'. Perfect is itself a superlative.
7. (b) Replace 'which' by 'that'. What is followed by 'that' instead of 'which'.
8. (c) Replace 'were' by 'was'. Statesman and politician refers one person.
9. (b) Delete 'to'.
10. (c) Put 'from' before 'being'. Prevented is followed by preposition 'from'.

Exercise 4

Read the following sentences to find error. The error will be in one part of the sentence. If there is no error, then the answer is E

1. I dislike (a)/my child (b)/watching T.V. (c)/all the time. (d)
2. These people (a)/get their bath water (b)/from the river (c)/and their drink water from a well. (d)
3. It was evident (a)/to me that there (b)/was any mistake (c)/in that account. (d)
4. He does not seem (a)/to be aware (b)/as to (c)/his merits. (d)
5. He declared (a)/at the top of his (b)/voice that (c)/it was not possible. (d)
6. Crossing the road (a)/a car knocked (b)/him down. (c)
7. The captain (a)/with all his team (b)/were held responsible. (c)
8. Bangladesh has come (a)/into existence (b)/thirty years ago. (c)
9. No sooner did (a)/she saw me (b)/than she came up (c)/and spoke to me. (d)
10. No monument in the world (a)/is so beautiful (b)/as the Taj Mahal. (c)

Solutions

1. (b) Replace 'my child' by 'child's'.
2. (d) Replace 'drink' by drinking.
3. (c) Replace 'any' by 'some'. Some is used in affirmative.
4. (c) Replace 'as to' by 'of'. Aware is followed here by preposition 'of'.
5. (E) No error.
6. (a) Replace 'Crossing the road' by. When he was crossing the road. This is the problem of unrelated participle.
7. (c) Replace 'were' by 'was'. Subject of the verb : captain is singular.
8. (a) Change 'has come' to 'came'.
9. (d) Replace 'saw' by 'see'.
10. (E) No error.

Exercise 5

Read the following sentences to find error. The error will be in one part of the sentence. If there is no error, then the answer is E

1. Many a man (a)/have been (b)/working under me. (c)
2. I told him (a)/the story (b)/in details (c)/to make him understand it fully. (d)
3. Different authorities (a)/defines (b)/intelligence in different ways. (c)
4. The old man (a)/told his sons (b)/that there was no such thing (c)/like luck. (d)
5. Everyone knows (a)/that the tiger (b)/is faster (c)/of all animals. (d)
6. Sakshi wrote an essay (a)/so well that (b)/her teacher was (c)/very pleased with her. (d)
7. The conference was (a)/attended (b)/by more than one hundred delegates (c).
8. This is (a)/one of the most (b)/interesting book (c)/I have ever read. (d)
9. Ram was happy (a)/that Rita and her sister was going (b)/by the same train (c)/the next day. (d)
10. The only criteria (a)/to judge (b)/a person (c)/is to observe his behaviour. (d)

Solutions

1. (b) Replace 'have' by 'has'. 'Many a' is followed by singular verb.
2. (c) Replace 'details' by 'detail'.
3. (b) Replace 'defines' by 'define'. Subject, 'authorities' is plural.
4. (d) Replace 'like' by 'as'. 'Such is usually followed by 'as'.
5. (d) Replace 'of all animals' by 'than any other animal'.
6. (a) Replace 'an essay' by 'the essay'. Here essay becomes particular.
7. (E) No error.
8. (c) Change 'book' to 'books'. One of is always followed by plural noun.
9. (b) change 'was' to 'were', as the subject 'Rita and her sister' is plural.
10. (a) Change 'criteria' to 'criterion', criteria singular criterion.

Exercise 6

Read each sentence to find out whether there is an error. The error, if any, will be in one part of the sentence. The number of that part is the answer. If there is no error, then the answer is E **(Bank PO)**

1. No country can long endure (a)/if its foundations (b)/were not laid deep (c)/in the material prosperity. (d)
2. Mahatma Gandhi did not solve (a)/all the future problems (b)/but he did solve (c)/problems of his own age. (d)
3. We now look forward for (a)/some great achievements (b)/which to some extent (c)/can restore the country's prestige once again. (d)
4. While Mahendra was away (a)/on a long official tour (b)/his office receive an important letter (c)/which was marked 'Urgent'. (d)
5. We will pack not only (a)/the material properly (b)/but will also deliver it (c)/to your valued customers. (d)
6. We cannot handle (a)/this complicated case today (b)/unless full details are not given (c)/to us by now. (d)
7. According to one survey (a)/only those forests which were (b)/not under village management (c)/succumbed from fires recently. (d)
8. Our school is making (a)/every possible effort (b)/to provide best facilities (c)/and personal attention for each child. (d)
9. We have done everything (a)/that could be done (b)/to avert the storm (c)/which is now coming on. (d)
10. Jayesh loved his Guru immensely (a)/and gave him fullest loyalty, (b)/yet he had his own (c)/independent way of thinking. (d)

Solutions

1. (c) Change 'were not' to 'are not'.
2. (b) Change 'all the future problems' to 'the problems of the future'.
3. (a) Change 'forward for' to 'forward to'.
4. (c) Change 'receive' to 'received'.
5. (a) Change Part (a) to 'We will not only pack'.
6. (c) Avoid using double negative. Part (c) should be 'unless full details are given'.
7. (d) Change 'from' to 'to' Part (d) should be 'succumbed to fires recently'.
8. (d) Change 'for' to 'to'. Part (d) should be 'and personal attention to each child'.
9. (E) No error.
10. (d) Delete independent. Part (d) should be 'way of thinking'.

Exercise 7

Read each sentence to find out whether there is any error in it. The error, if any, will be in one part of the sentence. The number of that part is the answer. If there is no error, then the answer is E **(Bank PO, RRB)**

1. This laboratory of physicists is (a)/not only equipped with (b)/all state-of-the-art instruments (c)/but also with outstanding physicists. (d)

2. No method of making other (a)/ people agree to (b)/your view point is (c)/as effective as this method. (d)
3. I was pretty sure that (a)/he would support me (b)/for changing the age-old (c)/and static structure of our organization.(d)
4. I did not like his (a)/comments on my paper (b)/but I had no alternative (c)/as I had agreed to keep quiet. (d)
5. The report is candid in admitting (a)/that the investment by the government (b)/in health and family planning (c)/have eroded considerably. (d)
6. He tried as he could (a)/but Naveen did not (b)/succeed in getting (c)/his car to start up. (d)
7. Foolishly Madhu threw (a)/some water on the electric heater (b)/when it catches fire and (c)/she got a shock. (d)
8. Rajesh was expecting (a)/a telegram from his uncle (b)/which would inform (c)/him whether he went or not. (d)
9. Either of the plans (a)/suits him and therefore (b)/he decided not to (c)/go out yesterday. (d)
10. Inspite of the rumors (a) of an impending takeover (b)/by the government, (c)/Ramlal bought more shares of that company. (d)

Solutions

1. (d) The word 'physicists' is meaningless.
2. (a) Change Part (a) to 'No other method of making'.
3. (c) Change Part (c) to 'in changing the age-old'.
4. (E) No error.
5. (d) Change 'have' to 'has' the verb should agree with the subject 'investment'.
6. (d) Change 'his car to start up' to 'his car start up'.
7. (c) Change 'when it catches fire' to 'when it caught fire'.
8. (d) Change 'he went or not' to 'he had gone or not'.
9. (b) Change 'suits him and therefore' to 'suited him therefore'. Superfluous use of and. Incorrect use of tense.
10. (E) No error.

Exercise 8

Read each sentence to find out whether there is any grammatical or idiomatic error in it **(*TC, RRB Kolkata*)**

1. Our housing society comprises (a)/six block and thirty flats (b)/in an area of (c)/about thousand square meters. (d)
2. They took to (a)/reading times (b)/for better knowledge (c)/of the facts. (d)
3. As I was to reach early (a)/I preferred train (b)/instead of (c)/bus. (d)
4. He did not go (a)/to the city on foot (b)/he went there (c)/by the train. (d)
5. One of the most (a)/widely spread (b)/bad habit (c)/is the use of tobacco. (d)
6. Myself and Ramanujam (a)/will take care of (b)/the function (c)/on Saturday. (d)
7. All the doctors (a)/were puzzled on the (b)/strange symptoms (c)/reported by the patient. (d)
8. India is in no way (a)/inferior than the USA (b)/in the fertility of soil (c)/and richness of resources. (d)
9. The visitors (a)/complained at (b)/the poor accommodation (c)/they were given. (d)
10. Amit's habit of (a)/delaying his work (b)/put his colleagues (c)/to a lot of trouble. (d)

Solutions

1. (b) Replace six block and thirty flats by six blocks and thirty flats six is plural so write blocks.
2. (c) Replace for better knowledge by for the better knowledge. 'knowledge' is particularised in the sentence.
3. (c) Change 'instead of' to 'to'. Preposition 'to' is used with prefer, senior, junior, etc.
4. (d) Replace by the train by 'by train'. In phrases like by train, by water, by bus etc. We should not make any change.
5. (c) Replace 'bad habit' by 'bad habits'. After one of, noun will be in plural form.
6. (a) Replace Myself and Ramanujam by Ramanujam and I.
7. (b) Change 'puzzled on' to 'puzzled over'. Wrong use of preposition.
8. (b) Change 'inferior than' to 'inferior to'. Wrong use of preposition. Since, inferior, superior, senior, junior, prefer etc. take preposition 'to' instead of 'than'.
9. (b) Change 'complained at' to 'complained about'. Wrong use of preposition.
10. (E) No error.

Exercise 9

One part of following sentences has an error, point out the portion carrying error in the answer sheet. In case no error is there mention accordingly

(*RRB Patna, Mumbai, ASM*)

1. I have been to a few of his lectures (a)/but understood little of (b)/what he has said. (c)
2. Not only the bandits robbed (a)/the traveller of his purse (b)/but also wounded him grievously. (c)
3. The old woman has had the best medical facilities available (a)/but she will not be cured (b)/unless she does not have a strong desire to live. (c)
4. Frozen foods are so popular today (a)/that many people wonder (b)/how they ever lived without them. (c)

5. We should never be (a)/cent percent sure of our success (b)/in any walk of our life. (c)
6. Smith including (a)/all the members of his family (b)/goes to the church every Sunday. (c)
7. The students of now-a-days (a)/hesitate to talk (b)/to their teachers. (c)
8. If you would have (a)/practised regularly (b)/you would have won the match. (c)
9. Kanchenjungha is one of the (a)/beautiful peak (b)/of the (c)/Himalayan range. (d)
10. He is one of the (a)/most intelligent (b)/student (c)/I have ever taught. (d)

Solutions

1. (c) Change 'what he has said' to 'what he said'. Wrong use of tense.
2. (a) Change 'Not only the bandits robbed' to 'The bandits not only robbed'. Improper placement of conjunction.
3. (c) Change 'unless she does not have a strong desire to live' to 'unless she has a strong desire to live'. Avoid double negative.
4. (E) No error.
5. (b) Change 'cent per cent' to 'hundred per cent'. Cent percent is a wrong expression.
6. (c) Delete 'the' before church. Wrong use of article 'the'.
7. (b) Replace talk by talking.
8. (a) Change 'would have' to 'had'. See the structure of conditional sentence.
9. (b) Change 'peak' to 'peaks'. After of noun is pluralised in such sentences.
10. (c) Change 'student' to 'students'. After 'of' noun is pluralised in such sentences.

Exercise 10

Read each sentence to find out whether there is any error in it. The error, if any, will be in one part of the sentence. The number of that part is the answer. If there is no error, then the answer is E

(RRB Secunderabad, ASM/TC)

1. Radha with (a)/her brothers (b)/and sisters (c)/are present here. (d)
2. Men (a)/proposes (b)/but God (c)/disposes. (d)
3. He gets (a)/up (b)/early at (c)/the morning. (d)
4. The house (a)/is built (b)/in an (c)/attractive manner. (d)
5. She worn (a)/a necklace (b)/studded (c)/with diamonds. (d)
6. None (a)/of these (b)/students (c)/was there. (d)
7. He (a)/was not (b)/blind (c)/from birth. (d)
8. I said (a)/that a interesting (b)/face could (c)/also be pretty. (d)
9. He love (a)/his father (b)/and his father (c)/also loved him. (d)
10. Milking used (a)/to be a task (b)/or a duty cost (c)/on him. (d)

Solutions

1. (d) Change 'are' to 'is'. When two nouns are joined by the conjunction 'with', 'as well as', 'together with', 'besides' etc., the verb should agree with the first noun.
2. (a) Change 'Men' to 'Man'.
3. (c) Change 'early at' to 'early in'. Wrong use of preposition.
4. (E) No error.
5. (a) Change 'worn' to 'wore'. Wore is the past form of wear.
6. (E) No error. None can be used as singular and as plural also.
7. (d) Change 'from' to 'by'. Wrong use of preposition.
8. (b) Change 'a' to 'an'. Wrong use of article.
9. (a) Change 'love' to 'loved' or 'used to love'. Wrong use of verb tense.
10. (c) Change 'a duty cost' to 'a duty cast'.

Exercise 11

Read each sentence to find out whether there is any error in it. The error, if any, will be in one part of the sentence. The number of that part is the answer. If there is no error, then the answer is E

1. The doctor (a)/did not (b)/ask Mohan (c)/the time. (d)
2. How do (a)/Vinoba appeal (b)/to the (c)/landlords ? (d)
3. Bats are (a)/sometime seen (B)/ in our (c)/houses. (d)
4. I am glad (a)/Rox never saw (b)/a trained (c)/police dog jump. (d)
5. His (a)/son met (b)/him (c)/on the door. (d)
6. The plane (a)/was to (b)/take of (c)/at 6 a.m. (d)
7. This is (a)/our attitudes (b)/towards (c)/Ahimsa and Truth. (d)
8. I caught him (a)/from the hand (b)/and began (c)/to plead. (d)
9. We ought (a)/not to (b)/speak ill (c)/for others. (d)
10. Radha works (a)/harder than (b)/I did (c)/her age. (d)

Solutions

1. (d) Change 'the time' to 'about the time'. Wrong use of preposition.
2. (a) Change 'How do' to 'How did'. Wrong use of tense verb.

3. (b) Change 'sometime' to 'sometimes'. Wrong use of word.
4. (d) Change 'police dog jump' to 'police dog jumping'.
5. (d) Change 'on the door' to 'at the door'. Wrong use of preposition.
6. (c) Change 'of' to 'off'. Wrong use of phrase.
7. (b) Change 'attitudes' to 'attitude'.
8. (b) Change 'from the hand' to 'by the hand police'. Wrong use of verb phrase.
9. (d) Change 'for' to 'of'. Wrong use of preposition.
10. (d) Change 'her age' to 'at her age'.

Exercise 12

Read each sentence to find out whether there is any error in it. The error, if any, will be in one part of the sentence. The number of that part is the answer. If there is no error, then the answer is E

1. Krishna is (a)/the taller (b)/boy (c)/in the class. (d)
2. Bhima was (a)/the man (b)/who all (c)/the Indians loved. (d)
3. I can (a)/neither read (b)/or speak (c)/Hindi. (d)
4. I have been (a)/suffering from (b)/fever since (c)/three days. (d)
5. The committee (a)/is devided (b)/over (c)/this issue. (d)
6. The Planning Commission expects (a)/the Gross Domestic Product to (b)/grow by a satisfactory (c)/rate during the year. (d)
7. The language used for writing text books (a)/differs from other forms of writing (b)/in its preference on (c)/simplicity over style. (d)
8. One of the basics of good writing (a)/is to have a (b)/clear understanding of the target audience (c)/and its requirements. (d)
9. This is an (a)/excellent site for (b)/a stadium which we (c)/should like to acquire. (d)
10. If you absent (a)/from college, your (b)/name is likely to be (c)/struck off the rolls. (d)

Solutions

1. (b) Change 'taller' to 'tallest'. Wrong use of degree of adjective.
2. (c) Change 'who' to 'whom'. Wrong use of pronoun.
3. (c) Change 'or' to 'nor'. Wrong use of conjunction.
4. (c) Change 'since' to 'for'. For used for period of time.
5. (b) Change 'is decided' to 'are decided'. Here committee is not used as collective noun.
6. (E) No error.
7. (c) Change 'in its preference on' to 'in its preference to'. Wrong use of preposition.
8. (E) No error.
9. (d) Change 'should like to acquire' to 'would like to acquire'.
10. (a) Change 'If you absent' to 'If you absent yourself'. Absent is used reflexively.

Exercise 13

There is a mistake in each of the following sentences. Find out the part in which the mistake occurs

(*RRB Bhubaneshwar, ASM*)

1. The man (a)/is (b)/a (c)/social animal. (d)
2. Twenty five kilometers (a)/from Bhubaneshwar to Cuttack (b)/are (c)/a long distance. (d)
3. The institute (a)/imparts training (b)/in (c)/the French. (d)
4. Looking forward (a)/to meet (b)/you (c)/soon. (d)
5. Pass on (a)/the salt, (b)/please, (c)/do you ? (d)
6. He is (a)/a mason (b)/who (c)/built my house. (d)
7. I cannot (a)/make from (b)/what you are saying (c)/about him. (d)
8. What (a)/you will think (b)/if school boys (c)/make fun of you ? (d)
9. The minister's speech (a)/has been reported (b)/to the newspaper. (c)
10. No sooner (a)/we reached there (b)/than it started raining. (c)

Solutions

1. (a) Delete 'The'. Wrong use of definite article 'The'.
2. (c) Change 'are' to 'is'. Wrong use of verb. Here twenty five kilometers is used as a unit, so singular verb is used.
3. (d) Change 'the French' to 'French'. Do not use definite article 'the' before name of language.
4. (b) Change 'to meet' to 'to meeting'. Wrong use of infinitive.
5. (d) Change 'do you' to 'won't you'. It is a request.
6. (b) Change 'a mason' to 'the mason'. Wrong use of article.
7. (b) Change 'make from' to 'make out'. Wrong use of preposition or phrasal verb .
8. (b) Change 'you will think' to 'will you think'. Proper use of inversion is necesary in questions.
9. (E) No error.
10. (b) Change 'reached there' to 'did we reached there'. Wrong use of inversion.

Exercise 14

The following sentences contain errors in grammar, usage, diction (choice of words) and idiom. Some sentences may be correct. No sentence has more than one error. Select the numbered part that according to you contains the error. Its number is the answer

(*RRB, Mumbai*)

1. Being a very cold day (a)/I would (b)/not go out for (c)/a morning walk. (d)
2. Such an act of cruelty (a)/had never (b)/be commited (c)/before. (d)
3. If you will (a)/insist upon (b)/challenging me, (c)/I will fight it out alone. (d)
4. Fifty years (a)/have passed (b)/since (c)/Subhash Chandra Bose had died. (d)
5. A good house (a)/and a good bank (b)/account is what (c)/he wants. (d)
6. Of all the (a)/other teachers the (b)/students respected the history (c)/teacher the most. (d)
7. He is one of those persons (a)/who listen (b)/to all advice but keep (c)/his own counsel. (d)
8. No one but (a)/he knew (b)/who was (c)/setting the question paper. (d)
9. A box (a)/of apples are (b)/in (c)/the car. (d)
10. The principal threatened to (a)/inform to (b)/his father about (c)/his misdeeds. (d)

Solutions

1. (a) It should be 'It being a very cold day'. This is the problem of dangling participle.
2. (c) Change 'be' to 'been'.
3. (c) Change 'will insist' to 'insist'. Do not use will after if in such conditional type of sentences.
4. (d) Delete had. It should be Subhash Chandra Bose died.
5. (c) Change 'is' to 'are'. Wrong use of singular verb. When two nouns are joined with the conjunction 'and' use plural verb.
6. (d) Delete 'the' before most. Wrong use of article 'the'.
7. (d) Change 'keep his' to 'keep their'. Pronoun their refer to 'those persons' not 'he'.
8. (E) No error.
9. (b) Change 'are' to 'is'. Wrong use of plural verb with singular subject 'box'.
10. (b) Delete 'to' after 'inform'.

Exercise 15

Read each sentence to find out whether there is any error in it . The error, if any , will be in one part of the sentence. The number of that part is the answer. If there is no error, the answer is E. ***(Stenographers Exam)***

1. Sharad was entrusted with (a)/the task of co-ordination yesterday (b)/but due to certain difficulties (c)/he does not do it. (d)
2. One should make (a)/his best efforts if (b)/one wishes to achieve (c)/success in this organisation. (d)
3. Having deprived from their (a)/homes in the recent earthquake (b) they had no other option but (c)/to take shelter in a school. (d)
4. The technician reminded (a)/them to have a (b)/throughly cleaning of the (c)/machine after use. (d)
5. The villager told (a)/us where was the (b)/temple and even led (c)/us to the spot. (d)
6. The person who (a)/they are referring (b)/to is none other (c)/than my close friend. (d)
7. Mahesh was kind enough (a)/to inform us about the (b)/conspiracy but declined to (c)/name the person behind it. (d)
8. He told the policeman (a)/that he would rather (b)/starve to stealing to get (c)/what he had been aspiring for. (d)
9. In spite of the workload yesterday (a)/Nitin manages to play (b)/it cool and continued (c)/with his work as usual. (d)
10. The demand of the workers' (a)/union that the dismissed (b)/employee to reinstated, has (c), been accepted by the management. (d)

Solution

1. (d) Change 'he does not do it' to 'he did not do it'. Wrong use of tense.
2. (b) Change 'his best' to 'one's best'. Wrong use of pronoun.
3. (a) Change 'deprived from' to 'deprived of'. Wrong use of preposition.
4. (c) Change 'throughly' to 'through'. Unnecessary use of adverb.
5. (b) It should be : The villager told us where the temple was and even led us to the spot.
6. (d) Change 'than' to 'but'.
7. (E) No error.
8. (c) Change 'to' to 'than'.
9. (b) Change 'manages to play' to 'managed to play'. Wrong use of tense verb.
10. (c) Change 'to reinstated' to 'be reinstated'.

Exercise 16

(i) In this section a number of sentences are given. The sentences are divided in three separate parts and each one is labelled (a), (b), (c). Read each sentence to find out whether there is an error in any part. No sentence has more than one error. When you find an error in any one of the parts [(a), (b) or (c)] indicate your response. You may feel that there is no error in a sentence. In that case letter (d) will signify a 'No error' response.

(ii) You are to indicate only one response for each item. (If you indicate more than one response, your answer will be considered wrong.) Error may be in grammar, word usage or idioms.

There may be a word missing or there may be a word which should be removed.

(iii) You are not required to correct the error. You are required only to indicate your response.

(CDS)

1. Thinking that he has finally found (a)/someone with similar interests, (b)/the scholar tried to strike up a conversation. (c)/No error. (d)
2. Earlier this year, (a)/Constantan had entered the news via a video-tapted interview (b)/telecasted by commercial television channel. (c)/No error. (d)
3. If you permit me to speak the truth, (a), I shall say without hesitation (b)/that you have done a mistake. (c)/No error. (d)
4. My friend is so rich that (a)/he is having six houses in Mumbai (b)/and four in Pune, (c)/No error. (d)
5. He asked me (a)/if I am ill (b)/and I answered that I was not. (c)/No error. (d)
6. He lost his new knife (a)/shortly after (b)/he bought it. (c)/No error. (d)
7. The ultimate problem of Physics (a)/is to reduce matter by analysis (b)/to its lowest condition or divisibility. (c)/No error. (d)
8. By the time (a)/she finished typing (b)/it was not hardly ten. (c)/No error. (d)
9. He like (a)/his companions (b) were deceived. (c)/No error. (d)
10. He told me that you had left the school (a)/a year ago (b)/and seeking for a job. (c)/No error. (d)

Solutions

1. (a) It should be 'Thinking that he had finally found'. The sentence is in past tense so to use present perfect is incorrect.
2. (c) It should be 'telecast by a commercial television channel'. The past of telecast is telecast.
3. (c) It should be 'that you have made a mistake' or 'you have committed a mistake'.
4. (b) It should be 'he has six houses in Mumbai'. Generally the verb 'have' is not used in continuous form.
5. (b) It should be 'if I was ill'. If the reporting verb is in past, the tense of the reported speech will also be past.
6. (c) It should be 'he had bought it'. For the action completed first, use past perfect tense.
7. (b) It should be 'is to reduce matter by an analysis'. Use article a/an before countables.
8. (c) It should be 'it was hardly ten'. Hardly has negative meaning. Avoid using double negative.
9. (c) It should be 'was deceived'. If two nouns are joined with; like , in addition to, together with, etc., the verb will be as per the first noun.
10. (c) It should be 'and were seeking a job'. Use past verb before seeking.

Exercise 17

(i) In this section, a number of sentences are given. The sentences are divided in three separate parts and each one is labelled as (a), (b), and (c). Read each sentence to find out whether there is an error in any part. No sentence has more than one error. When you find an error in any one of the given parts 9(a), (b) or (c)] indicate your response. You may feel that there is no error in a sentence. In that case letter (d) will signify a 'No error' response.

(ii) You are to indicate only one response for each item. (If you indicate more than one response, your answer will be considered wrong.) Errors may be in grammar, word usage or idioms. There may be a word missing or there may be a word which should be removed.

(iii) You are not required to correct the error. You are required only to indicate your response.

1. As I prefer coffee than tea (a)/my friends always take the trouble (b)/to get a cup of coffee, whenever I visit them. (c)/ No error. (d)
2. There has been (a)/little change in the patient's condition (b)/since he was moved to the special ward. (c)/No error. (d)
3. The king was perturbed (a)/to found evidence (b)/against his own queen. (c)/No error. (d)
4. They begged her (a)/not to go but she was determined (b)/ and left the castle. (c) /No error. (d)
5. They cook meal, (a)/lay the table, (b)/clean the house and iron the clothes. (c)/No error. (d)
6. No sooner did (a)/the doctor enter the house (b)/then the patient died. (c)/No error. (d)
7. The drawing room was a mess (a)/with all the furnitures (b)/scattered in total disarray. (c)/No error. (d)
8. The gap between what he preaches (a)/and what he practises is too wide (b)/to be accepted by anyone. (c)/ No error. (d)
9. While flying over India (a)/we had glimpses of the two sources of her culture (b)/Ganges and Himalayas. (c)/No error. (d)
10. This picture (a)/is the best (b)/of the two. (c)/No error. (d)

Solutions

1. (a) Part (a) should be: 'As I prefer coffee to tea'. Prefer always take preposition 'to'.
2. (d) No error.
3. (b) Part (b) should be : '.....to find evidence.....'
4. (d) No error.
5. (d) No error.
6. (c) Change 'then' to 'than'. Than is used here in conjunctions.
7. (b) Noun 'furniture' cannot be pluralised as 'furnitures'. Part (b) should be : '.....with all the furniture'.
8. (d) No error.
9. (c) Insert definite article 'the'. 'The Ganges and the Himalayas'.
10. (b) Change to 'is the better.....'. For the comparison of two, use comparative degree.

Exercise 18

In this section, a number of sentences are given. These sentences are marked in three parts indicated by the letters (a), (b) and (c). Read each sentence to find out whether there is an error in any part of it. No sentence has more than one error. When you find an error in any one of the parts (a), (b) or (c), select that part as your answer. You may feel that there is no error in a sentence. In that case letter (d) will signify a 'No error' response.

Errors may be in grammar, word usage or idioms. There may be a word missing or there may be a word which should be removed.

1. Finishing the work (a)/he was allowed rest (b)/for half an hour. (c)/ No error (d)
2. The pirates, who had hidden the treasure on the island, (a)/went back again (b)/because they thought they can now remove it with safety. (c)/No error. (d)
3. In those early days (a)/the West paid lip-service (b)/to United Nations. (c)/ No error. (d)
4. Ten Shillings (a)/was charged (b)/by him for the service. (c)/No error. (d)
5. To an amusing degree (a)/he was addicted to read the jokes in punch aloud (b)/even when he was alone. (c)/No error. (d)
6. Why not stop the first man you meet next and ask, (a)/"could you tell me (b)/what the time is?" (c)/No error. (d)
7. The invention of the internal combustion engine (a)/is considered to be (b)/a most unique development. (c)/No error. (d)
8. Put off (a)/the fire (b)/quickly. (c)/No error. (d)
9. A fight (a)/took place (b)/on the board of the ship. (c)/No error. (d)
10. Hardly the rains started (a)/when a child in the corner (b)/sent out a piercing wail. (c)/No error. (d)

Solutions

1. (a) Change Part (a) to 'After he finished the work'.
2. (c) Change 'can' to 'could' as. 'Because they thought that they could now remove it with safety'. The sentence is in past tense.
3. (c) Insert 'the' before United Nations.
4. (b) Change 'was' to 'were'.
5. (b) Part (b) should be, 'he was addicted to reading the jokes in punch aloud'. Gerund form is used in such sentence structure.
6. (a) Use either first or next in the sentence. Part (b) should be, 'Why not stop the first man you meet and ask' or 'Why not stop the man you meet next and ask'.
7. (c) 'Unique' cannot be compared. Part (c) should be, 'a unique development'.
8. (a) Put out means to extinguish. Part (a) should be, 'Put out.'
9. (c) Part (c) should be, 'on the deck of the ship'.
10. (a) Always use auxiliary had after hardly. Part (a) should be, 'Hardly had the rains started'.

Exercise 19

(i) In this section, a number of sentences are given. The sentences are in three separate parts and each one is labelled (a), (b) and (c). Read each sentence to find out whether there is an error in any of these part. No sentence has more than one error. When you find an error in any one of these parts choose that part as your response. You may feel that there is no error in a sentence, in that case choose (d) as your response.

Errors may be in grammar, word usage of idioms. There may be a word missing or a word which should be removed.

1. Don't think you can say unpleasant things (a)/about someone behind his back (b)/and not found out. (c) /No error. (d)
2. The Americans speak (a)/different from us (b)/ though our grammar is the same (c)/No error. (d)
3. This is an instance (a)/of the blind (b)/leading the blinds. (c)/No error. (d)
4. He took to drink (a)/to lessen (b)/his mental worries. (c)/No error. (d)
5. My father could lead (a)/a full and happy life (b)/without spending lot of money. (c)/No error. (d)

6. All India Radio broadcasted (a)/a very good programme (b)/this morning. (c)/No error. (d)
7. There were so much cattle (a)/on the road that (b)/it was difficult to drive safely. (c)/No error. (d)
8. What, could have provoked him to behave (a)/in such a rude manner (b)/at dinner last night? (c)/No error. (d)
9. They were rich zamindars in the thirties (a)/but now they have fallen on the evil days (b)/and have lost much of their property. (c)/No error. (d)
10. The foreign ambassador was (a)/both noted for his charming manners (b)/as well as his wide knowledge of languages. (c)/No error. (d)

Solutions

1. (c) Change 'and not found out' to 'and are not found out'. Use of 'verb' is necessary here.
2. (b) Change 'different' to 'differently'. Incorrect use of verb in place of adverb.
3. (c) Change 'leading the blinds' to 'leading the blind'. The blind means the blind people.
4. (a) Change 'took to drink' to 'took to drinking'.
5. (c) Change 'lot of money' to 'a lot of money' as 'A lot of' is a phrase.
6. (a) Change 'broadcasted' to 'broadcast'. Broadcasted is the past of broadcast.
7. (a) Change 'much' to 'many'. Much is used for uncountables.
8. (a) Change 'What, could have provoked him' to 'What provoked him'. Incorrect use of perfect tense.
9. (a) Change 'They were rich zamindars in thirties' to 'They had been rich zamindars in thirties'.
10. (c) Change 'as well as' to 'and'. Incorrect use of conjunction as well as.

Exercise 20

(i) In this section, a number of sentences are given. The sentences are divided in three separate parts and each one is labelled (a), (b) and (c). Read each sentence to find out whether there is an error in any part. No sentence has more than one error. When you find an error in any one of the given parts [(a), (b) or (c)] indicate your response according. You may feel that there is no error in a sentence. In that case letter (d) will signify a 'No error' response.

(ii) You are to indicate only one response for each item. (If you indicate more than one response, your answer will be considered wrong. Errors may be in grammar, word usage or idioms. There may be a word missing or there may be a word which should be removed.

(iii) You are not required to correct the error. You are required only to indicate your response.

1. The news of the disturbance (a)/was braodcasted (b)/the same evening. (c)/ No error. (d)
2. Everyone visiting the house asked the young girl (a)/how could she kill the wolf (b)/single handed and without a weapon. (c)/No error. (d).
3. While walking slowly in the park (a)/on a quiet summer afternoon (b)/a mad dog suddenly attacked him from behind (c)/No error. (d)
4. Since the attachment of air-conditioned sleeping cars to all important trains. (a)/travelling became very pleasant (b)/especially during the summer season. (c)/No error. (d)
5. It is the newspapers (a)/that exposes us to the widest range (b)/of human experiences and behaviour. (c)/No error. (d)
6. The method suggested in the lecture (a)/enables a student to learn more quickly (b)/and to have remembered for a longer period of time. (c)/No error. (d)
7. Last month we celebrated (a)/the wedding of our sister for whom (b)/we have been looking for suitable alliance for three years. (c)/No error. (d)
8. A leading textile manufacturer, one of the fastest growing in the industry. (a)/is looking for a marketing manager (b)/to look up the marketing network of the company. (c)/No error (d)
9. There was very heavy rain last night. (a)/and the rivers have over flown their banks. (b)/ causing severe hardship to the people living by them. (c)/No error. (d)
10. The government warned the shopkeepers (a)/that if they persist in charging unfair prices (b)/ their licences would be cancelled. (c)/No error. (d)

Solutions

1. (b) Change 'broadcasted' to 'broadcast'.
2. (b) Change 'how could she kill' to 'how she could kill'. Incorrect use of inversion in indirect speech.
3. (a) Change 'While walking slowly in the park' to 'While he was walking slowly in the park'. This is a problem of unrelated participle.
4. (b) Change 'travelling became very pleasant'. to 'travelling has become very pleasant'. Incorrect use of tense.
5. (b) Change 'exposes' to 'expose'. Incorrect use of singular verb.
6. (c) Change 'and to have remembered for' to 'and to remember for'. Incorrect use of perfect tense.

7. (c) Change 'we have been looking for' to 'we had been looking for'. Incorrect use of tense.
8. (c) Change 'look up the marketing' to 'look after the marketing'. Incorrect use of phrasal verb.
9. (b) Change 'have overflown' to 'have overflowed'. Part (b) should be 'and the rivers have overflowed their banks'.
10. (b) Change 'persist' to 'persisted'. The sentence structure is in past.

Exercise 21

Read each sentence to find out whether there is any error in it. The error, if any will be in one part of the sentence. The number of that part is the answer. If there is no error, the answer is (E). (Ignore the errors of punctuation, if any)

1. Kamlesh asked the dealer (a)/what was the price (b)/of that bicycle and whether (c)/it is really made in Germany ? (d)/No error. (E)
2. While luminaries of the dance world (a)/has no dearth of opportunities to display their art, (b)/upcoming dancers suffer from (c)/an unfortunate lack of exposure. (d)/No error. (E)
3. Scarcely had I (a)/finished washing the car (b)/than the master came (c)/and asked me to clean the floor of the house. (d)/No error. (E)
4. The job is much worse than I expected (a)/if I would have realised (b)/how awful it was going to be (c)/I would not have accepted it. (d)/No error. (E)
5. I am trying to finish (a)/this letter for the last one hour (b)/I wish you would (c)/go away or stop disturbing me. (d)/No error.(E)
6. I offered him part-time work (a)/ but he turned it over (b)/saying that he would (c)/rather wait for a full-time job. (d)/No error. (E)
7. He fixed a metal ladder (a)/for the wall below his window (b)/so as to be able to (c)/escape if there was a fire. (d)/No error. (E)
8. The foremost criteria of selection we adopted (a)/were the number of years of training (b)/a dancer had received (c)/under a particular guru. (d)/No error. (E)
9. He refused to disclose to his friends (a)/whether he will leave (b)/for England immediately (c)/after finishing his studies. (d)/No error.
10. Despite for her protests (a)/I decided (b)/to buy the saree (c)/which she did not like. (d)/No error. (E)

Solutions

1. (d) Change 'it is really made' to 'it was really made'. Incorrect use of tense in indirect speech.
2. (b) Change 'has no dearth of' to 'have no dearth of'. Incorrect use of verb.
3. (c) Change 'than' to 'when'. Incorrect use of than with 'scarcely'.
4. (b) Change 'if I would have realised' to 'if I had realised'. See the structure of conditional sentences.
5. (a) Change 'I am trying' to 'I have been trying'. Incorrect use of tense.
6. (b) Change 'but he turned it over' to 'but he turned it down'. Incorrect use of phrasal verb.
7. (b) Change 'for the wall below' to 'against the wall below'. Incorrect use of preposition.
8. (a) Change 'criteria' to 'criterion'. Criteria is plural of criterion.
9. (b) Change 'will' to 'would'. The sentence structure is in past.
10. (a) Delete 'for'. Incorrect use of preposition.

Exercise 22

Read each sentence to find out whether there is any grammatical or idiomatic error in it. The error, if any, will be in one part of the sentence. The number of that part is the answer. If there is no error, the answer is (E). (Ignore the errors of punctuation, if any.)

1. The principal of equal justice (a)/for all is one of (b)/the corner stones of our (c)/democratic way of life. (d)/No error. (E)
2. The trust has succeeded (a)/admirably in raising (b)/money for (c)/future programmes. (d)/No error. (E)
3. Honesty, integrity and being intelligent (a)/are the qualities which (b)/we look for when (c)/ we interview applicants. (d)/No error. (E)
4. In order to save petrol, (a)/motorists must have to (b)/be very cautious (c)/while driving along the highways. (d)/No error. (E)
5. If the by-stander had not been (a)/familiar with first-aid techniques, (b)/the driver which had met (c)/with the accident would have died. (d)/No error.(E)
6. Not one of the children (a)/has ever sang (b)/on any occasion (c)/in public before. (d)/No error. (E)
7. Neither the earthquake (a)/nor the subsequent fire (b)/was able to dampen (c)/the spirit of the residents. (d)/No error. (E)
8. The customer scarcely had (a)/enough money to pay (b)/to the cashier (c)/at the cash counter. (d)/No error. (E)
9. The apparently obvious solutions (a)/to most of his problems (b)/were over look by (c)/many of his friends. (d)/No error. (E)
10. By arresting the local criminals (a)/and encouraging good people (b)/we can end (c)/hostilities of that area. (d)/No error. (E)

Solutions

1. (a) Change 'principal' to 'principle'. Incorrect use of word.
2. (d) Change 'future programmes' to 'its future programme'.
3. (a) Change 'Honesty, integrity and being intelligent' to 'Honesty, integrity and intelligence'.
4. (b) Change 'must have' to 'have to' or 'must'.
5. (c) Change 'which' to 'who', 'who' is used for living persons.
6. (b) Change 'sang' to 'sung'. Incorrect past participle of verb.
7. (c) Change 'was able to' dampen to 'could dampen'.
8. (b) Change 'enough money' to 'any money'.
9. (c) Change 'were overlook' to 'were overlooked'. In passive structure third form of the verb is used.
10. (d) Change 'hostilities of that area' to 'hostilities in that area'.

Exercise 23

In this section ten sentences are given. Each sentence has three parts, indicated by (a) ,(b) and (c). Read each sentence to find out whether there is an error. If you find an error in any one of the parts, [(a), (b) or (c)]. Indicate your response by blackening the letter related to that part in the answer sheet provided. If a sentence has no error, indicate this by blackening (d), which stands for 'No error'. Errors may be in grammar, appropriate word usage or idioms ***(NDA)***

1. The flicker of light from the gas lamps (a)/indicated that the night (b)/was barely passed. (c)/ No error. (d)
2. India was committed to keep maintaining peace (a)/and solving all outstanding prob lems (b)/ with her neighbours through dialogue. (c)/No error. (d)
3. Being the second Saturday of the month, (a)/he got up late and spent the whole day at home, (b)/doing his share of the household chores. (c)/No error. (d)
4. As economic restructuring in Central and Eastern Europe progresses, (a)/an estimated 15 million people may be out of work (b)/by the end of the year. (c)/No error. (d)
5. Such of those who have not paid the fees, (a)/the circular says, (b)/will not be permitted to attend classes. (c)/No error. (d)
6. There is a good British Library in the city (a)/and anyone interested in books (b)/can avail of the facility (c)/No error. (d)
7. Those who are excessively careful (a)/for their health (b)/are not generally healthy (c)/ No error. (d)
8. Once we have agreed on (a)/the fundamentals, there will hardly be (b)/anything left to discuss about, (c)/No error. (d)
9. I did ask him (a)/where you were (b)/but he didn't tell me, (c)/No error. (d)
10. I will wait for you (a)/at the office (b)/till you will finish your work, (c)/No error. (d)

Solutions

1. (c) Change 'was' to 'had'. Incorrect use of tense.
2. (a) Change 'to keep maintaining' to 'to maintaining'.
3. (a) Change 'Being the second' to 'It being the second'. It is a problem of unrelated participle.
4. (d) No error.
5. (a) Change 'Such of those who have not paid the fees' to 'They who have not paid the fees'.
6. (c) Insert himself after avail. Avail is used reflexively.
7. (b) Change 'for' to 'of' '.... of their health...'
8. (c) Omit 'about'. Part (c) should be : '....anything left to discuss.'
9. (b) Change pronoun 'you' to 'he'. Part (b) should be : '..... where he was.'
10. (c) Part (c) should be : '...... till you finish your work.' In such type of sentences do not use will after when, as soon as, till, after, as, etc.

Exercise 24

Read each sentence to find out whether there is any grammatical or idiomatic error in it . The error, if any, will be in one part of the sentence. The number of that part is the answer. If there is no error, the answer is (E). (Ignore the errors of punctuation, if any)

1. We had swam (a)/across the river (b)/before (c)/ sunset. (d)/No error. (E) ***(SBI PO)***
2. Madhuri is (a)/more prettier (b)/than her (c)/younger sister. (d)/No error. (E) ***(SBI PO)***
3. A cell (a)/is the smallest (b)/identifiable unit of life and cannot be (c)/seen with a naked eye. (d)/No error. (E)
4. If a student needs advices about (a)/careers, (b)/he or she should consult (c)/the Career officer. (d)/No error. (E)
5. Had they have been in (a)/my condition, (b)/they would have felt (c)/miserable and thought of committing suicide. (d)/No error (E) ***(RRB, Kolkata)***
6. The Secretary of the worker's union (a)/remarked that the present government is so selfish (b)/that it cared very little (c)/about solving anyone else's problem. (d)/No error. (E) ***(RRB, Kolkata)***

7. He don't know (a)/the difference between (b)/a ship and a submarine. (c)/No error. (d) ***(SSC Clerical)***
8. Yesterday I met an old friend (a)/when I are going (b)/to the market. (c)/No error. (d) ***(SSC Clerical)***
9. Cattles (a)/were grazing (b)/in the meadows (c)/near our farm. (d)/No error (E) ***(BSRB Clerical)***
10. You are really (a)/senior than (b)/me (c)/in age. (d)/No error (E) ***(BSRB Clerical)***

Solutions

1. (a) Replace 'swam' by 'swum'. Third form of swim is swum.
2. (b) Delete 'more'. Avoid using double compartives in a sentence.
3. (d) Replace 'A' by 'The'. 'With the naked eyes' is correct expression.
4. (a) Replace 'advices' by 'advice'. Advice is an uncountable noun we cannot pluralise advice as such (advices).
5. (b) Delete have after 'they'. This is a conditional sentence with following structure.
   Had they invited me, I would have attended the function.
6. (b) Replace 'is' by 'was'. Reporting verb is in past so the reported speech will also be in past.
7. (b) Replace don't by 'does not'.
8. (b) Replace 'are' by 'was'. The sentence structure is in past.
9. (a) Replace 'cattles' by 'cattle'. Cattle is itself in plural.
10. (b) Replace 'than' by 'to'. Superior, senior, junior, inferior, prior, etc take preposition 'to'.

Exercise 25

Read each sentence to find out whether there is any grammatical or idiomatic error in it . The error, if any, will be in one part of the sentence. The number of that part is the answer. If there is no error, the answer is (E). (Ignore the errors of punctuation, if any)

1. Make haste (a)/lest (b)/you should not miss (c)/the train. (d)/No error. (E) ***(BSRB Clerical)***
2. Many of us (a)/do not know (b)/to swim (c)/at all. (d)/No error. (E) ***(BSRB Clerical)***
3. His car is (a)/more bigger than (b)/that of any of us. (c)/No error. (d) ***(SSC Clerk)***
4. One of my uncles (a)/is a doctor / in America. (c)/No error. (d) ***(SSC Clerk)***
5. This machine looks (a)/good but is very (b)/badly designed (c)/and doesn't work good. (d)/No error. (E)
6. He is well-known for both (a)/his kindness (b)/as well as (c)/his understanding. (d)/No error. (E)
7. Ramu closely (a)/resembles to his father (b)/not only in physical features (c)/but also in habits. (d)/No error. (E) ***(SBI PO)***
8. After he had read the two first chapters (a)/of the novel (b)/he felt like reading (c)/the book at one sitting. (d)/No error. (E) ***(SBI PO)***
9. India is (a)/one of the leading (b)/film producing country (c)/in the world. (d)/No error. (E) ***(CSRB, Patna)***
10. Hardly had (a)/I left the house (b)/then it began (c)/to rain. (d)/No error. (E) ***(CSRB, Patna)***

Solutions

1. (c) Delete 'not'. Avoid double negative.
2. (c) Place 'how' before 'to'.
   (i) I do not *know how to* swim.
   (ii) I don't *know how to* play carrom.
   (iii) I do not *know where to* go.
3. (b) Delete 'more'. Double comparatives should be avoided.
4. (d) No error.
5. (d) Replace 'good' by 'well'.
6. (c) Replace 'as well as' by 'and'. The structure of the sentence is 'Both ..... and'.
7. (b) Delete 'to' after 'resembles'.
8. (a) Replace 'the two first' by 'the first two'.
9. (c) Replace 'country' by 'countries'. After 'one of, most of'use noun in plural.
10. (c) Replace 'then' by 'when'. 'Hardly', 'scarcely' takes conjunction 'when'.

Exercise 26

Read each sentence to find out whether there is any grammatical or idiomatic error in it . The error, if any, will be in one part of the sentence. The number of that part is the answer. If there is no error, the answer is (E). (Ignore the errors of punctuation, if any)

1. He told me (a)/that he wrote a letter (b)/to his superior (c)/for a certain reason. (d)/No error. (E) ***(BSRB Clerical Bhopal)***
2. The teacher told the boys (a)/that one (b)/ought to work hard (c)/to earn one living (d)/No error. (E) ***(BSRB Clerical Bhopal)***
3. The obstacles to which (a)/Gandhiji had to surmount (b)/were mostly (c) on the moral and spiritual grounds (d)/No error. (E) ***(BSRB, Lucknow)***
4. Unless you do not (a)/take care of your health (b)/you will continue (c)/to suffer (d)/No error. (E) ***(BSRB, Lucknow)***
5. After Ravi (a)/read the (b)/magazines and newspapers, and watched the TV programme, he decided (c)/to go out and meet some old friends. (d)/No error. (E) ***(RRB, Kolkata)***

6. Everyone agrees that (a)/the Ganga is the holiest (b)/of all other rivers (c)/of India (d)/No error. (E) **(BSRB, Bhopal Clerical)**
7. The issues are (a)/complex and (b)/has been obscured (c)/by other factors. (d)/No error. (E) **(CSRB, Patna)**
8. The bus was (a)/hired by (b)/the ladies (c)/for its picnic. (d)/No error. (E) **(CSRB, Patna)**
9. If (a)/it snowed tomorrow (b)/we'll go (c)/skating. (d)/No error. (E) **(SBI PO)**
10. A quarrel arose between the five members (a)/and for a time (b)/it appeared as if the party (c)/had been heading for a split. (d)/No error. (E) **(SBI PO)**

Solutions

1. (b) Replace 'he wrote' by 'he had written'.
2. (d) The correct expression is one's living.
3. (a) Use of 'to' is superfluous.
4. (a) Use of 'do not' is wrong. 'Unless' is itself negative.
5. (b) Place had before 'read'.
   (i) After he had reached the station, the train arrived.
   (ii) The patient had died before the doctor reached here.
6. (c) Use of 'other' is superfluous.
7. (c) Replace 'has' by 'have'. Subject 'The issues' is plural.
8. (d) Replace 'its' by 'a'. 'For a picnic' is correct phrase.
9. (b) Replace 'snowed' by 'snows'. The use of future and past like this is an incorrect combination.
10. (a) Replace 'between' by 'among'.'Between' is used for two and 'among' for more than two.

Exercise 27

Read each sentence to find out whether there is any grammatical or idiomatic error in it . The error, if any, will be in one part of the sentence. The number of that part is the answer. If there is no error, the answer is (E). (Ignore the errors of punctuation, if any.)

1. They had swam (a)/across the river (b)/before (c)/the sun sets. (d)/No error. (E) **(SBI PO)**
2. She is (a)/more prettier (b)/than her (c)/friend Sheela. (d)/No error. (E) **(SBI PO)**
3. Everyone of (a)/the staff members present here (b)/has given a day's pay (c)/as their contribution to the fund. (d)/ No error. (E) **(CSRB, Patna)**
4. Found guilty (a)/on murder (b)/the accused was (c)/sentenced to death. (d)/No error. (E) **(CSRB, Patna)**
5. The criminal was (a)/sentenced to death (b)/and was hung for his crime. (c)/No error. (d) **(SSC Clerical)**
6. He said that (a)/he will help me (b)/secure a decent job. (c)/No error. (d) **(SSC Clerical)**
7. The recent symposium on censorship (a)/indicated that to refrain with saying or writing (b)/something, others might object, (c)/to, is a form of self-censorship. (d)/No error. (E) **(RRB, Kolkata)**
8. The Indian way (a)/of thinking is superior (b)/to most of the (c)/countries of the world. (d)/No error. (E) **(RRB, Kolkata)**
9. I am certain that none (a)/of these two books (b)/is useful to the (c)/students of the 8th standard. (d)/No error. (E) **(BSRB Lucknow)**
10. The lawyer asked me (a)/where had I (b)/kept clothes (c)/before taking a dip in the river. (d)/No error. (E) **(BSRB Lucknow)**

Solutions

1. (a) Replace 'swam' by 'swum'.
2. (b) Delete 'more'. Avoid using double comparitives in a sentence.
3. (d) Replace 'their' by 'his'. With 'everyone, everybody, anyone, anybody' always use singular possessive pronoun (his or her).
4. (b) Replace 'on' by 'of'.
5. (c) Replace 'hung' by 'hanged'. Verb 'hang' has two forms and two meanings as per following :

Ist form	IInd form	IIIrd form
Hang	hung	hung
Hang	hanged	hanged

6. (a) Replace 'don't by 'does not'. Subject 'He' is third person, singular number.
7. (b) Use 'from' after refrain instead of 'with'.
8. (c) Place that of after 'to'.
9. (a) Replace 'none' by 'neither'.
10. (b) Replace 'where had I' by 'where I had'. In 'Indirect narration' the sentence changes from interrogative to assertive.

Exercise 28

Read each sentence to find out whether there is any grammatical or idiomatic error in it . The error, if any, will be in one part of the sentence. The number of that part is the answer. If there is no error, the answer is (E). (Ignore the errors of punctuation, if any)

1. Like most young (a)/women living at homes, I can't really (b)/talk about my ideas or what I really feel, to my parents. (c)/No error. (d)
2. The minister conferred /(a) with his colleagues (b)/and agreed that the new projects on education (c)/should be sanctioned immediately. (d)/No error. (E) **(RRB, Kolkata)**
3. Sunil is (a)/a best student (b)/in our class (c)/at present. (d)/No error. (E) **(CSRB, Patna)**

4. It is in 1929 (a)/that we first (b)/flew to (c)/the United States. (d)/No error. (E) ***(CSRB, Patna)***
5. Being a (a)/fine day we went out (b)/for picnic (c)/at Okhla. (d)/No error. (E) ***(BSRB Clerical)***
6. Many a man (a)/have been (b)/working (c)/under me. (d)/No error. (E) ***(BSRB Clerical)***
7. Please explain to me (a)/how is a digital computer (b)/different from (c)/an analog computer. (d)/No error. (E)
8. I'll work for you (a)/as long as (b)/you'll pay (c)/well. (d)/No error. (E)
9. Had you informed me earlier (a)/I would have (b)/certainly purchase (c)/the car for you. (d)/No error. (E) ***(BSRB, Lucknow)***
10. It was seven o'clock (a)/in the evening that (b)/the train steamed (c)/into the station. (d)/No error. (E) ***(CSRB, Patna)***

Solutions

1. (b) Replace 'homes' by 'home'. 'at home' is a phrase.
2. (E) No error.
3. (b) Replace 'a' by 'the'.
4. (a) Replace 'is' by 'was'. The whole sentence reflects action in the past.
5. (a) Place It before 'being'. This is the problem of unrelated participle.
6. (b) Replace 'have' by 'has'.
7. (b) 'is' will be used after 'a digital computer'. This is an assertive sentence, not an Interrogative one.
   (i) I do not know where he lives.
   (ii) I know what he says.
8. (c) Replace 'you'll pay' by 'you pay'.
9. (c) Replace 'purchase' by 'purchased'. This is a Conditional sentence with the following structure : Had + Sub + V-III .... + would have + V-III?
10. (E) No error.

Exercise 29

Read each sentence to find out whether there is any grammatical or idiomatic error in it . The error, if any, will be in one part of the sentence. The number of that part is the answer. If there is no error, the answer is (E). Ignore the errors of punctuation, if any)

1. Even if he had been driving more slowly (a)/it will have been quite impossible (b)/to avoid the accident. (c)/No error. (d) ***(Investigators Exam)***
2. Would you please (a)/stop from smoking (b)/while the ceremony (c) is in progress. (d)/No error. (E) ***(Investigators Exam)***
3. When I offered him to help (a)/which he needed, (b)/he persisted in refusing it (c)/so I left him to his fate. (d)/No error. (E) ***(BSRB Clerical)***
4. He reminded me (a)/that he has (b)/often told me not to (c)/play with fire. (d)/No Error. (E) ***(BSRB Clerical, Bhopal)***
5. Our country need (a)/a number of (b)/self sacrificing and (c)/devoted political leaders (d)/No error. (E) ***(CSRB, Patna)***
6. Instead of (a)/his busy and hard life (b)/he still retains (c)/freshness and robustness (d)/No error. (E) ***(CSRB, Patna)***
7. The smuggler yielded (a)/for the tempatation (b)/and fell into (c)/the police trap. (d)/No error. (E) ***(CSRB, Patna)***
8. The girl said (a)/that she preferred (b)/the blue gown (c)/than the black one. (d)/No error. (E) ***(CSRB, Patna)***
9. Of the two principles (a)/he put forward, the last one (b)/was the more (c)/difficult to understand. (d)/No error. (E)
10. All of us (a)/surprised (b)/to see an old man of (c)/sixty taking part in the Marathon held last month. (d)/No error. (E)

Solutions

1. (b) Replace 'will' by 'would'. When the sentence reflects an action in the past it is incorrect to use will.
2. (b) 'from' is superfluous.
3. (a) Place to before 'help'.
4. (b) Replace 'has' by 'had'.
5. (a) Replace 'need' by 'needs'. Subject 'our country' is singular.
6. (a) Replace 'Instead of' by 'In spite of'.
7. (b) Replace 'for' by 'to'.
8. (d) Replace 'than' by 'to'. Remember use 'to' after senior, junior, prefer, prior instead of 'than'.
9. (b) Replace 'last' by latter.
   (i) Ramesh and Suresh are friends. The latter is an engineer.
   (ii) Ramesh, Suresh and Medha are friends. The last is a banker.
10. (b) Place were before 'surprised'. This is a passive structure.

Exercise 30

Read each sentence to find out whether there is any grammatical or idiomatic error in it . The error, if any, will be in one part of the sentence. The number of that part is the answer. If there is no error, the answer is (E). (Ignore the errors of punctuation, if any)

1. The new railway line will greatly improve (a)/transport and communication (b)/in eastern part of the country (c)/No error. (d) ***(SSC Clerical)***

2. The receptionist asked me (a)/who do I want (b)/to meet in the office. (c)/No error. (d) ***(SSC Clerical)***
3. At last (a)/he was married (b)/with a poor girl (c)/No error. (d) ***(BSRB Clerical)***
4. She said (a)/that she will help me (b)/whenever I was in difficulty. (c)/No error. (d) ***(BSRB Clerical)***
5. Neither Rakesh (a)/nor I are leaving (b)/for Hyderabad. (c)/No error. (d) ***(SBI PO)***
6. Death (a)/is preferable (b)/than life. (c)/No error. (d) ***(SBI PO)***
7. We were still talking (a)/about what we should do (b)/when we heard (c)/the children shouting. (d)/No error. (E) ***(BSRB Clerical, Bhopal)***
8. As soon as the peon rings (a)/the first bell (b)/then all the students assemble (c)/on the playground for prayer. (d)/No error. (E) ***(BSRB Clerical, Bhopal)***
9. Have you (a)/turned detective (b)/that you keep your eye (c)/on me like this ? (d)/No error. (E) ***(BSRB Clerical, Bhopal)***
10. She asked him (a)/what it was that made him (b)/so much stronger and braver (c)/than any man. (d)/No error. (E) ***(BSRB Clerical, Bhopal)***

Solutions

1. (c) Place the before 'eastern'.
2. (b) Replace 'who do I want' by 'whom I wanted'. In indirect narration the sentence is changed to Assertive.
3. (c) Replace 'with' by 'to'.
4. (b) Replace 'will' by 'would'. The tense of the reported speech changes accordingly.
5. (b) Replace 'are' by 'am'.
6. (c) Replace 'than' by 'to'.
7. (E) No error.
8. (c) Use of 'then' is superfluous.
9. (E) No error.
10. (d) Place other after 'any'.

Exercise 31

Read each sentence to find out whether there is any grammatical or idiomatic error in it . The error, if any, will be in one part of the sentence. The number of that part is the answer. If there is no error, the answer is (E). (Ignore the errors of punctuation, if any)

1. Being that he (a)/is interested in getting himself examined (b)/by a heart specialist (c)/we must try our best to take him to a reputed doctor. (d)/No error. (E) ***(RRB, Kolkata)***
2. The college is (a)/hoding special lectures for their students (b)/and teachers so that they (c)/may get enlightened about the economic problems (d)/No error. (E) ***(RRB, Kolkata)***
3. A cell (a)/is the smallest (b)/identifiable unit of life and cannot be (c)/seen with a naked eye. (d)/No error. (E)
4. If he needs advices about (a)/carreer, (b)/he should consult (c)/the Career officer. (d)/No error. (E)
5. Being a (a)/rainy day we went out (b)/for a picnic (c)/to Nehru Kendra. (d)/No error. (E) ***(BSRB Clerical)***
6. Many a man (a)/have been (b)/participating (c)/in the competition. (d)/No error. (E) ***(BSRB Clerical)***
7. To our surprise (a)/we noticed that (b)/every soldier and every sailor (c)/was in his place (d)/No error. (E) ***BSRB Lucknow)***
8. Neither he nor I (a)/was able to (b)/finish the task within (c)/the time limit. (d)/No error. (E) ***(BSRB Lucknow)***
9. No sooner we entered (a)/than he got up (b)/and left the room. (c)/No error. (d) ***(SSC Clerical)***
10. The villagers fled away their houses (a)/when they saw (b)/the flood water rising. (c)/No error. (d) ***(SSC Clerical)***

Solutions

1. (a) Replace 'Being' by 'That, Because, Since, or As'. In this question Being is used in place of That or Because or Since or As.
2. (b) Replace 'their' by 'its'.
3. (d) Replace 'A' by 'The'. 'with the naked eyes' is correct expression.
4. (a) Replace 'advices' by advice.'advice' is uncountable. We cannot pluralise advice as such (advices).
5. (a) Place It before 'being'. This is the problem of unrelated participle.
6. (b) Replace 'have' by 'has'. 'Many a' takes singular noun and singular verb.
   (i) Many a pen is on the stool.
   (ii) Many a person comes here daily.
7. (E) No error.
8. (E) No error.
9. (a) Place 'had' after 'No sooner'. This is the question of inversion.
10. (a) Use of away after 'fled' is superfluous. This is the question of superfluous expression.

Exercise 32

Read each sentence to find out whether there is any grammatical or idiomatic error in it . The error, if any, will be in one part of the sentence. The number of the part is the answer. If there is no error, the answer is (E). (Ignore the errors of punctuation, if any)

1. I know (a)/he is having (b)/a lot of books (c)/on how to improve English. (d)/No error. (E)
2. The theory of relativity is (a)/so complicated (b)/as we cannot describe (c)/it in a few sentences. (d)/No error. (E)
3. After the brief appearence before the waiting crowds, (a)/he was taken (b)/to the Governor chamber (b)/for the swearing in ceremony. (d)/No error. (E) **(RRB, Kolkata)**
4. Congress dissidents and (a)/a wide range among the (b)/opposition has mounted a (c)/campaign to have the President renominated. (d)/No error. (E) **(RRB, Kolkata)**
5. If I would have (a)/worked regularly (b)/I would have passed (c)/the examination. (d)/No error. (E) **(CSRB, Patna)**
6. The gentleman (a)/together with his (b)/wife and daughter (c)/were drowned. (d)/No error. (E) **(CSRB, Patna)**
7. No man (a)/in our country (b)/is as rich (c)/as he is. (d)/No error. (E) **(BSRB Clerical Bhopal)**
8. The teacher remarked (a)/very angrily yesterday (b)/that the boys have (c)/all done it very badly. (d)/No error. (E) **(BSRB Clerical Bhopal)**
9. A letter of recommendation (a)/from the principal and (b)/the head of English department have helped him to (c)/get this lucrative job. (d)/No error. (E)
10. An Indian driver or carpenter has to work (a)/about two hours to buy kilogram of rice (b)/while his counterparts in Austria, the Netherlands and Switzerland (c)/need work only fifteen minutes for it. (d)/No error. (E) **(RRB, Kolkata)**

Solutions

1. (b) Replace 'is having' by 'has'.
2. (c) Replace 'as' by 'that'. Structure is 'so....that'.
   (i) He is so poor that he cannot buy a pen.
   (ii) She is so weak that she cannot climb up the stairs.
3. (c) Replace 'Governor chamber' by 'Governor's chamber'. This is the question of use of apostrophe.
4. (c) Replace 'has' by 'have'. Subject 'Congress dissidents and a wide range' is plural. If the subject is plural, verb is plural.
5. (a) Replace 'would have' by 'had'. This is a Conditional sentence with specific structure : If + Subject + had + V-III + Would have + V-III.
6. (d) Replace 'were' by 'was'. If this subect is singular, verb is singular. If subject is plural, verb is plural.
7. (a) Place other after 'No'. While making comparison the item (being compared) is required to be excluded. As :
   No other girl of this class is so/as beautiful as Rani.
8. (c) Replace 'have' by 'had'. Reporting verb is in past tense.
9. (c) Replace 'have' by 'has'. Subject 'A letter' is singular.
10. (b) Place a before 'kilogram'. Kilogram is a countable noun.

Exercise 33

Read each sentence to find out whether there is any grammatical or idiomatic error in it. The error, if any, will be in one part of the sentence. The number of that part is the answer. If there is no error, the answer is (E). (Ignore the errors of punctuation, if any)

1. The vehicle which is stopped (a)/by the policeman (b)/contained a number (c)/of smuggled watches. (d)/No error. (E) **(BSRB, Lucknow)**
2. One should look for his (a)/own faults first (b)/and then those (c)/of others (d)/No error. (E) **(BSRB, Lucknow)**
3. Sitting under the shade (a)/of a tree for a while (b)/made us fresh (c)/for the further journey (d)/No error. (E) **(BSRB, Lucknow)**
4. Although it is summer (a)/yet the weather at the (b)/hill station was (c)/quite pleasant (d)/No error. (E) **(BSRB, Lucknow)**
5. The smuggler yielded (a)/for the tempatation (b)/and fell into (c)/the police trap. (d)/No error. (E) **(CSRB, Patna)**
6. The girl said (a)/that she preferred (b)/the blue gown (c)/than the black one. (d)/No error. (E) **(CSRB, Patna)**
7. Cattles (a)/were grazing (b)/in the meadows (c)/near our farm. (d)/No error. (E) **(BSRB, Clerical)**
8. You are really (a)/senior than (b)/me (c)/in age. (d)/No error. (E) **(BSRB, Clerical)**

Solutions

1. (a) Replace 'is' by 'was'. The sentence reflects an action in the past.
2. (a) Replace 'his' by one's.
3. (a) Replace 'under' by in.
   Sit in the shade of a tree.
   Sit under a tree.
4. (c) Replace 'was' by 'is'.
5. (b) Replace 'for' by 'to'.
6. (d) Replace 'than' by 'to'. After, senior, junior, prefer, prior etc., always use 'to' instead of 'than'.
7. (a) Replace 'cattles' by 'cattle'.
8. (b) Replace 'than' by 'to'.

Unit 43

Exercises : Synonyms and Antonyms

Exercise 1

Choose the word which is most near to the meaning as the word given in capital letters
(*Bank of Maharashtra Specialist Officers*)

1. OSTENTATION
   (a) Calmness (b) Equianimity
   (c) Deception (d) Declaration
   (e) Pageantry
2. PENITENT
   (a) Eccenric (b) Profound
   (c) Remorseful (d) Observant
   (e) Blameless
3. SATIATE
   (a) Direct (b) Gratify
   (c) Manage (d) Defeat
   (e) Expose
4. MUSE
   (a) Ponder (b) Infect
   (c) Appease (d) Taint
   (e) Hold
5. PROFANE
   (a) Assert (b) Benefit
   (c) Lengthen (d) Desecrate
   (e) Advance

Solutions

1. (e) 2. (c) 3. (b) 4. (a)
5. (d)

Exercise 2

Choose the word which is most nearly the same in meaning as the word given in capitals letters **(*AIMT*)**

1. INTERPOLATE
   (a) Clarify
   (b) Investigate
   (c) Reverse
   (d) Insert
2. CAULDRON
   (a) Computer term (b) Pot for boiling
   (c) Static electricity (d) Laser fusion
3. INSOLVENT
   (a) Flourishing (b) Bankrupt
   (c) Soluble (d) Opprobrious
4. OFFICIOUS
   (a) Pushing (b) Modest
   (c) Stubborn (d) Mystic
5. VERACITY
   (a) Mendacity (b) Truth
   (c) Imperfection (d) Judgement

Solutions

1. (d) 2. (d) 3. (b) 4. (a)
5. (b)

Exercise 3

Choose the word which is most nearly the same in meaning as the word given in capitals letters **(*IITM*)**

1. VIA MEDIA
   (a) By the way
   (b) Through communication
   (c) A middle course
   (d) Thereverse order
2. IN TOTO
   (a) In the heart
   (b) In peace
   (c) Within the walls
   (d) Entirely
3. RESUME
   (a) A summary
   (b) To carry on after interaction
   (c) A report of the work done
   (d) A review

Solutions

1. (c) 2. (d) 3. (a)

Exercise 4

Read the list of word given below and choose from the options (a) to (e) the word that is similar in meaning to the word given in capital letters ***(Bank PO)***

1. EXIGUOUS
(a) Tall (b) Large
(c) Wide (d) Scanty
(e) Broad
2. RECREANCY
(a) Recreation (b) Recuperation
(c) Bravery (d) Cowardice
(e) Obstinate
3. PROSCRIBE
(a) To nominate
(b) To be supportive of
(c) To give early warning signals
(d) Outlaw
(e) None of the above
4. INGEST
(a) Enrag
(b) Invigorate
(c) To absorb
(d) Burn up completely
(e) To stir up
5. MONTICULE
(a) A small river (b) A small hut
(c) A lane (d) A small hill
(e) A small plane
6. COMPENDIOUS
(a) Comprehensive (b) Illustrative
(c) Unbearable (d) Elaborate
(e) None of the above
7. NADIR
(a) Asylum (b) Heaven
(c) Depth (d) Nebulous
(e) None of the above
8. SOMNAMBULISTIC
(a) Sleep walking
(b) Ghost dancing
(c) Women's group activity
(d)Colourful scenario
(e) Over-eating
9. PRIMORDIAL
(a) Feeling of elation
(b) Original
(c) Elementary
(d) Daunting
(e) None of the above
10. SOMBRE
(a) Causing sleep
(b) Squalid
(c) Gloomy
(d) Complacent
(e) Malicious

Solutions

1. (d)	**2.** (d)	**3.** (e)	**4.** (c)
5. (d)	**6.** (a)	**7.** (c)	**8.** (a)
9. (c)	**10.** (c)		

Exercise 5

In this section, you will find a number of sentences, parts of which are underlined. You may also find only a group of words which is underlined. For each underlined part, four words/ phrases are listed below. Choose the word/ phrase nearest in meaning to the underlined part ***(CDS)***

1. We were taken aback at the fulsome praise heaped upon his former enemy.
(a) elaborated (b) extravagant
(c) excessive (d) exorbitant
2. You may think at first that it is queer to talk of having too much paper money and that money is so nice and useful that you cannot have too much of it.
(a) ridiculous (b) absurd
(c) anomalous (d) odd
3. The Government is under no obligation to offer contracts to companies which choose to flout guidelines.
(a) condemn (b) ignore
(c) defy (d) neglect
4. Soon he felt uncomfortable, for the coach was now moving over a rugged road.
(a) rough (b) narrow
(c) dusty (d) sturdy
5. Indians exhibited a remarkable solidarity at the time of war.
(a) coalition (b) cooperation
(c) unification (d) unity
6. A great statesman is actuated by love for his country.
(a) compelled (b) induced
(c) impelled (d) persuaded
7. The cutting curved sharply, and in the darkness the black entrance to the tunnel loomed up menacingly.
(a) harmfully (b) imminently
(c) dangerously (d) threateningly
8. Had he delivered his speech without a long and winding preamble, people would have understood him better.
(a) digression
(b) introduction
(c) explanation
(d) background
9. His impeccable style caught the attention of all critics.
(a) faultless (b) inoffensive
(c) upright (d) harmless

10. We should not look down on people who are not educated.
(a) dislike (b) despise
(c) disown (d) denounce

Solutions

1. (c) 2. (d) 3. (c) 4. (a)
5. (d) 6. (c) 7. (d) 8. (b)
9. (a) 10. (b)

Exercise 6

In the following questions, out of the four alternatives choose the one which best expresses the meaning of the word given in capital letters and mark it on the answer sheet **(SSC Stenographers)**

1. OBJECT
(a) Disapprove (b) Challenge
(c) Deny (d) Disobey
2. UNTIE
(a) Unfold (b) Unchain
(c) Undo (d) Unhinge
3. ALERT
(a) Energetic (b) Observant
(c) Intelligent (d) Watchful
4. MOVING
(a) Taking (b) Toying
(c) Shifting (d) Turning
5. RECKLESS
(a) Courageous (b) Rash
(c) Bold (d) Daring

Solutions

1. (b) 2. (b) 3. (d) 4. (c)
5. (b)

Exercise 7

Choose the word which is most near to the meaning as the word or group of words given in capital letters **(Bank PO)**

1. LAUNCH
(a) Review (b) Begin
(c) Propel (d) Push
(e) Force
2. RELIED
(a) Emphasised (b) Depended
(c) Convinced (d) Followed
(e) Referred
3. OBTAINED
(a) Combined (b) Procured
(c) Acquired (d) Conquered
(e) Attained

Solutions

1. (b) 2. (b) 3. (e)

Exercise 8

In this section, you will find a number of sentences, part of which is underlined. You may also find only a group of words which is underlined. For each underlined part, four words/phrase are listed below. Choose the word nearest in meaning to the underlined part **(Indian Bank PO)**

1. In spite of his best efforts the officer could not redeem his prestige.
(a) recover (b) raise
(c) extend (d) fulfil
2. There is abundant supply of water for the crops.
(a) considerable (b) plentiful
(c) adequate (d) sufficient
3. All his attempts to win the favour of his boss proved infructuous.
(a) meaningless (b) unnecessary
(c) redundant (d) fruitless
4. As she had never been in such a situation before, her apprehension was understandable.
(a) eagerness (b) fear
(c) hesitation (d) excitement
5. You should not get paranoid about what others think of you.
(a) flattered by (b) influenced by
(c) obsessed with (d) upset by
6. I wonder if his intervention in the dispute will be of any help.
(a) interception (b) interruption
(c) mediation (d) meddling
7. A strange mental aberration often made her forget her own name.
(a) eccentricity (b) insaniti
(c) disorder (d) illusion
8. He treats with disdain anyone who goes to him for help.
(a) contempt (b) disgust
(c) insolence (d) displeasure
9. He spoke impromptu on the occasion.
(a) eloquently
(b) without preparation
(c) without enthusiasm
(d) with great force
10. The perpetual noise made it impossible for them to concentrate on the problems.
(a) irritating (b) constant
(c) unlimited (d) recurrent

Solutions

1. (d) 2. (a) 3. (a) 4. (b)
5. (c) 6. (a) 7. (c) 8. (b)
9. (a) 10. (d)

Exercise 9

In this section, you will find a number of sentences, part of which is underlined. You may also find only a group of words which is underlined. For each underlined part, four words/phrase are listed below. Choose the word nearest in meaning to the underlined part

(UPSC, APFC)

1. It is possible for a writer to be copious in his words, and at the same time, to give the reality of a natural form.
   (a) scanty (b) plentiful
   (c) repetitive (d) arrogant
2. The security arrangements made for the visiting dignitary were impeccable.
   (a) flawless (b) elaborate
   (c) grand (d) tight
3. Even today many people are guided by abstruse moral values.
   (a) dangerous
   (b) impracticable
   (c) obscure
   (d) irrational
4. The workers tried their best to thwart the plans of the management.
   (a) embarrass (b) embitter
   (c) frustrate (d) hasten
5. The prisoners of war signed the document under coercion.
   (a) compulsion (b) confusion
   (c) supervision (d) security

Solutions

1. (b) 2. (a) 3. (c) 4. (c)
5. (a)

Exercise 10

In this section, you will find a number of sentences, part of which is underlined. You may also find only a group of words which is underlined. For each underlined part, four words/ phrase are listed below. Choose the word nearest to the opposite of the underlined word or phrase

(UPSC, APFC)

1. The proposal was denounced by one and all.
   (a) announced (b) pronounced
   (c) appraised (d) commended
2. Where ignorance is sometimes bliss, illiteracy is always considered a curse.
   (a) erudition (b) experience
   (c) education (d) information
3. The news brought by the maidservants authentic.
   (a) authoritative (b) baseless
   (c) ridiculous (d) vacuous
4. The doctor said that there is no improvement in the condition of the patient.
   (a) depression (b) deterioration
   (c) change (d) degradation
5. He plunged into the turbid waters of the stream.
   (a) deep (b) muddy
   (c) clear (d) fresh

Solutions

1. (d) 2. (a) 3. (b) 4. (b)
5. (c)

Exercise 11

In this section, you will find a number of sentences, part of which is underlined. You may also find only a group of words which is underlined. For each underlined part, four words/phrase are listed below. Choose the word nearest opposite in meaning of the underlined part

(CDS)

1. His repulsive behaviour could not be ignored by the members of the jury.
   (a) lovely (b) mild
   (c) admirable (d) attractive
2. He is an amateur photographer.
   (a) average (b) experienced
   (c) professional (d) skilled
3. The witness affirmed on oath that he was an eyewitness to the crime under study.
   (a) contradicted (b) opposed
   (c) disputed (d) denied
4. On the hillside, he could see the vague shapes of sheep coming through he mist.
   (a) clear (b) transparent
   (c) plain (d) apparent
5. His casual remarks were taken note of by all members of the board.
   (a) careful (b) sincere
   (c) precise (d) flawless
6. If you pamper the child you will regret it.
   (a) scold (b) scorn
   (c) discourage (d) neglect
7. These rules are meant to prevent further appointments.
   (a) facilitate (b) accelerate
   (c) expedite (d) aggravate
8. The artist led a very austere life.
   (a) luxurious (b) boisterous
   (c) exciting (d) eventful
9. The new boss is well-known for his rigid approach to all problems.
   (a) swift (b) logical
   (c) sympathetic (d) flexible
10. Adversity is the source of numerous vices.
   (a) Wealth (b) Prosperity
   (c) Luxury (d) Money

Solutions

1. (d) 2. (a) 3. (a) 4. (b)
5. (b) 6. (c) 7. (c) 8. (d)
9. (a) 10. (d)

Exercise 12

Choose the word which is opposite in meaning to the word given in capital letters **(PO)**

1. CHRONIC
(a) Acute (b) Fleeting
(c) Irregular (d) Temporary
(e) Recurring
2. LETTING
(a) Demanding (b) Permitting
(c) Disallowing (d) Refusing
(e) Rejecting
3. INTEGRATE
(a) Isolate (b) Analyse
(c) Distinguish (d) Mark
(e) Distribute

Solutions

1. (d) **2.** (c) **3.** (a)

Exercise 13

Choose the word which is opposite in meaning to the word given in capital letters ***(SSC Stenographers)***

1. CONFESS
(a) Refuse (b) Deny
(c) Contest (d) Contend
2. ABSOLUTE
(a) Deficient (b) Faulty
(c) Limited (d) Scarce
3. VALUABLE
(a) Invaluable (b) Worthless
(c) Inferior (d) Lowly
4. HINDRANCE
(a) Aid (b) Persuasion
(c) Cooperation (d) Agreement
5. ALIEN
(a) Native (b) Domiciled
(c) Natural (d) Resident

Solutions

1. (b) **2.** (c) **3.** (b) **4.** (a)
5. (a)

Exercise 14

Each question below consists of a word in capital letters followed by four alternatives. Choose the alternative that is most nearly opposite in meaning to the word given in capital letters

(Tourism Management Entrance)

1. GARBLE
(a) Enjoy (b) Rinse
(c) Clarify (d) Accept
2. FORTITUDE
(a) Timidity (b) Laxity
(c) Placidity (d) Ambition
3. PERNICIOUS
(a) Precious (b) Healing
(c) Swerving (d) Conservative
4. ANATHEMA
(a) Appreciation (b) Blessing
(c) Protection (d) Obstacle
5. CONCUR
(a) Pertain (b) Reveal
(c) Oppose (d) Delay

Solutions

1. (c) **2.** (a) **3.** (b) **4.** (b)
5. (c)

Exercise 15

In this section, each item consists of a word or a phrase which is underlined in the sentence given. It is followed by four words or phrases. Select the word or phrase which is closest to the opposite in meaning of the underlined word or phrase ***(CDS)***

1. My brother is very sensitive about hurting animals.
(a) callous (b) senseless
(c) indifferent (d) inconcerned
2. He did it purposely.
(a) half-heartedly (b) timidly
(c) unintentionally (d) hesitatingly
3. After a week-long strike, the workers took to the path of collision when the chairman intervened.
(a) retaliation (b) atonement
(c) reconciliation (d) expiation
4. He yielded to temptation.
(a) succumbed (b) rescinded
(c) skirted (d) resisted
5. The dishevelled appearance of the two men on the street made everyone take notice of them.
(a) composed (b) tidy
(c) confident (d) complacent
6. He has penchant for writing satirical poems.
(a) dislike (b) bias
(c) repulsion (d) hatred
7. The lawyer was convinced that his client had made a/an authentic statement.
(a) absurd
(b) false
(c) unreasonable
(d) ridiculous
8. He was on pins and needless while his wife was undergoing an operation.
(a) unexcited (b) at rest
(c) undisturbed (d) relaxed
9. The coach was too lax about the training of the team.
(a) stern (b) strict
(c) firm (d) steadfast

10. The rebels <u>held out</u> in the face of stiff odds.
(a) gave in (b) deserted
(c) fled away (d) betrayed

Solutions

1. (a) 2. (c) 3. (c) 4. (d)
5. (b) 6. (c) 7. (b) 8. (d)
9. (d) 10. (a)

Exercise 16

To answer the following questions, choose the alternative that is nearly opposite in meaning to the word given in capital letters **(AIMT)**

1. LACONIC
(a) Terse (b) Loquacious
(c) Curt (d) Sagacious
2. RENEGADE
(a) Traitor (b) Heretic
(c) Loyalist (d) Fugitive
3. ADIPOSE
(a) Corpulent (b) Glutinous
(c) Thin (d) Oleaginous
4. PUTRID
(a) Fresh (b) Rancid
(c) Recondite (d) Choleric
5. VULGAR
(a) Plebeian (b) Aristocratic
(c) Impervious (d) Licentious

Solutions

1. (b) 2. (c) 3. (c) 4. (a)
5. (b)

Exercise 17

To answer the following questions, choose the alternative that is nearly opposite in meaning to the word given in capital letters **(MAT)**

1. SANCTIMONIOUS
(a) Holy (b) Realistic
(c) Humble (d) Callous
(e) Pessimistic
2. MUNIFICENT
(a) Miserly (b) Faulty
(c) Perplexing (d) Rudimentary
(e) Grandiose
3. OPAQUE
(a) Vague (b) Firm
(c) Transparent (d) Poor
(e) None of the above
4. RESTIVE
(a) Unrestrained (b) Communicate
(c) Peaceful (d) Quarrel
(e) Disturbing
5. CATAPULT
(a) Reach great heights
(b) Downfall
(c) Caterpillar
(d) Gaining
(e) Losing
6. ENIGMATIC
(a) Industrious (b) Mysterious
(c) Enthusiastic (d) Straightforward
(e) Sincere
7. TRAIPSE
(a) Walk (b) Stroll
(c) Crawl (d) Run
(e) None of the above
8. PIQUANT
(a) Jovial (b) Merry
(c) Blunt (d) Rigorous
(e) Shocking
9. BIGOTED
(a) Dignified (b) Tolerant
(c) Wide (d) Contrite
(e) Sincere
10. OBLIQUITY
(a) Thin (b) Frank
(c) Self-righteous (d) Depreciation
(e) Conformity

Solutions

1. (d) 2. (a) 3. (c) 4. (c)
5. (b) 6. (d) 7. (c) 8. (a)
9. (a) 10. (e)

Exercise 18

To answer the following questions, choose the alternative that is nearly opposite in meaning to the word given in capital letters **(Bank PO)**

1. DENOUNCE
(a) Accept (b) Accuse
(c) Condemn (d) Faith
2. DIPSOMANIAC
(a) Alcoholic (b) Teetotaller
(c) Sick (d) Lunatic
3. PRECIPITOUS
(a) Rash (b) Steep
(c) Thoughtful (d) Rain
4. MAGNANIMOUS
(a) Generous (b) Giving
(c) Stingy (d) Greedy
5. INCOMMODE
(a) Cause trouble (b) Comfortable
(c) Inconvenience (d) Small
6. EXPLICIT
(a) Clear (b) Straightforward
(c) Hidden (d) Closed

7. CHURLISH
(a) Ill-mannered (b) Rude
(c) Pleasant (d) Decent

8. ASTATIC
(a) Dynamic (b) Unstable
(c) Stable (d) Directionless

Solutions

1. (a) 2. (b) 3. (c) 4. (c)
5. (b) 6. (c) 7. (d) 8. (c)

Exercise 19

To answer the following questions, choose the alternative that is nearly opposite in meaning to the word given in capital letters

1. MOTLEY
(a) Homogeneous (b) Deadly
(c) Gloomy (d) Concise
(e) Dreary

2. BELITTLE
(a) Allure (b) Disturb
(c) Entangle (d) Ascend
(e) Magnify

3. PREMEDITATION
(a) Compression (b) Impromptu
(c) Audacity (d) Succession
(e) Terminal

4. PEEVISH
(a) Dreamy (b) Acquisitive
(c) Genial (d) Decorous
(e) Conscious

5. FORBID
(a) Appeal (b) Dispose
(c) Examine (d) Permit
(e) Obtain

Solutions

1. (a) 2. (e) 3. (b) 4. (c)
5. (d)

Exercise 20

In the following questions choose the alternative which is almost the same in meaning to the word given in capital letters ***(RRB, Bhopal Non-Tech)***

1. INCLEMENT
(a) Pleasant (b) Stormy
(c) Feeble (d) Dignified

2. AFFECTATION
(a) Hypocrisy (b) Simplicity
(c) Antipathy (d) Harmony

3. LATENT
(a) Apparent (b) Dormant
(c) Ample (d) Illegal

4. VANITY
(a) Humility (b) Pride
(c) Ostentation (d) Pity

5. LAUD
(a) Lord (b) Eulogy
(c) Praise (d) Extolled

Solutions

1. (a) 2. (b) 3. (a) 4. (a)
5. (c)

Exercise 21

Rewrite the following sentences, selecting the most appropriate word from the ones given in the brackets ***(IFS)***

1. The story of his escape was very (excitable/exciting/excited).
2. The (scene/scenery) around here is very beautiful.
3. I have been studying English (since/for) ten years.
4. The old man asked if we had any articles of (cloth/clothes/clothing).
5. If you annoy the god it is (apt/liable/likely) to bite you.

Solutions

1. exciting 2. scene 3. for
4. clothes 5. likely

Exercise 22

Choose the word which is most nearly the SAME in meaning ***(RRB, Kolkata)***

1. COMMEMORATE
(a) Boast (b) Harmonise
(c) Manipulate (d) Remember

2. CONNOISSEUR
(a) Lover of art (b) Interpreter
(c) Delinquent (d) Ignorant

3. LETHAL
(a) Unlawful (b) Sluggish
(c) Deadly (d) Smooth

4. NEBULOUS
(a) Tiny (b) Vague
(c) Insignificant (d) Dead

5. ELICIT
(a) Induce (b) Divulge
(c) Insignificant (d) Dead

6. PROLIFIC
(a) Plenty (b) Competent
(c) Predominant (d) Fertile

7. EXORBITANT
(a) Odd
(b) Excessive
(c) Ridiculous
(d) Threatening

8. DILIGENT
(a) Industrious (b) Energetic
(c) Modest (d) Intelligent
9. ADMONISH
(a) Support (b) Praise
(c) Appeal (d) Reprove
10. BOUNTY
(a) Gift (b) Donation
(c) Pleasure (d) Reward

Solutions

1. (d) 2. (a) 3. (c) 4. (b)
5. (b) 6. (d) 7. (b) 8. (a)
9. (d) 10. (a)

Exercise 23

From the given words, choose a word which means the same as the word given in capital letters ***(RRB, Bhopal)***

1. UNCOUTH
(a) Ungraceful (b) Rough
(c) Slovenly (d) Dirty
2. LYNCH
(a) Hang (b) Madden
(c) Killed (d) Shoot

Solutions

1. (b) 2. (c)

Exercise 24

Choose the nearest to similar meaning of the words/phrase ***(RRB, Kolkata, ADM)***

1. To come round
(a) To get well
(b) To reach a roundabout
(c) To succeed
(d) To complete a circle
2. A white elephant
(a) An elephant with white skin
(b) A costly thing
(c) A costly and useful thing
(d) A costly but useless thing

Solutions

1. (d) 2. (d)

Exercise 25

Choose one word which is similar in meaning to the key-word given in capital letters ***(RRB Tech Trivendrum)***

1. BLITZ
(a) Concentrated attack
(b) News
(c) Happiness
(d) Fall
2. DROOP
(a) Straight (b) Curved
(c) Hanging down (d) Line
3. FALLACY
(a) False opinion (b) Deep fall
(c) Dream (d) Death
4. INFER
(a) To conceive (b) To deduce
(c) To attack (d) To take away

Solutions

1. (a) 2. (c) 3. (a) 4. (b)

Exercise 26

In the following questions, choose the word similar in meaning to given words given in capital letters ***(RRB, Ajmer)***

1. WORTH
(a) Merit (b) Fright
(c) Anger (d) Pity
2. TOUCHSTONE
(a) Kill (b) Criterion
(c) Precious (d) Roll
3. TRADUCE
(a) Trade (b) Defame
(c) Dance (d) Dunce
4. TRAIL
(a) Drag (b) Defame
(c) Dance (d) Die
5. SWATH
(a) Envelop (b) Gallant
(c) Blanket (d) Wholesale

Solutions

1. (a) 2. (b) 3. (b) 4. (a)
5. (a)

Exercise 27

Choose the word which is most nearly the same in meaning given in capital letters ***(RRB, Guhati)***

1. ESTABLISH
(a) Prove (b) Hold on
(c) Removed (d) Set up
2. CONFERRED
(a) Offered (b) Divulged
(c) Damaged (d) Advised
3. COMMAND
(a) Consolation (b) Order
(c) Amendment (d) Assignment
4. POWER
(a) Training (b) Electricity
(c) Authority (d) Drive

5. ELEMENT
(a) Prime (b) Component
(c) Particle (d) Persons

Solutions

1. (d) 2. (a) 3. (b) 4. (c)
5. (b)

Exercise 28

In following questions, choose from the alternatives a word which is similar in meaning to the word given in capital letters ***(RRB, Trivendrum)***

1. IMPROMPTU
(a) Offhand (b) Unimportant
(c) Unreal (d) Effective
2. RABBLE
(a) Mob (b) Noise
(c) Roar (d) Rubbish
3. TROUPE
(a) Fast (b) Group
(c) Medium (d) Energetic
4. MAYHEM
(a) Jubilation (b) Havoc
(c) Excitement (d) Defeat
5. TEPID
(a) Hot (b) Warm
(c) Cold (d) Boiling

Solutions

1. (a) 2. (a) 3. (b) 4. (b)
5. (b)

Exercise 29

To answer the following questions choose the alternative that is nearly opposite in meaning to the word given in capital letters ***(MBA Entrance)***

1. LACONIC
(a) Terse (b) Loquacious
(c) Curt (d) Sagacious
2. RENEGADE
(a) Traitor (b) Heretic
(c) Loyalist (d) Fugitive
3. ADIPOSE
(a) Corpulent (b) Glutinous
(c) Thin (d) Oleaginous
4. PUTRID
(a) Fresh (b) Rancid
(c) Recondite (d) Choleric
5. VULGAR
(a) Plebeian (b) Aristocratic
(c) Impervious (d) Licentious

Solutions

1. (b) 2. (c) 3. (c) 4. (a)
5. (b)

Exercise 30

Choose from the alternatives, provide a same in meaning for each of the following words given in capital letters ***(RRB Secundrabad)***

1. BUSY
(a) Active (b) Quiet
(c) Secure (d) Bold
2. DENY
(a) Negate (b) Differ
(c) Disagree (d) Vary
3. GRIEF
(a) Cheerful (b) Happy
(c) Sorrow (d) Injury
4. FAITH
(a) Cordial (b) Woe
(c) Noble (d) Belief
5. CLEVER
(a) Novel (b) Talented
(c) Insane (d) Useful
6. GENEROUS
(a) Friendly (b) Liberal
(c) Cordial (d) Graceful
7. REGARD
(a) Civil (b) Grateful
(c) True (d) Respect
8. QUARREL
(a) Rough (b) Secure
(c) Dispute (d) Grief
9. SHELTER
(a) Cover (b) Secure
(c) Repose (d) Pity
10. WORSHIP
(a) Yield (b) Retain
(c) Adoration (d) Differ
11. UNHAPPY
(a) Timid (b) Dispute
(c) Agreeable (d) Sad
12. SUITABLE
(a) Strong (b) Brief
(c) Benefit (d) Fit
13. FAME
(a) Reputation (b) Modesty
(c) Right (d) Majestic
14. ABOLISH
(a) Desert (b) Forsake
(c) Eradicate (d) Perform
15. AFRAID
(a) Rage (b) Frightened
(c) Mean (d) Accuse

Solutions

1. (a) 2. (a) 3. (c) 4. (d)
5. (b) 6. (b) 7. (d) 8. (c)

9. (a) 10. (c) 11. (d) 12. (d)
13. (a) 14. (c) 15. (b)

Exercise 31

In each of the following questions four words are given below the numbered word. Choose the word/phrase which is most nearly similar in meaning to the numbered word given in capital letters

(RRB, Mujaffarpur)

1. INTEGRITY
(a) Edifice (b) Honesty
(c) Essence (d) Embodiment
2. MONUMENTAL
(a) Upright (b) Indefinite
(c) Confusing (d) Memorable
3. PLOY
(a) Entrance (b) Composure
(c) Device (d) Investigation

Solutions

1. (b) 2. (d) 3. (c)

Exercise 32

Choose the word which is most opposite in meaning of the word given in capital letters

(BPO)

1. FOLLY
(a) Right (b) Exact
(c) Mistake (d) Action
(e) Wisdom
2. HEIGHTEN
(a) Widen (b) Decrease
(c) Strengthen (d) Dissolve
(e) Disappear
3. LETHARGIC
(a) Immobile (b) Indolent
(c) Unpleasant (d) Irresponsible
(e) Hyperactive
4. DRAWS
(a) Pushes (b) Extracts
(c) Spends (d) Replenishes
(e) Recharges

Solutions

1. (e) 2. (b) 3. (e) 4. (d)

Exercise 33

In the following questions choose the word or words which is closest in meaning to the keyword or words given in capital letters

(RRB, Clerk Bhopal)

1. CONSOLE
(a) Comfort
(b) Control
(c) Sole of a container
(d) Sole of self
2. PERSONNEL
(a) Belonging to oneself
(b) Belonging to one person
(c) Group of persons
(d) Staff employed in an institution
3. ON PURPOSE
(a) Deliberate (b) Selfish
(c) For one's self (d) Biting one's aim
4. HUE AND CRY
(a) Desperate (b) With discovered
(c) Sad (d) Public outcry
5. INVINCIBLE
(a) Unseen (b) Undiscovered
(c) Defeated (d) Unconquerable

Solutions

1. (a) 2. (d) 3. (a) 4. (d)
5. (d)

Exercise 34

Select the word which is most nearly the same in meaning to the word given in capital letters

(RRB, Mumbai)

1. DEMISE
(a) Result
(b) Default
(c) Death
(d) Apprehension
2. DISPARITY
(a) Distaste (b) Dissimilarity
(c) Criticism (d) Distinction
3. FORUM
(a) An Assembly
(b) Place Of Public Discussion
(c) An Application
(d) Rss
4. DISMANTLE
(a) Take Apart (b) Destroy
(c) Shatter (d) Upset
5. CURTAIL
(a) Decorate (b) Celebrate
(c) Cut Short (d) Deprive

Solutions

1. (c) 2. (b) 3. (b) 4. (b)
5. (c)

Exercise 35

Choose the correct antonym for the words given in capital words, out of the four choices given under each

(RRB Chandigarh)

1. ADAGE
(a) Motto (b) Harangue
(c) Proverb (d) Heresy

2. COMPLIANCE
(a) Condone (b) Clamour
(c) Resistance (d) Condense
3. Exhilarate
(a) Depress (b) Elate
(c) Ambiguous (d) Serene
4. GRUESOME
(a) Disgusting (b) Attractive
(c) Grisly (d) Stern
5. MACABRE
(a) Gruesome
(b) Attractive
(c) Splendour
(d) Trash

Solutions

1. (d) 2. (c) 3. (a) 4. (b)
5. (b)

Exercise 36

In the following questions choose the alternative which is opposite in meaning to the word given in capital letters ***(RRB Non-Tech Bhopal)***

1. INCLEMENT
(a) Pleasant (b) Stormy
(c) Feeble (d) Dignified
2. AFFECTATION
(a) Hypocrisy (b) Simplicity
(c) Antipathy (d) Harmony
3. LATENT
(a) Apparent (b) Dormant
(c) Ample (d) Illegal
4. VANITY
(a) Humility (b) Pride
(c) Ostentation (d) Pity

Solutions

1. (a) 2. (b) 3. (a) 4. (a)

Exercise 37

Choose the word which is opposite in meaning to the word given in capital letters ***(RRB Kolkata)***

1. VENERATE
(a) Accuse (b) Abuse
(c) Criticise (d) Defame
2. CAPACIOUS
(a) Changeable (b) Limited
(c) Caring (d) Foolish
3. DOUR
(a) Cheerful (b) Active
(c) Young (d) Radical
4. WRATH
(a) Solace (b) Delight
(c) Peace (d) Cheer
5. DEFIANCE
(a) Obedience (b) Suspicion
(c) Dismay (d) Anxiety
6. VAGUE
(a) Known (b) Published
(c) Popular (d) Definite
7. CROWDED
(a) Empty (b) Lonely
(c) Deserted (d) Barren
8. CONVENE
(a) Adjourn (b) Contact
(c) Dissolve (d) Postpone
9. DORMANT
(a) Ancient (b) Modern
(c) Permanent (d) Active
10. SHAME
(a) Exaltation (b) Glory
(c) Dignity (d) Enshrine

Solutions

1. (b) 2. (b) 3. (a) 4. (a)
5. (a) 6. (a) 7. (c) 8. (a)
9. (d) 10. (c)

Exercise 38

Choose the word which is most opposite in meaning to the word given in capital letters ***(RRB Telecom Bhopal***

1. VISIONARY
(a) Pragmatic (b) Practical
(c) Realist (d) Pragmatist
2. INFALLIBLE
(a) Unreliable (b) Dubious
(c) Untrustworthy (d) Erring

Solutions

1. (a) 2. (d)

Exercise 39

In Questions 1 and 2 choose the correct antonym of the words given in capital letters ***(RRB, Chandigarh***

1. ANONYMOUS
(a) Desperate (b) Expert
(c) Known (d) Written
2. CURTAIL
(a) Lengthen (b) Shorten
(c) Entail (d) Close

Solutions

1. (c) 2. (a)

Exercise 40

Choose the correct antonym of the key word from the four alternative to the word given in capital letters ***(RRB Tech Trivendru***

1. VICE
   (a) False (b) Fool
   (c) Wrong (d) Virtue
2. PRIDE
   (a) Jealously (b) Prestige
   (c) Humility (d) Pride

Solutions

1. (d) 2. (c)

Exercise 41

In the following questions, choose the word or hrase which is opposite in meaning to given word in apial letters : **(RRB, Ajmer)**

1. CRYPTIC
   (a) Tomblike (b) Secret
   (c) Famous (d) Candid
2. CLOUDY
   (a) Shadowy (b) Murky
   (c) Ominous (d) Illuminating
3. CURB
   (a) Encourage (b) Discourage
   (c) Repress (d) Restrain
4. CURTAIL
   (a) Shortened (b) Enlarged
   (c) Robust (d) Active
5. CONFESS
   (a) Grant (b) Conceal
   (c) Concede (d) Acknowledge

olutions

1. (d) 2. (d) 3. (a) 4. (b)
5. (b)

xercise 42

In this section each item consists of a word or a rase which is underlined in the sentence given. It is lowed by four words or phrases. Select the word or rase which is closest to the opposite in meaning or the derlined word or phrase **(CDS)**

1. An obscure traveller was found dead on the road.
   (a) A decent (b) An affluent
   (c) A famous (d) A respectable
2. We have carefully studied your explanation and it sounds plausible.
   (a) incoherent (b) unconvincing
   (c) undesirable (d) impertinent
3. Only a pragmatic approach to these problems can solve them.
   (a) practical (b) diplomatic
   (c) theoretical (d) idealistic
4. In the olden days the prisoners were kept in dark, and dank cells.
   (a) small (b) old
   (c) dry (d) dingy
5. My father is a very stern man.
   (a) liberal (b) emotional
   (c) indulgent (d) lenient
6. The pleasures of life are eternal.
   (a) brief (b) transient
   (c) occasional (d) periodical

Solutions

1. (c) 2. (b) 3. (c) 4. (c)
5. (d) 6. (b)

Exercise 43

In the following questions, choose the word opposite in meaning to the word given in capital letters **(RRB Trivendrum)**

1. EQUANIMITY
   (a) Resentment (b) Dubiousness
   (c) Duplicity (d) Excitement
2. DENSITY
   (a) Rarity (b) Intelligence
   (c) Clarity (d) Brightness
3. DEFIANCE
   (a) Anxiety (b) Obedience
   (c) Suspicion (d) Dismay
4. BASE
   (a) Climax (b) Height
   (c) Top (d) Roof
5. PATCHY
   (a) Attractive (b) Uniform
   (c) Simple (d) Clear

Solutions

1. (d) 2. (a) 3. (b) 4. (c)
5. (b)

Exercise 44

Choose the word which is nearly opposite in meaning to the word given in capital letters **[RRB (ASM) Patna]**

1. CLANDESTINE
   (a) Dim (b) Clear
   (c) Open (d) Congested
2. ONEROUS
   (a) Light (b) Tough
   (c) Heavy (d) Dark
3. LACKADAISICAL
   (a) Dull
   (b) Sensible
   (c) Hopeful
   (d) Enthusiastic
4. TURGID
   (a) Fair (b) Rough
   (c) Tall (d) Smooth

Solutions

1. (c) 2. (a) 3. (d) 4. (d)

Exercise 45

Choose from the alternatives provided an antonym (opposite in meaning) for each of the words given in capital letters **(RRB, Secundrabad)**

1. ABOVE
   (a) Retreat (b) Shallow
   (c) Deep (d) Below
2. ATTRACT
   (a) Differ (b) Deny
   (c) Repel (d) Exit
3. RISE
   (a) Rash (b) Smooth
   (c) Pride (d) Fall
4. INFERIOR
   (a) Shame (b) Superior
   (c) Senior (d) Narrow
5. PERMIT
   (a) Prohibit (b) Partly
   (c) Profane (d) Polite
6. SAINT
   (a) Complex (b) Polite
   (c) Sinner (d) Rough
7. MISER
   (a) Spiritual (b) Foreign
   (c) Villain (d) Spendthrift
8. FLOAT
   (a) Loose (b) Sink
   (c) Empty (d) Follow
9. CHEAP
   (a) Dull (b) Fair
   (c) Dear (d) False
10. COMMON
   (a) Rare (b) Light
   (c) Easy (d) Ugly

Solutions

1. (d) **2.** (c) **3.** (d) **4.** (b)
5. (a) **6.** (c) **7.** (d) **8.** (b)
9. (c) **10.** (a)

Exercise 46

In each of the following sentences, four words or phrases are given below the numbered word. Choose the word which is nearly opposite in meaning to the numbered word given in capital letters
[RRB (ASM) Mujjafarpur]

1. MOLEST
   (a) Evade (b) Abolish
   (c) Mislead (d) Inspire
2. PLENARY
   (a) Restricted (b) Confidential
   (c) Mysterious (d) Basic

Solutions

1. (d) **2.** (a)

Exercise 47

Choose the word opposite in meaning to the word given in capital lettrs **(Stenographers Allahabad)**

1. ENMITY
   (a) Friendship (b) Agreement
   (c) Amity (d) Cooperation
2. FRUGAL
   (a) Charitable (b) Extravagant
   (c) Generous (d) Gaudy
3. PERILOUS
   (a) Innocuous (b) Healthy
   (c) Safe (d) Fine
4. VIVACIOUS
   (a) Languid (b) Open
   (c) Strong (d) Bright
5. OBVIOUS
   (a) Isolated (b) Celebration
   (c) Ancient (d) Illusion

Solutions

1. (a) **2.** (b) **3.** (c) **4.** (a)
5. (d)

Exercise 48

Each of the following items contains a word given in capital letters, followed by four words or phrases. Select the word or phrase most nearly opposite in meaning to the capital letters **[RRB (ASM) Bhuvneshwar]**

1. ADAPTABLE
   (a) Adoptable (b) Flexible
   (c) Yielding (d) Rigid
2. BUSY
   (a) Occupied
   (b) Engrossed
   (c) Relaxed
   (d) Engaged
3. FLIMSY
   (a) Frail (b) Filthy
   (c) Firm (d) Flippant
4. RELINQUISH
   (a) Abdicate (b) Renounce
   (c) Possess (d) Deny
5. MOUNTAIN
   (a) Plainte (b) Plateau
   (c) Precipice (d) Valley

Solutions

1. (d) **2.** (c) **3.** (c) **4.** (
5. (d)

Exercise 49

Select the word which is most nearly opposite in meaning to the word given in capital letters

(RRB, Mumbai)

1. CONCISE
   (a) Wrong (b) Smooth
   (c) Precise (d) Wordy
2. LETHARGIC
   (a) Alert (b) Careless
   (c) Prudent (d) Promising
3. DISINTERESTED
   (a) Avid (b) Related
   (c) Opposed (d) Partial
4. ACQUIT
   (a) Disclose
   (b) Convict
   (c) Adjudge
   (d) Sentence
5. SCAR
   (a) Sacred (b) Transpire
   (c) Abundant (d) Excellent

Solutions

1. (d) **2.** (a) **3.** (d) **4.** (b)
5. (c)

Exercise 50

Choose the word which is most nearly the SAME in meaning as the word given in capital letters **(Bank PO)**

1. Vexed
   (a) Annoying (b) Recurring
   (c) Unresolvable (d) Complex
   (e) Dangerous
2. Evolve
   (a) Introduce (b) Start
   (c) Develop (d) Abandon
   (e) Establish
3. Reinforced
   (a) Strengthened (b) Re-examined
   (c) Replaced (d) Reconstructed
   (e) Restructured
4. Unabated
   (a) Unsympathetic
   (b) Unaltered
   (c) Unparalleled
   (d) Uncompromising
   (e) Unexpected

Solutions

1. (a) **2.** (b) **3.** (c) **4.** (d)

Unit

44

Exercises : Choosing Appropriate Words

Exercise 1

Fill in the blanks choosing appropriate word from the options given below

1. My mother upset the kettle of boiling water and ...... her right hand badly. ***(SSC Clerks)***
(a) scorched (b) burn
(c) woulded (d) scalded

2. Please do not .... an offer made by the chairman. ***(Income Tax)***
(a) refuse (b) deny
(c) refrain (d) refuge

3. The government is confident that the standard of living will begin to .... again soon. ***(Income Tax)***
(a) rise (b) lift
(c) flourish (d) revive

4. On second reading his poems strike us as singularly .... of sublime emotions. ***(CDS)***
(a) attributive (b) significative
(c) symptomatic (d) evocative

5. Health is too important to be .... ***(Asstt Grade)***
(a) neglected (b) discarded
(c) dispised (d) detested

6. Even a .... glance will reveal the mystery. ***(Hotel Management)***
(a) crude (b) cursory
(c) critical (d) curious

7. Like any other country India has its .... share of superstitions. ***(Central Bureau)***
(a) abundant (b) fair
(c) proper (d) peculiar

8. Hindus believe that .... from the cycle of birth and rebirth can be attained only by good deeds. ***(CDS)***
(a) bondage (b) deliverance
(c) delivery (d) retirement

Solutions

1. (d) **2.** (a) **3.** (a) **4.** (d)
5. (a) **6.** (b) **7.** (b) **8.** (b)

Exercise 2

Each of the following sentences has a blank space and four words given after the sentence. Select whichever word you consider most appropriate for the bank space and indicate your choice on the answer sheet **(CDS)**

1. An employment advertisement should .... the number of vacancies.
(a) provide (b) declare
(c) contain (d) specify

2. The family gave father a gold watch on the .... of his fifteenth birthday.
(a) time (b) event
(c) occasion (d) celebration

3. The passengers were afraid but the captain .... them that there was no danger.
(a) promised (b) advised
(c) assured (d) counselled

4. It's very kind of you to .... to speak at the meeting.
(a) comply (b) agree
(c) accept (d) concur

5. I haven't seen you............a week.
(a) within (b) since
(c) for (d) from

6. Do you know............?
(a) where she comes from
(b) where does she come from
(c) where from she comes
(d) from where does she come

7. The battalion operating from the mountain was able to .... three enemy divisions.
(a) tie up (b) tie down
(c) tie on (d) tie with

8. She .... a brief appearance at the end of the party.
(a) put on (b) put in
(c) put across (d) put up

9. Once he has signed the agreement, he won't be able to ....
(a) back up (b) back in
(c) back at (d) back out

10. .... of old paintings is a job for the experts.
(a) Resurrection
(b) Retrieval
(c) Restoration
(d) Resumption

Solutions

1. (d) **2.** (c) **3.** (c) **4.** (b)
5. (c) **6.** (a) **7.** (b) **8.** (b)
9. (d) **10.** (c)

Exercise 3

From the four alternatives given under each questions, find the one that fits into the blank space most appropriately) **(*Tourism Management*)**

1. The terrorists made a vain attempt to .... the bridge.
(a) blow down (b) blow up
(c) blow over (d) blow out

2. The finance minister may new proposals in his budget speech.
(a) bring out (b) bring forward
(c) bring round (d) bring forth

3. The main suspect in the Rajiv Gandhi assassination are still ....
(a) under a cloud (b) at daggers drawn
(c) at large (d) at sea

4. The building was so old and dilapidated that it was not ....
(a) habitation (b) habitat
(c) habitant (d) habitable

5. Polyster shirts are more .... than the cotton ones.
(a) durably (b) duration
(c) durability (d) durable

Solutions

1. (b) **2.** (b) **3.** (c) **4.** (d)
5. (d)

Exercise 4

Pick out the most effective word from the given words to fill in the blank to make the complete meaningful **(*SBI PO*)**

1. Leadership define what the future should like and .... people with that vision.
(a) encourages (b) develops
(c) trains (d) aligns
(e) transforms

2. We upset ourselves by responding in an .... manner to someone else's actions.
(a) invalid (b) irrational
(c) arduous (d) arguable
(e) unabashed

3. All the people involved in that issue feel a great .... to his suggestion.
(a) contradiction (b) adherence
(c) indifference (d) objection
(e) erepugnance

4. These election will be remembered as much for its anti-incumbency mood as for its .... mandate.
(a) invincible (b) rational
(c) unprecedented (d) deliberate
(e) pervasive

5. How do you expect us to stay in such a .... building even if it can be hired on a nominal rent?
(a) scruffy (b) desperate
(c) fragmented (d) robust
(e) damaging

6. .... efforts from all concerned are required to raise the social and economic condition of our countrymen.
(a) Perpetual (b) Dynamic
(c) Massive (d) Exploring
(e) Penetrative

7. Many companies see technology as a .... for a whole host of business problems.
(a) consideration (b) preference
(c) linking (d) craving
(e) panacea

Solutions

1. (d) **2.** (e) **3.** (e) **4.** (c)
5. (a) **6.** (a) **7.** (e)

Exercise 5

In the following questions, sentences are given with blanks to be filled in with an appropriate word (s). Four alternatives are suggested for each question. Choose the correct alternative out of the four and indicate on the answer sheet **(*Stenographer Grade*)**

1. He admired precision in everything, but it never hampered his quick........... .
(a) decision (b) action
(c) dealing (d) finalisation

2. .... you meet my son in the market, ask him to come home at once.
(a) Should (b) Would
(c) While (d) Will

3. The proud king turned a deaf ear to the .... of wise counsellors.
(a) advices (b) advises
(c) advise (d) advice

4. I shall not desert him .... all the world.
(a) for (b) by
(c) from (d) with

5. The judge acquitted the prisoner .... the charge of murder.
(a) from (b) about
(c) with (d) of

6. More than twenty years have now passed .... I had my first flight.
(a) when (b) since
(c) while (d) as

7. .... being hard-working he is thoroughly honest.
(a) Along with (b) Besides
(c) Over and above (d) Although

8. Through perseverance and hard work we can keep the .... of liberty burning even during dark and trying times.
(a) light (b) goal
(c) lamp (d) flame

9. He became the governor of a province ....
(a) by and large (b) in course of time
(c) at times (d) little by little

10. You're coming to the movie, ... ?
(a) isn't it (b) won't you
(c) aren't you (d) can't you

11. While strolling on Janpath, I chanced to meet .... European.
(a) one (b) the
(c) an (d) a

12. Because of the heavy rain, the match was ....
(a) set aside (b) called off
(c) fallen off (d) broken off

13. Usually the ascent of mountain face is much easier than the ....
(a) fall (b) decent
(c) descent (d) descend

14. This is a .... translation of the speech.
(a) literal (b) literary
(c) verbal (d) verbatim

15. I spend much of my time .... writing letters and memos.
(a) in (b) to
(c) on (d) at

Solutions

1. (b) **2.** (a) **3.** (d) **4.** (a)
5. (d) **6.** (d) **7.** (a) **8.** (d)
9. (b) **10.** (c) **11.** (b) **12.** (b)
13. (c) **14.** (a) **15.** (a)

Exercise 6

Each of the following sentences has a blank space and four words given after the sentence. Select whichever word you consider most appropriate for the blank space **(CDS)**

1. The .... effect of suitably chosen firms on children's minds cannot be overestimated.
(a) educative (b) debilitating
(c) baneful (d) educational

2. A number of scientists in the country think that they are on the .... of a major breakthrough.
(a) frontier (b) threshold
(c) gateway (d) periphery

3. .... from the campaigns have been used to buy medical supplies, food and educational materials.
(a) Revenue (b) Profit
(c) Proceed (d) Proceeds

4. When I joined the flying club, my instructor gave me the first lecture on the ....of flying.
(a) foundations (b) basics
(c) need (d) theory

5. You must .... your house in order before you venture to offer advice to others.
(a) arrange (b) bring
(c) get (d) organise

6. Fact is often stranger than ....
(a) fancy (b) fiction
(c) imagination (d) dream

7. It is becoming increasingly difficult for a housewife to pick up a genuine article from the crowd of the .... ones in a store.
(a) fake (b) duplicate
(c) counterfeit (d) spurious

8. His rustic and robust humour was an embarrassment to the .... sensibility of the young ladies.
(a) fragile (b) delicate
(c) soft (d) sober

9. His teacher said that his comments on his performance was not demoralise him but to .... him to do still better
(a) encourage (b) persuade
(c) instruct (d) goad

10. Diseases are .... through contact with infected animals.
(a) transmitted (b) transported
(c) transferred (d) transplanted

Solution

1. (a) **2.** (b) **3.** (d) **4.** (b)
5. (c) **6.** (a) **7.** (b) **8.** (b)
9. (c) **10.** (a)

Exercise 7

Fill in the blanks in the following sentences with the most appropriate word from among those given in brackets after each sentence **(IFS)**

1. Our charming hostess was very .... to all her guests. (graceful, gracious, grateful)
2. There was nothing unusual about the man .... he smiled, but that happened only (except, except for, except that)
3. The doctor .... the woman that her son would recover. (ensured, assured, insured)
4. I like .... music. (classic, classical, classics)
5. I don't think I dare ask for a .... at the moment. (raise, rise, arise)

Solutions

1. grateful 2. except that 3. assured
4. classical 5. rise

Exercise 8

Fill in the blanks in the following sentences with the most appropriate word from among those given in brackets after each sentence **(CDS)**

1. An .... man is sure to be successful.
(a) industrus (b) indistrious
(c) industrious (d) indestrious
2. Students will go on an ....
(a) excusion (b) excurtion
(c) ascursion (d) excursion
3. You cannot leave without ....
(a) permision (b) premission
(c) purmission (d) permission
4. It is difficult to cross the ....
(a) barier (b) berrier
(c) borier (d) barrier
5. Ravi was .... from the school.
(a) expeled (b) espelled
(c) expilled (d) expelled

Solutions

1. (c) 2. (d) 3. (d) 4. (d)
5. (d)

Exercise 9

Fill in the blanks in the following sentences with the most appropriate word from among those given in brackets after each sentence

1. After a recent mild paralytic attack his movements are........restricted, otherwise he is still very active. **(BSRB)**
(a) frequently (b) not
(c) nowhere (d) slightly
(e) entirely
2. The prisoner was relased on.......for good behaviour. **(RRB Ajmer)**
(a) parole (b) bail
(c) probation (d) guarantee
(e) guarantee
3. Rajeev is too.......as far as his food habits are concerned. **(Bank PO)**
(a) enjoyable (b) fastidious
(c) curious (d) interesting
(e) involved
4. My father keeps all his.......papers in a lock and key. **(BSRB)**
(a) required
(b) necessary
(b) useful
(c) confidential
5. The brilliant students will be.........scholarships.
(a) honoured (b) rewarded **(RRB)**
(c) awarded (d) forwarded
6. Several of our players were injured so our losing the match was almost........ **(Central Bureau)**
(a) necessary (b) indispensable
(c) inevitable (d) inexcusable
7. My friend says that he drinks tea because it is the best.........in the world. **(Asstt Grade)**
(a) fluid (b) drink
(c) beverage (d) liquid
8. Life is to death as pleasure is to......... **(CDS)**
(a) suffering (b) pain
(c) poverty (d) anguish

Solutions

1. (d) 2. (a) 3. (b) 4. (d)
5. (c) 6. (c) 7. (c) 8. (b)

Exercise 10

Fill in the blanks in the following sentences with the most appropriate word from among those given in brackets after each sentence **(Bank PO)**

1. These essays are intellectually........and represent various levels of complexity.
(a) modern (b) revealing
(c) superior (d) demanding
(e) persistant
2. The soldiers were instructed to.....restraint and handle the situation peacefully.
(a) control (b) exercise
(c) prevent (d) enforce
(e) remai
3. Since one cannot read every book, one should be content with making a ......selection.
(a) normal (b) standard
(c) moderate (d) judicious
(e) imposed
4. He is too........to be deceived easily.
(a) strong (b) modern
(c) intelligent (d) kind
(e) honest

5. There has been a..........lack of efficiency in all the crucial areas of the working of Public Sector Undertakings.
(a) positive (b) surprising
(c) conspicuous (d) stimulating
(e) insignificant

Solutions

1. (b) 2. (b) 3. (d) 4. (c)
5. (c)

Exercise 11

Fill in the blanks in the following sentences with the most appropriate word from among those given in brackets after each sentence

1. I write a letter to you tentatively........the dates of the programme. ***(BSRB)***
(a) involving (b) indicating
(c) guiding (d) urging
(e) propagating
2. Contemporary economic development differs....... from the Industrial Revolution of the 19th century. ***(Bank PO)***
(a) naturally (b) markedly
(c) literally (d) usually
3. Ravi had to drop his plan of going to picnic as he had certain .... to meet during that period.
(a) preparations (b) observations ***(SBI PO)***
(c) urgencies (d) commitment
(e) transactions
4. It was....hot that day and the cable suffered the brunt of the heat. ***(SBI PO)***
(a) treacherously (b) acceptably
(c) unfailingly (d) unbelievably
(e) uncompromisingly
5. ....eye-witness, the news reporter gave a graphic description of how fire broke out. ***(Indian Bank PO)***
(a) reporting (b) observing
(c) seeing (d) quoting
(e) examining
6. His life consists of........of drinking punctuated by periods of drunken sleep. ***(Central Excise)***
(a) barrels (b) bouts
(c) bowls (d) pints
7. When the morning......the murder was discovered.
(a) occured (b) came ***(Asstt Grade)***
(c) arrived (d) happened
8. He lives in the world of...... ***(Hotel Management)***
(a) allusions (b) illusions
(c) conclusions (d) delusions
9. There was a serious .... between the two brothers. ***(Hotel Management)***
(a) altieration (b) alteration
(c) altercation (d) aberration

Solutions

1. (b) 2. (b) 3. (d) 4. (d)
5. (d) 6. (b) 7. (c) 8. (b)
9. (c)

Exercise 12

Fill in the blanks in the following sentences with the most appropriate word from among those given in brackets after each sentence

1. The primary purpose of modern weapons is .... to prevent a particular course of action by a specific threat.
(a) deterrent (b) prognostic
(c) minatory (d) hegemony
2. As for the free world, trade with Cuba as been taking place on a modest scale despite the .... opposition of the United States.
(a) casual (b) independent
(c) clandestine (d) overt
3. The basic structure of the living cell is a problem whose .... can be judged by reference to the difficult exploration of the structure of the atom.
(a) importance (b) universality
(c) complexity (d) antiquity
4. The endless battle to modernise the .... structure of work rules on the nation's railroads appears destined to reach the showdown stage with a strike at one minute after midnight tonight.
(a) anemic (b) impracticable
(c) archaic (d) streamlined
5. Cyprus is still not economically viable, and though.............. important, it is militarily weak in its own right.
(a) necessarily (b) strategically
(c) scarcely (d) independently
6. He's gone through a .... He is not at all the man be was when he was a combat officer.
(a) metamorphosis (b) crisis
(c) frustration (d) surveillance
7. It was Jacob Grimm who transformed philology from an .... study in to an exact science.
(a) abstruse (b) alleged
(c) esoteric (d) errant
8. As the waves rose and the ship tossed, many of the passengers felt............
(a) lethargic (b) subdued
(c) tremulous (d) queasy
9. Although advertising men often complain that their industry is hemmed in by government regulations, the fact remains that a/an .... attitude toward Madison Avenue continues to exist in this country.
(a) laissez faire (b) savoir faire
(c) bete noire (d) idee fixe

10. The knockout wallop travelled only seven or eight inches and, admittedly, did not look like much. But boxing experts, and .... scientists, will attest that punches that travel more than a foot lose much of their initial force.
(a) nuclear (b) biological
(c) electronic (d) kinetic

11. Are not the youngsters, viewing such war films, hypnotised by .... thrills and the elders, especially the veterans, deluded into identifying themselves with the hero breed?
(a) sensational (b) specious
(c) auspicious (d) vicarious

12. It is fascinating to note how many travellers return from their gastronomic tours of Europe with a .... of la grande cuisine and a haunting hunger for the simplicity of local dishes.
(a) memory (b) suspicion
(c) surfeit (d) superfluity

13. To avoid any outside influences, the judge has wisely decided to .... the jury.
(a) admonish (b) preclude
(c) sequester (d) dismiss

14. The remarkable thing about Spoon River Anthology is the way its .... little autobiographies merge into a unity.
(a) desparate (b) undeveloped
(c) superficial (d) concatenated

15. The general scientific assumption is that any amount of radiation, however small, will cause genetic damage that will appear as .... in the future.
(a) mutations (b) disabilities
(c) diseases (d) handicaps

Solutions

1. (a)	2. (d)	3. (c)	4. (c)
5. (b)	6. (a)	7. (c)	8. (d)
9. (a)	10. (d)	11. (d)	12. (c)
13. (c)	14. (a)	15. (a)	

Exercise 13

In the following questions, sentences are given with blanks to be filled in with an anpropriate word (s). Four alternatives are suggested for each question. Choose the correct alternative

1. The problems that India's economic development faces are ....
(a) enormous (b) great
(c) myopic (d) morbid

2. She refused to wear the new dress as she felt it to be ....
(a) odd (b) uncouth
(c) outmoded (d) unfashioned

3. Leah Robin saw him .... his tranformation from warrior to peacemaker.
(a) off (b) through
(c) about (d) up

4. Few countries can .... India in variety, colour and the richness of dance forms.
(a) rival (b) depict
(c) prevail (d) perform

5. The magistrate sent a ....of fifty policemen to the village where disturbances had occurred.
(a) team (b) force
(c) battalion (d) cover

6. Take possession of the records immediately so that they are not ....with.
(a) destroyed (b) manhandled
(c) tampered (d) mishandled

7. Having lived a .... life for 40 years, he is not able to take any independent decision
(a) happy (b) successful
(c) safe (d) cloistered

8. I like listening to the radio but I am not always impressed .... the quality of the programmes.
(a) with (b) at
(c) about (d) on

9. I saw a man .... the wire and walking away.
(a) picked (b) having picked
(c) picking (d) picking up

10. Sometimes truth is stronger than ....
(a) falsehood (b) lies
(c) fiction (d) history

11. It is felt that India, even with limited .... and funds, could still become a reckoning force in the art world.
(a) resources (b) sources
(c) wealths (d) enthusiasm

12. According to the recent .... made by the Govermment of India, the target of foodgrains production for this year is 190 million tonnes.
(a) inferences (b) statistics
(c) accounts (d) estimates

13. Gopal Krishna Gokhale's patriotic speeches .... people to dedicate their lives for the nation.
(a) forced (b) inspired
(c) inflamed (d) prompted

14. There have been quite a large number of .... in the Himalayas now and some of them have been extremely successful.
(a) attempts (b) journies
(c) expeditions (d) attractions

15. We though that the Sadhu had miraculous powers but we soon found out that we were ....
(a) wronged (b) mistaken
(c) befooled (d) deceived

Solutions

1. (a)	2. (c)	3. (b)	4. (a)
5. (b)	6. (c)	7. (d)	8. (a)
9. (d)	10. (c)	11. (a)	12. (d)
13. (b)	14. (c)	15. (d)	

Exercise 14

In the following you find a number of sentences, parts of which are printed in bold type. You may also find only a group of words which is printed in bold type. For each part printed in bold type, four words/phrases are listed below. Choose the word nearest in meaning to the part printed in bold type

1. He displayed a distinct tendency to **long winded** speeches when asked how he was.
(a) boring (b) repetitive
(c) circumlocutory (d) hyperbolic
2. The data is **misleading.**
(a) illusory (b) deceptive
(c) misplaced (d) misinformative
3. This library was built with donations from the **munificent** citizens of this city.
(a) well-to-do (b) generous
(c) respectable (d) learned
4. Some satirists are known for their **trenchant** style.
(a) sharp (b) critical
(c) aggressive (d) incisive
5. Many educationists think that the classroom instruction should be made more **vigorous.**
(a) serious (b) brisk
(c) lively (d) active
6. Medical science is yet to come out with a **panacea** for cancer.
(a) remedy (b) medicine
(c) treatment (d) drug
7. The navy gave **tactical** support to the marines.
(a) sensitive (b) strategic
(c) expedient (d) expert
8. Businessmen who lack **acumen** cannot be expected to be very successful.
(a) cleverness (b) sharpness
(c) keenness (d) smartness
9. In modern hospitals computers **check** the patients before they see the doctor.
(a) screen (b) protect
(c) cover (d) stop
10. A genius tends to **deviate** from the routine way of thinking.
(a) dispute (b) disagree
(c) differ (d) distinguish

Solutions

1. (d) 2. (b) 3. (b) 4. (d)
5. (d) 6. (a) 7. (b) 8. (a)
9. (a) 10. (c)

Exercise 15

In the following you find a number of sentences, parts of which are printed in bold. You may also find only a group of words which is printed in bold. For each bold part, four words/phrases are listed below. Choose the word/phrase nearest in meaning to the part and choose the corresponding space on the answer sheet **(NDA)**

1. The tacher **reiterated** the importance of steady and hard work for getting through the examinations.
(a) emphasised (b) stressed
(c) repeated (d) furthered
2. There is **affectation** in the way he talks.
(a) beauty (b) sincerity
(c) artificiality (d) sadness
3. He is in the habit of using **obsolete** words.
(a) difficult (b) outdated
(c) wrong (d) simple
4. He talked on a passage from Hamlet; the **explication** was lucid.
(a) discussion (b) explanation
(c) argument (d) description
5. The books supplied by the shop were not only rare, they were also **invaluable.**
(a) valueless (b) priceless
(c) useless (d) cheap

Solutions

1. (c) 2. (c) 3. (b) 4. (b)
5. (b)

Exercise 16

The most appropriate word/phrase to fill in the blank in each of the following sentences is given as one of the four alternatives under it. That is your answer. Mark it on the answer sheet **(Hotel Management)**

1. He is very keen .... going abroad for higher studies.
(a) for (b) at
(c) over (d) on
2. You are not justified .... laying the blame .... my door.
(a) in, over (b) in, at
(c) at, at (d) over, at
3. What you have done .... no excuse.
(a) admits (b) admits to
(c) admits about (d) admits of
4. Timid by nature the doctor who was alone in his house was frightened ....
(a) out of wits
(b) out at his wits
(c) at his wits end
(d) out of his wits
5. His approach to work is so .... that none of his colleagues considers him dependable.
(a) uninteresting (b) low
(c) casual (d) common

6. He has full facts .... but is deliberately hiding them.
(a) up his sleeves (b) in his sleeves
(c) under his sleeves (d) upon his sleeves

7. Their faults are .... by their masters.
(a) winked after (b) winked at
(c) winked out (d) winked

8. Having had .... crops for the last two years, the government is falling short of storing space.
(a) bloated (b) bumper
(c) booming (d) blooming

9. Having been set .... he is now free to go anywhere he likes.
(a) at freedom (b) freedom
(c) at liberty (d) liberty

10. .... come to my rescue I would have been killed by the bandits.
(a) If he had not (b) If he did not
(c) Having not (d) He having not

Solutions

1. (d)	**2.** (b)	**3.** (d)	**4.** (d)
5. (c)	**6.** (a)	**7.** (b)	**8.** (b)
9. (c)	**10.** (a)		

Exercise 17

The most appropriate word/phrase to fill in the blank in each of the following sentences is given as one of the four alternatives under it. That is your answer. Mark it on the answer sheet ***(Hotel Management)***

1. The child kept on crying while it ....
(a) is bathed (b) is being bathed
(c) was bathed (d) was being bathed

2. He has such good manners that he can easily .... a gentleman.
(a) pass out (b) pass on
(c) pass in (d) pass for

3. Shivaji .... a plan to escape from jail.
(a) hit upon (b) hit out
(c) hit about (d) hit against

4. We chose to .... our views in the light of the new information made available to us.
(a) disclose (b) revive
(c) diagnose (d) revise

5. Although the Rajput army was out numbered, the brave general refused to ....
(a) give away (b) give over
(c) give in (d) give out

6. Having earned a lot of money in business, Mr. Sharma .... his poor cousins.
(a) looks down upon (b) hits upon
(c) shows off (d) looks upon

7. The price of gold as well as silver .... risen.
(a) are (b) have
(c) has (d) is

8. The building was so old and dilapidated that it was not ....
(a) habitable (b) habitat
(c) habitability (d) habituating

9. Your son had promised to call you to USA, ... ?
(a) didn't he (b) did he
(c) hadn't he (d) had he

10. A large majority of students .... absent from the college yesterday.
(a) was (b) were
(c) has been (d) had been

Solutions

1. (d)	**2.** (d)	**3.** (a)	**4.** (d)
5. (c)	**6.** (a)	**7.** (c)	**8.** (a)
9. (b)	**10.** (a)		

Exercise 18

In the following sentences are given with blanks to be filled in with an appropriate word (s). Four alternatives are suggested for each. Chosse the correct one

1. Dowry is no longer permitted by law even in .... marriages.
(a) natural (b) love
(c) conventional (d) polygamous

2. Family planning is essential for curbing the rapid .... in population.
(a) spurt (b) augmentation
(c) spread (d) growth

3. The transfer to territories could not take place because one State .... the findings of the Commission.
(a) disputed (b) rejected
(c) questioned (d) objected

4. Kings have few things to desire and many things to ....
(a) crave (b) long
(c) fear (d) apprehend

5. Vikram shouted .... her at the top of his voice, but she did not hear and went on.
(a) at (b) to
(c) against (d) for

6. The winding road was no doubt a .... climb and, though at every steep turn the car groaned, we finally reached the top.
(a) tortuous (b) easy
(c) fast (d) slow

7. A light breeze...........the forest fire and made it more dangerous.
(a) blew (b) ignited
(c) fanned (d) lit

8. Take care of the .... and the hours will take care of themselves.
(a) days (b) years
(c) seconds (d) minutes

9. The way Dara kept knocking over things, he was more like a bull in a ....
(a) english (b) china
(c) cattle (d) grocery

10. Though he took a leap in the .... when he invested all his savings in Reliance shares, he later on found that it was well worth the risk.
(a) abyss (b) dark (c) light (d) hole

Solutions

1. (c) 2. (d) 3. (a) 4. (c)
5. (b) 6. (a) 7. (c) 8. (d)
9. (b) 10. (b)

Exercise 19

Fill in the blanks in the following sentences with the most appropriate word from among those given in brackets after each sentence

1. The committee's appeal to the people for money .... little response. ***(CDS)***
(a) provoked (b) evoked
(c) gained (d) provided

2. Colgate has also got an ambitious aim of .... an eight percent value share of the tooth paste market by the end of the first year. ***(MBA Entrance)***
(a) keeping (b) distributing
(c) cornering (d) soliciting

3. He is very .... on meeting foreigners and befriending them.
(a) anxious (b) find ***(SSC Clerk)***
(c) insistent (d) keen

4. If a speech is full of prompous words, it is ...... ***(MBA Entrance)***
(a) verbose (b) bombastie
(c) grandiose (d) grandiloquent

5. We don't know what .... him to commit this crime.
(a) excited (b) roused ***(SSC Clerk)***
(c) prompted (d) attracted

6. He is like a body without a soul, an eye without light or flower without .... ***(Insurance)***
(a) smell (b) fragrance
(c) petal (d) colour

7. It is difficult to believe what he tells us because his account of any event is always full of ...... of all sorts.
(a) discretions (b) differences ***(CDS)***
(c) discrepancies (d) distinction

8. The country needs a .... government to tackle the challenges it faces today. ***(SSC Clerk)***
(a) sustained (b) stable
(c) stationary (d) stagnant

9. .... an accident the train will arrive in time.
(a) despite (b) accepting ***(SSC Clerk)***
(c) besides (d) barring

Solutions

1. (b) 2. (c) 3. (d) 4. (d)
5. (c) 6. (b) 7. (c) 8. (b)
9. (a)

Exercise 20

In the following questions, sentences are given with blanks to be filled in with an appropriate word (s). Four alternatives are suggested for each question. Choose the correct alternative

1. The rank and .... of the party had turned against the leader.
(a) file (b) class
(c) officers (d) people

2. After being caught in the act, Rajneesh knew that he was in .... trouble.
(a) intense (b) dreaded
(c) terrible (d) dire

3. Zairian health officials said that 93 people have died .... the Ebola virus so far.
(a) of (b) for
(c) from (d) on

4. Owing to their unruly behaviour, some members of the cricket team were ....
(a) excluded (b) exempted
(c) banned (d) Putlawed

5. It is not the right .... to ask for my help; I am far too busy even to listen to you.
(a) opportunity (b) sistuation
(c) circumstance (d) moment

6. The government has agreed to pay compensation .... damaged crops, land and cattle.
(a) to (b) through
(c) for (d) of

7. As the driver swerved violently at the turning, the wheel came off, as it was already ....
(a) lose (b) loose
(c) loss (d) lost

8. The interior of the concert hall is a .... feast to the eye.
(a) veritable (b) hopeless
(c) delicious (d) visual

9. If you have already paid your dues, please do not take .... of the letter.
(a) note (b) notice
(c) care (d) consideration

10. The writer, like a spider .... a web; the creatures caught in the web have no substance, no reality.
(a) writes (b) catches
(c) spins (d) compiles

Solutions

1. (a) 2. (d) 3. (c) 4. (a)
5. (d) 6. (c) 7. (b) 8. (a)
9. (b) 10. (c)

» Unit

45

Double Blanks in a Sentence

In many competitive examinations, the question paper of English has five or ten questions with two blank spaces. Candidates are required to fill up these blank spaces out of the four or five choices given. On filling up these blank spaces, the sentence takes a meaningful shape. The candidates are required to fill up the appropriate pair out of the given choices. The knowledge of appropriate use of words and good command over vocabulary will help the candidates in solving such type of questions.

» Exercises

Exercise 1

Directions (Q. 1-5) : *In each of the following sentences, there are two blank spaces. Below each sentence there are five pair of words denoted by numbers (a), (b), (c), (d) and (e). Find out which pair of words can be filled up in the blanks in the sentence in the same sequence to make the sentence meaningfully complete.*

1. Our latest battle plan .... some projects .... at saving the earth's biological diversity.
(a) finishes, stirring (b) covers, aimed
(c) finances, looking (d) encloses, looked
(e) excludes, arriving

2. Unless the authorities adopt the principle.........., the strategies cannot become.......... .
(a) whole-heartedly, successful
(b) fully, defunct
(c) finally, obsolete
(d) legitimately, noteworthy
(e) logically, trivial

3. Trying to..........a team without a good and simple system is like trying to drive a car without a steering wheel.......... .
(a) form, working
(b) place, exploratory
(c) organise, empowering
(d) make, guidance
(e) achieve, developmental

4. ....members of a group often.......... influence the outcome of a consensus forecast.
(a) Fixed, exert
(b) Majority, rightly
(c) Oral, legitimately
(d) Minority, inadvertently
(e) Dominant, unduly

5. Transforming..........bureaucracies into dynamic, this task of customer-driven organisations is..........under prevailing circumstances.
(a) ideal, important
(b) lazy, undesirable
(c) inefficient, challenging
(d) civilised, ineffective
(e) lethargic, insurmountable

Solutions

1. (b) **2.** (a) **3.** (a) **4.** (e)
5. (c)

Exercise 2

Directions (Q. 1-10) : *In each of the following sentences there are two blank spaces. Below each sentence there are four or five pair of words denoted by numbers (a), (b), (c), (d) and (e). Find out which pair of words can be filled up in the blanks in the sentence in the same sequence to make the sentence meaningfully complete.*

1. The deputy manager........to resign because all his proposals were......down by his superiors. **(Bank PO)**
(a) planned, thrown (b) gave, held
(c) began, kept (d) willing, knocked
(e) threatened, turned
2. The counter clerk was very busy and.........not pay.......to Sameer's request. **(Bank PO)**
(a) can, help
(b) could, cooperation
(c) had, cash
(d) did, attention
(e) certainly, acceptance
3. He was initially.............at the suggestion but was soon..........it himself. **(SBI PO)**
(a) anger, rejecting
(b) shocked, advocating
(c) impressed, negating
(d) thrilled, propagating
(e) suspicious, trusting
4. Shalini was not..........by the criticism and paid no............even when her best friend talked against her. **(SBI PO)**
(a) bothered, attention (b) troubled, brained
(c) threatened, warning (d) deterred, heed
(e) shaken, indication
5. She was..........because all her plan had gone............ . **(Asst. Grade)**
(a) happy, selected
(b) dejected, splendidly
(c) distraught, awry
(d) frustrated, magnificently
6. He preaches liberal views but in practice, he is not...............and is..........narrow minded than almost any other person. **(Bank PO)**
(a) tough, openly
(b) tolerant, more
(c) ambitious, hardly
(d) acceptable, genuinely
(e) approachable, less
7. Ravi.........a bit........he was not invited by his friend to attend the party. **(Bank PO)**
(a) annoyed, before
(b) angered, since
(c) expressed, than
(d) grumbled, when
(e) surprised, about
8. He is...........to...........any kind of work with due sincerity. **(BSRB Clerk)**
(a) fond, perform
(b) reluctant, entrust
(c) determined, undertake
(d) eager, avoid
(e) willing, ignore
9. Children are more........than adults, it is........their quickness in learning a new language. **(Indian Bank PO)**
(a) intelligent, disproved by
(b) adaptable, reflected in
(c) conservative, seen in
(d) susceptible, demonstrated in
(e) resourceful, proportionate to
10. ......of crops was due to continuous............. .
(a) Loss, draught (b) Ruin, draft
(c) Failure, drought (d) Depreciation, drift

Solutions

1. (e)	**2.** (d)	**3.** (b)	**4.** (a)
5. (c)	**6.** (b)	**7.** (d)	**8.** (c)
9. (b)	**10.** (c)		

Exercise 3

Directions (Q. 1-9) : *In each of the following sentences there are two blank spaces. Below each sentence there are four or five pair of words denoted by numbers (a), (b), (c), (d) and (e). Find out which pair of words can be filled up in the blanks in the sentence in the same sequence to make the sentence meaningfully complete.*

1. Prabha's .... in athletics yielded rich ...... as she got a scholarship. **(SBI PO)**
(a) performance, money
(b) defeat, results
(c) behaviour, appreciation
(d) excellence, dividends
(e) failure, disappointment
2. The police .... any attempt of arson by ..... at the trouble spot quite in time. **(SBI PO)**
(a) squashed, surrounding
(b) made, encircling
(c) predisposed, visiting
(d) thwarted, presenting
(e) pre-empted, arriving
3. The ...... imposed for non-payment was too ...... for it to bring in improvement in collection. **(SBI PO)**
(a) fine, severe (b) toll, simple
(c) penalty, low (d) damage, cruel
(e) punishment, harsh
4. Somesh ...... me coming to his table, he smiled and .... me a chair. **(Bank PO, Maharashtra)**
(a) found, signalled (b) met, sat
(c) looked, gave (d) saw, offered
(e) welcomed, took
5. The leaders were ..... needed by those to ..... they addressed. **(Bank PO)**
(a) angrily, who (b) readily, which
(c) scarcely, whom (d) rarely, where
(e) joyfully, when

6. I am not.....to sell you my house unless you offer a more.......price. (*Asst Grade*)
(a) agree, better (b) prepared, realistic
(c) ready, correct (d) having, actual

7. Due to.......rainfall this year, there will be........cut in water supply. (*BSRB Clerk*)
(a) scanty, substantial (b) meagre, least
(c) sufficient, no (d) surplus, abundant
(e) abundant, considerable

8. In a changing and........unstructured business environment, creativity and innovation are being.........demanded of executives. (*MBA Entrance*)
(a) excessively, rapidly
(b) highly, extremely
(c) increasingly, moderately
(d) progressively, increasingly
(e) highly, speedily

9. We are.......to have him.....here to make this function a great success. (*Bank PO*)
(a) happy, have (b) unhappy, arrive
(c) sure, come (d) pleased, over
(e) wonderful, again

Solutions

1. (d) 2. (e) 3. (c) 4. (d)
5. (c) 6. (b) 7. (a) 8. (d)
9. (d)

Exercise 4

Directions (Q. 1-18) : *In each of the following sentences there are two blank spaces. Below each sentence there are four or five pair of words denoted by numbers (a), (b), (c), (d) and (e). Find out which pair of words can be filled up in the blanks in the sentence in the same sequence to make the sentence meaningfully complete.*

1. To ...... yourself from ....., wear warm clothes. (*BSRB Officers*)
(a) prohibit, heat (b) protect, cold
(c) save, heat (d) suffer, cold
(e) prevent, ice

2. We.........him with many promises, but nothing would.....him. (*Bank PO*)
(a) tempted, influence
(b) provoked, desiccate
(c) attracted, fascinate
(d) gave, deprive
(e) negotiated, please

3. In his......., he followed the.....course. (*SBI PO*)
(a) agony, funny
(b) ignorance, wrong
(c) hurry, diversified
(d) predicament, proper
(e) bewilderment, appropriate

4. The construction of the hall has been.......because of the....... of cement in the market. (*Bank PO*)
(a) held, non-availability
(b) denied, restrictions
(c) hampered, shortage
(d) prevented, supply
(e) completed, disappearance

5. Only when..........failed, the police resorted to..... (*Bank PO*)
(a) efforts, power
(b) arrests, imprisonment
(c) persuasions, force
(d) power, punishment
(e) manipulations, arrests

6. The partners broke off as they found each other......of......breach of promise.
(a) faulty, severe (b) responsible, serious
(c) guilty, flagrant (d) accused, rigid

7. They wanted to....all these books, but they could not find.....time to do so. (*BSRB Clerk*)
(a) cover, almost (b) pursue, necessary
(c) dispose, some (d) read, sufficient
(e) buy, some

8. Though he is reputed for his technical...., his books were sadly........of the work of others as he lacked originality. (*Bank PO*)
(a) advice, unconscious
(b) skill, independent
(c) knowledge, ignorant
(d) expertise, derivative
(e) dependence, indicative

9. He had managed to........several times, but was finally........by the police.
(a) deceive, cheated (b) defend, acquitted
(c) escape, arrested (d) cheat, robbed
(e) abscond, kidnapped

10. The candidate's ....at the polls was.....as he won with a striking margin. (*SBI PO*)
(a) claim, unrealistic
(b) victory, overwhelming
(c) image, real
(d) strategy, unsuccessful
(e) candidature, inappropriate

11. In......of international matters, there is always an element of risk in.....one might do. (*Bank PO*)
(a) view, whichever (b) many, doing
(c) defence, wrong (d) case, whatever
(e) spite, whatever

12. We must prevent endangered wild animal species from becoming.....in order that our future generation may.....the great diversity of animal life. (*Bank PO*)
(a) rare, escape (b) outdated, know
(c) volatile, notice (d) powerful, protect
(e) extinct, enjoy

13. We cannot....such a/an.....act of violence.
(a) tolerate, insipid (SBI PO)
(b) consider, important
(c) commit, magnificent
(d) pardon, egregious
(e) neglect, insignificant

14. The secretary.........the society's funds,.....he was dismissed. (Asstt-Grade)
(a) misplaced, soon (b) rolled, thus
(c) pirated, therefore (d) misappropriated, so

15. The.......words of the mother comforted the........child. (SBI PO)
(a) harsh, naughty
(b) sweet, happy
(c) soft, energetic
(d) melodious, playful
(e) salty, sad

16. Santosh looked very happy and.........when he heard that his proposed scheme was.......by the committee. (SBI PO)
(a) energetic, rejected
(b) elated, accepted
(c) satisfied, stalled
(d) disconsolate, approved
(e) overwhelming, received

17. It is indeed........that fifty years after independence, we have failed to.......a suitable education or examination system.
(a) bad, produce
(b) improper, create
(c) sad, evolve
(d) objectionable, present

18. The bandit..........the traveller of his purse, gold and.......him grievously. (BSRB Clerk)
(a) snatched, hurt (b) stole, injured
(c) demanded, beat (d) robbed, wounded

Solutions

1. (b)	**2.** (a)	**3.** (b)	**4.** (c)
5. (c)	**6.** (c)	**7.** (d)	**8.** (d)
9. (c)	**10.** (b)	**11.** (d)	**12.** (e)
13. (d)	**14.** (d)	**15.** (d)	**16.** (b)
17. (c)	**18.** (d)		

Exercise 5

Directions (Q. 1-17) : *In each of the following sentences there are two blank spaces. Below each sentence there are four or five pair of words denoted by numbers (a), (b), (c), (d) and (e). Find out which pair of words can be filled up in the blanks in the sentence in the same sequence to make the sentence meaningfully complete.*

1. It is.......for every tax payer to.....the tax returns to the Income Tax Department. (RBI)
(a) necessary, lodge (b) binding, pay
(c) obligatory, submit (d) possible, remit
(e) worthwhile, evade

2. The.....of glory lead but to the...... .
(a) ways, happiness
(b) acts, prosperity
(c) paths, grave
(d) achievements, suffering

3. If we do not take........care in our industry, we will have to........a grave problem.
(a) normal, experience (b) proper, face
(c) adequate, catch (d) intensive, aggravate
(e) preventive, solve

4. He shifted to his late parent's house not because of the.....it provided but for purely.........reasons.
(a) convenience, sentimental
(b) satisfaction, aesthetic
(c) reasons, monetary
(d) comforts, personal
(e) benefit, extraneous

5. The increasing revival of dramatic classics is to one critic.......; it seems to him a sign of ....of the modern theatre. (MBA Entrance)
(a) auspicious, resurgence
(b) tragic, anaemia
(c) incomprehensible, paradox
(d) astounding, liveliness

6. The activities of the association have.........from the.........objectives set for it in the initial years. (SBI PO)
(a) grown, simple (b) deviated, original
(c) details, grand (d) emerged, total
(e) increased, perverse

7. Those suffering from glaucoma find that their.......vision is.......and that they can no longer see objects not directly in front of them. (MBA)
(a) optical, distorted
(b) peripheral, impaired
(c) prephrastic, demurred
(d) peripatetic, diminished

8. ....the broker had warned him that the stock was a..........investment, he insisted on buying a thousand shares. (SBI PO)
(a) Because, prudent
(b) Since, negligible
(c) Because, speculative
(d) As, vulnerable
(e) Although, precarious

9. Due to......rainfall this year, they had to.....cut in water supply. (BSRB)
(a) scantly, lift (b) heavy, regulate
(c) regular, clamp (d) sufficient, enforce
(e) inadequate, impose

10. He is so.....that everyone is always......to help in his work. (RBI)
(a) helpful, reluctant
(b) aloof, cooperative
(c) adamant, enthusiastic
(d) miserly, ignorant
(e) magnanimous, eager

11. Instead of.........prove your worth by......something. ***(Bank PO)***
(a) begging, demanding
(b) talking, doing
(c) worrying, paying
(d) writing, reading
(e) donating, demanding

12. The great scientist........himself with ability and moderation all......the conference. ***(Bank PO)***
(a) felt, about (b) displayed, in
(c) disclosed, besides (d) conducted, through
(e) presented, though

13. The speech........with subtle threats has resulted in........tension in the sensitive areas of the city. ***(Bank PO)***
(a) started, reduced (b) replete, increased
(c) full, escalating (d) forced, dissolving
(e) followed, continuous

14. The minister felt that the........made by the committee was.....even though similar schemes had worked earlier.
(a) decision, gainful
(b) choice, profitable
(c) acceptance, approved
(d) election, acceptable
(e) recommendation, infeasible

15. We can.......to travel by air, but we.......train journey. ***(SBI PO)***
(a) spend, enjoy (b) desire, commute
(c) afford, prefer (d) decide, undertook
(e) decome, accept

16. He was convinced that people were driven by........motives that he believed there was no such thing as a purely........act. ***(SBI PO)***
(a) personal, vengeful
(b) personal, eternal
(c) altruistic, praiseworthy
(d) ulterior, selfless
(e) sentimental, divine

17. I don't.........I shall be........to go. ***(Bank PO)***
(a) know, able (b) consider, desirous
(c) think, able (d) believe, liking
(e) feel, available

Solutions

1. (c)	**2.** (c)	**3.** (b)	**4.** (a)
5. (a)	**6.** (b)	**7.** (b)	**8.** (e)
9. (e)	**10.** (e)	**11.** (b)	**12.** (d)
13. (b)	**14.** (e)	**15.** (c)	**16.** (d)
17. (c)			

Exercise 6

Directions (Q. 1-6) : *Each sentence below has two blanks, each blank indicates that something has been omitted. Beneath the sentence there are four alternatives. Choose the alternative that best fits into the meaning of the sentence as a whole.*

1. The......tactics of the party drove the community......and all hell broke loose.
(a) dilatory, berserk (b) timely crazy
(c) opportune, wild (d) apposite, excited

2. The chief........him of his administrative powers and...........him to the Bahamas.
(a) invested, shipped
(b) augmented, deported
(c) incremented, sent
(d) divested, deported

3. They feared that they might.......develop the.........raiding activity of the tribe into regular operation.
(a) abruptly, spontaneous
(b) incidentally, resplendent
(c) knowingly, spurious
(d) inadvertently, spurious

4. She denounced the fiendish pronouncements of the General as the........schemes of..........and power-crazy radical.
(a) spurious, lenient
(b) radical, beguiled
(c) loose, morals
(d) beneficial, high-strung

5. Already...........tensions between the ethnic group and the refugees were..........last week after fresh riots broke out.
(a) reducing, toned down
(b) low, sparked off
(c) attenuated, driven away
(d) escalating, aggravated

6. The spirit of the New year Eve's celebrations was...........by the downpour of rains, much to their............. .
(a) aggravated, delight (b) fired up, joy
(c) dampened, chagrin (d) blown out, valour

Solutions

1. (a)	**2.** (d)	**3.** (d)	**4.** (b)
5. (d)	**6.** (c)		

Exercise 7

Directions (Q. 1-7) : *Each sentence in the questions has two blanks, each blank indicates that something has been omitted. Beneath the sentence there are four alternatives. Choose the alternative that best fits into the meaning of the sentence as a whole.*

1. He cleverly drew upon the.......... motives of his colleagues and made them contribute to the .... fund.
(a) miserly, sincere
(b) insular, relief
(c) craven, justice
(d) altruistic, dubious

2. The world is ...., its suffering.......... .
(a) perfect, sincere (b) just, scarce
(c) diverse, sparse (d) imperfect, random

3. There were two baskets kept for the garbage's disposal, one was marked..........and one was marked .... to simplify matters.
(a) low, high
(b) upward, downgraded
(c) parasitic, renewable
(d) biodegradable, recyclable
4. The task of the special committee was to put a ....to the accelerating spread of the highly contagious disease across the .... states.
(a) spur, far-flung
(b) hold, warring
(c) brake, contiguous
(d) clamp down, factions
5. Aimed at putting a check on .... disruptions to the WTO proceedings, the Riot Guards made it clear that they can match the protestors' efforts stone by stone,..........
(a) rational, bridge by bridge
(b) justified, day by day
(c) putrid, hour by hour
(d) irrational, brick by brick
6. Our initial days at Rockford were..........,quite surprising, the head boy was the biggest.........., and we earned the nickname of the 'Peevish Batch'.
(a) calm, mediator
(b) tempestuous, dissenter
(c) turbid, arbiter
(d) sane, leader
7. To the dismay of her friends, her father......... shouted at the authorities and hurled......... abuses at them.
(a) vociferously, vituperative
(b) gently, decibel
(c) malignantly, carnal
(d) cowardly, harsh

Solutions

1. (d)	2. (d)	3. (d)	4. (c)
5. (d)	6. (c)	7. (a)	

Exercise 8

Directions (Q. 1-10) : *Each sentence in the questions has two blanks, each blank indicates that something has been omitted. Beneath the sentence there are five alternatives. Choose the alternative that best fits into the meaning of the sentence as a whole.*

1. A ....is a.................... .
(a) norm, standard (b) knowledge, mistake
(c) student, school (d) doctrine, follower
(e) thesis, superstition
2. A ....shade of distinction is a................ .
(a) beautiful, vindication
(b) complete, profanity
(c) subtle, nuance
(d) thorough, prejudice
(e) entire, paradox
3. ....flattery is known as.....................
(a) Regular, maturity
(b) Indiscriminate, encomium
(c) Servile, adulation
(d) Unasked for, gratitude
(e) Cowardly, temerity
4. At some private schools, pupils are under the .... of a ....
(a) guidance, palladium
(b) tutelage, preceptor
(c) coaching, verity
(d) assiduity, palladium
(e) consensus, mentor
5. A large.............centre is a/an............ .
(a) district, affliction
(b) transport, automobile
(c) civic, utarchy
(d) shopping, emporium
(e) educational, indignity
6. ....persons are inclined to............. .
(a) Obese, corpulence
(b) Generous, leanness
(c) Domineering, temperance
(d) Vacillating, determination
(e) Cowering, effrontery
7. A ....is a temporary................ .
(a) deviation, rest
(b) shambles, journey
(c) respite, relief
(d) paradox, enchantment
(e) feint, spell
8. ....language may also be termed............. .
(a) Eloquent, exiguous
(b) Frenzied, placid
(c) Abusive, scurrilous
(d) Contumelious, flattering
(e) Denunciatory, peripatetic
9. A.............of small stones is called a ....
(a) design, numismatist
(b) collar, tiara
(c) seller, connoisseur
(d) mound, lithograph
(e) pattern, mosaic
10. Suzerainty is.............control over a .... state.
(a) full, democratic
(b) domestic, backward
(c) central, unified
(d) political, dependent,
(e) economic, federate

Solutions

1. (a) **2.** (c) **3.** (c) **4.** (b)
5. (d) **6.** (a) **7.** (c) **8.** (c)
9. (e) **10.** (d)

Exercise 9

Directions (Q. 1-11) : *Each sentence in the questions has two blanks, each blank indicates that something has been omitted. Beneath the sentence there are five alternatives. Choose alternative that best fits into the meaning of the sentence as a whole.*

1. To encourage colonial peoples in their aspirations to attain independence before it is ....proved that a..............state will evolve instead of anarchy is unforgivable.
(a) unchanged, formidable
(b) certainty, sympathetic
(c) succinctly, redoubtable
(d) incontrovertibly, viable
(e) unequivocally, mobile

2. Human memory is not.............especially on ancientry happenings that smack of the ....
(a) infallible, mythological
(b) dependable, simple
(c) confidant, fanciful
(d) reliable, inventive
(e) noteworthy, fanciful

3. Athletes have so perfected their techniques in track and field events that the .... becomes .... before record books can be published.
(a) announcement, public
(b) meet, official
(c) time, authentic
(d) fantastic, common place
(e) result, universal

4. Like the .... part of an iceberg, much of what is really interesting in the capital is not......
(a) inner, known (b) submerged, visible
(c) greater, dangerous (d) upper, viable
(e) lower, penetrable

5. Hence the word sophistry has an unfavourable .... and means arguing deceitfully, attempting to turn a poor case into a good one by means of clever but .... reasoning.
(a) denotation, ingenuous
(b) meaning, ingenious
(c) connotation, specious
(d) significance, vague
(e) impact, cogent

6. He warned the workers against supporting these anti-social policies, which he declared would ....rather than............the plight of the common people.
(a) rescue, destroy (b) encourage, defy
(c) aggravate, alleviate (d) empower, improve
(e) protract, inhibit

7. We have criticised our university students for preferring the security of political silence and the safety of............to the excitement of social .... and humanitarian action.
(a) acquiescence, dissent
(b) college, adventure
(c) concealment, revolution
(d) tolerance, antagonism
(e) security, insecurity

8. The practice of painting slogans on rock faces, once a thriving industry in Britain, has fallen into ....but there has recently been a/an .... in County Antrim.
(a) oblivion, demand (b) misuse, artisan
(c) disfavour, puheaval (d) mediocrity, surfeit
(e) disuse, recrudescence

9. Curiously enough the very passages, which set out to clarify only ....; the details are served up in .... three-page paragraphs which stupefy the reader.
(a) adumbrate, excessive
(b) obscure, succinct
(c) mystify, stimulating
(d) disturb, compact
(e) obfuscate, monolithic

10. Oddly enough .... the prestige of the United States in such countries as Britain, France, and Italy is considered important here, Congress has been .... about supplying funds to the U.S. Information Agency in these countries.
(a) inasmuch as, chary (b) since, delaying
(c) while, generous (d) whereas, wasteful
(e) although, niggardly

11. The increasing revival of dramatic classics is, to one critic, ... ; it seems to him a sign of the .... of the modern theatre.
(a) Inconceivable, revival
(b) deplorable, anaemia
(c) suspicious, resurgence
(d) astounding, uselessness
(e) incomprehensible, fatuousness

Solutions

1. (d) **2.** (a) **3.** (d) **4.** (b)
5. (c) **6.** (c) **7.** (a) **8.** (e)
9. (e) **10.** (e) **11.** (b)

Exercise 10

Directions (Q. 1-11) : *Each sentence in the questions has two blanks, each blank indicates that something has been omitted. Beneath the sentence there are five alternatives. Choose the alternative that best fits into the meaning of the sentence as a whole.*

1. It is a well-known .... that the lover of the sea craves for dry land, the age-old.......to be where we are not.

(a) belief, antipathy
(b) anomaly, demiurge
(c) credo, inspiration
(d) contention, duplicity
(e) paradox, yearning

2. Why should a university..............the values which are supposedly basic to its functioning and give an honorary doctorate to one who has not distinguished himself in a/an .... manner?
(a) deflate, scholarly
(b) foretell, worldly
(c) vilify, collegiate
(d) abuse, doctrinaire
(e) debase, academic

3. Such stalling tactics are...........to all fans and cannot be...........
(a) repugnant, condoned
(b) anathema, ascertained
(c) injurious, explained
(d) unfair, superseded
(e) understandable, countenanced

4. The..........of democratic freedom is dialogue and the .... interchange of diverse ideas.
(a) deterioration, untrammeled
(b) height, restrained
(c) essence, unhampered
(d) alienation, compulsory
(e) epitome, discriminating

5. Although there were...........circumstances in this particular violation of the law, the judge ruled that there had to be strict............or there would be no law at all.
(a) extraordinary, complaisance
(b) specific, obedience
(c) tantalising, adherence
(d) extenuating, compliance
(e) questionable, observation

6. In spite of all...........,in spite of penalties for examinees when cheaters were caught, there is evidence of the ..... of the rigid rules of external help on civil service tests.
(a) threats, encompassment
(b) surveillance, vulnerability
(c) temptation, flouting
(d) precautions, circumvention
(e) discouragement, acceptance

7. Hungarians may grumble about the difficulty of acquiring cars, but they point quickly to a compensation: the..............look of their tree-lined avenues and the absence of .... exhaust fumes.
(a) calm, superfluous
(b) otiose, poisonous
(c) tranquil, copious
(d) anomalous, fetid
(e) uncluttered, noxious

8. In architecture, much more than in any of the other fine arts, there is a marked time lag between the .... of ideas and their .... in the shape of completed building.
(a) settlement, fruition
(b) creation, welcoming
(c) tradition, modernization
(d) dawn, practicability
(e) emergence, application

9. In analyzing the............teenage population, Madison Avenue has decided that it is eminently receptive to the .... of advertising.
(a) proliferating, buncombe
(b) ubiquitous, mystique
(c) diminishing, fantasy
(d) burgeoning, blandishments
(e) viable, syndrome

10. No matter how .... the Russians are of wish to appear, they, as well as we, know that to survive it is necessary to reach agreements which may .... mutual sacrifices.
(a) fatuous, necessitate
(b) bellicose, evade
(c) refractory, obliterate
(d) indifferent, subsume
(e) intransigent, entail

11. Into the limited space given him a headline writer must compress the .... of the news and he must do it without ....
(a) synopsis, reservations
(b) gist, ambiguity
(c) magnitude, distortion
(d) totality, hedging
(e) bias, apology

Solutions

1. (e)	**2.** (e)	**3.** (a)	**4.** (c)
5. (d)	**6.** (d)	**7.** (e)	**8.** (e)
9. (d)	**10.** (e)	**11.** (b)	

Exercise 11

Directions (Q. 1-12) : *Each sentence in the questions has two blanks, each blank indicates that something has been omitted. Beneath the sentence there are four or five alternatives. Choose the alternative that best fits into the meaning of the sentence as a whole.*

1. For some years past, French governments had been...............and divided, and French parliaments had been incoherent and........... .
(a) inarticulate, responsive
(b) untenable, domineering
(c) weak, inchoate
(d) many, few
(e) vacillating, irresponsible

2. Scientific imagination is a specific intellectual power that is .... in every population that

has learned to be................about the mechanisms governing the physical world.
(a) encouraged, wary
(b) evoked, self-deprecatory
(c) latent, curious
(d) growing, self-possessed
(e) language, diffident

3. In diplomatic ....the................ sought by on government from another to the name of a proposed ambassador is known as an 'agreement'.
(a) dealing, understandings
(b) parlance, assent
(c) circles, permission
(d) channels, condition
(e) language, interpretation

4. Camille Pissarro, eldest of France's great impressionist................that included Monet, Manet, Rennoir, and Degas, was both the movenment's .... and its saint.
(a) cabal, doyen (b) sodality, gadfly
(c) entity, defector (d) hierarchy, patriarch
(e) brotherhood, demon

5. The westerlies normally cross the United States at altitudes from 10,000 to 50,000 feet along the Canadian border, acting as a...............to Arctic winds and giving the Middle Atlantic States relatively.............winters.
(a) counterpart, unsettled
(b) propellant, mild
(c) counterpart, settled
(d) buffer, temperate
(e) deterrent, cold

6. But even Mr. Moses, one of the most .... public servants of our time, is at a loss to convey in words the size, the imaginative engineering............ that built this contribution to the welfare of family and industry.
(a) tongue-tied, miracle
(b) dedicated, appositeness
(c) unappreciated, technique
(d) public-spirited, skill
(e) articulate, ingenuity

7. Among the younger people there are complaints that the sight of ex-Nazis flourishing recommends.........to youth, that it instills, instead of needed moral values, the dubious precept that .... is the best policy.
(a) precepts, intolerance
(b) desperation, dishonesty
(c) emulation, honesty
(d) cynicism, expediency

8. Even as.................machines free men from drudgery, they....................displace men from jobs.
(a) automated, simultaneously
(b) robotlike, unwillingly
(c) animated, ineluctably
(d) accelerated, seemingly
(e) antiquate, understandably

9. To cross the Rubicon means to take a final ....step which may have dangerous ....
(a) hazardous, precedent
(b) unwarranted, potentialities
(c) inconsequential, concomitants
(d) well-considered, implications
(e) irrevocable, consequences

10. Though the Oxford English Dictionary is undoubtedly the greatest dictionary ever ...., it is designed for scholars and research workers rather than for the .... dictionary user.
(a) assembled, assiduous
(b) demonstrated, amateur
(c) projected, omniscient
(d) published, professional
(e) compiled, casual

11. For nearly a century the...........travellers chech has been the nearest thing to an internationals currency yet devised by man, and has guided generations of Americans and other tourists through the ...... of foreign exchange.
(a) useful, excesses
(b) surreptitious, complexities
(c) plausible, maze
(d) sacrosanct, fluctuations
(e) ubiquitous, labyrinth

12. If it were true that enduring lesson are learned from................errors, Broadway would be the repository of.......... theatrical wisdom.
(a) accidental, occult (b) egregious, sublime
(c) dubious, profound (d) dramatic, lasting
(e) stupid, attenuated

Solutions

1. (e)	2. (c)	3. (b)	4. (d)
5. (d)	6. (e)	7. (d)	8. (a)
9. (e)	10. (e)	11. (e)	12. (b)

Unit 46

Exercises : Ordering of Sentences

In most of the competitive examinations, five or ten questions of ordering of sentences are appeared.These sentences are part of a paragraph. The candidates are required to place these sentences in proper sequence. In some examinations, first and the last sentences of the paragraph are given and the candidate is required to place the given four middle sentences in proper sequence. In some question papers all the five or six given sentences are required to be placed in logical sequence to construct a coherent paragraph. In some examinations you are asked to find the first, second or third sentence. Such questions are meant to judge the compositional and organising capability of the candidate.

Exercises

Exercise 1

Directions (Q. 1-2): *Sentences given in each question, when properly sequenced, form a coherent paragraph. Each sentence is labelled with a letter. Choose the most logical order of sentences from among the given choices to construct a coherent paragraph.* **(*CAT*)**

1. (A) But this does not mean that death was the Egyptians'only preoccupation.
(B) Even papyri come mainly from pyramid temples.
(C) Most of our traditional sources of information about the Old Kingdom are monuments of the rich like pyramids and tombs.
(D) Houses in which ordinary Egyptians lived have not been preserved, and when most people died they were buried in simple graves.
(E) We know infinitely more about the wealthy people of Egypt than we do about the ordinary people, as most monuments were for the rich.
(a) CDBEA (b) ECDAB
(c) EDCBA (d) DECAB

2. (A) Experts such as Larry Burns, head of research at GM, reckon that only such a full hearted leap will allow the world to cope with the mass mootorisation that will one day come to China or India.
(B) But once hydrogen is being produced from biomass or extracted from underground coal or made from water, using nuclear or renewable electricity, the way will be open for a huge reduction in carbon emissions from the whole system.
(C) In theory, once all the bugs have been sorted out, fuel cells should deliver better total fuel economy than any existing engines.
(D) That is twice as good as the internal combustion engine, but only five percentage points better than a Diesel hybrid.
(E) Allowing for the resources needed to extract hydrogen from hydrocarbon, oil, coal or gas, the fuel cell has an efficiency of 30%.
(a) CEDBA (b) CEBDA
(c) AEDBC (d) ACEBD

Solutions

1. (c) **2.** (a)

Exercise 2

Directions (Q.1-3) : *Sentences given in each question, when properly sequenced, form a coherent paragraph. Each sentence is labelled with a letter. Choose the most logical order of sentences from among the given choices to construct a coherent paragraph.* **(CAT)**

1. (A) He felt justified in bypassing Congress altogether on a variety of moves.
(B) At time he was fighting the entire Congress.
(C) Bush felt he had a mission to restore power to the presidency.
(D) Bush was not fighting just the democrats.
(E) Representative democracy is a messy business, and a CEO of the White House does not like a legislature of second guessers and time wasters.
(a) CAEDB (b) DBAEC
(c) CEADB (d) ECDBA

2. (A) The two neighbours never fought each other.
(B) Fights involving three male fiddler crabs have been recorded, but the status of the participants was unknown.
(C) They pushed or grappled only with the intruder.
(D) We recorded 17 cases in which a resident that was fighting an intruder was joined by an immediate neighbour, an ally.
(E) We, therefore, tracked 268 intruder males until we saw them fighting a resident male.
(a) BEDAC (b) DEBAC
(c) BDCAE (d) BCEDA

3. (A) In the west, Allied Forces had fought their way through Southern Italy as far as Rome.
(B) In June 1944, Germany's military position in II World War appeared hopeless.
(C) In Britain, the task of amassing the men and materials for the liberation of Northern Europe had been completed.
(D) The Red Army was poised to drive the Nazis back through Poland.
(E) The situation on the eastern front was catastrophic.
(a) EDACB (b) BEDAC
(c) BDECA (d) CEDAB

Solutions

1. (d) **2.** (a) **3.** (b)

Exercise 3

Directions (Q.1-5) : *In this section, each question consists of six sentences. The first and the sixth sentences are given in the beginning. The middle four sentences in each have been removed and jumbled up. These are labelled P, Q, R and S. You are required to find out the proper sequence of the four sentences from the given alternatives (a), (b), (c) and (d).* **(CDS)**

1. S_1 : In 1945, America faced two powerful enemies in the world war.
S_6 : This was the weapon that ended the second World War.
P : America found conventional weapons insufficient to crush them.
Q : These were Germany and Japan who posed strong opposition to America.
R : The result of this was the production of the Atom bomb.
S : The government ordered scientists to conduct research and produce a new, deadly weapon.
The proper sequence should be :
(a) Q P S R (b) P Q R S
(c) Q P R S (d) P Q S R

2. S_1 : Advertising is also advantageous to the consumer in that if it increases the sale of goods, industry prospers and prices may be reduced.
S_6 : Advertising of this particular kind is planned to stimulate new wants or to induce buyers to change their habits.
P : There is no obvious connection, for example, between a picture of a smiling girl and a certain brand sweets.
Q : The advertiser's assumption is that by looking at such pictures, the consumer would be influenced to buy his products.
R : On the other hand, much of the canvassing of which the consumer is the object does not convey information but endeavours merely to draw the public attention to certain products.
S : But most people like looking at pictures of pretty girls.
The proper sequence should be:
(a) R Q S P
(b) S P R Q
(c) R P S Q
(d) S Q R P

3. S_1 : We are living in an age in which technology has suddenly 'annihilated distance'.
S_6 : In that event, we should be dooming ourselves to wipe each other out.
P : We have never been so conscious of our variety as we are now that we have come to such close quarters.
Q : Physically we are now all neighbours, but psychologically we are still strangers to each other.
R : Are we going to let this consciousness of our variety make us fear and hate each other?
S : How are we going to react?
The proper sequence should be :

(a) Q P S R (b) Q P R S
(c) P R Q S (d) S R P Q

4. S_1 : Mom was pleased to receive your wishes on her birthday.
S_6 : Your Mom has forgotten all the bitterness and sends her blessings to you.
P : Girl! wishes are more powerful than any other thing in the world.
Q : Both of us had forgotten the day.
R : Your letter holds a proof of it.
S : It was your letter and the card which reminded us of it.
The proper sequence should be :
(a) P S Q R (b) Q R S P
(c) R Q S P (d) Q S P R

5. S_1 : A century ago, the cinema was just a mechanical toy.
S_6 : Finally it has evolved as the century's most potent and versatile art form.
P : Thus it gained respectability and acceptance.
Q : It gradually came to be considered as an art form of the new era.
R : By the 1920s, even its worst critics had to take it seriously.
S : Later it was viewed as an extension of photography.
The proper sequence should be :
(a) P Q R S (b) S Q R P
(c) S P Q R (d) Q R S P

Solutions

1. (a) **2.** (c) **3.** (b) **4.** (d) **5.** (d)

Exercise 4

Directions (Q. 1 to 5) : *Rearrange the following four sentences (A), (B), (C) and (D) in the proper sequence to form a meaningful paragraph and then mark the correct sequence as your answer.*

(Agriculture Officers' BSRB)

1. (A) It also gives rise to a feeling of animosity among the different sections of society.
(B) In a democratic system, frequent use of power is never desirable, it on the part of government or the people.
(C) Therefore, citizens should never resort to violent ways and means in democracy, though they have the right to oppose the government.
(D) It destroys the stability and security in public life.
(a) DBAC (b) BDAC
(c) BDCA (d) DACB
(e) DCBA

2. (A) He was so busy with them that he did not get time to eat.
(B) Thousands of people came to him and asked different types of questions.
(C) No one cared to see that he had his food or rest that night.
(D) Swami Vivekanand once stayed in a small village.
(a) BCDA (b) CBAD
(c) DBAC (d) DBCA
(e) ABCD

3. (A) The facts speak for themselves so they need exposition only, not demonstration.
(B) At the present moment, it is widely recognised that India holds the balance in the world wide competition between rival ideologies.
(C) It is not, of course, only in geographical sense that India is in a key position.
(D) India's key position simply needs pointing out.
(a) DACB (b) CDAB
(c) BCDA (d) BDAC
(e) DABC

4. (A) This feeling of an extensive group gives rise to a fellow feeling, a feeling of brotherhood among the citizens.
(B) This feeling takes up beyond the bounds of family, caste, religion and region and helps us develop a broad perspective that we all of us together constitute an extensive group called the nation.
(C) National integration is the feeling among all the citizens of a country that they are all a part of one nation.
(D) We do not then limit our thinking to our own caste or religion but think about all our fellow citizens.
(a) CDAB (b) CABD
(c) CDBA (d) CBDA
(e) CBAD

5. (A) The peasant, the shoemaker, the sweeper and such other lower classes of India have much greater capacity for work and self-reliance than you.
(B) Remember that the nation lives in the cottage.
(C) They are producing the entire wealth of the land without a word of complaint.
(D) This process of production is going through long ages.
(a) BDAC (b) BDCA
(c) DCBA (d) BACD
(e) ADCB

Solutions

1. (b) **2.** (c) **3.** (c) **4.** (e)
5. (d)

Exercise 5

Directions (Q.1-5) : *In this section, there are six sentences marked S_1, S_6, P, Q, R, S in each question. The positions of S_1 and S_6 are fixed as the first and the last sentence of the passage. You are required to choose one of the four alternatives given below, which would be most logical sequence of the sentences P, Q, R, S in the passage.* ***(NDA)***

1. S_1 : His wrist watch had gone out of order.
S_6 : His estimate appeared reasonable.
P : He took it to a watch repairer.
Q : He gave an idea of the likely cost of the replacement based on the examination of the watch.
R : He found that some parts needed replacement.
S : The repairer opened the outer case and checked the parts.
The proper sequence should be :
(a) P Q S R (b) R Q S P
(c) P S R Q (d) R P S Q

2. S_1 : Now-a-days, soap is going almost out of use as a washing agent.
S_6 : There are better washing agents than soap,but scientists are not yet sure if their use is harmless to man.
P : They produce lather due to the presence of calcium salts in water.
Q : Its place has been occupied by a new range of chemicals, called detergents.
R : So they are called soapless soap.
S : Detergents are not soap because they are not sodium or potassium derivatives of fatty acids, as the normal soap is.
The proper sequence should be :
(a) S Q R P (b) Q S R P
(c) S Q P R (d) Q P R S

3. S_1 : Our house is high up on the Yorkshire coast, and close to the sea.
S_6 : Between the two, shifting backwards and forwards at certain seasons of the year, lies the most horrible quicksand on the shores of Yorkshire.
P : One is called the North spit and one the South.
Q : The sand hills here run down to the sea, and end in two stretches of rock, sticking out opposite each other.
R : This one leads through a dark plantation of fir-trees, and brings you out between low cliffs to the loneliest and ugliest little bay on all our coast.
S : There are beautiful walls all around us in every direction except one.
The proper sequence should be :
(a) S Q R P (b) Q S P R
(c) Q P S R (d) S R Q P

4. S_1 : Unhappiness and discontent spring not only from poverty.
S_6 : We suffer from sickness of spirit and hence we should discover our roots in the eternal.
P : Man is a strange creature fundamentally different from other animals.
Q : If they are undeveloped and unsatisfied, he may have all the comforts of the wealth, but will still feel that life is not worthwhile.
R : He has far horizons invariable hopes, spiritual powers.
S : What is missing in our age is the soul, there is nothing wrong with the body.
The proper sequence should be :
(a) P R Q S (b) S P R Q
(c) S P Q R (d) P R S Q

5. S_1 : Before we left Bareilly jail, a little incident took place which moved me then and is yet resh in my memory.
S_6 : This spontaneous act of courtesy and the kindly thought that prompted it touched me and I felt very grateful to him.
P : He told me the packet contained old German illustrated magazines.
Q : The Superintendent of Police of Bareilly, an Englishman, was present there, and as I got into the car, he handed to me rather shyly a packet.
R : I had never met him before, nor have I seen him since and I do not even know his name.
S : He said that he had heard that I was learning German and so he had bought these magazines for me.
The proper sequence should be :
(a) R Q P S (b) Q P S R
(c) Q P R S (d) R Q S P

Solutions

1. (c) **2.** (d) **3.** (d) **4.** (b)
5. (c)

Exercise 6

Directions (Q.1-5): *Each passage consists of six sentences. The first and the sixth sentences are given in the beginning. The middle four sentences in each have been removed and jumbled up. These are labelled P, Q, R and S. You are required to find out the proper order for the four sentences.* ***(Engineering Service)***

1. S_1 : Our ancestors thought that anything which moved itself was alive.
S_6 : Therefore some scientists think that life is just a very complicated mechanism.
P : This philosopher Descartes thought that both men and animals were machines.
Q : But a machine such as a motorcar or a steamship moves itself, and as soon as machines which moved themselves had been made, people asked, 'Is man a machine ?'

R : And before the days of machinery that was a good definition.

S : He also thought that the human machine was partly controlled by the soul action on a certain part of the brain, while animals had no souls.

The proper sequence should be :

(a) P R S Q (b) R P Q S
(c) P S Q R (d) R Q P S

2. S_1 : On vacation in Tangier, Morocco, my friend and I sat down at a street cafe.

S_6 : Finally a man walked over to me and whispered, 'Hey buddy/ this guy's your waiter and he wants your order.'

P : At one point, he bent over with a big smile, showing me a single gold tooth and a dingy fez.

Q : Soon I felt the presence of someone standing alongside me.

R : But this one wouldn't budge.

S : We had been cautioned about beggars and were told to ignore them.

The proper sequence should be :

(a) S Q R P (b) S Q P R
(c) Q S R P (d) Q S P R

3. S_1 : The heart of the pump of life.

S_6 : All this was made possible by the invention of the heart lung machine.

P : They have even succeeded in heart transplants.

Q : Now-a-days surgeons are able to stop a patient's heart and carry out complicated operations.

R : A few years ago it was impossible to operate on a patient whose heart was not working properly.

S : If the heart stops we die in about five minutes.

The proper sequence should be :

(a) S R Q P (b) S P R Q
(c) S Q P R (d) S R P Q

4. S_1 : In 1934, William Holding published a small volume of poems.

S_6 : But Lord of the flies which came out in 1954 was welcomed as 'a most absorbing and instructive tale'.

P : During the World War II (1939-45) he joined the Royal Navy and was present at the sinking of the Bismarck.

Q : He returned to teaching in 1945 and gave it up in 1962, and is now a full-time writer.

R : In 1939, he married and started teaching at Bishop Wordsworth's School in Salisbury.

S : At first his novels were not accepted.

The proper sequence should be :

(a) R P Q S (b) R P S Q
(c) S R P Q (d) S Q P R

5. S_1 : Sunbirds are among the smallest of India birds.

S_6 : Our common sunbirds are the purple sunbird, the glossy black species and purple rumped sunbird, the yellow and maroon species.

P : Though they are functionally similar to the hummingbirds of the New World, they are totally unrelated.

Q : They do eat small insects too.

R : They are also some of the most brilliantly-coloured birds.

S : Sunbirds feed on nectar mostly and help in pollination.

The proper sequence should be :

(a) S Q P R
(b) R P S Q
(c) Q P R S
(d) P S R Q

Solutions

1. (c) **2.** (c) **3.** (a) **4.** (a)
5. (a)

Exercise 7

Directions (Q.1-5) : *In this section, each question consists of six sentences. The first and the sixth sentences are given in the beginning. The middle four sentences in each have been removed and jumbled up. These are labelled P, Q, R and S. You are required to find out the proper order for the four sentences.* **(CDS)**

1. S_1 : There are numerous kinds of superstitions in different parts of the country.

S_6 : A dog's howling predicts death—this is a typical superstition.

P : But people go on respecting it through force of blind custom.

Q : Most of them have a bearing on "luck"—good or bad.

R : Superstitions usually have their origin in fear and ignorance.

S : Nobody remembers now how a superstition first started in remote ages.

The proper sequence should be :

(a) Q P R S (b) R S P Q
(c) R S Q P (d) Q S P R

2. S_1 : Society in every country shapes itself out of its own initiative.

S_6 : And our Indian women are as capable of doing it as any in the world.

P : No one can or ought to do this for them.

Q : Our part of duty lies in imparting true education to all men and women in society.

R : Woman must be put in a position to solve their own problems in their own way.

S : It will not be then necessary to pull down or set us anything in society by coercion.

The proper sequence should be ;

(a) S R Q P (b) Q R S P
(c) Q S R P (d) S R P Q

3. S_1 : Many people believe that it is cruel to make use of animals for laboratory studies.

S_6 : It is in view of these facts that the Government of India has banned the export of monkeys to America.

P : They point out that animals too have nervous systems like us and can feel pain.

Q : These people, who have formed the Anti-vivisection Society, have been pleading for a more humane treatment of animals by scientists.

R : Monkey, rabbits, mice and other mammals are used in large numbers by scientists and many of them are made to suffer diseases artificially produced in them.

S : We can avoid such cruelty to animals if we use alternative methods such as tissue culture, gas chromatography and chemical techniques.

The proper sequence should be :

(a) Q P R S (b) P R Q S
(c) Q R S P (d) P S Q R

4. S_1 : A spider's web, after a shower of rain, is a very beautiful thing.

S_6 : They are also feared because their bites may have unpleasant effects like a rash on the skin.

P : his explains partly why spiders are thoroughly disliked.

Q : But no poet has ever sung of the beauty of the spiders, for most spiders are not beautiful.

R : On the contrary, most of them are rather unattractive, if not ugly!

S : Poets have sung about the beauty of the spider's webs, comparing the water drops on them to ropes of pearls.

The proper sequence should be :

(a) S P Q R (b) Q S R P
(c) Q R S P (d) S Q R P

5. S_1 : We are what our thoughts have made us.

S_6 : If good impressions prevail, the character becomes good, if bad it becomes bad.

P : And so take care of what you think.

Q : Every man's character is determined by the sum total of these impressions.

R : Every work we do, every thought that we think, leaves an impression on the mind.

S : Thoughts live, they travel far.

The proper sequence should be :

(a) S P R Q (b) R Q S P
(c) P R S Q (d) R Q P S

Solutions

1. (d) **2.** (c) **3.** (a) **4.** (d)
5. (a)

Exercise 8

Directions (Q. 1-8) : *In each of the questions below four sentences are given which are denoted by (A), (B), (C), (D). By using all the four sentences you have to frame a meaningful para. The correct order of the sentences is your answer. Choose from the five alternatives the one having the correct order of sentences and mark it as your answer.* ***(SBI PO)***

1. (A) Now under liberated economy they are learning to compete domestically and globally.

(B) In India corporations until recently achieved success by avoiding competition, using protected and regulated domestic markets.

(C) The trend is irreversible.

(D) Business leaders are preparing themselves to meet competitive challenges, and to avoid being swept away.

(a) ABDC (b) BDCA
(c) BDAC (d) CDBA
(e) BADC

2. (A) Recovery was given inadequate attention and consequently some bank branches regularly incurred heavy losses and their parent bodies had to bale them out.

(B) As a result, banks indulged in extensive lending to borrowers who had little or no potential to make repayments.

(C) To fulfil the social objectives laid down by the masters of nationalisation, banks were asked to lend to identified priority sectors.

(D) 1992-93 results showed that the loss making branches of public sector banks increased from 10,000 to 13,000 and the quantum of losses showed at Rs.3,360 crores.

(a) BACD (b) DABC
(c) CBAD (d) BCAD
(e) CDBA

3. (A) However, different rulers and governments dealt with the different groups in a compartmentalised manner.

(B) Various situational and political changes have taken place over the past three and half centuries.

(C) This tendency resulted in deeply embedded fragmented South American Society which became even more prominent in the period 1948 until the commencement of the new constitution on 19 May 1994.

(D) South Africa is a racially divided society since the first European settlers arrived in 1652.

(a) BDAC (b) DBAC
(c) CABD (d) ACDB
(e) BACD

4. (A) Such a system will help identify and groom executives for positions of strategists.
(B) Evaluation of performance is more often than not done for the purpose of reward or punishment for past performance.
(C) They must become an integral part of the executive evaluation system.
(D) Even where the evaluation system is for one's promotion to assume higher responsibilities, it rarely includes items that are a key for playing the role of strategists effectively, eg, the skills for playing the role of change agent and creative problem solving.
(a) DBAC (b) DCBA
(c) ABCD (d) BDCA
(e) CDBA

5. (A) Finally the bureaucratic organisation took over from the pioneering enterprise.
(B) The nineteenth century was the age of entrepreneur, the self-made man.
(C) Thoughtful business administration took over from action centred business entrepreneurship.
(D) In the twentieth century the rational executive took command.
(a) DBAC (b) CABD
(c) BDCA (d) BCDA
(e) DBAC

6. (A) But categorisation schemes are not always helpful in determining what one can do with or about organisational culture.
(B) Much of the literature on organisational cultures is focused on categorising types of cultures.
(C) It has taken the understanding of corporate culture far beyond what used to be called the informal organisation.
(D) This literature is both interesting and informative.
(a) BDAC (b) BADC
(c) BCDA (d) DABC
(e) DBAC

7. (A) Much of the argument that goes on around the alternative solution occurs because people hold different perceptons of the problem.
(B) One of the reasons that Japanese managers are perceived as making superior decisions compared to Western managers is that they spend a great deal of effort and time determining that the problem is correctly defined.
(C) Unfortunately, too often in the West, managers assume that the initial definition of the situation is correct.
(D) Up to half the time in meetings is spent in asking 'Is this the real problem?'
(a) BDCA (b) BCDA
(c) CBDA (d) ACDB
(e) ABCD

8. (A) Participation involves more than the formal sharing of decisions.
(B) Through anticipation, individuals or organisations consider trends and make plans, shielding institutions from trauma of learning by shock.
(C) Innovative learning involves both anticipation and participation.
(D) It is an attitude characterised by cooperation, dialogue and empathy.
(a) BCAD (b) ABCD
(c) DACB (d) CBAD
(e) ACBD

Solutions

1. (e)	2. (c)	3. (b)	4. (d)
5. (c)	6. (a)	7. (b)	8. (d)

Exercise 9

Directions (Q. 1-5) : *Rearrange the following five sentences (A), (B), (C), (D) and (E) in the proper sequence so as to form a meaningful paragraph and then answer the questions given below them.* **(Bank PO)**

(A) A study to this effect suggests that the average white-collar worker demonstrates only about twenty-five per cent listening efficiency.
(B) However, for trained and good listeners it is not unusual to use all the three approaches during a setting, thus improving listening efficiency.
(C) There are three approaches to listening; listening for comprehension, listening for empathy, and listening for evaluation.
(D) Although we spend nearly half of each communication interaction listening, we do not listen well.
(E) Each approach has a particular emphasis that may help us to receive and process information in different settings.

1. Which sentence should come SECOND in the paragraph ?
(a) A (b) B (c) C (d) D
(e) E

2. Which sentence should come FIFTH in the paragraph ?
(a) A (b) B (c) C (d) D
(e) E

3. Which sentence should come FOURTH in the paragraph ?
(a) A (b) B (c) C (d) D
(e) E

4. Which sentence should come FIRST in the paragraph ?
(a) A (b) B (c) C (d) D
(e) E

5. Which sentence should come THIRD in the paragraph?
(a) A (b) B (c) C (d) D
(e) E

Solutions

1. (e) 2. (a) 3. (d) 4. (c)
5. (b)

Exercise 10

Directions (Q. 1-5) : *Rearrange the following five sentences (A), (B), (C), (D) and (E) in the proper sequence to form a meaningful paragraph, then answer the questions given below them.* ***(Bank PO)***

(A) The history of mankind is full of such fightings between communities, nation and people.
(B) From the primitive weapons of warfare, man has advanced to the modern nuclear weapons.
(C) Ever since the dawn of civilisation, man has been fighting with man.
(D) A modern war is scientific in character, but the effect is the same, wiping human existence out of this earth.
(E) The only difference now seems to be in the efficiency of the instruments used for killing each other.

1. Which of the following should be the FIRST sentence ?
(a) A (b) B (c) C (d) D
(e) E

2. Which of the following should be the SECOND sentence ?
(a) A (b) B (c) C (d) D
(e) E

3. Which of the following should be the THIRD sentence ?
(a) A (b) B (c) C (d) D
(e) E

4. Which of the following should be the FOURTH sentence ?
(a) A (b) B (c) C (d) D
(e) E

5. Which of the following should be the FIFTH (last) sentence ?
(a) A (b) B (c) C (d) D
(e) E

Solutions

1. (c) 2. (a) 3. (b) 4. (d)
5. (e)

Exercise 11

Directions (Q. 1-7) : *In each of the following questions, the first and the last parts of the passage are numbered S_1 and S_6. The rest of the passage is split into four parts and named P, Q, R, S. These four parts are not given in their proper order. Read the sentences and find out which of the given four combinations is correct.* ***(SSC Clerks)***

1. S_1 : 'As a matter of fact', said the boy modestly, 'I'm a spaceman.'
P : 'You can't see it from here'.
Q : 'From another planet.'
R : 'I'm a spaceman', he said again.
S : George and Cathy stared at the boy.
S_6 : Cathy gasped, George gave a shout of laughter.
(a) PSRQ (b) QPSR
(c) RQPS (d) SRQP

2. S_1 : I suddenly began to climb swiftly, and the next I knew it was speeding eastward again till it became a speck in the blue morning.
P : I didn't know what force they could command, but I was certain it would be sufficient.
Q : My enemies had located me, and the next thing would be a cordon round me.
R : This made me do some savage thinking.
S : The aeroplane had seen my bicycle, and would conclude that I would try to escape by the road.
S_6 : In that case there might be a chance on the moors to the right or left.
(a) RQPS (b) QPSR
(c) PSRQ (d) SRQP

3. S_1 : His penance grew harder, he abjured even fruit.
P : Then the water, too, that the girl offered him in leaf-cups lay untouched.
Q : Birds pocked at them as they lay rotting at his feet.
R : She gathered wild blossoms and laid them humbly before him.
S : The girl mused in sorrow: "Is there nothing left for me to do."
S_6 : The ascetic took no notice.
(a) RQPS (b) SRQP
(c) QPSR (d) PSRQ

4. S_1 : In other words, grammar grows and changes, and there is no such things as correct use of English for the past, the present, and the future.
P : "The door is broke."
Q : Yet this would have been correct in Shakespeare's time!
R : Today, only an uneducated person would say, "My arm is broke."

S : For example, in Shakespeare's play Hamlet, there is the line.

S_6 : All the words that man has invented are divided into eight classes which are called parts of speech.

(a) PSQR (b) SPRQ
(c) QPSR (d) RSPQ

5. S_1 : There is no transportation system in any city that can compare in efficiency with the circulatory system of the body.

P : The larger one goes from the heart to the various parts of the body.

Q : If you will imagine two systems of pipes, one large and one small, both meeting at a central pumping station, you'll have an idea of the Circulatory system.

R : These pipes are called arteries, veins and capillaries.

S : The smaller system of pipes goes from the heart to the lungs and back.

S_6 : Arteries are blood vessels in which blood is going away from the heart.

(a) QSPR (b) PQSR
(c) RSQP (d) SPRQ

6. S_1 : Gandhiji's first political fast was made soon after his return from Africa.

P : He had also received help from their man's sister.

Q : This was when the poor labourers of the cotton mills of Ahmedabad were on strike.

R : He was a friend of the largest mill-owner.

S : Gandhi had made the strikers promise to remain on strike until the owners agreed to accept the decision of an arbitrator.

S_6 : He did not fast against the mill-owners, but in order to strengthen the determination of the strikers.

(a) SRPQ (b) QSRP
(c) RPQS (d) PQSR

7. S_1 : A certain young man was entrusted to the care of a teacher.

P : "This dullard will come to grief if I send him away without a single lesson," thought the teacher.

Q : He was so dull of the mind that he could not, even in three months' time, learn as much as a single lesson.

R : The young man came to ask the teacher's permission to go home.

S : "It's my business to provide a good education to my pupils to get on in life."

S_6 : The teacher asked him to wait.

(a) QPSR (b) PSRQ
(c) SRQP (d) RQPS

Solutions

1. (c) **2.** (d) **3.** (d) **4.** (b)
5. (a) **6.** (b) **7.** (a)

Exercise 12

Directions (Q. 1-7) : *In each of the following questions, the first and the last parts of the sentence are numbered S_1 and S_6 respectively. The rest of the sentence is split into four parts and named P, Q, R and S. These four parts are not given in their proper order. Read the sentence and find out which of the given four combinations is correct.*

1. S_1 : A study
P : success increases
Q : concludes that
R : and chances for
S : commitment to future tasks
S_6 : future success.

(a) RQPS (b) SRQP
(c) QPSR (d) PSRQ

2. S_1 : Putting it another way
P : What we see as our
Q : our goals throughout our lives
R : we are constantly resetting
S : in response to
S_6 : wins and losses.

(a) RQSP (b) QPRS
(c) PRSQ (d) RSQP

3. S_1 : Studies of Nobel laureates show that
P : or encounter professional
Q : and have strained relationship with friends and colleagues
R : they often publish less frequently
S : After winning the prize
S_6 : envy and rivalry.

(a) SRQP (b) RQPS
(c) QPSR (d) PSRQ

4. S_1 : There is
P : no such thing
Q : from one nation
R : as the gift
S : of independence
S_6 : to another.

(a) SPQR (b) PRSQ
(c) QPRS (d) RSPQ

5. S_1 : People who
P : are terrible
Q : no way of taking
R : there is
S : have no weaknesses
S_6 : advantage of them.

(a) PSQR (b) RSPQ
(c) SPRQ (d) QSRP

6. S_1 : There are
P : any other kind of
Q : more ants
R : land animal
S : than
S_6 : in the world.

(a) PSQR (b) RSPQ
(c) SPRQ (d) QSPR

7. S_1 : For some time
P : it was commonly assumed
Q : after the treaty of Versailles
R : that Germany had caused World War I by her aggressive acts
S : by scholars and laymen alike
S_6 : and by encouraging Italy in her aggression.
(a) PRQS (b) SPQR
(c) QPRS (d) QPSR

Solutions

1. (c) 2. (a) 3. (a) 4. (b)
5. (c) 6. (d) 7. (d)

Exercise 13

Directions (Q. 1-6) : *Put the given sentences in each of the following questions in proper order and find which of the four combinations is correct.*

1. (A) His mother was dead.
(B) They had not sent him the sad information.
(C) Probably they knew his deep love for her.
(D) When Gandhi returned to India his son Hiralal was four.
(a) dCab (b) dabc
(c) dbac (d) dcab

2. (A) It results from a carefully revised plan.
(B) Men work together for a cause or purpose.
(C) Team work does not just happen.
(D) It must be clearly known to them.
(a) bcad (b) cbda
(c) bcda (d) cabd

3. (A) I will give you a copy of it.
(B) The book was published in New York.
(C) It is a very interesting book.
(D) It deals with mankind's political future.
(a) dcba (b) cbda
(c) bdca (d) dbca

4. (A) He had inherited that money from an uncle.
(B) Mr Maini was an innocent man.
(C) It was regarding investing ten thousand rupees in my firm.
(D) He agreed to my proposal.
(a) dcab (b) badc
(c) cdab (d) bdca

5. (A) His elbow was bleeding.
(B) He had a few bruises on his left hand.
(C) I went into the crowd and was relieved to see that he wasn't very badly injured.
(D) A crowd gathered around my brother before he could stand up.
(a) bcda (b) dabc
(c) badc (d) dcba

6. (A) They were generally fed in the afternoon.
(B) But father said that it was most interesting to see them being fed.
(C) Gopal wanted to see the tigers and the lions first.
(D) When we entered the gate it was difficult to decide which way to go first.
(a) acdb (b) dcba
(c) bcda (d) cbad

Solutions

1. (b) 2. (d) 3. (c) 4. (a)
5. (d) 6. (b)

Exercise 14

Directions (Q. 1-5) : *In each question below, rearrange given five or six sentences in the proper sequence so as to form a meaningful paragraph, then answer the questions given below them.*

1. (A) She said that she was a school teacher and a social worker.
(B) Then for sometime we discussed her plans for schooling of the children living in slums.
(C) Our conversation now took another direction.
(D) She also said that social work was her hobby only and not the job.
(E) I asked Meena about her occupation.
(i) Which of the following should be the SECOND sentence?
(a) B (b) D (c) C (d) E
(e) A
(ii) Which of the following should be the FOURTH sentence?
(a) E (b) A (c) B (d) C
(e) D
(iii) Which of the following should be the FIRST sentence?
(a) A (b) C (c) D (d) E
(e) None of these
(iv) Which of the following should be the FIFTH sentence ?
(a) C (b) D (c) B (d) E
(e) None of these
(v) Which of the following should be the THIRD sentence ?
(a) A (b) B (c) C (d) D
(e) E

2. (A) But he added that there was a good deal to be said in favour of it.
(B) Govind asked what it was.
(C) Gopal told Govind that India would not progress until the caste system was abolished.
(D) Govind expressed his surprise on hearing that there was a good deal to be said in favour of it.
(E) Gopal observed that there was truth in what he said.

(i) Which of the following should be the FFTH sentence?
(a) A (b) B (c) C (d) D
(e) E

(ii) Which of the following should be the FIRST sentence?
(a) A (b) B (c) C (d) D
(e) E

(iii) Which of the following should be the SECOND sentence?
(a) A (b) B (c) C (d) D
(e) E

(iv) Which of the following should be the FOURTH sentence?
(a) A (b) B (c) C (d) D
(e) E

(v) Which of the following should be the THIRD sentence?
(a) A (b) B (c) C (d) D
(e) E

3. (A) Seema's parents died in her early childhood.
(B) Her uncle who had been kind to her was dead.
(C) She spent most of her first ten years with her unkind aunt.
(D) She always treated her wickedly and not as a loving niece.
(E) Her three cousin sisters also treated her as servant.
(F) Despite such ill treatments, she grew up as sensitive and self-reliant lady.

(i) Which of the following should be the SECOND sentence?
(a) A (b) B (c) C (d) D
(e) F

(ii) Which of the following should be the LAST sentence?
(a) A (b) B (c) C (d) D
(e) E

(iii) Which of the following should be the FIRST sentence?
(a) B (b) C (c) D (d) E
(e) F

(iv) Which of the following should be the FIFTH sentence?
(a) A (b) B (c) D (d) E
(e) F

(v) Which of the following should be the FOURTH sentence?
(a) B (b) C (c) D (d) E
(e) F

4. (A) It is fixed on Tuesday.
(B) We have, therefore, called him for interview.
(C) Due to his illness he lost that job.
(D) Ramesh was working in a factory.
(E) Hence he has applied for a job in my office.

(i) Which of the following should be the FIRST sentence?
(a) A (b) B (c) C (d) D
(e) E

(ii) Which of the following should be the SECOND sentence?
(a) A (b) B (c) C (d) D
(e) E

(iii) Which of the following should be the THIRD sentence?
(a) A (b) B (c) C (d) D
(e) E

(iv) Which of the following should be the FOURTH sentence ?
(a) A (b) B (c) C (d) D
(e) E

5. (A) Some of the world's highest peaks are in the Himalayas.
(B) The Himalayas are beautiful mountains to the north of India.
(C) Therefore, we call them the Himalayas of the 'abodes of snow'.
(D) The highest peak is Mount Everest.
(E) They stretch for two thousand miles from Kashmir to Assam.
(F) The top of the mountains are covered with snow.

(i) Which of the following should be the FIRST sentence ?
(a) B (b) E (c) C (d) A
(e) D

(ii) Which of the following should be the SECOND sentence ?
(a) B (b) C (c) E (d) D
(e) A

(iii) Which of the following should be the THIRD sentence ?
(a) B (b) D (c) A (d) E
(e) C

(iv) Which of the following should be the FIFTH sentence ?
(a) A (b) F (c) B (d) A
(e) C

(v) Which of the following should be the LAST sentence ?
(a) D (b) A (c) E (d) C
(e) B

Solutions

1. (i) (e) (ii) (d) (iii) (d) (iv) (c) (v) (d)
2. (i) (b) (ii) (c) (iii) (a) (iv) (e) (v) (d)
3. (i) (a) (ii) (d) (iii) (b) (iv) (b) (v) (d)
4. (i) (d) (ii) (c) (iii) (e) (iv) (b)
5. (i) (b) (ii) (c) (iii) (c) (iv) (b) (v) (d)

Unit

47

Sentence Improvement or Phrase Substitution

How to Improve Sentences or Substitute Phrases ?

In most of the competitive examinations you will find five or ten questions relating to sentence improvement or phrase substitution. In such questions a sentence is given in which a part of the sentence is incorrect, such incorrect part is to be replaced by the other phrase or part. From the choices given, so that the given sentence becomes grammatically correct. In such questions there is either some grammatical error or wrong use of verbs in the phrase or some other kind of error. Such error is to be detected and replaced with the correct option. The knowledge of grammatical rules and phrasal verbs will be of utmost help in solving such questions. Candidates must learn the grammar portion of this book well and do all the exercises given with each chapter.

Exercises

Exercise 1

Directions (Q.1-5) : *Which of the phrases (a), (b), (c) and (d) given below each sentence should replace the phrase printed in bold type to make the sentence grammatically correct ? If the sentence is correct as it is, mark (e) as your answer.*

1. My doctor knew that I would eventually recover and do the kind of work I **would be doing** before.
   (a) would have been doing
   (b) would have done
   (c) had been done
   (d) had been doing
   (e) No correction required
2. If you are thinking about investing overseas, **isn't make** sense to find an experienced guide ?
   (a) is it not making (b) doesn't it make
   (c) does it make (d) is it making
   (e) No correction required
3. In addition **to enhanced their reputation** through strategic use of philanthropy, companies are sponsoring social initiatives to open new markets.
   (a) of enhancing their reputations
   (b) to having enhance their reputation
   (c) to enhancing their reputation
   (d) to have their reputation enhancing
   (e) No correction required
4. Technology **must use to feed** the forces of change.
   (a) must be used to feed
   (b) must have been using to feed
   (c) must use having fed
   (d) must be using to feed
   (e) No correction required
5. The **crime has growth rapidly** in Russia since the disintegration of the communist system.
   (a) rapid crime has grown
   (b) crime has grown rapidly
   (c) crimes grow rapidly
   (d) crimes have been rapidly grown
   (e) No correction required

Solutions

1. (d) 2. (b) 3. (c) 4. (a)
5. (b)

Exercise 2

Directions (Q. 1-5) : *In the following questions, each sentence has an underlined word or phrase followed by four alternatives. You are to choose the one that best keeps the meaning of the original sentence if it is substituted for the underlined word or phrases.*

1. Veterinarians usually give dogs an anesthetic so that they don't cry out in pain.
   (a) gulp (b) flip
   (c) yelp (d) purr
2. City taxes are based on an estimate of the value of one's property.
   (a) appraisal (b) forecast
   (c) diagnosis (d) outline
3. Although buses are scheduled to depart at a certain hour, they are often late.
   (a) listed
   (b) requested
   (c) obligated
   (d) loaded
4. Because light travels faster than sound, lightning appears to go before thunder.
   (a) prolong (b) traverse
   (c) repel (d) precede
5. When students do not have time to read a novel before class, they read an outline of the plot instead.
   (a) an article (b) a synopsis
   (c) a critique (d) an essay

Solutions

1. (c) **2.** (a) **3.** (a) **4.** (d)
5. (b)

Exercise 3

Directions (Q.1-5) : *Which of the phrases (a), (b), (c) and (d) given below each sentence should replace the phrase printed in bold type to make the sentence grammatically correct ? If the sentence is correct as it is, mark (e) as the answer.*

1. The performance of our players was rather **worst than I had expected.**
   (a) bad as I had expected
   (b) worse than I had expected
   (c) worse than expectation
   (d) worst than was expected
   (e) No correction required
2. It is always better to make people realise the importance of discipline **than to impose them on it.**
   (a) impose it with them
   (b) impose them with it
   (c) imposing them on it
   (d) impose it on them
   (e) No correction required
3. The crops are dying, **it must not had rained.**
   (a) must had not (b) must not be
   (c) must not have (d) must not have been
   (e) No correction required
4. They **were all shocked at** his failure in the competition.
   (a) were shocked at all
   (b) had all shocked at
   (c) had all shocked by
   (d) had been all shocked on
   (e) No correction required
5. He is too impatient **for tolerating** any delay.
   (a) to tolerate
   (b) to tolerating
   (c) at tolerating
   (d) with tolerating
   (e) No correction required

Solutions

1. (b) **2.** (d) **3.** (c) **4.** (e)
5. (a)

Exercise 4

Directions (Q. 1-10) : *Look at the underlined part of each sentence. Below each sentence are given three possible substitutions (a, b, c) for the underlined part. If one of them is better than the underlined part, select that part as your response. If none of them improves, the sentence, choose (d) as your response. Thus a 'No improvement' response will be signified by the letter (d).*

1. Just before the commencement of the examination, the invigilator advised us from copying or indulging in any other malpractices.
   (a) against (b) upon
   (c) about (d) No improvement
2. The whole country is disappointed over the defeat of the cricket team.
   (a) on (b) above
   (c) by (d) No improvement
3. If he joins the coaching class so late, I am afraid i will be hard for him to catch up with the others.
   (a) speed up (b) join up
   (c) get in line (d) No improvement
4. If a definite cure for cancer is discovered in few years it is unlikely that it will be a simpler or safe affair than that of diabetes.
   (a) in some few years
   (b) in the next few years
   (c) after few years
   (d) No improvement
5. The tourists insured their luggage because the assumed it must be stolen.
   (a) will be (b) was going to be
   (c) might be (d No improvement

6. By the end of May each year the agricultural produce comprising wheat and gram goes to the market.
   (a) to markets (b) to market
   (c) into a market (d) No improvement
7. The old man looked with caution before he crossed the busy street
   (a) cautiously before (b) at cautiously when
   (c) cautiously when (d) No improvement
8. Make haste lest you should not be caught in the storm.
   (a) that you should not be
   (b) you can be
   (c) you should be
   (d) No improvement
9. The contesting candidates agreed to seek a common platform while canvassing for votes.
   (a) have (b) share
   (c) find (d) No improvement
10. The new bank clerk kicked off a row with a colleague.
   (a) out a (b) on to a
   (c) up a (d) No improvement

Solutions

1. (a)	2. (c)	3. (d)	4. (b)
5. (c)	6. (a)	7. (a)	8. (c)
9. (b)	10. (d)		

Exercise 5

Directions (Q. 1-10) : *Look at the underlined part of each sentence. Below each sentence are given three possible substitutions for the underlined part. If one of the alternatives (a), (b), or (c) is better than the underlined part, indicate your response accordingly against the corresponding letter (a), (b), or (c). If none of the substitutions improves the sentence, indicate (d) as your response. Thus a 'No improvement' response will be signified by the letter (d).*

1. Other countries have eradicated this disease ten years ago.
   (a) eradicated
   (b) had eradicated
   (c) did eradicate
   (d) No improvement
2. We were not the wiser for all his effort to explain the case to us.
   (a) none (b) neither
   (c) nevertheless (d) No improvement
3. If I stood alone in defence of truth, and the whole world is banded against me and against truth, I would fight them all.
   (a) will be banded (b) were banded
   (c) banded (d) No improvement
4. During his long discourse, he did not touch that point.
   (a) touch at (b) touch on
   (c) touch of (d) No improvement
5. He died in the year 1960 at 11 p.m. on 14 July.
   (a) on 14 July in the year 1960 at 11 p.m.
   (b) in the year 1960 on 14 July at 11 p.m.
   (c) at 11 p.m. on 14 July in the year 1960
   (d) No improvement
6. For all our powers of reason and understanding we know a little about life's secrets.
   (a) a little of life's secrets
   (b) little about life's secrets
   (c) nothing about life's secrets
   (d) No improvement
7. You have come here with a view to insult me.
   (a) to insulting me
   (b) of insulting me
   (c) for insulting me
   (d) No improvement
8. This matter admits of no excuse.
   (a) admits to
   (b) admits for
   (c) admits
   (d) No improvement
9. He has not and can never be in the good books of his employer because he lacks honesty.
   (a) has not and cannot be
   (b) has not and can never been
   (c) has not been and can never be
   (d) No improvement
10. The logic of the Berlin Wall already had been undermined, but when the news came through that the wall itself had been opened I jumped into a car.
   (a) had been undermined already
   (b) had already been undermined
   (c) had been already undermined
   (d) No improvement

Solutions

1. (a)	2. (a)	3. (b)	4. (b)
5. (c)	6. (b)	7. (a)	8. (d)
9. (c)	10. (b)		

Exercise 6

Directions (Q. 1-7) : *In each of the following questions some part of the sentence is underlined. Five choices numbered (a), (b), (c), (d) and (e) rephrasing the underlined part follow each sentence. If the original part itself seems better than the alternatives and 'no change' is desired, choose answer (a) and if not, choose one of the others.*

For each sentence, consider the requirement of standard written English. Your choice should be correct and, with effective expression, not awkward or ambiguous. If a choice changes the meaning of the original sentence, do not select it.

1. If the present trend continues, the cost of a good personal computer system even can be as low as Rs. 15,000 soon.
   (a) No change
   (b) even soon can be as low as Rs.15,000
   (c) can soon be as low as Rs.15,000
   (d) as low as even Rs. 15,000 soon can be
   (e) as low can soon be even Rs. 15,000
2. As the message of the freedom struggle could not be spread over the government controlled radio, it effectively was carried to the masses by the press.
   (a) No change
   (b) it was effectively carried to the masses by the press
   (c) by the effective press it was carried to the masses
   (d) it was carried to the effective masses by the press
   (e) to the effective masses it was carried by the press
3. From a study of University enrolment figures over the past decade, evidence is that women are increasingly opting for professional courses.
   (a) No change
   (b) the increasingly opting for professional courses by women is evidence
   (c) evidently it is increasing the enrolment of women in professional courses
   (d) it is evident that women are increasingly opting for provisional courses
   (e) women are increasingly opting for professional courses, that is evident
4. The new draft legislation seeks to ensure that some of the profits form the commercialisation of bio diversity goes to the know how actually possessed by local communities.
   (a) No change
   (b) goes to the actual communities who possess the local know how
   (c) actually goes to the communities that possess the know how locally
   (d) to the local communities that possess the know how actually
   (e) goes to the local communities that actually possess the know how
5. The rapid fall in birthrate achieved by China over the 1980s is placing a retiring strain on many old workers who must retire now from the workforce.
   (a) No change
   (b) places a strain on the old workers as they retire from the workforce
   (c) is placing a strain on the workforce now as many old workers retire
   (d) is placing many old workers on a strain as they must retire from the workforce
   (e) is placing many old workers who must retire as a strain on the workforce
6. A recently carried out mega-analysis of two decades of published research does not suggest that there should be an association between coffee drinking and coronary ailments.
   (a) No change
   (b) suggests that there is no association between coffee drinking and coronary ailments
   (c) suggests for no association between coffee drinking and coronary ailments
   (d) any association between coffee drinking and coronary ailments is not suggests
   (e) shows that coffee drinking should not be suggested to have an association with coronary ailments
7. In relation to the forthcoming parliamentary election the EC clarified that as no legislation had been formulated, there was no question of raising the official ceiling on election expenses of candidates.
   (a) No change
   (b) raising the ceiling on official election expenses of candidates could not be questioned
   (c) no question had been raised regarding the official ceiling on election expenses of candidates
   (d) the official ceiling on election expenses of candidates should be raised, there is no question
   (e) there was no need to question the official ceiling on election expenses of candidates

Solutions

1. (c)	2. (b)	3. (d)	4. (e),
5. (c)	6. (b)	7. (a)	

Exercise 7

Directions (1-10) : *Which of the phrases (a), (b), (c) and (d) given below each sentence should replace the phrase printed in bold type to make the sentence grammatically correct ? If the sentence is correct as it is, mark (e) as the answer.* **(Bank PO)**

1. It is true that there **has been a considerable decline** in rural poverty.
   (a) has been considerably declining
   (b) was considerably a decline
   (c) have been considered decline
   (d) has a considerable decline
   (e) No correction required

2. They **have been attending** classes since the term began.
(a) would attend (b) had attended
(c) would be attending (d) should attend
(e) No correction required

3. He considers the new assignment as more challenging than **much of the other** assignments.
(a) none for the other's (b) most of the other
(c) more of the other (d) rest of the other
(e) No correction required

4. Resolutions must **be introducing quickly to repeal** the outdated laws.
(a) be introducing to quick repeal
(b) have to be introduced to quick repealing
(c) be quickly introduced to repeal
(d) be quick introducing to repeal
(e) No correction required

5. The driver **didn't accede at the demand** of the people as he was aware of the risk involved in it.
(a) was not accede at the demand
(b) didn't accede at demanding
(c) was not acceded by the demand
(d) didn't accede to the demand
(e) No correction required

6. Though his actions **were severe criticism**, he didn't lose his temper.
(a) were severely criticised
(b) had severely criticised
(c) were at severely criticising
(d) had severe criticised
(e) No correction required

7. Yogic exercises and meditation **seems to be of help** modern men and women deal effectively with anxiety.
(a) seem to help
(b) seems to be helping
(c) seem to have help
(d) seems to help
(e) No correction required

8. Despite all the complaints against him, we must admit that his behaviour with others **has always courteous.**
(a) had always courteous
(b) have always courteous
(c) has always been courteous
(d) has always been courteously
(e) No correction required

9. **Whom did you intend to** offer the job besides the two young boys?
(a) Who are you intending to
(b) Whom do you intended to
(c) Who do you intend for
(d) Whom had you been intended for
(e) No correction required

10. She always behaves **as if she has not** care at all about my feelings.
(a) as though she will not
(b) as if she doesn't
(c) as far as she doesn't
(d) like if she does not
(e) No correction required

Solutions

1. (e)	2. (e)	3. (b)	4. (c)
5. (d)	6. (a)	7. (a)	8. (c)
9. (e),	10. (b)		

Exercise 8

Directions (Q. 1-15) : *Look at the underlined part of each sentence. Below each sentence are given three possible substitutions for the underlined part. If one of the alternatives (a), (b) or (c) is better than the underlined part, indicate your response against the corresponding letter (a), (b) or (c). If none of the substitutions improves the sentence, indicate (d) as your response. Thus (a) 'No improvement' response will be signified by the letter (d).*
(CDS)

1. Being given to understand that there is a vacancy of an assistant in the firm, an application was submitted by me.
(a) an application has been submitted by myself
(b) an application by me was submitted
(c) I submitted an application
(d) No improvement

2. She drives her car at eighty miles each hour.
(a) an hour (b) every hour
(c) hourly (d) No improvement

3. I hope it will not rain when they have started their journey.
(a) they will have started their journey
(b) they will start their journey
(c) they start their journey
(d) No improvement

4. After a six-hour marathon session, the two political parties are united together.
(a) joined (b) together
(c) united (d) No improvement

5. I gave my niece **a** children's very colourfully illustrated encyclopaedia.
(a) a very colourfully illustrated children's encyclopaedia
(b) a child's very colourfully illustrated encyclopaedia
(c) an illustrated child's very colourful encyclopaedia
(d) No improvement

6. Nearly everyone suffers when unemployment rises.
(a) Everyone nearly (b) Nearly all
(c) Nearly each one (d) No improvement

7. If you wrote to me earlier, I would have easily solved your problem.
(a) were writing (b) had written
(c) have written (d) No improvement
8. Can't you never understand what has been said ?
(a) ever understand (b) rather understand
(c) at all understand (d) No improvement
9. The limestone formations suggest that in the distant past, the area was a vast sea filled with creatures that absorb calcium compounds from the water.
(a) absorbs (b) absorbed
(c) had absorbed (d) No improvement
10. He asked me where was my book.
(a) my book was (b) my book is
(c) is my book (d) No improvement
11. Suddenly she became conscious regarding the presence of a stranger in the room.
(a) about (b) of
(c) over (d) No improvement
12. This is the first time in my memory that the river has overflown the banks.
(a) overflew
(b) has overflowed
(c) overflowed
(d) No improvement
13. What I learned is that freedom is really the result of how you will remove obstacles.
(a) you would remove (b) you can remove
(c) you remove (d) No improvement
14. The workers are waiting for their pay packets since morning.
(a) would be waiting (b) were waiting
(c) have been waiting (d) No improvement
15. Ensure to contact with as many teachers as possible.
(a) contact (b) contact on
(c) contact to (d) No improvement

Solutions

1. (c)	2. (a)	3. (c)	4. (c)
5. (a)	6. (d)	7. (b)	8. (a)
9. (b)	10. (a)	11. (b)	12. (b)
13. (c)	14. (c)	15. (a)	

Exercise 9

Directions (Q. 1-6) : *Look at the bold part of each sentence. Below each sentence are given three possible substitutions for the bold part. If one of the alternatives (a), (b) or (c) is better than the bold part, indicate your response on the answer sheet against the corresponding letter (a), (b) or (c). If none of the substitutions improves the sentence, indicate (d) as your response on the answer sheet. Thus a ' No improvement' response will be signified by the letter (d).* **(NDA)**

1. I can't tackle this problem which with all its complications **have** confused me.
(a) has (b) had
(c) will have (d) No improvement
2. My friend **would have missed** the train if he had not hurried.
(a) had missed (b) has missed
(c) missed (d) No improvement
3. We have plenty of time, **isn't it** ?
(a) haven't we (b) have we
(c) is it (d) No improvement
4. The criminal as well as his accomplice **was** arrested.
(a) were
(b) are being
(c) have been
(d) No improvement
5. The world's population will continue to grow **when** the birthrate exceeds the death-rate.
(a) as long as
(b) unless
(c) until after
(d) No improvement
6. Until he **does not ask for** an apology, I am not going to reinstate him.
(a) does ask for
(b) asked for
(c) asks for
(d) No improvement

Solutions

1. (a)	2. (d)	3. (a)	4. (d)
5. (a)	6. (c)		

Exercise 10

Directions (Q. 1-10) : *Which of the phrases (a), (b), (c) and (d) given below each sentence should replace the phrase printed in bold type to make the sentence grammatically correct ? If the sentence is correct as it is, mark (e) as the answer.* **(Bank PO)**

1. All the members of the club **were assembled to celebrate** the 50th anniversary of the club.
(a) had assembled to celebrate
(b) were assembling to celebrate
(c) had been assembled for celebrating
(d) assembled to celebration
(e) No correction required
2. **Increased productivity necessary** reflects greater efforts made by the employees.
(a) Increase in productivity necessary
(b) Increased productivity is necessary
(c) Increase of productivity necessary
(d) Increased productivity necessarily
(e) No correction required

3. The earnest appeal by the staff members that the salaries be subjected to **upward revision were rejected** by the industrialist.
   (a) upwardly revision was rejected
   (b) upward revision was rejected
   (c) upward revising were rejectable
   (d) upwardly revision was rejectable
   (e) No correction required
4. Speculations and **hypothesising are** the most essential and well known aspects of inventions.
   (a) hypothesis has been
   (b) hypothesising needs
   (c) hypothesis makes
   (d) hypothesising confronts
   (e) No correction required
5. The **alarming report** of the building collapse made everyone spell bound.
   (a) alarmed report
   (b) alarmed reporting
   (c) reporting alarm
   (d) reported alarm
   (e) No correction required
6. Your good gestures **will highly appreciate.**
   (a) will be highly appreciate
   (b) will be high appreciative
   (c) will be highly appreciated
   (d) would be high appreciation
   (e) No correction required
7. Yogic exercise **seems to be help** urban population deal effectively with stress.
   (a) seems to be helpful
   (b) seems to be helped
   (c) seems to help
   (d) seemed to be of helping
   (e) No correction required
8. They **fell very proudly** that their team had won the match.
   (a) feel very proudly (b) felt very pride
   (c) feel very pride (d) felt very proud
   (e) No correction required
9. The pedestrians **must to be** very cautious while crossing the road.
   (a) should have to be
   (b) must be
   (c) should have
   (d) are required to be
   (e) No correction required
10. I am sure that he has recovered from his illness **and he will accompany** us to the picnic spot.
   (a) and that he will accompany
   (b) and that he will be accompanied
   (c) but he will accompany
   (d) although he will accompany
   (e) No correction required

Solutions

1. (a)	**2.** (d)	**3.** (b)	**4.** (e),
5. (e)	**6.** (c)	**7.** (c)	**8.** (d)
9. (b)	**10.** (a)		

Exercise 11

Directions (Q. 1-10) : *In the following questions, which of the phrases (a), (b), (c) and (d) given below each sentence should replace the phrase given in the sentence to make the sentence grammatically meaningful and correct. If the sentence is correct as it is and no correction is required, mark (e) as the answer.* ***(Indian Bank PO)***

1. He will be greatly surprised if he **was felicitated** by his staff members.
   (a) if he will have felicitated
   (b) unless he was felicitated
   (c) if he is felicitated
   (d) if he would have felicitated
   (e) No correction required
2. Did you know when **shall he be leaving** for higher studies to the USA?
   (a) should he be left (b) he would be leaving
   (c) he would be left (d) would he have left
   (e) No correction required
3. The labour contractors reported that they **had finished** the work of building the stone wall.
   (a) had been finished (b) was finished
   (c) could be finished (d) has finished
   (e) No correction required
4. For want of financial resources, he was **unable to continue** his studies.
   (a) unabled to continue
   (b) unable to be continued
   (c) unable to have continued
   (d) unable to continuing
   (e) No correction required
5. He complained **of being unjustly treatment.**
   (a) of being unjustly treated.
   (b) for being injustice in treatment.
   (c) that unjust treatment being given.
   (d) for being unjustly treatment.
   (e) No correction required
6. The donation amount was **such that as I was expected** him to donate.
   (a) so that as I expected
   (b) such that I expected of
   (c) such as that I expect
   (d) exactly as I had expected
   (e) No correction required
7. It is pity that no one in the family **disapproves by his getting up** late.
   (a) disapproved by his getting up
   (b) disapproves of his getting up
   (c) disapproved that he is getting up
   (d) disapproved why he got up
   (e) No correction required

8. He is less likely to win **unless he practised** rigorously and regularly.
(a) until he practised
(b) unless he practise
(c) unless he practises
(d) unless he does not practise
(e) No correction required

9. Because it was a stormy night, **he dare not to go** out in the dark.
(a) dared not to go
(b) dare not went
(c) dared not to have gone
(d) dare not goes
(e) No correction required

10. **Just when they reach** the station, the train had departed.
(a) Just before they reach
(b) After they just reach
(c) Just when they had reached
(d) Just before they reached
(e) No correction required

Solutions

1. (c)	**2.** (b)	**3.** (e),	**4.** (e),
5. (a),	**6.** (b),	**7.** (b)	**8.** (c)
9. (a)	**10.** (d).		

Exercise 12

Directions (Q. 1-15) : *In the following questions look at the underlined part of each sentence. Below the sentence are given three possible substitutions for the underlined part. If any one of the substitutions (a), (b), or (c) is better than the underlined part, choose that substitution as your response. If none of the substitutions improves the sentence, choose (d) as your response. Thus a 'No improvement' response will be signified by the letter (d).* **(CDS)**

1. The sun was shining such brightly that Leela had to put on her sun-glasses.
(a) very (b) too
(c) so (d) No improvement

2. If I were you, I would report the matter at once.
(a) be (b) am
(c) was (d) No improvement

3. The document is concerning your health and that of your family.
(a) concerns with (b) is concerned with
(c)concerns (d) No improvement

4. The lady laid out a special dinner for her husband on his birthday.
(a) laid (b) laid up
(c) laid by (d) No improvement

5. Epidemics are likely to break off in the areas from where flood-water has receded.
(a) break out (b) break up
(c) break in (d) No improvement

6. There is no objection to him joining the party.
(a) on him (b) to his
(c) upon his (d) No improvement

7. You are too big to go out alone.
(a) big enough
(b) so big
(c) very big
(d) No improvement

8. One of my old friends has invited me for tea in the evening.
(a) to take tea (b) to tea
(c) on tea (d) No improvement

9. Hardly had he saddled the horse than the mare broke loose and galloped down the hill.
(a) that (b) when
(c) then (d) No improvement

10. The speaker tried to work up the emotions of his audience.
(a) round (b) off
(c) in (d) No improvement

11. Until the sky is overcast, I take my raincoat with me.
(a) When (b) Even if
(c) Whenever (d) No improvement

12. His discourse about the meteorology was very stimulating.
(a) on (b) of
(c) concerning (d) No improvement

13. Mira told her brother that she had made a mistake.
(a) said to (b) pleaded to
(c) admitted to (d) No improvement

14. You don't want a beggar to look happy, isn't it ?
(a) aren't you ?
(b) do you ?
(c) don't you ?
(d) No improvement

15. The instructor told the student to hold the club lightly, to keep his eye on the ball but should not use too much force.
(a) and not (b) and not to
(c) still not to (d) No improvement

Solutions

1. (c)	**2.** (d)	**3.** (b)	**4.** (a)
5. (a)	**6.** (b)	**7.** (a)	**8.** (b)
9. (b)	**10.** (d)	**11.** (c)	**12.** (a)
13. (d)	**14.** (b)	**15.** (b)	

Exercise 13

Directions (Q. 1-11) : *In the following questions look at the italicised part of each sentence. Below the sentence are given three possible substitutions for the italicised part. If any one of the substitutions (a), (b), or (c) is better than the italicised part, choose that* *substitution as your response. If none of the substitutions improves the sentence, choose (d) as your response. Thus a 'No improvement' response will be signified by the letter (d).*

1. *It is no good to cry* over (spilt milk.) **(NDA)**
   (a) It is no good crying
   (b) It is of no good to cry
   (c) It is of no good crying
   (d) No improvement
2. He has been working *off and on* for several years to compile a dictionary. **(NDA)**
   (a) on or off (b) on and off
   (c) regularly (d) No improvement
3. Rohit assured Sunita that he *would look* at her work while she was on leave. **(RRB)**
   (a) would overlook (b) would look after
   (c) will look (d) No improvement
4. Newton wanted to *know why did the apple fall* to the ground. **(CBI)**
   (a) know that why did the apple fall
   (b) know why the apple fell
   (c) know that why the apple fell
   (d) No improvement
5. He was extremely unhappy because of *the inordinately delay.* **(CDS)**
   (a) the inordinate delaying
   (b) the inordinate delay
   (c) the inordinately delaying
   (d) No improvement
6. *There is no more room* for you in this compartment. **(Section Officer)**
   (a) There is no more accommodation
   (b) There is no more space
   (c) There is no more sear
   (d) No improvement
7. When he arrived to attend the wedding of his brother, he *had been dressed* in dark suit. **(NDA)**
   (a) dressed
   (b) was dressed
   (c) had dressed
   (d) No improvement
8. I can always *count on him* in times of difficulty.
   (a) count at him (b) count on he **(CDS)**
   (c) count him on (d) No improvement
9. Sunita told me that she would not mind *to stand and eating* the lunch. **(Income Tax)**
   (a) to stand and eat (b) standing and eating
   (c) standing and eat (d) No improvement
10. Modern industrialised communities have lost touch with the soil and do not experience that joy which nature gives and the rich glow of health that *which comes from contact with* mother earth. **(CBI)**
    (a) which comes from contact with
    (b) which comes out from contact with
    (c) which flows how from contact with
    (d) No improvement
11. He has been receiving no other message than an urgent telegram *asking him to rush his village* immediately.
    (a) asking him rushing at his village **(Income Tax)**
    (b) asked him to rush his village
    (c) asking him to rush to his village
    (d) No improvement

Solutions

1. (a)	2. (d)	3. (b)	4. (b)
5. (b)	6. (d)	7. (b)	8. (d)
9. (b)	10. (a)	11. (c)	

Exercise 14

Directions (Q. 1-7) : *In the following questions look at the italicised part of each sentence. Below the sentence are given three possible substitutions for the italicised part. If any one of the substitutions (a), (b), or (c) is better than the italicised part, choose that substitution as your response. If none of the substitutions improves the sentence, choose (d) as your response. Thus a 'No improvement' response will be signified by the letter (d).*

1. Each of our *students pay their* tuition fee at the beginning of the month. **(Asst Grade)**
   (a) student pay their (b) students pays their
   (c) students pays his (d) No improvement
2. I told him clearly that he *hadn't ought to do* that to me.
   (a) ought not to have done **(NDA)**
   (b) ought not done
   (c) ought not has done
   (d) No improvement
3. The fast train *come a halt to before* crossing the bridge. **(CBI)**
   (a) came before to a halt
   (b) came to a halt before
   (c) came to halts before a
   (d) No improvement
4. I took the cycle *which he bought yesterday.* **(Stenographers)**
   (a) that he bought yesterday
   (b) that he had bought yesterday
   (c) that which he had bought yesterday
   (d) No improvement
5. The practical importance of the role of the industrialist in the establishment of the new order is greater than *the economist and the politician.*
   (a) of the economist and politicians **(RRB)**
   (b) that of the economists and the politicians
   (c) that of the economist and the politician
   (d) No improvement
6. The poor villagers *have waited* in the bitter cold more than four hours now. **(IES)**
   (a) has been waiting (b) had waited
   (c) have been waiting (d) No improvement

7. They succeeded *without hardly making* any effort. **(CBI)**
   (a) hardly without making
   (b) with hardly making
   (c) without making
   (d) No improvement

Solutions

1. (c) 2. (a) 3. (b) 4. (d)
5. (c) 6. (c) 7. (c)

Exercise 15

Directions (Q. 1-6) : *In the following questions look at the italicised part of each sentence. Below the sentence are given three possible substitutions for the italicised part. If any one of the substitutions (a), (b), or (c) is better than the italicised part, choose that substitution as your response. If none of the substitutions improves the sentence, choose (d) as your response. Thus a 'No improvement' response will be signified by the letter (d).*

1. He was urgently in need *to get his eye operation.* **(CBI)**
   (a) of an eye operation
   (b) for operation on eye
   (c) for eye to be operated
   (d) No improvement
2. *By definition, make a map* is to select certain features as relevant and ignore others.
   (a) To make a map by definition
   (b) In making a map, the definition
   (c) Map making is defined as
   (d) No improvement
3. We demonstrated to them how we *were prepared* the artistic patterns. **(CDS)**
   (a) are prepared (b) have prepared
   (c) had prepared (d) No improvement
4. Asking me *why was I absent, I was punished by the Headmaster.* **(CBI)**
   (a) why was I absent, was I punished by the Headmaster
   (b) why I was absent, was I punished by the Headmaster
   (c) why I was absent, the Headmaster punished me
   (d) No improvement
5. Do you *remember to meet her* at my house last year ? **(UDC)**
   (a) remember of meeting her
   (b) remember about meeting her
   (c) remember having met her
   (d) No improvement
6. If you had attended the meeting, you *would have benefitted* a great deal. **(Stenographers)**
   (a) would benefit (b) could benefit
   (c) benefitted (d) No improvement

Solutions

1. (a) 2. (c) 3. (c) 4. (c)
5. (c) 6. (d)

Exercise 16

Directions (Q. 1-8) : *In the following questions look at the italicised part of each sentence. Below the sentence are given three possible substitutions for the italicised part. If any one of the substitutions (a), (b), or (c) is better than the italicised part, choose that substitution as your response. If none of the substitutions improves the sentence, choose (d) as your response. Thus a 'No improvement' response will be signified by the letter (d).*

1. *Although partially destroyed, the experts were able to infer* from what remained that the treasure was buried in the cave. **(Income Tax)**
   (a) Although partially destroyed, the experts had inferred
   (b) Destroyed partially, the experts were able to infer
   (c) Although it had been partially destroyed, the experts were able to infer
   (d) No improvement
2. The Principal lamented that though a detailed report was submitted to the management a month ago, *no action is being taken* so far.
   (a) no action had taken
   (b) no action has been taken
   (c) any action had been taken
   (d) No improvement
3. May I know *who did accompany you* to the bus station ?
   (a) who accompanied you
   (b) must be
   (c) whom did you accompany
   (d) No improvement
4. *Leaving aside little room for* misinterpretation, the senior politician offered clarification about his role in the past elections.
   (a) Leaving less room for
   (b) Leaving little room for
   (c) Having left less room for
   (d) No improvement
5. We should take up the first item, let *us begin this song.* **(UDC)**
   (a) this song begin us
   (b) us begin with this song
   (c) this song begin with us
   (d) No improvement
6. *Any able bodied man is* eligible for the job. **(NDA)**
   (a) Any able bodied men are
   (b) Each able bodied man is
   (c) Any able bodied men have been
   (d) No improvement

7. *I, your brother and you* will be partners in the business. **(NDA)**
(a) I, you and your brother
(b) You, your brother and I
(c) You, I and your brother
(d) No improvement

8. While we would like that *all Indian children* to go to school, we need to ponder why they do not.
(a) all Indian children **(CDS)**
(b) that all the Indian children
(c) if all the children of India
(d) No improvement

Solutions

1. (c) **2.** (b) **3.** (a) **4.** (b)
5. (b) **6.** (d) **7.** (b) **8.** (a)

Exercise 17

Directions (Q. 1-5) : *In the following questions look at the italicised part of each sentence. Below the sentence are given three possible substitutions for the italicised part. If any one of the substitutions (a), (b), or (c) is better than the italicised part, choose that substitution as your response. If none of the substitutions improves the sentence, choose (d) as your response. Thus a 'No improvement' response will be signified by the letter (d).*

1. *I think in my opinion that* all those who claim to be honest are not really so. **(CBI)**
(a) In my opinion (b) It seems to me
(c) It is my believing (d) No improvement

2. Will you *lend me few rupees* in this hour of need.
(a) borrow me a few rupees ***(Section Officers)***
(b) lend my any rupees
(c) lend me a few rupees
(d) No improvement

3. Hold *hands of your child* while crossing the road. **(CBI)**
(a) your child's hands (b) your child's hand
(c) hand of your child (d) No improvement

4. *Have you not reached* in time, we would have lost our lives? **(CDS)**
(a) Had you not reach
(b) If you have not reached
(c) Had you not reached
(d) No improvement

5. You must *accustom yourself with* new ideas. **(NDA)**
(a) accustomed with (b) accustom to
(c) accustom yourself to (d) No improvement

Solutions

1. (a) **2.** (c) **3.** (b) **4.** (c)
5. (c)

Exercise 18

Directions (Q. 1-10) : *In the following questions look at the italicised part of each sentence. Below the sentence are given three possible substitutions for the italicised part. If any one of the substitutions (a), (b), or (c) is better than the italicised part, choose that substitution as your response. If none of the substitutions improves the sentence, choose (d) as your response. Thus a 'No improvement' response will be signified by the letter (d).* **(CDS)**

1. The climate of Delhi is somewhat *like Jaipur*.
(a) like Jaipur's (b) as Jaipur's
(c) as Jaipur (d) No improvement

2. His brother *never has* and never will be dependable.
(a) never had (b) never has been
(c) was never being (d) No improvement

3. If you *would have remembered* to bring the map, we would not have lost our way.
(a) had remembered (b) were remembering
(c) remembered (d) No improvement

4. You must *carry on* my order.
(a) carry off (b) carry out
(c) carry of (d) No improvement

5. The boat *was drowned*.
(a) was drown (b) were drowned
(c) was sunk (d) No improvement

6. Now I must *beg leave of you*.
(a) beg your leave (b) beg of your leave
(c) beg off your leave (d) No improvement

7. *When describing* the accident he was in tears.
(a) In describing
(b) When he was describing
(c) As describing
(d) No improvement

8. The two thieves distributed the loot *between themselves*.
(a) among themselves (b) amongst themselves
(c) with themselves (d) No improvement

9. The *preservation of peace* is necessary.
(a) maintenance of peace
(b) establishment of peace
(c) persuasion of peace
(d) No improvement

10. The spirit of democracy had *sped into* our way of thinking.
(a) leaked into (b) permeated
(c) soaked into (d) No improvement

Solutions

1. (a) **2.** (b) **3.** (a) **4.** (b)
5. (c) **6.** (d) **7.** (b) **8.** (d)
9. (a) **10.** (b)

Unit 48

Cloze Test/Passage

How to Attempt ?

In many competitive examinations the question paper of English encompasses cloze passage/test questions. In a cloze passage/test usually a passage is given with ten or twelve blank spaces. Candidates are required to fill in the blanks from the given choices. The purpose of the cloze test is to judge the grammatical knowledge, vocabulary power and the common sense of the candidate.The candidate must go through the whole passage before starting to answer the questions. Sometimes one or two blanks appear somewhat difficult to answer or seem to have more than one correct answer.The answer of these blanks may have some links with the next sentences, so it is always better to read out the whole passage first. It must well be understood that good knowledge of grammar and good command on vocabulary will be of utmost help in answering such questions.

Exercises

Exercise 1

Directions (Q. 1-6) : *Fill up the blanks in the passage given below with the most appropriate word from the options given for each blank.*

"Between the year 1946 and the year 1955, I did not file any income tax returns." With that (1)...... statement, Ramesh embarked on an account of his encounter with the Income Tax Department. "I originally owed Rs. 20,000 in unpaid taxes. With (2)...... and (3)...... the 20,000 became 60,000. The Income Tax Department then went into action, and I learned first hand, just how much power the Tax Department wields. Royalties and trust funds can be (4)...... automobiles may be (5)......, and auctioned off. Nothing belongs to the (6)...... until the case is settled." **(CAT)**

1. (a) devious (b) blunt (c) tactful (d) pretentious

2. (a) interest (b) taxes (c) principal (d) returns

3. (a) sanctions (b) refunds (c) feet (d) fines

4. (a) closed (b) detached (c) attached (d) impounded

5. (a) smashed (b) seized (c) dismantled (d) frozen

6. (a) purchaser (b) victim (c) investor (d) offender

Solutions

1. (b) **2.** (a) **3.** (d) **4.** (c) **5.** (b) **6.** (d)

Exercise 2

Directions (1-4) : *Fill up the blanks in the passage given below with the most appropriate word from the options given for each blank.*

At that time The White House was as serene as a resort hotel out of season. The corridors were (1)...... in the various offices. (2)...... gray men on waistcoats talked to one another in low-pitched voices. The only color or choler, curiously enough, was provided by President Eisenhower himself. Apparently, his (3)...... was easily set off; he scowled when he (4)...... the corridors. *(CAT)*

1. (a) striking (b) hollow (c) empty (d) white
2. (a) Quiet (b) Faded (c) Loud (d) Stentorian
3. (a) laughter (b) curiosity (c) humour (d) temper
4. (a) paced (b) strolled (c) stormed (d) prowled

Solutions

1. (c) 2. (a) 3. (d) 4. (d)

Exercise 3

Directions (Q. 1-10) : *Fill up the blanks in the passage given below with the most appropriate word from the options given for each blank.*

Someone (1)........at the door. A lady opened it. A stranger was standing at the (2)........He said, "Madam, please excuse me for.......... (3) you. May I ask you something ? I (4)......by your house everyday on my (5).........to work, I have (6).........that every day you hit your son on (7).........head with a loaf of bread." The lady replied, "Yes, that's (8)........" The stranger asked, "This morning, I saw you (9)......him with a chocolate. Why (10)......? The lady replied, "Today is his birthday. Therefore I hit him with a sweet thing."

1. (a) pointed (b) knocked (c) looked (d) moved (e) stood
2. (a) fence (b) gate (c) compound (d) door (e) step
3. (a) disturbing (b) harassing (c) asking (d) enquiring (e) worrying
4. (a) wait (b) watch (c) stand (d) pass (e) connect
5. (a) office (b) steps (c) legs (d) journey (e) way
6. (a) decided (b) felt (c) noticed (d) remembered (e) surprised
7. (a) your (b) his (c) my (d) our (e) fore
8. (a) right (b) obvious (c) surprising (d) clear (e) funny
9. (a) feeding (b) bestowing (c) giving (d) hitting (e) offering
10. (a) bread (b) then (c) so (d) change (e) thus

Solutions

1. (b) 2. (b) 3. (a) 4. (d) 5. (e) 6. (c) 7. (b) 8. (a) 9. (d) 10. (c)

Exercise 4

Directions (Q. 1-15) : *Fill up the blanks in the passage given below with the most appropriate word from the options given for each blank.*

Erosion in nature is a beneficent process without which the world would have died long ago. The same process (1).....by human mismanagement has become one of the most (2).....and destructive forces that had ever been (3).....by man. What is (4).....known as (5).....erosion or denudation is a universal (6).....which through thousands of years (7).....carved the earth (8).....its present shape. Denudation is an early and (9).....process (10).....soil formation where by the (11).....rock material is continuously broken (12).....and sorted out by wind and water until it becomes (13).....for colonisation (14).....plants. Plants by the binding (15).....of their roots bring denudation almost to a standstill. *(CDS)*

1. (a) started (b) accelerated (c) adopted
2. (a) drastic (b) degrading (c) vicious
3. (a) produced (b) released (c) caused
4. (a) normally (b) generally (c) usually
5. (a) geological (b) ocological (c) natural
6. (a) aspect (b) phenomena (c) experience
7. (a) has (b) had (c) have
8. (a) to (b) in (c) into
9. (a) inevitable (b) important (c) accurate
10. (a) at (b) in (c) for
11. (a) basic (b) early (c) original
12. (a) up (b) down (c) off
13. (a) natural (b) necessary (c) suitable

14. (a) of (b) by
(c) for
15. (a) forces (b) effect
(c) powers

Solutions

1. (b) 2. (c) 3. (a) 4. (b)
5. (b) 6. (b) 7. (a) 8. (c)
9. (a) 10. (c) 11. (c) 12. (a)
13. (c) 14. (a) 15. (a)

Exercise 5

Directions (Q. 1-10) : *Fill up the blanks in the passage given below with the most appropriate word from the options given for each blank.*

The king of Rampur was not (1)...... The following story proves that. Once he paid a (2)........to a town away from his capital.

The king's staff governing the town welcomed the king. As per the king's desire a (3)........of the renowned people of the town was called at night. The people (4)........the king and bestowed their praise on him and all sat down to listen to (5).......the king had to tell them.

Suddenly the lantern gave away. It became very dark. "Light the lantern !" ordered the king to his servants. Five minutes passed. The king shouted to know why there was (6).......in lighting the lantern. "My Lord, I am (7).........to lay my hand on the match box. It is so dark!" replied the servant . "Fool !" screamed the king (8).......... . If that is the case, why (9)........you light the candle first? You can certainly (10)......the match box with the help of the candle.

1. (a) kind (b) cruel
(c) generous (d) wise
(e) brave
2. (a) homage (b) visit
(c) donation (d) fund
(e) contribution
3. (a) meeting (b) majority
(c) procession (d) survey
(e) list
4. (a) bowed (b) surrendered
(c) greeted (d) offered
(e) complained
5. (a) carefully (b) about
(c) which (d) all
(e) what
6. (a) difficulty (b) time
(c) patience (d) delay
(e) haste
7. (a) unable (b) looking
(c) confident (d) ready
(e) trying
8. (a) loudly (b) angrily
(c) anxiously (d) happily
(e) pertinently
9. (a) must (b) should
(c) don't (d) did
(e) do
10. (a) watch (b) try
(c) touch (d) light
(e) locate

Solutions

1. (d) 2. (b) 3. (a) 4. (c)
5. (e) 6. (d) 7. (a) 8. (b)
9. (c) 10. (e)

Exercise 6

Directions (Q. 1-10) : *Fill up the blanks, in the passage given below with the most appropriate word from the options given for each blank.*

Tea prices in the domestic (1).....continue to rule high in the (2).....year despite the expectation of a (3).....production as compared to the previous year. According to a preliminary assessment (4).....on the weather (5).....in recent months. Tea output in 1990 may reach 740 million kg as (6) .....700 million kg last year. During the past three months, tea prices have generally shown an (7)..... . Unlike last year, when tea prices rose dramatically, this year, prices seem to have (8).....at a rather high level. In the subsequent four months, the (9).....average price showed a downtrend but in September the prices have (10).....hardened to a considerable extent. ***(Asstt Grade)***

1. (a) sector (b) production
(c) area (d) market
(e) flour
2. (a) last (b) first
(c) second (d) current
(e) general
3. (a) higher (b) maximum
(c) optimum (d) large
(e) lower
4. (a) conducted (b) based
(c) shared (d) strategy
(e) carried
5. (a) outbursts (b) outbreak
(c) conditions (d) forecast
(e) pattern
6. (a) above (b) per
(c) to (d) compared
(e) against
7. (a) downtrend (b) increment
(c) reduction (d) uptrend
(e) upgrade
8. (a) increased (b) surfaced
(c) synchronised (d) moderated
(e) stabilised

9. (a) monthly (b) weekly
(c) daily (d) annualy
(e) quarterly
10. (a) then (b) never
(c) again (d) since
(e) now

Solutions

1. (d) 2. (d) 3. (a) 4. (b)
5. (c) 6. (e) 7. (d) 8. (e)
9. (a) 10. (c)

Exercise 7

Directions (Q. 1-10) : *Fill up the blanks in the passage given below with the most appropriate word from the options given for each blank.*

Each species has its special place or habitat. An (1).....bird-watcher can look at (2).....forest, meadow, lake, swamp or field and (3).....almost exactly what birds he (4).....find there (5).....birds are found all over the world; other (6).....themselves to certain areas. Still (7).....migrate from one country to another in (8).....in search of warmth and (9).....and then return in spring (10).....the season is more favourable.

(SSC Stenographer Grade C)

1. (a) experience (b) expert
(c) advanced (d) active
2. (a) the (b) some
(c) a (d) certain
3. (a) predict (b) suggest
(c) prophesy (d) calculate
4. (a) should (b) must
(c) might (d) will
5. (a) more (b) some
(c) most (d) all
6. (a) keep (b) entrust
(c) confine (d) involvé
7. (a) some (b) others
(c) few (d) all
8. (a) winter (b) summer
(c) spring (d) autumn
9. (a) seeds (b) crops
(c) fruit (d) food
10. (a) while (b) until
(c) after (d) when

Solutions

1. (b) 2. (c) 3. (a) 4. (c)
5. (b) 6. (c) 7. (b) 8. (a)
9. (d) 10. (d)

Exercise 8

Directions (Q. 1-20) : *Fill up the blanks, in the passage given below with the most appropriate word from the options given for each blank.*

I noticed George Ramsay at the restaurant. He was staring into space. He looked as though the burden of the whole world sat on his shoulders. I (1).....at once that his unfortunate brother (2).....trouble again. I suppose every family has a black (3)..... . Tom had been a (4).....trial to his family (5).....twenty years. He had begun life decently enough he went (6).....business, married and had two children. The Ramsays were (7).....respectable people, and there was every (8).....to suppose that Tom Ramsay would have a useful and (9).....carrier. But one day without warning, he (10).....that he did not like to work, and that he was not suited (11).....marriage. He wanted to enjoy (12)..... He would listen (13).....no advice. He left his wife and his (14)..... He had (15).....money and he spent two happy years in the various capitals of Europe. Rumours of his (16).....reached his relations from time to time and they were (17)..... He certainly (18).....a very good time. They shook their heads and asked what (19).....when his money was spent. They soon found out that he was broke and wanted to (20).....home. ***(MBA)***

1. (a) believed (b) suspected
(c) agreed
2. (a) had been causing (b) was causing
(c) will cause
3. (a) goat (b) sheep
(c) wolf
4. (a) sore (b) bitter
(c) sweet
5. (a) since (b) for
(c) in
6. (a) into (b) for
(c) to
7. (a) utterly (b) perfectly
(c) wholly
8. (a) reason (b) cause
(c) point
9. (a) profitable (b) bad
(c) honourable
10. (a) said (b) announced
(c) wrote
11. (a) to (b) for
(c) with
12. (a) himself (b) idleness
(c) others
13. (a) to (b) in
(c) with
14. (a) job (b) house
(c) relatives
15. (a) a little (b) little
(c) no
16. (a) habits (b) doings
(c) whereabouts

17. (a) deeply (b) shocked
(c) disappointed
18. (a) has (b) had
(c) will have
19. (a) would happen (b) happened
(c) will happen
20. (a) come back (b) go
(c) settle

Solutions

1. (b)	2. (b)	3. (b)	4. (b)
5. (b)	6. (a)	7. (b)	8. (a)
9. (a)	10. (b)	11. (b)	12. (a)
13. (a)	14. (a)	15. (a)	16. (b)
17. (b)	18. (b)	19. (a)	20. (a)

Exercise 9

Directions (Q. 1-10) : *In the following passage there are blanks each of which has been numbered. These numbers are printed below the passage and against each five words are suggested one of which fits the blank appropriately. Find out the appropriate word in each case.*

Desire and action are often coordinated in, that desire may (1)....the person to action or that desire may be (2).....from action . If P is seen as trying to do X, it is often inferred that P desires X. However, desire and action are not (3).....coordinated. The person may desire X without (4).....in any action directed towards the attainment of X. This event happens when X appears (5).....or when the other effects resulting from the action (6).....to attain X are sufficiently undesirable as to (7).....the desire for X. Sometimes, of course, no action is necessary; the desire may or may not be (8).....quite independently of P's action. Furthermore, a given desire may lead to different actions, depending upon the environmental requirements. Actions are (9).....not only by desire but also by the way the person (10).....the causal structure of the environment. **(*SBI PO*)**

1. (a) dampen (b) hinder
(c) indulge (d) arouse
(e) prohibit
2. (a) expelled (b) ceased
(c) abstained (d) refrained
(e) inferred
3. (a) invariably (b) hopefully
(c) deliberately (d) purposely
(e) negatively
4. (a) wanting (b) associating
(c) engaging (d) supporting
(e) exhibiting
5. (a) manageable (b) valuable
(c) unattainable (d) reachable
(e) approachable
6. (a) hostile (b) necessary
(c) incidental (d) insensible
(e) detrimental
7. (a) express (b) appreciate
(c) reciprocate (d) damage
(e) negate
8. (a) realised (b) hypothesised
(c) verbalised (d) criticised
(e) actualised
9. (a) projected (b) determined
(c) controlled (d) galvanised
(e) pronounced
10. (a) downgrades (b) fabricates
(c) develops (d) sees
(e) enlarges

Solutions

1. (d)	2. (a)	3. (a)	4. (c)
5. (c)	6. (b)	7. (a)	8. (a)
9. (a)	10. (d)		

Exercise 10

Directions : (Q. 1-15) : *In the following passage there are blanks each of which has been numbered. These numbers are printed below the passage and against each three words are suggested one of which fits the blank appropriately. Find out the appropriate word in each case.*

One day while I was discussing a new strategy to locate the wild dogs, a forest guard at Sariska informed me that about 15-16 metres to the right of Pandupole road, a Chital lay killed apparently by wild dogs. This was difficult to (1) .... because wild dogs usually do not leave (2) ...... any kill. They finish it (3) ..... to the bone. Still an examination would (4) .....interesting information and vital clues about the (5) ...... So I proceeded in the direction pointed (6) ..... by the guard, Scanning the area I (7) .....across the dead Chital. The (8) ..... had been opened but not (9) ..... eaten. Its owner had (10) ..... dressed the dinner ready for eating. I looked about for marks and (11) ..... I found them, the marks (12) ..... indicated the presence of a canine. But (13)... Jackals or wild dogs ? Since Jackals were active in Sariska independently (14) ..... Chital-kills, the actual presence, (15)... the wild dogs still remained doubtful. **(*CDS*)**

1. (a) presume (b) believe
(c) know
2. (a) behind (b) away
(c) after
3. (a) up (b) over
(c) off
4. (a) prove (b) reveal
(c) involves
5. (a) predator (b) chital
(c) man-eater

6. (a) out (b) to
(c) at
7. (a) found (b) located
(c) came
8. (a) body (b) corpse
(c) carcass
9. (a) now (b) yet
(c) at all
10. (a) probably (b) surely
(c) really
11. (a) when (b) where
(c) which
12. (a) frankly (b) openly
(c) clearly
13. (a) what (b) which
(c) who
14. (a) having (b) hunting
(c) making
15. (a) about (b) of
(c) regarding

Solutions

1. (b)	2. (a)	3. (a)	4. (b)
5. (a)	6. (b)	7. (c)	8. (c)
9. (c)	10. (a)	11. (a)	12. (c)
13. (b)	14. (a)	15. (b)	

Exercise 11

Directions (Q. 1-10) : *In the following passage there are some blanks, each of which has been numbered. Below the passage you are given a choice of three words (a), (b), (c) for each blank one of which is the most appropriate. Choose the best word as your answer.*

It is one of the tragic ironies of our age that the rocket which could have been a symbol of humanity's aspirations for the stars, has become one of the weapons threatening to destroy civilisation. This state of affairs has (1).....a difficult moral problem to (2).....wishing to take an active (3).....in the development of astronautics, (4).....almost all research on rockets (5).....now carried out by military (6).....and is covered by various (7).....classifications. The technical problems involved (8).....designing long-range guided missiles are (9).....identical with those involved in the (10).....of reconnaissance rockets.

(UPSC APF)

1. (a) produced (b) caused
(c) presented
2. (a) those (b) others
(c) men
3. (a) part (b) position
(c) interest
4. (a) when (b) for
(c) where
5. (a) was (b) are
(c) is
6. (a) establishments (b) officers
(c) centres
7. (a) secret (b) security
(c) defence
8. (a) in (b) with
(c) for
9. (a) hardly (b) never
(c) practically
10. (a) launching (b) construction
(c) deployment

Solutions

1. (b)	2. (a)	3. (a)	4. (a)
5. (c)	6. (a)	7. (a)	8. (a)
9. (b)	10. (a)		

Exercise 12

Directions (Q. 1-10) : *In the following passage there are blanks each of which has been numbered. These numbers are printed below the passage and against each, five words are suggested, one of which fits the blank appropriately. Find out the appropriate words in each case.*

New industries supported by foreign interests (1).....offer (2).....salaries to their employees at all levels of responsibility than (3).....locally-owned industries. They need (4).....people and are (5).....to pay high wages to (6).....them. Local industries often (7).....the high salaries offered by foreign-supported industries, arguing that this will (8).....raise all wages to an excessive level. Workers in local industries, seeing the sharp (9)..... in job-pay will agitate for an improvement in their salaries. This eventually will drain the resources and (10).....their profitability.

(Bank PO Madras)

1. (a) hardly (b) reluctantly
(c) seldom (d) never
(e) usually
2. (a) disproportionate (b) better
(c) proportionate (d) comparable
(e) unreasonable
3. (a) did (b) could
(c) do (d) their
(e) does
4. (a) local (b) several
(c) more (d) talented
(e) less
5. (a) willing (b) bound
(c) forced (d) reluctant
(e) authorised
6. (a) entertain (b) retain
(c) enrich (d) hire
(e) bribe

7. (a) uphold (b) imitate
(c) protest (d) pay
(e) accept
8. (a) hardly (b) considerably
(c) not (d) unreasonably
(e) artificially
9. (a) difference (b) cut
(c) hike (d) decrease
(e) injustice
10. (a) augment (b) fulfil
(c) enhance (d) lower
(e) check

Solutions

1. (e) 2. (b) 3. (c) 4. (d)
5. (a) 6. (b) 7. (c) 8. (d)
9. (a) 10. (d)

Exercise 13

Directions (Q. 1-10) : *In the following passage there are blanks, each of which has been numbered. These numbers are printed below the passage and against each five words are suggested, one of which fits the blank appropriately. Find out the appropriate words in each case.*

Belief systems the framework upon which cultures and societies function. It is the bond that (1).....civilizations together, and it is the small voice (2).....each of us that urges us to be (3).....to what we have been taught. We cannot (4).....our spiritual teachings from our learning, nor can we separate our beliefs about who and what we are (5).....our values and our behaviours. We ask that educational systems (6).....our right to religious freedom and our right to live in harmony tribal beliefs vary, as does the (7).....to which a tribe embraces (8).....traditional cultural beliefs (9).....tribal group has distinct and unique beliefs that are basic to that tribe's culture. Most tribes cling to the old teachings because they know that once gone it means the (10).....of their culture. ***(Bank PO)***

1. (a) compels (b) holds
(c) makes (d) breaks
(e) completes
2. (a) outside (b) around
(c) about (d) inside
(e) near
3. (a) true (b) habitual
(c) accurate (d) graceful
(e) upright
4. (a) see (b) separate
(c) upset (d) distinguish
(e) search
5. (a) near (b) on
(c) from (d) about
(e) across
6. (a) recognise (b) destroy
(c) diminish (d) reach
(e) infer
7. (a) capacity (b) nearness
(c) practise (d) extent
(e) principle
8. (a) for (b) their
(c) itself (d) about
(e) its
9. (a) many (b) all
(c) one (d) several
(e) each
10. (a) mark (b) regeneration
(c) death (d) tradition
(e) mistake

Solutions

1. (b) 2. (d) 3. (a) 4. (b)
5. (c) 6. (a) 7. (d) 8. (e)
9. (e) 10. (c)

Exercise 14

Directions (Q. 1-10) : *In the following passage there are blanks each of which has been numbered. These numbers are printed below the passage and against each five words are suggested, one of which fits the blank appropriately. Find out the appropriate word in each case.*

Faced with an (1).....number and variety of products on the market, managers are finding it more difficult to (2).....demand and plan production and orders (3)..... . As a result, (4).....forecasts are increasing and along with them, the costs of those errors.

Many managers today, (5).....speed is the (6).....have turned to one or an other popular production scheduling system. But these tools tackle only part of the problem. (7).....really needed is a way to (8).....forecasts and simultaneously redesign planning processes to (9).....the impact of (10).....forecasts.

1. (a) equal (b) exact
(c) optimum (d) unanimous
(e) unprecedented
2. (a) ignore (b) meet
(c) predict (d) accept
(e) register
3. (a) immediately (b) quickly
(c) accordingly (d) positively
(e) spontaneously
4. (a) inadequate (b) buoyant
(c) frequent (d) inaccurate
(e) exorbitant
5. (a) consider (b) neglecting
(c) visualising (d) believing
(e) notwithstanding

6. (a) problem (b) answer
(c) source (d) outcome
(e) lacuna
7. (a) One (b) That's
(c) What's (d) Managers
(e) Companies
8. (a) ignore (b) obtain
(c) vitiate (d) negate
(e) improve
9. (a) rationalise (b) substantiate
(c) minimise (d) counter
(e) tolerate
10. (a) dangerous (b) absolute
(c) unpredicted (d) erroneous
(e) popular

Solutions

1. (e)	2. (c)	3. (c)	4. (d)
5. (d)	6. (b)	7. (c)	8. (e)
9. (c)	10. (d)		

Exercise 15

Directions (Q. 1-10) : *In the following passage there are blanks, each of which has been numbered. You are given a choice of three words marked (a), (b), (c) for each blank. Choose the best word from these three and indicate your choice.*

From that moment his life became intolerable. He passed his days in apprehension of each succeeding night; and (1).....night the vision (2).....back again. As soon as he (3).....locked himself up in his room he (4).....to struggle; but in vain. An (5).....force lifted him up and pushed him (6).....the glass, as if to call the phantom, and before long he saw it (7).....in the spot where the crime was (8).....lying with arms and legs outspread the way the body (9).....found. Then the dead girl (10).....and came towards him with little steps just as the child had done when she came out of the river.

1. (a) all (b) each
(c) every
2. (a) comes (b) come
(c) came
3. (a) had been (b) had
(c) was
4. (a) strives (b) strived
(c) strove
5. (a) compelling (b) irresistible
(c) overwhelming
6. (a) upon (b) towards
(c) against
7. (a) laid (b) lying
(c) laying
8. (a) perpetrated (b) done
(c) committed
9. (a) has been (b) had been
(c) was
10. (a) stood up (b) raised up
(c) rose up

Solutions

1. (c)	2. (c)	3. (b)	4. (c)
5. (b)	6. (b)	7. (b)	8. (c)
9. (b)	10. (a)		

Exercise 16

Directions (Q. 1-10) : *In the following passage there are blanks each of which has been numbered. These numbers are printed below the passage and against each five words are suggested, one of which fits the blank appropriately. Find out the appropriate word in each case.*

Do women (1).....leadership differently from what men do ? And if so, will feminine leadership (2).....where (3).....leadership does not ? A recent study suggests somewhat paradoxically that female managers (4).....their male (5).....even when the personal characteristics of both are very (6).....of the two schools of thought, the structuralist theory argues that men and women do not receive the same treatment in the workplace and that stamping out (7).....bias would stamp out the observed (8).... . In contrast, the socialisation theory contends that men and women experience work differently because men seek work as more (9).....to their lives. These (10).....explanations, apart, today business appears to be undergoing a feminisation of leadership. ***(Bank PO)***

1. (a) exercise (b) undertake
(c) authorise (d) empower
(e) tolerate
2. (a) affect (b) succeed
(c) compete (d) progress
(e) dominate
3. (a) traditional (b) charismatic
(c) masculine (d) benevolent
(e) authoritarian
4. (a) outlive (b) outcast
(c) outwork (d) outstand
(e) outdo
5. (a) employees (b) subordinates
(c) managers (d) counterparts
(e) superiors
6. (a) minimal (b) distinct
(c) unique (d) similar
(e) constant
7. (a) employment (b) culture
(c) gender (d) class
(e) category
8. (a) variations (b) discriminations
(c) resemblances (d) distortions
(e) equalities

9. (a) needy (b) desperate
   (c) preliminary (d) trivial
   (e) central
10. (a) contradictory (b) corresponding
   (c) discriminating (d) analogical
   (e) identical

Solutions

1. (a) 2. (b) 3. (c) 4. (e)
5. (d) 6. (d) 7. (a) 8. (b)
9. (e) 10. (a)

Exercise 17

Directions (Q. 1-6) : *In the following passage at certain points you are given a choice of three words, one of which is the most appropriate. Choose the best word out of the three words. Mark the letter, viz, (a), (b), (c) relating to this word.*

Smallpox, the most devastating and feared pestilence in human history, is making its last stand in two remote areas of Ethiopia, one in the desert and one in the mountains.

As of the end of August (1).....five villages had experienced cases (2).....the preceding eight weeks. More (3)..... and necessary, the onset of the last (4).....case was on 9th August. (5).....man is the only known (6).....of the smallpox virus, the disease should be eliminated forever when the last infected person recovers. ***(NDA)***

1. (a) rarely (b) the
   (c) only
2. (a) in (b) about
   (c) of
3. (a) necessary (b) important
   (c) urgent
4. (a) found (b) remembered
   (c) known
5. (a) Because (b) When
   (c) While
6. (a) culprit (b) reservoir
   (c) producer

Solutions

1. (c) 2. (c) 3. (c) 4. (a)
5. (a) 6. (b)

Exercise 18

Directions (Q. 1-10) : *In the following passage there are blanks, each of which has been numbered. The numbers are printed below the passage and against each five words are suggested, one of which fits the blank appropriately. Find out the appropriate word in each case.*

The world economy is in recession, the deepest and the most widespread (1).....the 1930s. There are (2).....of (3).....in the industrial countries, but most serious economic (4).....anticipate the rates of growth and levels of economic activity will remain low.

In all that has been written about world (5).....the (6).....have been overwhelmingly and narrowly economic. Few have (7).....the human consequences in more than a superficial manner. Not a single international study has (8).....the recession's (9).....on the most vulnerable half of the world's population—the children.

The need for (10).....clearly the contrast between world economic conditions and child welfare has thus become even more urgent in the last few years. The world scale of current child distress also makes it artificial to restrict the analysis of causes to the national level.

1. (a) in (b) for
   (c) by (d) before
   (e) since
2. (a) risks (b) glimmers
   (c) studies (d) tips
   (e) histories
3. (a) development (b) downfall
   (c) recovery (d) slackness
   (e) impact
4. (a) analysts (b) journalists
   (c) surveys (d) findings
   (e) students
5. (a) development (b) economy
   (c) wars (d) recession
   (e) conflicts
6. (a) emphasis (b) aims
   (c) glimpses (d) supposition
   (e) preoccupations
7. (a) delved (b) taught
   (c) propagated (d) investigated
   (e) manifested
8. (a) understood (b) analysed
   (c) highlighted (d) prepared
   (e) planned
9. (a) analysis (b) undercurrents
   (c) impact (d) overtures
   (e) study
10. (a) chalking out (b) curbing
   (c) bringing out (d) implementing
   (e) propagating

Solutions

1. (e) 2. (a) 3. (d) 4. (a)
5. (b) 6. (b) 7. (a) 8. (b)
9. (c) 10. (c)

Exercise 19

Directions (Q. 1-10) : *In the following passage there are blanks each of which has been numbered . The numbers are printed below the passage and against each four words are suggested, one of which fits the blank appropriately. Find out the appropriate word in each case.*

Many parents greet their children's teenage years with needless dread. While teens (1)......assault us with heavy-metal music (2)......outlandish clothes and spend all (3)......time with friends, such behaviour (4)......adds up to full scale revolt. Teenage (5)......according to psychologist Laurence Steinberg, has been (6)......exaggerated. Sociologist Sanford Dornbusch agrees. "The (7)......that teenagers inevitably rebel is a (8)......that has the potential for great family (9)......"says Dornbusch. He believes the notion can (10)......communication during this critical time for parents to influence youngsters. ***(Assistant Grade)***

1. (a) can (b) must (c) may (d) should
2. (a) show (b) dress (c) put (d) flaunt
3. (a) her (b) his (c) their (d) our
4. (a) sporadically (b) always (c) infrequently (d) scarcely
5. (a) rebellion (b) subversion (c) mania (d) revolution
6. (a) always (b) never (c) greatly (d) hardly
7. (a) complaint (b) surmise (c) accusation (d) idea
8. (a) myth (b) story (c) fact (d) reality
9. (a) ruin (b) downfall (c) harm (d) defeat
10. (a) destroy (b) suffocate (c) damage (d) injure

Solutions

1. (c) **2.** (d) **3.** (c) **4.** (b) **5.** (a) **6.** (c) **7.** (d) **8.** (a) **9.** (a) **10.** (b)

Exercise 20

Directions (Q. 1-5) : *In the following passage there are blanks each of which has been numbered. The numbers are printed below the passage and against each five words are suggested, one of which fits the blank appropriately. Find out the appropriate words in each case.*

Nations which have (1)....programmes of economic development often run into unsuspected barriers which threaten, and often (2)....the (3)....needed growth of the economy. Industrialisation (4)....productivity fails to respond and the nations goals of rising standard of living for its people are (5).... . ***(Bank PO)***

1. (a) decided (b) progressed (c) insisted (d) embarked (e) initiated
2. (a) activate (b) deteriorate (c) halt (d) cut (e) enlighten
3. (a) positively (b) hopefully (c) alarmingly (d) deceptively (e) desperately
4. (a) falters (b) deviates (c) fluctuates (d) lowers (e) dissolves
5. (a) postponed (b) frustrated (c) suspended (d) criticised (e) fulfilled

Solutions

1. (d) **2.** (d) **3.** (e) **4.** (a) **5.** (b)

Exercise 21

Directions (Q. 1-10) : *In the following passage there are blanks each of which has been numbered. The numbers are printed below the passage and against each four words are suggested, one of which fits the blank appropriately. Find out the appropriate word in each case.*

For generations man has (1)......against the wilds to create a world where only he (2)......whether animals and plants survive or are (3)......out. Earlier we accepted as self-evident that any (4)......in our environment brought about by science and technology must be improvements (5)......the world of our (6)...... . However, many people all over the world have begun to feel that (7)......are going too far, and that we should try to (8)......some of the world's original life before we find it (9)......too late. The same science which had led us away from nature is now (10)......the miracle of creation. ***(Delhi Police)***

1. (a) faced (b) stood (c) struggled (d) challenged
2. (a) decides (b) thinks (c) advises (d) observes
3. (a) taken (b) wiped (c) put (d) thrown
4. (a) differences (b) increments (c) changes (d) replacements
5. (a) in (b) at (c) over (d) for
6. (a) aborigins (b) ancients (c) successors (d) ancestors

7. (a) ourselves (b) we
(c) us (d) some
8. (a) demolish (b) cherish
(c) save (d) renovate
9. (a) occurs (b) sounds
(c) seems (d) gets
10. (a) unfolding (b) discussing
(c) arguing (d) narrating

Solutions

1. (c) 2. (a) 3. (b) 4. (c)
5. (a) 6. (d) 7. (b) 8. (c)
9. (d) 10. (a)

Exercise 22

Directions (Q. 1-10) : *In the following passage there are blanks each of which has been numbered. These numbers are printed below the passage and against each five words are suggested, one of which fits the blank appropriately. Find out the appropriate word in each case.*

The latest stage of the continuing (1)....between India and the United States on the nuclear issue is now punctuated with pleasing diplomatic observations. Our latest round of talks with the American Deputy Secretary of State is "positive and encouraging". The US Deputy Secretary of State remarked that none or us are pleased to have any clouds over the (2)..... We in India know that these clouds have (3)....towards the subcontinent from the West. The US can easily disperse the clouds if it wants. But the economic sanctions are still in place. The US is only (4)....trying to come to terms with the fact that the nuclear weapons are not the (5)....of the Permanent Members of the Security Council. If they do not recognise India as a nuclear power, then what is it that they are (6)....to ? India will not (7)....by their derecognising the nuclear tests both sides can happily close (8)....eyes and agree to (9)....what has happened. The fact that India is a sovereign nation entitled to take decision beneficial for its own security, has not been altered by the tests. The US has come round to (10)....that India has some say in this matter. ***(Bank PO)***

1. (a) adversaries (b) negotiations
(c) strifes (d) strategies
(e) disputes
2. (a) relationship (b) struggle
(c) matter (d) talks
(e) countries
3. (a) formed (b) eclipsed
(c) ruined (d) covered
(e) floated
4. (a) spontaneously (b) generously
(c) grudgingly (d) gracefully
(e) willingly
5. (a) threats (b) creations
(c) properties (d) monopoly
(e) possession
6. (a) prepared (b) objecting
(c) pointing (d) clinging
(e) planning
7. (a) gain (b) differ
(c) flourish (d) suffer
(e) develop
8. (a) their (b) our
(c) naked (d) inward
(e) both
9. (a) imitate (b) undo
(c) cherish (d) reiterate
(e) ignore
10. (a) expecting (b) suspecting
(c) accepting (d) advocating
(e) rejecting

Solutions

1. (b) 2. (a) 3. (e) 4. (c)
5. (d) 6. (b) 7. (d) 8. (a)
9. (e) 10. (c)

Exercise 23

Directions (Q. 1-10) : *In the following passage there are blanks each of which has been numbered. These numbers are printed below the passage and against each five words are suggested, one of which fits the blank appropriately. Find out the appropriate word in each case.*

Although John Wisdom's writings in philosophy show clearly the influence of Wittgentstein, they nevertheless also display a (1)....originality. Despite the (2)....and difficulty of his style, a careful reading of Wisdom is seldom (3)..... He is unique kind of genius in philosophy.

This essay is an excellent example of Wisdom's repeated attempts to (4)....the ultimate bases of philosophical perplexity. A great deal of the time Wisdom is (5)....interested in finding out why metaphysicians feel (6)....to utter such strange sentences eg, "Time is unreal", "There are no material things", etc. According to Wisdom such sentences are both false (and perhaps meaningless) and hardly (7).... Even more than Wittgenstein, Wisdom has stressed the 'Therapeutic conception of philosophy, a view that comes out clearly in this essay where he emphasises that analogy between philosophical and neurotic distress (8)....them with other kinds of problems.

The reader who is interested in gaining a fuller (9)....with Wisdom's thought is referred to his famous article 'gods' in Philosophy and Psycho-analysis. Other Minds is Wisdom's most....(10).... discussion of a single topic and in many ways his finest work. ***(Bank PO)***

1. (a) concise (b) virtual
(c) marked (d) limited
(e) relative

2. (a) individuality (b) novelty
(c) originality (d) complexity
(e) creativity
3. (a) unprofitable (b) useful
(c) advantageous (d) unreliable
(e) durable
4. (a) jettison (b) delimit
(c) augment (d) fortify
(e) explore
5. (a) admirably (b) primarily
(c) advertently (d) reluctantly
(e) happily
6. (a) depressed (b) confined
(c) alluded (d) compelled
(e) adapted
7. (a) illuminating (b) damaging
(c) confusing (d) critical
(e) unreliable
8. (a) compelling (b) associating
(c) contrasting (d) describing
(e) advocating
9. (a) comparison (b) analysis
(c) agreement (d) elaboration
(e) acquaintance
10. (a) projected (b) sustained
(c) prolonged (d) prolific
(e) attributed

Solutions

1. (c) 2. (d) 3. (a) 4. (e)
5. (b) 6. (b) 7. (a) 8. (b)
9. (e) 10. (b)

Exercise 24

Directions (Q. 1-6): *In the following sentences there are some blanks each of which has been numbered. You are given a choice of three words for each blank. Choose the best word out of the three . Mark the letter, viz, (a), (b) or (c) relating to this word on your answer sheet.*

One summer a Brazilian farmer took his donkey, Pele, with him to town (1)....the market place, a small boy began (2)....Pele with a stick, and the donkey struck (3)....injuring the boy with a kick on the head. The police chief (4)....the farmer arrested. The (5)....wept so profusely in the jail cell that the police chief changed his mind and locked up the (6)....instead. The charge against the animal was attempt to murder.

1. (a) at (b) on
(c) in
2. (a) teaching (b) tormenting
(c) playing
3. (a) back (b) backward
(c) forward
4. (a) has (b) ordered
(c) had
5. (a) donkey (b) boy
(c) farmer
6. (a) donkey (b) boy
(c) farmer

Solutions

1. (c) 2. (b) 3. (a) 4. (c)
5. (c) 6. (a)

Exercise 25

Directions (Q. 1-15): *In the following passage at certain points, you are given a choice of three words marked (a), (b), (c). Choose the best word from these three.*

The most attractive and unique feature of crossword puzzle is that it is a game one can play alone! There are several kinds of crossword puzzles. One kind is the prize competition in which the (1)....who finds the correct answers gets a big prize (2)....the answers are very hard to find, since several (3)....appear equally appropriate : bad, mad or sad for (4)....in the clue sentence, people are seldom popular. Such (5)....attract people who are fond of gambling because by (6)....a small entry fee, they can win big prizes. The (7)....type of crossword puzzle is one in which (8)....is only one possible answer to every clue. But (9)....answer is elusive and calls for some detective work (10)....our part. The clue gives only hints about the word. A (11)....like 'Mate changes to flesh for food' (12)....elude you till you realise that by changing the (13)....of 'mate' you get 'meat'. Your comprehension and your (14)....knowledge are put to the test. The effort to (15)....such crossword is an intellectual exercise. ***(CDS)***

1. (a) person (b) actor
(c) persons
2. (a) though (b) although
(c) but
3. (a) letters (b) words
(c) alphabets
4. (a) assumption (b) illustration
(c) example
5. (a) competitions (b) puzzles
(c) races
6. (a) paying (b) buying
(c) giving
7. (a) another (b) second
(c) two
8. (a) this (b) their
(c) there
9. (a) am (b) this
(c) any
10. (a) on (b) in
(c) upon

11. (a) puzzle (b) word
(c) clue
12. (a) will (b) did
(c) shall
13. (a) lettering (b) words
(c) spelling
14. (a) general (b) overall
(c) common sense
15. (a) solve (b) dissolve
(c) think of

Solutions

1. (a)	2. (c)	3. (b)	4. (c)
5. (b)	6. (a)	7. (b)	8. (c)
9. (b)	10. (a)	11. (a)	12. (c)
13. (c)	14. (a)	15. (a)	

Exercise 26

Directions (Q. 1-15): *In the following passage at certain points, you are given a choice of four words marked as (a), (b), (c) and (d). Choose the best word out of these four.*

Our scientific spirit must be shocked not only by the (1)......of fabulous (2)......and (3)......poverty, but also by those of intense holiness and (4)......superstition. In our relations with one another, we have (5)......to apply scientific and social wisdom. The failure is (6)...... large (7)......our society. Some social (8)......like untouchability are (9)......simply because the spirit in us is oppressed by the force of (10)...... . These are practised by (11)......kindly persons, who have ceased to feel and whose understanding is (12)......any tradition. There are millions in our country today who use scientific (13)......and yet (14)......superstition as mystical revelation and adhere to absured social customs (15)..the name of tradition. ***(Assistant Grade)***

1. (a) phenomenon (b) contrasts
(c) existence (d) comparison
2. (a) property (b) prosperity
(c) resources (d) wealth
3. (a) common (b) rampant
(c) grovelling (d) growing
4. (a) religious (b) blind
(c) popular (d) prevailing
5. (a) attempted (b) refused
(c) succeeded (d) failed
6. (a) writ (b) written
(c) wrought (d) wrapped
7. (a) in (b) on
(c) among (d) for
8. (a) abuses (b) ceremonies
(c) function (d) obligations
9. (a) allowed (b) approved
(c) tolerated (d) resisted
10. (a) opinion (b) habit
(c) society (d) custom
11. (a) fairly (b) very
(c) otherwise (d) somewhat
12. (a) stupefied (b) sanctified
(c) subsidized (d) substantiated
13. (a) discoveries (b) devices
(c) apparatus (d) machines
14. (a) consider (b) decry
(c) declare (d) revere
15. (a) on (b) for
(c) in (d) with

Solutions

1. (c)	2. (c)	3. (d)	4. (a)
5. (d)	6. (a)	7. (b)	8. (a)
9. (c)	10. (b)	11. (a)	12. (b)
13. (b)	14. (a)	15. (c)	

Exercise 27

Directions (Q. 1-10): *In the following passage at certain points, you are given a choice of five words marked as (a), (b), (c), (d) and (e). Choose the best word out of these five.*

There is an old story told (1)......a man who (2)......into a drunken sleep. His friend stayed by him as long as he (3)......but being compelled to go and fearing that he might be in want, the friend hid a (4) ......in the drunken man's garment. When the drunken man (5)......not knowing that his friend had (6)......jewel in his garment he wandered about in (7)......hungry. A long time afterwards the two men met again and the friend told the poor man about the jewel and advised him to look(8)......it. Like the drunken man of the story people (9)......about suffering in this life of birth and death (10)......of what is hidden away in their inner nature. Pure and untarnished, the priceless treasure of God. ***(Bank Clerk)***

1. (a) of (b) to
(c) with (d) by
(e) that
2. (a) left (b) felt
(c) fail (d) fell
(e) gone
3. (a) might (b) can
(c) would (d) had
(e) could
4. (a) garment (b) drink
(c) jewel (d) treasure
(e) sleep
5. (a) slept (b) recovered
(c) covered (d) drinking
(e) realised
6. (a) taken (b) presented
(c) substituted (d) replaced
(e) hidden

7. (a) vain (b) search
(c) sleep (d) poverty
(e) persuit
8. (a) for (b) to
(c) at (d) in
(e) with
9. (a) search (b) wonder
(c) wander (d) trouble
(e) unknown
10. (a) conscious (b) unconscious
(c) knowingly (d) expected
(e) useless

Solutions

1. (a)	**2.** (d)	**3.** (e)	**4.** (c)
5. (b)	**6.** (e)	**7.** (a)	**8.** (a)
9. (c)	**10.** (b)		

Exercise 28

Directions (Q. 1-12) : *In the following passage, at certain points, you are given a choice of five words marked as (a), (b), (c), (d) and (e). Choose the best word out of these five.*

The (1)......of a survey by the National institute of (2)......health give (3)......for (4)...... . According to the survey about 14 million people in India are affected (5)......mental (6)......at any point of time. In the case of mentally ill, it is (7)......enough difficult to (8)......them, let alone (9)......them. The most (10)......are those in the (11)......areas, for whatever (12)......for the mentally sick exist are concentrated around major urban centres.

1. (a) verdicts (b) decisions
(c) judgements (d) measures
(e) findings
2. (a) spiritual (b) psychical
(c) social (d) physical
(e) mental
3. (a) food (b) cause
(c) purpose (d) support
(e) reinforcement
4. (a) alarm (b) discontent
(c) fear (d) dissatisfaction
(e) vexation
5. (a) dangerous (b) strong
(c) serious (d) fatal
(e) important
6. (a) disorder (b) perturbation
(c) dislocation (d) confusion
(e) involvement
7. (a) seldom (b) occasionally
(c) often (d) hardly
(e) never
8. (a) cure (b) recognize
(c) identify (d) select
(e) rehabilitate
9. (a) facilitate (b) guide
(c) cure (d) advice
(e) treat
10. (a) indifferent (b) neglected
(c) careless (d) abandoned
(e) serious
11. (a) urban (b) rural
(c) forest (d) suburban
(e) metropolitan
12. (a) facilities (b) advantages
(c) avenues (d) remedies
(e) solicitations

Solutions

1. (e)	**2.** (e)	**3.** (b)	**4.** (a)
5. (c)	**6.** (a)	**7.** (c)	**8.** (c)
9. (c)	**10.** (b)	**11.** (b)	**12.** (a)

» Unit

49

Report Writing

How to Write a Good Report ?

What Is a Report ?

A report is a factual description of some incident, or a consolidated statement of some plan or scheme either existing or being implemented, based upon some logics collected verbally or in writing.

Reports can be classified in four categories :

1. Official report
2. Report to a newspaper by a reporter
3. Report for a specific purpose
4. Technical/Research report

Official Report An official report is prepared usually on a matter of public importance or official interest. It is submitted by an official to a higher authority or to a committee. An official report is quite formal. While submitting the report it begins like this .. "The report is submitted by.... to ......". In an official report only the immediate and practical aspects of the subject matter need discussed. In an official report its subject and scope is limited upto the official terms of reference. When a report is submitted by a junior officer in respect to any happening, the immediate and practical aspects of the subject matter are discussed in it and suitable suggestions and his recommendations are also given.

Report to a Newspaper by a Reporter A correspondent or a reporter prepares such reports for the publication in a newspaper. He is either deputed for the purpose or the incident about which he is submitting his report, pertains to his area of operation. Usually, he is well acquainted with the situation or event. This report should reflect the detailed study made by the reporter.

A reporter who reports on an event, say an accident, a riot, a strike, a rally etc, collects facts and figures from a number of persons involved in that particular event. From their accounts he prepares his report, but he must make sure that the facts and figures submitted in the report are correct.

This reporter should be objective, impersonal and unbiased in his report.

Report for a Specific Purpose Sometimes a reporter is deputed for preparing a report on a specific subject or he himself suo motto prepares a detailed report. Such report is not in respect to any incident like accident, fire or terrorist attack etc. but it usually covers the after effects of an official policy or is in respect to a long prevailing problem being faced by the society, country etc. The data and information collected are not only on verbal basis but also from official records. While analysing the figures in preparing the report the personal bias must be avoided.

Technical Report These reports are prepared by economists/engineers /scientists and other technical persons as a part of their duty. Such reports help the policy makers to take major decisions. While preparing such reports the reporter is required to base his reports on the basis of all the relevant data and the conclusions must be drawn very sincerely, meticulously, as the conclusions may have far reaching effects.

Essentials of a Good Report

1. **Factual description:** Report must be factual and free from personal prejudices. All the data and information collected should be relevant and unbiased.
2. **Clear, compact and concise :** The object of the report should be clear. The suggestions and recommendations submitted should also be very clear. The report should not be unnecessarily detailed and should not cover irrelevant points. In short, it should be clear, compact and concise.
3. **Purpose :** The purpose of the report is very important. A good report must contain relevant points as per the purpose of the report.
4. **Simple and logical :** The language used should be simple and not be couched in typical or unnecessary technical words. No round about statement should be used while making recommendations or giving suggestions. All the report and the final conclusion must be logical and to the point.

Look at the following Original Reports taken from a Newspaper :

Economic Times, dated 04-01-200....

Sensex Rise Makes MF Investors Junk Debt

Mumbai, 4 January
Financial Correspondent

Equity culture is making deeper inroads due to the rising sensex. Mutual fund investors who have been traditional debt schemes takers are opting for the riskier equity oriented schemes to crash into the sensex party, Puja Mehra reports from New Delhi. Historically, MF investors in India have had a huge debt bias. Total share of assets under management in equities, however, has grown gradually but steadily, over the past few months. As per latest data, the share of assets deployed in equities has risen to 21.6% against 16.0% in 03. Significantly, the jump in the equity share has come despite the blow of net outflows from existing equity schemes. These schemes suffered heavy redemption pressures from investors booking profits. Investor preference for equities, however, is most visible in subscriptions to new equity schemes launched by domestic funds.

Economic Times, dated 04-01-200....

SC Notice to Govt on Soft Drink PIL

Our Delhi Bureau
New Delhi, 3 January

The Supreme Court today stepped up pressure on the government to review the contents of soft drinks marketed in the country. The court issued a notice to the Centre on a petition seeking a thorough examination of the contents of soft drinks on the ground that they pose 'health hazards'. This follows the court's observation earlier last month when it dismissed petition filed by soft drink makers Pepsi and Cocacola, challenging a Rajasthan High Court order asking them to print on containers, the extent of pesticide residues in their products. In its latest salvo, a Bench comprising Chief justice R.C. Lahoti and justice G. P. Mathur issued the notice on a petition by the Centre for Public Interest Litigation (CPIL) alleging that the government which has a duty to protect the life of citizens, has not taken any initiative in this regard despite several researches finding soft drink contents to be harmful, especially for children. The petitioner requested the court to direct the Centre to constitute an expert technical committee to evaluate the harmful effects of soft drinks on human health, particularly children and put in place a regulatory regime to control and check the contents of particular chemical additives in foods and soft drinks. It also requested the court to make it mandatory for soft drink manufacturers to disclose the contents and the quality of their products including appropriate warning about ingredients and their harmful effects.

Economic Times, 31-12-200....

Fresh Tsunami Fear Causes Alert

Chennai, 30 December

Fresh panic swept the Tsunami ravaged coasts of southern India as the government today issued a high alert against more titanic waves a possible quake near Australia could generate. The warning issued after an emergency meeting of the home ministry's crisis management team, triggered fresh fears as the already traumatised people along the southern and south-eastern coastline scurried for safe ground. The warning was flashed through television, whereby the administration asked the people to vacate their homes in the more vulnerable villages. In some areas, loudspeakers were also used to relay the alert. But, despite the warnings, Prime Minister Manmohan Singh's aides said he was not cutting short his tour of the affected areas. All coastal states and union territories, especially the worst hit Tamil Nadu and the Andaman and Nicobar Islands, were asked to be on the highest alert for the next 48 hours for tidal waves hitting Indian coasts. This is barely four days after Sunday's giant waves generated by a huge undersea quake off Sumatra ravaged seven South and South-east Asian nations including India and swallowed up large tracts of coast claiming at least 60,000 lives. Amid experts fears of an ominous tectonic sea bed shift around Australia, heightened sea turbulence was being reported from the 1,000 km. East Coast of Tamil Nadu and people were being warned to keep off the shore. Choppy conditions and sea incursions of upto 10 metres have been reported Thursday morning from the Thiruvanmiyur beach in south Chennai and rough sea has been reported also at Chennai's Marina beach. Large ripples were said to be hitting the Kalpakkam and Cuddalore coast once again besides the Kanyakumari coast. Based on inputs from experts and weather-men, the home ministry directed immediate evacuation of people to safer places and all shorelines to be made in accessible to the public.

Economic Times, 30-12-200....

NC Leader Among 9 killed in Valley

Masood Hussain

Srinagar, 29 December

In a sudden escalation in violence, militants killed a National Conference (NC) leader in old city. Another incidents claimed eight lives including that of a soldier in other areas of the State. Police said they have busted a number of hideouts in border Poonch-Rajouri region where a few militants were also killed. Police said unidentified militants shot dead Farooq Ahmad Zargar, provincial president of the Youth NC in old city's Kawdara locality around noon. Massive protests were reported from South Kashmir Tral township after reports of soldiers raining bullets on a passenger bus spread like wild fire. Residents resorted to brick-bating and damaged many government buildings and vehicles. Details revealed that when Rashtriya Rifles-42 stopped a Srinagar bound passenger bus in Lalgam village in Tral, a militant alighted from the bus and shot at one of the soldiers. This led to an encounter in which three passengers and the militant were killed. Four other commuters received serious bullet injuries and they were admitted to hospitals. Some of them are stated to be critical. Police said the slain militant Abdul Rashid Bhat was a Hizb-ul Mujahideen cadre who was set free after two years detention in October last. Defence spokesman Lt. Col. V. K. Batra said the soldiers were attacked by the militant who was killed in retaliatory fire. Asked about civilian casualties, the spokesman said it was actually a BSF party that was passing through and opened fire on the bus. However, a BSF spokesman said their party reached around 30 minutes after the incident had taken place. In Sopore, militants shot dead a BSF man Anuraj Kumar near the local bus stand and fled with his rifle. A hitherto unknown outfit Al-Khandak has staked the claim for the attack. Reports from Jammu said police recovered the corpse of civilian Ali Mohammed whom militants had kidnapped a day earlier from Sarwara belt in Rajouri. In neighbouring Darhal belt, soldiers killed a militant whose identity was not immediately known.

Economic Times, 30-12-200....

More Hooch Victims Pour in Hospitals

Our Political Bureau
Mumbai, 29 December

Municipal hospitals across Mumbai continue to register more casualties in the Hooch tragedy. The toll from the spurious liquor tragedy in suburban Vikroli along has mounted to 65 with seven more persons succumbing to the lethal drink. The condition of a majority of the over 80 people undergoing treatment is reported to be serious. Of the 174 affected individuals admitted to the Rajawadi hospital in Ghatkopar, 49 succumbed to internal haemorrhage caused by the spurious liquor. "Ten persons were brought dead," said hospital dean Dr V. B. Shukla. In Sion hospital, six of the 34 persons admitted died, hospital sources said. Over 80 people are still undergoing treatment in the hospitals while some have been discharged. Taking stern action against the erring officials the State Government on Tuesday suspended 27 officials including five from the excise department and 22 policemen. The Police also arrested 24 persons in neighbouring Thane and Nhava Sheva for their alleged involvement in the illicit liquor trade. Taking a serious note of the tragedy, the Maharashtra Government today decided to hand over the probe into the spurious liquor tragedy, to the CID, "The CID will conduct a thorough probe into the illicit liquor tragedy, once the present probe being handled by an officer of the rank of Additional Police Commissioner is completed," State Deputy Chief Minister R.R. Patil, who also holds the home portfolio. Following the twin Hooch tragedy, massive raids have been conducted over the last two days at various places in Navi Mumbai, Raigad and Thane said the deputy CM. He said that a large stock of illegal liquor had been destroyed. He attributed the tragedy to the small number of licenced liquor shops and availability of cheaper illegal liquor. Interestingly, the proposal to legalise bootleggers, by offering them country liquor licences was raised during the winter session in Nagpur. However, it is believed that the political parties were divided on this front, which is why the subject was not brought up for discussion at the cabinet meeting today. The Deputy CM also gave a clean chit to city police chief A.N. Roy, whose transfer was sought by opposition leader Narayan Rane holding him responsible for the incidents. "The Police Commissioner had directed police officials to take precautionary measures," said Patil.

» Exercises

(1) ***You are Ankit, working as the news correspondent for the Times of India, Mumbai. You are invited by the organisers to cover the programme of the National Film Award. Write a report giving necessary details in not more than 100 words.***

Soumitra, Priyamani Won the Best Awards

Mumbai, 10th June, 200.... (From our news correspondent Mr Ankit)

The much awaited 54th National Films Awards 200....... were announced yesterday. The auditorium was fabulously decorated with dazzling light and an electronical effect was given to the stage, to welcome the film stars. The Chief Minister of Maharashtra graced the occasion as Chief Guest. A large gathering cheered the respected leader and the film stars. The awards were given for the best film in Hindi and other regional languages. The best film actor and actress award was conferred on Soumitra and Priyamani. Other awards included the best director, character actor, music director and the best film. When the function was closed, people crowded the stars to get their autographs. The function was a grand success.

(2) *As a staff reporter of the Hindustan Times, who witnessed a multiple collision of a Maruti car, a scooter and a tourist bus in a road accident, write a report in not more than 100 words.*

Two Dead, Six Injured in Road Accident

New Delhi, 10th May, 200.... (From our staff reporter)

It was perhaps the most unfortunate and saddest day of many people who witnessed a multiple collision of a Maruti car, a scooter and a tourist bus near ITO, New Delhi. A tourist bus of U.P. Roadways, full of passengers, was on a picnic to India Gate. When it reached near ITO, it hit a Maruti car from the left side and a scooter from the back. The two young boys in their teens, on the scooter were thrown on the road and died on the spot. The dead bodies were lying on the road in a pool of blood. The scooterists were not wearing helmets so they succumbed to the head injury caused in the accident. Even the driver of the Maruti car lost his sense, hit a wall, but didn't get hurt. Passengers in the bus got a sudden jerk. Six passengers seriously injured. All were crying for help. There was a loud hue and cry. The injured were taken to hospital for immediate medical aid. The whole traffic came to a standstill. The police arrived in no time and registered a case for negligent driving and homicide against the bus driver.

(3) *You are Mohan, a staff reporter of The Times of India. You have witnessed a severe road accident involving a Truck and a Maruti car. Write a report including details about number of people injured and extent of damage caused to the colliding vehicles in not more than 100 words.*

Truck Hits Maruti, One Dead

New Delhi, 16th September, 200.... (From our staff reporter Mohan)

A serious accident took place near Naraina in which a truck bearing Registration No. DLI 023, D 4573 suddenly jumped the red light and turned to right. It was about to collide with a Maruti car Registration No. DLJ 012, J 1572, but the driver was very smart and careful. He saw the impending danger and took a turn to the left, but could not escape fully. The Truck hit the Maruti and lost its balance and hit the wall in the right. The truck was overturned causing serious injuries to the passengers sitting in the cabin. The driver was thrown out and his head struck against the wall and died on the spot. The three passengers sitting in the cabin of the truck were badly injured, two suffered minor injuries. The Maruti driver got minor injuries. The traffic came to a standstill. The injured were removed to hospital. Police rushed to the spot and a case was lodged against the Truck driver.

(4) You are Nisha working as a newspaper reporter for the Hindustan Times. Yesterday, you were invited to attend a press conference convened by the Union Minister for Parliamentary Affairs on the proposed changes in the Constitution of India. Write a report for publication in the newspaper in not more than 150 words.

Constitutional Amendments Necessary for Stability : Minister

New Delhi, 24th March, 200.... (By Miss Nisha, staff reporter from H.T. New Delhi)

The Union Minister for Parliamentary Affairs convened a press conference at his residence on the proposed changes in the Constitution of India in order to provide a stable government to the country. Here, in India, Members of the Parliament are elected to run the government. In case any political party fails to get a clear majority to form a government, it has to get the support of other political parties to form a government. Thus a coalition government takes place. At present we are having a coalition government, but its success is neither certain nor admirable, as the allied parties in general force their motives and decisions on the government. This creates great hurdles in the smooth functioning of the government. Sometimes the coalition partners start working against the Government. In order to put a check over such practice, certain changes in the Constitution are under process. The majority party shall be allowed to form a government. In the first instance no candidate should be allowed to change a party after winning the election. On the issues of national interest all parties have to give their consensus. There should be only four political parties which have secured at least 20% votes in the last three elections. Once accepted as coalition partner that party shall not be allowed to withdraw the support. Once a government is formed, that cannot be thrown out unless a majority of two-thirds of the total membership put a demand in writing to the President, and a no-confidence motion is passed by the same majority. When asked about the feasibility of such a move the Minister replied that it is well in the interest of the nation and for the peace and progress, stability is must.

(5) Paresh Tonk, a correspondent from the Statesman, was asked to submit a report on Environment Pollution. Write a report on Environmental Pollution in 80-100 words.

Environmental Pollution

New Delhi, 25th Oct., 200.... (From our special correspondent Mr Paresh Tonk)

Environmental Pollution has assumed alarming proportion resulting in a serious health hazard now-a-days. Not only air but also water has become dangerously polluted. Smoke pollutes air, sewage pollutes water and solid wastes (garbage and junk etc.) pollute land. Population explosion, urbanization and industrialization are the biggest causes of the present pollution. Industrial units throw their wastes and chemicalized water in the rivers. Sewage of big cities is being dumped into rivers. This has resulted into spreading of harmful chemicals in the environment which are harmful for the living creatures. Plants, animals and human beings are suffering from many known and unknown diseases because of this pollution. The polluted water causes cancerous diseases like cholera, jaundice and diarrhoea etc. The smoke coming out of the chimneys of the factories and vehicles causes serious health problems. We regularly breathe the polluted air and as a result headache, nausea and many diseases of lung and heart take place. This is a serious health hazard to all of us. The public be made aware to the harms and the problems caused due to environmental pollution. Public be advised to use anti-pollutant instruments in their vehicles and regular tuning and pollution check to be made compulsory. Industrial Units be forced to take anti-pollution measures. A proper arrangement for dumping of industrial and sewage wastes be made. Use of polythene bags be banned. A mass awareness programme be launched by the Governmental and non-governmental agencies. To save the younger generation from the side-effects of the environmental pollution it is necessary to take immediate and proper action.

(6) *You are Mr Ashok Jain. You have seen a student demonstration near Moti Nagar, New Delhi. Write your report in about 80-100 words for the newspaper.*

Students Demonstrated against Fees Hike

New Delhi, 29th August, 200.... (From our special correspondent Mr Ashok Jain)

The students of senior classes of Government School, Moti Nagar walked out of their classes and held massive demonstration against the hike in board fees. They were raising slogans against the government decision for increasing Board fees and abolishing the compartment examinations altogether. They were having hand bills and many posters. They were shouting slogans for restoring the compartment examination and maintaining the status quo in the matter of Board fees. This peaceful procession proceeded towards the office of Education Minister. Approximately 20,000 students gathered at the office of the Education Minister from all corners of Delhi. The police tried to disperse the students but they did not budge even a single inch. There was complete chaos and the traffic was jammed. The Minister arrived on the spot and had discussion with the student leaders. After discussion, he assured the students for prompt and positive action. The situation was thus controlled and then the students left the place winningly and peacefully.

(7) *You are Sarla. You visited the Industrial Exhibition at Pragati Maidan. Your teacher has asked you to write a report for the school magazine. Write your report in about 100 words.*

A Report on Exhibition

Delhi, 25th Dec., 200.... (Report by Miss Sarla, a staff correspondent)

A national level exhibition commenced at Pragati Maidan today, inaugurated by the Home Minister. On the inauguration the Home Minister said, "Exhibitions are the reflections of a country's progress in toto and this exhibition is unique in which all the States and the Union Territories are participating." Every year many exhibitions and trade fairs are organised by the Governmental and Non governmental Agencies. This year a specific industrial exhibition was held in Pragati Maidan. All the States participated in this exhibition. It attracted a throng of visitors from all over the country. It reflects that India has made an exemplary progress in the field of industry. People could be seen in long queues before the different pavilions. At the machinery section, one could not find a place to keep foot on. Agricultural implements of Punjab were in great demand. Handmade Galichas and dresses of Kashmir also attracted a lot of visitors. The pavilion of Rajasthan was also very interesting as it had very cheap and beautiful items of clay and mud. Some of the stall-keepers distributed hand-bills to the visitors. People were walking here and there in an enthusiastic mood. Small children were enjoying the merry-go-rounds, horse and camel rides. The refreshment corner was also full of hustle and bustle.

(8) *You are Bhawani Dev, a correspondent from the Indian Express. You were an eye witness to an Electioneering campaign in Ahmedabad. Write a report for the newspaper in about 100 words.*

Elections Held Peacefully

Ahmedabad, 25th Nov, 200.... (Report by Bhawani Dev, a correspondent from Indian Express)

India being the largest democracy of the world a great emphasis is laid on the free and fair elections. In Gujarat, the election commission declared elections and the schedule of filing and withdrawing nominations as well as the date of election was also announced. Electronic Voting Machines will be used in the elections. All preparations were made in advance. More than thirty candidates filed their nomination papers for Ahmedabad (North) assembly seat. After date of withdrawal there were ten candidates in the fray. Accordingly different symbols were allotted to the contesting candidates. The candidates arranged meetings and put forth their charter of manifesto. Every candidate was trying to tempt and woo the voters through his oily and sweet slogans and speeches. Posters and slogans were decorating the walls. Several meetings of many high profile leaders and film stars were organised during the campaign. Hand bills were being circulated among the residents. The candidates were holding corner meetings under a certain code of conduct. The election campaign came to a standstill 48 hours before the date of polling. On the polling day tight security arrangements were made. The voters came in great number and there were long queues in the beginning. The voting started at 7.00 p.m. and continued till 5.00 p.m. The counting was scheduled after three days. It was started in the presence of the candidates and their agents as per the scheduled programme. The returning officer declared the result then. The elections were held peacefully and in a congenial atmosphere.

(9) *Imagine you are posted as SDM in a district, prepare a report on the Pulse Polio Programme carried out in the district.*

From :

Sub Divisional Magistrate
District ....

To,

The Chief Secretary,
Govt of ....
....

Sub : *Pulse Polio Programme*

Sir,

Under National Programme of Polio Eradication, we have carried out the Pulse Polio Campaign on 15th August in the district. A good advance publicity campaign was launched to make the general public aware of the Programme and about the date 15th August, the day of vaccination. A wide publicity was made not only in the city area but in the remote rural areas also.

Forty teams of doctors and nurses, fifteen for the city area and twenty-five for the rural areas were deployed on the vaccination day to provide polio drops to every child. Male and Female nurses were deployed to visit door to door and give the drops to the children wherever possible. More than twenty thousand children were given the polio drops on that day.

We are planning to repeat this campaign in the month of October again. This time we shall be covering only the rural areas of the district. Our target for the district is 90,000 children. We have already covered twenty thousand plus forty thousand (in earlier camps) total sixty thousand children so far. We hope not only to achieve our target but also to exceed the same. Every child will be given the drops positively. We are determined to make the Polio Eradication programme a grand success positively.

R. K. Purohit
S.D.M.

23rd August, 200....

(10) *You are posted as District Family Planning Officer in the district. Submit a report to the Director, Medical and Health of the State in respect to the Family Planning Campaign launched in your district.*

From :

District Family Planning Officer
District ....

To,

The Director,
Medical and Health Department
....
....

Sub : *Family Planning Campaign in the district of ...*

Sir,

As per the instructions received from your office via letter No. RJ/FP/103/200.... dated 25th Dec. we launched the Family Planning Campaign on 20th January, 2006.

All the staff of our department was deployed for the purpose. Various voluntary organisations including Panch, Sarpanch and the respected persons of each village were motivated to make the campaign a grand success. In city area the public is well aware to the advantages of adopting family planning measures, but in rural area, more awareness is required to be created.

During this campaign, 315 operations were done and 3,000 packets of condoms were distributed.

To make this programme a regular feature, I like to suggest that at least two Mobile Operation Van be made available for the district to cover the rural areas. We want to fix a day for every village, on which the pending cases and the interested cases may be operated on a regular basis.

However we will be achieving our targets positively.

P. K. Sharma 22nd Jan., 200....

D F P O

(11) ***You are posted as Assistant Collector in a district. Flood has caused a lot of damage in the district, submit a factual report to Chief Secretary of the State, stating therein the measures taken by you to control the situation and your recommendations to assist the flood affected people.***

From :

Assistant Collector

District ....

To,

The Chief Secretary,

....

....

Sub : *Flood in the district of ....*

Sir,

I have personally visited the area affected by the recent flood. The villages lying in the path of river 'Sone' are the worst affected. As there had been little rain during the last three-four years so the people started settling nearby the river. The sudden rains have overflooded the river and all the huts and houses within approximately one km range of the river were completely washed away and destroyed. Flood water entered the houses. People have taken shelter in hills. A huge damage to properties have been done. Two persons died in Takupaka village. An acute shortage of eatables, drinking water and dry firewood, is being faced. We have taken all measures to help the flood victims. Packets of food, bottles of drinking water, wheat flour, kerosene etc, are being supplied to the people, with the assistance of the generous people and the NGOs and other voluntary organizations and selfless clubs. To check the spread of any epidemic diseases CMHO was called to take necessary measures immediately. A team of doctors was dispatched to every affected village to take care of spreading of any water borne or any other kind of diseases.

We are taking all possible measures to assist the flood affected people. But looking at the heavy damage caused by the flood, more funds are required immediately.

You are requested to arrange at least five crore rupees urgently, so that the relief work can be carried out effectively.

J.C. Bhagat Sept. 19, 200....

Assistant Collector

(12) *Suppose you are Collector of a district. Submit a report to the Chief Secretary of the State in respect to the drought situation in the district. Inform the remedial measures taken by you and what further measures required to control the situation.*

From :

Collector

District ....

To,

The Chief Secretary,

Govt of................

....

Sub : *Havoc caused by the drought in the district of ...*

Sir,

Our district has been suffering from the shortage of rains regularly for the last four years. Due to scanty rainfall, the water level in whole of the district has gone down tremendously. Without water in the wells, and no rainfall, all the crops have dried up thus causing huge loss to every farmer. Our agriculture depends mainly on rainfalls. The dams and ponds are also fully dried up. An acute shortage of water is being faced. Cattle are either sold by the farmers or left to die for the shortage of water and fodder. The cost of fodder has increased tremendously. This drought has so far claimed 120 lives of cattle and affected more than 600 villages of the district with a population of 78 lacs.

'No rains' and 'shortage of water' have created famine like conditions. The drought has rendered lacs of villagers jobless. The dead bodies of animals are stinking in the fields and creating a health hazard. The danger of spreading an epidemic is immense.

I have visited almost all the affected villages. I found the situation very alarming. We are arranging fodder from the nearby state. Water is being supplied in tanks from the city area. Loans are being arranged for the farmers for deepening of wells and electrification of wells. The CMHO is instructed to check the spreading of any disease. Free dry wood is made available for the cremation of dead animals.

We have also taken assistance of voluntary organisations, NGOs and other generous people to help the affected people.

The situation is under control, yet lot of fund is needed to help the affected people. We need at least 150 crore rupees to start relief work in a proper manner.

Please arrange the necessary funds so that the situation caused due to the drought may be checked effectively.

Piyush Dixit

28th Aug., 200....

District Collector

(13) *As a newspaper correspondent of a national daily, write a report for your paper on the destruction caused by flood and the relief measures have been taken by the administration.*

The Editor

The Indian Express

Bahadur Shah Zafar Marg

New Delhi–110002

Sir,

I hereby submit to you a report on the flood situation in district Ropar of Haryana. Floods have become a common feature in our country during rainy season. This time it has affected many areas of Haryana but the situation in district Ropar is the worst. Thousands of people have been rendered homeless. At least twenty-two persons are reported to have been drowned. Thousands of people have been marooned owing to heavy rainfall. One railway track is badly damaged and many roads are under knee-deep water. Property worth crores of rupees has been washed away.

The people of the area are facing the calamity bravely. The Haryana Government is handling the situation on a war footing. The rescue and relief operations are going on in full swing. The medicines, clothes and other necessary articles are being supplied to the flood-stricken people by the Government and voluntary organisations. Many boats have been pressed into service to rescue the marooned people. The Chief Minister of Haryana is personally supervising the relief operations and he has announced an outlay of Rs. 250 crores to rehabilitate the affected people. Many voluntary organisations from neighbouring States Punjab, Rajasthan and Delhi have sent men and materials to assist the relief work. The Government has exempted the farmers from payment of land revenue and postponed the repayment of loans. The situation now appears to be quite under control though most of the areas in the district are still submerged in water. An active team of policemen and two battalion of military soldiers have been keeping round the clock vigil on strategic points. Due to active role played by the political leaders and vigilance of the Government machinery a lot of sufferings of the affected people have since mitigated. It is hoped that, in a week or so, there will be a remarkable improvement in the situation.

XYZ

Correspondent

(14) ***Imagine that you have conducted a survey of teenagers in your city and the television programmes they watch. Write a report for a newspaper about the survey, your findings and your critical remarks.***

The Editor
The Indian Express
New Delhi

Sir,

I have conducted a survey of TV- watching teenagers about their preferences. A peculiar similarity was observed in the likings of the present teens. A few important points which are universally applicable to all the children who fall between the age of thirteen and nineteen are being discussed here under.

A few special traits and tendencies govern their minds. The teenagers generally select those TV programmes which are action oriented or have love triangle. They prefer adventurous stories, serials involving love, romance and separation, detective episodes, comedy serials and some other programmes like cartoon films etc. They do not relish things of lofty and sublime nature. They enjoy funny, imaginative, romantic and tragedy items, which can make them jump and find in themselves one of the heroes of the serials. Some serials which show conflict with the society in the matter of love and marriage are also liked by the teenagers very much. They do not need things of intellectual nature.

I think such type of tendencies are not good for their real development. They are living in imaginations and dreams. They are being carried away by the imaginatives of the serials and unable to understand the reality of the life, of the world. They should be inspired to watch different programmes connected with political, social, religious and economic subjects. It is must for the healthy development of the teenagers. The parents should check the children and try to discuss with them and quench their querries. Something radical should be done to raise the level of teenagers' thinking. In fact the parents can play a vital role in this matter.

I request you to publish this survey report in one of the columns of your leading daily and oblige.

Yours faithfully,

Rajesh Prassanna

A free lancer

(15) ***Imagine that you have travelled by train and as a result of derailment of the train all the passengers were delayed and faced many kinds of problems. Write a report for newspaper describing the problem the passengers faced. Narrate the accident as an eye witness.***

The Editor
The Hindustan Times
New Delhi
Sub : *A report on Train Accident.*

Sir,

Hardly had the Meerut Shuttle travelled about 20 Kms, when suddenly its three bogies and the engine derailed about 7.15 a.m. on Saturday, the 20th December 200.... Nine passengers were reportedly died on the spot and 85 injured, some of them were serious.

The Ghaziabad-Meerut Administration of U.P. Government started rescue and relief operations immediately. The nearby local residents helped in the rescue work. The policemen and military jawans have rushed to the place of accident. The injured were taken to Ghaziabad and Meerut hospitals where they are being given treatment.

Senior Police Officers and the District Magistrate have already reached the accident site. They are personally supervising the relief work. But still the accident victims are facing a number of problems. Some dead bodies are still lying in the wreckage.The arrangement of power crane could not be made for five hours. In the hospital some patients are complaining against the lack of up-to-date facilities and prompt attention. The relatives of the seriously injured are not able to meet them. Proper arrangements of food, medicines etc., are not being made. However, the Chief Minister of U. P. is in constant touch with the local administration. He has announced a compensation of Rs. 5 lacs to next of kin of the dead and Rs fifty thousand for the injured. I hope that the situation will come back to normalcy within two or three days. Further developments will be communicated to you in the next despatch.

Yours sincerely,

XYZ

(16) ***You participated in an inter-college debate competition as a contestant, organized by the Lions Club of your area, in which you spoke in favour of the motion and stood first. The topic for the debate was, "In the opinion of the house, free education upto secondary level should be the fundamental right of every Indian Child." Write a report in not more than 120 words for publication in your college magazine.***

Jaipur, 15th August, 200.... (From Rajdeep TDC IInd Yr. Sc.)

Yesterday an inter-college debate competition was organised by Lions Club in our college. Total twelve participants spoke in favour of the topic that free education upto the secondary level should be the fundamental right of every Indian child. Simultaneously twelve contestants spoke against the motion. Many college lecturers, students and parents were there to listen to the different ideas. I was also one of the contestants. I pleaded that without education a man is just like a devil who can disrupt the life of a nation. It is the education that ennobles our souls and remove darkness from our minds. Education is a window that opens channels to achieve the highest learning. It joins us with the master minds of other nations, whose achievements can be made use of, in the best possible way. Getting education upto secondary level should be a Fundamental Right of every child of India. The government should see that every school going child must attend the school. It is the education that provides wisdom, wealth, prosperity and what not. The audience clapped time and again when I cited many examples supporting my contentions. When the result was declared, I was adjudged as the best contestant. The function was a grand success. Chief Guest, the District Collector, exhorted the president of the Lions Club to organise such type of competitions on regular basis, as such debate opens the minds of the students and make them a good citizen.

(17) *You are a reporter from the Times of India News service. Being an eye witness to AN-52 aircraft, which crashed near Delhi airport. Draft a report of the crash in about 150 words.*

New Delhi, 21st Sept., 200.... (By a staff reporter)

An Indian Air Force transport aircraft crashed near the upcoming Dwarka township in South-West Delhi on 21st Sept., killing 22 persons including all the 17 IAF officials and the pilot on board and injuring seven. The UK built AN-52 first hit electric wires strung across two poles, with one of its wheels breaking off after hitting a concrete structure. It burst into flames after hitting a ten-feet high boundary wall and finally crashed into an under construction DDA water tank. As per one eye witness the pilot sayed the residential area by slightly changing the direction of the plane, otherwise a huge loss to the lives and the property could have taken place. The accident took place at about 7:20 a.m. Besides the IAF Men, a 60 year old mason, two children of another mason and two passers-by were also killed due to the burning fuselage of the aircraft. The aircraft's fuselage lay embedded in the water-tank with parts of its engine, wings, scattered on top of the structure. Broken wings of metal and the debris of the aircraft were spread over an area of around 500 metres around large stretches of vacant land. IAF sources said a court of inquiry has been constituted. The Government of Delhi has also ordered a judicial enquiry into the cause of accident.

(18) *You are working for The Times of India as a reporter. Last week, you attended a seminar on 'Pleasures of Eye-Donation', organised by the Medical Association of your district. Write a report of this seminar in not more than 120 words for publication in the Newspaper.*

New Delhi, April 29, 200...: (By a staff reporter of The Times of India)

Last week, a seminar on 'Pleasures of Eye Donation' was organised by the Medical Association of out district at the Andrew's Community Centre on 27th April. A large number of residents attended the seminar. The President of the Association Mr J.H. Jha, stressed the need for protection of our eyes and emphasised the pleasures of Eye donation, "*We can provide eyes to the blind and the others who need eyes.*" People can mention in their will that their eyes can be taken for the benefit of others after their death. It will be a great source of pleasure for the departing soul. They will provide light to the needy people. Much of our generation fail to get proper light and become prematurely blind. It is our duty to help them. Stressing the need of the eye donation the Chief guest of the function Sh. Vijay Dutta said, "*By donating eyes we can give support and light to others.*" It is said, "*Eyes are the greatest Blessings on Earth. We can help others even after our death.*" More than a thousand rose to register their names for eye donation after their death. Such functions can solve the problems of blinds to a great extent.

(19) *You are a reporter of the Hindustan Times. One day you happened to attend a seminar on 'Case for Reducing the Retirement Age in the Public Sector from 60 to 55', organised by the 'Society of Public Sector Employees'. Write a report on this seminar in not more than 100 words for publication in the Newspaper.*

New Delhi, 25th June, 200... (From our staff reporter)

A very exhilarating seminar on reducing the retirement age in Public Sector from 60 to 55 was organised at Sapru House yesterday by the 'Society of Public Sector Employees'. Eminent jurists and legal experts participated in the seminar and spoke vehemently against the reduction of the retirement age and they compared the employees with the politicians who have no age limit for their retirement. They advocated that they can work with more zeal and zest,with more responsibility and sincerity than the modern youth and the politicians. On the other side government advocated that by reducing the retirement age, they will be opening avenues for unemployed youths. The employment among the youth rather posed a greater threatening to the nation. They can never be compared with politicians as after retirement they can too join politics. It was also pleaded that this will be less costly for the exchequer to recruit new men in the Public Sector. After a heating debate, a consensus was arrived at to fix the retirement age in Public Sector to 58. The recommendations will be sent to the Government for being looked into. The society also asserts that if the Government does not agree to the consensus arrived at, the association of the public sector employees can go to the court and resort to the strikes and other direct actions in the matter.

(20) ***On International Women's Day, different women activists organised functions, seminars etc, in the capital. Being a reporter from the Indian Express News Service you attended one of the programmes. Draft a report in about 150 words.***

New Delhi, 9th March, 200... (By a staff reporter, The Indian Express)

From workshops to burning of effigies of politicians and seminars to puppet shows, women activists organised a wide range of programmes in the capital to mark 'International Women's Day' on Monday. The 'Joint Action Forum for Women' organised a seminar on 'Necessity of Women's Empowerment for the Development of the Nation', in which Union Human Resource Development Minister was the Chief Guest. Several other political leaders also graced the occasion with their presence. Most of the speakers asserted the need of passing the bill on providing Women's reservation in Parliament and State Assemblies. The minister informed that the bill on reservation had already been introduced in this budget session of Parliament and the government is trying to get the bill passed with support of the opposition. He also informed that some political parties are opposing the bill just for the sake of opposition. The member activists exemplify the role of women in the freedom struggle and in the development of the nation. The president of the forum Mrs Kidwai told that by giving 33% reservation for women, no political party is doing any favour to the women. Women constitute 50% of the total population. A demand for free education for women upto graduation, making judiciary more quick in disposing the cases of crimes against the women was also made. Though participants expressed jubilation at the progress women have made in several fields, but the crude statistics of crime against women and low literacy among women bothered many.

Many politicians stressed the need that the women and the girls should avoid invitational and inciting fashions which resulted in the increase in the crimes against the women and girls. The necessity of moral and ethical values was also emphasised in the education of the young generation. The seminar was a grand success.

(21) ***Pollution has become a problem for all. Write an article on Environmental Pollution in Metropolitan cities. Suppose you are a correspondent of a local newspaper.***

Environmental Pollution in Big Cities

New Delhi, 15th Feb., 200.... (By a correspondent)

Preservation of environment is one of the most alarming problems of today. Most of the big cities are suffering from the problem of conservation and preservation of purity of environment. Our atmosphere is being polluted by various factors like smoke, noise, dirt, dust, chemicals and gases. Even water has become polluted. We need a safer and healthy environment for our survival and for the survival of the young generation. Water, air and food are the basic necessities of life that all are becoming polluted day-by-day. The rapid industrialisation has made everything polluted, no care has been placed for the safe drainage of the chemical wastes, safe exhaling of the gases. The nature has provided a very balanced and correct system for our survival. For example, we inhale oxygen and exhale carbon-di-oxide. This carbon gas is absorbed by plants. Still we need care to preserve our environment. The recent decisions and directions of the Supreme Court that the vehicles run by the CNG should replace the vehicles run by the petrol and diesels is very important in keeping the air pure and inhalable in big cities. We as a member of the civic society should also not spoil it by spreading unhygienic items, eg, garbage and rubbish that produce foul smell. We can save our atmosphere by applying and paying careful attention for their proper disposal. It will help us in stopping the spread of dangerous diseases and pollution of the atmosphere. So it is a sacred duty of all to preserve our environment for our survival. We should also adopt the motto. " Keep clean and Remain clean."

(22) *English is a link language and opens a gateway to knowledge. Write a case on 'Importance of English in Education'. Write your description in about 100 words.*

Importance of English in Education

Meerut, 26th Jan., 200.... (From special correspondent)

India became free on 15 August, 1947. The Britishers ruled over India, they left their imprint on us. Since then English forms an important part of our educational system. All the technical, medical and professional courses are taught in English. The literature of these subjects are available in great abundance written in English. Without English our education seems to remain incomplete. It has opened a way to see the world in its entirety. It has become a universal language. In every country, we find people speaking, talking and understanding English. In reality, English has become a link language and we cannot do without it. It paves our way to understand the culture, customs and other activities of different nations. In this period of globalization it is but necessary to learn writing and speaking good and correct English.

(23) *'Drug Addiction' has become a great menace against the society. Write an article for your college magazine on Drug Addiction in about 100 words.*

Drug Addiction

Mumbai, 15th March, 200.... (By Kapil Nagar)

The word 'addiction' implies to be habitual to something and it is generally applicable in bad sense. Of course, addiction to anything is bad but drug addiction is the worst of all. The modern scientific research has proved the harmful effects of regular use of a particular drug. It not only damages our digestive system but also spoils our nervous system. In reality it is a breeder and an invitation to death. It is a slow poison, degrades one to the lowest level. All our energy and vitality is sucked like a bacteria sucks our blood. The user becomes hollow just like a coconut. The addict person loses his moral values and to get the drug he can commit any crime like theft, dacoity, even the murder. He cannot do anything properly, can't work, can't rest, can't play, even can't sleep without taking drugs. Addiction to smoking, wine, smack, hashish and heroine distort the mental ability, agility, confidence, propriety of any decision of a drug addict. We should avoid use of such narcotics.

(24) *As the correspondent of a local daily, write a report for the paper on need of vocational education in India.*

Vocational Education

Hisar, 30th April, 200.... (From Local Correspondent)

The Britishers provided us a very outdated and defective system of education. That system produces clerks and white collar job-seekers. India is facing a great problem of educated unemployment because of this educational system. After Independence many changes have taken place in our educational system. The Kothari and Chattopadhaya Commissions have strongly recommended for the vocationalisation of education. Many vocational schools or colleges find place in our society. Vocational Education helps us in controlling unemployment. Above all, vocational education gives us a sense of dignity of labour. We can stand on our foot without feeling any work ignoble. It is a high time that Government and our society should come forward to open more and more such vocational institutions so that the youth do not feel frustrated after completion of their studies and get employment or can start their own ventures.

(25) ***You are a correspondent of a local daily, you find very unhealthy craze among the students for the foreign goods. Write an article for a newspaper in about 100 words.***

Craze for Foreign Goods

Chandigarh, 12th May, 200.... (From Local Correspondent)

A general tendency is now-a-days seen among the students that they are attracted by foreign goods, whether good or bad, but whatever they purchase should be originated from a foreign country. This idea never enters into our brains that Indian goods are not in any way inferior. We have advanced to such an extent that many items are being exported by us. Our goods are of the superb quality. Still we have a sensation to buy a foreign make. We are admired in construction, utility and acclaim its worth. In some of the cases, even our manufactured items are labelled as made in foreign, eg, Japan, England and Germany etc. We never try to examine its worth, utility and consumption. Gone are the days when even from the smallest needle to the highest implement was imported from England or USA. This led to a habit of liking for the foreign goods. It is also a worth mentioning fact that foreigners do not like to purchase foreign goods. They believe in purchasing their own national goods. Let us come forward and initiate steps to buy own *Swadeshi* goods. Consuming goods made in our own country saves very precious foreign exchange.

Unit 50

Comprehension

"Comprehensions judge your capability and ability of understanding the passage, your power of analysing the problem in proper perspective and your ability of presenting your answers systematically".

Verbal comprehension measures your ability to read and understand the written passage. Through the comprehension exercise you are asked to answer questions about the passage.

In answering the questions based on the reading passage, it is important that you answer the questions only according to the information given in the passage. If you have information from your own experience and knowledge, you should not use it to answer a question of this type. Even if you think that there is a mistake in the reading passage, you must still answer the question on the basis of the information given in the reading passage.

There are certain techniques that will help you do well on reading comprehension questions.

Here is a summary of the most important techniques

(a) Use your pencil : To begin with, use your pencil as a pointer. Using the pencil to guide your eye along a line of text, helps you to focus on the details in the reading; it holds your attention to the precise words in the passage. In a long test, attention may weaken. Fatigue may blunt your attention to details. But using your pencil as a pointer will help to preserve your attention to details.

(b) Another benefit of using the pencil as a pointer is that it will probably speed up your reading. The steady flow of the pencil across the page with each line of text draws the eye along at a steady pace. Do not go faster than you can grasp the text, but do try to keep your reading going at a steady pace set by the pencil.

(c) Circle key words and phrases : Remember, you are not reading for just a vague general understanding of the passage. You usually have to read for detailed understanding. There will be individual words which are important for grasping a point exactly. Circling key words or phrases will enable you to zero in on precise points needed to answer a question.

(d) Keep forging ahead : Do not get bogged down if there is a word or sentence you do not understand. You may get the main idea without knowing the individual word or sentence. Sometimes you can sense the meaning of the word from the context. Sometimes the word or sentence may not be the basis of any question. If there is some idea you need to answer a question but do not understand, read it one more time. If you still do not understand it, move on. You can come back to this question later if you have more time at the end of the test.

(e) Another good reading comprehension strategy is to read the questions before starting the passage. This does not mean to read the answer choices at this time. By reading the questions, you will have an idea of what information you will need after reading the passage. This may alert you to certain details, ideas and specific areas in the paragraph where the questions are being drawn from.

Right approach to answer the questions

1. Questions are to be answered on the basis of the information provided in the passage, and you are not expected to rely on outside knowledge of a particular topic. Your own views or opinions may sometimes conflict with the views expressed or the information provided in the passage. Be sure that you work within the context of the passage. You should not expect to agree with everything you encounter in reading passages.
2. You should analyse each passage carefully before answering the accompanying questions. As with any kind of close and thoughtful reading, look for clues that will help you understand less explicit aspects of the passage. Try to separate main ideas from supporting ideas or evidence.
3. Note transitions from one idea to the next, and examine the relationships among the different ideas or parts of the passage. For example, are they contrasting? Are they complementary? Consider the points the author makes, the conclusions drawn, and how and why those points are made or conclusions are drawn.
4. Read each question carefully and be certain that you understand exactly what is being asked.
5. Always read all the answer choices before selecting the best answer.
6. The best answer is the one that most accurately and completely answers the questions being posed. Be careful not to pick an answer choice simply because it is a true statement. Be careful also not to be misled by answer choices that are only partially true or only partially satisfy the problem posed in the question.

» Exercises

Directions : *Each of the five passages given below is followed by a set of questions choose, the best answer to each question.* **(CAT)**

Passage 1

The painter is now free to paint anything he chooses. There are scarcely any forbidden subjects, and today everybody is prepared to admit that a painting of some fruit can be as important as painting of a hero. The impressionists did as much as anybody to win this previously unheard of freedom for the artist. Yet, by the next generation, painters began to abandon the subject altogether, and began to paint abstract pictures. Today the majority of pictures painted are abstract.

Is there a connection between these two developments? Has art gone abstract because the artist is embarrassed by his freedom. Is it that, because he is free to paint anything, he doesn't know what to paint? Apologists for abstract art often talk of it as the art of maximum freedom . But could this be the freedom of the desert island? It would take too long to answer these questions properly. I believe there is a connection. Many things have encouraged the development of abstract art. Among them has been the artists' wish to avoid the difficulties of finding subjects when all subjects are equally possible.

I raise the matter now because I want to draw attention to the fact that the painter's choice of a subject is a far more complicated question than it would at first seem. A subject does not start with what is put in front of the easel or with something which the painter happens to remember. A subject starts with the painter deciding he would like to paint such-and-such because for some reason or other he finds it meaningful. A subject begins when the artist selects something for special mention. (What makes it special or meaningful may seem to the artist to be purely visual, its colours or its form.) When the subject has been selected, the function of the painting itself is to communicate and justify the significance of that selection.

It is often said today that subject matter is unimportant. But this is only a reaction against the excessively literary and moralistic interpretation of subject matter in the nineteenth century. In truth the subject is literally the beginning and end of a painting. The painting begins with a selection (I will paint this and not everything else in the world); it is finished when that selection is justified (now you can see all that I saw and felt in this and how it is more than merely itself).

Thus, for a painting to succeed it is essential that the painter and his public agree about what is significant. The subject may have a personal meaning for the painter or individual spectator, but there must also be the possibility of their agreement on its general meaning. It is at this point that the culture of the society and period in question precedes the artist and his art. Renaissance art would have meant nothing to the Aztecs and vice versa. If, to some extent, a few intellectuals can appreciate them both today it is because their culture is a historical one: its inspiration is history and therefore it can include within itself, in principle if not in every particular, all known development to date.

When a culture is secure and certain of its values, it presents its artists with subjects. The general agreement about what is significant is so well established that the significance of particular subject accrues and becomes traditional. This is true, for instance of reeds and water in China, of the nude body in Renaissance, of the animal in Africa. Furthermore, in such cultures the artist is unlikely to be a free agent he will be employed, for the sake of particular subjects and problems, as we have just described it will not occur to him.

When a culture is in a state of disintegration or transition the freedom of the artist increases, but the question of subject matter becomes problematic for him as to choose for society. This was the basic of all the increasing crises in European art during the nineteenth century. It is often forgotten how many of the art scandals of the time were provoked by the choice of subject (Gericault, Courbet, Daumier, Degas, Lautrec, Van Gogh, etc).

By the end of the nineteenth century, there were roughly speaking two ways in which the painter could meet this challenge of deciding what to paint and so choosing for society. Either the identified himself with the people and so allowed their lives to dictate his subjects to him; or he had to find his subjects within himself as painter. By people I mean everybody except the bourgeoisie. Many painter did, of course, work for the bourgeoisie according to their copy-book of approved subjects, but all of them filling the Salon and the Royal Academy year after year and now forgotten, buried the hypocrisy of those they served so sincerely.

1. In the sentence, "I believe there is a connection" (second paragraph), what two developments is the author referring to ?
(a) Painters using dying hero and using a fruit as a subject of painting
(b) Growing success of painters and an increase in abstract forms
(c) Artists gaining freedom to choose subjects and abandoning subjects altogether
(d) Rise of impressionists and an increase in abstract forms

2. When a culture is insecure, the painter chooses his subject on the basis of
(a) the prevalent style in the society of his time
(b) its meaningfulness to the painter
(c) what is put in front of the easel
(d) past experience and memory of the painter

3. In the context of the passage, which of the following statements would not be true?
(a) Painters decided subjects based on what they remembered from their own lives
(b) Painters of reeds and water in China faced no serious problem of choosing a subject
(c) The choice of subject was a source of scandals in nineteenth century European art
(d) Agreement on the general meaning of a painting is influenced by culture and historical context

4. Which of the following views is taken by the author?
(a) The more insecure a culture, the greater the freedom of the artist
(b) The more secure a culture, the greater the freedom of the artist
(c) The more secure a culture, more difficult the choice of subject
(d) The more insecure a culture, the less significant the choice of the subject

5. Which of the following is NOT necessarily among the attributes needed for a painter to succeed?
(a) The painter and his public agree on what is significant
(b) The painting is able to communicate and justify the significance of its subjects selection
(c) The subject has a personal meaning for the painter
(d) The painting of subjects is inspired by historical developments

Answers

1. (c) **2.** (b) **3.** (a) **4.** (a) **5.** (d)

Passage 2

Recently I spent several hours sitting under a tree in my garden with the social anthropologist William Ury, a Harvard University professor who specialises in the art of negotiation and wrote the best-selling book, Getting to Yes. He captivated me with his theory that tribalism protects people from their fear of rapid change. He explained that the pillars of tribalism that humans rely on for security would always counter any significant cultural or social change. In this way, he said, change is never allowed to happen too fast. Technology, for example, is a pillar of society. Ury believes that every time technology moves in a new or radical direction another pillar such as religion or nationalism will grow stronger-in effect, the traditional and familiar will assume greater importance to compensate for the new and untested. In this manner, human tribes avoid rapid change that leaves people insecure and frightened.

But we have all heard that nothing is as permanent as change. Nothing is guaranteed. Pithy expressions, to be sure, but no more than cliches. As Ury says, "people don't live that way from day-to-day. On the contrary, they actively seek certainty and stability. They want to know they will be safe."

Even so we scare ourselves constantly with the idea of change. An IBM CEO once said "We only restructure for a good reason, and if we haven't restructured in a while, that's a good reason. We are scared that competitors' technology and the consumer will put us out of business so we have to change all the time just to stay alive. But if we asked our fathers and grandfathers, would they have said that they lived in a period of little change? Structure may not have changed much. It may just be the speed with which we do things."

Change is over-rated, anyway, consider the automobile. It's an especially valuable example, because the auto industry has spent tens of billions of dollars on research and product development in the last 100 years. Henry Ford's first car had a metal chassis with an internal combustion, gasoline-powered engine, four wheels with rubber tyres, a foot operated clutch assembly and brake system, a steering wheel, and four seats, and it could safely do 18 miles per hour. A hundred years and tens of thousands of research hours later we drive cars with a metal chassis with an internal combustion gasoline-powered engine, four wheels with rubber tyres, a foot operated clutch assembly and brake system, a steering wheel, four seats and the average speed in London in 2001 was 17.5 miles per hour!

That's not a hell of a lot of return for the money. Ford evidently doesn't have much to teach us about change. The fact that they're still manufacturing cars is not proof that Ford Motor Co. is a sound organisation, just proof that it takes very large companies to make cars in great quantities—making for an almost impregnable entry barrier.

Fifty years after the development of the jet engine, planes are also little changed. They've grown bigger, wider and can carry more people. But those are incremental, largely cosmetic changes.

Taken together, this lack of real change has come to mean that in travel—whether driving or flying—time and technology have not combined to make things much better. The safety and design have, of course, accompanied the times and the new volume of cars and flights, but nothing of any significance has changed in the basic assumptions of the final product.

At the same time, moving around in cars or aeroplanes becomes less and less efficient all the time. Not only has there been no great change, but also both forms of transport have deteriorated as more people clamour to use them. The same is true for telephones, which took over hundred years to become mobile, or photographic film which also required an entire century to change.

The only explanation for this is anthropological, once established in calcified organisations humans do two things: sabotage changes that might render people dispensable and ensure industry-wide emulation. In the 1960s, German auto companies developed plans to scrap the entire combustion engine for an electrical design. (The same existed in the 1970s in Japan, and in the 1980s in France) So for 40 years we might have been free of the wasteful and ludicrous dependence on fossil fuels. Why didn't it go anywhere? Because auto executives understood pistons and carburettors, and would be loath to cannibalise their expertise, along with most of their factories.

1. Which of the following views does the author fully support in the passage?
   (a) Nothing is as permanent as change
   (b) Change is always rapid
   (c) More money spent on innovation leads to more rapid change
   (d) Over decades structural change has been incremental

2. According to the passage, which of the following statements is true?
   (a) Executives of automobile companies are inefficient and ludicrous
   (b) The speed at which an automobile is driven in a city has not changed much in a century
   (c) Anthropological factors have fostered innovation in automobiles by promoting use of new technologies
   (d) Further innovation in jet engines has been more than incremental

3. Which of the following best describes one of the main ideas discussed in the passage?
   (a) Rapid change is usually welcomed in society
   (b) Industry is not as innovative as it is made out to be
   (c) We should have less change than what we have now
   (d) Competition spurs companies into radical innovation

4. According to the passage, the reason why we continued to be dependent on fossil fuels is that
   (a) auto executives did not wish to change
   (b) no alternative fuels were discovered
   (c) change in technology was not easily possible
   (d) German, Japanese and French companies could not come up with new technologies

Answers

1. (d) **2.** (d) **3.** (b) **4.** (a)

Passage 3

Fifty feet away three male lions lay by the road. They didn't appear to have a hair on their heads. Nothing the colour of their noses (leonine noses darken as they age, from pink to black), Craig estimated that they were six years old-young adults. "This is wonderful!" he said, after staring at them for several moments. "This is what we came to see. They really are maneless." Craig, a professor at the University of Minnesota, is arguably the leading expert on the majestic Serengeti lion, whose head is mantled in long, thick hair. He and Peyton West, a doctoral student who has been working with him in Tanzania, had never seen the Tsavo lions that live some 200 miles east of the Serengeti. The scientists had partly suspected that the maneless males were adolescents mistaken for adults by amateur observe. Now they knew better.

The Tsavo research expedition was mostly Peyton's show. She had spent several years in Tanzania compiling the data she needed to answer a question that ought to have been answered long ago: why do lions have manes ? It's the only cat, wild or domestic, that displays such ornamentation. In Tsavo she was attacking the riddle from the opposite angle. Why do its lions not have manes? (Some "maneless" lions in Tsavo East do have partial manes but they rarely attain the real glory of the Serengeti lions'.)

Does environmental adaptation account for the trait? Are the lions of Tsavo, as some people believe, a distinct subspecies of their Serengeti cousins?

The Serengeti lions have been under continuous observation for more than 35 years, beginning with George Schaller's pioneering work in the 1960s. But the lions in Tsavo, Kenya's oldest and largest protected ecosystem have hardly been studied. Consequently legends have grown up around them. Not only do they took different, according to the myths, they behave differently, displaying greater cunning and aggressiveness. "Remember too," Kenya: The Rough Guide warns, "Tsavo's lions have a reputation of ferocity." Their fearsome image became well-known in 1898, when to males stalled construction of what is now Kenya Railways by allegedly killing and eating 135 Indian and African labourers. A British Army officer incharge of building a railroad bridge over the Tsavo River, Lt. Col. J.H. Peterson, spent nine months pursuing the pair before he brought them to bay and killed them. Stuffed and mounted, they now glare at visitors to the Field Museum in Chicago. Petterson's account of the leonine reign of terror, the Man-Eaters of Tsavo, was an international best-seller when published in 1907. Still in print the book has made Tsavo's lions notorious. That annoys some scientists.

"People don't want to give up on mythology. "Dennis King told me one day. The zoologist has been working in Tsavo off and on for four years. "I am so sick of this man-eater business. Petterson made a helluva lot of money off that story, but Tsavo's lions are no more likely to turn man-eater than lions from elsewhere."

But tales of their savagery and wiliness don't all come from sensationalist authors looking to make a buck. Tsavo lions are generally larger than lions elsewhere, enabling them to take down the predominant prey animal in Tsavo, the Cape buffalo one of the strongest, most aggressive animals of Earth. The buffalo don't give up easily: They often kill or severely injure an attacking lion, and a wounded lion might be more likely to turn to cattle and humans for food.

And other prey is less abundant in Tsavo than in other traditional lion haunts. A hungry lion is more likely to attack humans. Safari guides and Kenya Wildlife Service rangers tell of lions attacking Land Rovers, raiding camps, stalking tourists. Tsavo is a tough neighbourhood, they say, and it breeds tougher lions.

But are they really tougher ? And if so, is there any connection between their manelessness and their ferocity ? An intriguing hypothesis was advanced two years ago by Gnosake and Peterhans. Tsavo lions may be similar to the unmaned cave lions of the Pleistocene. The Serengeti variety is among the most evolved of the species—the latest model, so to speak—while certain morphological differences in Tsavo lions (bigger bodies, smaller skulls, and may be even lack of a mane) suggest that they are closer to primitive ancestor of all lions. Craig and Peyton had serious doubts about this idea, but admitted that Tsavo lions pose a mystery to science.

1. The sentence which concludes the first paragraph, "Now they knew better," implies that
(a) the two scientists were struck by wonder on seeing maneless lions for the first time
(b) though Craig was an expert on the Serengeti lion, now he also new about the Tsavo lions
(c) earlier, Craig and West thought that amateur observers had been mistaken
(d) Craig was now able to confirm that darkening of the noses as lions aged applied to Tsavo lions as well

2. The book 'Man-Eaters of Tsavo' annoys some scientists because
(a) it revealed that Tsavo lions are ferocious
(b) Petterson made a helluva lot of money from the book by sensationalism
(c) it perpetuated the bad name Tsavo lions had
(d) it narrated how to male Tsavo lion were killed

3. Which of the following, if true, would weaken the hypothesis advanced by Gnosake and Peterhans most?
(a) Craig and Peyton develop even more serious doubts about the idea that Tsavo lions are primitive
(b) The maneless Tsavo East lions are shown to be closer to the cavelions
(c) Pleistocene cave lions are shown to be far less violent than believed

(d) The morphological variations in body and skull size between the cave and Tsavo lions are found to be insignificant

4. According to the passage, which of the following has NOT contributed to the popular image of Tsavo lions as savage creatures?
(a) Tsavo lions have been observed to bring down one of the strongest and most aggressive animals—the Cape buffalo
(b) In contrast to the situation in traditional lion haunts, scarcity of non-buffalo prey in the Tsavo makes the Tsavo lions more aggressive
(c) The Tsavo lion is considered to be less, evolved than the Serengeti variety
(d) Tsavo lions have been observed to attack vehicles as well as humans

Answers

1. (c) **2.** (c) **3.** (c) **4.** (c)

Passage 4

Throughout human history the leading causes of death have been infection and trauma. Modern medicine has scored significant victories against both, and the major causes of ill health and death are now the chronic degenerative diseases, such as coronary artery disease, arthritis, osteoporosis, Alzheimer's, muscular degeneration, cataract and cancer. These have a long latency period before symptoms appear and a diagnosis is made. It follows that the majority of apparently healthy people are pre-ill.

But are these conditions inevitably degenerative? A truly preventive medicine that focused on the pre-ill, analysing the metabolic errors which lead to clinical illness, might be able to correct them before the first symptom. Genetic risk factors are known for all the chronic degenerative diseases, and are important to the individuals who possess them. At the population level, however, migration studies confirm that these illness are linked for the most part to lifestyle factors—exercise, smoking and nutrition. Nutrition is the easiest of these to change, and the most versatile tool for affecting the metabolic changes needed to tilt the balance away from disease.

Many national surveys reveal that malnutrition is common in developed countries. This is not the calorie and/or micronutrient deficiency associated with developing nations (Type A malnutrition): but multiple micronutrient depletion, usually combined with calorific balance or excess (Type B malnutrition). The incidence and severity of Type B malnutrition will be shown to be worse if never micronutrient groups such as the essential fatty acids, xanthophylls and flavonoids are included in the surveys. Commonly ingested levels of these micronutrients seem to be far too low in many developed countries.

There is now considerable evidence that Type B malnutrition is a major cause of chronic degenerative diseases. If this is the case, then it is logical to treat such diseases not with drugs but with multiple micronutrient repletion, or pharmaco-nutrition'. This can take the form of pills and capsules—'nutraceuticals', or food formats known as functional foods'. This approach has been neglected hitherto because it is relatively unprofitable for drug companies—the products are hard to patent—and it is a strategy which does not sit easily with modern medical interventionism. Over the last 100 years, the drug industry has invested huge sums in developing a range of subtle and powerful drugs to treat the many diseases we are subject to. Medical training is couched in pharmaceutical terms and this approach has provided us with an exceptional range of therapeutic tools in the treatment of disease and in acute medical emergencies. However, the pharmaceutical model has also created an unhealthy dependency culture, in which relatively few of us accept responsibility for maintaining our own health. Instead, we have handed over this responsibility to health professionals who know very little about health maintenance or disease prevention.

One problem for supporters of this argument is lack of the right kind of hard evidence. We have a wealth of epidemiological data linking dietary factors to health profiles/disease risks, and a great deal of information on mechanism: how food factors interact with our biochemistry. But almost all intervention studies with micronutrients, with the notable exception of the omega 3 fatty acids, have so far produced conflicting or negative results. In other words, our science appears to have no predictive value. Does this invalidate the science? Or are we simply asking the wrong questions?

Based on pharmaceutical thinking, most intervention studies have attempted to measure the impact of a single micronutrient on the incidence of disease. The classical approach says that if you give a compound formula to test subjects and obtain positive results, you cannot know which ingredient is exerting the benefit, so you must test each ingredient individually. But in the field of nutrition, this does not work. Each intervention on its own will hardly make enough difference to be measured. The best therapeutic response must, therefore, combine micronutrients to normalise our internal physiology. So do we need to analyse each individual's nutritional status and then tailor a formula specifically for him or her? While we do not have the resources to analyse millions of individual cases, there is no need to do so. The vast majority of people are consuming suboptimal amounts of most micronutrients, and most of the micronutrients concerned are very safe. Accordingly, a comprehensive and universal program of micronutrient support is probably the most cost-effective and safest way of improving the general health of the nation.

1. Tailoring micronutrient-based treatment plans to suit individual deficiency profiles is not necessary because
   (a) it is very likely to give inconsistent or negative results
   (b) it is a classic pharmaceutical approach not suited to micronutrients
   (c) most people are consuming suboptimal amounts of safe-to-consume micronutrients
   (d) it is not cost effective to do so
2. The author recommends micronutrient-repletion for large-scale treatment of chronic degenerative diseases because
   (a) it is relatively easy to manage
   (b) micronutrient deficiency is the cause of these diseases
   (c) it can overcome genetic risk factors
   (d) it can compensate for other lifestyle factors
3. Why are a large number of apparently healthy people deemed pre-ill?
   (a) They may have chronic degenerative diseases
   (b) They do not know their own genetic risk factors which predispose them to diseases
   (c) They suffer from Type-B malnutrition
   (d) There is a lengthy latency period associated with chronically degenerative diseases
4. Type-B malnutrition is a serious concern in developed countries because
   (a) developing countries mainly suffer from Type-A malnutrition
   (b) it is a major contributor to illness and death
   (c) pharmaceutical companies are not producing drugs to treat this condition
   (d) national surveys on malnutrition do not include newer micronutrient groups

Answers

1. (c) **2.** (b) **3.** (d) **4.** (b)

Passage 5

The viability of the multinational corporate system depends upon the degree to which people will tolerate the unevenness it creates. It is well to remember that the 'New Imperialism' which began after 1870 in a spirit of Capitalism Triumphant, soon became seriously troubled and after 1914 was characterised by war, depression, breakdown of the international economic system and war again rather than Free Trade, Pax Britannica and Material Improvement. A major reason was Britain's inability to cope with the by-products of its own rapid accumulation of capital; ie, a class-conscious labour force at home; a middle class in the hinterland; and rival centres of capital on the Continent and in America. Britain's policy tended to be atavistic and defensive rather than progressive—more concerned with warding off new threats than creating new areas of expansion. Ironically, Edwardian England revived the paraphernalia of the landed aristocracy it had just destroyed. Instead of embarking on a 'big push' to develop the vast hinterland of the Empire, colonial administrators often adopted policies to arrest the development of either a native capitalist class or a native proletariat which could overthrow them.

As time went on, the centre had to devote an increasing share of government activity to military and other unproductive expenditures; they had to rely on alliances with an inefficient class of landlords, officials and soldiers in the hinterland to maintain stability at the cost of development. A great part of the surplus extracted from the population was thus wasted locally.

The new Mercantilism (as the Multinational Corporate System of special alliances and privileges, aid and tariff concessions is sometimes called) faces similar problems of internal and external division. The centre is troubled: excluded groups revolt and even some of the affluent are dissatisfied with the roles. Nationalistic rivalry between major capitalist countries remains an important divisive factor. Finally, there is the threat presented by the middle classes and the excluded groups of the underdeveloped countries. The national middle classes in the underdeveloped countries came to power when the centre weakened but could not, through their policy of import substitution manufacturing, establish a viable basis for sustained growth. They now face a foreign exchange crisis and an unemployment (or population) crisis—the first indicating their inability to function in the international economy and the second indicating their alienation from the people they are supposed to lead. In the immediate future, these national middle classes will gain a new lease of life as they take advantage of the spaces created by the rivalry between America and non-American-oligopolists striving to establish global market positions.

The native capitalists will again become the champions of national independence as they bargain with multinational corporations. But the conflict at this level is more apparent than real, for in the end the fervent nationalism of the middle class asks only for promotion within the corporate structure and not for a break with that structure. In the last analysis their power derives from the metropolis and they cannot easily afford to challenge the international system. They do not command the loyalty of their own population and cannot really compete with the large, powerful, aggregate capitals from the centre. They are prisoners of the taste patterns and consumption standards set at the centre.

The main threat comes from the excluded groups. It is not unusual in underdeveloped countries for the top 5 percent to obtain between 30 and 40 percent of the total national income, and for the top one-third to obtain anywhere from 60 to 70 percent. At most one-third of the population can be said to benefit in some sense from the dualistic growth that characterises development in the hinterland. The remaining two-thirds, who together get only one-third of the income, are outsiders, not because they do not contribute to the economy, but because they do not share in the benefits. They provide a source of cheap labour which helps keep exports to the developed world at a low price and which has financed the urban-biased growth of recent years. In fact, it is difficult to see how the system in most underdeveloped countries could survive without cheap labour since removing it (eg, diverting it to public works projects as is done in socialist countries) would raise consumption costs to capitalists and professional elites.

1. According to the author, the British policy during the 'New Imperialism' period tended to be defensive because
   (a) it was unable to deal with the fallouts of a sharp increase in capital
   (b) its cumulative capital had undesirable side-effects
   (c) its policies favoured developing the vast hinterland
   (d) it prevented the growth of a set-up which could have been capitalistic in nature
2. In the sentence "They are prisoners of the taste patterns and consumption standards set at the centre." (fourth paragraph), what is the meaning of 'centre'?
   (a) National government
   (b) Native capitalists
   (c) New capitalists
   (d) None of these
3. The author is in a position to draw parallels between New Imperialism and New Mercantilism because
   (a) both originated in the developed Western capitalist countries
   (b) New Mercantilism was a logical sequel to New Imperialism

(c) they create the same set of outputs—a labour force, middle classes and rival centres of capital
(d) both have comparable uneven and divisive effects

4. Under New Mercantilism, the fervent nationalism of the native middle classes does not create conflict with the multinational corporations because they (the middle classes)
(a) negotiate with the multinational corporations
(b) are dependent on the international system for their continued prosperity
(c) are not in a position to challenge the status quo
(d) do not enjoy popular support

Answers

1. (a) **2.** (b) (3) (d) **4.** (d)

Passage 6

Directions (Q. 1 to 15) : *Read the following passage carefully and answer the questions given below. It certain words are printed in bold to help you to locate them while answering some of the questions.*

(Indian Bank PO)

Can India make it to a leadership position in the new millennium or will it retain the 'fast train-going-slow' image of the last 50 odd years ? Most people believe that the potential for our country to succeed is huge. They are also disappointed at the inability to convert the natural advantages we possess into tangible benefits. The recent success of our infotech industry globally has reinforced the belief that when we put our mind to it we can succeed. Now, the expectation is that this success will be replicated in other areas.

There is no doubt that India's further will be driven by the intellectual capital of its people. Even though many of the billion Indian people are and will continue for the foreseeable further to live in a third-world setting, there are many Indians with the skills, ability and aspiration to prosper and flourish in a first-world environment. It is, therefore, likely that India will, at the same time, belong to both the first and the third worlds.

That first-world environment will be powered increasingly by knowledge workers and brainware India clearly has the numbers. It needs to invest in training and skill-building and also encourage entrepreneurship and risk-taking.

I have no magic recipe to convert India's people power into a competitive advantage on global basis. Also, I am nowhere near qualified to address macro issues like universal education and school curricula. Therefore, I have to shrink the issue into a familiar framework of 'growing our people.'

It is imperative that Indian business pay more than lip service to the empowerment of their employees. We have to break the 'do-as-you are told' mentality which inhibits creativity and promotes the culture of servitude long after our 'foreign masters'are gone. Together with empowerment, there has to be a culture of personal accountability so that everyone realises the necessity of valuing commitment.

In all areas of activity, seniority and hierarchies (if any) must be based purely on merit. **Seniority, like respect, must be earned** and not 'termed,' ie, based on the length of service.

Future organisations will be based on communities and interaction between individuals and teams both within and outside the organisation. The work environment both with respect to physical space and culture, must be barrierless/boundryless, allowing the **impromptu** and regular interaction across workgroups/teams.

Organisations must accept that empowerment and personal accountability should go hand in hand with a degree of tolerance for mistakes and failures. Mistakes and failures are good learning opportunities for our people and should be regarded as such unless repeated. Tolerance would also provide a safety net for those prepared to take risks, a quality rarely seen among Indian executives today but crucial to succeed in the new economy.

Organisations must be as transparent as possible with their employees. Both good and bad news must be shared. Often organisations and their leadership wrongly believe that the employees aren't interested in certain information or, more arrogantly, decide that information is best withheld as it is beyond the comprehension of their employees.

Knowledge sharing must be pushed at all levels through a carrot-and-stick approach. Those who continuously hoard knowledge must be weeded out. Everyone must come to work thinking that they will learn and add to their skills.

Performance management must be institutionalised to give everyone a clear understanding of organisational goals, team goals, the individual's role or goals within a team, rewards which follow from meeting goals, and career opportunities in the organisation.

Encourage a sense of commitment to the community among your employees. Apart from making them feel good about themselves it also affords opportunities for them to work as teams in a non-work environment.

Above all, make work fun. If people, however talented, show up at work because it is a job', then they are unlikely to realise their full potential.

The above is not an exhaustive list for each organisation to get the best out of its people. But if each organisation addresses some of these issues then people will grow individually and collectively. Thus is bound to have a beneficial effect on harnessing and driving their intellectual capital.

1. The author attributes success of India in infotech industry to
(a) do-as-you are told mentality
(b) lazy and intolerant attitude of Indians
(c) growing global economy
(d) realising the latent intellectual capital
(e) None of the above

2. Which of the following is the best way for organisations to be transparent?
(a) Share both good and bad news at all levels
(b) Share only that information which employees can understand
(c) Share only good news and withhold bad news
(d) Only relevant information should be shared
(e) None of the above

3. The carrot-and-stick method will realise which of the following objectives ?
(a) The accountability of the employees will improve
(b) The confidential information will remain as guarded secret
(c) There will be improvement in the skill of employees
(d) The free flow of knowledge and information will improve
(e) None of the above

4. Which of the following measures, if adopted, according to the passage will make employees value commitment ?
(A) Strengthening the skills
(B) Giving necessary instructions
(C) Fixing accountability
(a) All A, B and C
(b) Only B and C
(c) Only A and C
(d) Either A or B and C
(e) None of the above

5. What does the word 'impromptu' communicate in the passage ?
(a) The communication should be unprovoked
(b) Employees interaction should be spontaneous and natural
(c) The work groups should be prompted to talk less, work more
(d) Work groups and teams should interact only if it is necessary
(e) None of the above

6. The phrase 'fast-train-going-slow' in the passage refers to
(A) Following the old policies of governance
(B) Not realising the inbuilt potential
(a) Only A
(b) Only B
(c) Either A or B
(d) Neither A nor B
(e) Both A and B

7. According to author, which of the following factors inhibits creativity?
(a) Giving more emphasis on seniority
(b) Less emphasis on team work
(c) Asking employees to follow directions only
(d) Liability of organisation to address macro issues
(e) None of the above

8. According to the passage which of the following is predicament of Indian business ?
   (a) The core issues of universal education are not addressed
   (b) The Government policies are not favourable
   (c) While strengthening employees potential the policies are more talked implemented
   (d) The field of competition is uneven
   (e) None of the above
9. To realise the full potential of the talent, what are recommendations of the passage?
   (a) Making the working place as funny as possible
   (b) Love your job even if you hate to work
   (c) Make clear difference between job and work
   (d) Make your work as interesting as if it is fun
   (e) None of the above
10. Which of the following provides good learning opportunities?
   (a) High level of tolerance for failure
   (b) Repeating the mistakes till learning takes place
   (c) Overlooking the mistakes of the employees
   (d) Making efforts not to do the same mistake again
   (e) None of the above
11. The phrase 'seniority, like respect, must be earned'........refers to
   (A) the seniority must reflect the expertise and knowledge
   (B) the earning of seniority should be related to length of services
   (C) merit should decide seniority
   (a) Only A and C (b) Only A and B
   (c) Only B and C (d) All A, B and C
   (e) None of these
12. What is the expectation of the author from the Indians?
   (a) They will realise their potential in areas other than Information Technology
   (b) Despite being slow they will think fast
   (c) They will stop working if forced to work like 'do as you are told'
   (d) Indians will turn natural disadvantage into advantage
   (e) None of the above
13. Which of the following is not true in the context of the passage?
   (a) India has huge potential to succeed
   (b) To empower its employees Indian business pay more for the services of the employees
   (c) The seniority should not be based on age
   (d) India should encourage the risk taking behaviour
   (e) Business bodies of future will have more knowledge workers
14. Which of the following best describes the word 'framework' as used in the passage?
   (a) Working within frame
   (b) Fixing frame for the assigned work
   (c) The basic premise
   (d) Divising a defined work culture
   (e) None of the above
15. How does sense of commitment to community among employees help people?
   (a) It develops competition feeling in them
   (b) People learn risk-taking even in non-work situation
   (c) It encourages accountability in them
   (d) People start perceiving opportunities for them to work as teams in non-work situation also
   (e) None of the above

Passage 7

Directions (Q. 16 to 25) : *Read the following passage carefully and answer the questions given below it. Certain words are printed in bold to help you to locate them while answering some of the questions.*

(Indian Bank PO)

Many people believe that science and religion are contrary to each other. But this notion is wrong as a matter of fact, both are complementary to each other. The aim of both these institutions is to explain different aspects of life, universe and human existence. There is no doubt that the methods of science and religion are different. The method of science is observation, experimentation and experience. Science takes its recourse to progressive march towards perfection. The rules of religion are faith, intuition and spoken word of the **enlightened.** In general, while science is inclined towards reason and rationality, spiritualism is the essence of religion.

In earlier times when man appeared on earth, he was over-awed at the sight of violent and powerful aspects of nature. In certain cases, the usefulness of different natural objects of nature overwhelmed man. Thus began the worship of forces of nature—fire, the sun, the rivers, the rocks, the trees, the snakes, etc. The holy scriptures were written by those who had developed harmony between external nature and their inner self. Their object was to ennoble, elevate and liberate the human spirit and mind. But the priestly class took upon itself the monopoly of scriptural knowledge and interpretation to its own advantage. Thus the entire human race was in chains. Truth was **flouted** and progressive, liberal and truthful ideas or ideas expressing doubt and skepticism were suppressed and their holders punished. It was in these trying circumstances the science emerged as a saviour of mankind but its path was not smooth and safe. The scientists and free thinkers were tortured. This was the fate of Copernicus, Galileo, Bruno and others but, by and by science gained ground.

16. Why does man worship the force of nature?
(a) The holy scriptures advocate the worship of forces of nature
(b) The worship elevates and liberates the human spirit and mind
(c) The worship makes man believe in faith and intuition
(d) Forces of nature reach us spiritualism
(e) None of the above

17. Which of the following statements is true in the context of the passage?
(a) Science and religion are antagonistic to each other
(b) Science encourages worshipping of nature
(c) Religion is essential for external peace and harmony
(d) Regimental religion was replaced by scientific principles
(e) Science is essential for inner peace of mind.

18. According to the passage science and religion both
(a) rely on the spoken word of the enlightened
(b) emerged out of the fear of man
(c) emerged from the desire of man to worship the forces of nature
(d) employ different methods of enquiry
(e) work at the cross-purpose of each other

19. Why is it said in the passage that, "science emerged as a saviour of mankind"?
(a) Many great thinkers contributed to the progress of science
(b) Science takes recourse to progressive march towards perfection
(c) Science is inclined towards reason and rationality
(d) Man was bound in chains by religious orthodoxy
(e) The free thinkers and enlightened men were tortured

20. Which of the following statements is not true in the context of the passage?
(a) Man worships the forces of nature
(b) Methods of science and religion are different
(c) Regimental religion got degenerated into orthodoxy
(d) Galileo and Bruno were disciples of Copernicus
(e) The holy scriptures were written by people who had tremendous inner strength

21. Choose the word which is most nearly the same in meaning as the word "flouted" as used in the passage.
(a) Mocked (b) Nourished
(c) Expressed (d) Deflated
(e) Concealed

22. According to the passage science and religion
(a) are contrary to each other
(b) have the same origin
(c) are supportive to each other
(d) have the same aim of controlling universe
(e) do not allow any deviation from their rules

23. According to the passage, at the present juncture, there is a need to
(a) encourage spiritualism as much as possible
(b) teach people to worship the forces of nature

(c) free man from all sorts of bondages
(d) explain to the people different aspects of life and universe
(e) judiciously mix the principles of science and true spirit of religion

24. What was the object of the authors of the holy scriptures?
(a) To teach man the methods of worshipping nature
(b) To advocate the progressive and liberal ideas
(c) To educate and raise the human spirit and mind
(d) To develop harmony between external nature and their inner self
(e) None of the above

25. Choose the word which is most opposite in meaning of the word **"enlightened"** as used in the passage.
(a) Uninformed
(b) Derogatory
(c) Downtrodden
(d) Educated
(e) Authority

Answers

1. (d)	**2.** (a)	**3.** (c)	**4.** (c)
5. (b)	**6.** (b)	**7.** (c)	**8.** (c)
9. (d)	**10.** (a)	**11.** (a)	**12.** (a)
13. (b)	**14.** (c)	**15.** (d)	**16.** (b)
17. (d)	**18.** (d)	**19.** (d)	**20.** (d)
21. (a)	**22.** (c)	**23.** (e)	**24.** (c)
25. (a)			

Passage 8

Directions (Q. 1 to 10) : *Read the following passage carefully and answer the questions given below it. Certain words/phrases are printed in bold to help you to locate them while answering some of the questions.*

(Bank PO)

In modern time Abraham Lincoln stands as the model of a compassionate statesman. He showed this quality not only in striving for the emancipation of the American blacks but in the dignity with which he conducted the American Civil War.

Lincoln did not fancy himself as a liberator. He thought it would be better for all if emancipation was a gradual process spread over many years. He proposed compensation for slave-owners in US bonds and grants for the rehabilitation of blacks—'colonisation' as he called it. But fate was to deem otherwise. The haste with which the South wanted to break away from the Union with the North, compelled him to move faster than he expected, perhaps more than most men of his time he had thought through the issue of slavery. "We must free the slaves", he said, 'or be ourselves subdued." Before reading he first draft of the proclamation of Emancipation, he told his colleagues. "In giving freedom to the slaves, we assure freedom to the free."

On September 22, 1862 Lincoln set his hand on the Proclamation of Emancipation declaring that on the first day of January 1863, all persons held as slaves within any state "shall the then, and forever free."

Lincoln's revulsion for slavery left him without any moral indignation or passion against the slave-owners. The guilt of the slave-owners, he felt, should be shared by the whole country the North and the South, for it seemed to him that everyone in the nation was an accomplice in perpetuating that system. To have whipped up any hatred against slave-owners would, to him, have been an act of malice.

"I shall do nothing in malice", he wrote, "what I deal with is too vast for malicious dealing." As the Civil War was coming to a successful conclusion, a Northerner demanded of Lincoln, "Mr President, how are you going to treat the Southerners when the war is over ?" Lincoln replied, "As if they never went to war ?"

When the news came of the Victory of the Northern against the Confederate forces, someone suggested that the head of the Confederation Administration, Jefferson Davies, really ought to be hanged. "Judge not, that ye be not judged", Lincoln replied, as to the demand for the prosecution of rebels, "We must extinguish our resentments if we expect harmony and union." This was his last recorded utterance.

1. The sentence : 'In giving freedom .... to the free' (last sentence of para 2) means
   (a) by freeing slaves, we are honouring the concept of freedom
   (b) by freeing slaves, we are safeguarding our own interests
   (c) if we give freedom to the slaves, they will serve us better
   (d) if we do not give freedom to the slaves, they will free themselves
   (e) None of the above
2. What came in Lincoln's way of carrying out emancipation as a gradual process ?
   (a) The haste of the South to break away from the Union with the North
   (b) The inadequate compensation given to slave-owners
   (c) His own over-enthusiasm to complete the process fast
   (d) His proposition to give grant for the rehabilitation of slaves
   (e) None of the above
3. Which of the following makes Abraham Lincoln a compassionate statesman ?
   (a) His hesitation in striving for emancipation of American blacks
   (b) His indifference in conducting the American Civil War
   (c) His efforts to force the American blacks from slavery
   (d) His efforts to conclude the American Civil War without dignity
   (e) None of the above
4. The term 'colonisation' as used in passage means
   (a) making separate dwelling arrangements for slave-owners
   (b) rehabilitation arrangements made for slave-owners
   (c) efforts made by American blacks to free themselves
   (d) handing over slaves to the slave-owners
   (e) None of the above
5. The incidents in the passage prove that Lincoln was
   (a) not a firm administrator
   (b) afraid of the majority of slaves
   (c) unduly concerned for the safety of the rebels
   (d) sympathetic and kind-hearted statesman
   (e) unreasonably in favour of slaves
6. The author of the passage seems to be
   (a) a staunch and biased critic of Abraham Lincoln
   (b) an advocate of the system of slavery
   (c) an opponent of the system of slavery
   (d) indifferent to Lincoln's remarkable achievements
   (e) impressed with Lincoln's good qualities
7. According to Lincoln, the culprits of the system of slavery were
   (a) the slaver-owners alone
   (b) the slaves alone
   (c) both the slaves and the slave-owners
   (d) all the people in the country
   (e) None of the above
8. Which of the following statements is TRUE in the context of the passage ?
   (a) Lincoln hated the demand of hanging Jefferson Davies
   (b) Lincoln turned down the demand of the prosecution of rebels
   (c) Lincoln wondered how mere compassion could lead to harmony
   (d) The Civil War was fought by the Northerners and Southerners against the enemies
   (e) None of the above
9. Lincoln didn't have any hatred for the slave-owners because
   (a) they were in a vast majority
   (b) they all belonged to upper caste
   (c) they would have treated him with malice
   (d) they were not guilty at all
   (e) None of the above
10. Lincoln's reply to the Northerner's question regarding the treatment to Southerners proves that
   (a) the Southerners were wicked in their dealings
   (b) Lincoln did not have revengeful attitude towards the Southerners
   (c) the Northerners were in favour of the Southerners
   (d) Lincoln did not like the Southerner's act of breaking away from the Union with the North
   (e) Lincoln could control his anguish against the Southerners while expressing himself

Answers

1. (a)	**2.** (a)	**3.** (e)	**4.** (e)
5. (d)	**6.** (e)	**7.** (d)	**8.** (b)
9. (e)	**10.** (b)		

Short Passages

Passage 1

Directions (Q. 1-5) : *Read the following passage and answer the questions based on it.* **(CDS)**

At low tide he walked over the sands to the headland and round the corner to the little bay facing the open sea. It was inaccessible by boat, because seams of rock jutted out and currents swirled round them treacherously. But you could walk there if you chose one of the lowest ebb tides that receded a very long way. You could not linger on the expedition, for once the tide was on the turn, it came in rapidly. For this reason very few people cared to explore the little bay and the cave at the back of it. But the unknown always drew this man like a magnet. He found the bay fresh and unlittered, as it was completely covered by the sea at high tide. The cave looked mysteriously dark, cool and inviting, and he penetrated to the farthest corner where he discovered a wide crack, rather like a chimney. He peered up and thought he could see a patch of daylight.

1. According to the writer, the bay could not be reached by boat, because
(a) it had numerous layers of rocks
(b) there were too many eddies
(c) it was facing the open sea
(d) there were seams of rock and treacherously swirling currents

2. One could visit the bay
(a) at any time one chose
(b) on certain specified occasions
(c) when there was a low tide
(d) during the evening walk

3. It was not possible to "linger on the expedition" because
(a) the water rose rapidly
(b) the tide turned quickly
(c) the tide turned sprightly
(d) the water rushed in with a great force

4. He found the bay "fresh and unlittered" because
(a) the sea water had receded
(b) he was the first visitor there
(c) the high tide had just washed the litter away
(d) it was not frequented by people who would pollute it

5. While passing through the cave, the writer discovered a
(a) cool and secluded corner
(b) large opening
(c) chimney-shaped rock
(d) big crack through which light came in

Passage 2

Directions (Q. 6-10) : *Read the following passage and answer the questions based on it.* **(CDS)**

Regular physical activity provides numerous health benefits—from leaner bodies and lower blood pressure to improved mental health and cognitive functioning. As the school physical education programme promotes physical activity and can teach skills as well as form or change behaviour, it holds an important key to influencing health and well-being across the life span. To improve the fitness of students, we need to rethink the design and delivery of school-based physical education programme. Adults in the United States think that information about health was more important for students to learn the content in language arts, mathematics, science, history or any other subject. Deposite this high ranking, most schools devote minimal curriculum time to teaching students how to lead healthy lives. Our first step might be to consider ways to increase curriculum time devoted to physical education. In addition, schools need to thoughtfully analyse the design and delivery of school physical education programme to ensure that they are engaging, developmentally appropriate, inclusive and instructionally powerful.

6. According to this passage, regular physical activity is needed to
(a) control one's blood pressure
(b) lose one's weight
(c) improve one's cognitive skills
(d) improve one's physical as well as mental health

7. In order to tone up the physical education programme
(a) it should be made compulsory at school
(b) an assessment of the existing programme should be made
(c) a committee should be set up in every school
(d) the programme should be reoriented and implemented

8. According to the Americans, health education is more important than teaching
(a) social sciences
(b) liberal arts
(c) any subject
(d) natural sciences

9. The author wants the reoriented physical education programme to be
(a) given minimal curriculum time
(b) very comprehensive
(c) relevant to the modern society
(d) thoughtful

10. In order to improve the physical education programme, we should, first of all
(a) allot more time to the teaching and learning of physical activity
(b) decide on the number of activities to be taught
(c) employ qualified instructors
(d) increase the teaching load of instructors

Passage 3

Directions (Q. 11-15) : *Read the following passage and answer the questions based on it.* **(CDS)**

The highbrows reverse the numerical argument and imply that, because they are so few, they must therefore be right but where they chiefly offend is in their excessive self-congratulation and contempt for others. In the past, the highbrows were alone in expressing a feeling of superiority; the lowbrows humbly accepted the position assigned to them. Recently, however, there has been a change, and the lowbrows now adopt towards the highbrows exactly the same attitude as the highbrows adopted towards them.

11. The reversal of the numerical argument in the context of the passage means that the highbrows
(a) have no regard for the majority
(b) respect the majority
(c) are indifferent to numbers
(d) have regard for the minority

12. A highbrow is
(a) a liberal minded person
(b) a believer in conservative values
(c) a self-opinionated intellectual
(d) a democrat

13. The phrase 'self-congratulation' can best be replaced by
(a) self-effacement
(b) self-admiration
(c) self-negation
(d) self-criticism

14. The attitude of the lowbrows towards the highbrows in the past was one of
(a) violent rejection
(b) resentful acceptance
(c) open rebelliousness
(d) unprotesting submission

15. The recent change in the attitude of the lowbrows towards the highbrows suggests that
(a) the lowbrows have rejected the superiority of the highbrows
(b) the lowbrows have become highbrows
(c) the lowbrows have become indifferent to the highbrows
(d) the highbrows have become meek and humble

Passage 4

Directions (Q. 16-20) : *Read the following passage and answer the questions based on it.* **(CDS)**

Crude mineral oil comes out of the earth as a thick brown or black liquid with a strong smell. It is a complex mixture of many different substances, each with its own individual qualities. Most of them are combinations of hydrogen and carbon in varying proportions. Such hydrocarbons are also found in other forms such as bitumen, asphalt and natural gas. Mineral oil originates from the carcasses of tiny animals and from plants that live in the sea. Over millions of years, these dead creatures form large deposits under sea-bed and ocean currents cover them with a blanket of sand and slit. As this material hardens, it becomes sedimentary rock and effectively shuts out the oxygen, so preventing the complete decomposition of the marine deposits underneath. The layers of sedimentary rocks become thicker, and heavier. Their pressure produces heat, which transforms the tiny carcasses into crude oil in a process that is still going on today.

16. Marine deposits under the sea do not get decomposed because they
(a) become rock and prevent oxygen from entering them
(b) are covered by the sand and slit brought by the current
(c) contain a mixture of hydrogen and carbon
(d) are constantly washed by the ocean current

17. Sedimentary rock leads to the formation of oil deposits because
(a) it becomes hard and forms into rocks which produce oil
(b) its pressure produces heat and turns the deposits of animal carcasses and plants into oil
(c) it turns heavy and shuts out the oxygen
(d) it becomes heavy and hard, and applies pressure to squeeze oil

18. In order to have mineral oil, hydrogen and carbon are combined in
(a) equal proportions
(b) fixed proportions
(c) varying proportions
(d) the proportion of two and one

19. The time it takes for the marine deposits to harden into rocks is
(a) a few years
(b) thousands of years
(c) hundreds of years
(d) million of years

20. The most apt title for the passage is
(a) Crude mineral oil
(b) How sedimentary rock is formed ?
(c) How mineral oil is formed ?
(d) Marine deposits under the sea

Passage 5

Directions (Q. 21-25) : *Read the following passage and answer the questions based on it.* **(CDS)**

To avoid the various foolish opinions to which mankind is prone, no superhuman brain is required. A few simple rules will keep you free, not from all errors, but from silly errors. If the matter is one that can be settled by observation, make the observation yourself. Aristole could have avoid the mistake of thinking that women have fewer teeth than man, by the simple device of asking Mrs Aristotle to keep her mouth open while he counted. Thinking that you know when in fact you do not is a bad mistake, to which we are all prone. I believe myself that hedgehogs eat black beetles, because I have been told that they do; but if I was writing a book on the habits of hedgehogs, I should not commit myself until I had been one enjoying this diet. Aristotle, however, was less cautious. Ancient and medieval writers know all about unicorns and salamanders; not one of them thought it necessary to avoid dogmatic statements about them because he had never seen one of them.

21. The author portrays mankind as
(a) very intelligent
(b) having superhuman qualities
(c) nervous and weak
(d) by and large, lazy and ignorant

22. The author is in favour of drawing conclusions on the basis of
(a) reasoning
(b) study of eminent thinkers
(c) empirical evidence
(d) discussion and consultation

23. According to the author, unicorns and salamanders
(a) existed in the past but now have become extinct
(b) are invisible
(c) never really existed
(d) have caused strange stories to be written about them

24. The author implies that
(a) hedgehogs eat black beetles
(b) hedgehogs do not really eat black beetles
(c) he is writing a book about hedge hogs
(d) he has never seen a hedgehog eating beetles

25. The attitude of the author is
(a) philosophical (b) scientific
(c) cultural (d) commonsensical

Passage 6

Directions (Q. 26-30) : *Read the following passage and answer the questions based on it.* **(CDS)**

Long ago Emperson wrote: "A man's task is his life-preserver." This seems to be remarkably correct in our modern life. The man without task is like a ship without a ballast and anchor, he is all too often merely a drifter. Few men seem to have initiative enough to choose a task for themselves if they do not need to work. When the inevitable disappointments come, as they assuredly will, they are completely overwhelmed. But the man who has his task has no time for vain regret, he escapes the disastrous fate which overtakes his less fortunate brother.Work is one of the greatest safety-valves which was ever invented, and youth especially needs it.

26. It seems to be remarkably correct in modern life that
(a) a man has enough leisure
(b) youth needs less work and more rest
(c) the correct choice of the task preserves one's life
(d) men fail to choose a task for themselves

27. The expression 'safety-valve'means
(a) something which blows up safety
(b) an outlet for rent-up energy
(c) something which guarantees safety
(d) a leaf of a folding door

28. A ship without ballast and anchor
(a) is in great danger
(b) merely drifts
(c) is very safe
(d) may not go in the right direction

29. A man who suffers from vain regrets must have
(a) chosen his life's work rather carelessly
(b) met with disastrous fate
(c) been a victim of adverse circumstances to do
(d) lived a preserved life

30. A person who has chosen the right task has no time to regret because he
(a) is engrossed in his work
(b) has too much to do
(c) has succeeded in life
(d) has a safe and secured life

Answers

1. (d)	**2.** (c)	**3.** (c)	**4.** (c)
5. (d)	**6.** (d)	**7.** (d)	**8.** (c)
9. (d)	**10.** (d)	**11.** (c)	**12.** (c)
13. (b)	**14.** (d)	**15.** (a)	**16.** (b)
17. (b)	**18.** (c)	**19.** (d)	**20.** (c)
21. (d)	**22.** (c)	**23.** (c)	**24.** (d)
25. (b)	**26.** (c)	**27.** (c)	**28.** (d)
29. (a)	**30.** (b)		

Passage 7

Directions (Q. 1-5) : *Read the following passage and answer the questions based on it.*

(SSC Stenographer)

Mountaineering is now looked upon as the king of sports. But men have lived amongst the mountains since prehistoric times and in some parts of the world, as in the Andes and Himalayas, difficult mountain journeys have inevitably been part of their everyday life. However, some of the peaks there were easily accessible from most of the cities of Europe. It is quite interesting that while modern mountaineers prefer difficult routes for the greater enjoyment of sport, the early climbers looked for the easiest ones, for the summit was the prize they all set their eyes on. Popular interest in mountaineering increased considerably after the ascent of the Alpine peak of Matterhorn in 1865 and Edward Whymper's dramatic account of the climb and fatal accident which occurred during the descent.

In the risky sport of mountaineering the element of competition between either individuals or teams is totally absent. Rather one can say that the competition is between the team and the peaks themselves. The individuals making up a party must climb together as a team, for they depend upon one another for their safety. Mountaineering can be dangerous unless reasonable precautions are taken. However, the majority of fatal accidents happen to parties which are inexperienced or not properly equipped. Since many accidents are caused due to bad weather, the safe climber is the man who knows when it is time to turn back, however, tempting it may be to press on and try to reach the summit.

1. Mountaineering is different from other sports because
(a) it is risky and dangerous
(b) it can be fatal
(c) it is most thrilling and exciting
(d) there is no competition between individuals

2. People living in the Andes and the Himalayas made mountain journeys because
(a) it was a kind of sport
(b) they had to undertake them in their day-to-day life
(c) they lived in pre-historic time
(d) of the challenge offered by the difficult journey

3. Mountaineers climb as a team because
(a) the height is too much for one individual
(b) the competition is between the team and the peak
(c) they have to rely on each other for safety
(d) there is no competition among them

4. ".....the summit was the prize they all set their eyes on". In the context of the passage, this means
(a) reaching the top was their exclusive concern
(b) they kept their eyes steadily on reaching the summit
(c) they cared for nothing but the prize of reaching the summit
(d) they chose a route from which they could see the summit clearly

5. "to press" in the last sentence of the passage means
(a) to struggle in a forceful manner
(b) to force upon others
(c) to work fearlessly
(d) to continue in a determined manner

Passage 8

Directions (Q. 6-10) : *Read the following passage and answer the questions based on it.*

(SSC Stenographer)

On the morning of August 31, 1573; 3000 horsemen of the imperial Mughal army paused at the banks of the Sabarmati. The rebels, they were after, lay just beyond the swollen river but the soldiers were exhausted: they had traversed 960 kilometres of difficult terrain in nine days, riding almost continuously. Suddenly a warrior on a chestnut charger plunged into the raging torrent. As man and horse struggled on to the opposite bank, a thrill ran through the army. It was the emperor, Jalaluddin Akbar! With a roar, the soldiers followed him across and within two days, they had put down the rebellion so thoroughly that Gujarat remained in Mughal hands for the next 185 years.

6. The rebels were camped
(a) across the Sabarmati river
(b) on the banks of Sabarmati river
(c) in Gujarat
(d) in imperial Mughal courts

7. The expression "swollen river" means
(a) a river in flood
(b) a calm and serene river
(c) a deep river
(d) a shallow river

8. The Mughal soldiers didn't cross the river because
(a) they were cowards
(b) they had joined hands with the rebels
(c) they were waiting for the king to arrive
(d) they were tired after a difficult journey

9. The sudden arrival of King Akbar
(a) surprised the soldiers
(b) angered the soldiers
(c) dismayed the soldiers
(d) enthused the soldiers

10. The attack on the rebels turned out to be
(a) a dismal failure
(b) a grand success
(c) of no particular significance
(d) an ordinary affair

Passage 9

Directions (Q. 11-15) : *Read the following passage and answer the questions based on it.*

(SSC Stenographer)

He saw nothing he had no knife or sharp instrument, the grating of the window was of iron and he had too often assured himself of its solidity. His furniture consisted of a bed, a chair, a table, a pail and a jug. The bed had iron clamps, but they were screwed to the wall and it would have required a screwdriver to take them off.

Dantes had but one resource which was to break the jug and with one of the sharp fragments attack the wall. He let the jug fall on the floor and it broke in pieces. He concealed two or three of the sharpest fragments in his bed, leaving the rest on the floor. The breaking of the jug was too natural an accident to excite suspicion, and next morning the gaoler went grumblingly to fetch another, without giving himself the trouble to remove the fragments. Dantes heard joyfully the key grate in the lock as the guard departed.

11. Dantes was in
(a) a hostel
(b) a dining room
(c) an army barracks
(d) a prison

12. Dantes was planning to
(a) carve his name
(b) make his escape
(c) tease the guard
(d) call for breakfast

13. The guard left the fragments because he
(a) didn't notice them
(b) wished to punish dantes
(c) was too lazy to bother
(d) wanted Dantes to clear up

14. Dantes probably broke the jug
(a) in the morning
(b) during the night
(c) after breakfast
(d) at exactly 3 p.m.

15. Dantes heard the key grate in the lock when the
(a) cell door was shut
(b) cell door was opened
(c) storeroom was opened
(d) storeroom was shut

Passage 10

Directions (Q. 16-20) : *Read the following passage and answer the questions based on it.*

(SSC Stenographer)

Wild peacocks live together in large flocks in the forests of Central Africa. They scratch about in the ground during the day for seeds to eat and at nightfall they fly up to the trees where they perch and sleep. Every peacock has several wives, known as peahens. The female birds build their nests on the ground and lay from four to six whitish, sometimes spotted eggs. During the mating season the male utters a harsh raucous cry.

16. Why do peacocks live in flocks ?
(a) They are frightened of wild animals
(b) They cannot fly very well
(c) They can get more food
(d) The passage does not tell us

17. 'Perch' in the passage means
(a) rest
(b) nest
(c) climb
(d) fly

18. Peacock eggs are
(a) pure white
(b) whitish
(c) spotted
(d) both 'b' and 'c'

19. "Harsh raucous cry" in the passage means
(a) loud cry (b) deep cry
(c) roaring cry (d) loud and hoarse cry

20. A suitable title for the passage could be
(a) Peacock Eggs
(b) The Habitat of the Peacock
(c) Wild Peacocks
(d) Wild Birds of Africa

Answers

1. (d)	**2.** (b)	**3.** (c)	**4.** (a)
5. (d)	**6.** (b)	**7.** (a)	**8.** (d)
9. (d)	**10.** (b)	**11.** (d)	**12.** (b)
13. (c)	**14.** (b)	**15.** (a)	**16.** (d)
17. (a)	**18.** (d)	**19.** (d)	**20.** (b)

Passage 11

Directions (Q. 1-9) : *Read the following passage carefully and answer the questions given below it. Certain words/phrases are given in bold to help you to locate them while answering the questions.*

(Reserve Bank of India)

Alleviation of rural poverty has been one of the primary objectives of planned development in India. Ever since the inception of planning, the policies and the programmes have been designed and redesigned with this aim. The problem of rural poverty was brought into a sharper focus during the Sixth Plan. The Seventh Plan too emphasised growth with social justice. It was realised that a sustainable strategy of poverty alleviation has to be based on increasing the productive employment opportunities in the process of growth itself. However, to the extent the process of growth bypasses some sections of population, it is necessary to formulate specific poverty alleviation programmes for generation of a certain minimum level of income for the rural poor. Rural development implies both the economic betterment of people as well as greater social transformation. Increased participation of people in the rural development process, decentralisation of planning, better enforcement of land reforms and greater access to credit and inputs go a long way in prospects for economic development improvements in health, education, drinking water, energy supply, sanitation and housing coupled with attitudinal changes also facilitate their social development.

Rural poverty is inextricably linked with low rural productivity and unemployment, including underemployment. Hence, it is imperative to improve productivity and increase employment in rural areas. Moreover, more employment needs to be generated at higher levels of productivity in order to generate higher output. Employment at miserably low levels of productivity and incomes is already a problem of far greater magnitude than unemployment as such. It is estimated that in 1987-88 the rate of unemployment was only 3 percent and inclusive of the underemployed, it was around 5 percent. As per the currently used methodology in the Planning Commission, poverty for the same year was estimated to be 30 percent. This demonstrates that even though a large proportion of the rural population was working it was difficult for them to eke out a living even at subsistence levels from it. It is true that there has been a considerable decline in the incidence of rural poverty over time. In terms of absolute numbers of poor, the decline has been much less. While this can be attributed to the demographic factor, the fact remains that after 40 years of planned development about 200 million are still poor in rural India.

1. According to the passage, rural poverty is associated with which of the following one or more factors ?
1. Want of effectiveness of productive efforts
2. Dearth of employment opportunities
3. Better sanitation and housing facilities

(a) Only 1 (b) Only 2
(c) Only 3 (d) 1 and 2 only
(e) 2 and 3 only

2. Which of the following statements is/are TRUE in the context of the passage?
1. There has been a significant increase in the number of the rural poor.
2. Before the Sixth Plan, the policies regarding alleviation of rural poverty were almost nonexistent.
3. Social change coupled with financial upliftment is implied in rural development.

(a) Only 1 (b) Only 2
(c) Only 3 (d) 1 and 2 only
(e) 1 and 3 only

3. Under which of the following circumstances is employment a greater problem than unemployment ?
(a) There cannot be such circumstances
(b) In rural areas where employment opportunities are less
(c) In urban areas where sanitary conditions are subnormal
(d) In areas where magnitude of unemployment is more serious
(e) None of the above

4. Which of the following is NOT mentioned in the passage as an important factor for rural development ?
(a) Better enforcement of land reforms
(b) Greater access of credit and inputs
(c) Transferring planning from central to local authorities
(d) Involvement of rural folk in the development process
(e) Enhancing production in the various new industries in rural areas

5. The passage deals mainly with.........
(a) the shortcomings in the implementation of poverty alleviation
(b) improvement in industrial growth strategies
(c) alleviation of rural poverty
(d) methodology of Planning Commission
(e) the growth rate of unemployment

6. Which of the following necessitates formulation of specific poverty alleviation programmes ?
(a) Certain sections are not covered in the process of growth
(b) The sharper focus given in the Sixth Plan
(c) Extension of social justice to rural areas
(d) To keep the rural population outside the periphery of growth
(e) None of the above

7. Which of the following inferences can be drawn from the passage ?
(a) The number of the rural poor people in India is quite substantial
(b) The development activities during the past 40 years had all been futile
(c) Alleviation of rural poverty needs a strong political will
(d) The unemployment situation in the country has been worsening year after year
(e) None of the above

8. What is the desired probable impact of formulation of specific poverty alleviation programmes?
(a) Provision of good sanitation and housing for the rural poor
(b) Ensuring certain minimum income for the rural poor
(c) Change in attitude of the rural masses
(d) Increased involvement of the rural people in developmental activities
(e) None of the above

9. Which one or more of the following statements show/shows a striking paradox ?
(A) In 1987-88, the rate of unemployment was only 3 percent and inclusive of underemployment it was 5%

(B) Unemployment together with underemployment was 5% whereas the poverty was 30%
(C) More employment needs to be generated at higher levels of productivity in order to generate higher output
(a) Only A (b) Only B
(c) Only C (d) A and B only
(e) B and C only

Answers

1. (a)	**2.** (c)	**3.** (d)	**4.** (a)
5. (b)	**6.** (b)	**7.** (c)	**8.** (b)
9. (c)			

Passage 12

Directions (Q. 1-9) : *Read the following passage carefully and answer the questions given below it. Certain words/phrases in the passage are given in bold to help you to locate them while answering the questions.* ***(Bank PO)***

Globalisation, liberalisation and free market are some of the most significant modern trends in economy. **Most economists** in our country seem **captivated** by the spell of the free market. Consequently, nothing seems good or normal that does not accord with the requirements of the free market. A price that is determined by the seller or, for the matter, established by anyone other than the aggregate of consumers seems **pernicious**. Accordingly, it requires a major act of will to think of price-fixing as both normal and having a valuable economic function. In fact, price fixing is normal in all industrialised societies because the industrial system itself provides, as an effortless consequence of its own development, the price-fixing that it requires. Modern industrial planning requires and rewards great size. Hence a comparatively small number of large firms will be competing for the same group of consumers that each large firm will act with consideration of its own needs and thus avoid selling products for more than its competitors charge is commonly recognised by **advocates** of free-market economic theories. But each large firm will also act with full consideration of the needs that it has in common with the other large firms competing for the same customers. Each large firm will thus avoid significant price cutting, because price-cutting will be prejudicial to the common interest in a **stable** demand for products. Most economists do not see price-fixing when it occurs because they expect it to be brought about by a number of **explicit** agreements among large firms; it is not.

Moreover, those economists who argue that allowing the free-market to operate without interference is the most efficient method of establishing prices have not considered the economics of non-socialist countries. Most of these economies employ intentional price-fixing, usually in an **overt** fashion. Formal price-fixing by cartel and informal price-fixing by agreements covering the members of an industry are common place. Were there something peculiarly efficient about the free market and inefficient about price-fixing, the countries that have avoided the first and used the second would have suffered drastically in their economic development. There is no indication that they have.

Socialist industry also works within a framework of controlled prices. In the early 1970's the Soviet Union began to give firms and industries some flexibility in adjusting prices that a more informal evolution has accorded the capitalist system. Economists in the USA have hailed the change as a return to the free-market. But the then Soviet firms were not in favour of the prices established by a free-market over which they exercised little influence; rather, Soviet firms acquired some power to fix prices.

1. The author's primary objective of writing the passage seems to
(a) belie the popular belief that the free market helps enhance development of industrial societies
(b) advocate that price-fixing is unavoidable and it is beneficial to the economy of any industrialised society
(c) explain the methodology of fixing price to stabilise free-market
(d) prove that price-fixing and free market are compatible and mutually beneficial to industrialised societies
(e) create awareness among the general public regarding combating price-fixing by large firms

2. Which of the following statements (1), (2), and (3) is/are TRUE in the context of the information given in the passage ?
The information in the passage is helpful to
1. know some of the ways in which prices can be fixed
2. identify the products for which price-fixing can be more beneficial
3. differentiate between the economies of various countries
(a) Only (1)
(b) Only (2)
(c) Only (3)
(d) Only (1) and (2)
(e) None of these

3. Considering the literal meaning and connotations of the words used in the passage, the author's attitude towards "most economists" can best be described as
(a) derogatory and antagonistic
(b) impartial and unbiased
(c) spiteful and envious
(d) critical and condescending
(e) indifferent

4. The author feels that price fixed by seller seems pernicious because
(a) people don't have faith in large firms
(b) people don't want the Government to fix prices
(c) most economists believer that consumers should determine prices
(d) most economists believe that no one group should determine prices
(e) people do not want to decide prices

5. Which of the following statements is definitely TRUE in the context of the passage ? Price fixing is
(a) a profitable result of economic development
(b) an inevitable result of the industrial system
(c) the joint result of a number of carefully organised decisions
(d) a phenomenon uncommon to industrialised societies
(e) a result of joint venture of the Government and industry

6. According to the passage, price-fixing in non-socialistic is generally
(a) intentional and widespread
(b) illegitimate but beneficial
(c) conservative and inflexible
(d) legitimate and innovative
(e) conservative and scarce

7. What was the result of the then Soviet Union's change in economic policy in the 1970's ?
(a) They showed greater profits
(b) They had less control over the free-market
(c) They were able to adjust to techno advancement
(d) They acquired some authority to fix prices
(e) They became more responsive to free market

8. The author's primary concern seems to
(a) summarise conflicting viewpoints
(b) make people aware of recent discoveries
(c) criticise a point of view
(d) predict the probable results of a practice
(e) prepare a research proposal

9. Which of the following statements about the socialist industry is/are false ?
1. It works under certain price restrictions
2. It has no authority to determine price
3. It hails the strategy of price fixing, as a major deviation
(a) Only (1)
(b) Only (2)
(c) Only (3)
(d) (1) and (2)
(e) (2) and (3)

Answers

1. (b)	**2.** (a)	**3.** (b)	**4.** (c)
5. (b)	**6.** (a)	**7.** (e)	**8.** (a)
9. (c)			

Passage 13

Directions (Q.1-5) : *Read the following passage carefully and then answer these questions based on what is stated or implied therein.* **(MAT)**

Are the 1980s and 1990s the era of colour ? According to some people, they are. Now you can buy radios and electric fans in lavender and pink. Restaurants have an emphasis on flowers and colourful plates. Cars are coming out in pink and aqua. Even bathroom fixtures are being made in "honeydew" and "blond". Part of the importance of the colour of an object is that the colour affects the way one feels about it. You want a vacuum cleaner to look light and easy, which is why it may be coloured in pastels and light colours. But gardening equipment and athletic equipment you want to look powerful. You would never find a lawn mower in pink, but red would be fine. Not very long ago, sheets were always white and refrigerators commonly came in colours like "old gold" "avocado green" and "coppertone". Now those are thought of as old-fashioned, popular colours change because fashion influences everything. In fact, new colours often spring from the fashion industry. It's a lot cheaper to make a blouse or skirt than a sofa. After people get used to seeing new colours on clothing or towels, they are ready to accept those colours in carpeting, refrigerators, or cars. Colour- analysis consultants have been very successful in recent years. People want to choose the most flattering colours for make up and clothing. Some car designers are even saying that people may begin buying cars of the colour that goes with their skin colouring. This sounds too extreme. It's hard to believe that people are that impressionable.

1. The main subject of the passage is
(a) popular colours today
(b) colour consultants
(c) the influence of colour
(d) colours that flatter people

2. The word "era" in line I could best be replaced by which of the following words?
(a) Season
(b) Age
(c) Epic
(d) Generation

3. According to the author which of the following is not popular now ?
(a) Coppertone
(b) Colourful cars
(c) Pastels
(d) Colourful bathroom fixtures

4. According to the author, why would red be a good colour for a lawn mower ?
(a) Because it is strong
(b) Because it is cheap
(c) Because it is light
(d) Because it is pastel

5. In this passage which of the following are not used names for colours?
(a) Fruit (b) Hair colour
(c) Minerals (d) Drinks

Answers

1. (c) **2.** (b) **3.** (a) **4.** (a) **5.** (a)

Passage 14

Directions (Q. 1-5) : *Read the following passage carefully and then answer the questions based on what is stated or implied therein.* ***(MAT)***

If life exists on Mars, it is most likely to be in the form of bacteria buried deep in the planet's permafrost or lichens growing within rocks, say scientists from NASA. There might even be fossilised Martian algae locked up in ancient lake beds, waiting to be found.

Christopher Mckay of NASA's Ames Research Centre in California told the AAAS that exobiologists, who look for life on other planets, should look for clues among the life forms of the Earth's ultra-cold regions, where conditions are similar to those on Mars.

"Lichens, for example, are found within some Antarctic rocks, just beneath the surface where sunlight can still reach them. The rock protects the lichen from cold and absorbs water providing enough for the lichen's need," said Mckay.

Bacteria have also been found in 3-million-year-old permafrost dug up from Siberia. If there are any bacteria alive on Mars today, they would have had to have survived from the time before the planet cooled more than 3 billion years ago. Nevertheless, McKay is optimistic, "It may be possible that bacteria frozen into the permafrost at the Martian South Pole may be viable."

McKay said, "Algae are found in Antarctic lakes with permanently frozen surfaces. Although no lakes are thought to exist on Mars, they might have existed long ago. If so, the dried-out Martian lake beds may contain the fossilised remains of algae." " On earth, masses of microscopic algae form large, layered structures known as stromatolites, which survive as fossils on lake beds, and the putative," Martian algae might have done the same thing," said Jack Farmer, one of McKay's colleagues.

The researchers are compiling a list of promising Martian lake beds to be photographed from spacecraft," said Farmer. Those photographs could help to select sites for landers that would search for signs of life, past or present". "If we find algae on Mars, I would say the Universe is lousy with algae," McKay said, "Intelligence would be another question".

1. The passage is primarily concerned with
(a) the possibility of life on Mars
(b) selecting sites for landers on Mars
(c) research on Mars
(d) findings of Christopher McKay on Mars

2. Lichens survive in the extreme cold conditions of Antarctica on earth for all the following reasons, except
(a) some Antarctic rocks protect lichens beneath their surface
(b) bacteria in the Antarctic frost protect lichen from the residual cold after the rock absorbs water
(c) sunlight penetrates the surface of the Antarctic rock where lichen grows
(d) the Antarctic rocks protect the lichen from cold by absorbing water and leaving enough for the lichen's needs

3. Which of the following statements is not true ?
(a) If any bacteria are alive today on Mars, they must have survived from the time before the planet cooled
(b) Space photographs of Martian craters should reveal to the explorers signs of life there
(c) Bacteria frozen into permafrost at the Martian South Pole may be viable
(d) On digging up, more than 3 million years old Siberian permafrost has revealed bacteria

4. The most primitive forms of life likely to exist on Mars are all the following except
(a) villus and spare (b) bacteria
(c) algae (d) lichen

5. Exobiologists might find on Mars algae similar to stromatolites on earth because
(a) on our planet stromatolites are formed by microscopic algae
(b) Martian lake beds may contain fossilised remains of algae similar to stromatolites on earth
(c) there is evidence that photosynthesis which takes place in earth's algae can be found in Martian algae
(d) All of the above

Answers

1. (a) **2.** (b) **3.** (b) **4.** (a)
5. (d)

Passage 15

Directions (Q.1-5) : *Read the following passage carefully and then answer the questions based on what is stated or implied in the passage.* ***(MAT)***

A jolly musicologist by the entirely unobjectionable name of Henry Pleasants has written a book called "The Agony of Modern Music". That word "Agony" is right. Much of it is just not written down but improvised. Much of what passes for music of these times is raucous noise and the excuse for persisting with it is that every common youngster understands and likes it. The pleasant fellow concedes that "serious" music is virtually dead. This may be dismissed as yet another pleasantry which the undirected young indulge in. Paul Hindesmith, possibly one of the last of the classical giants. Once said that some composers tended to develop an oversublimated technique "which produces images of emotions that are far removed from any emotional experience a relatively normal human being ever has. That is just the point. High art can never be totally democratised. There is a barrier between the egghead and the hoipolloi and it would be lazy idealism to ignore this. When Bach played and beethoven roared, who was then the gentleman? The pity of it is that while talking music to the masses, all known rules are broken and **improvisation** becomes king. That, roughly speaking is how jazz was born; by dropping discipline, inspiration, deep personal emotions and every element of creative art, and adopting improvisation as its main rationale. Why, they even tried to smuggle bits of jazz into serious music so that the composer could somehow survive. Now they are going one step further : learn it by ear, don't write down the stuff, make it up as you go along and hope, by these shoddy techniques, that everyone present will applaud and, thus, provide the composer and the performers with their daily bread.

1. The author uses the word 'improvisation' to suggest
(a) making the original more sublime
(b) tampering with the original
(c) rendering the original more popular
(d) simplifying the original

2. According to the author high art cannot be democratised because
(a) high art is oversublimated
(b) people differ in their emotional experience
(c) masses cannot be expected to appreciate what only the few intelligent can
(d) democratising necessarily involves improvisation

3. They tried to introduce bits of jazz in serious music so that
(a) music might survive
(b) the masses could take to serious music
(c) the new composers might survive
(d) music is democratised

4. Which of the following words can best replace the word 'raucous' in the paragraph?
(a) shrill (b) soothing
(c) pleasant (d) popular

5. Speaking of the techniques of some composers Paul Hindesmith said that they evoked image of emotions
(a) not experienced by normal people
(b) felt only by subnormal people
(c) never felt by masses
(d) not experienced by eggheads

Answers

1. (b) **2.** (c) **3.** (c) **4.** (a) **5.** (a)

Passage 16

Directions (Q. 1-5) : *Read the passage given below carefully and then answer the questions based on what is stated or implied in the passage.* *(MAT)*

One simple physical concept lies behind the formation of the stars : gravitational instability. The concept is not new. Newton first perceived it late in the 17th Century. Imagine a **uniform**, static cloud of gas in space. Imagine then that the gas is somehow disturbed so that one small spherical region becomes a little denser than the gas around it so that the small region's gravitational field becomes slightly stronger. It now attracts more matter to it and its gravity increases further, causing it to begin to contract. As **It** contracts its density increases, which increases its gravity even more, so that it picks up even more matter and contracts even further. The process continues until the small region of gas finally forms a gravitationally bound object.

1. The primary purpose of the passage is to
(a) describe a static condition
(b) support a theory considered outmoded
(c) depict the successive stages of a phenomenon
(d) demonstrate the evolution of the meaning of a term

2. It can be inferred from this passage that the author views the information contained within it as
(a) lacking in elaboration
(b) original but obscure
(c) speculative and unprofitable
(d) uncomplicated and traditional

3. With which of the following words can you replace the word 'uniform' as given in this passage ?
(a) Uniting
(b) Varying
(c) Gaseous
(d) Unvarying

4. What does the underlined word 'it' stands for in the passage ?
(a) Gravitational instability
(b) Cloud of gas
(c) Small spherical denser region
(d) Matter

5. The author provides information that answers which of the following questions ?
(A) What causes the disturbances that changes the cloud from its original static condition?
(B) How does this small region's increasing density affect its gravitational field ?
(C) What is the end result of the gradually increasing concentration of the small region of gas?
(a) 1 only
(b) 2 only
(c) 2 and 3 only
(d) 1, 2 and 3

Answers

1. (c) **2.** (d) **3.** (d) **4.** (c) **5.** (c)

Passage 17

Directions (Q. 1-4) : *Read the passage given below carefully and then answer the questions based on what is stated or implied in the passage.* ***(UPSC Assistant PF Commissioners)***

A great deal of the world's work is neither producing material things nor altering the things that Nature produces, but doing services of one sort or another.

Thoughtless people are apt to think a brickmaker more of a producer than a clergyman. When a village carpenter makes a gate to keep cattle out of a field of wheat, he has something solid in his hand which he can claim for his own until the farmer pays him for it. But when a village boy makes a noise to keep the birds off he has nothing to show, though the noise is just as necessary as the gate. The postman does not make anything—the policeman does not make anything—the doctor makes pills sometimes; but that is not his real business, which is to tell you when you ought to take pills, and what pills to take, unless indeed he has the good sense to tell you not to take them at all, and you have the good sense to believe him, when he is giving you good advice instead of bad. The lawyer does not make anything substantial—they are all in service.

1. Thoughtless people think a brickmaker more of a producer than a clergyman because
(a) a clergyman is an idler
(b) a brickmaker produces something solid which he can keep with him till he gets its price
(c) a brickmaker, being physically stronger than a clergyman, can naturally produce more
(d) he cannot understand the philosophical lectures of the clergyman

2. According to the author of the passage, a large number of persons
(a) are producing material things
(b) are altering the things that Nature produces
(c) are doing nothing in particular
(d) offer services

3. The writer thinks that
(a) both the doctor and the patient are sensible when one makes pills and the other buys them
(b) the doctor is sensible and the patient is insensible
(c) the doctor is insensible and the patient is sensible
(d) both the doctor and the patient make sense when one offers and the other receives a service

4. The writer's description of the doctor's business
(a) strengthens the main argument of the passage because the doctor's business is to make pills
(b) is irrelevant to the main argument of the passage
(c) weakens the main argument of the passage
(d) illustrates the difference between producing something and offering a service

Answers

1. (b) **2.** (d) **3.** (d) **4.** (d)

Passage 18

Directions (Q. 1-6) : *Read the given passage carefully and answer the questions which are based on what is stated or implied in the passage.* ***(MAT)***

Since the world has become industrialised, there has been an increase in the number of animal species that have either become extinct or have neared extinction. Bengal tiger, for instance, which once roamed the jungle in vast numbers, now number only 2300 and by the year 2025 their population is estimated to be down to zero. What is **alarming** about the case of Bengal tiger is that this extinction will have been caused almost entirely by poachers who according to some sources, are not interested in material gain but in personal gratification. This is an example of the callousness that is part of what is causing the problem of extinction. Animals like the Bengal tiger, as well as other endangered species, are a valuable part of the world's ecosystem. International laws protecting these animals must be enacted to ensure their survival, and the survival of our planet. Countries around the world have begun to deal with the problem in various ways. Some countries, in order to circumvent the problem, have allocated large amount of land to animal reserves. They then charge admission to help defray the costs of maintaining the parks, and they often must also depend on world organisations for support. With the money get, they can invest in equipment and patrols to protect the animals. Another solution that is an attempt to stem the tide of animal extinction is an international boycott of products made from endangered species. This seems fairly effective, but it will not, by itself, prevent animals from being hunted and killed.

1. What is the author's main concern in this passage ?
(a) Problems of industrialisation
(b) The Bengal tiger
(c) Endangered species
(d) Callousness of man

2. According to the passage, poachers kill for
(a) material gain
(b) personal satisfaction
(c) both
(d) none of these

3. Which of the following words is closest in meaning to the word 'Alarming'?
(a) Serious
(b) Dangerous
(c) Distressing
(d) Frightening

4. Certain species are becoming extinct because of
(a) industrialisation
(b) poaching
(c) love of products made from them
(d) All of the above

5. The phrase 'Stem the tide' means
(a) save (b) stop
(c) touch (d) spare

6. Which of the following best describes the author's attitude ?
(a) Concerned (b) Vindictive
(c) Surprised (d) Generous

Answers

1. (c) **2.** (b) **3.** (d) **4.** (d)
5. (b) **6.** (a)

Passage 19

Directions (Q. 1-6) : Read the given passage carefully and then choose the best answer for each question. ***(MAT)***

The conservative is not an extreme individualist. He may be willing to concede numerous arguments of the unqualified individualists, for his own respect for the dignity of the individual is not surpassed by that of any man. Yet he cannot agree to the full implications of individualism, which is based so he thinks on an incorrect appraisal of man, society, history, and government. In his own way, the individualist is as much a perfectionist as the Socialist, and with perfectionism the conservative can have no **truck**.

In particular, the conservative refuses to go all the way with economic individualism. His distrust of unfettered man, his recognition to groups, his sense of the complexity of the social process, his recognition of the real services that government can perform all these sentiments make it impossible for him to subscribe to the dogmas and shibboleths of economic individualism : laissez-faire, the negative state, enlightened self-interest, the law of supply and demand, the profit motive. The conservative may occasionally have kind word for each of these notions, but he is careful to qualify his support by stating other, more important social truths. For example, he does not for a moment deny the prominence of the profit motive, but he insists that it be recognised for the selfish thing it is and be kept within reasonable, socially imposed limits.

1. The conservative is
(a) a perfectionist
(b) an economist
(c) a socialist
(d) None of these

2. The conservative is against Economic Individualism for all the following reasons except
(a) he does not trust free men
(b) he believes in the authority of the government
(c) he believes in groups
(d) he feels that social processes are important

3. The author mentions all the following catchwords of economic individualism except
(a) free trade
(b) the profit motive
(c) balance of trade
(d) the negative state

4. Which of the following words can replace the word 'Truck'?
(a) Dealing
(b) Bargain
(c) Debate
(d) Transport

5. Which of the following statements is true ?
(a) The socialist and the individualist tend to be broadly similar in their views
(b) The conservative believes that profit motive originates in selfishness
(c) The conservative is also an extreme individualist
(d) None of the above

6. Which of the following could be an appropriate title for the passage ?
(a) Anarchy and Freedom
(b) Progress and The Conservating
(c) A Conservative Apology
(d) The Conservative Stand

Answers

1. (d) **2.** (d) **3.** (a) **4.** (a)
5. (b) **6.** (d)

Unit
51

The Art of Writing an Elegant 'Precis'

What Is a Precis?

'Precis' is a French word derived from the latin word '*praecisum*' which means 'to cut short' or 'abridge'. As per the Oxford dictionary it means, a concise or abridged statement, a summary. *Precis is a summary or a condensed composition of bare facts. Precis denotes a brief, concise, clear and well connected abstract, summary or gist of a given passage.*

It is a summary of the essential and important ideas of a longer composition; the basic thought of a passage is reproduced in miniature, retaining the mood and tone of the original. It must possess clear, emphatic diction and effective sentence construction. Its unity and coherence should be maintained through smooth, unobtrusive transitions.

In a composition, we may find figurative speech, synonyms, ornamental language, proverbs etc, which does not find place in precis-writing. Precis must be terse, simple and lucid but at the same time, meaningful, and complete. The elegancy of a precis lies in the fact that the reader, without going through the original composition, can understand the gist of the composition.

From these definitions, it is clear that precis-writing means the art to cut short a composition in such a way as to make it precise, exact and well connected gist of the given text.

Essentials of a Good Precis

A precis (pronounced pray-see) is a kind of summary that encompasses an exact reproduction of the logic, organisation and emphasis of the original text. It reflects the relative order, proportions and relationships of the original parts of the given composition. An effective precis retains the logic, development and argument of the original in a much shorter form. There is no single perfect precis of any article, simply versions that fulfil various functions. The writer's job is to become skilled in the art of precis writing and in highlighting essential aspects relating to his purpose.

1. **Brevity or Conciseness** *Brevity is the soul of a good precis.* A precis is a shortening, in your own words, of a text or written work. You are to describe as accurately and briefly as possible the substance or main ideas contained in a text.
2. **Completeness or Comprehensiveness** Precis must have the complete idea of the passage. A well-written precis should be a serviceable substitute for the original work. The goal is to preserve the core essence of the work in a manner that is both clear and concise. At a minimum, the precis should include the topic or main thesis, the purpose of the research, what was studied, what methods were used, what results (or insight) were gained, and a conclusion.
3. **Compactness or Well connected** The sentences must be well connected and the whole precis should reflect a necessary compactness. The paragraphs must be joined together congenially. The precis should not reflect any jerk or discontinuity.
4. **Clarity or Lucidity** Precis should be clear and free from any ambiguity or obscurity. In

an attempt to shorten the passage you must take care that the sentences constructed by you are free from any error; like improper use of words.

5. **Preciseness or Accuracy** It must be understood well that a precis is not a personal interpretation of a work or an expression of your opinion of the idea; it is, rather, an exact replica in miniature of the work, often reduced to one-third of its size, in which you express the complete argument.
6. **Grammatically correct or Purity of language** After you've completed a draft, read your precis and check for accuracy. Correct grammar, spelling, and punctuation errors, looking particularly for those common in your writing.

Length of the Precis

No rigid rule can be laid down as regards the length of the precis. Normally the length of the precis must be one-third of the original composition. The length indeed depends upon the nature of the matter and the purpose of the precis.

How to Write a Good Precis?

1. **Reading and studying of the passage** First read the passage thoroughly, not too slowly, just to get the idea of the passage.Normally one reading is not sufficient for the purpose. Read again in order to get the exact meaning or the gist of the passage. Read the passage, sentence by sentence and word by word. Detail study of this kind is required because a phrase or a sentence or even a single word may be of prime importance and misunderstanding of it may lead to write wrongly.
2. **Writing Heading or title** Normally students are asked to supply a suitable title or heading to the precis.While reading the passage think of some word , sentence or a phrase that sums up the main idea or theme of the passage. Sometimes title is found in the key sentence itself. The key sentence is usually found either at the beginning or at the end of the passage. This is not always true, sometimes the key sentence is typically found in the middle. A good title reflects the subject or the theme of the passage.
3. **Distinguish between essentials and non-essentials** Now you are to decide which parts of the passage are essential .The selection of the essentials points is to be done very carefully. Do not select in a haphazard manner or randomly. You can underline the sentences or the phrases in the original passage. You will be able to do it correctly if you are able to understand the theme of the passage clearly and unambiguously. Now jot down the essential points in your own words.
4. **Prepare the rough draft** Prepare a rough draft of the precis with the help of the essential points jotted down by you. Do not use the wording of the original except for certain key words which you may find indispensable. If you cannot translate the idea into language of your own, you do not understand them very well. Be especially careful not to rely too much on the topic sentence. Do not add any opinions or ideas of yours. **It is not likely that your rough draft will be a complete success.** The draft may be too long and that may require further shortening.You are to make the selection again out of the rough draft prepared by you. Abridge it further if needed. This draft may be revised by making necessary improvements in the sentences and arranging the sentences in proper sequence. If you find any error or ambiguity in sentence construction, correct it.
5. **Finalising the precis** After revising the first draft prepared by you, read it again and see if further improvement is required. Read once again the original passage to see that all the essential points have been incorporated in your precis. Now write out the final precis in its finally revised form. Use of good handwriting counts here also as everywhere else.
6. **Spelling check and word count** Now comes the last stage, check spellings and count the words. See that it is as per the required parameters and every word is correctly spelled.

Some Important Points to Keep in Mind

1. As per the accepted norms, a precis should always be written in indirect speech.One should not write any sayings or quotation in

Direct Speech. For example if the original text contains the following:

Jacob said, "The USA is right in protecting the interests of its citizens."

While writing precis the above sentence must be changed into Indirect Narration and you may write it as following :

Jacob argued in favour of the USA.

2. The precis should be written in third person. If the passage contains pronouns; I, we, you, these may be changed to; he, they, she, as per the sense of the sentence.

For example :

Mr Ramaiyya said to Situben, "I will take care of your son."

This can be changed in the precis as following:

Mr Ramaiyya assured Situben that he would take care of her son.

3. If the reporting verb in direct speech is in the past tense then remember to change all the verbs of the reported speech in their corresponding past tense. (Don't forget the exceptions when the tense of the reported speech does not change.)

4. There is no room in a precis for circuitous expressions or verbosity. No need to use any type of ostentatious, pompous or oratorical language. All kinds of redundancy must be done away with. A precis must be simply worded and grammatically correct.

Art of Reducing the Words

Brevity is the soul of a good precis. How to abridge the original passage upto the desired number of words, is an art.

After sorting out the essential points, as described earlier, now learn how to reduce the number of words as per the demand of the question.

1. Try to shorten each and every sentence individually, or if two or more sentences refer to the same point, shorten them jointly by using appropriate conjunction or by using the technique of transformation of sentences.
2. Use one word substitution technique, if many words can be substituted by a single word.

See the following examples.

Sentence shortening :

1. He betrayed his country and this was to his eternal disgrace.
   To his eternal disgrace he betrayed his country.
2. Besides his father giving him money, his mother also did the same.
   His parents gave him money.
3. He was unlucky and therefore he met with an accident on the eve of his examination.
   Owing to ill-luck he met an accident on the eve of examination.
4. The boy made a mistake. His teacher punished him severely for committing such a mistake.
   The teacher punished the boy for comming a mistake.
5. He succeeded although he was not expecting the success.
   He succeeded unexpectedly.
6. He could afford to lose something but he lost somewhat more.
   He lost more than he could afford.
7. He is something of a poet, but rather more of a philosopher.
   He is more a philosopher than a poet.
8. A fox once met a man. The fox had never seen a man before.
   A fox who never had seen a man before met one.
9. A man and his wife had a hen. The hen laid an egg every day. The egg was golden.
   A man and his wife had a hen which laid a golden egg daily.
10. She was not there. I spoke to her parents for that reason.
    She was not there so I spoke to her parents.
11. I shall not oppose your design. I shall not however approve of it.
    I shall neither oppose nor approve of your design.

One Word Substitution

1. He was a farmer. He did not know reading and writing even his name.
   He was an illiterate farmer.
2. He did not take any intoxicating drinks.
   He was a teetotaller.
3. He renounced the throne with his sweet will.
   He voluntarily abdicated the throne.

4. He was very much particular about the purity of his language.
   He was a purist.
5. He never cared for the pleasure or pain of life.
   He was a stoic.
6. He was always fearing the failures and so never hoped to get success.
   He was a pessimist.
7. She was a maid servant. Her husband died in her young age.
   The maid servant was a young widow.
8. He not only looks and behaves but also sounds like a woman.
   He is an effeminate.
9. He is a good dancer. He does it for the sake of his hobby. He is not a professional dancer.
   He is an amateur dancer.
10. He was a soldier. He killed the king. He was charged with it.
    The soldier was charged with regicide.
11. He was a professor. He did not believe in existence of God.
    The professor was an atheist.

Remember that writing a precis is an art, not easy to learn by reading the rules or tricks but it requires practice. Practise again and again for having perfection.

Do's and Don'ts of Precis Writing

(a) Start your precis by stating the main idea of the passage.

(b) Do not use the words "in this article." Use the style "Jacob argues that the most significant contribution of the Iraqies was . . "

(c) When writing about history, use the past tense.

(d) Do not use abbreviations or contractions.

(e) Avoid words like big, good, bad, little, and a lot. Also, do not use the phrase "throughout history." This is cliché.

(f) Count your 'ands.' Avoid use of 'ands' unnecessarily.

(g) Title of text should be put in italics or underlined.

Most Essential : Help Yourself

1. Nothing but your own knowledge helps you the most.
2. Your knowledge of English Grammar will be of utmost help.
3. Your command over the vocabulary helps you understand the words and the theme of the passage. Good knowledge of synonyms and one word substitutes helps you in using your own words and reducing the words while writing a precis.
4. Your command over writing, joining the sentences, using conjunctions or using the technique of transformation of sentences etc, will give you perfection in the art of writing precis.

Examples

Exercise 1

Make a precis of the following passage, about one-third of its length. As far as possible, the precis should be in your own words. Also suggest a suitable title for the precis.

People moan about poverty as a great evil; and it seems to be an accepted belief that if people only had plenty of money, they would be happy and useful and get more out of life. As a rule, there is more genuine satisfaction and more is obtained from life in humble cottages of the poor men than in the palaces of the rich. I always pity the sons and daughters of the rich men, who are attended by servants and governesses; at the same time, I am glad to think they do not know what they have missed.

It is because, I know how sweet and pure and happy the home of honest poverty is, how free from perplexing care and from social envies and jealousies, that I sympathise with the rich man's boy and congratulate a poor man's son. It is for these reasons that from the ranks of the poor so many strong, eminent, self-reliant men have always sprung and always must spring. If you read the list of the great men and women of the world, you will find that most of them have been born poor. (192 Words)

Essential Points

1. Poverty-regarded an evil.
2. It is believed that money is essential for being happy and useful.
3. The poor man living in cottages are found comparatively happier and contented than the rich.
4. A rich man's children brought up by the servants miss a lot of valuable things in life about which they are unknown.
5. A poor man is usually free-from irritating care, social envies and the jealousy .
6. Going through the list you find that most of the great men are emerged from the world of the poor.

Rough Sketch

Poverty is usually regarded as an evil. It is believed that money is essential for a happier life. The poor man living in cottages are found comparatively happy and contented to the rich. A rich man's children brought up by the servants miss a lot of valuable things in life about which they are unknown. A poor man is usually free-from irritating care, social envies and the jealousy. Most of the great men are so emerged from the world of the poor.

Precis 1 : Poverty—a Blessing

People curse the poverty as evil. They think, money is essential for making life happier. A poor man indeed leads a contented life free from irritating overcare and social jealousy. Children of the rich, brought up by the servants miss many valuable things, while the children of the poor turn out to be great and self made, as evident from the list of great men. (65 words)

Exercise 2

Make a precis of the following passage, about one-third of its length. As far as possible, the precis should be in your own words. Also suggest a suitable title for the precis.

Two of the most obvious of the merits of newspapers are cheapness and readability. The penny newspaper, even in its abbreviated form of today, is remarkable value for money. We can think of no other product, which is sold for so small a sum. The readers of penny newspaper clearly find in it something that satisfies their reading needs. They find a brightly coloured kaleidoscopic picture of the world day by day. They find exciting incidents home and abroad; they find pathos and tragedy mingled with sentiments and comedy; they find personal gossip about the great or the notorious but have caught the popular imagination for the moment; they find well produced photographs of people or places. Great affairs of national or international importance may not always get the space or the dispassionate treatment that is their due but they are not neglected; nor are serious features lacking even if the lighter ones predominate. In the quality Press, important questions whether national or international, are handled seriously and if the presentation of events and the treatment of personalities are not untinged with partisanship, these newspapers do succeed on the whole in conveying to their reader a clear picture of the conflict of issues in the world today. A mass of materials upon which considered judgement on crucial problems, national and international, can be built up, will be found in their pages and if such papers are few in number, than it is open to the public to increase their circulation.

(250 words)

Essential Points

1. Important features of Newspaper—cheap and readable.
2. Even the small newspapers provide full value for their price.
3. People find exciting domestic and foreign news including comedy gossips and interesting photographs of persons and places.
4. Gives news and views about people, places and events of national and international importance.
5. Though quality newspapers deal seriously with the national and international questions yet they are sometimes not free from the bias.
6. If the newspapers could present the events unbiased , they really convey the true position to their readers and thus get more circulation.

Rough Sketch

Two important features of Newspaper are that they are cheap and readable. Even the small newspapers provide full value for their price. People find exciting domestic and foreign news including comedy gossips and interesting photographs of persons and places. Gives news and views about people, places and events of national and international importance. Though quality newspapers deal seriously with the national and international questions yet they are sometimes not free from the bias. If the newspapers could present the events unbiased, they really convey the true position to their readers and thus get more circulation.

Precis 2 : Merits of Newspapers

Two most discerning features of a newspaper are its inexpensiveness and readability. Newspapers cater to the diverse reading needs of people with diverse tastes. It provides, news and views about events of national and international importance. They may have biased opinion about some issues, but they never neglect them. Though quality press deals with the issues seriously yet not impartial. A few newspapers present the events analytically and unbiased, they deserve to get their circulation increased. (76 words)

Exercise 3

Make a precis of the following passage, about one-third of its length. As far as possible, the precis should be in your own words. Also suggest a suitable title for the precis.

There were many obstacles in the development of commerce during the Middle Ages. Dangers by land and sea had to be considered by the merchant who wished to send his goods to some distance part; but as the towns grew and multiplied, the resolution and ingenuity of man rendered it possible for commerce to increase steadily, till by the dawn of the modern period every country in Western Europe had felt its beneficent influence. When we think of the poorness of communication, the vast forests, the inferior roads, the unbridged rivers and the innumerable foes lining the trade routes, it would seem at first sight, almost an impossibility for merchants in the North of Europe to have intercourse with those of the South.

Then again, the narrow spirit of the Middle Ages, the survival of feudalism offered a difficulty which was almost as prohibitive to the transportation of merchandise as the robbers and pirates, noble and ignoble, who lay in wait for the trembling merchant.

There was an elaborate system of dues and tolls which made most goods, when they arrived safely at their destination, a luxury beyond the means of the average man; furthermore, it was the practice for governments in those days to prohibit and prevent passage through their countries. Yet, in spite of all difficulties the groups of towns which were developing in Northern and Southern Europe and the manufacturing centres of the East and West, steadily increased their wealth and prosperity. (245 words)

Essential Points

1. Commerce faced obstacles during middle age, on account of dangers at land and sea routes, but with the growth of towns and improved ability of the men the commerce increased.

2. Due to lack of proper infrastructure it seemed impossible for the trade to grow.
3. The presence of robbers and narrow mindedness of the middle age along with survival of feudalism were the main hindrances in the development of commerce.
4. Custom of charging dues and tolls and the practice of governments preventing the passage of goods further hindered the commerce.
5. In spite of all these obstacles, the developing groups of towns enhanced their prosperity all over the Europe.

Rough Sketch

Commerce faced obstacles during middle age, on account of dangers at land and sea routes, but with the growth of towns and improved ability of the men the commerce increased.

Due to lack of proper infrastructure it seemed impossible for the trade to grow and the presence of robbers and narrow mindedness of the middle age along with survival of feudalism were the main hindrances in the development of commerce. Moreover the custom of charging dues and tolls and the practice of governments preventing the passage of goods further hindered the commerce. In spite of all these obstacles, the developing groups of towns enhanced their prosperity all over the Europe.

Precis 3 : Commerce During the Middle Ages

During the Middle Ages commerce faced obstacles due to dangers at land and sea routes. Moroovor lack of proper infrastructure, presence of robbers and narrow mindedness of the Middle Age alongwith existence of feudalism also created hurdles. Also the custom of extracting charges and the practice of governments preventing the passage of goods hindered the commerce. In spite of all these obstacles,the commerce grew steadily and the developing groups of towns could enhance their wealth and prosperity in Europe. (80 words)

Exercise 4

Make a precis of the following passage, about one-third of its length. As far as possible, the precis should be in your own words. Also suggest a suitable title for the precis.

Speech is regarded as a great blessing but it can also be a great curse, for, while it helps us to make our intentions and desires known to our fellows, it can also, if we use it carelessly make our attitude completely misunderstood. A slip of the tongue, the use of an unusual word or of an ambiguous word, may create an enemy where we had hoped to win a friend. Again different classes of people use different vocabularies. The ordinary speech of an educated man may strike to an uneducated listener as showing pride; unwittingly we may use a word which bears a different meaning to our listener from what it does to mean to our own classes.Thus speech is not a gift to use lightly without thought but one which demands careful handling. Only a fool will express himself alike to all kinds and conditions of men. (148 words)

Essential Points

1. Speech is a blessing and a curse also.
2. A slip of tongue or single inappropriate word may create ambiguity and enmity.
3. Different peoples use different types of words that may mean differently to different types of people. That may be understood by an illiterate as our pride.
4. So speech is such a gift that should be used carefully.

Rough Sketch

Speech is a blessing as well as a curse. A slip of tongue or single inappropriate word may create ambiguity and enmity. Different people use different types of words that mean differently to the different people. That may be misunderstood by the illiterate as our pride. So speech should be used carefully by us.

Precis 4 : Speech a Gift

Speech is a valuable gift. It must be used carefully, otherwise we may be misunderstood and turn our friends into foes. Words don't always mean the same thing to the literate and illiterate. A wise man uses the gift of speech, with great caution in order to avoid undesired effect. (49 words)

Exercise 5

Make a precis of the following passage, about one-third of its length. As far as possible, the precis should be in your own words. Also suggest a suitable title for the precis.

In difficulty the man who has to face it either come better or worse. Encounter with it will train his strength and discipline his skill. The road to success may be steep to climb, but it puts to proof the energies of him who would reach the summit. By experience a man soon learns how obstacles are to be overcome by grappling with them. Thus difficulties often fall away of themselves before the determination to overcome them.

In nine cases out of ten if marched boldly upon they will flee. Like thieves they often disappear at a glance. What looked like insurmountable obstacle like some great mountain chain in our way, is found to become practicable. When approached, and even the paths formerly unseen, though they may be narrow and difficult, themselves open a way for us through the hills. (140 words)

Essential Points

1. In difficulty the strength and skill of a man is judged.
2. Road to success is not an easy one, it tests the strength of a person.
3. Experience teaches us to overcome obstacles.
4. Difficulties if faced boldly, themselves flee away. What once looks insurmountable soon becomes very easy.
5. Even the unknown paths give us way automatically. When we overcome obstacles, we will achieve success.

Rough Sketch

In difficulty the strength and skill of a man is judged. Road to success is not an easy one, it tests the strength of a person. It is the experience that teaches us to overcome obstacles. Difficulties if faced boldly, themselves flee away. What once looks insurmountable soon becomes very easy. Even the unknown paths give us way automatically.

Precis 5 : Overcoming Difficulties

Difficulties try the strength and talent of a person. Success doesn't come easily, it requires proven strength. Conquering difficulties successfully comes with the experience. Obstacles once look insuperable gives away the solution themselves to the bold and determined. (45 words)

Solved Exercises for Practice

Exercise 6

Make a precis of the following passage, about one-third of its length. As far as possible, the precis should be in your own words. Also suggest a suitable title for the precis.

When our childhood has fallen behind us and taken on some of the glamour of distance we often ransack our memories in order to call up to our mind's eye the picture of the children we were. Then we are surprised to discover how little we remember of our earliest days; they have gone for ever and seemingly have left nothing behind them. All is lost in haze, and no definite image rewards our efforts to recapture the incidents of infancy.

Some, however, can recall more than others; one may remember something that happened when he was only a child of two, while another may find his memory blank a clean sheet of paper as far as anything is concerned which befell him before he was five. Yet, perhaps as regards things generally, the memory of the latter may be stronger than that of the former, it is only in regard to his early childhood that the first man's memory is stronger.

To account for these variations is not easy : there are so many factors to be taken into account. Nature and circumstances have to be considered. One may be markedly introspective, unconsciously looking into himself from his earliest days : another may have had an accident which could not fail to impress itself on his memory. Again, one man may remember earlier events because his memory is a visual one, while another looks not so far back because his memory is more of the mind and a child's mind is of slower development than his sight. (259 words)

Precis 6 : Memory of Childhood

After some years, if we look back to our earliest days of childhood, we would find that we remember very little. The memories of some however can go back farther than that of others. It is not necessarily the stronger memory that does it. It is the nature of a man and his circumstances, that determine the extent of his memory. A man with visual memory may have better memory than others. (72 words)

Exercise 7

Make a precis of the following passage, about one-third of its length. As far as possible, the precis should be in your own words. Also suggest a suitable title for the precis.

It is possible to score goals and lose the game. It is possible to win battles and lose the campaign. It is possible to make money and miss a fortune. The short-sighted man suffers, no matter where he is found; he may see some things with excessive clarity, but he fails to get the true perspective which will enable him to arrive at wise conclusions. He gains one thing, but he loses something better.

This is a very common error. The student makes it when he forgets the life-goal in thinking of the medal or the scholarship. The saint forgets it when he thinks of to-day and forgets the greater to-morrow. The business man misses his way when he choses a present gain and forfeits ten times as much in the future. The youth makes such a mistake when he marries good looks, and forgets the character which will be necessary to command his respect for forty years to come.

Man was made to think and unless he uses his brain he will stumble into no end of unseen morasses. There is a future, and it cannot be evaded; and when it is reached it cannot be changed, for we are just deciding what it shall be. We are our own destiny-makers. It is well to face the future with care and caution . (225 words)

Precis 7 : Disadvantages of Short-Sightedness

Winning and losing, are parts of life. A short-sighted person loses the greater future gain for an immediate small gain. The student misses his life-goal for a medal, the saint ignoring future bliss for the present achievement, the business man foregoing a larger fortune for the present gain and the youth marrying a beautiful girl rather than one of character, all are short-sightedness of the respective fellows. We are the architect of our destiny; we should face it carefully. (71 words)

Exercise 8

Make a precis of the following passage, about one-third of its length. As far as possible, the precis should be in your own words. Also suggest a suitable title for the precis.

How many apparent defeats, Enthusiasm has transformed into victories ? It is one of the most vital elements in all successes, but in the sphere of religious activity its value cannot be over-estimated. Nevertheless it must be admitted, that enthusiasm is not something that can always be had merely for the asking.

In the first place, to be effective, enthusiasm must be genuine. Simulated enthusiasm is a weak, vapid thing that soon dies. People do not become enthusiastic merely by wanting to be. It is not something that can be thrust upon others at will. Nothing could be more ridiculous than for someone to rise before a large gathering and say, "I move them all and they became enthusiastic!" Enthusiasm is not necessarily a noise or shouting or even feverish activity. These may be, and sometimes are, manifestations of its presence, but not necessarily so. Often, indeed, such symptoms are merely spurious imitations, and as far from the genuine articles as the counterfeit money from the real money.

All genuine, lasting enthusiasm must be built upon knowledge. This is the true fountain from which it bubbles up, and nothing will take its place. People cannot be lastingly enthusiastic about that of which they know nothing." (210 words)

Precis 8 : The Power of Enthusiasm

Enthusiasm is very important element to achieve success. Enthusiasm has turned many sure tumblings into victories. But it must be genuine for being effective otherwise it dies soon. We should distinguish real from false enthusiasm which consists in noise, shouting or feverish activity. Genuine enthusiasm can be built upon knowledge alone. To be genuinely enthusiastic about a thing, people should acquire complete knowledge. (64 words)

Exercise 9

Make a precis of the following passage, about one-third of its length. As far as possible, the precis should be in your own words. Also suggest a suitable title for the precis.

When in the course of human events it becomes necessary for people to dissolve the political bonds which have connected with one another and to assume among the powers of the earth a separate and equal station, a decent respect for the opinions of mankind requires that they should declare the causes which impel them to separation.

We hold truth to be self evident that all men are created equal; that they are endowed by their creator with certain inalienable rights; that among these are life, liberty and the pursuit of happiness; that to secure these rights, governments are liberty and the pursuit of happiness; that to secure these rights, governments are instituted among the, deriving their just powers from the consent of the governed; that whenever any form of government becomes destructive of these ends, it is the right of the people to abolish it and to institute a new government, laying its foundation on such principles and organising its power in such form, as to them shall seem most likely to effect their safety and happiness.

Prudence will dictate that governments long established should not be changed for light and transient causes and accordingly all experience hath shown that mankind are more disposed to suffer while evils are sufferable than to right themselves by abolishing the forms to which they are accustomed. But when a long train of abuses and usurpations, pursuing invariably the same object, evinces a design to reduce them under absolute despotism it is their duty to throw off such government, and to provide new guards for their future security. (267 words)

Precis 9 : The People and the Government

Whenever people force to break political bonds, assuming an independent status of a separate nation, the causes of such separation should be declared.

All men are created equal and they possess certain inalienable rights. Governments are created by the people to protect these rights. If a government fails to secure these, the people have a right to change that government. Prudence requires that long-established governments should not be changed for trivial causes. Only when constant abuses and usurpations threaten to bring them under despotism, then such a government should be thrown off for better future. (88 words)

Exercise 10

Make a precis of the following passage, about one-third of its length. As far as possible, the precis should be in your own words. Also suggest a suitable title for the precis.

Trading is a social activity. Whoever undertakes to sell any kinds of goods to the public, does what affects the interest of other persons and of society in general. Thus his conduct, in principle, comes within the jurisdiction of society. Accordingly, it was once held to be the duty of governments, in all cases which were considered of importance, to fix prices, and regulate the process of manufacture. But it is now recognized, though not till after a long struggle, that both the cheapness and the good quality of commodities are most effectively provided for by leaving the producers and sellers perfectly free, under the sole check of equal freedom to the buyers for supplying themselves elsewhere. This is the so-called doctrine of Free Trade, which rests on grounds different from, though equally solid witty, the principle of individual liberty. Restrictions on trade or on production for purposes of trade are indeed restraints; and all restraints, as restraint, is evil. But the restraints in question affect only that part of conduct which society is competent to restrain and those are wrong solely because they do not really produce the results which it is desired to produce by them. As the principle of individual liberty is not involved in the doctrine of Free Trade, so neither is in most of the questions which arise respecting the limits of the doctrine : as, for example, what amount of public control is admissible for the prevention of fraud by adulteration; how far sanitary precautions, or arrangements to protect work-people employed in dangerous occupations, should be enforced on players. Such question involves considerations of liberty, only in so far as leaving people to themselves is always better than controlling them. (285 words)

Precis 10 : Control over Trade

Trade affects society. Earlier Governments controlled prices and the manufacturing processes. For making available cheap and good quality things, buyers and sellers should have freedom to deal with freely. It's Free Trade, which may or mayn't have personal freedom. Restraints for the sake of restraint, over trade are unjustified. Imposition of restraints by the society itself are improper if it doesn't give desired results. Control enforcement to prevent adulteration and protecting people from health hazards again involves the point of liberty . So it's always better to left the people free and let them control themselves. (92 words)

Exercise 11

Make a precis of the following passage, about one-third of its length. As far as possible, the precis should be in your own words. Also suggest a suitable title for the precis.

Although our age far surpasses all previous ages in knowledge yet there has been no correlative increase in wisdom. The agreement between the two ceases as soon as we attempt to define 'wisdom' and consider means of promoting it. I want to ask first what wisdom is, and then what can be done to teach it.

There are, I think, several factors that contribute to wisdom. Of these, I should put first a sense of proportion : the capacity to take account of all the important factors in a problem and attach to each its due weight. This has become more difficult than it used to be owing to the extent and complexity of the specialised knowledge required of various kinds of techniques. Suppose, for example that you are engaged in research in scientific medicine. The work is difficult and is likely to absorb the whole of your intellectual energy. You have no time to consider the effect which your discoveries or inventions may have outside the field of medicine. You succeed (let us say) as modern medicine has succeeded, in enormously lowering the infant death-rate, not only in Europe and America but also in Asia and Africa. This has the entirely unintended result of making the food supply inadequate and lowering the standard of life in the most populous parts of the world. To take an even more spectacular example, which is in everybody's mind at the present time : You study the composition of the atom from a disinterested desire for knowledge and incidentally place in the hands of powerful lunatics the means of destroying the human race. In such ways the pursuit of knowledge may become harmful unless it is combined with wisdom; and wisdom in the sense of comprehensive vision is not necessarily present in specialist in the pursuit of knowledge.

Comprehensiveness alone, however, is not enough to constitute wisdom. There must be also, a certain awareness of the ends of human life. This may be illustrated by the study of history. Many eminent historians have done more harm than good because they viewed facts through the distorting medium of their own passions. Hegel had a philosophy of history which did not suffer from and lack of comprehensiveness, since it started from the earliest time and continued into an indefinite future. But the chief lesson of history which he sought to inculcate was that from the A.D. 400 down to his own time Germany had been the most important nation and the standard-bearer of progress in the world. Perhaps, one could stretch the comprehensiveness that constitutes wisdom to include not only intellect but also feeling. It is by no means uncommon to find men whose knowledge is wide but whose feelings are narrow. Such men lack what I am calling wisdom. (514 words)

Precis 11 : Knowledge Versus Wisdom

Our age is far ahead of previous ages in the matter of knowledge but not so in case of wisdom. Wisdom means a sense of proportion. It further means to analyse a problem in the light of all the related factors. Comprehensiveness itself does not mean the 'wisdom'. Technical knowledge about medicines and atomic energy does not bother about the far-reaching consequences of its use. So, there should be wisdom to control and guide the use of knowledge. Besides comprehensiveness, wisdom includes the awareness about the ends of our lives. The study of history well threw light on this point. Some historians distorted the facts of history because of their personal passion and interest. Indifferently pursuing for acquiring the knowledge may result in its misuse, if used by a man having no wisdom. A man with wide knowledge but no feelings is a man without wisdom. (157 words)

Exercise 12

Make a precis of the following passage, about one-third of its length. As far as possible, the precis should be in your own words. Also suggest a suitable title for the precis.

What is a perfectly free person ? Evidently a person who can do what he like, when he like and where he like, or do nothing at all if he prefers it. Well, there is no such person; and there never can be any such person. Whether we like it or not we must all sleep for one-third of our lifetime; wash and dress and undress; we must spend a couple of hours eating and drinking; we must spend nearly as much in getting about from place to place. For half the day we are slaves to necessities which we cannot shirk, whether we are monarchs with a thousand servants or humble labourers with no servants. And the wives must undertake the additional heavy slavery of child-bearing if the world is still to be full of people.

These natural jobs cannot be shirked. But they involve other jobs which can. As we must eat we must first provide food; as we must sleep, we must have beds and beddings in houses with fireplaces and cool; as we must walk through the streets, we must have clothes to cover ourselves. Now, food, houses and clothes can be produced by human labour. But when they are produced they can be stolen. If you like honey you can let bees produce it by their labour, and then steal it from them. What you can do to a bee you can also do to a man or a woman or a child if you can get the upper hand of them by force or fraud or trickery of any sort, or even by teaching them that it is their religious duty to sacrifice their freedom for yours.

So beware if you allow any person, or class of persons, to get the upper hand of you, they will shift all that part of their slavery to Nature that can be shifted on to your shoulders; and you will find yourself working form eight to fourteen hours a day when, if you had only yourself and your family to provide for, you could do it quite comfortably in half the time or less. The object of all honest governments should be to prevent your being imposed on in this way. But the object of most governments is exactly the opposite. They enforce your slavery and call it freedom. But they also regulate your slavery, keeping the greed of your master within certain bounds. They promise that in future you shall govern the country for yourself. They redeem this promise by giving you a vote, and having a general election every five years or so. At the election, two of their rich friends ask for your vote : and you are free to choose which of them you will vote for to spite the other—a choice which leaves you no freer than you were before, as it does not reduce your hours of labour by a single minute. But the newspapers assure you that your vote has decided the election, and that this constitutes you a free citizen in a democratic country. The amazing thing about it is that you are foolish enough to believe them. (530 words)

Precis 12 : Perfect Freedom

Perfect Freedom is an illusory thing. None, including the Kings and the labourers are perfectly free. They have to obey the natural calls of sleeping, eating, clothing, drinking, etc. For fulfilling these calls, we need food, beddings, produced by human labour, which can be stolen also. Likewise, man exploits other weak people through force or fraud. Strong are the slaves of nature. They in turn, enslave the weak by forcing them to work from eight to fourteen hours daily. This exploitation should have been stopped by the governments, but instead of stopping, government perpetuate slavery in the name of freedom. By extending a right to vote, they hoodwink the people with the idea of self-governance by choosing their rulers themselves. But the choice is limited because the poor have to choose one rich man every time, who doesn't bother to give any relief to them.The newspapers also make the people feel that they have chosen their leaders. They are befooled to believe that they are free citizens of a democratic country.

(170 words)

Exercise 13

Make a precis of the following passage, about one- third of its length. As far as possible, the precis should be in your own words. Also suggest a suitable title for the precis.

Disarmament assumes a very special importance for us, overriding all other issues. For many years past, there have been talks on disarmament and some progress has undoubtedly been made in so far as the plans and proposals are concerned. Still we find that the race of armaments continues, as also the efforts to invent even more powerful engines of destruction. If even a small part of these efforts was directed to the search for peace, probably the problem of disarmament would have been solved by this time. Apart from the moral imperative of peace, every practical consideration leads us to that conclusion. The choice today in this nuclear age is one of utter annihilation and destruction of civilization or of some way to have peaceful co-existence between nations. There is no middle way. If war is an abomination and an ultimate crime which has to be avoided, we must fashion our minds and policies accordingly. In order to achieve peace we have to develop a climate of peace and tolerance and to avoid speech and action which tend to increase fear and hatred. It may not be possible to reach full disarmament in one step, though every step should be conditioned to that end. Much ground has already been covered in the discussion on disarmament. But the sands of time run out, and we dare not play about with this issue or delay its consideration. This, indeed, is the main duty of the United Nations today and if it fails in this, the United Nations fails in its main purpose. (260 words)

Precis 13 : Importance of Disarmament

Disarmament has acquired a special significance today. In spite of talks, plans and proposals to stop it, mad race for armament and search for more destructive weapons continue. In this Nuclear Age we are to choose either total destruction or an atmosphere of peaceful coexistence. To create a peaceful environment we must avoid speeches and talks, mounting tensions, fear and hatred. Total disarmament is not possible in one step, but gradual move towards this goal can be fruitful. In order to prove its utility the UNO must endeavour to achieve this goal. (88 words)

Exercise 14

Make a precis of the following passage, about one-third of its length. As far as possible, the precis should be in your own words. Also suggest a suitable title for the precis.

If the rule of reason in the region of thought is the aim of science, the rule of equality in the region of behaviour is the aim of democracy. Democracy is not a political arrangement or a form of government. It is a pattern of life, an active conviction which informs and inspires every thought, word and deed. Our present constitution of society induces in its more fortunate members far too great readiness to accept privilege as though it were inherent in the social order as though it were normal and even proper and just.

If we are sincere in our professing of democracy, we should not shut our eyes to the most obvious defects of the present social order. A system which does not offer security and decent employment to multitudes of trained young men suffers from fundamental vice. Society is in danger of splitting to pieces if the few who have the benefits of civilization are not willing to share them with the rest. No state is stable unless it procures for all its members the essentials of a good life. We acknowledge that health is better than disease, sufficiently better than poverty, shelter better than cold and exposure, ease of mind better than racking anxiety. It is our duty to obtain these essentials of civilised life or the mass of the population to work for basic economic justice for all, if necessary; by the imposition of higher taxes on incomes, land, property and inheritance. Riches were created by the maker for being spent on social purposes. It was Blackstone, not Lenin, who wrote; "The law not only regards life and protects every man in enjoyment of it, but also furnishes him with everything necessary for its support. For there is no man so indecent or wretched but that he may demand a supply sufficient for all the necessities of life from the more opulent part of the community. (325 words)

Precis 14 : Essentials of Democracy

Democracy aims to establish rule of equality in the behavioural conduct of society. Democracy is not simply a form of government but a way of life, an important mode of conduct. In the prevailing order of our society a few classes flourish but masses suffer.

Unless the inequality is not removed, and States provide security, employment, shelter, economic justice etc and other essentials of civilised life to all citizens, it cannot be called truly democratic. No affluent can be safe if the masses are wretched. For its own existence, it's the foremost duty of the State to protect the basic rights of the poor and to provide economic justice to all. (108 words)

Exercise 15

Make a precis of the following passage, about one-third of its length. As far as possible, the precis should be in your own words. Also suggest a suitable title for the precis.

We talk so much about democracy, without going into ancient records. Parliamentary democracy, roughly speaking, is something of the growth of the last 150 or 200 years. We might remember that, say in England and in other countries too, this parliamentary democracy and the system of giving the franchise to the people was very strictly limited. Till quite recently, some 20 to 30 years ago relatively small number of people had the vote. Even now in quite advanced countries, half the population consisting of women do not have the vote. Therefore, democracy in those countries is presumably thought of in terms of 'male democracy' not female.

When we talk about democracy in the nineteenth century it was a democracy which was limited very strictly to certain classes and gradually after great struggles it widened out; the franchise went wider and wider. Then again after a good deal of trouble, the actual representatives, who were chosen, also spread out from certain limited classes to other. It is a relatively slow process. Therefore, it is only in the last, I believe, thirty years or so, that adult franchise has come into being in a number of countries. That clearly is long enough, I suppose, and yet it is not long enough really to tell us what the ultimate effects of this are likely to be in solving problems etc. because the ultimate test, of course, is how far a system of government solves the problems which the country had and the people have to face. Any broadly theoretical approach to this question, good as it may be, does not take you very far if the best of these fails to solve the problems that the country has to face. Of course, the problems are solved not merely by good machines, the structure of government, but by many other things, by the quality of human beings, by their training, by their education, by their education, by their character and any number of other things. All that the machine can do is to make it easier to these qualities to develop and remove any element of suppression and actually encourage them to grow.

Now, we talk about democracy again. Democracy has been spoken of chiefly, in the past, as political democracy, roughly represented by every person having a vote. This is a substantial idea but it becomes obvious that a vote by itself does not represent very much to a person who is down and out, to a person, let us say, who is starving or hungry or has no other resources. He is much more interested in getting food to eat than a vote a part from some few individuals who might be. Therefore, political democracy, by itself, is not enough except that it may be used to obtain a gradually increasing measure of economic democracy, equality and the spread of the good things of life to other and removal of gross inequalities. That process has, no doubt, continued for some time in countries where there is political democracy and brought about a lessening of these differences, and because of the growth in other ways it lessened internal tensions, though not completely. (440 words)

Precis 15 : Parliamentary Democracy

Parliamentary democracy is a product of gradual growth of 150 to 200 years. In the past, franchise was limited in many countries to a few people. Even now there are countries where women do not have any franchise. It was after a long drawn struggles that the right of voting was extended to others. But the ultimate effect of this change has to be seen not simply in the kind of government that it promises to introduce but in the way it helps the people in solving their economic and other problems. A vote by itself has no value for a starving person. For true political democracy it is necessary that it leads to economic equality, equal distribution of wealth among the people, and to the lessening of their social and economic differences and all round gradual growth with little internal tensions.

(141 words)

Unit

52

The Art of Writing Expansions and Paragraphs

How to Write an Expansion?

What Is an Expansion ?

Expansion means an enlargement of the topic/theme or the statement given. It is therefore, precisely opposite in nature to precis writing where we have to compress and concise the given passage. In Expansion, a sentence or a short statement has to be enlarged into paragraphs by elaborating in detail, adding therewith illustrations, examples or proofs etc. The exercise of expansion practically amounts to writing a miniature essay on the subject or topic given. No strict rule can be laid down as to the length of the expansion, it should be neither too short nor so large as to become an essay.

Normally, a proverb, maxim or a statement packed with meaning is given for expansion, eg, A stitch in time saves nine; Rome was not built in a day; Honesty is the best policy etc.

Some Important Tips

1. First of all try to understand the precise meaning, significance and implications of the statement or the topic, given for expansion. Devote a few minutes.
2. Having grasped the subject and meaning of the given sentence or statement, proceed to expand it by adding illustrations, examples, and other relevant details etc, until it becomes a mini essay.
3. Arrange your ideas and note down the important points in the order to be mentioned. Mention only those points that are relevant to the subject.
4. If you are given a metaphor, describe its full meaning in plain language, and give reasons to support it.
5. Do not use or begin your expansion with such stereotyped or uninteresting phrases, as; The meaning of the saying is', or 'This proverb means', or 'These lines teach us', or 'Instances are not wanting to prove the truth of this statement', or 'It is a common saying and does not require any explanation'. Such opening are 'dull, flat and unproductive',and indicate lack of originality. Begin your expansion in some striking way.
6. Write simply and to the point. Use grammatically correct language, taking care, if a limit has been set, not to exceed it.
7. Finally, examine your composition. Your expansion should read as a complete piece of composition couched in good English.

Avoid

1. Misunderstanding the subject, or not understanding it fully.
2. Lack of arrangement, and consequent confusion in the expression of ideas.
3. Repetition of ideas/arguments.
4. Inclusion of irrelevant matter.
5. Writing too little or too much.
6. Inaccurate illustrations.
7. Grammatical and spelling errors.

(1) Familiarity Breeds Contempt

(PCS)

Familiarity means closeness, means lack of formalities, means knowing all the ins and outs of others, means lot of expectations that all results in arising of causes of dispute and breeding reasons for quarrel or contempt, as expectations can't be calculated and very difficult to be fulfilled in this world where everyone is busy in his own affairs. On the other hand in formal acquaintances we know little about others and take more formal care and pay more formal respect so there is little cause of quarrel or contempt. A reasonable distance in relations so is necessary to avoid quarrel and contempt. Rightly said, "A hedge between keeps the friendship green and familiarity breeds contempt."

(2) Romance Is the Magic of Distance

(PCS)

One likes to acquire what is not within one's ambit. Any rare thing once possessed, lost charm of having it but a thing of whatever quality till not acquired is a rare thing and so has its importance. There is a saying : 'Distant bells are charming.' The future is always more charming because that is far from the present. A man generally pines for distant objects and moments in the hope of getting imaginative pleasure. We often discover an element of magic in the distant objects. Romance vanishes as soon as the object of Romance is achieved or acquired by us. The fact is that the element of distance casts some magical spell on us. All human faces, and distant objects look romantic till they are at a distance. Keats has so rightly said, "Heard melodies are sweet, but those unheard are sweeter."

(3) God Helps Those Who Help Themselves

(Asst Grade)

God has gifted the man with such wonderful and tremendous powers that he can achieve anything. A person who is sincere and dedicated to his task gets success. In time of distress, when one aspires some divinely help to get one free from the period of distress, the divine help comes only to those who help themselves. God only helps those who do not lose heart and fight tooth and nail to get success. One who is hard working, sincere and devoted honestly to one's work is certain to achieve his goal and get success and to such fellows God is there to come to their aid and rescue. So one must not keep oneself idle and waste one's time in the hope of any divine help as God helps those who help themselves. Everyone pushes the moving cart but none lifts the bogged down one.

(4) They Also Serve Who Only Stand and Wait

(Asst Grade)

This is one of the crucial line from Milton's snnet 'On His Blindness'. This is a concluding and proverbial sentence of the poem means that God does not require any active service from his creatures. What He requires from man is obedience and His commandments. Those who only stand and wait at His service also serve Him as do His trusted angels. It means those who surrender themselves to His will and act as per the wishes of the Almighty are also doing a service. The persons who are though not putting any active service yet always at the call of Him are not lesser devotees.

(5) Man Is a Social Animal

(Asst Grade)

The functions of Man and other animals are to a great extent similar. Man has a developed brain while other animals do not have such a developed brain. So man is also an animal. The natural impulses like hunger, thirst, sex and pugnacity are found in all animals alike. Because of the gift of brain possessed by the man, he is superior and created a world of its own, developed families, societies, towns, cities, countries. Man acts and live for the welfare of his family, society. All the actions of the man are oriented for the good causes and for the welfare of the human being, while other animals live only for themselves. Therefore, man is called a social animal.

(6) The Fruits of Labour Are Sweeter Than the Gifts of Fortune

What is received in gift or what is inherited from the parents is never as charming or important as the things achieved by us by our own efforts, by our own labour. The sweet acquired through 'sweat' will be much sweeter than the sweet given to us by someone. Nothing tastes so sweet as that is earned by hard labour. 'By the sweat of thy brow thou shalt earn thy bread', was the divine wish. The things achieved by hard work shall be more permanent, more delicious, more lovable, more enjoying and render us real happiness.

Anything acquired by the grace of God or by luck will not give us the real enjoyment and real respect, because this fortune does not have anything your own. The history remembers those who change the path of adversity by their hard labour. The world adores those who make their own fortune and create examples for others. Abraham Lincoln, Dhiru Bhai Ambani etc, are several examples of persons who achieved the success by their sheer hard work and so they are adored today. 'Honest labour bears a beautiful face.'

(7) Fame Is the Last Infirmity of a Noble Mind

Fame does not make a man noble, nobility makes a man famous. If a noble mind becomes sensitive to the fame, he is no more noble. Noble means doing everything without any ambition. Nobility does not require or aspire any reward. A noble mind works with selfless, detached spirit and considers work to be its own reward. Milton, the author of this quotation, has well said that a noble soul may conquer all weaknesses but he cannot override the desire to acquire fame. But whatever said or done by anybody, it is undoubtedly true that the day the noble mind gets influenced by the lust of fame, his nobility diminishes upto the degree the lust is there. It is right that desire of getting famous is a great desire which an ordinary man cannot over-ride but for a noble man nothing is more important than the nobility in real terms.

(8) Character Is Destiny *(Asst Grade)*

A fatalist believes in destiny. According to him fate is a pre-written thing, can't be changed or made by the human being. Such people believe that a man's fate is preordained by God, and man has no power over his fate. To such people, destiny is character. While many persons believe that man is the maker of his own destiny and fate. A man who wins, is the man, who thinks he can. A man can change his fate, create his fortune, who believes in himself, has positive attitude, strong will, firm determination and zeal to achieve the goals. Character is nothing, but these qualities, which shapes the conduct of a person. So character is the real destiny and it is wrong to think that destiny is somewhat a prewritten thing. God also helps those who help themselves.

(9) Attack Is the Best Form of Defence

(Asst Grade)

Defence is necessary for a happy living. The imperialistic persons try to grab the neighbour's territory and so attack him. Under such circumstances it is better to make first attack instead of waiting for the attack and then defend. All the planning be made in advance considering the imminent attack by the enemy. It also does not mean that one should not resort to the peaceful means to avoid war, but after exhausting all the solutions of maintaining peace, if the war seems definite then it is always better to attack than to wait for attack and defend. Attack is the best defence in such circumstances.

(10) To Thine Owns Self Be True

Most of the persons find faults with others and blames other for all the wrongs and troubles of the present day. We never judge ourselves, we don't analyse our actions, but always find solace in searching faults or mistake of others. We ignore our inner voice when we do something wrong. This is the reason why everybody is unhappy and suffering from one or other infirmity. If we want to live in peace with real happiness, we should try to perform our duties. Society consists of individuals and if each individual takes care for his conduct most of our troubles will cease to exist. The above quotation from Shakespeare's 'Hamlet' is a maxim which should be followed by all. One must be true to his own conduct.

(11) Poverty Is the Mother of All Crimes *(IAS)*

A hungry man can commit any sin or crime. He knows no morality no ethics. How can we expect from a hungry man to think of good or bad, reasonable or unreasonable action when his own existence is at stake. Right to life is the paramount right. Rightly said that poverty is the mother of all crimes. A poor person can commit any crime to save his family from the clutches of illness, hunger etc. When a person finds that his wife and children are starving to death, he can resort to any measure to save his wife and his children. Crimes like theft, robbery, dacoity, pick-pocketing are generally committed by those whose means of living are very meagre. The poor parents cannot afford to educate their children. They fail to teach them what is right and what is wrong. A poor man, in fact, has no idea of ethics. It also does not mean that all the crimes are committed by the poor. Now-a-days the abductions—murders, kidnapping, rapes, high-jacking and all other heinous crimes are being committed by the rich, who have never seen the face of poverty. They commit such crime not for the sake of hunger of stomach but hunger of power, hunger of more and more money. In the present world the above saying should be amended to some extent to mean that the poverty is not alone a cause of crime.

(12) Spare the Rod and Spoil the Child

What is good and what is bad can't be understood by a child. He tries to do what he feels good and enjoyful. Sometimes he puts unreasonable demands and presses upon it to get it fulfilled by all the means he knows. If we fulfil such demands it means we are not sincere to our child in real terms and spoiling his habits, making him peevish and obstinate. To make a child disciplined and hard working we have to put a check on the wrong demands, wrong actions of the child. Even if we are to use some force we must not hesitate because if we spare the rod we spoil the child. Unjustified and wrong demands must be nipped in the bud.

(13) Time and Tide Wait for None

Time and tide have their own course, their own routine as per nature's rule. They do not wait for anyone. They come and go their own ways. A wise man makes the best use of his time. The time once gone never comes back. Those who do not make a proper use of opportunity often repent later on. One should siege the opportunity whenever it is within one's reach. If you loose, other fellow will grab it and then you will be blaming your luck or anything else for your losing such a good opportunity. Time and tide wait for none and they will not wait for us also.

(14) All That Glitters Is Not Gold

Guided by the appearance can be disastrous. In this world of deception and deceit, what is seen outwardly, is not the reality. Often the glittering appearance, hide the foulness of wickedness. When advertisements display, showiness, have all become the day of life and the judgement of the reality have become very difficult. The good looking innocent people are the perfect cheat of the day. The only way to save ourselves from such hypocrites is to be very attentive and careful in life with good observance.

What is exhibited and displayed outwardly should not be taken, as creditworthy. Visual appearances are commonly deceptive. The quality of a thing can only be judged by its use only. In many cases, a thing that appears to be very durable and cheap may turn out a duplicate. Duplicates or imitations commonly have more shining or glittering than the original one.

A person can be judged by his deeds, attitude and aptitude towards show off others. A coarse man may be more helpful and co-operative than a person of pleasant countenance. A well dressed, gentlemanly looking person is apt to deceive you by his outward looks. What he intend to show, may not be his actual intention. Appearance may be delusory and misleading. Try to ascertain his motives, and analyse his actions. Keep a close vigil. What appears to be gold, may turn out a yellow metal, a polish of Gold on iron, a fake colour of gold on brass. So beware of the appearance, judge the things from its original contents, 'All that glitters is not Gold'.

(15) As You Sow So Shall You Reap

In other words, you shall harvest what you plant, spiritual or natural, as God said that if you sow the flesh, you shall reap corruption, but if you sow the spirit of love for all, you shall reap life everlasting. God is the great paymaster, we are under his workmanship. We are the clay and he is the potter, so do something for the God, who made you and he will not forget the things that you do but you shall receive your pay, good or bad.

The theory of Karma is spoken about in many of the sacred texts of all the religions in the world and is implied in the Golden Rule : Do unto others as you would have them do unto you. The implication: as you treat others, so you will be treated.

Every tragedy we live through is the result of some terrible wrongs we did in our past life. A child who dies of an illness at an early age, for example, might simply have chosen to experience the birth and young adult stages of life before deciding what he wanted to do with his life as an adult in his next incarnation.

Karma is inescapable. Your actions do return to you. It may not be in this lifetime, but it certainly will return in some way. 'As you sow, so shall you reap', has relevance in today's competitive market place as well as in the timeless arena of human relationships. At every juncture, in all times, this theory of karma (As you sow so shall you reap) is well respected and well observed.

(16) Delayed Justice No Justice

Many Chief Justices, Judges of the Supreme Court, the High Courts, The Law Ministers, the Law Commission, the media, the great writers and thinkers have all lamented over the delay in the dispensation of justice. The inordinate delay in the provision of relief amounts to the virtual denial of any relief found in number of cases.

The litany of woes caused by delay in the administration of justice is disastrous. A layman does not want and understand that he has the right to get the justice and that is too within reasonable time. An aggrieved, if doesn't get the justice within reasonable time, then all his sufferings and hardships because of such delay, is like a punishment inflicted on him for no fault of his own.

Delayed justice is the biggest cause of prevalent corruption in the country. Many political leaders are enjoying the chairs of Ministers while a number of cases are pending against them. Are our courts not their accomplice ? It is unimaginable that how much loss our nation be suffering from ethical and moral point of view at least, because of the delay in disposing of the cases. Innocent person is the worst affected unfortunate, who has to take shelter of the courts for getting justice, which he can never calculate as to when that so called justice be finally arrive. None can compute his worries and the frustrations. Such sufferings and hardships made him to conclude that Delayed Justice is no Justice.

(17) Diligence Is the Mother of Success

There can't be any short cut to success. The toil of years, the sweat of your brow, struggle you make, everything counts in achieving the goal. Looking at the biographies of greatmen we find that the most of the successful persons whether inventors, artists, scientists, technocrats, sculptures, thinkers, leaders and workers of any kind, owe their success to their indefatigable hard work and dedication. They were the men who achieved their successes with dedication, devotion and true hard work. This really holds that the secret of success consisted in being master of our subject. Such mastery is attainable through continuous application and study.

Those who work diligently not only achieve their goals and get success, but also remain happy, cheerful and active, which is itself a great reward even if the work does not bring success. Idleness or laziness is worse as it brings jealousy, gloom, frustration, depression which are more degrading than the failure itself.

No doubt diligence is very necessary for the success, but intelligent decision is again an important factor that can't be ignored. We know so many daily wage earners toiling hard day and night to earn their livelihood, can't be termed as successful, but a person putting little labour and managing the things properly, earning handsomely is a successful man. Thus not only *diligence but intelligentsia is also necessary for the success in life.*

(18) Educating A Girl Child Means Educating a Family

Today's girl child will be the mother of tomorrow. As a mother she can give her child a sound nursing and capable upbringing. A woman has the maximum impact on the social, economical decisions made in the family generally. At micro level, educated woman help in making the whole family including the older family members, understand the values and importance of education, and at macro level, educated women add to the social and economical development of the nation.

Girl's education is like sowing the seed which gives rise to green, cheerful and full grown family plant. In ancient time girl's education had a significant place in the society. Gargi and *Maitreyi* played very encouraging role in spreading the education to a great extent.

The educated girl can shoulder any kind of responsibility. See the example of Indira Gandhi, Kalpna Chawla, Kiran Bedi, Sonia Gandhi,

Sushma Swaraj, Uma Bharati, and so....., everyone has earned a name in the society in our country. Education for the girls is more important as she not only builds the home but all routine responsibilities are taken care of by her. An educated woman not only helps in nourishing the family in a better way but can also help in earning.

"One could judge the degree of civilization of a country by the social and political position of its women."

—*Charles Fourier*

Education for a girl child means making the next generation well educated, full of virtues, free from the useless superstitions, confident and capable to do something good for the family, for the society and for the country as a whole. The present day girl is the mother of tomorrow.

"Give me good mothers and I will give you a great nation."

—*Napolean*

(19) Failures Are the Pillars of Success

Every successful man fails at some time. Failure tells you about your weaknesses, shortcomings, lack of preparations, lack of efforts so if you can manage to learn from failures, you will definitely reach where you started out to go. Making a mistake is not a crime, the ability to learn from it contributes to lasting success. Extract the lesson to be learnt from failure and try again with redoubled vigour. Facing failure makes one strong, more wise and more resolute, spur them on to greatest efforts. There is no failure in truth save from within; unless we are beaten there, we are bound to succeed.

'Failures' means lack of preparation, lack of competitiveness, lack of analysing the things properly. Failures not only tell us that we couldn't prepare ourselves upto the level of success and reveal our shortcomings, but also give us encouragement to try again with more preparations, with more labour and with more hard work. Failures are the stepping stones to achieve success. Every successful man failed, not once but several times in their life, but they analysed the things in real perspective and tried again with more vigour and zeal and got success.

Abraham Lincoln failed many times in his life, but never got frustrated and fought with more determination, with full devotion and became the President of America. Indian freedom fighters including Mahatma Gandhi, Jawahar Lal Nehru, Vallabhbhai Patel, saw face of failures not once but several times, but never daunted or became desperate, they all had fought to attain the sacred goal of attaining freedom, and as a result, they attained it. Failures should not be allowed to create frustration, desperateness or disappointment, instead failure should be taken as a boon which gives you strength to fight back with fierce fortitude and invincible zeal.

"Failure is not fatal, it can be the stepping stone to success, if you can make 'the failure' to work for you."

"Failures are our best teachers, they are the mirrors who show us our real face."

(20) Fate and Coincidence

Many people believe that there is something bigger than us. There is a reason for everything. Some believe that everything is a coincidence. Some believe that coincidence is real and not fate. However, none of this can ever be truly proven. Coincidence is a seemingly planned sequence of accidentally occurring events. One might think the collision of events was fated to occur, but one is mistaken. It signified nothing. But searching like we all do for an explanation and a sense of importance, one creates his fate by spelling out meaning from a jumble of coincidences.

We've all had it happen to us. We think about someone who we haven't seen in a while, and later that same day, we bump into them. We have an ominous feeling that something bad is going to happen and it does. We have a dream that predicts our future. We look back at events in our lives and we see them fitting together like a puzzle.

If one thinks to oneself, "If I hadn't been in that exact place, at that exact moment, my life would have gone in a totally different direction. I wouldn't have met this or that person. I wouldn't have done this thing or that thing. I would have taken that job instead of this one. I would have married that boy instead of my husband."

Is it all connected somehow? Or Is it just a coincidence?

To many, fate only occurs on a personal level. Chain reactions exist, certainly, where one person's behaviour results in a massively far-reaching effect, but they are not ruled by fate. Incidents and chain reactions with a broader range of impact, such as the butterfly effect, have no intended purpose. It is fate that can play the triggering role within the intimate confines of a single person's life. Sometimes, there are certain events in our lives that are just meant to be happened. Those events happen for some reason in some person's lifetime meant to influence only the person they happen to.

No doubt coincidences happen too. Not every occurrence in a person's life is fated.

So what exactly is the difference between fate and coincidence? Rather, what evidence is there that fate exists in a world of randomness? That's where personal faith comes in.

(21) Habit : A Good Servant But a Bad Master

A habit is like a tree grown crouched. One cannot go to orchard and take hold of a tree grown such and straighten it and say now get straight and make it obey him. When one is young, he can acquire good or bad habits. One starts doing certain act for the sake of pleasure, for the sake of fun and if he is doing that thing, that particular act at regular or irregular intervals, he starts enjoying it and starts feeling the necessity of doing it again at that particular time and it gradually takes a form of a habit.

Every chain smoker or a habitual drunkard never starts smoking or drinking as a habit. He simply begins with such act for the sake of company for the curiosity of taste, or for the sake of fun in the company of his friends or otherwise and he starts smoking or drinking alcohol, now and then and afterwards, he consumes it often, these now become his necessity and then the habit is formed. Habit is cultivated slowly and gradually. Habit is nothing but a slow and gradual intake of something, performing of some act, slowly and gradually, when becomes a necessity, is called a habit.

People enjoy smoking, people enjoy drinking, but habit of smoking or drinking when becomes our master, we feel uneasy or wearisome, without smoking or drinking, it is felt bad. So rightly said, "Habit is a good servant but a bad master."

"Don't let the habits control you, conquer you, keep them your 'servants' and enjoy their company", is the secret of enjoying the life to the fullest extent.

(22) Ideas Rule the World

Ideas rule the world and thoughts decide the way of life. It is the mind which sculptures one's destiny. If one thinks positively, if one thinks in right direction, one achieves the goal, what one aspires for.

Life consists in what a man is thinking of all day. Ideas are nothing, but an outcome of one's detailed thinking. They shape and determine the destiny of human being, and contribute to the growth and well beings of the civilization. Every great achievement whether in the field of religion, science, medicine, space technology, information and communication sector or in any field, was at the first stage an idea. The most scintillating success, the astonishing scientific discovery, the splendid technological feats like splitting the atom, heart transplantation, cloning of sheep, unravelling the secrets of Mars, walking on the surface of Moon, have all the results of an idea in the beginning.

Have we ever think of the present revolution in Information Technology two decades back? It was the vision of Azim Hashm Premji, N.R. Narayan Murthy, as also the late Dewang Mehta who catapulted India among the super powers in IT sector, making the first two Mr Premji and Narayan Murthy, enter the elite Billionaire Club. Ideas with knowledge lead to action and success comes to you with hugging hands. Knowledge is power, when one applies his knowledge and understands the problems, analyses the prevailing situation with hard work and perseverance, the solution is not far to reach, and when one knows the answer, the success is yours.

The flash of new idea strikes to those who have worked hard and given full thoughts to the problem. See the historical example of Archimedes jumping out of his bathtub screaming 'Eureka' finding out the solution, the idea of a razor with a cheap disposable blade came to Gillette while he was shaving himself. It was the noble idea of Alfred Nobel inventor of Dynamite, to use his fortune for the establishment of annual awards to people, who contributed outstandingly in the field of Physics, Chemistry, Medicine, Literature, Economics and Peace. An idea just in mind or on paper without implementation is no idea, we are talking about.

How to handle and implement the new idea is the most important thing to realise the goal.

"Ideas are like rabbits, you get a couple, learn how to handle them and pretty soon you have a dozen."

—John Steinbeck

In brief it is the idea that rule the world and also the minds of people. Idea and determination to translate it in practice can do wonders.

(23) Knowledge Is Power

Knowledge means knowing the things in an appropriate and better way. A man of knowledge can understand the circumstances more wisely, so can decide the things favourably. Knowledge inspires confidence, courage, to act at a right time. A man of knowledge possesses immense influence in society. He has the capacity to lead the society, mould the society in a positive direction, keep away the society from the many social evils. A man of knowledge can turn the sleeping people into a thundering force.

Time has gone, when power of sword ruled the world. Even during that period, the power of sword alone never ruled, but the knowledge about enemy, knowledge about own strength and knowledge of the right time attack always had played a crucial role in grabbing the power. In other words, knowing what to do at what time—in what direction and how, are the various parameters that leads to sure success. Knowing the timings well, knowing our goals well, knowing our strengths and weaknesses well and shape them in right direction, we can achieve what we aspire to achieve. Knowledge gives power to mobilise the things in right direction and so it is said that knowledge is power.

If one ventures to establish any business, wishes to achieve any goal, he must acquire full knowledge of all the things including his own limitations and weaknesses. Knowledge gives one capacity and capabilities to know the result of his actions, probability of success and failure, propriety of his venture and so knowledge is said to be a power.

For a country knowledge about its friends and foes, knowledge about the capabilities of its enemies is very important. In the present world scenario many satellites and spy aircrafts are deployed for the purpose of gaining maximum knowledge of activities going on in other countries. A country having the maximum and accurate knowledge of other countries can use them for its advantage, it is the 'Knowledge' that rules the world.

Knowledge gives one immense power, so rightly said, 'Knowledge is Power.'

(24) Money Is a Good Servant, But a Bad Master

No doubt, Money is an essential, almost indispensable article in the present day world. It is the 'money' through which we can purchase all the necessary comforts and amenities of life. If you have money, you can obtain what seems impossible to others. It is the money which gives confidence, credit worthiness, credentials, capacity, capabilities and courage to a man. In present materialistic world, money has become very powerful. In the present day corruption, cut throat competition, callous degradation of moral and ethical values are for the sake of grabbing and accumulating more and more money. The prestige, respect, social status, commanded by a person is calculated as per his monetary status.

Money is regarded as omnipotent by a few people, particularly by the poor. As whatever one does not possess, one aspires it badly, and it becomes mono aim of achievement. For the rich that owe lots of money still craving to earn more and more by hook or by crook with fair or foul means without caring even for their own health, own family. They are the servants of money, earning money not for the sake of themselves but for the sake of money and a time comes they find themselves unable to use the money for their happiness. They are unable to eat, unable to taste the most delicious dish, unable to move, walk or enjoy because they suffer from many diseases which are the result of their undue craving for wealth at the cost of health.

Those who earn money simply to have more money, more balance in their accounts are no better than the proverbial miser king 'Midas'. Excessive love for money makes a man slave of money. Those who use money for fulfilling their necessities, acquiring reasonable comforts and for the welfare of a common good, are the masters of money. But those, who earn money just for the sake of increasing its volume and number, are slaves of the money. They are the most unfortunate creatures of God who know well that whatever money they are earning, can't be carried along an iota of that when they die even they are minting more and more money. What a paradox! Money has become their master and they are just slaves, having no peace of mind, no moral and ethical values, no inner satisfaction.

So it is rightly said that money is a good servant but a bad master. Let us earn the money for our comfort, not for the sake of money, minting more and more money.

(25) Preparedness for War for Preserving Peace

Very strange and paradoxical it seems that preparedness for war is essential for preserving peace. But the saying, appears to be true for if a country be well equipped with all the modern war gadgets and weapons, other nations will have to think twice before entering into any conflict with it. On the other hand, a weak nation becomes prey to the whims and aggressions of powerful neighbours. Balance of Power is must for preserving the peace.

Peace means freedom from war, but how can one preserve it unless or until you are well equipped you can't preserve your peace. A peace loving nation may not have the intention to enlarge its empire but who can guarantee the dictates of other neighbour countries.

What happened with our country when China attacked in 1962 ? We, being a fully peace loving country, never felt necessity till then to equip ourself with modern war gadgets and weapons. China, took the opportunity and attacked us, made encroachment on our land. What did UNO do? What other Super Power could have done ? In the present world your power decides your relation with neighbours.

Nothing but Power, your preparations to face any eventualities, your preparations to face any imperialistic whims, can guarantee you the peace. So it is the right conclusion that preparedness for war is necessary for preserving peace.

(26) The Child Is the Father of Man

This line which has since taken the shape of a proverb, really occurs in the famous poem 'My Heart Leaps when I behold' of Wordsworth, the great poet. It implies that the qualities and characteristics shown by a child often indicate, what the child is going to be as a grown up man. The childhood is the reflection of future personality. The habits, traits and qualities of a man are usually the development of the habits, traits, qualities he had as a child. A careful study of the characteristic and qualities in a child can help us to foretell his future prospects.

'The Child is the Father of Man', is proved true in many cases. See the example of Shivaji who during his childhood, loved so much to hear the stories of famous heroes of Ramayana and Mahabharat, became later a great warrior himself. Michael, the famous sculptor and painter, during his childhood used to make drawings on the pots, easels, stools and other things belonging to an old painter. The old painter said, "One day this boy will beat me." A young Italian lad, Titian, was very fond of painting pictures, but had no paints to colour with. He was so genius, he made his own paints. Nelson, the daring Naval Commander of British Navy, showed his traits of courage and fearlessness during his childhood.

Many more examples like that of Florence Nightingale, Macaulay, can be quoted to prove the veracity of the proverb that 'The Child is the Father of Man', but we can find hundreds and thousands other examples, where childhood of a man did not reflect anything about the grown up personality of the man. Sonia Gandhi, never thought to entangle in the political arena. In her childhood, none could imagine that one day she would be in a position to become the Prime Minister of India, the world's largest democracy. Though she did not accept the position of Prime Minister. Lal Bahadur Shastri never showed any such trait in his childhood. He was an average student from a poor and simple family. George Bernard Shaw was known as a hopeless dullard. Mahatma Gandhi was inclined to become a rich Barrister. Shelley, the great poet and writer never showed such traits during his childhood. Amitabh Bachchan, the great Super Star of Bollywood today, didn't show such traits and qualities in his childhood.

In spite of apparent exceptions, it is generally observed that the characteristics and qualities during childhood are developed in the grown up personality of a man. Circumstances can change the life of a person. Fate and coincidence play a great role in developing qualities of a person. The childhood ordinarily reflects the calibre of a person, but in changed circumstances, with several coincidences and the destiny, which i called predetermined can change everything. An average child can reach the highest position and a brilliant may have to survive in rectitude.

An old proverb, "As the twig is bent, so the tree will grow", endorses the saying "The Child is the Father of Man."

(27) Think Positive Win Positively

Positive thinking leads a man to success. One, who thinks that he can achieve the things will put his best to achieve, will not fetter by the problems in the path of success and one day he will win positively. Self-confidence, determination, perseverance, and hard work are the key factors of success. Every small or big, easy or complex problem have its solution. There is a way out of every labyrinth, there is an answer to every enigma. The only requirements are the confidence, hard work and determination and you get the answer.

Dedication, devotion to the task and positive thinking with determination have been the important factors of success of every successful celebrity.

A winner never quits and a quitter never wins shows that one who constantly tries to achieve something, one who endeavours hard incessantly to achieve something, he is the winner, later or sooner, but a quitter could never be a winner.

Your biggest assets are your enthusiasm that enriches with your positive thinking. Never lose hope, keep cheerful, put the best possible efforts with your total involvement, have confidence in you and you are the winner. Through positive hinking one can overcome the mountains. One who always thinks positively, even in adverse ircumstances, wins. 'Positive thinking always pays'. Life belongs to the ambitions.

28) Where There Is a Will There Is a Way

'Will' means not the ordinary desire but an nflinching, undaunting wish to achieve omething. If you have a will to achieve your goal, ou will positively overcome the difficulties that ome in your way. Every problem has its solution.

Whatever inventions are seen today were a roblem one day, but the will and hard work of e inventor found their solution. Impossible is ossible for the persons of strong will. Path of ccess runs through many labyrinth of failures. One who has a will to achieve the success, never gets frustrated by the odds and failures of the path. Every successful man failed many times but with his unshaken faith and strong will, he became successful one day. Think high, try your best, without being daunted by the odds of the path, success is yours.

One can certainly win and achieve one's goal, if one firmly believes in self and makes up one's mind to lead and succeed. The secret of success lies in the determination, dedication, perseverance of a man. A man who strides majestically with firm steps and unshaken faith, no matter what the odds and obstacle, is the man who actually finds his way and achieve success.

It is the unwavering faith and self-confidence that makes the man a winner. Faith brings miracle. It looks beyond all boundaries, transcends all limitations, conquer all obstacles and carries one to one's goal. Therefore, whosoever has resolution, indefatigable 'will' unfettered confidence and faith in himself will march ahead, onward, upward till he achieves his goal.

One step at a time and that well placed will take you to the grandest height. One seed at a time and the forest grows, one stone at a time and the palace rises, one drop at a time and the river flows, one word at a time and the great book is written.

The only thing is to start with firm determination strong and unfettered 'will' and the way is yours. So rightly said, "Where there is a will there is a way."

(29) Your Enemies Are Your Best Friends

(IIT)

Our enemies could be treated as friends, as they disclose our weaknesses and try to get benefit of our drawbacks. They teach us to remove our weaknesses and take care of our drawbacks. In this way we are bound to improve ourselves and thus the fear of enemy results in the overall improvements in ourselves and thus they really help us to get improved, so they are our friends.

If we don't have any enemy we shall not take care of our misdeeds and our shortcomings, as such we shall be losing. We will ignore our weaknesses as friends do not care to take benefit of our weaknesses. An enemy is, therefore, sometimes better than a friend. Moreover, it is because of enemies that we are cautious otherwise they may have the upper hand. We are forced to apply our best to give a strong reply to the enemy. Moreover competition and rivalry infuse enthusiasm and zest for better and greater work. So in this way too our enemies are our friends as they help us to improve and excel in the world.

(30) Better to Rule in Hell Than to Serve in Heaven *(IIT)*

King is always King even if the empire is small and far better than a servant of a large empire. This famous line is taken from the Milton's 'Paradise Lost'. Satan is the king of Hell. He prefers supremacy in Hell to subordination in heaven. The sovereignty is very important. Freedom of will is one of the most sought after things in man's life. Man is by nature does not like subordination to others.

Our Constitution guarantees equality to all. The Charter of UN also have the provisions of freedom from the dominance of the rich and developed over the poor and the under developed. Full sovereignty is guaranteed to all the nations. Why anyone would be slave to others ? It is because even poor and undeveloped nations cannot tolerate interference from other rich and developed countries. Such nations prefer policies of their own in spite of their limited resources. The same thing applies both to individuals and the nations. Even the luxuries of heaven are of no use if one is not independent there. The most important thing is that one must be free from any dominance so that one can feel free and enjoy life in one's own way.

(31) The Man, Who Makes No Mistakes, Does Not Usually Make Anything *(Income Tax Inspector)*

If one does something, one may or may not commit mistakes but a person who does not do anything will not at all commit any mistake. Committing mistakes is not a bad thing because a mistake today will lead us to do correct things tomorrow. It is natural that human beings commit mistakes. Errors and mistakes lead us to success. We should learn from the mistakes we make. Repeated errors compel us to do that particular work again and again resulting in ultimate success.

But a person, who for fear of committing mistake does not do anything, never succeed. It is always better to travel hopefully than to arrive. We shall have to take the initiatives otherwise laziness and idleness will overcome us and we shall be suffering from the indolence. Our friends will march ahead of us. It is better to make mistakes and lose than never to try at all. Failures are the stepping stones to success.

(32) Work Is Worship *(Asst Grade)*

We do worship because we want something from the Almighty. In fact it is work, which gives us everything we aspire for. Idleness or laziness could not bring us anything. Unless we work hard with dedication and devotion we can't achieve anything. Self-confidence, determination, perseverance, and hard work are the key factors of success.

Whatever inventions are seen today are the result of hard work. The will and hard work of the inventor found their solution. Impossible is possible for the persons having strong will. Path of success runs through many labyrinth of failures. So it is nothing but hard work that gives us all the things we aspire for or we desire or we think of. So, 'Work is worship'.

(33) Man Is Ruled by Nature *(Asst Grade)*

A fatalist thinks that a man's destiny is determined by the stars and everything is ordained by God, which for practical purposes, means the natural forces over which man has no control. Some people with logical and scientific temperament believe that the man is the master of his own efforts. According to them one can make one's destiny by the sheer force of his labour, energy and determination, and there is nothing like fate or destiny. Nature also plays an important role in making the things happen, in shaping the things. Sometimes the role of nature is so predominant in determining the course of events that the people who do not believe in the dominance of nature are bound to accept the role of nature in determining the fate of man. It is a very controversial issue and no conclusion can be drawn whether man is ruled by nature or whether man himself rule.

(34) If Winter Comes, Can Spring Be Far Behind ?

(Income Tax Insp, PCS, Asst Grade)

Day is followed by night and night is followed by day. Fortune and misfortune are part of life. Period of misfortunes is not a permanent one. Sooner or later the days of misfortunes and miseries will be over and the bright rays of hope and joy spread over. Man gets perturbed and disappointed when misfortune loom large on him, and feels totally dejected. One must realize the basic truth of life that after every patch of sorrow there comes a period of happiness and hope. Winter is a kind of misfortune, treated as gloomy days when everything is pale and in gloomy shape, is also followed by Spring which brings days of hope and happiness with all the bright colours and new leaves blooming. This is what the nature also tells us that don't be panicky during the bad days and pass this period with patience. The good days are ahead as Spring follows the winter. Rightly said if winter comes, can spring be far behind.

(35) Love Knows No Barriers

(Asst Grade)

Barriers of caste, creed, status and religion are generally imposed by the parents and the society on the lovers. But the history has witnessed that the true lovers do not accept any such barriers. The stories of Shiri-Farhad, Laila-Majanu, Sohni-Mahiwal are the best examples to support the above saying. But all this does not mean that others who sacrificed their love for the sake of parents or the society, were not true lovers. Love does not mean the love of lovers only. The point is that love is not started with a planning, so it does not accept any barrier as lovers are unable to know as to when they are entangled in love. Love is a great phenomenon, love is a bundle of emotions, love is unconditional. So we can say 'that love knows no barriers'.

(36) The Old Order Changeth Yielding Place To New

(Asst Grade, PCS)

Change is inevitable, it is the law of nature. Nothing in this world is perfectly stable, constant and permanent. Man is also mortal, the world itself is mortal. The civilization of today will finish one day and new civilization will take place. The present will become past and future will become present. This is the rule of nature. The old order changes and gives way to a new order. Old fashions, old customs, old traditions and old ways undergo natural and virtual change in the course of time. Ancient kingdoms and empires, old culture and civilization, ancient beliefs and superstitions give way to new kingdoms, new thoughts and new ideologies. Time is the great remedy of all changes, whatever seems inevitable once extinct, the world does not stop and runs with the same pace and people forget him after some days. A new system takes place as the older one changes.

(37) Only the Wearer Knows Where the Shoe Pinches

(Asst Grade)

It is very difficult to calculate the sufferings or problems of others without putting oneself entirely in others place. Looking from the outside a man of power like a king or a minister seems enjoying all the luxuries of life, but his problems and pains can't be understood by the people. The pains and the difficulties and responsibilities of enjoying position of authority are so immense that can't be realised until we are in the same position. Crown carries with it not only the power but also the liabilities and the responsibilities. So it is rightly said that only the wearer knows where the shoe pinches.

(38) Charity Begins at Home

(Asst Grade, PCS)

If we like to improve our society, bring some good changes in the society. We must first bring such improvements and changes in our own home itself. If you preach value of cleanliness to your neighbours and keep your own home dirty, it will not do to make others to follow you or to make others to accept your changes, it is always better to follow them first in your own life. Charity begins at home means that start all the good things from your home, so that others can follow you in letter and spirit.

(39) There is Nothing Good or Bad, But the Thinking Makes It So

(Asst Grade, PCS)

Good or bad lies in the eyes not in the things itself. Everything has two sides good or bad. It is in your eyes what you see. An artist will see art in a naked picture, while an ordinary man will find sex in it. A painter will find a beautiful object in such a picture, while a critic will see indecency in the nakedness. Every decision taken by the government is favoured by the ruling party MPs, while for the opposition every action is a point for criticism especially in India. The opposition do not find anything good in any decision of the government, while the government pro MPs find nothing wrong in that decision. Nothing is either good or bad. How is our approach, positive or negative, our thinking and our opinion will automatically framed accordingly. For an optimist a glass with half water is half filled glass, while for a pessimist it is half unfilled (blank) glass. The glass is same but how do we look upon it is important. So it is right that there is nothing good or bad, but the thinking makes it so.

(40) Politeness Costs Nothing, Gains Everything *(Asst Grade)*

Anger defeats itself is a well known proverb. History is evident of the fact that more works are done by politeness than by anger. We can't get anything with anger. Anger gets you nowhere. Instead of getting the favour we get disfavour. While with politeness we can win even our enemies. Politeness gets you favour and happiness while anger gets you disfavour and sorrow. Politeness does not mean cowardice, but it means maturity, it means your highness. It is wrongly believed that strong man rules the world, but to rule the hearts you have to be polite and generous. Any problem can be well solved with politeness, but nothing can be solved with hatred and anger. Politeness is the most important trait in the personality of a human being. It costs us nothing but it could gain us upto any extent.

(41) Virtue Is Its Own Reward *(PCS)*

Virtues and evils are what every being possesses. Evils generate miseries while virtues bring happiness in life. A man with virtues is contented, satisfied and really rich. Virtues are such good habits that bring peace in life, that bring happiness in life, that keep you happy, healthy and prosperous. The practice of virtue in the manner gives a peculiar spiritual satisfaction and saves man from disappointment and frustration. Whatever is needed by a man in life is achieved by him because of the virtues he possesses, and so it is more than correct to say that virtue is its own reward.

(42) United We Stand and Divided We Fall *(PCS)*

None but we Indians can well understand the value of Unity and the saying 'United we stand and divided we fall.' India was ruled by the British, who came to India as traders and because of the fractions and infighting here they became the ruler. A closed fist may be valued in lacs of rupees, but open hands are valueless. We can break a stick one by one but we can't break the bundle of these sticks whatever power we may enjoy. The unity of a nation depends not on the number of individuals but because these individuals have a natural feeling of sincerity and loyalty towards the nation. History is a witness to the fact that we were defeated by foreigners only when we were divided. So it is very correct to say that united we stand and divided we fall.

(43) Rome Was Not Built in a Day *(PCS)*

Hard toil for years is necessary to achieve anything great or everlasting. The city of Rome which ultimately became the wonder of the civilised world was not built in a day, it took many years to get it in this shape. Nothing important or great can be attained by a mere thought of attaining it, a serious planning, hard labour, dedication and positive thinking and a regular perseverance is required to get it. To reach the Moon, to reach the Saturn it took many many years of research and hard work.

We must remember that there is no royal road to anything and that the true success can be attained only by hard work. We must not yield to discouragement because our efforts are not crowned with success. Failures are the pillars of success. Nothing but hard work, dedication and perseverance is necessary to achieve the goal. Slow progress must not make us impatient and difficulties must not discourage us. We must remember that Rome was not built in a day.

(44) Look Before You Leap *(PCS)*

Check your pocket before you enter a hotel. Haste makes waste. Rash decisions are always dangerous. This is what the saying "Look before you leap" means. You must see the pros and cons of your decision before you act according to it. It is always better to find the merits and demerits of any venture, before entering into it. See where are you going to leap, it is always better to know the risk involved in it. History is full of such examples when the rashness costs a lot. Napolean decided to attack Russia without taken into consideration the fierce winter of that country. As a result of this rashness and miscalculation, his armies were trapped in the snows and thus lost the iron guard, the main strength of the army. One must have patience, must plan well, must see the risk involve and then act, he will positively get success. So it is true to say that look before you leap.

(45) Example Is Better Than Precept *(IFS, PCS)*

If you actually wish others to follow what you say, it is necessary that you yourself follow what you want others to follow. Mere words of advice, laying down rules of action and the like are of no use. People do not believe in the preaching or if some believe the strength is very meagre. Living examples, which the persons for whom they are meant can see before his eyes, can make better impression and have the desired end, being something concrete : but precepts, which are things only in abstract, do not make good impressions upon the mind or even if they make any impression at all, it lasts only for a short time. Mahatma Gandhi always believed in the saying that example is better than precept and so he had lacs of followers. He never did what he asked others not to do. He was an apostle of creating examples in real terms.

(46) Forgiveness Is the Noblest Revenge *(PCS, Asst Grade, IFS)*

If you want to destroy your enemy, forgive him, he will not be your enemy any more and so the enmity is destroyed and a friend takes birth. And in this way to destroy the enemy, forgiveness is the biggest tool. Revenge is an ordinary tool, does not destroy the enmity, it can cause some harm, physical or financial to the enemy but the enemy becomes more determined to avenge it. While the forgiveness not only makes him feel sorry and finishes the enmity but also makes you safe for ever and the enemy now becomes your friend. So to destroy the enemy forgiveness is the noblest revenge.

(47) Handsome Is That Handsome Does *(PCS)*

Outward looks or beautiful face does not makes a man really good or handsome. The inner virtues, and the good actions are the real beauty of a person. A person is considered to be handsome, if he has physical outwardly bright eyes, pointed nose, rosy cheeks, pearly teeth, curly hair and strong body. In reality, handsome is he whose deeds are handsome. The greatness lies neither in wealth nor in rank and nor in physical beauty but in our actions and our deeds. We can find number of beautiful prostitutes, but the deeds of these pimps are not worthful. The noble laureate Mother Teressa was not a handsome lady but her deeds made her so great. So if we want to make our life noble, dignified and handsome, we must do noble deeds.

Mahatma Gandhi, the father of the nation, was not good-looking but still he is regarded as the finest specimen of humanity because of his noble deeds. We must not judge a person from his outward looks but we must judge him from his character, thoughts and the most important his deeds.

(48) Capital Punishment

The punishment of criminals has always been a problem for society. Citizens have had to decide whether offenders such as first-degree murderers should be killed in a gas chamber, imprisoned for life, or rehabilitated and given a second chance in society. Many citizens argue that serious criminals should be executed. They believe that killing criminals will set an example for others and also get rid society of a cumbersome burden. Other citizens say that no one has the right to take a life and that capital punishment is not a deterrent to crime. They believe that society as well as the criminal is responsible for the crimes and that killing the criminal does not solve the problems of either society or the criminal.

(49) He Is Strong Who Conquers Others; He Who Conquers Himself Is Mighty

It is very easy to direct others to do this or that. It is also easy to use force to make others to obey you. It is also easy to use brutal force to subjudicate others, you may be a winner, but if you are asked to change your life style or to give up your habits or give up any kind of lust you are having, you will find it the most difficult task or impossible to do so. The sacrifices to be made to win over own self is really tremendous. For an ordinary man relinquishing the empire is not possible, but Gautam Buddha did it. Though Nadir Shah defeated a number of kings with his brute force, but he can't be equated with Gautam Buddha. Samrat Ashoka became great only when he renounced the throne, but not on defeating the Kalinga. Rightly said that the man who could conquer himself is indeed great and mighty and who conquers others is simply more powerful or strong.

(50) Slow and Steady Wins the Race

The story of the fast runner hare who was defeated by the slow running tortoise is a well known story. The saying teaches us three things—firstly, one should not believe in shortcuts and secondly, one should not rest until one achieves one's goal and thirdly, one should not underestimate the rivals. In this competitive world, we must be totally vigilant and put hard work and make all efforts or better efforts in order to excel others. 'Slow and steady wins the race' is not so relevant in this competitive world. In my opinion 'Fast but perfect wins the race', slow remains far behind now-a-days.

(51) A Little Knowledge Is a Dangerous Thing

(PCS, IFS, Asst Grade)

Superficial and shallow knowledge always leads to dangerous consequences. An incompetent doctor or surgeon may play with the lives of his patients; a teacher with shallow knowledge of his subjects will misguide his students; a lawyer without a thorough knowledge of law will ruin his clients; similarly an inefficient engineer will build bridges and buildings that could cause major accidents. These people expose the lives of others to serious risks. They are so conceited that they never realise their shortcomings and hence make no progress. We can find such people in every walk of life whether art, science or literature or economics or medicines and these are hazards for the common people.

One must, therefore, never rely on persons who are not thorough in their profession or vocation and be cautious to deal with such fellows.

(52) The Pen Is Mightier Than the Sword

(IES, PCS)

It has been a point of contention since long that what is more powerful, physical force or the intellectuality or who rules the world sword or the pen. During the primitive age, the Sword ruled the world and the maxim 'Might is Right' was accepted by all. In the civilised world of today, the pen is surely mightier and Sword is worked for the Pen. In today's world where every rule and law are coded and democratic values are being accepted the pen becomes more powerful.

The president of USA, who is regarded as the most powerful man of the world, is because of his power of pen, means the intellectuality prevails over the physical force. In the jungle where the animals rule prevails, only there the physical force is more important. An empire created by the physical force is of temporary nature, soon will crumbled to dust within some years, but the empire of literature is immortal. So in this civilised world the pen is mightier than the sword.

(53) Laugh and the World Laughs with You; Weep and You Weep Alone

In general, man does not like to share his sorrow with others, as sorrow is otherwise a private or personal affair. Happiness is a matter to be shared with all the relatives and friends, as happiness increases when you share it. Laughter is essentially a wonderful virtue and a great medicine for the depressed also. One never laughs alone, there are always friends and companions to share and increase your laughter.

It does not mean that the world is altogether indifferent to the sorrow. When we weep there are certain friends and relatives who share our sorrow. But a common man will not be ready to share your sorrow, he can only laugh with you.

(54) Our Sweetest Songs Are Those That Tell of Saddest Thought

Man's character and conduct are often largely governed by his environment and circumstances. The mixed threads of good and evil embedded in his nature are drawn out by the circumstances through which he has to pass. Experience shows that in times of prosperity, ease and luxury, man's base nature gets the upperhand whereas in adverse circumstances, the best in him comes to the surface. Nations which gave themselves up to a life of pleasure and indolence rapidly declined, whereas those which had to face ordeal after ordeal emerged harder and more powerful than before. It is in times of difficulty that a man exerts himself utmost, reaches unsuspected heights of endurance and perseverance, whereas in easy times the sturdier part of his nature remains dormant and begins to deteriorate. A rich man with plenty of money often gives himself up to sensual pleasures, but a poor man leads a blameless and straightforward life so that he may keep his body and soul together.

(55) It Is Always Better to Light One Little Candle Than to Curse the Darkness

Man is by nature a critic. He always tries to take the excuses for his failure instead of trying to solve the things. It is no use to blame the circumstances or the lacking of something for not getting anything done. Everybody knows there cannot be perfection anywhere, so to criticise the shortcomings is of no use. The right approach should be to find the solution instead of criticising. A winner always finds his way among the adverse circumstances. He does not blame the shortage or lack of infrastructure or any other thing for not getting the desired results but he actually finds the solution in the given circumstances. We should remember where there is a will there is a way. So it is always better to light a little candle than of cursing the darkness.

(56) A Thing of Beauty Is a Joy Forever *(PCS)*

If the beauty means simply the physical beauty of a thing or person, it is of very temporary nature. A beauty with aesthetic value is of permanent nature. But whatever kind of beauty it may be, it is very unreasonable to conclude that it will be the source of joy forever. Nothing in this world is so beautiful which can always give us happiness and joy.

The pretty face of a most beautiful woman of the world, the innocence smile of a child, any kind of beautiful scene of nature, the sculpture of Leonardo da Vinci, the paintings of Raphael, the music of Beethoven the plays of Shakespeare the verses of Kalidas the epics of Homer and Milton, the poetry of Keats or Tagore or anything else is so beautiful as to give joy forever. Even the loveliest of objects lose some of their charm with the period of time. Variety is necessary even in preserving the charm and appeal of beautiful objects. As such it is not true to say that a thing of beauty is a joy forever.

(57) Where Ignorance Is Bliss It Is Folly to Be Wise

It means that in cases happiness lies on the side of ignorance, it would be folly to be wise. Every ignorance is not bliss. Ignorance could be a cause of great loss, ignorance could be a cause of failure, ignorance could be resulted in the defeat of empire and so many very drastic and dangerous consequences may be the result of the ignorance.

But when knowing any thing may result in unhappiness, or result in a something drastic, then it is wrong to put efforts in knowing that thing.

Adam tasted the forbidden fruit of the Tree of Knowledge and was so expelled from the Garden of Eden. "He that increaseth knowledge increaseth sorrow" was the verdict of Solomon; and the experience of ages has confirmed the truth of the verdict.

(58) Do Unto Others As You Would Have Them Do Unto You

The theory of Karma is spoken about in many of the sacred texts of all the religions in the world and is implied in the Golden Rule : 'Do unto others as you would have them do unto you.' The implication: 'as you treat others, so you will be treated.'

Karma is inescapable. Your actions do return to you. It may not be in this lifetime, but it certainly will return in some way. How you deal with the return of this karmic energy determines whether or not you bring your soul further into balance or create more karmic energy that must be dealt with at a later stage. If you seek to learn from the seeming injustices in your life, chances are that you will be balancing your karmic books rather than increasing your karmic debt.

It is helpful to look at Karma as a sort of credit card. Each time we do something in our lives motivated by love, we are 'paying off' some of the karmic debts we have built up over our many lifetimes. Each time we act in selfish interest, we are charging something else to our credit card.

(59) The Heights by Great Men Reached and Kept Were Not Attained by Sudden Flight, But They, While Their Companions Slept, Were Toiling Upward in the Night

There can't be any short cut to success. The toil of years, the sweat of your brow, struggle you make, everything counts in achieving the goal. Looking at the biographies of greatmen, we find that the most of the successful persons whether inventors, artists, scientists, technocrats, sculptures, thinkers, leaders and workers of any kind, owe their success to their indefatigable hard work and dedication. They were the men who achieved their success with dedication, devotion and true hard work. This really holds that the secret of success consisted in being master of our subject. Such mastery is attainable through continuous application and study.

Those, who work diligently, not only achieve their goals and get success, but also remain happy, cheerful and active, which is itself a great reward even if the work does not bring success. Enthusiasm is the best asset of a person, self-determination and hard work, could achieve anything.

(60) A Man Who Wins, Is the Man Who Thinks, He Can

Confidence is the most important key to success. It boosts the morale and creates determination to attain a goal. The loss of confidence makes a man pessimist, coward or a dead man. A winner never quits and a quitter never wins, shows that one who constantly tries to achieve something, one who endeavours hard incessantly to achieve something, he is the winner, later or sooner, but a quitter could never be a winner. When Vallabhbhai Patel told that 'Swaraj is my birth right' so many people find it mere a slogan, but the incessant struggle put by all the freedom fighters supported the claim of Patel and we could win the freedom. Organising the efforts properly, in right direction, striking at the opportune time, are essential for achieving a target. Optimism, determination, undaunted will power makes every impossible task possible.

Your biggest assets are your enthusiasm that enriches with your positive thinking. Never lose hope, keep cheerful, put the best possible efforts with your total involvement, have confidence in you and you are the winner. Through positive thinking one can overcome the mountains. One who always think positively even in adverse circumstances wins. Positive thinking always pays. Life belongs to the ambitions.

Paragraph Writing

What Is a Paragraph?

A paragraph is a collection of related sentences dealing with a single topic or we can say that a paragraph is a unit of thoughts with one idea developed adequately. A paragraph should contain each of the following : Unity, Coherence, A Topic Sentence, and Adequate Development. All of these traits overlap so using and adapting them to our specific purpose will help us to construct effective paragraphs.

1. **Unity** : The entire paragraph should concern itself with a single focus. If it begins with one focus or major point of discussion, it should not end with another or wander within different ideas.
2. **Coherence** : Coherence is the trait that makes the paragraph easily understandable to a reader. Coherence can be created or maintained in your paragraphs by carrying over the same idea from sentence to sentence. These sentences are related to the main idea and give more information about the main idea. These sentences include, facts, details, explanations, reasons, examples, illustrations.
3. **A topic sentence (Main idea sentence)** : A topic sentence is a sentence that indicates in a general way what idea or thesis the paragraph is going to deal with. Although not all paragraphs have clear-cut topic or main idea sentences, and despite the fact that topic sentences can occur anywhere in the paragraph (as the first sentence, the last sentence, or somewhere in the middle), an easy way to make sure your reader understands the topic of the paragraph is to put your topic sentence near the beginning of the paragraph.

   A main idea sentence (Topic sentence) answers the following questions :

   What is the paragraph about?

   What is the main point I want to make?

   What do I want to say?
4. **Adequate development** : The topic (which is introduced by the topic sentence) should be discussed fully and adequately. Again, this varies from paragraph to paragraph, but it solely depends on the purpose of writing and demand of the examination.

Some Important Tips

1. Use examples and illustrations
2. Cite data (facts, statistics, evidence, details, and others)
3. Examine testimony (what other people say such as quotes and paraphrases)
4. Use an anecdote or story
5. Define terms in the paragraph
6. Compare and contrast
7. Evaluate causes and reasons
8. Examine effects and consequences
9. Analyse the topic
10. Describe the topic
11. Offer a chronology of an event (time segments) if need be.

1. The Value of Time

Time is very precious. We should not waste our time. Time once lost is lost forever. If you waste your time, time will waste you. Money spent can be earned again. It is not so with time. Time once spent is spent and gone. It can never be got back. Almost everything in the world can be purchased, but time lost cannot be purchased. As each second ticks away, that second moves from the present to the past. If you have not properly used that single second when it was in the present, it is a second wasted and it is already lost and becomes the past. No amount of crying or trying can bring you back the past. If you want success in life, make proper use of time. Mind the present and make full use of it.

2. I Won a Lottery

I am from a middle-class family. My life was going on easily. One day I was coming back from school. A lottery ticket seller came to me. He requested me to purchase a ticket. He told me the possibility of winning the first prize. He drew a very promising picture before me. I purchased a ticket in the name of God. On due date the draw was opened. Next day I saw the newspaper. I brought my ticket. I was surprised to see that I had won the first prize of Rs fifty lakh. At first I did not believe it. I was mad with joy. When luck favours, it knows no limits. I cried with happiness. My parents, brother and sisters came to me. They also checked the ticket number. They were extremely happy. My relatives and friends came to congratulate me. My father brought sweets from the market. We gave sweets to everyone who came to our house. Everyone was telling us that we were very lucky. I have no words to express my joy and feelings. That day really brought happiness to all of us.

3. Good Manners

Good manners are not born with us. They are learnt. Good manners help to make a man popular. They are the ornaments of a gentleman. They make a person a useful member of the society. They are a ladder to success. They are more important than the laws of the government. If a man has good manners, he is liked by all. People praise him and respect him.

Good manners cost nothing, but their effects are very valuable. Good manners give colour and grace to life. We should have good manners at home, at school and everywhere. We should respect our parents, neighbours, teachers and elders. We should have affection for those who are younger to us. We should respect the feelings of others. We should look to the comforts of each member of our family. Politeness is very necessary for good manners. We should not unnecessarily argue with others. We should not lose our temper. We should not hurt the feelings of others. We must remember that our rights are limited by the rights of others. Good manners bring you honour.

4. My Ambition in Life

Life without an ambition is like a ship without rudder. Man is the maker of his life. Those who aim at nothing get nothing. In fact, without aim, a man wanders about in dark. Life without aim is no life at all. Aim gives direction to the life. Ambitions differ from man to man. Some people aim at wealth, some at power and some at eminence.

The service to man is the service to God. I also want to serve human beings. My ambition is to become an ideal teacher. Teachers are the builders of nation . It is a peaceful job. A teacher is always young among the students. A teacher feels pleasure in teaching. A mother simply gives birth to a child, a teacher makes him capable. He wishes that his students should bring a good name to him and to his country. A true teacher does not run after money. A true teacher has a respectable position in the society. People respect a true teacher.

Students are the true wealth of a teacher. A teacher follows the principle simple living and high thinking. A teacher has morals and teaches morals to his students. So my ambition is to become a true teacher.

5. A Morning Walk

Walking is the best exercise. It is a natural tonic. It is good for the old and the young alike. It keeps the body healthy and strong. There is a saying "A healthy mind lives in a healthy body." It keeps our mind fresh and makes us active. Early rising is a good habit.

Nature is full of peace and beauty. Through morning walk we come into close contact with nature. We enjoy the beauties of nature. The air is cool and pleasant. We see that birds are singing. Flowers are laughing and leaves are dancing. We feel pleasure. We notice green trees and green fields. They look very beautiful. The air is fresh and full of natural fragrance. Peace prevails everywhere. It gives us pleasure and peace. We forget our worries. Noble ideas come to our mind. We are not in a hurry and walk slowly. We feel that God is really a big artist. We get free fresh air. It makes our lungs and heart strong and keeps illness away.

After some time, the sky begins to become red in the east. It shows that the sun is about to rise. Slowly the sun peeps out at the horizon. It looks like a big red ball. The scene of rising sun has its own charm. In short, we can say that morning walk is a boon.

6. Going to a Doctor

I detest the idea of being sick. However, sickness does not care for one's likes and dislikes. One day, I got up feeling quite uneasy. I thought it was the outcome of lack of sleep. When it persisted, my parents and I knew some sickness was in the offing. My father took me to Dr. Joshi, a well known physician of the town. There was a great rush at his clinic. The doctor was examining the patients one by one. We had to wait for over forty-five minutes. The doctor asked me to open my mouth and show him the tongue saying 'ah'. An assistant of the doctor took my temperature. The doctor told my father that I had a bad cold. He asked me to stay in bed for a week. I was asked to take light food only. The doctor prescribed me some capsules, some tablets and a cough syrup.

The behaviour of the doctor impressed my father and me a lot.

7. A Road Accident

It was on 21st December. I was going to my school. The road between Ashoka circle and Bhagat Singh Circle was very busy. Everybody seemed in a hurry. A young man on a motorcycle came. He was driving the bike at a great speed. A girl was going on a bicycle. The motorcyclist tried to control his speed but it was too late. There was a severe collision. He knocked down the girl. The girl started screaming with pain. Some people ran to help the girl. The motorcyclist and I took her to general hospital. I took the girl to 'Emergency'. The doctor on duty quickly examined the girl and gave her some tablets. I telephoned the parents of the girl. They immediately arrived and thanked me. The motorcyclist was very ashamed for the accident.

There has been a great rise in traffic recently. The number of road accidents is fast increasing. Rash driving and lack of effective traffic control are mainly responsible for it.

8. A Rainy Day

It was a cloudy day. Before I set off to office my mother insisted on taking an umbrella. So I took an umbrella along with my briefcase. Hardly had I started when it started drizzling. Within minutes the drizzle turned to heavy showers. The road was completely wet, with water gushing into the drains near the road. I took shelter in the varandah of a shop near the bus stop.

As I looked around, I saw boys and girls splashing water on one another. Little children were dancing and jumping with joy. One small boy was trying to float a little paper boat. Some people were fully drenched but did not care and went on walking. Buses, cars, rickshaws and scooters flashed past splashing water.

After about half an hour, the rain stopped and I set off to office.

9. My Hobby

Every person has some hobby. Hobbies differ from man to man. My hobby is gardening. It gives me pleasure and satisfaction. It also helps me to keep fit as physical labour is involved in it. Mostly I am free in the mornings. So I devote an hour every day for the sake of my hobby. I have grown a beautiful lawn in front of my house. This lawn is surrounded by flowering plants. I have a good variety of 'English roses' besides the seasonal flowers that I grow. I have collected a good number of fine species of cacti and crotons. In the evenings I sit in the lawn, see the blooming flowers and feel as if I am living in a garden of happiness. My parents like the hobby I pursue , and my neighbours praise me.

10. A Village Fair

I live in a village. Last Monday I went to see the fair of Baba Ramdeoji. I went there with my friends. Hundreds of men, women and children were there. They were in fine clothes. The ground looked like a sea of people. People were going and coming here and there in groups. Some women were singing songs. There were many beggars also. They were begging. There were some scouts and policemen to help the people.

There were many stalls. They were selling toys, bangles, rings, ear-rings, combs, clothes, balloons and many other things. There was rush on every stall. Stall-keepers were doing good business. There were some stalls selling sweets, namkins and tea. We were also enjoying the fair. We saw a small boy weeping. He had lost his parents. We took him to the police-chowki. His parents were waiting there. They were very sad. When they saw the boy with us, they were very happy. They thanked us.

We went to temple. There was a long queue of people. We also stood in the queue. After some time we had 'darshan' of Baba. We took one more round of the fair. We were tired. We went to a tea stall. We took a some 'chat' and tea. There were some merry-go-rounds. They were attracting many people. We went there. We also enjoyed them.

It was evening. I purchased some toys and balloons for my younger brother. We came back to our houses. I was very happy. I cannot forget this fair in my life.

11. Importance of Trees

Trees are called 'GREEN GOLD'. It means trees are as valuable as gold. We get wood from trees. Wood is used in making furniture, houses and other useful things. Trees give us fruits, spices and many useful medicines. They give fodder to animals. Trees breath out oxygen. We breathe in oxygen and so are alive. Every country is suffering from air pollution. Trees help in reducing air pollution. Many industries depend on trees.

Trees attract clouds, and clouds bring rain. Trees check soil erosion. Wild animals and birds live in forests. They are useful in many ways.

Trees are our helpful and useful friends. In reality trees are the valuable gifts of nature to man. We should honour and preserve trees.

12. The Importance of Newspapers

Newspaper is a mirror which reflects the political, economical and the social conditions of the country. Newspapers try to give us the latest news about the country and the world. Newspapers are the windows through which we see the happenings of the world and the country.

They increase our general knowledge. They have educational value. They serve the society in many ways. We should inculcate the habit of reading newspapers.

The government programmes and policies are made public through newspapers. If a particular policy is good people appreciate it; and if it is harmful, a cry against it can be raised in newspapers. They are an eye-opener for the government. In this way newspapers are very important for democracy. A good newspaper is a watchdog of democracy.

13. An Indian Wedding

Marriage is a social necessity. It is said that marriages are settled in heaven and celebrated on the earth. Indian weddings are colourful.

Last month I attended the marriage ceremony of my friend. The house was decorated with colourful lights and paper-flags. In the evening his friends and relatives gathered at his house. All were in fine dresses. Ladies were singing songs. My friend put on a special dress. He sat on a decorated mare. There was a band-party with the '*barat*'. We went to the bride's house. On the way, his friends danced at places .

The house of the bride was also decorated. The relatives of the bride welcomed us. There was a tent and there were chairs. We took our seats. The groom went at the gate. The bride came in a fine dress. She was looking very beautiful. They garlanded each other.

They served us tasty dinner. We enjoyed it. The groom also took food. Then he was taken into the house. There was a '*Pandit*'. The bridegroom and the bride sat side by side. The '*Pandit*' chanted out some promises. The bride and bridegroom repeated them. The pair took seven rounds of the holy fire. The ceremony took about two hours. Now they were husband and wife. Next, morning the '*barat*' came back to the bridegroom's house with the bride. They were welcomed there.

14. A Visit to a Museum

It was Sunday. The college was closed for the day. Weather was cloudy and the breeze was blowing. My friend Ramesh came from my native village to meet me. We made a programme for visiting the museum. We spent about two hour there, and saw many wonderful things. There were works of art, paintings, sculpture, pottery, embroidery; clay models of various scenes from the village life, of social and religious ceremonies, were very interesting. Among the most interesting articles, we saw, were the antiquities of the stone and bronze periods, consisting of daggers, swords, shields and early pottery and sculptural urns, and weapons and personal ornaments of that period. In one room we noticed several old coins of India and fine brass articles.

The dresses worn by the people of that time; and the dresses of the ancient Rajput and Sikh warriors of this country were amazing to be seen. Old swords, shields and armours of the old inhabitants of this country were nicely arranged and attracted the sight of the visitors. The models of the Kohinoor, the Taj Mahal, the Golden Temple and the Bhakra Dam pleased us greatly.

Passing into another room, we saw, thousands of years old, big statues of Gautam Buddha and some other Budhist saints. We saw the history of India written on stone and paper by hand. We also saw the pillars on which were recorded the edicts of Asoka. All these carried us into the past.

The most interesting thing that caught our eyes, was an Egyptian mummy—a man in a glass case wrapped in a hundred yards of cloth. The Egyptians did not bury their dead, but preserved them from decay with salts and spices and other chemicals.

The museum contained many things of interest and instruction. One could learn much from an inspection of its treasures and also derive amusement from the various curiosities stored therein. It was a fine, memorable and educative visit.

15. A Walk by the River Side

It was a little before sunset on a hot evening that I, with two of my friends, went out for a walk by the river side. The sight was charming and eye catching. The trees spreading out their branches to catch the breezy air, the flowers 'tossing their heads in sprightly dance'in the cool and mild breeze, the birds with their variegated plumes singing on the trees; the buterflies flitting from one flower to another , the children also enjoying in their own way, the acquatic birds swimming and diving, the boys rowing and larking, and the fish coming up here and there in the river water all presented a fascinating and mesmerizing sight. The blue vault of the sky, reflected in the transparent water, was beautiful to behold. The whole landscape was captivating; scenery all round was charming. Wonderful was the whole ramp show of the Nature. It filled our hearts and minds with peace and exhilarating excitement.

The dusk fell, the stars started showing their twinkling lights and the smiling moon rose in the sky. The twinkling stars were reflected beautifully in the calm water of the river; the moon sailing through the clouds in the sky, now smiling upon us, now blushing, and bathing trees, flowers, buildings and gardens, in her light blue silvery beams, presented a beautiful scene. Every thing seemed asleep in the soothing beams of the moon. The sight was too mesmerizing to forget.

16. Caught in a Shower of Rain

The clouds which have been gathering on the horizon for a long time, have become dark and the rain started pouring down heavily. Those who were caught in, ran in all directions, some laughing and some yelling.

I always find particular amusement in such sudden helter-skelter. It seems as if each person, taken by surprise, loses the personality which he poses to the world and now appearing in his true colours. For example, that big man with deliberate steps, who suddenly forgot his indifference made to order, and ran like a schoolboy. He is a thrifty gentleman, who, with all his fashionable airs, is afraid of spoiling his hat.

That pretty lady, on the contrary, whose looks are so modest, and whose dress is so elaborate, slackens her pace with the increasing storm. She seems to find pleasure in braving it, and does not think of her valvet cloak spotted by the hail. She is evidently a lioness in sheep's clothing.

Here a young man who was passing, stops to catch some of the hailstones in his hand, and examines them. By his quick and businesslike walk just now, you would have taken him for a commercial traveller on his rounds. And those schoolboys who left their ranks to run after the sudden gusts of whirlwind; those girls, just now so demure,who flew with bursts of laughter; those guardsmen, who quit the martial attitude of their days of duty, and took refuge under a porch! The sudden rain storm has caused all these transformations.

17. The Postman

Postman is a very humble member of our society. His work looks very simple but it's indeed very important and valuable work. His work facilitates us to know about our near and dears.

He symbolises what duty is. He performs his duty even in odd weather. It may be raining in torrents, thunder and lightning, the day may be blazing hot or stormy, he is ever punctual in delivering letters. He is a very sincere and dedicated worker and is strictly devoted to his duties. He is a fountain head of good humour, contentment and happiness, and ever comes with a smiling face. He is an embodiment of the virtues of obedience, courtesy and civility.

And when we think of what he carries in his bag from door to door along the streets of the city, or through the jungles and along mountain paths to distant villages, he seems to be the messenger of good luck. People wait for him anxiously, with mixed feelings, some with hope, some in dread, for he carries messages. In his bag, may be the long-expected letter from a soldier in a far-off country to his anxious parents; the letter that will tell a newly married girl about the date of arrival of her husband; the letter that will tell a poor widow of the death of her only son; the letter informing an anxious candidate of his success or failure in an examination; letters of joy and sorrow, complaint and request, success and failure, upbrading and praise, death and life, fortune and ruin. And the humble postman, all unknowing, passes on indifferently scattering all sorts of news.

With the advent of other sources of communication, now a lot of role of the postman is taken over by courier-man, telephones, mobiles etc, yet the importance of postman in rural area is still high.

18. Disarmament

Disarmament assumes a very special importance for us, overriding all other issues. For many years past, there have been talks on disarmament and some progress has undoubtedly been made in so far as the plans and proposals are concerned. Still, we find that the race for armaments continues, as also the efforts to invent ever more powerful engines of destruction. If even a small part of these efforts was directed to the search for peace, probably the problem of disarmament would have been solved by this time. Apart from the moral imperative of peace, every practical consideration leads us to that conclusion. The choice today in this nuclear age, is one of utter annihilation and destruction of civilization or of some way to have peaceful co-existence between nations. There is no middle way. If war is an abomination and an ultimate crime which has to be avoided, we must fashion our minds and policies accordingly. In order to achieve peace, we have to develop a climate of peace and tolerance and to avoid speech and action which tend to increase fear and hatred. It may not be possible to reach full disarmament in one step, though every step should be conditioned to that end. Much ground has already been covered in the discussion on disarmament. But the sands of time run out, and we dare not play about with this issue or delay its consideration. This, indeed, is the main duty of the United Nations today and if it fails in this, the United Nations fails in its main purpose.

Unit

53

Letter Writing

How to Write Good Letters ?

Letter writing is an art. A well written letter not only conveys your message to the receiver in clear terms but also reflects on him about your over all personality. Everyone has to write letter of some sort in his life so one must learn the art of letter writing.

· **Letters can be classified broadly in two categories.**

(1) Personal or friendly letters, including invitational letters

(2) Business letters,including letters to government or semi government officials, letters to newspapers , letters of application etc.

All letters in general consist of following parts:

1. The Heading
2. The Greeting
3. The Body
4. The Complimentary close
5. The Signature line

Personal Letters

Personal letters, also known as **friendly** letters, normally have five parts.

1. The Heading This includes the address, line by line, with the last line being the date. Skip a line after the heading. If using pre-addressed stationery, just add the date.

The heading of a friendly letter contains the return address followed by the date.

If the correspondents are familiar enough and the recipient knows the writer's address, or if the stationery is imprinted with the return address, then the return address may be omitted. (Although another reason for the return address is a backup in case the envelope gets damaged...) But don't forget to include the date. For example:

129, South West Block,
Alwar (Rajasthan)
August 24, 2006

(Most writers skip a line between the address and the date.)

2. The Greeting (Salutation) The greeting always ends with a comma. The greeting may be formal, beginning with the word "dear" and using the person's given name or relationship, or it may be informal if appropriate.

Formal : Dear Uncle Jimmy, Dear Mr. Walker,
Informal : Hi Joe, Greetings,

The greeting in a friendly letter capitalises the first word and any noun. It normally ends with a comma, though it might be all right to end with an exclamation point when writing to someone with whom you are very familiar and the emphasis is appropriate. (Occasionally very personal greetings may end with an exclamation point for emphasis.)

3. The Body The body of the letter contains the main text. This includes the message you want to write. Normally in a friendly letter, the beginning of paragraphs is indented. If not indented, be sure to skip a space between paragraphs. The block style (no indented paragraphs) is considered too formal for a friendly letter, so each new paragraph should be indented.Skip a line after the greeting and before the close. Skipping a line between paragraphs, especially in typed or printed copy, helps the reader.

4. The Complimentary Close (The subscription) This short expression is always a few words on a single line. The complimentary close begins with a capital letter and ends with a comma. It should be indented to the same column as the heading. Skip one to three spaces for the signature line.

Sincerely yours
Truly yours

5. The Signature Line Type or print your name. The handwritten signature goes above this line and below the close. The signature line and the handwritten signature are indented to the same column as the close.

Unless there is great familiarity between the correspondents, the signature should be in blue or black ink. For example:

Truly yours,
(*Signature goes here*)
Suresh Gupta

Postscript : If your letter contains a postscript, begin it with **PS** and end it with your initials. Skip a line after the signature line to begin the postscript.

Punctuating Letters

Commas

Use commas after the salutation (also called the greeting) and after the complimentary closing in all letters. eg,

(i) Salutation :
Dear Ram,
My dearest Hina,

(ii) Closing :
Sincerely,
Truly yours,

Colons in Special Cases

1. Numerical expressions of time.
eg, : 5:31 p.m.
The colon goes between the hour and minute. If seconds are noted, a colon goes between the minute and second also.

2. Colons follow labels that identify important ideas meant to get attention.

Warning: To be opened by authorised personnel only.

Capitals in Letters

There are two additional rules for capitalising when writing letters.

1. Capitalise the first word and all nouns in the salutation (or greeting). eg,
Dear Sir,
My dearest Aunt,
Greetings!

2. Capitalise the first word in the complimentary closing. eg,
Sincerely yours,
Truly yours,
With best wishes,

Q. 1. Write a letter from a father giving advice to his son who has taken admission in a college.

Answer.

1/42, Aravali Vihar
Rajgarh (Alwar)
July 14, 2....

My dear Son,

This is the first letter I am writing to you after you left home for higher studies at the college. You have been a very sincere and hard working student so far. You are at the threshold of making and shaping your future career. If you would be sincere to your studies, you could get what you desire. These four years of sincerity and devotion to the studies are very important in shaping the career of a student. You are venturing into a new life where you find everything to decide yourself. There is none to tell you to study or play or watch T.V. You are to manage all your time yourself.

I know that you will not disappoint me with respect to your studies, but you are in your youth, and know little of the temptations and allurement with which youth is beset now-a-days. The bad habits and evils which might catch during this period can spoil not only your own career but also destroy the aspirations of the parents.

Companions influence one's character greatly : good companions make good one's character and bad companions mar one's career. Choose the friends who are sincere, honest and industrious. Education plays very important role in the formation of character. Morals are of greater importance in life than the subjective knowledge.

Indolence is the worst habit a student can form. Remember that doing nothing may do you even more harm. You may find plenty of books in your college library. Read history and biography, both for instruction and amusement and if you feel inclined for something lighter.

I don't want to say anything more.You are also a wise boy. Remember :

Heights by the great men reached and kept,,
Were not attained by sudden flight,
But while their companions were slept,
They were toiling upwards in the night.

Write to me regularly and unreservedly. Always look upon me as your best friend, hiding nothing, not even your mistakes or faults.

Your mother conveys you her fondest love.

Your affectionate father,
SC Gupta

Q. 2. Write a letter to your friend congratulating him on his success in the RAS examination.

Answer.

32/31, West Patel Nagar
Jaisalmer
July 23, 20..

My dear Pramod,

I am glad to see your result in the *Rajasthan Patrika* of today that you have been successful in the RAS examination and secured good rank. I conveyed this happy news to my father who was sitting beside me. He too was overjoyed.

I thank God for His kindness and wish you a bright future. I know well that you have been intelligent and diligent in your school and college days. Certainly your success is due to God's grace as well as your hard work and also timely guidance of your respected parents.

Please convey my respectful compliments to your parents. Again congratulations to you.

Yours sincerely,
Raj Kumar

Q. 3. Write a letter to your friend who has recently lost his mother.

Answer.

10, Barkat Nagar
Jaipur
May 4, 20..

My dear Mahesh,

It is really a very sad news that you have lost your mother. I knew your mother was ill but the illness was not so serious. The news of your mother's death came to me as a shock. I know you will feel it deeply for you always thought so much of your mother and loved her very much. I also feel it as a personal loss to myself. She was always very kind and loving to me. I can't forget her love and affection for me and her motherly care and worries for me. She was such a good and noble woman.

In such sorrow we are always alone. Words, I know can't soothe your wounds. May God give you strength to bear this uncompensationable loss.

Yours sincerely,
Kailash Jaiman

Q. 4. Write a letter of apology to a friend for not keeping an appointment.

Answer.

29, Janta Colony
Jaipur
June 19, 20..

My dear Pradeep,

I am sorry I could not join you at dinner last night. You must have waited for me and cursed me as well for not keeping the appointment. But this lapse on my part was due to the fact that I met with an accident while coming over to your place.

Near Ghat Gate a motor cycle came from the opposite direction. It was without lights. It hit my scooter. I fell off the scooter and lay on the road. My left arm was badly injured. Some people took me to hospital. I was allowed to leave the hospital only after midnight. My arm was plastered. I hope you will excuse my absence.

Yours sincerely,
Ashok

Q. 5. Write a letter to your younger brother advising him to take part in evening games.

Answer.

12, South West Block
Alwar
February 15, 20..

My dear Tapan,

I met your class teacher yesterday. He told me that you stood first in the class. I was glad to hear it. But he also told me that you have become a bookworm. You do not take part in any kind of games. It is not good. It will affect your health.

I suggest you to take part in evening games. Do not study at the cost of your health. Play hockey or football. Play any game at least for an hour. It will refresh your mind and keep you physically fit. This will help you in your studies. Do study hard, but do play a while. Always remember the saying *'Work while you work and play while you play; that is the way to be happy and gay'*.

With love,

Yours affectionately,
Prakash Gupta

Q. 6. Write a letter to your elder brother from the town in which you have just joined a new appointment describing the important features of the town, of the people with whom you are associated.

Answer.

13, Mayur Colony Bhilwara
April 25, 20...

My dear Brother,

I am glad to receive your loving letter and happy to learn that everyone is fine at home. You have asked me to give you a brief description of this town. I like this town and the people here. 9 A.M. sure that the description as follows will make you like the place and fill you with a longing to see it.

It is a big trade centre. There are two cloth mills here which supply cloth to the whole of the country. There is a large cloth market where you can buy cloth of all qualities and designs. There are four Boys' Colleges and eight Senior Secondary Schools.There are two Girls' College also. There are three Government Hospitals, one for male, other for female and child and several private nursing homes. Besides these, there is a charitable eye hospital also. It is a Railway junction. Three beautiful Picture Halls are also situated in the town. There is one Engineering and one Dental College too in the town, located in the Industrial Area about 8 Km. far from the town. The most interesting feature of the town is its magnificent temples where hymns are sung and cymbals are clashed daily in the morning and evening.

People are nice, honest, straight forward, hardworking and trustworthy. They are not addicted to any vices as drinking and gambling. My colleagues are also very cooperative and of helping nature. The General Manager of my company is a thorough gentleman and takes keen interest in the welfare of the staff. He is very kind and sympathetic to all the employees.

I am fine here. Everything is going on here nicely as per scheduled routine. Regards to Daddy and Mom.

Yours affectionately,
Maneesh

Q. 7. Write a letter from a student to his friend, telling him about the first impression of the college.

Answer.

215, Aravali Vihar
Near Jain Temple
Alwar (Raj.) 301001

Dear Shankar,

As you know, I got admission in Rajasthali Commerce College, Alwar Rajasthan this year. You have asked me to tell you about my new college.

The atmosphere and the environment of the college is entirely different from that of our schools. The discipline in the college is not as strict as in our school. No bindings of wearing any uniform. The professors treat us in very friendly way. There is no terror of the teachers as in school . Professors just come in the class, deliver the lectures and generally do not bother to ask any question from the students. They are not worried whether any student follow them or not. All kinds of facilities like library, sports, games and canteen are available in this college.

Students enjoy the freedom of college life. Everyone is at liberty to go wherever he likes, do whatever he likes, and speaks what he has in his mind within some limits. There is none to check the students. They can spoil or they can make their lives.

I can't afford to waste my time in useless things and have started making notes, consulting the library books for the last one week.

I have to do a lot of hard work to achieve good marks.Tell me about you.

Convey my regards to your parents.

Yours sincerely,
Dinesh

Q. 8. Write a letter to your elder brother writing him the reasons of your failure in Public Service Commission Examination.

Answer.

304, Shastri Nagar
Jodhpur (Raj.)
Jan. 16, 20......

My dear brother,

I am in receipt of your letter. You have asked me the reasons of my failure in Public Service Commission Examination. I do not like to take any excuse but believe in narrating the facts of my failure as per my imaginations. As you also know, this was not an easy exam. I made full preparations for all the four papers, but the time table of my exams was very cumbersome. I had to take three papers continuously. The Economics paper was on 12th Jan. from 3 P.M. to 6 P.M. and the paper of Statistics-I was scheduled on 13th Jan. from 10 A.M. to 1 P.M. and after that I had to take the paper of Statistics-II from 3 P.M. on the 13th Jan, itself. This all caused a lot of tension to my mind. I couldn't sleep even for a minute on the night of 12th Jan. and so when I went to the examination hall on 13th Jan., I could take the paper of Statistics-I satisfactorily but I could not take the paper of Statistics-II properly and so in this paper I got only 31 marks out of 100 marks and that spoiled my percentage. I did very good preparations for all papers, but to whom can I blame, it is my hard luck or say I was unfortunate as the time table was so uneasy and tedious.

This is the first time when all the students who opted Economics and Statistics have suffered a lot because of such time schedule. I am myself not happy with the result but nothing can be done now. I am determined to take this examination again with more hard work. I remember your words *"A man who wins, is the man who thinks, he can."*

Convey my regards to Papa and Mummy.

Yours loving brother,
Prakash

Q. 9. Write a letter to your uncle thanking him for the birthday gift you have received from him.

Answer.

105, Mangal Vihar
Alwar
February 28, 20..

My dear Uncle,

Yesterday was my birthday. I received many gifts, but your gift was the best. You have sent me a beautiful wrist watch. Everybody liked it. I thank you very much for such a lovely gift.

Your gift is very precious to me. I was often late for school. Now I shall be punctual. This watch will help me during my examination days also.The watch is a token of your love for me. I shall always keep it with me. Once again I thank you.

Convey my regards to Aunty.

Yours lovingly,
Harsh

Q.10. Write a letter to your father asking for some money.

Answer.

415, Lajpat Nagar
Alwar (Rajasthan)
February 23, 20...

My dear father,

I hope this letter will find everybody at home in the best of health and happiness. I am well here. You might have received my progress report from the school. You will be glad to know that I secured first position in my terminal examination. I assure you that I will maintain this position in the Annual Examination also. As you know my dues for the next quarter are due, kindly send me Rs. 1100/- by draft at the earliest.

Please pay my respects to dear mother and convey my love and affection to Puppy and Raju.

Yours loving son,
Raman

Q. 11. You are Putin. Your sister, Ragini, has just completed X standard and has sought your advice in the matter of opting Science or Commerce group. Write a letter advising her to select the group in XI standard.

Answer.

KH-3, South West Block
Near Eid Gah
Alwar (Raj.).
18th March, 20......

Dear Ragini,

I am in receipt of your letter dated 15th March. You have sought my advice in the matter of opting Science or Commerce group in your XI standard.

First of all, I like to tell you very frankly that whatever stream you opt, you are to put hard to achieve success. In the present competitive world, poor show in any stream is of no use. In Science group, you can opt either Engineering or Medical. If we compare Engineering and Medical profession, the medical profession is more suitable, particularly for female candidates. On the other hand, through Commerce stream, you can become a Chartered Accountant, ICWA, Company Secretary and can also go for MBA. Along with Commerce stream, you are required to take computer training also, because now-a-days all business is being carried through the computer. As such commerce also opens new vistas of career opportunities to you.

So if you are interested in becoming an Engineer or a Doctor, you should opt for the Science stream and if you are interested in the work of accounting nature, the Commerce stream is more suitable to you. Any way, choice is yours.

Whatever may be your decision, please convey me positively. I also like to tell you that you should also improve your English alongwith your academic achievements. English is very important for acquiring higher qualifications.

Everything is normal at my end. Do write for any work.

Convey my regards to Mummy and Papa.

Yours loving brother,
Putin

Q. 12. You are Sweta living in the hostel of PQR School, New Delhi. Write a letter to your sister, Rashmi, describing your hostel life.

Answer.

Indira Hostel
PQR School
New Delhi
25th March 200......

My dear Rashmi,

I received your loving letter three days ago, but because of my preoccupation in making preparations for the annual function of our hostel, I could not spare time to reply you.

I feel pleasure in informing you that I stood first in the quiz competition and our team stood second in folk dance competition held during the annual function programmes. As I am staying in the hostel, I am devoting more than two hours daily in improving my General Knowledge and General Awareness in addition to course studies. Ours is a very good hostel. Most of the students are well disciplined and sincere. Our hostel warden Mrs. Savita Vermani is a very strict lady. She keeps close watch on every student. All the students are required to attend the morning and evening prayers daily and both the time attendance is marked.

The quality of food being served is very good, consisting of two vegetables, curd and salad, with Tawa chapatis and a sweet dish. Breakfast is served at 8 A.M., after that I go to school and take lunch at 12 P.M. and dinner is served from 7 P.M. to 9 P.M. In the evening we play games like badminton, hockey, cricket in the hostel playground from 4 P.M. to 7 P.M. As such I find this hostel a well maintained one, with everything of good quality and caring.

What about you ? How are your studies going on ? Do write to me for any help or work.

Convey my regards to mummy and love to Sunny.

Yours loving sister,
Sweta

Q. 13. You are Sarwesh living at 1215, Qutab Enclave, New Delhi. Write a letter to your father telling him of your plan to go to a village with a group of students to teach illiterate villagers.

Answer.

1215, Qutab Enclave
New Delhi
22nd April, 200......

Respected Daddy,

I received your affectionate letter three days ago, but I was busy in my examinations so I could not reply earlier. I am very happy to note that Sonu has been selected in IIT with very good rank. Please congratulate him on my behalf . He deserves the kudos.

As I informed you earlier that my annual examination will be over on 29th April. On 30th April I along with a team of ten students are planning to go to a nearby village Hatina to educate the illiterate villagers. The team will be headed by our professor Dr. Pannikaran. We will teach them how to read and write our mother tongue Hindi. We will also train them to write their signatures.

Illiteracy is a curse in our society. Many problems and hardships are faced by the poor villagers because of the illiteracy. Our tour will not only help the villagers but it will also be beneficial for us to get the first hand knowledge of rural problems. I will write you about our detailed programme later on. Every other thing is fine at my end. I am preparing well for my annual examinations.

Convey my deep regards to Mom and heartily congratulations to Sonu.

Yours loving son,
Sarvesh

Q. 14. You are Girish living in a hostel of BTR School, New Delhi. Write a letter to your friend Mohan, telling him about an interesting weekend that you spent at your friend's house recently.

Answer.

Subhash Hostel
BTR School
New Delhi
30th March, 20......

Dear friend Mohan,

I have been thinking to write to you for the last several days about my short but enjoyful stay at my friends. As you are aware that I am well settled in the hostel now. I have got some very good friends here. I wrote you earlier about my friend Pankaj who belongs to Kolkata. The school was closed for winter vacations. Pankaj took me with him to Kolkata. His father is an Executive Engineer in PHED. He owns a big house and a small farm house. Kolkata is a large metropolitan city. We visited National Library, Victoria Palace and New A.C. market. We also travelled in tram, a small train with two coaches. It was really thrilling to visit zoo and Birla Planetarium there. I also visited Bara Bazar, a commercial market. I purchased two shirts and a wrist watch from the Madaan Market at very economical prices.

I really enjoyed my short stay with Pankaj. His parents are very generous and amiable. Every family member gave me love and affection. Their love and affection will always be fresh in my mind.

What about you ? When are you going to London ? Please write me your exact programme, so that I may plan to visit you accordingly.

Yours truly,
Girish

Q. 15. You are Anubhuti. Write a letter to your friend Reena about the futility of exploding crackers on Deepawali.

Answer.

1876, Mount Villa
Mount Abu
24th May, 200......

Dear friend Reena,

Hope this letter finds you happy and enjoying the leisure after examinations. You know that the festival of Diwali is approaching fast. I like to inform you that in our town, I along with my four friends decided to make the people aware of futility of using crackers on Diwali.

I do not find any reason for wasting so much money on firing and exploding crackers which not only pollutes the atmosphere but also causes outbreak of fire on many occasions. Many times the fire caused by the crackers endangers human lives and destroys huge properties. On the one side people are wasting money in exploding crackers and on the other side people are not having sufficient food to eat and clothes to cover their bodies. We have decided to collect rupees fifty from every house to distribute sweets and clothes to the poor. I think by this way we will be celebrating this festival in real sense. Tell me what you think about our plan of celebrating Diwali as in such manner.

Convey my regards to your parents.

Yours friend,
Anubhuti

Q. 16. Your are Prakash. Write a letter to your friend Ramesh asking him about his studies for competitive examinations.

Answer.

103, Narpat Colony
Near Ahimsa Circle
Jaipur (Raj.) 302015
15th March, 200......

Dearest Ramesh,

I haven't heard from you since long. It seems that you are very busy in preparing for the State Service Commission Examinations or something else ? Anyway, tell me about your preparations. I think you should have completed all the optional papers so far. I like to tell you only one thing that whenever you start revising your papers, try to prepare short notes, so that you can revise the same again during examination period. This will help you in making several revisions and you will be able to secure good marks. A good percentage in theory papers means your selection is almost confirm.

I know you must be putting all your strength and wisdom as you are a very hard working and devoted guy. I wish to see you among the first fifty candidates.

I am doing my job well. My good wishes for the exams.

Do write for any deserving service.

Yours truly,
Prakash

Q. 17. Write a letter to your father explaining him the reasons of your not securing good marks in English paper.

Answer.

24, Subhash Hostel
WXT College
Jaipur
March 26, 200......

Respected Papa,

I received your letter today in the morning. You have asked me the reasons of my securing poor marks in English paper.

First of all I like to tell you that I put very hard labour in English. As you are aware that I am not good at Grammar, so I couldn't attend the Grammar portion so well. I need tuition for English Grammar. I have talked with our Grammar teacher who has consented to give me tuitions for two months only. Without good command over English Grammar, it is not possible to secure good marks in English. Please allow me to take English tuition so that the problem of English is finished for ever.

You can see that in other subjects I have secured more than 85% marks, but in English I could not manage to secure more than 40%.

Convey my regards to Mom, and Grandmom.

Yours loving son,
Jaipal

Q. 18. Write a letter to your elder brother telling him about the discomforts of a railway journey without reservation.

Answer.

214, Nehru Nagar
Ambala
3rd March, 200......

Dear brother,

As I informed you telephonically also I reached here safe and sound yesterday.

I like to tell you about the discomfort I suffered because I had no reservation. As you know I could not get the reservation so I had to travel in second class general compartment. The journey was very tiring and cumbersome. First of all the train was late by two hours. As soon as the train arrived I managed to push myself into the general compartment. It was overcrowded, but after one hour I got half a seat, just managed to sit on the corner of a seat. Six persons were sitting on a seat for three, but it was comparatively comfortable. It was not possible to take rest or sleep the whole night, but I had no option.

However the night passed and the train reached Ambala at 5 a.m. I found myself safe and sound but extremely tired. I took a lesson to plan the journey in such a way that either get a reservation or if not better travel by bus.

How the things are going at your end. Convey my regards to Mom and love to Tini.

Yours younger brother,
Pulkit

Business Letters

Ingredients of Business Letters

A business letter is more formal than a personal letter. It should have sufficient margin (at least one inch) on all four edges. It is usually written on 8½" x 11" unlined stationery. There are six parts to a business letter.

The Heading The heading of a business letter contains the return address with the date on the last line. If the stationery is imprinted with the return address, then the return address may be omitted. Sometimes a line after the address and before the date may include a phone number, a fax number, an E-mail address, or the like.

Often a line is skipped between the address and date. If you are using stationery with the return address already imprinted, need not to write return address above the date.

eg,

Lacme Stores
140-B Ganesh Apartment
Mansarovar, Jaipur
(0141)2760795
July 18, 200....

The Inside Address This is the address you are sending your letter to. It should be complete. Include titles and names if you know them.

This is always on the left margin. If an 8½" x 11" paper is folded in thirds to fit in a standard 9" business envelope, the inside address can appear through the window in the envelope.

An inside address also helps the recipient route the letter properly and is of much help, should the envelope be damaged and the address become unreadable.

Skip a line after the heading before the inside address. Skip another line after the inside address before the greeting. eg,

Dr Govind Raghvan
Cross Country Coach
Dept. of Athletics
University of Jodhpur
Jodhpur (Rajasthan)

The Greeting It is also called the salutation. The greeting in a business letter is always formal. It normally begins with the word "Dear" and always includes the person's last name.

It normally has a title such as Mr., Mrs., Dr., or a political title. Use a first name only if the title is unclear. The greeting in a business letter may end in a colon or comma.

Names and Titles of People

Use the full name in standard writing unless the person uses an initial as part of his or her name. For eg,

George Smith,

Robert E. Lee

(The initial is fine here because that is the name he went by.)

Social titles before a proper name are capitalised. All but Miss and Master are abbreviated and end with a period.

Social titles: Mr., Master, Mrs., Miss Ms.
Mlle., Mme., M. Messrs., (Plural of Mr. or M.)
Mmes. (Plural of Mrs., Ms., Mme.)

The Body The body is the main letter. It is written as text. A business letter is usually typed . Depending on the letter style you choose, paragraphs may be indented. Regardless of format, skip a line between paragraphs. The first line of a new paragraph is indented in the semiblock style. The block and modified block style have all lines of the body to the left margin.

Skip a line between the greeting and the body. Skip a line between the body and the close.

The Complimentary Close (Subscription) This short, polite closing ends with a comma. It is either at the left margin or its left edge is in the center, depending on the Style that you use. It begins at the same column the heading does. The complimentary close begins with a capital letter and ends with a comma.

The Signature Line Skip two lines and type out the name to be signed. This customarily includes a middle initial, but does not have to. Women may indicate how they wish to be addressed by placing Miss, Mrs., Ms. or similar title in parentheses before their name.

The signature line may include a second line for a title, if appropriate. The term "By direction" in the second line means that a superior is authorising the signer. Sign the name in the space between the close and the signature line, starting at the left edge of the signature line. eg,

Sincerely,
(Signature goes here)
(Mrs.) Ben Jackson
Sincerely yours,
Director of Acquisitions
Prakash Jha
By direction : General Manager (Finance)

The signature should start directly above the first letter of the signature line in the space between the close and the signature line. Use blue or black ink.

Business letters should not contain postscripts.

Some Important Basics of Good Business Letters

Following phrases are usually found in any standard business letter. By using these standard phrases, you can give a professional touch to your business letters. These phrases are used as a kind of frame and introduction to the content of business letters.

The Beginning

Dear Personnel Manager,

Dear Sir or Madam (use if you don't know who you are writing to)

Dear Mr, Mrs, Miss or Ms (use if you know who you are writing to, and have a formal relationship with—VERY IMPORTANT use Ms for women unless asked to use Mrs or Miss)

Dear Frank (use if the person is a close business contact or friend)

The Reference

With reference to your advertisement in *The Times of India*,
Your letter of 3 rd May,
Your phone call today,
Thank you for your letter of March 25 th .

The Reason for Writing

I am writing to....
enquire about
apologize for
confirm

Requesting

Could you possibly ...?
I would be grateful if you could ...

Agreeing to Requests

I would be delighted to...

Giving Bad News

Unfortunately ...
I am afraid that ...

Enclosing Documents
I am enclosing...
Please find enclosed...
Enclosed you will find...
Closing Remarks
Thank you for your help.
Please contact us again...
if we can help in any way.
there are any problems.
you have any questions.
Reference to Future Contact
I look forward to...
hearing from you soon.
meeting you next Tuesday.
seeing you next Thursday.
The Finish
Yours faithfully, (If you don't know the name of the person you're writing to)
Yours sincerely, (If you know the name of the person you're writing to)
Best wishes,
Best regards, (If the person is a close business contact or friend)
Some Useful Letters

Q. 19. Write a letter from M/s V.K. Gupta & Sons Jaipur to M/s Arihant Prakashan, Karol Bagh, New Delhi, requesting them to supply the books.

Answer.

M/s V.K. Gupta & Sons
University Road Jaipur

Ref:Un/

Date 08/3/20......

M/s Arihant Prakashan
106, Karol Bagh
New Delhi 110013

***Sub** : Supply of books.*

Dear Sir,

We are sending herewith draft No. 1478952 dated 25/01/05, drawn on Punjab National Bank, favouring yourselves payable at New Delhi for Rs 15000/- in advance against the supply of the following books :

1. 60 Days Grammar By S.C. Gupta 200 copies
2. Objective Physics By Sharma & Gupta 150 copies

Please send the above books through Jaipur Golden Transport Company, duly packed with polythene. Please send the bill after allowing discount as usual.

Thanking you.

Yours faithfully,
V.K. Gupta
Partner
V.K. Gupta & Sons

Q. 20. Write a letter to the retailer from whom you purchased a TV but its picture tube is not functioning well. Write him to get it changed.

Answer.

15, Ganesh Colony
Alwar (Raj)
Aug 25, 20......
M/s Preeti Electronics
Jayanti Market
Jaipur

Sub : *Replacement of TV.*

Dear Sir,

I have purchased a T.V. make BPL-21FSTW from you vide bill No. 2581 dated 1/7/200.... for Rs. 11300/-.

The picture tube of the T.V. is not functioning properly. You have sent the mechanic twice to check the same, but of no avail.

As the T.V. is under one year guarantee period, so you are requested to get the T.V. changed immediately. I think you will not make any excuse in the matter and the T.V. be replaced without any delay.

Thanking you.

Yours faithfully,
Vikas Sharma

Q. 21. Write a letter to M/s Jaipur Publications returning the book wrongly supplied by him and asking him to supply the proper books.

Answer.

R.K. Book Depot
155, Nangali Circle, Alwar

Dated 16/3/20......

Ref : Po/
M/s Jaipur Publications
Chaura Rasta
Jaipur

Sub : *Supply of Proper Books.*

Dear Sir,

Today we have received the parcel of books sent by you. We are surprised to find that you have sent all the twenty books of English Grammar written by some Mr. Sarraff, while we have ordered for the English Grammar written by Mr. Gupta & Gupta.

We are returning the books. You are requested to supply the books of English Grammar written by Mr. Gupta & Gupta.

Please be kind enough to supply the proper books immediately. The parcel be packed properly with polythene.

Thanking you.

Yours faithfully,
R.K. Jain
Partner

Q. 22. As Principal of a college, place an order for supplying some sports items to M/s Sports & Sports Ludhiana.

Subhash Gandhi College

Lucknow (U.P.)

Ref : Ord/sport

Dated 18/4/20......

M/s Sports & Sports
Lal Bazar, Ludhiana

Sub : *Supply of Sports items.*

Dear Sir,

You are requested to supply the following sports goods at the rates mentioned by you in your quotation dated 10/3/200.......

Name of items		Quantity
(1) Cricket Bats	—	12 Pieces
(2) Volley Balls	—	12 Pieces
(3) Badminton Rackets	—	12 Pieces

Please dispatch the above items duly packed to avoid any damage in transit.
Thanking you.

Yours faithfully,
R.P. Ojha

Q. 23. You are Anil Shah, General Manager of M/s Cement Associates, Karol Nagar, Nimbahera. Mr. R.K. & Sons has placed with you an order for two thousand bags of cement. Please write a letter asking them to send 50% amount in advance by draft and also to submit you two references as this is the first dealing.

Ans. **M/s Cement Associates**

Karol Nagar, Nimbahera

Ref : Adv/

Dated 27/8/20......

Mr. R.K & Sons
Akbar Nagar
Shri Ganganagar (Rajasthan)

Sub : *Supply of 2000 bags of cement.*

Dear Sir,

We thankfully acknowledge your order No. 1841 dated 21/8/200..., for supplying of two thousand bags of cement.

Please be informed that this is our first dealing and as per our business policy, yours being a new firm, need to send 50% advance payment by draft and also two references for all future dealings.

For your ready reference, we are attaching herewith list of firms in Rajasthan who are registered with us.

We hope you will get these formalities fulfilled at the earliest.

Thanking you.

Yours faithfully,
Anil Shah
General Manager

Q. 24. You are the dealer of Pakija Biscuits for the State. Due to strike of Transport operators, your supply of biscuits has been disrupted. One of your distributors has asked you to arrange the supply of biscuits at whatever cost. Draft a letter to your distributer telling him regarding increase in the supply rates.

Answer. **Bengal Bakeries Ltd.**

Registered Office,181, Nanitalla Lane
Kolkata—700023

Dated 17/4/20......

Ref : Supply/ad/

M/s Priya Distributers
Asansol (W.B.)

Sub : *Supply of Pakija Biscuits.*

Dear Sir,

We are in receipt of your urgent call for supplying the biscuits at whatever cost.

As you are aware due to strike of transport operators it has become impossible to supply the biscuits by trucks.

We are sending you biscuits with our sales executive Mr. P.V. Vardhan by passenger train as per your requirements.

You are requested to pay him Rs 350 /- extra, as excess charges borne by us in supplying the biscuits through train.

Thanking you.

Yours faithfully,
Kamal Bose
Marketing Executive

Letters to/from Bank

Q. 25. You are Rajesh. You have deposited a cheque for collection in your current account. Even after passing more than one month, the amount of cheque has not been credited in your account so far. Write a letter to the Manager of the Bank, to get the amount of cheque deposited in your account and make a demand for payment of interest for the delayed period.

Answer.

The Manager,
Quick Bank,
New Delhi

Sub. : *Non-crediting the proceeds of cheque.*

Dear Sir,

I had deposited a cheque bearing No. 175896 dated 25/03/200...... for Rs 56200 /- drawn on State Bank of India, Alwar for collecting the proceeds in my Current Account No. 7816 with your branch.

I regret to note that even after passing of more than a month, the amount of cheque has not been credited in my account so far.

You are requested to look into the matter and arrange to get the amount of cheque credited in my current account immediately along with the interest for the delay as per norms.

Thanking you.

Yours faithfully,

Date

Rajesh

27.4.20......

Current A/c No. 7816
12/7, Vikas Nagar, New Delhi

Q. 26. As manager of a Bank, write a letter to a customer that his cheque has been dishonoured.

Answer.

Quick Bank Ltd.
Ram Nagar Jaipur
29th April, 20......

Ref : Com/05/

Mr. Rajesh Sharma
12/7, Vikas Nagar
Jaipur

Sub : *Dishonour of your cheque No. 175896 dated 25/03/200.. for Rs 56200 /- drawn on SBI Alwar.*

Dear Sir,

In reference to your letter dated 27.4......, we beg to inform you that your above cheque was received back by us for the following reason :

1. Funds Insufficient.

The cheque has since been sent to you by Registered Post on dated 29.04.200..... at your residential address.

We are always at the service of our clients.

Thanking you.

Yours faithfully,
T.K. Bose
Sr. Manager

Official Letters, Applications and Complaints

Q. 27. Write a letter to the Postmaster complaining that your sister at Ambala has not received the parcel sent by you last month.

Answer.

129, South Block
Alwar (Raj.)
26/4/200......
The Postmaster,
Head Post Office,
Alwar

Sub : *Non-receipt of parcel sent on 25/03/20...*

Dear Sir,

I had sent a Registered Parcel to my sister Jaya at House No. 16, Sector 5, Ambala on dated 25/3/200.... vide your receipt No. 1479. The parcel has not so far been received by her. More than two months have since passed. It appears either the parcel is delivered to somebody else or it has been lost in transit.

You are requested to enquire into the matter and apprise us the factual position without any further delay. Your early action is highly appreciated.

Thanking you.

Yours faithfully,
S.K. Gupta

Q. 28. Draft a First Information Report regarding theft of your Scooter.

Answer.

15, Kalindi Market
Near University
Jaipur
28/5/20......
The S.H.O.
University Road Thana
Jaipur

Sub : *FIR regarding theft of scooter.*

Dear Sir,

I have to lodge an FIR for the theft of my scooter from the University Road. It was about 1 P.M. I went to the market to make some purchasing. I locked my scooter as usual and parked it outside the shop of M/s K.K. & Sons, University Road, Kalindi Market. After about half an hour I came out of the shop was shocked to find that my scooter was missing. I made enquiries from the nearby shopkeepers but of no avail. The scooter was of 2003 model, Priya, blue coloured 100 cc, self start bearing registration No. RJ 02, C 2879.

I request you to lodge the FIR and arrange to trace the Scooter at the earliest. Your immediate action in the matter is solicited.

Yours faithfully,
Pramod Jhalani

Q. 29. There is an advertisement in the local newspaper for the post of Office Assistant. Make an application and write your biodata.

Answer.

The General Manager
Tilak Associates
Faluja Road
New Delhi

Sub : *Application for the post of Office Assistant.*

Dear Sir,

With reference to your advertisement in the Indian Express dated .... for the post of 'Office Assistant' I am sending my biodata with this application. My biodata contains all the details regarding my qualifications and experience.

I like to assure you that if I am given a chance to serve in your esteemed organisation, you will positively feel satisfied with my attitude and working.

Bio-Data

(1) Name : R.K. Sharma

(2) Father's Name : Mr. P.K. Sharma

(3) Address : 4/47, Shah Nagar Near Nai Mandi New Delhi—110007

(4) Telephone No. : 011—22094521 (R)

(5) E-mail : rksharma_147@yahoo. com

(6) Date of Birth : 25th April 1984

(7) Qualifications :

Degree	University	% Marks	Year of Passing
B.A.(Maths)	University of Delhi	78%	2001
M.A. (Economics)	University of Delhi	75%	2003

(8) Experience : One year at M/s Sandeep Associates as cashier-cum-Accountant (Experience certificate enclosed).

(9) Hobbies : Playing cricket, Reading Newspapers,

(10) Extra : (1) English Typing speed on computers 60 wpm.

(2) Hindi Typing speed on computers 40 wpm.

(3) Well versed in Tally 5.4 and 6.3 versions

(4) Have good knowledge of MS Word, MS Excel .

I hope you will find my bio-data as per your requirements.

Your faithfully
R.K. Sharma

Q. 30. Write an application to the Principal of your college/school requesting him to grant you fee concession.

Answer. The Principal

....

....

Sub : *Concession in Fee.*

Sir,

Most humbly I beg to state that I am a student of class B.Com. II Year B of your college. My father is a retired clerk. He is getting a pension of Rs 1800 /- P.M. I have two younger brothers. They are also studying in this college. There is no other source of income. My father is unable to pay my fee. Last year too, your goodness granted me 100% concession in my fee. This year too I request you to grant me 100% concession in my college fee, so that I shall be able to continue my studies. I like to apprise you that I secured 83% marks in B.Com I Year.

Please be kind enough to grant me full fee concession.

Thanking you.

Dated
24/03/20......

Yours obediently,
Saurabh

Q. 31. Send a reply to the following advertisement in a newspaper. Indicate to which post you are applying for. Include your Bio-Data. Suppose you are Satish Pradhan from New Delhi.

Advertisement

Wanted male/female Marketing Executives, Accountants, well qualified, experienced. Salary no constraint for the right candidate. Apply to General Manager, XYZ Company, New Delhi within seven days.

Answer. The General Manager
XYZ Company
New Delhi

Sir,

With reference to your advertisement published in the Hindustan Times, dated January 28, 200......, for the posts of Marketing Executives, Accountants etc. I offer myself as a candidate for the post of Accountant. As far as my academic and other qualifications are concerned, these are indicated in the bio-data attached herewith :

Bio-Data

(1) Name	:	Satish Pradhan
(2) Father's Name	:	Shiv Kumar Pradhan
(3) Date of Birth	:	11.7.82
(4) Educational Qualifications	:	M.Com.
(5) Nationality	:	Indian
(6) Marital Status	:	Unmarried
(7) Experience	:	One year experience of working in a private company
(8) Reference	:	(a) Mr. P.K. Mishra (Bank Manager) 142, Nehru Nagar, New Delhi-18 Tel. : 011-25761081
	:	(b) Sh. S .R. Sharma, MBBS (Councillor) 145, Patel Nagar, New Delhi-11
(9) Extra	:	Apart from the above mentioned Bio-Data, I have an additional record of extra-curricular activities. I participated in debates, dramas and sports and had won many prizes from time to time.

In light of the above mentioned facts, I request you to consider my application favourably. I like to assure you, that you will never feel disappointed with my work and attitude. I believe in working with full dedication and positive attitude.

Yours faithfully,
Satish Pradhan

Date 30/01/200,..

Q. 32. Write a letter to the District Education Officer, Jaipur, applying for the post of a temporary teacher.

Answer.

231, Arya Nagar,
Alwar,
February 14, 20.

The District Education Officer
Jaipur District
Jaipur

Sir,

I have come to know through some reliable sources that the post of a teacher of English is lying vacant in one of the schools under your control. I beg to apply for the same. As regards my qualifications and experience, I submit as follows :

I passed the Matriculation Examination from the D.S. High School, Jaipur in the year 1994, securing 87% marks and stood first in the school. I passed the B.A. Examination from D.S. College, Jaipur in 1998 with 76% marks. I took my M.A. Degree in English from University of Rajasthan, Jaipur with first division securing 61% marks in 2000, and stood first in the University in the B.Ed. Examination in 2002.

I have seven months experience of teaching English in a Higher Secondary School. The experience certificate is enclosed herewith for your kind perusal.

I like to assure you that if I am selected, I shall do my best for the students and everybody concerned shall feel satisfied with my conduct and devotion.

Yours faithfully,
Vijay Kumar

Q. 33. You have read an advertisement in 'The Hindustan Times' about the application of appointment of teachers. Write an application to the Director of Education, Rajasthan, Jaipur asking for a job as a teacher in an educational institution.

Answer. The Director of Education,
Rajasthan,
Jaipur.

Sir,

With reference to your advertisement published in 'The Hindustan Times' dated 15th January for the post of teachers, I beg to offer my services as a candidate for one of them.

Relevant particulars of my career are given below :

Name : Bahadur Khan
Age : 27 years (Date of Birth 1.1. 1978)

Examinations	**Division**	**Year**
High School	2nd	1990
Intermediate	2nd	1992
B.A.	2nd	1995
B.Ed.	2nd	1996

Experience : Working as a temporary teacher of English in a private college since July, 2002.

I am enclosing photocopies of my qualifications and the experience certificate for your kind perusal. A favourable decision will oblige me.

My address :
Bahadur Khan,
S/o Mr. Rashid Khan,
20, Nai Basti,
Jaipur (Rajasthan)

Yours faithfully,
Bahadur Khan

April 25, 200..

Complaints and Letters to the Editor

Q. 34. Write a letter to the editor of Newspaper, complaining against the increasing nuisance of beggars in the city.

Answer.

S.K. Joshi
17, Mahabir Colony
Asansol (W.B.)
Jan. 23, 200......
The Editor
The Times of India
New Delhi

Sub : *Increasing nuisance of beggers.*

Dear Sir,

Through the columns of your esteemed newspaper, I like to draw the attention of local authorities towards the increasing nuisance of beggars in our city.

Now-a-days, the population of beggars has abruptly increased in the city. Everywhere in the city, whether market, park or outside a restaurant or even in every street and on Red Light stoppage, you will find such obstinate beggars who can't be easily put off. The pity is that most of them are physically fit. Begging is their well thought of profession.

Some of them must be involved in other crimes also. Some of the beggars also suffer from highly infectious diseases such as leprosy and TB etc., and while begging they come in contact with general public. It is necessary that such cases be taken care of and be treated in General Hospital and other able bodied beggars be taken to the task. Either they be given jobs or they must not be allowed to make the begging their profession.

I am sure the authorities will positively take care of this increasing nuisance of beggars at the earliest.

Thanking you.

Yours faithfully,
S.K. Joshi

Q. 35. Write a letter to the Editor of a newspaper about very irregular and short water supply in your locality.

Answer. The Editor
The Times of India
New Delhi

Sub : *Irregular and short water supply.*

Dear Sir,

I crave the hospitality of the 'HELP LINE' columns of your esteemed newspaper to draw the attention of local authorities, particularly the authorities of "Water Works Department".

For the last one month the water supply in our colony has become very irregular and scanty. Out of the seven days, the supply was given on three days only and that too for one hour to 90 minutes.

On yesterday and day before yesterday, the water was supplied only for 35 minutes. When contacted the Assistant Engineer in the matter, he replied that due to some electric problem the water supply had become irregular. His reply was very evasive. I was not satisfied with the reply. It appears that the concerned A.En. is not taking the problem seriously.

In the summer season, water is of utmost necessity. I hope you will be kind enough to publish this letter in your daily, so that the higher authorities take notice and solve this acute problem immediately and warn those who are responsible for it.

Dated

Yours faithfully,
28/4/20......
Ram Chand
21/7, Janakpuri Road, New Delhi 1100031

Q. 36. Write a letter to the District Collector drawing his attention to the nuisance caused by loudspeakers in the city during examinations days.

Answer. The District Collector
Hoshiyarpur (Punjab)

Sub : *Nuisance caused by the loudspeakers during examination days.*

Dear Sir,

I beg to draw your kind attention to the problem of nuisance being caused by the loudspeakers in the city.

Now-a-days students are preparing for their examinations. The loud noise of loudspeakers is causing a lot of problems to the students. Every year, a prohibitive order is issued by your office banning the use of loudspeakers during the days of examination, but this year no such action has been taken so far.

I request you to ban the use of loudspeakers totally for the period of two months so that the students can prepare well for the ensuing examinations and not suffer due to the unwarranted noise of loudspeakers.

Hope to get your immediate attention.

Thanking you.

Yours faithfully,
P.K.Mehra

Date : 15th March, 20..

Student of B.E.
(Computers) III Year
17, Janta Colony
Hoshiyarpur (Punjab)

Q. 37. Write a letter, in not more than 200 words, to a national daily about the neglect of priceless Historical Monuments in and around your city. Suggest ways and means to preserve them.

Answer. The Editor
The Hindustan Times
New Delhi

Sub : *Neglect of Historical Monuments.*

Sir,

Through the esteemed columns of your prestigious newspaper I like to draw the attention of the general public on the neglectful and miserable conditions of Historical Monuments which are the evidential witnesses of our past glory and grandeur. They are the proven records of our past history, but have fallen victims to the criminal neglect of the officials. I had earlier tried to bring it to the notice of the department of Archaeological Survey of India, Government of India, but there was no response. This callous indifference on the part of concerned authorities has compelled me to approach you through this letter.

Sir, if you personally visit some of the monuments like the Humayun Tomb, Tughlak Kila, Qutab Minar, etc you will realise that they are gradually losing their shape and are getting dilapidated day by day in the flames of times. Their walls are mouldering, their roofs are getting cracked, their bricks and stone pieces are losing plaster and the top corner of walls have already crumbled. All this is due to the lack of proper maintenance and criminal neglect by the government servants. These monuments are the heritage of the glorious period of our past history. We must realise that even the present will be past one day. I was shocked to witness the sight of these worn and torn monuments.

I request you to publish this letter in your esteemed paper so that the concerned authorities are awakened in time, and the priceless Historical Monuments are saved and preserved.

Thanking you.

Yours truly,
XYZ

Q. 38. Write a letter in about 200 words to the Municipal Corporation of you city describing the miserable condition of roads in your locality, also suggest some remedies for improvement.

Answer. The Commissioner
Municipal Corporation
New Delhi.
Sub : *Miserable condition of roads.*

Sir,

I would like to attract your kind attention to the miserable conditions of roads in my locality, Nehru Nagar, Near Subzi Mandi, Delhi. The roads are broken at many places. One can't drive the vehicle for ten minutes regularly without making adjustments with the broken roads. The buses, trucks, cars, three-wheelers and two-wheelers, all have to halt at every five to seven minutes just to adjust with the road breaks and pits. It has been repeatedly brought to the notice of P.W.D. but all in vain. There is always a traffic problem on the roads. The first showers of monsoon will put the things in its worst shape. The residents are in deep distress on this account and they have repeatedly expressed their resentment through Press as well as through written complaints but nothing has so far been done. People have also staged demonstrations last month and the authorities have assured to take necessary action in the matter but so far all the assurances are proved only the assurances for the sake of assurances.

I request you to get the roads constructed without any further delay lest the anger of the public should explode. I hope to get immediate attention of you.

Yours Sincerely,
Secretary
(S.R.K. Tyagi)

Date : 25th Aug., 200...

Nehru Nagar Residents Society
Near Subzi Mandi
Delhi

Q. 39. You are a resident of Indira Nagar a posh colony of DDA. There are no street lights on the main road leading to this colony. The road gets so dark after seven in the evening that the possibility of some major accident cannot be ruled out. Write a letter to the Editor of a Daily, drawing attention of the authorities to this serious problem. *(in not more than 200 words).*

Answer. The Editor
The Hindustan Times
New Delhi
Sub : *Provision for street lights on the main road.*

Sir,

Through the columns of your esteemed newspaper I want to draw the attention of the authorities concerned towards the provision of street lights on the main road leading to Indira Nagar. I like to apprise that Indira Nagar is a posh colony of DDA and inhabited by more than 3500 flats on both the sides of the road. The electricity board has installed poles on either side of the road to supply light to the residents, but they are just poles without the electricity. The civic authority is lacking in providing basic amenities to the residents.

During these days of winter, after seven there is pitch dark. There is every possibility of occurrence of some major accident because of the heavy traffic passes over this road round the clock. The necessity of electrification requires no emphasis. In addition to accidents, cases of thefts and robbery can also not be denied. Darkness may lead to any kind of mishappening. It may also be stated that many residents go on pouring into their flats even after late hours in the night. The residents pay house tax to the

Municipality regularly but facility of street lights are denied to the residents. The matter has been taken up with the authorities again and again, every time mere assurances were given but problem still persists in the same way.

I hope, if the letter is published in your esteemed newspaper, the authorities shall be awakened from the slumber and the problem will be finally solved.

Thanking you.

Yours faithfully,
XYZ (A Resident of Indira Nagar)

27th Oct. 200... 152, Indira Nagar,New Delhi.

Q. 40. You are a resident of the 'Aparna Apartments', Mayur Vihar, Delhi. There is no bus-stop within the radius of 2 km from the apartments, causing a lot of inconvenience to the residents. Write a letter to the Editor of The Hindustan Times drawing attention of the government to this problem.

Answer.

271, Aparna Apartments,
Mayur Vihar, New Delhi
23rd Jan, 200...
The Editor,
The Indian Express
New Delhi.

Sub : *Providing nearby Bus-stops.*

Sir,

Through the columns of your esteemed newspaper I like to attract the attention of the concerned Government officials and the leaders representing the public, towards the problem of bus nonavailability stop in surrounding area, near Mayur Vihar Aparna Apartments. These apartment are spread within the radius of at least 4 km and are situated on the main road of Mayur Vihar. One can notice the running of buses on the main road in all the directions of Delhi after every five minutes. But it is very strange to note that the Government has not provided enough bus stops to cover all the apartments and colonies on the road. The residents have to run more than 2 km. to catch a local bus. Hiring of a rickshaw or three-wheeler is very costly for all of us in order to reach the bus stand. The chilly or the hot rough weather often puts the passengers in a great dolldrum. This also wastes time, energy, stamina and strength of a traveller.

For lady passengers it is all the more awesome from the safety point of view. No investment or no financial burden be passed on to the government in making more bus stops keeping in view the necessities and the convenience of the residents. It being fully residential area, it is need of the hour to provide bus stops at the most near points in this area instead of having a bus stop at a distance of more that 2 km.

I hope the government would definitely consider our difficulty and provide enough bus stops for the convenience of the passengers. It will provide relief to all of us as moving to a long distance of 2 km. in winter and hot summer is very troublesome and tiresome.

Hoping for doing the needful.

Yours faithfully,
XYZ

Q. 41. You are resident of Mangal Vihar Colony, Alwar. Write a letter to the Editor, Rajasthan Patrika, about the misuse and poor maintenance of the public park in your area.

Answer.

118-A, Mangal Vihar Colony,
Alwar
December 15, 200......
The Editor
Rajasthan Patrika
Alwar

Sub : *Poor maintenance of public Park.*

Sir,

Through the columns of your esteemed daily, I want to draw the attention of the authorities concerned towards the poor maintenance of the public park in our area.

Public Parks are the lungs of the locality where residents come and refresh their tired and fatigue minds. But in our colony, the park is not well maintained or say not at all maintained. The park suffers from the utter neglect of the authorities. The residents of a nearby basti are using the area as public convenience. Some rowdies create disturbance and obstruct in proper upkeeping of the park. The park has become the favourite halting place of stray cattle, dogs and pigs. Miscreants sit and gamble here in the broad daylight. They create disturbance and affect the normal health and hygiene of the common man. In reality, the park has become a safety heaven for all types of evil characters.

If no immediate actions are taken, the park will turn into a devil's den and a cause of nuisance for the colony.

I hope the authorities concerned will take immediate steps in the matter.

Yours faithfully,
XYZ

Q. 42. You are a resident of South West Block, Alwar. Write a letter to the Superintendent of Police about the unauthorised construction of a block of three shops adjacent to the public park.

Answer.

329-South West Block
Alwar
15th Dec, 200.....
The Superintendent of Police
Alwar (Rajasthan)

Sub : *Unauthorised construction adjacent to the public park.*

Sir,

May I lodge a complaint against Sh. Ram Nath who has constructed a block of three shops adjacent to the Nehru Park in our colony. The construction was completed in the late hours of night when there was none to oppose. In the morning, a block of shops was found disfiguring the park area. This has created a good example for others to occupy the government land, in any way one likes. There is complete "Goonda Raj" in this area. Powerful men are usurping the property of the Government for their own benefits. It is not out of place to mention that the saying "Might is Right" stands true here. In the morning some residents opposed but instead of listening to their voice, he threatened them to shoot. There is complete chaos and an atmosphere of fear prevails in the area.

It looks he has got good relations with high ups. If this remains the state of affair, a day will come when others will also occupy the available land. This is the only main park where children can play and rest in the morning and evening.

Please take action and protect the park from the miscreants spoiling its use and beauty.

Yours faithfully,
XYZ

Q. 43. You are Pralay Kumar of 125, Jahangir Road, New Delhi. Write a letter to the Police Commissioner (Traffic) about inadequate parking facility in the Connaught Place area of New Delhi.

Answer.

125, Jahangir Road
New Delhi
20th Aug, 200......
The Police Commissioner (Traffic)
Connaught Place, New Delhi

Sub : *Inadequate parking facility at Connaught Place.*

Sir,

Connaught Place is the heart and soul of our capital. It is the most busiest and cleanest site of the capital. It attracts a large number of businessmen, foreigners and tourists daily. Being the centre of trade, there is great hustle and bustle in the market. During the peak hours one cannot park his car at a safe place here because the parking facilities are very much inadequate. If one has to park his vehicle, he has to look here and there for safety of vehicle and availability of a parking place. If a suitable site is available by chance, it becomes difficult to get one's vehicle back because of the shortage of sufficient space. Under these circumstances it is imperative on the part of the authorities to make sufficient spots available for parking the vehicles.

I hope you will definitely realise the inconvenience caused to all as above. Please take suitable steps to solve this genuine problem.

Thanking you.

Yours faithfully,
Pralay Kumar

Q. 44. You are Tek Chand of 115, Subhash Nagar, Jaipur. Write a letter to The Postmaster complaining about the irregular delivery of letters and parcels etc.

Answer.

115, Subhash Nagar
Jaipur
25th August, 200......
The Postmaster
General Post Office
Jaipur (Rajasthan)

Sub : *Irregular Delivery of Letters.*

Sir,

I want to draw your kind attention towards the negligent working style of Mr. P.K.Verma, the postman of this area. He is very irregular and negligent in his work. He does not deliver the letters and parcels on daily basis. He never comes in time. He often throws the letters either in the "Ganda Nala" or delivers them to the small children playing in the streets. Many times the letters are lost and the business is also hampered due to irregular and late delivery of letters. This is a matter of great concern and can cause a great loss. On many occasions he has been warned to mend his ways but he paid a deaf ear to the requests of the residents.

Kindly take necessary action in this matter and Mr. Verma be immediately transferred to some other area, lest he should take revengeful action against some of the residents.

Thanking you.

Yours faithfully,
Tek Chand

Q. 45. You have visited the general hospital by chance. You find the condition of the hospital very pathetic. Write a complaint letter to the CMHO, Jaipur Hospital in this matter.

Answer.

12, Gurunanakpura
Adarsh Nagar
Jaipur
24th September, 200......
The CMHO
General Hospital
Jaipur (Rajasthan)

Sub : *Uncleanliness and negligency of the staff in the General Hospital.*

Sir,

May I lodge a simple but very important complaint to draw your attention towards the poor facilities available in the General Hospital and the neglectful attitude of the medical staff. The nurses hardly attend to their duties and generally busy in gossiping. Even the low priced tablets and medicines remain out of stock in the hospital. The toilets are never found clean, always emit a very foul smell. Yesterday an attendant took her mother to toilet, the nauseating smell made her nervous and she fainted. A complaint was also lodged with the staff nurse on duty, she took no care of the complaint.

The electric wiring is lying uncovered and tubes don't emit proper lights. The sweepers even leave the rubbish in the small corners. Everywhere a foul smell, uncleanliness, dust and negligence prevail. I don't know how the staff is so indifferent and working in such unhygienic conditions.

I hope you will take steps to improve the conditions and proper arrangements to keep the hospital clean be made immediately.

Thanking you.

Yours faithfully,
XYZ

Q. 46. You are Dipti Sharma of 110, Raja Park, Jaipur. Write a letter to the General Manager, Rajasthan Roadways, Jaipur, complaining about rude and irresponsible behaviour of the drivers and the conductors.

Answer.

110, Raja Park,
Jaipur
25th June, 200......

The General Manager
Rajasthan Roadways
Jaipur (Rajasthan)

Sub : *Complaining about rude and irresponsible behaviour of the drivers and the conductors.*

Sir,

I want to draw your kind attention towards the rude and irresponsible behaviour of both the drivers and the bus conductors with the commuters. They look towards the passengers with indifference and behave with them in a very strange and absurd way. They lack etiquettes and use filthy language.

Generally the bus drivers do not stop the bus at the fixed stops, they rather disdain the travellers and stop before or after the stop so the passengers have to run after the bus. The passengers hardly approach the bus when it starts. In this way many commuters fall and feel lot of irritation and insult.

No less irresponsible is the behaviour of conductors. They never bother whether the passengers have got into the bus or not but they are bent on blowing the whistle. The bus moves while passengers have only one foot on the foot board. This leads to the falling of the poor passengers and sustaining by them injuries several times.

They have forgotten the elementary duties of a good driver and conductor and behave indecently. They show no courtesy and sympathy towards the senior citizens and the ladies.

It is my humble suggestion that at the time of their recruitment and during the initial training they must be taught how to deal with the passengers. Regular training in this matter may help them to understand the problems of the commuters. Presently, they must be instructed and advised suitably to mend their ways and a surprise checking in this respect also be done.

Yours faithfully,
Dipti Sharma

Q. 47. Write a suitable letter in reply to the following advertisement signing yourself as "Somebody".

Found a Suitcase

A suit case is found in Jammu Mail on 28/02/200...., the owner should contact the Station Master, Delhi Cantt. with proof of belongings.

Answer.

B-423, Man Singh Park
New Delhi
April 27, 200....
The Station Master
Delhi Cantt

Sub : *Missing suitcase.*

Dear Sir,

Please refer to your advertisement published in the 'Times of India' on dated 23.3.200...., regarding the suitcase found in the Jammu Mail on 28.2.200...., I want to bring to your kind notice that the suitcase belongs to me.

It is a VIP Suitcase-22 inches, of grey colour. My name 'ABC' is pasted on it. It contains three white shirts, two trousers, one blue-coloured pant, one towel, a comb and one ball pen and some coins also. It also contains my original certificate (Matric and M.A. Economics) with attested copies, one issue of 'Akhand Jyoti ' monthly, as well as a newspaper of that day. I had returned on that day from Kanpur after attending an interview.

I shall feel obliged if the same is returned to me. Please let me know the date and the time, convenient to you, when I may collect my suitcase.

Yours faithfully
Somebody

Office Circulars

Q. 1. As the Head of your office, draft a circular for the staff outlining the need and value of punctuality in keeping office hours and quick disposal of writs and other work.

Answer.

Office of Dy. Commissioner Commercial
Taxation Hasan Khan Mewat Nagar Alwar
Circular

Ref. No. KB/14/15/20... Date : 27th Sept, 20......

For All the members of the staff including the Officers :

All the members of the staff including the officers are instructed to adhere to the punctuality in coming to the office and leaving the office. Hence attendance in the office is desired upto 10.00 A.M. positively. It has been noticed that some of the employees including the officers are habituated of coming late and leaving the office before time that is before 5 P.M. This causes great inconvenience to the public. Lack of punctuality and leaving the office before time is an act of indiscipline and it leads to delay in disposing of the files and hinders smooth working. Intentional delay and keeping the work pending must be stopped forthwith. All the officers are instructed to dispose off all the pendency within a week and apprise the undersigned in the matter positively on next Monday.

Noncompliance on the part of any staff including the officers shall be viewed by the undersigned seriously.

XYZ
Dy. Commissioner (Administration)

Q. 2. Draft a circular from the Government of Rajasthan, Department of Civil Supplies, addressed to all District Supply Officers advising the steps to be taken for proper distribution of essential commodities from fair price shops.

Answer.

Government of Rajasthan
Secretary Department Civil Supplies, Jaipur

Circular Ref : Civil Sup/26/200.. Date : 15th July, 200......

Sub : *Distribution of essential commodities through Fair-price shops.*

For : All District Supply Officers

It has come to the notice of the Government that some fair-price shop dealers are not making the proper distribution of the essential commodities, instead they are selling the commodities in open market. Some fair price shops are not being opened on regular basis. In rural areas specially the shops remain either closed or the commodities are not distributed to all the people, which frustrates the aim and objective of opening these fair price shops. People are facing great problems in getting the commodities from these shops and the dealers are getting undue advantages by selling the commodities in open market. The matter was discussed in a meeting presided over the Minister for Civil Supplies and a very serious view was taken of the situation.

I therefore, advise you to make all our efforts to make the supply regular in a proper manner.You are also being advised to implement the following measures agreed upon in the meeting :

(1) The Enforcement Inspectors should visit personally all the fair price shops and should also meet the Panch or the Sarpanch of the villages. Not only this, reports and views of the general should also be taken and noted in their daily diary to ascertain the factual position.

(2) The DSOs should also make a point to visit at least 15 fair price shops in a month and verify the daily diary of the enforcement Inspectors invariably. Out of the 15 fair price shops 10 must locate in rural areas.

(3) Action including the suspensions and termination of licence of the dealer of the fair price shop should be resorted to, in the first instance. In second chance the dealership of the fair price shop must be terminated and legal action should also be initiated as per the advice of the legal cell.

(4) Periodical inspection report and the visit reports are be submitted to my office on the monthly basis.

Intimate the compliance to the undersigned within seven days.

S.K. Mahajan
Secretary Civil Supplies

Q. 3. Draft a Circular to all Commissioners and District Collectors working as District Election Officers to make adequate arrangements for the free and fair General Assembly Election.

Answer.

Office of The Election Commissioner
Government of Rajasthan, Jaipur

Phone : 23334512,
Fax.:2334511

Circular Ref : EC/3/05 Date : 21/9/ 20......

Sub : *Election Urgent.*

For : All Commissioners/Dist.Collectors

As per instructions and guidelines received from the office of the Chief Election Commissioner Government of India, New Delhi vide Cir .No CEC/GE/2/03dated 15/9/0...... and in compliance of the same, you are hereby instructed to make proper arrangements, planning and preparations for conducting the free and fair Assembly Elections.

Please get all the voterlists updated and printed timely. Ensure to get the Photo-identity card issued to all voters. Get the Ballot boxes checked if required get the same repaired and new ones ordered. Marking and mapping of polling stations and polling booths are also to be done. Sensitive areas be marked and requisition for additional Police Force be sent in advance.

Lists of Zonal Magistrates, Presiding officers, Polling Officers and employees for election duty be chalked out in advance. In all circumstances the elections must be conducted in free and fair atmosphere. Compliance be made under intimation to the undersigned. This should be treated as most urgent.

XYZ
Election Commissioner

Q. 4. Draft a circular from the Finance Secretary, Government of Rajasthan, to all Departments, District Officers and Commissioners requesting them to adopt measures of further economy.

Answer.

Government of Rajasthan
Office of the Secretary Finance, Jaipur

Circular No.F 348/26/20035 Date : 28.8.20....

Sub : *Economy Drive.*

For : All Head of Depts., Commissioners, and District Collectors.

To review the drought and famine conditions prevailed in the State, a High Power Committee has instituted under the Chairmanship of Chief Minister. The Committee has decided in its last meeting held on 23rd August to adopt some thrift measures as per following :

(1) An overall cut of 20% in all non-plan expenditure with immediate effect.
(2) All unnecessary and avoidable TA bills be reduced by 25% with immediate effect.
(3) Expenses on Office purchase be stopped forthwith. No expenditure will be made on office purchase without the permission of the Deputy Secretary of the respective Ministry.
(4) All the Medical Bills be thoroughly checked before making the payments.

All the concerned Departments under your jurisdiction be informed of the instructions immediately.

Compliance of the order be submitted to the undersigned within three days.

KK Jha
Finance Secretary

Memorandums

Q. 5. As Deputy General Manager of a Private Limited Company, write a memo to the General Manager informing him about the damage caused by fire in the factory.

Answer.

Kotsons Mills Pvt. Ltd.
Mall Road, Mumbai

Ref. No. GM/26/0..... 23rd Aug. 20....

Memorandum

From : Dy. General Manager
To : The General Manager

Sub : *Damage caused by Fire.*

It was on 22nd August 200...... a fire broke out in the Mills Showroom at about 3 o'clock in the night. It seems to be caused by short circuit and the entire showroom was in full blazes within minutes. It took nearly four hours by the two fire brigades to control the fire. The total damage estimated is not less than Rs. One crore, as some goods lying in the adjacent godown also caught fire, lot of the goods was saved by the timely arrival of the fire brigades. The Insurance Company has since been informed and a requisite claim for the damage will be submitted within three days.

I am trying to chalk out the plans and the measures to be taken to prevent such happenings in future. A detail report will be submitted to you at the earliest.

Sd/-
Dy. General Manager

Q. 6. As Deputy Secretary in the Ministry of Home Affairs, Central Government, New Delhi, write a memorandum to be sent to all the State Home Ministers, expressing the Government's concern about police excesses in the States.

Answer.

Government of India
Ministry of Home Affairs, New Delhi

Ref No. HM/SHM/5/0........ 18th July, 20..

Memorandum

Sub : *Police Excesses in States.*

Undersigned has been directed to apprise all the State Home Ministers that the entire Lok Sabha has expressed its sincere concern and taken a serious view of the excesses committed by the police more or less throughout the country. The department of Police comes under the State List, so it is the sacred responsibility of all the States to check the recurrences of any such cases. Cases of deaths in police custody, indiscreet firing, cases of violence and rape against the women and similar other cases of indecent and torture, have been reported frequently by the Press. Human Rights violation is a crime even committed by a government deptt. The honourable Home Minister has expressed great concern over the situation and he has earnestly desired that the police ought to be sensitise and police officials be trained to deal with common mass politetly and should exercise the powers within their limits. Strong and strict action must also be initiated against the criminals irrespective of their status in the society.

Therefore it is urgently required that a meeting of all the Superintendents of Police of the States be called to discuss the ways and means to check this social evil. A report be sent to the Ministry at the earliest.

Ram Dhari Dinkar
Deputy Secretary

Copy to :
All the Home Ministers of All States.

Unit

54

Essay Writing

How to Write an Excellent Essay ?

'Essay writing is an art. One may have thorough knowledge of a topic or a subject, but to put this knowledge in a logical and coherent way is a task that requires skill, practice and subtle technique'.

What Is an Essay ?

The word 'essay' means an 'attempt'. For an attempt to be crowned with success, certain techniques, methods and perseverance are necessary. An essay is an organised collection of ideas, facts and figures about the topic, nicely written and elegantly presented.

In other words, the essay must be well structured, organised, well planned and presented in a way that the reader finds it clear and easy to follow. It must look tidy and not present any obstacle to the reader. It must have a clear readable interesting style. But, above all, it must consist of ideas, facts and figures relevant to the subject.

An essay can have many purposes, but the basic structure is the same, no matter what the subject or the topic is. You may be writing an essay to argue for a particular point of view or to explain the steps necessary to complete a task. Either way, your essay will have the same basic format. If you follow a few simple steps, you will find that the essay is almost written itself. You are to supply ideas, facts and figures, which are the important parts of the essay anyway.

Classification of Essays

(1) Narrative Essays Narrative Essays consist of the narration of some events about historical facts or eminent personalities. Such events may be:

(a) Historical or legendary events
(b) True or imaginary stories
(c) Biographical sketches

(2) Descriptive Essays Descriptive Essays consist of the description of some place or thing. These may be about:

(a) Countries, islands, mountains, seas, rivers
(b) Aspects and phenomena of nature
(c) Towns and buildings

(3) Reflective Essays Reflective Essays consist of reflections upon some topic, which are generally of an abstract nature. These may be in respect to:

(a) Habits, qualities, etc
(b) Social, political, economical or domestic affairs

(4) Expository or Argumentative Essays These consist of the exposition or explanation of a saying, or a thesis.

As : "Truth always triumphs".
"I am the maker of my destiny"
"Get started"!

These simple steps will guide you through the essay writing process.

1. Select the topic.
2. Prepare an outline of your ideas.
3. Write the introduction.
4. Write the body.
5. Write the main points.

6. Write the subpoints.
7. Elaborate on the subpoints.
8. Write the conclusion.

Select a Topic for Your Essay

Selection of topic out of the given topics is an important task. Evaluate each topic. You must simply consider each one individually. Select the topic about which you have detailed facts and figures. You must be sure it is a subject about which you are particularly well-informed. You must be sure it is a subject about which you are at least moderately passionate. Of course, the most important factor in choosing a topic is the number of ideas you have about that topic. Even if none of the topic you find particularly appealing, in that case select a topic which may not be selected by other candidates or select a topic which is selected by only a few candidates, that will minimise the chances of immediate comparison of the essay written by you with others.

Before you are ready to move on in the essay-writing process, look one more time at the topic you have selected. Once you have determined that your topic will be suitable, you can move on.

Organise Your Ideas

The purpose of an outline or diagram is to put your ideas about the topic on paper, in a moderately organised format. A well thought-out structure is the heart of every good essay.

Outline

1. Begin your outline by writing your topic at the top of the page.
2. Next, write the Roman numerals I, II, and III, spread apart down the left side of the page.
3. Next to each Roman numeral, write the main ideas that you have about your topic, or the main points that you want to make. If you are trying to persuade, you write your best arguments.If you are trying to explain a process, you write the steps that should be followed.You will probably need to group these into categories. If you have trouble grouping the steps into categories, try using Beginning, Middle, and End. If you are trying to inform, you write the major categories into which your information can be divided.
4. Under each Roman numeral, write A, B, and C down the left side of the page.
5. Next to each letter, write the facts or information that support the main idea.

Now you have finished, you have the basic structure for your essay and are ready to continue.

Introduction

The introduction should be designed to attract the reader's attention and give him an idea of the essay's focus.

Begin with an attention grabber : Which attention grabber you use, is up to you, but here are some ideas.

(a) Startling information : This information must be true and verifiable. It could simply be a pertinent fact that explicitly illustrates the point you wish to make. If you use a piece of startling information, follow it with a sentence or two of elaboration.

(b) Anecdote : An anecdote is a story that illustrates a point. Be sure your anecdote is short, to the point, and relevant to your topic. This can be a very effective opener for your essay, but use it carefully.

(c) Dialogue or Quotation : An appropriate dialogue or quotation does not have to identify the reader, but the reader must understand the point you are trying to convey.

Write the Body Paragraphs

In the body of the essay, all the preparation up to this point comes to fruition. The topic you have chosen must now be explained, described, or argued. Each main idea, that you wrote down in your outline, will become one of the body paragraphs. If you had three or four main ideas, you will have three or four body Paragraphs.

Each body paragraph will have the same basic structure.

1. Start by writing down one of your main ideas, in sentence form.
2. Next, write down each of your supporting points for that main idea.
3. In the space under each point, write down some elaboration for that point. Elaboration can be further description or explanation or discussion.

Write the Conclusion

Now, you need a tight, powerful conclusion, which is the logical consequence of everything that has gone before.The conclusion brings closure of the essay to the reader, summing up your points or providing a final perspective on your topic. All that the conclusion needs is three or four strong sentences which do not need to follow any set formula. Simply review the main points (being careful not to restate them exactly) or briefly describe your feelings about the topic. Even an anecdote can end your essay in a useful way. The conclusion completes the paragraphs of your essay.

Remember

If your essay is badly written, you will be losing marks. And, in the outside world, you would be a failure. It is very important to write in a crisp, clear style, with good sentence construction and proper punctuation. Needless to say, spelling mistakes also fail to impress.

Some 'Tips' on Writing an Excellent Essay

1. Use Simple Words Rather Than Complex Words

Keep your writing style simple. Follow the standard rule in all editing: prefer the simpler word to the complex word. This means writing 'extra' or 'more' rather than 'additional'; 'help' rather than 'assistance'; 'use' rather than 'utilise'. Although you might need specialist or technical words, depending on your subject, you should choose the simpler word instead of the more difficult word, whenever you can.

"When something can be read without effort, great effort has gone into its writing."

Enriqe Jardiel Poncela

Your essay should be interesting but also easy to read. As well as the advice to use the simpler word to the complex word, you can also make your essay read much better if you cut down on heavy words.

2. Structure Your Essay to Help Your Reader

All documents need a start, a middle and an end. Traditionally, we think of the Introduction, Body and Conclusion as the key parts of an essay. Logically, this helps us set the context for the essay (introduction), present the facts and develop the arguments (body) and summarise the main points or the answer to the question set (conclusion).

3. Writing Introduction

This introduces the main idea of your essay and draws the reader into the subject. A good introduction gets to the heart of the subject and captures the interest of the reader. Most students write poor introductions that needlessly repeat information and turn off the reader with too much background information. If you want to gain a top grade for your essay, you have to start strongly and gain your reader's attention immediately.

4. Writing the Body of Essay

This consists of supporting paragraphs, logically arranged to develop your main ideas. List the points you wish to develop, place each point in its own paragraph, and expand on each point with supporting facts, details and examples. Each paragraph should clearly present the relevant information, discuss and evaluate information and opinions, and develop an argument based on the information and a review of opinions. This is 80-90 percent of the essay and must satisfy the reader's appetite. To do this, the body of the essay must reflect solid research, show a clear understanding of the subject, and develop your points logically.

5. Writing Conclusion

The conclusion is vital. It is the last impression, the reader has of the essay. Use it well, making sure your essay doesn't fizzle out. Make it a strong statement, confidently answering the question, summarising the position, and reviewing the topic. If you are in doubt what to put in the conclusion, think about the key information or argument the essay has presented and repeat it in a short, direct form.

"Do not write so that you can be understood, write so that you cannot be misunderstood."

—Epictetus

1. Is Consumerism a Curse ?

Consumerism is a term that describes the relations between personal happiness and possessing of the material things. Consumerism is also associated with the belief that the free choice of consumers should dictate the economic structure of a society. The theory of consumerism dictates that an increasing consumption of goods is economically beneficial. It also means to a movement that advocates greater protection of the interests of consumers.

Consumerism is economically manifested in the chronic purchasing of new goods and services, with little attention to their true need, durability, product origin or the environmental consequences of manufacture and disposal. Consumerism is driven by huge sums spent on advertising designed to create both a desire to follow trends, and the resultant personal self-reward system based on acquisition. Materialism is one of the end results of consumerism.

Consumerism interferes with the workings of society by replacing the normal common-sense desire for an adequate supply of life's necessities, community life, a stable family and healthy relationships with an artificial ongoing and insatiable quest for things and the money to buy them with little regard for the true utility of what is bought. An intended consequence of this, promoted by those who profit from consumerism, is to accelerate the discarding of the old, either because of lack of durability or a change in fashion.

The traditional cultural values of Western society are degenerating under the influences of corporate politics, the commercialization of culture and the impact of mass media. Society is awakening from its fascination with television entertainment to find itself stripped of tradition, controlled by an oppressive power structure and bound to the credit obligations of a defunct dream.

Consumerism is the myth that the individual will be gratified and integrated by consuming. The public fetishistically substitutes consumer ideals for the lost acculturating experiences of art, religion and family. The consumer sublimates the desire for cultural fulfillment to the rewards of buying and owning commodities, and substitutes media-manipulated undulations in the public persona for spiritual rebirth. In the myth of consumerism, there is no rebirth or renewal. And there are no iconic symbols to evoke transcendent truths.

While consumerism offers the tangible goal of owning a product, it lacks the fulfillment of other cultural mythologies. Consumerism offers only short term ego-gratification for those who can afford the luxury and frustration for those who cannot. It exists as an incomplete and inadequately engineered system of values substituted for a waning cultural heritage.

The egocentricity of Western society made it an easy target for the transition to a consumer society. As deceptive advertising and academic nihilism gutted culture of its subjectively realized values, the public was easily swayed onto the path of consumerism. The reduction of cultural values to economic worth has produced a situation in our 'enlightened' society where product availability, as opposed to survival needs, becomes ethical justification for political oppression.

Self-worth is gauged by buying power. The acts of buying and owning reinforce self-worth within consumer society. You can see it in the haughty and demanding attitude of the consumer as he stands before the cashier. No longer does the purchase have to be justified by purpose.

Mass media perpetuates the myth of consumerism as a priority of the New Capitalism. The corporate profiteers are very quick to substitute the lure of material luxury and consumer gratification for the fading spirit. Media advertising sells an image—an empty shell.

As we become acclimated to life around the television set, collectively striving for a media-produced image, our choices are made for us. Choice is reduced to brand name. We sacrifice self-knowledge for consumerism. Consumerism, like communism and fascism, is a secular religion restricting freedom of choice.

In the era of consumerism, self-awareness and self-worth have been distorted. We are what we wear. In the New Capitalism's seduction of the television audience, the individuating personality identifies with advertising fantasies and consumer ideals. Who we are merges with roles and images portrayed in the media. Ever so subtly we are losing our ability to act independently of the justifications of consumerism. This constitutes a qualitative loss to the individuation process. The affront on human values by mass media advertising has left a well actualized consumer but a poorly individuated personality.

Consumers are only beginning to realize the political power they wield as a collective buying force. This potential has been tested on a small scale by union pickets and grassroots economic boycotts. It is expected that a day will come when the public tires of the shallow gratifications and empty promises of consumerism, it will turn to large scale boycotts to control the abusive tactics of corporate policy.

2. Invasion of Privacy Through Phone Tapping

There is no denying the fact that invasion of privacy through phone tapping is undertaken the world over for reasons of national security or serious crimes, but in not a single democratic country the invasion of privacy through phone tapping is as easy as in India.

In India there is no legislation or law that guarantees an individual's privacy. The Supreme Court has broadened the ambit of **Article 21 of the Constitution,** which talks about an individual's right to life and liberty so as to include the right to privacy. The Honb'le Supreme Court in the case of **Kharak Singh vs State of UP** and others took this position. Kharak Singh had lodged a complaint that the police made domiciliary visits to his place of dwelling at odd hours and as such harassed him and invaded his privacy. This was the first time that the court upheld an individual's right to privacy as a fundamental right.

The subsequent development of the right has seen it being invoked in cases, ranging from the right of a prisoner not to be interviewed to the right of confidentiality of an HIV-infected person. More significantly from the perspective of the employee's right to privacy, the Supreme Court has held that 'technological eavesdropping' is also a violation of the right to privacy in the case of *People's Union for Civil Liberties vs Union of India* in 1997.

The case arose out of a challenge to Section 5(2) of the Telegraph Act, 1885, which permits the interception of messages in cases of public emergency or in the interest of public safety. The court held that the right to privacy included the right to hold a telephone conversation in the privacy of one's home or office and that tapping of phone, infringed this right.

The Information Technology Act, 2000 in Section 71, makes a reference to privacy in Section 72, where securing access to any electronic correspondence, without the consent of the person concerned, and disclosing such information to any other person has been made an offence punishable with **imprisonment for two years, or with a fine of one lakh rupees**. The provision would not protect the employee from undesirable electronic surveillance by the employer, if the employer does not disclose the information that he has intercepted to anyone else. It is interesting to note that in no country does the right to privacy enjoy constitutionally guaranteed status.

The problem is that since the right to privacy has been equated with a fundamental right, an individual can only bring action against the State and not another private individual or organisation. This is because fundamental rights are guaranteed against the state.

The Universal Declaration of Human Rights, in article 12, states:

No one shall be subjected to arbitrary interference with his privacy, family, home or correspondence, nor to attacks upon his honour and reputation. Everyone has the right to the protection of the law against such interference or attacks.

The truth is that virtually anybody in a position of authority can tap anybody's phone in India. Never mind the police, IB and RAW. The enforcement authorities can do it. So can the income tax people. Or the customs department. Or the CBI. Or a state intelligence outfit. Or anybody with a grudge.

Unfortunately, most telephone tapping is undertaken for political or personal reasons. The latest bout of **'tu tu, mein, mein'** has been sparked off by the alleged tapping of the telephone of the Samta Party General Secretary, Amar Singh. The high-profile SP leader has accused the Congress Party boss, Sonia Gandhi, personally of ordering the phone-tapping. It was alleged that the tapping was part of a larger conspiracy to sack every non-Congress government in the country. First, Samajwadi Party leader Amar Singh's phone was proven to be tapped and then Tamilnadu Chief Minister Jayalalitha Jayaram alleged that her phone has been tapped as well. In a country that touts itself as the world's largest democracy, such incidences prove that the very important fundamental right of privacy of an individual is in jeopardy.

Quite clearly, there is far more than meets the eye in the phone-tapping incident. But, be it as it may, it underlines the fragility of citizen's right to privacy and dignity in a manner which recent sting operations carried out in the name of public interest have most unfortunately failed to do.

Fortunately, Prime Minister Manmohan Singh has done well to have honestly acknowledged that "phone-tapping is a very serious matter". Asked to comment on the Samta Party's charge, he also asserted : "Phone-tapping should not be there". There are no two views on it". Clearly, there is an urgent need to shore up public confidence by prescribing a fresh set of guidelines barring the Government from tapping phones of its rivals. Or else it could turn into a scandalous "political tool and trade practice'.

The need for a comprehensive legislation on sting operations and illegal phone tapping cannot be exaggerated. It is time for political sagacity and not political confrontation. After all the issue is not one of political sloganeering but concerns the right of individuals and their freedom.

We must not make the mistake of arguing that all surveillance is unnecessary. In present time when terrorists activities are at a helm, necessary surveillance through phone tapping can't be denied to safeguard the interest of the nation. But we should consider the case that if some tapping is inevitable, why can't we follow the international practice and have some safeguards and checks ?

That is a stronger case. And in the current climate of judicial activism, we might even be able to get the judges to do what the politicians won't : put a new regulatory system in place.

3. Yoga : A Way of Life

Yoga is a way of life. It is virtually concerned with maintaining a state of equanimity at all costs. The Yoga emphasize the importance of the mind remaining calm, because as the saying goes, only when the water is still you can see through it.

The basic idea of yoga is to unite the atma or individual soul with the paramatma or the Universal Soul. According to Yoga philosophy, by cleansing one's mind and controlling one's thought one can achieve the state, when the individual self was nothing but a part of the Divine Self. The aim of the yogi is to be capable to perceive the world in its true light and to accept that truth in its entirety.

In Sanskrit, the term 'yoga' stands for 'union'. A yogi's ultimate aim is to be able to attain this 'union' with the Eternal Self with the help of certain mental and physical exercises. For all extant knowledge of yoga and its practices, such as yogasanas and pranayama, the entire credit goes to Maharishi Patanjali.

'Patanjali' the founder and father of Yoga, systematized the various yogic practices and traditions of his times by encapsulating them in his Yoga Sutra. In this momentous work, he describes the aim of yoga as knowledge of the self and outlines the eight steps or methods of achieving it. These are:

1. Yamas or eternal vows,
2. Niyamas or observances,
3. Yogasanas or yoga postures,
4. Pranayama or breath control exercises,
5. Pratyahara or withdrawal of the senses from distractions of the outside world,
6. Dharana or concentration on an object, place or subject,
7. Dhyana or the continuance of this concentration-meditation and
8. Samadhi or the ultimate stage of yoga meditation.

The collation of these eight steps is known as **Patanjali's Ashtanga Yoga**

Patanjali, lived around three centuries before Christ, and was a great philosopher and grammarian. He was also a physician and a

Yoga is an art and takes into purview the mind, the body and the soul of the man in its aim of reaching Divinity. The body must be purified and strengthened through various practices. The mind must be cleansed of all gross and the soul should turn inwards if a man should become a yogic adept. Study purifies the mind and surrender takes the soul towards God.

The human mind is subject to certain weaknesses which are universal. Avidya-wrong notions of the external world, asmita-wrong notions of the external world, asmita-wrong notions of oneself, raga-longing and attachment for sensory objects and affections, dweshad is like and hatred for objects and persons, and abinivesha or the love of life are the five defects of the mind that must be removed. Constant meditation and introspection eradicate these mental flaws.

The human body is a vehicle for journeying this life. It must be kept in proper form if the mind should function well. For this, there are practices too, but Patanjali does not elucidate on them.

Results of Several Researches

"Academy of Research in Physical Culture, Warsaw, conducted studies and investigations on physiological and psychological aspects of Yoga system of exercises. The result of these investigations lead us to the conclusion that the judicious and progressive follow-up of yogic practices brings about higher and higher conditioning of limbic system which is thought to be responsible for regulation of ANS, endocrinal system and the practitioners gradually begin experiencing greater and greater volitional control over the metabolic and the autonomic functions of the body which leads to the recovery of homeostatic dysfunction in the case of the sick and towards perfection of biological equilibrium in the case of normal persons. How such changes are brought about is still not so very clear and requires further investigations regarding the mechanism through which yogic exercises produce physiological and mental effects."

Yoga has been gaining immense popularity now a days due to the short-term as well as long-term benefits that it provides. The aims of the yoga practitioners are extremely varied. Some are particularly inspired by the Spiritual Element that yoga provides; others by the increased Fitness and Flexibility that it results in. Some people find solutions to suffering from varied Health Disorders and there are others who achieve an All-Round Development of a calm, stress-free mind and a fit body.

Whatever may be the reason, it is proved beyond doubts that Yoga gives one inner satisfaction, mental calmness, good health and long life.

4. Leisure

"What is this life, if full of care
we have no time to stand and stare."

W.H. Davies

Leisure in life is immensely important. Both work and relaxation are important ingredients of life. How we use our leisure is equally as important to our joy as our occupational pursuits. Proper use of leisure requires discriminating judgment. Our leisure provides opportunity for renewal of spirit, mind, and body.

Leisure is not idleness. The Lord condemns idleness. He said, "Thou shalt not idle away thy time, neither shalt thou bury thy talent" Idleness in any form produces boredom, conflict, and unhappiness. It creates a vacancy of worth, a seedbed for mischief and evil. It is the enemy of progress and salvation.

We are living in a machine age which provides numerous labour-saving devices and leaves plenty of time at our disposal. Some of us do not know what to do with all this leisure. In future, as life grows more mechanised, man will become more confused as to how to spend all the extra time. An idle mind is a devil's workshop. No wonder more and more people get involved in gambling, drinking and other useless activities.

The proper use of leisure brings us pleasure. It is beneficial for everyone to cultivate a suitable hobby to help in the proper channelising of free time. Great men in the past have realised the importance of this. It is said that Stalin found pleasure in shoe-making and Winston Churchill spent so much of his leisure in painting that he became a good painter.

The leisure time of children must be constructively directed to wholesome, positive pursuits. Too much time viewing television can be destructive, and pornography in this medium should not be tolerated. It is estimated that growing children today watch television over twenty-five hours per week.

Leisure time in student life, if made proper use of, would help to strengthen character and make life more enjoyable and fruitful. In the campus, if student bodies were to organise group activities, students could be made to cooperate and channelise their collective energies to promote social welfare. What immense good youthful energy and talent could be put to, if only leisure is well utilised.

Remember, leisure is a pleasure, always to be treasured.

5. Smoking : A Health Hazard

Almost everyone knows that smoking causes cancer, emphysema, and heart disease; that it can shorten our life by 14 years or more; and that the habit can cost a smoker thousands of rupees a year. So how come people are still lighting up? The answer, in a word, is addiction.

Almost no smoker begins as an adult. Statistics show that about nine out of 10 tobacco users start before they're 18 years old. Some teens who smoke say they start because they think it helps them look older. Others smoke because they think it helps them relax. Some light up as a way to feel rebellious or to set themselves apart. Some start because their friends smoke or just because it gives them something to do.

Some people, especially girls, start smoking because they think it may help keep their weight down. The illnesses that smoking can cause, like lung diseases or cancer, do cause weight loss but that's not a very good way for people to fit into their clothes!

Another reason people start smoking is because their family members do. Most adults who started smoking in their teens never expected to become addicted. That's why people say it's just so much easier to not start smoking at all.

The cigarette ads from when your parents were young convinced many of them that the habit was glamorous, powerful, or exciting even though it's essentially a turnoff: smelly, expensive, and unhealthy. Cigarette ads still show smokers as attractive, sophisticated and elegant, or rebellious and cool. The good news is that these ads aren't as visible and are less effective today than they used to be: Just as doctors are more savvy about smoking today than they were a generation ago, teens are more aware of how manipulative advertising can be. The government has also passed laws limiting where and how tobacco companies are allowed to advertise to help prevent young kids from getting hooked on smoking. Today we're more aware about how bad smoking is for our health. Smoking is restricted or banned in almost all public places and cigarette companies are no longer allowed to advertise on buses or trains, billboards, TV, and in many magazines.

There are no physical reasons to start smoking the body doesn't need tobacco the way it needs food, water, sleep, and exercise. In fact, many of the chemicals in cigarettes, like nicotine and cyanide, are actually poisons that can kill in high enough doses. The body's smart and it goes on the defense when it's being poisoned. For this reason, many people find it takes several tries to get started smoking: First-time smokers often feel pain or burning in the throat and lungs, and some people feel sick or even throw up the first few times they try tobacco.

The consequences of this poisoning happen gradually. Over the long term, smoking leads people to develop health problems like cancer, emphysema (breakdown of lung tissue), organ damage, and heart disease. These diseases limit a person's ability to be normally active and can be fatal. Each time a smoker lights up, that single cigarette takes about 5 to 20 minutes off the person's life.

Smokers not only develop wrinkles and yellow teeth, they also lose bone density, which increases their risk of osteoporosis (pronounced: ahs-tee-o-puh-row-sus, a condition that causes older people to become bent over and their bones to break more easily). Smokers also tend to be less active than nonsmokers because smoking affects lung power. Smoking can also cause fertility problems in both men and women and can impact sexual health in males. The consequences of smoking may seem very far off to many teens, but long-term health problems aren't the only hazard of smoking. Nicotine and the other toxins in cigarettes, cigars, and pipes can affect a person's body quickly, which means that teen smokers experience many problems.

Smoking Is Expensive Too

Not only does smoking damage health, it costs an arm and a leg. Depending on where you live, smoking a pack of cigarettes a day can cost about lacs of rupees a year. That adds up. It's money you could save or spend on something for yourself and for the society.

We must realise the dreadful effects of smoking and enlighten the people about its dangerous consequences. 31st June is being observed as the day to say no to tobacco throughout the world.

6. Cable TV : A Blessing or A Bane

With rapid development of information and technology the visual media in the shape of cable TV, with multitudes of domestic ad foreign channels have reached in almost every house, plays vital role in moulding the public opinion in various ways. It plays very crucial role in educating, and entertaining the masses. The cable TV has changed the means and modes of entertainment, education. Sitting before a TV, one can pass and enjoy his free time, listening music, viewing movie, learning techniques of body building, hearing sermons of religious saints, learning about lives of wild animals, birds, water creature, knowing about space, and what not. During election period, one can know the positions of political parties, their leaders, happenings in all parts of the country and their impact on the election campaigning and all facts of electioneering, just sitting before the TV.

Youngsters and teenage students are now a days seen viewing the channels, as per their likings, if some are viewing the music, some are seen quenching their thrust of knowledge, viewing channels like 'discovery' or National Geography or History etc. The image on the small screen thus have a significant impression on all, more particularly on the gullible children and on the teens. The young mind takes the reel as real and thus more often and more easily moulded and motivated by the visual media. The present-day fashion, hair dressing, sexual liberties, dating and awakening towards the right of children, awareness among the women to their rights are because of the role visual media is playing in the society.

In a hysterical effort to excel from others, some channels are showing such scenes and images, which are of no importance and have an adverse effect on the mind of viewers. Showing of sexual and rape cases, with minute details by the anchor, and showing brutal scenes of murder, the channels have crossed the limit of ethics and morality. The TV coverage of massacre of Gandhi Nagar Akshardham, Godhra's burnt railway bogies, with burnt and charred bodies of victims lying in the bogies and outside coaches, create feeling of hatred among the communities, and motivate others to wreak vengeance. Obsessed by the monoaim of making fast bucks, the channels are competing with one another to stoop to any kind of absurdity, without considering even for a minute as to what effect such visuals have on the society.

The Cable T.V, is a boon or bane depends upon the impact it has on the society. Some of the programmes shown are healthy and some are very obscene.The government should control the cable tvs so that the unhealthy programmes are not telecasted.

7. Value Education : The Need of the Hour

In the present competitive era, one can notice that value education has become an odd item. There is no emphas is in the present education to uplift the students moral, ethical and spiritual values. There is of course much impact on academic knowledge but spiritual and moral etiquettes find no place in our curriculum.

The high ranking politicians, professors, educationists forget their duty of making the next generation sound in all aspects. Illegal and unfair means are in vogue to get the things done.

The sharp fall in ethical and moral values all round, the callous disregard of common man's interests, the increasing hypocrisy and double talk have cumulatively caused deterioration that is truly alarming. The prevalence of corruption in all walk of life, the worst type of human exploitation, the accumulation of wealth by any means has ruined the basic fabric of the country which was once known for its high values. The moral and ethical values, performance of duty, regard and consideration for fellow men, sympathy and compassion seem to have gone with the wind and are among major casualties of the post independence period. A closer assessment indicated that the degradation has started from the roots and society is decaying. Our great leaders like Gandhi, Subhash, or RadhaKrishnan have all spoken for the "crisis of character" but all have become the victims of the same phase. Dr. Radhakrishnan pointed out that civilisations are not built with brick and mortar, steel and machinery, they are built with men and women, having high values and character.

No steps were taken by the high ups because they themselves are corrupt, dishonest, greedy and lover of luxuries. It is the urgent need of the hour for the intellectuals to arrest this unethical escalation of value degradation, if we like to save our country from going into the pathos of crime and corruption.

8. The Present Day Fashion

In recent times, fashion has acquired new dimensions. The spawning satellite channels have opened the floodgates for a cultural invasion and fashion is holding the centre stage at the moment.

Fashion is synonymous with rapid changes. Fashion has taken a dangerous dip into the realms of vulgarity and lasciviousness. One is not considered 'hip-and-happening' if he or she doesn't sport the in-thing like boot cuts, bell bottoms, tight fits, parallels, tank tops and low cuts. The industry has become lucrative for lot of youngsters and models. But the emphasise on carnal beauty is effecting the moral and ethical values.

The clothes that men wear and even their shoes and wrist-watches keep changing with every passing day. But the changing fashion in the men's world is more to do with the utility in day-to-day life. But that is not so with the women's world of fashion. The fashion in their world is more to do with attracting others than utility. If skin is God's gift then beauty is only skin deep. Over exposure is nauseating at times. Women do not realise that beauty comes with good health, body condition, behaviour and etiquette and not with style and over exposure. Some people take the concepts of women empowerment and gender equality in the wrong route of scantily clad fashion shows. Fashion now days has exceeded the cultural limits. Over-exposure is the latest trend in fashion, and that is a gross social violation. The skin is God's gift that goes to the dust with us, whereas character is talked of even after death. So that is more important. Girls should be cautious while dressing, as provocative dressing could land them in trouble. Wearing dangerously low-cut tight jeans would certainly call for a few superlatives like 'wow' and 'sexy', but that is not what our culture prescribes. Dignity should not be compromised at any cost.

People perceive how they find us and we Indians are known for the strong culture that we inherit. The young generation, of late, is lured by the burst of fashion shows and video albums in the electronic media. It's better to spend the same time in doing something useful like studies. To look good or to get noticed one need not wear exposing costumes. To arrive at Vision 2020 of a developed nation, the younger generation should concentrate on creative and constructive ideas and not on such fashions that will take us nowhere.

The younger generation likes to associate itself with the American culture more than the rich culture that they have inherited. They tend to forget that our culture is not only the oldest but also more evolved than any other culture in the world. Fashion is an integral part of human civilization.

The so-called designers are churning out outfits that are bizarre by the very look but still they carry a tag of creativity. The glitter of the ramp and modelling world is luring our young generation. They argue that wearing trendy and scanty outfits aping the Westerners is modernity. If we are really moving in to a modern age then why are women being harassed in the name of dowry and other things? This only strengthens the fact that we are changing physically and not mentally. One should realise that mental change is more important for the development of the nation. The ride on two cultures is leading us to a chaotic situation. The only way out is by imbibing the good features of modernity while sticking to our own culture and tradition.

The growth of fashion consciousness is both a boon and a bane. On the positive side, it has led to the flourishing of the fashion industry. The developments in fashion technology have led to the starting of new courses of study, which has led to a consequent rise in employment potential.

Someone said that, "Beauty belongs to the soul but not to the body". But the fashion world believes in just the opposite. The fallout of this is that youngsters believe that "only beauty has the right to exist on the earth, to demand dignity and to possess self-confidence". This apart some persons are over-dieting and over-exercising and falling a prey to various health problems.

The skin-fit and short outfits not only provoke undesirable thoughts in the opposite sexes but may also drag them into the vicious circle of committing mistakes. One should remember Gandhiji's words of wisdom, "Youth is a priceless possession which should not be squandered away in a moment of excitement and in miscalled pleasure". Fashion is the reflection of one's taste and ideologies. It should be explored with certain moral 'lines of control'. After all simple living and high thinking is the principle that we Indians are known for.

9. Reservation in IIMs, IITs

"No doubt there has been social injustice for a majority of the people in our country. It has to be set right. We already have reservation for scheduled castes (SC) and scheduled tribes (ST). Expanding it is not the right solution,", **N R Narayana Murthy—Chairman Infosys Technologies.**

"Reservation is not the right way to move forward"

—Ratan Tata

One thing that the politicians have learnt is to reserve quotas in education and employment for all those communities that stick together to form vote banks. So the communities that are very well-knit such as the tribals, many occupational castes, and the lucrative chunk of Muslims get covered.

The politicians are just trying again to divide the castes further in the name of reservations. The Congress tells Muslims that Hindus are ill-treating them; BSP, RJD, DMK etc. tell the "lower" castes that they have to fight the "higher" castes; regional parties ask their people to fight those from other states such as Shiv Sena is against Biharis; and DMK asks the Tamilians to fight Hindi-speaking North India!

And yet we have the temerity to harp on "Unity in Diversity". Whither unity? With what in mind are we flooding every page of school textbooks with this meaningless phrase "Unity in Diversity"?

The new fever to have gripped India is Arjun Singh's or Congress Party's yet another silly gimmick. Hiking reservations to 49% in IIMs, IITs and Central Universities—the cream of the country.

There are presently reservations in these institutions, but hiking them to 50% of the total seats will lead to incredible devaluing of the country's top institutes. If students were denied seats on merit, that is the greatest injustice in humanity next to denying food. Education is the birthright of every citizen of the world, more so in India where it is valued highly.

Supposing students are denied seats based on merit and admitted based on their caste, this will greatly dilute the talents in the IITs and the IIMs. The presently well-regarded institutes will fall in the eyes of all Indians as well as the world. It has become quite a common headline to read of the high starting salaries that IIM graduates are paid.

But now the recruiting companies may start to discriminate against the lower castes because they gained an IIM degree through the back door. Or world-renowned universities may stop admitting IIT graduates because their quality is no longer assured.

On the other hand, reservations have done a great deal of good to India. They have levelled the playing field for the SCs and STs and even the BCs. Now we see more and more of the so-called 'lower' castes in mainstream education and employment, not only in govt. but also in private.

But then again, our crass politicians have been digging Indians yet another hole by declaring OBCs, MBCs etc. and including more and more castes in these 'lower' caste groups to gain petty votes during elections. And we also see the caste leaders lobbying for their caste to be called 'lower'.

Due to OBC reservations, now some caste like YADAV have highest percentage in government jobs, MLAs and MPs in comparison of upper castes. Some sections of OBC (for example Yadav's) are enjoying power of administrations and politics since last one decades. They should be treated as upper caste otherwise there is no meaning of reservations for OBC or social justice.

It is just a paradox that the participations of majority of castes of OBC still looking for social justice because of all the benefits of reservations only taken by the some upper castes of OBC. The Center's recent decision to implement additional reservations for economically and socially impaired classes, is drawing widespread reactions from diverse media. The general feeling about reservations appears to be that they are necessary, but should be limited and phased out, as Dr Ambedkar himself had advocated many years back. IIT or IIM coursework is quite challenging and fastpaced.

Many of the SC/ST candidates though hard working and sincerely tried to keep up, but it is quite challenging for them to compete with the general category students. Often, they take additional semesters to complete the four year course. On one hand, there is an impact on their self-esteem, if they end up at the bottom of the class, on the other, they have the inherent guarantee of graduation and a good job, that many equally qualified or more deserving students never experience in their lives. In addition, the reserved class students also sail pretty easily through IIM after graduation from IIT. It is also a point to be recognised that there are a couple of talented SC/ST students who later lament coming through the reservation system, because they don't wish their calibre to be diminished by the stigma of the quota-based admission.

The resident doctors of five medical colleges in the national capital began an indefinite hunger strike to protest the proposed reservations for OBCs in higher educational institutions. The agitation has affected normal medical services. However, emergency services are being run by senior doctors in these hospitals. The doctors, who are demanding rollback of the quota proposal and appointment of a judicial committee to review the existing reservations, claimed to have faxed their demands thrice to the PMO. The government has issued notices to the junior and senior resident doctors asking them to come back on duty or face break in service," Delhi Health Secretary D S Negi said. Meanwhile, countering the ongoing agitation against reservation in elite educational institutions, several activists demonstrated in favor of quota saying it was the only way to ensure quality education for poor students. Activists of the OBC Mahapanchayat and All India Pasmanda Muslim Mahaj (AIPMM) staged a sit-in at Jantar Mantar shouting slogans and waiving placards demanding implementation of Center's proposal to introduce quotas of OBCs.

"Reservation for OBCs is justified. It will facilitate the poor students get quality education," said Chattar Singh, convener of OBC Mahapanchayat. The Prime Minister Manmohan Singh has set up an informal committee of three senior ministers; Informations to be updated to defuse the growing tension and work out the details of what the Government had said will be a "mechanism to satisfy all sections of the society." The situation is very tensed, no solution in sight. Neither the government nor the doctors are ready to give up.

Are college reservations the right solution? Isn't it better to have programs that develop competencies at younger age so that a larger target group can compete effectively with general stream students, rather than provide a lame stick to a few SC ST/tribal individuals?

Its high time to findout lower cast OBCs to give them benefits of reservations inspite of just showing them lollypop of OBC reservation. For this, the leaders who belong to the upper caste OBC must come forward in favour of Lower caste OBC, and ask the government to exclude the upper caste of OBC from reservations benefit as they don't not need this support and give the reservation benefits to the lower caste of OBC.

Many elite academicians, professionals and alumni of various institutes have cried foul saying that at least premier institutes like the IITs and IIMs should be kept away from the backward caste-based reservation system, even though most other institutes in the country are already burdened with such reservations. This is the very attitude that breeds casteism.

It must be understood well that reservation can't be a solution to the problem of social justice. The SC/ST and OBC may be given all the facilities and economic aid to make them fully competitive and capable so that the stigma of being inefficient is no more attached with them and they also join the main stream with full self-esteem.

10. Transparency in Public Administration (Right to Information)

"In a democratic country like ours, where all the agents of the public must be responsible for their conduct, there can be few secrets. The people of this country have right to know every public act. The denial of the right to know which is derived from the concept of freedom of speech and expression, though not absolute yet is a factor which should make one worry"—*Supreme Court.*

Transparency means, knowing the reasons, logics and basis of the decision taken by the administration. Transparency in public administration in legal terms means, that a citizen of India has a right (legal or fundamental) to have access to the information about government's actions. Denial of such information to the public by the public authorities without appropriate reasons, would be offence under the law. Though Supreme Court has recently gave a constitutional status for the right to know. Yet under the guise of Official Secrets Act 1923, and Section 123, of Indian Evidence Act 1872, the executive can withhold the records from production in the court of law. The laws were framed by the British with the sole purpose of protecting the interest of the British executives and keep them out of the purview of the scrutiny of court. The laws as exist today corrupts officials and protect them from the public exposure.

Undisputedly, Transparency in Public administration, will make the executive more responsible and people friendly. The red tapism prevailed in the administration will be minimised as the public become more powerful. Transparency will positively result in wiping out the authoritarianism and whimsical way of working of the so called powerful bureaucrats under the patronage of politicians. The discretions enjoyed by bureaucrats and the ministers also comes into focus, as soon as the Transparency in Public Administration is restored. Though Supreme Court has decided in several cases that discretions enjoyed must be used reasonably and decisions taken under the discretion must be based on reasoning, yet the things are not so smooth as it appears.

Transparency or right to know or right to get information, emanates from the fundamental rights; Right to speech and expression guaranteed under Article 19(i)(a) of the Indian constitution. Denial of information means a restriction on Right to free speech and expression.

In a democratic set up like India, the right of franchise is not suffice, but right to know the affairs of the state is necessary, says an eminent thinker. Mr. Justice Krishna Iyer rightly observed, "the essential measure to ensure a responsible political system is to grant the right to information without which an intelligent participation is not possible in a democracy".

Right to Information Act 2005

The much touted and even heralded National Right to Information Act came into force on 12 October. It is being implemented both at the Central level for access to records of departments and agencies under control of the Union government, and also independently by the State governments for their own departments and agencies. Not surprisingly, bureaucracies across the nation are ushering in the new law in a manner that can only be termed as 'unwilling'.

Right to Information

The right to information includes an access to the information which is held by or under the control of any public authority and includes the right to inspect the work, document, records, taking notes, extracts or certified copies of documents/records and certified samples of the materials and obtaining information which is also stored in electronic form.

The Information Which Is Exempt from Disclosure

The Right to Information Act, 2005 under Sections 8 and 9 exempts certain categories of information from disclosures. These include:

- Information, disclosure of which would prejudicially affect the sovereignty and integrity of India, the security, strategic, scientific or economic interests of the State, relation with foreign State or lead to incitement of an offence.
- Information which has been expressly forbidden to be published by any court of law or tribunal or the disclosure of which may constitute contempt of court;
- Information, the disclosure of which would cause a breach of privilege of Parliament or the State Legislature;
- Information including commercial confidence, trade secrets or intellectual property, the disclosure of which would harm the competitive position of a third party, unless the competent authority is satisfied that larger public interest warrants the disclosure of such information;
- Information available to a person in his fiduciary relationship, unless the competent authority is satisfied that the larger public interest warrants the disclosure of such information;
- Information received in confidence from foreign Government; information, the disclosure of which would endanger the life or physical safety of any person or identify the source of information or assistance given in confidence for law enforcement or security purposes;
- Information which would impede the process of investigation or apprehension or prosecution of offenders;
- Cabinet papers including records of deliberations of the Council of Ministers, Secretaries and other officers;
- Information which relates to personal information the disclosure of which has no relationship to any public activity or interest, or which would cause unwarranted invasion of the privacy of the individual.

Fee/Cost to Get the Information

A request for obtaining information under Section 6(1) of the Act needs to be accompanied by an application fee of Rs.10 by way of cash against proper receipt or by DD or bankers' cheque.

Who Can Ask for Information?

Any citizen can request for information by making an application in writing or through electronic means in English/Hindi/official language of the areas, in which the application is being made together with the prescribed fees.

Who Will Give Information?

Any public authority would designate Central Asst. Public Information Officer (CAPIO at various levels, who will receive the requests for information from the public and necessary number of Central Public Information Officers (CPIO) in all administrative units/office who will arrange for providing necessary information to the public as permitted under the law. The public authorities are also required to designate authority (ies) senior in rank to CPIO, as Appellate Authorities, who will entertain and dispose of appeals against the decision of the CPIO a required under the Act. Any person who does no receive the decision from CPIO wither by way of information or rejection within the time frame may within 30 days from the expiry of perio prescribed for furnishing the information or 3 days from the date of receipt of the decision prefer an appeal to the Appellate Authority.

The Role of Central Public Information Officers (CPIO)

The CPIO will receive the application/request for information under the Act and process the request for providing the information and dispose of the same; either by providing the information or rejecting the request, within a period of 30 days from the date of receipt of request.

Dr Wajahat Habibullah has just taken charge as India's Chief Information Commissioner. He retired very recently as Secretary to the Government of India at the Ministry of Panchyati Raj. Dr Habibullah appears to be progressive minded enough to write an article recently in the *Financial Express* on citizens using power to effect change. "The Right to Information Act of 2005 will guarantee the other essential elements of good governance: transparency and accountability", he wrote. In Karnataka, the former Chief Secretary K K Misra took charge as the State Information Commissioner. In Maharashtra, a current civil servant, Dr Suresh Joshi, Metropolitan Commissioner of the Mumbai Metropolitan Regional Development Authority (MMRDA) is slated to take over as Information Commissioner.

With virtually all IC positions being given to former bureaucrats, the National Campaign for the People's Right to Information has sounded an alarm on the dangers of extending a bureaucratic culture and legacy into the very offices that hold primary charge of overseeing enforcement.

The new law specifies that "The Chief Information Commissioner and Information Commissioners shall be persons of eminence in public life with wide knowledge and experience in law, science and technology, social service, management, journalism, mass media or administration and governance." None of this seems to matter to the heads of our governments. The credibility of the government is likely to suffer serious damage if appointments of "independent" ICs are largely restricted to serving or retired bureaucrats, say Shekhar Singh and Aruna Roy.

The law has now come into force, in the broad light of media attention and some early filings. One thing seems certain. As was the case when the state laws were used, the new national law will also see most of the serious work of operationalisation and implementation only henceforth, and with citizen pressure. How much light is shed on the workings of government by the new law will only become known in the months ahead?

11. Adulteration : Crime Against Society

"Adulteration thrives in India, in the name of 'Sab Kuchh Chalta Hai'. Such belief encourages and allures even the so far honest traders to resort to it to make quick bucks. The unholy nexus between merchants of death and corrupt officials, has allowed this heinous crime go on since long".

What do we find pure or unadulterated nowadays? False branding of ghee, adulterated petrol, turmeric mixed with chromate powder, Chilli powder mixed red colour, dal blended with stones bits, dust tea garnished by saw dust, white powder in salt, milk with water or synthetic milk, mustard oil with argemone are known examples of adulteration. Even fruits, vegetable and cereals sold in market, reportedly contain high level of toxic metals like lead, nickle, cadmium A survey conducted recently by a private agency revealed that all the cold drinks, Pepsy, Cocacola etc, are found adulterated with unhygenic substances. National Dairy Development Corporation also conducted a survey, which revealed that 90% of the edible oils available in the market contain highly intoxicated elements.

Food adulteration has become the order of the day and consumer education is the need of the hour, assert experts. "A common mistake committed by most consumers is to blindly pick up any product without reading the label, which includes details like batch number, expiry date, manufacturer's name and address. Adulteration like corruption has become rampant. Every citizen, every government department is well known to the fact, that 90% spices, dals, milk, ghee, sugar, tea, sold in our rural area are adulterated. We have laws against adulteration, but like any other social legislation, it is rarely enforced. Adulteration has become a way of life,the negligent government officials, indifferent society, are awakened, only when a tragedy take place.

Can't we forget the death of 54 people in the Capital because of dropsy triggered by the consumption of adulterated mustard oil? Dropsy is caused by a toxin called sanguinarine, found in the seeds of common weed, prickle poppy argemone mexicama. Its seeds have been used in recent times to adulterate mustard seeds for a 'zing' taste. It was claimed that 'zing' having been lost in some of the high yielding hybrid varieties of mustard, so some unscrupulous oil mill owners have started adding an overdose of 'argemone' to restore the 'zing' punch, the taste liked by many consumers. It was a pity that a major cooperative giant, like NDDB (National Dairy Development Board), Which supplies, mustard oil under the brand name of 'Dhara' was also in the list of adulterated oils.

The story of the adulterated 'Dal' mixed with 'Kasari Dal' is so not so old, that we could forget. Hundreds of people disabled in M.P, who had consumed this adulterated Dal. But those who commit this crime, have gone scot free. Don't we remember the recent finding of pesticides and other non edible items in the cold drinks of renowned brands, even the 'Dhara' vegetable oil was found adulterated? what action was taken ? After a lapse of a little period, every thing is in the same shape, no change, no action? Neither the government nor the public at large is worried of the things. So rightly observed about India, Sab Kuchh Chalta Hai Yahan.

Despite amendments to the Prevention of Food Adulteration Act, 1954, the level of adulteration in food products in Vadodara was found to be 8.16 per cent. About 37 of the 453 food samples collected by the Food & Drugs Laboratory in 2002-2003 were adulterated. If loopholes in law have emboldened erring manufacturers, the lack of consumer awareness has made things worse. "Most consumers are not brand conscious. They are ignorant about PFA standards and pick up cheaper products by compromising on quality and subsequently health too. And those who look for label details like the manufacturer's name, expiry date and batch number do not make an effort to lodge a complaint on finding spurious or substandard food products. At the most, they would avoid buying these things themselves," said Arun Kagadwala of Jagrut Nagrik, a consumer protection organisation.

"The penalty for selling substandard products is a meagre sum of Rs 500 to Rs 1,000, which every trader can pay. Also, the fact that one is rarely put behind bars for food adulteration is also a reason why people have no fear of law,"

There is hardly any item in the Indian market, which is pure. Adulterators spare nothing to make quick money. Reports, have come to light that empty water bottles are used to supply well known brand names of mineral water. Every year thousands of people die after consuming spurious liquor. Every time, when the tragedy takes place, some arrests are made and actions are initiated just to pacify the public agitations. The production of spurious liquor can't be possible without knowledge and support of local police, but never any action is initiated against the police. There is no system to check or punish the known ignorance of such police or other officials.

It is the duty of the State to improve the food testing facilities. The Inspectors, Drug Inspectors, Police Officials, Food Analyst should be taken to task and must be made accountable if any incidence of adulteration in found in their area of jurisdiction.Unless they be held responsible, they will not be worried of the happenings and adulteration will thrive with more pace and speed.

The Health Ministry must also make I S I or AgMark certification mandatory for all edible items. Every citizen should also be made aware that consuming any adulterated item may prove to be more dangerous than their imaginations. The indifferent attitude of general mass towards the hygienic values is also responsible for prevalence of such crime. Unless the common people be conscience to the hygienic values, and protest against the spurious and adulterated items, the adulteration will not be checked, as the law takes its own time. If we like to remain healthy, we shall have to act at our own and wherever and whenever availability of such items come to our notice, the matter must be brought to the notice of officials through letters and newspapers Unless we care for the health of ours and health of our family members, nothing can be changed. A social awakening against adulteration can only check such a crime.

12 : AIDS : A Horrendous Disease

AIDS, Acquired Immune Deficiency Syndrome has assumed alarming proportions in the last few years, though it has been surreptitiously developing over a number of years.

AIDS is a collection of symptoms and infections in humans resulting from the specific damage to the immune system caused by infection with the human immunodeficiency virus (HIV). The late stage of the condition leaves individuals prone to opportunistic infections and tumors. Although treatments for AIDS and HIV exist to slow the virus's progression, there is no known cure.

HIV is transmitted through direct contact of a mucous membrane or the bloodstream with a bodily fluid containing HIV, such as blood, semen, vaginal fluid, preseminal fluid, and breast milk. This transmission can come in the form of anal, vaginal or oral sex, blood transfusion, contaminated needles, exchange between mother and baby during pregnancy, childbirth, or breastfeeding, or other exposure to one of the above bodily fluids.

AIDS is the most severe manifestation of infection with HIV. HIV is a retrovirus that primarily infects vital components of the human immune system such as CD4+ T cells, macrophages and dendritic cells. It directly and indirectly destroys CD4+ T cells. CD4+ T cells are required for the proper functioning of the immune system. When HIV kills CD4+ T cells so that there are fewer than 200 CD4+ T cells per microliter of blood, cellular immunity is lost, leading to AIDS.

There is currently no vaccine against HIV or AIDS, the only known methods of prevention are based on avoiding exposure to the virus or, failing that, on antiviral treatment directly after a highly significant exposure. Also, not a single case has been documented in which systemic HIV infection has been cured and even on the theoretical level, no plausible way of eradicating HIV infection has so far been found. Treatment for HIV can suppress viral replication to a degree sufficient to apparently stop disease progression, but success is critically dependent on the patients ability to keep perfect adherence to their drug schedule, which many people will fail to achieve. Also, modern combination therapy has been around for merely ten years, so it is not presently known whether treatment failure or inacceptable long-term side effects can be avoided in the majority even of perfectly compliant patients over a time-span of potentially many decades. However, it is known that without major medical and scientific breakthroughs, HIV will not have any problem surviving combination therapy for said decades. Still, in western countries, most patients survive many years following diagnosis because of the availability of the highly active antiretroviral therapy (HAART). In the absence of HAART, progression from HIV infection to AIDS occurs at a median of between nine to ten years and the median survival time after developing AIDS is only 9.2 months. HAART dramatically increases the time from diagnosis to death, and treatment research continues.

Owing to the rapid pace, it spread all over the world, it has earned a veritable state of Pandemic. The HIV has multiplied a hundred times in less than a decade. The situation is very grave in the USA, Thailand, and many African, Central American and East Asian countries. It is estimated that the developing countries accounts for 84% of the total HIV infectants.

The lower strata of the society are more prone to the HIV, due to poverty, illiteracy, lack of access to the proper counselling and medical facilities. Despite the best efforts of NGOs and voluntary, social workers, people living in villages are oblivious of the dreaded effects of the AIDS.

India has launched a national campaign to fight the HIV/AIDS epidemic. The Prime Minister inaugurated the first ever national convention of the elected representatives on HIV/AIDS in New Delhi on July 26,2003. The two day convention was organised by the newly formed parliamentarians forum on HIV/AIDS in collaboration with the Ministry of Health and UNAIDS. The prime Minister called for greater openness in the community. He wanted the younger to be more enlightened about AIDS so that they could protect themselves and the community. He emphasised the need to ensure that there was no prejudice towards those affected by the disease. Ms. Sonia Gandhi leader of opposition who delivered keynote address, called for efforts to provide AIDS education to adolescent girl both school going and those out of school and for measures to include drug therapy as part of the national AIDS control programme.

Mr. Peter Piot executive director of UNAIDS, emphasised the need for special efforts to address the problem of stigma and discrimination faced by HIV patients. Humanity has rarely witnessed as dreaded a scourge as AIDS. As of today, there is no cure for AIDS. So by imbibing the maxim: 'Prevention is better than the cure' and as such educating the public about the ways and modes of transmission of this horrendous disease. We may hope to check the rampaging HIV.

13. Are Events Like 'Beauty Contests' an Insult to Womanhood?

"Globalization today means exploitation of natural and human resources from a third country like India, by transnational corporation to reap huge profits, when it enters our daily life and seeks to capture our personal values and gender perceptions into commodities".

The point of holding events like beauty contests was not of culture, but it is more of economical, in this commercial world. The corporate dealing in cosmetics are always in search of virgin markets to enhance their profits. Nothings can facilitate market expansion than fashion parades, fashion shows, and beauty pageants.

The organisers of beauty contests all over the world have intermingled the beauty with brain. The girls are reportedly selected Miss World, Miss Asia, Miss Universe not only in reference to their beauty parameters but also with their way of answering some trimmed questions to judge their I.Q. They are given several crowns with specific features like Miss Beautiful Hair or Miss Photogenic, Miss Beautiful smile etc, to sell the multitude of products spewed out the beauty industry.

It can't be taken as a mere coincidence that most of the beauty queens nowadays are discovered in the developing countries, with vast population and a good market potential to sell the products meant for females.

No doubt that beauty shows prototype the female form and women's body language and determine bodily movements to satisfy the lustful craving of the male eyes. The women are being publicly judged on the basis of her vital statistics amounted to an insult to woman hood to some extent. Several women's organisations and feminists group opposed the holding of such pageant in Bangalore on several grounds, not all related with women. Politics, morality, nationality are intermingled in a pot pourri of hysteria. These women group never opposed the holding of such contests out of India, But made much hue & cry when the same kind of event was being held in India. How and why could they hold, Indian woman more pure, their dignity a bone of contention if a bunch of adolescents were paraded semi nude in the country ? It was also argued that such semi nude dressing girls, could also be seen at sea shores for example in Goa, Cochin etc.

Beauty pageants are an exercise to dovetail the female behaviour with the likings of males, so the premium were placed on the synthetic smile, smooth movements of body, made up face and moisturised skin with beautiful hair.

The present boom in electronic media, the vast coverage of such contests, have accelerated the commercial viability of such pageants. A beauty is acceptable only if the demands of a particular market are met, if the packaging is proper and promotion is up to the mark. Beauty in short is what the beauty business defines. Crowning girls from developing countries as Miss world, Miss Asia, Miss Photogenic is all part of this commercial game.

All the violent protests and destructive approach taken by the opponent of the beauty pageant, did more harm than good to the feminist cause by giving an impression that these protestors were restricted to a reactionary and lunatic frenzy.

There were feminists who argued that beauty contests provide an opportunity for women to express their femininity and part of the sexual freedom for which she is entitled as human being. Some argued that opposing to holding such contests in India, is like chaining the Indian women in the old traditional values and ethics which are not at all acceptable to the modern Indian girls.

Since our country is a democracy, which guarantees several fundamental rights to the citizens, so opponents of the event have right to oppose, the organisers have right to organise, the contestants have right to contest. In brief, holding such events, does not constitute an insult to the womanhood. The ill is not in holding such contests but ill is in the minds and thoughts of an individual or group.

14. Brain Drain & Brain Circulation

"The brain drain has been a curse for developing countries like India. Throughout the post World War II era, the "best and brightest" routinely left for the economic opportunities and higher standards of living in the West. Entire graduating classes from the elite Indian Institutes of Technology emigrated during the 1970s and 1980s".

'Brain Drain' means, migration of highly trained manpower from one country to another. Shri P.N. Haksar once remarked, "A society, which cannot place the highest value on knowledge and its acquisition, inevitably alienates it self from creating transmitting and applying knowledge." The alienation leads partly to the visible brain drain, that in migration and invisible brain drain means loss of morale and creativity among those who still stay in India. Both visible and Invisible brain drain produce a great national loss, which can't be calculated in terms of money.

A brain drain of highly-skilled professionals to well paid jobs in the first world costs Asia billions of dollars each year but the traffic is not all one way, a UN report found. The United Nations Development Programme's (UNDP) Human Development Report 2001 estimates India loses $2 billion a year in resources because of the emigration of computer professionals to the United States alone.

These emigrants often achieve impressive professional and economic successes abroad. For example, in 1998 Indian engineers were running more than 775 technology companies in California's Silicon Valley that accounted for $3.6 billion in sales and 16,600 jobs. But the connections between these Non-Resident Indians (NRIs) and their home country rarely extended beyond holiday visits.

Indian policymakers now have an opportunity to transform the brain drain from a curse into an asset. Changes in the structure of competition in information technology (IT) industries have not only allowed the growth of software development in India, but also create the possibility of economic leapfrogging of a sort that was not possible in an earlier era. In many parts of the world, the "brain drain" is giving way to a process of "brain circulation" as talented immigrants who have studied and worked abroad increasingly return to their home countries to pursue promising opportunities there. As engineers and other professionals return home—either temporarily or permanently—they transfer not only technology and capital, but also managerial and institutional know-how to formerly peripheral regions. They also link local producers more directly to the market opportunities and networks of more advanced economies.

The policymakers in India must learn from the experience of Taiwan, where brain circulation was critical to its shift from a peripheral source of cheap labour to a global leader in IT production. The challenge for India's information technology (IT) sector is to upgrade the software industry, an industry that currently produces primarily low-value added services for export markets. As in Taiwan, Indian policymakers can accelerate the process of industrial upgrading by creating incentives for engineers to return to India both as policy advisors and as investors, entrepreneurs, and managers.

It should be understand well that this can only be a first step for India. The expansion of external linkages is essential to competitiveness in a global economy. However this must be accompanied by concerted efforts to develop the domestic market to insure that the benefits of the new industries contribute to a wider process of economic development.

For years now products of the Indian educational system, students and professionals have been going abroad in search of distant horizons. It's now India's turn to reverse the 'brain drain'.

The Ministry of Human Resource Development has taken the strategic initiative to "internationalise Indian education in a big way." As part of the this overall drive the Ministry, with the assistance of Educational Consultants India Limited (Ed.CIL), today launched an educational portal www.educationindia4u.com at India International Centre.

What we are looking to provide is comprehensive information at the students' fingertips who are living abroad, "said Dr.Yajulu Medury", Chairman of Ed.CIL, adding: "We want to act as long-term career guides to foreign students not just a one-time facility."

Currently around 161 educational institutions are a part of this portal which includes names like Indian Institute of Technology (IITs), Indian Institute of Management (IIMs), Regional Engineering Colleges, Madras University, Pune University etc.

According to the Secretary, Department of Secondary and High Education, Mr. Maharaj Krishen Kaw, the portal which this year is targeting students of countries of Africa as well as others like Mauritius, Gulf region, Malaysia and Indonesia, is a step taken in the "larger diplomatic interest of forging closer relations with these countries." He explains "We have also instructed universities to have a 15 percent quota for foreign students with priority to people of Indian origins."

But there are a few academicians who express a note of warning. "We shouldn't be too euphoric at the creation of the site thinking it would bring a cascade of foreign students to India. There is need for aggressive advertising of this portal abroad" cautioned Mr. Syed Shahid Mahdi, Vice-Chancellor of Jamia Milia Islamia.

"If you go back with reasonable expectations you are not going to be disappointed", says Susheel Chandra. There is always a possibility that people may not like the new situation, but the decision to return should not be cast in stone "you've got to keep your options open."

"In the end, people will go where the jobs are...There are exciting new opportunities opening up in India and so the trend is in reverse gear"

15. Capital Punishment

Capital Punishment is the legal infliction of death as a penalty for violating criminal law of the land. Since time immemorial people have been put to death for various forms of wrongdoing. Methods of execution have included such practices as crucifixion, stoning, drowning, burning at the stake, impaling, and beheading. Today capital punishment is typically accomplished by lethal gas or injection, electrocution, hanging, or shooting.

In modern world the death penalty is the most notorious severe practice. Other harsh, physical forms of criminal punishment also referred to as corporal punishment have generally been eliminated in modern times as unsophisticated and unnecessary. In the majority of countries, contemporary methods of punishment, such as imprisonment or fines, no longer involve the infliction of physical pain. Although imprisonment and fines are universally recognized as necessary to control the crime.

The nations of the world are split on the issue of capital punishment. About 80 nations have abolished the death penalty and an almost equal number of nations retain it.

An accepted principle of a just society is that every person has an equal right to "life, liberty, and the pursuit of happiness." Within that framework, an argument for capital punishment can be formulated along the following lines: some acts are so vile and so destructive of community that they invalidate the right of the committor to membership and even to life. The privilege of living and pursuing the good life in a society is not absolute. It may be negated by behavior that undermines the nature of a moral community. To live in a community requires from each citizen to honor the rightful claims of others. The utter and deliberate denial of life and opportunity to others forfeits ones own claim to continue membership in the community. The preservation of moral community demands that the shattering of the foundation of its existence must be taken with utmost seriousness. The preciousness of life in a moral community must be so highly honored that those who do not honor the life of others make their own right to membership 'null and void '. Those who violate the person hood of others, especially if this is done persistently as a habit must pay the ultimate penalty. This punishment must be inflicted for the sake of maintaining the community whose foundation has been violated. The point of contention is whether capital punishment even in such case is justified or not?

An ideal community would be made up of free and equal citizens devoted to a balance between individual self-fulfillment and the advancement of the common good. Communal life would be based on mutual love in which equality of giving and receiving was the norm of social practice. Everyone would contribute to the best of ability and each would receive in accordance with legitimate claims to available resources.

What action should a community based on this kind of love take with those who commits brutal acts of terror, violence, and murder? Taken in negatively, it would govern by the philosophy of "an eye for an eye, a tooth for a tooth, and a life for a life." Those who had shown no respect for life would be restrained, permanently if necessary, so that they could not further endanger other members of the community. But the purpose of confinement would not be vengeance or punishment. Rather an ideal community would show mercy even to those who had shown no mercy. It would return good for evil. The aim of isolation is reconciliation and not revenge. It is ever hopeful that even the worse among us can be redeemed so that their own potential contribution to others can be realized.

In brief, such are the arguments for and against capital punishment, one founded on justice and the nature of moral community, the other resting on love and the nature of an ideal spiritual community. If we stand back from this description and make an attempt at evaluation, one point is crucial. The love ethic requires a high degree of moral achievement and maturity. It is more suitable for small, closely-knit communities in which members know each other personally and in some depth. Forgiveness and reclamation flourish best in a community in which people can participate in each other's lives. It becomes an ethic of non-resistance to evil, unqualified pacifism, and self-sacrifice in which self-interest is totally abandoned.

The conclusion of the matter is that the present practice of capital punishment is regarded by many a moral disgrace. The irony is that the very societies that have the least right to inflict it are precisely the ones most likely to do so. The compounding irony is that the economic malfunctions and cultural diseases in those same societies contribute to the violence that makes it necessary to unleash even more repression and brutality against its unruly citizens to preserve order and stave off chaos. To the degree that society provides opportunities for all citizens to achieve a good life in a sensible culture, it is reasonable to believe that the demand for capital punishment will be reduced or eliminated. It points to the shallowness of our dedication to solving the basic problems of poverty, moral decay, meaninglessness, and social discord.

16. Computer : A Boon or A Bane ?

"Computer is not a magical device. It possesses no IQ or intelligence of its own. It's IQ is zero. It has to be told what to perform and in what sequence. Hence only the user can determine what task a computer will perform. A computer can't take any decision at its own without it is programmed to do so. These are some mechanical deficiency of the computers, but in addition to these technical flaws, the invention of computer has adversely effected the human life, the social economic fabric of the nations."

Today hardly any corner of our life is left untouched by the computers. In school, banks, shops, hospitals, restaurants, post offices, government offices, railway or bus reservation counters, travel companies and all such utility service departments, we find the computers everywhere.

For the last two decades, the world seems to have undergone a computer revolution. Initially, computers were designed to solve the complicated scientific problems, but now a days, computers are becoming indispensable day by day. Necessity is the mother of invention, the saying holds true for computers, as computers were initially invented for fast and accurate calculations. The word computer comes from the word "Compute", that means to calculate. So a computer was normally considered to be a calculating device that can perform arithmetic calculations at an enormous speed and with perfect accuracy. But now a days more than 80% of the work done by computers is of non mathematical or non-numerical nature. Hence to define a computer merely a calculating machine does not hold good in present day situation. To be correct and more precise, a computer may be defined as a device that operates upon information or data. The fact that the computers process data is so fundamental that many people have started calling it a data processor. The name data processor is more comprehensive as it includes not only the work of computing but also perform other functions with the data like, processing, merging, sorting, printing etc.

Today the computer has become cornerstone of our industrial and scientific development. The computers have shrank the world into a room. In all walks of life from manufacturing of a small item, to exploration of ocean and space, computers are being used extensively..Robots are being used in study of volcanoes, in space research, in medical science, remotely commanded by the computers. This omnipotent device, has taken entry into such diverse areas like sports, agriculture, medicine, business, space, ocean that has become an indispensable gadget.

But Is Computer a Boon or a Bane ?

No works of art or any great scripture or the Shakespearean tragedies have had so spasmodic effect on human society than the computer, which has made the present world totally dependant on it. Rightly said by someone that since the existence of human an earth, it has never encountered anything as complex and ingeniously designed, as named computer. **"Computer is a person, unable to walk, but its mind transcends the barriers of space"**, retorted Dr. Stephen. It is indeed an example of the excellence of human mind, which had done wonders and made the creator its slave to a great extent.

Characteristics of Computers

Speed : Computer is such a fast working device, that can perform in records the amount of work that a human being can't do in an entire year.

Accuracy : The accuracy of the computers is unparalleled or unchallengeable. Each calculation is performed with same accuracy.

Diligence : Unlike human being, a computer is totally free from monotony, tiredness, lack of concentration, boredom etc. and so a computer can work regularly, for any longer period of time, without creating any error and without feeling boredom or monotonousness.

Versatility : Versatility is one of the most wonderful characteristics of a computer. At one moment it is preparing bills of electricity the next moment it can generate result of university, and the next moment it can trace an important file. All that is required to give appropriate instruction to the computer. A computer is capable of performing almost any task without getting irritated, provided the task can be reduced to a series of logical steps.

Memory : A computer can store and recall any amount of information because of its secondary storage capability. Every piece of informations can be retained as long as desired by the user and can be recalled as and when required. Even after several years, the information recalled will be as accurate as on the day when it was fed into the computer.

With such important and wonderful characteristic computers has ushered in all aspects of business, science, research and daily routine of human being.

Shortcomings

But every invention has its merits and demerits, and so the computer is no exception. Computer is a device have no feelings. It is devoid of emotions and instincts, as it is simply a machine, have no soul or heart. Computer can't make any judgement at its own. The judgement is based on the instructions given to it by the user. Although men have succeeded in building a memory for the computer, but no computer possesses the equivalent of a human heart. A computer can't judge good or bad effects of its decision.

Moreover computer is not a magical device. It processes no I.Q. or intelligence of its own. It's I.Q. is zero. It has to be told what to perform and in what sequence. Hence only the user can determine what task a computer will perform. A computer can't take any decision at its own without it is programmed to do so.

As already mentioned, a computer can perform the work with such accuracy and speed that many number of persons can't perform even in years. The problem of unemployment faced by so many countries including our own country is further worsened by the use of computers in various offices, departments.

The invention of nuclear weapons, weapons of most destructive nature, warships, space ships have been possible with the invention of computers. The use of missiles, dropping of nuclear bombs, destroying the basic amenities, communication system of any nation has become so easy to such developed nations, that they have started using them for aggrandisement of their imperialistic motives.

Yes, indeed, the computers, on the one side helped the mankind to solved many crucial problems, on the other side put the world at the verge of destruction. In spite of that it is not at all the fault of the computers itself. It is a machine, which obeys the orders of the user. The fault lies with the user not with the computers.

Summarily, computers has solved humanity's most pressing problems like energy crisis, cancer research, water purification, and helped man to explore the space, ocean and other hidden secrets of the world. The computer is a boon or a bane depends, on its use. If used for the benefits of the mankind, its a boon, if used for the evil purpose, its a bane. Remember the story of Alladin and genie, genie obeys order of Alladin, whether wrong or right, good or bad, in the same way, the computer obeys the orders, instructions of its user.

17. Corruption v/s Economic Growth

"Corruption free government is not a necessary condition for rapid economic development. If the corporate and institutions work, and uncertainty is checked, progress is possible". ***S. Swaminathan***

Corruption in any form is treated as an incurable disease, a cause of many social and economical evils in the society and it damages the moral and ethical fibres of the of the civilisation. Indisputably, it is correct that corruption breeds many evils in the society and once corruption starts taking place, slowly and gradually, whole country passes into its net and it becomes after some time an incurable disease. From the point of view of economic growth, there seems to be no clear cut correlation, between corruption and the economic growth of a country.

We can find, several countries having corrupt regime, but yielding excellent economic results, and other countries, with clean regime, showing very poor results in terms of economic prosperity & growth.

Transparency International Publishes every year, lists ranking corruption in various countries. It has just come up with a list of the 10 most corrupt rulers. According to reasonably authoritative local estimates. Numero Uno is Indonesia's 'Suharto' who is estimated to have skimmed off $15-35 billion. He is followed by the Phillippines Marcos ($5-10 billion), Zaire's Mobutu ($5 billion), Nigeria's Abacha ($2-5 billion), Serbia's Milosevic ($1 billion), Haiti's Duvalier ($300-800 million), Peru's Fujimori ($600 million), Ukraine's Lazarenko ($114-200 million), Nicargua's Alemai ($100 million) and the Phillippines Estrada ($78-80 million).

This list in neither complete, nor exhaustive. Saddam Hussein and his cronies might have skimmed more than some of the above rulers.

Now the point of discussion is : Why do some corrupt regimes do very well others badly ?

If we take the case of Indonesia, we see the income of Indonesian's quadruple to $1000 per capita under the regime of Suharto. Indonesia's economy during 1980-1990, showed miraculous uptrend, graduating from a mere commodity producer it became a big exporter of manufacturers. During this golden period under Suharto, poverty, infant mortality and fertility plummeted, while the literacy soared high. The era ended in ruins during the Asian Financial Crisis, but that event upended regimes from Korea to Bangkok. The achievements during the period had remained impressive and remarkable.

On the other hand, Mobutu left Zaire poorer and in more desperate condition than ever, like Nigeria and Haiti, where too, no progress was made. Marcos and Fujimori tried to rebuild the collapsing economies amidst lot of praise for their efforts, but the prevailing corruption and maladministration eroded the initial gains seriously.

If we took, at transparency international's list of 133 countries ranked in order of corruption, we will find that the well-off western countries all figure in the top of 35. Singapore the most successful developing country, ranks at 5, Botswana, Africa's star performer, ranks at 30, the Scandinavians are generally regarded the most honest (Finland is no 1) and the USA comes a bit lower at 18. Paradoxically, some of the poorer countries are also among the most corrupt and some of the less corrupt are progressing.

Again it is difficult to find any correlation between corruption and economic growth. Some of the fastest growing counties in the world are also in the bottom half of the corruption list. China, stands at 66, India at 83 (along side Malawi) Russia at 86 (alongside Mozambique) Vietnam at 100 (alongside Guatemala and Kazakhstan).

Corruption in long run may destroy the whole society, morally, ethically and economically. May be in the long run, a country needs clean government to reach the top of the income ladder, May be rapid income growth by itself induces better accountability and governance, may be corruption in long run degenerates the society into several misfortunes and evils. But one fact still stands out : Clean government is not a necessary condition for rapid economic growth.

Bangladesh stands at the last of list of 133, yet it has been growing at five percent annually for a decade. Italy the most corrupt country in Western Europe has been one of the fastest growing economy. Corruption is often a good predictor of eventual economic crisis, yet when Argentina (92) went bust, the ensuing financial crisis, also consumed its neighbours Uruguay, which ranks at 33.

The puzzle to ponder is why does corruption coexist with both good and bad economic performance ? Why has India over the decades grown more slowly than Indonesia, despite less corruption ?

The quality of institutions seems to be the most important factor for the growth of a country. If the institutions work even moderately well, progress is possible even if money is skimmed off at the top. But if the institutions are incapable of enforcing any rights, corruption will hasten economic collapse.

So far Indian economy is concerned the slow progress is the result of lack of decision making at higher levels. Many politicians, who takes money, but could not enforce their will, because of powerful lobby of bureaucrats at many places and in a democracy like India, voice of media, voice of opposition could suppress the wish of the leader. Ours is a peculiar democracy, where politicians are corrupt but not authoritative, ours is a multi-party system, where leg pulling for no cause, accusation without any evidence is common. Instability in political system is also responsible for the slow economic progress, where the Prime Minister is always busy in satiating the coalition partners to keep attached. So far quality of institutions are concerned. We are having well matured corporate and the fast development reflected during the last years, is became of stability in the country and good relations with the neighbouring nations.

India's economic growth on an average 6% GDP despite considerable corruption, is because of the stability and the liberalisation measures taken by the present government, gradual privatisation of various sector, reducing bureaucratic intervention in routine work and other like measures adopted by the government. It is important to note that growth in some States, where institutions are strong and decision making is least arbitrary, is faster than other states.

In brief it can well be concluded that corruption and economic growth has no clear correlation. Strong institutions, political stability, fast and reasonability in decision taking are some of the requirements for fast economic growth.

18. Elimination of 'Female Foetus' (Murder of Unborn Girls)

"In India, we have inherited the cultural legacy of strong son-preference among all communities, religious groups and citizens of varied socio-economic backgrounds. Patri-locality, patri-lineage and patriarchal attitudes manifest in women and girls having subordinate position in the family, discrimination in property rights and low-paid or unpaid jobs. Women's work is limited to house hold duties. At the time of marriage, dowry is given by the bride's family to the groom's for shouldering 'the burden of the bride'. In many communities female babies are killed immediately after birth either by the mother or by elderly women of the households to relieve themselves from the life of humiliation, rejection and suffering"

Social discrimination against women results in systematic neglect of women's health, from womb to tomb. Female infanticide and female foeticide are widely practiced in many states. The reason of female infanticide can be traced to the evil of dowry, hypergamy, prevailed in our society. A more degrading and disparaging feature of the society came into existence for the last two decades is the immense love for male child and elimination of female foetus. With invention of new technologies to monitor the 'Foetal' health, it was expected that these will be used for taking care of the health of the unborn child, but these became terminator of female foetus. Are female foetus being deliberately eliminated or aborted, is the question?

To a great extent, yes! is the answer.

Are the technologies (ultrasonography, amniocentesis, chorian villi biopsy, foetoscopy, material serum analysis etc) assisting in this systematic elimination ? Again the answer is; yes, to a great extent.

The answer is well supported by the trends that surfaced in the 2001 Census. The following statistics reveal the truth :

Census	Girl child/male child ratio in 0-6 agegroup
1981	962 Girls/1000 Boys
1991	945 Girls/1000 Boys
2001	927 Girls/1000 Boys

Biologically girls are stronger and with all the thrust on the well being of the girl child, the 1981 trends should have atleast continued, but in 20 years the ratio has dropped considerably.

While there can be no moral or ethical justification for elimination of female foetuses, it continues to be practiced. In fact sex determination which was mainly restricted to metros now, is prevalent in villages. If sex determination tests are allowed to proliferate, and the elimination female foetuses allowed, the society would have to pay for this sin, after a gap of around two decades.

The greatest supporters of a child (whether male or female) are the natural parents. If a girl has a father who loves her and grants her all her fundamental rights, that girl is inviolable. Fathers often provide material comforts, but deny daughters, their right to choose their life partner. A few lines from a poem come to the mind, when one thinks of the way a girl fears her father.

> Oh haste, thee haste, the lady cries
> Though tempests round us gather
> I will face the raging of the skies
> But not an angry father.
>
> (From Lord Ullin's Daughter)

For a daughter there can be no greater misery, than the knowledge that she does not have her father's support. What can be more demeaning than the feeling that one is nothing more than a contraceptive failure?

Some months back, Delhi University Students and teachers came out of their class rooms to support the amendment to the Pre-Natal Diagnostic (PNDT) Bill which was tabled in Parliament, recommending more stringent measures against doctors who selectively abort female foetuses.

The amended PNDT Bill suggests certain important modifications in the existing 1994 PNDT Act, which make, it mandatory not only to register all kinds of techniques but to maintain records of every such scan. It also enhances the penalties for violation of the act. Of course a powerful lobby of doctors resisted the amendments.

Since 1979, when the first private sex determination clinic was set up in Punjab, such clinics have proliferated rapidly. By the early eighties, such diagnostic centers had mushroomed even in rural areas, offering sex determination for a few hundred rupees.

According to 'Saheli' a Delhi based women's group, between 1978 and 1982, 78000 female foetus were aborted. During 1987-88, an estimated 13000 sex determination tests were done in seven Delhi clinics only.Today the north western states, where such clinics first appeared have the lowest sex ratio. Punjab has 793 girls for every 1000 boys, Haryana 820 girls/1000 boys and Delhi follows with 845 girls/1000 boys.

The decline in ratio in urban areas is more than twice that in the rural areas. It is true that women should have the right to abort their unwanted foetus, but if the technology is being used only to eliminate the female foetus, then we need to question its use.

The amendment to PNDT Bill is one of the means towards an end. We must build a nation wise campaign again gender discrimination and inequities. The root cause for elimination of female foetus is to be traced. Unless the evil of forced marriages, dowry, illiteracy among the females are done away with, lives of women will not improve. Banning prenatal sex determination tests might add a feather in the caps of rights activists; it will not materially improve the lives of women. A social awakening is required, for true respect to the girls, a lot of honest work with full political 'will' can only solve the problem.

19. Environmental Pollution

It is paradoxical, that the man, who needs the environment most, is destroying its sanctity and purity for present monetary gains, and endangering its own generation.

Never before in the history, the environment pollution has drawn such attention of policymakers, academicians, and the court, at least in India. A lot of research has done during the last few years to find out a suitable linkage between economic activities and the environment and a need for new technologies has felt in order to save the environment from the ever increasing pollution.

Because of the rapid industrial growth, the most precious heritage of mankind, the natural environment is in danger of becoming polluted and chemicalised. Earlier most of the economic activities, development policies, were centered towards the motive of benefits or gain, but for the last few years, it has been sincerely realised that, investment on environmental conservation and pollution control measures enhance and improve the productivity. It is necessary to save the mankind from revenge of the nature, if pollution continues like in the past.

Environmental pollution causes Global Warming a threat to the whole civilisation. In 1992, the United Nationals Framework Convention on Climate Change (UNFCCC) was adopted. It recognized that industrialized countries were mostly responsible for increased Green House Gases, concentration in the Earth's atmosphere and should be the first to act against climate change.

The present concern for preservation and conservation of environment arises from the hazardous impact on the environment, due to human actions. Human demands are increasing day by day, with the growth of population and modernisation, but the resources are limited. Reckless and regular exploitation of nature resources is causing serious impact on the purity of environment. The spread of many diseases like dengu, viral fevers, like endemic, soil erosion, floods, droughts, earth quakes, urban congestion and threat of extinction of many species of plants, birds and animals, are the visible impact of environment pollution.

It is paradoxical, that the man, who needs the environment most, is destroying its sanctity and purity for present monetary gains, and endangering its own generation. Indiscriminate and unplanned industrialisation has affected the environment to a great extent. It pollutes the air by releasing gases, smoke, fumes and dust. It pollutes the water by discharging wastes in rivers, wetlands. It also causes ruinous effects on the forest. The indiscriminate mining in forest area has ruined many surrounding forests in Alwar, Makrana, Kishangarh, Raj-Samandh, areas of Rajasthan, Dehradun in U.P. and several other places, which has disturbed the eco-balance of the nature seriously. Environmental pollution has become serious health hazards of today.

India has been quick to realise the hazards of environment pollution. The Govt. of India for the first time asserted its concern in the fourth five year plan (1969-74). A department of environment was established at the centre level in 1980, to act as nodal agency for conservation and protection of environment. The successive plans also emphasised the necessity and importance of environmental protection. In 1982, International conference on environmental education was held in New Delhi. Which stressed the need for a massive programme of environmental education, research and monitoring. The conference specifically emphasised that environmental education must start from primary classes. World Charter on Nature, adopted by U.N.General assembly on 28th Oct, 1982, declared that nature shall be respected and its essentials shall not be impaired. Conservation of nature should be a part of all economic plannings. National Environment Advisory Committee was constituted in 1983, to identify and highlight the environmental issues and to advise on measures for the implementation of environment policy, and to organise public debate on national issues of environmental importance. In 1992, the central government made the Environmental Audit compulsory. Industries are now required to submit Environmental Audit Report from the fiscal year 1993.

In our country, the Supreme Court has played very crucial role in preserving the pollution in city area and preserving the forests of our country. The various decision has forced the government to stop mining in forest areas of the country. The Supreme Court has forced the government to adopt strict vehicular emission norms in the principal metropolitan cities. The Apex court has also insisted on the use of preferred technologies-such as CNG for buses and autos, in order to limit the pollution levels that were chocking the key cities. It is good to see that the government has given green signal for the development of Hydrogen fuelled vehicles that have zero pollution capabilities. A High Power Committee has established in June 2003, to draw up a blue print for developing Hydrogen as an alternative fuel in India. The focus of present day policies is to use emission free technologies for preserving and conserving the precious natural environment.

Though government is quite serious to protect the environment now, yet it is the duty of every industrialist, every citizen to understand well the necessity of preserving the nature and purity of environment not only for ourselves but also for our own generation.It is the environment where from we get the first basic requirements for our existence; Air, Water, and we are bent upon to pollute them, isn't it like hitting our own head!

20. Euthanasia : Mercy Killing

"Euthanasia is understood as an action which aims at taking the life of another at the latter's expressed request. It concerns an action of which death is the purpose and the result." This definition applies only to voluntary euthanasia and excludes the non-voluntary or involuntary euthanasia, the killing of a patient without the patient's knowledge or consent. Some call this "life-terminating treatment."

Euthanasia can be either active or passive. Passive euthanasia allows one to die by withholding or withdrawing life supporting means. This is a tricky area because ordinary and extraordinary means of supporting life come into the picture. Ordinary means, such as nutrition and hydration, are never to be withheld since they are one's basic right in order to survive. However, one is not obligated to use extraordinary or 'disproportionate' means to sustain life. Due to complexity, each situation needs to be looked at individually when discussing extraordinary means. However, as a rule, one can discontinue "medical procedures that are burdensome, dangerous, extraordinary, or disproportionate to the expected outcome." One can not intend death by withdrawing or withholding treatment, but should, however, obey God and let one die a natural death. To withdraw a treatment as a condition worsens is letting one die and not a direct killing. In this case, it is the disease that is doing the killing and not the one who withdraws the treatment.

Active euthanasia or 'mercy killing' pertains to the Dr. Kevorkians' of the day. This is the direct intentional killing of a patient with either their consent (voluntary), without their consent when impossible (non-voluntary), or without consent but not sought (involuntary). Advocates of this murder have covered their ears to the command of the Lord: Thou shall not kill! The goal is to eliminate or relieve suffering by an evil means of death. Many patient's are in immense suffering and may be led to choose death as the answer by these 'doctors', friends or relatives. The culpability for the patient, in these cases may be lessened, but, this act of killing can never be justified as a means. These patients, whether having an incurable disease, being elderly, or suffering in other ways, are crying out for help and love. Palliative care, not death, is the answer. Medical personnel, friends and family must reach out and comfort the afflicted. Suffering and pain is manageable, especially today, with so many different medicines and treatments available. Painkillers can be used as long as there is no danger or intention of death. Consciousness of the patient is strongly encouraged, so that if dying, one may prepare to meet God.

We can not do whatever we please to our bodies, since they are not our own. God made us and knows what we need here on earth, so that we, someday, may enter into eternity. If Christ endured immense suffering, then why do we expect any less? We are called to be imitations of Christ and to share in His Passion. Is my life really mine? "If we live, we are responsible to the Lord, and when we die we are responsible to the Lord. Both in life and death we belong to the Lord." God has a plan, and, each human person having an eternal destiny has a dignity. God, being the author of life, alone has the right to create and take life. No human person has this right to take innocent human life, no matter how one tries to justify it. Thou shall not kill is still a command and not a suggestion, as many seem to believe.

There are many reasons why Euthanasia is gravely immoral, some of which, have already been discussed. Suffering has many benefits, especially suffering in the last days of one's life. In addition to sharing in Christ's Passion, one may find peace in God, reconciliation with family and friends, and acceptance of death. One also may be undergoing temporal punishment here on earth through suffering; a sort of 'purgatory on earth'. There are many benefits and advantages to suffering. However, in a pragmatic society as ours, we tend to look past the positives and see only the negative side. This type of reasoning has led many to see death as the answer to suffering, regardless of the consequences.

Euthanasia, whether active or passive, is immoral and contrary to God's law. Within passive euthanasia, what is considered extraordinary means of sustaining life may not always be clear, but ordinary means, such as hydration and nutrition, must be provided. We must look past the suffering in this world and look towards our eternal home with God. As humans we can not always see the answers, and for that reason, it is not we to decide about the death of a human being, God has not given us this authority. We must also ask ourselves concerning euthanasia; Where will it end? If we allow the elderly or incurable to be assisted in suicide, what other groups will be given this 'right'. Will the handicapped or mentally retarded be next? Will teenagers, who are the leading age group of suicide, also have this 'right to die'? The answer rests in our hands as a people. If we continue to disrespect human life and its Creator, God, then we will destroy ourselves. A right is a moral claim and since we do not have a claim on death, which has a claim on us, we have no 'right to die'. Perhaps Mother Teresa was right when she said that "if a mother can kill her own child, what is there to stop you and me from killing each other?" There is no way to stop this culture of death, unless, we get back to God's law and speak out, boldly, against the horrors and injustices of the day!

21. Fright and Hardship of Working Women

"Today there is no sphere of life in which the women have not shown their worth. From holding highest public office in bureaucracy to holding highest political position, the women have shouldered all kinds of responsibilities with grand success. A lot of change has taken place, in the role of women, in the position of women in this man dominated society now. With this gradual transition from household life to working women, the sufferings of women have actually doubled."

With the political emancipation of India, the women of free India ushered into a new role. Today the women enjoy equality of status, equality of opportunity with men. Today there is no sphere of life in which the women have not shown their worth. From holding highest public office in bureaucracy to holding highest political position, the women have shouldered all kinds of responsibilities with grand success. A lot of change has taken place, in the role of women, in the position of women in this man dominated society now. With this gradual transition from household life to working women, the sufferings of women have actually doubled. She became financial independent, she became economically sound, she became the major decision taker, she became the policy makers in various new fields thus she taken one more burden in addition to her household duties. She ventured into outer field, but the traditional views about her role as home maker, about her so called sacred duties of Mother, Sister, Wife, are still kept on demanding on her. The women are divided between her official work and home duties. Her duties start from early in the morning with many responsibilities on her shoulder before going to office, like preparing break fast, lunch, getting kids ready for school etc. During office hours she has to work equally or say more sincerely than her male counterparts. After back from office in stead of hers all fatigue and exhaustions, she has to fulfil her duties at home. Her pathetic position, working at home as well as at office, is not admired, even by her husband or mother in law or father in law. The support and cooperation, if extend by her husband in household work is at his sole desertion. Husband is free to take excuses of over burdened work, pressure of official exigencies, but wife is expected to be found fresh and amiable all the time. The men consider the household work, as sole responsibility of the women. He considers working at home below his dignity and if he does some thing, it is done as per his wish and convenience.

The working atmosphere in the offices particularly for the women is also not so congenial. Most of the male counter part treat the women an easy scape goat for fulfilling their sexual desires. The incident of intentional touching, using double meaning dialogues, making unwarranted comments, piercing in her private affairs are same of the common examples which create lot of irritation and make the women unnecessarily defensive. The incidents of sexual advancement by the boss, staring at her body parts, alluring her with quick promotion in return are generally to be faced by a working woman. With women entering into new fields, she become more vulnerable to the dangers like eve-teasing, sexual advancement of her bosses, transfers, etc. The women can only explain have frights and hardships experienced by her, while working in office.

In the present male dominated, patriarchal society, people find it difficult to accept the women as independent personality. In addition to these hardships, the women are bound to play the traditional role of child bearing and child rearing. She can't desist from her role as a mother, as a wife. So while performing these natural roles, she had to be out of office for a long period, which causes adverse effects on her career, though not openly but in reality. One more peculiar problem, a woman has to face is keeping the children with her, in case her husband in transferred out of town, and she is unable to shift being a working woman, as children prefer to stay with mother. Now she has to play the role of both the parents and her duties are trebled.

It has become irrelevant to talk as on date, that traditional role played by the women, was a better course. The woman of today, has her own personality, more confident, financially independent, accepting any kind of challenge, can no longer remain under the illogical dominance of man, but at the same time suffers mentally and physically divided between home and office.

The situation demands effective measures to protect the career women in her official environment from the lust and greed of male bosses and colleagues. There is an urgent need to make new amendments to provide extra legal teeth to IPC section 292 (Sale of obscene books), section 293 (Sale of obscene objects to young) Section 294 (obscene acts and songs) and to the indecent representation of women (Prohibition) Act 1986 and other laws. Educational serials and programme must be launched to educate the society through audio and visual media, so that the women could feel safe in her office and live, peacefully with dignity. Unless man's attitude towards woman changes, any kind of law however strict and stringent can change the conditions of career women in our society.

Our society had been a male dominated society, the changes are gradually being digested. With necessity of time, absence of joint families, the financial independence of women, are making the male absorb the change slowly but gradually. The actions initiated by the government against the eve-teasing, sexual harassment of career women, have also brought a lot of favourable change in the life of career women. In spite of all the hardships, being faced by the career women, it must be noted that women have fought a great battle and are still fighting at their own against the fright and hardships faced by them and got remarkable success in every field of life.

22. Government Employees 'Rights to Strike'

"India is perhaps a unique country where one witnesses a bandh almost every other day."

A foreign Press reporter.

Our constitution guarantees the basic rights to every citizen of the country in the chapter on Fundamental Right. It is also a virtual fact that fundament rights of people as a whole cannot be subservient to the fundamental rights of a group, or section of the people. There cannot be any right to strike, which interferes in the lives of common people, and also causing huge loss to the national economy.

In a democracy, government employees are part and parcel of the government machinery and so owe duty and responsibility towards the society. Too many strikes and bandhs are very disastrous for the smooth running of government and cause lot of hardships to the common people. In our country everyone is fond of talking of his rights in democracy, but he forgets the fundamental duties enshrines in the same constitution.

From workers point of view, strikes are ultimate weapons, which are only resorted to by them when all other means of struggle and negotiation have been exhausted. Denial of this right would lead to a massive deterioration of the bargaining power of workers, which has already been weakened by various macroeconomic processes such a global integration and the withdrawal of the state from important areas of regulation and provision. In any society, the socio-economic rights of all citizens, including workers, have never really been freely gifted by the state or employers; their recognition and implementation have always been the result of prolonged struggle on the part of workers and other groups.

It is a fact that over the years, under the patronage of politicians or under the banner of political parties, the trade unions or organisations have begun to feel themselves so powerful and perversive that they do not mind neglecting their work, but at the same time will like to demand for more perks and facilities. The frequency with which various trade unions resort to strikes has resulted in a heavy toll on the socio-economic fabric of the country. All the political parties, taking excuse for their vote-banks never resort to take any tough action against such striking employees.

Fortunately the Judiciary has intervened at the right time to underscore this reality. On Aug 6, 2003 the verdict came from the Supreme Court, that ruled that government employees had no fundamental, legal, moral or equitable right to strike work. The Divisional bench of the Supreme Court made the observation while disposing of a writ appeal and petitions challenging the Madras High Court's dismissal of the petitions against the summary dismissal of Government employees in Tamil Nadu under the Tamil Nadu Essential

Services Maintenance Act (TESMA) 2002, as amended by an ordinance on July 4, 2003. Lacs of Government employees and teachers in the State launched an indefinite strike on July 2, 2003. About two lacs of them were dismissed from service on July 4, 2003 under the provisions of TESMA.

The supreme Court Observed that "strikes hold the state to ransom" and "cause heavy loss of Man-days". The Supreme Court also observed that strike was the most misused weapon in the country. The Supreme Court made it quite clear that, the employees have no fundamental right to resort to strike. Quoting the judgement in a case relating to an all India strike by bank employees, the Bench said that the Supreme Court had specially held that even very liberal interpretation of sub clause (c) of clause (i) of Article 19, cannot lead to the conclusion that trade unions have a guaranteed rights to an effective collective bargaining or to strike either as part of collective bargaining or otherwise.

Thus, the Court had not rejected the employees right to form an association. Indeed it made it clear that government employees can have their legitimate grievances addressed through different statutory provisions. In making the arguments the court further observed that the government employees can legitimately enjoy their rights as long as this enjoyment does not endanger the well being of the largest democracy.

In Indian context, when the economy is at verge of taking flight, the trade unions and the labour class must realise that the future of the country depends on "an all out effort to improve the quality of working and raise the standard of living of each and every citizen of this country". Only then the nation can make rapid progress. The government should also create an impartial machinery to redress the genuine grievances of its employees. The service rules should be unambiguous and transparent. Nepotism and corruption should not have any place in recruitment, transfer and promotional matters of employees.

It is the duty of both employees and the employer to avoid the conflicts and try to sort out the things with open mind, keeping in view the good and welfare of the society and the nation as a whole.

23. Human Cloning : A Dangerous Invention

Cloning is an advance technological invention for producing a genetic twin of a living thing, an organism that starts life with the same genes as its parents. In mammals, DNA is taken from an adult animal and then it is inserted into an egg cell from another animal. This egg then divides into an embryo. The embryo is then transplanted into a surrogate mother and grown to term. This process has worked in animals like cows, sheep, goats, mice, pigs, while such attempts could not succeed in rabbits, rat, cat, dog, monkey and horse.

In 1997, researchers at Scotland's Rosline Institute, led by embryologist Ian Wilmat reported that they had successfully cloned a sheep-named Dolly, from the cell of an adult ewe. In 1998, scientists at the University of Hawaii, cloned a mouse, creating not only dozens of copies, but three generations of cloned clones. In the same year two research teams succeeded in growing embryonic stem cells.

In November 2001, the scientists were able to clone the first human embryo. From pure scientific analysis, it was unprecedented mile stone in the field of genetic engineering technology, but the news created a fetter among the moralists, governments. US president Mr. George W. Bush condemned human cloning as "morally wrong" "We should not as a society grow life to destroy it," said the President "The use of embryos to clone is wrong".

Many US states, including California, have banned cloning and congress is also considering to impose such a ban. The company Advanced Cell Technology (ACT) in Worcester Massachusetts USA, which claimed to clone the first human embryo, said, "This corporation(ACT) is creating human embryos for the sole purpose of killing them and harvesting their cells". This announcement of ACT, provoked angry reactions across Italy and inside the Vatican. Mr Girolamo Sirchia, the Italian

Health Minister, described human cloning as a crime against humanity. The Vatican Archbishop said that the church opposes any form of human conception that was not born from an act of love between husband and wife.

Scientists at ACT said that the experiments were aimed at aiding stems cells research to treat a wide range of diseases providing hope for people with spinal injuries, heart diseases, and other ailments, according to Dr. Robert P. Langa one of the scientists at ACT, this latest experiment "sets the pace for human therapeutic cloning as a potentially limitless source of immune compatible cells for tissue engineering and transplantation medicine." When stem cell research could be so beneficial in curing various diseases in human being, then why human cloning is being condemned. The crux of the matter is human cloning shall not be stopped at stem cell research; its potential for gross abuse will make it a virtual Frankenstein.

The opponents of human cloning say that an embryo at any stage of development is a human life, worthy of protection, and any kind of research that entails destroying an embryo is immoral, unethical, no matter, how worthy the intent is. It involves using human being as means, it turns human life into a commodity and fosters a culture of dehumanization. Another group of anti moralists find, such making of fuss against cloning is unreasonable and illogical they ask point blank, why do we permit abortion ? We permit in vitrofertilisation which creates nine or ten embryos, of which all but one will be destroyed. Worse things are happening is our country where lacs of female foetuses are destroyed by parents, eager to have a male child, with the connivance of doctors.

The scientists have now started talking of designer babies, which make it theoretically possible to genetically engineer our children, with added height or intelligence and removing defective genes or disabilities such as crystic fibrosis or alcoholism. The advocates of human cloning gave number of arguments as to how cloning could take modern society forward, it could prove a panacea for several diseases.

Every such invention have merits and demerits. Human cloning could be misused to destroy the existing humanity and civilisation. We have seen the proliferation of weapons of mass destruction and the spectrum of germs and chemical warfare. Scientists, philosophers, thinkers, philanthropists from all over the world spoke out against human cloning, prompted by fears that the world has taken a step further towards nightmare of humans replicated in the lab. The human cloning can tear the society to pieces, it can endangers the very existence of human being in this world.

24. Human Right Violations

"It is the obligation of the State to ensure everyone has the right to adequate food, education and enjoyment of highest attainable standards of physical and mental health. These rights have to be respected and made available to the citizens by the State"

Justice Anand Chairperson Human Rights Commission

Human rights violation have become very common now a days. The Newspapers and T.V. tell us that every day and at every moment, somewhere in the world, Human Right are being violated. Broadly speaking 'Human Right' means right to life, liberty, equality and the dignity of an individual irrespective of caste, creed or sex. These human right are natural right, required to be protected for the peaceful existence of a person. Our constitution safeguards the human rights, but inspite of all provisions in law, the violation of these right is very frequent. The protection and preservation of Human Rights has become a great challenge to every country in the world. Cases of violence, murder, torture, rape, child abuse, death due to starvation, death due to dowry, sexual harassment, custodial death have become rampant in the society.

The National Human Rights Commission (NHRC) has been able touch the tip of iceberg of the problem of Human Rights violation. But NHRC can't be blamed, when the entire society is culpable in respect of Human Rights violations in one way or the other. It is not possible to keep vigil on every human being in any country.

The Chairperson of the National Human Rights Commission, Dr. Justice A.S. Anand has emphasized that it is the obligation of the State to ensure everyone has the right to adequate food, education and enjoyment of highest attainable standards of physical and mental health. These rights have to be respected and made available to the citizens by the State, said Justice Anand while inaugurating the two-day Capacity Building Workshop on "Economic, Social and Cultural Rights" jointly organized by the National Human Rights Commission and the Indian Institute of Public Administration.

Under the International Covenant on economic, social and cultural rights a State party is obliged to use all steps to achieve progressively full realization of the rights recognized in the covenant, Justice Anand said, these include adoption of legislative means, which are to be exercised on a non-discriminatory basis.

India being a signatory to Universal Declaration of Human Rights, International Covenant on Economic, Social and Cultural Rights and other international instruments, is legally as well as morally committed to ensure basic human rights to all its citizens and enact laws accordingly, he said.

With every passing year, conviction has grown in the Commission that for right to live with human dignity, it is essential to focus in equal measures on economic, social and cultural rights and civil and political rights. The indivisibility and interrelated nature of both these rights is a reality and there is a symbiosis between them. Those in the field must, therefore, ensure that the concern and anxiety, which they show for political and social rights, are also manifested in economic, social and cultural rights, he said.

The abject poverty prevailed in the country, denies basic Human Rights to millions of poor in our country. Poverty is the natural cause of various Human Rights violations. Child labour, bonded labour, Illiteracy, are various forms of Human Rights violation. The Human Rights of women are violated from birth to death. Even the rights of girl to born is taken away by Sex determination tests, with termination of girl foetus. Girl infanticide is common in certain parts of the country even as on date. Sexual abuse of female children, dowry deaths, flourishing flesh trade, rape cases, pitiable conditions of widows living in Vrindawan and Varanasi are some flagrant examples of violations of the Rights of the fair sex. Ours is a male dominated society, where women are being treated as their subordinates. Most of the women in real terms, do not enjoy any rights at all, they are just living first as per wish of their parents, and after marriage as per whims of their husband and in the old age, as per convenience of their sons and daughters in-law.

The NHRC, has tried to check the human rights violations in wide range of spheres. The commission has asked the States and Union Territories in April 2000, to compulsorily video film the post-mortem examination in all cases of custodial deaths. The NHRC also taken up the cases of victimised women in all perspective. It has also recommended that the maintenance allowance for divorced women be increased to Rs.5000 per month, from the existing Rs.500 per month. Cases of violation of children's right, like trafficking in children, imprisonment of juveniles, child marriage, have also taken up by the NHRC. NHRC also taken up cases of rape, death and detention of undertrials without trials, vehemently. Recently the NHRC has taken up the case of Best Bakery in Gujrat and moved an application to Supreme Court. The Apex court heard the matter and found that the State carried out the investigation and prosecution in a manner which ruled out conviction.

The Chairperson of the National Human Rights Commission, Dr. Justice A.S. Anand stressed the need for making human rights the focal point of good governance. He called for greater role for National Human Rights Commissions in the work of United Nations, its treaty bodies and specialized agencies, stressing the need to further develop cooperation between them.

He made these observations while delivering a Statement to the 60th Session of the Commission on Human Rights at Geneva on 14th April 2004.

He emphasized that the protection of human rights not only requires vigilance by various agencies but also sustained cooperation at regional and international levels.

No commission or no police station can police every nook and corner of the country. No NGO, no any other agency can be present every where to protect the Human Rights. It is the we people, it is the duty of every civilised person to rise to the occasion. This can be brought about only through general awakening, which make everyone understand the eternal values of life and dignity of an individual irrespective of caste, creed or sex. In the word of Swami Vivekanand that the "Self in you is the Self everywhere."

25. Menace of Drug Addiction

The problem of Drug addiction has gradually been taken an alarming proportions. Today there are more than 1,00,600 drug addicts in Bombay alone. Five of them die each day owing to repeated intake of lethal drugs. The parents of nearly all young addicts never imagined that their sons or daughters could fall victims to this dangerous vice. We all thought that drug addiction was an evil of the West. It is here now-right in our midst.

Drug addiction is a very complicated and complex illness. It is characterized by compulsive, at times uncontrollable drug craving, seeking and use that persist even in the face of extremely negative consequences. For many people, drug addiction becomes chronic, with relapses possible even after long periods of abstinence.

The path to drug addiction begins with the act of taking drugs. Over time, a person's ability to choose not to take drugs can be compromised. Drug seeking becomes compulsive, in large part as a result of the effects of prolonged drug use on brain functioning and, thus, on behavior.

Various reasons are assigned for the drug addiction :

1. Emotional, Insecurity, Lack of Love : Lack of parental love at home, impaired and tense relationships between parents and dictatorial handling of children have been traced out as significant root causes.
2. Misuse of Money-Lack of Guidance : Easy availability of and access to money lead to habits such as cigarette-smoking the first step to drug addiction. The next stage, hash-smoking sets in easily. The 'culture mix' you belong to, will make you try more and more 'harmless' experiments. Proper guidance is required.
3. Curiosity of Experimentation is the most common cause.
   Just to taste as to how it tastes many times leads the beginning.
4. Peer Pressure : The pressures of Bosses or other friends just for the sake of company also leads the beginning.

Most drug addicts are male, but there are several girls hooked on the drug too. Most girls on the drug are persuaded by their boy friends to try it. Few try it out of frustration. The ratio is 1:25.

Drug addiction or the compulsion to use drugs can take over the individual's life. Addiction often involves not only compulsive drug taking but also a wide range of dysfunctional behaviors that can interfere with normal functioning in the family, the workplace, and the broader community. Addiction also can place people at increased risk for a wide variety of other illnesses. These illnesses can be brought on by behaviors, such as poor living and health habits, that often accompany life as an addict, or because of toxic effects of the drugs themselves.

Because addiction has so many dimensions and disrupts so many aspects of an individual's life, treatment for this illness is never simple. Three decades of scientific research and clinical practice have yielded a variety of effective approaches to drug addiction treatment. Extensive data document that drug addiction treatment is as effective as are treatments for most other similarly chronic medical conditions. In spite of scientific evidence that establishes the effectiveness of drug abuse treatment, many people believe that treatment is ineffective. In part, this is because of unrealistic expectations. Many people equate addiction with simply using drugs and therefore expect that addiction should be cured quickly, and if it is not, treatment is a failure. In reality, because addiction is a chronic disorder, the ultimate goal of long-term abstinence often requires sustained and repeated treatment episodes.

A variety of scientifically based approaches to drug addiction treatment exists. Drug addiction treatment can include behavioral therapy (such as counseling, cognitive therapy, or psychotherapy), medications, or their combination. Behavioral therapies offer people strategies for coping with their drug cravings, teach them ways to avoid drugs and prevent relapse, and help them deal with relapse if it occurs. When a person's drug-related behavior places him or her at higher risk for AIDS or other infectious diseases, behavioral therapies can help to reduce the risk of disease transmission. Case management and referral to other medical, psychological, and social services are crucial components of treatment for many patients. The best programs provide a combination of therapies and other services to meet the needs of the individual patient, which are shaped by such issues as age, race, culture, sexual orientation, gender, pregnancy, parenting, housing, and employment, as well as physical and sexual abuse.

Nearly all addicted individuals believe in the beginning that they can stop using drugs on their own, and most try to stop without treatment. However, most of these attempts result in failure to achieve long-term abstinence. Research has shown that long-term drug use results in significant changes in brain function that persist long after the individual stops using drugs. These drug-induced changes in brain function may have many behavioral consequences, including the compulsion to use drugs despite adverse consequences in the defining characteristic of addiction.

The criminal justice system refers drug offenders into treatment through a variety of mechanisms, such as diverting nonviolent offenders to treatment, stipulating treatment as a condition of probation or pretrial release, and convening specialized courts that handle cases for offenses involving drugs. Drug courts, another model, are dedicated to drug offender cases. They mandate and arrange for treatment as an alternative to incarceration, actively monitor progress in treatment, and arrange for other services to drug-involved offenders.

The most effective models integrate criminal justice and drug treatment systems and services. Treatment and criminal justice personnel work together on plans and implementation of screening, placement, testing, monitoring, and supervision, as well as on the systematic use of sanctions and rewards for drug abusers in the criminal justice system. Treatment for incarcerated drug abusers must include continuing care, monitoring, and supervision after release and during parole.

Family and friends can play very crucial role in motivating individuals with drug problems to enter and stay in treatment. Family therapy is important, especially for adolescents. Involvement of a family member in an individual's treatment program can strengthen and extend the benefits of the program.

More than ever before, India's future depends on the strength and dynamism of its youth. In a fast-changing world accelerated by new advances in electronic technology only a dynamic exuberant generation can put India on a strong footing. A strong religious base combined with strong family ties and high morals can help wrench out this evil from our society. Both, preventive and Rehabilitation procedures depend strongly on these factors. Save youth from drugs, save India.

26. Politics without Ethics

'On 15th August 1947, when India after centuries of foreign domination, started breathing fresh air of freedom, none would have thought then that this very fresh air would turn foul and with the passes of time get so much contaminated that it would poison the whole of the country's democratic set up and the persons to whom the responsibility of governing the country be given, would be the fountain head of such poisonous contaminated air'.

The present day politicians, the leaders governing the country, are obsessed with the monomania to loot the country and fill their own coffers, could be seen fighting for the bone like the snarling stray dogs on the street. Power by hook or by crook in their only motto, and this power leads to conspiracy, murder, forging a network of like minded politicians and bureaucrats and mafias. Nowadays politics has become such a lucrative profession, wherein prior investment of money and muscle power to grab the chair once, is sufficient to feed the several generations and gives one the status and respectful position in society. Which another profession could be so rewarding ? Politicians of today are very much willing to liaise with any political party or group so long it serves their interest. The trading and defection among the political parties have become a very common thing. See the recent case of Mr. Jogi, Ex Chief Minister of Chhattisgarh caught red handed with audio tapes, alluring the MLA's of BJP to join his party. Number of scam cases are pending before the courts, relating to misappropriation, frauds, corruptions, in which the present day politicians are shamelessly involved. The definition of corruption has since modified by these politicians, tearing the every fabric of morality and ethics. Now unless the final court decides a politician as corrupt, he is corrupt, otherwise he is more honest than an individual, even after jailed for months, on corruption charges.

Talking of ethics, in terms of politicians, is the most traumatic joke of the day. In every big scandal, whether, Telgi Stamp Case, Jain Dairy Case, Bank Security Scam, Tehelka Case, Hawala Case, Fodder Scam, we find wires connected to some powerful politicians. When the office of Prime Minister during Rao regime, was in question, what can be talked of lower rank politicians ? Many politicians has reached the nadir of immorality, when as a last ditch effort to grab power, they resort to booth capturing and rigging with the help of criminals and dreaded gangsters. Many politicians are winning the elections, just because they wield huge muscle power and openly threaten the common people either to vote for them or get ready to be wiped out.

Impact of Unethical Politicians on the Common People

A leader in office, has the authority to direct the course of the nation's socio-economical development. He enjoys the power to make policies for the developmental activities to be initiated at macro level. His decisions have far reaching effect in the developmental process of the country. But he himself become corrupt, spells unethical and immoral acts, it can wreck havoc on the country. The ills of communalism, casteism, nepotism has gradually become the necessity of political arena. Nine five year plans, have since been completed, and tenth five year plan is on the anvil yet the development is not up to the mark. Rightly observed by Sh. Rajeev Gandhi, the then Prime Minister, that out of 100 only 17% is actually spent on developmental work, and the rest goes into the pockets of officials & politicians. Today our country could not progress so rapidly, our country has acquired many, ills, like corruption, communalism, casteism, all because the leaders have forgotten their moral and ethical duties towards the Mother Land and have but one motto, to grab the power and earn money, by hook or by crook.

People have lost their faith in the leaders. The youth are disillusioned, they are going to west for higher education for being settle there permanently. Voters have also become increasingly indifferent towards the process of election. They have to choose between the corrupt and the more corrupt and so the turnout is very thin in recent elections. The situation is undoubtedly very grave. Everyone seems frustrated, unhappy, find none who can improve the things.

It is not appropriate to blame the politicians alone. It is the public, that is responsible to a great extent, in making the politicians; corrupt, unethical, goons. If the people use their right of vote in favour of a gentleman, in favour of an honest leaders, and devote some time to make him, winner, an example be set and the corrupt and goons would have to think twice to fight election, but it is not the case.

It is not to conclude that all the politicians, all our leaders are corrupt, unethical. The hope lies with only such honest, dedicated and devoted politicians, who have sacrificed a lot for the welfare of this nation. It is high time that we enforce a code of conduct to stem the rot and this exercise must begin right now. A transparency in the working is very urgently needed. Responsible opposition, the media, can play very important role in exposing the unethical and immoral corrupt practices. The people are also becoming aware that unless they will use their right to vote in favour of a better leader, the future of the nation is dark, and they themselves have to suffer because of their own wrong judgement. Let us hope, the people of the country will use their vote in this Lok Sabha elections, in favour of dedicated, sincere and honest leaders for the good of themselves and for the welfare of this great grand nation.

27. Proper Infrastructure Necessary for Growth

Proper infrastructure is the base for rapid development of an economy. The development of infrastructure is calling for expansion, technological modernisation, scientifical tuning.

Our country needs good roads, better transport facilities, better railway facilities, reliable air travel, more telecommunication linkage, better facilities at ports, better and sufficient power supply, planned urbanisation, housing and particularly in respect to rural area, basic infrastructure of road, power supply, education, water etc.

Indian, now a country of one billion people, out of which 70% people live in rural area. It is strange that even after fifty six years of independence, the shape and form of the rural sector have not changed prospectively. Lot many problems of metro cities is the result of lack of infrastructural facilities, job opportunities in rural area. The increasing number of slum areas in metros is the result of no facilities, no job opportunities, no development in our rural sector. Despite progress made by the country in various fields like communication, manufacturing, industrial segment, space technology, information technology, the rural sector has not made any significant progress. The planning has since been oriented towards the development of infrastructure in cities industrial areas, and so the rural segment remain far behind in growth parameters.

Things are not so pessimistic and bleak. Slowly and steadily improvements are taking place. Infrastructure facilities are being developed. The newly laid down expressway between Mumbai and Pune that has reduced the travelling time from seven hours to just two & a half hour. We are proud of the sleek and modern international airport at Nedumbassery near Kochi. The various flyovers being constructed in Delhi will positively reduce the problem of transportation in the metro.

Indian Economy has significantly grown in the recent years. Both social and economic indicators have reflected their respective positive impact for the development of the Economy. In the Social sector the best example today is 108 million children attend primary schools in India by making the country's education system the second largest in the world after China. In the economic sector Gross Domestic Product (GDP) in nominal terms of US$692 billion in 2004, has made the country the world's tenth largest economy. Real GDP grew by 6.9 percent in 2004/05 compared to 8.5 percent a year earlier. Prospects for real GDP growth for 2005-06 is 6.5 to 7 percent. External position of the economy is becoming significantly stronger. Exports have grown, especially exports of services, which grew by 105 percent in 2004-05. Growth in services has largely been fueled by the information technology boom in which India is emerging as a world leader.

India needs new airports for Navi Mumbai, Bangalore, Hyderabad, Chennai and others. Economic viability and feasibility reports have since finalised. Government is considering to start the work in joint venture. As regards power India needs around 31000 mw of power under greenfield projects upto 2007. India would require Rs. 800,000 crore investment for adding another 100,000 MW of power capacity over the next years, out of which government expects Rs. 80,000 crores from the private sector or Foreign Direct Investments (FDI). Indian railway too is suffering from poor infrastructure and shortage of coaches etc. The Rakesh Mohan committee report pointed out "If the railway is to survive as an ongoing transportation organisation it has to modernise and expand its capacity to serve the emerging needs of the economy.

The approach to the 10th plan considers the decline of railways revenue from the transportation is because of some policy distortions, like overcharging freights, in order to subsidise ordinary passenger fair. Moreover the investment strategy of railways put more emphasis on opening new lines for passenger traffics and no care to tap the area which have potential of commercial traffic. The decisions are based on political needs. The commercial angle is given second thought. This resulted into alarming deterioration in the financial condition of the railway and so unable to undertake investments to improve railway transport services.

Development of infrastructure is the basic requirement for the rapid growth of the Indian economy. The present government has taken care to provide road communication in the vast countryside. Under personal Hygiene, cleanliness of the home and environmental sanitation all hinges on personal attitude awareness, education and economic status of the families. The concept of sanitation was expanded in 1993 to include the personal hygiene, home sanitation, safe water, garbage and excreta and waste water disposal. The programme was further restructured from April 1999, and greater emphasis has now laid on community involvement under what is called total sanitation campaign.

A comprehensive self employment programme entitled Swaran Jayanti Gram Swarojagar Yojana was launched on April 1, 1999, with an aim to develop large number of micro-enterprises for individuals or groups or self help groups.

Despite all the rural development programmes, rural India is in a malign state. The most challenging task is to check the misappropriation of funds meant for the rural development. With corruption becoming an integral part of governance from panchayat level upwards, the real impact of different schemes for the development of rural segment is not insight. A nexus between 'Babus' politicians, contractors, take away more than 60% of the funds meant for the development.

Had the funds meant to develop the rural segment would have been utilised for the actual cause, the growth of Indian economy might have reflected a more flourishing state. The efforts put by the government for the development of infrastructure in rural area are required to be strengthen further. Without proper infrastructure, the pace of growth of Indian economy can't be accelerated.

Infrastructure does not mean just the development of roads, raid, and air traffic or power etc. It will be folly to ignore any single component in either economic o. social infrastructure. They are complementary in nature. The development of infrastructure involves not only the government agencies, but also the private sector, the NGO's and the heartily involvement of the people at large. Without foundation of necessary infrastructure, how can we think of building an edifice of economic growth ?

28. Women's Reservation : A Forlorn Hope

"An International Labour Organisation study shows that "while women represent 50 percent of the world adult population and a third of the official labour force, they perform nearly two-third of all working hours, receive a tenth of world income and own less than one percent of world property." Therefore, reservation for women is not a bounty but only an honest recognition of their contribution to social development".

Every political party for the last many years has been assuring its support to the Bill which disarms women activists. And then a farce rather than a tragedy is played out by so-called radical politicians, jumping into the well of the House, tearing copies of the Bill and making impossible for proceedings to continue - the House gets adjourned, the Bill is thrown into the dustbin till it is revived in subsequent years with the same result. It is time this mockery stopped, considering that the Congress, the BJP and Left parties proclaim that they are for the Bill in the present form, and really want it to become a law.

The Women's Reservation Bill (WRB) providing 33% reservation for women in the Lok Sabha and state legislatures has been a non-starter through seven Lok Sabhas, from 1996 onwards. Successive governments have placed it on the floor of the house, only to have it shelved.A hasty retreat is no solution. The bill is now firmly on the national political agenda and political parties know that sooner or later, something will have to be done. It is for this reason that proposals and counter-proposals are being suggested by our political leaders to show that at least publicly they are not hostile to the bill.

It is difficult for the existing bill to be passed since the majority of male MPs believe that introducing 33% reservations will, along with reservations for scheduled castes and tribes, make 50% of seats unavailable to them. Which body of men will give up their seats to allow women to take over? As one MP from the Telugu Desam said, "Why should we agree to sign our own death warrant?" Patil's suggestion, made at a recent meet called by the Lok Sabha speaker Manohar Joshi to arrive at a consensus on this subject, has received the support of the BJP top brass. Vijay Kumar Malhotra, BJP MP, echoing the view of his party, also believes "the suggestion needs to be studied seriously since there is no harm in increasing the number of seats in Parliament".

The Election Commission had also put up a proposal making it mandatory for political parties to nominate 33% women candidates with a state as a unit for the Lok Sabha and the district as a unit for the state assemblies. This would mean that in a state where there are 40 Lok Sabha seats, the party would have to nominate at least 13 women candidates, and in the state assembly elections, it would have to nominate one-third women candidates at the district level. The Election Commission's suggestion has the advantage that it does not bear the 'quota' tag. Nor will they be faced with the problem of rotation of constituencies. Politicians however are not very receptive to the Election Commission's suggestion either. The Shiv Sena is opposed to it and Mulayam Singh Yadav is not willing to concede more than 20% seats for women. He has argued time and again that reservations will only favour elite, English-speaking women and will not empower backward or low-caste women, especially since the majority are present in Parliament by virtue of family connections forged either by birth or by marriage.

Even IK Gujaral had moved a private member's bill in 1995, making it compulsory for parties to nominate women on the basis of their strength in Parliament. The CPI (M) has issued a statement saying that it will support the women's bill in its present form and is not open to alternative suggestions. This is the stand that has been taken by the women's organisations which have spearheaded the whole movement to ensure greater representation of women in parliament. As Mohini Giri, former chairperson of the National Commission for Women said, "We do not want any more discussions on the bill".

While the struggle for women's empowerment goes on, one must however not forget that though numbers and percentages are important, it is ultimately numbers coupled with the correct world-view that can go a long way to strengthen the movement for women's liberation. Hence, it is finally the struggle of the working class and the toiling women that must benefit from women's quota. For the women who have made history without portfolios and reserved seats, where women would be the contestants would expose better, the politics of 'by women, of women, for women'.

It is to be realised by the Indian politicians that they can no longer ignore the justified demand of reservation for the women in Parliament and State Ligislature. Till the parliament is dominated by such MPs and lack of 'will' of determination with ruling party and no support form the other parties the 33% reservation for the women will remain a 'Forlorn Hope'.

29. Can the Corruption Be Eradicated from Our Society ?

'With materialistic values at the toppest priority, moral and ethical values at lowest span of ladder, every fibre of society indulged in self aggrandisement, where in not only the credibility of politicians and bureaucrats but also of the judicial officers are at stake, it is very difficult and ridiculous to dream of a corruption free society'.

In present spectrum, an honest man, is like a drop in the ocean, which loses its identity, as soon as mingles virtually in the salt water of ocean, Corruption has become, a common practices, a way of life.

It is a matter of shame, that even after 56 years of independence, India figures among the first thirty most corrupt countries. The Virus of corruption has crept into all walks of life and it can endanger the body politic of our nation.

Corruption always existed in human society in one form or other. In primitive period, the scope of public administration was minimum, as a result the scope of corruption was also limited. After independence, with the concept of welfare state coming into existence, the scope of being corrupt widened. At the juncture of

Independence a statesman like C. Rajagopalachari called the PWD (Public Works Department) as the first enemy of the country in terms of the prevailed corruption in that department. Today every department has become a Public Works Department. Today the corruption has crept into every fabric of society in such a way that it was the theme of speeches made by the President, the Prime Minister, the Speaker of Lok Sabha, during the Golden Jubilee celebrations of our independence. Every Chief Election Commissioner since Mr. Sheshan hold the office, has advocated the dire necessity of electoral reforms to strike at the root of corruption. When the highest placed leaders, and bureaucrats join the bandwagon of corruption, who is there to watch the interests of the common people.

Causes of Corruption

A peculiar face of corruption in our Country is that it goes upstream not down stream and so most of the fundamental policies and decisions about big purchases, contracts, projects etc. are distorted at the top level.

The delay in disposing of the cases of corruption, is one of the important causes of flourishing of corruption. Corrupt officials even if caught can manage to go scot free, in due course of time by manipulations and otherwise.

Possessing of vast discretionary powers by the political leaders, bureaucrats is also one of the important reasons of being corrupt. Discretionary powers in appointments, nominations to various bodies, allotment of Petrol Pumps, and other agencies resulted into favouring the kith or kin and because of other self interest.

Huge election expenses necessarily incurred by the vested interests, whether by the private companies or by the private people to be later on gained with the aid and assistance of such political leaders, who now enjoy the chair, because of their investing the money, is a fundamental reason of politicians being corrupt. Politics has become such a lucrative business, that once you occupy the chair by hook or by crook, you become rich for ever, with many perks and facilities through out the life.

One more reason can be advanced to the existence of corruption, is the present inflationary trend, which make an employee difficult to maintain his family. He finds corruption an attractive preposition.

The taxation system, takes away the thirty percent of income of an individual, which renders the person in such hapless state that he can't live happily, if does not fulfill his needs by other means.

The foremost reason of flourishing of corruption is, the virtual change in the thinking of the people, a total disregard to the moral and ethical values, making the self aggrandisement the sole reason of all activities. Attaining the things, by any means, whether wrong or right, has encouraged most of the generation to adopt easy preposition of corruption.

Preposition of Corruption

The basic question is—can the corruption be eradicated? "Nothing is impossible", can be said by an enthusiastic social leader but, eradication of corruption is next to impossible thing in the present spectrum of affairs. When whole of the body politic is effected by the virus of corruption, then to eradicate it in toto, is a Herculean task. Corruption is a multifaceted, hydraheaded colossus problem, required to be dealt with several measures simultaneously.

(1) Full transparency, in official dealings be adopted.

(2) Discretion, be minimised at the barest possible level. Whenever discretion is used, should be based on reasoning and reasons must be recorded in writing. Unreasonable use of discretion could be reversed back, such provisions should be included in the system.

(3) Judiciary system to try the cases of corruption must be accelerated and it should be time bound. Whatever expenses needed to establish separate courts for the trial of the cases of corruption, must be incurred and it must be given top most priority in future planning. The loss incurred by the nation due to corruption is much more than the expenses required in establishing such courts. Appeal in such cases, should be discouraged, if allowed in some cases, then the appeal must also be given toppest priority for disposal. The penally imposed under IPC must be suitably enhanced, in order to check the corruption in social life.

The bodies like CVC, CBI, Lok Ayukta, etc. must be headed by the persons of high integrity and must be made autonomous truly. The budgetary allocation to these bodies should be liberal and no hinderance of any kind be allowed in their functioning.

Elections Expenses must not be allowed to crossed the limits. The loopholes like making expenses by other persons are not included in party expenses must be plugged. The political parties have to be sincere and honest to fight the cancer of corruption. The chief hurdle is the unwillingness and lack of determination of politicians to eradicate the corruption. All the policies, rules and regulations are framed by the leaders, they do not wish to chain themselves by making laws so stringent and fool proof, so that they themselves are entangled. So the eradication of corruption is not seems possible.

The people and the society can play very important role in fighting the gigantic animal of corruption. The general awakening can make the politicians and bureaucrats to use their discretion fairly. The common men must cast their votes, not on the basis of caste or creed or party, but on the basis of values and character of the candidates. In a democracy the actual power lies with the voters. The politicians, use their caste affiliations, religion, to woo the innocent voters in their favour. The common must use their vote wisely in favour of the honest and dedicated candidate.To eradicate the corruption from the society all have to fight it, it is the most powerful, most dangerous monstrous evil, which doubles and troubles itself with the passes of time.

30. Caste Politics in Elections

'Caste has polarised the national politics and caste politics breed caste parties. Not a single party, however avowedly opposes casteism, is free from the dominant influence of caste. During election time, when the question of number games becomes most important, candidates seek to mobilise the support of not only their own caste members but also those belonging to backward caste and the Dalits.'

Caste is a gift of centuries of history whose origin goes back to 3 or 4 millennia in. It goes back to a past when like all other humans, the tribal Aryans roamed the plains of Central Asia before reaching India.

Castes always differentiate themselves from other castes on multiple fronts : on how they get married, how they conduct their funeral ceremonies, the cuisines they cook and prefer, and even on the basis of gods that they each castes considers to be special to its members. Each caste has a clear idea of which caste it considers to be below it and which ones roughly equal. Endogamy, or marrying within one's jati, is a strict rule that all castes hold dear. It is not at all true that poorer castes are less punctilious in observing their caste norms. Each caste inspires its own variety of caste patriotism for which reason jati puranas, or origin tales, are such an important aspect of their cultural legacy and heritage. All dominated castes explain their subjugation, not on the basis of purity and pollution, but on the basis of lost wars, chicanery and deceit by kinsmen and fair weather friends. Sometimes the Gods too are blamed for being fickle, inconstant and temperamental in bestowing their favours. The distinguishing characteristic of the caste order is the discrete character of its constituent units that resist being forced into a single hierarchical frame. As these castes are discrete and semaphore their separation on multiple fronts, caste competition is built in at various levels. It is only by accepting the reality of multiple hierarchies that we can conceptually make room for the existence of caste politics. If one were to go by the traditional understanding of a single hierarchy of purity/pollution, with brahmans at the top, then any evidence of caste conflict should have meant the dissolution of the caste order.

It is not true that caste politics is a recent phenomenon. All through traditional and medieval India castes have fought and slaughtered each other to gain worldly preeminence. The difference between traditional and modern displays of caste politics is not that there were no power struggles between communities in the past, but that the format for such competition and strife has now changed.

Democracy and commerce have created new avenues that were not available to caste antagonists even in early colonial India.

If one is to understand caste politics in its vivacity and depth it is necessary to appreciate that in the caste situation there are multiple nodes. Jats are against Gujars, together they are against urban castes; Kolis are against Patidars; Thevars oppress Pallars or the Devendrakula vellalas; the Vanniyars torment Adi dravidas, even as many of them may be against, or for, Brahmans in their local settings.

Caste alliances such as the KHAM (Kshatriya, Harijan and Muslim) and AJGAR (Ahir, Jat, Gujar and Rajput) are made and then cast aside. Consequently, caste politics would be imbued with a logic quite different from what obtains in racist politics. It is because many members of India's literati did not quite appreciate this and, perhaps unconsciously, applied the race model to caste politics that they let the Mandal recommendations pass without too much opposition.

In the view of these pro-Mandalites, caste politics in India is really between powerful brahmans and the oppressed rest, just as in race politics it is whites versus blacks. In fact, brahmans do not always occupy the top spot in most hierarchies. And whenever brahmans hold such a position it is because they have economic and political power to match. But this would still be a very small and a typical part of the entire caste and politics scenario. If caste politics is seen only in terms of superior brahman versus the suffering rest then the atrocities that yadavas inflict on ex-untouchables, what thevars do to pallars, and what rajputs did to the jats, would be unnoticed and brushed aside. This would impoverish and distort our understanding of caste politics in India and would allow for the intellectual acceptance of dangerous and retrograde policies such as those recommended by the Mandal Commission.

The casteism has penetrated in Indian Politics so deeply, as to shape and reshape not only the political parties, but also, their manifestos for the elections. The various caste groups, like Nair, the Christian and Ezhava in Kerala, the Brahmin and non-Brahmin in Tamil Nadu, the Khamma and Reddy in Andhra, the Vokkaliga and Lingayats in Karnataka, the Maratha and Mahar in Maharashtra, the Patidar and the Rajput in Gujrat, the Jat, Rajput, Meena, Brahmin and Vaisya in Rajasthan, formed likewise in all states and determine the political scenario in the states to a great extent.

In Bihar there is a communal triangle formed by the Bhumihara, the Rajput and the Kayastha. Caste politics in U.P varies from region to region. The Thakurs from the majority community nurture strong anti Brahmin feelings. Not only the group among the caste, a strong lobby of Dalits and Non-Dalits are further exists nowadays with the active support of their so-called Dalit leaders, making propaganda, against so called Manuwadis or other Castes.

Caste has polarised the national politics and caste politics breed caste parties. Not a single party, however avowedly oppose casteism, is free from the dominant influence of caste. Even the National parties, whether Congress or BJP while allocating tickets to the candidates, allocating portfolios to the Ministers, a proper analysis of caste factor is done. Caste tends to determine electoral nominations, voting behaviour now a days. Numerous castes has started making numerous demands, whether for reservation, or categories them in OBCs etc, vitiating the representative principles envisaged and emphasised under the democratic pattern of our country.

Every Government oriented its policies on caste on caste lines, as it was found most convenient and politically expedient keeping the caste factor in view, not only while forming ministeries, but also while deciding the placement of individual members in Government organizations and institutions.

Caste, which has a past of three thousand years in our country, can't be abolished altogether. The future of democracy and the system of parties in this country depends upon the willingness of the society to change according to the demands of democracy. Illiteracy among the backward castes, poverty among the downtrodden, lack of awakening among the rural folk are some of the factors responsible for the prevalence of casteism in elections. The so-called Dalit leaders or caste Headmen are encashing the votes of their fellow caste members as per their vested interests.

Political parties have an enormous role to play in the social awakening of India on democratic pattern. Instead of being influenced by caste and their current interests, they must endeavour to educate the people as per the ethics and demand of democracy and organise public opinion to regularise the progressive changes and withdrawal of privileges based on castes. For the real success of democracy, casteism is a big obstacle.

31. Communalism a Threat to India's Unity and Democracy

All kinds of communalism are dangerous. Just before 1947, the main damage to national unity was inflicted by Muslim Communalism, which led to the partition of India. After 1947, it is the Hindu Communalism which poses great threat to India's Democracy and it's Unity.

A Thinker.

India is a secular state. Secular means non-religious, but in the context of Indian polity, it means the co-existence of all religions without any kind of discrimination. Thought our constitution provides safeguards for the minorities, the actual implementations of the provisions is a complex one. Indian people are generally known for their non-violence, tolerance, brotherhood characters, that is why number of religion has flourished in Indian society. After the traumatic partition and the blood shed, during the partition period, has given the political parties, several inflammable issues for exploiting communal passions for their political gains. Not only the politicians, but also the religious heads of minorities and majority community instead of trying to mitigate the communal frengy, flared it up time and again, with their speeches and actions. The destruction of Babri Masjid and burning alive the Hindu Kar Sewak in Godhra (Gujrat) and the incidences of violence in Gujrat after Godhra massacre, have torn the Secular Fabric of Indian Democracy to uncountable pieces. One incidence after another creates more hatred, more incidences, more Communalism in the country.

During struggle for independence, several reformers and freedom fighters were committed to the task of modernising the religious practices in India, but, what is seen now-a-days? Communal violences have become the order of the day. The socio economic backwardness, illiteracy, poverty of the vast population of our country, both Hindus and Muslims, have always remain a fertile ground for fanaticism, and communal hatred. The hard-liners or extremists on both sides, never try to educate the common people, about the demerits of their communal feelings, so that they may Continue to exploit them for their vested interests. Such attitude of these religious leaders, contributed to a great extent in the growth and development of communalism in Indian society.

In India, throughout the past century, communal forces have tried to capture the political centrestage, time and again. By various means,they have sought to disrupt the unity and integrity of the country, tried to gnaw at the very secular foundations of Indian culture and history. But everytime they have failed. Yet, the consequences of such thought have often been traumatic. One has to but mention the holocaust of 1947, assassination of Mahatma Gandhi, demolition of the Babri Mosque at Ayodhya and the riots accompanying it etc. to get a feel of the trauma. The Muslim fundamentalists have made it an issue of their identify and existence. The Hindu fundamentalists are also not behind inciting the gullible masses, to rise against the Muslims, by making them believe that Hindus in Hindustan are being treated as second class citizens.

The Rashtriya Swayamsevak Sangh (RSS) and the Sangh Parivar, which is an umbrella sheltering and nurturing organisations like Bhartiya Janata Party (BJP), Vishwa Hindu Parishad (VHP), the Bajrang Dal, the Shiv Sena and others of their ilk, is such a conglomerate. The backbone of the now infamous 'Saffron Brigade' i.e. the organisations following a militant Hindu Fundamentalist agenda and fascist principles, is the RSS. In fact the 'family' came into being because the RSS was rejected by people after the assassination of Mahatma Gandhi and thus chose to remain in background.

The basic fabric of Indian society and polity, which is heterogeneous, composite and democratic, came under attack by Rashtriya Swayamsevak Sangh (RSS) and its various children in different guises. The most important of these is BJP. The politicians or religious leaders of BJP, VHP, RSS, and Bajrang Dal might have some good reasons in reviving the past glories of Hinduism, but the cruel fact is that their efforts for such revival are creating communal tensions among Muslims. After independence, all the political parties, have exploited religion and caste sentiments in furthering their political goals.

Over the past years, the Muslim community in India has been demonised in both subtle and overt ways. There Hindu right is obsessed with sexuality and power, obsessions which manifested themselves in most gruesome form during the riots via both the systematic attacks on Muslim women and the widespread - and false - stories circulating that Hindu women were being abducted and raped by Muslim men. The second key obsession is with 'nation'. It is telling that immediately after the burning of the Sabarmati the deputy prime minister LK Advani said that the event was Pakistani-inspired, in the absence of any evidence. Although some claimed that this was to divert blame away from the local Muslim community, the record of the Sangh Parivar, and Advani in particular, shows that the fundamental motivations are quite the opposite - to call the nationality of Indian Muslims into question.

Creating strong associations between the notion of 'Muslim' and the notion of 'foreigner' is a part of the Sangh Parivar project of the construction of India as a Hindu state. During the riots it is common for mobs to chant the verse "there are only two places for Muslims - Pakistan or the cemetery (kabrastan)". Traditionally secular forces in India have attempted to undermine these notions by stressing the 'Indianness' and 'loyalty' of Indian Muslims, the role of so many in the freedom struggle, etc.

All groups, whether Hindu or Muslim, which encourage narrow communal identities are adding to the problem. The reality is that real people's identities are fluid and complex, whereas the project of ethnic nationalism requires the construction of narrow identities, and then the use of those identities to mobilise people. In this way, the apparently innocent encouraging of religious identity can be part of a process which culminates in violence. Riots are rarely spontaneous events. Probably the most incorrect caricature of the recent violence is of spontaneous tit-for-tat violence. To highlight the organised nature of the violence is not to brush away the difficult questions of where exactly mass violence and mass sexual violence come from, and how these are connected with authoritarianism and sexual repression.

In a country like India, with so much plurality and diversity, talking of Hindu state, or Hindustan for Hindus, shall be a dangerous sign, totally against the well established, secular fabric of Indian Constitution. Unless an all out attempt is made to contain the Communal forces, the very unity of India is in danger. A total ban on all types of Communal Organisations must be put forth. A social and cultural movement should be launched to awaken the people about the reality of the Communal violences and their effects on them and on the country as a whole. The process has to start from top. All political parties and religious organisations must stop delivering inflammatory speeches and inciting the general messes in the name of religion. A wrong action on the part of a community cannot be equalise by another wrong action on the part of another community.

For the survival of the country, secularism has to be survived, for the survival of secularism, religious friendship, togetherness and tolerance is must. Communalism, can only destroy the unity and integrity of the nation, it can't help in creating friendship, fraternity or togetherness.

32. Criminalisation of Politics

"As per Election Commission estimates 1,500 candidates in the 1996 parliamentary election had criminal records and 40 of them got elected to the 11th Lok Sabha. In the state legislatures, the picture is even more distressing. Out of the 4,072 sitting MLA's in all the states, more than 700 have criminal records."

Criminals enter Politics to become Politicians and then patronise other criminals. The dire consequences of this unholy alliance between Criminals and Politicians, is that at every level from bottom, Panch at Panchayat level to Chief Minister or Ministers at State and Central level, Criminals are being elected and appointed to the positions of power.

The reason many criminals enter politics is to gain influence and ensure that cases against them are dropped or not proceeded with. They are able to make it big in the political arena because of their financial clout. Political parties tap criminals for funds and in return provide them with political patronage and protection. As the Times of India points out: "Indeed, today, far from shrinking at the thought of harboring criminal elements, parties seek them out, judging the muscle and money combination they represent to be of enormous value. Rough estimates suggest that in any state election 20 percent of candidates are drawn from criminal backgrounds. For the parties, it means overflowing coffers and unlimited funds to fight elections and for the criminals it means protection from the law and respectability in the eyes of society."

Another reason why political parties are not averse to fielding mafia dons is that winnability, not merit or experience, determines who gets to contest elections. And mafia dons and other powerful gangsters have shown that they can convert their muscle power into votes, often at the point of the gun.

An indomitable Mr. T.N. Sheshan tried his best to cleanse the system, but he failed. Mr. Sheshan's successor, Mr. Gill faced the same problem. The next Chief Election Commissioner Mr. Lingdoh also find himself in such a pitiable position, that he has no concrete remedy to cleanse the system, but to appeal the voters : Not to vote for the criminals.

A virtual impression seems have gained ground that you could commit crime and get away with it, if you have Political patronage at the proper level. The police dare not to proceed against you or if having initiated an action shall drag away their feet to defeat the ends of justice. With politics and crime intertwined, bureaucracy and the police have also become part of nexus. This unholy affinity is having a malignant effect over the public life and poses a threat to the democratic structure of the country.

Until recently our laws did not sanction Election officials asking candidates for detailed information about their criminal and financial backgrounds, let alone making this information available to citizens before the polls began.

But as India went to her largest election exercise over this year, the balance has perhaps begun to shift in favour of voters. India's 2004 elections are the first and the largest national election exercise that are being fought under the new election disclosure rules instituted in 2003. Candidates for Parliament and State Assemblies are now required to submit sworn affidavits along with their nomination papers giving information about their criminal, financial, and educational backgrounds.

Nationwide, citizens wanting to know more about their candidates have a better opportunity at this before casting their ballot. To the cynics, this is a drop in the ocean and may not lead to much. The others, this may be the beginning of a new era in Indian democracy; an era of opportunity for citizens' initiatives to mobilize around publicly available information.

During the current elections cycle, the Election Commission opened the gates for the media and citizens to collect copies of candidate affidavits from Returning Officers and the District Election Officers. Ten states are having some form of election watch campaign, indicating a broad-based nationwide civil society initiative to give teeth to the EC rules. Some state election commissions have already made candidate disclosures public on their websites and election watches have been distributing analyses to the media and citizens.

In a nation crying for reforms in our electoral system, process of power and judiciary, this verdict and people's right to know must be the starting point of democratic reform. This is also a moment for us to reflect. Once again, the resilience of our democratic system, the inherent strength of institutions, and the constitutional checks and balances stand as testimony to the maturity and vibrancy of our governance system. We congratulate the advocates who marshalled the arguments ably on behalf of citizens and helped the court form its conclusions. Millions of Indians, several organizations and media all have fought this battle for democracy and liberty in keeping with glorious traditions of citizen assertion and people's sovereignty. We salute those sentinels of freedom.

We are confident however, that our parties and legislators will exhibit the requisite courage, wisdom and foresight to accept this verdict of the Supreme Court and use it as a launching pad for engineering far-reaching and vital electoral and governance reforms.

The enormous problem of the nexus between criminals and politicians cannot be ignored any longer. The submission of affidavit may have some deterrent effect, but seems as it will also result in a futile exercise as in India, votes are being cast on the basis of caste, creed and religion.The poor illiterate people of this country still vote to their caste man or to the man of fellow religionship, or to the fellow who belongs to their region. Moral values and ethics have long been vanished from the political arena of our country, but we cannot have such an indifferent attitude. We shall have to find a solution to eradicate the menace for which we are overselves also responsible to a great extent.

In a democratic country, all the powers lies in the hands of the voters that is the general public. An awakening among the general mass can only show the right place to such criminal politicians.

33. Democracy in Theory and Practice

If one view as a source of solutions for the country's economic and social problems, the Indian polity is increasingly seen by political observers as the problem. Law and order have become increasingly tenuous because of the growing inability of the police to curb criminal activities and quell communal disturbances. Indeed, many observers bemoan the 'criminalization' of Indian politics at a time when politicians routinely hire 'muscle power' to improve their electoral prospects, and criminals themselves successfully run for public office. These circumstances have led some observers to conclude that India has entered into a growing crisis of governability. When populist political appeals stir the passions of the masses, government institutions appear less capable than ever before of accommodating conflicts in a society mobilized along competing ethnic and religious lines. The democracy is at a stake.

India became sovereign Democratic Republic at 10:18 a.m. on January 26, 1950, with the inauguration of the Constitution. India's last Governor General, C. Rajagopalachari, read the proclamation announcing the birth of the new Republic.

If we look at the political and social history of the last 55 Years, we found a dramatic change in the democratic setup of our country. Since independence, our country has fastly deteriorating to become the 'wild west'. In fact, the present state of the things makes one wonder, it the country has any Constitution or Laws at all. The democratic values preserved and practised by the founding Fathers, have consigned to dustbin and the institutions meant to safeguard the democratic fabric have been undermined and devalued. The educationists or the freedom fighters must be wondering, whether this is the democracy, we gave to ourselves?

The answer is simple, 'Blame not anything else, blame ourselves', for we have not risen to the lofty ideals our founding fathers have incorporated into our constitution. It is the cumulative failure of all ; the politicians, the bureaucrats, the traders, the professionals and the people from different walks of life. Let us not blame the institutions and Statutes that reinforced the foundation of our democracy. Who is to blame if a State Assembly becomes a replica of a street scene in Mumbai, where hoodlums are seen exchanging stones and missiles? Who is to blame if MPs rush up to a Minister only to tear off the Bill he is going to introduce i Lok Sabha?

Some analysts contend the prevailed problems are the result of the maturation of civil society and the emergence of new, more democratic political practices. Backward Classes, the Dalits, and tribal peoples increasingly have refused to rest content with the patronage and populism characteristic of the 'Congress system'. Mobilization of these groups has provided a viable base for the political opposition and unraveled the fabric of the Congress. Since the late 1970s, there has been a proliferation of non-governmental organizations. These groups made new demands on the political system that required a substantial redistribution of political power, economic resources and social status.

The constitution of India draws extensively from Western legal traditions in its outline of the principles of liberal democracy. It is distinguished from many Western constitutions, however, in its elaboration of principles reflecting the aspirations to end the inequities of traditional social relations and enhance the social welfare of the population. According to constitutional scholar Granville Austin, probably no other nation's constitution "has provided so much impetus toward changing and rebuilding society for the common good." Since its enactment, the constitution has fostered a steady concentration of power in the central government—especially the Office of the Prime Minister. This centralization has occurred in the face of the increasing assertiveness of an array of ethnic and caste groups across Indian society. Increasingly, the government has responded to the resulting tensions by resorting to the formidable array of authoritarian powers provided by the constitution. Together with the public's perception of pervasive corruption among India's politicians, the state's centralization of authority and increasing resort to coercive power have eroded its legitimacy. However, a new assertiveness shown by the Supreme Court and the Election Commission suggests that the remaining checks and balances among the country's political institutions continue to support the resilience of Indian democracy.

The present political scenario in our country is alarmingly pathetic. Politics has tattered and tainted with crime. The moral values of our politicians, policemen and criminals are inseparable from one another. Even the thin dividing line between the politicians and criminals has disappeared giving rise to criminal politicians nexus. Politics has been criminalised and crime politicised. The people have lost faith in political parties and the promises of the leaders have proven hollow.

Free and fair elections constitute the foundation of Parliamentary Democracy. The Constitution provides sacred provisions for free and fair election. The increasing role of money power and muscle power have rendered the election process a mockery of our democracy. The role of caste and creed in fielding the candidates and allocating the ministries, have made the fun of fundamental rights envisaged in our constitution. The misuse of official machinery, mobilising the electorate with false promises, or assuring the benefits based on caste and creed have further weaken the democratic fabric of our constitution. From Sheshan and Gill, Mr. Lingdoh and then Mr. Krishna Murthy have tried their best to make the election process free and fair, but whether they succeeded? The dishonest and corrupt politicians with criminal backgrounds winning the seats with the assistance of money and muscle power.

The Judiciary has played a very important role as the watch dog of our democratic system. Politicians have tried time and again to undermine the judiciary, by providing out of turn promotions to the Judges and making transfers and postings keeping in view their political philosophy. But kudos to the Supreme Court, which has put check on various nefarious acts of the politicians. The contribution of Supreme Court in upholding Constitutional values, rule of law, personal liberty, and human rights, gender justice and democratic values has been quite significant.

The election of 1999 has proved that the voters won't accept any idea of toppling a democratic government without any concrete reason, thereby reinstalling Mr. Atal Bihari Vajpayee as Prime Minister of India. Now the elections of 14th Lok Sabha have surprised everybody. The much advertised India Shinning and Feel Good Factor have thrown to winds by the electorate and again the Congress was give mandate to form the government. Therefore, it is wrong to say that democracy in India has failed utterly, but we can conclude that to make the democracy success in real terms, our politicians have to make lot of sacrifices and people of India must use their votes in favour of honest, incorrupt and dedicated leaders so that the values preserved by our Founding Fathers could be restored.

34. Job Reservation in Private Sector

"It is a bitter truth, that reservation has resulted in mediocrity and repudiation of quality. With the help of legislative support of reservation, the not eligible have climbed to the high posts and the better qualified, with high marks, have just been looking the injustice being done with them, for no fault of theirs."

The basic concept of providing reservation to drown trodden society called schedule caste and schedule tribe, initially through our constitution has altogether changed now. Reservation might have provided some relief to the people from poor and down trodden sections, who had scarce opportunities, but the same could have been provided through subsidised better education and other support services. Once a concession or any kind of privilege is extended to a particular class, it is impossible for any government to withdraw it, in a democracy, where voting decides the fate of any party.

Indian democracy is called by some thinkers as mobocracy, where the illiterate mob, decides the fate our the political parties. The privilege of reservation once given, was extended every time, as to withdrawing this privilege means, definite removal of that party from the power in the next election. The opposition party or other regional parties can assure to grant the privilege, if voted for power. This issue of reservation has become a political concession to garner vote banks.

Now the point of extending reservation to the private sector is also being raised from the political platform, little realising the disastrous consequences for the country. It is argued by protagonists of extending reservation in private sector also, that with the globalization and due to rapid narrowing of the state sector on account of privatisation, and the withdrawal of state from many spheres under the liberalisation regime, the little room is left for the reserved class to get jobs. If the prevalence of economic discrimination is the justification for reservation in public sector, why can it not be the reason for reservation in private sector. In countries like U.S., Northern Ireland, Malaysia and others in Latin America, affirmative action was developed from the very beginning both in public and the private sector. As such the demand for introducing reservation in the private sector is being raised in order to set off the long injustice to the reserved category or so called untouchables. It is further demanded that India must enact an Equal Employment Opportunity Act (as in United States) so as to provide safe guards against discrimination. This could be supplemented by affirmative action in terms of reservation in some categories of jobs and other markets.

So far private sector is concern, it is purely a commercial concern, set up to earn profits or investible surplus to earn more profits. The objective of the private sector to earn profit can't be achieved if it is forced to run by less competent people. This is an age of globalization, liberalization, where no business can be successful if it is has less competent, less efficient manpower . Winning in the competition require highly skilled, most competent, most dedicated and result oriented working class, not the people who has been supported with the stick of reservation. Everyone knows that any private enterprise grow with the support and hard work of the specialized and technically trained, well educated, highly motivated manpower. How can a company be expected to carry on with the staff employed under the reservation quota. Not only from the point of efficiency, competence, are important, it must also be kept in mind, that for the last 56 years, the general class candidates have been suffering a lot because of the reservation provided to their counterparts.

During the short regime of Mr. V.P. Singh, the then P.M., several youth lost their lives against the recommendations of Mandal Commission. It is a bitter truth, that reservation has resulted in mediocrity and repudiation of quality. With the help of legislative support of reservation, the not eligible have climbed to the high posts and the better qualified, with high marks, have just been looking the injustice being done with them, for no fault of theirs.

"Reservation is against the fundamental principles of humanity, it is against the dictates of reason that a man should by reason of birth, be denied or given extra privileges" Mahatma Gandhi.

This is the demand of time, that the present policy of reservation even in public sector should be reviewed honesty, without considering its political repercussion, for the real good of the general public. So far reservation in private sector is concern, it is neither justified nor have any propriety keeping in view the objectives of the private concern.

If India shinning is to be changed to India downing, only then the reservation in private sector should be considered. Providing any kind of facilities, subsidies, financial aid, can be justified, but reservation in private sector shall ruin the business competence, efficiency & growth of the economy totally.

35. Necessity of Police Reforms

'Our Police is functioning under the outmoded Police Act of 1861, framed by the British to perpetuate their colonial rule and subjugate the natives. The olden Act has since allowed to prevail in spite of recommendations of National Police Commission in 1977 and the State Police Commissions and several other committees, perhaps that the present politicians find the olden Act serving their purpose nicely.'

It is a known fact that the image of the police has fallen to abyss in recent years. People want an efficient Police, which serves them in need. The poor want reforms because they are the crude victims of oppression, and dictates of the powerful, rich and so they need the true services of the police for their rescue. The National Human Rights Commission demands reforms, because it is overwhelmed by public complaints against the police that ranges from death, rape and torture in custody, to the refusal to file FIR, manipulation coercion and threats to witnesses and demands for money to register, neglect or pursue a case. The Supreme Court pulled up the police inefficiency, neglect and corruption prevailed in many cases and passed serious strictures against the functioning of the police.

Despite demands from all quarters, and necessity to reform the Police force, no concrete or resulting action has so far initiated by any Government since independence. Paradoxical all it appears, that a country which so emphatically threw off the British yoke is satisfied to be ruled by a colonial Act, whose main objective was to subjugate the population. Every successive government avoided so far, the necessary reforms in police force, indicate, the obnoxious nexus between the Police, and politicians, the police and the executives and a belief that if the reforms be made, the benefits being derived by them from the police will no more be available.

In 1977, the National Police Commission recommended, analysing carefully the problems of the police and pressures faced by the police force. The recommendations mainly dealt with two aspects, one insulating the police from undue political pressure and accountability of the police to law alone and not to any person. The Rebeiro Committee has also given its recommendations along similar lines to the NPC, as also the Padmanabhai Committee. The Vohra Committee indicated in very clear terms that the Police-Politicians Mafia nexus is ruining the governance, yet nothing has been done so far.

Immediate Police reforms are too important to neglect and too urgent to delay further. The vicious culture of crime especially under the patronage of politicians, against the women which has gripped the entire nation, and increasing day by day, have reduced the civil people into helpless victims.

The Godhra incidence, the Telgi scam, the involvement of DGP Mr. R.K. Sharma in a murder, and so many other cases can reveal the obnoxiety of the functioning of the police force.

It would be wrong to undermine the efficiency of the Police force. The quick and effective action at Akshardam by the Gujrat Police is acclaimed by every one. The brilliant action of Punjab Police in wiping out the terrorists from the state, are worthy of praise. The fault is not with the police functioning but with the system which is to be scrutinised. Under the present circumstances, the Police is accountable only to MLA, MP or the party workers of a ruling party. One can not obviously expect the Police to go by the rule book of the Police Manual; they are to go by the rule book of the party in Power. This the reason why the police in India has earned a bad image among the general public. The general public do not understand that this image is not self created; it is the reflection of the moribund system under which the police functions.

There in U.K., the policeman is nobody's valet, and it is the duty of the Commissioner of police as it is of every chief constable to enforce the law of the land and he is answerable to none but law and law alone. In India, a policeman is like a football to be kicked about by any one and when he is needed no more he could be dispensed with like a disposable item. The plight of the Police shows the sorry plight and predicament of the entire system. Let us not blame the police if the system, the political and administrative system within which they have to operate has become rotten to the core.

Whatever is argued by anybody, it is undisputable, that reforms in Police is the need of hour. It is ridiculous that our police force is still being governed by the outdated Police Act 1861. If police reforms are delayed further, there will be no end to the trauma of the ordinary people, especially those who have no Godfather, no political support.

36. The Non Aligned Movement

"NAM, born with the farsighted vision of Jawaharlal Nehru, Marshal Tito of Yugoslavia and Colonel Abdel Nasser of Egypt in the fifties today presents the miserable spectacle of an aged eutherian struggling to find a way out of the complex political forest. With the end of the Cold War the pious concept of non-alignment seems to have become totally irrelevant and redundant, but by no means eliminated the causes that warranted concerted action by the ever enlarging non-aligned club to fight common problems engulfed their economies. Peace, disarmament and development are still the vital issues that should be tackled with the same sense of urgency as the issues flowing from globalisation that have crucially benefit the already affluent North and create new problems in the economies of the South. But strangely enough, many of the NAM members, preoccupied with the bitterness emanating from festering bilateral disputes (as between India and Pakistan and as between Iran and a few Arab countries) misuse the NAM forum to settle scores with each other."

The NAM traces its origins to a meeting in 1955 of 29 Asian and African countries at which heads of state discussed common concerns, including colonialism and the influence of the West. A meeting in 1961 set up the criteria for NAM membership. It ruled that member countries could not be involved in alliances or defence pacts with the main world powers. In this way the NAM sought to prevent its members from becoming pawns in Cold War power games and distanced itself from the Western and Soviet power blocs.

NAM member countries represent many shades of political opinion :

The first summit of NAM heads of state took place in the Yugoslav capital Belgrade in 1961 at the instigation of Yugoslav President Tito. Twenty-five countries were represented and the threat of war between the US and the Soviet Union dominated the summit.

The NAM says it aims to protect the right of nations to 'independent judgement' and to counter imperialism. The movement is also committed to restructuring the world economic order.

Since the collapse of the Soviet Union, the NAM's preoccupations with global politics and the Cold War have given way to concerns about globalisation, trade and investment, debt, Aids and international crime.

The NAM's February 2003 summit in Malaysia was dominated by the issues of weapons of mass destruction in Iraq and North Korea, and the possibility of US-led military action against the former.

The NAM does not have a constitution or a permanent secretariat. Its highest decision-making body is the Conference of Heads of States or Government, which usually meets once every three years. At this time the post of NAM chair is passed to the host country of the summit.

Malaysia assumed the chair of the NAM at the Kuala Lumpur summit in February 2003. Cuba will take up the post in 2006. South Africa's Thabo Mbeki has called on the NAM to take a bolder stance.

The NAM chair takes on the administrative burden of running the movement. Because much of the NAM's work is undertaken at the United Nations in New York, the chair country's ambassador to the UN is expected to devote time and effort to NAM matters. The NAM's Co-ordinating Bureau, also based at the UN, is the main instrument for directing the work of NAM task forces, committees and working groups.

The NAM says all its members have a decision-making role, regardless of size or influence.

With 116 diverse member nations, consensus-building is no easy task in the NAM. Some member nations, including India and Pakistan, have been at loggerheads with each other for many years.

The relevance of the NAM since the collapse of the Soviet Union has also been questioned, with some commentators speculating whether the organisation has outlived its usefulness.

In 2003, Thabo Mbeki, President of South Africa—the NAM chair country at the time—warned that the movement's future depended on its response to global challenges. He called on the NAM to take stronger resolutions on issues of concern.

The issue of alleged mistreatment of Iraqi prisoners by United States and British soldiers will be "touched upon" during the Non-Aligned Movement ministerial committee meeting on May 13. Foreign Minister Datuk Seri Syed Hamid Albar said the coalition forces should not resort to giving excuses or justification for their troops' behaviour, photographs of which have angered most of the Islamic world. "Our stand is that there must be respect for the rule of law. A country which has respect for the rule of law and democratic process cannot give excuses or justification for the actions of their own soldiers under whatever circumstances.

"It is important that the two countries do not sweep the allegations under the carpet. The whole issue must be investigated thoroughly," he told reporters after attending his ministry's staff monthly meeting at Wisma Putra. He said there had been previous reports accusing some of the people working in Iraq as having "very condescending and obnoxious attitudes" towards the locals. "Whatever investigations carried out by the US or British authorities must not be about to find justification. This is against international law and rules of engagement," he said. Syed Hamid said the meeting, which was called specially to discuss the current situation in Iraq, should be coming out with at least one declaration on the recent revelations. "It will be touched upon during the NAM meeting," he said.

In the present international scenario, the dominancy of USA and the other developed countries is gradually increasing. The American hegemony be viewed not only in the United Nation's meetings, but also in alleged intervention all over the world. Under these circumstances, NAM has to play an important role in revitalising the UNO, so that it may remain a major entity in solving the international problems.

Almost all the countries are facing the threat of terrorism today. NAM has been endeavouring for peace and complete nuclear disarmament ever since its inception. It always asserts that disarmament is closely related with the very survival of humanity. The rise of religious fanaticism, ethnic nationalism and internal conflicts are other crucial problems facing the world today. NAM can play effective role in drawing the attention of the world towards the present day problems. NAM's conference has laid stress on many such aspects, but got little success. NAM has to work more vigorously to achieve its goal. NAM is facing many challenges in the present world scenario. NAM is an International movement, may have some shortcomings, but as a foreign policy, it has great value and will always enjoy great importance.

To say that NAM has lost its relevance is a wrong conclusion. It is argued, that NAM couldn't get any positive success so far, still the voice raised by NAM on so many issues forced the Super Powers to vindicate their actions. The US or other developed countries were bound to reply the points raised by NAM. "With the Non Aligned at its heart, the U.N. can at last serve the people of the world as they must be served. Together we can turn 21st century into a time of truly revolutionary change", said Dr. Boutros Boutros Ghali.

In nutshell, it can, so be concluded that NAM has not lost its relevance. It has stood test of adverse circumstances. It has served an important purpose of protecting and preserving the interests of third world countries.

In the words of R. Venkataraman (Former President of India):

"NAM is not an 'ism'. It cannot become outdated anymore than common sense can become outdated. No national, no group of nations can disregard the NAM. It must today rase its voice against the injustices and inequities of the current decade and the emerging 21st century."

37. Is The United Nations Redundant ?

"The brutal, unabashed aggression on Iraq by the USA and Britain, the cofounding members of United Nations, have thrown to wind the basic principals on which the United Nations was formed and rendered this organisation a monuments of no relevance."

The preamble of United Nations Charter says, "we the people of the United Nations determined to save succeeding generations from the scourge of war, which twice in our life time has brought untold sorrow to mankind and..."

"To reaffirm faith in fundamental human rights, in the dignity and worth of the human person, in the equal rights of men and women and of nations large and small and..."

Not to talk of human rights of men and women, the basic reason for which the formation of United Nation's necessity was felt, that is to save the mankind from the scourge of war, was torn to pieces, by the aggression of USA and U.K., on the Iraqi people.

'Might is Right', Who can challenge or stop the wrong actions or doings of the super power, the USA. Some calls USA, the 'United States of Arrogance', but who cares! The USA and Britain very systematically used the various resolutions of United Nations to cripple the Iraq's military power, economic and social structural with the covert aim to change the regime of Saddam Hussain.

When Saddam Hussain captured and annexed Kuwait, the USA coalition, blessed with the several UN's resolutions, liberated Kuwait with its military might, But after the Gulf war I, the USA's planning to change the regime of saddam Hussain, started taking shapes. There is no place for any provision to change of regime in any country in the charted of the United Nations. Who could stop the USA and Britain in doing so. An ultimatum was served by Mr. Bush on Mr. Saddam and his sons, to quit Iraq or face war, within 48 hours. This ultimatum had no sanction of United Nations. All the appeal of the Secretary General, were laid on deaf ears, even the protest march, denouncing USA action by various countries were all in vain. Every country was using very cautious words, as mild as possible words to lodge their protest against the action of the 'Super Power'.

USA first tried to get a resolution passed from the security council against Iraq. The other permanent and non permanent members of the security council refuse to oblige USA, even this couldn't deter the USA and the U.K. from waging war against Iraq. U.S.A. and Britain had already made all out preparation for this aggression, started sending troops and aircraft carriers, bomber planes and battle ships to the strategic points. Even the reports of U.N. inspectors mentioned that the Iraq officials were fully cooperating in their inspections work, and asked for more time to complete their inspection work, acted against the wishes of Mr. Bush to launch quick assault on Iraq.

The invaders proclaimed and propagated brazenly to use the weapons never used before in order to liberate the Iraqi people, In such attempt of liberation, thousands of innocent civilians killed and huge loss was caused to the Iraq's economic and social infrastructure. The barbarity of the so called war for liberation of Iraq can only be compared to the savagery of the war fought during the period of Alexander the Great. What could have been done by the UNO, NAM? Where have gone the so called champions of Human Rights? None could prevent this war and the basic principles on which the United Nation was found were blew to winds. Every nation kept silence, just to see the outcome of the one sided war. Not a single voice was heard to call an emergency meeting of General Assembly to condemn the assault and to stop the war.

On March 19, 2003, the U.N. Secretary General Mr. Kofi Annan, did say that Iraq's essential infrastructure to provide basic necessities of clean water, health and education has totally devastated by two decades of war and conflict.

A special meeting of U.N. Security council was convened on 27th march, 2003, when the US led military action come in for severe criticism, questioning the legality of the action and Iraq calling it a barbaric aggression.

The hypocrisy of USA and Britain came to light when they asserted their right to destroy a country and then rebuild it on humanitarian ground. It amounts to breaking a sick persons limb and legs and them offering him artificial limb freely.

The US led aggression on Iraq has sent a message to every civilized country, that neither UNO, nor NAM or any such forum can save you from the whimsical aggression of the mighty powers. Unless country is itself powerful to face the challenges, it is not safe. The basic principles a United Nations, the respect to the sovereignty of Nations, equality of Nations, are just principles for the sake of goodness.

If the United Nations does not act strongly, or to say if the member nations do not act unitedly against such blatant aggressions, the fate of United Nations can't be other the fate of United league.

The United Nation has become simply a platform to discuss the general issues. The main task for which United Nations was structured, has become irrelevant as such as the super powers want to discard it for their own benefits. The adage Might is Right, is true even in this civilized world, which has made the United Nations redundant so far the basic principles, on which it was formed, are concerned.

38. Global Warming : (A Grave Threat to Ecology)

The Earth has a natural system of balancing the absorption and release of heat, that it absorbs from the sunlight, but for the - last some years, the balance seems to be under severe threat. There have been enormous increase in gases like carbon di oxide, methane, nitros oxide etc.

As the temperature rises, there will be a rise in sea level, due to melting of glaciers and the ice sheets of Greenland and Antarctica. While sea level is expected to rice almost every year but a considerable variation is seen nowadays. In some regions, the rise in sea level, may be almost nil, but other might experience a rise of as much as twice the global average. The predictions are that the rise in sea level in some parts of north pacific and to the west of Greenland may be comparatively more and it can spoil the ecological balance of the respective region.

As per the latest report of U.K. Met office's Hadley centre for Climate Prediction and Research, global warming over the next century might turn out to be much worse than estimated earlier. If the Green House Gas (GHG) emissions are stabilised, which means immediate cut of 60-70% emission of carbon dioxide globally, even then the rise of atmospheric temperature would be 10°C and rise in sea level would be approximately 1Meter. Based on the finding of the Intergovernmental panel on climate change (1PCC), the centre predicted that warming overland could lead to a 60°C rise in temperature by 2100, that is 20°C higher than the earlier estimates.

As per the findings of a joint study conducted by Indian Institute of Technology New Delhi and Hadley Centre, the global warming may also cause a good increase in rainfall over western coast line of India.

Effects of Afforestation

It is assumed that planting more trees will solve the problem, as the trees absorb more carbon dioxide, but it is a wrong presumption. Planting more trees will absorb carbon dioxide from the atmosphere in some parts of the world, but in other parts, global warming may hamper the growth of trees or even may cause their death. Therefore, afforestation may not be a perfect solution to this problem. One important point to note is that forest area is usually darker than the other areas, especially when the surface is snowclad and being darker absorbs more sunlight comparatively. Hence it might accelerate warming. Different forests reflects different amount of sunlight, dark green forests absorbs more solar radiation than land surface and so the benefits of their carbon intake could be reduced and in some areas be reversed by this darkening effect. Dying forests might result in greater emission of carbon di oxide, thus changing the climate to our peril.

The Hadley centre reported that average temperature in 1999 was lower than that of 1998, but the year 1999 was still the fifth warmest year since global records began in 1860. The centre has further discovered that by 2050, the trees and soils will start falling and perishing, which will result in less absorption of carbon dioxide.

Global warming due to sunlight is likely to be set off or reduced to some extent by volcanic aerosols. During the 21 century, large scale reduction in the amount of rainfall is being expected in some areas such as southern Africa, Australia, Central America and the northern region of south America. The highest increase in precipitation over land may occur in East Asia, Central Africa, Eastern South America and at high latitudes.

The Hadley centre has also predicted that Antarctica ice may have all but melted away by 2100, if urgent precautionary measures are not taken to cut down emission of green house gases. The melting of ice is due to warming of water of the North Atlantic, as well as due to rising air temperatures in the region. Melting ice from the frozen continents shall increase the level of sea. Melting of sea ice can further accelerate global warming as the ocean surface would not now reflect as much sunlight as ice sheets.

According to world meteorological organisation, deaths from heat waves in big cities are expected to double world wide over the next two decades, if no measures are taken to check the global warming. In the largest cities of USA, an average of 1500 deaths take place every year. It is expected to increase such death to 3000-4000 by 2020.

A study conducted by Indian Ocean Experiment (INDOEX) reveals that the effect of aerosols in the atmosphere will magnify the warming over several developing countries. The study indicates that precipitation might change over tropical regions due to aerosols. Aerosols have both a warming and cooling effect in the climate. On average estimation, aerosols are expected to have cooling effect, as they indirectly help in formation of cloud droplets, making clouds more bright and more reflective.

In 1992, the United Nationals Framework Convention on Climate Change (UNFCCC) was adopted. It recognized that industrialized countries were mostly responsible for increased Green House Gases, concentration in the Earth's atmosphere and should be the first to act against climate change.

In 1997, United Nation's conference on global warming was held in the ancient Japanese Capital of Kyoto for ten days, the climate change meet lay deadlocked,as none was ready to take initiative to check the further damage to planet earth. USA, and 37 other industrial nations agreed to binding reduction in their Green House Gas emission by 2012, setting out a target of five percent below 1990 levels. The next meeting held at Buenous Aires, where it was agreed on Nov.14,1998, to set a time table for discussing by 2000 the many issues that still need to be settle.

Actually, the USA and Europe want that other developing countries like, India, China, should act as per the accord signed at Kyoto, but India, China have their own reasons, as in these countries, industrialization has just began, while developed countries who are actually responsible for the global warming must act fast to have some remedial measures.

In nutshell the global warming has became a grave threat to the ecological balance of the earth. The civilisation is moving slowly towards a dooms day. All the nations, particularly the most industrialized, developed countries have to be active to take immediate action in the matter, otherwise, the human race shall have to face an unimaginable peril, and that day is not too far.

39. Terrorism

Millions of innocent people and thousands of cops have lost their lives fighting terrorism but the thirst for human blood of the creators and fumigators of terrorism has not been quenched so far.

Terrorism has now become a world wide phenomena. Terrorism can be defined as an organized way of intimidation and violence especially for political purpose. political frustration, political necessities, religious and Racial fanaticism and personal political interests are some of the main causes of Terrorism. Terrorists are encouraged by the interested countries, external powers, to create instability in certain country or region. Terrorists indulge in looting, kidnapping, murdering, shooting, arson and other unlawful activities to serve their very purpose of creating instabilities or deter the innocents, so that either they support them or don't support the legal government machinery.

As far as India is concerned, terrorism has become endemic here since early 1980s. India has been fighting the cross border terrorism on its own for the last 20-30 years. India has been the worst sufferer of global terrorism, having lost more than 65000 people during the last 20 years. The terrorism in India is mainly nurtured by external agencies, especially Pakistan, in the bordering states of Kashmir and Punjab. In North-Eastern states, ULFA and NSCN like organisations have also indulged in terrorist activities.

The much talked about 'Global war against Terrorism' is one of the most cruel jokes of present time. It is ironical that Pakistan, the epicenter of Global Terrorism, is the greatest ally of USA, fighting Global Terrorism. India has regularly been drawing the attention of the US and other countries to the atrocities committed by the terrorists, trained and funded by Pakistan but of no avail.Rightly said by someone 'Only the wearer knows where the shoe pinches'. USA realised the danger of terrorism only when terrorists struck at its heart, on 11th Sept, 2001, when twin towers of 'World Trade Centre', New York were reduced to debris by suicide squads of terrorists. USA, that boasted of its Super Power status, military might and intelligence, suddenly was forced to realise its vulnerability. USA feared that its fortress was also not impregnable and therefore wanted to eliminate the kingpin, the notorious dreaded Osamabin Laden and its Al-Queda. But President Bush couldn't identify the God-Father of all the mischief in the terrorist world, Gen. Pervez Mushrraf, instead joined hand with Mr. Musharraf to fight the terrorism globally. The removal of Osamabin Laden from Afganistan, has not eliminated the threat of terrorists attack on USA. The American people even today are living under the long shadow of fear. The military might and word's most powerful intelligence agency CIA could no longer eliminate the fear from the general American's mind. The tapes of Osamabin Laden released by Al Zazira again threaten the USA Government of his laden's determination to teach a lesson to the US Government.

Every person entering USA, is being frisked by the authorities thoroughly. There have been thousands of instances when passengers are out loaded on strength of suspicion. Once bitten, twice shy, they don't want to leave anything to chance. But inspite of all that, insecurity prevailed among the minds of Americans? The US ambassador to India has time and again asserted that global Terrorism will not end until the problem of trans border terrorism across India's borders is tackled. The crux of the story is that the USA is having double standard in dealing with terrorism and formulating its foreign policy to suit its interest. In the name of destruction of WMD (Weapons of Mass Destructions), US destroyed the Iraq, ousted the Saddam and till date, not even a trace of Biological, Chemical or Nuclear weapons has been found there. Indian government time and again drew the attention of US' appeasement policy towards Pakistan. Appeasement of devilish elements can result in more unforeseen catastrophe.

India has to fight on its own with the terrorism, being funded and encouraged by the neighboring countries. How can we expect that USA or Britain will feel the pinch of terroristic attack in India? To look for support from either of them would be a folly. Just like any other country, we have to empower ourselves, we have to tackle our problems in our own way. Terrorism has to be dealt firmly with determined efforts and indomitable political will, with the full and all out support of all political parties and every citizen.

40. Basic Structure of Constitution

The phrase 'basic structure' itself is not found in the Constitution. The Supreme Court recognised this concept for the first time in the historic Kesavananda Bharati case in 1973. Ever since the Supreme Court has been the interpreter of the Constitution and the arbiter of all amendments made by Parliament.

According to the Constitution, Parliament and the state legislatures in India have the power to make laws within their respective jurisdictions. This power is not absolute in nature. The Constitution vests in the judiciary, the power to adjudicate upon the constitutional validity of all laws. If a law made by Parliament or the state legislatures violates any provision of the Constitution, the Supreme Court has the power to declare such a law invalid or ultra vires. This check notwithstanding, the founding fathers wanted the Constitution to be an adaptable document rather than a rigid framework for governance. Hence Parliament was invested with the power to amend the Constitution. Article 368 of the Constitution gives the impression that Parliament's amending powers are absolute and encompass all parts of the document. But the Supreme Court has acted as a brake to the legislative enthusiasm of Parliament ever since independence. With the intention of preserving the original ideals envisioned by the constitution-makers, the apex court pronounced that Parliament could not distort, damage or alter the basic features of the Constitution under the pretext of amending it. In Kesavananda Bharati case, the judges explained the concept of basic structure that included :

- supremacy of the Constitution
- republican and democratic form of government
- secular character of the Constitution
- separation of powers between the legislature, executive and the judiciary
- federal character of the Constitution
- unity and integrity of the nation
- sovereignty of India
- democratic character of the polity
- unity of the country
- essential features of the individual freedoms secured to the citizens

Some judges also opined that the fundamental rights of the citizen belonged to the basic structure and Parliament could not amend it.

In summary the majority verdict in Kesavananda Bharati recognised the power of Parliament to amend any or all provisions of the Constitution provided such an act did not destroy its basic structure. But there was no unanimity of opinion about what amounts to that basic structure.

Again, in Indira Gandhi Election case, each judge expressed views about what amounts to the basic structure of the Constitution that included;

- sovereign democratic republic status
- equality of status and opportunity of an individual
- secularism and freedom of conscience and religion
- 'government of laws and not of men' i.e. the rule of law

As such the the term basic structure limits the power of the parliament to amend the constitution.

41. India's Claim to Security Council of United Nations

The permanent members were originally drawn from the victorious powers after World War II: the Republic of China, France, the Soviet Union, the United Kingdom, and the United States. In 1971, the People's Republic of China was awarded the Republic of China's seat in the UN by UN General Assembly Resolution 2758. In 1991, the Russian Federation acquired the seat originally held by the Soviet Union, including the Soviet Union's former representation in the Security Council.

There has been discussion of an increase in the number of permanent members. The countries who have made the strongest demands for permanent seats are Japan, Germany and India. Indeed, Japan and Germany are the UN's second and third largest founders, respectively, while Germany and India are among some of the largest contributors of troops to UN mandated peace-keeping missions.

India's claim is quite justified for permanent membership in the expanded UN Security Council as it is the world's largest democracy, a rapidly growing economic power and a major contributor to the peacekeeping operations. On any objective grounds, India is well qualified for permanent membership.

Moreover the Third World and other developing countries are underrepresented when it comes to policy and decision-making at the UN Security Council, especially with the absolute and imperative veto power of the permanent members. The inclusion of India is necessary in order to promote balance of power and interests between western industrial nations and developing nations in the world's legislative body. This would equip the Security Council to confront the grave challenges that confront the international community in the 21st century.

42. India : A Secular State

According to our Constitution, India is a "sovereign, socialist, secular, democratic republic. India adopted secularism primarily to counter the threat of prevailing communal discord after partition. It was however expected that there would not be any distinction in society on the basis of religion when plural India with a number of social orders mingled into one political unit. But the then political leadership of the country viewed the individual not as a citizen but a member of a particular religious group, which gradually legitimised the communal identity of Muslims in secular India. A large majority of Indian Muslims still feel that secularism is a ploy to impose Hinduism upon them.

Agitation against preferential treatment to Muslims in respect of their religion became a prime agenda of Hindu nationalists, who raised the issue time and again for their political gains. Religious obstinacy of Muslims in one hand and its challenge by Hindu nationalists on the other generated a social confrontation between the two largest religious communities in the country. This resulted in communal clashes in different states.

Since Indian secularism is not defined in categorical or clear terms, Indian Muslims can accept or reject secular state and secularism as suited to Islamic law. Muslim orthodoxy, which believes to live only in a country under Darul Islam (abode of Islam) - is never ready to divorce religion from politics and thereby cannot play a meaningful role to secularise its mindset. Even singing a song like 'Vande Mataram' to demonstrate loyalty to motherland is not acceptable to them. Any voice if raised by non-Muslims against Muslim orthodoxy, is opposed with the plea that secularism is in danger. Whenever there was any attempt by the state to rationalise the civic life of Muslims it was viewed by them as anti-secular.

Political parties especially the parties in power can be seen vying with one another to prove their secular credentials to the muslim community. The appointment of Banerjee Commission to re-probe Godhra riots, the advocacy of providing reservation to the Muslims on the basis of religion, inspite of the known fact that our constitution does not permit any reservation based on religion are examples of brazen attempts to appease the Muslims. The politics of vote bank has made the concept of secularism a musical instrument that can be played by anyone in their own way.

43. Unemployment Problem Facing India

India's labour force is growing at a rate of 2.5 per cent annually, but employment is growing at only 2.3 per cent. Thus, the country is faced with the challenge of not only absorbing new entrants to the job market (estimated at seven million people every year), but also clearing the backlog.

India as a nation is faced with massive problem of unemployment. Unemployment can be defined as a state of worklessness for a man fit and willing to work. It is a condition of involuntary and not voluntary idleness. The special features of unemployment in India can be summarised as under :

1. The incidence of unemployment is much higher in urban areas than in rural areas.
2. Unemployment rates for women are higher than those for men.
3. The incidence of unemployment among the educated is much higher than the overall unemployment.
4. There is greater unemployment in agricultural sector than in industrial and other major sectors. The unemployment in agriculture or rural sector is called hidden unemployment, which means that more number of persons are working on a job than the actual requirement.

Open unemployment is not a true indicator of the gravity of the unemployment problem in India, characterised as it is by large-scale underemployment and poor employment quality in the unorganised sector, which accounts for over 90 per cent of the total employment. The organised sector contributes only about 9 per cent to the total employment.

Underemployment in various segments of the labour force is quite high. For instance, though open unemployment was only 2 per cent in 1993-94, the incidence of under-employment and unemployment taken together was as much as 10 per cent that year. This, in spite of the fact that the incidence of underemployment was reduced substantially in the decade ending 1993-94.

The problem of unemployment has becoming a colossal. Various problems have caused this problem. There are individual factors like age, vocational unfitness and physical disabilities which restrict the people. External factors include technological and economic factors. There is enormous increase in the population. Every year India adds to her population afresh. More than this every year about 5 million people become eligible for securing jobs. Business field is subject to ups and downs of trade cycle and globalization. Economic depression or sick industries are often close down compelling their employees to become unemployed. Technological advancement contributes to economic development. But unplanned and uncontrolled growth of technology is causing havoc on job opportunities. The computerization and automation has led to technological unemployment. Strikes and lockouts have become inseparable aspect of the industrial world today. Due to these industries often face economic loses and production comes down. Since workers do not get any salary or wages during the strike period they suffer from economic hardships. They become permanently or temporarily unemployed.

Today young people are not ready to take jobs, which are considered to be socially degrading or lowly. In India, the spectra of frustration, of misery and hunger, of fallen hopes and barren dreams, of bitter pain and dark despair, haunts the unemployed. The youth of India today seems to belong to that lost generation and if it is true that the future of a country depends on the ability and the mental attitudes of its young men and women, then India has already lost the will to develop. If India allows her young men to be gripped by insecurity and frustration, she will have to pay for modernisation and rapid advancement with several years of stagnation.

Our educational system has its own irreparable defects and its contribution to the unemployment is an open truth. Our education does not prepare the minds of young generation to become self-employed on the contrary it makes them dependent on government vacancies which are hard to come. Our State right from the beginning of Five year plans has introduced several employment generating schemes and programmes over the years but in the absence of proper implementation and monitoring have failed to achieve the required targets.

In the light of this, the task of harnessing the unemployed should be put on a war footing. Massive urban recruitment will be useless, as the cities which have got along well enough without the recruits, can certainly continue to do so. Besides, massive urban recruitment will be inflationary and hence, is impracticable. The unemployed population should be mobilised for rural reconstruction, especially as the villages lack technical know-how and also that 70 per cent of India's population lives there.

Recently UPA Government has come up with Rural Employment Guarantee program which aims to provide minimum days of employment to people living in the villages. This is a laudable programme if implemented sincerely because it will provide employment to people during natural calamities like drought, floods etc. The remedial measures for reducing unemployment may lay greater emphasis on creation of opportunities for self-employment, augmentation of productivity and income levels of the working poor, shift in emphasis from creation of relief type of employment to the building up of durable productive assets in the rural areas and instead of attempting to revert somewhat to protectionist policies the pace of privatization may be accelerated.

44. Necessity of Sex Education in India

Failure to provide appropriate and timely information "misses the opportunity of reducing the unwanted outcomes of unintended pregnancy and transmission of STDs (Sex Transmitted Diseases), and is, therefore, in the disservice of our youth," the report called Effects of Sex Education on Young People's Sexual Behavior says. This report was commissioned by the Youth and General Public Unit, Office of Intervention and Development and Support, Global Program on AIDS, and the WHO.

Kids need the right information to help protect themselves. Teenagers suffer from sexually transmitted diseases (STDs) including HIV, and premarital pregnancy due to lack of knowledge and hesitation to discuss her problem with somebody who does not teach her lesson of morality, ethics and social bindings etc.

A study conducted by the National Institute of Health and Family Welfare says that a quarter to a third of India's young people indulge in premarital sex. The study, surveyed premarital sexuality and unmet contraceptive needs among school and college students, young working men and women, and young people aged 15-24 years living in slums in Delhi and Lucknow. It concludes that premarital sex varies from 17% among schoolchildren to 33% among young workers in the typical north Indian population. Premarital sex was more common in Lucknow than in Delhi. About a third of the respondents were found lacking in awareness of unsafe sexual encounters. Interestingly, 30% of respondents (54% men and 20% women) stated that, although they did not have premarital sex, their friends did. Eighteen per cent of male respondents had sex with strangers or commercial sex workers. Only a fifth of the respondents experienced guilt after sex. Homosexuality was declared by 5% of respondents. A greater percentage of males (59%) than females (35%) in Delhi stated that kissing, caressing, and dating had become common among young people. Unsafe sex was more common among less educated young people and unskilled workers. The use of contraceptives ranged from 55% among young workers to 75% among university students. The percentage of respondents who never used a condom was quite high—50% of females and 45% males. The use of a condom "always" was higher among males (19%) than females (9%). Overall, 46% never used condoms, 22% sometimes, and 17% always.

Such findings reveal a continuing denial in government speak about the reality in our society. Central and state governments are taking a moralistic position on this issue and have refused to recognise the magnitude of the problem. Ignorance and sex can be a troubling and sometimes deadly mix for young people and people living under suffocating societal demands. In the midst of all this, non-governmental organisations have been trying to produce and distribute their own guidebooks to address what they see missing in the school syllabus on sex education, but their efforts have met with opposition.

Most parents in India are not aware of their role in imparting sex education, explains a well-known sex counsellor; "Sex education doesn't even figure at all in the priorities of the Indian parents." Most parents are not just unwilling to discuss sex with their children, but even more aghast if it is suggested that they share information on birth control. "There's no need to now," says a mother, who is terrified to even mention the S-word aloud.

"We need to acknowledge the social change happening—with so many late marriages taking place due to both men and women building their careers, we can't expect them all to indulge in sex only after marriage," says an eminent Gynaecologist. "But we should make it safer for them."

Although the researchers emphasised the unmet contraceptive need of the youngsters, the study highlighted the need for sex education felt by 70% of the respondents. The study recommended that the reproductive health needs of young people should be given more priority by opening clinics for adolescents and counselling centres in schools, colleges, professional institutions, and working places.It is need of the hour that the parents should understood the problems of their children and be friendly with them. Instead of just telling them no for sex it is better to tell them about problems due to unsafe sex. Sexual activity among youngsters is on the rise—as is the rising number of young women seeking abortions. Unfortunately, persistent negative social attitudes towards adolescent sexual activity make it harder for young people in the city to obtain reproductive health information and family planning services, leading to a higher risk of unwanted pregnancy. With changing time and values it is the need of the hour to start sex education from schools level in India.

45. Indian Population

The world has a population of 6 billion. As of March 2001, the total population of India was a little over 1 billion—1,027,015,247 to be exact (531,277,078; female: 495,738,169). Of this number, 157,863,145 are children up to the age of six years (81,911,041 males and 75,952,104 females).

India is presently the second most populous country in the world. By the year 2050 India's population is expected to surpass that of China. Like most countries, which have experienced the population explosion, India's population has skyrocketed because of consistently high fertility rates despite falling mortality rates. Over the last fifty years the expectation of life at birth rose from 32 years to around 60 years at present. This results in reproduction over the replacement rate, which in turn results in rapid (exponential) population growth. It is commonly professed that, for the benefit of society and the earth's resources, fertility rates must eventually be curbed to equal the replacement rate.

Despite the fact that India was the first country in the world to have a population policy, not much has been achieved in terms of population control. India is facing an intense crisis of resources. There is fierce competition for the nation's limited natural resources leading to quarrels between states, between communities and even families. Our land and water resources are being exploited to the hilt. The exploitation of mineral resources is threatening forests, nature reserves, and ecology. Seventy percent of the energy resources need to be imported putting constant pressure on us to export more or face currency devaluation. Over use of resources is contributing to natural disasters occurring more frequently and with greater devastation.

For many Indians, life is a big struggle just to put together the bare essentials for survival, and shortages of resources works most against the poor and underprivileged. Even as sections of India's middle-class struggle with scarcities, it is the poor and vulnerable sections of society who suffer most. It is well known that the biggest curse to the lives of millions of Indians is poverty. Though the rural poor have always been a deprived lot, their urban counterparts are not an inch better off. Having migrated to towns and cities in search of better life, they now survive under the most appalling of living conditions, with scant regard to the basics of cleanliness and hygiene. Awareness of healthy living habits is woefully lacking, so that, though the mortality rate has fallen over the years, epidemics and killer diseases continue to claim lives that could easily be saved. Infant mortality and deaths related to childbirth are still disturbingly common all over India, with large sections of the female population and a fair section of the male yet to receive their first lessons in literacy. With illiteracy rampant among the impoverished majority of the country, it is not difficult to understand why the rich easily exploit the poor, and corruption seems to have become a way of life. Indian life presents a classic example of being trapped in a vicious circle of poverty, from which there appears to be no escape. Nevertheless, a close inspection of the nature of these ills and inequalities reveals a single root cause lying at the core of the great entangled mass of our national life: viz. Population.

Population is the only non-depleting resource and a parameter of a country's development. In a country like India where the factors contributing to population growth far outweigh the factors for development, population is no longer a resource but a burden to society. India's population policy has been guided by the perception that a growing population is a serious impediment to development efforts. At the time, census figures showed a Crude Birth Rate (CBR) of over 45/1,000 population—every year; over 45 children were born for every 1,000 people. Many couples have large families as insurance against multiple infant and child deaths. The National Population Policy 2000 notes that only 44 per cent of India's 168 million couples in the reproductive age group use effective contraception. Reproductive health and basic health infrastructure and services often do not reach the villages.

When India became independent, population growth was seen as a major impediment to the country's socio-economic development and population 'control' was seen as integral to the development process. Population growth was seen as an urgent problem related to economic development with limited resources. At the same time, family planning would benefit both individual families as well as women's health.

The pressing need of the day is to at create ideal conditions for acceptance of the need for stabilizing the population and how it is an essential element of human welfare and development. The solution to this lie in spreading of education and enlightenment, and in the empowerment of women. Birth control programmes should also be integrated with medical and public health services to make them popular among the masses.

46. India and Globalisation

A most common measure of globalisation is openness to trade and a country's participation in trade. By this measure, the extent of India's globalisation is insignificant—it is one of the lowest in the world. India's share in world trade is a meagre 0.7 per cent or so. If a map of the world were drawn on the scale of a country's participation in trade, India with a population of more than 1,000 million will occupy a smaller area than Singapore with a population of only 3 million. You would need a magnifying glass to locate India on that map!

A second commonly used measure of globalisation is a country's participation in international capital flows, particularly Foreign Direct Investment (FDI). As you know, annual flow of FDI across the globe is more than $1 trillion, ie, $ 1,000 billion. Annual FDI inflows into India is $ 3—4 billion only or 0.3—0.4 per cent of the total—that is all. Same is true of Foreign Institutional Investment (FII).

It should be well understood that despite all the talk, we are nowhere even close to being globalised in terms of any commonly used indicator of globalisation. In fact, we are still one of the least globalised among major countries. An equally important point is that whether the so-called globalisation is considered to be good or bad for a country depends crucially on the sense in which the word is used. The word may be used in a purely descriptive sense to describe a "shrinkage" of distance among nation states due to technological changes in transport and communication and closer integration of product and financial markets across the world.

Another sense in which the word may be used is the effect of such changes on different countries or groups of countries, such as, developed and developing. In yet another sense, the word may also represent a "globalisation of ideas or ideology" and may be used as a synonym for triumph of capitalism or dominance of unfettered markets.

In discussing the issue of globalisation in the Indian context, we should understood the meaning of this word i.e. the technological changes, and associated policy changes, that have brought the world economies closer and made them more integrated with each other. In this particular sense, the changes that have occurred in the patterns of trade and capital flows in recent years are to India's advantage, although, unfortunately, so far we have not made much use of it. Today, in terms of the potential benefits of globalisation, India is in a very different position than would have been the case 50 or even 20 years ago.

This is because the sources of what economists call "comparative advantage" have changed dramatically in India's favour in the 1990s because of the technological revolution. In the old days, comparative advantage was largely determined by "factor endowments", i.e. land, labour and capital. Geographical location and early starts in industry also conferred greater advantages.

Thus, at one time, a country's trade pattern, was determined by its natural resources and the productivity of its land. Leaving aside political and institutional factors, a country's level of income was also largely determined by the global demand for its natural resources and its relative efficiency in exploiting them. The importance of land as a source of comparative advantage, however, changed dramatically after the industrial revolution. Today, it is almost insignificant. Thus, except for the United States, countries accounting for a predominant share of the world GDP have a relatively small share of global land area.

Today, availability of capital and productivity are still crucial in determining a country's growth rate. However, there has been a dramatic change in the global mobility of capital, and national boundaries are no longer important determinants of sources and uses of capital. A dramatic illustration of this is the fact that the most developed country in the world, which enjoyed unprecedented growth during the 1990s, is actually a capital-importing country, i.e. the United States. Similarly, the fastest growing developing country, i.e. China, is one of the largest recipients of capital from outside.

Similary, labour is no longer an important element in cost of production and in determining a country's comparative advantage. In most manufacturing industries in the world, it is no higher than 1/8th of total costs. In India, it may be somewhat higher because of our domestic laws, but the important fact to note is that India no longer needs to specialise only in the production of labour-intensive plantation crops or primary commodities.

A related development which is linked to the above changes, is the "Services Revolution". The focus of attention in conventional economics, was on production of goods—manufactured products and agricultural commodities. It was, of course, recognised that the services sector (which includes transport, communication, trade, banking, construction and public administration, etc.) was an important source of income and employment in most economies. However, overall, the growth of services was perceived at best as a by-product of developments in the primary and secondary sectors, and at worst as a drag on the prospects for long-term economic growth.

In the last few years, there has been a phenomenal change in the conventional view of services and their role in the economy. This change has been facilitated by unprecedented and unforeseen advances in computer and communication technology. As a result, the development of certain services is now regarded as one of the preconditions of economic growth, and not as one of its consequences. The boundary between goods and services is also disappearing. Many industrial products are not only manufactured, but they are also researched, designed, marketed, advertised, distributed, leased and serviced. An important aspect of the "services revolution" is that geography and levels of industrialisation are no longer the primary determinants of the location of facilities for production of services. As a result, the traditional role of developing countries is also changing – from mere recipients to important providers of long-distance and high value services.

Another consequence of recent global trends is the greater vulnerability of national economies to developments outside their own borders. A crisis in any one or a group of countries, can be transmitted to other countries which may not have any strong economic linkages with crisis-affected countries. While we must be careful, on the whole, the death of distance, the services revolution, and the mobility of capital which characterise globalisation present unprecedented opportunities for India. The primary source of comparative advantages today are : skills and ability to adapt and change. India has the advantage of skills, entrepreneurship and managerial competence in taking advantage of these changes.

Inspite of all these favourable parameters then, why are we not jumping with joy and optimism? Why are we so "unglobalised" in terms of our share in trade, investment or communication?

Transition from a closed to a vibrant, open and a more globally dominant economy will certainly take time and will not be painless.

As of now, we also have much greater tolerance for waste, non-work and survival of the inefficient, and the self-seeking than other fast growing countries. Somehow to make this transition from a less productive and less challenging economy to a more work-oriented and competitive economy is the real challenge of globalisation.

If we continue in our old ways, we can witness real social problems and inequalities emerging in our society. We will have islands of prosperity and excellence – IT, beauty parades and media entertainment amidst growing disparity, rising unemployment and immiserisation. And as has happened in several countries in the 1990s, including Turkey and Argentina just now, those who are with us today will be the first to leave.

The principal lesson of recent economic and technological developments, and growing tensions and inequalities within and across countries, is that our fate is in our hands. Our public policies have to respond to our own requirements rather than to any fixed global ideology or a pre-determined and internationally prescribed model of economic progress. We must face the realities of "globalising" world, keeping India's interest, its integrity, its indivisibility and its future potential close to our hearts and our minds. We can very well hope that if we are able to adapt ourselves with the challenges of globalisation, India of 2025 will be a very different place, and a much more dominant force in the world economy, than was the case twenty five years ago or at the beginning of the new millennium.

47. Poverty in India

Poverty is one of the main problems which have attracted attention of sociologists and economists. It indicates a condition in which a person fails to maintain a living standard adequate for his physical and mental efficiency. The term poverty is a relative concept. It is very difficult to draw a demarcation line between affluence and poverty. According to Adam Smith Man is rich or poor according to the degree in which he can afford to enjoy the necessaries, the conveniences and the amusements of human life.

Even after more than 56 years of Independence India still has the world's largest number of poor people in a single country. Of its nearly one billion inhabitants, an estimated 260.3 million are below the poverty line, of which 193.2 million are in the rural areas and 67.1 million are in urban areas. More than 75% of poor people reside in villages. Poverty level is not uniform across India. The poverty level is below 10% in states like Delhi, Goa, and Punjab etc whereas it is below 50% in Bihar (43) and Orissa (47). It is between 30-40% in Northeastern states of Assam, Tripura, and Mehgalaya and in Southern states of TamilNadu and Uttar Pradesh.

Poverty has many dimensions changing from place to place and across time. There are two inter-related aspects of poverty-Urban and rural poverty. The main causes of urban poverty are predominantly due to impoverishment of rural peasantry that forces them to move out of villages to seek some subsistence living in the towns and cities. In this process, they even lose the open space or habitat they had in villages albeit without food and other basic amenities. While a select few have standards of living comparable to the richest in the world, the majority fails to get two meals a day. The causes of rural poverty are manifold including inadequate and ineffective implementation of anti-poverty programmes. The overdependence on monsoon with non-availability of irrigational facilities often result in crop-failure and low agricultural productivity forcing farmers in the debt-traps. The rural communities tend to spend large percentage of annual earnings on social ceremonies like marriage; feast etc.

Since the 1970s the Indian government has made poverty reduction a priority in its development planning. Policies have focused on improving the poor standard of living by ensuring food security, promoting self-employment through greater access to assets, increasing wage employment and improving access to basic social services.

The participation of civil society organizations in poverty reduction efforts, especially those directed to women, has increased social awareness and encouraged governments to provide better services. Cooperatives such as the Self-Employed Women's Association provide credit to women at market rates of interest but do not require collateral; they also allow flexibility in the use of loans and the timing of repayments. These civil society organizations have not only contributed to women's material well being; they have also helped empower them socially and politically. Such credit initiatives, by bringing women out of the confines of the household, are changing their status within the family and within village hierarchies. The demands of civil society organizations for better social services have spurred the government to launch campaigns to increase literacy and improve public infrastructure. And their calls for greater accountability and real devolution of power are increasing the likelihood that expenditures for poverty reduction will reach the needy, especially women.

The Indian government has undoubtedly failed in its responsibilities towards its citizens over the past many years. There is a need for the state to move out of many areas and the process has been started with economic liberalization. The process of decentralization should devolute lot more powers, both functional and financial, to panchayats. The lack of transparency and accountability has hampered our economic development at all levels. The problem of poverty persists because of a number of leakages in the system. New laws have to be evolved to ensure more accountability. Bodies like the Planning Commission should be modified into new constitutional bodies that can hold governments accountable for their failure to implement development programmes. A strong system of incentives and disincentives also needs to be introduced. The encouragement of non-governmental organizations and private sector individuals in tackling poverty is imperative, as the state cannot do everything.

48. Gender Inequalities in India

Gender differentiation is evident in every culture and society in the world. Some things are masculine others are feminine, some work is women's work, some responsibilities are women's responsibilities, even major religions of the world assign different social responsibilities to men and women. Sociologically the word gender refers to the socio-cultural definition of man and woman, the way societies distinguish men and women and assign them social roles. The distinction between sex and gender was introduced to deal with the general tendency to attribute women's subordination to their anatomy.

India has witnessed gender inequality from its early history due to its socio-economic and religious practices that resulted in a wide gap between the position of men and women in the society. The origin of the Indian idea of appropriate female behavior can be traced to the rules laid down by Manu in 200 B.C. : "by a young girl, by a young woman, or even by an aged one, nothing must be done independently, even in her own house". "In childhood a female must be subject to her father, in youth to her husband, when her lord is dead to her sons; a woman must never be independent." Women's lives are shaped by customs that are centuries old. "May you be the mother of a hundred sons" is a common Hindu wedding blessing. Statistics reveal that in India males significantly outnumber females and this imbalance has increased over time. The sex ratio according to 2001 census report stands at 933 per 1000 males. Out of the total population, 120 million are women who live in abject poverty. The maternal mortality rate in rural areas is among the world's highest. From a global perspective India accounts for 19% of all live births and 27% of all maternal deaths. The deaths of young girls in India exceed those of young boys by over 300,000 each year and every 6th infant death is specifically due to gender discrimination. Women face discrimination right from the childhood. Gender disparities in nutrition are evident from infancy to adulthood. In fact, gender has been the most statistically significant determinant of malnutrition among young children and malnutrition is a frequent, direct or underlying, cause of death among girls below age 5. Girls are breast-fed less frequently and for a shorter duration in infancy. In childhood and adulthood, males are fed first and better. Adult women consume approximately 1,000 fewer calories per day than men according to one estimate. Nutritional deprivation has two major consequences for women: they never reach their full growth potential, and suffer from anemia which are risk factors in pregnancy. This condition complicates childbearing and results in women and infant deaths, and low birth weight infants. The tradition also requires that women eat last and least throughout their lives even when pregnant and lactating. Malnourished women give birth to malnourished children, perpetuating the cycle. Women receive less healthcare facilities than men. A primary way that parents discriminate against their girl children is through neglect during illness. As an adult they tend to be less likely to admit that they are sick and may wait until their sickness has progressed far before they seek help or help is sought for them. Many women in rural areas die in childbirth due to easily preventable complications. Women's social training to tolerate suffering and their reluctance to be examined by male personnel are additional constraints in their getting adequate health care.

The Constitution of India ensures gender equality in its preamble as a fundamental right but also empowers the state to adopt measures of positive discrimination in favor of women by ways of legislation and policies. India has also ratified various international conventions and human rights forums to secure equal rights of women, such as ratification of Convention on elimination of all forms of discrimination against women in 1993. Women have been finding place in local governance structures, overcoming gender biases. Over one million women have been elected to local panchayats as a result of 1993 amendment to the Indian Constitution requiring that 1/3 rd of the elected seats to the local governing bodies be reserved for women. The passing of Pre-natal Diagnostic Tech Act in 1994 also is a step in removing gender discrimination. This Act seeks to end sex-determination tests and female foeticide and prohibits doctors from conducting such procedures for the specific purpose of determining the sex of the fetus. The Government also announced the National policy for empowerment of women in 2001 to bring out advancement, development and empowerment of women. The Government has also drawn up a draft National policy for the empowerment of women which is a policy statement outlining the state's response to problems of gender discrimination.

As persistent gender inequalities continue we need to rethink concepts and strategies for promoting women's dignity and rights. UN Secretary General Kofi Annan has stated, "Gender equality is more than a goal in itself. It is a precondition for meeting the challenge of reducing poverty, promoting sustainable development and building good governance." There is a need for new kinds of institutions, incorporating new norms and rules that support equal and just relations between women and men. Today women are organizing themselves to meet the challenges that are hampering their development.

49. Child Labour in India

Millions of children in today's world are suffering from the worst forms of child labour which includes Child Slavery, Child prostitution, Child Trafficking, Child Soldiers. In modern era of material and technological advancement, children in almost every country are being callously exploited.

ILO estimated that 250 million children between 5 and 14 work for a living, and over 50 million children under age twelve work in hazardous circumstances. United Nations estimate that there were 20 million bonded child labourers worldwide. Based on reliable estimates, at least 700,000 persons to 2 million, especially girls and children, are trafficked each year across international borders. Research suggests that the age of the children involved is decreasing. Poor children between the ages of 13 and 18, and very young children even babies, are also caught up in this horrific trade.

India has the dubious distinction of being the nation with the largest number of child labourers in the world. The child labours endure miserable and difficult lives. They earn little and struggle to make enough to feed themselves and their families. They do not go to school; more than half of them are unable to learn the barest skills of literacy. Poverty is one of the main reasons behind this phenomenon.

In India the emergence of child labour is also because of unsustainable systems of landholding in agricultural areas and caste system in the rural areas. Bonded labour refers to the phenomenon of children working in conditions of servitude in order to pay their debts. The debt that binds them to their employer is incurred not by the children themselves but by their parent. The creditors cum employers offer these loans to destitute parents in an effort to secure the labour of these children. The arrangements between the parents and contracting agents are usually informal and unwritten. The number of years required to pay off such a loan is indeterminate. The lower castes such as dalits and tribal make them vulnerable groups for exploitation in India.

In India a large number of children work in industries, such as cracker making, diamond polishing, glass, brass-ware, carpet weaving, bangle making, lock making and mica cutting to name a few. 15% of the 100,000 children work in the carpet industry of Uttar Pradesh. 70-80% of the 8,000 to 50,000 children work in the glass industry in Ferozabad. In the unorganized sector child labour is paid by piece-by-piece rates that result in even longer hours for very low pay.

Inadequate schools, a lack of schools, or even the expense of schooling leaves some children with little else to do but work. The attitudes of parents also contribute to child labour; some parents feel that children should work in order to develop skills useful in the job market, instead of taking advantage of a formal education.

Article 24 of the Indian constitution clearly states that "No child below the age of fourteen years shall be employed to work in any factory or mine or employed in any hazardous employment." The Bonded Labour System Act of 1976 fulfills the Indian Constitution's directive of ending forced labour. A Plethora of additional protective legislation has been put in place. There are distinct laws governing child labour in factories in commercial establishments, on plantations and in apprenticeships. There are laws governing the use of migrant labour and contract labour. A recent law The Child Labour (Prohibition and Regulation law) of 1986 designates a child as a person who has not completed their 14th year of age. It purports to regulate the hours and the conditions of child workers and to prohibit child workers in certain enumerated hazardous industries. However there is neither blanket prohibition on the use of child labour, nor any universal minimum age set for child workers. All of the policies that the Indian government has in place are in accordance with the Constitution of India, and all support the eradication of Child Labour. The problem of child labour still remains even though all of these policies are existent. Enforcement is the key aspect that is lacking in the government's efforts.

Child labour is a global problem. If child labour is to be eradicated, the governments and agencies and those responsible for enforcement need to start doing their jobs. The most important thing is to increase awareness and keep discussing ways and means to check this problem. We have to decide whether we are going to take up the problem head-on and fight it any way we can or leave it to the adults who might not be there when things go out of hand.

50. Domestic Violence

Domestic violence can be described as when one adult in a relationship misuses power to control another. It is the establishment of control and fear in the relationship through violence and other forms of abuse. It is basically an abuse of power. The abuser tortures and controls the victim by calculated threats, intimidation and physical violence. Although men, women and children can all be abused, in most cases the victims are women.

Violence within the home is universal across culture, religion, class and ethnicity. The abuse is generally condoned by social custom and considered part and parcel of marital life. An example of this can be seen through the gist of a popular Spanish riddle: Question: What do mules and women have in common? Answer: A good beating makes them both better."

The statistics reveal grim picture of the realities prevalent in developing and developed countries alike.

In the United States a women is beaten every 18 minutes; between 3 million and 4 million are battered each year, but only 1 in 10 cases of domestic violence is ever reported. In the United Kingdom, 1 in 3 families is a victim of assault and

1 in 5 a victim of serious assault, according to a recent report by the home office. In India the records of National Crimes Bureau, Ministry of Home Affairs government of India revealed a shocking 71.5% Increase in cases of torture and dowry deaths during the period from 1991 to 1995. In 1995, torture of women constituted 29.2% of all reported crimes against women.

The question arises why women put up with the abuse in the home? The answer lies in their unequal status in society. They are often caught in a vicious circle of economic dependence, fear for their children's lives as well as their own, ignorance of their rights before the law, lack of confidence in themselves and social pressures. These factors effectively force women to a life of recurrent mistreatment from which they often do not have the means to escape. The sanctity of privacy within the family also makes authorities reluctant to intervene, often leads women to deny they are being abused. This is equally common in the higher as well as in the lower segments of a society. A woman who files a charge of abuse is often forced to drop it by her husband's family if she wants an uncontested divorce. Social prejudices reinforce domestic violence against women. They are treated as their spouses' property; husbands assume that this subordinate role gives them right to abuse their wives in order to keep them in their place. Against this background is the tradition of dowry, an expectation of gifts and cash from the bride's family, one can imagine the anxiety these expectations may cause to a woman and the consequences she has to face if it is inadequate. Women's physical and mental health is often permanently damaged or impaired and in some cases violence can have fatal consequences as in the case of dowry deaths in India. Physical torture as well as mental torture usually occurs on a regular basis causing suffering and inflicting deep scars on the psyche of the victims and their families. Many assault incidents result in injuries ranging from bruises and fractures to chronic disabilities.

Domestic violence has devastating repercussions on the family. Mothers are unable to care for their children properly. Often they transmit to them their own feelings of low self-esteem, helplessness and inadequacy. Violence against women is the most pervasive human rights violation in world today. We need to think and ponder as how this form of degradation of women can be stopped. It needs support from all quarters be it government, NGOs and women themselves. There is also a need to improve women's economic capacities that include access to and control of income and assets and also share in the family's property. The government should strengthen and expand training and sensitization programs.

51. Judicial Activism

The term judicial activism is explained in Black's law Dictionary, Sixtieth Edition, [Centennial Edition (1891-1991)] thus, "Judicial philosophy which motives judges to depart from strict adherence to judicial precedent in favour of progressive and new social policies which are not always consistent with the restraint expected of appellate Judges. It is commonly marked by decisions calling for social engineering and occasionally these decisions represent intrusions in the legislative and executive matters."

Though it is the legislature, which makes the Law, the Judgments rendered by the Supreme Court and High Courts give the Law a concrete shape, which the people understand better as the Law. Hence, there is importance of the decision making process. In the Common Law, development is permitted, if not expected in Stature law, there must be at least a presumption that Parliament has on the topic it is dealing with, said all that it wanted to say, Justice V. R. Krishana Iyer, the greatest activist Judge, India has so far seen, feels, judicial activism is a device to accomplish the cherished goal of social justice. He said," After all, social justice is achieved not by lawlessness process,but legally tuned affirmative action, activist justicing and benign interpretation within the parameters of Corpus Juris".

It may be emphasized here that, Law and justice are, however, two district concepts. No doubt, they are interrelated but each has district sphere of its own.

The concept of Justice is even older than that of law. Justice is the legitimate end of law. It must, therefore, necessarily precede law because people thought of law as they wanted justice. Justice is a social value. Therefore, it is said that "it is not the words of law but the internal sense of it that makes the law. Letter of law is nobody, sense and reason of law is the sole." These, in my view, are the established principles in judicial philosophy.

No one will dispute that judiciary has to perform an important role in the interpretation and enforcement of human rights inscribed in the fundamental law of the country. Therefore, it is necessary to consider what should be the approach of the judiciary in the matter of constitutional interpretation. An approach must be a creative and purposive approach in the interpretation of various rights embodied in the Constitution. With a view to advancing human rights jurisprudence and social justice.

Once Chief Justice Ahmedi [as he then was] has said in his interview of the week to The Sunday observer dated April 20-26, 1997. The query was "There is much talk about judicial activism. What does that mean? How far should it be carried in democracy?" to which he answered. "I have always disapproved of this label of judicial activism because it gives the impression that the Court was earlier passive, which is incorrect. What is known as activism is where the judiciary takes decisions in sensitive cases, which are sensationalized by the media. When the media highlights the case of an influential person, it often pets referred to as activism. But the role of the court is limited.

The concept of judicial activism and public interest litigation are connected. This started in the Seventies. The legal aspect of PILs is the waiver of the rule of locus standi. The normal rule is that only the aggrieved party can move the court. But the court found in certain cases that the aggrieved party was so placed because of economic constraints or lack of awareness of rights that it could not move the court. So the count said that even if a third party moved it, the locus standi rule would be waived, if the petition had substance. In a situation where a mass of people would benefit, the court may not insist upon the locus standing rule. Then it becomes public interest litigation. This is sometimes described as activism or assertive action." In this context, it would be appropriate to recall the words of Dr. B. R. Ambedkar in context of the Constitutional provisions touching to the core of the role of the Supreme Court. On the day of the adoption of Constitution of India, Dr. Ambedkar said, ".....Constitution of our country would be found to be bulky........... . It would be difficult for those who have been through it to realize its silent and special features."

Speaking about Article 32 of the Constitution, Dr. Ambekar said, "........If I was asked to name any particular article in this constitution, as the important as one, without which this constitution would be nullity, I would not refer to any other article except this one........"

He further said, "........It is the very sole of the Constitution and very heart of it......."

Judicial approach is increased partially in every walks of life, cleaning up from politics to environment. There cannot be any dispute that the courts are bound to evolve, affirm and adopt principles of interpretation which will further and hot hinder the goals set out in the Directive Principles of State Policy, which forms integral part of fundamental rights as per the Constitutional wisdom. To conclude, judicial activism is justice personified. What is inherent in the body of the Judiciary has come on surface, to do justice and to stop miscarriage of justice. It has shed its shyness of adolescence and has learnt to face bravely the odds put by the Establishment. It has realized that it has a Third Eye of Lord Shiva to burn what is injustice. For that, every constitutional judge must be active and never passive or negative. Judicial activism is a blood cell of the Judiciary. Therefore, the phraseology "Judicial activism" is nothing but a new facet and expanded meaning to judicial interpretation and its implementation within permissible limits cannot be termed as a mere fiction inasmuch as with passage of time basic meaning do not change, but expansions are given new colour to the meaning.